THE
BRITANNICA
ENCYCLOPEDIA
OF
AMERICAN
ART

A Chanticleer Press Edition

THE BRITANNICA ENCYCLOPEDIA OF AMERICAN ART

A special educational supplement to the Encyclopaedia Britannica

Published by Encyclopaedia Britannica Educational Corporation, Chicago

World Book Trade Distribution by Simon and Schuster, New York

Chanticleer Staff

President:	Paul Steiner
Editors	
Editor:	Milton Rugoff
Project Editor:	Constance Sullivan
Associate Editors:	W. Jeffrey Simpson and Susan Weiley
Copy Editor:	Lucy Rosenfeld
Research Assistant:	Ingrid Wiegand
Design	
Art Director:	Ellen Hsiao
Assistant Art Director:	Roberta Savage
Production	
Production Manager:	Gudrun Buettner
Assistant Production Managers:	Ursula Amrain and Ruth Charnes

Published in the United States by Encyclopaedia Britannica Educational Corporation, Chicago.
World book trade distribution by Simon and Schuster, New York.

Manufactured in Milan, Italy, by Amilcare Pizzi S.p.A.

ISBN 0-87827-160-0
Library of Congress Catalog Card Number: 73-80529

10 9 8 7 6 5 4 3 2 1

Planned and produced by Chanticleer Press, Inc., New York

A Message From Senator William Benton

Just before his sudden death in March 1973, Senator William Benton, for three decades Publisher of the Encyclopaedia Britannica, and a noted collector of American art, wrote the following comment:

The Editors of the Encyclopaedia Britannica are pleased to present this distinguished and unique encyclopedia of American art, the first complete evaluation of what has become the world's dominant art expression. In its biographies of painters, sculptors, architects and workers in the graphic arts, in its histories of various movements and trends, in its illuminating description of different styles, this volume is, I believe, the most authoritative reference work of its kind. It makes an invaluable guide to America's contribution to the world of art. I am proud to associate our name with it.

Wm Benton

Foreword

American painting, sculpture, architecture and photography have come of age. At the same time, American decorative arts and handcrafts have acquired new importance and value. American art has, in the last fifty years, broken free of European domination and the result has been a burgeoning of the visual imagination, a virtual flood of creativity that has spread its influence all over the world.

The diversity and vigor of the arts have inspired a number of surveys and histories. But now, for the first time, an entire company of the most highly qualified specialists has recorded America's remarkably rich artistic achievements in one volume.

We have selected thirty-two critics, historians and curators of art to do justice not only to American painting and sculpture but also to architecture, glass, silver, furniture, printmaking and folk art as well as photography and handcrafts. Into these pages these experts have compressed an entire library of books and articles. They have, moreover, supplemented the biographical and historical data with interpretations and evaluations, balancing currently accepted estimates with personal judgments.

The decisions about what artists, movements and styles were to be included, and at what length, were made in consultation with our staff of contributors. Informed readers will note omissions, especially of the work of younger artists whose reputations have yet to stand the test of time. Such omissions are inevitable, even in a volume of this size, and while we regret them, we offer no apology for a book that spreads before the reader such an extraordinary record of creative activity.

The Editors

Contributors and Editors

Managing Editor: **Milton Rugoff**
Project Editor: **Constance Sullivan**
Advisory Editor: **David W. Scott**
Consulting Editor: **Lloyd Goodrich**

Painting

Colonial to 1830
Charles Coleman Sellers. Formerly Librarian of Dickinson College. Author of *Charles Willson Peale.*

Middle 19th Century
Hermann W. Williams, Jr. Formerly Director, Corcoran Gallery of Art. Author of *Mirror to the American Past: A Survey of American Genre Painting.*

Later 19th Century
Lloyd Goodrich. Consultant, and formerly Director, Whitney Museum of American Art. Author of *Thomas Eakins, Winslow Homer,* and *Albert P. Ryder.*

Later 19th Century
Theodore E. Stebbins, Jr. Curator of American Painting and Sculpture, Yale University Art Gallery.

Later 19th and Early 20th Century
David W. Scott. Consultant, National Gallery of Art. Formerly Director, National Collection of Fine Arts. Author of *John Sloan.*

1920–1940
Alfred V. Frankenstein. Art Critic, San Francisco *Chronicle.* Author of *After the Hunt* and *The World of John Singleton Copley.*

1940 to date
H. H. Arnason. Vice-President, Art Administration, the Guggenheim Foundation. Formerly Chairman, Art Department, University of Minnesota. Author of *History of Modern Art* and *Philip Guston.*

1940 to date
Eugene C. Goossen. Chairman, Department of Art, Hunter College of the City University of New York. Author of *Stuart Davis, Art of the Real,* and *Ellsworth Kelly.*

Sculpture

Colonial to 1920
Wayne Craven. H. F. du Pont Professor of Art History, University of Delaware. Author of *Sculpture in America.*

1920 to date
Dore Ashton. Head of Art History Department, Cooper Union. Author of *Modern American Sculpture* and *A Reading of Modern Art.* Contributing Editor, *Studio International.*

1950 to date
James Monte. Associate Curator, Whitney Museum of American Art.

1950 to date
Carter Ratcliff. Critic. Advisory Editor, *Art International.* Instructor, School of Visual Arts, New York City.

Architecture

Colonial to 1870
Paul F. Norton. Professor of Architectural History, Department of Art, University of Massachusetts, Amherst.

1870–1930
Alan Burnham. FAIA, Director of Research, Landmarks Preservation Commission, City of New York. Editor of *New York Landmarks.*

1930–1960
David Gebhard. Professor of Art and Director of Art Galleries, University of California at Santa Barbara. Author of *Schindler* and *Purcell and Elmslie, Architects.*

Contributors and Editors

1960 to date
C. Ray Smith. Critic. Formerly Features Editor, *Progressive Architecture.* Author of *The New Designs: Supermannerism.*

Landscape
Henry Hope Reed. Curator of Parks, New York City. Author of *Central Park: A History and a Guide.*

Folk Art
M. J. Gladstone. Formerly Director, Museum of American Folk Art.

Prints
Sinclair Hitchings. Keeper of Prints, Boston Public Library.

Riva Castleman. Curator of Prints and Illustrated Books, Museum of Modern Art.

Photography
Van Deren Coke. Director, Art Museum, University of New Mexico. Formerly Director, George Eastman House, Rochester. Author of *The Painter and the Photograph.*

Thomas F. Barrow. Assistant Director, George Eastman House, Rochester.

Dennis Longwell. Assistant Curator, Department of Photography, Museum of Modern Art.

Furniture
1650–1790
Charles F. Hummel. Curator, H. F. du Pont Winterthur Museum. Author of *With Hammer in Hand.*

1799–1920
Marilynn Johnson Bordes. Associate Curator of the American Wing, Metropolitan Museum of Art.

1920 to date
Dianne H. Pilgrim. Research Consultant, American Paintings and Sculpture Department, Metropolitan Museum of Art.

Silver
Martha Gandy Fales. Honorary Curator of Silver, Essex Institute. Author of *Early American Silver.*

Glass
Paul Perrot. Assistant Secretary, Museum Programs, Smithsonian Institution. Formerly Director, Corning Museum of Glass.

Jane Shadel Spillman. Assistant Curator, Corning Museum of Glass.

Ceramics
J. Jefferson Miller II. Curator of Ceramics History, National Museum of History and Technology, Smithsonian Institution.

Pewter
Ledlie M. Laughlin. Author of *Pewter in America.*

Contemporary Handcrafts
Rose Slivka. Editor-in-chief, *Craft Horizons.* Editor of *The Crafts of the Modern World* and author of *The Persistent Object.*

Contents

Notes on Use of the Encyclopedia

This encyclopedia—the first to summarize the scope of American art—includes all the arts in one alphabetical sequence. In addition, the *Guide to Entries by Arts* on page 622 gives an alphabetical list of the entries in each art.

A cross reference is indicated by an asterisk following a term.

Museums and public collections containing a substantial number of American works of art are listed, and their major holdings noted, in the *Guide to Museums and Public Collections* on page 628.

A glossary of three hundred terms from all the arts appears on page 634.

The initials at the end of longer entries are those of contributors listed at the front of the book.

The Britannica Encyclopedia of American Art

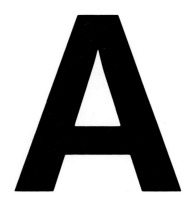

Abbey, Edwin Austin (1852–1911). Illustrator and muralist. Abbey was born in Philadelphia, where he attended the Pennsylvania Academy of the Fine Arts. From 1871 he did illustrations for *Harper's Weekly,* then for *Scribners,* specializing in historical subjects. In 1878 he went to London, and settled there, winning fame as the illustrator of classics by such authors as Herrick, Goldsmith, and Shakespeare. He greatly admired the work of such pre-Raphaelite painters as D. G. Rossetti and J. E. Millais and was distinguished by his archeological accuracy. His illustrations of 17th- and 18th-century English scenes were precise in detail and drawn with a graceful, finely spun technique that influenced the illustrative style in his day. His most famous mural work is the series depicting *The Quest for the Holy Grail* (completed in 1902, Boston Public Library). (D.W.S.)

Abbott, Berenice (1898–　). Photographer. Born in Springfield, Ohio, she attended Ohio State University for a year and a half before studying to be a sculptor in New York City in 1918–21. Like many young artists of the 1920s, she became an expatriate. Studies with the French sculptor Émile-Antoine Bourdelle and at the Kunstschule in Berlin led her to the Paris studio of the American artist Man Ray* and eventually to a successful career as a portrait photographer. Among her sitters were Jean Cocteau, André Gide, André Maurois, and James Joyce. Her first one-man show was held in Paris in 1926. Struck by the simplicity and strength of Eugene Atget's photographs (which she saw in Man Ray's collection), Abbott managed to meet this little-known photographer shortly before his death in 1927. The following year she acquired the contents of his studio, she brought it to America and spent much time promoting awareness of Atget's genius. The Abbott-Levey Collection of Atget photographs is now in the Museum of Modern Art.

Abbott returned to America in 1929 and, between commercial assignments, began to document Manhattan Island as Atget had done Paris. Using a view camera on a tripod, she made over three hundred superb photographs from about 1935 to 1939 for the WPA Federal Art Project's* "Changing New York" program. A book with this title was published in 1939 and many regard it as the finest photographic documentation of New York ever made. So thorough was her coverage that it might be possible to reconstruct the essential city on the basis of these photographs alone. Like the work of Walker Evans,* these photographs transcend the merely documentary through their specificity of detail, breadth of intelligence, and excellent print quality. The negatives and prints of this vast series are in the Museum of the City of New York.

About 1940 Abbott began experiments that enabled her to show photographically the normally invisible basic principles of physical science. This work was published in the 1960s in textbooks dealing with magnetism, motion, and gravity. A major retrospective of her career was held at the Museum of Modern Art in 1970–71. Since 1968 she has lived and photographed in Maine. (D.L.)

Abstract Art.
Perhaps the most significant single contribution of 20th-century artists to the arts of painting and sculpture. During much of the 19th century there was a movement away from the concept that a work of art is necessarily an imitation of something else—of a human figure, a landscape, a still life, or a battle scene—and toward the idea that it could exist as an entity in itself, without specific reference to the world of nature. This emerging conviction took various forms: simplification, an emphasis in painting on the two-dimensional picture plane, color used arbitrarily rather than descriptively. These tendencies can be observed in the painting of the French impressionists and post-impressionists, of Monet, Seurat, Gauguin, van Gogh, and above all, in the late works of Cézanne.

The exploration of a nonnaturalistic art was pursued early in the 20th century by painters such as Henri Matisse and more specifically by Pablo Picasso, Georges Braque, and the other cubists. Picasso and Braque in 1907 asserted for the first time the principle that the figure or still life subject could be distorted, cut up, transformed into a series of flat color planes. From this discovery it was only a short step to the realization that a painting might exist as an abstract arrangement of lines and colors integrated in various ways on the picture surface. Sculptors such as Raymond Duchamp-Villon and Jacques Lipchitz* were demonstrating by 1914 that sculpture also could abandon specific subject matter.

Cubism,* which constituted an entire new vocabulary for artists, characteristically retained residues of recognizable subjects and therefore could not properly be equated with abstraction.

There is still some question as to which artist first consciously created a totally abstract painting or sculpture. The Russian expressionist Vasily Kandinsky may have been the first abstract painter who realized the implications of his nonrepresentational, expressionist works. In a watercolor dated 1910 he eliminated all recognizable subject.

The term "abstract," understood as something abstracted from nature, has always been a matter of controversy, perhaps because of the implication that to "abstract" something is to lessen or demean it. Nevertheless, while literature and the visual arts of painting and sculpture have been conceived throughout history as imitative arts, music and architecture have always been recognized as abstract arts. It may be for this reason that Kandinsky and other early abstractionists continually offered musical analogies for their abstract paintings. Various efforts were made to find a more satisfactory name for the waves of nonimitative paintings and sculptures that the 20th century has produced. The terms "concrete" and "nonobjective" have been used, but no really satisfactory substitute has been found.

Perhaps because of the predominance of cubism in France between 1910 and 1920, pure abstraction developed primarily in other European countries, notably Holland and Russia, as well as in Germany. It is conceivable that the almost total absence of experiment in Russian art before 1910 made certain Russian artists, aware of experiments in France and other countries, feel that their only path to a new art was the most violent revolution against the dominant academic past. Only a few artists were involved—among the painters, Mikhail Larionov, Natalia Goncharova, Kasimir Malevich, El Lissitzky, and, of course, Kandinsky; among the sculptors, Vladimir Tatlin, Alexander Rodchenko, Naum Gabo,* and his brother, Anton Pevsner—but their influence was crucial for all subsequent 20th-century art. More than any other individual, Malevich first took cubist geometry to its logical conclusion of absolute geometric abstraction. In 1913 he exhibited a picture consisting merely of a black square on a white field, the first example of the style to which he gave the name "suprematism." In this work he felt that he had finally freed art from the burden of subject matter.

In sculpture the exploration of abstraction led to the new formal and technical concept of constructivism* in which, for the first time, sculpture, rather than being carved from masses of stone or modeled in clay, was constructed of elements of wood, metal, glass, or plastic. Picasso created a cubist construction in 1912 and the Russians Tatlin, Rodchenko, Pevsner, and, above all, Gabo, created constructions in which all residues of subject were eliminated.

In Holland during the first world war there emerged a parallel movement in abstraction led by Piet Mondrian and Theo van Doesburg to which the name "neoplasticism" was attached. The forms of abstract painting and constructed sculpture rapidly affected the design of modern architecture, and by 1920 abstract art had become one of the great, established new directions in the visual arts. Since that time abstraction has taken many different forms, from the geometric tradition of Mondrian and Malevich to the organic or expressionist traditions of Kandinsky and the sculptor Jean Arp. The concept of motion has been added to abstract constructions, particularly in the mobiles of the American Alexander Calder,* and entire schools using mechanized motion, light, and optical illusion have emerged during the last thirty years. During the 1940s and 1950s abstract expressionism* was the predominant new movement in American painting, and during the 1960s and early 1970s abstract color painting and constructed sculpture assumed new forms and a monumental scale never before achieved.

Thus, abstract art, a vocabulary created by visual artists during the early 20th century, continues to play a major role in the art of our own time.

(H.H.A.)

Abstract Expressionism.

The dominant movement in experimental American painting during the 1940s and 1950s and doubtless the most significant independent direction in the history of American painting. The term was first used in 1919 to describe certain paintings by the Russian expressionist painter Vasily Kandinsky and was used in the same context by Alfred Barr, critic and museum director, in 1929. The critic Robert Coates applied the term to a number of younger American painters in 1946, particularly to Willem de Kooning,* Jackson Pollock,* and their followers. The critic Harold Rosenberg coined the phrase "action painting" to describe the same tendencies, and the more neutral term "New York School" has also been used for the ferment among American painters during the 1940s and 1950s. Although none of these terms is particularly satisfactory, "abstract expressionism" is the most generally accepted.

There is still some obscurity and controversy concerning its origins. These origins in a sense encompass the whole expressive wing of modern art, from van Gogh and Gauguin through the fauves,* German expressionists, dadaists, futurists, and surrealists. Impressionism* played an important part. Also involved is the entire history of the acceptance of modern expressionistic and abstract art in the United States. This had begun even before World War I with the Armory Show* of 1913 and through contact with European movements by a few pioneers such as Max Weber,* Marsden Hartley,* John Marin,* and the synchromists. Before 1940, European experimental art was promoted in America by Alfred Stieglitz'* "291" gallery, Katherine Dreier's Société Anonyme, A. E. Gallatin's Gallery of Living Art, the Museum of Modern Art, the Solomon R. Guggenheim Museum, and a few other museums throughout the United States. The Museum of Modern Art's exhibitions during the 1930s of cubism* and abstract art and of dada* and surrealism* were of particular importance, as were the many Kandinskys in the Guggenheim Museum. During the 1920s and 1930s, the American precisionists attempted to combine European abstract structure with American realism. In 1935, the Whitney Museum held its first exhibition of American abstract art, and in 1936, the American Abstract Artists* group was organized.

Despite all these agencies, the progress of experiment in art in the United States was extremely slow. At the beginning of World War II, the dominant styles of painting were still social realism and regionalism (see American Scene Painting). Because America was at war, much emphasis was placed both by artists and art journals on art as war documentation. At the same time, the war created in 1942 in New York a ferment that actually made possible the victory of abstract and expressionistic art in America. The catalyst was the presence in New York of an extraordinary group of great European artists. Even before the war, Marcel Duchamp,* Laszlo Moholy-Nagy, Josef Albers,* and Hans Hofmann* had come to America. The war brought Piet Mondrian, sculptors Jacques Lipchitz* and Naum Gabo,* painters Marc Chagall, Max Ernst, Yves Tanguy, Salvador Dali, Matta, André Masson, and poet André Breton. It also brought Peggy Guggenheim* back from Europe to start in 1942, along with Howard Putzell, the

Abstract Expressionism

gallery Art of This Century. It became a meeting place for Europeans and younger American painters trying to find a new direction. Between 1943 and 1946, Art of This Century gave one-man shows to Jackson Pollock, Hans Hofmann, Robert Motherwell,* Mark Rothko,* Clyfford Still,* and William Baziotes.* During these years abstract expressionism was launched.

The relations of the new movement to surrealism—with its emphasis on automatism,* free association, and intuition—and particularly to the organic surrealism of Miró, Masson, and Matta —are obvious. However, in tracing its origins one must also look to Kandinsky, to the later style of Picasso, and to Soutine. American pioneers like Marin, Weber, Arthur Dove,* Mark Tobey,* and Arshile Gorky* in some sense anticipated where they did not directly influence the movement. Nevertheless, no artistic movement, and least of all abstract expressionism, can be understood simply as an accumulation of influences. In 1942, abstract expressionism was not even a movement, but between that time and its official recognition in the Museum of Modern Art's 1951 exhibition, "Abstract Painting and Sculpture in America," it developed, as noted above, into the most powerful original movement in the history of American art. During this period, the artists involved were conscious of their participation in an exciting, if loosely defined, development. A few critics, notably Clement Greenberg, championed the new movement; and a few dealers, such as Betty Parsons, Charles Egan, and Samuel Kootz, began to present the artists in their galleries. Recognition by major museums and by major art journals, which were heavily committed even after the war to social realism, art-as-documentation, Latin American art, and finally, reestablishment of contact with European art, came more slowly.

When the paintings done around 1950 by a number of the pioneer abstract expressionists are reexamined, their tremendous diversity is at once apparent. The surging labyrinth of what is now called a "classic period" drip painting by Jackson Pollock is entirely different from the slashing virtuosity of Willem de Kooning's brushstroke, even though both have the immediacy and participation in the act of painting embraced by the concept of action

1

2

3

5

4

Abstract Expressionism
1. *William de Kooning.* The Visit, *1967.*
   Knoedler Gallery, N.Y.
2. *Robert Motherwell.* Elegy to the
   Spanish Republic *XXXIV, 1954.*
   Albright-Knox Art Gallery, Buffalo,
   N.Y. (gift of Seymour H. Knox).
3. *Hans Hofmann.* The Conjurer, *1959.*
   Städt Galerie, Munich.
4. *Mark Rothko.* Number 10, *1950.*
   Museum of Modern Art, N.Y.
5. *Jackson Pollock.* Cathedral, *1947.*
   Dallas Museum of Fine Arts (gift of
   Mr. and Mrs. Bernard J. Reis).

painting. Franz Kline's* mature paintings are great black and white constructions combining an architectural structure with a large, rugged, but controlled brushstroke. The paintings of Robert Motherwell or Adolph Gottlieb* presented more isolated shapes or signs with a suggestion of symbolic content that might justify the term "image." In the same way, the great unified color shapes of Rothko or the vast color planes of Barnett Newman,* divided or joined by his characteristic vertical "line" (which is itself a color plane or shape), are certainly subject pictures in the overpowering impact of color and of expanding or contracting space.

The period between 1951 and 1961 was marked by the spread and enlargement of abstract expressionism throughout the United States and indeed throughout the world. Many of the original pioneers continued to grow as artists; some found a formula they continued to refine. In the late 1940s and early 1950s other established artists turned to abstract expressionism, and by now they are themselves considered pioneers. During the same period and on into the late 1950s many of these artists were sought after as teachers in art schools and university art departments throughout the country. Here their influence became enormous, and in the last few years their students have moved into the New York scene as still another generation of abstract expressionists.

Although abstract expressionism as a movement passed its peak by 1960, many of the major painters in it continue to work energetically and productively. Pollock, Kline, Rothko, William Baziotes, Bradley Walker Tomlin,* Barnett Newman, Ad Reinhardt* are all dead, most of them prematurely; but of the other pioneers, de Kooning, Motherwell, Philip Guston,* Gottlieb, Clyfford Still, James Brooks,* and Conrad Marca-Relli* constantly enlarge their image. Reinhardt, Newman, Rothko, and Motherwell have had a particular influence on the color-field* painting of the 1960s and 1970s. (H.H.A.)

Action Painting, see Abstract Expressionism.

Adams, Alice (1930–).
Weaver of free-hanging three-dimensional fiber constructions using a variety of materials and on- and off-the-loom techniques to achieve sculptural form. She was among the vanguard of weavers who took tapestry off the wall, gave it (with knots and ends showing) equal importance esthetically and visually with the image in front, and expanded this concept to outside-inside forms. Born in New York, N.Y., she studied painting at Columbia University, receiving a B.F.A. in 1953. Through a French government grant and a Fulbright Fellowship, she studied tapestry techniques at Aubusson, France. After her return to America she specialized in woven panels that included fibers and, occasionally, such elements as stained glass. Around 1960, her weaving became free-hanging and rounded or tubular, constructed of such innovative materials as aluminum and steel cables, link fencing, telephone wire, and plastic, gridlike modules. The dimensions of these pieces increased from six to twelve feet in length. (R.S.)

Adams, Ansel Easton (1902–).
Photographer. Born in San Francisco, Cal., he grew up in the then unpopulated Golden Gate area. Although he received his first camera, a box Brownie, when he was fourteen, his ambition was to become a pianist. By the time he was eighteen he was studying piano with Frederick Zech but also acting as custodian of the Sierra Club's conservation headquarters in Yellowstone Valley. In this summer job he developed many of his basic attitudes towards the natural environment. The friends he made among the members had a similar influence. With Cedric Wright in Yosemite during 1927 he made one of his best-known mountain photographs: *Monolith, the Face of Half-Dome.* This was also the year that Albert Bender helped him to publish *Parmelian Prints of the High Sierras,* the first and now rarest of Adams' portfolios. His next major project was with the writer on Indian life, Mary Austin, on what would become a beautifully printed book, *Taos Pueblo* (1930); it contained twelve reproductions from photographs of the architecture and residents of Taos.

After a meeting in 1930 with the photographer Paul Strand* in New Mexico, Adams decided to become a photographer instead of a pianist. In 1932 he became a founding member of the photographic group f64.* The following year he began a tour of the United States that culminated in a meeting

1

2

3

1. **Ansel Easton Adams.** Mount Williamson: Clearing Storm, *1944, photograph. George Eastman House, Rochester, N.Y.*
2. **Herbert Adams.** Adeline Valentine (Pond) Adams, *1888, marble. Hispanic Society of America, N.Y.*
3. **Aetatis Sue Limner.** Thomas Van Alstyne, *1721. New-York Historical Society, N.Y.*

with the photographer Alfred Stieglitz who gave him a one-man show at his New York gallery, An American Place, famous for its avant-garde exhibitions. In 1935 the publication of Adams' book *Making a Photograph* was the beginning of his immense influence on the technique and esthetics of American photography, and especially in making the unretouched, untoned "straight" photograph acceptable. Adams' Wagnerian visual approach—towering storm clouds, majestic rock formations, and woodland grottoes—to the natural environment has remained much the same for thirty years, a steadfastness that has made a tremendous impression on those who care for our environment. Technically, his detailed investigations into the use of large and small cameras have made his books the most useful and intelligent of photography manuals.

Adams has published over twenty other books and portfolios, including five portfolios of original photographs, and he has collaborated with numerous authors, most notably Nancy Newhall, who wrote the text for *Death Valley* (1954), *Mission San Xavier del Bac* (1954), and *This is the American Earth* (1960).   (T.F.B.)

Adams, Herbert (1858–1945).
Sculptor. He spent his youth in New England and attended the Massachusetts Normal Art School. In 1885 he went to Paris, where he studied at the École des Beaux-Arts. There he learned the lively new Parisian manner of modeling, so different from the smooth, carefully controlled modeling of neoclassicism* that earlier generations of American sculptors had learned in Italy. Because of this influence, his works display a greater spontaneity and a richer surface effect than do those of Horatio Greenough* or Hiram Powers.* In this, Adams was following Augustus Saint-Gaudens,* who had introduced the Parisian style to American sculpture in the 1870s. The new style is evident in the bust of *Adeline Valentine Adams* (1888, Hispanic Society of America, New York); the model was to become his wife and also a noted art critic. The delicate, almost effeminate quality of that bust is found again in his *Primavera* (1893, Corcoran) and his *Saint Agnes,* and late in his career in his "Debutante" series. An innovation was the light polychroming on some of his marble busts, as in his *La Jeunesse* (1893,

Metropolitan). The influence of Saint-Gaudens and of 15th-century Italian Renaissance relief sculpture is evident in *Singing Boys* (1894, Metropolitan). Adams participated in the sculptural work on the Dewey Arch in New York (1898) by producing the *Winged Victory,* and he was represented at the Pan-American Exposition at Buffalo in 1901 by an allegorical group, *The Age of Enlightenment.* Both of these works were executed in staff material (plaster and straw) and disintegrated soon after outdoor exposure. Adams also did several important portrait statues, among them *William Ellery Channing* (1902) for Boston, *Professor Joseph Henry* (1911) for the Library of Congress, and *William Cullen Bryant* (1911) for Bryant Park, behind the New York Public Library. Also among his better known works are the bronze doors (c. 1901–02) of St. Bartholomew's Church in New York City. Between about 1890 and 1920 he was one of the leaders in American sculpture: but as a thoroughly academic artist he resisted the abstract art introduced into America after 1913.
                    (W.C.)

Adler, Dankmar (1844–1900), see Louis Henri Sullivan.

Aetatis Sue Limner (active c. 1715–24). The first and most prolific of the anonymous portrait painters working in the upper Hudson River area in the early 18th century is identified by the words "Aetatis Sue" in many of the portrait inscriptions. In addition to such inscribed paintings from both New York and Virginia, a considerable number of uninscribed works from the same areas and Newport have been ascribed to him stylistically so that his known oeuvre is put at over sixty portraits, among them *Mr. Thomas Van Alstyne* (1721, New York Hist.). These include portraits of leading merchants and farm owners in which the technique involves layers of paint sometimes overlaid with transparent glazes. Portraits of less influential sitters are characterized by a much more direct painting method in which the ground layer appears as part of the finished picture surface. Although this technical variation and the broad geographic distribution of his works have suggested the hands of as many as nine artists, the inscriptions, stylistic kinship, and recurrent detail speak strongly for a single source.   (M.J.G.)

7

2

3

1

1. *Peter Agostini.* Baby Doll and Big
   Daddy, *1967, plaster.*
2. & 3. *Josef Albers. Two paintings from
   the* Homage to the Square *series.
   Metropolitan Museum of Art, N.Y.*

Agostini, Peter (1913–   ).
Sculptor, best known for his plaster-casting technique in which he was able to encompass the humor and intentions of surrealism* while still working in an abstract mode. He was born in New York, N.Y., and studied sculpture at the Leonardo da Vinci School. He learned the traditional sculptural skills there, which he later turned to advantage when he undertook his parodic castings of objects during the late 1950s. His exhibitions in New York from 1959 on frequently included what he called "frozen" life: such things as a clothesline hung with trousers frozen in plaster, or a still life of tin cans cast most delicately. During the 1960s, Agostini frequently used enormous inner-tube castings to produce full-blown, pneumatic visions of clustered forms. At times these sculptures verged on the grotesque. He was also capable of lighter humor, as in a suggestive carousel piece. Agostini has been exhibited in numerous group shows both here and abroad, and in 1964 he was awarded the Brandeis Creative Arts Award. In the same year, he was commissioned to make a piece for the New York World's Fair.   (D.A.)

Albers, Anni (1899–   ).
Weaver using loomed construction with emphasis on thread as a linear element. She was born in Berlin, Germany, and studied at the famous design institute, the Bauhaus* (1922–30), where she developed a reduction of elements suited to a machine esthetic, although she continued to make experimental weavings on the hand loom. She and her husband, the painter Josef Albers,* have been the most influential proponents of the rectilinear heritage, especially in America, where both have taught and lectured extensively. Characterizing the severe beauty of her works is *Tikal,* a pictorial weaving of cotton in plain and leno weaves, 35½ by 29½ inches (Johnson Coll.). Its closely related blues, yellows, and greens are arranged in vertical and horizontal rectangular modules. She is the author of *Anni Albers: On Designing* (1959 and 1962–66) and of *Anni Albers: On Weaving* (1965). In 1961 she was awarded a gold medal from the American Institute of Architects.   (R.S.)

Albers, Josef (1888–   ).
Painter. Albers was one of the original teachers in the German Bauhaus,* which revolutionized art training by combining the teaching of fine arts with the study of crafts, and emphasizing functionalism. He has achieved most of his worldwide reputation since emigrating to America in 1933. Born in Bottrop, Germany, he studied at the Royal Art School, Berlin, 1913–15; the School of Applied Art, Essen, 1916–19; Academy of Fine Arts, Munich, 1919–20; and the Bauhaus, Weimar, 1920–23. Entering the Weimar Bauhaus as a student, he, along with the geometric painter Laszlo Moholy-Nagy (1895–1946), took over teaching the foundation course. Albers was an instructor at the Bauhaus in Weimar, Dessau, and Berlin from 1923 until it was closed by the Nazis in 1933. He also taught furniture design, drawing, and calligraphy. In the United States he taught at Black Mountain College in North Carolina, 1933–49, and had his first New York one-man show in 1949. He was chairman of the Department of Design at Yale University from 1950 to 1960.

The basic course at the Bauhaus dealt largely with formal pictorial problems of space, light, color and their interactions both in the art of the past and the abstract arts of the 20th century. Through his research for this course, and his early apprenticeship in a stained-glass workshop, Albers developed his lifelong interest in problems of light and color set within geometric frames. In his glass paintings of the 1920s one can observe the transition from free-form composition of glass fragments to a rigid, rectangular pattern in which the relationships of each color strip to all the others are meticulously calculated. The transparency of glass also led him to investigate perspective illusion in which geometric shapes reverse themselves. The approach can be summarized in a painting first created in glass in 1931 and then recreated in tempera about 1935: it consisted of a black ground with straight white lines enclosing areas of white and of light and dark gray. Typical of his studies in black and white is the lithograph *Ascension* (1942, Modern Museum). In François Bucher's book on Albers' graphic constructions, *Despite Straight Lines* (1961), Albers describes precisely the many mutations of surface and the vertical and in-depth visual movement stimulated by these figures. These exercises in optics and perception were rooted in cubist concepts of simultaneity and fragmentation of vision, as well as in explorations of non-perspective pictorial space by the European geometric abstractionists Theo Van Doesburg, Piet Mondrian, and Kasimir Malevitch. A major influence in the training of American artists, architects, and designers, he is also an important theoretician on basic aspects of contemporary abstract art. Like Mondrian and Malevitch, he has sought to reduce the elements of geometric abstract painting to essences that state the elements and fundamental problems of nonobjective art. In this search he has, since the 1950s, settled on a formula that he has entitled "Homage to the Square," in which he has explored endlessly the relationships of color squares within squares, as in *Homage to the Square: Apparition* (1959, Guggenheim). By juxtaposing different hues generally of the same close values and intensities within his radiating squares, he demonstrates again and again how through association colors are modified in the spectator's eye.

His scientific theories and rational approach in both teaching and writing have almost obscured the fact that in his studies Albers has created works of art important not only for their influence on geometric abstractionists and optical painters, but also for their beauty and value in themselves. The importance of his experiments lies in his statement in the clearest terms of the problem—"How do we see the third dimension when created as an illusion by the artist in terms of lines, flat shapes, and colors on the two-dimensional surface?" Like Mondrian, he is one of the founders of that entire direction in modern painting concerned with geometric abstraction, color-field, and the ramifications of optical art. In the latter area, his influence has extended not only to painting but also to many of the color and illusionistic experiments of sculptural constructivism.*   (H.H.A.)

Albright, Ivan Le Lorraine (1897–   ).
Painter. Born in Chicago, Ill., he is the son of a painter who had studied under Thomas Eakins.* Albright studied at Northwestern University and at the University of Illinois. During World War I he served as a medical illustrator in an army hospital, an experience which doubtless influenced his later style. After the war he enrolled in the Museum School of the Art Institute of Chicago and, upon graduation, attended the Pennsylvania Academy of the Fine Arts and the National

Academy of Design in New York City.

In 1927, Albright established himself in Warrenville, Ill., near Chicago, where he still lives. Financially independent, he has been able to work very slowly, producing relatively few pictures. His early works were rugged portraits of local characters in harsh light, with somber earth tones and faded blues. Gradually his flesh areas, which he had described as "corrugated mush," took on a varicose, putrescent quality; his color became more garish and his contrasts of light and shade more violent. He also began to use long, poetic titles, such as *Heavy the Coat for Him Who is Weary, Heavy the Oar, Heavy the Sea.* In the 1930s he did a series of still lifes wherein the objects, studied with Flemish meticulousness, seem to be in turmoil in a bath of lurid light. In 1943 he went to Hollywood to paint the final, utterly corrupted picture of Dorian Gray for the motion picture based on Oscar Wilde's story.

Albright is a moralist in paint, and he has used his merciless artist's scalpel on himself in at least two remarkable self-portraits. His work is a continuous *memento mori,* whether or not it is based on the traditional subject matter of that theme. Typical of this treatment is *That Which I Should Have Done I Did Not Do,* (1941, Chicago), in which a hand places a funeral wreath on a battered old door. (A.F.)

Alexander, Cosmos (c.1724–c.72). Scottish portrait painter who toured the American colonies, 1766–71. He brought with him a first reflection of the new style of the English portrait painter Sir Joshua Reynolds, marked by informality of pose, delicacy of color, and greater emphasis on character, at a time when American artists were still painting in the more stately and stilted conventions. In Newport, R.I., he took the fourteen-year-old Gilbert Stuart* into his home as pupil and assistant. Master of a sophisticated if not highly sensitive style, he had a formative influence on Stuart, whom he later brought back with him to Edinburgh.

Alexander, Francis (1800–80). Painter of portraits, genre, and still life. He grew up in poverty on a Connecticut farm and was past twenty when he decided on a career in art. He studied briefly with Alexander Robertson at the Academy of Fine Arts in New York, and

1

3

2

1. *Ivan Le Lorraine Albright.* That Which I Should Have Done I Did Not Do, *1941. Art Institute of Chicago.*
2. *Ivan Le Lorraine Albright.* Fleeting Time Thou Hast Left Me Old, *1930. Metropolitan Museum of Art, N.Y. (George A. Hearn Fund).*
3. *Washington Allston.* Moonlit Landscape, *1819. Museum of Fine Arts, Boston (gift of Dr. W. S. Bigelow).*
4. *John White Alexander.* Isabella; or The Pot of Basil, *1897. Museum of Fine Arts, Boston (gift of Ernest Wadsworth Longfellow).*

4

was encouraged by John Trumbull,* who gave him a letter to Gilbert Stuart* in Boston. Stuart, too, was encouraging, recognizing in the young man's work a ready insight into human character and a talent for portraying it. Alexander opened a studio in Boston at about the time of Stuart's death; in Boston he learned from Washington Allston's* example a richer tonality in portraiture. For twenty-five years he was one of the city's most successful painters. In 1853 he settled with his family in Florence, Italy, where he spent the remainder of his life. The subtlety and charm of his portraiture is superbly expressed in his *Prudence Crandall* (Cornell University), a revealing study of the courageous Quaker schoolteacher of Connecticut. (C.C.S.)

Alexander, John White (1856–1915). Portrait and mural painter. Born in Allegheny, Pa., he showed early talent and at eighteen became a periodical illustrator for *Harper's Weekly.* He saved enough to go to Germany to study, entering the circle of Walter Shirlaw* and Frank Duveneck.* Proceeding to Venice, he met and was influenced by James Whistler.* To support his travels, he continued to send drawings to *Harper's.* He returned to America to work as an illustrator but then went to Paris in 1890 and remained eleven years as a successful portrait painter. During his subsequent career in the United States he was acclaimed as a painter of portraits and of murals (the Carnegie Institute, Pittsburgh, and the Library of Congress, Washington). He was a member of some twenty art societies, the recipient of virtually every art award, Knight of the French Legion of Honor, and president of the National Academy. His portraits were in great demand, and among his many sitters were leading actors, sculptors, and authors, including Mark Twain, Thomas Hardy, and Walt Whitman. His portraits and figures were characterized by brilliant improvisation and emphasized flowing lines and broad patterns, reflecting the decorative tendencies of the art noveau.* (D.W.S.)

Allston, Washington (1779–1843). Painter. Born in Georgetown County, S.C., he decided at an early age to become an artist and took no interest in the careers considered suitable for a gentleman. His family sent him to New-

port, R.I., in the hope that northern sea air would invigorate him and end his passion for painting. Instead, he haunted the Newport shop of portrait painter Samuel King, and became a friend of young Edward Greene Malbone,* who was to become America's greatest miniaturist. After graduating from Harvard in 1800, he went to London and entered the Royal Academy as a pupil of Benjamin West.* A graceful, high-spirited young man, poetry stirred him deeply and he was stimulated by the Gothic novel—two art forms to which he would later make his own contributions. He was an incarnation of that spirit of romanticism that would dominate the art life of his time.

After three years with West, he went to Paris, joining his colleague, John Vanderlyn.* He studied at the Louvre, then moved to Italy. In Rome he met Washington Irving and Samuel Taylor Coleridge, whom in some ways he much resembled as a romantic figure. His years in Italy were productive and happy; his work was highly dramatic, recalling the landscapes of Poussin with romanticized ruins and stormy skies. When he sailed for England, in 1811, he had with him a pupil of his own, Samuel F. B. Morse.* Illness, followed by the death of his wife, brought on a lingering mood of depression, yet these years in England marked the height of his productivity. Much of his work was a brilliant continuation of that of West, whom he might have succeeded as president of the Royal Academy had not his patrimony become exhausted in 1818. He returned to Boston, where ten friends contributed $1000 each to enable him to complete his large and already widely acclaimed painting, *Belshazzar's Feast* (begun 1817, Detroit). This was not an act of charity. The contributors had the example of the financial success of Rembrandt Peale's* similar *Court of Death* (1820), then on tour at an admission charge. But Allston's picture became a crushing burden on his conscience as he sought to repaint, in a style that would please his backers, a work conceived in the old grand manner of West. This romantic and colorful style had become alien to Allston, and he struggled in the inhospitable climate of Cambridge to recapture the poetry of his Italian period. His work lost much of its grandeur and romantic flavor. At his death, *Belshazzar's Feast* was still unfinished. It had a strong, dramatic quality, but Allston was at his greatest in a more softly poetic vein, such as *The Spanish Girl* (1831, Metropolitan) or *The Flight of Florimell* (1819, Detroit), one based on a poem of his own, the other on Spenser's *Faerie Queen*. As his biographer, Edgar P. Richardson, has pointed out, Allston was "the first American painter whose art was an exploration of the visions within his own mind." He was a painter who had been able to see the great masters of Venice in terms of the music of color and form and of emotional excitements; from these sources came such wholly original, haunting, and deeply personal works as his *Elijah Fed by the Ravens* (1818), and *Moonlit Landscape* (1819; both at Boston).

Allston's importance in the art world of Boston was considerable. He not only influenced many young painters, but he guided sculptors Horatio Greenough* and Thomas Crawford.* His career appeared to the young artists of his time to sum up the dilemma of the painter in America, and many of them thereafter chose to live as expatriates in Rome or Paris. (C.C.S.)

Amelung, Johann Friedrich (1741–98). Glass manufacturer of German origin. Arriving in America in 1784 with his family and sixty-eight glass workers, Amelung founded the settlement of New Bremen, Md., and set up his "Glassmanufactory." He was unique among 18th-century American glass manufacturers in that he had previous glass-making experience. His furnace was in operation by early 1785; he built a second, larger one before 1790 and continued glass manufacture until approximately 1795.

According to contemporary advertisements, Amelung's production included window glass and bottles of all types, optical glasses, and drinking glasses with cut "Devices, Cyphers and Coats of Arms." Excavation on the site of the glass works has shown that he probably also produced simple blown and pattern-molded glasses* repeating continental designs. Approximately thirty elaborately engraved presentation pieces, signed and/or dated, can now be attributed to him. For example, the *Bremen Pokal* (Metropolitan), probably made for Amelung's financial backers in Bremen, Germany, is engraved "New Bremen Glassmanufactory/ 1788/North America State of Mary-

land" and "Old Bremen Success and the New Progress." The shape of this goblet and that of another major piece, a large covered tumbler made in 1788 as an anniversary present for his wife (Corning), typify his "luxury production." The simple but massive proportions and the high-domed feet of the goblets follow forms made in German provincial factories earlier in the 18th century. The metal of Amelung's glass is usually colorless with a slight smoky tinge, and most of the pieces so far tested are of nonlead glass. Although colored fragments were excavated on the factory site, only two engraved colored pieces are known.

Initially financed by German merchants, Amelung was encouraged by such Americans as Franklin, Adams, and Jefferson in the hope that he could wean Americans away from their dependence on imported glassware. But Congress would not vote high tariffs on imported glassware, and he found it difficult to compete with English and German manufacturers. A fire partially destroyed his factory in 1790, and by 1795 he was advertising his establishment for sale. Despite his brief period of operation, Amelung was the first American to make fine engraved wares; and his production was far more sophisticated than that of his American predecessors, Caspar Wistar* and Henry W. Stiegel.* His presentation pieces stand unequaled in the history of American glass before 1820. (J.S.S.)

American Abstract Artists.
A group organized in 1936 following the Whitney Museum's first exhibition of American abstract art* in 1935. Throughout the late 1930s and early 1940s the group held annual exhibitions dedicated to the promotion of every form of abstraction, with particular emphasis on the geometric abstraction that was then the prevailing style in the Paris art world. Among the artists originally in the group were Ilya Bolotowsky,* Karl Knaths,* Ad Reinhardt,* Balcomb Greene,* and George McNeil.* By 1939 many other artists had become members, including Josef Albers,* Fritz Glarner,* Burgoyne Diller,* Irene Rice Pereira,* Jackson Pollock,* William de Kooning,* and David Smith.* In 1940 members of the American Abstract Artists group picketed the Museum of Modern Art, demanding that it show American art.

American Artists, The Society of.
Established in 1877 to provide a more liberal exhibition policy than that of the National Academy of Design.* The Academy, jealous and somewhat suspicious of the numerous young artists who were returning from Munich and Paris and threatened to dominate the Academy exhibition that year, determined to reserve prime space for its own members. Walter Shirlaw,* Wyatt Eaton,* and Homer Saint-Gaudens were among those who decided to found a more democratic society based exclusively on merit and committed to giving equal showing to all work that passed the jury. The first exhibition was held in 1878, with twenty-two members. John La Farge* was elected president and some of the more liberal painters of the older generation— George Fuller,* Eastman Johnson,* George Inness,* Alexander Wyant,* and Elihu Vedder*—joined with the younger men, who included Albert Ryder,* Frank Duveneck,* Abbott Thayer,* William Chase,* Theodore Robinson,* John Twachtman,* and J. Alden Weir.* The Society grew rapidly, reaching a membership of about a hundred by 1890, but found difficulty in achieving the prestige of the Academy, which it tended to supplement rather than rival. In 1892 it acquired a permanent home on New York's 57th Street together with the Art Students League* and the Architectural League. The addition of William Merritt Chase,* a leader of the artists dissatisfied with the National Academy, to the faculty of the Art Students League strengthened the dissidents. Its viewpoint, however, was becoming progressively more conservative, and in 1898, The Ten* seceded from it to stage their own exhibitions. Finally, the membership of the Society and Academy became so interlocking that in 1906 the Society, while holding its thirtieth exhibition, merged quietly into the older institution. (D.W.S.)

American Art-Union.
An organization which successfully provided for the distribution of original paintings to the public by lottery beginning in 1839. The Art-Union was founded in 1844, succeeding the Apollo Association and was dissolved in 1852 when the courts declared it illegal. In its heyday, it played an important role in patronizing living American

painters both famous and unknown, creating demand for original art, and shaping American taste. In 1849, for example, the Art-Union had nearly nineteen thousand subscribers, who for their five dollars received an original steel engraving and a chance to win one of the 460 works distributed that year. It helped to popularize American paintings, in particular genre pieces and landscapes. Among the pictures distributed to the membership were prints after *The Jolly Flatboatmen* by George Caleb Bingham* and *Voyage of Life—Youth* by Thomas Cole.* The Art-Union was based upon similar European organizations, and its success led in turn to a number of smaller American art unions. (T.E.S.)

American Scene Painting (also called Regionalism).

An ill-defined term most often used for artists of the early 20th century, many of whom rejected current modes of lyricism and abstraction to paint the urban and rural America of their time. In the days of Thomas Cole,* the American wilderness was regarded as a special American cultural asset, quite distinct from if not superior to the long-inhabited, carefully barbered landscape of Europe. Cole and his era regarded this American wilderness with awe, frequently with religious sentiment; wilderness was a sign of the hand of God. This sense of awe and wonder carried over into the American Scene Painting of the 1920s, especially that dealing with Manhattan Island. Brooklyn Bridge took the place of Niagara Falls as a symbol of wonder; the Woolworth Building succeeded Pike's Peak. The leaders of what might be called the Brooklyn Bridge school were Joseph Stella* and John Marin,* both of whom painted the bridge innumerable times, both of them in styles beholden to cubism.* Interpretation of the big city on canvas is, in fact, a special branch of American cubism, and even expatriate Americans like Lyonel Feininger* give it strong expression. Charles Demuth* and Max Weber* are other early exponents of this theme. In the 1930s the leader of the movement was Charles Sheeler,* who brought it a unique emphasis upon photographic exactitude (he was, in fact, an outstanding photographer) blended with cubist abstraction and great delight in gigantic machines, grain elevators, smoke stacks, and

other heroic manifestations of American industry. Painters like Niles Spencer* and Ralston Crawford* might be bracketed very roughly with Sheeler, although each has his own personal approach, his own themes, and his own palette. With them all, however, America is seen in her "proud and soaring" aspects, to paraphrase the pioneer modern architect Louis Sullivan.*

Meanwhile a very different trend was at work in the 1930s, especially in the paintings of Edward Hopper* and Charles Burchfield.* Here the emphasis is upon an old America, full of ancient, crowded loft buildings like those still numerous in lower Manhattan, of unpainted frame shacks in industrial towns, rusty railroad tracks, and so on. Although Hopper painted Manhattan at the same time as Marin and Sheeler, one would never gather from his work that a single skyscraper existed there; nevertheless his work, like theirs, is deeply beholden to cubism in its exploitation of rectilinear forms. Unlike any of the other painters mentioned above, Hopper stresses the human figure in urban surroundings, almost always with much emphasis on loneliness and isolation in the midst of the crowded city.

The urban world of Burchfield is that of Buffalo and its environs; it is less a world of oppressive old masonry and more a world of oppressive old Victorian gimcrackery; often a high degree of fantasy, lyricism, and the macabre characterize his handling of both city and rural subjects.

Regionalism, contemporary with American Scene Painting in the 20th-century sense of the term, may be regarded as its midwestern branch. It is associated very largely with the work of Grant Wood,* John Steuart Curry,* and Thomas H. Benton.* Benton had begun his career in Paris as a disciple of abstract synchromism* but after his return to America he reacted violently against abstract art and became enormously interested in the pictorial representation of western history. All three of these midwesterners did a great deal of mural painting on local themes, Benton at the State Capitol in Jefferson City, Mo., Curry at the Kansas Capitol in Topeka, Wood in various schools and public buildings.

Benton's style, for all the midwesternism and anti-Europeanism of his public statements, goes back to the

1

2

American Scene Painting
1. *Charles Sheeler.* Upper Deck, *1929. Fogg Museum of Art, Harvard University, Cambridge, Mass.*
2. *Charles Burchfield.* Ice Glare, *1933. Whitney Museum of American Art, N.Y.*

1

2

tormented, elongated mannerism of El Greco; Wood was indebted in equal parts to the precisionism of Jan van Eyck and the stylization of the Chinese willow plate pattern. There is a large element of satire in both Wood and Benton, and some of Wood's paintings, like *Daughters of Revolution* (Cincinnati), aroused resentment among patriotic societies.

A southwestern regionalism, centered in New Mexico and associated with the work of Andrew Dasburg* and Ernest Blumenschein, dealt with the landscape and the Indian life of that area. Regionalism of lesser celebrity has flourished in the Deep South, in California, in Hawaii, and in New England; indeed, any consistent or persistent painting of any local landscape is essentially regionalism. In this sense, there is much regionalism in the work of such contemporary painters as Andrew Wyeth,* with his Pennsylvania farm scenes, and Richard Estes, with his paintings of New York City store fronts.   (A.F.)

Ames, Ezra (1768–1836).
Self-taught portrait painter. A native of Framingham, Mass., he worked as a carriage painter, miniaturist, engraver, and decorator, first in Worcester, Mass. (1790–93) and later in Albany, N.Y., where he continued a long and successful career. Portraits on canvas and ivory, hair work in the gold cases of the miniatures, signs, and other odd jobs, were all combined with banking interests and a prominent place in the Masonic fraternity. His portrait of the vice-president, *George Clinton* (1812, New York Hist.), is a fine example of his solid, vigorously realistic work. His paintings of the governors, legislators, and aristocracy of New York State numbered over 450 and were faithful records of the important figures of Albany in the early 19th century.

Anderson, Alexander (1775–1870).
Founder of the art and industry of wood engraving in the United States. As a boy, Anderson taught himself drawing and copperplate engraving. Trained as a doctor, at his father's request, he also continued to engrave and found a ready market for his work. He greatly admired the tiny, cameo-like wood engravings that the English wood engraver and illustrator Thomas Bewick was making, and was responsible for

making Bewick's style prevail in American wood engraving for more than a generation. Working on the surface of the wood block, he used Bewick's "white line" technique, allowing the incisions or lines cut on the block to define his design. He thus departed radically from the traditional woodcutter's technique of leaving a design by cutting away the wood around its edges. After the loss of his wife and son in a yellow fever epidemic in New York City in 1798, Anderson gave up the practice of medicine and devoted his life to wood engraving. He made approximately six thousand engravings and was active as late as 1868. While he did some original work, most of his engravings were after the work of other artists. He copied several sets of Bewick's designs, including three-hundred wood engravings for the first American edition of Bewick's *General History of Quadrupeds* (1804). His tiny vignettes for almanacs, tracts, and books have charm; some of them interest historians today for their flavor of American life in the time of horse-drawn plows and of sowing and reaping by hand.   (S.H.)

André, Carl (1935–   ).
Sculptor. Born in Quincy, Mass., he attended Phillips Andover Academy, N.H., studying with Patrick Morgan and forming a close friendship with the painter Frank Stella* and the photographer/filmmaker Hollis Frampton. By the late 1950s he was living in New York City, writing poetry and making drawings and small sculptures. His earliest objects were small pieces of wood that he either charred or wire-brushed. Later, under the influence of the Romanian abstract sculptor Brancusi, he began cutting directly into building timbers (1959). Shortly after, he turned to the radial arm saw to create a series of mechanically notched and stacked wooden objects. Among these were the great "Pyramids"— which foreshadow his later assemblages of modular units. From 1960–64 André worked for the Pennsylvania Railroad, although he continued to produce poems—now composed of words grouped in various shapes on the page. His sculpture of this period ranged from found objects to assemblages* of tiny rolled steel modules to form "I's", "T's", and "L's", to collage-paintings, incorporating old gloves,

3

4

American Scene Painting
1. *Edward Hopper.* Manhattan Bridge Loop, *1928. Addison Gallery of American Art, Phillips Academy, Andover, Mass.*
2. *Thomas Hart Benton.* Mural No. 2— Arts of the West, *1932, New Britain Museum of American Art, Conn.*
3. **Ezra Ames.** George Clinton, *1812. New-York Historical Society, N.Y.*
4. **Carl André.** *Installation view of* Scatter Piece *at the Dwan Gallery, N.Y., 1966, plastic.*

umbrellas, and a whole lettuce, all covered with glossy enamel, and to vulgar slices and piles of concrete. In 1964 he was asked to reconstruct a "Pyramid" for an exhibition held at the Hudson River Museum; after this, André's work received considerable acclaim. One of the features of this work was that it became sculpture only when assembled by the artist; after the exhibition it might be taken apart and used as ordinary beams.

In 1965 André had his first one-man show in New York; it consisted of simple, monumental constructions of stacked styrofoam planks. The following year he placed ordinary firebricks on the floor of the gallery, producing eight arrangements of 120 bricks each—an early manifestation of the avante-garde interest in mathematical combinations and permutations. Successive exhibitions presented squares of different metals formed into larger squares on the floor and meant to be walked on. André has continued to form his pieces out of standardized, interchangeable units, but he has also turned to the materials of nature, such as rocks, and to scrap. In 1967 he produced his first "Scatter Piece"—its form determined by the random spilling of small pieces of plastic. Originally considered a minimal artist, in recent years André has become involved in politics and concept art.* (E.C.G.)

Anshutz, Thomas (Pollock) (1851–1912).
Painter and teacher, born in Newport, Ky. He studied in 1873 at the National Academy and then the Pennsylvania Academy of the Fine Arts, and in Paris in 1892 with the French academic painter Bouguereau. Thomas Eakins* was the principal influence on both his painting and teaching, for Anshutz continued Eakins' serious approach to factual accuracy and his method of demonstrating anatomy by building clay muscles on a skeleton. Anshutz assisted Eakins at the Academy, then taught with him, and in 1886 succeeded him as director.

Anshutz' own figure paintings and portraits, though solidly constructed, lacked the strength and spirit of Eakins' work. In one memorable small canvas, *Steelworkers Noontime* (c.1882), Anshutz brought his concern for everyday scenes and anatomical structure sharply to bear on an objective rendering of a working-class subject, anticipating the social realism of his student John Sloan.* Anshutz is now remembered chiefly as a teacher. Many of his students became prominent artists, among them Robert Henri,* Everett Shinn,* John Marin,* and Charles Demuth.*
(D.W.S.)

Antonakos, Stephen (1926–   ).
Best known for his sculpture employing neon tubing. Born in southern Greece, Antonakos moved to New York City at an early age. He studied at Brooklyn Community College and later taught at the Brooklyn Museum School. His earliest works were paintings influenced by the cut, stitched and sewn canvases of the Italian artist Antonio Burri. His first one-man show, in New York in 1958, displayed large sewn collages,* which he called "sewlages." These were expanded to assemblages as he widened his range of materials to include wood scraps sewn, nailed, and wired to the canvas. As these grew larger, they became free-standing sculptures, often incorporating fragments of furniture, even whole chairs. In 1962–63 he made a series of pillows whose surfaces were covered with buttons or nails, or slit to reveal enigmatic "found objects." Some were covered with words: "Yes," "No," "Dream." These were exhibited at the Contemporary Arts Museum in Houston in 1971. Several of the pillow sculptures employed neon lighting, which has become his sole material since the mid-1960s. Beginning with a one-man show in New York City in 1965, he has arranged neon tubing to modify space. Parallel lines of neon will accentuate the meeting of floor and wall. Widely spaced lines will extend from wall to wall across an upper corner, or jut into space in a series of right angles. These works are usually timed to flash on and off in segments, thus modifying space in different ways throughout a cycle of illumination. Recently, Antonakos has placed X's or ovals in corners, exchanging flashing, animated form for calm, stable presences. (C.R.)

Anuszkiewicz, Richard (1930–   ).
Born in Erie, Pa., he studied at the Cleveland Institute of Art and Kent State University; then worked with Josef Albers* at Yale where he came in contact with such theories as "the interaction of color." By 1963 he was producing his own color experiments in paintings that bordered on the visual demonstrations of perceptual psychologists. Within two years such work would be subsumed under the banner of optical art.* Anuszkiewicz's paintings typically consist of a mosaic of color-circles (blue, green) placed against a background color (red) in such patterns as to achieve the maximum optical mixing. Mechanical (set) responses of eye and brain insure that the spectator will perceive the illusion of movement by means of alternating positive and negative patterns, with oscillating and sometimes painful vibrations of color, and an after-image when he finally turns away from the work. The public is usually fascinated by these hypnotic and dizzying effects, and Anuszkiewicz remains a master of such optical devices. (E.C.G.)

Apple, Billy (1935–   ).
Sculptor and multi-media experimentor. Born in Auckland, New Zealand, Apple studied at the Royal College of Art, London, in 1959–62. In 1960–62 he participated in numerous group shows in England under his given name, Barrie George Bates. One of his earliest works after he took his new name in 1962 was *Live Stills* (shown in London in 1963), a series of photographic self-portraits silkscreened on fabric. Coming to New York in 1964, he had his first American one-man show, *Neon Rainbows;* it contained his first experiments with neon tubing, which have continued through the present. Especially notable are his *U.F.O.'s* (Unidentified Fluorescent Objects), shown in New York in 1967. These use flexible neon tube which the viewer can reshape at will. In 1969 he exhibited a series, *Neon Floors,* at his own gallery in New York, which he opened to provide space for experimentation in environmental art. From 1969 on, he employed other technological media, including laser beams and video tape. He has expanded his interests from environments to activities in such works as *Sleeping, Window Cleaning,* and *Floor Painting* (all 1971). With the wide range and variety of his works, Apple is outstanding among artists who have expanded modern art beyond its traditional media. He employs activities and materials with a combination of wit, sophistication, and insight. (C.R.)

1

2

3

1. **Thomas Anshutz.** Steelworkers Noontime,
   c.1882. Collection Dr. and Mrs.
   Irving F. Burton, Michigan.
2. **Richard Anuszkiewicz.** Primary Contrast,
   1965. Sidney Janis Gallery, N.Y.
3. **Stephen Antonakos.** Walk On Neon,
   1968. Fischbach Gallery, N.Y.

Arbus, Diane (1923–71).

Photographer, born in New York, N.Y. she worked with her husband, a fashion photographer, for many years. In 1959 she studied with the documentary photographer Lisette Model at the Ethical Culture School. When she began working on her own, she photographed bizarre subjects with a poet's power of observation. She sought to compare, in metaphorical terms, what are considered to be unusual people with what we accept as normal people. With directness and compassion she photographed midgets and circus folk, nudists and transvestites, triplets and twins. She was an astonishingly objective observer but not a social critic. Her photographs were reproduced in *Esquire, Show, Harper's Bazaar, Infinity, Artforum,* and *Sunday Times Magazine* (London). She received Guggenheim Fellowships in 1963 and 1966. In 1967 twenty of her photographs were included in the Museum of Modern Art pioneering exhibition "New Documents." In 1972 a large selection of her work was exhibited in the American Pavilion at the Venice Biennial, and in a retrospective exhibition at the Museum of Modern Art.

(V.D.C.)

Architecture Since 1540.

When the first European colonists arrived in America the only structures they saw were the simple dwellings of the Indians—wigwams, tepees, dugouts, and pueblos. These shelters had no permanent influence on the development of American architecture. Construction in the colonies, whether in New England, the South, or the West, was influenced by the building styles and techniques of the countries of the colonists' origin. Because settlers were without money and craftsmen, they could not live elegantly. Thus, with very few exceptions, the design of their houses and public buildings derived from the ordinary structures of town and country with which they were familiar. While English lords lived in Elizabethan mansions ornamented in the latest Italianate styles, the artisans of England and America contented themselves with medieval town houses characterized by half-timbered construction, overhanging second stories, and leaded-glass windows, and with country cottages featuring clapboard-covered walls and steeply pitched, thatched roofs.

1. **Diane Arbus.** A young Brooklyn family going for a Sunday outing, N.Y.C., 1966, *photograph. Collection Doon Arbus.*

2. **Diane Arbus.** Lady bartender at home with a souvenir dog, New Orleans, 1964, *photograph. Collection Doon Arbus.*

Toward the end of the 17th century, some colonists became prosperous enough to build substantial houses and towns more in keeping with European standards of taste. This meant replacing the medieval with the classic Renaissance forms developed by Inigo Jones in England nearly a century earlier. The pilaster, the column, the entablature, and the balanced, axial, rectilinear proportions of classicism began to appear, although sometimes they were clumsily grafted onto buildings of an older style. Once tempted, the builders applied classical ornament to structures with increasing frequency, until the medieval style disappeared altogether. By the first quarter of the 18th century the rich merchant of New Bedford was no longer satisfied with a cramped medieval house; he wanted his residence to represent his station in life. As communication improved, it became easier to stay in touch with changing European fashions. But in spite of their affluence, the new mercantile class could not persuade professional architects to leave London or Paris and settle in colonial outposts. No architects came to America until the end of the 18th century, although there were some men of taste who designed many buildings of surprisingly high quality. These amateurs had little acquaintance with the fine architecture of Europe and depended upon English guidebooks which became readily available to Americans only after 1750.

In the 18th century the English Renaissance style dominated architecture along the east coast, but in areas where the Dutch, Swedes, and French played a major part in colonization, their styles of plans and decorations dominated. As the colonies became unified, the qualities distinguishing the architecture of each area gradually decreased. Able men like William Buckland* and Richard Taliaferro* in the South, Robert Smith* in Philadelphia, and Richard Munday* and Peter Harrison* in the North, emerged as a consequence of improving economic conditions and a desire for progress in the arts.

Changes brought about by colonial victory in the Revolutionary War were less drastic for architecture than politics. Nevertheless, a conviction existed that quality in architecture, as in the other arts, was essential to a country emerging from subservience and hoping to win confidence in itself. Public buildings constructed with durable materials by the federal government and later by state governments from the designs of professional architects soon lined the streets of major cities. In 1801, John Davis, an English traveler at the presidential inauguration, noted: "When I had heard the speech of Mr. Jefferson, there was nothing more to detain me among the scattered buildings of the desert." But after the War of 1812 new construction flourished, and Anthony Trollope could later declare "the beauty and majesty of the American capitol might defy an abler pen than mine to do it justice. . . . The magnificent western façade is approached from the city by terraces and steps of bolder proportions than I ever before saw."

While there were in America a few talented amateur architects such as Thomas Jefferson and Peter Harrison, and an increasing number of skilled builder-architects, it was not until the influx of European-trained architects that the profession of architecture was recognized. From 1785 to 1820 several architects came from France (Maximillian Godefroy, Stephen Hallet, Pierre Charles L'Enfant, Joseph Jacques Ramée) seeking political asylum, and others from England (George Hadfield, B. H. Latrobe, John Haviland), where business was slack. The amateurs and builders had relied mainly on building tradition and books for their designs, whereas the professionals were more imaginative, independent, and open to new solutions to the problems of living in America.

The critical moment in American architecture came about 1800 with a shift from provincial, generally vernacular construction to an international style spurred by the arrival of the professional architects. Before this, American architecture had been fifty to one hundred years behind the English style, but a Londoner arriving in Philadelphia after this time would find houses and public buildings designed in exactly the same style as at home, that is, in Greek revival. Though not as ambitious in size or as richly decorated, American buildings were as advanced as many in England in the use of classical ornament and in adapting ancient temple designs. Builders' guidebooks and sumptuous British volumes filled with measured drawings of Greek and Roman architecture remained the bibles of decoration. Classical styles more than two thousand years old were convincingly adapted in spanning railroad tracks with arches and in designing banks. But classical design was only the first of many styles revived before the Civil War. The Gothic style, so satisfactory in spirit for medieval cathedrals, was resurrected not only for religious use but also, less appropriately, for mansions, factories, kiosks, and prisons. Soon the Egyptian, Chinese, Islamic, so-called French mansard, and other styles were called into use. No standard of appropriateness to purpose existed, though there were leanings. For instance, the Gothic was frequently preferred for churches, the classic for public buildings, the Italian Villa and the French mansard, along with picturesque medieval cottage, for houses, but the boundaries were by no means definite.

Some underlying structural inventions were, in a way, of greater significance than the exterior style. The popular notion of 19th-century buildings being picturesque, quaint, grotesque, or lavish, does not take into account such important innovations as fireproofing by the use of iron and iron surrounded by masonry, and the strengthening of structure with iron members in place of wood. The industrial revolution made possible the introduction of inventions such as the balloon frame (quickly and cheaply mass produced), the elevator, ferro-concrete, and improved glassmaking. These aids to greater safety and permanence were vital to architectural development. By the time the American Institute of Architects was founded in 1857, architecture had gone through an amazing development. Americans had accepted the principle of architectural design as an art, admitted the need for a profession of architecture, and welcomed fundamental changes in materials and engineering. By banding together, the professionals in the Institute were able to define professional ethics, promote architectural education, establish materials and engineering standards, and publish their findings. These developments contributed enormously to gaining public confidence in the profession.

Colonial South (17th Century)
Settlers in the southern colonies (the areas that became Maryland, Virginia, North and South Carolina, and Georgia) were mostly people seeking to own

1

plantations or ready to work in communities dominated by aristocrats such as they had known in England. They were merchants, county squires, sons of peers, professional men, artisans, and indentured servants. Since this more or less homogeneous group was Royalist, Virginia soon became a crown colony with a royal governor. Unlike their sister colonies in New England, the southerners were faithful to the Church of England and believed that people, government, and church should form a single social unit working for the common good. Thus the architecture of the South has characteristics that link it directly with English building tradition and yet distinguish it from that of other colonies. The churches were like the English parish church, not the meeting house of New Englanders. Plantation houses along the tidewater rivers resembled, if on a smaller scale, the aristocratic country houses built of brick and stone by English peers.

In the first permanent settlement, at Jamestown, Va., in 1607, the colonists initially lived in tents, small cabins, and even dugouts. By 1615 there were two rows of two-story timber-framed houses, making thirty-four dwellings, all surrounded by a sturdy palisade for protection from Indians. Other early towns must have had the same rugged frontier character, with few amenities in the form of architectural decoration. However, as soon as the plantation owners were able, they began to build extraordinarily fine residences. The timber-framed house was the earliest substantial type of building, and the most common. No 17th-century example has survived in this warm, humid climate. Between the vertical and horizontal timbers of the frame a filler of clay mixed with straw or brick nogging was inserted. Over this basic wall, clapboards (weatherboards) were fastened horizontally. Small houses had a chimney (first of wood plastered with clay and later of brick) at one end while larger houses had one at each end. The simple gable roof, the most common, was covered with thatch and, later, wood shingles. The Orr House (c.1725, but following 17th-century models), restored at Williamsburg, Va., is framed and bracketed by brick chimneys and has an axial plan. Since wood was plentiful and easier and quicker to build with, one might ask why the southerners used so much brick. The most likely

reasons are the impermanence of wood in that climate and the greater distinction that brick imparts to masonry houses. The brick houses varied from simple one-room cottages to more complex two-story houses. Perhaps the most interesting was only a single room deep but had a cross plan formed by a projecting doorway entering a hallway that led directly to a similar rear projection containing a stairway. At the central point in the hallway, doors opened on one side into a parlor, and on the other into a general kitchen and living room. The Adam Thoroughgood House, Princess Anne County, Va., exemplifies the simpler type. Bacon's Castle, Surry County, Va., nearly conforms to the basic cross pattern. Balanced by a central doorway and leaded, diamond-shaped casement windows on either side, these houses were frontier folk or vernacular architecture at its best.

The South also imitated the home country in its religious architecture. The brick churches are no more than small English parish churches: a central tower over the entryway, a nave and chancel in one room, and both Gothic and early Renaissance decorative elements. For instance, St. Luke's Church (1632), Smithfield, Va., has a square tower ornamented with quoins (squared stones set at the angles of a building) that descend from Renaissance styling, but the pointed windows, wall buttresses, and basic plan and tower are Gothic.

Log cabins were introduced some time in the late 17th century; since none of these early wood structures survives, they are best represented by 18th-century examples.

Colonial New England

The first settlers of New England, the Pilgrims, reached Plymouth so late in 1620 that the only shelters they could contrive for the first winter were extremely crude. Having seen how easily the Indians erected their wigwams, the Pilgrims imitated them, putting up what are called English wigwams. The Indian wigwam was rectangular, with an entrance at one end and a roof of pliable poles bent to form an arch like a quonset hut. The English simply added a brick chimney at the end opposite to the door. By the end of 1621 there were seven houses, four storehouses, and a meeting house. These were all of timber-frame construction; none remains today. Other settlements were

Colonial South
1. Orr House, Williamsburg, Va., 1725.
Colonial New England
2. House of the Seven Gables, Salem, Mass., 1668.
3. Parson Capen House, Topsfield, Mass., 1683.

2

3

1

soon established at Salem, Mass., Weathersfield, Conn., and Providence, R.I.

Throughout these New England settlements, timber frame was by far the most common kind of construction. It derived from English medieval practices, even to decoration. Oak and pine were plentiful for frames, and brick was used for chimneys. The frame was secured by cutting off the ends of timbers to form elaborate joints; these were held by wooden pegs. The spaces between the framing were filled with a mixture of clay (daub) pressed into and over interwoven sticks and boughs (wattle), or with bricks set into a mixture of clay and straw (nogging). Roofs were either gable, as in the Capen House, or gambrel, as in the Fairbanks House. Originally many of the houses were thatched, but the thatch was gradually replaced by shingles of wood or slate. The exterior walls were covered with clapboards. A second-story overhang, as in the Capen House, had been a feature of houses in medieval towns, but in America it was often used in country houses. The casement windows had diamond-shaped panes set in lead. Other decoration included drop-like ornaments depending from the overhang, pilastered chimneys, and brackets—all of medieval derivation. The entrance was at the center of a symmetrical plan, and just in front of the stairs. On one side was the living-room, and on the other the hall for cooking and general use. As families required more space, they added a lean-to with a less steep roof at the rear.

The same frame construction was used for larger buildings such as meeting houses. The Boston Town House was framed like an English town hall of the Middle Ages. By 1640 there were twenty frame construction meeting houses in Massachusetts, primarily for worship. Less widely used was plank construction. Planks from two to three inches thick sawn from timber and fitted into grooves cut in the major framing beams or posts were placed vertically or horizontally. Spaces between the planks were filled with a mixture of clay and straw. As in the framed houses, clapboards covered the exterior, protecting the clay and adding insulation. No log cabins were built until the Swedes introduced them in the central colonies, where they settled in 1638. Only in the 18th century did log cabins become common elsewhere.

As the colonists began to expand their economy, more and more buildings were constructed of brick, since clay was available in many parts of New England and fuel for kilns was plentiful. Few buildings were erected with stone because it was generally too expensive to quarry and haul.

Colonial Dutch-Flemish

The Dutch and Flemish who came to America in the 17th century settled along the Hudson River Valley, on Long Island, and in northern New Jersey. The most important contingent, mainly farmers, established New Amsterdam inside a protective stockade on Manhattan Island in 1625. Thirty bark-covered houses and some dugouts were habitable by 1626 and a town church in 1633, and by 1633–35 there was a guardhouse, governor's house, barracks, and three windmills within the stockade. Eighteen languages were spoken in New Amsterdam in 1643, but the architecture was consistently Dutch. With its waterfront close to the sea, its buildings of brick, its open public gardens and curving avenues, and even canals, the town resembled old Amsterdam. The Dutch loved to build with brick even when other material was as plentiful or cheaper, and the colony had brick kilns by 1628. In old prints of New Amsterdam the essential features of the architecture are distinct: rather tall brick buildings with stepped gables and end chimneys, and casement or double-transomed windows. Each outpost on the Hudson River used the same kind of construction whether for farm or town buildings. Fort Carilo, Rensselaer, N.Y. (c.1642), the administrative center for the great patroonship of Kiliaen Van Rensselaer, for example, was a massive building of brick laid in Dutch cross bond with "saw-tooth" work along the gable edges (bricks laid at right angles to the gable) and a red tile roof. Batten shutters covering narrow casement windows give it a heavy, gloomy look. Smaller in scale and typical of the Hudson Valley group is the Leendert Bronck House, West Coxsackie, N.Y. (c.1738). The brick walls are laid in English bond, the steeply pitched roof contains an attic granary, the inner beams are fastened to exterior walls by anchors of iron, batten shutters guard the windows, and heavy interior joists are held on protruding curved brackets. A curi-

2

3

ous linear design characterized many Dutch houses; thus the plan of the Senate House, Kingston, N.Y. (1675–95), shows three rooms in a line, two having outside doors. Some houses fitted a hood over the front door and most had a horizontally divided door. Clapboards or shingles filled the gable ends when the stone or brick did not reach the peak. The chimneys at each end are within the walls, not projecting through or even flush with the exterior wall.

The Flemish settlers on Long Island, in southern New York, and northern New Jersey were also farmers, but their architecture differed in several ways from that of the Dutch settlers. Wood was extensively used for framing, and clapboard or shingle sheathing was common. Sandstone was also used for exterior walls along with clay, and, later, lime mortar. Thatch roofing was gradually replaced by tile and shingles. The Wyckoff House, Brooklyn (1639–c.41) is wood-framed and shingle-covered, but, with later additions, has an up-flaring roof line projecting beyond the wall. This feature, which often occurs in the Flemish area, was supposed to protect walls having clay mortar, but the roof swoop became a tradition and was retained after clay was no longer used. Another Flemish feature is the gambrel roof.

Octagonal in form, with high peaked roofs, the Dutch-Flemish Protestant churches were unique in America. The pulpit was placed opposite the front door and the interior was an austere white, relieved only by blue paint on the window frames and other details of woodwork. None now remains as it was built.

Colonial Spanish
(17th–18th Century)
The Spanish colonization of America was ill-planned for permanent settlement. But the Spaniards left a strong architectural heritage in the Southwest. By 1513, they were exploring Florida and within a few years had penetrated as far as California. Actual colonization started when Franciscan and Dominican monks began founding missions. In Florida, the Spanish built fort after fort at St. Augustine, only to have them burned by marauders until, in 1672, they began the large limestone Castillo de San Marcos (completed 1756). Little else survives from the Spanish occupation of Florida.

1

2

3

The survival of Spanish architecture in New Mexico, along the Rio Grande, is confined to missions. No true colonization took place. The missions were extraordinarily beautiful because of their blending with the natural forms of the area and their use of Indian means and materials. They built with adobe (molded and sun-baked clay) and stone. These materials, particularly the adobe, lent themselves to large, flat-surfaced rectangles broken only by small doors, a few windows, and the ends of the log roof beams. All exterior surfaces, whether stone or adobe, were covered with an adobe plaster. Using Indian labor, the missionaries adopted the native system of construction; but colonists, employing more sophisticated tools, were able to build with greater speed and to use wood-carving and squared timbers. The missionary zeal for construction brought about one innovation: clay was formed into adobe bricks by sun-drying in wooden boxes. The mission church of San Estevan, Acoma, N.M. (c.1642), aside from its bell towers, closely resembles Pueblo Indian construction. The interior has Spanish baroque ornaments of Christian content, as well as Indian symbols —an unusual mixture. This type of mission church continued to be built until Mexico became independent of Spain in 1821.

An offshoot of the New Mexico enterprises were the early 18th-century missions in Texas, mainly near San Antonio, a center of government. The Alamo (1744–57), a mission for educating Indians, the Church of San José (1720–31), and the Governor's Palace (1749) were all built of stone and are far more imposing than the missions in New Mexico. Brilliant decorations, derived from the Spanish baroque of Mexico, are attached to the entrance-ways and towers, while inside the churches the builders constructed stone vaults and lavished baroque forms on the sanctuary.

Owing to frequent burnings by Indians, the missions of Arizona were unsuccessful. But one mission church, San Xavier del Bac, near Tucson (1784 –97), still stands. It was built of brick, stuccoed, and decorated profusely in the baroque manner. Gaudy and quaint, its striking forms are a far cry from the more disciplined Spanish prototypes.

The Spanish settlements in California

were established primarily by Franciscan missionaries along the coast from San Diego to San Francisco. Twenty-one missions were built between 1769 and 1836, and served as community centers for converted Indians, a thousand of whom lived and worked in them. The missions were mainly of adobe brick coated with whitewashed lime-sand stucco. Kiln-made bricks were used for chimneys, arches, domes. Roofs were at first of thatch, but later of red tiles on a wooden frame. Stone was used sparingly because it was difficult to quarry and cut. To found missions quickly, the fathers were content to build simply. The arch form is common, and while it was primarily functional, it also contributed to the decorative effect. Facades reflect Spanish Renaissance precedents, but in their sparing use of the exuberant baroque, these missions stand apart from the Texan and Mexican designs of earlier generations.

Colonial French

The French occupation of America formed a great arc from the mouth of the St. Lawrence River westward through the Great Lakes and south along the Mississippi to New Orleans. Waterways were its roads. What remains of French architecture in the United States today is scanty. Hampered by home rule and royal administrators, the French colonists were easy prey for the English, and their vast territory remained French a relatively short time. The extant buildings attributable to the 17th and 18th centuries were mainly trading posts and forts. Tadoussac on the St. Lawrence was settled in 1600, followed by Quebec (1608) and Montreal (1611). At the other end of the arc, New Orleans was founded more than one hundred years later (1718), and half a century later the French and Indian Wars concluded French colonization in America.

Timber frame is the construction most frequently seen in the French territory, but because of the great distances between the settlements, there was no typical French construction. At Quebec, the buildings were quite different from those in New Orleans. The Villeneuve house at Charlesbourg, near Quebec (c.1690), had fieldstone walls and a central chimney. The owner kept sheep in half the basement, the ground floor was one large room around the fireplace, and the second

4

5

Colonial Spanish
1. *Alamo, San Antonio, Tex., 1757.*
2. *Governor's Palace, San Antonio, Tex., 1749.*
3. *San Xavier del Bac, near Tucson, Ariz., 1797.*
Colonial French
4. *Cahokia Courthouse, Cahokia, Ill., c.1737.*
5. *Parlange Plantation, New Roads, La., 1750.*

1

2

floor, under the roof, served as a bed-room. The roof was of the mansard type, sloping steeply at the sides and almost flat on top, with windows and wood framing. Brightly painted wood-work and narrow casement windows were about the only decorative ele-ments of this vernacular house.

South along the Mississippi, timber-frame houses were at first constructed of heavy vertical planks set about three feet into the ground, a type called *poteaux-en-terre*. Later the system called *poteaux-sur-sole* was used: a foundation of stone holding a wooden sill upon which the vertical planks were set. Spaces between the planks were filled with a clay-grass or clay-hair mix-ture and given a coating of lime plaster. the Cahokia Courthouse (formerly a house), Illinois (c.1737, rebuilt 1939), is as typical as any in the Mississippi Valley; a single story surrounded by a gallery or verandah for outside access to rooms, it has plank walls on stone foundations and a double-pitch hip roof. Thatch was a common roofing material at first (in New Orleans pal-metto leaves served for thatch) but later tile was used because it was more durable.

Larger buildings have generally dis-appeared except in New Orleans where the Ursuline Convent is a re-minder of the French occupation even though it is much altered today. The first Convent building (1734) was de-signed by DeBatz in Paris; quite medie-val in appearance, with timber framing and cross braces filled with brick and clay, its late date is belied by its sym-metry, the cupola on the hip roof, and the Renaissance entrance arch. The structure that replaced it (also by De-Batz, 1748–52), much more advanced in design, is in the style of Louis XV. Though much remodeled, it still stands. The Louisiana plantation house usually has a ground floor of stuccoed brick and a second floor of wood. It has a gallery in front or in front and in back, or even all the way around. The second-floor gallery, which gives these houses some distinction, is held up by brick columns, while the gallery roof is sup-ported by wooden colonnettes.

Colonial Georgian
(18th Century to the Revolution)
Probably the most important change in architecture about 1700 in all the En-glish colonies was the shift from a medieval building tradition to designs

Colonial Georgian
1. *Vassall-Longfellow House, Cambridge, Mass., 1759.*
2. *Corbit House, Odessa, Del., 1774.*

in keeping with contemporary English architecture. By the early 18th century, English architects had made Italian Renaissance style the basis of their own designs. First Inigo Jones, then Sir Christopher Wren and a host of others, produced elegant variants on Italian design that were suitable to the English climate and way of life. At a second remove from its Italian origin, the Renaissance style dominated in America until the formation of the Republic. Always some decades behind the English, architecture took on new characteristics after 1700. Whether in New England or the South, the intent was to introduce classical ornament (meaning Greek and Roman ornament as interpreted by the Italian Renaissance and reinterpreted by the English) both inside and out, and a refined symmetry in plan and elevation. Classicism arrived in America mainly through builders' guidebooks, particularly plentiful after 1750, and a few translations of Italian theoretical works. In addition, plans for specific projects were brought from England, carpenters and builders migrated, and educated travelers produced their own designs. No professional architects came to America until the end of the 18th century.

The materials chosen for construction still depended on what was cheapest and available. When cost was of little concern, brick or stone was selected. In New England many of the finest buildings were wood-framed and clapboard-covered, but an increasing number, particularly public buildings, were of brick. In the central colonies stone was common, and in the South brick was almost always used for substantial houses and public buildings.

The tentative, sparing use of classical motifs in the early period is well illustrated by the Capitol (begun 1701) and the Governor's Palace (begun 1706) at Williamsburg, Va. With brick walls and steeply pitched roofs characteristically medieval, they have the charm of simplicity. Cupolas sit on top of their hip roofs to herald the new era, but the tall chimneys on the Palace remind one of medieval usage. Archways and circular windows, a captain's walk, and a perfect symmetry on the exterior, give a serene, vaguely classical feeling.

A rich merchant, Colonel John Foster, arriving in Boston in 1675, built his house (c.1688, demolished 1822) with pilasters, balustrade, balcony, cupola, and a classical symmetry; it was probably viewed with incredulity by Bostonians. As the use of classical architectural language became general, local differences were eradicated, so that by 1776 a Southern mansion, a Philadelphia residence, and a New England home were more alike than not. Moreover, as opposition to overseas rule grew, the colonies developed a consciousness of their own resources and dignity. What better way to demonstrate their equality with England than by building according to English style and standards? This was not easy in a country of tradesmen and farmers, but it was made possible by English builders' guidebooks, which allowed American builders to mimic without exactly copying. The Vassal-Longfellow House, Cambridge (1759) exhibits most of the elements which make up this highly developed colonial style. The symmetrical, rectangular proportion of the house as a whole is echoed by the projecting central bay, by the door and windows, and the chimneys. Pilasters giving a strong vertical accent, are nicely counteracted by the horizontal clapboards, eaves line, and captain's walk. Although later houses had more and daintier decoration, none improved on the proportions of the Vassall House. Other outstanding examples of the style are Mount Pleasant, Fairmont Park, Philadelphia (1761–62), where stone is substituted for wood, and the Corbit House, Odessa, Del. (1772–74). It is a great tribute to the architecturally untrained American builders of the 18th century that they were able to create such able designs in a country quite unprepared for graceful living.

Early Republican or Federal (1785–1820)

The victory in the Revolutionary War did not change the style of colonial architecture; nevertheless, a certain change did take place because the English style was itself changing. English architectural fashion, modified by Pompeian decoration and Roman ruins, produced a new trend in American architecture. Although English builders' books remained a basic reference source, American architects began publishing their own books, beginning with Asher Benjamin's* The Country Builder's Assistant (1797). However, such books could not create a new architecture. For this reason Washington, Jefferson, and other officials sought to find architects who would design public buildings for the new federal city on the Potomac. Competitions were held for the Capitol and White House, but since there were no professional architects in America, it was necessary to choose foreigners. Pierre Charles L'Enfant,* a Frenchman, was the first government appointee. He was to plan the city. Then Stephen Hallet, another Frenchman, was hired in 1793 to erect the Capitol from the winning designs of an amateur, William Thornton.* But the French influence was slight because neither architect designed a single building in Washington and only L'Enfant made a few designs elsewhere.

At this critical stage, several architects arrived from England—George Hadfield* (1794), B. H. Latrobe* (1796), John Haviland* (1816), William Jay* (1817)—and a few from France—Maximilian Godefroy* (1805), Joseph Mangin (c.1795), and Joseph J. Ramée* (1811). Of this group only Latrobe and Haviland made lasting impressions: Latrobe, who introduced the latest English manner, including the fetish for Gothic and Greek designs, and Haviland through his comprehensive builders' book, designs for prisons, and use of Grecian orders for residential architecture. Hadfield quit architecture early, Jay stayed in Charleston, S.C., Godefroy and Ramée returned to France, and Mangin's last design was made in 1809. The idea of professionalism in architecture was planted, but no firm national style developed until after 1820. Instead, we find the gentleman-architect Charles Bulfinch* in Boston, filling his city with mediocre designs in brick, culled from earlier British sources, and Samuel McIntire,* the woodcarver and builder of Salem, tastefully decorating the streets of his town. Characteristic of their work is the delicate interior ornament stemming from the popular English style of Robert Adam, who had been inspired by Roman decoration. Bulfinch's exteriors are flat, bland, and largely undecorated. The late buildings by McIntire are similar. Wherever the French architects worked, mainly in New York and Baltimore, there are traces of the Louis XVI style, but its intricacies never really caught the fancy of Americans.

The architectural work of Thomas Jefferson,* self-trained in the art, comprises a group of buildings that stands

1

2

3

alone in America and yet is the essence of the Early Republican period. His natural talents and enthusiasm for good architecture helped him establish a local style of high order. His designs were artfully drawn from Palladio (17th-century Italian architect and writer on architecture) and English pattern books. He gave his buildings a more modest scale than those in Europe, built in brick instead of stone, applied wood decorations painted white, and often devised rooms irregular in plan, like the oval rooms he had adored while living in France. The end of his personal renaissance of classicism came with his design for the University of Virginia; the library, domed like the Pantheon in Rome, and its adjoining buildings were intended as a lesson in architectural style.

By this time, individual architects were becoming influential. The man most successful in the profession as a designer was B. H. Latrobe. He had studied in the London office of an eminent architect, and had practiced briefly. He had accomplished very little before he arrived in America, but his native intelligence, confidence, and broad education enabled him to assume leadership quickly. For large public or commercial ventures, Latrobe used Greek orders and a Roman dome; for institutions, a simplified Georgian; for churches, Gothic or Georgian; and for residences, almost any style that could be reduced to the clarity and precision of Greek architecture and still meet the requirements of contemporary living. Most influential for the future was his direct application of Greek orders in the proportions used in antiquity.

By 1820 the colonial styles had almost disappeared, not to be revived until the end of the century, and the new Greek revival was beginning to prevail. It was the first style to be associated directly with the republican principles of the founding fathers.

Greek Revival (1820–60)

This style was not invented in America but for forty years it proved highly suitable to all types of American buildings. Its origins were European: German, French, and English artists and intellectuals had become romantically interested in the remains of ancient Greek and Roman civilization. A belief that Greek culture was superior to the Roman created a partiality for

4

5

Early Republican or Federal
1. Benjamin Henry Latrobe. Baltimore Cathedral, Baltimore, 1821.
2. Samuel McIntire. Derby Teahouse, Danvers, Mass., 1792.
3. Thomas Jefferson. Monticello, Charlottesville, Va., 1809.
Greek Revival
4. Salem City Hall, Salem, Mass., 1837.
5. Nicholas Biddle House, Andalusia, Pa., 1833.

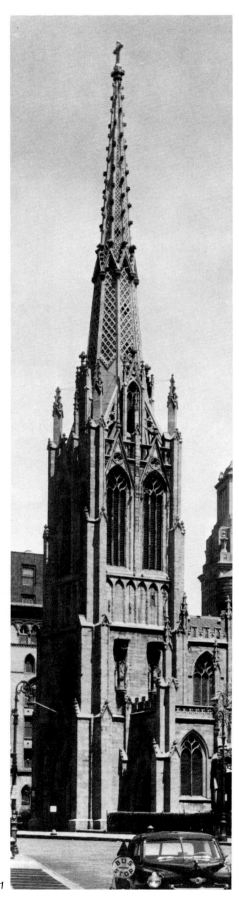

things Greek. And after James Stuart and Nicholas Revett, English architects, published *The Antiquities of Athens* (1762), filled with measured drawings of ancient buildings, it became clear that for beauty of proportion, workmanship, and correct ornament, Greek architecture was vastly superior to that of any other Mediterranean nation. Stuart and Revett were also the first to erect buildings in England that attempted to imitate large decorative portions of Greek temples, especially entrances consisting of a four- or six-column portico.

The first Greek revival buildings in America were designed by Latrobe in 1798. He had just arrived from England, where he had received architectural training and had built two houses using Greek orders for porticoes. The reasons for the success of Greek Revival are largely American. The founders of the new republic—Washington, Jefferson, etc.,—saw a genuine value in emphasizing an architecture related to the virtues of ancient Greek freedom and democracy. Soon American architects were publishing designs that adapted Greek style to houses, banks, hotels, and stores. Even before many books were available, Robert Mills,* William Strickland,* Alexander Parris,* and several others had developed a mature style acceptable to all. These, together with English and American builders' guidebooks, provided thousands of carpenters, masons, and builders with what they needed to know.

At the beginning of the Greek revival, an attempt was made to recover the remote past in all its imagined glory. Nicholas Biddle surrounded his monotonous old house with a grand Greek Doric colonnade as though it were an Athenian temple. Soon Greek Revival could be seen in the architecture of thousands of small homes, banks, and even gravestones, in every town. The style was revived for the sake of form, not for the meaning attached to it, and the original reason for use of the Greek style was almost totally disregarded. As one sage commentator said in 1841: "He . . . who would rival the Greek temple, must imitate, not the temple, but the Greek."

Gothic Revival

The revival in the mid-19th century of the Gothic style was in a sense the high point of an extended resurgence of medievalism. In fact, there was hardly a decade of the 19th century when a Gothic house or church was not built in America, nor did the building of Gothic cease with the coming of the 20th century. As used here, however, Gothic revival refers to the period from about 1830 to 1875, when the style accommodated a great variety of architectural projects.

In the early decades, Gothic appeared in apparent harmony with the Greek revival style. Architects sometimes submitted two sets of plans to a client: one Gothic and one classic. Later both styles were sometimes combined, creating a somewhat ludicrous effect. With the Civil War, the Greek revival waned, while the Gothic lost its vigor after the Philadelphia Centennial Exposition of 1876.

The origin of American Gothic in its revived form is mainly English. London-trained Latrobe, who built the first Gothic revival house in America, was well aware of the frequent use of Gothic in English country estates. Charles Bulfinch, who put Gothic windows in an essentially Georgian church, had seen Gothic buildings abroad and had books on Gothic, but he was particularly attached to classical design. The French architect Godefroy built a Gothic chapel in Baltimore but made little or no impression.

Like the Greek revival, the Gothic revival had its emotional basis in romanticism. Many Englishmen had tried to recapture the Middle Ages by recasting their architectural environment to resemble a duke's castle, abbot's house, or monk's cloister. Churches were frequently built in Gothic and conformed to the requirements of medieval liturgy. This became the most serious aspect of the revival, disrupting church tradition and arousing some opposition from the Church of England. The American attitude was less romantic: it did not matter much whether a building was correct in style as long as it pleased the eye and served its purpose. The ordinary American house was virtually without style until A. J. Downing showed readers of his books how a humble cottage could be made into a building of distinction by abandoning a plain box shape and adding some medieval ornament. His wooden Gothic cottages sprang up overnight. Larger houses of stone were developed for well-to-do clients, and finally mansions and castles for wealthy merchant princes were designed by Downing's followers.

The essentials of the Gothic revival style were pointed arches for windows and doors (or at least a hood molding over these openings), a vertical exterior form accentuated by a steep roof with high chimneys, and a picturesque irregularity. Many decorative details were added, some unknown in the Middle Ages; others were fanciful and simply ornamental. Only large Gothic churches preserved any genuine connection with medieval religious thought. Small wooden churches usually showed nothing more than a shift from classic to Gothic shapes—Greek columns gave way to clustered piers, rectangular windows were pointed, clear glass was stained, and towers bristled with finials and crockets instead of classical urns, pilasters, and pediments. Architects who had begun their profession as colonial or Greek revival designers were often forced in their later years to offer clients designs in the latest Gothic fashion, so that, in general, mid-century architects produced a curiously wide variety of designs. Richard Upjohn,* primarily a designer of Gothic churches, often did classical plans, and James Renwick,* known for his grasp of the essence of Gothic, turned to other styles when occasion demanded. Thus the Gothic style is more distinct than its practitioners. (P.F.N.)

Architecture 1860–1920

Structural and mechanical developments from 1860 to 1920 enabled architecture to achieve some of its most spectacular advances in this period. These included new building heights, made possible by the introduction of the steel skeleton, the elevator, and electricity.

Before the end of the Civil War, revival styles had had nationwide influence. The Greek revival, followed by the romantic styles, was a reaction against generations of classical formality, symmetry, and a limited design vocabulary. The new romanticism of the 1850s introduced freedom of plan, asymmetry, picturesque profiles, and a wealth of stylistic ornament. The Gothic revival and the Italiante coexisted with a multitude of lesser styles, all of them manifestations of this romantic reaction.

The new architecture that emerged after the Civil War was most nearly akin to the Italianate but found its inspira-

2

1. *Gothic Revival.* James Renwick, Jr. Grace Church, N.Y., 1846.
2. *1860–1920.* Victorian Gothic. Calvert Vaux. Jefferson Market Courthouse, N.Y., 1877.

1

2

3

1860–1920

1. *Romanesque Revival. Frank Freeman. Old Brooklyn Fire Headquarters, 1892.*
2. *Renaissance Eclectic. McKim, Mead & White. Racquet and Tennis Club, N.Y. 1918.*
3. *Chicago School of Architecture. Louis Sullivan. Auditorium Building. Chicago, 1889.*
4. *French Second Empire. Richard Morris Hunt. Belcourt, Newport, R.I., 1893.*
5. *Queen Anne House, Berkeley, Cal., c.1890.*
6. *Victorian stairway, Berkeley, Cal., c.1890.*

tion in the contemporary European style of the French Second Empire.* Many fortunes had been made during the Civil War and the parvenus sought formality and an opportunity to display their newfound wealth in architecture. In this they were inspired by the Paris of Napoleon III and the Empress Eugénie, a city reborn under the genius of the Emperor's architect, Baron Haussmann. Avenues through the old city were lined with handsome limestone facades of uniform height—a planner's dream city, superseding the random picturesqueness of the past.

Compared with what had gone before, the post-Civil War era was an age of mass production. Many items of stock design could be selected for use over and over again in the long rows of brownstone houses rising in every city. Slate mansard roofs were crowned by handsome mass-produced iron crestings, and cast-iron balustered handrailings for stoops could be bought by the yard. It was up to the architect to combine all these purchasable elements into a design in which the traditional crafts of the mason and carpenter were retained. Once designed, a fine town house would be reproduced in seemingly endless rows built by "jerry-builders."

Many French Second Empire designs came to the United States via England, particularly those for great hotels and country houses. The country villa with tower was usually symmetrical at the front, and was marked by an air of formality. Covered carriageways at the entrance, mansard roofs with iron crestings, and towers proclaimed the wealth of their owners. Even the arrangement of the grounds became more formal, with axial vistas terminated by gazebos and cast-iron urns. Gone were the asymmetrical rambles and constantly changing vistas once made popular by the books of A. J. Downing. As transatlantic travel became more dependable, Americans could see for themselves the glories of Paris, including Garnier's new opera house. The French Second Empire style was thus a formula ready-to-hand, and one that could be produced by the yard or by the mile. Once the pattern had been set by the architect, it was primarily a builder's style. Yet, after 1850, architects emerged in ever greater numbers and began to achieve standing as professionals. They were not pleased with the

4

5

6

Architecture

French formula and although they did design cast-iron commercial structures and certain public buildings in the style, they sought something more expressive in the use of materials and design. For a brief period they were won over by the structural expressionism of Henri Labrouste, a French architect working since 1840 in a style referred to as neo-Grec.* The style was not particularly Greek except in its ornamental externals, but it was a genuine attempt to reconcile the use of cast iron, glass, and masonry with the technology of the day. This "new look," replacing the rather heavy French Second Empire style, was, however, stopped short by the panic of 1873. Toward the end of the 1860s, architects were entering a new phase of romanticism that was to continue up to the new classicism of the World's Columbian Exposition (Chicago, 1893). One abortive phase of that romanticism, Victorian Gothic,* with its polychromy and structural expressionism,* ran concurrently with the neo-Grec and was also cut off by the panic of 1873. By the time it had picked up again in the 1880s, architecture had moved on to new developments, materials, and styles, including Romanesque revival* and Queen Anne.*

Not since the Gothic revival and the Italianate styles of the 1850s had America indulged itself in such a wave of romanticism; but the difference was that whereas that of the 1850s was the expression of an almost morbid literary yearning for something the young country had never experienced before, that of the 1880s was robust and joyous, fulfilling a quest, in architecture, for a cozy domesticity. The Queen Anne and Richardsonian Romanesque* architectural styles infused architecture with a new spirit. The asymmetrical plan reemerged and structural expressionism came into its own. The new houses combined brick, shingles, and half-timbering and, with their porches, balconies, and towers, created picturesque profiles. Wrought iron replaced cast iron, while in doors, natural wood replaced painted surfaces. Oriental and scatter rugs on polished wood floors displaced grandma's flowered carpeting, and the Living Hall, where the family foregathered, took the place of the Best Parlor. The Arts and Crafts* movement, which had originated in England with William Morris, found

1860–1920
Early skyscraper. Burnham & Root.
Reliance Building, Chicago,
1895.

expression in a new awareness of the beauty of household objects, replacing the ready-made bric-a-brac of the French Second Empire. The emphasis had shifted from Victorian formality to a desire for livability.

Successive phases of architectural development generally involve a swing away from romanticism and back again. The most notable exception to this pattern was a swing back to classicism precipitated by a single event: the World's Columbian Exposition in Chicago in 1893. Remembered as "The Great White City," the exposition's lagoons, surrounded by imposing classical and Renaissance buildings, gave visitors an insight into the order and dignity that might replace the ugliness of the average Main Street. This architectural revolution was introduced by the architects who controlled the Fair, Richard Morris Hunt* leading the eastern architects while Daniel Hudson Burnham* marshalled his western confreres. Nevertheless, a few were even sharply critical of the architecture of the Fair. Louis Sullivan,* whose Transportation Building was conspicuously not classical, declared: "The damage wrought to this country by the Chicago World's Fair will last half a century."

After the Fair, no bank was considered respectable unless it stood behind four white columns. The demand for classical buildings required that architects train legions of draftsmen in the proper use of "the orders" and of classical and Renaissance detail. This new self-conscious architecture inaugurated the age of eclecticism.* Designs were borrowed from the treasure trove of Europe and adapted to the needs of a rapidly developing America.

Americans, unwilling to await the gradual development of an indigenous architecture based on local requirements and native materials, accepted the pronouncements of established "men of taste," whether in the construction of a railway station, a state capitol, or a private residence. Such pioneers as Louis Sullivan,* Frank Lloyd Wright,* and the Chicago school of architecture* found only a very limited local acceptance of their work all through the first quarter of the 20th century.

The period from 1860 to 1920 saw practically every major technological development that has made possible the architecture of today. Before the Civil War, framed wood construction and masonry-bearing wall construction were the two principal methods of building. The steel skeleton, or frame, itself supporting an outer veneer of masonry, revolutionized America's system of building in the 1880s. The seeds of this development had been planted in the 1850s, when cast-iron building fronts were first developed.

Among the important developments in the amenities were lighting, with gas replacing kerosene lamps, then electricity replacing gas. In heating, cast-iron stoves were supplanted by furnaces and boilers using coal, oil, or gas and, finally, electrical units. Ventilation, which began with rudimentary gravity systems, developed into elaborate forced-air duct systems. Town planning and zoning introduced much needed controls at the turn of the century. Planning was given new impetus by the "City Beautiful" movements inaugurated by the Chicago Fair, while zoning of urban districts, and set-back and height requirements for skyscrapers, all contributed to the preservation of minimum standards.

The controlling forces in architectural development have been periods of economic depression and boom. World War I, which concluded an era, actually accelerated certain types of building in war-affected communities where housing developments were introduced on a scale thitherto unknown. It was the economic crash at the end of the 1920s that brought one of the most acute periods of stagnation. It created a hiatus that would be followed by a new architecture, new forms, and new ways of building. (A.B.)

The 1920s

American architecture of the 1920s seemed to be simply a little more of the modes that had prevailed during the first two decades of the century. The dominant note, whether in a downtown business district or in suburbia, was that of period-revival styles ranging from the neoclassic and Gothic for commercial structures, to colonial and English Tudor for houses. The prestige of the Paris École des Beaux-Arts was even greater than it had been before World War I. In the core of large cities, the pre-1914 enthusiasm for the skyscraper* became almost an obsession. And yet, for all of its strong ties with the preceding two decades, the 1920s was basically different. In scale, proportion, and details, its revival architecture was more correct historically and more refined and simplified. Large public buildings in the neoclassical mode relied increasingly for impact on their basic form, not on the use of classically inspired details. While some large-scale neoclassic country houses were built, the more intimate scale and interior spaces of the English Georgian or the Spanish Colonial revivals were preferred.

Although the imagery of most buildings of the 1920s was that of a historic style, their planning, construction, and mechanical cores were technologically up-to-date. Large office skyscrapers became cities within cities, with garages for automobiles and their own restaurants, shops, recreation facilities, and terraced gardens. More efficient heating, air conditioning, and vastly improved electric lighting allowed a building to create its own little world, ignoring the traditional need for natural light and air. While the middle-class American in his single-family detached house in the suburbs generally preferred a traditional image in his dwelling, he devoted more and more expenditure to its mechanical core—to automatically controlled central heating, more elaborate electric lighting, more adequate bathrooms, and a kitchen that was a "machine for living." His love affair with the automobile not only meant two cars in many a garage, but also an automobile entrance that was often virtually the main entrance. The freedom conferred by the automobile meant that more of the American landscape began to be covered with highways, and suburbia and the urban core itself had to be continually modified to accommodate the new device. The majority of suburban houses were put up by contractor-builders relying for design on popular home magazines and plan books and not directly on architects. Increasingly, suburban houses were built not singly but in large numbers, as part of a singly financed and organized "development."

The ideal seemed to be the establishment of a universal middle class with everyone enjoying a middle-class income. While Americans were fascinated by the city as a machine (of industry and business, not government) and by the machine in general, their basic commitment was to a romantic view of nature and to living in suburbia.

1

2

The 1920s

1. *Frank Lloyd Wright. Aline Barnsdall Residence, Hollywood, Cal., 1920.*
2. *Rudolph Schindler. Lovell Beach House, Newport Beach, Cal., 1926.*
   1931–42
3. *Rockefeller Center, N.Y., 1935.*
4. *Detail, Rockefeller Center, N.Y., 1935.*

Aside from America's interest in the freestanding suburban house and its furnishings, the buildings that exercised the greatest attraction during the 1920s were the skyscraper and the motion picture house. From the public's point of view the three outstanding architectural events of these years were the completion of Bertram Goodhue's* Nebraska State Capitol Building (Lincoln, 1916–28), a stripped neoclassic skyscraper set on the prairie; the Gothic-spired Chicago *Tribune* Tower (1922–24) by Howell & Hood, and the competition at the end of the decade to build the tallest skyscraper, won by the Empire State Building (New York City, 1930–31) of Shreve, Lamb & Harmon.

The stripped and cleaned-up neoclassicism of Goodhue enjoyed an increased popularity during the 1920s and with the interest in historic styles, it was only natural that many architects should eventually turn to America's indigenous architecture, that of pre-Columbian Mexico and Central America, and the motifs and forms of the Pueblo Indians of New Mexico and Arizona. The impact of these was felt not only by period-revival architects, but also by avant-garde designers such as Frank Lloyd Wright, his son Lloyd Wright, and Rudolph Schindler.*

The 1920s also witnessed the development of programatic architecture—commercial structures that adopted the form of the object being merchandised. Hot-dog stands in the form of a frankfurter, ice-cream stands as ice-cream cones, and so forth, began to crop up, especially in the less traditional world of southern California. With the increased reliance on the automobile, it was also this decade that saw the first major examples of drive-in architecture, ranging from markets to motels.

In the 1920s the exponents of modern architecture were divided into three related but distinct groups. In the early years there was a small but recognizable expressionist group centered in southern California. Second was the early or zigzag moderne,* and finally, the International style,* which never loomed large on the American scene, but still brought forth two great monuments: Schindler's concrete-frame Lovell Beach House (Newport Beach, Calif., 1922–26) and Richard J. Neutra's* steel and "gunite" Lovell House (Los Angeles, 1929). (D.G.)

1931–42

This brief period was marked, especially in its first years, by the Depression, which threw innumerable architects out of work and almost entirely halted new construction. One might assume that such a social and economic catastrophe would undermine, or at least modify, the convictions underlying American architecture of the 1920s, but such was not the case. Almost the opposite occurred—the ideal of suburbia and the freedom provided by the automobile became more influential than ever, and faith in technology, increasingly symbolized in machines and machine-made products, came to dominate. While the federal government emerged as the major client for architecture, the middle-class citizen was as distrustful as ever of bureaucracy and "big" government. He might accept a new WPA (Works Project Administration) post office or courthouse, but he was perhaps more interested in the newly developed FHA (Federal Housing Authority) with its guaranteed low-interest loan that could enable him to purchase his own suburban house. Federally sponsored low-cost housing did solve some of the pressing housing needs of the period, but construction was generally of regimented quality because of economic stringencies, and this made them only marginally effective as places to live. The notable exception was Richard Neutra's Channel Heights public housing (San Pedro, Cal., 1942), where a fine site plan was coupled with convincing imagery in the International style.

Period-revival architecture continued, but was somewhat transformed. Gothic and classical revival buildings were likely to be stripped and simplified, with less and less historic detail, and streamlined moderne* design elements began to appear, especially in interior details. Perhaps out of nostalgia, the early 18th-century American colonial style became the ideal for domestic architecture and for smaller buildings such as schools, post offices, and libraries. Later in the 1930s the colonial revival house tended to be modified by International style and streamlined moderne elements. Out of such a blend several regional styles developed.

The stripped neoclassicism of Bertram Goodhue and other architects of the 1920s became a set style—the

3

4

"neo-Babylonian," as one critic labeled it. The fondness for stripped neoclassicism was not restricted to the Franklin D. Roosevelt administration, but was almost worldwide. In Hitler's Germany it became the style of major public buildings. More traditional in their adherence to Roman Renaissance classical precepts, and also more popular, were such buildings as the National Gallery of Art (Washington, D.C., 1936–37) and the controversial Thomas Jefferson Memorial (Washington, D.C., 1937), both designed by James Russell Pope (1874–1937).

By the mid-1930s the International style, already the accepted high-art avant-garde mode, was in close competition with streamlined moderne. In the East, the International cause was fostered by the Museum of Modern Art in its exhibits and publications. But for the general public it was too cold and antiseptic, and the moderne (streamlined and otherwise) dominated at the Chicago World's Fair of 1933 and at the 1939 fairs in New York and San Francisco.

Although in the 1930s (as compared to the 1920s) only a few skyscrapers were built in the United States, the most widely discussed group of buildings was Rockefeller Center (New York, 1931–39), designed by a consortium of architects led by Reinhard and Hofmeister, and including Corbett, Harmon and MacMurray, and Hood and Fouilhoux. As imagery, the stiff monumentality of the Center was really quite old fashioned, but some aspects of the buildings, such as the interior of Radio City Music Hall (designed by Donald Desky), were approximately streamlined moderne, and the whole complex was most impressive.

The visual importance of the commercial vernacular, particularly the architecture of the roadside strip, came to dominate even more of the urban landscape. Shopping centers, drive-in supermarkets, drive-in hamburger stands, and motels became common on the urban and suburban scene. The motion picture house of the 1930s was less monumental, its exterior and interior imagery became almost exclusively streamlined moderne, and in many instances it was oriented to a parking lot or drive-in shopping center.

The dominant figures in architecture of the late 1930s and early 1940s were Frank Lloyd Wright, William Lescaze,* Richard J. Neutra, and Edward Durell

Stone,* but it should be added that the major commissions for both business and government buildings continued to go to business-oriented architectural firms, not to the figures who dominated the high-art scene in architecture.

1945–59

The fantasy world of the future suggested by the streamlined moderne of the 1930s was replaced by the here-and-now world of the late 1940s and 1950s. The fifteen years 1945–59 were boom years for the United States and this was clearly reflected in architecture. America's corporations commissioned innumerable skyscrapers, low-rise office buildings, factories and stores utilizing almost exclusively the imagery of the International style. The federal government, never before overly receptive to new architecture, embarked, under the presidency of Dwight Eisenhower, on a building program that used, for its embassies abroad, the talents of such major modern architects as Eero Saarinen* and Walter Gropius.* At home, Skidmore, Owings & Merrill,* the giant of American architectural firms, was commissioned to design the new Air Force Academy at Colorado Springs (1960). The skyscraper craze of the 1920s was equalled and eventually surpassed by the number and size of new high-rise buildings that began to transform all large American cities from New York to San Francisco. As in the 1920s, the large, business-oriented architectural firms were best able to work with the great corporations. Out of this corporation-dominated world emerged such firms as Skidmore, Owings & Merrill, Eero Saarinen, I. M. Pei,* Minoru Yamasaki,* and Victor Gruen (1903–   ).

The architectural imagery used by these and most other architects quickly developed into a set academic version of the International style, specifically the steel-frame, curtain-walled building the best example of which is probably the Seagram Building on Park Avenue, New York (1956–59), designed by Mies van der Rohe* and Philip Johnson.* These thinly clad, rather impermanent-looking buildings were succeeded in the late 1950s by more substantial-appearing structures either of reinforced concrete, using unfinished concrete in the manner of the new brutalism,* or by making the steel frame more three-dimensional so that it dominated the metal and glass skin applied to it.

1

2

3

1945–70
1. Ludwig Mies van der Rohe and Philip Johnson. Seagram Building, N.Y., 1959.
2. Buckminster Fuller. United States Pavilion, Expo '67, Montreal, 1967.
3. Frank Lloyd Wright. Solomon R. Guggenheim Museum, N.Y., 1960.

1945–70

1. Eero Saarinen. Auditorium Building, Massachusetts Institute of Technology, Cambridge, 1955.

2. Skidmore, Owings & Merrill. Manufacturers Hanover Trust Company, N.Y., 1961.

Saarinen's expressionistic TWA Terminal at Kennedy International Airport (New York, 1956–62) exemplifies this use of concrete, while Skidmore, Owings & Merrill's Alcoa Building (San Francisco, 1964) set a heavy criss-cross metal frame in front of its glass and metal sheathing.

As the middle class began a mass exodus from the city, domestic architecture continued to reflect the passion for suburbia. Older cities such as New York and Chicago were succeeded by a sprawling non-city such as Los Angeles. With this spreading of population, the most reasonable means of transportation was the automobile, so the new urban-suburban pattern reflected an increasing reliance on the automobile. Great "freeways" dominated the landscape, and the business centers of older cities and towns were succeeded by smaller, automobile-oriented shopping centers. Some of these, for example the Southdale Shopping Center, designed for Minneapolis (1954) by Victor Gruen & Associates, are totally enclosed capsules set in the midst of vast parking lots. Completely unplanned and visually more dominant was the roadside-strip commercial architecture, with more and more buildings completely transformed into an advertising sign. The reliance on lights, particularly neon lights, revealed that these buildings were meant to be seen at night; during the day they often looked tired and tawdry.

The popular form for the suburban house of the late 1940s and the 1950s was the loose, informal California ranch house. Like the bungalow craze of the early 1900s, the ranch house was low and conveyed an attachment to its site. Its interior space was oriented around the family room—an informal living, television, and dining space oftentimes opening directly into the kitchen. These single-floor houses were built by the thousands in large-scale suburban developments, and were financed through a rather easy-going credit system that required only a small down payment and relatively low rates of interest.

With the notable exception of Mies's version of the International style, high-art architecture retreated into its own secluded world after 1945. Frank Lloyd Wright continued to build his small (and expensive) "Usonian" houses, and in his larger commissions, such as the Guggenheim Museum (New York,

1942–60) and the Marin County Administrative Center (San Rafael, Cal., 1959–71), carried on his own highly personal version of the streamlined moderne of the previous decade. R. M. Schindler produced increasingly agitated designs, while Richard Neutra worked out innumerable variations on his classic International style buildings of the 1930s. The major maverick of these years was Bruce Goff, who projected a futuristic fairytale world that at times seems more unreal than Disneyland. And in a way, it could be argued that Disneyland itself was one of the architectural monuments of the post-World War II years.

More down to earth, but equally removed from the conventional world of building was the Mies-styled "Case Study" program of John Entenza and his *Arts and Architecture* magazine (Los Angeles). The program presented some of the most impressive examples of Mies's mode: the Charles Eames House of 1949, and the numerous houses designed by Raphael S. Soriano (1904–   ), Craig Ellwood (1922–   ), and Pierre Koenig (1925–   ). Other architects also continued to explore the Miesian box shape; Walter Gropius, Eliot Noyes (1910–   ), Edward L. Barnes,* and Hugh Stubbins (1912–   ) worked out their own personal interpretation of the steel frame, glass-and-metal-sheathed building.

The federal government and a number of large corporations had flirted with metal and other types of prefabricated houses in the 1930s. Immediately after World War II, two new approaches attracted attention: the Dymaxion House (1946) of R. Buckminster Fuller* and the more conventionally designed Lustron House, designed by Carl Strandlund beginning in 1946. Fuller's house was by far the more revolutionary, with its circular flying-saucer shape suspended from a central mast—the whole using the vocabulary of the streamlined moderne of the 1930s. The houses were to be manufactured at former wartime aircraft production plants in Kansas and Ohio. The Fuller product remained in the prototype stage; the Lustron House was produced in limited quantity for several years, but it could not overcome consumer resistance to its machine-made appearance and it was also confronted by other problems: finan-

cial, organizational, local building laws, and the opposition of building trades unions.

By 1959 it was evident in the world of high architecture that the former commitment to the esthetic ideals of the International style was waning. Edward Durell Stone, Walter Gropius, and others were slowly turning to the discipline of classical architecture, with its reliance on symmetry, elegance, and the axial arrangement of exterior and interior spaces. The pavilion mode, so elegantly expressed in the work of Stone and in the lacy tracery of Minoru Yamasaki, was to present major competition to the Miesian mode during the decade of the 1960s. (D.G.)

1960–70

During the decade of the 1960s there had been a crisis in architecture. So great were the needs of a rapidly expanding population, so diverse the interests and directions, and so varied was the design vocabulary, that the architecture profession was fragmented. The result was not merely esthetic diversity and eclecticism, but such divergent preoccupations as formal planning and building systems, social concerns, business and procedural emphasis, legislation, codes, and computers. Architects were no longer responsible for all of the art of architecture and certainly not for all the crafts of building; they were responsible for only five percent of the houses started during the decade. Despite mass education, the public made no distinction between architecture and mere building. In terms of esthetics, as the 1960s opened, the International style was, on the one side, approaching a peak of classical refinement, and on the other side a new "sensual" flamboyance in structural design was challenging the very validity of its achievement. One of the principal currents was the continuation and purification of Bauhaus* and International style as minimal architecture. Foremost among architects whose work was minimal* were Skidmore, Owings & Merrill's New York office; Eero Saarinen, in selected works; I. M. Pei; Harry Weese's* public projects; Edward L. Barnes; and the interior designers Florence Knoll Bassett,* Alexander Girard,* Benjamin Baldwin,* and Ward Bennett. However, with the completion of a substantial body of Miesian designs in the United States by the end of the 1950s, the goals of that

1

2

group were established and it became time to move on to something new. "Functionalism" had been usurped by the market place; the design world was ready for the revolution in progress.

First came some convoluted sculpturing that proclaimed independence from Mies's rectangle and from the taboo against ornamentation: Eero Saarinen used curvilinear, birdlike forms in the TWA Terminal in New York; Minoru Yamasaki and Edward Durell Stone flaunted their architectural lacework and Gothic tracery; Philip Johnson unfurled a quasi-Chinese parasol over a shrine called the Roofless Church. As the closest of Mies's disciples, Johnson continued to shock with his exploitation of Miesian principles, including the Founders' Room at the Museum of Modern Art, N.Y., where he brought the exterior I-beam mullion motif indoors, painting it white and using it frankly as interior decoration. This kind of parody, however, was not enough to constitute a total revolution. Louis Kahn* was a convincing rebel with his combining of clarity in planning and richly sculptured walls. In 1962 came the catalyst: Robert Venturi* began to lecture at Yale—even as the Art and Architecture building by Paul Rudolph* began to take shape there. The designs of Charles Moore* erupted in architectural publications. The vitality of Venturi's architectural theories and the startling perversities of the design work of Moore, Venturi, and their colleagues became the sensation of the 1960s.

A trademark of their work was the diagonal that cut across established traditions—breaking out of the rectangular, International style boxes, expanding the "architecture of squares." The new movement came to be called supermannerism.* It was a rebellion against the stilted formality of the past—the minimalist purity that had created monotonous "pigeon crates." They wanted to establish an involvement in a fuller range of architectural acitivity than previous decades of architects had encompassed—a reliance on architect as contractor, entrepreneur, and developer—and a super-expansion of design vocabulary. By the early 1970s, the general public had only begun to hear of this revolution in architecture, but its effects were internationally visible in graphics, advertising, and interior design.   (C.R.S.)

3

4

1960–70
1. *Charles Moore. Sea Ranch Condominiums, Gualala, Cal., 1965.*
2. *John M. Johansen. Goddard Library, Clark University, Worcester, Mass., 1968.*
3. *Venturi and Rauch. Lieb House, Long Beach Island, N.J., 1969.*
4. *Philip Johnson. Altar for Roofless Church, New Harmony, Ind., 1960.*

1

2

1960–70
1. *Harry Weese & Associates. Milwaukee Center for the Performing Arts, Wis., 1970.*
2. *Paul Rudolph. S.E. Massachusetts Technical Institute, North Dartmouth, 1966.*

Architecture, Landscape, see Landscape Architecture.

Armory Show, The.
The popular name for the International Exhibition of Modern Art, presented at New York's 69th Regiment Armory in 1913. It is the best-known and most influential exhibition ever held in America. The idea for the show was conceived at meetings held by four artists—Walt Kuhn,* Jerome Myers,* Elmer MacRae, and Henry Fitch Taylor—in December, 1911, to organize a society for "exhibiting the works of progressive and live painters, both American and foreign—favoring such work as is usually neglected by current shows and especially interesting and instructive to the public." Soon the four were joined by nine others, including sculptor Gutzon Borglum,* and painters Arthur B. Davies,* William Glackens,* Ernest Lawson,* Jonas Lie,* and George Luks.* The name "American Painters and Sculptors" was adopted (later incorporated as the "Association of American Painters and Sculptors"), and the membership was expanded to include, among others, Robert Henri,* George Bellows,* Maurice Prendergast,* John Sloan,* Childe Hassam,* Jo Davidson,* and Mahonri Young.* The members saw their society as progressive but not revolutionary. A number of them were also members of the National Academy of Design,* and the election of the liberal but long-established J. Alden Weir* as president represented a desire to retain harmony between the organizations. When the press presented the new body as at war with the older academy, Weir resigned. Arthur B. Davies was persuaded to accept the post.

In the summer of 1912, Davies and Kuhn went to Europe to select works by foreign artists. They were aided by expatriate artists Alfred Maurer* and Walter Pach, who was also a critic and a member of Parisian avant-garde circles. By the end of November, they had selected an extraordinarily full and discerning representation of the modern movement in Europe. Some thirteen hundred works of art were put in place in time for a press preview on February 16, 1913. The papers found the exhibit "something like a miracle." Whatever the critics might have thought of individual works, it was evident that American art was placed in a new perspective and "would never be the same again." The exhibition included over three hundred artists, of whom about one-third were foreign, beginning with Goya, Ingres, and Delacroix, continuing through the realists and impressionists, and culminating in the post-impressionists and cubists. Contemporary European artists such as Cézanne, Gauguin, van Gogh, Redon, and Matisse were extensively represented, along with the English painter Augustus John, but the popular sensations, caricatured across the country, were Marcel Duchamp's* Nude Descending a Staircase and Constantin Brancusi's sculpture, Mlle. Pogany. The American section included a few older painters (J. A. M. Whistler,* Childe Hassam, J. Alden Weir, and Albert Ryder*), a fairly strong representation of The Eight* and their associates, several Henri students, such older modernists as Oscar Bluemner* and Maurer, and a number of progressive younger men (Patrick Henry Bruce,* Arthur B. Carles,* Stuart Davis,* Marsden Hartley,* John Marin,* Morgan Russell,* Charles Sheeler,* Morton Schamberg,* Joseph Stella,* Abraham Walkowitz,* Edward Hopper,* and Lionel Feininger*).

The success of the exhibition may be judged by the quality of the selections, seen in retrospect, or by the undeniable impact of the post-impressionists and cubists on subsequent American painting. It was also evident from the waves of praise and protest that swept through the press and from the lines of people that formed to see it—close to 70,000 paid admissions in New York alone. A compact version went to Chicago, and although that city was less receptive to "insurgent art" than New York, the attendance came to nearly 190,000. A still more condensed version went to Boston, which was even more shocked and less understanding than Chicago.

In the aftermath, the Armory Show's success contributed to the demise of the group that had initiated it. The American artists, who had initially sought a way to show their own work effectively, were overshadowed by the foreign section, and Davies, who had worked so diligently to assemble and arrange financing for the show, had at the same time been high-handed, as well as vague about the sources and status of funds. When a post-exhibition members' meeting was finally held,

Henri, Sloan, Luks, Bellows, and others resigned. The Association did not recover from the quarrel, and the organization survived only until it wound up the business of its one great show.

(D.W.S.)

Arneson, Robert (1930–   ).

Ceramist. Born in Benicia, Cal., he studied ceramics at the California College of Arts and Crafts, and is considered the leader of the funk art* movement among ceramists. Deriving from the abstract expressionist ceramics of the late 1950s and from pop art* in general, Arneson came into prominence in the mid-1960s with his depiction of banal objects of modern life as vehicles of social commentary. Typifying his wit are A Toaster with fingertips emerging from one slot, Typewriter with bright red fingernails for keys, and a wide range of bathroom fixtures, usually with sexual implications. Most of his works are in polychrome, low-fire clay, roughly hewn and with shiny surfaces. A 1971 exhibition in San Francisco included a six by six-foot tableau with plates with portions of a smorgasbord molded on each, and also a self-portrait, all in white earthenware clay. Arneson has a wide following among young ceramists, and with his teaching has encouraged the proliferation of funk art. (R.S.)

Art Deco.

The style in design and the decorative arts of the period between art nouveau* and World War II; it is identified particularly with the 1920s and 1930s. The name comes from the 1925 Paris "L'Exposition Internationale des Arts Décoratifs et Industriels Modernes." In its origins it was strongly influenced by the later art nouveau and by the abstract devices of cubism* and related movements of 1910–20. Art deco includes an exotically decorative side, but also a streamlined, machine-inspired geometry. It affected architecture, interior design, industrial design, fashions, craft work, and graphic design; its influence can be traced in the Chrysler Building (New York, 1930); in the sculptural styles of the American Lee Lawrie and the Yugoslav Ivan Meštrović; and in the paintings of Joseph Stella* and Eugene Savage.* A revival of art deco forms began at the end of the 1960s, with designers and

graphic artists turning back to the style and painters such as Frank Stella* and Roy Lichtenstein,* incorporating in their work "nostalgia for the 1930s."

(D.W.S.)

Art Glass.

A colored and decorated glassware made in the last quarter of the 19th century and usually characterized by more than one color and type of decoration on each piece. One of the earliest examples was the "satin glass" produced in quantity in Europe and America from about 1880. Often mold-blown to give a diamond-quilted or herringbone pattern, the bowls and vases generally have three layers of colored and colorless glass, a ruffled rim, and sometimes gilt or enameled decoration.

Many glasses of this period are characterized by color shading produced by the action of heat and certain chemicals in the glass. Thus, a gold ruby glass is yellow when first made, but when reheated turns dark red. If this reheating is carefully controlled, only the hottest portions of the glass will "strike" or turn color. The earliest shaded glassware produced by this technique was Amberina, patented by Joseph Locke of the New England Glass Company in 1883 and made by them until 1888. It was reissued around 1917 by their successors, the Libbey Glass Company of Toledo, Ohio. Hobbs, Brockunier & Company of Wheeling, West Va., made Amberina under license from the New England Glass Company and eventually developed its own varieties of shaded glass, many of them pressed.

The sale of Mrs. Mary Morgan's Chinese porcelain "Peachblow" vase for $18,000 in 1886 produced a boom in imitations of its shading, and several companies made "peachbloom" or "peachskin" glass. Hobbs produced a copy called "Coral" glass, basically an Amberina glass lined with a layer of opaque white glass to give it a porcelain-like appearance. This shading of red to yellow, a natural by-product of making ruby glass, was made by other factories in the United States and Europe during the period of its popularity.

Between 1883 and 1888, the New England Glass Company also made Plated Amberina (which had an opaque white glass lining); Wild Rose, a peachblow type glass; Pomona, glass with a roughened surface and floral decoration; and Agata, a shaded glass with a mottled surface. The Boston & Sandwich Glass Company did not make shaded wares, but produced opaque white blown glass with enamel and gilt decoration and colorless glass in the frilly Victorian style. Probably the largest firm making art glass was the Mt. Washington Glass Company in New Bedford, Mass., which advertised itself as headquarters for art glass in America. In addition to decorated opaque white glassware, they produced Burmese, a pink-to-yellow shaded opaque glass; Rose Amber, their version of Amberina; Peachblow, an opaque glass which shaded from blue-gray to pink; Royal Flemish and Crown Milano, both enameled glasses; and many other varieties.

Art glass was hand made and expensive in its day. Much of it was well-made, reflected a sophisticated technological development, and, more important, satisfied the fanciful taste of the late Victorians. To modern eyes, the ruffled rims, elaborate applied decoration, and ornate metal holders tend to "torture" the glass, and it is only recently that the style has regained popularity with collectors. Today, an increasing number of imitations of this glass is being produced in the United States and abroad.　(J.S.S.)

Art Nouveau (in architecture).

Originally not an architectural style, art nouveau was developed from designs inspired by the "useful arts"—ceramics, glassware, ironwork, and hardware. The name derives from a shop that opened in Paris in 1895 and specialized in modern design. Probably the greatest architectural influence in this direction was the German architect Victor Horta (1861–1947), who practised largely in Belgium, designing several buildings in the 1890s in which the plastic, curvilinear quality of the designs was reminiscent of plant forms. From Scotland a more cubist version of the style came from the artist-designer Charles Rennie Mackintosh (1868–1928). Another source of inspiration was Oriental art, a style long familiar to most art nouveau artists.

Art nouveau never took the lead in architecture as it did in the decorative arts. Thus, Tiffany's, with its "Favrile" glassware, and Yale & Towne, with its

hardware, were both important in bringing the style to the attention of the general public. Robert D. Kohn (1870–1953), one of the few American architects who saw the possibilities in this style, combined sculpture with a fine art nouveau design in his New York Evening Post Building on Vesey Street. See also Art Nouveau (in glass).
(A.B.)

Art Nouveau (in glass).

A late 19th-century style of decoration leading to a fashion for glass that reacted against both elaborately decorated "art" glass and the heavy brilliant-cut glass. These styles are now considered overdecorated and alien to the inherent qualities of glass. Emile Gallé of Nancy, France, led the revolution in Europe; and Louis Comfort Tiffany, of the New York family of jewelers, was instrumental in developing the style in the United States. Tiffany (1848–1933) established his reputation with stained glass and mosaics before creating his "Favrile" glasses in the 1890s. Favrile resulted from his fascination with the iridescence that ancient glasses developed from being buried for centuries in damp soil. The Tiffany Furnaces, opened at Corona, Long Island, in 1893, produced Favrile pieces both in classical styles and in plantlike shapes reflecting the art nouveau affinity for natural forms. Tiffany also made lamp shades that related to his earlier work in stained glass.

Frederick Carder* (1863–1963), an Englishman who helped to found the Steuben Glass Works in Corning, N.Y., in 1903, became another leader in the production of art nouveau glass. Interested in glass technology, he soon developed an enormous range of glass color formulas and methods of decoration. His iridescent gold or blue "Aurene" resembled Tiffany's glass, but Carder proved that he had perfected his formula independently. He manufactured, cased, cut, and acid-etched glasses; glasses with bubble inclusions (for example, Cluthra and Cintra); and, after his semiretirement in 1933, cast glass sculptures and architectural glass.

In the first decade of the 20th century, three other firms produced glass that were of high technical quality but imitated Tiffany's in form and decoration. In 1901 Martin Bach, a Tiffany employee, started the Quezal Art Glass

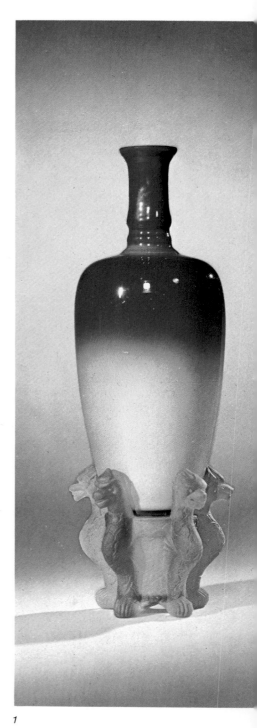

1

2

4

3

5

Art Glass
1. Hobbs, Brockunier & Co. The Morgan Vase, "Peachblow" or "Coral" glass, free-blown, c.1890's, pressed stand of amber glass. Corning Museum of Glass, Corning, N.Y.
2. Frederick Carder. Various pieces made from 1916 to 1930 at the Steuben Glass Works, Corning, N.Y., blue and gold "Aurene" and etched **glass. Smithsonian Institution, Washington, D.C.**

Art Nouveau (in glass)
3. Frederick Carder. Various pieces made from 1905 to 1920s at the Steuben Glass Works, Corning, N.Y., gold "Aurene". Smithsonian Institution, **Washington, D.C.**
4. Tiffany table lamp. Wisteria, c.1900. Collection Lillian Nassau, N.Y.
5. Tiffany table lamp. Trumpet-flower shade, c. 1900. Collection Lillian Nassau, N.Y.

and Decorating Company of Brooklyn, employing former Tiffany workers. Following this firm's closing in 1924, Martin Bach, Jr., and a number of Quezal workmen joined Victor Durand's Vineland (New Jersey) Flint Glass Works, which marketed a decorated iridescent glass as Durand Art Glass from about 1925 to 1931. Under the direction of Julian de Cordova, the Union Glass Works of Somerville, Mass., manufactured Kew Blas glass from about 1900 probably until the factory closed in 1924. During the period between World War I and the Depression, most of the companies making art nouveau glass suffered financial reverses and a loss of public interest in their product. The Tiffany furnaces closed in 1928, and Steuben Glass ceased manufacturing colored glasses in 1932. Until the development of the studio glass movement in the 1960s, American glass production was limited almost entirely to commercial lines and few new designs or techniques were introduced. See also Art Nouveau (in architecture).

(J.S.S.)

Art Students League of New York.

A school organized as a drawing and sketching class in 1875 by members of the National Academy of Design's* art school, which had closed temporarily. Even after the Academy school reopened in 1877, Walter Shirlaw* and others continued the League's classes, reflecting the younger artists' desire for independence that had led to their founding the Society of American Artists.* The Society and the League were closely allied, and the ties were strengthened in 1878, when William Merritt Chase,* a leader of those dissatisfied with the National Academy, initiated his class in painting at the League. The growth of both the Society and the League led in 1892 to the construction of a building on West 57th Street to house both organizations and the Architectural League. By the late 1890s the school boasted nearly a thousand students and eventually it took over the entire structure.

The Art Students League, unlike the art school of the National Academy of Design, has had no set course of studies and no requirements. Students attend classes of their choice and are represented on the governing board, which in turn appoints instructors and sets fees. The system has enjoyed

marked success, for the school over the years has attracted a distinguished teaching staff and a number of serious, dedicated students. Many of America's most famous artist-teachers have served as instructors there, including Chase, Thomas Eakins,* Robert Henri,* and John Sloan.* Its list of former students contains a high percentage of the best-known American artists of the 20th century.

(D.W.S.)

Arts and Crafts Movement.

Founded by the British pre-Raphaelite poet and painter William Morris (1834–96), its aim was to revive the handcrafts in an increasingly mechanized age. It emphasized the need for integrating beauty into everyday life and encouraged the return in the decorative arts of the artistic craftmanship that marked the Middle Ages. In 1861 Morris, along with several painters, designers, and architects, began his own London firm (Morris, Marshall, Faulkner & Company) to promote his ideas. The first Morris wallpapers were produced in 1862, and he went on to learn weaving and dye-staining and to design fabrics, furniture, and eventually books.

Several similar organizations were founded at that time, and in 1888 the Arts and Crafts Exhibition Society held its first show. During the 1890s crafts activity flourished, and the movement exerted a widespread influence throughout Europe. Many of the movement's ideals were continued by Walter Gropius in the Bauhaus* school in Germany long after the crafts enthusiasm had waned.

In America in 1895 Elbert Hubbard modeled his Roycroft shops in East Aurora, N.Y., after Morris' workshop. Hubbard also worked to revive handcrafts, particularly furniture-making and printing. The first American Society of Arts and Crafts was organized in Boston in 1897. The influence of the crafts movement was evident also in the early furniture that the architects Frank Lloyd Wright* and Henry Hobson Richardson* designed for their own buildings. (See Furniture Since 1650.)

Ash Can School, The.

A term loosely applied to the first American art movement of the 20th century, begun soon after 1900 by the realistic painters of The Eight* and their associates. Robert Henri,* John Sloan,* and George Luks* advocated the por-

trayal of daily life as it actually appeared, even if such everyday subjects were considered "vulgar." Several had been newspaper illustrators, and they found the New York scene an inspiring point of departure. Everett Shinn* (in his earlier work), Jerome Myers,* and such students of Robert Henri as George Bellows,* who portrayed slum scenes on occasion, and William Glackens,* who sometimes painted views of docks and cafés, did not, however, stress social content. Indeed, none of the artists placed consistent emphasis on the seamy aspects of city life or used their art as a vehicle for a social message, as did the "social realist" artists of the 1930s. They painted very few ash cans and actually formed no "school." As advocates, in varying degree, of realism, they have been termed more accurately "New York realists"; the colorful "Ash Can School" designation has stuck, however, with both public and critics ever since it first appeared in a book by Holger Cahill and Alfred Barr in 1934.

(D.W.S.)

Assemblage.

A term used in the early 1960s to designate an effort to integrate art and environment by assembling objects of everyday experience; it was borrowed from the French painter Jean Dubuffet, who used it for "all forms of composite art and modes of juxtaposition." Assemblage was rooted in the experiments of early 20th-century artists who sought to redefine the nature of painting and sculpture. Rejecting all previous theories of unity of composition, Braque, Picasso, Picabia, Duchamp, and scores of other artists before World War I tried to dissect forms and reconstitute them in unaccustomed juxtapositions. Although modern assemblage drew on the cubist experiment initially, it differed from these traditions because its raw elements are recognizable objects from the environment, such as photographs, old letters, weathered wood, automobile parts, leaves, dolls eyes, etc., arranged in less predetermined configurations.

The works of assemblage that began to appear frequently in the early 1950s drew upon several 20th-century traditions, notably surrealism,* with its juxtaposition of different conceptions and its exhaustive exploration of the meaning of objects in new psychological contexts. The surrealists had been primed by their dada* origins, in which objects familiar to the bourgeoisie were ridiculed, cast in new roles, and often used to produce a wry laugh. The "readymades" of Marcel Duchamp,* as well as the photomontages of George Grosz* and the objects and collages of Raoul Hausmann and Kurt Schwitters, led to the surrealist adventures of the 1920s and 1930s, such as Meret Oppenheim's *Fur-Covered Cup, Saucer and Spoon* (1936) or Joan Miró's *Object* (1936), with its stuffed parrot perched above a woman's stockinged leg standing on a man's hat. Surrealist objects, writes George Hugnet, one of the founders of the movement, "are the automatic, reasonless and yet material expression of inhibited wishes, anthropomorphic vegetations of the permanently unpredictable in man."

It was both the use of disassociated materials and the psychological need to explore the unpredictable in man that emerged in the assemblages of the 1950s and 1960s. Joseph Cornell,* an early practicioner of the method, pleased the younger generation with his poetic juxtapositions of objects and images set in uniquely crafted boxes; Marcel Duchamp also became a hero among young assemblagists during those years. To some degree, the three-dimensional objects of the period had been stimulated by abstract expressionism*—a primarily philosophical movement in which all canons of painting and sculpture were challenged and artistic liberty was declared limitless. The abstract expressionists were deeply urban in their attitudes, and frequently alluded to the importance of the city with all its crowded diversity and endless detritus. When the young assemblagists began, one of the first items of exploration was precisely the "junk culture" of New York. Richard Stankiewicz* compiled his sculptures from bits of machinery and household items found in junkpiles. John Chamberlain* used the chassis of abandoned automobiles. Ed Kienholz* used such items as mannequins' heads and discarded baby carriages in his satiric tableaux. All of these artists spurned the old associations of sculpture as an isolated object on a base and tried to move out into the environment, meeting, as many of them suggested, reality halfway.

The assemblage approach made it possible for Lee Bontecou* to make deep reliefs out of ordinary burlap and bits of found metal. The change in attitude accomplished by the assemblage period later implemented broad experimentation in plastics and other materials developed by technology. Those who in 1961 were interested, for instance, by the "combines" of Robert Rauschenberg* in which bits of paper, cloth, photographs, and even spoons and quilts were included in paintings, could easily follow him when he branched out into larger environments with the help of technologists. The assemblage protagonists were important in changing attitudes toward what constituted sculpture. (D.A.)

Atelier 17.
A printmaking workshop founded by the English painter Stanley William Hayter (b. 1901) in Paris in 1927 and moved to New York in 1940. The Atelier was associated with the New School for Social Research until 1945, when it moved to its own quarters on Eighth Street. After Hayter's return to Paris in 1950 and until its closing in the late 1950s, the workshop continued under the direction of several members, including Karl Schrag*and Peter Grippe. Hayter rediscovered and developed techniques of copper and zinc plate engraving and etching. Like Hayter, many of the artists belonging to the workshop worked in surrealist style. Marc Chagall, Max Ernst, Jacques Lipchitz,* André Masson, Matta, Joan Miró, and Yves Tanguy made prints there during their stay in the United States. Their presence, as well as Hayter's developments in the use of free line engraving, deep etching and drilled plates, had considerable influence on the members of the workshop, including Jackson Pollock,* Robert Motherwell,* Louise Nevelson,* Mauricio Lasansky* and Gabor Peterdi.* Lasansky and Peterdi and their students have carried on Hayter's methods. Publications containing prints made at the workshop include *VVV Portfolio (1942), Brunidor Portfolio No. 1* (1947), *Laurels Album* (1947), and *21 Etchings and Poems* (1960). The latter publication includes the only etchings by Franz Kline* and Willem de Kooning,* as well as poems by poets who visited the Atelier such as Frank O'Hara, Theodore Roethke, Dylan Thomas, and William Carlos Williams. Work from Atelier 17 was the subject of an exhibition at the Museum of Modern Art in 1944. (R.C.)

Atterbury, Grosvenor (1869–1956).
Architect and inventor. He was born in Detroit, Mich., attended Yale University and the Columbia School of Architecture, and in 1895 went to the École des Beaux-Arts in Paris. He returned to the United States and settled in Shinnecock Hills, Long Island, N.Y.

Because he was interested in socioeconomic problems, Atterbury combined his invention of a prefabricated system of building with low-cost housing. About 1907, he developed a nailable concrete block and a hollow concrete slab, eight by four feet; produced in precast concrete, this was used for many of the English Tudor houses he designed for Forest Hills Gardens—a model, parklike community in Queens County, New York. The streets, open spaces, and building lots had been laid out by the successors of the noted landscape architect, Frederick Law Olmsted,* in 1911. His work also included model tenement houses, hospitals, museums and many Long Island estates. This contemporary work contrasted with his historically correct restoration of the New York City Hall (1907–20) and demonstrated his versatility as an architect. He received the gold medal of the New York Chapter, American Institute of Architects, in 1953 and served as president of the Architectural League in 1915–17. He was consultant in architecture at Johns Hopkins University and taught at the Yale University School of Architecture. (A.B.)

Audubon, John James (1785–1851).
America's most famous painter of wildlife. He was born in Haiti, the natural son of a French father and a French Creole mother. Educated in France, where he was taken by his father after his mother's death, he studied drawing for a few months with the famous French painter David. In 1803 he was sent to live on his father's estate in Mill Grove, Pa., but he revisited France in 1805–06. On his return to the United States, he became the proprietor of a general store in Louisville, Ky., but it failed largely because he spent much of his time hunting, collecting specimens, and drawing wildlife. Several other business ventures met with a similar fate and after 1808, following his marriage, he taught drawing and painted portraits to help support his family. However, his passionate interest in natural history continued. Using

1

2

New Orleans as a base, he began in about 1820 the ambitious task of painting the birds of America with the intention of publishing them, expressing his urge thus: "Nothing . . . could ever answer my enthusiastic desires to present nature, except to copy her in her own way, alive and moving!"

To pursue his studies he traveled extensively from 1820–26 in the United States and even went to Labrador in search of specimens. Failing to find an American publisher, he went to England in 1826 and found support for his great undertaking in the form of individual subscribers. There, for the next decade, interrupted by three trips home to obtain additional specimens and subscribers, he painstakingly oversaw the production of his magnum opus. *The Birds of America* was conceived on a grand scale and there was no stinting of expense. It was published by subscription in eighty-seven parts between 1826 and 1838 as a huge "double elephant" folio, containing 435 life-size hand-colored aquatints, most of which were executed by Robert Havell, Jr., a gifted English engraver, after Audubon's original watercolors. The plates represent 1065 birds of 489 supposedly distinct species of American birds. While all the plates were widely admired then as now, his magnificent *Wild Turkey Cock* is certainly the rarest and the most sought after, and is generally considered his masterpiece. Audubon also published a smaller octavo edition containing five hundred plates, which went through three editions and several reprintings between 1840 and 1870. The elephant folio was never republished in its entirety, but after his death, 106 plates were reprinted in New York in 1860.

The text to accompany the plates appeared in five other volumes under the title *Ornithological Biography* (1831–39). The ornithological descriptions were edited by the distinguished Scotch naturalist, William MacGillivray, as Audubon, despite his ability to make accurate notes and studies in the field, had neither a classical nor a scientific education. However, the charm of this publication rests, not on the scientific records, but on the vivid account of his experiences of pioneer life in the Ohio and Mississippi valleys between 1808 and 1834.

Audubon was almost unknown when he arrived in England, but he was soon recognized as a peer by the ablest scientific and literary figures. His watercolors of American birds were greatly admired and he was proclaimed an American genius. His engaging personality and magnetism shortly made him a social lion. He was elected a member of the Linnaean Society in 1828 and became a fellow of the Royal Society in 1830.

Having accomplished his great undertaking, he returned to the United States in 1839. In 1842 he settled in New York City, purchasing an estate of some thirty acres at Washington Heights on the Hudson. His abundant energy, however, impelled him to undertake yet a further project, *The Viviparous Quadrupeds of North America.* It was similar in format to the *Birds,* except that the color plates were reproduced by the quicker, less expensive process of lithography. It appeared in thirty parts in 1845–46 and contained 150 plates in imperial folio. A smaller, octavo edition was published in 1849–54 with 155 plates. The text was written by Audubon's friend John Bachman and appeared in three octavo volumes in 1846–54. On this project Audubon was aided by his two talented sons, Victor (1809–60) and John Woodhouse Audubon (1812–62), both of whom had been trained by their father as artists and naturalists. *The Quadrupeds* has never enjoyed as much success as the *Birds,* partly because of the different medium used. In 1843 he embarked on his last trip to the wilderness, going to the upper Missouri and Yellowstone rivers to collect specimens.

Audubon was primarily a watercolorist but he occasionally painted in oil. In his early days, for example, he turned out a few portraits to help support his family. Later, especially after he went to England, he made oil copies of his watercolors of birds, many of which he gave to influential friends in the expectation of return favors. Other oil copies were painted to raise funds to pay his engraver, Havell. A typical, handsome example is *Hawk Pouncing on Quail* (1827, University of Liverpool). It is his watercolors, however, that sustain his reputation. More than four hundred of the original watercolors for the bird series are in the New-York Historical Society. Their importance rests on the fact that they combine keen observation of nature and accuracy of detail with great originality in composition.

Thus they communicate a feeling for living nature that raises them far above mere ornithological reportage.

Audubon was a handsome and romantic figure and he did nothing during his lifetime to dispel the aura of mystery surrounding him. Rumors were circulated that he was the Lost Dauphin of France. His portrait by the American painter Henry Inman* (1833, location unknown), for example, depicts him as the archetypal frontiersman, with long, flowing hair, a shirt open at the neck, and wrapped in a cloak. In fact, he clung to his colorful frontier dress and somewhat unorthodox conduct to give a picturesque impression of his wilderness life. He found such showmanship expedient in his constant need to meet the costs of engraving and publishing his bird prints. There is no other American artist with whom Audubon may be compared: for Alexander Wilson (1766–1813), who also published bird prints, was first and last an ornithologist. Audubon thus fills a unique role as the genius who devoted himself to one highly specialized subject. Not only are his masterly compositions esthetically satisfying, but also they preserve images of American nature in its pristine state. (H.W.W.)

Augur, Hezekiah (1791–1858).
One of the earliest American sculptors, and the first to carve full-length figures in marble. In the early 1820s Augur gave up a career in the drygoods business in New Haven, Conn., to become a woodcarver. He had no formal training, but by 1827 had turned to working in marble. In that year he did a bust of Professor Alexander M. Fisher (Yale); other early pieces include idealized neoclassical marble busts of Apollo and Sappho. Such subjects were clearly inspired by the classical revival then in vogue in Europe and America. Augur's most famous work, the neoclassical marble group, *Jephthah and His Daughter* (1828–30, Yale), attracted much attention when it was exhibited in several cities on the East Coast. The art of sculpture was only vaguely known in America at that time, and it was a curiosity indeed to see two full-length marble figures executed by a native artist.

Augur's career seems to have ended about 1832, after he executed a marble bust of Chief Justice Oliver Ellsworth for the U.S. Capitol. (W.C.)

3

4

1. *John James Audubon.* Purple Grackle, pub. 1827.
2. *John James Audubon.* Blue-winged Teal, pub. 1836. Both, aquatint engravings of the original watercolors. New-York Historical Society, N.Y.
3. *Hezekiah Augur.* Jephtha, 1830, marble.
4. *Hezekiah Augur.* Daughter of Jephtha, 1830, marble. Both, Yale University Art Gallery, New Haven, Conn.

Austin, Henry (1804–91).
Architect. Born in Mt. Carmel, Conn. In 1819 he became a carpenter's apprentice. Soon after, he moved to New York, where he worked in the office of Ithiel Town,* whose large library aided him greatly. About 1837 he opened his own office in New Haven and had a large practice for the next fifty years. Austin's practice began at the height of the Greek revival* style, but he was inspired by the so-called Italian Villa style introduced to America by John Notman and A. J. Davis. A. J. Downing's *Cottage Residences* (1842) provided Austin with illustrations of picturesque houses, which he adapted for his own generation, introducing Italianate features and raising the height of the first story. From 1840 to 1860 Austin's popularity in Connecticut was based on his lively villa designs, the most important of which were the Wallis Bristol House, Norton House, and Dana House, all in New Haven; and the Moses Yale Reach House, in Wallingford. His finest house, built with rich materials and considerable ornamentation in the Italian Villa style, is Victoria Mansion, erected for Ruggles Morse in Portland, Me. (1859). His railroad station for New Haven (1848–49, demolished) had an exotic skyline and Moorish details. He also built the New Haven Savings Bank; Eton School; the New Haven City Hall (c.1860), and Yale University Library (1842), both of the latter in Gothic revival* style; Kent Congregational Church (1848); the Egyptian Revival Gate to the Grove Street Cemetery, New Haven (1848); and Danbury First Congregational Church (1858).

Austin had a large number of pupils. He wrote little, although he probably intended to publish the two volumes of watercolor drawings now in the Yale Library (dated 1839–51).

(P.F.N.)

Autio, Rudy (1926–).
Ceramist known for applying abstract expressionist concepts to hand-built utilitarian stoneware objects. Autio was born in Butte, Mont. From 1952–56 he worked at the Archie Bray Foundation in Montana with Peter Voulkos,* and during that time abandoned traditional functional potting for the freedom and expressiveness his work shares with that of Voulkos. The sophisticated "crudeness" with which he handles clay and his relating of glazes to surface character have been highly influential. Like Voulkos, Autio has applied himself to welded-steel sculpture in recent years.

Automatism.
Behavior that is not initiated or directed by conscious thought processes. In philosophy the concept may be traced to the theories of René Descartes and Thomas Hobbes in the 17th century. In the 19th century Thomas Henry Huxley contended that "our mental conditions are simply the symbols in consciousness of the changes which take place automatically in the organism." Most 20th-century scientific exploration of automatism belongs in the province of psychology.

Ideas of free association and the intuitive sources of art may be traced throughout history. An oft-quoted passage from Leonardo da Vinci refers to the images or associations the artist may draw from a changing cloud form or from the cracked and broken surface of an old wall. Intuition, irrationality, and, in a sense, automatism gained strength in 19th-century romantic painting and literature. The nonrational approach recurs in cubist collages and in paintings of the futurists (see Futurism). It was with dada,* however, during World War I, that automatism emerged as a major instrument of expression in art and literature. Dada poems and manifestations were based largely on free association and accident. Jean Arp experimented with collages organized by chance. André Breton, the pioneer and high priest of surrealism,* learned about Sigmund Freud's ideas during World War I and even visited Freud. Breton and the surrealists attempted to systematize the irrational and various forms of automatic expression. Thus, they explored the possibilities of hypnotic trance, and Breton's famous definition in 1924 of surrealism described it as "pure psychic automatism."

In literature, automatism, in the form of free association or stream-of-consciousness techniques, was basic to the experiments of James Joyce, Gertrude Stein, and many others. In the 1920s, Joan Miró and André Masson in painting, along with Jean Arp in sculpture, were exposed to surrealist ideas of automatism and developed abstract organic or biomorphic surrealism. From this point forward, automatism, intuition, free association, and improvisation became central to much of the experimental art of the 20th century. American abstract expressionists such as Robert Motherwell* and Jackson Pollock* were probably more affected by the ideas of automatism than by other surrealist concepts. From the 1940s to the present a very large percentage of all abstract painting and sculpture throughout the world has been rooted in one or another form of automatic expression.

(H.H.A.)

Avedon, Richard (1923–).
Photographer, born in New York, N.Y. He left high school during World War II and received his first formal training in photography while serving in the merchant marine. Beginning in 1946 he attended Columbia University and studied under Alexey Brodovitch at the New School for Social Research. He began his professional career in photography as a studio assistant at *Harper's Bazaar* but soon moved up and became known for his fresh and inventive fashion photographs and for his tart portraits of such famous personages as the Reverend Billy Graham, President Eisenhower, and Bertrand Russell; in these studies every pore and facial blemish is exaggerated by shooting close-up with a wide-angle lens. The result is powerful photographs that capture the subject in a very revealing but not essentially unkind manner. In addition to *Harper's Bazaar*, Avedon's work has appeared in *Vogue, Life, Look,* and *Graphics.* In 1950 he received the highest achievement award at the Art Director's Show. His photographs were published in *Observations* (1959), with a text by Truman Capote, and in *Nothing Personal* (1964), with a text by James Baldwin.

(V.D.C.)

Avery, Milton (1893–1965).
One of the few 20th-century American painters who has constantly been reevaluated with each development in American painting. Born in Altmar, N.Y., he studied briefly at the Connecticut League of Art Students, but learned most from his personal studies of European fauvism* and expressionism.* His earlier figure drawings and his paintings of the 1930s suggest relationships with German expressionists such as Ernst Ludwig Kirchner, but increasingly during the 1940s he devel-

1

oped a style of broad, simplified, delicately modulated color planes whose closest parallel is to be found in works of the modern French master Henri Matisse. The influence of Matisse is also evident in many of his figure drawings and paintings including figures such as *Swimmers and Sunbathers* (1945, Metropolitan).

During much of his career Avery moved in a world of American art dominated by social realism and regionalism, but stood apart from it in his expression of a personal poetry through delicate yet powerful arrangements of flat color shapes. Although his paintings always involved a recognizable subject—figures in an interior or on a seashore, still lifes, and landscapes—they are highly abstract in impact, for example *Green Sea* (1954, Metropolitan). In the earlier landscapes he frequently used an overall pattern of lines or color dots, but he increasingly simplified this to color shapes that were essentially abstract. The extremely subtle balance that he achieved between nature and abstraction, both always permeated by a mysterious inner sensibility, defines the peculiar world of his works. The colors are generally laid on thinly and transparently. Despite the strength of the formal structure of his oil paintings, his gifts in the fluid medium of watercolor are always apparent. Avery is an important bridge in American painting between the pioneer European color masters such as Matisse and the abstract imagists and color-field painters of the 1960s. Mark Rothko,* a close friend, continually acknowledged the great debt that he and his generation owed to the "sheer loveliness" of Avery's work, the "inner power in which gentleness and silence proved more audible and poignant." To him Avery was a "great poet-inventor who had invented sonorities never seen nor heard before. From these we have learned much and will learn more for a long time to come." Younger painters, such as Helen Frankenthaler,* acknowledge a comparable debt. (H.H.A.)

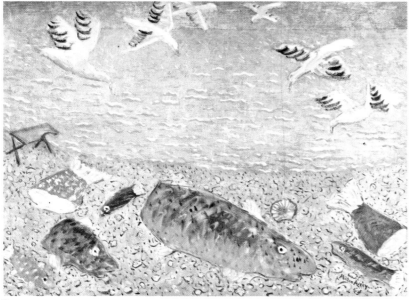

2

1. ***Milton Avery.*** Seated Girl with Dog, *1944. Collection Roy R. Neuberger, N.Y.*
2. ***Milton Avery.*** Sea Gulls, Gaspé, *1938. Addison Gallery of American Art, Phillips Academy, Andover, Mass.*

B

Bacon, Peggy (1895–   ).
Painter and printmaker. Primarily a caricaturist, she has contributed to the *New Yorker, Town and Country, Vanity Fair,* and other periodicals. Born in Ridgefield, Conn., she studied with John Sloan* at the Art Students League.*

She has published eighteen books of her own work (including poems and short stories) and illustrated sixty-four with text by others such as poets Carl Sandburg and Louis Untermeyer. The artist often accompanies her portraits and genre caricatures with verbal comment. The following verbal self-portrait is a good example of her style in both words and line: "Pinhead, parsimoniously covered with thin, dark hair, on a short, dumpy body; small features, prominent nose, chipmunk teeth, and no chin, conveying the sharp, weak look of a little rodent. Absent-minded eyes. Prim critical mouth. Personality lifeless, retiring, snippy."

She has had numerous exhibitions of her work in New York galleries. She held a Guggenheim Fellowship in 1934 and has taught at the Art Students League and at the Fieldston Ethical Culture School. She works in etching, drypoint, pastel, and pen-and-ink as well as oil.   (A.F.)

Badger, Joseph (1708–65).
Portrait painter. A native of Charlestown, Mass., he moved to Boston in 1731, where he worked as a house painter and glazier. Portraiture was a sideline, begun in around 1740, in which he prospered only because the decline and death of John Smibert* freed him from competition. His drawing is bad, his coloring dull, and his compositions imitative, owing much to mezzotint prototypes.* Thus, his *Mrs. John Edwards* (1750–60, Boston) may be related to the British mezzotint of Isaac Newton, adopted by many American painters as an appropriate pose for

worthy old age. His work, however, has the charm of the primitive—it is literal, labored, and naive. Like other minor artists he was often called upon to depict children, and these pictures, now the greater part of his surviving oeuvre, have always held a special appeal. His *Jeremiah Belknap* (c.1758, Cleveland) and *James Badger* (1760, Metropolitan) are examples.   (C.C.S.)

Baldwin, Benjamin (1913–   ).
Architect and designer of the purest, most minimal interiors of the 1960s, and an inspirational leader in design. Born in Montgomery, Ala., he studied painting with Hans Hofmann,* and architecture at Princeton University (M.F.A. 1938) and Cranbrook Academy of Art in Michigan. He worked (1939–40) with Eliel Saarinen* and Eero Saarinen,* was in architectural partnership (1940–41) with his brother-in-law Harry Weese, and helped to establish the interior design function of the architectural firm of Skidmore, Owings & Merrill* in New York (1945–47). Independent practice in New York, Alabama, and Chicago brought him commissions for furniture, textiles, and industrial design, and for office and residential interiors that he created in the most tranquil and refined architecture of the minimal style.* He was sought after because of the sophisticated, almost oriental chasteness of his designs, by such architects as Louis Kahn* (for the library and dining hall at Phillips Exeter Academy, Exeter, N.H., 1972), I. M. Pei* (for a residence in Texas, 1969), and Edward L. Barnes* (for a residence in Minnesota, 1968).   (C.R.S.)

Ball, F. Carlton (1911–   ).
Ceramist important as a teacher and also known for the surface textures and size of his pots. Born in Sutter Creek, Cal., Ball was one of the first university-educated potters, having studied under

Glenn Lukens* at the University of Southern California from 1932–35. While a student he also studied advanced sculpture, jewelry, and silversmithing, all of which he has practised and taught. His pots have been as much as six feet tall, and their rough textures, often with stamped or incised designs, have an oriental flavor. He teaches at the University of Puget Sound in Washington.

Ball, Thomas (1819–1911).
Sculptor, born in Charlestown, Mass. After commencing as a painter in Boston, Ball turned to sculpture about 1850. Like many American sculptors of this period, he had no formal training, and his style grew out of the naturalism which then dominated American art. As is evident in his statuettes of Daniel Webster (1852) and Henry Clay (1858), naturalism was to remain the basis of his art in the many busts and statues he would produce in the next thirty years. In 1854 Ball left for Italy where, like other expatriate American sculptors, he believed his art could develop better. He returned to America to model what is probably his most famous piece, the equestrian statue of Washington in Boston's Public Garden. He then returned to Florence, where throughout the 1870s his busy studio produced a procession of undramatic portrait statues, notably the marble *Governor John Andrew* (1871) for the State House, Boston, the bronze *Daniel Webster* (1876) for Central Park, New York City, and the bronze *Charles Sumner* (1878) for the Public Garden, Boston. Ball did not often attempt symbolic works, probably because his prosaic naturalism in portraiture was so satisfactory to his patrons. But his bronze *Emancipation Group,* showing Abraham Lincoln freeing a Negro from his chains, was erected in Washington in 1875. In the late 1890s the sculptor

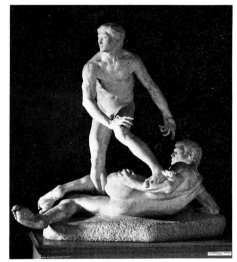

1. *Joseph Badger.* James Badger, 1760. *Metropolitan Museum of Art, N.Y. (Rogers Fund).*
2. *George Grey Barnard.* Struggle of Two Natures in Man, *1893, marble. Metropolitan Museum of Art, N.Y. (gift of Alfred Corning Clark).*

sold the Villa Ball, built on a hillside overlooking Florence, next to the property of his friend, the sculptor Hiram Powers,* and returned to America to live.   (W.C.)

Bannard, Darby (1931–   ).
Painter, born in New Haven, Conn., and educated at Princeton University. His earliest paintings, dating back to 1961, were absolutely simple, yet sophisticated: usually a single geometrical shape against a plain background—both painted in pastel shades of ordinary housepaint. Shortly after these paintings were first exhibited in 1964, his style became increasingly illusionistic. After a 1965 series in which geometric forms were bent forward and back in space, he turned to the manipulation of paint, contrasting matte and gloss finishes and adopting such abstract expressionist devices as paint splatters and dribbles and the illusion of soak-stain forms. Bannard's abstractions fall entirely within the tradition of easel painting and have had wide public acceptance, as attested by his numerous shows in New York, Toronto, London, and Paris.   (E.C.G.)

Barbizon School.
A group formed around 1830 by several French painters who, in order to work directly from nature, painted in the Forest of Fontainebleau and around the village of Barbizon. Reacting to the romantic generalizations of the day, they saw nature as intimate and humane, to be painted subjectively but with an eye for carefully observed detail. They were fascinated with the color and mood of changing seasons and times of day and with the effects of light playing on the landscape. Among the painters in the School were Charles-François Daubigny, Théodore Rousseau, Jean-François Millet, and, briefly, Jean-Baptiste Camille Corot. These painters opened the door to realism by exploring the effects of sensitive interpretation of objective reality. Their influence became international with the 1885 "Exposition Universelle" of Paris.

Among the American painters influenced particularly by Corot were George Inness,* Homer D. Martin,* and Alexander Wyant.* Millet's American followers included Wyatt Eaton* and William Morris Hunt,* both of whom spent periods at Barbizon living near Millet.   (D.W.S.)

Bard, James (1815–97) and **John** (1815–56).
New York City twins who as self-taught artists collaborated on more than 350 carefully detailed and accurate paintings of contemporary steamboats and sailing vessels. James probably supplied the drawings and John the color, figures, and backgrounds. After John's death James continued to work in the same vein with a total production that has been placed at four thousand paintings and which constitutes an incomparably rich record of Hudson River shipping of the 19th century. An example of their joint work is a painting of the ship *America* (c.1850, Smithsonian).

Barnard, George Grey (1863–1938).
Sculptor. Born in Bellefonte, Pa., he attended the Chicago Art Institute, where he was influenced by the plaster casts of Michelangelo's powerful figures that were used in drawing classes. In 1884 he went to Paris to study at the École des Beaux-Arts, and in 1886 he received his first important commission—to put his statue titled *Boy* into marble. This was soon followed by a monument to the poet Severin Skovgaard, for Langesund, Norway. These pieces reveal the influence of Rodin, then the most famous and controversial sculptor in Europe; they are already marked by the emotional turmoil that was to dominate much of Barnard's work, making him probably the most thoroughly romantic of all 19th-century American sculptors. This is evident in his *Struggle of Two Natures in Man,* modeled in Paris, blocked-out at the marble quarry at Carrara, Italy, and exhibited at the Salon of 1894, where it caused great excitement. Equally reminiscent of Michelangelo and Rodin are *Brotherly Love* (1892) and *The Elements* (1894), both in marble and containing powerful human forms expressive of emotional, turbulent spirits. More gentle passions are found in *The Hewer* and his mate, *Primitive Woman* (1902), which were placed on the Rockefeller estate in Pocantico Hills, N.Y., and in the bronze *Pan* (1896–1900, Columbia University), a languishing gigantic figure recalling Michelangelo's work.

Barnard's work had quickly made him famous, but an exhibition of his sculpture in New York in 1896 was not as well received as it had been in Paris. Nevertheless, he established his studio

1

2

1. *George N. Barnard.* View of Con-
federate Lines, Near Chattanooga
R.R.—Looking South, *1865, daguerre-
otype. Library of Congress,
Washington, D.C.*
2. *Edward Larrabee Barnes.* St. Paul's
School, student cafeteria, Concord,
N.H., 1970.

in New York and from 1900–04 taught at the Art Students League.* In 1902 he was awarded his largest commission—the sculptures for the new State Capitol at Harrisburg, Pa. Large groups of symbolic nude figures were designed to stand on blocks flanking the main entrance. Barnard must have conceived of his commission as comparable to Michelangelo's sculptures for the Medici Chapel or Rodin's *Gates of Hell.* Two groups were to represent "man's destiny on earth": *The Broken Law* contains writhing, tormented men; *The Unbroken Law* shows tranquil figures. The sculptures were unveiled in October, 1911. Barnard's last major sculpture was the controversial *Abraham Lincoln,* which was cast in bronze and erected in Cincinnati in 1917. Critics objected that it portrayed Lincoln as a disheveled dolt, but Barnard claimed he wanted to show his subject as an ordinary man deep in thought. His only effort at public portrait statuary, it was slow to win appreciation.

During his many years in France, Barnard had formed a large collection of medieval antiquities. These were purchased from him in 1925 by John D. Rockefeller, who later presented them to The Cloisters in New York to form the basis of that museum's collection. Barnard was approaching the end of his career in the 1920s, but he continued to dream and design in grandiose manner. His last great project was a colossal Rainbow Arch that he hoped to erect near The Cloisters. It was to be 60 feet across at its base and 100 feet high, with a tomb of a soldier beneath it, but his death ended the project.

Barnard's place in American sculpture is a special one because he embraced neither neoclassicism* nor the academic style of the École des Beaux-Arts, as nearly all his contemporaries had done. He created an individual and powerful style that was at once romantic, passionate, expressive, and naturalistic. (W.C.)

Barnard, George N. (1819–1902).
A pioneer daguerreotypist who became America's first news photographer and a celebrated documentor of the Civil War. Born in Connecticut and raised in Nashville, Tenn., Barnard began photographing at the age of twenty-three. By 1847 he had opened a portrait studio in Oswego, N.Y. When a fire destroyed the massive grain elevators

there in 1853, Barnard's camera recorded the event. These full-plate daguerreotypes (now at the International Museum of Photography, Rochester, N.Y.) are the first "spot news" photographs known to historians. In 1854, Barnard moved to Syracuse, N.Y., where he worked until the famous photographer Mathew Brady* employed him to photograph Lincoln's inauguration in 1861. Barnard was present at the Battle of Bull Run, but it is his photographs of Sherman's "March to the Sea," that are best known. These sixty-one photographs, published in portfolio in 1865 as *Photographic Views of Sherman's Campaign,* recording the ravaged buildings and deserted streets of Georgia and South Carolina, are mute and terrifying testaments to the mindless brutality of war.

Barnard established a studio in Chicago and when it was destroyed in the great fire of 1871, he used equipment hastily borrowed from others to record the event. Fire also razed his studio in Charleston, S.C. In the 1880s Barnard helped George Eastman, founder of the Eastman Kodak Company, introduce the dryplate process. His last known studio was in Painesville, Ohio, where he worked from 1884 to 1886. Barnard died in his daughter's home in Onondaga County, N.Y., a few miles from his first studio. (D.L.)

Barnes, Edward Larrabee (1915–   ).
Architect. Born in Chicago, he studied at the Harvard Graduate School of Design under Walter Gropius.* After graduation in 1942 he worked until 1946 for the United States Navy on the design of submarines. He then joined the industrial design office of Henry Dreyfuss, where he remained until he set up his own architectural practice in 1947. His early work, such as the Reid House (Purchase, N.Y., 1951), was pure International style,* with flat roofs, individual facades divided up into Mondrian-like squares and rectangles, and rooms declared as separate containers.

As early as 1950, in his Osborn Studio project, Barnes departed from the strict right-angle geometry of the International style. Here and elsewhere, he employed a single-pitch shed roof with glass areas on the gable ends following the angled roof line. The effect of his Dooneief House (1960, but never built) and the small informal buildings at the Haystack Mountain School of Arts and

Crafts (Deer Island, Me., 1960) recall the Scandinavian designers of that time, particularly Arne Jacobson. In the mid- and late-1960s, Barnes began to break up his rectangular planes with diagonal walls, as in his Beach House (Fisher's Island, N.Y., 1967). In this work he appreciably modified the closed horizontal space of the classic International style by building up vertical layered space within his buildings. This approach can be seen in his Walker Art Center Building (Minneapolis, Minn., 1970–71); here the major exhibition levels are connected, visually and actually, as a series of steps, in a fashion reminiscent of the European work of Adolf Loos during the 1920s or the California designs of R. M. Schindler* in the 1920s and 1930s. (D.G.)

Baroque Style.
European baroque, with its reworking of classic forms into a style of new energy, movement, profuse detail, and princely splendor, had run its course for more than a century in painting, sculpture, architecture, and decorative arts before its appearance in America. There all the factors of colonial life tended to dilute and weaken it further, though its influence may be traced in painting, buildings and furniture, 1700–50. It is early, and profusely, evident in the portraits of Justus Engelhardt Kuhn,* a painter of the middle colonies, where sophistication and European influences were relatively strong and Protestant inhibitions were weak. More than any other source, the mezzotint prototype* tended to bring the grandiose baroque of the virtuoso portraitist, Sir Godfrey Kneller, and his school into American art. From the same models, it had a wild flowering in the early 18th-century work of the patroon painters* of the Hudson River Valley. Later, it is reflected with more restrained elegance in some of the history paintings of Benjamin West* and the works of John Trumbull.* (C.C.S.)

Bartlett, Paul Wayland (1865–1925).
Sculptor. Son of the teacher and sculptor, Truman Bartlett, he was born in New Haven, Conn., but in 1874 was sent to Paris for his education. In 1879 he began studying at the École des Beaux-Arts and later worked in the studio of Emmanuel Fremiet, where he became a specialist as an *animalier,* or

1

animal sculptor. He quickly learned the Parisian manner of modeling, marked by richer surfaces and greater spontaneity than the prevailing neoclassical* style, and he retained this style throughout his career. The style is evident in his first important work, a bronze, *The Bear Tamer* (1887, Corcoran), which he sent to the Paris Salon, where he exhibited regularly. Exhibited at the Columbian Exposition of 1893 in Chicago, it brought him to the attention of America. His next important piece was the dynamic bronze figure of *Michelangelo* (late 1890s, Library of Congress). Bartlett worked mainly in France throughout his career, and it was there that he created what is probably his most famous statue, the equestrian *Lafayette* (1899–1908, garden of the Louvre, Paris). It is thoroughly French in its emphasis on impressionistic surface treatment rather than on contour and mass as in the neoclassicists. In 1908–09 Bartlett assisted J. Q. A. Ward* in making models for the sculptures of the pediment of the New York Stock Exchange Building. He then began work in 1909 on his own pedimental group, representing the flourishing of the American people under the benevolent guidance of democracy, for the House of Representatives wing of the U.S. Capitol. Bartlett's work is more picturesque and has greater emphasis on embellishment than the Senate pediment sculptures by Thomas Crawford.* The sculptor's last major project was the group of six heroic figures personifying philosophy and history (1915) for the facade of the New York Public Library. He died in France, the recipient of numerous honors.   (W.C.)

Bascom, Ruth Henshaw (1772–1848). Wife of a Franklin County, Mass., clergyman, who in middle age started to make profile likenesses of neighbors and relations in crayon and chalk, often embellishing them with bits of metal foil for realistic detail, as in the gold paper spectacles she pasted onto one portrait.

Baskin, Leonard, (1922–   ).
Printmaker, sculptor, book designer. Born in New Brunswick, N.J., the son of a rabbi. In 1937–39 he studied with the sculptor Maurice Glickman and in 1939 had his first one-man show in New York. He attended New York (1939–41) and Yale (1941–43) universities and then

served in the U.S. Navy during World War II before continuing his studies at the New School for Social Research in New York. The year of his graduation (1949) Baskin began making prints. In 1950 he went to Paris and studied at the Académie de la Grande Chaumière, and the following year to Florence to work at the Accademia di Belle Arti. Baskin's traditional training and his conviction that art should serve one's fellow man made him a rather unique figure during the 1950s, when abstraction and the expression of one's personal feelings held sway. Rather than experimenting with new formal structures, media, or techniques, Baskin developed a mastery of old techniques —woodcarving, woodcuts, etching, and lithography—and determined to use his work for social ends. During the 1950s he began a series of full-length standing figures of "dead men" in stone, bronze, and wood. Related to these are his "Birdmen" (human figures with bird heads that are reminiscent of certain statues of Egyptian gods) and his "Oppressed Men" (often featuring an owl—another favorite theme—standing on the head of a man). All of these figures represent "universal man" struggling with the problems of life and death, aspiration, immortality, and corruption.

In his prints Baskin extends the psychological overtones of his sculpture even further, frequently producing powerful brooding, and even tortured, images. Much of the strength of these works derives from his bold cutting technique, which exploits the texture of the wood, and from his mastery of black and white. Perhaps the two greatest influences on Baskin's work are Japanese calligraphy and German expressionism (the artists he admires most are Kaethe Kollwitz and Ernst Barlach). Defending the so-called "literary" or "journalistic" qualities of his work, Baskin has noted: "All art is propaganda. . . . The communication of an artistic idea is an act of propaganda." He has stated that for him the most important subject is "anxiety-ridden man, imprisoned in his ungainly self," and has illustrated this theme in such prints as *Hanged Man, Angel of Death,* and *Oppressed Bird with Human Aspects.* Like his black ink drawings on white paper, Baskin's graphics are technically brilliant. His most recent work is a series of bronze sculptures—many with

1. **Paul Wayland Bartlett.** The Bear Tamer, *1887, bronze. Corcoran Gallery of Art, Washington, D.C. (gift of Mrs. Paul Wayland Bartlett).*
2. **Florence Shust Knoll Bassett.** Knoll Interior, *1950's.*
3. **Leonard Baskin.** Tilrust, *1967, ink. Private collection.*

an elegiac air—on the usual themes of death and compassion, and like all his work they display an odd combination of sophistication with the seemingly "primitive." Baskin is often termed a "romantic humanist," perhaps a result of his disavowal of the "purely decorative" and "the private world of the artist."

He has long been interested in book illustration and founded the Gehenna Press, Northampton, Mass., which prints and publishes limited editions. A typical volume would be *Horned Beetles and Other Insects,* for which Baskin has provided thirty-four etchings; however, his interest extends beyond illustration into total book design: the integrating of type, paper, illustrations, and binding to form an esthetic object. Baskin has taught at Smith College since 1953 and has won numerous awards including the Printmaking Prize at the São Paulo Biennial (1961) and medals from the American Institute of Graphic Arts (1965) and the National Institute of Arts and Letters (1969).

(E.C.G.)

2

Bassett, Florence Shust Knoll

(1917–   ).

One of the most influential contemporary designers of furniture and interiors. Born in Michigan, she studied under Eliel Saarinen* and Eero Saarinen* at Kingswood School and Cranbrook Academy of Art in Michigan, then with Mies van der Rohe* at the Illinois Institute of Technology, graduating in 1941. After several years with architectural firms in Boston and New York, she joined Knoll Associates, a pioneer in modern furniture manufacture. She married Hans Knoll* in 1946, and upon his death in 1955, carried on as president of the firm.

Through the Knoll Planning Unit—the interior and furnishings design group she had formed—she helped to popularize the International style* and set the pace for sophisticated interior design throughout America. Her work demonstrated an impeccable sense of clean detail, a deft manipulation of domestic scale for institutional spaces, precise juxtaposition of pure forms, and a crisp yet rich orchestration of textures. She was responsible for the interiors of banks, university dormitories, showrooms, and office buildings, among the most influential of which were the Connecticut General Life In-

3

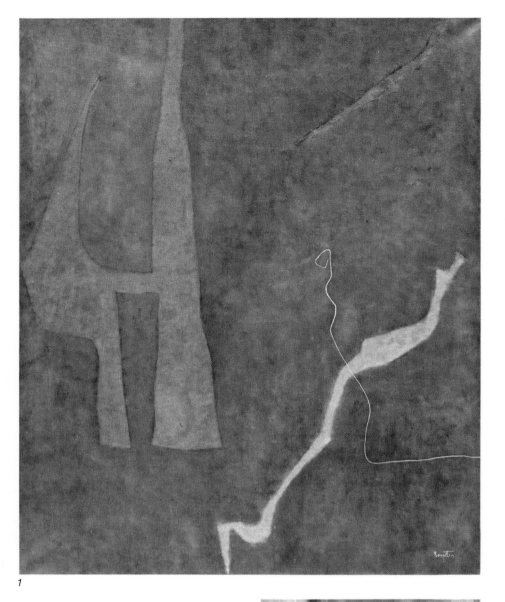

1

1. **William Baziotes.** Dusk, 1958. Solomon R. Guggenheim Museum, N.Y.
2. **Cecilia Beaux.** Man with the Cat (Henry Sturgis Drinker), National Collection of Fine Arts, Smithsonian Institution, Washington, D.C.

2

surance Building, in collaboration with Skidmore, Owings & Merrill,* and the CBS headquarters. She married Harry Hood Bassett in 1958 and resigned from Knoll in 1965. She continues her design work from studios in Florida and Vermont. (C.R.S.)

Bauhaus.
A school founded in Weimar, Germany, in 1919 by the architect Walter Gropius.* The name has since become synonomous with the functional style it introduced in design and architecture. Influenced by the Dutch De Stijl movement and Russian constructivism,* the anti-expressionist esthetic of the Bauhaus encouraged abstraction in art and a purity of line and design in furniture and architecture. One of Gropius' aims was to reunite all the arts—specifically the fine and the applied arts—under the discipline of architecture. He believed that an artist or architect should also be a craftsman, and courses both in theories of form and design and in materials and craftmanship were given. Among the subjects included in the school's curriculum were furniture design, metalworking, ceramics, photography, typography, and advertising. Gropius invited leading artists to teach at the school, including Paul Klee (1920–30), Lyonel Feininger* (1919–33), Oskar Schlemmer (1921–29), Vasily Kandinsky (1922–33), and Laszlo Moholy-Nagy (1923–28).

In 1925, pressure from conservative elements of Weimar society forced the Bauhaus to close. The school was moved to Dessau, and a new building, designed to house the school, was completed in 1926. During this period (1926–32) its orientation shifted toward an even more geometric and generally functional esthetic. Additions to the staff included former students Marcel Breuer* and Josef Albers.* Gropius resigned in 1928, and was succeeded by Hannes Meter and then by Ludwig Mies van der Rohe.* The rise of Nazism forced the Bauhaus to move to Berlin in 1932, and finally, to close in 1933. Several members—including Feininger, Gropius, Mies van der Rohe, and Albers—emigrated to the United States. The new Bauhaus, under the direction of Moholy-Nagy, was established in Chicago in 1937. The Bauhaus esthetic has had a profound influence on all of the American arts, including industrial design.

Baziotes, William (1912–63).
Painter. Born in Pittsburgh, Pa., Baziotes received an academic training from the portrait painter Leon Kroll* at the National Academy of Design (1933–36). He worked on the WPA Federal Art Project* (1936–41). He also taught at New York University and the Brooklyn Museum School (1949–52), the Museum of Modern Art, N.Y. (1950–52), and Hunter College (1952–63). He was cofounder of a school, "Subjects of the Artist," with Robert Motherwell,* Barnett Newman,* and Mark Rothko* in New York in 1948. He exhibited throughout the United States and his works are in major American museums. A retrospective of his paintings was held at the Guggenheim Museum in 1965.

Baziotes' first one-man exhibition took place in 1944 at Peggy Guggenheim's* Art of This Century gallery in New York, which introduced key figures in the movement known as abstract expressionism.* Although he was associated with the beginnings of American abstract expressionism, Baziotes had his stylistic origins in the abstract surrealism* of Joan Miró or André Masson, interpreted at times through Arshile Gorky.* His style, which remained remarkably consistent throughout his career, is characterized by shifting, fluid, luminous color into which are worked biomorphic shapes drawn with great sensitivity and always suggesting a form of microcosmic or marine life, as in *The Beach* (1955, Whitney). His obsession with marine life is manifest in many of his titles: *Aquatic, The Sea, Waterform, Waterflower.* The space of his paintings suggests the density and flow of water and his color has the delicate shifting qualities of water penetrated by light, color, and shadow. In the early 1940s Baziotes explored the automatism* of the European surrealists, many of whom had migrated to New York during World War II. Although he was taken with the surrealist concepts of improvisation, his art sought more fundamental roots in the world of prehistory, the domain of animals and minerals; he always, however, related these to strange, erotic and at times even monstrous manifestations of humanity. He was always primarily an individual romantic painter with a personal fantasy expressed through strange shapes and delicate, sensuous color, as in *Red Landscape*

(1957, Minneapolis). His influence extends to many of the artists of the 1960s and 1970s who are exploring what is known as lyrical abstraction.* (H.H.A.)

Beard, James Henry (1812–93) and **William Holbrook** (1824–1900).
Brothers popular for their genre and animal paintings. Raised as backwoodsmen in Ohio, James Beard worked chiefly in Cincinnati before moving to New York in 1870 and William traveled to Europe in the 1850s and then lived mainly in Buffalo prior to coming to New York in 1860. Both painted portraits and traditional genre scenes, but are best remembered for the wry, telling humor and implicit social criticism of paintings where animals act out the roles of people. Although neither was a craftsman of the highest level, both were original and imaginative. William Beard typically portrayed wild animals, especially bears, as in *The Bears of Wall Street Celebrating a Drop in the Market* (c.1880, New York Hist.), while James' favorite subject in his early work was the realistic depiction of the privations of the poor and social scenes, as in *The Long Bill* (Cincinnati). (T.E.S.)

Beardsley Limner, The (active c.1785–1800).
Folk artist. Real name unknown. He was designated the Beardsley Limner after the pair of portraits of Mr. and Mrs. Hezekiah Beardsley (Yale). He was active in South Carolina and along the Boston Post Road from New Haven to Boston from about 1785 to 1800. His early works, like those of other folk artists, are characterized by flattened space, detailed interiors, strong patterning, and bright color relationships. Later portraits show increasing sophistication, with a concentration on facial details and diverse poses and backgrounds. Although over a dozen portraits by his hand are now known, the name of the artist has not yet come to light.

Beaux, Cecilia (1863–1942).
Portrait painter. She was born in Philadelphia, Pa., and studied with William Sartain. In 1885 she won an award at the Pennsylvania Academy of the Fine Arts for *Les derniers jours d'enfance,* which was shown at the Paris Salon in 1887. Subsequently she went to Paris to study at the Académie Julien. In 1891 she settled in New York,

where she was recognized as one of the most able portrait artists of the day. Her work is distinguished by bold, fluent brushwork and a flair for lively composition and characterization; often compared to that of John Singer Sargent,* it developed independently but reflected the same art currents and social milieu, as in *Man with the Cat* (National Coll.). Among her sitters were Theodore Roosevelt and Georges Clemenceau. She won many prizes and honors, and is represented in European as well as American museums. (D.W.S.)

Beaux-Arts Eclectic Style.
A very individual but widespread architectural style fostered by the French École des Beaux-Arts. It offered a rather free interpretation of classical architecture, interesting combinations of forms, and profuse ornament. The plan was meticulously laid out according to logical principles taught at the École, with the straight axis a principal feature of the plan. Symmetry usually governed, although it might be enlivened by corner pavilions and by projected central portions crowned by mansard roofs. There was an almost plastic quality in these designs. Large glass areas, reminiscent of exposition buildings, were often skilfully introduced into the masonry walls, with wrought-iron grilles, statuary, and low-relief sculpture to adorn them. (A.B.)

Bel Geddes, Norman (1893–1958).
Stage designer turned industrial designer and then architect. His name became synonymous with the streamlined building and industrial product of the 1930s. Born in Adrian, Mich., his formal education was limited to the Cleveland School of Art and the Museum School of the Chicago Art Institute. In the 1910s and 1920s he designed numerous stage sets for plays and for several early films. In 1927 he established his own industrial design firm. Soon he was producing streamlined designs for everything from ships, trains, and airplanes to cars, and by 1930 he was applying aerodynamic streamlining to stoves, scales, and other industrial products. He designed "The House for Tomorrow" (1931) for the *Ladies' Home Journal;* and a revolving aerial restaurant for the Chicago Fair of 1933 (not built). At the end of the 1930s he produced the General Motors

Futurama Building at the New York World's Fair with its famous "City of Tomorrow." The building with its curved surfaces looks like a streamlined ship, and his "City" presents skyscrapers and other buildings bearing more than a passing resemblance to bumpers, fenders, and grills of the streamlined cars of the period. Bel Geddes published two influential books: one, *Horizons* (1932), contains a rationale for streamlining, while his *Magic Motor Ways* (1940) advocates the multilevel city, freeways with elaborate interchanges, and the automobile as a key to maximum mobility. While Bel Geddes declared that the styling or design of an object should always result from its function, he was nevertheless one of the first to argue convincingly that "surface qualities" should be distinct from structural and/or functional qualities. (D.G.)

Bell, Larry (1939–   ).
Painter and experimenter with glass boxes. Born in Chicago, Ill., Bell studied at the Chouinard Art Institute in Los Angeles, 1957–59. During the late 1950s and early '60s his paintings appeared in numerous West Coast exhibitions, including a one-man show in 1962. In 1965 he was still exhibiting shaped canvases, but he had also begun to explore the possibilities of three-dimensional art. *Untitled Construction* (1964), a twelve-inch cube of mirrored and painted glass, was one of Bell's earliest experiments with optics and reflections. By the following year he was producing his boxes of mineral-coated glass framed by metal strips and set on pedestals. The development in his work has been toward an increasingly pristine, industrially-manufactured look, but his structures are really more involved with optical effects than with elegant sophistication. The volumes framed by his transparent planes are filled with light and air, and there is a wealth of reflected color effects on the glass surface. Despite its sense of cool detachment, Bell's work is a polar opposite from that of the literalists: he has dematerialized sculpture and pushed it in the direction of illusionism and optical effects. (E.C.G.)

Bellows, George Wesley (1882–1925).
Painter and lithographer. He was born in Columbus, Ohio, and attended Ohio State University, where he developed talents in music, athletics, and as an artist on the school paper. He left college in 1904 to study art in New York. After working for two years with Robert Henri* at the New York School of Art, he took a studio and began serious painting. In a short time he received signal honors: a prize at the National Academy in 1908, and election as an associate academician the following year—the youngest in the institution's history. In 1910 he was invited to teach the life class at the Art Students League.*

The paintings of these first years were striking. A series of landscapes of the Hudson River and New York bridges combined sweeping breadth of concept and brilliance of execution, as in *North River* (1908, Pennsylvania). However, even more exciting were his raw, savagely dramatic prizefight paintings, such as *Both Members of This Club* (1909, Washington). His later landscapes and figures seldom achieved such effective freedom and spontaneity.

Bellows was vigorous and gregarious, and he participated fully in the art life of his day. He helped stage the Armory Show* of 1913, and was a founding director of the Society of Independent Artists.* His work began to reflect something of his friend Rockwell Kent's* vision of the stark drama of the northern coasts. He painted park and dockside scenes in New York, the circus in Montclair, and portraits in Columbus—winning awards all the while. Occasional commissions for illustrations for books and magazines led to some memorable characterizations, such as his studies of the evangelist, *Billy Sunday on the Sawdust Trail* (1915).

Bellows began working in lithography in 1916, and about that time increased his emphasis on pictorial structure, treating individual figures more simply and geometrically. The adjustment of all principal lines to conform to a grid of horizontals, verticals, and diagonals came to a climax in 1918, when he and Henri engaged in serious study of Jay Hambidge's theories of composition based on the geometrical system termed "dynamic symmetry."

During the last half-dozen years before his death of appendicitis in 1925, he did a number of landscapes, portraits, and figure compositions. The landscapes were often restlessly crowded with heavily textured and modeled forms, sometimes with theatrical back-lighting and lurid greens and blues. A popular and dramatic favorite is *The White Horse* (1922, Worcester). The portraits, which tend to be simpler and more selective in their massing and textures, are among his finest works. He has left memorable records of his family—mother, aunt, wife, and daughters singly and together, carefully composed, drawn, and modeled (*Portrait of My Mother,* 1921, Chicago). The figure compositions, taken as a group distinct from the portraits, are varied and curiously eclectic, ranging from a melodramatic crucifixion and prizefights to nude lovers wandering in idyllic landscapes.

Although he was somewhat slow at first in finding a market for his paintings, Bellows enjoyed unusual success with the public, the juries of art shows, and critics. He has been regarded as the most American of artists, partly because he did not go abroad and was little influenced by European modernism, and also because he was so completely representative of American temperament of his day—restless, vigorous, pragmatic, humorous, adventurous, healthy, assertive, inclined to bravura. His paintings had a youthful, uninhibited quality, but the tendency to overstate effects of light, weather, color, and compositional movement, widely regarded as reflecting "red-blooded American masculinity," led increasingly to mannered and forced dramatics. Nevertheless, he has left us paintings that vividly reflect his milieu and generation. (D.W.S.)

Belluschi, Pietro (1899–   ).
Architect, born in Ancona, Italy. He studied architectural engineering at the University of Rome and graduated in 1922. In 1923 he came to the United States and received a degree in civil engineering from Cornell University (1924). He joined the Portland, Ore., firm of A. E. Doyle in 1925 and was its chief designer from 1927 until he established his own practice in 1943. From 1951 to 1965 he was dean of the School of Planning and Architecture of Massachusetts Institute of Technology. He has since served as an architectural consultant on numerous large buildings and has carried on his interest in designing churches and smaller buildings. He received the gold medal of the American Institute of Architects in 1972.

Belluschi emerged in the late 1930s, along with William W. Wurster,* Gardner Daily, and Harwell H. Harris, as a regional West Coast exponent of a soft and woodsy version of modern architecture. The low-pitched gable roof of the Kerr House at Gearhart, Ore. (1941) keeps it closely attached to its grass-covered dune overlooking the Pacific Ocean. The often-illustrated Sutor House in Portland, Ore. (1938) is almost classic in its gabled, columned porch, yet its general quality is that of the vernacular. Other of his pre- and post-World War II buildings, such as the St. Thomas More Church, Portland (1939), his Zion Lutheran Church, Portland (1951), or his First Presbyterian Church, Cottage Grove, Ore. (1951), represent a similar attempt to blend the open plan and horizontal geometry of the modern International style* with the wood vernacular buildings of Oregon, especially barns and rural architecture.

A major departure from these buildings occurred in his steel-and-glass-caged Equitable Building in Portland (1948). This building, with its smooth, flat, and modular skin of green glass and aluminum, placed Belluschi fully in the camp of the post-World War II International style designers. His work of the 1950s and 1960s continued this sharp division. Thus his smaller buildings, such as the Unitarian Church at Rockford, Ill. (1966, designed with C. Edward Ware), used the low-scaled, much more traditional approach to design and "warm" materials such as brick, stone, and wood. In his larger buildings the design grammar of the International style prevails. This can be seen in his finely detailed and well-proportioned Juilliard School at Lincoln Center, New York (1958–1970, designed with Eduardo Catalano and Helge Westermann and others), certainly the most successful building at the Center, and in other buildings such as the Bank of America, San Francisco (1969), where he served as a consultant to a group of other architects.   (D.G.)

Belter, John Henry (1804–63). Furniture-maker. Born in Germany, he was apprenticed as a cabinetmaker and carver in Württemberg. By 1844 he was in New York at 40½ Chatham Square and by 1846 he had moved to Broadway, where his business was listed at four addresses in less than twenty years. From 1856 he also had a factory

1. *George Wesley Bellows.* Both Members of This Club, *1909. National Gallery of Art, Washington, D.C. (Chester Dale Collection).*

2. *George Wesley Bellows.* Portrait of My Mother, *1921. Art Institute of Chicago.*

1

2

1. *Henry Benbridge.* Captain and Mrs.
John Purves. *Henry Francis du Pont
Winterthur Museum, Winterthur, Del.*
2. *Henry Belter.* Victorian love seat in
Rococo revival style, mid-19th
century. *Metropolitan Museum of
Art, N.Y. (gift of Mrs. Charles
Reginald Leonard).*

at Third Avenue and 76th Street. Belter
is remembered chiefly for his extravagantly ornamented version of the rococo revival style. The curving backs of
chairs and sofas, and the aprons of
tables, were achieved by a lamination
process, which, though he did not invent it or use it exclusively, he greatly
improved, patenting his improvements
from 1847 to 1858. In his method, layers of wood were placed together—
much as in modern plywood—with the
grain running at right angles. The number of layers varied from four to sixteen
but was usually six or eight. The wood
was pressed in steam molds to make it
curve and then pierced and carved;
often more carving was glued on for
extra depth. According to the notes of
Ernest Hagen, an old New York cabinetmaker, in a manuscript in the Winterthur Library, Belter's contemporary,
Charles A. Baudouine, infringed on
Belter's patent "by making the backs
out of 2 pieces, with a center joint, and
this way got the best of Belter, who
died a very poor man." The company
went bankrupt in 1867, a few years
after Belter's death. Although virtually
all high-style American rococo revival
furniture has been called "Belter,"
other firms also worked in this style,
including Joseph Meeks and Son* and
Charles Klein of New York, and Ignatius
Lutz of Philadelphia. A small group of
labeled or documented Belter furniture
survives, including a handsome suite
in the Museum of the City of New York,
made for Carl Vietor. A center table of
this group bears Belter's label with the
date of 1856 to 1861. Belter also
sometimes stamped his furniture with
the notice of his patent.   (M.J.B.)

Benbridge, Henry (1743–1812).
Portrait painter in oils and miniature.
He came from a substantial Philadelphia family, distantly related to Benjamin West.* He may have met young
West and caught some of his enthusiasm for painting as a noble avocation.
When in 1758 John Wollaston* came to
Philadelphia and painted a portrait of
Alexander Gordon, Benbridge's stepfather, the boy left school in order to
take lessons from him. Wollaston soon
moved on, leaving his pupil busy painting allegorical murals and portraying
members of his family.

Benbridge sailed to Italy to study in
1764, as West had done five years
earlier. In 1769 he went on to London,

bringing his masterly portrait of the Corsican patriot, General Paoli, which he had painted on commission from James Boswell. In 1770 he returned to Philadelphia bearing letters of high commendation from West and Benjamin Franklin; he married Letitia Sage, a miniature painter, and in 1771 settled at Charleston, S.C. There, through the next twenty years, he enjoyed excellent patronage, though he did few portraits and painted little after 1790. He was in Norfolk, Va., in 1801, where he gave lessons to young Thomas Sully.* He died in Philadelphia.

Before returning to America Benbridge had written that he was "not long in painting a Picture, having studied an expeditious way and at the same time a correct one." This may be one factor in the uneven quality of his work. His best portraits are done with unusual sensitivity and grace, while others are awkward in pose and occasionally weak in draftsmanship. He excelled at group portraits. His subjects include numerous Revolutionary figures of the South, among them *Captain Charles Cotesworth Pinckney* (Washington) and *Captain and Mrs. John Purves,* posed together (Winterthur).   (C.C.S.)

Benjamin, Asher (1773–1845).

Carpenter-architect and writer of builders' guides. Probably born in Hartland, Conn., he worked as a carpenter in several Connecticut valley towns: Greenfield and Northampton, Mass., Suffield and Hartford, Conn., and Windsor, Vt., before going to Boston in 1802, where he is listed in directories until 1845. Because Benjamin's builders' guides were so popular, many New England houses look as though designed by him. Those buildings that are almost certainly his are: Hatch and Jones houses, and the South Congregational Church, Windsor, Vt.; Baldwin House, Brookfield, Mass.; Hinckley House and Old Congregational Church (burned), Northampton, Mass.; Center Church, New Haven, Conn., with Ithiel Town (1812–14); West Church, Boston (1806); J. P. Cushing House, Belmont, Mass. (1840); Olive St. Meeting House, Nashua, N.H.; Coleman-Hollister House, Greenfield; and the Academy, Deerfield. His importance derives mainly from his builders' guides. He compiled them by culling material from various English guides but gave them an American flavor by changing propor-

tions to fit the materials and lower standards of American construction. While keeping good proportion and harmony in his early Republican style, Benjamin liked to elongate classical orders. By publishing new editions he kept up with the changes in English taste. *The Country Builder's Assistant* (1797) was the first original American work on architecture. After it came such other volumes as *The American Builder's Companion* (1806), *The Practice of Architecture* (1833), and *The Elements of Architecture* (1843). A portfolio of Benjamin's early drawings is at the Society for the Preservation of New England Antiquities, Boston.   (P.F.N.)

Benson, Frank Weston (1862–1951).

Painter and member of The Ten.* Benson was born in Salem, Mass., and attended the Museum of Fine Arts school, Boston, for three years before going to Paris in 1883 to attend the Académie Julien. Returning to America in 1885, he taught art in Portland, Me., then in his own studio in Boston, and later, for many years, at the Boston Museum School.

Benson was one of the first generation of American painters to come under the spell of impressionism.* During the 1890s he painted glowing, graceful young ladies relaxing in sunny gardens and orchards, such as *Summer* (1890, National Coll.). His compositions were informal and easy; his brushwork was sometimes broad, sometimes broken, but always virtuoso. His manner was allied to that of his friend and fellow Bostonian, Edmund Tarbell,* but even more than Tarbell, Benson seems to have been the victim of his facility. His mural decorations for the Library of Congress are of slight interest, and for many years after the lively sparkle of his impressionism had faded he continued to turn out cleverly painted, well-composed canvases of still lifes and sporting scenes, and etchings of hunting fowl.   (D.W.S.)

Benton, Thomas Hart (1889–   ).

Painter. Born in Neosho, Mo., Benton was the son of a United States Congressman and grandnephew of a famous senator. His youth was filled with discussions of the issues that were shaping the Midwest. He studied at Western Military Academy (1906–07) and drew sketches and cartoons for a local newspaper. In 1907, he took classes at the

Chicago Art Institute, and in 1908 he left for Paris, spending three years at the Académie Julien. He was briefly influenced by cubism* and synchromism,* but the conservative tradition in which he was brought up militated against his absorbing deeply the revolutionary modernist esthetics that were sweeping Europe. The most lasting impression left by his European visit was of the monumental works of the Italian Renaissance and the paintings of El Greco, especially the distortions of the human figure. Returning to the United States, he settled in New York, and in 1916 he participated in the important "Forum Exhibition of Modern American Painting." He showed paintings in which Michelangelo figures were stylized into compositions dominated by strong, linear rhythms and with color playing a subordinate, reenforcing role.

In 1918, Benton was employed as a draftsman at the Norfolk, Va., Naval Base, and his attention turned to more realistic themes that reflected his rural and small-town background. The following year, he embarked on a series of paintings that he later called the "American Historical Epic." In these works, to which he devoted the next decade, he sought to forge an American art which would draw its themes from the history, folklore, and daily life of common American experience, and in which modernist principles would figure only to the extent that they contributed to a graphic clarity of style easily grasped by everyone. At first strongly influenced by the Russian Revolution and by the environmentalist theory of art propounded by the French historian, Hippolyte Taine, Benton's attitude deepened when he returned to Missouri for a visit shortly before his father's death in 1924; he began sketching and collecting material from life.

By the end of the 1920s, he had crystallized his style and attitude, and throughout the 1930s he was one of the most popular and influential of American scene,* or "regionalist" painters, whose numbers also included John Steuart Curry* and Grant Wood.* A parallel movement in literature was represented by such writers as Sinclair Lewis and Sherwood Anderson. Benton's ambitious mural cycles—in the New School for Social Research, New York (1930–31); Whitney Museum of American Art (1932); University of Indiana, Bloomington (1933); and Missouri State

1

2

Capitol, Jefferson (1936)—created wide interest in regionalist painting. They influenced the policies of governmental art programs during the Depression, although Benton himself never completed any work for federal programs. An articulate spokesman for the regionalist point of view, Benton remained an outspoken critic of Parisian "modernism"; contrary to common belief, he regarded his histories as nonpolitical in nature, and he was scathing in his criticism of "social realists" who saddled their art with specific causes.

In the mid-1930s, Benton left New York to direct the Kansas City, Mo., Art Institute, and he continues to live in that city. His work since the late 1930s has been characterized by a new interest in textural qualities, and a greater refinement of color and clarity of design patterns. He worked briefly on a series called "Perils of War" during World War II, but he later returned to American scene subjects, and to biblical and legendary themes reinterpreted in vernacular terms. His most recent paintings have dealt with the Far West. (A.F.)

Berman, Eugene (1899–   ).
Painter and stage designer. Born in St. Petersburg, Russia, he studied there with various academic masters. But his most important training was under Pierre Bonnard at the Académie Ranson in Paris, where he went in 1918 when the Russian Revolution cut off his contacts with his native country. In Paris he was associated with the group known as the neoromantics, along with Pavel Tchelitchew.* The emphasis of this group, as its name indicates, was on poetic subject matter, with nostalgic, surrealistic, and fantastic overtones.

Berman came to the United States in 1935. He has held two Guggenheim fellowships for work in Mexico and has lived for extended periods in New York and Los Angeles. Since 1968 he has made his home in Rome in what the critic Russell Lynes describes as "a private museum, an extraordinary collection of sculpture and paintings, of ceramics and glass, thousands (literally) of objects from Egypt and Mexico, from Gothic churches and baroque churches, from tombs and temples, from the Gold Coast and Oceania, and Etruscan mounds, and hundreds of drawings and paintings"—the last presumably his own. The archeological bent manifest in this collection is strongly evident in Berman's own work, which draws on Piranesi for the grandeur of ruins and on Italian Renaissance architecture, landscape architecture, and sculpture, and uses strange perspectives, suffused with ruin and melancholy, and often spattered to suggest the luster of age in the painting itself as well as in the subject. Berman is also an excellent portrait painter, and he has designed enough stage sets to justify a special exhibition of them at the Museum of Modern Art in New York. He is especially well known for the sets and costumes he has designed for the Metropolitan Opera Company, notably for Mozart's *Don Giovanni,* and Verdi's *La Forza del Destino* and *Rigoletto.*

(A.F.)

Biddle, George (1885–   ).
Painter and lithographer. Born in Philadelphia, Pa., he was trained at the Pennsylvania Academy of the Fine Arts and the Académie Julien in Paris, and is also a Harvard graduate. After service in World War I he went to Tahiti, where he worked for two years at painting, printmaking, and sculpture. He spent the years 1922–25 in Paris but returned to the United States convinced that an American painter needs to work in an American setting.

In the early 1930s, inspired by Mexico's example of art for the masses, Biddle anticipated the American government's support of mural painting by organizing artists to revive this form of expression, but his ideas found little patronage. When the government initiated its WPA Federal Art Project* in 1935, Biddle took an active part in its affairs. He was also active in the Artists Union and the Artists Congress, and campaigned for a Federal Department of Fine Arts. In 1935, he received his most important mural assignment, for the Department of Justice Building in Washington. He also painted murals for the Supreme Court building in Mexico City. After World War II he took an increasing interest in American genre subjects, frequently treating them satirically. He published his autobiography, *An American Artist's Story,* in 1939.

(A.F.)

Bierstadt, Albert (1830–1902).
Landscape painter. He was born in Solingen, Germany, but was brought to the United States in 1832 and spent his childhood in New Bedford, Mass. He

3

4

1. ***Thomas Hart Benton.*** Persephone, *1939. Collection Thomas Hart Benton.*
2. ***Thomas Hart Benton.*** Cradling Wheat, *1938. City Art Museum of St. Louis.*
3. ***Albert Bierstadt.*** Autumnal Scene, *1898. Kennedy Galleries, N.Y.*
4. ***Albert Bierstadt.*** Thunderstorm in the Rockies, *1859. Museum of Fine Arts, Boston.*

exhibited a few youthful works in Boston in 1851 and again in 1853. When he was twenty-three he went to Germany, where he studied painting at the Düsseldorf Academy, and then to Rome where he painted for one winter with Worthington Whittredge,* well-known American landscape painter. In 1857 he returned to New Bedford. The next year he went west with Colonel Lander's surveying expedition to map an overland route from St. Louis to the Pacific. Bierstadt left the party to sketch the Wind River and Shoshone country and then returned to New York in 1859. He settled in New York City, and exhibited one of his first Western landscapes, *Thunderstorm in the Rocky Mountains* (1859, Boston). The next year he was elected to the National Academy of Design. From this auspicious beginning he began to build a national reputation as a landscape painter. This he accomplished by working his western sketches into large and impressive exhibition paintings that were avidly sought by wealthy collectors. Shortly after the outbreak of the Civil War he traveled to the South, where he painted several historical and genre works, such as *Attack on a Union Picket Post* (1862, Century Association, N.Y.), and *The Bombardment of Fort Sumter* (c.1862, Union League of Philadelphia), a large, high-keyed painting empty of people, and monumental in its stark, sun-drenched simplicity.

He made another trip west in 1863 with Fitzhugh Ludlow, the journalist, who published an account of the journey in *The Heart of the Continent* (1870). Bierstadt had reached the peak of his career, his works commanding the highest prices ever paid for American paintings. Critical acclaim was international. He built a thirty-five-room house at Irvington-on-Hudson, and in 1867–69 he and his wife traveled through Europe on a government commission. He returned home to the White Mountains and Boston area and then spent 1871–73 on the Pacific Coast, occupying for a time a studio in San Francisco. Congress purchased his characteristic landscape, *The Discovery of the North River by Hendrick Hudson* (1875), which hangs in the Capitol. In 1878–81 the Bierstadts were again in Europe, then in Canada, and finally in the Bahamas. When their palatial home at Irvington was destroyed by fire, they moved to

New York City. Bierstadt's spectacular critical and financial success began to decline, and his work fell into disfavor. In 1889 his now-famous *The Last of the Buffalo* (c.1889, Corcoran), was refused by a jury of New York artists who were selecting American paintings for the Paris Exposition; they considered it out of step with French academic painting then in vogue. He visited the Canadian Rockies and Alaska in 1889 and again made several trips abroad but his fortune and artistic popularity declined steadily.

Bierstadt's principal contribution to American art is his vast, monumental, and panoramic landscapes of the West such as *Mount Corcoran* (1875–77, Corcoran) and *The Rocky Mountains* (1863, Metropolitan). They impressed the public in the post-Civil War era by their scale and their lavish detail. Unfashionable in the early years of this century, they have now regained some of their former popularity. Of late, his small oil sketches, painted directly from nature, have also been much admired: for example, *Buffalo Trail: The Impending Storm* (1869, Corcoran), in which the intensity of observation highlights the beauty of the Western mountain landscape perhaps better than do his grandiose panoramas. Bierstadt's best canvases capture the poetry of the wilderness and bring 19th-century American landscape painting to a grand climax.   (H.W.W.)

Bingham, George Caleb (1811–79).
Genre and portrait painter. He was born on a plantation near Charlottesville, Va., but in 1819 moved with his family to Franklin, Mo., which was then on the frontier. Aided by the portrait painter Chester Harding,* who had gone to Missouri to paint Daniel Boone, he became as early as 1833 a professional portrait painter. His early portraits are rather stiff and semi-primitive in style. Bingham studied briefly at the Pennsylvania Academy of the Fine Arts in 1837. He lived in Washington, D.C. from 1840–44, painting many prominent public figures, especially politicians: however, these efforts added little to his reputation as a portraitist. After this lengthy absence he returned to Missouri and began to paint the genre scenes on which his fame rests. In 1856–58 and again in 1859 he went abroad with his family and studied at the Academy in Düsseldorf. Coming home, he settled

permanently in Missouri, where he was active both as painter and politician.

Bingham was consciously a social historian, setting himself the task of painting what he described as "our social and political characteristics." In practice he concentrated on just two facets of life in Missouri: political campaigns and life along the great rivers. Surprisingly, he showed little of the middle class: the bankers, merchants, and politicians in Missouri's towns and cities—the circles in which he himself moved. Bingham was the first American genre artist raised in the West and it was his paintings of the picturesque life of the frontier region that brought him fame. In choosing western themes, he was plainly aware of the public's appetite, whetted by the accounts of travelers, for renderings of the scenes and denizens of the Missouri and Mississippi rivers.

In 1845 Bingham submitted two Western genre paintings to the American Art-Union,* both of which were quickly purchased. One of these was *Fur Traders Descending the Missouri*, (1845, Metropolitan), probably esthetically his most distinguished work. The following year his *The Jolly Flatboatmen* (1846, private collection) was a nationwide success, reproduced by colored aquatint engraving and distributed by the American Art-Union to its ten thousand members. He was at once hailed the unrivaled master of western genre.

Bingham took the greatest care in creating his paintings, not only technically but in working out a conception that conveyed mood and atmosphere. Like William S. Mount,* he was a master of his craft, especially skilled in figure drawing and giving expressive power to his images. Not until after his 1856–59 stay in Düsseldorf, where he embraced the theory and style of its Academy too wholeheartedly, did his paintings fail to be compelling representations of America's Western man.

The effectiveness of his genre paintings is evident in such examples of his best period as *Raftsmen Playing Cards* (1847, St. Louis) and *Shooting for the Beef* (1850, Brooklyn). In the 1850s he experimented with depicting night scenes, as in *Wood-Boatmen on a River* (1854, Boston). These extended his range but lacked the visual appeal of his daytime subjects. Bingham's series on political subjects, by far his most ambitious paintings, involving many figures, alone would be sufficient to establish his place as an outstanding American painter. *The County Election* (1851–52, St. Louis) and *The Verdict of the People* (1854–55, R. W. Norton Art Gallery, Shreveport, La.) are major works. He undoubtedly lavished so much effort on these subjects as a result of his long involvement in local politics. Several times a candidate, he was elected to the Missouri legislature in 1848 after a hectic campaign. The succession of political jobs he held, especially after the Civil War, sharply diminished his productivity as a painter.

Bingham's habit was to make careful drawings of individual figures, building up a file of characters from which he cast his compositions. His stock of "river rats," squatters, and townspeople, while precisely delineated, were types, not individuals; and yet they were truly representative figures. Like Mount, Bingham painted for the many, not the few. His greatest talent may have been his ability to set down figures in a composition with a maximum of precise detail and yet to subordinate each detail to the total scene. This skill in formal composition stems from his respect for the traditional devices of European masters which he absorbed by studying prints of their works. Inspired by a natural affinity for his subjects, his scenes convincingly convey the spirit of the region and the age.   (H.W.W.)

Birch, Thomas (1779–1851).
Marine and landscape painter. At fifteen he came from England to Philadelphia with his father, William Russell Birch (1755–1834), a miniaturist and engraver. They arrived in time to participate in the World's Columbian Exhibition of 1893 in Chicago. The father showed engravings and miniatures on enamel (an art he introduced into America), and Thomas was represented by drawings of scenes near London and of the Pennsylvania countryside. Thomas aided his father in making a series of topographical engravings, *Views of Philadelphia* (1798–1800). He joined John Wesley Jarvis* and other young artists in sketching tours, recording his impressions in watercolor. River and harbor scenes interested him; the engravings of Claude Joseph Vernet's views of the seaports of France were a major influence.

Birch brought to the New World a direct reflection of English romantic

1

2

1. *George Caleb Bingham.* Fur Traders Descending the Missouri, *1845. Metropolitan Museum of Art, N.Y. (Morris K. Jesup Fund).*
2. *Thomas Birch.* Naval Engagement between the United States and the Macedonian, *1813. Historical Society of Pennsylvania, Philadelphia.*

realism and of the new English interest in landscape and watercolor. With the War of 1812, the victories at sea of his adopted country fired his imagination and established his reputation as a marine painter. Landscape, however, still held a favored place, together with occasional portraits and miniatures on enamel in his father's technique. Of the battle pieces, the earliest are still the best, notably his painting *Naval Engagement Between the United States and Macedonian* (1813, Historical Society of Pennsylvania). His later seascapes celebrate the romantic wildness of storm and shore, always with the drama of ship against wave. He also painted highly imaginative shipwrecks.

(C.C.S.)

Bischoff, Elmer (1916–).
Painter who studied at the University of California at Berkeley, receiving an M.A. in 1939. He taught at the California School of Fine Arts (1946–52 and 1956–63) and, since 1963, at Berkeley. Bischoff is a leading member of the California school of realist expressionists that includes Richard Diebenkorn* and the late David Park.* He works in a freely representational manner that has affinities with the German and Austrian expressionists, particularly Oskar Kokoschka, as well as American realist expressionists such as Edward Hopper.* Like Hopper, his world is one of figures isolated in a lonely environment, presented in rich and varied color. Again like Hopper, his figures are organized within a classical, architectural space, although his use of heavily-loaded brush texture brings him closer to the tradition of Kokoschka and, in another context, that of American abstract expressionism.*

(H.H.A.)

Bishop, Isabel (1902–).
Painter. Born in Cincinnati, Ohio, she studied at the New York School of Applied Design, and at the Art Students League with Kenneth Hayes Miller.* Miller's work strongly influenced her choice of themes, which characteristically center on New York City subjects and especially working girls. Her paintings are usually executed in mixed media, combining soft lighting and resonant shadows in a style inspired by the sketches of Rubens. In addition to city and genre paintings such as her *Subway Scene* (1957–58, Whitney), she is known for her sensitive, moody paintings of the nude female figure.

Bissell, George Edwin (1839–1920).
A sculptor who began his career as a stonecutter in his father's stoneyard in Poughkeepsie, N.Y. His talent for ornate carving encouraged him to become a sculptor, and in 1875 he went to Paris to study for a year. But Bissell, unlike Saint-Gaudens* and others, never really mastered the new impressionistic modeling practiced in Parisian studios, and although his work dates mainly from the last quarter of the 19th century, his style is that of mid-century naturalism, dry and often prosaic. This quality marks his bronze statue *President Chester A. Arthur* (1899, Philadelphia). Perhaps his finest piece is the bronze statue of *Chancellor Kent* (c.1899) for the Library of Congress. Like many of his contemporaries Bissell was called upon to create bronze war memorials, such as his *Soldiers' Monument* (c.1876, Waterbury, Conn.). His career had come to an end by World War I.

(W.C.)

Bitter, Karl Theodore F. (1867–1915).
Sculptor. He was a native of Vienna where he studied at the Academy of Fine Arts before emigrating to America when he was twenty-one. He developed a special ability in decorative sculpture for architecture and later for memorials and expositions. After working for Richard Morris Hunt,* executing decorative architectural carvings for millionaires' mansions, Bitter's first big commission came when Hunt chose him to create a set of bronze doors (1891–94) for Trinity Church, New York City. In 1892 he again assisted Hunt by making the sculptural decorations for the Administration Building at the World's Columbian Exposition (Chicago, 1893). Bitter's style, like Hunt's, was essentially highly decorative and innovative in a neo-baroque manner but with eclectic tendencies that could, in 19th-century Romantic fashion, lead to variations on any historical style. Bitter rose to the forefront of American sculpture, and was commissioned to make four heroic-scale figures personifying the arts for the façade of the new Metropolitan Museum of Art.

In 1901 he was chosen to direct the extensive sculptural program at the Pan-American Exposition at Buffalo. His administrative abilities proved so exceptional that he was invited to direct the sculptural work at the Louisiana Purchase Exposition (St. Louis, 1902–

Ronald Bladen. *The X, 1967, wood mockup. Fischbach Gallery, N.Y.*

04) and the Panama-Pacific Exposition (San Francisco, 1912–15). In each of these he had as many as fifty of the nation's finest sculptors working under his direction. Bitter's studio in Weehawken, New Jersey, was also constantly busy with other commissions, mainly bronze portrait figures such as *Carl Shurz* (1913, New York City) and *President Andrew White* (1915, Cornell University). Bitter succeeded Daniel Chester French* as president of the National Sculpture Society in 1906.

(W.C.)

Black, Starr & Frost (1876–1929).

A New York silver firm, an outgrowth of a business begun by Frederick Marquand in 1826 and continued by Ball, Thompkins & Black. One of the leading producers of fine silver at the end of the 19th century, it made outstanding presentation trophies as well as ecclesiastical silver, although the names of the individual designers received little notice.

Blackburn, Joseph (active in America 1753–63).

English portrait painter who came from Bermuda to New England about 1754. In Newport, R.I., he painted companion portraits of Margaret (Mrs. David Chesebrough) and Mary Sylvester (1754, Metropolitan), with Mary posed in stilted grandeur as a beribboned shepherdess with attendant lamb. He was active in Boston, 1755–60, and worked in both Boston and Portsmouth, N.H., 1760–62, returning then to London. Blackburn's life elsewhere is a mystery. Probably he was an assistant in various London studios, acquiring some facility in the elegant portrait mode of the time, as well as in the painting of drapery, but never enough to compete for patronage with English masters such as Joseph Highmore or Thomas Hudson. Nevertheless, he was a success in Boston, where his delicate rococo portraits commanded the best patronage and profoundly influenced the development of young John Singleton Copley.* His *Isaac Winslow and His Family* (1755, Boston) and *Mary Warner* (c.1760, Warner House, Portsmouth, N.H.) contrast interestingly with Copley's later work on the same subjects. Copley's subsequent success may have forced Blackburn to leave America in 1763 to seek his fortune elsewhere.

(C.C.S.)

Bladen, Ronald (1918–).

Sculptor, whose bare, monumental pieces, defying the principles of gravity, loom large in any setting. Born in Vancouver, British Columbia, where he studied at the Vancouver School of Art, Bladen emigrated to the United States to study at the California School of Fine Arts in San Francisco. He later became a naturalized citizen. He was a painter for several years before he developed his minimal* sculptural style. His first exhibition was in 1956 in San Francisco, and his next in 1962 in New York, where his work was widely praised. Toward the mid-1960s Bladen began constructing huge wood forms, basically geometric, but skewed in such a way as to suggest queer spatial disequilibrium. In his 1967, 1970, and 1971 shows in a New York gallery, Bladen chose to incorporate the entire gallery space, either by means of a few related forms spaced evenly in the rectangular room, or by placing a single enormous shape, such as an inverted triangle, in such a way that the four corners of the room served as imaginary planar limits to the form. Bladen has exhibited in group shows in Europe and the United States.

Blakelock, Ralph Albert (1847–1919).

Painter of poetic and visionary landscapes. Blakelock was born in New York City, studied in the public schools, and entered the Free Academy of the City of New York (now the City College) in 1864. By the time he was eighteen he had begun painting landscapes independently, and he left college after three terms to begin a career in art. After attending Cooper Union, where he quickly mastered the conventional technique of the late Hudson River School,* he left academic training and in 1867 began exhibiting at the National Academy of Design*. His early work, literal in detail, reveals the love of lonely and wild landscape vistas that marked his work throughout his life.

It was characteristic of his romantic attachment to wilderness that he pursued his studies not in Europe, like most of his contemporaries, but by himself in the West. Between 1869 and 1872 he traveled through the western mountains, the Indian lands, California, and down the Pacific Coast to the Isthmus of Panama. A few of his early landscapes, such as *Peace Among the Nations* (c.1872), derive directly from the journey.

As art historian Lloyd Goodrich wrote of Blakelock, "What he retained from the West was the primeval forest, seen poetically" and "the vision of a primitive race living in harmony with nature." Throughout his career he often drew on Indian motifs and signed his name within an arrowhead, but he painted no specific western setting or Indian tribe.

The evolution of Blakelock's art is not easy to trace because few of his paintings are dated, but during the mid-1870s he developed a distinctly subjective manner. Perhaps because his paintings were too exploratory or too unconventional in their subjective approach he ceased exhibiting at the Academy from 1874 to 1878. The paintings that date to 1879, such as *The Chase* (1879, Worcester), are imaginative visions very different from those of the earlier part of the decade. During the 1880s Blakelock's painting came to full maturity and he exhibited frequently with the National Academy and the Society of American Artists.* He received uncertain, sometimes damning, critical response, and he fell into increasingly serious financial difficulty.

He described his approach to painting in terms of a philosophic subjectivism similar to that of French symbolism:* "The laws of painting are the laws of the creator . . . when knowledge is obtained, then we may trust our emotional nature or spirit to create, and then, upon comparison, we find them like nature." Inspiration came to him from observing random patterns in objects—wood grains, the worn enamel of a bathtub—and from playing the piano, upon which he created "pictures" through fluent improvisations. His typical subject matter was a moonlit landscape, in which the dark foliage of foreground trees formed a lacy decorative pattern through which distant woods, sky, and moon glowed in a silvery-green tonality. There were also daylit scenes charged with a similar magical atmosphere, and occasionally sunset paintings in a rich, "musical" coloration. His surfaces were built up slowly, painted, varnished, scraped, repainted, and rubbed down until their sensuous textures and fragmented images satisfied Blakelock's exacting sensibility. His subjective and poetic approach was similar to that of Albert Ryder,* but less broad in range. The two artists also employed similar methods of painting, well fitted for realizing

their intuitive visions but unsound technically, a dependence on bitumen and varnish which resulted in the ruin of some of their finest works.

As the 1880s wore on, Blakelock's financial situation grew worse. In December, 1890, *The Collector* described Blakelock's situation thus: "Neglected by a public which did not understand him; unnoticed by a criticism which dared not have any idea of its own; poor, burdened, depressed and often desperate, this man of ideals and vision never swerved upon his path." In 1899 he suffered a severe mental breakdown and was hospitalized for most of the rest of his life. By a cruel irony, recognition and sales of his work followed hard upon his breakdown, but neither he nor his family benefited. In 1900 a painting of his, shown in Paris by a collector, won his first (and only) prize; in the same year another collector arranged his first one-man show. Soon no collection of American painting was complete without a Blakelock. Between 1912 and 1916, as his condition became known, and his work scarce, his paintings set new records for auction prices of work by a living American and he was elected an associate of the National Academy of Design. Finally, a fund was raised, guardians appointed, and he spent most of his last years in a private sanatorium in the Adirondacks.

(D.W.S.)

Blanck, Jurian, Jr. (c.1645–1714). New York's earliest native silversmith. He was the son of a goldsmith and worked from about 1668 to 1714. A covered two-handled cup (Winterthur) made for a Van Cortlandt marriage in 1691, shows the skill and subtlety of his craftsmanship. The maker also of a Dutch-type of tall beaker for both domestic and ecclesiastical use, Blanck engraved them with strapwork borders and vignettes representing Faith, Hope, and Charity. He also made tankards and such diverse items as wine tasters, baptismal basins, casters, porringers, and ceremonial spoons.

Blashfield, Edwin Howland (1848–1936). Foremost late 19th-century mural painter after William Morris Hunt* and John LaFarge.* Born in New York, N.Y., he was educated in Boston, where he entered the Massachusetts Institute of Technology, intending to become an en-

gineer or architect. His interest in painting led him to seek out Hunt, who instructed him briefly and urged him to go to Paris, which he did in 1867. His principal instructor there was Léon Bonnat. By 1874 he was exhibiting at the Salon and becoming known as an easel painter, and it was as an easel painter that he set up a studio in New York in 1881. With the success of his mural decoration at the World's Columbian Exposition in Chicago (1893), followed by his work on the dome of the Library of Congress, however, he became nationally known as a muralist. Commissions for decorations of state capitols, libraries, and universities poured in from Wisconsin, Minnesota, Iowa, Illinois, Michigan, Ohio, Pennsylvania, New York, and Massachusetts.

A highly literate and literary man, the author of *Mural Painting in America* (1913), he edited Vasari's *Lives of the Artists.* He enjoyed classical borrowings, mixing Renaissance allegory with late 19th-century idealized female types, always keeping his eye on the grand style. Compared to the murals of his contemporaries, his work was marked by somewhat stronger drawing and more carefully developed composition. Its shortcoming, all too evident today, lies in its sentimental and eclectic academicism, which was most acceptable to official patrons of his time.

(D.W.S.)

Blown-Three-Mold Glass.
A method of glass manufacture, employed principally from about 1815 to 1840, in which the molten glass was blown into full-size, multi-part metal molds which imparted both pattern and shape to the glass. This technique enabled the manufacturer to produce a decorated glassware without the labor necessary for applied decoration, cutting, engraving, or enameling.

The early geometric patterns, produced about 1815, copied cut glass designs of the period and were probably heavily influenced by cut wares from England and Ireland. As designs became slightly more original in the 1820s, patterns appeared with gothic arches and baroque motifs. Because of the increasing popularity of the cheaper pressed glass* in the 1830s, however, glass companies decreased production of blown-three-mold wares by about 1840.

The most important factories known

1

2

1. **Ralph Albert Blakelock.** The Chase, 1879. Worcester Art Museum, Mass.
2. **Ralph Albert Blakelock.** Indian Encampment, 1906. Metropolitan Museum of Art, N.Y. (George A. Hearn Fund).

1

2

1. **Peter Blume.** Light of the World, 1932. Whitney Museum of American Art, N.Y.
2. **Blown-Three-Mold Glass.** Left to right: celery glass, attributed to Coventry Glass Works, Conn.; footed bowl, clear lead glass, Boston & Sandwich Glass Co.; pitcher with applied handle in cobalt blue; pair of decanters with stoppers; decanter with stopper, fern and concentric rings on base. All, Toledo Museum of Art, Ohio.

to have made this glass included Boston & Sandwich Glass Company, founded 1825; New England Glass Company, founded 1818; Mt. Vernon Glass Company in Mt. Vernon, New York, 1810–44; Coventry, Conn. Glass Works, founded 1813; the glasshouse on Marlboro Street in Keene, N.H., founded 1815; and the Kent (c. 1823–34) and Mantua (1821–29) glasshouses in Ohio. The Brooklyn Flint Glass Works, founded 1823, and several factories in Pittsburgh also advertised the ware.

Blown-three-mold glass appears most commonly as drinking vessels and serving pieces; colored items are relatively scarce. (J.S.S.)

Blume, Peter (1906–   ).
Painter. Born in Russia but brought to the United States at the age of five, Blume studied at the Art Students League* and the Beaux-Arts Institute of Design. He began in the precisionist manner of Charles Sheeler,* but soon ironic elements began to manifest themselves in his work, as in *Parade* (1930, Modern Museum), which shows a workman carrying a suit of armor on a pole past a group of factory buildings. He came to prominence in 1934 when his *South of Scranton* (1931, Metropolitan) won the first prize at the Carnegie International. This painting, a composite of landscape, architectural, and genre elements, including a group of sailors doing improbably high leaps from the deck of a cruiser, was one of the first American surrealist paintings (see Surrealism).

Blume caused controversy in 1939 when his painting *The Eternal City*, (1934–37, Modern Museum) was rejected by the Corcoran Gallery Biennial as too inflammatory in subject matter; it was directed at Mussolini, who is depicted as a green–headed jack-in-the-box lording it over a surrealist vision of Italian life and religion while American tourists look on. The years spent in the painting of this picture are typical of Blume's extremely painstaking method. He prepared each large canvas through innumerable sketches and labored tirelessly over the final result; his output is therefore very small. Other notable works of his in public collections are *Light of the World* (1932, Whitney) and *The Rock* (1945–48, Chicago). Blume has received two Guggenheim fellowships as well as numerous other awards. (A.F.)

Blumenau, Lili (n.d.–   ).
Leading weaver-designer and teacher. Born in Berlin, Germany, she first studied painting at the Academy of Fine Arts there; then, while studying painting in Paris, she was apprenticed to a weaver. After coming to the United States she studied weaving at the old New York School of Textile Technology and with Joseph Albers* at Black Mountain College in North Carolina. Since 1950 she has taught weaving at Columbia and New York universities and at the Fashion Institute of Technology, all in New York City. Blumenau has worked with textile manufacturers as a consultant and designer. Her designs tend towards the geometric and are enhanced by the detail and ingenuity of open or tightly woven constructions.

Blythe, David Gilmore (1815–65).
The foremost American satiric genre painter of his generation, Blythe was born in East Liverpool, Ohio. Apparently self-taught, he displayed an early aptitude for drawing. At sixteen he was apprenticed to a woodcarver, Joseph Woodwell, in Pittsburgh. There he designed and carved shop signs and did cabinetwork. His interest in art was encouraged by his easy access to the studio-shop of J. J. Gillespie, a meeting place for local artists and visiting portraitists.

Blythe visited New Orleans about 1834 and then served from 1837–40 in the U.S. Navy as a ship's carpenter. He then returned to Pittsburgh and became an itinerant portraitist. He also began to paint genre scenes of the city. His portraits were stiff and primitive; but his genre painting was marked by humor and anecdotal realism. In about 1852 he carved a heroic statue of General Lafayette for the Fayette County Court House in Uniontown, Pa. About this time, Blythe also tried making a living by means of a traveling panorama but met with the same failure that attended many other similar attempts. The panorama, the precursor of the movie travelog, was a popular specialized form of painting prevalent in the United States in the first half of the 19th century. Usually it was painted on a continuous strip of canvas and was mounted on large rollers so that only one section at a time was exposed to view. Sometimes the whole was displayed around a large room. Viewers paid an entrance fee. After being dis-

3

4

3. **David Gilmore Blythe.** Trial Scene. *Rochester Memorial Art Gallery, University of Rochester.*
4. **David Gilmore Blythe.** The Post Office, *c.1860. Museum of Art, Carnegie Institute, Pittsburgh.*

played in Cumberland, Md., in Winchester, Va., and in Baltimore and Pittsburgh in 1851, Blythe's panorama, which showed the Allegheny Mountains from Virginia to the Ligonier Valley in Pennsylvania, was sold in sections for stage scenery.

The Civil War had a profound effect on Blythe. He followed the 13th Pennsylvania Volunteers in the field and produced numerous sketches of army life as well as some of his most important paintings. His *Battle of Gettysburg* (1863–65, Boston) is one of his masterpieces. Free of any satirical overtones, it is one of the most powerful paintings of the war, conveying dramatically and convincingly the tumult, terror, and excitement of battle. Also noteworthy are his *General Abner Doubleday Watching His Troops Cross the Potomac* (c.1863, National Baseball Hall of Fame and Museum, Cooperstown, N.Y.) and *Libby Prison* (1863, Boston), a somber rendering of the fetid, overcrowded conditions in that Confederate jail. While Blythe's war subjects made up a large part of his total production from 1856 to 1865, the period of his greatest productivity, he is nevertheless best known for his satirical scenes of Pittsburgh life, its courts, taverns, prisons, and other urban institutions. He delighted in deriding the squalor, venality, pettiness and coarseness in the city he knew so well. No other American painter up to that time had satirized his fellows in such scathing terms. Only Thomas Nast's cartoons and drawings later in the century were equally virulent in their response to vice and corruption. Of Blythe's Pittsburgh scenes, *The Post Office* (1856–65, Carnegie) and *The Hideout* (c. 1850–60, private collection) are outstanding.

Using a low-keyed palette, Blythe was not a great colorist, but his paintings have a warm, mellow tone and against their rather dark, brownish backgrounds his touches of color glow with muted brilliance. And he was one of the earliest Americans to deliberately distort the human figure to convey a satiric message. Although in his lifetime his fame was definitely local, he has since been recognized as a precursor of the social realists of the next century.

(H.W.W.)

Bodmer, Karl (1809–93).
Painter of American Indians, born in Riesbach, Switzerland, and educated in Paris. He received his early train-

1

2

1. *Karl Bodmer.* Interior of a Mandan Indian Earth-Lodge near Fort Clark, *1833. Joslyn Art Museum, Omaha (Natural Gas Company Collection).*
2. *Aaron Bohrod.* Landscape Near Chicago, *1934. Whitney Museum of American Art, N.Y.*

ing as a painter from his uncle J. J. Meyer von Meilen. He came to the United States with a German naturalist, Maximilian, Prince of Wied, as the documentary artist of the expedition the prince had organized. On the expedition, which in 1832–34 traveled up the Missouri River to Fort McKenzie, he did many richly colored watercolors of the Indians of the Great Plains and of the landscape. They include scenes of Indian encampments, sketches of individual Indians and the native fauna, as well as delightful pure landscapes along the river. Eighty-two of these attractive views were engraved as aquatints and published as illustrations in Maximilian's book, *Reise in das innere Nord-Amerika in den Jahren 1832 bis 1834* (1839). Bodmer returned to Europe in 1834 and lived first in Paris, where he worked with the finest Parisian artists to make the eighty-two engravings. After 1849 he lived in Barbizon, where he died. Bodmer was an excellent draftsman, a rich colorist and a well-trained observer. His views of the wilderness and of Indian life on the Plains, such as *Interior of a Mandan Indian Earth-Lodge near Fort Clark* (Joslyn), are not only fascinating documents but also works of considerable artistic merit. Although he was not an American artist he belongs to that small company of visitors whose work has become an enduring part of the record of the American past.   (H.W.W.)

Bogardus, James (1800–74).
Inventor and architect in iron. Born in Catskill, N.Y. Apprenticed to a watchmaker at fourteen, he learned engraving, die-making, and the use of precision instruments. Moving to New York about 1825, he worked as a machinist and soon produced such inventions as a chronometer clock and a metal-cased lead pencil. Bogardus went to England in 1836, received an award of $2000 for inventing an engraving machine for postage stamps in 1839, and returned to New York in 1840. There his most important work was in fabricating iron buildings. Although not the first to construct a facade of cast iron, he exploited the idea by prefabricating parts and thereby building quickly. A drugstore in New York, Bogardus' first building in iron, was erected in three days in 1848. His own factory at Centre and Duane streets (1848–50) was an advertising model for his product. He claimed

it was completely of iron, but it is questionable whether the inner members of this five-story building were iron. Public response was slow because of fears of iron melting in fires, of inadequate strength, decay, and lack of esthetic qualities. Bogardus persisted and eventually received orders for cast prefabricated buildings from many American cities. *The Sun* Building, Baltimore (1850–51), and Harper and Brothers Building, N.Y. (1854), were spectacular examples of his work.

Of more lasting importance—though Bogardus could not know this—was his construction of fire-bell towers in New York in 1851, culminating in a design for the New York Crystal Palace exhibition; although not accepted, the design showed the possibilities of iron construction. Curiously it was a scheme for erecting a shot tower for a Mr. McCullough on Centre Street, New York (1855), that contained the clues to the tall buildings to come. Bogardus erected a frame of cast iron and then filled the interstices with brick, relying on the iron to support the brick as in the masonry covering of skyscrapers of the 1880s. In another shot tower (1881) he sheathed the entire tower with brick so that the metal parts were protected from weather. Much of his work has disappeared, but the E. H. Laing Store, Washington and Murray streets, New York (1849), still stands although bereft of much of its original ornament.
                                              (P.F.N.)

Bohrod, Aaron (1907–   ).
Painter and ceramist. Born in Chicago, Ill., he studied at the Chicago Art Institute and at the Art Students League* in New York, where he came under the influence of John Sloan.* He began his career with numerous paintings of the Chicago scene, emphasizing architecture and everyday incident, occasionally with elements of caricature, as in *Landscape Near Chicago* (1934, Whitney). A Guggenheim Fellowship in 1936 enabled him to extend his range to the Far West and then to the East Coast.

Bohrod served as a war correspondent-artist for *Life* in the South Pacific and in Europe during World War II. In 1948 he succeeded John Steuart Curry* as artist-in-residence at the University of Wisconsin, Madison, a position he still holds. His first creative efforts there were directed toward the local scene; gradually his interest shifted to

meticulously rendered, often symbolic still lifes, generally in *trompe l'oeil* style, and he has concentrated on these since 1954. He has also painted covers for *Time,* and he has enjoyed a long collaboration in ceramics with ceramist F. Carlton Ball* at the University of Wisconsin and at Southern Illinois University. Bohrod has been awarded prizes at the Carnegie International and at the Art Institute of Chicago. He is the author of *A Pottery Sketchbook* (1959) and of *A Decade of Still Life* (1966).
                                              (A.F.)

Bolotowsky, Ilya (1907–   ).
Painter, born in St. Petersburg, Russia. he emigrated to America in 1923 and entered New York's National Academy of Design, studying there until 1930. In 1933, after seeing a canvas by the Dutch modernist Piet Mondrian, he began producing the geometric paintings and constructions that have characterized his work. From Mondrian he derived a horizontal-vertical format and the use of primary colors plus black, white, and gray, although he sometimes adds diagonal lines or other hues for a more dynamic effect. His pictures are completely abstract, consisting of square and rectangular forms worked into elaborate tensions and balances resolved by way of color and composition. Bolotowsky writes: "In my paintings I avoid all associations. I try for perfect harmony, using neutral elements. I want things absolutely pure and simple. . . ." During the early 1930s he was a member of The Ten,* a group that included Mark Rothko* and Adolph Gottlieb.* In 1936, however, he was converted to "pure plastic art" and became one of the founders of the American Abstract Artists,* a group whose early members included Ibram Lassaw,* Ad Reinhardt* and George L. K. Morris.

Bolotowsky exhibited his work at the New Art Circle, New York City, in 1946 and 1952, and had nine one-man shows from 1954 to 1970. He has never altered his basic style despite the ascendance of abstract expressionism* and later trends, although he did add tondo-, diamond-, and rhomboid-shaped canvases and "sculpture" to his repertoire. These "shaped canvases"* often result in rectangular forms that are cut off in odd ways at the edges, while his "sculpture" is an extension of the paintings into the third dimension, as, for example, in *Columns,* where paintings wrap

Bontecou

around all four sides of rectangular constructions. Bolotowsky has designed a number of murals and he has made many experimental films. He taught at Black Mountain College, N.C. (1946–48), the University of Wyoming (1948–57), and New York State University at New Paltz.

(E.C.G.)

Bontecou, Lee (1931–   ).
A sculptor who has consistently demonstrated her originality not only in her use of unusual materials, such as her early reliefs in rough canvas, wire, and leather, but also in her motifs, which nearly always refer to natural forces. She was born in Rhode Island, and her early years were spent in Nova Scotia, Canada. Her initial training was at the Art Students League in New York, where she studied with William Zorach* and John Hovannes. She spent two years in Italy and Greece on a Fulbright Fellowship (1957–58) experimenting with terra-cotta, often fashioning animal effigies, and learning the subtleties of bronze casting. Her first exhibition in 1959 consisted of bronze sculptures. Soon after, she embarked on an adventure which startled and impressed her viewers. Gathering discarded army canvas, old steel rods, and wire, she built the deep reliefs which first gained her serious attention. They presented somber, even disquieting images, with impenetrable dark apertures and tautly stretched surfaces suggesting fearful experiences. At times they had anecdotal overtones, such as the allusion to war experience in a gas-mask image and the prickly extrusion of small wires recalling barbed wire.

Toward the mid-1960s, she began building elaborate welded armatures, like the frame of a ship, to support forms in far deeper relief. The planes of stretched canvas were now cleverly tilted and graded to suggest the illusion of great depth. The forms themselves were less aggressive and adhered to the cubist principles of recession. At times, she colored her surfaces brightly, reenforcing the vivacity of movement in the reliefs. All of her canvas reliefs were developed in concert with her study of natural form. For years Bontecou has rendered insects, flowers, and marine life with delicate and precise naturalism. Her drawings in charcoal or soot nearly always indicate specific characteristics, while retaining the visual mystery that she finds inexhaust-

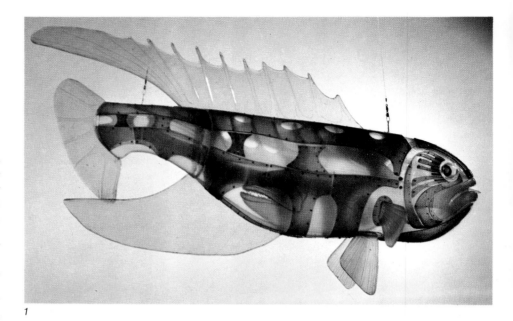

1

2

1. **Lee Bontecou.** Untitled, 1970, vacuum-formed plastic. Private Collection.
2. **Lee Bontecou.** Untitled, 1966, mixed media. Private Collection.

ible in nature. These studies were the basis for numerous abstract forms in her sculptures, and for her fine graphics.

After exhibiting her canvas assemblages in New York in 1960, 1962, and 1966, she began to work with clear and tinted plastics, developing a more naturalistic vocabulary but retaining her unusually inventive forms. These were exhibited in 1971. The exquisite poise of a towering flower, its petals smoky but transparent, its tall stem enclosing flowing strands within, its stamens falling luxuriously into space, was startlingly effective. Flowers, snails, and fish were shaped in elaborate patterns of light, their interiors dimly secreting other forms.

Lee Bontecou has exhibited throughout the world, including personal exhibitions in Germany and Holland, and has participated in numerous international shows, among them the São Paulo Biennial in 1961 and Documenta in Kassel, Germany in 1964. She has received numerous awards.   (D.A.)

Borglum, Gutzon (1867–1941).

A sculptor best known for his colossal presidential portraits on Mount Rushmore, S. Dakota. He was born in Idaho and was the older brother of Solon Borglum.* Most of the period from 1887 to 1903 he spent in Paris, where he studied at the Académie Julien and was greatly impressed by the work of Rodin. After establishing his studio in New York he gained national recognition when he exhibited his bronze *Mares of Diomedes* (Metropolitan) at the Louisiana Purchase Exposition in St. Louis in 1904. Early in his career Borglum found pleasure in doing animal and western subjects, executing them in the rich modeling, but without the decorative quality, of the Parisian manner. After creating the twelve Apostles for the facade of St. John the Divine, New York City, he turned increasingly to portraiture, at times on an enormous scale. The latter tendency first manifested itself in the six-ton marble head of *Abraham Lincoln* placed in the U.S. Capitol in 1908. This was followed by a commission to carve a colossal portrait of General Robert E. Lee from the live rock of Stone Mountain, near Atlanta; Borglum's vision of this project expanded until he planned a relief two thousand feet long with hundreds of figures. By 1917 he had begun work, however World War I interrupted him; when he returned

to the project it was surrounded by dissension, ending in Borglum's dismissal in 1925. Not to be denied his desire for a truly colossal sculpture, he commenced the Mount Rushmore portraits of presidents Washington, Jefferson, Lincoln, and Theodore Roosevelt (1930–41), "carved" from the live rock with dynamite and jackhammers. The project, paid for by Congress, cost about $1,520,-000. Meanwhile, Borglum had done numerous other life-size portraits, such as those of Alexander Stephens (1927) and John C. Greenway (1930) in Statuary Hall of the U.S. Capitol. Of his large memorials, *Texas Cowboys* (1920s, San Antonio) and *Wars of America* (1925–26, Newark, N.J.), are noteworthy.   (W.C.)

Borglum, Solon Hannibal (1868–1922).

A sculptor like his older brother Gutzon Borglum,* he was born in Utah and grew up in Nebraska, where he worked as a cowboy. The American West remained forever a part of his work, and he is best known for his bronze sculptures of cowboys and Indians and their horses. He first studied with his brother and then at the Art Academy of Cincinnati before going to Paris to attend the Académie Julien, where he worked with Fremiet, the animal sculptor. Naturalism remained the basis of his style, enriched with his first-hand knowledge of cowboy and Indian life. He returned to America and in the late 1890s produced several bronzes, among them *Little Horse in the Wind* (Cincinnati). Among his best known works is *On the Border of White Man's Land* (1900, Metropolitan), which shows an Indian, dismounted, peering over a ridge at a white man's settlement. Similar pieces were included in the Pan-American Exposition (1901, Buffalo) and the Louisiana Purchase Exposition (1904, St. Louis). Borglum's heroic exploits with the French army in World War I won him the Croix de Guerre. On his return to America he became a respected teacher. His book, *Sound Construction* (1923), contains hundreds of his illustrations.
(W.C.)

Bourgeois, Louise (1911–).

Sculptor. One of America's distinguished stone carvers, she has worked in nearly every medium. She was born in Paris, and as a child in France she helped her parents restore medieval tapestries, later studying at the Sor-

bonne, Académie Ranson, Académie de la Grande Chaumière, and with Fernand Léger. In 1938 she married Robert Goldwater, the art historian, and settled in the United States. Ten years later she held her first one-man exhibition at a New York gallery, where she exhibited large, fetish-like wood figures, sometimes grouped. Toward the mid-1950s, these wooden carvings became even more abstract, and were clustered together like a jostling crowd, their painted and stained surfaces forming continuities of considerable intricacy.

In the early 1960s, she temporarily abandoned wood, turning to plaster and papier-mâché to create irregular abstractions in which hovered the spirit of her early fetishistic works. Soon after, she devoted herself to stone, carving the large clusters of rounded verticals in varying degrees of finish, using the polished surfaces only for carefully gauged accents and letting the forms spring up from rough carved bases. These extremely arresting groups of forms, often regarded as phallic, earned Bourgeois a special place in American sculpture. Few have been able to work in a traditional medium with such force and invention.

Louise Bourgeois has had innumerable exhibitions in both America and Europe, and she is represented in major museums of the United States.   (D.A.)

Boyle, John J. (1851–1917).

Sculptor. He was born in New York City but grew up in Philadelphia, Pa. After commencing his career as a stonecutter he studied at the Pennsylvania Academy of the Fine Arts and in 1877 went to Paris to attend the École des Beaux-Arts. In 1880 he returned to Philadelphia and soon produced a sculpture that brought him national recognition: a bronze, *Indian Family, or The Alarm* (City of Chicago.) Shortly thereafter his most famous bronze group—*Stone Age in America* (1866–88)—was commissioned for Philadelphia. Boyle was drawn to subjects of primitive life, and his style shows the rich detail, lively surfaces, and active masses of sculpture in Paris in the 1870s and 1880s as opposed to the static volumes and smooth surfaces of neoclassicism.* The recipient of numerous honors, Boyle moved to New York City in 1902, where he occasionally undertook commissions for portraits and bronze memorial figures.   (W.C.)

1

1. *Edward Augustus Brackett.* Washington Allston, *1844, marble. Metropolitan Museum of Art, N.Y. (gift of children of Jonathan Sturges).*

Mathew Brady and Company
2. U.S. Christian Commission Storehouse, Washington, D.C., *c.1864, daguerreotype.*
3. "Pine Cottage," Winter Quarters at Fort Brady near Dutch Gap-canal, *Virginia, 1864, daguerreotype.*
4. Dead Confederate Soldier in the Trenches of Fort Mahone, Petersburg, Va., *1865, daguerreotype. (attributed to Brady's assistant Thomas C. Roche). All, Library of Congress, Washington, D.C.*

Brackett, Edward Augustus (1818–1908).

Portrait sculptor, he was born in Vermont but grew up in Cincinnati and made his first sculptures there. At age twenty-one he moved to New York City, where he began exhibiting portraits, including a bust of William Cullen Bryant, at the National Academy of Design. Finding little patronage in New York he settled permanently in Boston in 1841, and although several fellow-artists recognized his talent, patronage was far from munificent. Probably his best known portrait of this period is that of Washington Allston,* which shows Brackett at his best. His style was an uncomplicated naturalism which in portraits of less distinguished men could become rather prosaic. Entirely self-taught, Brackett only occasionally tried anything more ambitious than portrait busts. A full-length statue of *Hosea Ballou* (1857) may be seen in Mt. Auburn Cemetery, Cambridge, Mass., and one of his rare attempts at ideal works, the *Shipwrecked Mother and Child* (1851), is at the Worcester Art Museum. In the 1860s Brackett gave up sculpture for employment in the conservation of wildlife, serving for twenty-seven years as head of the Massachusetts Fish and Game Commission. (W.C.)

Bradford, William (1823–92).

Born in Fairhaven, Mass., he was a landscape and marine painter who specialized in Arctic views. After trying various occupations, including storekeeping, he turned to painting about 1854. His early work consists of ship portraits and harbor scenes near New Bedford painted in a detailed style suggesting the influence of Fitz Hugh Lane* and his teacher and collaborator, the Dutch painter Albert Van Beest (1820–60). In the 1860s, he went on numerous trips to Labrador and the Arctic, on which he made many sketches and photographs of icebergs. His work was widely collected and acclaimed both in America and in England, which he visited in 1872; it was English patronage that made possible his ambitious book of 1873, *The Arctic Regions.* He was based in New York in the following decades, but he traveled widely and painted in the West. During the same period, his style loosened and his palette grew more intense as he executed some powerful northern scenes, such as *Icebergs in the Arctic,* 1882, which stand out in an uneven oeuvre. (T.E.S.)

Brady, Mathew B. (c.1823–96).

Perhaps the most important figure in America's photographic history, Brady was born of Irish immigrant parents in Warren County, N.Y. As a youth he studied art with the painter William Page,* whom he accompanied to New York City in the late 1830s. By 1843 he was a manufacturer of the leather cases used to protect the delicate daguerreotype images introduced into America in 1840. By 1844 Brady had opened his own daguerreian studio at Broadway and Fulton Streets. For the next twenty years he was the most successful daguerreotypist in the city, attracting wealthy New Yorkers and visiting celebrities to sit for his camera. In 1853 Brady opened a fashionable "branch" studio on Broadway and Tenth Street. Almost from the beginning, Brady realized the importance of preserving the images of notables who visited his studio. He also began to amass a collection of portraits that he later called his "Gallery of Illustrious Americans," and he published many of them in *Leslie's Illustrated Weekly* and *Harper's Weekly.*

Brady's historical sense (he referred to the camera as "the eye of history") combined with the tragedy of the Civil War to make possible the vast body of photographs upon which his reputation rests. Brady's third studio, established in Washington, D.C. in 1849, was unsuccessful. Alexander Gardner,* an excellent Scottish photographer, managed the Washington studio. At the outbreak of war, Brady—with the help of Gardner, T. H. O'Sullivan* and, at one point, no fewer than twenty teams of photographers—began to record the conflict. Most of his time was spent in directing his vast staff, but he himself did make photographs at Bull Run in 1861, he was at Antietam and Fredericksburg in 1862, he recorded the aftermath of Gettysburg, he saw the bombardment of Confederate defenses at Petersburg, and at the close of the war he photographed Robert E. Lee in Richmond. Brady's photography diminished in quality as the financial responsibilities for this self-imposed project increased and his eyesight, never very strong, began to fail. It should be noted that while Brady was the most important photographer of this period,

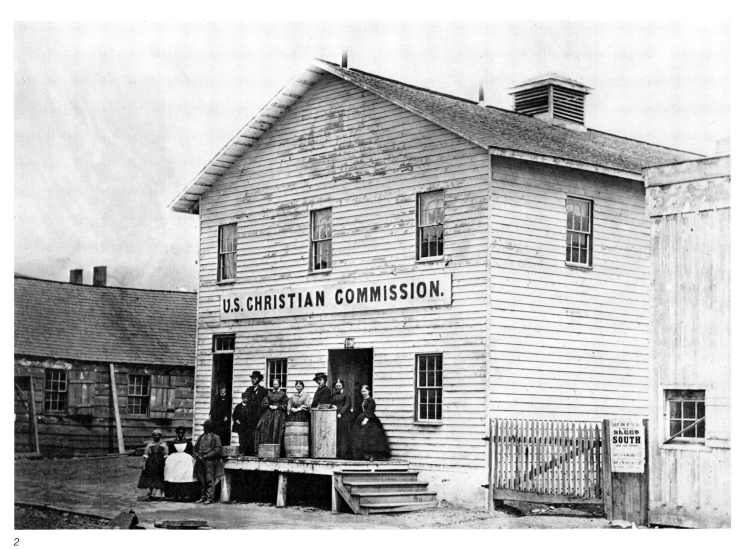

2

4

3

others surpassed him in ability.

Brady declared that he spent over $100,000 to secure this visual record of the war; this outlay, combined with an unwise choice in business partners, brought him to bankruptcy in 1873. A year later Congress purchased 5,712 of Brady's glass-plate negatives for $2500 and in 1875 they voted Brady $25,000 for a clear title to the collection. This money allowed him to keep his Washington studio going until 1881, when foreclosure shut its doors forever. For the next fifteen years, Brady worked for other photographers; he died in a charity ward in New York City and was buried in an unmarked grave in the Congressional Cemetery in Washington, D.C. His priceless legacy is today in the Library of Congress. (D.L.)

Breer, Robert (1926–   ).
Sculptor and filmmaker, born in Detroit, Mich., he attended Stanford University. Although he is known primarily for his animated films, his work with moving or kinetic sculpture* dates back to the early 1960s. Breer's first kinetic pieces were based on rotation. By 1966, the date of his first one-man show, he had turned to "crawling objects." Here basic geometric shapes—small rectangles, triangles, and semicircles—were cut out of styrofoam plastic and propelled slowly around the room by means of hidden battery-driven wheels. Formally, they are like children's toys, but the effect of all these little objects creeping over a rug is disconcerting. Breer sees his groups as a composition which changes its configuration as the objects move. The patterns are unpredictable since the little "floats" are in constant motion and change direction whenever they encounter an obstacle.

Breuer, Marcel (1902–   ).
Architect, born in Pécs, Hungary. He first studied painting and sculpture at the Art Academy of Vienna and then at the famous Bauhaus* in Weimar, Germany. After graduation from the Bauhaus in 1924, he became director of the school's furniture department. In 1928 he opened his own office in Berlin. With the rise of the Nazi regime in Germany, Breuer went to England where he formed a partnership with F. R. I. Yorke, and later, in Switzerland, with Alfred and Emith Roth. In 1937 he joined Walter Gropius* (former head of the Bau-

1

2

1. **Marcel Breuer.** Office Building for the Department of Housing and Urban Development, Washington, D.C., 1968.

2. **Marcel Breuer.** Whitney Museum of American Art, N.Y., 1961.

haus) at Harvard and formed a partnership with him. In 1941 he opened his own office.

Before he came to the United States, Breuer's major contribution was in furniture design. His classic 1925 tubular metal chairs and tables represent one of the earliest and most successful design developments in modern furniture. His buildings designed at the end of the 1920s and through the early 1930s were as meticulously detailed as his furniture. His "House for a Sportsman" at the Berlin Building Exhibition of 1931 utilized storage walls to divide a rectangular space. The Harnischmacher House in Wiesbaden (1932) and the Doldertal Apartments in Zurich (1934) are elegant examples of the mature International style,* with crisp white walls, horizontal bands of windows and balconies, and thin columns that make the building seem to hover over its site.

The architectural designs which he and Gropius produced before World War II, such as the Chamberlain House, Wayland, Mass. (1940) or the Ford House, Lincoln, Mass. (1939), softened the hardness of the International style by using warmer, more traditional materials such as stone and wood. Stone, wood, and brick continued to appear in his post-1945 houses. The juxtaposition of machine surface and traditional materials can be seen in his own house in New Canaan, Conn. (1947), or in such later work as the Stillman House II, Litchfield, Conn. (1965–66).

Since moving to New York in 1946 he has maintained a highly successful practice. In 1952, Breuer, the Italian architect Pier Nervi, and the French architect Bernard H. Zehrfuss were selected to design the Unesco Building in Paris (1958). The main complex of the Secretariat formed an eight-story curved "Y" reflecting the site on the Place Fontenoy. In classical International style the auditoriums were separated from the main building and housed in a splayed low rectangular block. As in all of Breuer's work, meticulous attention was paid to basic proportions and to details both within and without. A year later construction was started on his large Saint John's Abbey and University at Collegeville, Minn. (1953–68), and in 1956 he was commissioned to design the new Whitney Museum of American Art in New York. Both buildings illustrate how strongly

Breuer has been influenced by the late work of Le Corbusier and the new brutalism.* The cantilevered stripped design of the Whitney goes directly back to Breuer's urban projects of the late 1920s, especially the Elberfeld Hospital in Germany (1928). Such later buildings as the Armstrong Rubber Co. Building, West Haven, Conn. (1965–69), and the Engineering and Applied Sciences Building of Yale University (1965–69) are also of reinforced concrete, but in these structures the rectangular geometry of the surfaces is more in the spirit of the earlier International style. In 1966 Breuer, together with Herbert Beckhart, submitted a project for the Franklin D. Roosevelt Memorial in Washington, D.C. Although never built, this project sums up Breuer's approach to design. Its pinwheel layout of seven angular slabs that interpenetrate one another reveals the influence of abstract painting and sculpture; while the monumental stone slabs, the pattern of the pavement, and the central granite cube demonstrate that many of the major modern architects have returned to more traditional high-art architectural values.   (D.G.)

Brewster, John, Jr. (1766–1846).
Deaf mute miniature and portrait painter born in Hampton, Conn., who worked as an itinerant artist along the New England coast as far east as Maine. Brewster's painting may reflect his infirmity—in the intense concentration he fixes on his sitter's eyes and in a pervasive aura of stopped time, as if the image were a silent, remembered one. The quality is never more touchingly exemplified than in his portrait of Sarah Prince at her pianoforte (c.1801, Kaplan Coll.), holding the score of a popular song that the artist could never have heard.

Bricher, Alfred Thompson (1837–1908).
Marine and landscape painter born in Portsmouth, N.H. Becoming interested in art while engaged in business in Boston, he used his leisure time between 1851 and 1858 to study painting at the Lowell Institute. He then became a professional artist and during the next decade lived and painted in Boston and Newburyport. In 1868 he moved to New York where, apart from sketching and painting trips along the coast of Massachusetts and the offshore islands of Maine in the summer months, he

spent the remainder of his life.

Bricher represents the last developments in the cult of nature which had earlier stimulated the painter Thomas Cole* and the poet William Bryant. His work relates to that of Martin Johnson Heade,* Frederic Edwin Church,* and William Stanley Haseltine, all of whom shared an interest in the pictorial effects of light and air. Bricher portrayed the New England coast from Grand Manan Island and Mount Desert, Me., to the coastal areas of Massachusetts, Rhode Island and New York. A luminist (see Luminism), he was especially successful in capturing the translucent appearance of the sea in its constant movement and in conveying atmospheric perspective, as in *Marine Landscape* (1880s, Metropolitan). Almost forgotten by art historians and collectors until fairly recently, he has now emerged as one of the better marine artists of the late 19th century. (H.W.W.)

Bridges.
As a man-made object in the landscape, bridges, along with such other engineering monuments as dams and such transportation machines as ships, trains, automobiles, and airplanes, have often been referred to as the great works of the 19th and 20th centuries—the modern equivalent of the Greek temple or the Gothic cathedral. The bridge, as an expression of man's ability to master his environment, has often been sharply contrasted with what has seemed to be the caprice and aimlessness of 19th- and 20th-century architectural fashions. Thus a great bridge may achieve a magnificence and a graceful embodiment of function that makes it a work of art as well as a medium of transportation.

As with other engineering innovations in the 19th century, America began by taking over the new forms of bridge construction which had originated in Europe, especially in England and France. By the mid-19th century American bridges were comparable in inventiveness, if not from a purely esthetic point of view, with their French and English counterparts.

Bridges emerged as a major building type in the 19th century only after new materials were made available, such as cast iron, and, later, steel and reinforced concrete, after new methods of construction and calculation had been developed, and finally when new demands (as for railroads and, later, highways) had to be met. While iron bridges had been built in England long before 1800, the first iron bridge in the United States was a small structure over a creek in Brownsville, Pa. in 1836–39. And in 1845 the Philadelphia and Reading Railroad, using trusses, constructed, at Manayunk, Pa., the first iron railroad bridge.

After the Civil War, a self-trained engineer, James B. Eads, proposed a high bridge over the Mississippi at St. Louis; it was completed in 1874. Steel was used to create its three gentle arches, each over 500 feet long. The Eads bridge was followed by numerous steel-arched bridges during the 19th century, a classic example being the double-arched Washington Bridge (1884–89) over the Harlem River in New York, designed by William R. Hutton, with Edward H. Kendell as architect.

Many variations were rung on the form of the steel truss bridge in the late 19th and early 20th centuries. On the whole, these bridges are successful as a direct expression of skeletal engineering, but as visual forms they are generally weak or just plain dull. Occasionally, as in the Galveston Harrisburg and San Antonio Railroad Bridge over the Pecos River near Comstock, Texas (1891–92), the tenuous tower supports and the narrow horizontal road bed created a spectacular composition, particularly when set in a dramatic natural setting. Later bridges, like the Queensboro Bridge, New York (Gustav Lindenthal, 1901–08), the Hell Gate Bridge, New York (Lindenthal, 1907–17), and the Pulaski Skyway Bridge at Jersey City (Sigvald Johannesson, 1930–32) are all impressive feats of engineering, but are only marginally successful in their visual symbolism.

The suspension bridge, certainly the most appealing structural form for the bridge, was another 18th-century European innovation. It entered the American scene in 1801 in a small bridge over Jacobs Creek in Uniontown, Pa. Designed by James Finley, it employed wrought-iron chains and smaller wrought-iron suspenders which held up the wood trusses of the bridge. In 1841–42, Charles Ellet designed his thin, delicate Schuylkill River Bridge, 350 feet long, at Philadelphia using wrought-iron cables and wire rope suspenders. At Wheeling, W. Va., (1846-

4

1

2

3

5

6

7

Bridges
1. *Old Franklin Ave. Bridge, Philadelphia, 1697.*
2. *Eads Bridge. James Eads, St. Louis, 1874.*
3. *Suspension Bridge, Charles Ellet, Wheeling, W.Va., 1848.*
4. *George Washington Bridge. Othmar Ammann & Cass Gilbert, N.Y., 1931.*
5. *Brooklyn Bridge. John Roebling, N.Y., 1883.*
6. *San Mateo Creek Bridge. San Mateo, Cal., 1969.*
7. *Verrazano Narrows Bridge. Othmar Ammann & Charles Whitney, N.Y., 1964.*

48) Ellet designed a suspension bridge (1010 feet long) over the Ohio River, and in 1847–48 he started his spectacular Niagara Falls suspension bridge (770 feet long), which was completed by John Roebling. Roebling's own masterpiece was the famous Brooklyn Bridge, with a main span of 1595 feet and total length of 3455 feet. Its inauguration created unparalleled excitement and it soon became a symbol of American engineering genius, energy, and vision. It has been celebrated in poetry such as Hart Crane's *The Bridge,* in paintings by Joseph Stella,* John Marin* and others, and in countless photographs, including several striking interpretations by Walker Evans.* Soaring out from among the wharves and massed buildings of lower Manhattan, the bridge remained a major focal point of the New York skyline until the skyscraper* began to eclipse it in the 1920s.

During the 20th century the suspension bridge retained its distinction as the most handsome form for a bridge. The 3500-foot span George Washington Bridge (1927–31) over the Hudson River (Othmar H. Ammann, engineer; Cass Gilbert,* consulting architect), provided a form which dominated the natural cliffs to each side. Even more dramatic in its site and in its power to establish its presence is the Golden Gate Bridge (Joseph B. Strauss; O. H. Ammann, Moisseiff, and Derleth, 1933–37) which in much of its detailing is pure streamlined moderne.*

The collapse of the Tacoma Narrows Suspension Bridge in 1940, a year after it was completed, was the result of an effort to create a tenuous visual form, with structure reduced to an absolute minimum.

Founded on sounder aerodynamics have been the numerous suspension bridges built since 1945. Foremost among these are the 3800-foot Mackinac Straits Bridge in Michigan (David B. Steinman, 1954–57) and the even longer (4260 feet) Verrazano Narrows Bridge in New York (Ammann and Charles S. Whitney, 1959–64). Although these are magnificent structures, some critics feel that their larger structural members and architectural detailing make them less visually striking than the pre-1940 bridges.

Concrete for bridge construction was used sparingly in 19th century America. The small span footbridge built in Prospect Park in Brooklyn in 1871 was the first concrete bridge in the United States. In 1889 an engineer, Ernest L. Ransome, designed the Alvord Lake Bridge in Golden Gate Park, San Francisco, the first reinforced concrete bridge in America, but with the concrete sheathed in stone and an English 18th-century grotto effect underneath the arch. In 1898 reinforced concrete rib and girder bridges were introduced into America and after 1910 concrete was increasingly preferred for highway bridges. The parabolic arch of the Westinghouse Memorial Bridge (George T. Ray), spanning the Turtle Creek Valley near Pittsburgh, is effective in its conservative monumentality, with an effect similar to that of a Roman aqueduct. Since 1945 there has been an increased use of pre-stressed concrete especially for expressway bridges. The longest of these now being designed is the Potomac River Crossing Bridge (Howard Needless, Tammen and Bergendorf) which promises to be the most graceful structure of its kind in America. Another new engineering form, the stayed girder bridge, where the roadway is supported by tension guys suspended from high towers, is exemplified in the new John O'Connell Memorial Bridge (Alaska Department of Highways) at Sitka Harbor, Alaska.

American architects, especially in this century have been infatuated with the size and form of the bridge. During the 1920s many architects, including Raymond Hood,* proposed urban bridges as megastructures, housing apartments and offices. In 1948 Paolo Soleri* proposed an imaginative undulating slab bridge of concrete, and in the following year Frank Lloyd Wright* designed a low butterfly-wing bridge which was to cross the lower part of San Francisco Bay. However, none of these has thus far been realized.　(D.G.)

Bridges, Charles (active in Virginia, 1735–40).
British portrait painter. An elderly artist whose refined style was acceptable to the planter aristocracy, he produced courtly decorative work of provincial Virginians. Very little is known of him, and his work has been variously identified. The portraits attributed to him owe much to mezzotint prototypes.* The portrait, *Maria Taylor Byrd* (c.1724, Metropolitan), which for many years was attributed to Bridges, is now thought to be of European origin. Composed often with suavity and grace, Bridges' portraits express a mood of remote and romantic interest appropriate to their subjects and to the rooms of the old Tidewater mansions.　(C.C.S.)

Brook, Alexander, (1898–　　).
Painter. Born in Brooklyn, N.Y. He contracted infantile paralysis at the age of twelve and, while bedridden, began to draw and paint. He enrolled at the Art Students League* in New York in 1915 and remained there for four years, studying with Kenneth Hayes Miller* and winning nearly every scholarship the school had to offer. He was assistant director of the Whitney Studio Club from 1924 to 1927 and in this capacity assisted many artists in finding an outlet for their work. After 1923, when he had his first New York gallery show jointly with his wife, Peggy Bacon,* Brook exhibited almost constantly for a quarter of a century. In 1929 he won first prize in the annual American show at the Art Institute of Chicago, and the following year he also won first prize at the Carnegie International.

Brook might be described as a lyrical academician. His early work, emphasizing still-life subjects and the half-draped female figure, is notable for its fragile moods and its radiant color-light. In the 1930s he broke away from set studio themes to investigate landscape and the human environment in general; the moods of these later works are more dramatic and their color and chiaroscuro more sharply contrasted than in the earlier paintings. Brook has also had great success as a portraitist. He is in the permanent collections of many American museums.　(A.F.)

Brooks, James (1906–　　).
Painter, born in St. Louis, Mo. He studied at Southern Methodist University, Texas, the Dallas Art Institute, and the Art Students League,* New York. He has taught extensively at art schools and universities, including Columbia University and Yale, and has exhibited widely in the United States and Europe. The Whitney Museum gave him a retrospective exhibition in 1963 and his works have been featured in exhibitions of American abstract expressionists at major museums.

After his essentially academic training, Brooks began in the 1940s to experiment with a curvilinear, free version of

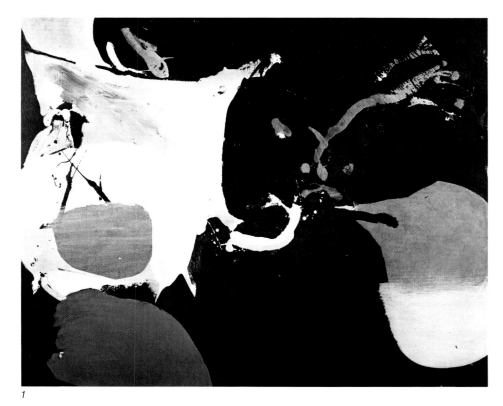

1

2

cubism* obviously aimed at rationalizing fragmented cubist shapes with the free, color expressionism of Jackson Pollock.* Following these free cubist works, Brooks moved to a more monumental but still lyrical-coloristic form of expression in which large masses of color were integrated with a delicate linear pattern, as in *Ainlee* (1957, Metropolitan). Although historically he has been associated with abstract expressionism,* he has always been primarily a colorist, concerned with the creation of large, coloristic harmonies rather than the violent discords with which action painting or abstract expressionism is normally associated. During the 1960s his color shapes became larger and more open, so that he should perhaps be associated with the contemporary school of color painters.　(H.H.A.)

Browere, John Henri Isaac (1792–1834).
Sculptor, best known for life-masks of famous men that he converted into portrait busts. Born in New York, he studied in Paris in 1816–17 and there learned to make plaster masks. After returning to America he settled in New York but traveled to other cities to take the masks of famous men, among them Lafayette and Gilbert Stuart.* Once he had made the mask of a face, he worked it into a portrait bust, the shoulders usually being draped with a toga. The manner in which the facial likeness was made resulted in a highly naturalistic style, but this was tempered by the classical element of the toga. His best-known portrait is that of Thomas Jefferson, who nearly died during the making of the mask in 1826. Browere was never fully accepted as an important sculptor, and his work remained in obscurity until around 1900.　(W.C.)

Brown, George Loring (1814–89).
Landscape painter born in Boston, Mass. As a youth he was apprenticed to a wood engraver and made a living illustrating children's books until G.P.A. Healy,* a prolific portraitist, encouraged him to become a painter. He made his first European trip in 1832, going to London and later studying in Paris with L. G. E. Isabey, French genre painter. In Paris he was captivated by the work of Claude Lorrain, and many of his later paintings are adaptations of Lorrain's rich coloring and formal composition.
He was back in Boston working as a

1. *James Brooks.* Cullodon, *1967. Martha Jackson Gallery, N.Y.*
2. *George Loring Brown.* The Public Garden, Boston, *c.1869. Museum of Fine Arts, Boston (Karolik Collection).*

1

2

painter in 1834 and, after a year in New York, again in the Boston area in 1838. He sailed to Europe in 1839 and spent most of the next twenty years in Florence and Rome, where he was a well-known member of the expatriate art colonies. In 1859 he returned to America and was in New York in 1862 and in the Boston area after 1864. He exhibited fairly regularly at the Boston Athenaeum, the National Academy of Design,* and the Pennsylvania Academy of the Fine Arts.*

Brown was highly regarded as a landscape painter especially in Boston; an early expatriate, he was also the best-known American landscape painter living abroad. A friend of Nathaniel Hawthorne, Brown is mentioned favorably in Hawthorne's *The Marble Faun* and in *The Journal*. His reputation today rests largely on his landscapes, especially those classed in the romantic-realist style. The less successful results of his emulation of Claude Lorrain seem merely ponderous today. He belongs among the American luminists (see Luminism) whose interest was in reproducing precise atmospheric effects. Most of the landscapes he painted between 1840 and 1859 are of Italian scenes, such as *View at Amalfi, Bay of Salerno* (1857, Metropolitan); his American landscapes were either early works or were painted after his return, such as *The Public Garden, Boston* (c.1869, Boston).   (H.W.W.)

Brown, Henry Kirke (1814–86).
A leading American sculptor of the mid-19th century, he was born in Leyden, Mass. He was apprenticed in 1832 to portrait painter Chester Harding* in Boston and then moved to Cincinnati in 1836, where he turned to sculpture. After modeling a number of portrait busts he departed for Italy in 1840 and spent two years in Florence and two more in Rome. He eventually returned to America, unlike such expatriate sculptors as Horatio Greenough* and his close friend, Hiram Powers.*

He had long believed that America should have a national art of her own rather than an adopted Italianate neo-classicism.* After establishing his studio in New York, his first major piece was *Aboriginal Hunter* (1846). One of the first sculptures to be cast in bronze in the United States, it depicted an Indian, a choice that in itself caused comment. After 1850, Brown produced mainly busts and full-length portraits. His most

important project in the 1850s was the equestrian statue of George Washington, a calm but heroic interpretation that he modeled with the help of his young assistant, John Quincy Adams Ward.* Erected in Union Square, New York City, in 1856, it established Brown as one of the nation's foremost sculptors. In 1851 he assumed an active role in the National Academy of Design* in New York. Brown completed several portrait statues for Statuary Hall in the U.S. Capitol. In all of these a direct and forthright naturalism dominated the sculptor's style. Other commissions included bronze equestrian statues of General Winfield Scott and General Nathanael Greene for Washington, D.C., and the sculptures for the pediment of the State House in Columbia, S.C. (destroyed during the Civil War). Brown moved permanently to Newburgh, N.Y., in 1861. By 1880 his position of leadership had been taken over by younger men such as Augustus Saint-Gaudens* and Daniel Chester French.*   (W.C.)

Brown, J. (active 1807–12).
Itinerant portraitist working in western Massachusetts and to the north and possibly the east. His three extraordinary signed and dated portraits of *Mercy Barnes Hall* and *Calvin Hall* (Abby Aldrich Rockefeller) and of their daughter *Laura Hall* (New York Historical Association), painted in Cheshire in 1808, have won him a firm position in scholarly considerations of early 19th-century folk painting. The stern and suspicious expressions of the affluent Hall parents (who are portrayed in three-quarter length pendant canvases) are in contrast to the somewhat shy seductiveness in the full-length portrait of their daughter. The sinuous hairdo of the ladies, which along with their dresses points to the rapid dissemination of French Empire style influence, is echoed somewhat more softly in Mr. Hall's modishly fringed bangs.   (M.J.G.)

Brown, Mather (1761–1831).
Portrait painter. The son of a Boston clock-maker and descended from Cotton and Increase Mather, he received in 1773 his first lessons in painting from Gilbert Stuart.* In 1777 he toured across Massachusetts to New York, selling wine and painting miniatures. Having earned enough in this way to go abroad for study, he sailed for France in 1780;

1. *J. Brown.* Mercy Barnes Hall, *1808.*
2. *J. Brown.* Calvin Hall, *1808.*
   Both, Abby Aldrich Rockefeller Folk Art Collection, Va.
3. *Henry Kirke Brown.* General George Washington, *c. 1850, bronze. Union Square, N.Y.*
4. *Francis Bruguière.* Double Portrait, *c.1925, photograph. George Eastman House, Rochester, N.Y.*

3

4

he reached London in 1781 and became a student of Benjamin West.* The rest of Brown's life was spent in London and provincial English cities as a moderately successful portrait painter. Early in his career he had painted one successful historical composition, had enjoyed some royal patronage, and was patronized also by visiting Americans. His *John Adams* (Boston Athenaeum) and *Thomas Jefferson* (1786, private collection, Mass.) are fine examples of his crisply authoritative yet graceful style. (C.C.S.)

Bruce, Patrick Henry (1881–1937).
Expatriate painter who spent much of his life in France and developed a distinctive form of geometric abstraction. Born in Virginia, Bruce studied with Robert Henri* in New York (1902–03) and Henri Matisse in Paris (1907); he was influenced by Robert Delaunay in 1912–14 (see Orphism). He exhibited in the Armory Show* and at the Paris Salon d'Automne. During the period 1914–18 he developed a vigorous style of geometric abstraction. His most characteristic paintings are still lifes dating from the 1920s in which carefully arranged, severely geometrical objects are painted in flat, bold colors. The flattened structure of his work was highly original, but never received public approval. He became increasingly withdrawn and embittered, and ceased painting in 1932. He destroyed most of his work before returning to New York and committing suicide in 1937. (D.W.S.)

Bruguière, Francis (1880–1945).
Photographer. Born into a wealthy San Francisco, Cal., family, Bruguière traveled in Europe in his twenties to develop his talents as a pianist and painter. He returned to New York in 1905, met Alfred Stieglitz* and became a member of the Photo-Secession movement in 1909. He studied photography with Frank Eugene, another member of the Secession group, and then returned to San Francisco to continue his work in painting and music. He was represented by four photographs in the Photo-Secession exhibition at Buffalo's Albright Art Gallery in 1910, and in 1918 he published his first book, *San Francisco*. His illustrations were mostly a soft-focus, journalistic paean to the city, but did convey his sensitivity to camera vision.

His private income was diminished severely the same year and in 1919 he opened a studio in New York City. During his next nine years, he was extremely productive, both in his own painting and photography and in a tremendous body of work as the photographer of the Theatre Guild, where he collaborated with producers and designers, including Robert Edmund Jones, Lee Simonson, and Norman Bel Geddes.* In 1924 the book of Geddes' unproduced play *Divine Comedy* was published with Bruguière's photographs of the stage model; remarkably lit through the use of unusual light angles and grids, they are typical of much of his later light experimentation. He also began to produce and direct an allegorical film *The Way,* but it was left unfinished when one of the actors died; only still photographs remain. A large exhibition of Bruguière's paintings and photographs in New York City in 1927 was generally well received. He moved permanently to London in 1928. In *Beyond This Point* (1929), his slightly figured, ambiguous images, derived from cut-paper light-modulators and multiple exposures, complement a text by Lance Sieveking on the basic human crises of Death, Jealousy, and Ruin. He and Oswald Blakeston collaborated on a film, *Light Rhythms,* released in 1930. One of his last major projects was giant photo murals, symbolic of England's cultural life, for the British Pavilion at the 1937 Paris International Exposition.

The unique quality of Bruguière's photographic work is its exhaustive exploration—as early as 1912—of the sculptural quality of light. Playing lights upon cut forms he created effects that resembled much of his later theatrical work. Little of this early work survives; the largest body of his remaining work dates from the late 1920s and is at George Eastman House, Rochester, N.Y. His later work with light borders on the mystical: in one of his last projects he photographed filaments of light bulbs in an attempt to capture pure light.

(T.F.B.)

Brush, George De Forest (1855–1941). Painter of American Indians and madonnas. Brush was born in Tennessee but spent his boyhood in Connecticut. After studying at the National Academy of Design, he went to Paris to enter the studio of Gérôme. whose literal aca-

1

2

1. *Charles Bulfinch. State House, Boston, 1797.*
2. *George De Forest Brush.* Mother and Child, *1895. Museum of Fine Arts, Boston (William Wilkins Warren Fund).*

demic style Brush applied to smoothly painted American Indian subjects during the 1880s, as in *The Moose Hunt* (1888, National Coll.). After his marriage, he turned to mother and child paintings, often using his own wife and children as models, as in *Mother and Child* (Boston). Unlike such contemporaries as J. Alden Weir,* John Twachtman,* and Abbott Thayer,* he did not move from a dark, precise academic manner toward brighter color or freer brushwork, but turned for strength to the study of the composition and modeling of the Italian Renaissance. In his best work he achieved a personal style that made a virtue of conservatism and transcended eclecticism with the impressive clarity and gravity of the characterizations. When he fell short of this, his work was dull and sentimental.

(D.W.S.)

Brutalism, New.

An architectural term apparently coined by the British architectural team of Peter and Alison Smithson in the mid-1950s, but popularized by the critic Reynar Banham. It originally referred to an effort to cleanse the International style of its nonfunctional design elements and return to the principle of necessity as the governing factor. Thus in the Huntstanton School (Norfolk, England, 1954) by the Smithsons the steel frame and brick infill walls are almost crude in their detailing and placement, and ostentatiously reveal the insides of the building—the pipes, electrical conduits, etc. Externally it was quite Miesian (see Mies van der Rohe), though it carefully avoided the finesse of detail that has characterized all of Mies' work.

Slowly this puritanism of necessity gave way to primitivism and crudeness of form as ends in themselves. In the popular mind the new brutalism came to be associated with concrete buildings whose surfaces were left as they came out of the wood frame, and with massive concrete members whose form often seemed completely arbitrary. In England, the Smithsons, together with the architect James Stirling, have continued to follow their original path. In Japan, Kenzo Tange and Kunio Maekawa are its leading exponents. In the United States its strongest representative is Louis Kahn,* but almost every major architect seems to have played with the mode—often without embracing or fully comprehending its ideology.

Probably the most prominent example of the new brutalism in the United States is Kahn's Richards Medical Research Laboratory Building, University of Pennsylvania (Philadelphia, 1957–61). Here, the laboratory and related areas were declared separate entities, emphasizing their symbolic as well as functional independence. (D.G.)

Buckland, William (1734–74).

Carpenter-architect. Born at Oxford, England, he was apprenticed in 1748 to an uncle who was a London joiner. He moved to Maryland in 1755 as an indentured servant of a Maryland plantation owner. He immediately set to work finishing Mason's house, Gunston Hall, in Charles County. After completing his four-year contract he began his own building practice.

His commissions were mainly the rebuilding and remodelling of Maryland and Virginia plantation houses, such as Whitehall (c.1765–73), Tulip Hill (c.1756–73), and Montpelier (c.1765–73). About 1762 he probably moved to Richmond County, Va., to work with John Ariss, who had established a practice there. At Annapolis, Md., he finished a house for Upton Scott (c.1762) and this may have led to Buckland's settling there in 1772. Buckland did his best work at Annapolis, where he designed a complete house: the large and costly Hammond-Harwood House (1773–74). For the design he drew, as always, on English pattern books such as Swan's *British Architect.* The Chase-Lloyd House (1771–72) and the Brice House (1772–73) are also fine examples of his work. Buckland invariably used a style of red brick with highly decorative white wood trim. All his work was handsome, well-balanced, and firmly built. Unfortunately he died at the height of his career. (P.F.N.)

Buffington, Leroy Sunderland (1847–1931).

Architect, remembered chiefly as the first patentee of iron-framed, masonry-covered buildings. Born in Cincinnati, Ohio, he studied architecture and engineering at the University of Cincinnati, graduating in 1869. He began his architectural apprenticeship with a local firm and in the early 1870s worked for the firm of A. M. Radcliffe in St. Paul, Minn. He opened his own office in Minneapolis in 1873.

An article written in 1885 by Major

W. L. Jenney, a Chicago architect, about a tall building he had completed, may have led Buffington to investigate the possibilities of designing a building with a "skeleton of iron" that could carry exterior masonry walls on continuous iron brackets (shelf angles), floor by floor. On May 22, 1888, he finally took out a patent for such a "cloudscraper." It shows a twenty-eight-story building with a handsome masonry envelope sketched by his talented designer, Harvey Ellis. Unfortunately for Buffington, Major Jenney had built his skeleton-framed Home Insurance Building in Chicago by 1885, and Holabird & Roche had also preceded him, in 1887, with their similarly constructed Tacoma Building in Chicago. Although as late as 1929 Rufus Rand of Minneapolis paid Buffington a royalty for the "Rand Tower," Buffington apparently received no other royalties on his patent, despite the many lawsuits he initiated. Buffington's solid-steel square columns, built up of steel plates riveted together, hardly formed the basis for a patent, since the columns used by other architects, though much lighter and more conventional in cross-section, were similar to his.

Buffington's office designed the first state capitol building of North Dakota (1883–89); the West Hotel in Minneapolis (1884), in which he followed the fashionable Queen Anne style; and, between 1878–87, flour mill buildings and residences for the Pillsbury family in Minneapolis. He later produced some attractive Romanesque revival* buildings (designed by Harvey Ellis), of which Pillsbury Hall (1887) at the University of Minnesota is the outstanding example. (A.B.)

Bulfinch, Charles (1763–1844).

Architect and public administrator. Born in Boston of a wealthy family, he studied at Boston Latin School, graduated from Harvard (1781), and took an M.A. there (1784). No architectural course was available at Harvard, so it was not until he traveled to Europe (1785–87) that he realized his own interest and talents.

Although much of his time was spent on city affairs as chairman of the board of selectmen for Boston and superintendent of police, his fame rests mainly on his architectural accomplishments. Lacking formal training, he relied on observation and books. His drawings, confined to plans and elevations, reveal his lack of training, and for detailed working drawings he appears to have depended upon carpenters and stone masons. Although he was talented by American standards, much of his work is unimaginative, rather stiff and plain, and too directly related to English pattern books. His designs were gentlemanly, and their rigidity was more appropriate to city streets than to the country. His sense of proportion and use of ornament were derived from architects of the previous generation, such as Robert Adam and William Chambers, and he made constant reference to recent editions of the great 16th-century Italian Palladio rather than to those of his English contemporaries. Since Bulfinch was an arbiter of taste in Boston, his insensitivity to contemporary trends resulted in the persistence of the time lag between American and English style.

The preserved drawing for his first design, the wooden Hollis Street Meeting House, Boston (1787–88, burned 1897), shows how dependent he was on drawing instruments. During the 1790s he built many columnar and pilastered houses for Boston's elite, but his major public project was the Connecticut State House in Hartford (1793–96), austere on the exterior but more cheerful within. Bulfinch sponsored the theater in Boston by helping to remove the ban on public performance and by providing the plans for a theater (1793–94). The Tontine Crescent, Boston (1793–94) was row housing for more affluent families; it resembled its predecessors at Bath, England. It was his most ambitious scheme and he worked hard to promote it commercially, but it ultimately cost him his fortune.

A major public building of his design was the State House, Boston (1795–97), a small version of Chambers' Somerset house, London. The design produced more problems than Bulfinch could solve: the horizontal main front appears to carry a complete little building on its back, and in turn the little building somehow holds up a large golden dome. Of the very few houses surviving from the 1790s, the Otis House, 141 Cambridge Street, Boston (1795–96), is the best and most typical of Bulfinch's plain style.

During the decade beginning in 1800, Bulfinch was very busy as an architect. The second Otis House (1800–02), on Mount Vernon Street, one of his best, introduces the segmental arch motif over the windows, but lacks a central theme. The New North Church (1802–04, now St. Stephen's) still stands and, though restored, retains its Bulfinch flavor. The houses he built in Boston are substantial and well built, with interiors often handsomer than exteriors, but few are of major decorative interest. Stoughton Hall at Harvard (1804–05) is large but undistinguished. Of historical as well as practical importance was the enlargement of Faneuil Hall (1805–06): he satisfied commercial interests and saved the building from demolition. The Federal Street Church (1809; demolished) had the distinction of being the first Gothic revival* building in New England. It was really a Georgian church with a few Gothic elements. Although altered, much of his original Massachusetts General Hospital Building can still be seen.

After B. H. Latrobe* resigned as architect of the Capitol in Washington, Bulfinch was appointed by President Monroe to complete the central structure, which he did by 1827. His design modified Latrobe's by raising the dome, making it less like the Roman Pantheon and more in keeping with his own leaning toward Renaissance modes. He returned to Boston in 1830. His last major work was the Maine State House, Augusta (1829–32). Although similar in conception to the Boston State House, it was smaller and, freed of some of the awkward features of the Boston building, it seemed more unified.

Though all of Bulfinch's designs exhibit his lack of professional training, his diligence and love for the art raised the standards of New England architecture immeasurably. (P.F.N.)

Bullock, Wynn (1902–   ).

A photographer whose awareness of time and space in the natural world has led to images of exceptional beauty and has extended the philosophic boundaries of photography. Bullock was born in Chicago, Ill., but soon moved to southern California with his parents. After high school, he embarked on a career as a concert singer, studying first in New York City, where he supported himself by singing leading tenor roles in Irving Berlin's *Music Box Review.* In 1929 he continued his musical training in Paris and began to give concerts. Fascinated by the French impressionist paintings at the Louvre and the abstract, manipulated imagery of Laszlo Moholy-Nagy, the naturalized French photographer and painter, he began to photograph.

When the Depression ended his singing career, he returned to the United States in 1931 and managed his family's real estate business in Clarksburg, W.Va., until 1938. He continued to photograph, however, and was particularly interested in the mysterious effects he created by "solarizing" his prints. This technique—exposing either the film or photographic paper to light while it is being developed—reverses the normal tonal relationships in a photograph: light areas become gray or even black; edges appear etched in silver; shadows glow eerily. Although he was later to repudiate the process as being more painterly than photographic, he often employed it in his early work, and he held patents for his methods of solarization.

In 1938 Bullock moved again to California and studied photography for two years under Edward Kaminski at the Art Center School in Los Angeles. The Los Angeles County Museum of Art gave him a one-man show of experimental photographs in 1941. In 1942 he enlisted in the army, but was soon discharged in order to do photographic work for the aircraft industry. After World War II he moved to Monterey, Cal., and opened a commercial studio. A meeting with Edward Weston* in 1948 inspired him to devote more of his time to personal work. Edward Steichen* included several of his photographs in the exhibition "The Family of Man" at the Museum of Modern Art in 1955. Since then, Bullock's work has been shown in many one-man exhibitions throughout the world.

Bullock's mature work is characterized by an extreme clarity and rich tonality based on straightforward contact prints of eight by ten inch negatives. Although he has achieved notable results in color photography of enlarged abstractions, his major contribution has been in black-and-white revelations of what he terms "space-time." Objects, for Bullock, are events that happen in space and time; and photography, through such techniques as time exposures, can reveal this ongoing process. Bullock has written: "My favorite forest backgrounds are the wild and untouched areas, or areas with

1. **Wynn Bullock.** 1950s, photograph.
2. **Wynn Bullock.** 1960s, photograph.
   Both, Light Gallery, N.Y.

1

1. **Gordon Bunshaft.** Lever House,
N.Y., 1952.
2. **Charles E. Burchfield.** Church Bells
Ringing, Rainy Winter Night, *1917.*
Cleveland Museum of Art (gift of
Mrs. Louise M. Dunn in memory of
Henry G. Keller).

old deserted buildings almost returned to nature. In such an environment the human figure, the trees, plants, ferns and flowers manifest the cyclic forces of life and death in various characteristic stages of development. All blend into my experience, not just as objects with external physical qualities, but as events in time and space. Since I experience everything as events, I want my photographs to express events." In his photograph *Erosion* (1959, Modern Museum), for example, living trees on a hillside send naked roots down into soil that rain, wind, and time have worn away. Layers upon layers of subsoil are mysteriously visible, as is the final bedrock, the time of earth's beginning. (D. L.)

Bultos, see Santos.

Bunshaft, Gordon (1909–   ).
Architect. Born in Buffalo, N.Y., he received a B.A. (1933) and M.A. (1935) in architecture from the Massachusetts Institute of Technology and then went to Europe on a fellowship. In 1936 he worked in the office of Edward Durell Stone,* then briefly with Raymond Loewy before joining Skidmore, Owings & Merrill.* The firm was moderately successful during the late Depression years, and did much design work (the Westinghouse Building, the American Gas Association Building, etc.) for the 1939 New York World's Fair.

Bunshaft's first major work after World War II—and the building that firmly established the preeminence of the firm—was Lever House on Park Avenue in New York City (1952). It impressively assimilated the design lessons of the International style* of the late 1920s and 1930s. The thinly clad metal and glass tower of the building occupied only a small part of the site, and the street level was opened up to public use. In contrast to the characteristic International style skyscrapers of the 1920s and 1930s it came far closer to the imagery one expected of the machine. Its thin glass and metal walls, made up of repeated identical units, suggest the mass production potential of the machine in the same manner as the assembly-line automobile. Its success among both architects and businessmen set a worldwide fashion in skyscraper* office buildings that is still with us. Bunshaft worked out numerous variations of the steel-framed and glass-

and metal-sheathed skyscraper, the best known of which are the Hanover Trust Building on Fifth Avenue (1961), the Pepsi Cola Building on Park Avenue (now the Olivetti Building, 1960), and the Chase Manhattan Building (1961, all in New York City). The use of richer, more traditional material has characterized his later skyscraper towers such as the 140 Broadway Building (1967) and the 1114 Avenue of the Americas Building (1972).

Increasingly during the 1960s, the firm's New York office replaced many direct symbols of the machine with more traditional architectural elements, such as the use of brick and stone. Bunshaft's marble-sheathed Beinecke Rare Book Library (1963, Yale University, New Haven), suggests a precious Islamic jewel box gracefully suspended over a Renaissance plaza. His monumental L. B. Johnson Library at the University of Texas (1971, Austin) is solidly set upon a raised classic podium; while his doughnut-shaped Hirshhorn Museum and Sculpture Garden (1969–74, Washington, D.C.) reveals the same fascination with pure geometric forms one finds in the late 18th-century French designs of fantasy of Ledoux and Boulée. Currently, Skidmore, Owings & Merrill, led by Bunshaft, is designing the New York Convention and Exhibition Center, which promises to do for the western rim of mid-Manhattan what Rockefeller Center did for the center of the city in the 1930s.

Although Skidmore, Owings & Merrill has had a remarkably talented group of designers, much of its success and its reputation has undoubtedly been due to Bunshaft's contributions. In its administration of large-scale projects, its understanding of available technology, and in its consistently high standard of design, the firm has been unequalled. (D.G.)

Burchfield, Charles (1893–1967). Painter. Born in Ashtabula, Ohio, he was raised in Salem, Ohio, and began to paint as an adolescent while working in a metal-fabricating plant. From 1912 to 1916 he studied at the Cleveland Institute of Art, mainly with Henry G. Keller. After a brief, unsatisfactory period at the National Academy of Design in New York City, he returned to Salem and the metal plant but also began his career as an artist, drawing and

2

doing watercolors in his spare time.

His Salem pictures combine a fascination with nature—the woods and streams around the town—with an obsessive, macabre quality reflecting a profound psychological disturbance; he saw visions of evil faces in flowers, heard strange sounds, and attempted to translate sound—both the normal sounds of nature and the others as well —into pictorial form. His *Conventions for Abstract Thoughts* is a group of symbols for "Fear, Morbidness, Dangerous Brooding, Insanity, Menace, Fascination of Evil," and so on, and these were to turn up repeatedly in his painting for some years thereafter, as in *Church Bells Ringing, Rainy Winter Night* (1917, Cleveland).

Burchfield served in the army for seven months in 1918, and this experience had a pronounced effect on his art, as it turned his attention from nature to the small town. However, he now combined the theme of the fantastic with that of the drabness and squalor of small industrial cities. A reading of the realistic studies of smalltown people in Sherwood Anderson's *Winesburg, Ohio* had much to do with this change.

In 1921 Burchfield married and moved to Buffalo, N.Y., where he became head designer in a wallpaper factory. In 1925 he settled in Gardenville, a suburb of Buffalo, and remained there until his death. He left the wallpaper factory in 1929, after arranging with a gallery in New York to sell his paintings. For the first time in his life he was on his own as an artist. Buffalo, with its docks, bridges, and industrial areas, offered him a much broader field of operations than the small towns he had known. At the same time he broadened his artistic ability. Although he was certainly interested in oil—and some of his best works, such as *Old House by Creek* (1932, Whitney), are in that medium. He was particularly fond of watercolor, and he began to do works of exceptionally large size in that medium, often piecing together several watercolor papers to secure a surface large enough for his conception. The Buffalo pictures are largely of workaday aspects of the industrial scene, as in *Black Iron* (1935, Whitney) or of the shabbily Victorian aspects of the city, as in *Rainy Night* (1930, Fine Arts Gallery of San Diego), but the smalltown motif and the fascination with nature remained. A persistent motif throughout this pe-

1

2

1. **Daniel Hudson Burnham.** *Railway Exchange Building, Chicago, 1905.*
2. **Benjamin Burt.** *Silver tankard for presentation to Richard Devens, director of the building of the Charles River Bridge (depicted on the piece), 1786. Museum of Fine Arts, Boston (Karolik Collection).*

riod is water and snow, suggesting the redeeming powers of nature as against man's degradation of his environment. In his last years, Burchfield gave up the urban scene entirely and returned to the woods and fields of the landscapes of his youth; in fact, he resurrected many of his old pictures and repainted them, so that a work such as the *Sun and Rocks* (Albright) bears the date 1918/50. In general, he greatly expanded the scale of the older pictures in the reworking, emphasizing a mysticism or lyricism of nature that was monumentally expressed. The old macabre note was only rarely sounded.

In the 1950s Burchfield taught at the University of Minnesota, the Buffalo Fine Arts Academy, the University of Buffalo, and Ohio University. He received numerous awards.   (A.F.)

Burgis, William (active 1716–31).
English gentleman-adventurer and topographical draftsman who designed some of the earliest American prints. He was in New York from about 1716 to 1722, and there drew a detailed view of the city, which was engraved in London and published about 1721. The engraving is more than six feet across and consists of four joined sections, each printed from a separate copperplate. From 1722 to 1731 he was in Boston, where he drew a large view of the "Great Town" (engraved in London and published in 1722), the first view of Harvard College (1726), a map of Boston engraved there by Thomas Johnston* (1728), and a view of Boston Light House (1729), the second American mezzotint,* which he himself engraved. A small view of Boston and a view of Castle William in Boston Harbor are also attributed to him. He returned to New York about 1730 and continued his career with engraved views of Fort George and of the New Dutch Church.   (S.H.)

Burnham, Daniel Hudson (1846–1912).
Architect and city planner. He was born and raised in Henderson, N.Y. In 1855 his family moved to Chicago, where he spent most of his life. Despite a slow start and the lack of a college degree, Burnham achieved major goals. During a brief apprenticeship with the architectural firm of Carter, Drake & Wight in 1872, he met the talented designer and musician, John Wellborn Root, and formed a partnership with him. From

1873 on, Burnham & Root took advantage of the devastation wrought by the Chicago fire of 1871 to produce a large number of new buildings there.

Burnham organized and directed the great World's Columbian Exposition in Chicago in 1893, recruiting the most imposing array of artistic and architectural talent ever assembled in this country. The architectural success of the fair was due largely to the energy of Burnham as chief of construction. It was he who brought five outstanding eastern architects, under the leadership of Richard Morris Hunt,* along with five Chicago architects, into the fold. He later did much to promote the cause of the "City Beautiful" in America, and became a noted planner of cities in the grand manner. He was appointed chairman of a committee for the development of Washington, D.C.; it moved the Union Station out of the Mall and sought to recreate the plan, with its diagonal axes, laid out by Pierre Charles L'Enfant* under George Washington. Burnham also developed plans for Manila, capital of the Philippines, and for Baguio, the summer capital of the Philippines, not to mention master plans for Chicago and San Francisco.

Burnham was an organizer with the vision and ability to inspire others with his own enthusiasms. To a group of Chicago businessmen he once said: "Make no little plans . . . let your watchword be order and your beacon beauty."

Burt, John and **Samuel, William,** and **Benjamin.**
John Burt (1693–1746) was the first of a family of important silversmiths in colonial Boston. He probably received his training from John Coney.* Most of his work is in the early rococo style with little surface ornamentation other than engraved decoration. He is noted for the silver he made for churches and for silver associated with Harvard College. The latter included a pair of octagonal candlesticks and a pair of chafing dishes presented to tutor Nicholas Sever in 1724, and a grace cup purchased by the college. Of his domestic silver, a hexafoil salver (Harrington Coll.) and a punch bowl with three hoof feet (Jeffords Coll.) are unusual.

John Burt had three sons who were silversmiths: Samuel (1724–54), William (1726–51), and Benjamin (1729–1805). Few examples survive of William's workmanship since he died only

a few years after completing his training. Samuel's career was also short, but he is known to have made flagons for the First Church in Marblehead, and domestic silver including a tankard, cream pot, and sauceboats.

Benjamin Burt was the most prolific son, finishing his training about 1750, and thereafter fashioning silver for many New England churches. He was patronized by the Browns of Providence, R.I., as well as the Derbys of Salem, Mass., and worked in both the florid rococo and early neoclassical styles. He was the maker of presentation silver, his most interesting piece being a tankard (Boston) made in 1786 for Richard Devens, special director of the building of the Charles River Bridge, which is depicted in an engraved vignette on the side of the tankard. There are many examples of his work at Yale University.

Bush-Brown, Henry Kirke (1857–1935).
A sculptor, he was the nephew and adopted son of the sculptor Henry Kirke Brown,* with whom he studied before attending the National Academy of Design in New York City. He studied and worked in Paris and Florence in the late 1880s but returned to America in time to exhibit his large sculpture, *Buffalo Hunt,* at the World's Columbian Exposition in Chicago (1893). He rose to prominence in the late 1890s with his bronze equestrian statues of generals George G. Meade and John F. Reynolds for Gettysburg, Pa. In 1898 he did the figure of Commander Hall for the Dewey Arch in New York City and then a figure of the Roman emperor Justinian for the Appellate Court Building, also in New York, thus participating in two of the most prestigious sculptural projects of the period. After 1910 he worked in Washington, D.C., completing many memorials.   (W.C.)

Buttersworth, James E. (1817–94).
English-born marine painter who came to America about 1850. He may have been a relative of the earlier English ship painter, Thomas Buttersworth; their styles were related, both men creating tight compositions of small groups of ships on choppy seas. James Buttersworth's best-known work is probably the *Clipper Ship "Great Republic"* (1853, Peabody) which was the subject of one of the many popular lithographs made from his paintings by Nathaniel Currier (see Currier and Ives).

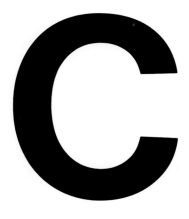

Cadmus, Paul (1904–   ).
Painter and etcher. Cadmus was born in New York City, where his father was a commercial lithographer and watercolorist and his mother was an illustrator. He studied at the National Academy of Design from 1919–26, and later for two years at the Art Students League,* where his teachers were Joseph Pennell and Charles Locke. Cadmus began to paint seriously in the early 1930s while living on the island of Mallorca during a prolonged stay in Europe. After returning to the United States, he did murals for the WPA Federal Art Project* and the U.S. Treasury Department (1934–37); in 1938, he designed sets and costumes for Ballet Caravan, a ballet company.

Cadmus is best known for paintings that depict perverse scenes of sex and horror, often in an everyday setting and in a precise style—a combination that has been termed "magic realism." He has worked in oil, but most of his paintings are executed in egg tempera. His most notable paintings include *Fantasia on a Theme by Dr. S.* (1946) and *Sailors and Floozies* (both, Whitney Museum).   (A.F.)

Calder, Alexander (1898–   ).
World-famous for his unique development of sculptures in motion. In these hanging sculptures, known as mobiles, Calder developed his interest in the movement of colored forms in space as governed by the delicate balance of the pieces and by air currents.

Son of two generations of sculptors, Calder was born in Lawnton, Pa. Perhaps to distinguish himself from his father, Alexander Stirling Calder,* and his grandfather, A. Milne Calder,* young Alexander studied mechanical engineering. In 1919 he graduated from Stevens Institute of Technology with a Master of Engineering degree and began his career in jobs ranging from draftsman and logger to fireman on a freighter. In 1923 he registered at the Art Students League* in New York, where he studied for two years. With his natural flair for line drawing he got a job as illustrator for the *National Police Gazette.* In 1926 he went to Europe, where he spent several months drawing at the Grande Chaumière in Paris. He soon took a small studio and began fashioning figures and animals in wire and wood, gradually assembling a whole menagerie. Calder's ingenious performances with his circus characters of wire and wood—tumblers, trapeze artists, clowns, trained dogs—soon brought visits from outstanding artists and intellectuals, among them the French painter Jules Pascin, who later wrote the introduction to Calder's first Paris exhibition (1929). From wood-and-wire figures Calder branched out, fashioning caricatures entirely in linear wire, among them his celebrated figure of the jazz singer, Josephine Baker. Some of the wire sculptures were exhibited in his first New York exhibition (1928). Other exhibitions in Paris, Berlin, and New York before 1930 established him as an important young artist who was appreciated largely for his irrepressible humor.

Early in 1930, Calder returned to Paris from one of his frequent voyages to America and settled down not far from the studio of the Dutch abstractionist Piet Mondrian. His first visit to Mondrian, as he has said, "gave me a shock that started things." He immediately began painting abstractions. Although he soon reverted to things he could "twist or tear or bend," he henceforth worked largely with abstract forms. At this time he became acquainted with many prominent abstract artists, such as painters Fernand Léger, and Theo van Doesburg, and sculptor Jean Arp. They helped him focus on the new problems he faced in his sculpture— the organization of contrasting movements and changing relations of forms in space. In 1930 his moving sculptures were still motivated by either manual or motor apparatuses, but he was already formulating the approach that would lead to his wind-driven pieces. He wrote: "Disparity in form, color, size, weight, motion, is what makes a composition. . . . It is the apparent accident to regularity which the artist actually controls by which he makes or mars a work."

In 1931, Calder exhibited a group of wire heads and abstract constructions; he was introduced in the catalogue by Fernand Léger as "one hundred per cent American." Among the early mobile sculptures (so named by Marcel Duchamp*), there were several in which small spheres of different sizes, painted in primary colors, moved up and down on thin wires at different speeds. These, according to James Johnson Sweeney, Calder's first biographer, went beyond anything done by the Russian constructivists (see Constructivism). By 1934, when he exhibited in New York, Calder had already launched his mobiles in which "nature and chance began to replace the mechanical and calculable as motive forces." These carefully balanced works, with their almost naturalistic, petal-like shapes turning slowly in space, established Calder as a genuine innovator. Numerous critics saw in them a release from all previous sculptural traditions. Calder's incorporation of chance as an element in sculpture set a precedent, which after World War II was exploited by artists everywhere.

Besides mobiles, Calder continued fashioning a variety of occasional pieces, cutting large sheets of steel in vigorous patterns for outdoor sculptures (dubbed stabiles by Hans Arp). He also worked on a very small scale, producing figurines and jewelry that were

1

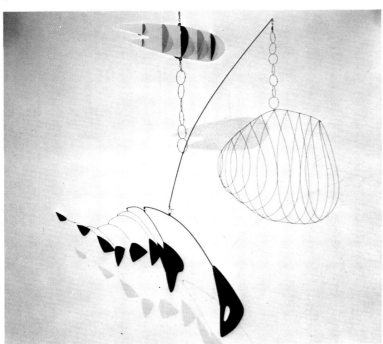

1. *Alexander Calder.* El Sol Rojo, *1968, painted steel. XIX Olympiad, Mexico City.*
2. *Alexander Calder.* Lobster Trap and Fish Tail, *1939, hanging mobile. Museum of Modern Art, N.Y.*

2

1

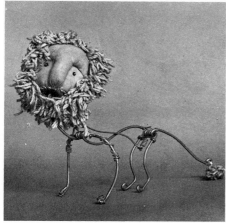

2

exhibited in New York in 1940. By 1943, Calder's reputation was already large enough to warrant his first retrospective exhibition, at the Museum of Modern Art in New York City.

After World War II, Calder was given several large commissions, among them a stabile for the American Consulate in Germany (1955); a mobile, *The Whirling Ear,* for the Brussels World's Fair (1959); a giant mobile for New York's Kennedy airport (1958) and one for UNESCO in Paris (1959). His exhibitions all over the world continued at an astonishing rate—he is a prodigious worker—and he was honored with a retrospective at the Guggenheim Museum in New York (1964), and one at the Musée National d'Art Moderne in Paris (1965). Calder's many awards include prizes at the São Paulo Biennial and the Venice Biennial. (D.A.)

Calder, Alexander Milne (1846–1923). Sculptor. Father of Alexander Stirling Calder* and grandfather of Alexander Calder,* he was born in Aberdeen, Scotland. He learned to carve from his father, a gravestone cutter, and studied in Edinburgh, London, and Paris before coming to America in 1868. He settled in Philadelphia, Pa., where he did decorative carving in collaboration with architects. After four years his great opportunity came when he was asked to model and supervise the execution of hundreds of sculptures for the new Philadelphia City Hall. Calder's first-hand knowledge of the Second Empire style in Paris, particularly the additions to the Louvre, which he had seen in 1867, specially qualified him for the project. The modeling, enlarging, casting in plaster and carving in stone required a small army of assistants, and occupied Calder for most of the years between 1872 and 1892. In fact, he created only a few other works; the most notable of these is his bronze equestrian statue, *General George G. Meade* (1881, Fairmount Park, Philadelphia). (W.C.)

Calder, Alexander Stirling (1870–1945). Sculptor. Son of A. Milne Calder* and father of Alexander Calder,* he studied at the Pennsylvania Academy of the Fine Arts, (1886–90) with Thomas Eakins,* and attended the Académie Julien and the École des Beaux-Arts in Paris. At first he worked in the Beaux-Arts

style, as seen in the fountain he produced for the University of Pennsylvania in the mid-1890s or his Depew Fountain (c.1915) in Indianapolis. In 1910 he moved his studio from Philadelphia to New York City and was soon at work on two enormous groups, *The Nations of the East* and *The Nations of the West,* for the Panama-Pacific Exposition (San Francisco, 1915). These plaster and straw groups represented the epitome of Beaux-Arts style of exposition sculpture in their rich modeling, colorful imagery, and grandiose conception. By 1918, however, Calder's style was strongly influenced by the modern movement; he began to simplify and abstract natural forms. Although he never totally converted to abstract art,* much of the flamboyant character of the Beaux-Arts style is gone, for example, in his Swann Memorial Fountain (1924, Philadelphia). The element of abstraction appeared in his sculpture of a group, *George Washington with Wisdom and Justice* (1918, for a pier of the Washington Arch, New York.) In the 1920s and '30s Calder's compromise between nature and abstraction became academic—as may be seen in his bronze statue, *Leif Ericson,* which was presented by America to the people of Iceland in 1932, or in his *Native Dance* (1938) in Brookgreen Gardens, S.C., perhaps his most abstract work. One of the few sculptors to bridge the academic tradition and the new modernism, Calder received many commissions and awards. (W.C.)

Callahan, Harry (1912–   ). Photographer and teacher. Born in Detroit, Mich., Callahan began photographing as a hobby in 1938. Soon he began to get guidance from the photographer Todd Webb. Callahan had no formal photographic education other than occasional lectures at the Detroit Photo Guild in the early 1940s, but there he saw and was influenced by the photographs of Ansel Adams.* In 1946 he joined the photography department at the Institute of Design in Chicago, and in 1949 he became its head. He was included in Museum of Modern Art, N.Y., exhibitions in 1948 and 1952. At this time Callahan met the photographer and director of photography of the Museum of Modern Art, Edward Steichen.* It was also in this year that he met the photographer Aaron Siskind* and began a friendship that shows its influ-

1. *Alexander Calder. The Exotic Dancer from Calder's* Circus, *1932, wire, cloth, beads, rhinestones.*
2. *Alexander Calder. The Lion from the* Circus, *1932, wire and cloth. The* Circus *is on extended loan to the Whitney Museum of American Art, N.Y.*
3. *Harry Callahan.* Chicago, *photograph.*
4. *Harry Callahan.* Eleanor: Chicago, *1956, photograph. Both, Light Gallery, N.Y.*

3

4

ence in both men's work. A 1956 Graham Foundation Award in the fine arts enabled him to spend a year photographing in Aix-en-Provence, France. The George Eastman House in Rochester, N.Y. gave him a retrospective exhibition of over three hundred prints in 1950 and another major exhibition in 1971. In 1961 Callahan became head of the department of photography at the Rhode Island School of Design.

Callahan continues to be one of the major influences in photography through his teaching and even more through his photographs, which reveal a tremendous range of inventiveness. He was one of the earliest photographers to utilize extremely high contrast (black and white with the gray midtones eliminated) to isolate objects and destroy their dimensionality. His explorations of the creative possibilities of multiple exposure to indicate states of time (past, present, becoming) and to develop random, overall patterns are comprehensive.

His most recent work has emphasized architecture in a variety of ways, the sheer density of urban structures and, simultaneously, a serial portrayal of the frame houses of Providence, R.I. Finally, he is one of the finest printmakers in photography, which is almost certainly due to his constant experimentation with the extreme limits of the tonal scale of the silver print. Several monographs have been published.

(T.F.B.)

Calverley, Charles (1833–1914).
Sculptor of bas-relief medallions and portrait busts. Born in Albany, N.Y., Calverley served an apprenticeship under a local marble cutter before becoming a studio assistant to Erastus Dow Palmer,* a position he held for fifteen years. One of his earliest works is a medallion of the painter, *Charles Loring Elliott* (1863, Metropolitan). That year he moved to New York City. He reportedly executed 250 portrait busts and profile relief medallions during his New York period; his style was a dry, unexciting naturalism, competent in its likenesses but weak in its formal qualities. So far as is known he produced only two pieces that were more ambitious than bust-length portraits; these were the bronze figure of *Robert Burns* (1890, Albany) and a personification of *Meditation* (Albany Rural Cemetery). His bronze bust of *Sir Walter Scott* (1896) is owned by Yale University.   (W.C.)

Carder, Frederick (1863–1963).
Glass designer, founder of Steuben
Glass Works, Corning, N.Y. Carder was
born in Brockmoor, Stafford, England.
At fourteen he went to work in his family's pottery, meanwhile studying chemistry and metallurgy at Dudley Merchants' Institute. A brilliant student, he
won awards for designing and sketching. In 1881, Carder was hired by Stevens and Williams Company of Brierly
Hill to design shapes and applied decorations for a line of glass. In 1891 he
began teaching at Wordsley Institute
while still art director for Stevens and
Williams. In 1902, while traveling in
America, observing technical education and manufacturing, he decided to
open a factory in Corning, N.Y., and
soon incorporated Steuben Glass
Works with Thomas G. Samuel, and
Townsend de M. Hawkes. An academician by training, Carder produced glass
for Steuben in all the late Victorian
styles, including Chinese, and made
interesting contributions to art nouveau* and to the revival of neoclassicism.* (See also Glass; Art Nouveau
Glass.)   (R.S.)

Carles, Arthur B. (1882–1952).
Painter. Carles was born in Philadelphia, Pa. and studied with Henry McCar-
ter at the Pennsylvania Academy of the
Fine Arts from 1900–07 and with William M. Chase.* Scholarship trips to
Europe (1905 and 1907) enabled him to
seek out the circle of Matisse, Picasso,
and Delaunay, and he formed friendships with Rodin and John Marin.* Other
trips took him to France in 1910 and
Rome in 1911. By this time he was painting landscapes that combined strong,
broadly painted forms with a fauve-like
freedom of brushwork and color. Alfred
Steiglitz* included him in an exhibit of
"Younger American Painters" at the gallery "291" in 1910 and gave him a one-
man show in 1912. In 1913 Carles exhibited in the crucial Armory Show.*
During the next twenty years he painted
a number of still lifes, particularly of
flowers, with brilliant, resonant color
and rhythmic, richly plastic form, as in
Bouquet Abstraction (c.1930, Whitney). In the course of the 1930s he
changed from this lyrical style to toughly
painted geometric abstractions.

Carles stopped painting after a paralytic stroke in 1941. He had discontinued teaching at the Pennsylvania
Academy in 1923 and had practically

1

2

1. *Arthur B. Carles.* Bouquet Abstraction, c.1930. Whitney Museum of
   American Art, N.Y.
2. *Arthur (Espenet) Carpenter.* Rolltop
   desk, 1970, walnut and muteyne
   wood. National Collection of Fine
   Arts, Smithsonian Institution,
   Washington, D.C.

retired from public life, discouraged by the limited acceptance of his work. But during his last invalid years he was recognized as a pioneer of modernism in Philadelphia, the city which had been so discouraging to progressive art during the first decades of the century.

(D.W.S.)

Carousel Figures.
Carved and polychromed animals and chariots produced for American carousels and now recognized and collected as a significant expression of national folk art. The history of the carousel has been traced to 12th-century equestrian games of Asia Minor, later transplanted to France and Italy by returning Crusaders, and evolving into a widespread European sport in which horsemen tried to lance a suspended ring. By the 18th century, wooden horses had replaced live ones and the game had become a favorite at fairs, parks, and marketplaces. The first American carousel patent was filed in 1850, and within twenty-five years major steam-operated examples had been constructed in Philadelphia, Atlantic City, and Brooklyn, and at Cabin John on the Potomac near Washington, D.C. The wooden horses of the prototype were joined, and occasionally replaced, by a menagerie of carved creatures including pigs and poultry, dogs and dragons, lions, tigers, whales, frogs, ostriches, giraffes, and camels—alone or in tandem, stationary or moving up and down on vertical posts. Among major American firms producing these figures were those of William H. Dentzel, Allen Herschell and Spillman Engineering Corporation, and the Philadelphia Toboggan Company. Examples of their work have been acquired by such institutions as the Smithsonian Institution, the Shelburne Museum, and the Circus World Museum in Baraboo, Wis. (M.J.G.)

Carpenter, Arthur, known professionally as **Espenet** (1920–   ).
Outstanding maker of wood furniture and accessories with simple, rounded forms, sensitively articulated joinery, and richly grained woods. One of the early post-World War II group of American craftsmen, Espenet was born in New York, N.Y. With a B.A. from Dartmouth College in 1942, and after four years in the navy, he decided he wanted "a physical job, some kind that would allow me to express myself creatively."

He moved to San Francisco, bought a lathe and began making wooden bowls and other treen ware. Within a few years his bowls were being sold at select stores across the country, and when his work was chosen for the New York Museum of Modern Art's "Good Design" exhibits in 1950, Carpenter slowly taught himself the necessary skills and acquired the machinery for making furniture—wooden forms with greater creative possibilities. By the mid-1950s his custom furniture business employed six people and was becoming too large and successful for Espenet's taste. He then moved to Bolinas, Cal., where he built himself a circular house, in which he now works. His music stands, stools, desks, and chairs owe much to art nouveau* and the work of the late Wharton Esherick.* Carpenter believes his life as a craftsman enables him to use all the skill and knowledge he possesses. To him, "There's no reason why you shouldn't have a good education and still be a carpenter or be a bricklayer if you want . . . the better education you have . . . the better you can do it . . ." (R.S.)

Carrère & Hastings.
Architectural firm, founded in 1885 when John Merven Carrère (1858–1911) and Thomas Hastings (1860–1929) formed a partnership stemming from the friendship they formed in Paris at the École des Beaux-Arts in the early 1880s. They served joint apprenticeships with the New York firm of McKim, Mead & White* from 1884 to 1885. The formation of their own firm came about when Henry M. Flagler, developer of the east coast of Florida, commissioned young Hastings to design his first great hotel, the Ponce de Leon (1887), in St. Augustine. They then enjoyed a succession of commissions that lasted for over thirty years, sharing architectural dominance of the eastern states with McKim, Mead & White.

The architecture produced by the firm was largely influenced by that late phase of French renaissance style developed during the 17th and 18th centuries. It included many fine city and country residences. Their outstanding city residence was designed in 1912 for Henry Clay Frick at 70th Street and Fifth Avenue in New York City in a modified version of the Louis XVI style. It now houses the Frick Collection. The country house designed by the firm in 1903

for Murray Guggenheim at Elberon, N.J., won the gold medal of the American Institute of Architects, New York Chapter. This spectacular house, modeled on the Petit Trianon at Versailles, was flanked by Italian loggias embracing a wide terrace reflected in a formal pool.

In its early years, the firm designed a series of overly ornate office buildings, and later, such imposing classical structures as the Senate office building (1905) and the House of Representatives office building (1906) in Washington, D.C., and the New York Public Library (1898–1911). In 1922 Hastings was awarded the gold medal of the Royal Institute of British Architects. (A.B.)

Casilear, John William (1811–93).
Engraver and landscape painter. Born in New York, N.Y., Casilear went to study with the engraver Peter Maverick (1780–1831) when he was fifteen. He became a successful engraver of bank notes as well as of landscape, and was elected to the National Academy in 1835. In 1840–43 he traveled to Europe with Asher B. Durand* and John F. Kensett,* both of whom influenced his style. Durand encouraged him to abandon engraving in favor of landscape painting, and in 1854 he opened a studio in New York. As a landscape painter he was highly regarded in his day. His unassuming, placid, pastoral views were praised by his contemporaries for their silvery tone and truth to nature, as in *Distant View of the Catskills* (1891, Metropolitan), although today they seem rather cold and colorless.

Cassatt, Mary (1845–1926).
Expatriate American painter, member of the impressionist (see Impressionism) group in Paris. She was born on the outskirts of Pittsburgh, Pa., the daughter of a prosperous businessman, but spent much of her childhood (1851–58) in France and Germany with her family. In 1858 the Cassatts moved to Philadelphia, Pa., where she attended the Pennsylvania Academy of the Fine Arts* (1861–65). A strong individualist, she left for France after the Civil War; she studied briefly in Paris with the academic painter Charles Chaplin but worked largely on her own. She began to sell some of her work in the United States, to which she returned in 1870 at the outbreak of the Franco-Prussian War.

Cassatt was slow in reaching maturity as a painter. Only after she went back to Europe in 1872 did she make rapid progress in evolving a personal style. In that year she went to Parma, Italy, where she attended the Art Academy and studied the work of Correggio. From Italy she sent a painting to the Paris Salon of 1872. The next year she traveled to Seville, where she developed stronger brushwork under the influence of Velásquez and the Spanish realists (*Toreador,* 1873, Chicago), and to the Low Countries, where she studied Rubens and Hals. In Paris that year she began a lifelong friendship with Louisine Elder, the future Mrs. Havemeyer, who at fifteen was so stimulated by Mary Cassatt's enthusiasm for Courbet and Degas that she purchased a pastel by the latter and initiated the great Havemeyer collection.

For five years (1872–76) Mary Cassatt exhibited at the annual Salon in Paris, but as her paintings moved into the higher impressionist key, she met with criticism, and in 1877 she was rejected. In the same year Degas, who had been struck by her Salon entry in 1874, *Portrait of Mme. Cortier,* invited her to join the small group of advanced painters called the impressionists. This appealed to her independent temper: she stopped sending to the Salon and showed with the impressionists in their exhibitions of 1877, '79, '80, '81, and '86. Meanwhile, she began sending paintings to exhibitions in the United States, for although she was to visit this country only infrequently, she considered herself definitely American. The two paintings she sent to show at the Society of American Artists* were perhaps the first examples of impressionism displayed in the United States and were severely criticized.

The interest that Degas took in her paintings led to one of the rare friendships of that sarcastic and cynical aristocrat. She worked closely with him and was much influenced by his demanding standards of drawing and composition. In her brilliantly designed *Little Girl in a Blue Armchair* (1878, private collection), one of the first paintings to reveal her potential strength, Degas painted part of the background. For several years Cassatt bathed her works in glowing impressionist atmosphere, as in *Dans la Loge* (1879, private collection), although she had relatively little interest in the landscape subjects and ex-

terior lighting favored by such typical impressionists as Monet, Sisley, and Pissarro. Her concerns were closer to those of Manet and Degas, and by the mid-1880s this was apparent in her stronger patterning and firmer outlines. As with Degas, she was inspired in this direction by Japanese prints, and after visiting the large Japanese print exhibition in Paris in 1890, she produced a brilliant, highly original set of ten color prints of her own, including *Maternal Caress* (1891).

In 1892 her friend, the Chicago patroness of the arts, Mrs. Potter Palmer, commissioned her to paint a mural decoration for the 1893 World's Columbian Exposition in Chicago. Unfortunately, the mural is lost, but the effect of working on a broad scale left lasting results in *The Boating Party* (1893, Washington), a work which shows her at the height of her power—it is firmly drawn, boldly patterned, and brilliantly colored. Her more customary subjects deal with the everyday lives of women, most often caring for babies, but also at their toilette, reading, and at the opera.

Gradually during the 1890s her work grew drier in technique and less imaginative in concept. In 1901 she traveled to Italy and Spain with the Havemeyers, advising them on purchases for the collection that was to go to the Metropolitan Museum. Her brothers also bought a few paintings upon her recommendation. They were well able to, since one was the president of the Pennsylvania Railroad; however, the Cassatt family generally had little interest in art. In 1904 she was made a chevalier of the Legion of Honor, and won many American awards. But her career as a painter was drawing to a close. After a last visit to America in 1908–09, she began to suffer increasingly from eye trouble and ill health, and ceased painting by 1914. Bitter and practically blind, she lived on into the mid-1920s. She did not know that an old painter-friend, J. Alden Weir,* had included her work in the Armory Show,* nor would she have appreciated being one of that company, for she was hostile to 20th-century developments in art. This was ironical, for no woman artist of her age had won a firmer place in the history of that development. (D.W.S.)

Cast Iron.
Objects made of a non-malleable iron alloy by pouring molten metal into

molds. Such castings were made in American ironworks as early as the 17th century. Because of the decorative potential of the molds and because the brittle nature of the hardened metal determines the varied thickness of a worked surface, even the most utilitarian cast iron is likely to be embellished with decorative forms that have been recognized as a folk expression of their time.

The first American ironworks, established in Virginia in 1619 was soon destroyed by Indians, but a more successful venture begun at Saugus, Mass., in 1646 is known to have produced sand castings of large pots and the firebacks that reflected fireplace heat and insulated chimney walls. In general, it can be said that almost all American cast-iron productivity before the 19th century was addressed to cookery and heating, but the bas relief ornamentation of stove plates, firebacks, and andirons shows remarkable variety. A very sophisticated fireback sold by Joseph Webb of Boston in 1781 (Winterthur) and a later "Liberty" Franklin stove in the same collection suggest that contemporaneous coins were the models, while a Mary Anne Furnace stoveplate in the Pennsylvania Farm Museum of Landis Valley in Lancaster, Pa., offers a direct relief translation of the painted tulip motifs of contemporaneous taufscheine.*

In the 19th century a wide range of small cast-iron objects like trivets, boot jacks, and hitching posts and larger objects like garden furniture and ornamental sculpture illustrate the richness of Victorian decorative invention. The material reaches its summit of expression, however, in 19th century architectural forms, especially the lacy grillwork of Charleston, S.C., and New Orleans, La., and the facades of commercial buildings in the North. In New York City the section immediately south of Houston Street (now sometimes referred to as Soho) has been publicized as the Cast Iron District and designated a landmark area. (M.J.G.)

Castle, Wendell (1932–).
Woodworker known for large organic furniture designs in laminated wood. Born in Emporia, Kan., Castle studied sculpture and industrial design. The woodwork of Wharton Esherick* has been most important to the development of his own shapes, and Esherick's

1

3

2

1. **Mary Cassatt.** The Boating Party, *1893.*
2. **Mary Cassatt.** Woman with a Red Zinnia, *1890s. Both, National Gallery of Art, Washing-* ton, D.C. (Chester Dale Collection).
3. **Mary Cassatt.** Dans la Loge, *1879. Collection Mrs. William Coxe Wright, N.Y.*

1

2

attention to the grain and color of wood is reflected in a typical Castle furniture-sculpture, which often accommodates several furniture functions in one piece. A table-chair of afrormosia wood (1968, Johnson Coll.) resembles a long-necked bird within the compact dimensions of 29 x 16 x 30 inches. The head is flattened on top to serve as a table; the neck grows from the table to the floor to provide support; the body sweeps upward along the floor and is concave to provide the chair's seat. The flowing unit of the piece is comprised of many laminations, which heighten the colors and grain of the afrormosia. The laminations also free Castle to work with exotic shapes and otherwise impossible varieties of dimensions within a single piece. In recent years he has introduced molded forms in plastic, to be made and sold in editions. (R.S.)

Catlin, George (1796–1872).
Miniaturist and portraitist best known for his paintings of the American Indian. Born in Wilkes-Barre, Pa., Catlin studied law at Litchfield, Conn. in 1817–18 and practiced it briefly. He then taught himself to paint and worked as a portrait miniaturist in Philadelphia from 1820 to 1825. While living in Philadelphia he saw a group of Plains Indians on their way to Washington and was inspired to plan the monumental project of painting all the Indian tribes between the Alleghenies and the Rockies. He went to New York and worked there from 1825 to 1829. He was elected a member of the National Academy of Design in 1826, but never exhibited in their annual exhibitions. In 1829 he moved to Richmond, Va.

In 1832 he arrived in St. Louis and traveled up the Missouri river, painting the daily activities of the Indian tribes he encountered. He was in the Southwest in 1834, and in 1835–36 he went to the upper Mississippi river and the Great Lakes areas. In 1837–38 he traveled to South Carolina to depict the Seminoles. In all, during six years (1832–38) he visited forty-eight different tribes and completed almost five hundred canvases of Indian life, individual Indians, and wildlife. These provided the pictorial images for his *Illustrations of the Manners, Customs and Conditions of the North American Indians* (1841). From 1837 to 1851 he traveled with his "Indian Gallery" and a troupe of Indians —he was thus a precursor of Buffalo

1. *George Catlin.* Indian Troop, *1844. Gilcrease Institute, Tulsa, Okla.*
2. *George Catlin.* Buffalo Bill's Back Fat (Head Chief, Blood Tribe), *1832. National Collection of Fine Arts, Smithsonian Institution, Washington, D.C.*

Bill's Wild West Show—touring Central and South America in 1852–57 and Europe in 1858–70. He returned to the United States in 1870 and died in Jersey City. Some six hundred of his paintings are in the Smithsonian Institution and others may be found in numerous other American museums.

Catlin appears to have been too busy recording what he saw to devote the effort to make his paintings the finished work of which he was capable. As a result, his paintings were sometimes almost pictorial shorthand, slipshod, and crude. His Indian portraits generally were more carefully painted than most of his pictures. *Kee-O-Kuk, Chief of the Sauk and Foxes* (1832) and *Black Hawk* (1832, both in the Smithsonian), and *The Dakota Chief: One Horn* (1832, Chicago Natural History Museum), for example, were among his most decorative and strongest Indian portrayals. That he had talent is clear, and some of his obviously hasty oil sketches, such as *Prairie Fire* (1832, Smithsonian), show a feeling for the power of nature. Although he was not an accomplished student of the subject to which he devoted his life, he remains the best-known painter of the American Indian, whose popular image he did much to establish. (H.W.W.)

Cavallon, Georgio (1904–   ).
Painter born in Sorio, Italy. Arriving in America in 1920, he studied at the National Academy of Design* (1925–30) with Charles Hawthorne* as well as with Hans Hofmann* (1935–36). In 1930 he returned to Italy for three years. He taught at Pratt Institute, was visiting critic at Yale University, and an original member of the American Abstract Artists* group between 1936 and 1957. Like most American artists of his generation, he worked the WPA Federal Art Project* during the 1930s, both in mural and easel painting, specifically as an assistant to Arshile Gorky.* He teaches at the University of North Carolina at Greensboro. He has exhibited at museums throughout the country.

Cavallon has maintained a remarkably persistent style of lyrical abstraction since about 1950, embodying large, light color shapes freely organized in vertical-horizontal patterns of rose, pinks, light blues, reiterating in general the frame of the canvas. Despite the freedom of the forms, a sense of two-dimensional pattern in most of his works

combines a tradition of European geometry, specifically that of the modern Dutch master, Piet Mondrian, with American free abstraction. This sense of openness, nonobjectivism, unified color, and two-dimensional geometry becomes more and more apparent in his works of the late 1960s and 1970s, in which small dark window panels at the edges frequently control the large unified rectangles of light color. The free geometry of Cavallon, particularly in the late works, as, for example, *Untitled* (1959, Whitney), suggests the most abstract color images of the early work of Henri Matisse. (H.H.A.)

Ceramics to 1900.
Derived from *keramos*, the Greek word for earthenware, the term "ceramics" applies to the art or technique of shaping and firing clay as well as to the objects themselves.

Earthenwares
Up to about the time of the American Revolution, nearly all of the fine ceramics used in the colonies were imported. There was no shortage of colonial potters but, with few exceptions, their trade was restricted to supplying nearby markets with useful household wares such as milk pans, storage jars, and pitchers. Most of these ceramics were made of earthenware fired in simple kilns at low temperatures and frequently covered with a lead glaze. There were limited attempts at decoration, usually by incising lines in the clay before it was fired, by painting a design in a contrasting color with slip (a liquid clay), or by adding splashes of color to the clear lead glaze. Forms and decorative styles generally were derived from English prototypes. Most of the colonial efforts were prosaic, but at times the early American potters were capable of producing wares that were of artistic merit, both in form and decoration. A few early potters have been identified, and some rather imprecise regional characteristics occasionally make it possible to assign pieces from unknown sources to various parts of the eastern United States.

When a large German colony settled in eastern Pennsylvania during the 18th century, they brought with them a rich tradition in the decorative arts that differed markedly from the English modes. The vigorous Pennsylvania-German culture produced especially fine earthenwares during the last quarter of the

3

4

5

Ceramics to 1900
3. Red earthenware crock with incised bands and wavy lines, early 18th century. Probably from Essex County, Mass.
4. Red earthenware plate with sgrafitto of vase and flowers, 1815. Pennsylvania-German.
5. Porcelain. Bonnin and Morris, Sweetmeat dish with blue underglaze, c.1772.
All, National Museum of History Washington, D.C.

18th and the first quarter of the 19th century. In addition to a wide range of utilitarian ceramics, colorful decorative pieces were made. The more elaborate of these were *sgrafitto* decorated, a technique in which a redware piece was covered all over or in part by one or more liquid clays (slips). After the slip dried, the potter incised a picture or design in the slip, uncovering the contrasting red clay body beneath. The piece was then fired, given a clear lead glaze, and fired a second time. The folk art of western and southern Germany is revealed in these *sgrafitto* pieces. Favored decorative motifs were flowers, birds, animals, and occasionally patriotic designs or mounted horsemen. Frequently, German inscriptions circle the borders and dated pieces are not uncommon. A number of the craftsmen who made these wares have been identified through signed pieces or other documentation. Georg Hübener, John Leidy, David Spinner, and Johannes Neesz can be included among the more proficient Pennsylvania-German potters of the period 1775–1825. Though the German style persisted in parts of eastern Pennsylvania, an interesting transposition occurred at the end of the 18th century in the Moravian settlements in the Salem, N.C., area. There, the Moravian potters Rudolph Christ and Gottfried Aust produced fine, cream-colored earthenwares in imitation of the English ceramics of the type extensively used in America at this time.

From about 1840 on, the independent local potter who had made hand-thrown earthenwares was increasingly replaced by large potteries located in ceramic centers such as Trenton, N.J., and East Liverpool, Ohio. These potteries made molded wares in large quantities. The various types of earthenwares produced included "yellow wares," made of buff-colored clays, and "Rockingham," which was earthenware glazed with a mottled brown glaze. The latter, named for an English pottery that used this type of glaze, became very popular. These wares are today often mistakenly called "Bennington." Though the Lyman & Fenton Pottery in Bennington, Vt., made fine Rockingham wares, ceramics of this type also were produced by many other American potteries. The D. & J. Henderson Pottery (established in 1828) in Jersey City, N.J., made Rockingham wares, as did the E. & W.

Ceramics to 1900

1. Red earthenware plate with sgrafitto of flowers and heart, 1816. Pennsylvania-German. Original in Metropolitan Museum of Art, N.Y.
2. Gray and tan stoneware jug, 1844. From Pennsylvania. Private collection.

Both, Index of American Design, National Gallery of Art, Washington, D.C.

Bennett Pottery (established in 1848) in Baltimore. Although figures and useful wares of many kinds were made with Rockingham glazes, perhaps most typical of American Rockingham were the houndhandle pitchers made at Bennington and by numerous other potteries from the East Coast to Ohio.

Stoneware

Salt-glazed stoneware had long been favored throughout Europe as a durable, tough ceramic especially suitable for storage purposes and for drinking vessels. Stoneware was being made in America in the 18th century but it was not until the first half of the 19th century that its decoration attracted interest. The accepted convention for decoration probably derived from German stonewares exported to America. Before firing, a simple design—often a flower or a bird—was incised in the piece and cobalt (which gives a blue color) was applied to the incised lines. Often there was no incised decoration and the design was simply painted in blue. During the firing, common salt was thrown into the kiln, the sodium in the salt combining with the silica and alumina in the clay to give a clear "salt glaze" beneath which was the blue, incised design. Of the many American makers of salt-glazed stonewares in the mid-19th century, perhaps the producer of the most elaborate pieces was the J. & E. Norton Pottery of Bennington, Vt. The large water-coolers made at Bennington were the most spectacular of the American stonewares, but countless jugs and storage jars made in hundreds of small potteries were also decorated in the same manner. The stonewares of this type comprise one of the few groups of American ceramics that might be said to have distinctive national characteristics.

Porcelain

While the technology of earthenware and stoneware was not difficult, the production of porcelain was far more demanding. Porcelain is a high-fired, vitrified, translucent ceramic that can be manufactured only from certain clays and demands a more complex technology in kiln construction. Commerical manufacturing of porcelain in Europe commenced around the beginning of the 18th century. Andrew Duche, a potter of Savannah, Ga., seems to have experimented with porcelain-making about 1741. He possibly succeeded in making porcelain, but the evidence is

3

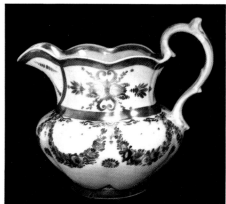

4

5

6

Ceramics to 1900
3. *Art Pottery. Rookwood Pottery, pitcher, plate, and vase, 1880s.*
4. *Porcelain. William Ellis Tucker, pitcher, early 1830s.*
5. *Art Pottery. Chelsea Keramic Art Works, teapot, 1880s.*
6. *Porcelain. Knowles, Taylor & Knowles, vase, late 19th century. All, National Museum of History and Technology, Smithsonian Institution, Washington, D.C.*

inconclusive. In 1771, when the great art of the German porcelain manufacturing center of Meissen already had declined and when the French royal porcelain factory of Sevres had reached its zenith, the first substantial production of porcelain in the New World took place. This attempt was a short-lived and unsuccessful one lasting only two years, but from it came the earliest documented American porcelain. In 1771 Gousse Bonnin and George Morris established a small porcelain manufactory in Philadelphia. To date, little more than a dozen pieces of Bonnin and Morris porcelain have been identified, all of it modestly decorated in underglaze blue more or less in the manner of the blue and white porcelain made at Bow, Lowestoft & Worcester in England at the same time. As art, Bonnin and Morris porcelain has no great merit. It is derivative and uninspired. With few exceptions, prior to 1900, American ceramics—from either an artistic or technical standpoint—have consistently relied on European styles and fashions and have usually been inferior to their European counterparts. One area in which American ceramics, as an art form, has assumed international leadership is that of 20th-century studio pottery.

It was not until about 1826 that porcelain-making gained a permanent foothold in the United States. In that year William Ellis Tucker established a porcelain factory in Philadelphia. Tucker porcelain was a hybrid, having some qualities of English bone china but more closely resembling French porcelain. In form and decoration, Tucker porcelain generally imitated the fine French porcelains of the period. Most Tucker porcelain was unmarked and much of it may be confused with the less rare French porcelain that was exported to the United States in quantity at the time. Tucker died in 1832, but the factory continued for six more years. The importance of the Tucker endeavor is that for the first time high-quality porcelain had been produced in the United States. From the 1840s onward a number of American porcelain-makers appeared, though it must be said that in nearly all cases the porcelains manufactured in the United States were inferior to the best then being produced in the Orient and Europe. Some of the more important porcelain manufacturers were the Southern Porcelain Manufacturing Company near Aiken, S.C. (1856); the Ott & Brewer Company of Trenton, N.J., which in about 1882 seems to have been the first American pottery to make the eggshell-thin porcelain known as "Belleek"; and the Union Porcelain Works in Greenpoint, Long Island, N.Y., which made fine porcelains after about 1865. An outstanding midwestern manufacturer was the pottery of Knowles, Taylor & Knowles Company of East Liverpool, Ohio, established in 1870. During the last quarter of the 19th century, this firm produced a variety of fine porcelains including their lotus ware, a soft, white, bone china that usually was given a brilliant painted decoration in gold and enamel colors.

Parian Ware

During the second half of the 19th century, one of the most expressive mediums of ceramic art was so-called "parian ware." Named for the fine Greek marble from the island of Paros that it imitated, this white, porcellaneous stoneware was highly esteemed by the Victorians. The semi-mass production techniques available to some American potteries enabled parian statuary, usually of a size suited for a mantlepiece, to be made in quantity and sold at reasonable prices. Thematically, sentimental figures and busts of historic figures were popular. Parian pitchers, boxes, vases, and plaques were made in volume. If unmarked, it is often difficult to differentiate between the American, French, and English pieces. Parian wares were made by many American potteries, some of the more competent manufacturers being the United States Pottery Company in Bennington, Vt., the Chesapeake Pottery in Baltimore, Md. (established in 1881), and Ott & Brewer Company of Trenton, N.J. Isaac Broome, a sculptor and professor of art, modeled a number of figures and impressive groups for Ott & Brewer in 1876. These were produced in parian and exhibited at the Centennial Exhibition held in Philadelphia that same year.

Tiles

Tiles form a rather special category of the ceramic art. Toward the end of the 19th century, a number of competent tile manufacturers appeared on the American scene as the architectural use of ceramics was extended to floors and interior and exterior walls. In 1878 John G. Low founded the Low Art Tile works in Chelsea, Mass. Here numerous techniques were used to produce fine decorative tiles, many of them designed by a talented artist, Arthur Osborne. Other major tile manufacturers of the period included the American Encaustic Tiling Company, begun in Zanesville, Ohio, in 1875 and the Cambridge Art Tile Works, established in Covington, Ky., in 1887. The Moravian Pottery and Tile Works of Doylestown, Pa., founded in 1900 by Henry C. Mercer, produced some of the most interesting American tiles. Using a mosaic technique, Mercer made colorful, decorative architectural tiles—pictures that, when installed, complemented the eclectic nature of the interior and exterior architecture of the time.

Art Pottery

During the last twenty years of the 19th century the United States was provided with an important movement in the ceramic art that was not primarily derivative. This was "art pottery," which came about essentially as a reaction to the inferior quality of products from the factory system. A new concept embodying high standards of workmanship and a more refined esthetic started a return to quality production under the direction of artists. This approach reflected elements of the craft movement inspired by the English designer and poet, William Morris, and indeed applied many of its tenets. The result was, in most cases, the creation of potteries that used modern techniques but were more concerned with craftsmanship, design, and decoration. Inevitably, a number of these potteries were drawn to the art nouveau* style of the late 19th century, and their products must be considered a particularly appropriate expression of that style.

Perhaps the most important of the art potteries was the Rookwood Pottery founded in about 1880 in Cincinnati, Ohio. This concern, which survived until 1960, was the creation of a group of women led by Maria Longworth Nichols. Their inspiration seems to have been ceramics from Europe and the Orient shown in the 1876 Philadelphia Exhibition. As the Rookwood Pottery became successful and increasingly professional, its wares were made in a wider range of form and decoration. Mat and shiny glazes were used and naturalistic decorative motifs were favored. The colors most usually associated with Rookwood are shades of brown, green, and creamy-yellow. Many other art potteries, roughly contemporary with Rookwood, sought the same objectives. The wares of these potteries were often quite distinctive, though in most cases there was the common bond of a generalized art nouveau taste. In the Boston area the Chelsea Keramic Art Works (c.1868–1894) achieved a limited production of fine ceramics that can only be termed Victorian eclectic. Other major American art potteries were the S.A. Weller Pottery in Zanesville, Ohio (1872–1948), the Grueby Faïence Company in Boston, Mass. (1891–1907), which developed a special mat glaze, and the Newcomb Pottery in New Orleans, La. (1897–1940).

In the 20th century there has been a continuation of prevailing trends. Although technically advanced, commercially made American ceramics remain, for the most part, dependent upon European taste. However, in the area of studio pottery, that is, of pieces made as objects of art by individual artist-craftsmen, American artists have assumed a prominent role. (For contemporary ceramics see Handcrafts, Contemporary.)   (J.J.M.)

Chalfant, Jefferson David (1846–1931).

Painter. Born in Lancaster, Pa., Chalfant began his career as a cabinetmaker and came to Wilmington, Del., to work on the cabinetry of the elaborate railroad cars of the period. He began to paint, without training, as an avocation, but was so successful that he became a full-time artist around 1880. Most of the still lifes on which his present reputation rests were painted during the next ten years. He went to Paris in 1890 and spent two years studying with Adolphe William Bouguereau and Jules Lefèvre, but this experience seems not to have changed his style to any degree.

Chalfant spent the rest of his life in Wilmington, painting still lifes, genre, and portraits. His still life work closely parallels that of William Michael Harnett;* in fact, he sometimes even appropriated Harnett's subjects and titles, as in *Old Violin* (1888, Delaware Art Center, Wilmington). Chalfant's color is somewhat drier than Harnett's and his composition is likely to be simpler; he is nevertheless closer to Harnett stylistically than to any other painter. Recently, collectors have begun to show

Jefferson David Chalfant, Old Violin, *1888. Wilmington Society of the Fine Arts, Delaware Art Center.*

interest in Chalfant's genre—he painted cobblers at work, black boys playing musical instruments, models posed nude before art classes, and so on—as well as his still lifes.   (A.F.)

Chamberlain, John (1927–   ).
A sculptor of the generation of younger artists affected by the liberating notions of the abstract expressionists. His best-known works are the baroque, abstract sculptures he created from the discarded chassis of automobiles, in which he assembled the parts freely and used the original colors in his compositions.

Born in Rochester, Ind., Chamberlain studied sculpture at the Museum School of the Chicago Art Institute for two years and then attended Black Mountain College, North Carolina (1955–56), where he was exposed to the vanguard theories of both artists and poets. When he moved to New York in 1958 he began developing his method of assemblage,* using found parts first in small models and later in larger versions of bent and twisted steel. At first he seemed to have been impressed by the compilation methods of David Smith,* who also relied a great deal on found parts, but Chamberlain later showed a preference for larger masses. His work stressed the deep volumes and eccentric folds he managed to get when he squeezed and compressed old body parts from automobiles. In the late 1960s, he turned for a while to painting, using an enamel automobile finish, and to plastic sculpture, using mineral-coated plexiglass.

Chamberlain has exhibited widely, including one-man shows in New York, Chicago, Boston, Los Angeles, and London, and has been included in important international exhibitions. In 1971, he was given a retrospective exhibition at the Guggenheim Museum in New York City.   (D.A.)

Chambers, Thomas (1815–after 1866).
One of the major untrained romantic painters, best known for his seascapes. Very little is known about his life other than the facts of his birth in England and his appearance in the directories of New York (1834–41, 1858–59, 1861–66) and Boston (1843–51), where he was listed as a landscape, marine, or portrait painter. From 1852–57 he worked in the Hudson Valley. Chambers' paintings are often based on

prints, and they were seldom signed or dated; his style was distinguished by a bold sense of composition and brilliant coloring, often with an enamel-like finish. An unusually romantic atmosphere and striking composition are evident in *The Constitution and the Guerriere* (c.1845, Metropolitan).

Chandler, Winthrop (1747–90).
Itinerant portraitist and decorator born in Woodstock, Conn., who may have studied in Boston and is thought to have been apprenticed to a house and sign painter. He developed a distinctive style which appears to have influenced a succession of limners working mainly in Connecticut. Chandler's large figures tended to press against the upper and lower limits of his canvas but he also found room for decorative embellishment and detailed allusion to his sitter's life and material comfort, as in *Rev. Ebenezer Devotion* (1770, Brookline Historical Association, Mass.) which pictures the sitter in his library.

Chapman, John Gabsby (1808–89).
Painter, printmaker, and illustrator born in Alexandria, Va. As a young man Chapman studied under George Cooke and Charles Bird King.* After establishing himself as an artist in Winchester, Va., in 1827, he studied briefly at the Pennsylvania Academy of the Fine Arts and then in Italy. When he returned in 1831 he worked as a portrait and historical painter, dividing his time between Washington, D.C. and New York City. He published in 1847 the *American Drawing Book,* which went through many editions, and he also provided some fourteen hundred illustrations for Harper's popular *Family Bible* (1846). He again went abroad in 1848 and remained until shortly before his death.

Chapman was perhaps best known as a figure painter and as an illustrator for magazines and gift books, and his large mural *The Baptism of Pocohantas* (1837–42) in the rotunda of the U.S. Capitol was highly esteemed. In recent years, however, more positive recognition has been accorded him for his landscapes and color etchings of the Roman Campagna, which are sensitive and at the same time strong in color. He was one of the first Americans to produce etchings (1843). His early works in this medium are closer in appearance to engravings than those of his later years, which are more fully developed and characterized by a freer line.

Among his few paintings in public collections is *Pines of the Villa Barberini* (1856, Boston), an attractive, if somewhat awkwardly composed, landscape, and his portrait of the pioneer American wood engraver, Alexander Anderson, is in the National Academy of Design, New York City.   (H.W.W.)

Charlot, Jean (1898–   ).
Painter. Born in Paris, Charlot spent a year at the École des Beaux-Arts until his studies were interrupted by service in World War I. In 1920 he left France for Mexico, where he was to remain for nine crucial years. There he was swept into the Mexican mural movement along with Rivera, Orozco, Siquieros, and others. He painted the murals for the Preparatory School and the Ministry of Education in Mexico City and spent three years as staff artist for the Carnegie Archeological Expedition in Yucatán. In 1929 he came to the United States, and the following year joined the faculty at the Art Students League in New York and at Columbia University. He was artist-in-residence at the University of Georgia in 1941–44. During that time he created murals for university and government buildings and he was awarded a Guggenheim Fellowship (1945) to write a book on the Mexican mural movement. During the 1940s and '50s he also published several books of lithographs. In 1947 Charlot headed the school of the Colorado Springs Fine Arts Center; then, after a year at Yale, he joined the faculty at the University of Hawaii.

Although he has produced many easel paintings, Charlot is primarily celebrated as a muralist who deals with historic, religious, and mythological themes in heroic style, but with a remarkable and very special tenderness in the handling of the figures of chilren; the round-headed Charlot child is almost his signature. In addition to his murals at the University of Georgia, he has painted walls in New York, Ohio, Michigan, Kansas, at the University of Hawaii, and in various churches in the Hawaiian Islands.   (A.F.)

Chase, William Merritt (1849–1916).
Versatile painter and influential teacher. Chase was born in Williamsburgh, Ind., and grew up there and in Indianapolis, where he clerked in his father's shoe store and painted portraits when he could find a patron. In 1868 he be-

1. **William Merritt Chase.** A Friendly
   Call, *1895. National Gallery of Art,
   Washington, D.C.*
2. **John Chamberlain.** Mr. Press, *1961,
   welded auto material with fabric.
   Collection Donald Judd, N.Y.*
3. **Winthrop Chandler.** Captain Samuel
   Chandler, *1780. National Gallery of Art,
   Washington, D.C. (Garbisch Collection).*

1. **Frederick Edwin Church.** Rainy Season in the Tropics, *1866. Collection J. William Middendorf, II, N.Y.*
2. **Chicago School of Architecture.** *Louis Sullivan. Gage Building Group, Chicago, 1899.*

gan art studies with a local artist, Benjamin F. Hayes, and two years later went to New York to study, eventually attending the National Academy of Design.*

In 1871 he returned to his parent's home (then St. Louis) where his meticulous still lifes awakened the interest of some local patrons, who enabled him to study in Europe. Going to Munich in 1872, he studied with Alexander Wagner, then with Karl von Piloty, while responding, like his fellow-American Frank Duveneck,* to the influence of Wilhelm Liebl. His technique matured rapidly, and his local reputation mushroomed as he won award after award at the Munich Academy. When Duveneck returned to Munich in 1875, the two young Americans took a studio together, and Chase did increasingly skillful paintings in the dark, richly-pigmented Munich style. In 1877 he spent nine months with Duveneck and John H. Twachtman* in Venice, where his landscape sketches took on a new luminosity. On his return to America the same year, he was represented in the National Academy show in New York and attracted attention in Philadelphia, Pa., where he won a medal at the Centennial exhibition.

In 1878 he moved emphatically back into the New York scene. His studio on Tenth Street became famous for its art life, exotic furnishings, and his paintings of interiors—brilliantly brushed records of eclectic taste on a grand scale. He then entered upon three decades of exceptional activity and influence. He taught extensively; he traveled to Europe every summer; and he painted copiously, mastering a variety of technical approaches to portrait, landscapes, and still-life painting.

Beginning in 1881, he spent three summers in Spain, studying Velásquez and picking up some of the technical tricks of Fortuny. Passing through Paris, he encountered J. Alden Weir* and influenced him to purchase two important Manets. In 1885 he visited Whistler* in London and during a brief, warm friendship painted his famous Whistleresque portrait, *James A. McNeill Whistler* (1885, Metropolitan). Honors began to come his way regularly: he was elected to the National Academy in 1890 and won no less than three gold medals in 1901. He was president of the Society of American Artists from 1885–95. He pursued an extraordinary teaching career: at the Art Students League* and in his studio for thirty-five years, at his summer school in Shinnecock, Long Island, N.Y., for eleven years; at the Chase School, which he opened in New York City in 1896; at its successor, the New York School of Art for ten years beginning in 1898; at the Pennsylvania Academy of the Fine Arts for thirteen years; in summer classes abroad; and in a final summer session in Carmel, Cal., in 1914. He was sought after as a master of technique, but above all because he gave zest to the process of painting. His list of students ranged from Alfred Maurer* to Kenneth Hayes Miller,* Marsden Hartley,* Edward Hopper,* Rockwell Kent,* Charles Demuth,* Charles Sheeler,* and Georgia O'Keeffe.*

Chase's restless, active personality was evident in his painting, which was rapidly and freshly executed, and tended to be eclectic, reflecting in various ways his enthusiasm for Velásquez, Chardin, Whistler, Sargent, and Japanese prints. He alternated landscapes in a loosely-brushed impressionist key with still lifes of fish painted in a 17th-century Dutch tonality. The vigor, vitality, and skill of his work went far toward compensating for the eclecticism and overemphasis on surfaces; and his sheer joy in painting still communicates itself effectively through canvases of a wide variety, marked by sumptuous texture and muted harmony.   (D.W.S.)

Chicago School of Architecture, The.
The name given to the group of architects who practised in and around Chicago from 1900 into the 1920s. Their work had an indigenous quality in its use of materials, while the designs, although original, displayed a cubist monumentality. Chicago School design was a rebellion against borrowing from Europe and past cultures. It attempted to solve each problem in terms of the conditions that controlled it and the uses to which it would be put. These architects evolved new standards, a new type of design, the "prairie style" house, and a highly original type of ornament.

Louis H. Sullivan* was the originating genius. He inspired a host of followers, including Frank Lloyd Wright,* who referred to him as "Lieber Meister" and worked in his office. Sullivan's *Kindergarten Chats,* which appeared serially in the *Interstate Architect & Builder* magazine, challenged the thinking of a generation of young architects seeking an honest expression for their work. Later, Wright, through his writings, reached Holland and Germany, and had a profound influence in America through his Fellowship at Taliesin in Spring Green, Wis., and in the winter in Scottsdale, Ariz. Among the other original members of the School were George G. Elmslie, Dwight Perkins, Robert Spencer, George Maher, Hugh Garden, Arthur Heun, and Walter Burley Griffin.   (A.B.)

Chryssa (1933–   ).
Sculptor. Born in Athens, Greece, she studied at the Académie de la Grande Chaumiere, Paris (1953–54) and the California School of Fine Arts, San Francisco (1954–55). Chryssa's first exhibition of sculpture was held at a New York Gallery in early 1961, followed by a second one-man exhibition later that year at the Guggenheim Museum. Her work of that period consists of ironic translations of letters, signs, and advertisement layouts into plaster, bronze, and aluminum reliefs. The subdued surfaces of these works faintly echo the formal sources of commercial layout and sign craft from which they derive. Chryssa introduced the use of neon tubing in an aluminum construction *Times Square Sky* (1962, Walker). In this work the commercial sign letters are laid one upon another in a jumbled series capped by the word "air" rendered in neon tubing, which became the dominant material in her art through the mid-1960s. Fragments of specific letters are used in these works as purely formal elements as well as to spell out words.

Chryssa's neon pieces have been in numerous group exhibitions, including the Carnegie Institute, 1961; the Whitney Museum Annual Exhibition of Contemporary American Sculpture, 1966 and 1970; and the "American Sculpture of the '60's" exhibition at the Los Angeles County Museum of Art, 1967.   (J.M.)

Church, Frederic Edwin (1826–1900).
Leading landscape painter of the mid-19th century, Church led the American school in depicting the great sights of the world in a realistic style. Born in Hartford, Conn., son of a prosperous insurance man who acceded to his son's wish to study art, Church received his

first instruction from Alexander H. Emmons (1816–?) and Benjamin H. Coe (1799–after 1883). From 1844–48 he studied with the acknowledged founder of the American landscape school, Thomas Cole.*

Church's early works recall Cole's style; they are painterly in technique, emotional, and often have religious or Catskill subjects. Yet as early as his painting of *Hooker and Company Journeying Through the Wilderness* (1846), Church reveals new interests: the New World, rather than the Old, and the reality of light rather than the creation of picturesque storms.

By 1850, Church had been living in New York for several years; he was a full member of the National Academy of Design, already had his first student, and was well on his way to being accepted as Cole's successor. Unlike almost all American artists before him, he felt no need to go to Europe, but instead began to travel in the summers over the United States in search of subjects both native and heroic. In 1850, for example, he traveled through Vermont, New Hampshire, and to Mt. Desert Island, Me. In 1851, he visited Virginia, Kentucky, and the upper Mississippi region, and then journeyed to Grand Manan Island, the Bay of Fundy, and again to Mt. Desert. The growth of Church's style paralleled his ever-widening travels. In the early 1850s he threw off the didactic and religious elements of Cole's approach. He began to paint wilderness in a dramatic yet realistic manner, for like the Transcendentalists of American literature he felt that moral perfection could best be approached in the solitude of nature.

Church first traveled abroad in 1853, accompanied by Cyrus Field. He did not choose Europe and the lessons of past art, but rather South America and her archetypal mountainous wilds. On his return he began to paint South American scenes on the basis of many pencil and oil sketches he had made, and in 1855 he produced *The Andes of Ecuador* (Reynolds House, Winston-Salem, N.C.), perhaps his first full-scale masterpiece.

In 1856 Church visited Niagara Falls and after making many studies of it, he painted the large *Niagara* (1857, Corcoran), which established him as the leading landscape painter in America. After a second trip to South America, he completed his South American master-

piece, the huge *Heart of the Andes* (1859, Metropolitan), which was sold for $10,000, the highest price up to that time for a painting by a living American artist. He then set off again, searching for heroic subjects, this time along the coast of Labrador. This resulted in a book by his traveling companion, Rev. L. L. Noble, called *After Icebergs with a Painter* (1861), with sketches and paintings of the far north by the artist.

Church reached his peak in his *Twilight in the Wilderness* (1860, Cleveland). In this taut view of the Maine woods he brought to a culmination a decade of wilderness paintings. In the searing reds and yellows of the sky and the quiet water, Church directly influenced the other painters in New York; in the anguish and power of the painting he spoke moreover for a nation on the verge of civil war. Though major paintings followed in this decade, the moment of his most intense energy was gone. By 1866, his work had lost its fine balance between high realism and overblown melodrama; the latter prevails in his *Rainy Season in the Tropics* (1866, Metropolitan).

Church went to Europe for the first time in 1867, and then spent several months visiting Egypt, Jerusalem (which he painted), Beirut, Cyprus, and Constantinople, before returning to Rome.

By 1870 he had begun construction of his great villa "Olana" near Hudson, N.Y.; this house, with the artist's furnishings and collections, is still intact. In the 1870s he continued to paint his favorite subjects, though his skills had declined noticeably; thus his *Morning in the Tropics* (1877, Washington) has none of the excitement of observation and discovery of his tropical views of the 1850s. In these years Church spent much time at his camp near Mt. Katahdin, Me., which he painted many times, the last in 1895. In the 1880s and 1890s he visited Mexico repeatedly. After his death in 1900 he was honored by a memorial exhibition at the Metropolitan Museum. (T.E.S.)

Church, Henry (1836–1908).
Self-taught artist of Chagrin Falls, Ohio, who at the age of forty-two abandoned the family blacksmith trade and devoted himself to painting, sculpture, and hunting. Squaw Rock, a monumental bas-relief carving of an Indian woman surrounded by a serpent (symbolizing

Church Silver
1. Hull and Sanderson. *Communion Cup.*
2. Cornelius Vanderburgh. *Beaker.* Both, Yale University Art Gallery, New Haven, Conn. (Mabel Brady Garvan Collection).
Circus Wagons
3. Lion and Mirror Bandwagon, originally with life-size St. George and the Dragon, which telescoped into the wagon between parades; converted into a bandwagon for Ringling Brothers Circus, 1879.
4. Gollmar Mirror Tableau Wagon, railroad car, 1903.
5. Orchestmelochor Wagon, designed to house the Barnum and London Circus' band organ, 1882. All, Circus World Museum, Baraboo, Wis.

the rape of Indian America by the white man) is a northern Ohio landmark once attributed to prehistoric Indians, but executed by Church in 1885. A fantastic crouching stone lion, also his work, marks his grave in the Chagrin Falls cemetery. Most of Church's paintings were burned by his daughter after his death, but those remaining point to the artist's spiritualist bent and illustrate a complicated symbolism that is expressed in composition as well as in clearly stated and hidden figures. (M.J.G.)

Church Silver.

From the middle of the 17th century, silver vessels were made by American silversmiths for presentation to the Protestant churches in the colonies. Often consisting of domestic forms and even used in homes prior to presentation, these vessels included standing cups, caudle cups, beakers, tankards, and mugs, as well as specifically ecclesiastical forms such as flagons, patens, baptismal basins, and alms basins. In general, early American church silver closely followed the designs of English or Dutch silver. Myer Myers* made scroll bells or Rimonim, a protector, and possibly a silver pointer for use in synagogues in the 18th century.

During the Gothic revival in the 19th century, church silver, particularly in Anglican churches, became more ecclesiastical and less domestic in design. Cooper & Fisher of New York made the iconographically-enriched communion service for Trinity Chapel in 1855. Gorham* made the Romanesque silver for St. Agnes' Chapel in 1892, which *The Ecclesiologist* called one of the richest sets ever made in America. Both Gorham and Tiffany* excelled in neo-Gothic* church silver, including altar crosses and candlesticks in the last decade of the 19th century. (M.G.F.)

Circus Wagons.

Vehicles made for transporting circus personnel and animals, particularly the extravagantly carved carriages and tableaux that were created in the late 19th and early 20th century as dramatic elements of the circus parade. Such introductory parades of men and animals date back to ancient Rome, but 19th-century American showmanship brought them to resplendent heights in which the sculptured parade elements equaled, and in some instances may have even outshone the actual cir-

3

4

5

cus features. Beginning in 1846, when Isaac Van Amburgh's circus passed down New York City's Broadway with a twenty-foot bandwagon variously described as a "Roman Chariot" and an "Imperial State Carriage and Throne," American wood carvers were regularly called upon either to invent or execute increasingly baroque fancies to add to the drama of the parade scene. Van Amburgh's wagon boasted a canopy topped by a carved eagle and supported on each side by a dolphin. A year or two later, the New York City carving shop operated by John L. Cromwell from 1838–55 created for the Welch, Delevan & Nathan National Circus an "Armamax or Imperial Persian Chariot," advertised as being modeled on the vehicles of Cyrus the Great but with scrollwork "in the style of Louis XIV, decorated with eagles, equestrians, stars, and flowers, wrought in gold and silver," and with a driver "borne along between the expanded wings of two mighty dragons, apparently of massive gold." This mammoth wagon drawn by thirty horses soon inspired an "Apollonicon" dedicated to "The Spirit of '76" and drawn by forty horses, four abreast. The latter introduced a half-century of tableaux wagons produced for a succession of American circuses by such firms as Fielding Brothers and the Sebastian Wagon Company, with carvings largely from the shop of Samuel A. Robb.*

The subject span of the tableaux is considerable, ranging from nursery figures (*Mother Goose, Cinderella, The Old Woman Who Lived in a Shoe*) to historic periods (*The Age of Chivalry*) and symbolic geography (*Africa, Europe*). In most of these works enormous wooden figures, gessoed and polychromed or gilded, rode in florid surroundings of curlicues, swirls, cartouches, and rococo shell forms. Like Robb's show figures, his circus carvings show enormous stylistic variety. The realism that is such an important factor in Victorian stone sculpture is represented, but many of the bas-reliefs have a quality of formal restraint, and the monumental scale and the imaginary nature of many of the figures further distinguishes them. The models for many of the tableaux were pictorial, but in at least one instance, Robb's *Europe* wagon, the figures are based on those at the corners of the Prince Albert Memorial in Hyde Park. Many of the great circus wagons are preserved at the Circus World Mu-

seum in Baraboo, Wis. Parts of others have been acquired by other major American museums, and the monumental figures from the *Europe* wagon are now in the collection of the Smithsonian Institution, Washington, D.C.

(M.J.G.)

Claypoole, James, Jr. (c.1743–c.1800). Portrait painter. He was a son of James Claypoole (1720–96) of Philadelphia, "limner and painter in general." Both the son and a nephew, Matthew Pratt, became more proficient than their master. Young James figured in the art life of the city as early as 1761, when he engraved a view of the Pennsylvania Hospital. His prominence as a portrait painter was noted by Charles Willson Peale* in 1762. After the death of his young wife and child, Claypoole determined to visit his friend, the expatriate painter Benjamin West,* in London. Landing in Jamaica, he remained there, however, until his death, a successful portrait painter and (like his father) a dealer in artists' materials. His masterpiece is his *Memorial to E. R.* (1774), a full-length painting of a young woman being led through a funerary grove by the figure of Fame, while cherubs drape her tomb with flowers.

(C.C.S.)

Clevenger, Shobal Vail (1812–43). Sculptor. Born in Middletown, Ohio, he saw his first examples of sculpture in Cincinnati, where Hiram Powers* was commencing his career and was soon to depart for Italy. Clevenger found employment as a carver of gravestones while he modeled portrait busts of prominent local citizens. Inspired by Powers, he was eager to go to Italy; however, a wealthy patron, Nicholas Longworth, insisted that he first spend a few years as a portrait sculptor in the major eastern cities. Somewhat bitter, the young sculptor went to Washington, D.C. By 1838 he had received commissions to do busts of such national leaders as Henry Clay and Daniel Webster. By 1839 he had moved to Boston; his works at the Boston Athenaeum portray such eminent men as the artist Washington Allston* and Senator Harrison Grey Otis. From a New York trip came portraits of Mayor Philip Hone and the poet William Cullen Bryant. These likenesses rely on the forceful naturalism* of a self-taught artist largely untouched by any historic style such as neoclassicism.* Although he was successful as a

portraitist he was impatient to get to Italy; only there, he believed, could his abilities be nourished. In 1840 he and his family joined Hiram Powers in Florence. Although he was moved by the great ancient statuary he saw, it had little affect on his work. His reputation rested on his portrait busts, his true talent being his ability to capture likenesses of veracity and vitality. Stricken with tuberculosis, he sailed for home in 1843, but died while at sea. (W.C.)

Clonney, James Goodwyn (1812–67). Genre, landscape, and miniature painter as well as lithographer. Clonney, who is believed to have been born in either Edinburgh, Scotland, or Liverpool, England, emigrated to the United States and worked as a lithographer for the firm of Child and Inman in Philadelphia, Pa., from about 1830 to 1833. By 1834 he had set himself up as a painter of portrait miniatures in New York City. When competition from the increasingly popular daguerreotype cut into his income, he began about 1841 to devote himself to paintings of everyday life and an occasional landscape. From 1844 to 1852 he worked in New Rochelle, N.Y., and then moved to Cooperstown in upstate New York.

It is probable that in New York City he became familiar with the genre work of William Sidney Mount.* Mount's influence can be detected in Clonney's preference for subjects that lent themselves to humorous treatment. In one instance he appears actually to have borrowed one of Mount's comic devices: a sleeping Negro is tickled by a straw in Mount's *Farmer's Nooning* (1836, Suffolk Museum and Carriage House) and in Clonney's *Waking Up* (1851, Boston). Most of Clonney's genre paintings have a comic touch; typical are *Militia Training* (1841, Pennsylvania), which is one of his early works and may reflect the influence of the English genre painter Sir David Wilkie, and *The Happy Moment* (1847, Boston). *In the Cornfield* (1844, Boston) was, on the other hand, a serious work representing a departure from usual genre painting in its objective realism, unusually low horizon that silhouettes figures against the sky, and in its sympathetic rendering of the Negro.

Clonney exhibited regularly at the Pennsylvania Academy of the Fine Arts, New York's National Academy of

Design, the American Art-Union, and the Apollo Association. Many of his preparatory sketches are in the Karolik Collection in Boston. (H.W.W.)

Codman, Charles (1800–42).
Landscape and marine painter of Portland, Me. The art critic John Neal* dining comfortably at the Elm Tavern in Portland had been struck by the attractive quality of the wall decorations around him. "They were masterly, and I lost no time in hunting the artist up. I found him in the midst of his workshop, half buried in signs, fire-buckets, and all sorts of trumpery." Neal's encouragement brought Codman a spectacular and immediate rise from local job painter to the galleries of the Boston Athenaeum and New York's National Academy, and to prosperity under a distinguished patronage. Codman had a flair for the detailed rendering of vegetation with an effective use of perspective and of small figures in harmony with his theme but always subordinate to it. As in his *The Bathing Pool* (c.1830, Boston), he could create with much skill an atmosphere of restful and romantic charm. (C.C.S.)

Cogdell, John (1778–1847).
One of the earliest sculptors of the American school, he was a lawyer and banker by profession and an artist by avocation. His works were seldom more ambitious than portrait busts of friends or literary personalities, the major exception being the neoclassical wall monument in St. Philip's Church in his native Charleston, S.C. A member of South Carolina's legislature, Cogdell was also an organizer, with Samuel F. B. Morse,* of the South Carolina Academy of Fine Arts in 1821. Although self-taught, Cogdell was very much influenced by neoclassicism,* especially as found in the work of the Italian sculptor Canova, (whose studio he visited in Rome) and the English sculptor John Flaxman. (W.C.)

Coin Silver.
The name given to silver made in the first half of the 19th century, generally very thinly rolled and fashioned into spoons with fiddle handles. Early silver was frequently made from coins that had been melted down, but with the establishment of the first banks in the United States after the Revolutionary War, this practice became less common as refineries made rolled sheets of metal available. To indicate that their wares were of a quality equal to that of coins, the silversmiths stamped their products COIN.

Cole, Thomas (1801–48).
The ablest of early American landscape painters, Cole is often considered the founder of the native landscape school. He was born in Bolton-le-Moors, an English industrial center. He was apprenticed at fourteen to a designer of calico prints in Nottinghamshire and later to an engraver at Liverpool. In 1818 the Cole family moved to America, settling in Steubenville, Ohio. There, about 1820, Cole received brief instruction in painting from a portraitist named Stein. For several years thenceforth, Cole worked in the Ohio area as an itinerant portrait painter. In 1823, Cole and his family moved to Pittsburgh, where he worked in his father's "floorcloth manufactory" and began to make pencil sketches of scenery along the Monongahela River, beginning a lifelong habit of doing studies from nature. He soon moved to Philadelphia, where for two years he studied painting intermittently at the Pennsylvania Academy of the Fine Arts.

By 1825, Cole was a landscape painter. When he moved to New York that year, he was an almost immediate success, for his work was purchased by three powerful members of the New York art world, John Trumbull,* Asher B. Durand,* and William Dunlap.* In 1826, Thomas Cole became a founder of the National Academy of Design.* William Dunlap's *History of the Arts of Design* (1834) echoed American sentiment of the time in describing Cole as "one of the first painters in landscape . . . that the world possesses."

Though much of Cole's work seems overly laden with didactic sentiment, there is no doubt about his power as an artist. In his fluid, often luxuriant, brushwork and his strongly romantic imagination, he stands apart from his contemporaries. His early paintings of American scenery are dramatic and colorful; with religious awe he gave heroic visual expression to the vast wilderness that Americans were just coming to appreciate. Yet almost from the beginning, Cole was pulled in two directions: his patrons often wanted him to paint recognizable American scenes, while the artist himself increasingly preferred moralizing compositions that could display the virtuosity of his technique and his intellect. Thus, in 1827 he painted a large *View in the White Mountains, New Hampshire* (Wadsworth) in a realistic, nearly topographical style, and at nearly the same time completed the spectacular, imaginary *Expulsion from the Garden of Eden* (1827, Boston).

In 1829, Cole left for Europe. He spent nearly two years in England, and in 1831 went on to Florence, staying in the same house as Horatio Greenough,* the sculptor. He returned to New York in 1832. One immediate result of the trip was a change in his subject matter from Catskill, White Mountain, and Hudson landscapes to more sophisticated views of Italian scenery. More important was the maturation of Cole's theory of art, in particular his concept of doing a series of broad allegorical pictures that would develop a single theme. While still in Europe, he planned a cycle of five paintings—"to be the History of a Scene, as well as an Epitome of Man"; on his return to New York, he met the patron and collector, Luman Reed, who commissioned this series, *The Course of Empire* (New York Hist.), completed in 1836. Commenting upon human history and vanity, he painted landscapes depicting the evolution of a civilization from its savage state to its climax and eventual destruction.

During the 1830s, Cole was at the height of his powers. He went on to other elaborately allegorical series: *Departure* and *Return* (1837, Corcoran), and *The Voyage of Life* (1840, Proctor). He traveled widely in the eastern United States and he lectured, wrote essays and poetry, and occasionally practiced architecture, entering the competition for the Ohio State Capitol in 1838. Cole continued to paint American views, such as *The Oxbow (The Connecticut River near Northampton)* (1836, Metropolitan). He regarded realistic pictures like this one as hackwork, and he regretted the popular taste that made them profitable; yet both in his own time and today, critics and public have preferred these easily understood native scenes to the more complex allegorical pictures. For both types of painting, Cole believed in making extensive oil and pencil sketches from nature; yet he never painted on the spot and for the final composition he would combine sketch and memory, relying upon "a vivid picture in the mind's eye." After a

1

2

1. **Thomas Cole.** The Voyage of Life:
Youth, *1840.*

2. **Thomas Cole.** The Voyage of Life:
Old Age, *1840.*

Both, Munson-Williams-Proctor
Institute, Utica, N.Y.

second European trip (1841–42), he turned increasingly to religious subjects, and particularly to another great allegorical series, *The Cross and the World,* which was never completed. At the same time, Cole was painting some of the purest and most luminous landscapes of his life, such as *American Lake Scene* (1844, Detroit). In 1844 he also accepted his only formal pupil, Frederic E. Church,* and it was Church who, a decade later, confronted the same artistic dichotomies as had Cole: between the romantic and the real, the reportorial and the didactic.

Cole's death was considered "a national loss," which was a tribute to his success in popularizing landscape painting and in making a new place for art and the artist in America. (T.E.S.)

Collage.

Term (from the French, *coller,* to paste or stick) for a technique consisting of cutting and pasting natural or manufactured materials on a painted or unpainted surface. As early as 1908, Picasso had pasted a small piece of paper on the center of a drawing to make what is probably the first papier collé, or collage. In 1910 both he and Georges Braque superimposed words and letters on paintings, and Braque particularly had already used *trompe-l'oeil* wood-grain effects. This insertion of elements of visual realism into the increasingly abstract cubist paintings was part of the artist's concern with the central problem: what is illusion and what reality? Is reality in the eye of the spectator? Or is it the absolute of the canvas? This concern led logically not only to the introduction of imitations of observed nature in painted passages, but also to the application to the work of pieces of newspapers, restaurant menus, etc.—that is, elements of collage or, specifically, papier collé—to act as "real" themes in counterpoint to the abstract structure built up by the paint.

Picasso's *Still Life with Chair Caning* (1911–12) is his earliest integrated collage. In it he used a piece of common oilcloth with a design of simulated chair caning, and then worked over it a particularly free and bold pattern of still-life shapes. Even the oval shape of the work—a shape that many cubists were exploring in reaction against the dominant rectangle of Renaissance painting—and the rope frame, contribute to

the complication of the different levels of "reality" with which Picasso was playing. In 1912, too, Picasso had made of sheet metal and wire a construction that was a three-dimensional projection of a painted cubist guitar. In 1913 and 1914 he again translated cubist still-life paintings into constructions of wood, paper, and other materials, obviously in an investigation of the three-dimensional implications of cubist painted space. Although cubist collages continued the sense of subject that persisted in cubist painting, they were known to the Russian constructivist Vladimir Tatlin, whose abstract construction (as well as those of the other Russian constructivists) they affected (see Constructivism). During 1914 Picasso carried his constructions further in a wood-and-metal assemblage of musical instruments in which he opened up the potentials of construction for new concepts of sculptural space and abstract design.

The expansion of collage into sculpture was further developed by the Italian futurist Umberto Boccioni, who spoke of "sculpture as environment." He insisted on the use of every kind of material—"glass, wood, cardboard, iron, cement, horsehair, leather, cloth, mirrors, electric lights, etc., etc." Carlo Carra, among the Italian futurists, used collage for expressionist purposes in his *Patriotic Celebration* (free word painting) of 1914, a work that anticipated the expressionist use of collage by the dadaists and surrealists.

In 1916–17, sculptor Jean Arp produced some collages of torn pieces of colored papers scattered in a vaguely rectangular arrangement on a paper ground. At the same time he devised a type of relief consisting of thin layers of wood, with shapes suggesting plants, exotic vegetables, encrustations, or swarming amoebae; brightly painted, they suggested life, growth, and metamorphoses.

Among the German dadaists, Kurt Schwitters was the master of collage (*merzbilden* and *merzbau*) utilized for essentially fantastic effects. Max Ernst in 1919–20, collaborating with Jean Arp, produced collages and photomontages that demonstrated a genius for suggesting metamorphoses or the double identity of objects. As a result of the influence of Ernst and Arp, collage became a fundamental technique of fantasy in the development of Paris

dadaism* and surrealism* after 1919.

The entire movement of abstract constructivism in sculpture may be said to have emerged originally from the ideas of collage. In 1925 Max Ernst began to make drawings that he termed "frottage," or rubbing, in which he used the child's technique of placing a piece of paper on a textured surface and rubbing over it with a pencil. The resulting image was largely a consequence of the laws of chance; the transposed textures were then reorganized in new contexts, and new and unforeseen associations were aroused. Not only did frottage provide the technical basis for a series of unorthodox drawings; it also intensified Ernst's perception of the textures in his environment—wood, cloth, leaves, plaster, and wallpaper.

In sculpture, collage developed into the concept of the "found" object—everyday objects from the environment—in works by Boccioni and Picasso (for example, *Bull's Head,* 1943).

American painters in the early 20th century, such as Arthur Dove* and Stuart Davis,* experimented with effects of collage or relief sculpture involving found objects. Since the mid-1900s, collage and its offshoots have become major approaches in painting and sculpture both in Europe and the United States. Among American abstract expressionists, Robert Motherwell* and Conrad Marca-Relli* have developed collage into monumental forms. Much of the painting and sculpture of the 1960s throughout the world has involved the assemblage of different materials to a point where it is difficult to apply the terms "painting" and "sculpture" to them. "Assemblage,"* a word coined by Marcel Duchamp* to indicate the broadening of the base of collage, has expanded to include three-dimensional environments and happenings.* Thus Picasso's miniature 1908 collage has developed into one of the major art forms of the 20th century.

(H.H.A.)

Colman, Samuel, Jr. (1832–1920).
Landscape painter and watercolorist born in Portland, Me. His father, a bookseller and publisher, moved to New York City while Samuel, Jr., was still a boy. In New York, young Colman studied under Asher B. Durand.* He exhibited his first painting, *Morning,* at the National Academy of Design in New York City at age eighteen. Colman

made two trips abroad (1860–62 and 1871–75) to study and paint. In later years he lived in Irvington-on-Hudson and in Newport, R.I., but moved to New York City prior to his death.

In his work before 1870 Colman may be considered a second generation member of the Hudson River School* of landscape painters. In his later work French influence is apparent, and he developed a bold style, making use of a thick impasto and hot, raw color. His specialty was picturesque landscapes of Europe, especially Italy, and of the American West. Typical of his western landscapes is *Ships of the Plains* (1872, Union League Club, New York City). Convincingly honest, his views of the West are an important documentation of America's expansion.   (H.W.W.)

Color-Field Painting.

The French impressionists (and especially Monet in his late pictures of water lilies) were the first to create an oeuvre based on all-over brushwork. Such works lacked any central focus, and the most radical did not even emphasize the part-to-part relationships within the work that formed the basis of traditional composition. Instead, the impressionist painters arrived at a uniformly articulated "field" of color strokes. Between 1920 and 1950 the surrealists experimented with "automatism" (letting the pencil wander freely over the page) as a means of releasing creative expression, and such methods also led to the even distribution of images over the entire field. During the early 1940s Mark Tobey* experimented with a field-type painting that he called "white writing," derived from oriental sources. By 1947 Jackson Pollock* (who had employed "automatic writing" as early as 1941–42) was producing "all-over" compositions on a vast new scale in his drip paintings. Because of their physical size and the single, unified image, such works tended to encompass the spectator and become his total environment since they occupied his entire field of vision.

By 1950 other artists such as Barnett Newman* and Mark Rothko* were combining Pollock's field concept with their interest in color, and by reducing their forms to a few simple shapes and vastly increasing the size of their canvases, they were often able to achieve the effect of a field of pure color. Both Newman and Rothko ultimately arrived

at an art based on pure optical sensation, and both stressed the continuity of the color field by articulating their surfaces with the narrowest possible horizontal and vertical divisions between colors. Their simplified format, heroic scale, and the luminous, atmospheric, saturated color were soon taken over by artists such as Kenneth Noland,* Morris Louis,* and Jules Olitski.* Color-field also became the point of departure for the more "optical" field paintings of Gene Davis* and Larry Poons,* while its radical simplification and tendency to relate its internal shapes to the rectangular format of the canvas helped lay the groundwork for minimal art.*   (E.C.G.)

Concept Art.

A term derived from a definition in 1913 by the French painter Marcel Duchamp* of the role of the artist as one of selecting for esthetic consideration rather than one of manipulating materials. In his "ready-mades" and in subsequent work he took the emphasis off technique, formalism, and the "romantic sensuality of painting," and turned to commonplace objects and ideas; ultimately Duchamp produced no art objects in the traditional sense; his life became his art. He had foreseen pitfalls for artists who stop being "creators" and turn into "performers" or manufacturers. Duchamp's oeuvre has been a continuing source of ideas for the flood of young "concept" artists in America in the very late 1960s, as well as for Robert Morris,* a sculptor of minimal* art, who earlier in the decade consciously imitated Duchamp (Morris's *Three Rulers* and *Location,* 1963, are more concerned with "ideas" than with form or technique).

An alternate source for concept art can be found in the nihilistic, anti-art movement, dada,* which came in with the spiritual exhaustion following World War I. Many younger artists in the 1960s seemed to feel a similar exhaustion, which, coupled with an anti-materialistic attitude, has often led to works of art with little or no physical form. One contribution to a 1969 exhibition was a small card with the words: "All the things I know but of which I am not at the moment thinking—1:36 P.M., 15 June 1969, New York."

One can trace the gradual elimination of "handicraft" in art down through industrially fabricated painting and

sculpture: and the gradual elimination of complicated forms, which led to minimalism. Concept artists, however, went one step further and sought to eliminate the art "product." This transformation of art from physical object to mental image is usually effected by means of photographs, "documents," specifications, formulae, or ordinary narrative prose—often with the "official signature" of the artist. As one critic has pointed out, the concept movement has replaced art with literature. Among the more interesting concept artists are Joseph Kosuth, who has published his "work" in newspapers (usually definitions from a dictionary), and Douglas Huebler, who has constructed elaborate "Duration Pieces," which are carefully documented on maps and drawings.

Perhaps the most obvious result of concept art is the elimination of a "product" created to be sold. By undermining the idea of "ownership" it attacked the museum as well as the private collector, and all standards applied to traditional works of art. Concept art is available to everyone, on whatever level he wishes to take it. Because the concept artist conceives of himself as a "mind" and not as a "craftsman," he is free to suggest almost anything as a work of art. His subjects can be general or specific, trivial or profound, real or abstract, grandiose or personal. The concept artist seems primarily involved in recognizing possible experiences, and then in transmitting the possibility of these (or related) experiences to others. Because his art has been so dematerialized, its ultimate "site" is the mind of the observer.   (E.C.G.)

Coney, John (1656–1722).

Outstanding among Boston's second generation of silversmiths, Coney received his training with John Hull* and Robert Sanderson.* He is highly regarded because of the variety and quality of his work in gold and silver. His biographer lists 112 examples of his work. In 1690 he may have engraved the first paper currency issued in Massachusetts. It is noticeably similar to the currency issued in 1702, which documentary evidence shows was engraved by Coney. He made silver for churches in Connecticut as well as Massachusetts, and made a splended monteith punch bowl for the Livingston family of New York. He made another of these scalloped-rim bowls for John Colman, a Boston merchant (Yale); with flat-fluted sides, cast lion masks holding ring handles, and elaborately created and wrought removable rim, it is one of the best expressions of the late baroque style in American silver.

Much of Coney's silver was decorated with armorial engraving. His covered caudle cup (Yale) with a bulbous body, reel-top lid, and caryatid handles, is engraved with one of the earliest American coats of arms, that of Isaac Addington. The maker of elegant embossed sugar boxes, chafing dishes, and salvers, as well as more mundane objects such as casters, cups, and spoons, Coney is noted also for the earliest American silver standish (Metropolitan). Triangular in shape and supported by three cast couchant lions, it was made for Governor Jonathan Belcher.

Coney is also known for the silver he made that is associated with Harvard. In 1701, Lieutenant-Governor Stoughton presented a massive grace cup to the College, fashioned by Coney in the baroque manner with a boldly gadrooned body, two tiers of gadrooning on its domed lid, and widely scrolled caryatid handles. For presentation to a tutor in 1716, he made a pair of faceted, octagonal candlesticks. A caudle cup made by Coney is believed to have inspired Oliver Wendell Holmes' "Ode on Lending a Punch Bowl." Among Coney's apprentices were the elder Paul Revere* and John Burt.* (M.G.F.)

Connelly, Pierce Francis (1841–after 1902).
Sculptor. He was born in Grand Coteau, La., however he spent his youth in Philadelphia, and then in Florence, Italy, and in England. He studied in Rome for several years before settling in Florence as an expatriate in the American colony. Early in his career he completed many portrait busts of the English aristocracy, but later he turned to allegorical works that demonstrated a romantic style and a minute attention to detail. Connelly's greatest exhibition was at the Philadelphia Centennial of 1876, when he showed eleven pieces, all representing subjects from history or literature; one of the most impressive of these was *Thetis Holding the Infant Achilles* (Metropolitan). Curiously enough, following the success of his exhibit, Connelly began to slip into obscurity. He sailed to New Zealand to paint landscapes. He returned to America, but little is recorded of any later sculptures. (W.C.)

Conner, Bruce (1933–   ).
Sculptor and filmmaker. Born in Pyramid Lake, Nev., he has been living on the West Coast since 1957. Conner has been strongly influenced by Wallace Berman's horrifying imagery; his earliest works are assemblages in which deformed figures in wax are wrapped in torn nylon and spotted with wax drippings. A trip to Mexico in 1961–62 led him to add images of commercialized religion to his art. These devotional subjects are often combined with pin-up nudes, illustrations from movie magazines, costume jewelry, lace, and human hair. Conner has said that he is not interested in transmuting his materials by means of traditional composition, thus setting himself apart from others who employ so-called "found objects." He has wanted to create a "primitive urban art" completely untouched by the ideals of high culture. By juxtaposing the sacred and the secular, the mass-produced and the decayed, he expresses both horror and nostalgia. *Couch* (1963) shows a disintegrated figure lying on a Victorian couch that is slit and smeared with grease.

Conner received a Ford Foundation grant to make films in 1964. Juxtaposing pornographic and children's movies, newsreels and his own footage, his films are similar in effect to his sculpture. Art critic Philip Leider has said that Conner's art reveals "a mentality which must obsessively recast all it observes into the imagery of the most unutterable horrors of our times." (C.R.)

Constructivism.
A movement of Russian origin, associated primarily with the sculptors Naum Gabo* and Antoine Pevsner. In 1913–14 these two brothers became acquainted with synthetic cubism* in Paris. Assimilating this style, they participated in the development of constructivism after their return to Moscow in 1917. Their theories appeared in 1920 in the manifesto of constructivism, titled the *Realist Manifesto,* which advocated an innovative, nonobjective art "based on two fundamental elements: space and time. . . . Dynamic and kinetic elements must be used to express the true nature of time." By 1923 both Gabo and Pevsner had moved to Germany, where Laszlo Moholy-Nagy soon carried constructivism to the Bauhaus,* the avant-garde school thoroughly in tune with Pevsner's desire to synthesize the plastic arts, including architecture.

The sculptural work of Gabo and Pevsner, geometric compositions of transparent materials and threads establishing planes in space, represent a typical aspect of constructivism, but the movement has been traced through very different plastic manifestations. The brothers' long-time friend, the Russian sculptor Alexander Archipenko, brought his cubist-and-constructivist-influenced figure style to the United States in 1923. Moholy-Nagy followed, and founded the New Bauhaus in Chicago in 1937. The next year Gabo himself visited America, and returned to live there following World War II.

The paths opened by constructivism have led to wide experimentation with geometric form in space, light, and motion by many American artists. For example, Gyorgy Kepes works in media ranging from painting to flashing lights; the sculptors Richard Lippold* and José de Rivera* are among many noted for their exploration of sculptural space; and painter Ellsworth Kelly* reflects constructivist concepts in his geometric panels creating colored environments. (D.W.S.)

Cooper, Peter (active 1717–25).
One of the first painters in Pennsylvania. His signed *South East Prospect of the City of Philadelphia* (c.1720, Library Company of Philadelphia) is not only a rare survival of early colonial landscape, but gives us a glimpse of the sign painters' art that brightened the aspect of every town in that day. The style is crude and indicates Cooper was probably an artisan by trade.

Cope, George (1855–1929).
Painter of still lifes whose best work is in the *trompe l'oeil* tradition. Cope was born near West Chester, Pa., where he spent most of his life. He began as a landscapist, but by 1890 had turned to still lifes of game birds, pipes, hunting costumes, and the like, frequently shown standing against flat backgrounds, as in *Fisherman's Accoutrements* (1887, Butler). These are often dramatic and are far more successful than his light-keyed, sometimes harshly colored tabletop still lifes.

Copley, John Singleton (1738–1815). Painter of portraits and historical subjects, acknowledged in his own day, as in ours, to be colonial America's leading artist. He was born in Boston, Mass., and in 1748 his widowed mother married Peter Pelham,* portrait painter, engraver, dancing master, and schoolteacher. He became the boy's instructor in painting and engraving, as Copley, in turn, became the teacher of his half-brother, Henry Pelham (1749–1806). In his formative years, Copley was influenced by Robert Feke,* John Greenwood,* and, most of all, by Joseph Blackburn.* He also made large and skillful use of mezzotint prototypes,* which he used as guides and to keep abreast of the latest fashions in portraiture. Above all, he dedicated himself to mastering techniques and to achieving material success. Portraiture was not enough. As a young man he thought of painting as "one of the most noble arts in the world," and hoped to win acclaim in its more admired branches, particularly historical subjects.

However, his livelihood in Boston came from portraiture, and at the age of fifteen his stiffly posed likenesses could hold their own with any in the homes of Boston. At nineteen he was a well-established professional. He had written to a Swiss pastelist, Liotard, asking for information on that medium, then making himself proficient in it. He worked skillfully in miniature. In his portraits he often depicted the sitter in a setting of his daily life. His style depended on careful drawing and the outlining of forms, the so-called "liney" manner for which he is known. Obviously looking forward to higher art forms, he had made careful studies of anatomy, and read widely in art theory. In 1765, he painted his *Boy with a Squirrel,* a portrait of Henry Pelham and, hopefully, sent it to London. He could not have dreamed of a more favorable response. Everyone—even the famous English portrait painter Sir Joshua Reynolds—praised the painting, declaring that it outshone all others in the Society of Artists exhibition, marveling that a work of such excellence should have come from the wilds of America. Benjamin West* wrote in congratulation, urging the artist to settle, as he himself had, in London. It was the first contact between these two, whose careers were to be curiously, but not happily, interrelated thereafter. Copley hesi-

tated. Here "I make as much as if I were a Raphael or a Correggio," he wrote. Unlike West, he made material rewards a first consideration. In 1769 he married and moved into a mansion on Beacon Hill. He was in New York and Philadelphia for the latter half of 1771. But not until 1774, when Revolutionary activity seemed to threaten his prosperity at home, did he sail for England. Placing art above politics, he remained neutral in the struggle, thus retaining his Boston properties and foregoing indemnities he might have received as a Loyalist refugee.

Before settling permanently in London he toured Italy, studying and copying its great masterpieces. Then he moved into historical painting, choosing subjects that would introduce him to good patronage as a portraitist also. These themes were of contemporary interest, and the characters portrayed well known. His dramatic *Watson and the Shark* (1778, Washington) celebrated the youthful adventure of a popular social and political figure. His *Death of the Earl of Chatham* (1779–80, Tate) showed a scene in the House of Lords with portraits of nearly fifty peers. Its composition was based upon West's enormously successful *Death of Wolfe* (1771), in which the viewer's eye is carried upward through the form of the fallen hero into an area of light. With this sensational picture Copley demonstrated that an artist could make a triple profit, exhibiting the work himself for an admission fee, selling rights of reproduction, and then selling the painting itself. He incurred, however, the ill-will of the Royal Academy, of which he became a member in 1776, for his refusal to exhibit it there. Also, some of the lords felt a loss of dignity in its being shown for private profit. Copley's finest historical work is his spirited *Death of Major Peirson* (1782–83, Tate), showing a young officer falling at the head of his charge against a raiding French force. These historical works shared the documentary interest and grandiloquence characteristic of many 18th-century popular works.

Copley's American style of portraiture, with that directness, intimacy, austerity and subdued coloring that strengthened the emphasis on human character, was one of the finest of early American art. In England, in his determination to win success, he moved into the more ornate and flowery rococo

manner and the bold brushstrokes that were in fashion. Thus the wide difference between such early works as *Governor and Mrs. Thomas Mifflin* (1773, Historical Society of Pennsylvania), *Mrs. John Winthrop* (1773, Metropolitan), *Samuel Adams* (1771, Boston), or *Paul Revere* (1765–70, Boston), and his later *Viscount Sidmouth* (St. Louis), or *Daughters of George III* (1785, Buckingham Palace). In his last years he was embittered by declining patronage, due in part to the slowness with which he worked and in part to his character.

(C.C.S.)

Cornell, Joseph (1903–73). Sculptor known for his poetic boxed ensembles and collages. Although one of the first American artists acknowledged by the Parisian surrealists and published abroad, his style remains totally personal and not readily associated with any specific art movement. Cornell was born in Nyack, N.Y., and attended Phillips Academy in Andover, Mass. In 1929 his family moved to Flushing, N.Y., to a very modest house, where he remained until his death.

His life during the 1920s was occupied partly with business and partly in the exercise of his strong interest in the arts, especially opera. In his trips to Manhattan, Cornell explored not only the museums and theatres, but also a downtown quarter rich in second-hand bookstores. He began collecting "Americana" and what he called "ephemera"—old books, engravings, and objects that evoked other eras, other times, other spaces.

In 1931, the surrealist movement, then prevalent in Europe, found a New York proponent in the art dealer Julien Levy. Cornell quickly became a regular at the gallery opened by Levy, where he met other young artists. There he also probably encountered Max Ernst's celebrated book of juxtaposed engravings, *La Femme 100 Têtes.* Ernst's sly juxtaposition of unrelated images, culled from books of old engravings, inspired Cornell to begin making collages. His earliest works were included in a group show in 1932, and later that year he exhibited the prototypes of all his forms—small boxes in which were juxtaposed memorabilia and objects, frequently Victorian bibelots. By 1936, when his works were included in the important exhibition "Fantastic Art, Dada and Surrealism," Cornell had estab-

1. **John Singleton Copley.** The Copley Family, c.1785. National Gallery of Art, Washington, D.C.
2. **John Singleton Copley.** Watson and the Shark, 1778. National Gallery of Art, Washington, D.C.
3. **John Singleton Copley.** Governor and Mrs. Thomas Mifflin, 1773. Historical Society of Pennsylvania, Philadelphia.

lished his inimitable form: the glassed box with its contents arranged to provoke free associations, repeatedly including a clay pipe, an egg shape, fragments of maps, signs of the zodiac, colored sand, and rings, He has also projected historic opera singers and ballerinas in boxed homages, and he has often dipped into art history as in *The Medici Slot Machine* (1942). In the latter he used a severe composition of rectangular divisions, the central portion dominated by a Moroni portrait of a Renaissance prince, the side divisions containing symbolic references to his life and its furnishings. Cornell's passion for the retrieval of history has led to many nostalgic evocations, such as boxes using the romantic names of hotels with hints of the ephemera of the period.

"Shadow boxes," he wrote in 1948, "become poetic theatres or settings wherein are metamorphosed the elements of a childhood pastime." In the early 1950s, however, Cornell's shadow boxes often transcended the idea of a stage setting and verged on pure abstraction. A number of boxes were made up of a white wood grid of small compartments in which white cubes moved freely. The mysteries of these boxes were matched by others in which he explored dovecotes and their suggested but unseen population of birds. Cornell's poetic allusions, sometimes printed on pieces of papers, sometimes contained in a title or a visual hint, have almost always related to 19th-century Romantic poetry. On the other hand, his exquisite play with materials, such as colored sands shifting freely in a box, or rings that slide along a bar, was decisively plastic. This unique fusion of literary and plastic means has won him his prominent position in American art.

Cornell's works have been exhibited internationally. He has had many special museum exhibitions, including at the Pasadena Art Museum, Cal. (1967), the retrospective at the Guggenheim Museum, New York City (1967), and a special room at the Metropolitan Museum, New York City (1970) was devoted to his work. Cornell was also the author of several celebrated films, some of which were compiled surrealistically with discarded Hollywood footage. (D.A.)

Cox, Kenyon (1856–1919).
Academic portrait and mural painter. Cox was born in Warren, Ohio, and re-

ceived his training in Paris with Gérôme and Carolus-Duran. Returning to the United States, he began painting large nude studies and symbolic figures in the manner of the Paris Salons, but he found relatively little encouragement for his academic productions until the World's Columbian Exposition in Chicago (1893) started a wave of mural decoration across the country. Cox was given commissions at Chicago, the Library of Congress, Bowdoin College, and the Appellate Court of New York. He placed great emphasis on line, using restrained color, and employed classically-derived types, poses, and compositions. His decorations were received with enthusiasm by eclectic architects and conservative critics, though today he no longer appears to have the impeccable draftsmanship and composition, or convincing sentiment he was once credited with. He became a most eloquent spokesman for the classic view, writing *The Classic Point of View* (1911) and *Concerning Painting* (1917), lecturing actively and denouncing realism, impressionism, and modern tendencies in general. Cox was also prominent as an illustrator and teacher. (D.W.S.)

Cram, Ralph Adams, see Period Revival.

Crane, Bruce (1857–1937).
Landscape painter. Crane studied with A. H. Wyant* and in Europe. His early work moved from a literal and detailed, Barbizon-school-influenced style to the tonalism that characterized the later works of such painters as Dwight Tryon* and J. Francis Murphy.* His range of mood and subject was, however, narrower than theirs; he was known particularly for scenes of Connecticut fields in autumnal grays and yellows. Crane joined the Society of American Artists* in 1881 and the National Academy of Design* in 1889. His greatest popularity began in the late 1890s, when he won the Webb prize at the Society of American Artists, the first of some ten major awards given him during the next two decades.

Crawford, Ralston (1906–   ).
Painter. Born in St. Catherine, Ontario, Crawford sailed all the Great Lakes as a boy and before he was fourteen had developed special affection for the industrial architecture of harbor cities. This ultimately became a leading theme

in his painting. In 1926–27 he also sailed the Caribbean and the Pacific on a tramp steamer; then he came ashore, studied at the Otis Art Institute in Los Angeles, and then worked at the Disney Studios. In the late 1920s Crawford studied at the Pennsylvania Academy of the Fine Arts and at the Barnes Foundation in Merion, Pa., where, as he said, his eyes were first opened to the possibilities of contemporary art. After spending two years abroad, he had his first one-man show, at the Maryland Institute of Art, in 1934. During the 1930s he began working in a more realistic manner, with emphasis on the rural scene. At this time he taught at the Art Academy of Cincinnati, Ohio, and at the School of Fine Arts in Buffalo, N.Y.

During World War II Crawford served as chief of the visual presentation unit of the Army Air Force Weather Division. In the 1940s and 1950s he returned to a cubist-precisionist manner, that is, to the use of flat colors, angular shapes, and crisp outlines, retaining an abstracted imagery of ships, grain elevators, factories, and machines. In 1947 he was guest director of the Honolulu School of Arts. During the 1950s and 1960s he became interested in the visual imagery of the jazz world and made many trips to New Orleans to photograph the musicians there.

In the early 1950s Crawford did intensive work in lithography in Paris and later taught at the University of Colorado and other schools. The Milwaukee Art Center gave him a retrospective show in 1958. (A.F.)

Crawford, Thomas (c.1813–57).
Sculptor. Trained as a stonecutter in the stoneyard of John Frazee* and Robert Launitz in his native New York City, Crawford became one of the most famous American sculptors of the mid-19th century. After about three years he went to Europe in 1835, believing, as many did, that the art of sculpture could be learned only in Italy. He settled in Rome, where he lived for nearly twenty years. Initially he did only occasional portrait busts, but his first serious attempt at a mythological subject, *Orpheus* (1839), brought him much acclaim in Europe and America. Crawford was very much influenced by Roman antiquities and the neoclassicism* of the famous Danish sculptor Berthel Thorwaldsen, his neighbor and good friend. During the 1840s Crawford's

work was stylistically even more neo-classical than that of the other two American sculptors working in Italy—Horatio Greenough* and Hiram Powers.* His *Hebe and Ganymede* (1842) is an example of his adaptation of classical themes and forms to his own purposes. By 1842 he had so many commissions that he employed numerous workers to do his carving; thus, his work was often lofty in conception but undistinguished in execution.

On returning briefly to America in 1849, Crawford won the commission for the Washington Monument in Richmond, Va. The statue, a bronze equestrian figure atop a central pedestal, was to be surrounded by six of Virginia's famous sons at the base. After it was cast in Munich the fame of the equestrian statue established him as one of the nation's foremost sculptors. He was deluged with other large commissions, such as the bronze *Beethoven* (1853–55) for Boston's Academy of Music. But his greatest commission was for the sculptures for the pediment of the Senate wing of the U.S. Capitol. Crawford's theme for this multi-figured composition was the triumph of a great civilization over a barbaric way of life. In his enormous studio in Rome he modeled the many groups of pioneers and Indians in clay and turned them over to Italian artisans to cast in plaster and then carve in marble. Meanwhile, he began work on the clay models for the bronze doors for the House wing of the U.S. Capitol, and on the model for the colossal figure of *Armed Liberty,* which now crowns the dome of the Capitol.

But by 1856 he was already experiencing the pains of a tumor behind his eye, and work soon became difficult. Within a year he died, leaving a host of large unfinished commissions. Randolph Rogers* completed the Washington monument in Richmond, William Rinehart* finished the bronze doors for the House of Representatives, and Clark Mills* supervised the casting in bronze of the *Armed Liberty.* Crawford, along with Horatio Greenough and Hiram Powers, occupies a special place in American sculpture as one of the pioneers who carried art beyond the artisan-craftsman tradition that dominated it before 1830. (W.C.)

Crayon, The.

The first American periodical devoted to art criticism. Even though its life span

1

2

1. *Joseph Cornell.* Orphans of the Storm.

2. *Joseph Cornell.* Sand Fountain, *1953. Both, Allan Stone Gallery, N.Y.*

Crewelwork

was a short one (1855–61), it had considerable impact on American taste. It numbered among its contributors leading figures in the arts and literature of both England and America. *The Crayon* included, besides art criticism, essays, letters, and romances, such important series as Asher B. Durand's* *Letters on Landscape Painting,* which expressed the esthetic of the Hudson River School.* The magazine and its editors were particularly devoted to realism and to the pre-Raphaelite* movement. Under the influence of the English pre-Raphaelites, the editor sought to explain and to champion their theories: that a higher moral and spiritual state was achieved by adherence to nature, intensity of thought, and elaborate finish and realism.

(T.E.S.)

Crewelwork.

This embroidery, popular among the upper classes in colonial America, derives its name from the twisted worsted yarn with which designs were stitched on cotton, linen, or wool, or on combinations of two of those fibers such as linsey-woolsey. Traditional motifs for crewelwork were derived from such Near Eastern patterns as paisley or "tree of life." In general American crewelwork of the 18th century is cruder and bolder than its English prototype and, perhaps because yarns were scarce in the colonies, tends to have larger unworked areas (making it especially attractive to the modern eye). As in England, crewel-embroidered fabrics were most often used as chair coverings or bed hangings. Good examples of the latter are preserved in the pink bedroom of the Prentis House at the Shelburne Museum in Shelburne, Vt.

(M.J.G.)

Cropsey, Jasper Francis (1823–1900).

Popular member of the Hudson River School,* best known for his autumnal landscapes. Cropsey was born on Staten Island, N.Y. At the age of fifteen he began a five-year apprenticeship to the architect Joseph Trench of New York, and during the same period also studied painting briefly. Failing to find architectural commissions, he devoted increasing time to painting scenes near Greenwood Lake, N.J., and in the White Mountains, the Catskills, and on the Hudson River. He made an extended trip to Europe in 1847–49, and in 1857

1

2

1. *Jasper Francis Cropsey.* Autumn on the Hudson River, *1860. National Gallery of Art, Washington, D.C. (gift of the Avalon Foundation).*
2. *Imogen Cunningham.* Portrait of Morris Graves, *1958, photograph.*

128

he began a six-year stay in London. He settled permanently in Hastings-on-Hudson, N.Y. in 1864.

Cropsey's early works are often dark and turbulent, and his rich handling of paint reflects the influence of Thomas Cole.* By the 1850s Cropsey had developed his own more sharply realistic style, in which he typically depicted pastoral, autumn landscapes. Although his paintings are repetitive in their composition and bright coloring, Cropsey gained considerable reputation in his own day both in America and in England, where his *Autumn on the Hudson River* (1860, Washington) was highly praised. The painter's style remained virtually static throughout his career, and he worked in the realistic mode into the 1890s. Cropsey was one of the best draftsmen of the Hudson River School; he is known both for his careful pencil studies and for his watercolors. In addition, he painted a few fine still lifes during the 1860s, and he continued to practice architecture; his best-known commissions in the latter field were his Sixth Avenue elevated stations in New York, which were executed in the high Victorian style. (T.E.S.)

Cubism.

A movement, centered in Paris, and headed by Pablo Picasso and Georges Braque, which passed through its initial period during the years preceding World War I but had a deep impact on most of the abstract painting of this century. Picasso had absorbed lessons from French symbolism* and African sculpture; Braque had passed through a period of vigorous simplification under the influence of fauvism.* Both Picasso and Braque were particularly influenced by the paintings of Paul Cézanne, who advocated seeing "in nature the cylinder, sphere, and cone," and distorted his forms to resolve them into planes related to the plane of the canvas. During cubism's "analytical" phase (roughly 1909–12), the painters progressively abstracted their subjects, reducing them to geometric planes that overlapped or were made transparent to indicate depth. Subjects were portrayed as if seen from several viewpoints simultaneously. Color was reduced to a limited scale, largely of browns and grays. Finally the subject (often a figure or still life) was dissolved in the lines or planes on the canvas, but the "motif" in nature remained as the starting point of the

cubist analysis; the paintings never became completely abstract or "non-objective."

The "synthetic" phase of cubism, which overlapped the analytic phase, involved the pasting of actual objects (printed papers and cloths, pieces of wood, etc.) on the picture, employing them as colored and textured shapes combined with forms abstracted from objects in nature.

Among the Americans, Max Weber* adopted cubist devices perhaps as early as 1911, and within the next two or three years, Marsden Hartley,* Arthur B. Davies,* Man Ray,* Morton Schamberg,* and Alfred H. Maurer* followed suit. Pursuing different paths but stemming from cubism's initial geometrical abstractions were Patrick Bruce* Lyonel Feininger,* Joseph Stella* John Marin,* Abraham Walkowitz* and Charles Demuth,* and the synchromists (MacDonald-Wright* and Russell*).

Meanwhile, in Paris, Picasso, Braque, Matisse, Gris, Léger, and others employed cubist elements in their works both before and after World War I. Geometric, more or less abstract lines and planes, often combined with strong, flat colors and expressive distortions, continued to be characteristic of the work of many European and American artists for two generations. In the diversity of contemporary art, cubism's heritage is still everywhere apparent, both as an attitude toward subject matter and as a grammar for the treatment of form and composition. (D.W.S.)

Cummings, Thomas Seir (1804–94).

Portrait and miniature painter. He was born at Bath, England, and brought to New York City as a child. There, in 1818, his drawings were praised by the wandering English painter, Augustus Earl, encouraging the boy to continue in a career in art. He became a student and, for a while, a partner of Henry Inman.* He was one of the founders, in 1826, of the National Academy of Design,* continuing as vice-president, teacher, and, in 1865, as the leading promoter of its building, which was long a landmark of the city. In 1866 he moved to Mansfield, Conn., and in 1889 to Hackensack, N.J. He was a portraitist of charm and technical skill. His works belong to the period when miniatures had become mainly portraiture rather than a distinct branch of painting. His miniature *The Bracelet: Portrait of the Artist's Wife*

(1835, Metropolitan) is as an excellent example of his work. (C.C.S.)

Cunningham, Imogen (1883–).

A photographer whose portraits rank among the most expressive of the 20th century. Born in Portland, Ore., she grew up in Seattle where, inspired by a magazine portfolio of Gertrude Käsebier's* work, she began to photograph in 1901. She entered the University of Washington in 1903 and majored in chemistry. An apprenticeship (1907–09) in the Seattle studio of the noted photographer of American Indians, Edward S. Curtis, made her a master of photographic techniques. She was awarded a scholarship in 1909 and studied photographic chemistry in Dresden, Germany. There she perfected a lead salt substitute for the expensive platinum print process. On the return trip to Seattle (where she opened a portrait studio in 1910) she met Alvin Langdon Coburn and Alfred Stieglitz,* whose pictorial ideas influenced her early style. The Brooklyn Institute in New York gave her a major exhibition in 1912, followed in March 1914 by the publication of a portfolio in the respected *Wilson's Photographic Magazine.* In 1915 she married the etcher Roi Partridge and moved to San Francisco in 1917, then to Oakland, Cal., in 1920.

Restricted by family duties, in the following decade she photographed primarily the plant forms in her small garden. Edward Weston,* whom she had met in 1917, selected ten of her plant photographs for the American section of the important exhibition, "Film und Foto," in Stuttgart, Germany, in 1929. Her friendship with Weston led to membership in the influential f/64* group and one-man exhibition in San Francisco at the de Young Memorial Museum in 1932. For *Vanity Fair* magazine she created (1932–34) a notable series of portraits of film stars, including James Cagney, Cary Grant, Spencer Tracy, and Wallace Beery. Characterized by a direct, intensely honest approach, her portraits probe the spiritual essence of the subject. Thus she photographed the West Coast painter Morris Graves in 1958 in a barren corner of a garden with the aridity of the sun-dappled rocks behind him echoing perfectly the asceticism of his thin, bearded face and haunted eyes.

1. **Currier & Ives.** Early Winter, *1869,*
lithograph. Museum of the City of
New York.

2. **John Steuart Curry.** Baptism in
Kansas, *1928. Whitney Museum of*
American Art, N.Y.

Cunningham's work has been exhibited in major museums, and important collections are held by the Smithsonian Institution, the Library of Congress, George Eastman House, and the Museum of Modern Art. She continues to live and work in San Francisco with customary gusto. In her late eighties she wrote to a friend, "Things change with the years, but as yet I do not think of any possibilities except those that might be good." (D.L.)

Currier & Ives (active 1835–1907).
The most popular and successful of American printmakers. The firm was founded in New York City in 1835 by Nathaniel Currier (1813–88), a lithographer. Currier was born in Roxbury, Mass., where he was apprenticed to a lithographer at fifteen. After five years in Boston, he went to Philadelphia, and then in 1834 to New York City, where he set up his own business. His graphic renderings of events which captured the public imagination—fires, shipwrecks, and the like—quickly became popular; the prints were handsome, and they filled a need for inexpensive art works whose subjects had universal appeal. Currier's early prints are usually marked "N. Currier" and carry the firm's New York address. The firm became "Currier & Ives" in 1857, when its bookkeeper James Merritt Ives (1824–95) became general manager and a partner. Born in New York City, where he learned lithography, Ives was a skillful draftsman, as can be seen, for example in his *Old Age The Season of Rest.* His keen sense of quality and saleability led to the heyday of the company; for many years thereafter, Currier and Ives accounted for perhaps three-quarters of the American print market. Pedlars and agents sold the lithographs all over the United States and in England at from $.20 to $3.00 apiece, depending on the size.

For many years (1866–96) the main workshop was located at 33 Spruce Street, New York City. The regular staff included one man who prepared the lithographic stones, up to seven lithographers, and perhaps a dozen women who tinted the prints with watercolors. Experiments were made in printing skies and backgrounds in color on some prints, but most continued to be made in black and white and then hand-colored, or sometimes, sold "plain." The designs for the prints came from various sources. Some were made by staff artists such as Mrs. Fanny Palmer (c.1812–76), whose name appears on a number of prints; others were designed by lesser painters, who received no credit. Many were based on well-known American paintings, both old and contemporary, including historical scenes and portraits by John Trumbull* and Gilbert Stuart,* and marine, landscape, and genre views by such well-known artists of the time as James Buttersworth,* Arthur F. Tait,* and George Durrie.*

Many of the most popular prints, such as *Home for Thanksgiving* (after Durrie), catered to the pastoral ideas of an increasingly urban middle class. Though the early prints played something of a journalistic role, reflecting current events, the later ones increasingly stressed only the happy, prosperous aspects of American life. The heyday of the firm was the mid-19th century; by the 1880s its hand processes had become outdated because of new, cheaper printing techniques such as chromolithography and photoengraving. Before the firm closed in 1907, it had produced about seven thousand different prints, of which the most common subjects were landscape views, historic events, sentimental or allegorical scenes, portraits, and sports—especially horse racing and boating scenes. Although Currier & Ives prints have been considered merely popular art, they provide a unique guide to American culture and taste in the 19th century; they are also rich in both the sources and echoes of the work of America's "serious" artists. (T.E.S.)

Curry, John Steuart (1897–1946).
Painter. Curry was born in Dunavant, Kan., the son of Scottish Presbyterian farm people, and he never forgot his midwestern roots. He studied at the Kansas City Art Institute and the Art Institute of Chicago, and, after successfully launching a career as magazine illustrator in the East, went to Paris in 1926 to study with the Russian academician, Basil Schoukaieff. On his return in 1927 Curry began a series of paintings on midwestern themes, including the famous *Baptism in Kansas* (1928, Whitney). This series, on which a considerable part of Curry's reputation still rests, had much to do with creating the school of midwestern regionalism of which Grant Wood* and Thomas Hart Benton* were other leading exponents.

In 1932, Curry toured with Ringling Brothers Circus, making a series of paintings on circus life, and in the same year he began teaching at the Art Students League and at Cooper Union. In 1936 he was appointed artist-in-residence at the Agricultural College of the University of Wisconsin and held that position until his death. In the 1930s and 1940s he also painted murals for the Department of Justice Building in Washington, D.C. and for the Kansas State Capitol and the University of Wisconsin. In the midwestern pictures of his finest period he is particularly concerned with the terror and spectacle of storm and flood and human tragedies that resulted in mass hysteria. (A.F.)

Cut Glass, see Glass Cutting and Engraving.

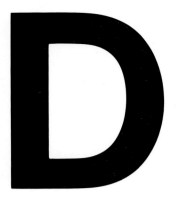

D

Dada.

An international movement that climaxed modernism's rejection of traditional art forms and expressed the disillusionment of many artists during World War I. Essentially a literary movement, dada incorporated all the arts in its antiesthetic, antirational nihilism. Its first center was in neutral Zurich, where, in 1916, the word "dada" was reportedly picked at random from a dictionary, and the first dada manifesto was published. The Zurich dada group (identified with the Café Voltaire, where they often met) included poets Hugo Ball and Tristan Tzara, and artists Jean Arp, Max Ernst, and Kurt Schwitters. By 1917 the movement had spread to Germany, and from 1920–22 its center was Paris. During the next two years many of its supporters joined the surrealist movement, headed by the French writer André Breton.

The first wave of dada in America was simultaneous with that in Zurich, though the group, led by Marcel Duchamp* in New York City, was much smaller. Duchamp had been one of the first to challenge all accepted concepts of art, and by 1916 Man Ray* and Morton Schamberg* were producing novel works reflecting his influence. In 1917 Duchamp submitted a urinal as a so-called "ready-made" to the exhibition of the newly-founded Society of Independent Artists,* and in the same year he produced dada publications with Ray, the French painter Francis Picabia, and collector Walter Arensberg.

Influenced by cubism* and futurism,* dada artists utilized "found objects," trash and paper in collages and assemblages, and exhibited ready-mades —objects from the every-day environment presented intact or slightly changed. Dada, because it liberated art from tradition and created a totally new way of seeing the ordinary, the accidental, and the intuitive, cre-ated the base upon which much of later 20th-century art was built.   (D.W.S.)

Daguerreotype.

The forerunner of modern photography, it was invented by Louis J. M. Daguerre (1787–1851), working with his partner, Nicéphore Niepce (1765–1833). When the daguerreotype was introduced in a publication of 1839, it caused an immediate, worldwide sensation; by the end of 1839, Daguerre's book on the process had been translated into many languages, including English. It was brought to America late in 1839 by Samuel F. B. Morse* and J. W. Draper, who themselves had been working on similar processes. Despite the bulky apparatus required, the complex process by which the silvered copper plates were developed over heated mercury, and the long exposures and bright sunlight that were necessary, the daguerreotype had considerable impact upon American painters. The process actually drove the portrait miniaturist out of business. It affected the way portrait painters saw their subject, and as the process improved, it was used by landscape painters such as Albert Bierstadt* and Fitz Hugh Lane.*   (T.E.S.)

Dallin, Cyrus Edwin (1861–1944).

Sculptor, best known for his sculptures of Indians. He was born in Utah and grew up surrounded by the West and its cowboys and Indians. In 1880 he went to Boston, where he studied with Truman Bartlett, and then to the Académie Julien in Paris. In Paris in 1889 Dallin produced the first of his four great equestrian Indian subjects, *The Signal of Peace* (bronze, Lincoln Park, Chicago). This brought him much attention, as did the second of the series, *The Medicine Man* (1898, Fairmount Park, Philadelphia), which won a gold medal at the Paris Exposition of 1900.

1

2

1. **Bruce Davidson.** *From photo essay,* *"Brooklyn Gang," photograph.* Magnum Photo Library, N.Y.
2. **Daguerreotype.** *Unknown photographer.*
3. **Daguerreotype.** *Unknown photographer.*
   Both, George Eastman House, Rochester, N.Y.

3

The third piece in the series, *The Protest,* was created in perishable staff (plaster and straw) material for the Louisiana Purchase Exposition in St. Louis in 1904, but the fourth of the group, *The Appeal to the Great Spirit* (1908, Boston), was cast in bronze. All of these are rendered with sympathetic feeling for the plight of the Indian and in a naturalistic style free of the decorative excesses that often characterized the work of Dallin's French contemporaries.

Dallin returned to Boston in 1900 and throughout his career continued to produce sculptures portraying the American Indian. One of his last major pieces was the bronze equestrian *Paul Revere* (1940, City of Boston). (W.C.)

Darley, Felix Octavius Carr (1822–88). One of the most prolific of American draftsmen. Born in Philadelphia, Pa., he lived in New York City after 1848. For forty years, beginning about 1845, he did book illustrations, beginning as a humorist but becoming a serious interpreter of history. He had a sure ability to imagine and dramatize scenes from the American past. In addition to his many magazine illustrations, he illustrated more than two hundred books. Some of his first designs were for lithographs; later he drew for both the steel engravers and wood engravers. He was the best known of the early American illustrators, and prominent among the artists who with pen, pencil, and brush (and with the collaboration of skilled engravers) produced a movement of distinction in American book illustration after 1840.

Dasburg, Andrew (1887–   ). Painter. Born in Paris, Dasburg was brought to the United States at the age of five. He studied at the Art Students League* with Kenyon Cox,* Frank Du Mond and Birge Harrison, and had additional instruction from Robert Henri.* In 1909 Dasburg returned to Paris, where he was much impressed by the work of Matisse and Cézanne. Returning to the United States two years later, he taught for several seasons at the Art Students League. He had two cubist paintings and one piece of sculpture (the only one he ever produced) in the Armory Show* of 1913.

Dasburg went to Taos, N.M., in 1916 to visit his friend, Maurice Sterne, and he returned there from New York for part of each year until 1933, when he settled there permanently. For a brief time he was involved there in the conduct of a Spanish-American Trading Post, which dealt in native weavings and works of art. In 1932 he was awarded a Guggenheim Fellowship to work in Mexico, but most of his effort since the 1930s has gone into somewhat Cézannesque interpretations of the southwestern scene, such as *New Mexican Village* (Santa Fe Art Museum) and *Road to Lamy* (Metropolitan), and many still lifes in the same manner. From 1935 to 1946 he was unable to work because of Addison's disease, but he resumed painting in 1946, and recently has produced a large number of semiabstract drawings of southwestern motifs.

Dasburg has received three awards at the Carnegie International and one at the Pan-American Exhibition in Los Angeles. In 1927, while serving on the jury for the Carnegie International, he was responsible for the first recognition granted John Kane, and thereby gave great impetus to the entire folk-art movement in the United States. (A.F.)

Davidson, Bruce (1934–   ). Photographer. Born in Oak Park, Ill. While in high school, he assisted a local commercial photographer. He studied photography at the Rochester Institute of Technology, N.Y., followed by courses in philosophy and graphic arts at Yale University with Alexey Brodovitch, Herbert Matter, and Joseph Albers.* After service in the U.S. Army, he free-lanced as a photographer in Paris and New York until 1958, when he was awarded a Guggenheim Fellowship to produce a study of the American Negro. His photo essays, such as "The Widow of Montmartre," "The Clown," "Brooklyn Gang," and "England," deal in straightforward but somewhat romantic terms with man's destiny as shaped by social and physical limitations imposed by society. He has had a number of one-man shows since 1965, including those at George Eastman House (1965), the Museum of Modern Art (1966), and the Smithsonian Institution (1971). He is a photographer of people, with a special interest in clarifying the relationships between the human condition and the milieu in which people live. His most extensive essay, published as a book, *East 100th Street,* conveys in beautifully made prints the pessimism of ghetto inhabitants and their resentment of the limitations of their existence. Throughout, he shows an acute sensitivity to the spiritual undercurrents of black and Puerto-Rican family life. (V.D.C.)

Davidson, Jo (1883–1952).

Primarily a portrait sculptor; in the period between the two world wars, he was one of the best of those working in a bold naturalistic style. Born in New York, N.Y., Davidson had little formal instruction, and even after going to Paris in 1907 he worked mainly on his own. He returned to New York and began specializing in portrait busts. In 1918 he commenced a series of portraits of wartime leaders of the Allies; among the finest of these are the likenesses of General Pershing and Marshal Foch. Fascinated with the personalities behind world events, he declared that sculpting portraits "became an obsession." Following the war he made portraits of world leaders who had gathered in Versailles for the peace treaties. In the course of his career his subjects included such eminent individuals as Mahatma Ghandi, Franklin D. Roosevelt, Woodrow Wilson, Gertrude Stein, Rudyard Kipling, and James Joyce. He also did full-length bronze statues of Will Rogers (1939, U.S. Capitol) and Walt Whitman (Bear Mountain State Park, N.Y.). In a period dominated by the rise of abstract and nonobjective art, he infused new vitality into the naturalistic tradition. (W.C.)

Davies, Arthur Bowen (1862–1928).

Painter and printmaker. He was born in Utica, N.Y., where he studied art at the age of fifteen with the landscape painter Dwight Williams. When his family moved to Chicago in 1878, he attended the Chicago Academy of Design, then went to Mexico to work as an engineering draftsman from 1880–c.82. Returning to Chicago, he engaged briefly in business while studying at the Art Institute. In 1886 he moved to New York City, where he made his living as a magazine illustrator and attended classes at the Gotham Art Students and Art Students League.*

Davies left most of his work undated and undocumented, but a few landscapes are assignable to this early period, and they show that from the beginning he worked in a highly sensitive and decorative manner (*Along the Erie*

Canal, 1890, Phillips). In 1893 the collector Benjamin Altman sent Davies to Europe for independent study. The young artist absorbed influences from romantic, poetic, and decorative painting wherever he encountered it—from the Venetians (especially Giorgione), from the primitives generally, from Delacroix and Puvis de Chavannes, Arnold Böcklin, the pre-Raphaelites, and James Whistler.* Davies henceforth drew on a wide variety of sources but characteristically painted dreamlike canvases of idealized figures in idyllic settings. The themes and titles often served as fragmentary or even mysterious allusions to poems or legends. After he returned from Europe, his richly-applied pigment and poetic approach recalled particularly the earlier Venetians and such contemporary romantics as Albert P. Ryder.* He had his first one-man show in 1896 and soon found enough patrons to enable him to spend all his time painting.

Gradually he worked toward elongated horizontal compositions punctuated by figures in dancelike poses, as in *Dancing Children* (1902, Brooklyn). and then "to precise and dainty design and to pearly tints diaphanously spread," the critic-painter Bryson Burroughs wrote. A less intuitive, more calculating design became evident in his paintings following a trip to California in 1905: these reflected the grandeur of the western landscape as in his famous *Unicorns* (1906, Metropolitan). His friezelike compositions of dancing figures culminated in a work such as *Crescendo* (1910, Whitney). The style and romantic sentiment of Davies' work through this period suggest a basic conservatism enlivened by touches of fantasy, but his nature was paradoxical. His art was both intuitive and intellectual; it was rooted in past styles but he was keenly interested in the avantgarde. His personality seemed in harmony with his mild, decorous manner but it hid totally unsuspected depths. His sympathy with the more adventurous younger men led to his exhibiting with The Eight* in 1908, though his art was at the opposite pole from New York realism. His deepest sympathies, in fact, lay with even more radical art, as he demonstrated when he accepted the responsibility for organizing the Armory Show* and chose the most significant manifestations of European modernism with a sure eye, while shaping the un-

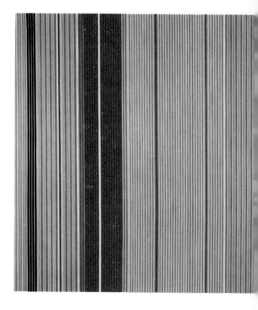

1. *Arthur Bowen Davies.* Crescendo, *1910. Whitney Museum of American Art, N.Y.*

2. *Arthur Bowen Davies.* Unicorns, 1906. *Metropolitan Museum of Art, N.Y. (bequest of Lizzy P. Bliss).*
3. *Gene Davis.* Blueprint for Riveters, 1967. *Fischbach Gallery, N.Y.*

wieldy exhibition with a firm hand. The affair came off triumphantly, but Davies' authoritarian and secretive manner subsequently led to serious rifts with fellow artists. The years 1912 and 1913 were largely taken up by Armory Show matters, and his painting soon reflected the influence of its cubist-related styles. Thus his figures were sometimes superficially faceted, sometimes broken into large geometric forms interpenetrated by curves sweeping across the canvas, as in *Day of Good Fortune* (1916, private collection). His experiments in abstraction affected all his subsequent work, strengthening the relationship of the inner rhythms of figures and their settings.

In 1918 he revived a long-standing interest in lithography, and some of his most successful and imaginative figure compositions were developed in this medium, or in aquatint and etching, which he also employed in his later years. During the 1920s his interest in a variety of technical processes led to work in chalk on black paper and to designs for rugs and tapestries for the Gobelins in France. At the same time, he explored theories about Greek art, and sometimes borrowed Greek motifs. In 1924, following a heart attack, he recuperated abroad. Thereafter until his death in 1928 he painted flowing, rhythmic landscapes in France and Italy: an example is *The Umbrian Mountains* (1925, Corcoran). (D.W.S.)

Davis, Alexander Jackson (1803–92).
Architect, born in New York, N.Y. He worked as a printer's assistant in Florida and New York, and in 1823 he drew a series of handsome architectural views for a New York bookseller, A. T. Goodrich. While apprenticed to the architect J. C. Brady, Davis traveled to New England in 1827–28, and there made further architectural renderings of the highest quality. Ithiel Town,* the New York architect, employed him as a draftsman, and finding him highly skilled, made him a partner in 1829. They undertook many jobs of considerable importance; outstanding was the New York Customs House (1832–42) on Wall Street, which they decorated with the Greek Doric order and a central dome. The firm also designed state capitols in North Carolina (1831), Indiana (1832–35), Illinois (1837, altered 1866), Ohio (with T. U. Walter and others, 1839), and other public buildings,

before Davis decided to establish his own office, in 1843.

Davis' innumerable commissions for houses, churches, and public buildings show excellent taste and an ability to scale ornamental details to fit the whole design. By studying the Greek orders and learning how to apply them to contemporary ends, he retained Greek simplicity and elegance while satisfying the functional needs of the time. During his long career he dabbled in various styles: in the 1830s and 1840s he did several Gothic buildings, and in the 1850s he designed some houses in the Italian Villa style and a few public buildings with Renaissance orders.

Davis was a founder of the American Institution of Architects in 1836, and, in 1857, its successor, the important American Institute of Architects. In a way, Davis' drawings are more important than his completed buildings because they are such exquisite works of art. Many of them are at the New York Historical Society and the Metropolitan Museum of Art. Davis referred to himself as an "architectural composer," accenting beauty of pictorial composition even more than structure and function. (P.F.N.)

Davis, Gene (1920–   ).
Painter. Davis was born in Washington, D.C., and spent most of the 1940s as a journalist there. He had no formal training in art and did not begin painting until 1950. It was not until 1958–60 that he developed the edge-to-edge paintings of vertical stripes that have become characteristic of his work. These early works were quite small and employed relatively subdued colors; Davis alternated them with paintings of horizontal stripes and with horizontal bar paintings made up of separate canvases. Ultimately, however, he settled on vertical stripes as his vehicle for color. He writes: "There is no simpler way to divide up a canvas than with straight lines at equal intervals. This enables the viewer to forget the structure and see the color for itself. I never vary the width of the stripes within a single painting. If I did, the eye would immediately become overly aware of the composition." Davis' stripes vary in width from one-half inch to eight inches, and in his later work he turned to much larger paintings—often twenty feet or more in length. Many of these later canvases employ vibrating color and optical ef-

fects. These larger paintings have resulted in increasingly complex rhythms and patterns of color, with Davis becoming more and more involved with placement and sequence. At the opposite end of the scale are his "micro-paintings" (1966), usually not larger than two inches square and often grouped on the walls of a room. Davis has had one-man shows at the Corcoran Gallery, the San Francisco Museum, and the Washington Gallery of Modern Art. (E.C.G.)

Davis, Joseph H. (active 1832–38).

Itinerant watercolor portraitist who worked around Dover, N.H., and nearby Maine. He is best known for his double portraits of man and wife seated in painted wooden chairs at either side of a boldly grained or marbleized table, but his style is also readily recognizable in pictures of single male and female standing figures. Davis' interiors were notable for brightly patterned floors, bowls of fruit often interlaced with greenery, and pictures surrounded by leafy garlands, as in his well-known work *James and Sarah Tuttle* (1836, New York Hist.). His sitters' profiles and features were carefully worked in pencil, and their names and other details of the sitting were often inscribed in varying calligraphic styles in the lower border of the picture, occasionally bearing the words "Joseph H. Davis, Left-handed Painter." (M.J.G.)

Davis, Stuart (1894–1964).

Painter. Born in Philadelphia, Pa., Davis was immersed almost from the beginning in the currents of change sweeping through American painting at the start of the 20th century. His father, Edward D. Davis, was art director of the *Philadelphia Press,* which counted among its employees John Sloan,* William Glackens,* Everett Shinn,* and George Luks,* who were soon to become the founders of the Ash Can School.* Davis' mother, Helen Stuart Foulke, was a sculptress.

The family moved to East Orange, N.J., in 1901, and in 1909 Davis left high school to study with Robert Henri* in New York. With Henri's other students, Davis stalked the city streets in search of scenes of everyday life to be drawn and painted in the raw. Eventually he reacted against Henri's insistence on the preeminence of subject matter over formal principles. But a feeling for

the minutiae of the common scene—its signs, symbols, and vivid colors, and for its tempo, rhythm, and dissonance remained, infusing his later abstract paintings with the vitality and pulse of 20th-century American life.

In 1913, Davis began drawing for *Harper's* and the radical *The Masses,* but he resigned from the latter when he found its commitment to social realism incompatible with the aims of his art. His aims began to crystallize in the same year, when he had his first encounter with modern European art at the Armory Show.* He was represented there with five small watercolors. He was particularly impressed with "the objective order, the broad generalizations of form and the nonimitative use of color in fauve painting (see Fauvism) and to a lesser degree in cubism.*

Davis's paintings of 1916–19 include a number of abstract landscapes that echo van Gogh's use of thickly textured paint, "all-over" composition, and multiple perspectives. During the next few years he experimented with collage* and with painted imitations of collage elements—package labels, cigarette papers, and so on. These form a link between the eccentric *trompe l'oeil* paintings of 19th-century artists like John Haberle* and modern pop art.* They also introduced a new flatness to his painting, as well as words and letters handled as elements of abstract design; these later became major elements in his visual vocabulary.

As early as 1918, Davis began to experiment with paintings that would synchronize views of landscapes and objects, seen at different times, into a "single focus," or simultaneous vision. Working at first in a relatively literal manner, Davis gradually simplified his forms until they became a series of geometric planes. An eggbeater set up in his studio in 1927–28 became the focus for a series of works in which he progressively generalized his shapes and the spatial relationships between them. He created compositions in which form, color, space, and movement are synchronized in a complex choreography of ambiguous relations between observed fact and constructivist abstraction. Davis later said that "the eggbeater idea" was the basis of everything he painted in after years.

Following the success of his first one-man show in 1927, Davis spent a year in Paris, where he painted street scenes

in which literal views of shop windows and sidewalk cafes were translated into schematic outlines against flat color planes. These somewhat "picturesque" works exerted a strong influence over commercial art for the next decade.

From 1930 to his death in 1964, Davis continued to refine and elevate the style he had developed in the 1920s, generally keeping a middle course between the abstraction of the "Eggbeater" series and the delineative emphasis of his Paris scenes. His paintings of the 1930s sometimes incorporate both types of views set side by side. The paintings after 1945 tend to drop references to external reality in favor of more purely pictorial structures. Many include letters or words that reflect his love for jazz and the American vernacular; so do many of his titles: *Pad, Rapt at Rappaport's, Ready to Wear, Something on the Eight Ball.* In his last years, the format of his work expanded and the forms took on larger dimensions. At the same time there is less movement and more stability than before.

During the 1930s, Davis executed a number of major murals under the WPA Federal Art Project* and as independent commissions, including *Men Without Women* at Radio City Music Hall in New York (1932), *Swing Landscape* at Indiana University (1938), and works for Radio Station WNYC in Manhattan and the New York World's Fair of 1939. He was active in the Artists' Union from 1933 to 1935 and was an officer of the later Artists' Congress, but resigned in 1940. In addition to painting and teaching, Davis was a prolific and effective writer on his own work and American art in general. His work won numerous prizes, and he was given major retrospective exhibitions. (A.F.)

Dawkins, Henry (active c.1753–80).

Engraver who came from England to New York about 1753, went to Philadelphia in 1757 to work as assistant to James Turner, and was active there until 1780 or later. His work included copperplate bookplates, maps, currency, and book illustrations. His engraving *The Paxton Expedition,* 1764, one of the earliest American caricatures, satirizes Benjamin Franklin.

Deas, Charles (1818–67).

Painter of genre, landscape, and the early West. Born in Philadelphia, Pa.,

1

2

1. **Stuart Davis.** Swing Landscape, *1938. Indiana University Art Museum, Bloomington.*

2. **Stuart Davis.** Colonial Cubism, *1954. Walker Art Center, Minneapolis.*

1

1. **Charles Deas.** The Death Struggle,
   1845. Webb Gallery of American
   Art, Shelburne, Vt.
   Decoys
2. Wooden decoy. Mid-19th century.
   Museum of American Folk Art, N.Y.
3. Charles E. (Shane) Wheeler. Sandhill Crane, c.1930. Stratford, Conn.

Deas passed his early years there and in the Hudson Valley. After failing in 1836 to be appointed to West Point, he decided upon a career as an artist. He studied art in New York City for a brief period and in 1838 exhibited his first painting, *Turkey Shooting,* at the National Academy of Design.* In 1839 he was elected to the Academy and exhibited there his only picture known to have been derived from a literary source, *The Devil and Tom Walker* (1839), taken from Washington Irving's *Tales of a Traveler.* In 1840 he visited his brother in Fort Crawford, Wis., and was so enthralled by life on the frontier that he remained there for seven years. Making St. Louis his headquarters, he spent several months each year sketching life among the mountain men and Indians west of the Mississippi. The curiosity of easterners concerning the exciting life in the West stimulated popular interest in Deas' paintings when they were exhibited in New York, Boston, and Philadelphia. The bloodcurdling representations of danger and sudden death evidently satisfied the appetite of sheltered city-dwellers for a glimpse of a life of action. In 1847 Deas returned to New York, where a few years later he suffered a nervous breakdown. His mental illness was permanent, and he died in an asylum.

Of the paintings of the early West, those by Deas are by far the most dramatic. Rather than paint an objective record of events, as Seth Eastman* did, he concentrated on fleeting moments of stress and danger. *The Prairie Fire* (n.d., Brooklyn) depicts two terror-stricken men and a woman caught in a conflagration, *The Death Struggle* (1845, Shelburne) depicts a frontiersman and an Indian plunging to their deaths over a cliff, and *The Voyageurs* (1846, Boston) shows fur trappers in an overloaded canoe battling dangerous rapids. Whatever may have been their basis in fact, the incidents are presented in such melodramatic terms that their credibility and consequently their power to move the beholder is weakened. (H.W.W.)

Decker, Joseph (1853–1924).
An important though still little-known still-life and figure painter of the late 19th century. Born in Würtemberg, Germany, Decker emigrated to America in 1867 and lived most of his life in Brooklyn, N.Y. Around 1880 he studied

in Munich; on his return he began to exhibit regularly at the Brooklyn Art Association, the Society of American Artists, and the National Academy of Design* (where he had studied for three years). In the 1880s, Decker attracted the attention of an important patron, Thomas B. Clarke, of New York, who employed him to repair Oriental vases. His still lifes of this decade, such as *Russet Apples on a Bough* (private collection) are sharp-edged, highly realistic, and have a "close-up" composition that suggests the influence of photography. The few genre scenes of the same period, equally original, are wry and disquieting paintings.

In the 1890s he painted numerous misty landscapes and marine views in a manner close to that of George Inness.* More important are the softly-painted, light-toned still lifes of the same period; often using tabletop compositions of fruit, Decker recalls the 18th-century French painter Chardin in his sensitivity. With these pictures, Decker gained some critical praise; however, he appears to have painted little after 1900, and at the time of his death he was listed only as a laborer.   (T.E.S.)

Decoys.

Man-made figures of birds used to attract live birds. Although game birds and water fowl appear in scenes as ancient as Egyptian wall paintings, no early Old World decoys have been found, and the American hunter learned the construction and use of the bird lure directly from the Indians. Prehistoric Indian decoys made from bulrush wrappings that were painted, embellished with feathers, and in some cases provided with stuffed heads, have been found at archeological digs, in particular the 1924 excavations at Lovelock Cave, Nevada, which revealed birds dating back to 1000 A.D. Late in the 16th century, John White made drawings of Indians hunting with decoys in what is now North Carolina, and a century later Indian decoys used around Lake Champlain were described by Baron Lahontan. Colonial adaptation of these Indian practices led to the carved and painted decoys that survive as a practical art form today.

The sophisticated detail and variety of 19th-century decoys is considerable, and collectors prize them as exacting expressions of a truly indigenous folk art. A large group of shorebird lures,

some only six inches long, includes sandpipers, yellowlegs, curlew, and plover, all mounted on sticks and set in the ground in lifelike groupings. Rarer shorebirds simulate such types as the black-necked stilt and ruddy turnstone. Floating decoys portray broad-beamed sea ducks, marsh ducks (for example, the Joel Barber *Mallard* in the Shelburne Museum), and the rarer mergansers. Goose decoys in swimming poses are not uncommon, nor are decoys simulating herons, bitterns, cranes, egrets, and swans. A remarkable example is the *Sandhill Crane* (Abby Aldrich Rockefeller) carved by the celebrated Charles E. Wheeler of Stratford, Conn.

Most of these decoys are carved in the round and realistically painted, but some are made of skin or lathing stretched over a frame, and others are cut from flat board or made of molded and enameled tin. While their makers are largely unknown, the work of some particularly expert carvers is readily identified and prized. Among the more celebrated are Albert Davids Laing (1811–86) of Connecticut, Lothrop T. Holmes, (1824–99), Joseph Whiting Lincoln (1859–1938), Anthony Elmer Crowell (1862–1951) of Massachusetts, and Henry Van Nuckson Shourdes (1871–1920) of New Jersey. In the late 19th century, several factories mass-produced decoys of good quality, the best known being the Mason birds from Detroit. A few major museums have acquired sizeable collections, particularly the Shelburne Museum and the Museum of American Folk Art in New York City.   (M.J.G.)

de Creeft, José (1884–   ).

Sculptor. Born in Guadalajara, Spain, he studied at the Bellas Artes in Madrid before going to Paris in 1905; there he soon learned of the experiments of the cubists and fauves. It was not until the early 1920s that he began direct carving in stone, the *taille direct* that led to his mature style; an early example is the *Maternity* (1922, Metropolitan). In 1929 he came to the United States where William Zorach,* Robert Laurent,* and John B. Flannagan* were already carving directly in stone; all four men had broken with the academic tradition and had set off independently to study the beauty of plastic form. De Creeft had one-man shows in New York, Seattle, and Chicago and became known from coast to coast. He worked at a prolific rate during the late 1930s, produc-

2

3

ing such pieces as the black granite head, *Maya* (1937, Wichita Art Association), *Astonishment* (1941, Metropolitan) and *I am Black but I am Beautiful* (1942). De Creeft converted the original shape of the rock into bold sculptural forms; this approach differed markedly from the 19th-century method in which the artist created only the clay model and then had assistants and stonecutters cast it in plaster and carve it in stone. In describing his interest in abstracting a sculptural form from the shapes of nature, de Creeft has said, "I see nature and I love it; it is the source of all my art." Later works include *The Poet* (1950, Fairmount Park, Philadelphia) and *Alice in Wonderland* (1960, Central Park, New York City). (W.C.)

de Kooning, Willem (1904–   ).
Painter, born in Rotterdam, Holland, and initially trained as a commercial artist and decorator. From 1916 to 1924 he was enrolled in the Rotterdam Academy of Fine Arts and Techniques. The school combined the traditions of the medieval craft guilds with those of the academies, so de Kooning was thoroughly trained in the techniques of painting while assimilating the influences of Renaissance art. In the early 1920s he came in contact with the de Stijl geometrical design movement led by Piet Mondrian and Theo van Doesburg in Holland as well as the cubist tendencies that dominated so much of early modern art. He has, nevertheless, never departed from his early conviction that painting and sculpture are continuing streams in which the artist is carrying on ideas and forms rooted in the entire history of past art. Like the medieval or Renaissance artist, de Kooning considered himself a craftsman. He was not only a designer and portraitist, but for a long period earned his living as a carpenter and house painter.

In 1926 he emigrated to the United States, where he supported himself by commercial art, sign painting, and carpentry. In New York City he became acquainted with the painter John Graham,* who introduced him to many of the personalities and ideas of the school of Paris, and with Arshile Gorky,* who long remained a close friend. A year spent on the WPA Federal Art Project* (1935) convinced him of his vocation as a painter, and during the 1930s he made various designs for murals and ap-

1

1. **Willem de Kooning.** Woman and Bicycle, *1953. Whitney Museum of American Art, N.Y.*
2. **Willem de Kooning.** Door to the River, *1960. Whitney Museum of American Art, N.Y.*
3. **Willem de Kooning.** Night Square, *1951. Collection Martha Jackson, N.Y.*

2

3

peared in a few New York exhibitions. Most of his earliest works have disappeared or been destroyed.

During the 1930s he was principally a figure painter producing many portraits of men, isolated in an ambiguous space, whose haggard faces and haunted eyes suggest the suffering of the unemployed during the Depression. The figures became increasingly flattened and fragmented during the late 1930s and early 1940s, suggesting the influence of curvilinear cubism* as well as the increasing force of automatism* that derived from the many European surrealists who were living in New York during World War II. Perhaps the principal influence on de Kooning during this time was still Gorky, who was then translating aspects of European surrealism* into a personal expressive idiom.

During the late 1940s de Kooning's paintings became explicitly nonfigurative although retaining suggestions of figure fragments, such as a torso or a shoulder. The "black paintings" of 1946–48, in which the artist limited himself to a palette of white lines on a black or dark gray ground, as in *Painting* (1948, Modern Museum), may be most closely associated with the tonal paintings of Picasso and Braque during their development of analytical cubism early in the century. Like the cubists, de Kooning has continued to explore problems of nonperspective space, of shifting vision, and ambiguous, simultaneously seen images. The principal difference in his use of cubism lies in the linear energy—the staccato movement of his lines and shapes on the surface and in and out of the pictorial space, an energy and movement related to the cubist variants of the Italian futurists as well as to the automatism* of surrealists such as André Masson. From this point on there is a tremendous sense of the jagged brush gesture, of the act of creation, of painting as a process of change and becoming. The artist revised constantly, never losing the force of instantaneous creation but still leaving an implication of something not entirely finished, an image out of which another image will inevitably grow. Around 1951 recognizable figures, as in *Two Women* (1952, Chicago), began to emerge once more in his work and then came the fantastic "Women" series of portraits that have dominated so much of his later works. These female images of the early 1950s are monstrous apparitions painted in full and lush color which, despite their violent distortions, stem from the great figure painting traditions of Rubens and Rembrandt. The same qualities of violent energy and garish but brilliant color characterize his abstract landscapes of the late 1950s, such as *Backyard on Tenth Street* (1956, Baltimore) and recur as the women figures emerge once more during the 1960s. The principal change in the more recent paintings of women is a delicacy of color, almost rococo in feeling, and a heightened sensuousness in which the underlying eroticism becomes ever more apparent.

De Kooning is the leader of that wing of gestural brush painting in American abstract expressionism which is known as action painting. He has had perhaps more followers and imitators than any of the other abstract expressionists, but the complexity of his vision, with its roots in the art of the Old Masters as well as in that of the pioneers of modern art—cubist, surrealist, and abstract—has proved impossible to imitate. He is not only one of the most important leaders of American painting, but also one of the international masters of 20th-century painting. (H.H.A.)

Delano & Aldrich (1903–1950).
Architectural firm that carried on the Beaux-Arts tradition in New York. It was conceived when Chester Holmes Aldrich (1871–1940) met William Adams Delano (1874–1960) in the office of Carrère & Hastings* in New York. They worked there for a year before leaving for Paris to study architecture at the École des Beaux-Arts. Aldrich graduated in 1900, Delano in 1902.

Athough they never reached the volume of work achieved by McKim, Mead & White,* they were known for a comprehensiveness of concept in which the plan of the house, even to the location of doors and windows, was often predetermined by the overall plan for the landscaping. In their residential work they favored the simple elegance of the Federal style, as exemplified in the town house designed for Willard D. Straight at 94th Street and Fifth Avenue, New York City (1914) and in the country estate of James A. Burden at Syosset, Long Island, N.Y. The firm also favored a very grand version of French manorial architecture, as in Otto Kahn's estate at Cold Spring Harbor, Long Island. Like

Carrère & Hastings, they also produced a formal type of low-roofed, balustraded house, but one that usually was Italian Renaissance in inspiration, instead of French. In New York City, the house of Harold I. Pratt at 68th Street and Park Avenue (1920), and in the country, the estate of Bertram G. Work at Oyster Bay, Long Island, best demonstrate this style. They designed many club houses, art galleries, institutional buildings and embassies, including the American Embassy in Paris (1933). An outstanding instance of municipal planning was the firm's classical design for the Post Office (1934) complex in Washington, D.C., where two "C-shaped" buildings, with handsome semicircular arcades, are set back to back.

Delano received the gold medal of the American Institute of Architects in 1953. Aldrich spent many years in Italy and was director of the American Academy in Rome in 1935–41. (A.B.)

Demuth, Charles (1883–1935).
A painter, Demuth grew up in Lancaster, Pa., somewhat sheltered because of lameness, in a family of means and artistic interests. In 1901 he entered the Drexel Institute in Philadelphia, and in 1905 the Pennsylvania Academy of the Fine Arts, where he studied with Thomas Anshutz* and William M. Chase.* In 1907 he spent a year in Paris before returning to the Pennsylvania Academy. Again in 1912 he went to Paris, spending two years at the Académies Moderne, Colarossi, and Julien. From these years he retained few works, but by 1912 his sensitively expressive figure style in watercolor was well developed. By 1915, when he held his first exhibition in New York, he was an incisive master of the medium. Demuth found precisely delicate, imaginative watercolors congenial to his temperament, and he worked on several series at once: flower pieces, scenes of vaudeville actors and acrobats, book illustrations, and landscapes. The intense feeling of the pieces, the expressionist movement of composition together with the almost painful sensitivity of line, has led to their being characterized as strangely sinister, as, for example, his *Acrobats* (1919, Modern Museum). The books Demuth chose to illustrate (his pictures were done not on commission, but as personal interpretations) were indeed sinister and often sexually morbid, including Zola's *Nana,*

James's *Turn of the Screw,* and Poe's *Masque of the Red Death.*

Another stylistic idiom began to appear in Demuth's paintings of buildings by 1916: a personal cubism,* projecting architectural planes and diagonal shafts cutting through compositions in which tree forms serve as an organic counterpoint to geometric elements. The landscapes grew in size and architectonic firmness, until by 1920 they had achieved impressive monumentality as compositions. They were built up in tempera, presenting a surface quite different from Demuth's mottled, fluent watercolors. Culminating examples of his architectural style are the tempera study of a colonial steeple titled *After Sir Christopher Wren* (1920, Worcester), and a later painting of grain elevators, *My Egypt* (1927, Whitney).

During the last fifteen years of his life he was often ill. However, he continued to paint architectural landscapes and brilliant watercolors of flowers and fruit. The fruit studies often incorporated deft allusions to the form-building techniques of Cézanne. In addition, Demuth painted several works which he called "posters"—pictures which incorporated symbols into his personal cubist style, and which were intended for friends. One of these, *I Saw the Figure 5 In Gold* (1928, Metropolitan), based on a poem by William Carlos Williams, is one of his most original and telling works. (D.W.S.)

Dennis, Thomas (c.1638–1706).
Born and trained in England as a carver and joiner, Dennis arrived in the colonies by 1663 and was listed as a resident of Portsmouth, N.H. In 1668 he settled in Ipswich, Mass. Recent studies indicate that much of the furniture attributed to his shop was made in Essex County, Mass., by joiners as yet unidentified. Attribution is difficult because there are no signed examples of 17th-century American furniture. Although the quantity of furniture attributed to Dennis has been drastically reduced, enough documentation exists to prove that he was a skillful craftsman who produced wainscot chairs, boxes, and chests-of-drawers. Their surfaces are usually covered with carved strapwork, guilloche, palmettes, S-scrolls, and split spindles. One of the best-documented examples of his work, a chest-of-drawers dated 1684, is also decorated with black, red, and white paint. (C.F.H.)

de Rivera, José (1904–   ).
A forceful and innovative proponent of the constructivist tradition in sculpture. Born in West Baton Rouge, La., he received no formal art training, but learned to deal with tools on his father's farm. For eight years he worked with tools and dies in factories and in foundries, and there learned the essentials of his craft. During the 1930s, he decided to be a professional artist and traveled in Spain, Italy, France, Greece, and Egypt, studying and drawing. In France, he sought out the major constructivist sculptor, Georges Vantongerloo, whose explorations of mathematical forms greatly impressed him.

Rivera's first exhibited sculptures in the 1930s were machine-age stylizations made from sheets of steel, usually with highly burnished curving surfaces. Gradually his fascination with Vantongerloo's theory of mathematical form began to be reflected in his works, and by the mid-1940s he had begun to experiment with the linear, arabesque forms for which he is best known. In the early 1950s, Rivera began to work almost exclusively with thick steel rods that he heated, forged, and hammered into parabolic curves that described virtual spaces as they turned slowly on their mechanized bases. Using steel, copper, or aluminum, Rivera burnished his surfaces until every millimeter was capable of reflecting light and suggested the fluid continuities he prized.

Rivera has won many awards. His work is in many major American museums, as well as the Tate Gallery in London. He has had works in group exhibitions all over the world, including the American National Exhibition in Moscow in 1959. Since 1930 he has been in more than seventy-five exhibitions in the United States.   (D.A.)

1. **Charles Demuth.** I Saw the Figure 5 in Gold, *1928. Metropolitan Museum of Art, N.Y. (Alfred Stieglitz Collection).*
2. **José de Rivera.** Construction No. 103, *1967, bronze. Collection Lionel Bauman, N.Y.*

Dewing, Thomas Wilmer (1851–1938).
Painter of delicately poetic studies of women. Dewing was born in Boston, Mass., and studied in Munich with Frank Duveneck* and in Paris at the Académie Julien. He was one of the younger men who exhibited in the National Academy of Design* and with the Society of American Artists,* of which he became a member in 1880. Dewing painted withdrawn, sensitive women in flowing gowns, seated in quiet rooms or straying in soft green fields. Gradually the figures emerged from warm-toned Victorian interiors, as in *The Spinet* (National Coll.)

1

2

1. **Edwin Dickinson.** The Fossil Hunters, *1928. Whitney Museum of American Art, N.Y.*
2. **Thomas Wilmer Dewing.** The Necklace, *c.1907. National Collection of Fine Arts, Smithsonian Institution, Washington, D.C. (gift of John Gellatly).*
3. **Richard Diebenkorn.** Man and Woman in a Large Room, *1957. Collection Joseph H. Hirshhorn, N.Y.*

3

to a still, cool world of dreamlike clarity, where precise accents hint at intense inner dramas, as in *The Necklace* (c. 1907, National Coll.). His themes may be related to those of his fellow Bostonians such as Abbott Thayer's* idealized females in flowing draperies or Edmund C. Tarbell's* women in light-flooded interiors, but his vision remained distinctly his own. Bloodless, repetitive, it is nonetheless haunting when his refined ladies do not cloy.

(D.W.S.)

Dexter, Henry (1806–76).

Portrait sculptor. Raised in Connecticut, he tried painting portraits before he began modeling them in 1836. His first commissioned bust was of Samuel Sweet (1837, Public Library, Newburyport, Mass.) and for nearly four decades he did little other than marble portraits, completing nearly two hundred of them. His style was a dry, often lifeless naturalism that found acceptance among mid-19th-century American patrons, who demanded little more than an accurate likeness. One of his most famous busts was that of Charles Dickens, modeled in 1841 when the author visited the United States; several replicas were produced. Dexter's most ambitious undertaking came in 1859–60, when he set out to model the portraits of all the state governors then in office; this enterprise carried him as far as Texas. Back in Boston he exhibited thirty-two plaster busts of governors, hoping his collection would become the basis of a national portrait gallery. But the Civil War intervened and nothing more came of the project. Dexter created a few ideal works, but he was better suited to copying likenesses. (W.C.)

Dickinson, Edwin (1891–   ).

Painter. Basically a realist, Dickinson has participated in his own way in many of the major movements of his time and lent distinguished personal insight to each. The son of a New England parson, he was born in Seneca Falls, N.Y. He studied at Pratt Institute, then at the Art Students League* under William M. Chase* and Frank V. DuMond, and then with Charles W. Hawthorne.* Dickinson has in turn taught at the Buffalo Academy of the Fine Arts, the Art Students League, Cooper Union, the Brooklyn Museum art school, Cornell University, and other institutions.

Dickinson's big museum pieces, such as *The Fossil Hunters* (1926–28, Whitney), are filled with complex perspectives and foreshortened bodies and objects placed in fantastic contexts. His imagination often invokes comparison with the "Gothic" romanticism of the 19th century: There are also surrealist overtones in the hallucinatory precisionism of his shapes and their dissolving one into another. His work sometimes possesses a highly macabre clarity as well. In some of his later works a fresh, open feeling for nature is expressed in small, quiet, highly controlled canvases.

(A.F.)

Dickinson, Preston (1891–1930).

Painter. Born in New York, Dickinson studied at the Art Students League* but regarded his five years in Europe (1910–15) as his real education. He studied the old masters in the Louvre Museum and the contemporary masters, especially the cubists, then active in Paris. Dickinson's early landscapes and still lifes adhere strictly to the principles of analytical cubism, but after his return to America he applied the cubist analysis of form more loosely and freely; this is especially true of the landscapes and city views he painted in and about Quebec, a metropolis and a province which he loved and to which he often returned. As his style developed, a Chinese influence superimposed itself upon his basic cubism,* manifested in strongly calligraphic draftsmanship and a light, transparent tonalism. He had only just achieved full maturity in the plastic use of color when he died, very suddenly, in Spain. He is represented in many museums and private collections. (A.F.)

Diebenkorn, Richard (1922–   ).

Painter. Born in Portland, Ore., he received an M.F.A. degree from the University of Mexico (1950–52). He taught at the California School of Fine Arts (1947–50) and later at Stanford University. Although Diebenkorn is normally considered an outstanding member of the California school of expressionist realism, he has moved back and forth between realism, abstract expressionism,* and recently, a form of abstract, geometric color painting. At the California School of Fine Arts he was influenced by David Park* and Clyfford Still.* His paintings of the early 1950s represent a form of abstract landscape, broadly and simply conceived, although with considerable emphasis on brush texture. In the later 1950s he turned to a more representational image in which, like Elmer Bischoff,* figures are isolated within a light-filled, coloristic, architectural space, as in *Woman in a Window* (Albright). The mood again is one of isolation in which the figures are in form highly coordinated with the space they occupy and yet separated from it. During the 1960s Diebenkorn's paintings again became increasingly abstract, although they continued to retain vestiges of landscape or interiors, for example *Landscape I* (1963, San Francisco). His works of the early 1970s are the most geometrically abstract, organized on a vertical-horizontal tradition like that of the Dutch abstractionist Piet Mondrian but still maintaining suggestions of landscape perspective space. (H.H.A.)

Diller, Burgoyne (1906–65).

Painter and sculptor. Although born in New York City, Diller grew up in Michigan and attended Michigan State College. He returned to New York to attend the Art Students League* (1928–33) and to study with Hans Hofmann.* He is credited with being the first American convert to the Dutch geometric De Stijl style (1934) and his compositions reflected the tenets of the Dutch abstractionists Piet Mondrian, and van Doesburg. During the early 1930s, few American painters were interested in "pure plastic art," and Diller soon became a member of the American Abstract Artists* group. Although his own work met with little success at this time, Diller occupied a succession of influential positions: head of the mural division (1935) and assistant technical director (1940) of New York's WPA Federal Art Project* (1940), and director of art for New York's War Service Section during World War II. By 1935, as director of the WPA art program, Diller was allocating jobs to such artists as Stuart Davis,* Arshile Gorky,* and Willem de Kooning.* Diller had a number of shows in a New York gallery between 1946 and 1951, yet his work continued to meet with little sympathy, owing perhaps to the rigor of his geometric abstractions.

Diller worked with only three themes during his lifetime: one was discrete rectangular or square elements as in *First Theme* (1962, Chicago); the second showed these elements "gener-

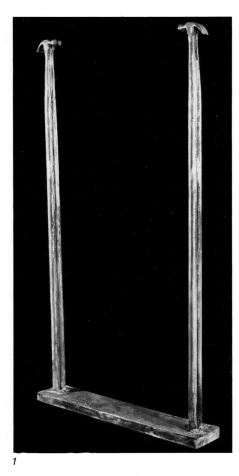

1

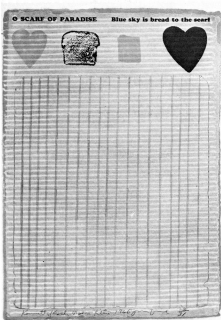

2

1. **Jim Dine.** The Hammer Doorway, *1967, cast aluminum. Collection Gene R. Summers, Chicago.*
2. **Jim Dine.** Kenneth Koch Poem Lithograph, *1966. Collection Tatyana Grosman, N.Y.*

ated by continuous lines"; and the third was these elements "submerged in activity." Despite these seemingly narrow limits, Diller was such a master of proportion and of mediating surface tensions with composition in depth that his work is never repetitive. Toward the end of his career he developed these themes in three dimensions, working with precisely finished formica solids; sometimes these "color structures" are over life-size. In 1961 a retrospective at a New York gallery revealed Diller as one of the best of the American neoplasticists and henceforth his work began to appear in important exhibitions and major museum collections. In addition to paintings and constructions, Diller produced a number of spontaneous collages and drawings.

(E.C.G.)

Dine, Jim (1935–   ).
Painter. Born in Cincinnati, Ohio. After studying at the University of Ohio, Dine moved to New York City in 1958. His earliest shows coincided with a period when the desire to go beyond abstract expressionism* was manifesting itself in various forms. A pioneer of happenings,* he presented four "performances" that combined painting, sculpture, drama, music, dance, and audience participation: "Smiling Workman," "Vaudeville," "Car Crash," and "The Shining Bed," the last three in New York City (1960). At the same time Dine exhibited drawings, easel paintings, and collage and construction paintings—the latter assembled from objects found in the streets. Dine's first one-man show came in 1961, where he emerged fully as a "new realist." The show consisted of pictures of neckties, coats, hats, and bandanas, painted in varying styles—expressionist, hard-edge,* trompe l'oeil—often with the actual article of apparel pasted onto the canvas and labeled with its name. Dine's huge pop art* ties in particular were tremendously popular, and indeed, the pop art movement, initiated by Jasper Johns* and Robert Rauschenberg,* was then in full swing. In his subsequent shows Dine moved increasingly toward "sculptural" and "theatrical" situations. A series of works from 1962 consisted of everyday objects placed in front of "paintings," such as a strand of *Pearls* (1961, Guggenheim), or as in *Lawnmower,* which stands on a pedestal before a canvas smeared with thick dabs of paint. In *Black Bathroom* a real bathroom sink emerges from a stretched canvas partially painted black. In most cases Dine used his objects graphically; the "painting" becomes a backdrop against which the object is seen, and this combination of the painted surface with real objects produces a theatrical effect.

In recent years Dine has turned to actual "sculpture." *Four Jobs Six Years After the First* (1969)—a ten-foot plank of wood placed across sawhorses, with paint rollers, electrical wires, and small pieces of wood sawed from the larger plank strewn on the floor—is both environmental and a foray into process art. In 1966 Dine designed costumes and sets for the San Francisco Actor's Workshop performance of *A Midsummer Night's Dream;* in 1966–67 he illustrated Apollinaire's *The Poet Assassinated;* and in 1969 he published his first book of poems. Dine has exhibited widely, including the Venice Biennial (1964, 1968) and Expo '67, Montreal. In 1970 his *Complete Graphics* was published, and he had a retrospective at the Whitney Museum.

(E.C.G.)

Di Suvero, Mark (1933–   ).
Sculptor. Born in Shanghai, China, he moved to the United States at an early age. He received a B.F.A. degree from the University of California. Constructing his sculpture from found objects of metal parts and weathered timber, Di Suvero has expanded the vigorous gestural thrust of action painting into three dimensions. He has worked on an ever-increasing scale since the early 1960s, exchanging expressiveness for structural complexity. His *XDelta,* shown in the 1970 "Whitney Sculpture Annual," is eighteen feet high. Its steel beams are held at opposing diagonals under tension while a metal platform that is suspended from one of the beams swings freely, initiating movement throughout the piece whenever it is stirred. Di Suvero's integration of delicacy and monumentality has received wide attention since his first one-man show at a New York gallery in 1960. He has had shows in Chicago, Los Angeles, and, in 1972, in the Netherlands. He was one of the founders of an important cooperative gallery (with Edwin Ruda, Robert Grosvenor, and Forrest Myers) in New York in 1963. Di Suvero has been included in numerous group shows, among them Documenta IV

in Kassel, Germany, and "New York Painting and Sculpture: 1940–70" at the Metropolitan Museum. He has had awards from several foundations. (C.R.)

Doughty, Thomas (1793–1856).
One of the first Americans to devote himself exclusively to landscape painting. Doughty was born in Philadelphia, Pa., and after being apprenticed to a leather merchant, turned to painting about 1820. He noted later in life that he had never received any instruction in oils. In 1822 he began exhibiting his landscapes regularly at the Pennsylvania Academy of the Fine Arts, of which he became a member in 1824. In later years he exhibited in Boston and at New York's National Academy of Design.* He lived in Philadelphia until 1826, then in Boston, but he later returned to Philadelphia. In 1837 he traveled to Europe and spent two years in England. Other than a second trip abroad in 1845–46, he spent the rest of his life in New York City. Working throughout the eastern United States, Doughty produced many quiet pastoral landscapes and gained a considerable reputation. His work at its best was charming and poetic, as in his *Nature's Wonderland* (1835, Detroit); more often, his compositions were repetitive and uninspired. He also is known for his lithography, particularly for the series of rural scenes published with his brother John Doughty in the Philadelphia periodical *Cabinet of Natural History and American Rural Sports* (1830–34).
(T.E.S.)

Dove, Arthur G. (1880–1946).
Pioneer abstract artist. He was born in Canandaigua, N.Y., attended Hobart College, and then studied art at Cornell University with Charles W. Furlong. Upon graduation in 1903, he went to New York City, where he did magazine illustration with some success, doing pastels in his spare time. On a trip to Paris, he was strongly influenced in 1908 by the painters known as the fauves (see Fauvism), as is apparent in *The Lobster* (1908, private collection), which attracted attention in the Salon d'Automne held in 1909.

When he returned to New York in 1909, Dove's independent spirit and bold talent were already manifest, and Alfred Stieglitz* invited him to show in the "Younger American Painters" exhibition at his gallery "291" in March, 1910.

3

4

3. *Mark di Suvero.* X Delta, *1970, steel. LoGuidici Gallery, N.Y.*
4. *Mark di Suvero.* Loveseat, *1965, steel, tires, and rope. Private collection.*

During that same year, Dove moved rapidly into his personal style. First he painted six small oil "Abstractions" and then, between 1911 and 1914, a group of larger pastels that Stieglitz later entitled "Nature Symbolized." These were included in his first one-man show, at "291," in 1912. As in the "Abstractions," the source in nature—landscape, house, sails—is sometimes clearly discernible, but at times the abstracting process is so complete that the subject is unidentifiable. Dove thereby comes in line with Vasily Kandinsky, Robert Delaunay, and Frank Kupka in his claim to have painted the earliest completely abstractionist pictures. The critics recognized the distinctive approach and handsome color of Dove's work. On the whole they treated him well, although one rhymester's observation, "To show the pigeons would not do/ And so he simply paints the coo," was instantly quoted. For over thirty years Dove continued to return to the same concerns in his art. He would start, he said, with a motif in nature but paint with "the means of expression becoming purely subjective." The motif was simplified "to color and force lines and substances." He sought for something he called "a condition of light . . . applied to all objects in nature . . . , which established them to the eye, to each other and to the understanding."

About 1912 Dove bought a farm in Westport, Conn., and struggled to support his family by farming and by raising chickens. He painted when he could, and for a brief time showed a strong cubist influence. In 1916 he exhibited in the Forum exhibition and in 1917 with the Society of Independent Artists.* Eventually he gave up farming and left his family, taking up residence about 1920 on a forty-two-foot yawl, cruising about in summer and spending cramped winters in Huntington (Long Island, N.Y.) Harbor. Though he continued to paint during the 1920s—with increased emphasis on sun, moon, and sea symbols—his most striking innovation was in the form of constructions or collages, small and witty compositions whose size was fitting for cabin life. They may be traced to precedents in cubism* and dada,* but they are transformed by Dove's unorthodox imagination, whimsy, and homespun humor, as in *Portrait of Ralph Dusenberry* (1924, Metropolitan). In 1925 Dove held the first of a series of exhibitions at Stieglitz' newly founded Intimate Gallery, and the next

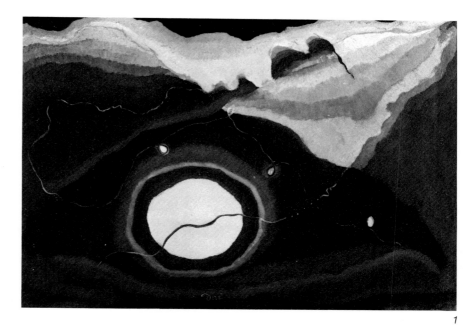

1

1. **Arthur Dove.** Rise of the Full Moon, *1937. Phillips Memorial Gallery, Washington, D.C.*

2. **Guy Pène du Bois.** Café du Dôme, *National Gallery of Art, Washington, D.C. (Chester Dale Collection).*

2

148

year his work was purchased by his first consistent patron, Duncan Phillips. In 1927 he began to show abstractions based on jazz themes and entered a brief calligraphic period.

During 1929–33 he lived on the upper floor of a yacht club at Halesite, Long Island, and the size and breadth of his painting soon reflected this spacious environment, as in *Sand Barge* (1930, Phillips). As he moved into a strong and richly mature phase of work, the pattern of his life was disrupted by his attempts to save the family properties in upstate New York. He managed to paint regularly in the face of lawsuits and foreclosures, but his health was undermined. During his last seven years he lived in an abandoned post office in Centerport, Long Island, painting vigorously when health permitted. He moved from poetic, rhythmic works often based on sun and moon symbols, such as *Rise of the Full Moon* (1937, Phillips), toward a style more geometric, angular, and hardedged as in *That Red One* (1944, William H. Lane Foundation).

Dove's work, from the time of his first abstractions, is unique, expressing "his inner self with sensuous and lyrical pictographs," to quote the critic-collector Duncan Phillips, who adds, "certainly in the realm of uncompromising and impetuous exploration Dove was the boldest American pioneer." (D.W.S.)

Downing, Andrew Jackson (1815–52). Architect, horticulturist, and landscape gardener. Son of a wheelwright and nurseryman, he was born and lived in Newburgh, N.Y. He had little formal education, the greater part of his knowledge coming from reading, correspondence with professionals, travel, and experience.

Downing published the results of his horticultural investigations in American and European magazines and in books. In 1841 he published his *Treatise on the Theory and Practice of Landscape Gardening,* which established his authority, and in 1846 he became editor of the *Horticulturalist.* At first he kept a nursery business, but he gave this up to take large projects from the federal government. Downing's abilities were soon recognized in England and highly praised by J. C. Loudon and John Lindley, English experts in landscaping. Because of the relationship of land to building, horticulture gradually led to architecture, so that several of his later

books are devoted to his deep, somewhat romantic concern for nature and man's relationship to it, particularly with respect to housing in the country. Thus *Cottage Residences* (1842) emphasized the need for a house to fit the site. Next came his *The Fruits and Fruit Trees of America* (1845), and then *Additional Notes and Hints to Persons about Building in this Country* (1849). For architecture his most important book was *Architecture of Country Houses* (1850), which contains his philosophy of building in the picturesque manner, various means of constructing cottages, farm houses, and outbuildings, and his view of the ideal country villa. With this complete guide finished, Downing went to England to meet English friends and to see the countryside. He returned with an assistant, Calvert Vaux, who soon became his partner and helped him with such projects as landscaping the Capitol and the White House grounds. At the age of thirty-seven, Downing died in a steamboat disaster on the Hudson River. His *Rural Essays* (1853) was published posthumously. Frederick Law Olmsted,* the outstanding landscape architect of the next generation, was much influenced by Downing's theories and practical good sense, as is reflected in Olmsted's wise planning of Central Park, New York City. (P.F.N.)

Du Bois, Guy Pène (1884–1958). Critic and painter. He was born in Brooklyn, the son of a literary and music critic, and he studied at the New York School of Art under William Merritt Chase,* Robert Henri,* and Kenneth Hayes Miller.* In 1905 he went to Paris to continue his studies under Alexandre Steinlin. Returning to New York, he worked as an art critic or reporter on various newspapers and for seven years as editor of *Arts and Decoration* magazine. His early works were in a style of social realism and he served as interpreter and spokesman for artists of the Henri group, as well as for the 1913 Armory Show,* in which he was represented as a painter. His autobiography, *Artists Say the Silliest Things,* appeared in 1940.

Du Bois' style changed little over the years. His canvases often show two or three simplified figures in frozen motion, like mannequins caught in a spotlight. His incisive characterizations distill art gallery, theater, and cafe so-

ciety into witty little tableaux, as in *Opera Box* (1926, Whitney). (D.W.S.)

Duchamp, Marcel (1887–1967). French avant-garde artist long an intermittent resident of the United States. The younger brother of the painter Jacques Villon and the sculptor Raymond Duchamp-Villon, Marcel was a precocious painter of impressionist canvases by his fifteenth year, and was equally accomplished in the manner of the fauves (see Fauvism) by 1910. In 1911 he developed a personal version of cubism* with an emphasis on portraying motion in painting through multiple images and in 1912 he painted his best-known work, *Nude Descending a Staircase* (second version, Philadelphia), which created a furor and became the most famous and notorious example of modern art in America when it was exhibited at the Armory Show* in 1913. Duchamp spent the years 1915–18 in New York City. From 1912 on he contemplated creating a new form of art, which would allow greater freedom and precision of expression of both imagination and intellect. By 1915 he had begun work on *The Bride Stripped Bare by Her Bachelors, Even* (also known as the *Large Glass;* 1915–23, Philadelphia), which was intended as his *chef-d' oeuvre* but was "brought to a state of incompletion" in 1923. The glass of the construction has since been broken.

Meanwhile, Duchamp had been pursuing other directions in questioning the accepted concepts of art and esthetics. In 1915, shortly after arriving in New York, he began to collect "ready-mades," commonplace objects such as a snow shovel, which he bought and nominated an artwork by virtue of the creative act of his selection. Two years later he carried this concept to its logical conclusion when he submitted for exhibition at the Society of Independent Artists* a urinal signed "R. Mutt." Duchamp had been a founding member of the new society, which proclaimed a "no-jury" policy. When the urinal was rejected, he resigned. The openly antiesthetic attitude of this episode served to establish him as a leader of the international dada* movement which had begun in Zurich during World War I. In New York, the French avant-gardist Francis Picabia, the painter Man Ray,* and the collector Walter Arensberg joined Duchamp in producing dadaist publications. After 1918 he ceased painting entirely, though he continued to make a variety of collages, constructions, casts, sketches, optical machines, and such. In 1920 Duchamp, together with the painter and patron Katherine Dreier, founded the Société Anonyme for the purpose of gathering an extensive representation of modern art to serve as a museum collection. This led to travel and various exhibitions, publications, and lectures for some twenty years before the collection was presented to the Yale University Art Gallery in 1941. (D.W.S.)

Dummer, Jeremiah (1645–1718).

The earliest native-born and -trained American silversmith whose work has been identified, Dummer was born in Newbury, Mass., and learned his trade from John Hull* and Robert Sanderson.* He worked in Boston and supplied numerous silver vessels for churches in Massachusetts and Connecticut. Over a hundred examples of his work have been listed. Working in late Renaissance and early Baroque styles, Dummer made items such as porringers, and tankards (including one with a cast lion thumbpiece), as well as less usual forms such as a two-handled bowl, a basin, candlesticks, and plates. A pair of candlesticks (Yale) were fashioned about 1686 of flattened silver in the form of cluster columns with square bases.

Dummer's tankards featured flat lids, slightly tapering straight sides, molded base bands, widely sweeping curved handles with a rat-tail drop under the top, and a cherub or shield-shaped handle ending. Occasionally, cutcard work —relief decoration cut from a thin sheet of metal and soldered to the surface— was added to the lid or body of the tankard. His earliest tankards had cusped thumbpieces, while the later examples had scrolled or dolphin-and-mask thumbpieces.

The colony of Connecticut engaged Dummer to engrave the plates for the first paper money printed there in 1709. He also served in Massachusetts in many public offices. His third wife was the sister-in-law of John Coney.* Dummer's apprentices included such well-known silversmiths as Edward Winslow* and John Edwards.* When he died on May 24, 1718, he was described by the Boston News-Letter as having enjoyed a long retirement and "having served his country faithfully in several Public Stations, and obtained of all that knew him the Character of a Just, Virtuous, and Pious Man." (M.G.F.)

Duncanson, Robert S. (1817–72).

Portrait, landscape, still-life, and genre painter, he was one of the first black artists to make an international reputation and a living as a painter. Born of a Negro mother and a Scotch-Canadian father in New York State, he spent his childhood in Canada, where he received a primary education. About 1841 he joined his mother in Mount Holly near Cincinnati, and was already sufficiently accomplished to exhibit three paintings there the following year. This probably resulted from a trip, at the expense of the Anti-Slavery League, to Edinburgh, Scotland, about 1840 to study painting. His first important commission was a series of mural landscapes (1848–49) for "Belmont," the home of Nicholas Longworth (now the Taft Museum, Cincinnati). In 1853 he went to Italy, France, and England to study landscape in company with the Hudson River School* painter William Sonntag and the Cincinnati painter John R. Tait. In 1863–66 he was in England, and he may have been in Scotland in 1870–71. Duncanson spent most of his life in Cincinnati, but lived in Detroit around 1849, and died there after a mental breakdown in 1872.

As a romantic-realist landscapist he may be considered a member of the second generation of Hudson River School* painters and he was especially close to Sonntag. His landscapes were similar to the idyllic works of George Inness,* notably in the effort to capture the effect of torpid, humid air. His best-known works are Blue Hole, Flood Waters, Little Miami River (1851, Cincinnati) and the murals now in the Taft Museum. He also painted portraits of some well-known residents of Cincinnati and Detroit. On the evidence of Drunkard's Plight (1845, Detroit) Duncanson was less successful as a painter of genre. On the other hand, his still lifes, such as Fruit Still Life (1848, Corcoran), show considerable talent. (H.W.W.)

Dunlap, William (1766–1839).

Painter and art historian. The close alliance between the arts of painting and drama, so marked throughout the 19th century, was a dominant influence in Dunlap's career. As a child in Perth Amboy, N.J., he lost the sight of one eye, but he could still enjoy and paint pictures, and was pointed toward the career of an artist. He first received lessons from Abraham Delanoy (c. 1740–90) and then in 1784 he went to London to study with Benjamin West.* Returning in 1787 almost as untrained as when he left, he attempted to earn his living as a portraitist. But he was soon active as theatrical manager and became the first American playwright with a serious professional concern. For more than fifteen years he did not paint. But when the Old American Company failed in 1805, he became an itinerant miniature painter and was often on the road from Virginia to Canada, doing portraits on canvas and ivory. In 1821, inspired by the success of Rembrandt Peale's* huge Court of Death, he painted a series of large pictures, mostly biblical scenes, borrowing liberally from the well-known works of West; he sent or took them on tour as a form of semidramatic popular entertainment. Dunlap's works were competent but had little depth or distinction, a fact he himself admitted. His The Artist Showing His Picture of a Scene from Hamlet to His Parents (1788, New York Hist.), painted just after his return from London, is perhaps his best.

In 1817 he was appointed librarian of the American Academy, and in 1826 joined a number of younger artists in founding the National Academy of Design.* His last years were given to the writing of his History of the American Theatre (1832); he also wrote some thirty plays. However, his History of the Rise and Progress of the Arts of Design in the United States (1834), a compilation of autobiographical statements and anecdotes about the artists of his time, is his most enduring work, remaining an invaluable primary source of American art history. (C.C.S.)

Durand, Asher Brown (1796–1886).

Widely regarded as a founder of American landscape painting, and a leader of the Hudson River School.* Durand was born in Jefferson Village (now Maplewood), N.J. He first studied engraving in the shop of his father, who was a watchmaker and silversmith. In 1812 he was apprenticed to the engraver Peter Maverick (1780–1831) in Newark, N.J., and in 1817 he became Maverick's partner. This partnership dissolved in 1820, when Durand was awarded a commission to engrave John Trumbull's* painting, The Declaration of Indepen-

dence (1786–97, Yale). This project occupied him for three years, and the print made his reputation as the leading engraver in America. From this time to the mid-1830s, he was busy as an engraver, doing portraits, landscapes, banknote vignettes, as well as such subjects as John Vanderlyn's* famous painting, *Ariadne* (1812, Pennsylvania; Durand's engraving: 1835, Metropolitan).

Durand turned to painting in the 1830s and produced in this decade a substantial body of portraits, genre, and history pieces, as well as a few landscapes. Exhibiting annually from 1826 to the 1870s at the National Academy of Design* (of which he was a founding member, and president from 1845–61), he quickly gained a reputation as one of New York's leading painters. He began to specialize in landscape about 1837, and he painted that subject almost exclusively after making a European "Grand Tour" in 1840. Returning in 1841, he came to be ranked with his friend Thomas Cole* as one of the chief American landscapists.

Durand's landscapes are precise and well-drawn. He was primarily a painter of mood and sentiment in nature, and working within a limited range of compositions, he achieved considerable variety in suggesting subtle variations of texture and light. His favorite subjects were individual trees, such as his splendid beeches; larger and more ambitious ideal views, influenced by Cole's work; forest interiors, particularly after 1845; and, later in his career, sunlit pastoral landscapes influenced by the French landscape painter Claude Lorrain's unusual lighting effects. Though his masterpiece is often considered to be *Kindred Spirits* (1849, New York Public Library)—where Cole was portrayed with his friend, the poet William Cullen Bryant—perhaps more representative of his majestic expressions of forest subjects is his *The Catskills* (1859, Walters).

More important than his paintings was his influence, both as an example and as a theorist, on the second generation of the Hudson River School. Together with Frederic E. Church,* he led the younger painters away from the moralizing passions of Thomas Cole toward a more straightforward realism based on the preaching of the critic John Ruskin* and the close observation of nature. His series of "Letters on Landscape Paint-

1

2

1. **Robert S. Duncanson.** Blue Hole, Flood Waters, Little Miami River, *1851. Cincinnati Art Museum (gift of Norbert Heermon).*

2. **Marcel Duchamp.** Nude Descending a Staircase, No. 2, *1912. Philadelphia Museum of Art (Louise and Walter Arensberg Collection).*

1

ing" published in an art magazine, *The
Crayon** (1855), outlined his theories,
and stressed particularly the use of
drawings, the study of engravings of
light and atmosphere, a knowledge
of botany and geology, and the need to
keep brushwork unnoticeable.   (T.E.S.)

Durand, John (active 1766–82).
Portrait and landscape painter. He came
of a Huguenot family whose name would
figure largely in later American art history. In 1767 he opened an art school
and ambitiously planned a series of historical paintings. He made his home in
New York City, but as a limner he traveled extensively, going southward to
Virginia and northward into Connecticut. He worked in a hard, flat, sign-painter's technique, yet with distinctive
bright coloring and elegance, and an
interest in surface pattern. The naive
charm of his style is at its best in his
*Rapalje Children of Garret and Helena
De Nyse* (c. 1768, New York Hist.). His
oeuvre may be considered a late flowering within the school of patroon painters.*   (C.C.S.)

Durrie, George Henry (1820–63).
Portrait, genre, and landscape painter
who is best known for his rural winter
scenes. Durrie spent most of his life in
New Haven, Conn. He and his brother
John Durrie (1818–?) studied with the
portraitist Nathaniel Jocelyn (1796–
1881) of New Haven, Conn. In the early
1840s, Durrie painted portraits in Virginia, New Jersey, Connecticut, and
upper New York State. During the same
period, he also painted fruit pieces,
genre scenes, and Shakespearean
scenes, but by the mid-1840s was devoting most of his energy to landscape.
He first exhibited winter scenes in 1844
at the New Haven Horticultural Society
and in 1845 at the National Academy of
Design* (where he exhibited fairly regularly until his death). His *East Rock*
(1857, New Haven Colony Historical
Society) and his *Winter Scene in New
England* (1862, Yale) typify his realistic
style, which always retained something of the untrained artist's meticulousness along with an often charming
lack of sophistication in design. His
winter scenes became particularly well
known in the 1860s, when a number of
them were published as lithographs
by Currier & Ives;* of these, the best
known was *Home for Thanksgiving,*

which remains an archetypal American memento of rural contentment.   (T.E.S.)

Duveneck, Frank (1848–1919).
Painter, an American exemplar of the Munich school. He was born in Covington, Ky. While still a youth he traveled around, working on church decorations. In 1870 he went to Munich just as the Royal Academy felt the impact of Wilhelm Leibl, a forceful objective realist and admirer of Hals and Courbet. Duveneck, studying with Wilhelm von Diez, quickly acquired a brilliant, vigorous style, working with a broad, loaded brush in a dark-brown ground. His figures retain a fresh liveliness to this day, as in *Whistling Boy* (1872, Cincinnati). When Duveneck returned home in 1873, however, there was little recognition of his achievement until he showed paintings in Boston in 1875; these met with immediate success and established his reputation nationally. He returned to Munich, where he established his own school in 1878.

A lively circle formed in Munich, including William Merritt Chase,* John Twachtman,* who had studied with Duveneck in Cincinnati, and "Duveneck's Boys"—his Munich pupils, of whom Joseph De Camp and John Alexander* were eventually the best known. Duveneck's colorful bohemianism dominated the group and became legendary. Chase and Twachtman went with him to Venice in 1877; after this excursion he decided to move the school to Italy (1879). Winters were spent in Florence, summers in Venice, and very shortly Duveneck's painting changed as he entered his "Italian phase." Landscapes and figure groups in sun-filled Italian settings replaced the dark Munich paintings. To capture the effects of light, he changed to a thinner, smoother application of paint and a higher color key.

Duveneck then entered a highly productive but perhaps less interesting period, painting large, picturesque genre scenes, studied portraits, and skillful etchings. Then, in 1888, his wife of two years died in Paris. He returned to Cincinnati, where he undertook a sculptured memorial to her and devoted much time to teaching at the Cincinnati Academy. Awards and honors followed—but he did little painting during his last thirty years.   (D.W.S.)

2

3

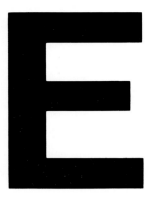

Eakins, Thomas (1844–1916).

Painter, teacher, and the foremost American realist of his period. The son of a writing-master, he was born in Philadelphia, Pa., where he spent most of his life. In 1861 he entered the Pennsylvania Academy of the Fine Arts, where he studied drawing, mostly from casts. He supplemented this meager education by studying anatomy at Jefferson Medical College, Philadelphia. In 1866 he went to Paris, where he went through three years of strictly academic training at the École des Beaux-Arts under Jean Léon Gérôme, with short courses under Léon Bonnat and the sculptor Augustin Alexandre Dumont. In the summer of 1868 he visited Italy and Germany; in 1869 he traveled to Spain, where he discovered the 17th-century Spanish masters, especially Velásquez and Ribera, whose naturalism was a revelation after the artificiality of academic French art. He spent six months in Seville, painting his first composition. In 1870 he returned to Philadelphia, and never went abroad again.

Eakins immediately began painting the life of his community in a completely realistic style: portraits of his family and friends, revealing a strong sense of character and deep emotional attachment; and scenes of outdoor life—rowers racing on the Schuylkill River, sailboats on the Delaware, hunters in the southern New Jersey marshes. These sporting pictures showed a strong structural sense, precise vision, and first-hand observation of outdoor light and color, though far from the impressionist palette.

Eakins combined artistic with scientific interests, and many of his friends were prominent scientists and doctors. His early paintings were constructed in exact perspective, involving higher mathematics. His knowledge of anatomy was as thorough as that of most

1. **Thomas Eakins.** Mrs. William D. Frishmuth, *1900. Philadelphia Museum of Art (gift of Mrs. Thomas Eakins and Miss Mary A. Williams).*
2. **Thomas Eakins.** Max Schmitt in a Single Scull, *1871. Metropolitan Museum of Art, N.Y. (Alfred N. Punnett Fund, gift of George D. Pratt).*
3. **Thomas Eakins.** The Gross Clinic, *1875. Jefferson Memorial College and Medical Center, Philadelphia.*
4. **Thomas Eakins.** Professor Henry A. Rowland, *1897. Addison Gallery of American Art, Phillips Academy, Andover, Mass.*

2

3

4

physicians. The masterpiece of his early years was *The Gross Clinic* (1875, Jefferson Medical College), representing the famous surgeon Samuel D. Gross operating before his students—a painting whose realism shocked the art world but which made the artist's reputation as a leader of naturalism in America.

An expert photographer, from the early 1880s Eakins used the camera as a visual aid to painting, and as a means of studying the body and its actions. In 1884 he worked with the pioneer photographer Eadweard Muybridge* in recording human and animal locomotion, improving on the photographer's method by using a single camera instead of a battery of cameras.

In addition to painting, Eakins practised sculpture, executing a number of pieces in the 1880s and early 1890s. Among his works were the horses for the Lincoln and Grant Monument in Brooklyn, N.Y. An influential and inspiring teacher, Eakins became an instructor at the Pennsylvania Academy in 1876; he was made acting head of the school in 1879, and director in 1882. Abandoning the old system of drawing from casts, he based his teaching on a thorough study of the nude, on anatomical lectures, and dissection. Another innovation was in having students paint in full color from the beginning. But his emphasis on the nude, and particularly his insistence on the completely nude male model in his lectures on anatomy, brought opposition from the more proper women students, and the Academy trustees forced his resignation in 1886. Many of his male students seceded from the school and started the Art Students League of Philadelphia, at which he taught for about seven years, without pay. He also lectured on anatomy at schools in other cities, but ran into the same opposition, so that his teaching career ended in the 1890s.

The Academy affair was a severe blow to Eakins. And although he had gained considerable reputation as a painter, he had attained little financial success: at thirty-six he had sold only nine oils and watercolors, for a total of $1,975. All of this may account for the fact that after the middle 1880s he abandoned outdoor and genre subjects, except occasionally, and concentrated on portrait-painting. But even as a portraitist he never achieved worldly success. Commissions were rare; almost all his sitters

were friends and students, or individuals who interested him by their qualities of mind—scientists, doctors, teachers, musicians, fellow artists, and churchmen. Most of his portraits were labors of love; he asked the sitters to pose, and often gave them the paintings. Uncompromisingly realistic, his portraits show no trace of flattery. His sure, strong sense of character, his command of the head, hands, and body, and his psychological insight give his portraits intense vitality (for example, *Miss Amelia Van Buren,* c.1889–91, Phillips; *Professor Henry A. Rowland,* 1897, Addison; and *The Thinker: Louis N. Kenton,* 1900, Metropolitan). Handsome or homely, his people exist. By contrast to the bodiless idealism of academic American portraitists, his portraits of women, such as *Mrs. Letitia Bacon* (1888, Brooklyn), have flesh-and-blood reality and a healthy sense of sex. Eakins' portraiture as a whole forms a pictorial record of the American people of 1870 to 1910 equal to Copley's record of colonial America.

But none of these qualities made for popularity. From the late 1880s Eakins suffered from increasing neglect, or from rejection, as in the case of the chief work of his middle years, *The Agnew Clinic* (1889, University of Pennsylvania)——again a great surgeon operating before his students. But his realism remained unchanged, while his mastery increased; some of his finest works were painted in the early 1900s, such as *Mrs. William D. Frishmuth* (1900, Philadelphia) and *Professor Leslie Miller* (1901, Philadelphia). In these years he finally received increasing recognition and a number of awards and honors.

Eakins was the strongest figure painter of his time in America. His art combined pure naturalism with great physical substance and power, and with sculptural form. It was essentially plastic: not merely the representation of reality, but the creation of round forms in three-dimensional pictorial space. His figure compositions, especially those based on the nude or semi-nude body, achieved design more fully realized than that of any American contemporary—except his opposite in every other respect, Albert Ryder.* Like all vital art, his art was founded on a deep sensuousness; but the prudery of his environment and his own realism prevented full development of his poten-

tiality in figurative design. Despite this limitation, his work was a monumental contribution to American art. (L.G.)

Eames, Charles (1907-   ).
Designer, internationally famous for his innovative furniture. A tireless experimenter with new materials and techniques, and with new means of communication, Eames has also contributed to such other fields as architecture, graphics, and photography. Born in St. Louis, Mo., he supported himself first as a delivery boy, then as a laborer, and later as an engineering draftsman. He attended Washington University on an architectural scholarship, and after a trip to Europe in 1929, where he became familiar with the work of architects Walter Gropius* and Mies van der Rohe,* he opened his own architectural office in St. Louis. In 1936 Eliel Saarinen,* architect, and director of the Cranbrook Academy of Art, offered him a fellowship. He remained at Cranbrook for several years, helping to develop an experimental design department. He also collaborated with Eliel's son, Eero Saarinen,* on a chair whose unique design, using plywood molded to fit the human body, won first prize in a competition at the Museum of Modern Art in 1940. The chair was never manufactured because of the high cost of the molding process. Eames fought to bring comfortable, quality furniture to the public at a reasonable price. In 1941 he and his wife Ray, who has collaborated with him, moved to California. He supported himself by designing movie sets in Hollywood, and in his spare time tried to develop an inexpensive molding process. During World War II he designed equipment for the United States Navy based on his molded plywood experiments. Out of all this work developed one of the great chair designs of the 20th century—a distinctive, artistic form that used new materials in a new way and could be mass produced. The chair consists of a separate molded plywood back joined to a seat by plywood or metal frames. The seat and back are attached to the frame with rubber shock mounts that give the chair greater resiliency and comfort. His plywood furniture was exhibited at a one-man show at the Museum of Modern Art in 1946.

Eames's interest in new materials and techniques led to experiments with plastics. In 1948 he and a group from the University of California, Los Angeles, won a prize in a Museum of Modern Art competition for low-cost furniture designs with a plastic chair reinforced with glass fibers. Fiberglass had never been used in domestic furniture. As in all his work, he stressed the natural surface of the material, leaving the plastic exposed and unupholstered. The chair allows for a choice of four leg structures and can be mass-produced at a reasonable price. In the same year he designed storage cabinets with interchangeable parts made of plywood, plastic, and metal, employing construction methods previously used only in industry. Eames has also experimented with chairs made of wire; inexpensive and light, upholstered in lightweight foam rubber, they stack for easy shipping. In 1956 he designed a maximum-comfort lounge chair and ottoman made of laminated rosewood "petals" joined by aluminum connectors, supported on a metal swivel base with down- and foam-filled leather cushions. More recently he has designed furniture of cast aluminum, and also unit furniture, such as the row-chairs at O'Hare (Chicago) and Dulles (Washington, D.C.) airports.

A monument to Eames' practical genius is the house that he and his wife built in Santa Monica, Cal., in 1949. He considered his major problem to be the enclosure of the maximum amount of space for the minimum amount of money. Designed as part of a research program in the use of prefabricated parts for the magazine *Arts and Architecture,* he used standard factory-produced windows, doors, and steel beams. The walls were broken up by bright-colored panels and transparent glass of various shapes and sizes, creating an extraordinary effect. The house can be constructed rapidly, is flexible, with interior space that can be rearranged, is inexpensive, allows for privacy and yet gives a feeling of space, light, and air.

During the last fifteen years Eames has become increasingly interested in photography, and has produced many educational films, including those shown at world's fairs in Brussels (1958), Moscow (1959), Seattle (1962), and New York (1964). In 1960 an international jury awarded Eames and his wife the first Kaufmann International Design Award of $20,000. They have won many awards in such other fields

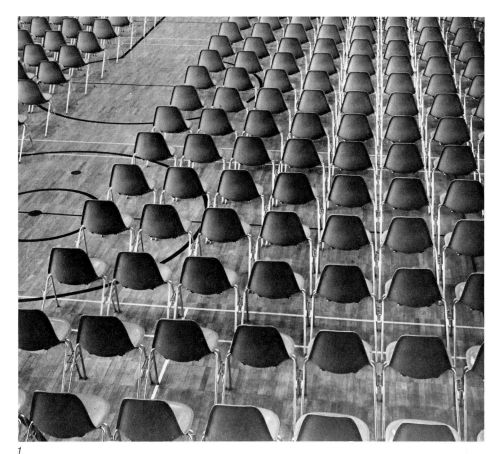

1

2

1. **Charles Eames.** Stack Chairs, c.1950, fiberglass and cast aluminum.
2. **Charles Eames.** Lounge chair and ottoman, c.1957, molded rosewood plywood, black leather, and cast aluminum. Museum of Modern Art, N.Y. (gift of Herman Miller, Inc.).

as architecture, exhibits, graphics, toys, stage and product design, and photography, and for the writing and directing of motion pictures. Eames has lectured and taught widely and was Charles Eliot Norton Professor of Poetry at Harvard University for 1970–71.

(D.P.)

Earl, Ralph (1751–1801).

Portrait and landscape painter. Born in rural Massachusetts, he set up as a painter of portraits in New Haven, Conn., in 1745. He and Amos Doolittle (1754–1832), fellow soldiers in the Governor's Foot Guard, marched to Boston in 1775, where Earl drew and Doolittle afterward engraved his four views of the battles at Lexington and Concord—the first news pictures in American art. Prompted by his Loyalist sympathies, however, Earl fled in 1778 to England, where he studied with Benjamin West* and remained for seven years, painting in London and the provinces and exhibiting at the Royal Academy. He returned to America in 1785, beginning a decade and a half of itinerant painting throughout Connecticut and New York.

Earl's portraits of this period responded to American taste by showing a greater simplicity and severity than his English work. Although rarely profound in delineation of individual character, he depicted the characteristic aspects of his place and time. Strongest in both aspects is his portrait of *Roger Sherman* (1777–79, Yale), a signer of the Declaration of Independence, the seated figure clad in red, stark, motionless, resolute. A more typical piece is *Chief Justice and Mrs. Oliver Ellsworth* (1792, Wadsworth), the two figures seated on each side of an open window in which their home acres are portrayed. Although Earl ventured into landscape painting, he is most interesting in this genre where it appears within a portrait, as here, or in his *Colonel William N. Taylor* (1790, Albright), showing his subject, an amateur artist, painting the view from his window. (C.C.S.)

Earth Art.

In 1968, when the first exhibition of "earthworks" was held in a New York City gallery, the very idea of sculpture being made of sod or earth seemed radical and new. Most of the works in this show simply employed natural materials as a medium, although it seemed a

1

2

1. ***Ralph Earl.*** Chief Justice and Mrs. Oliver Ellsworth, *1792. Wadsworth Atheneum, Hartford, Conn.*
2. ***Seth Eastman.*** Lacrosse Playing among the Sioux Indians, *1851. Corcoran Gallery of Art, Washington, D.C.*

big jump from the traditional arts of wood and stone-carving to Robert Morris'* pile of dirt or Robert Smithson's* boxes filled with chunks of rock. Within a short time it became evident that "earth art" constituted more than a change in medium: works were now being produced in out-of-the-way places, on a vast new scale, and often in deliberately impermanent form. The forces behind the movement have been a desire to subvert the commercial gallery-museum-collector syndrome, the new interest in landscape and ecology (along with the simultaneous disintegration of city life), and the nostalgia that is now felt for past ages: ruins, geology, prehistory. Perhaps the greatest single influence on these artists has been the "Great Serpent Mound" in Ohio; Smithson has literally borrowed the tail for his *Spiral Jetty* (1970) and others have been inspired by its mystery and monumentality. Unfortunately, such ritual and religious works usually have a deeper meaning, which most earth art lacks. As the movement has developed, its practitioners have gone off in many directions and additional forebears have been rediscovered: Gutzon Borglum's* carvings on Mount Rushmore; the sculptured-earth pyramid, spiral, and pool of Isamu Noguchi's* *Play Mountain* (1933); and Herbert Bayer's sodsculptures in Aspen, Col., meadows.

Among the earliest manifestations of earth art were Michael Heizer's *Nevada Depressions* (1968), a series of trenches dug in the desert that in overall configuration are strangely reminiscent of Bauhaus* composition. All of these works have subsequently disappeared. Similarly ephemeral is the work of Rafael Ferrer, who has dumped tons of leaves in New York galleries and museums, and of Dennis Oppenheim, who has cut patterns in snow and harvested a wheat field in the form of an "X". Unfortunately, such works as *Canceled Crop* (1969) are basically willful and destructive: instead of being made into bread, five hundred sacks of grain were exhibited in a Dusseldorf gallery and then abandoned. Even more explicitly destructive are such works as Heizer's smashing of the asphalt outside the Kunsthalle Museum in Berne, Switzerland, with house-wrecking machinery, and Christo's *Wrapped Coast* (1969). In the latter, a mile of Australian coastal cliffs was swathed in rope and plastic, displacing nesting birds and disrupting

the larger ecological scene, for the sole purpose of publicity. A more creative use of the natural environment has been made by artists like Hans Haacke, who has used flowing water and freezing cycles to build snow and ice configurations; Alexander Starkey, whose giant ring of birdseed (1971) was used to attract migrating birds; and Peter Hutchinson, whose plastic and glass containers filled with algae, fungus, and crystals present forms and colors of unexpected beauty without doing damage to the natural environment.

Developments related to earth art have appeared in painting, notably in the resurgence of poetic nature-images in the work of many "lyrical abstractionists," and even more explicitly in Larry Poons'* "cracked-earth" landscapes. Here layers of heavy impasto are used to create effects that approximate craggy plateaus and flowing lava—all seen from aerial views. And in architecture, Patricia Johanson* has designed a mile-long dirt loop-road to be used as a sunken circulation system through the grounds adjoining Con Edison's nuclear generating plant at Indian Point, N.Y.

The "earthworks" movement began as a revolt against traditional ways of making and marketing art, and a reinvolvement with the materials of nature, but it has moved off in many different, and often conflicting, directions, ranging from the production of heroic monuments to empty gestures. If its initial achievements have often been doubtful and disturbing, earth art nevertheless implies something more important in terms of the relationship between architecture, sculpture, and the environment.

(E.C.G.)

Eastlake Style (also called **Eastlakian**). A minor phase of American architectural development in the 1870s. It was inspired by furniture designs derived from the writings of the English painter and art critic Charles Locke Eastlake (1836–1906) and his influential book *Hints on Household Taste* (1868). Eastlake's furniture, in which natural or oiled wood, usually oak, was left unfinished to display the beauty of the grain, was intended to be an honest expression of the materials. A reaction against the pretentiousness of popular "period" furniture, it was a tour de force of structural expressionism in which every leg, bracket, or shelf proclaimed its usefulness to the eye.

The Eastlake style in architecture produced an assortment of small frame houses, often built from stock plans, and lesser structures such as boat houses, summer cottages, and stables. It was characterized by picturesque profiles and end gables, and was generally executed in wood-frame construction, with many balconies carried on conspicuous bracket supports. Often such buildings looked like Swiss chalets. Much of the building ornament was pierced boards or jigsaw cutouts.

Like the Victorian Gothic* style and the neo-Grec* style with which it coexisted, the Eastlake style was short-lived and did not long survive the panic of 1873, but it was still in evidence at the Centennial Exposition in Philadelphia in 1876. (A.B.)

Eastman, Seth (1808–75). Soldier, landscape painter, and painter and illustrator of Indian life. Born in Brunswick, Me., he entered the U.S. Military Academy in 1824 and was commissioned a second lieutenent in the Regular Army in 1829. His first posts were at Fort Crawford, Wis. and Fort Snelling, Minn. (1829 and 1831). There he sketched the western scene. After two years on topographical duty he was ordered back to West Point, where he taught drawing during 1833–40. During this period he began to exhibit at the National Academy of Design and was elected "honorary member amateur" of the Academy in 1839. As a nascent painter, Eastman received help from his colleague Robert W. Weir,* already a highly regarded artist, who had arrived at West Point in 1834. The paintings and watercolors of this period, with the exception of a genre work entitled *Sawing Wood* (lost), were all landscapes. A typical early work, *Hudson River With a Distant View of West Point* (c.1835, Butler), shows Eastman to have been a competent painter in the manner of the Hudson River School.*

From 1841 he saw service in the Seminole War in Florida and again until 1848 at Fort Snelling and in Texas (1848-49).

In Minnesota he became deeply interested in studying and recording without romantic distortion the Indian way of life. Because of his intimate knowledge of Indian life acquired in the course of twenty years, he was assigned in 1850 to the Bureau of the Commissioner of Indian Affairs in Washington, D.C., to illustrate the six volumes of Henry R.

Schoolcraft's monumental *History . . . of Indian Tribes of the United States.* He also completed *Lacrosse Playing Among the Sioux Indians* (1851, Corcoran) and *Sioux Indians* (1850, Joslyn), which show him at the height of his powers as a painter. After this special duty, which terminated in 1855, he returned to regular army life, and served throughout the Civil War. He retired in 1863, but nevertheless commanded various installations until 1867. In 1866 he reached the rank of brevet brigadier general. The following year, by joint resolution of the Congress, he was commissioned to paint two series of paintings for the government, including one on U.S. forts.

Eastman was probably the most talented of the artists who depicted the early West and Indian life. Although his paintings lack the zest, dramatic intensity, and romance of those by Charles Deas* and Alfred Jacob Miller, they are more faithful to everyday reality and are equally well painted. His best efforts, transcending mere reportage, stand as works of art of high quality.

(H.W.W.)

Eaton, Wyatt (1849–96).

Figure and portrait painter, born in Canada. He studied at the National Academy of Design* before going to France; at the École des Beaux-Arts he studied under Jean Léon Gérôme and then went to live near Jean François Millet at Barbizon. While in Europe he was influenced by both Millet and Bastien-Lepage. As one of the younger artists who, on his return to America, felt the limitations of the National Academy of Design, he helped found the Society of American Artists* in 1877 and served as the organization's first secretary. He painted quiet portraits and small, subjective studies of graceful female figures, such as *Ariadne* (National Coll.).

Eclecticism (in architecture).

A design approach that borrows freely from various architectural styles but does not usually combine them in one design. It was inspired by one of the most influential events in American architectural history—the World's Columbian Exposition of 1893 in Chicago. The great white classical buildings surrounding the Grand Basin of the Court of Honor left a lasting impression of what the "City Beautiful" might be. So overwhelming was the effect of this classical fairyland

that it overshadowed picturesque romanticism and any possibility that an indigenous architecture might have evolved out of it. The Fair and eclecticism brought a new order wherein the architect assumed control and, in his choice of styles, dominated the taste of a generation. The Fair was the concerted work of the leading architects of the country. Richard Morris Hunt* and four other eastern architects were invited to join their western confreres in designing the major buildings. Dominating the Fair grounds, Hunt's Administration Building was a pure evocation of Parisian Beaux-Arts elegance. Uniformity was achieved by the establishment of a uniform cornice line and by having all buildings in white. In addition, most of the buildings had colonnades or columns, which gave the fair a classical character even though many of the buildings were of Renaissance derivation. One nonconformist note was Louis Sullivan's* Transportation Building, the creation of a talented rebel.

Eclecticism was assimilative rather than creative. But it required great ingenuity to devise the plan for a building that would retain all the exterior characteristics of an Italian palazzo or a Roman temple. Proper design of the Roman orders (columns) called for much knowledge, a sense of proportion, and uncommon skills. Legions of draftsmen had to be trained to meet the demands of this new classical mode. The École des Beaux-Arts and, later, the American Academy in Rome, were called upon to train American architects and help adapt foreign styles to American requirements. Often referred to as the "Age of Eclecticism" or "American Renaissance," this basically classical development eclipsed the Queen Anne,* the Romanesque revival,* and other romantic styles. and held sway for thirty years. Most favored for large public and commercial buildings were designs derived from Roman, Romanesque, or Beaux-Arts sources. The Renaissance styles also found favor in these categories and in residential work. Gothic architecture was used in collegiate, commercial, and ecclesiastical buildings while the Federal and Georgian styles served for hotels, apartment houses, and private residences.

Because eclectic architecture followed an established set of rules, it produced splendid externals but made little

technological advance. This paved the way for the post-World War I invasion by foreign architects, who introduced the International style,* with its new structural systems and materials and the stripped architecture fostered by the economics of inflationary Europe. Just as the revivals gave way in 1893 to eclecticism, so eclecticism was gradually superseded in the 1930s by the International style. (See also Beaux-Arts Eclectic, French Classic Eclectic, French Renaissance Eclectic, Federal or Georgian Eclectic, Gothic Eclectic, Renaissance Eclectic, Roman Eclectic, Romanesque Eclectic.)

(A.B.)

Edmonds, Francis William (1806–63).

Painter of genre and of incidents from literature. Edmonds was born in Hudson, N.Y. Although he showed signs of considerable artistic talent, he embarked on a career as a banker. But in 1826, while working in a bank, he became a student at the National Academy of Design. His work was exhibited at the National Academy from 1836 to 1838 under the pseudonym E. F. Williams, but in subsequent exhibitions he resumed his own name. In 1840 he sailed for Europe, and there studied the Old Masters, especially in Italy. Several paintings, later shown in New York, were landscapes of Italian scenes. He was a productive painter and exhibited widely in all the regular exhibitions held in New York, Boston, Philadelphia, Baltimore, and on one occasion at the Royal Academy in London. His banking interests persisted at least until 1853, when he assisted in the establishment of the New York Clearing House and various artistic and civic organizations. He retired in 1855 and settled in a country home on the Bronx River, where he painted and exhibited at least until 1859.

His paintings are similar to those of his more famous contemporary, William Sidney Mount,* whom he must have known. A somewhat uneven painter, he was at his best in compositions involving few figures, such as *All Talk and No Work* (c.1856, Brooklyn). However, on occasion, such as in *The Image Peddler* (1844, New York Hist.), he handled a complex composition with considerable skill. He was an excellent draftsman and included in most of his canvases a variety of beautifully rendered still-life accessories. He often failed, however, to convey convincingly the psychological relationship between the actors in his scenes of everyday life. His older women are strongly individual, but his representations of young women were apt to be vapid stereotypes of the contemporary ideal of feminine beauty. (H.W.W.)

Edwards, John, and Thomas, Samuel, and Joseph, Jr.

One of colonial Boston's most illustrious families of silversmiths. The first of the family to practice the craft, John (1671–1746), was born in England but probably received his training here from Jeremiah Dummer,* and started working about 1692. He is noted for his church silver and a rare early standing salt.

John's two sons, Thomas (c.170l–55) and Samuel (1705–62), were also silversmiths. After John died in 1746, Thomas carried on the business. Most of his silver is in the simpler style of the early rococo period, although a teapot made at the end of his career is in the inverted pear form with repoussé decoration. His most beautiful pieces are the salvers he made with molded and incurving octagonal sides and engraved imbricated borders, or cast scroll and shell borders with elaborate armorial bearings (Winterthur).

Samuel was commissioned by the General Assembly to make presentation silver. In a major exhibition at the Boston Museum in 1956, he was represented by four items. A teapot in the rococo tradition and a fluted ladle by him are at the Winterthur Museum.

It was probably Samuel who trained Joseph Edwards, Jr. (1737–83), since he bequeathed Joseph some of his silversmithing tools. Joseph, Jr., was a nephew of Thomas and Samuel Edwards, and his work ranged from pocketbook clasps and tea tongs to porringers, casters, and marrow spoons. (M.G.F.)

Eichholtz, Jacob (1776–1842).

A native of Lancaster, Pa., who became a leading portrait painter of the Philadelphia and Baltimore area. As early as 1806 he was painting small profile oils as a sideline to his work as a coppersmith. Thomas Sully,* visiting Lancaster in 1808, gave him advice and encouragement. About three years later, a visit to Gilbert Stuart* in Boston gave Eichholtz further confidence. Determined to succeed, he read all authors on art he could find, filled a commonplace book with notes, and painted constantly, though

without formal training. His mature style was direct and strong, with the flat texture of the ornamental painter and a good sense of character, as in his *Self-Portrait* (c.1810, Pennsylvania). His full charm is evident also in his pendant portraits, *Judge and Mrs. Thomas Emlen Franklin* (1838, Franklin and Marshall College). His work includes also a few landscapes and subject pieces characterized by a naiveté of design and careful detail.
(C.C.S.)

Eight, The.

A group of eight painters who exhibited at the Macbeth Gallery in New York City in February, 1908. Robert Henri* was the leader; with him were four of his friends from Philadelphia days: William Glackens,* George Luks,* Everett Shinn,* and John Sloan,* and three other artists, Arthur B. Davies,* Ernest Lawson,* and Maurice Prendergast.* All had exhibited for a number of years, several were well established, and their average age was over forty. Henri himself was a member of the National Academy of Design.* They and their friends, however, had met with sufficient rebuffs to make them want to liberalize the art establishment and broaden opportunities to exhibit.

The group began to take shape in 1904 when all but Shinn and Lawson were included in a showing at the National Arts Club. In 1906, again, five of the eight exhibited at a private gallery, which subsequently failed. In December of that year Glackens, Luks, and Shinn were all rejected by the Academy. The following March, Henri, then a member of the Academy jury, fought to obtain a fair showing for his friends and students. There were tense scenes, and in the end Henri withdrew two of his paintings and failed to have a Luks canvas hung. Henri issued sharp statements and called his friends together to discuss an independent exhibition. The Academy, meanwhile, at their annual meeting rejected thirty-three of thirty-six nominees for membership, including Lawson and Davies. By mid-May the eight painters had agreed to stage a cooperative show the following February. The press featured the "rebellion" of "The Eight." Some were much later dubbed "The Ash Can School".* When the exhibition opened on February 3, 1908, attendance was heavy, and sales amounted to nearly $4000. The more sensational journalists

proclaimed the works shocking, and conservative critics found it eccentric and poor in drawing; but there were a number of favorable reviews, noting the show's liveliness, independence, and distinctive emphasis on the New York scene and on a more realistic approach. The city views of Glackens, Luks, Shinn, and Sloan gained national attention, and the exhibition has ever since been regarded as a milestone in the development of American realism. It was a milestone, also, in that it demonstrated that artists, critics, and public wanted other outlets than the traditional exhibitions and a fuller view of new movements.

The National Academy reacted by a temporary liberalizing of its exhibition policies and by electing to membership both Ernest Lawson and George Bellows,* a Henri student. Interest in the exhibition was such that The Eight sent their work on tour to Philadelphia and eight cities of the midwest and East Coast. No further action was taken until the spring of 1910, when another reactionary wave at the Academy again provoked an independent exhibition, this time organized along different lines (see Society of Independent Artists).
(D.W.S.)

Eilshemius, Louis Michel (1864–1941).

Painter who produced a large body of work, highly varied and often intensely personal, before he ceased painting about 1920. He was born near Newark, N.J., the son of a Dutch importer, and received schooling in Germany before attending Cornell University (1882–84). Turning to art, he studied in New York City with Robert Minor at the Art Students League,* and in Paris at the Académie Julien (1886). He traveled widely—to California in 1888, and during the following years to Europe, North Africa, Hawaii, and the South Seas.

Eilshemius sketched constantly and also wrote, composed music, and worked on inventions. An eccentric spirit, he adopted the pseudonym Mahatma and described himself as the "all supreme genius," "the World's mightiest mind," and "Scientist Supreme." During the 1930s his work began to receive belated recognition, but he became increasingly embittered. Eilshemius' painting was highly uneven, reflecting his eccentricity, but it was often visionary in character. It related to the poetic, introvertive tradition of Ralph Blakelock* and Albert Ryder,* but was more naive. Taken all together, it varied from academic to primitive, from objective travel notations to fantasies of naked nymphs in landscape settings. Broadly brushed, warmly colored, often crudely finished, it was slow to receive acceptance as serious art. An example is *New York at Night* (1917, on loan to Metropolitan). Marcel Duchamp* introduced Eilshemius' painting at the first Independents Exhibition in 1917, and together with the dynamic patron, Katherine Dreier, arranged for the artist's first one-man show at the Société Anonyme in 1920. Valentine Dudensing, a Parisian art dealer, and Duncan Phillips, a collector and writer on art, also became champions of his painting. (The signature on Eilshemius' earlier work very often took the form "Elshemus.") (D.W.S.)

Elfe, Thomas, Sr. (c.1719–75).
Very few 18th-century southern cabinetmakers have been identified. An exception is this Charleston, S.C., craftsman who was active from about 1747 to his death. There is evidence that in 1747 he spent £500 for slaves, indicating that he was already well established. An account book reveals that for the years 1768–75 alone, more than fifteen hundred pieces of furniture were produced in Elfe's shop. As was true of most cabinetmakers, the bulk of his production was side chairs (643), but he also made mahogany bedsteads (68), double chests of drawers (28), "half-drawers and dressing drawers" (51), mahogany desks (22), tea tables (52), "slab and side board tables" (41), dining tables (132), and just about every furniture form known to English colonists in the South. An inventory of his estate reveals that he used a great quantity of mahogany, with poplar, ash, cedar, and cypress among the secondary woods.

None of his furniture pieces is signed, but among those attributed to him are a library bookcase and desk and bookcase (MESDA), as well as a chest-on-chest (Heyward-Washington). Attributions have been based on a distinctive fret decorating case pieces, a cross-member running from front to rear in the center of large drawers, and ownership by families for whom Elfe is known to have worked.

Judging from the fact that Elfe had numerous apprentices, at least two partners, and employed nine slave-craftsmen, he must have had one of the largest cabinetmaking establishments in the South, if not in all of the colonies. His estate included large holdings of real estate, and each of his four children inherited a town house and £1000. His tools, benches, and three slave-craftsmen were left to Thomas Elfe (1759–1825), the only one of his sons trained as a cabinetmaker. (C.F.H.)

Elliott, Charles Loring (1812–68).
Portrait painter, born in Scipio, N.Y. Slated by his father to become an architect, his first exposure to art was in that field. However, architecture failed to hold his interest. Moving to New York City, he worked briefly with John Trumbull* before becoming, in 1829, a student of John Quidor.* He then became an itinerant portrait painter and traveled in central New York. After ten years he returned to New York City, where he soon won a reputation for achieving remarkable likenesses. From 1839 until his death, his portraits were regularly shown at the National Academy of Design.* Eminently successful in a highly competitive field, he produced in his lifetime almost seven hundred portraits. Many of these works depicted figures prominent in American arts and letters, the professions, and political life.

Elliott was one of the leading portraitists of his period. Unlike his contemporary, G. P. A. Healy,* who achieved both an American and an international reputation and clientele, he was content to be the recorder of prominent Americans. The advent of the daguerreotype and photography, which was eventually to supersede portraiture for all practical purposes, was already making its inroads in Elliott's day. Elliott used it as an aid—a not uncommon practice in that period—and often painted directly from photographs. In the process, he often lost the briskness and buoyancy that characterizes his work done directly from life.

Elliott's portraits showed little originality in pose, coloring and composition, and followed the traditional bust and full-length formulas. What made his paintings stand out was his ability, when faced with a challenging sitter, to obtain a likeness that had immediacy and force and made the subject come to life. The portraits of *Thomas Lorraine McKenny* (1856, Corcoran) and *Preston H. Hodges* (1850, Metropolitan) have this vitality.
(H.W.W.)

Ellsworth, James Sanford (1802–74).
Eccentric itinerant New England portraitist best known for his numerous pencil and watercolor miniatures. He was born in Windsor, Conn., and most of his sitters were from Connecticut, Massachusetts, eastern New York, Vermont, and New Hampshire. Nearly all were depicted half length with faces and figures in profile, surrounded by billowing, cloudlike nimbuses that, together with the fanciful Victorian chairs in which they sit, served as the artist's trademark. Many of the miniatures were on embossed papers produced for Valentine messages and were framed in the die-stamped metal cases that were mass-produced for daguerreotypes. Ellsworth's use of these materials, along with a variety of chair types and nimbuses, may ultimately allow a chronological reconstruction of his career. Several large oil paintings signed with his name are markedly different from the miniatures, which range from 2½ x 3 to 6 x 8 inches. (M.J.G.)

Elmer, Edwin Romanzo (1850–1923).
Folk painter born in Ashland, Mass. A farmer, and inventor of agricultural machines, he apparently began to paint in middle age with little formal training, although he did study briefly at the National Academy around 1895. Of his few known paintings, several explore the nature of reality and illusion with great originality, as in his *Mourning Picture* (c.1889, Smith College Museum of Art), painted to commemorate the death of his daughter. The elements of the composition are presented in great detail but appear, as in a collage, curiously isolated from each other. In another painting, the *Magic Glasses* (c.1891, Shelburne), a magnifying glass presented in an indoor milieu mysteriously shows us a fragment of outdoor landscape.

Emmes, Thomas (active c.1700).
Engraver of the first American portrait printed from a copperplate. The portrait, of Increase Mather, survives in two copies (Boston Library) of Mather's *Ichabod, Or A Discourse, Etc.* (1702, Boston). The crudely scratched image is based on a late 17th century English engraving. Little is known of Emmes.

Emmons, Nathanial (1704–40).
One of the earliest native-born artists. His obituary in the *Boston News-Letter*

1. **Edwin Romanzo Elmer.** Mourning Picture, c.1889. Smith College Museum of Art, Northampton, Mass.
2. **Louis Michael Eilshemius.** New York at Night, 1917. Metropolitan Museum of Art, N.Y. (bequest of Adelaide Milton de Groot).
3. **Charles Loring Elliott.** Thomas Lorraine McKenney, 1856. Corcoran Gallery of Art, Washington, D.C.

Environmental Art

praises his "admirable Imitations of Nature, both in faces, Rivers, Banks and Rural Scenes." All that have survived are a few small portraits in black and white, strongly influenced by the mezzotint prototypes.*

Environmental Art.

"Environmental" works have been part of a continuing 20th-century effort to break down the barriers between art and life—to replace the "illusionism" and "object" traditions of Renaisance painting and sculpture with direct experience by immersing the spectator in the work. During the 1950s, as abstract expressionist paintings grew larger and larger, viewers began to "experience" color rather than observe it in an intellectually detached way; they felt literally surrounded by the vast color-fields of Barnett Newman* and Mark Rothko.* At the same time, architects such as Frederick Kiesler were working on collaborations between painting, sculpture, and architecture; sculptor Louise Nevelson* was extending her bas-reliefs along entire walls; and Herbert Ferber was beginning to formulate his ideas about sculpture-rooms. By the late 1950s a number of younger artists had turned to "theater events" and happenings*—a form that had developed out of the large-scale environment implicit in the new American painting, as well as from a new emphasis placed on "performance" that can be traced back to the "action painting" of Jackson Pollock.*

Because they incorporated real people and real objects in living environments, "happenings" tended to lead to a new emphasis on the "total art environment" rather than the individual, isolated work of art. One of the earliest and most complete manifestations of the new attitude was Store (1961–62) by Claes Oldenburg.* Determined to make a totality out of art and life, the artist rented a real store, produced his wares in the back room, and then marketed his plaster and cloth sculptures in the front—displaying his "wares" in the show-window. During the same period he presented a number of "performances," which made use of gigantic props. After the mid-1960s, artists of all persuasions began turning their New York gallery shows into total "environments": Carl André* covered floors with firebrick; Les Levine* covered rooms with mylar or plastic modular units; Dan Flavin* structured rooms by colored fluorescent light. Perhaps the most brilliant "environmental" gallery show was Andy Warhol's* room of floating, helium-filled silver pillows; with the walls of another room displaying his pink, silk-screened "cow" wallpaper (1966). All of these "environmental" gallery shows were very clearly structured by the architecture of the exhibition space Tony Smith* has created his own architectural environments with his huge space-frame sculptures for the Corcoran Gallery (1967) and the World's Fair in Osaka, Japan (1971). In both cases the spectator moves through the sculpture, "experiencing" rather than "viewing" the work.

Among the consequences of environmental art has been the revived interest in three-dimensional form, a vast increase in scale, and a new sympathy for architecture and landscape. A number of younger artists, such as Peter Hutchinson and Hans Haacke, are attempting to change the environment itself by making changes in ecological conditions. Other artists are integrating their work into the natural environment, as in Cyrus Field (1970)—a seven-mile continuous line-sculpture by Patricia Johanson* that structures its woodland setting. Carrying even further the developments in "landscape sculpture" and the use of literal space, other artists have created earth art.*   (E.C.G.)

Esherick, Wharton (1887–1970).

Dean of 20th-century American woodworkers, originator of sculptural, organic furniture and furnishings. Esherick was born in Philadelphia, Pa., and trained as a painter. His preoccupation with woodcuts in the 1920s led to his experiments in wood—at first in fashioning frames for woodcuts—and to his impatience with the angularity of almost all furniture designs of that time. In the 1930s he built his landmark studio in Paoli, near Philadelphia, where he worked until his death. Every detail of the studio—floors, beams, ceilings, and the famous winding stairway—used wood as never before, while retaining an overall unity of design. During the making of the studio, his earlier, angular, and geometric designs evolved into his mature flowing style, which was influenced by art nouveau.* Beginning in the early 1930s, he accepted many commissions to design the interiors of private homes, the most important being

1

2

1. **Walker Evans.** Houses, Atlanta, Georgia, 1936, photograph. Library of Congress, Washington, D.C.

2. **Walker Evans.** Auto Parts Shop,
Atlanta, Georgia, *1936, photograph.
Library of Congress, Washington, D.C.*

the house of Judge and Mrs. Curtis Bok in Gulph Mills, Pa., in 1935–38, one of America's outstanding domestic interiors. Esherick's technique was to draw directly on a piece of wood, intuiting shapes from its grain, cracks, and knots. Knots were allowed to project slightly from the surface and any characteristic of the wood with tactile potential was drawn out. As his fame grew, Esherick introduced mechanical tools into his technique in order to meet the demand for his chairs, sofas, music stands, and tables. His studio was perhaps his epic work, as he constantly refined its parts, always using the woods he found in his immediate environs. As a source of free-form furniture design, his work and his ethos of woodworking was most important to younger woodworkers, particularly Sam Maloof* and Wendell Castle.* (R.S.)

Evans, Edward.

The life dates of this Philadelphia "joiner" are unknown, but he was evidently one of the earliest settlers of William Penn's "Green Town." There is evidence that he was London-trained and was given his freedom in 1674 or 1685. In 1702, Evans billed Pennsylvania's Governor Hamilton £8 for "joyners work." He made an "ovill table" for William Trent in 1703 and another, along with a stand, for James Logan in 1714. The latest record of his existence in Philadelphia is 1719. A walnut fall-front secretary desk (Williamsburg) in the William and Mary style bears his name and the date 1707. It is the earliest signed and dated piece of Philadelphia furniture and one of only a few pieces in the William and Mary style associated with a colonial American craftsman. (C.F.H.)

Evans, Walker (1903–   ).

Photographer, magazine editor, and teacher. Evans, whose taut, direct, and aristocratically pure vision counts as one of the major influences on American photography, was born in St. Louis, Mo., and grew up in Kenilworth, a suburb of Chicago, and in New York City. He was educated at Loomis and Andover academies and attended Williams College in Massachusetts for one year (1922–23). In 1926 he audited classes at the Sorbonne in Paris, returning to New York City a year later. After several temporary jobs he acquired, in 1928, a vest-pocket camera and decided to become a photographer. Like many before him, Evans visited Alfred Stieglitz,* the dean of American photographers, in 1929, seeking encouragement. Stieglitz was noncommital and the two never met again.

The main influence on Evans' work came from intellectuals, writers, and painters, not photographers. Lincoln Kirstein, publisher of the literary quarterly, *Hound and Horn,* introduced him to other creative men who, like himself, struggled in the midst of the Depression. He met Hart Crane and illustrated his book of poems, *The Bridge* (1930). He shared a Greenwich Village house with the painter and photographer Ben Shahn* about 1931–33. Later he became a friend of the writer and film critic James Agee, whose book, *Let Us Now Praise Famous Men,* he illustrated in 1941. His first one-man exhibition, "Walker Evans: Photographs of 19th Century Houses," was held at the Museum of Modern Art in 1933, the same year he illustrated Carleton Beals' book *The Crime of Cuba.* In 1935, he documented the Museum of Modern Art exhibition, "African Negro Art," with 477 photographs.

The most sustained creative period in Evans' career began in 1935, when he joined the historical unit of the Farm Security Administration.* In eighteen months he made hundreds of photographs that dramatized the plight of the rural poor and directly established the style of American documentary photography. A Museum of Modern Art exhibition of these photographs augmented by other work was published in his *American Photographs* (1938) and led to a Guggenheim Fellowship in 1940. About them Lincoln Kirstein has written: "The most characteristic single feature of Evans' work is its purity, or even its puritanism. It is 'straight' photography not only in technique but in the rigorous directness of its way of looking. . . . Every object is regarded head-on with the unsparing frankness of a Russian ikon or Flemish portrait. . . . The view is clinical." Additional exhibitions resulted in 1966 in two important publications: *Many Are Called* and *Message from the Interior.*

Evans became a contributing editor for *Time* in 1943. Two years later he joined *Fortune* magazine, and over the next twenty years produced twenty-eight photographic essays on the American landscape. In 1964 he was appointed professor of graphic design at Yale University, retiring in 1971, the year of his major retrospective exhibition at the Museum of Modern Art. (D.L.)

Evergood, Philip (1901–73)
Born in New York City, he was educated in England. He left Cambridge University in 1921 to study sculpture at the Slade School, then in 1923 he went to New York to study painting with George Luks* at the Art Students League,* and finally to the Académie Julien in Paris, where his teachers were André Lhote and Jean-Paul Laurens. He had his first one-man show in New York in 1927, exhibiting biblical subjects. After a stay in Spain in 1929, he settled in New York in 1931.

The Depression was then at its height and it affected Evergood profoundly. He abandoned biblical and literary themes for subjects drawn from life and involving social problems, racial discrimination, and political oppression. He was active in the American Artists Congress, the Artists Union, and other organizations concerned with the civil rights of artists. His three major murals (in the Richmond Hill, N.Y., Public Library, at Kalamazoo College in Michigan, and in the Post Office at Jackson, Ga.), all deal with labor on the land or in factories. During the period of the WPA Federal Art Project,* Evergood was supervisor of the Easel Painting Division in New York. Major examples of his social protest painting are *American Tragedy* (1937, Whitney), a large canvas commemorating a police attack on striking steel workers in Chicago, and *Don't Cry, Mother,* depicting two children and their mother contemplating empty plates on a table in a tenement (1938–44, Modern Museum).

Evergood was not by any means solely devoted to such direct social criticism. His work often took on symbolic or allegorical form, as in *The New Lazarus* (1954, Whitney), which has allusions to the crucifixion, racial turmoil, war, and the clownish phantasmagoria of modern society, all in one large canvas. Often his painting dealt with simple human themes, as in *Dream Catch,* with a little black fisherman and his huge fish (1946, Hirshhorn Collection), or *Woman at Piano* (1955, National Coll.). Like his subject matter, his style varied greatly from work to work, but despite frequent excursions into fantasy, it is characterized mainly by a down-to-earth bluntness recalling that of American primitive painters and sometimes the equally direct but complex manner of Max Beckmann.

Evergood taught at universities in New York, Iowa, Minnesota, and elsewhere, and he received many awards. (A.F.)

Expressionism (in architecture).
A style that emerged between 1915 and 1923 and was characterized by volumes, surfaces, and details that seem to purposely contradict traditional architectural values and to deny or ignore normal construction processes. The resulting buildings displayed walls that battered outward at the top, and angular surface patterns that seemed to be unrelated to the surface or utilitarian considerations. They all have in some degree a fanciful or even bizarre quality.

The leading expressionist architect in the United States was Frank Lloyd Wright.* Like Erich Mendelsohn in Europe, Wright was not consistently an expressionist, but a number of his realized buildings and many of his projected structures have completely unorthodox forms. Wright's first strong assertion of such visual values came in his Midway Gardens (1914, Chicago) and in his Imperial Hotel (1917–22 Tokyo). In his California work of the 1920s he imparted an expressionist quality to all of his precast concrete "block" houses as well as to his projects for large-scale developments in the mountains above Los Angeles, Cal., in the desert south of Phoenix, Ariz., and his Lakeshore scheme for Lake Tahoe, Cal. The details of his expressionist designs were self-consciously primitive and derived from the pre-Columbian architecture of Mexico and Central America and the Pueblo Indians of the Southwest. These elements were later taken over by Wright's close associates, his son Lloyd Wright (1890–   ), and by Rudolf M. Schindler.* Lloyd Wright's Sowden House (Los Angeles, 1926), with its mouthlike facade, is probably the extreme example of American expressionism. Equally removed from ordinary architectural reality were many of the 1920s projects of Bruce Goff,* and several designs of another midwesterner, Barry Byrne (1883–1967). None of these designers completely abandoned the expressionist quality in their work, and in the 1950s and 1960s expressionist elements surfaced again in the buildings of several designers, particularly those of Herb Greene (b.1929). (D.G.)

Expressionism (in art).
A type of painting, sculpture, or graphic art in which the artist uses exaggeration or distortion of form, color, or space to express turbulent emotion. The term refers to both a style in art and a 20th-century movement. Unlike the impressionists, who recorded their perceptions of light and surface movement, the expressionists often used light for dramatic purpose, and relied on movement to project emotion. Basically a personal and introspective style, it contrasts sharply with cubism* and impressionism,* which are analytical and descriptive.

Primarily a central European movement, expressionism originated in Germany and Austria. The three phases of the movement are associated with three groups of artists. The work of the group known as *Die Brücke* (The Bridge, 1905–14) stems from Vincent van Gogh, African sculpture, and fauvism* and is characterized by distorted figures and bold color. Members included Emil Nolde and Ernest Kirchner. Artists in *Der Blaue Reiter* group (The Blue Rider, 1911–14), such as Vasily Kandinsky, Paul Klee, and Lyonel Feininger,* were slightly more abstract. Their art, relating to that of Paul Gauguin and Robert Delaunay, is markedly rhythmic and emphasizes the interpenetration of forms and colors. The third group, *Die Neue Sachlichkeit* (The New Objectivity, 1920s), included such artists as Otto Dix and George Grosz.* More concerned with social commentary, their work was intensely emotional, bitterly realistic, and almost clinical in detail. Among other artists who are considered expressionist are James Ensor, Oskar Kokoschka, Gustave Klimt, Georges Rouault, Chaim Soutine, Edvard Munch, and Max Weber.* American painters who reveal an expressionist influence include Ben Shahn,* Ivan Albright,* Abraham Rattner,* Jack Levine,* Karl Knaths,* and Philip Evergood.* (See also Abstract Expressionism.)

Eyre, Wilson, Jr (1858–1944).
Architect. He was born in Florence, Italy, but came to Newport, R.I., at the

age of eleven. He studied architecture for two years at the Massachusetts Institute of Technology. He served his apprenticeship until 1882 with James P. Sims of Philadelphia, and then began his own practice there. In 1912 he took a partner, J. Gilbert McIlvaine, and adopted the firm name of Wilson Eyre McIlvaine.

A talented artist and musician, Eyre's architectural designs reflected his feeling for texture and color. He was influenced by the British designer and poet William Morris and by the work of Morris's architect, Philip Webb. Like Charles A. Platt* and Delano & Aldrich,* he allowed his country-house designs to develop out of a carefully studied scheme. As an architect, Eyre was an individualist, his buildings are distinctive and readily identified on stylistic grounds alone.

Aside from the City Trust (1888), an early office building in Philadelphia, where he introduced a gable facing the street, most of his work was residential. The gable theme was also used in the Philadelphia town house he remodelled in modified Gothic style for Dr. Louis Starr (1889) located on Rittenhouse Square, while the Clarence B. Moore House (1890) at Juniper and Locust streets, Philadelphia, was more explicitly Venetian Gothic. The C. L. Freer House (1890) at 71 East Ferry Street, Detroit, was a good example of his urban architecture. In his early period, the country house he designed for Craig Herberton (1888) at Camp Hill Station, Pa., exemplified the shingle style,* while the great country house for Walter B. Jeffords, Hunting Hill Farms (1915) at Glen Riddle, Pa., was typical of his later, more conservative and less distinctive designs. (A.B.)

1. **Philip Evergood.** The New Lazarus, 1954. Whitney Museum of American Art, N.Y. (gift of Joseph H. Hirshhorn).
2. **Expressionism** (in architecture). Frank Lloyd Wright. Midway Gardens, façade, Chicago, 1914.

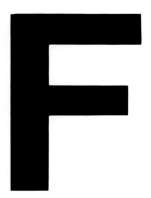

f/64.

The name of an informal group founded in San Francisco, Cal., by West Coast photographers Ansel Adams* and Willard Van Dyke to further the cause of simple and straightforward techniques in photography. These photographers used the large "stand" camera and a small aperture, f/64 (hence the name). Prints were usually made on smooth paper and great attention was given to achieving a maximum range of tones from black to white. Other members of the group that met from time to time at Van Dyke's studio in Oakland, were Imogen Cunningham,* Sonya Noskowiak, John Paul Edwards, Henry F. Smith, and Edward Weston.* In 1932 they held an exhibition at the M. H. de Young Memorial Museum in San Francisco, showing 64 prints by members of the group and 16 prints by Alina Lavenson, Consuelo Kanaga, Preston Halder, and Brett Weston, who shared their ideas. Before the group disbanded in 1935 the work of Peter Stackpole and Dorothea Lange* was also included in exhibitions in the Oakland gallery.

(V.D.C.)

Farm Security Administration (FSA) Historical Division.

An agency of the Resettlement Administration, Department of Agriculture, it was created in 1935 to acquaint city-dwellers with the living conditions of migratory workers, poor farmers, and the inhabitants of small towns in areas that suffered from drought and soil erosion. The FSA program was discontinued in 1943.

The head of FSA Historical Division was a Columbia University economist, Roy Stryker, a forceful administrator who believed in the social and political power of photographic documentation. Not only did he hope to create a historical record, but he also wanted the pictures to be used to gain support for

1

2

3

Farm Security Administration
1. *Russell Lee.* Tenant Purchase
   Clients at Home, *1939. Library of
   Congress, Washington, D.C.*
2. *Ben Shahn.* Family of Resettlement
   Administration Client in Doorway of
   Their Home, *1935. Library of Con-
   gress, Washington, D.C.*
3. *Dorothea Lange.* Tractored Out,
   *1938. George Eastman House,
   Rochester, N.Y.*
4. *John Vachon.* Front Porch, *1941.
   Library of Congress, Washington,
   D.C.*

4

New Deal social legislation. To carry out his plan, he hired a number of outstanding photographers, including Paul Carter, John Collier, Jr., Jack Delano, Walker Evans,* Theodore Jung, Dorothea Lange,* Russell Lee, Ed Locke, Carl Mydans, Gordon Parks, Arthur Rothstein, Ben Shahn,* Jonn Vachon, and Marion Post Wolcott. Generally only six photographers were working in the project at one time. Over 270,000 negatives were made, most of which are now on file at the Library of Congress. Prints from 200,000 of the negatives are in the Picture Collection of the New York Public Library. Initially restricted to pictures of the Midwest, Far West, and South, the project was later expanded to include virtually the entire country. Stryker indoctrinated the photographers in history, geography, politics, and economics, and suggested relevant books to be read and maps to be studied. The straightforward documentary approach of the photographers preserved for future generations a vivid sense of a period when thousands abandoned homes and unproductive farms and wandered jobless across the country, and when breadlines were common in industrial cities. The pictures have continued to be widely reprinted and organized into exhibitions. The content of the photographs was often made doubly effective by the esthetic sensibilities brought to the work by the remarkable group of photographers Stryker assembled. The body of work created under the FSA has had a profound influence on the history of photography because of the high quality and the direct approach of the photographs as well as the comprehensiveness of their coverage of American life from 1935 to 1943.　(V.D.C.)

Farnham, Paulding (n.d.–1927).
One of the chief designers of silver for Tiffany & Company,* he was thoroughly trained in the technology of silversmithing by that firm and worked as a sculptor as well, exhibiting a sculptural figure, *Phoenicia and the Wind,* at the National Sculpture Society exhibition in 1895. While much of his work was in jewelry, he designed and supervised the execution of the important pieces of silver that Tiffany exhibited in Paris in 1900 and at the St. Louis Exposition in 1904. In 1900 he designed the Adams Gold Vase for Tiffany in the Renaissance revival style, of which he

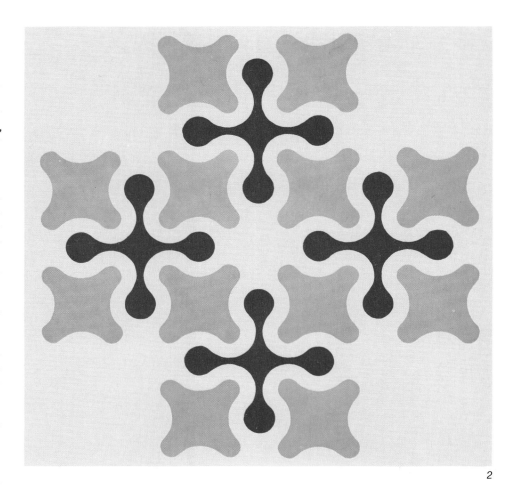

1. **Paul Feeley.** Gomelza, *1965. Whitney Museum of American Art, N.Y. (gift of the Friends of the Whitney Museum).*

2. **Lyonel Feininger.** Zirchow VII, *1918. National Gallery of Art, Washington, D.C. (gift of Mrs. Julia Feininger).*

was the chief proponent. This vase, symbolizing the importance of the cotton industry, illustrates the thoroughness of Farnham: he studied live models for all the American flora and fauna represented in the vase. The gold and all the gems used in the vase were mined in this country. He was also the designer of the gold Tiffany sword (U.S. Naval Academy Museum) presented to Admiral Dewey in 1899 in recognition of his victory at Manila Bay. Late in his career he made a bust of Tiffany.

(M.G.F.)

Fauvism.
A movement that emerged just after 1900 in Paris and included the painters Henri Matisse (1869–1954), Georges Rouault (1871-1958), André Derain (1880–1954), Maurice de Vlaminck (1876–1954), Raoul Dufy (1877–1953), and Georges Braque (1882–1963). By using bold, luminous color, often chosen intuitively and at times squeezed directly from the tube, the fauves sought to define space and distribute light and weight without reference to natural color. The work of Gauguin, van Gogh, and the pure color strokes of Seurat were major influences. Matisse, the catalyst and leader, used color to clarify and simplify composition, achieving chromatic brilliance more through placement and controlled interrelationships than through intensity. By 1905 he had attained a uniquely fauve balance of flat patterning and bright dots of color combined with audacious but highly expressive draftsmanship. Vlaminck, whose art represents the movement's opposite pole, applied his "hot" color almost at random for the sake of self-expression and release of energy.

Although several of the painters had occasional small exhibitions from 1902 on, they exhibited together for the first time at the Salon d'Automne in 1905, revealing the extent of the movement and its innovations, and shocking the art critic Louis Vauxcelles into terming the painters "les fauves," or "wild beasts." By 1908 and the emergence of cubism, the movement had lost its impetus, but the impact of its freely expressive style continued.

The work of several Americans who were in Paris between 1906 and 1909—including Arthur B. Carles,* Arthur G. Dove,* Maurice Prendergast,* Alfred Maurer,* John Marin,* Abraham Walkowitz,* and Max Weber*—reflected the

vigorous freedom and heightened color of the French painters. In 1908 Alfred Stieglitz* introduced Matisse to New York in his Photo-Secession gallery, and during the next two years most of the American fauves exhibited there. Americans were also exposed to European fauves in the 1913 Armory Show* in New York. (D.W.S.)

Federal Art Project, see WPA Federal Art Project.

Federal or Georgian Eclectic Style.
An architectural style. The brick tradition of this architecture was reintroduced at about the beginning of the 20th century by a revival of the Federal style. With its Flemish-bond brick walls set off by the stone details of the trim, it was well adapted to serve as a veneer for tall buildings. It was used for large hotels and apartment houses whose graceful parapets were adorned with stone urns, marble panels set above windows, and paneled lintels. In the residential field, the style was particularly well adapted to the individual row house in the city, and to the large country house. Many of these houses expressed the idiosyncrasies of their architects, who freely combined Georgian and Federal details. (A.B.)

Feeley, Paul (1910–66).
Painter. A native of Des Moines, Iowa, Feeley lived in California from 1922–31. Then, at the suggestion of his teacher, Hobart Jacobs, he moved to New York City, where he studied figure painting at the Art Students League* and portraiture with Cecilia Beaux,* and worked at the Beaux-Arts Institute of Design. During 1932–37 Feeley taught painting, sculpture, and drawing at Cooper Union, at one point serving as head of the industrial design department. He also worked as a commercial artist. In 1939 he moved to Bennington, Vt., and taught at Bennington College until his death. There his students included Helen Frankenthaler* and Patricia Johanson,* and he was responsible for early exhibitions of Jackson Pollock,* David Smith,* and Hans Hofmann.* Feeley's own work during these years moved through various expressionistic styles; however, his classical turn of mind and earlier training in drawing and industrial design demanded a sounder basis in structural principle. In New York in 1955, in his

first one-man show, the most notable of his paintings was The Red Blotch, a single, centered, loosely-brushed red shape against a green background. Although his work of the next few years retained vestiges of abstract expressionist brushwork, more and more he rejected personal expressionism, which he felt produced "jungles of movement and action," and sought an art of "sanity, joy, peace, and pleasure."

By 1957, in a second New York show, he consistently combined the sensuality of abstract expressionism* with a preconceived pictorial order, shapes in absolute stasis, and avoided any optical mixing of adjacent colors. Never interested in geometry as such, Feeley had managed to achieve an intricate balance between expression and design, between feeling and reason—an absolute and classical order. He often painted pictures in series, testing the effect of different colors on a given motif. In 1965 he began to project his color-shapes into three dimensions in a series of painted wood sculptures, each with two flat planes intersected at right angles. Most impressive of these pictorial "sculptures" is a nine-unit red, white, and blue Sculpture Court each rippling "column" twenty-one feet high. The work was executed posthumously. Feeley was one of the first artists to turn away from a strict formalism (he was always interested in ambivalence and extrinsic meanings) and he trained his form and color sense to values outside the immediate tradition of western painting. His approach was both original and objective, and he opened up a whole range of source materials—textiles, rugs, Spanish and Moroccan tiles—previously alien to his French-oriented contemporaries. In 1968 a memorial exhibition was held at the Guggenheim Museum, and a retrospective of his masterly drawings and watercolors was held at Bennington College. (E.C.G.)

Feininger, Lyonel (1871–1956).
Painter. Born in New York, the son of distinguished concert artists, he was trained as a violinist. "Music has always been the first influence in my life," he later acknowledged; "polyphony, paired with delight in mechanical construction, went far to shape my creative bias." In 1887, Feininger went off to Germany to study music, but he turned to painting, studying in Hamburg, Berlin,

and at the Académie Colarossi in Paris. From 1893 to 1907, his principal artistic activity was as an illustrator and satirical cartoonist for German periodicals, doing comic strips for the Chicago *Sunday Tribune,* and illustrating fanciful children's stories. He developed a flat, decorative, and distorted manner that he carried over into his early paintings.

Feininger spent the years 1906–08 in Paris, and became acquainted with such avant-garde painters as Jules Pascin and Robert Delaunay. In 1907 he began serious painting, soon reflecting influences of van Gogh, Cézanne, Delaunay, and (by 1911) cubism.* In 1912 he met members of the pioneer German expressionist group, *Die Brücke,* and in 1913 he exhibited with a young German group, *Der Blaue Reiter.* By then his work had developed toward cubist fragmentation of planes but he broke up surfaces less analytically and more dynamically and expressively than many of the early cubists, as can be seen in *Bridge I* (1913, Washington University). He experimented with light, color, and space as emotive forces, sometimes emphasizing movement by sequences of planes in the manner of futurism;* sometimes increasing tensions by distorting human figures; and sometimes, as in *Ascending Balloon* (1920, Pasadena), employing a pseudo-naive, symbolic approach similar to that of Paul Klee.

In 1918 he began working with woodcuts, a medium he was to employ for some of his most spontaneous and delightful work. Also in 1918, he met Walter Gropius,* the architect who was establishing the German center for design studies, the Bauhaus.* Gropius invited him to join the faculty, where he was soon to be joined by Paul Klee and Vasily Kandinsky; Feininger remained with the school, first as instructor and then as artist-in-residence, from 1919 until it closed in 1933. By 1921 he began to paint calmly monumental canvases of soaring steeples and expansive seascapes in which the forms of nature were dissolved into seemingly infinite, dematerialized planes of light (influenced by Delaunay's experiments in the analysis of light). It was a romantic style that fused aspects of cubism and expressionism (*Gelmeroda VIII,* 1921, Whitney).

In 1924 Feininger joined Kandinsky, Klee, and Alexej von Jawlensky in the group known as the "Blue Four," which exhibited widely. During the succeeding decade he was honored by major exhibitions in New York and various German cities. But as the German political climate changed in the mid-1930s he returned to America and in 1936 began teaching at Mills College in California. The following year, when his paintings were shown as "degenerate art" in Munich, he settled in New York City. Transplanting himself at sixty-six was not easy, and for several years he did little work. However, during the 1940s and early '50s he had another burst of creative activity in a more colorful, spontaneous style. The early, laboriously refined, superimposed transparent planes were replaced, as in *Church on the Hill* (1946, Fort Worth Art Association), by freely applied color areas usually overlaid by a drawing of quickly darting lines.   (D.W.S.)

Feke, Robert (c.1705–c.50).
Portrait painter of unusual sensitivity, Feke could bring both life and character into the rigid pattern of the formal portraiture of his day. Early works place him in 1741 in Boston and in Newport, R.I., in 1742-45. He seems to have been both seafarer and painter, and according to a family tradition was taken prisoner by the Spaniards during the War of Jenkins Ear (1739–41). An itinerant, as most early American painters were, he ranged between Boston, where he was influenced by the work of John Smibert,* and Philadelphia, where his response to the town's admiration may be read in the freedom and grace of portraits he painted there.

Considered among the best colonial artists, Feke was noted for his sophisticated baroque styles, particularly in portraits of women. His depiction of feminine charm is well represented in his *Unknown Woman* (c.1748–50, Brooklyn). In other portraits he was the first who sought to portray woman as sensual and graceful, rather than in the flat style of the limner tradition. Gentlemanly elegance was evident in his *Tench Francis* (1746, Metropolitan) and in *Captain Alexander Graydon* (Washington). His strongest characterization is his *Reverend Thomas Hiscox* (1745), also published as a mezzotint at Newport, 1775. Here he has departed from the conventional poses, accentuating the strong lines of the face by showing it from below.

His most important work historically is his *Benjamin Franklin* (c.1746, Harvard), the earliest of the innumerable portraits of Franklin. He has left one group composition, his *Family of Isaac Royall* (1741, Harvard), an early work, influenced by *The Bermuda Group* (1729) of John Smibert.* It is thought that he died at sea.   (C.C.S.)

Ferber, Herbert (1906–   ).
Sculptor. Born in New York, N.Y., he studied at Columbia University and graduated as a dentist. But he also attended the Beaux-Arts Institute of Design and his first exhibited work was shown at the National Academy of Design* in 1930. He went on to sculptures carved directly from wood, developing some of the wiry, undulating forms seen in his later work. (His first one-man show was in 1937.) By the 1940s Ferber was working exclusively in metals, partly under the influence of constructivism* and partly because his conceptions now required the spatial freedom of the new material. His sculpture ceased to deal with mass, turning instead toward openwork compositions of forms interacting with space. *Apocalyptic Rider* (1947), for example, is an energetic drawing in bronze with positive and negative spaces given equal weight. Like most artists of his generation, Ferber was affected by surrealism;* his forms frequently have sexual overtones and many are spiked and sinister. By the late 1940s he was a member of the abstract expressionist group, his work relating to that of the painters not only in his use of crude, passionate forms in ultimately resolved combat, but because he helped liberate American sculpture from representationalism. (He did a "portrait" of his friend Jackson Pollock,* viewed as a skeletal condor bursting through one maze after another.) During the 1950s Ferber received several commissions from the architect Percival Goodman. One of them, "*. . . And the Bush Was Not Consumed*" (1952), was installed on the façade of B'nai Israel Synagogue, Millburn, N.J., and other of his bristling compositions of copper, lead, and brass appeared on synagogues in Cleveland, Ohio and St. Paul, Minn. (1956). Almost baroque in conception is the design for the Jewish Chapel at Brandeis University (1955). Here a vigorously coiled, seven-branch candelabrum rises from the floor, while from the ceiling an

open spheroid—"Eternal Light"—hangs transfixed by scimitar-like shafts.

Around 1954 Ferber began experimenting with "roof" and "wall" forms that tended to place a "lid" on upward movement or create a restraining "frame" for the violent forces within. These open yet spatially defined sculptural structures probably derived from Giacometti's *The Palace at 4 A.M.,* in which figures and structures are in an open box of space. These "environments in miniature" ultimately led to room-size sculptural experiences. In 1961 the first of these was realized at the Whitney Museum, New York City. Here undulating forms of polyvinyl resin were cantilevered off walls, floor, and ceiling to create a dramatic sculptural environment. In his *Calligraphs* and *Homage to Piranesi* series he continued to work with defined (frequently "caged") spaces, activating them with twisting, surging forms. Other works are "pictorial"—essentially two-dimensional compositions assembled from linear elements—and tend to be seen as silhouettes. The surfaces of Ferber's sculpture are usually worked over or rough-textured to catch the light. All of his pieces seem charged with references and meanings, and yet they remain light, airy, and ultra-simple. His first retrospective exhibition was held at Bennington College, Vt., in 1958, and an environmental sculpture-room is permanently installed at Rutgers University in New Jersey.   (E.C.G.)

Ferriss, Hugh (1889–1962).

Architect most responsible for the skyscraper* style of the late 1920s and early 1930s. Although he was trained as an architect and served his apprenticeship in Cass Gilbert's* New York office, Ferriss did not practice on his own; instead, he became a highly skilled, visionary renderer of the architectural schemes of other architects. His drawings were very effective not only in selling individual buildings but also in making Americans receptive to the skyscraper city of the future. Beyond simply producing handsome drawings, he often functioned as a designer or made major modifications of a concept.

In his book *The Metropolis of Tomorrow* (1929), and in many drawings of buildings, Ferriss presented a vision of the high-density city dominated by a forest of megastructures. He showed the dark streets below not as almost

1

2

1. **Herbert Ferber.** Sculpture to Create an Environment, *1961, polyvinyl resin.* Rutgers University Art Gallery, New Brunswick, N.J.

2. **Robert Feke.** Portrait of Benjamin Franklin, c. 1746. Fogg Art Museum, Harvard University, Cambridge, Mass. (bequest of Dr. John C. Warren).

uninhabitable, but as romantic, mist-shrouded grottos; the upper elevated layers of streets are packed with vehicles, bumper to bumper, and the air around the buildings is thick with dirigibles and airplanes. A characteristic Ferriss building was a silvery elongated shaft whose verticality was accentuated by thin rows of windows separated by masonry piers. The whole had an atmosphere of mystery and awe reminiscent of a primitive Mayan or Egyptian pyramid.

Although Ferriss was identified with the perpendicular skyscraper style of the 1920s, many of his drawings anticipate the streamlined moderne* buildings, with their horizontal strip windows, curved façades, and glass bricks, which became prominent in the middle and late 1930s. During 1936–39, he was an architectural consultant to the New York World's Fair, and after World War II he was on the planning staff of the United Nations headquarters building in New York. In 1953 he published *Power in Building: An Artist's View of Contemporary Architecture,* in which he depicted the United States architectural scene between 1940 and 1953. (D.G.)

Field, Erastus Salisbury (1805–1900).
Folk painter of portraits and classical and biblical scenes. He returned to his family home in Leverett, Mass., after a very brief apprenticeship with Samuel F. B. Morse.* Field developed his own principles of portraiture, which he practiced as an itinerant in western Massachusetts and Connecticut and, in 1842–48, in New York City. Field was probably adept at taking likenesses before his association with Morse. In his early work (c.1839) the teacher's influence can be adduced, but in the next decade, Field emerged as a distinctive technician with sharp powers of observation that revealed much about his middle-class sitters. His works showed a great facility in capturing details of dress while rendering the larger forms with bold but sensitive economy. As Field recorded neighbors, friends, and relatives, hard-edged simplification (as in the 1830 portrait of *Mrs. Pearce of Hadley,* c.1830, Williamsburg), eventually gave way to more colorful work with an aura of wealth and wordliness, (as in the 1839 portrait of Clarissa Gallond, Shelburne). His move to New York in the 1840s brought this fruitful period of regional portraiture to an end,

and his entries in the annual "Fair of the American Institute of New York City" show a transfer of interest to landscape and subject paintings. As the newly imported daguerreotype technique attracted prospective sitters, Field mastered and practiced the technique, working with photography to circumvent sitting sessions and modifying his style until his portraits looked like colored photographs. After returning to Massachusetts in 1848, his most notable portraiture involved family groups with some members shown posthumously; it may be significant that in such compositions the camera could not compete with the painter. The subjects that Field depicted in his later years all have reference to popular prints of the time. *The Embarkation of Ulysses,* the *Taj Mahal,* and *The Visit of Ulysses Grant to India* were depicted with rich coloring and with tightly modeled forms inhabiting stagelike spaces. The decorated frames of some added to the quality of personal vision in spite of the familiar source material. His masterpiece was the tremendous 115" x 159" grisaille painting, *Historical Monument of the American Republic* (Springfield Museum of Fine Arts, Mass.), which was completed in 1876 (but with additions made in 1888) to commemorate the centennial of U.S. independence. The work is history in the grand manner: towers in different architectural stages rise high in the air, and each level of each tower is keyed to a major episode in American history, with every national hero represented. (M.J.G.)

Figureheads.
From earliest times, human or animal figures have been carved and placed at the prow of sailing vessels. The symbolic, polychromed carvings that graced American ships of the 19th century are, however, probably unique in their elaborate variety, and have long been prized as an important folk art expression of one of the nation's early industries. Although American carvers are recorded as having executed figureheads as early as the 17th century, no examples of their work are known. Extant 18th-century carvings adhere closely to English models for the most part, but a discernible national style emerges soon after the Revolution at the same time that the subject range expands to include symbolic figures; national heroes; ship owners; mytho-

1

1. *Erastus Salisbury Field.* Historical Monument of the American Republic, c.1876. Museum of Fine Arts, Springfield, Mass. (Morgan Wesson Memorial Collection).
Figureheads
2. *Emory Jones.* Figurehead for the George R. Scholfield, 1885. Mariners' Museum, Newport News, Va.
3. *Samuel McIntyre.* Female figurehead, c.1805. Peabody Museum, Salem, Mass.
4. Girl with Flowers, 19th century. *Index of American Design, National Gallery of Art, Washington, D.C.*

2

3

4

logical beings and literary characters; marine animal forms like serpents, dolphins, and alligators; and the national eagle. A few of the early carvers are known. Among the more important are the Skillin family of Boston and New York, Samuel McIntyre of Salem, and William Rush of Philadelphia. Later work of distinction was produced by John Bellamy of Portsmouth, N.H., celebrated especially for his eagles, and in New York City by such men as Samuel A. Robb (1851–1928).

The first known American figureheads tend to be small, with only the busts of human figures freestanding, like the *Female Figurehead* in the Peabody Museum, attributed to McIntyre, or the *Bust of Benjamin Franklin* (Yale), attributed to William Rush. Freestanding full figures followed, erect like the 1834 figure of *Andrew Jackson* (Museum of the City of New York), but leaning forward in accord with the sleek hulls of the clipper ship as the century progressed. Figures like that carved by Emory Jones of Freeport, Me., in 1885 for the *George R. Skolfield* (Mariners Museum), were almost horizontal. The last full-length figures were carved in the 1870s and 1880s. Billethead scrolls and eagles replaced them as the glory of the wooden sailing ship was eclipsed by metal hulls and steam power. Ship carvers turned their skills to making pilothouse figures for riverboats, such as Thomas V. Brooks's *Goddess of Liberty* from the *Mary Powell* (Smithsonian). To an even greater extent they devoted themselves to creating the wooden show figures that symbolized late 19th-century commercial activity and, later, to the florid decorations that embellished America's circus wagons* in their turn-of-the-century heyday. (M.J.G.)

Fisher, Alvan (1792–1863).

A pioneer of American genre, landscape, and animal painting. Born in Needham, Mass., Fisher grew up in nearby Dedham, and spent much of his life there. As a young man he studied with the Boston artist J. R. Penniman (1783–c.1832), and by 1814 Fisher was painting portraits "at a cheap rate," as he wrote to William Dunlap.* In 1818 he painted *Mishap at the Ford* (Corcoran), a pastoral scene that demonstrates his already mature style. In the following decade, Fisher traveled widely over the eastern United States, doing animal

1

2

1. **Alvan Fisher.** Activity at the River, *1815. Vose Galleries, Boston.*
2. **John B. Flannagan.** Triumph of the Egg, I, *1937, granite. Museum of Modern Art, N.Y.*

portraiture, landscapes, and a number of views of Niagara Falls (two fine examples of which are owned by the National Collection of Fine Arts, Washington, D.C.). He traveled to Europe for further study in 1825, and returned to set up a Boston studio in 1826. He was a successful, if unsophisticated, painter, for his notebooks record sales of nearly one thousand paintings (landscapes, story-telling pieces, and portraits) between 1826 and the time of his death. (T.E.S.)

Fisher, Jonathan (1768–1847).
Wood engraver, painter, and Congregationalist minister of Blue Hill, Me. His paintings and engravings reflect prodigious talent and accomplishment in such diverse fields as natural history, poetry, carpentry, architecture, surveying, and linguistics. Fisher, who was born in New Braintree, Mass., graduated from Harvard in 1792. He settled in Blue Hill in 1796 and remained there for half a century, in the course of which he built his own precisely planned house and recorded the surrounding landscape in oil. He also painted four intensely revealing self-portraits (one for each of his surviving daughters), installed his own wooden-works clock, and built his own furniture. He is most widely known for 142 highly varied wood engravings in a series entitled *Scripture Animals or the Natural History of the Living Creatures Named in the Bible,* published in 1834. Most of these are dependent on the English illustrator Bewick or contemporary travel books, but a few (such as "The Spider and the Little Brown Owl") are drawn from nature and demonstrate his power of observation. The original wood blocks are owned by the Farnsworth Museum in Rockland, Me. (M.J.G.)

Fitch, Simon (1758–1835).
Self-taught portraitist, born in Lebanon, Conn., who is best known for his large and powerful portraits, *Ephraim Starr* and *Hannah Beach Starr* (1802, Wadsworth). Fitch, who was an officer in the Conneticut militia from 1793 to 1799, is often referred to as "captain." His painting, which is characterized by fine preliminary drawing in oil and a thin application of paint, is closely related to the work of such contemporary Connecticut folk painters as William Jennys* and Reuben Moulthrop* and the Massachusetts painter J. Brown.*

Flagg, Ernest (1857–1947).
Architect. Son of the rector of a fashionable Brooklyn church, he was sent to the École des Beaux-Arts in Paris by Cornelius Vanderbilt, a relative, and was graduated in 1889. In 1891 he established a practice in New York and maintained it until his retirement in 1940. One of his first commissions, won in open competition, was for St. Luke's Hospital on 113th Street in New York. Another was for the Corcoran Art Gallery in Washington, D.C., commissioned in 1891 and done in classical Greek style. After these, he adopted his own version of French Beaux-Arts architecture, infusing it with a strong personal idiom expressed in symmetrical schemes with boldly featured central elements and large openings and bases, one or two stories high, rusticated for horizontal emphasis.

The ten-story Singer Building (1898) in New York at Broadway and Liberty Street, crowned with a mansard roof, was a good example of his Parisian style. In 1906–08 he raised the height of this building and added a tower, thus making it the highest on the New York skyline. Even more significant were his theories of zoning for height; he believed that a uniform cornice line should be established throughout the city, as in Paris, and that only towers should be allowed to rise above this level. Some of his ideas led to the enactment of zoning ordinances. His design for the Mills House, a hotel for working men on New York's Bleecker Street, was repeated at various locations in the city, and the model tenements he developed were a pioneer effort to solve the housing problems of the poor.

A great opportunity, involving a cluster of buildings, came to Flagg in 1899 with the commission for the United States Naval Academy at Annapolis, Md. The plan of these Beaux-Arts buildings served as a model for academic design in the grand manner. Flagg was a founder of the Society of Beaux-Arts Architecture in 1894 and its president from 1911 to 1913. (A.B.)

Flannagan, John Bernard (1895–1942).
Sculptor. One of the most gifted of the direct carving school of sculpture in the 1920s and 1930s, he was born in Fargo, N.D. After studying briefly at the Minneapolis Institute of Arts and serv-

ing in the Merchant Marine (1917–22), he was rescued from near starvation in New York by Arthur B. Davies,* who suggested wood carving to him. About 1923 he first tried wood carving and five years later made his initial attempts at taille direct, carving directly in stone. Often the shape of the stone itself, as found in the field, would suggest the subject of the piece. In such works as *Elephant* (1929–30, Whitney), *Jonah and the Whale* (1937, Virginia Museum of Fine Arts, Richmond), or *Triumph of the Egg* (1937, Modern Museum), the original shape of the stone may still be imagined. For Flannagan, part of the creative process was "seeing" the image in the original shape of the stone. He often worked in rural areas such as Woodstock, N.Y., or Ridgefield, Conn., where his raw material, fieldstone, was plentiful. The stones he found during his two years in remote areas of Ireland in 1930–31 and 1932 were of special inspiration to him; his granite *Goat* (Metropolitan) was made in Ireland in 1932, where he had returned on a Guggenheim Fellowship. As Flannagan sacrificed naturalism to obtain the beauty of sculptural form, his work became increasingly abstract. His career was marked by illness, poverty, and personal calamity, and in 1942, shortly before a retrospective show of his work opened in New York, he committed suicide. (W.C.)

Flasks.
Glass spirit containers, blown in full-size metal molds, constituted one of the staple products of 19th-century American glasshouses. From about 1790 to about 1870, flattened ovoid flasks or pocket bottles in various designs were popular containers for whiskey and other spirits. Until about 1850, they were made in most of the glasshouses in New England, in the Pittsburgh area, and by Dyott in Philadelphia. After 1850 production was centered in the Midwest, Connecticut, and New Jersey. Cheap to produce, flasks were usually blown from nonlead "bottle" glass, generally aquamarine or brownish amber in color, and almost never from the glass with which tablewares were made.

Although simple pattern-molded flasks had been produced since the mid-18th century, full-size molds imparting both pattern and shape came into use about 1815. In addition to decorating the forms, this innovation standardized the capacity of the flasks. "Sunburst" flasks, produced by several factories, were one of the earliest designs; but flasks bearing portraits of heroes and politicians had become popular by the 1820s. Washington appears on numerous examples, and political figures often joined his image to theirs. Other flasks commemorated such prominent personalities as William Henry Harrison, John Quincy Adams, Lafayette, Louis Kossuth, and Jenny Lind. The development of the railroad, the gold rush (symbolized by Pike's Peak), the Civil War, Masonic societies, and the "American System" of free trade all figured on flasks. An American folk art, flasks represent the skill of the moldcutter, for the development of the mold took the initiative out of the hands of the blower and gave it to the moldmaker. (See also Glass.)　　　　　(J.S.S.)

Flavin, Dan (1933–　　　).
Pioneer in light sculpture, born in Jamaica, N.Y. By 1957 he had begun to produce small drawings, watercolors, and paintings, and in 1961 in New York he had his first one-man show. He first used artificial illumination in his "icons" —painted, boxlike constructions with electric lights attached or simply flat surfaces framed in electric bulbs. By 1963 he was presenting fluorescent light fixtures as works of art. *The Diagonal of May 25, 1963* was a standard eight-foot-long tube that cast white light and its own shadow into the space around it. In the same year he placed a red neon tube vertically in the corner of a room, dissolving the architecture with its eerie theatrical effects. Flavin was acutely aware that he was moving toward environmental and optical concerns. He wrote: "I realized that the actual space of a room could be disrupted and played with by careful, thorough composition of the illuminating equipment . . .", that corners could be completely eliminated "by physical structure, glare, and doubled shadow" and "sections of wall could be visually disintegrated."

Flavin's art is contradictory in that he deals with illusionistic effects while presenting the physical light as an equivalent for more palpable kinds of form. His earliest fluorescent works were "minimal" in form, with standard tubes two, four, six, or eight feet long placed side by side or formed into sim-

1

2

1. **Dan Flavin.** Pink & Gold, *1968, fluorescent light, installation at Chicago Museum of Contemporary Art. Dwan Gallery, N.Y.*

2. **Thomas Fletcher.** Silver service presented to Commodore John Rodgers for his defense of Fort McHenry, 1817. Maryland Historical Society, Baltimore.

ple triangles or rectangles. Later, he began to "compose" in colored light, deploying his tubes so as to achieve color mixtures, reflections, and areas of greater and lesser intensity. Because his fixtures were usually located on a floor, ceiling, or walls, the exhibition space became an integral part of the work. Frequently, entire rooms were diffused with a single color—green, pink, gold, ultraviolet, or cool white—and occasionally the fixtures were placed on elaborate structures that extended out into, and effectively blocked, the space of a room. Unlike most of the other artists working with light, Flavin is not involved with technology or decorative effects. Rather, he uses light as a medium that must be transcended. He was not only one of the pioneers of neon-light sculpture; he also produced genuinely new experiences of artificial light. He has had numerous exhibitions, including an important show at the Museum of Contemporary Art, Chicago (1967), and a retrospective at the National Gallery of Canada (1969). (E.C.G.)

Fletcher, Thomas (1787–1866).

Philadelphia silversmith and leading producer of presentation pieces from 1812–38. Born in New Hampshire, Fletcher established himself as a jeweler in Boston in 1808 in partnership with Sidney Gardiner.* In 1811 they moved to Philadelphia. Only a pair of simple two-handled church cups (Boston) are known from their Boston period. Their alliance continued until Gardiner's death in 1827.

By 1812 Fletcher & Gardiner had established a sufficient reputation to be selected by a Philadelphia committee to make the large vase (Naval Historical Foundation) commemorating Captain Isaac Hull's victory in the *Constitution* over the *Guerrière.* Fashioned after an antique "pot-a-oille" by Napoleon's designers, Percier and Fontaine, it introduced naval motifs and an engraved view of the naval engagement. They made other presentation vases for Commodore Oliver H. Perry, Captain Jacob Jones, and Lieutenant James Biddle. All are large urns featuring eagle finials mounted on military or naval trophies, with scrolled handles above an antique ram's head or Neptune's head, and supported by a high square plinth and large, well-articulated paw feet. Fletcher & Gardiner made less imposing domestic wares. An enor-

mous dinner service was presented to Commodore John Rodgers in 1817 for his defense of Fort McHenry (Maryland Historical Society, Baltimore). Totaling fifty-two pieces, including silver plates, platters and pitchers of graduated sizes, sauceboats and tureens, the set cost $4000 and features gadrooned and nautical borders along with less bellicose motifs. The most handsome of their presentation silver is the pair of vases presented by New York merchants to De Witt Clinton for his part in the building of the Erie Canal (New York Chamber of Commerce). The vases have panels with views of the Erie Canal around the sides.

Apparently, Fletcher was the business head and designer of the partnership while Gardiner managed the shopwork. After Gardiner's death, Fletcher continued to supply customers throughout the country, from New Hampshire to New Orleans. The silver service given in 1838 to Nicholas Biddle by the Directors of the Second Bank was described by Philip Hone as "the most superb service of plate I ever saw . . . cost $15,000 . . . Nobody in this 'world' of ours hereabouts can compete with them in their kind of work." Only sketches of four designs for the Biddle service survive (Metropolitan).

After a short-lived association with Calvin W. Bennett and financial reverses, Fletcher continued to be listed as a silversmith in Philadelphia until 1849.

(M.G.F.)

Folk Art.

Three dissimilar veins of creative activity have been designated folk art. Each has its own collectors and collections and each with a separate literature. They are: the decorative tradition of a distinctive cultural group as expressed in its crafts—as fractur,* painted tinware,* or crewelwork* and patchwork;* the essentially anonymous painting and sculpture produced to meet practical needs—such as nameboards,* show figures,* trade signs,* gravestones,* weathervanes,* and decoys;* and the painting and sculpture of self-taught artists.

All of these folk arts may be said to have in common that they are produced outside the mainstream of fashion and that (with the exception of work by some well-publicized "naive" artists like Grandma Moses*) they are unlikely to be seen as "art" by the prevailing world of taste and opinion.

3

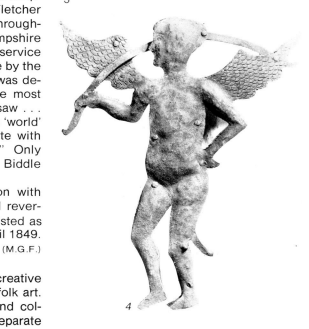

4

Folk Art
3. *Miss Liberty holding a flag and a liberty pole topped by its symbolic cap; the palm leaf in her right hand suggests victory over the oppressor; c.1815. Colonial Williamsburg, Va.*
4. *Ironmonger's trade sign, Cupid, 19th century, wrought iron. Collection Mr. and Mrs. Howard Lipman, Cannondale, Conn.*

1

2

3

Folk Art
1. Mahantango Valley Farm, c.1860. Artist unknown. National Gallery of Art, Washington, D.C. (Garbisch Collection).
2. The Dog, c.1860. Artist unknown. National Gallery of Art, Washington, D.C. (Garbisch Collection).
3. Painted chest, c.1770–85, made in Guilford, Conn. Index of American Design, National Gallery of Art, Washington, D.C.
4. Appliqué "Friendship" quilt, c. 1830, made in Middlesex County, Va. Index of American Design, National Gallery of Art, Washington, D.C.
5. American Flag Gate, 19th century, carved wood.
6. Fractur. Crucifixion, 1847, watercolor and pen on paper.
7. Gravestone rubbing. All, Museum of American Folk Art, N.Y.

4

6

5

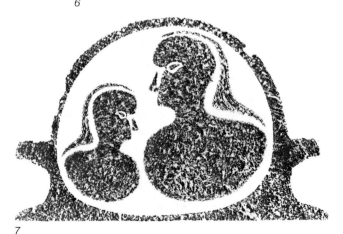

7

In America, early interest in folk art is closely related to interest in the rediscovery of the national past. The 19th century in particular produced a wealth of anonymous creative expression that provides more direct insight into surrounding life and popular customs than the work of traditionally acknowledged artists, and the efforts of artisans working against the tide of mass production and the industrial revolution have long been prized for their individuality. Folk painting was given its first genuine esthetic consideration in the 1930s, however, when the newly-formed Museum of Modern Art made special provision for study and collection in the field. The bulk of the Abby Aldrich Rockefeller Folk Art Collection, which was the nucleus of this activity, was subsequently transferred to Williamsburg, Va. The pattern established there, providing for both architectural restoration and the collection and study of relevant folk art has since been pursued in such centers as Old Sturbridge Village in Massachusetts, Greenfield Village in Dearborn, Mich., the Shelburne Museum in Shelburne, Vt., and the New York State Historical Association complex in Cooperstown, N.Y. In 1963, under the aegis of the late Joseph B. Martinson, the Museum of American Folk Art opened in New York City. It presented exhibitions covering a wide range of folk art interests and developed broad popular acquaintance with folk art examples of distinction. Within its own collection, the frequently reproduced 19th-century *Flag Gate* can serve as a neat symbol of the anonymity, ingenuity, beauty, and national historic significance of its sphere of activity. (M.J.G.)

Foster, John (1648–81).

First American printmaker. His woodcut portrait of the Reverend Richard Mather of Dorchester, in the Massachusetts Bay Colony, is believed to have been made about 1670. In 1675 he entered into competition with the long-established press in Cambridge, and set up the first printing press in Boston. His almanacs contain astronomical diagrams apparently cut by him on wood or metal. He made a woodcut Massachusetts seal, which was printed on official proclamations, and a woodcut map of New England (1677), the first printed map made in British North America. It was issued as frontispiece

to the Reverend William Hubbard's *A Narrative of the Troubles with the Indians in New-England* (Boston, 1677).

Fractur.

The illuminated calligraphy practiced by the Pennsylvania Dutch in the late 18th and 19th centuries, probably derived from the black-letter manuscripts of 11th-century German monks. The term is now used to designate the calligraphic technique as it appears in religious books and hymnals and on title pages and bookplates, and particularly the memorial certificates and framed blessings and prayers for which it was most frequently employed. By extension, it also referred to similar works executed outside Pennsylvania. Birth, baptismal, and marriage certificates and family records are probably the most common examples of fractur. Executed in ink and watercolor on paper, they frequently employ pomegranate and lotus-bud motifs intertwined with heraldic bird and animal forms and geometric elements that are reminiscent of Near Eastern decorative art. In Pennsylvania Dutch examples, the heart is a recurrent symbol, as in *Birth Certificate of Alexander Danner* (1804) and *Birth Certificate of Elizabeth Portzline* (1810) by Francis Portzline (both, Abby Aldrich Rockefeller). In late examples the black-letter forms give way to both German and italic script, and ultimately decorative printed certificates supplant the handmade Pennsylvania prototypes. In neighboring New Jersey and in New York, New England, Virginia, and North Carolina, illuminated ceremonial certificates also referred to as fractur are known to have been produced in the early 19th century. Although they probably have a functional relationship to the Pennsylvania Dutch examples, some (especially those with English rather than German texts) incorporate very different decorative elements that seem more closely connected to the then prevalent taste in art as taught in female seminaries.

(M.J.G.)

Francis, John F. (1808–86).

A still-life painter, he specialized in elegant Dutch style "luncheon type" works. Born in Philadelphia, Pa., he always had close ties there despite moving to a succession of small cities in Kentucky, Delaware, and Pennsylvania. The portraits with which he began in

the 1830s and 1840s are strongly characterized, and fall between the folk and academic styles. In the 1850s he turned increasingly to still life, and his work reflects the early still-life tradition of the Peales.* Using a limited range of subject matter, favoring strawberries, apples, pears, oyster crackers, wine bottles, and porcelain, glass, and silver jugs (only one flower painting is known), Francis demonstrated great interest in subtle tones and textures. *Luncheon Piece* (Newark) is a particularly fine example, and typically depicts a rich profusion of glassware and foodstuffs on a white tablecloth. He died in Jefferson, Pa., where he had lived after 1866.

(T.E.S.)

Francis, Sam (1923–   ).

Painter, born in San Mateo, Cal., he studied at the University of California, 1941–43, and received his M.A. in 1950. He was first influenced by the expressionist realism of David Park.* After serving in World War II he worked in Paris for seven years and traveled widely throughout Europe and the Far East, finally settling in Santa Monica, Cal. He was included in the 1956 exhibition "Twelve Americans" at the Museum of Modern Art, New York City.

As a result of his long association with Paris and his travels, Francis is one of the most international of American painters. The works of the 1950s are generally painted in a dense, unified organization of small color shapes that at one extreme may be associated with the paintings of Mark Tobey* and at another with those of his friend, the French-Canadian abstractionist, Jean-Paul Riopelle. Occasionally he experimented with light, spacious, atmospheric works, predominantly white, pale green, or light gray. In 1956–57, partly as a result of his contact with Japanese painting, he opened up the empty space as well as the scale of his canvases, accenting the space with a few accents of free textural brush and drip painting. In the late 1950s he began painting on a mural scale and his style alternated between that of vast white spaces controlled by the color accents of abstract expressionism* and equally huge organizations in which color accents, mainly in primary colors, took over, as in *Shining Black* (1958, Guggenheim). Although Francis has been a completely abstract painter since the early 1950s, his paintings since the late 1950s often have a hint of naturalistic images, sometimes landscapes and sometimes objects suggesting surrealist microcosms. Some of the paintings of the early 1960s, in which strange, circular organisms float through an infinite emptiness, suggest relationships with the organic-surrealist tradition of Miró.

Since 1960 Francis has emphasized the edges of his paintings. In many of these, brilliantly coloristic passages—again primarily red, yellow, and blue, presented in slashing brushstrokes or whipped spatters of paint—surround large white centers frequently composed of raw canvas. During the late 1960s and early '70s his paintings became increasingly spare, sometimes consisting of a total white space set within a minimal frame of vertical color strips. Francis has always been a so-called "color painter." The later paintings continue this tradition toward a form of lyrical abstraction related not only to the works of Helen Frankenthaler* but also to the color-field* tradition of Morris Louis.* Despite these influences, Francis is a brilliant painter with a very personal point of view that encompasses the entire contemporary international tradition of lyrical color experiment. Since the early 1960s he has also done watercolors and has become one of the new leaders in the revival of color lithography. (H.H.A.)

Frank, Robert (1924–   ).
Cinematographer and photographer. Born in Zurich, Switzerland, Frank began photographing in 1942 and served apprenticeships with Michael Wolgansinger in Zurich and Hermann Eidenbenz in Basel. He came to the United States in 1947, where he had various photographic jobs, including fashion photography for *Harper's Bazaar*. He was encouraged by an outstanding teacher, Alexey Brodovitch. In 1949–51 he photographed in France, England, Spain, and Wales, and went back to Europe the next year with Edward Steichen* to assist in collecting photographs for the Museum of Modern Art exhibition, "Post European Photographers" (1953). Frank received a Guggenheim Fellowship in 1955–56 to make the photographs that became one of the most influential books of the 1960s, *The Americans* (1959). Its ironic overview of the American culture after the McCarthy era of the 1950s seemed

Sam Francis. Shining Black, *1958. Solomon R. Guggenheim Museum, N.Y.*

1

2

devastating. Without any text, the problems and preoccupations of the people were clearly stated: the paradoxes of race relations, the escape amusements of the workingman, the compulsive attraction of the automobile, and finally an array of faces that was a palimpsest of American life.

Since 1958 he has almost ceased making still photographs and has concentrated on cinema-photography. His first film, *Pull My Daisy,* made with Alfred Leslie with a narration written and read by novelist Jack Kerouac, won first prize at the San Francisco Film Festival in 1959. His later films include *The Sin of Jesus* (1960), *OK End Here* (1963), *Me and My Brother* (1968), and *Conversations in Vermont* (c.1970).

(T.F.B.)

Frankenthaler, Helen (1928–   ).
Painter. Born in New York, N.Y., Frankenthaler attended Bennington College, where she studied with the painter Paul Feeley. By 1951 she had exhibited in a group show in a New York gallery and had her first one-man show, and the following year she painted one of the most remarkable pictures of the period, *Mountains and Sea,* after a summer of painting and sketching landscapes in Nova Scotia. Here Kandinsky's early "improvisations," Gorky's* graceful line, Marin's* watercolor feeling, and Pollock's* technique of spilling paint directly onto raw canvas were all brought together in a unique and highly personal synthesis. By thinning out her color and allowing it to soak into the weave of the canvas, Frankenthaler developed a technique—the "soak-stain"—that eliminated brushwork and paint texture, unified form and manner, and made a new kind of color painting possible. (Morris Louis* and Kenneth Noland* both carried this method over into their own work.) During the next seven years, with a rare lack of inhibition, she explored the possibilities of painting, producing works that ranged from the heavily-impastoed pictures of 1954–55 to huge colored line "drawings" such as "Nude" (1957). The majority of her work of this period, however, emphasized the expressive power of color, and was characterized by passion, lyricism, softness, and openness. Areas of flooded, saturated color in varying densities and modulations were pulled together with areas of unpainted canvas by means of structuring line. An early

1. **Robert Frank.** City Fathers, Hoboken, New Jersey, *1955, photograph.*
2. **Robert Frank.** Parade—Hoboken, New Jersey, *1955, photograph.*
3. **Helen Frankenthaler.** Mauve District, *1966. Museum of Modern Art, N.Y. (Mrs. Donald B. Straus Fund).*
4. **Helen Frankenthaler.** The Human Edge, *1967. André Emmerich Gallery, N.Y.*

study of cubism had left her with a thorough knowledge of pictorial structure, and the result was paintings that were both formal and intuitive, in moods that ranged from gaiety to violence. No matter how large the format, her paintings always evoke an intimate experience—perhaps because references to nature are never far beneath the abstract surface.

During the 1960s the image she created underwent radical simplification and many works took on a more obvious formal structure. Her use of acrylics, beginning in 1963, tended at first to harden the edges of her forms and eliminated the residual turpentine-halo so prominent in her earlier work. Also, the fragile color and ambiguous space of many of the 1950s paintings evolved into designed shapes, frequently painted in opaque hues that left no doubt as to their position in space. Paintings such as *Small's Paradise* (1964, Smithsonian) indicate her interest in symmetry and geometry, while *Virgo* and *Commune* (both 1969) each offer a single-centered color shape.

Some of her more recent pictures, beginning with *Five Color Space* (1966), explore pictorial tensions by pushing the shapes nearly off the edge of the canvas, so that a huge "empty" area is opened up in the middle. Other paintings develop this tautness through careful placement of the positive figures. All of Frankenthaler's pictures are planned during the painting process—not in prior sketches—thus the importance to her of careful selection and cropping. She is willing to risk everything on inspiration, but later judges her work with a keen intelligence. Out of this comes the poetic freedom of her personal vision, grounded in an unfailing pictorial sensibility. She has had solo shows throughout the world and retrospectives at the Jewish Museum (1960) and the Whitney Museum (1969) in New York City. She was included in the Venice Biennial (1966) and won first prize at the Paris Biennial of 1959.

Frankl, Paul T. (1887–1958).
Pioneer modernist in furniture design. Born in Vienna, he studied at the universities of Vienna and Berlin and at art schools in Paris and Munich. He arrived in America in 1914 with advanced European design ideas, but went unnoticed until the 1925 Paris decorative arts exposition awakened

3

4

1

Americans to new developments in interior decoration. Frankl set out to design furniture that would be distinctly modern and American, choosing as his model form the American skyscraper.* He became famous for his "skyscraper furniture," such as bookcases that were tall and stepped inward toward the top. He made much use of highly polished light woods, gold and silver leaf, and lacquers in red, blue, and black. Much of his furniture was in the moderne mode; it had an American bravado but was largely French-inspired and was sometimes undistinguished.

Frankl's furniture was featured by his own firm, a Madison Avenue art gallery. He lectured at the Metropolitan Museum of Art, at New York University, and later at the University of Southern California. He was a prolific writer whose articles expounded his views on rethinking and reshaping our life-styles.

(D.H.P.)

Franklin, Benjamin (1706–90).
The statesman, scientist, and author was first a printer and printmaker; he describes in his autobiography how he designed and printed paper currency for New Jersey in 1728. He may have made the first American political cartoon, *The Waggoner and Hercules,* a relief cut used in his *Plain Truth* (Philadelphia, 1747). One of the most successful American political symbols, a snake divided into thirteen parts to represent the thirteen American colonies, with the motto in type, "Join or die," is thought to be Franklin's design. It was first used as a relief cut in his newspaper, *The Pennsylvania Gazette,* in 1754, and was quickly copied in Boston and New York.

Franklin, James (1696–1735).
Boston printer and engraver, one of the older brothers of Benjamin Franklin. He advertised skills not only in letter-press printing but also in wood engraving and calico printing. His woodcuts are among the earliest American book illustrations. They include the portrait of Hugh Peter (copied from a London engraving of sixty years earlier) in the 1717 Boston edition of Peter's *A Dying Fathers Last Legacy* and the portrait of James Hodder in the 1719 Boston edition of *Hodder's Arithmetick.* Franklin returned from an apprenticeship in England to establish his own press in

1. **Ulrich Franzen.** Graduate Residence, Cornell University, Ithaca, N.Y., 1970.
2. **John Frazee.** Self Portrait, 1842, bronze. Pennsylvania Academy of the Fine Arts, Philadelphia.

2

Boston in 1717. He moved in 1726 to Newport, where he set up the first press in Rhode Island.

Franzen, Ulrich (1921–   ).
Architect, born in Germany. Although his works show a strong sense of form and refinement, he gave no priority to form over structure, mechanical systems, or theory, but attempted to base his designs on the context of each building. "The problem is the solution" is his guiding tenet. He studied at Williams College (1942) and Harvard University (1948) and worked (1950–55) with I. M. Pei.* In 1955 he opened his own office in New York. He was first recognized for a number of residences that demonstrated bold massing and crisp details. In the Agronomy Building at Cornell University (1968) he produced a laboratory in which the mechanical systems in service spaces between floors were combined with vertical venting towers on the perimeter; this led to vertical sculpturing of the brick exterior. He then designed the Alley Theater, Houston, Tex., (1968), one of the half-dozen most important regional theaters of the decade. It has a semicircular thrust stage and strong raked caliper stages alongside the audience. The exterior is treated as a gateway, with true clarity of circulation, and as a sculptural fortress, with turrets for venting. At the same time he showed his acceptance of the more permissive supermannerist* architecture for the decorative shops of a fashion chain (Paraphernalia Inc., New York, 1967–68). He went on to government commissions, such as the Harpers Ferry Center for the National Park Service (Harpers Ferry, W.Va., 1970), and to large-scale housing projects (Urban Development Corporation Housing, Utica, N.Y., 1972). His architectural development synthesizes the ideas and forms of his time into an individual product of his own.   (C.R.S.)

Frasconi, Antonio (1919–   ).
Printmaker. Born in Buenos Aires, Argentina, of Italian parents, Frasconi was raised in Montevideo, Uruguay, where he studied art and had his first one-man exhibition of paintings. He received a Guggenheim Fellowship in 1945, enabling him to go to New York and study at the Art Students League and the New School for Social Re-

search. He turned from painting to printmaking in 1943 and since that time he has concentrated on the woodcut. Like most South American artists working in that medium, he was influenced by the Mexican popular printmaker, José Guadalupe Posada. His work combines the discipline of Japanese technique with the vitality of the German expressionists. Ranging from simplified figurative vignettes in his many book decorations to multi-paneled views of American life, he utilizes the unique quality of his material as he pulls from it considerable variety of texture and form. Recipient of a Tamarind Fellowship in 1962, he completed a series of lithographs inspired by the work of the modern Spanish poet Garcia Lorca. As an illustrator he has both enlivened and expanded the art of book design by uniting simple form with highly literate and often witty conception.   (R.C.)

Fraser, Charles (1782–1860).
Miniature painter. He was a native of South Carolina who, like his compatriot and close friend, Washington Allston,* began his career in art in the face of family opposition. Yielding to pressures for a more respectable profession, he studied law and practiced it intermittently, 1807–18. Art prevailed after that, in his native Charleston and during summer visits to the northern cities, where he painted and exhibited successfully. He was a lifelong friend of the painter Thomas Sully* and the miniaturist Edward Greene Malbone* (1777–1807), and had an equally distinguished patronage. Though his style lacked the romantic grace of theirs, it was pleasant, competent, and mature. While known chiefly for his work on ivory, Fraser also painted portraits on canvas, and holds a respectable place in the landscape school of his time.   (C.C.S.)

Frazee, John (1790–1852).
One of the earliest of American sculptors, Frazee was born in Rahway, N.J., and at age fourteen was apprenticed to a bricklayer and mason. By 1818 he had moved to New York and established a stoneyard specializing in marble gravestones and mantlepieces, which were decorated with such classical motifs as pilasters and pediments. His first successful portrait in marble was the bust of John Wells (1824),

Freeman

which was placed atop Wells' wall monument in St. Paul's Chapel, New York. He was clearly influenced by neoclassical portraiture but, having had no formal training, his reliance on direct observation of nature led to a style that was predominantly naturalistic. Although Frazee was a major portrait sculptor on the eastern seaboard from 1825–35, his commissions were limited and he had to maintain his stoneyard business to supplement his income. Dating from these years are busts of John Jay, Lafayette, Daniel Webster, and John Marshall. In 1831 he took as his partner Robert Launitz,* who had studied with the famous Danish sculptor Berthel Thorwaldsen in Rome. After 1835 Frazee's interests turned in other directions. For a time he tried architectural design. Little is known of the last fifteen years of his life. (W.C.)

Freeman, Frank (1862–1940).
Architect, born in Hamilton, Ontario, Canada. After a stay in Winnipeg, where he began to develop his architectural talent, he moved to Brooklyn, N.Y., in 1884 and apprenticed himself to architect Francis H. Kimball. He soon established his own office (1886) in Manhattan but did almost all his urban work in Brooklyn. Despite his meager formal training, he designed some of the finest Romanesque revival* buildings in the country, and won the praise of Montgomery Schuyler, the architectural critic. He was one of the few architects who carried the style beyond the massive bearing-wall stage used by his predecessors. In his use of materials, such as Roman brick, tile, copper, terracotta, and carved brownstone, he displayed a sense of the appropriate, and he used a fine range of colors, including the darker shades of yellow, red, brown, and green. Such a tall building as his Hotel Margaret (1889) on Columbia Terrace in Brooklyn, with its low floor heights and extensive use of copper and glass, was a serious attempt to adapt Romanesque revival with its fine materials and rich ornamentation to a steel-framed building. He also used the style in the Thomas Jefferson Building on Court Square (1889) and in the Old Brooklyn Fire Headquarters (1892) on Jay Street. He then inaugurated a series of more conservative designs, culminating in the high Renaissance-style of the Crescent Athletic Club

(1904) at Clinton and Pierrepont streets, Brooklyn.

Shunning all publicity, he died almost forgotten by his profession; but those works that have survived have since won the praise of architectural historians and laymen alike. (A.B.)

French, Daniel Chester (1850–1931).
Sculptor. French grew up in the Concord, Mass., of Thoreau, Emerson, and the Alcotts, and had his first instruction in sculpture from Abigail May Alcott. Although he was far from a proven sculptor in 1873, Concord awarded him the commission for the now-famous *Minute Man;* it was modeled in Boston and unveiled to an admiring throng in 1875. By then, French was on his way to Italy. He studied with Thomas Ball* in Florence and was influenced by the antiquities of Rome and the fading neoclassical* style, but he returned to America after two years. At first there were only commissions for portrait busts, the finest of which is *Ralph Waldo Emerson* (1879); but then came larger, more challenging tasks, such as the full-length, seated bronze figure, *John Harvard* (1882), for Harvard University.

After a trip to Paris (1886–88), where he absorbed much of the new French style of the École des Beaux-Arts, he established his studio in New York City. In the 1880s he also began work in that area where he would gain his greatest fame—the allegorical figure representing the lofty goals of a proud nation. This opened a long period of intense activity that led French to the forefront of American sculpture alongside Augustus Saint-Gaudens.* Several choice assignments were given to him at the World's Columbian Exposition in Chicago in 1893, probably the best known being the colossal female figure, personifying the "Republic," which dominated the great lagoon. He also created allegorical figures for the famous Dewey Arch (New York, 1899) and for the new Appellate Court Building in New York. His memorial to the architect Richard Morris Hunt* (Central Park, 1898) combines portraiture and personification. For the New York Customhouse he created four richly symbolic personifications called *Four Continents* (1907). Important commissions of this sort came continually to French, and with the death of Saint-Gaudens he became the "dean" of

American sculptors. In winter he worked at his New York studio, in summer at "Chesterwood," a studio in the Berkshires, which is now a museum of his sculpture.

One of French's most famous works is the standing bronze *Lincoln* (1912) for Lincoln, Neb., showing the thoughtful figure of Lincoln in front of a stone slab inscribed with the Gettysburg Address. Even more famous is the great seated marble figure he did for the Lincoln Memorial in Washington (1922). This statue, eighteen feet high, was carved from nearly 200 tons of Georgia marble by the Piccirilli brothers of New York and was the crowning achievement of a career that earned him the admiration of the nation, countless awards, and several honorary degrees. French represented the very best of the academic tradition: allegorical and heroic themes sculptured in a naturalistic but elegant style. Midway through his long career that tradition was assailed by the revolutionary developments of modernism, but to the end of his life French was the standard-bearer of the academic tradition. (W.C.)

French Classic Eclectic Style.
An architectural style that ran the gamut from the rather heavy baroque interiors of Louis XIV to the delicate and stiff rectangularity of those of Louis XVI, and was epitomized in Marie Antoinette's Petit Trianon at Versailles (1762–68). It found its finest expression in the town house and was occasionally used for large country estates. Symmetry and formality ruled supreme, and such houses made the same appeal to the American tycoon of the early 1900s that the French Second Empire* house had made to the post-Civil War *nouveau riches* of forty years before.

French Renaissance Eclectic Style.
An architectural style that was derived from early French architecture in which a medieval house, such as that of Jacques Coeur in Bourges, France (mid-15th century), began to assimilate elements of the Italian Renaissance. It was a richly decorated style in which royal symbols such as the salamander and the *fleur de lis* were features of the ornament. In most of these designs there was a delicate balance between the outgoing Gothic and the incoming Renaissance. The early phase has a medieval asymmetry.

French Second Empire Style.

American architectural style of the 1860s that was a direct reflection of a contemporary European style, not a revival. The inspiration came from Paris, where Napoleon III and the Empress Eugénie were dazzling the continent with the elegance of a city that had been virtually redesigned by the emperor's architect, Baron Haussmann. With its École des Beaux-Arts and strong architectural tradition, Paris set an example, both in town planning and in design of individual buildings, that was emulated from Saint Petersburg to San Francisco.

In the United States, those who had acquired fortunes during the Civil War demanded a new formality and elegance in their architecture, and they turned eagerly to Paris for inspiration. The new style displayed all the trappings of wealth, with mansard roofs and towers crowned by ornamental iron crestings. Covered carriage entrances (porte cochère) graced the arrivals of glistening carriages. A new formality was also evident in the landscaping, where cast-iron fountains, urns, benches, and gazebos were set in formal circles or rectangles of plantings. In public and commercial buildings, broken pediments, coupled columns, and sculpture were conspicuous features.

The plan of country houses was generally symmetrical and designed primarily for formal entertainment. A series of drawing rooms were easily joined by opening their sliding doors, providing a vista of rooms with floral carpeting, tasselled chairs, and ormolu (bronze or gold gilding) tables. Great gilt pier glasses increased the sense of spaciousness. Large bay windows admitted a soft, glowing light through lace curtains framed with heavy velvet draperies crowned by gilt valances. Like the revival styles that preceded it, the French Second Empire style swept the country, bringing with it order and a symmetry and a formality to which the average American was unaccustomed.

(A.B.)

Friedlander, Lee (1934–　).

Photographer. He was born in Aberdeen, Wash., and began photographing in 1948. He later studied with Edward Kaminski at the Art Center in Los Angeles. He received Guggenheim Fellowships for photography in 1960 and 1962. Widely recognized, he had an

1. **French Renaissance Eclectic.** *Alwyn Court façade detail, N.Y., 1908.*

2. **French Second Empire.** *James Renwick, Jr. Main Building, Vassar College, Poughkeepsie, N.Y., 1864.*

exhibition at the George Eastman House in 1963, and was included in "The Photographer's Eye" at the Museum of Modern Art (1964) and in "Toward a Social Landscape" at George Eastman House (1966). In 1972 he had an exhibition, "Gatherings," at the Museum of Modern Art of his observations of wedding receptions, backyard barbecues, and other parties. He has also collaborated with the painter Jim Dine* on a portfolio, *Works from the Same House* (1969), with original photographs by Friedlander and etchings by Dine.

All of Friedlander's work derives from careful observation of everyday occurrences and, more recently, what might be described as "non-events." Filled with visual puns, pictures within pictures, and sometimes a Daumier-like recording of contemporary life, the photographic prints themselves have traditional qualities, full tonal range, and large depth of field, and are never manipulated in any way. His work has shown a steady growth and promises to become an incisive document of how life around us looks to a more than casual observer. (T.F.B.)

Frost, John Orne Johnson (1852–1928).
Self-taught artist of Marblehead, Mass., who began painting in his sixty-eighth year and diligently recorded his own youthful adventures at sea and the early history of his native village. Many of Frost's paintings were donated to the Marblehead Historical Society by his son but were not exhibited until more than ten years after the artist's death. General recognition came even later, after additional works by the artist were discovered nailed (face-to) to the walls of the Frost house. Panels such as *Mugford in the Franklin Capturing the Hope* (1923, Williamsburg) or *Marblehead Harbor* (c. 1925, Marblehead Historical Society, Mass.) typify the artist's very literal recreation of historic moments and his liberal use of annotation on the picture surface to clarify important details. (M.J.G.)

Frothingham, Benjamin, Jr. (1734–1809).
This Charlestown, Mass., cabinetmaker, born in Boston, was probably trained in his father's shop before producing his own works in about 1756. Surviving examples reveal that he worked in the

1

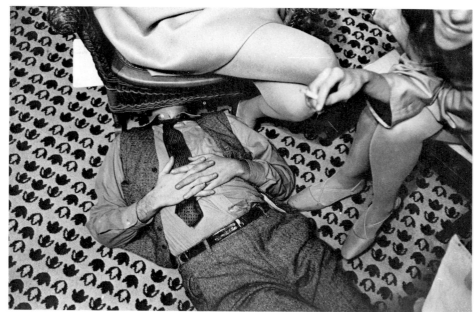

2

1. *John Orne Johnson Frost.* Mugford in the Franklin Capturing the Hope, 1923. *Colonial Williamsburg, Va.*
2. *Lee Friedlander.* Picture Made at Party Following Wedding of Old Friend, 1967, *photograph.*

Queen Anne, Chippendale, and Federal styles. An artillery major during the Revolutionary War, he was a good friend of George Washington. Frothingham's house and shop on Main Street were destroyed in 1775 when General Gage burned Charlestown; his losses included a bureau table and mahogany and walnut chests of drawers.

Frothingham's work exhibits most of the characteristics associated with Massachusetts Queen Anne and Chippendale furniture: slender cabriole legs; claw-and-ball feet with side talons raked back at a sharp angle; block-front case pieces with rounded tops on the block panels; carved sunburst fans on the drawers of case pieces; and tall, corkscrew finials atop case furniture. Furniture known to have been manufactured by Frothingham includes side chairs, chest-of-drawers, high chests-of-drawers, chests-on-chests, fall-front desks, desks and bookcases, sideboards, and card and dining tables. Solid, well-constructed pieces of good proportion and nice detail surely satisfied his customers' demands for beautiful and subtly appealing furniture.

(C.F.H.)

FSA, see Farm Security Administration.

Fuller, George (1822–84).
Painter of portraits and landscape, born in Deerfield, Mass., the son of a farmer. As a boy, he worked in a Boston grocery and a shoe store. His mother, whose father, brother, and sister were painters, did what she could to discourage his yearning to become an artist. At the age of nineteen he was in Albany, and later in Boston, sharing the studios of the sculptors Henry Kirke Brown* and Thomas Ball,* but returning in summers to the farm. His early career, as with so many other painters, was as an itinerant portraitist. He entered the National Academy life class in 1847 and by 1859 had become successful enough to travel in Europe, sketching in museums. In London he met the pre-Raphaelites Dante Gabriel Rossetti and William Holman Hunt. Returning the next year, he married and settled down on the home farm. He continued to paint, but for the next fifteen years remained out of touch with the art world.

In 1843 he had written to Brown, "I have concluded to see nature for myself, through the eyes of no one else, and put my trust in God, awaiting the result." It was a resolve characteristic of the New England of his day—personal and visionary, yet open also to chosen influences. The coloring and dreamy response of Washington Allston* to themes of the romantic movement had stirred him profoundly. The pre-Raphaelites had had some effect on him, but in his years of isolation he developed a manner of his own, ahead of his time. When farm crops failed in 1875 he endeavored to recoup by sending a group of paintings to Boston for exhibition and sale; they were received with surprise and enthusiasm and were an overwhelming success. His style had none of the precise realism then popular. It was blurred in outline, vague, mysterious, an impressionst technique independent of French impressionist influence, yet much like theirs and with light effects that would be compared to Corot's. A surprising variance from the accepted mode had launched Fuller into fame. Yet his success was due even more to his having touched a mood of romantic feeling deeply seated in American character, entering a tradition which would continue from Allston to Albert Ryder,* Arthur B. Davies,* and others of a later day. It is present in his landscapes, but even more poignantly in his figure pieces, such as *Evening-Lorette* (Corcoran) of 1882.

(C.C.S.)

Fuller, R. Buckminster (1895–   ).
Since the late 1920s, Fuller has occupied a unique position in the world of American architecture and design. Born in Milton, Mass., his formal education was sketchy. He spent two years at Harvard, 1913–15, served as a naval officer during World War I, and later occupied a number of positions in business and industry. In contrast to traditionally trained architects, his designs were never directly oriented toward the world of high art, but like other 20th-century designers he has been fully committed to the symbolism as well as to the fact of machine architecture. All of his work reveals the hand of a sophisticated stylist, but he has a unique ability to make these styles appear to be the result of functional considerations. His 1927 scheme for a Ten-Deck Building deliverable to its site by a dirigible, and his six-sided Dymaxion House supported by a central stem, were styled as machine constructivist objects (see

Constructivism). According to Fuller, the Dymaxion House and, indeed, all of his designs, are based upon three considerations: an understanding of the synergetic principles that govern the relation of parts to the whole; the expression of this understanding in the most economical way; and the expression of the way in which events and objects are related and accommodated to one another in time. His three-wheeled bullet-shaped Dymaxion Car (1927–34) and his prefabricated Dymaxion stainless steel bathroom units of 1937 fit perfectly into the 1930 streamlined moderne* design. His post-World War II metal prefabricated circular Wichita House (1946) clearly resembled the streamlined bulbous automobile designs of the late 1940s and early 1950s, while his much more famous geodesic dome (and its many variations since 1946) reflects the return to pure form for its own sake, which was then beginning to appear on the American architectural scene.

Fuller's classic dome is basically a network of spherical triangles laid out as arcs of three great circles. Fuller argues that the most economic design can never be realized by relying on straight lines, cubes, squares, and rectangles. Rather it is the triangle, especially the tetrahedron, which most closely approaches the reality of the world and its structure. His geodesic dome, composed of these very triangles, forcefully exemplifies these principles. Its strength and lightness is a result not of sheer bulk and weight, but of an efficient equilibrium obtained by relying on tension and compression. The dome is not only a handsome object, but is also economical in its use of materials, and simple enough to be built and assembled by a non-skilled amateur. Since 1949, numerous companies, ranging from makers of children's play equipment to large-scale commercial enterprises, have been licensed to produce variations of the dome. As a do-it-yourself building unit, the dome has become a favorite structure in communes all over America.

Although the geodesic dome has become common in world architecture, Fuller's major impact has been that of a thinker. In the 1950s he developed a world map (also based on the spherical triangle) that makes it possible to comprehend more realistically the size of the world's land masses and the propor-

1

2

1. **Buckminster Fuller.** *Dymaxion House,* model, 1929.
2. **Buckminster Fuller.** *Dymaxion Car,* 1933.

tional distances between places. More recently he devised a "world game" that uses the computer to establish the world's resources in relation to human needs. Through his writings (*Nine Chairs to the Moon,* 1938, and *Operation Manual for Spaceship Earth,* 1969) and innumerable lectures and teaching, he has imbued a whole generation of young architects and designers with his ideas. Fuller's theories and the forms derived from them have had an enormous appeal, especially for students and the young, because they seem to go directly back to nature for their source; because his large-scale views discard conventionally separate disciplines; because they argue that technology must be economically used to provide for contemporary needs; and, finally, because they address themselves to pressing problems ranging from historic nationalism to poverty and hunger.

The geodesic dome is impressive as a pure lacy form, but it is even more impressive as an expression of certain basic principles of nature; and finally, because it is a grand do-it-yourself "erector set." His current popularity is a result of the theory that his designs are based solely on processes and prototypes inherent in nature (micro-organisms, etc.), and equally upon his argument that we must examine and work with our total environment (the whole earth, etc.). He is one of the few who have been able to convincingly unite a deep feeling for nature with a passionate, almost science-fiction belief in the power of technology to control and remold our environment. In 1972 Fuller turned over much of his work to an organization he has founded, The Design Science Institute of Washington, D.C.

(D.G.)

Fulton, Robert (1765–1815).
Portrait painter and inventor. At seventeen he went from his home in Lancaster County, Pa., to Philadelphia to earn his living as an artist. He is listed in the directory of 1785 and advertised himself in June of the next year as "Miniature Painter and Hair Worker." Encouraged by Benjamin Franklin, he left soon after for study in London with Benjamin West.* During 1791–93, he was exhibiting portraits and historical subjects at the Royal Academy. In 1798 he brought Robert Barker's idea of the cyclorama to Paris, secured patent

rights to it, but sold them before a painting was begun. He used the money for the development in Paris of the inventions of the steamboat and the submarine, which had become his chief concern and prevented his attaining eminence as a painter.

Furness, Frank (1839–1912).
Architect. Born in Philadelphia, Pa., he was a leader of his profession there for forty-five years. At twenty, he became a student in the New York atelier of Richard Morris Hunt,* who trained some of the outstanding architects of the time. Furness was imbued with the teachings of various French and English theorists, such as Viollet-le-Duc and Ruskin.* After service in the Civil War, he returned to work again for Hunt. He set up his own office in Philadelphia in 1867 and then joined with George W. Hewitt in 1868 and with Allen Evans in 1875.

Furness' love of outdoor life may explain his ability to translate natural forms into ornament, an ability much admired by Louis Sullivan,* who worked for him as a draftsman. Furness' work represented a never-ending struggle to discover and express function and to find a suitable ornament for it. The results were often thought to be crude; and in this he anticipated the new brutalism* of recent years. His first great commission, for the Pennsylvania Academy of the Fine Arts (1876), shocked staid Philadelphians into an awareness of a new architecture in which structure itself became ornamental, and ornament ceased to be merely an exercise in genteel academicism. During the 1870s, his most creative decade, he also designed two Chestnut Street banks, the Guarantee Trust and Safe Deposit Company (1875), and the Provident Life and Trust Company Bank (1879), which in their boldness repudiated their more timid neighbors. He designed countless residences both in the city and, along the Main Line, in the country. The enlargment of the Broad Street Station for the Pennsylvania Railroad (1892–94) involved a bold use of terra-cotta ornament and the creation of one vast glass and steel train-shed with a clear span of 300 feet, which at the time was the largest in the world.

A founding member of the Philadelphia chapter of the American Institute of Architects, Furness was long an in-novative force in the world of Philadelphia architecture. (A.B.)

Furniture Since 1650.
Because American furniture, like much of early American art, was derived from European forms and especially from those popular in England, the subject is treated here in terms of European style periods. It would be a mistake, however, to believe that all American furniture from the 17th to the early 19th century was a slavish imitation of European counterparts. Local traditions, native woods, economic problems, matters of taste, morals, and philosophy, all influenced the design, execution, and decoration of furniture in America. As for considering furniture as an art, it should be noted that it was only a historical accident in the 15th and 16th centuries that separated "artists" from "artisans." Such furniture might indeed be thought of as utilitarian sculpture.

17th and 18th Centuries
The term 17th century refers to furniture made in the English-speaking American colonies between 1609 and 1700, or—because the furniture made by the first generation of settlers has not been identified—more precisely, between 1650 and 1690. Surviving forms include benches, or "formes" (a low bench on which people sat when dining), boxes (dressing, spice, and writing or "bible"), armchairs ("Brewster and Carver," slatback, and wainscot [a heavy oak chair with solid panels in back and seat], all frequently listed in inventories as "great" chairs), side chairs of the same types as armchairs but also including upholstered "Cromwellian" or farthingale types, chests (blanket, chest of drawers, and chest-on-frame), cupboards (court and press), stools, and lastly, tables (stretcher and trestle).

The construction of 17th-century furniture is closely related to medieval building practices and consists of fitting together, or "joining," members at angles of 30, 45, 60, or 90 degrees. Basic to this construction is the mortise and tenon joint, which is held together by wooden pegs or pins. This is why most 17th-century furniture craftsmen were called "joiners." Legs and stiles of seating furniture, however, were usually turned on the crude pole lathes commonly used in Europe by 1400, or on great wheel lathes. Craftsmen per-

3

4

17th Century
3. Slatback armchair with mushroom-shaped terminals on front posts, New England, late 17th century.
4. Joint stool, New England, late 17th century.
   Both, Henry Francis du Pont Winterthur Museum, Winterthur, Del.

1

2

forming this function were called "turners." Most available evidence indicates that, from earliest colonization in America, both furniture-making techniques were frequently practiced by the same artisan, especially in rural areas. This furniture is usually characterized as rectilinear, massive, solid, and sturdy. Oak was the primary wood employed, but pine, maple, and ash are also found. Surfaces were decorated with paint, shallow chip and incised carving, and chamfering. Applied moldings and bosses were often used for ornament and to break up large surfaces. Turnings consisted of ball, baluster, spiral, spool, columnar, and vase shapes. Chair seats were commonly made of rush or splints. Velvet and woolen cushions, sometimes tasseled and fringed, often provided comfort on seats, and leather and turkey-work (tapestry work imitating a textile from the orient) were common materials for upholstered chairs, stools, and benches.

Most of the evidence relating to 17th-century American furniture is supplied by pieces made in rural areas, but at least two chests of drawers have been identified as made in late 17th-century Boston. Although joiners in specific communities produced distinctive furniture, attributions to regional schools of joinery or areas of production are speculative. However, some differences can be observed in the materials and decoration of chests of drawers made in Boston and Ipswich, Mass., a press cupboard of the Hartford and Wethersfield, Conn., area, and a court cupboard probably made in Virginia.

A chest attributed to the Massachusetts shop of Thomas Dennis* has a surface broken into as many small, decorative areas as possible. Red oak, its primary wood, was used for much of American 17th-century furniture but not for English furniture of the time. Sycamore is also present in the Dennis chest, a secondary wood not usually found in furniture made in the other American colonies of this period. Maple split spindles and bosses were used on New England furniture but surviving examples in southern furniture are of walnut. Although it is generally believed that dovetails were first used in colonial America to construct drawers on furniture of the William and Mary period, this construction has also been found on earlier 17th-century furniture believed to have been made in Boston.

3

4

The presence of dovetails in an authentic piece of early 17th-century American furniture, therefore, could be a clue to its regional origin. Flat-carved tulip-and-sunflower designs frequently appear on cupboards and linen chests made in the Hartford and Wethersfield, Conn., areas and were apparently used nowhere else. The use of yellow pine (Pinus taeda) in 17th-century furniture is one reliable indication of southern origin.

Historians often say that 17th-century American furniture was old-fashioned even in its own time, and offer evidence of a "time-lag" between the introduction of customs and ideas in England and their adoption in the colonies. It must be noted, however, that furniture produced in America in the 17th century reflects the taste and values of English artisans and yeomen whose basic outlook was still medieval, regardless of where they lived. The furniture designs of Jan Vredeman de Vries (b.1527), published in Antwerp as early as 1588, or those in Oficina Arcularia (Amsterdam, 1642) published by Crispin de Passe (c.1597–1670), had virtually no impact on these groups before 1650. The Renaissance, a humanistic revival of classical design derived from Roman models and expressed in a flowering of the arts and the beginnings of modern science, began to stir England only as colonization started in America. Its impact on the arts was not felt by most Englishmen, including American colonists, for most of the 17th century.

Hadley Chests, 1675–1725
Hadley chests refer to a group of oak chests with pine lids and a distinctive type of shallow chip carving in a tulip-and-leaf pattern on the entire front surface of panels, stiles, rails, and drawer fronts. All have the initials of their original owners and a few have dates carved on them. The designation as Hadley chests resulted from the discovery of the first example in Hadley, Mass., in the late 19th century. They were produced in a section of Hadley, later called Hatfield, in the Connecticut River Valley. While a few such chests may have been a forerunner of modern "hope" chests, most were probably used to store family clothing and bedding. Chief makers of the more than one hundred known examples include John Allis (1642–91), his brother Samuel (1647–91), his son Ichabod (1675–1747), Samuel Belding (c.1633–1713),

17th Century
1. Thomas Dennis. Chest, red oak, carved and painted with decorations of split spindles, 1678. Henry Francis du Pont Winterthur Museum, Winterthur, Del.
2. Press cupboard with drawers, red oak and other native woods, carved, turned and applied jewelwork and strapwork, late 17th century. Yale University Art Gallery, New Haven, Conn.

3. Peter Blin (attributed). Tulip-and-Sunflower chest, Connecticut, ebonized split-spindle and other applied ornaments in Jacobean style, 1675–1725. Metropolitan Museum of Art, N.Y.
4. John Pease. Hadley chest, carved oak and pine in leaf and flower patterns, painted red and black, c.1714. Yale University Art Gallery, New Haven, Conn. (gift of C. Sanford Bull).

Furniture

and Samuel Belding, Jr. (1657–c.1737), all of Hatfield, and John Hawkes (1643–c.1721) of Hatfield and Deerfield.

Tulip-and-Sunflower Chests

Throughout the last quarter of the 17th century, a number of blanket chests and cupboards with a distinctive tulip-and-sunfower design were made in Connecticut. So many of them have been discovered around Hartford and Wethersfield that they are sometimes called Hartford or Connecticut chests. Like the Hadley chest, they make use of a tulip motif, but that is the only decorative similarity to chests made farther north along the Connecticut River. The shallow-carved designs of tulip-and-sunflower are confined to chest panels. The sunflowers are found only on the center panel, whereas the tulip and leaf designs usually appear on the flanking panels. Applied split spindles decorate the stiles, and bosses decorate the drawer fronts of examples found in Wethersfield. This decorative technique also distinguishes these pieces from Hadley chests.

For many years it was thought that Nicholas Disbrowe (c.1612–83), a joiner who came to Hartford from Saffron Walden, England, had made these chests. This is now doubted as a result of evidence that he was illiterate and could not have inscribed his name on the back of a chest allegedly made for Mary Allyn (Bayou Bend). Disbrowe was an important Hartford joiner, however, and it is likely that he made the elaborately carved wainscot chair used by Governor John Winthrop of Connecticut and owned by Wesleyan University, Middletown, Conn., since 1836.

Another candidate for credit as the joiner who produced these chests is Peter Blin (c.1724–25), who arrived in Wethersfield, Conn., in 1675. One account records his making a chest and trenchers (wooden serving platters) in 1681, which has been used as evidence that he had the equipment and skills to turn the split spindles on tulip-and-sunflower chests. All tulip-and-sunflower chests are so nearly identical that, unlike Hadley chests, it is almost certain that one joiner in the vicinity of Hartford and Wethersfield made this type of chest.

William and Mary

This style prevailed in the English-speaking colonies from 1690 to 1725. Some of the furniture designs, forms, and types of decoration of this period

William and Mary

1. Edward Evans. Fall-front desk, walnut with ball feet, 1707. Colonial Williamsburg, Va.
2. High chest of drawers, maple burl veneer, ball and vase turnings on legs, 1700–25. Henry Francis du Pont Winterthur Museum, Winterthur, Del.
3. Slatback side chair with baluster turnings on front legs, 1700–25. Connecticut Historical Society, Hartford.
4. "Boston Chair," armchair with cane back and seat, maple, 1700–25. Henry Francis du Pont Winterthur Museum, Winterthur, Del.

had been introduced to the English court with the restoration of Charles II in 1660. But the major influences on American furniture in this style undoubtedly occurred during the reign of William of Orange and his English wife, Mary (r.1689–1702). Baroque design and esthetic criteria are usually considered the major components of this style. It would be well to class baroque influence as playful rather than purely classical. Typically, rules and conventions were sacrificed to achieve the effect of grandeur and complexity. Another term for the design theories of this period would therefore be mannerism. In furniture as well as in buildings one finds boldly projecting and receding surfaces, broken pediments, twisted columns, and contrasted light and dark surfaces. The style has a sensuous and emotional spirit in contrast to the intellectual calm of pure classical art. Given the traditional reticence of Englishmen, the student of American furniture in the William and Mary style must be very sensitive to the baroque esthetic if he is to describe American furniture made between 1690 and 1725.

Many of the furniture forms produced in the 17th century continued to be made, but a number of new types were introduced. To seating furniture were added banister, tallback, cane, and easy chairs. Perhaps the earliest reference to furniture in the William and Mary style in colonial America is a listing of "six cane chairs" in the 1688 inventory of Giles Master, "the King's attorney" in Boston. Daybeds, called couches, were used for sitting or lounging. New developments in case furniture—furniture that functions as a repository for objects, for example desks, bookcases, etc.—included the chest of drawers, dressing table, desk-on-frame, and slant-top or fall-front desk (escritoire). Butterfly, gateleg, splay-leg, mixing, tavern, and tea tables complete the list of innovations in the form and function of furniture.

Tea drinking and caning were not the only practices introduced to the West from the Orient. A taste for Chinese lacquer objects developed in Europe and colonial America at this time. Partly in response to this demand, John Stalker and George Parker published *A Treatise of Japaning and Varnishing* (Oxford, 1688). As early as 1695 the inventory of a Captain Andrew Cratey's estate in Marblehead, Mass., listed "1

dozen of Lackered Cane Chears, 1 Japan case of draws, 1 ditto case for plate, and 1 Japan table."

While much William and Mary style furniture was still basically rectilinear in design, and masses of squares and rectangles were used to organize furniture surfaces, an attempt was made to lighten the heavy forms of the earlier period. Relief carving in the form of C- and S-shaped scrolls, leaves, and volutes (scroll-shaped ornaments) appeared on the crest rail and stretchers of chairs and daybeds. Curved and molded armrests contrasted with earlier, solid members. Baluster, vase, ball, and disc turnings became more slender and appear crisper. Bold trumpet turnings, while not common, came into use on legs of case pieces. The new appearance of turnings may have been due in part to the wider use of wheel lathes as against the less efficient pole lathe. Case furniture exhibited ball feet, and Spanish feet were common on chairs. All these innovations helped to reduce the massive character of furniture. Walnut and maple became the principal woods and beautiful burl or crotch-grained veneers of these species were bordered by herringbone-pattern inlays. As baroque painters learned to use the effects of light and shadow on their canvases, so cabinetmakers used marquetry, veneer, inlay, and bold moldings to make the viewer's eye dance over the surfaces of the furniture.

The term "cabinetmaker" first appeared during this period because more skill was required for veneer, inlay, dovetailing, and board construction than was usually possessed by a joiner. It is known that at least ten cabinetmakers worked in Boston between 1696 and 1725. So scant, however, is our knowledge of American furniture in this style that the work of only two cabinetmakers outside of Boston has been identified: Samuel Clements of Flushing, then a rural town in New York, and Edward Evans* of Philadelphia.

Queen Anne, 1725–80

Colonial furniture made in 1725–80 is said to be in the Queen Anne style, although the Queen died in 1714. Elements of this style were developed in England during the reign of Queen Anne (1702–14), George I (1714–27), and even of George II (1727–60). Conservative traditions in the American colonies caused the style to persist

Furniture

for almost a century, especially among country cabinetmakers.

The concept of massive furniture, favored by 17th-century joiners and only slightly altered by the William and Mary style, disappeared in the Queen Anne style. Between 1725 and 1760 cabinetmakers became dominant in furniture production and the period might well be characterized as an age of the elegant simplicity of curved forms. Two outstanding innovations marked furniture design during this era. Use of the S-curve, or *cyma-recta*, developed from earlier baroque concepts, was so pervasive that the English painter William Hogarth in 1754 designated it as the ultimate "line of beauty." A new curved leg, the cabriole, following the outline of the *cyma-recta*, dominated furniture design in Europe and America for more than half of the 18th century. This ancient classic shape was actually developed by the Dutch from the Chinese, with whom they traded, and the Dutch introduced it to England and America. On American seating furniture it was usually reserved for the front legs of chairs, but even the simplest rear leg curved or flared away from an upright stance. Case pieces and tables used it for all legs, front and rear.

The influence of curvilinear design in this period is seen in the use of yoke-back and hoop-back crest rails that flow into the stiles or vertical members of a chair that form the rear legs and back posts in one continuous piece. Backs of chairs, including their vase-shaped splats, were curved and shaped to provide more comfort. Chairs became shorter than those of the William and Mary period. Armrests often flowed in undulating curves, and arm supports frequently appear to be reverse cabriole legs. Even the previously rigid type of seat frame was curved to form horseshoe, balloon, or compass shapes. Curved pediments on desk and bookcases and high chests of drawers replaced earlier flat tops. The skirts of both case pieces and tables were also shaped with S-scrolls and volutes. Carved shells frequently appeared on the knees of all cabriole legs and elsewhere on chairs. Shells also appeared on high chests and dressing tables in natural, carved form or in a stylized version referred to as a fan or sunburst. Circular pad feet were the most common type of terminal, but claw-and-ball

feet were introduced about 1750.

Very few new furniture forms were developed during the Queen Anne period, perhaps because cabinetmakers were too busy modifying existing forms. Upholstered sofas and settees evolved from benches. Circular, dished-top candlestands and tea tables on cabriole-leg tripod bases appeared. Gaming tables were also introduced. Although no documented American bureau table of the Queen Anne period has survived, at least three Boston citizens owned such forms between 1739 and 1752. Similarly, Windsor chairs were in use in South Carolina and Pennsylvania as early as the 1730s. If the period of 17th-century furniture can be called the age of oak, the Queen Anne period is the age of walnut. Furniture was also made of maple, especially in New England and in Pennsylvania. Cherry was a favorite of Connecticut and New York cabinetmakers. The latter also preferred locally available red gum or bilsted, especially for use as a secondary wood. Mahogany was in the shop of a Philadelphia cabinetmaker, Charles Plumley, as early as 1708, but did not become a popular furniture wood until about 1750.

Probably because more is known about furniture of the Queen Anne and later periods, regional characteristics have been identified. The cabriole leg favored by Massachusetts cabinetmakers is often a marvel of lightness and sometimes appears inadequate to support a piece of furniture. Newport cabinetmakers preferred a sharp front edge to the knee of their cabriole legs while Connecticut craftsmen often shaped a distinctive notch below the knee. Circular pad feet were most common in New England, and variants of the pad foot were used in other colonies. New York cabinetmakers often used a broad, pointed "hoof." In Philadelphia, carved trifid, web, or long, pointed elliptical "slipper" feet were preferred. The rear legs of most New England chairs were made in a block-and-cylinder shape. New York chairs follow English chairs closely in having a rounded, tapered rear leg ending in a square-shaped platform or foot. A "stump" rear leg, that is, a block of wood with chamfered or rounded edges, was employed by Philadelphia artisans. The blocking of drawer fronts in either rectangular or rounded form is exclusively associated with New England cabinetmakers: the earli-

Queen Anne

1&2. *Upholstered easy chair with rolled arms, cabriole legs, and turned stretchers; front view showing upholstery in flame stitch wool embroidery; rear view showing a backing of crewel work embroidery, early or mid-18th century. Metropolitan Museum of Art, N.Y. (gift of Mrs. J. Insley Blair).*

3. *High chest, japanned by Thomas Johnston of Boston (attributed), with classical motifs used for the ornamentation and oriental forms and images on the surface, 1730-70. Metropolitan Museum of Art, N.Y. (bequest of Joseph Pulitzer).*

3

est surviving example is a desk and bookcase (Winterthur) signed in 1738 by Job Coit, Jr., of Boston. Broad, heavy, and sturdy pieces seem characteristic of New York Queen Anne furniture—attributes usually ascribed to Dutch influence. Finials of case pieces often varied, including the distinctive "corkscrew" type preferred in Massachusetts, a fluted urn with a carved "flame" atop used in Rhode Island, and the lavishly carved flame exhibited on Philadelphia furniture.

Townsend-Goddard, c.1737–1858

For over a century, twenty members of the Townsend and Goddard families supplied furniture to residents of Newport, R.I. Their cabinetwork spanned from Queen Anne to Victorian styles. These Quaker families have so dominated the imagination of collectors that their work is usually treated as synonymous with Newport or Rhode Island furniture. The best known of them working before 1790 includes Job Townsend, Sr. (1699–1765), John Goddard I (1723–85), James Goddard (1727–57), Job Townsend, Jr. (1726–78), John Townsend (1733–1809), and Townsend Goddard (1750–90). Considering the number of artisans in these families, surprisingly few documented examples of their work have survived. In public collections Job Townsend is represented by a labeled mahogany desk and bookcase in the Rhode Island School of Design, while a mahogany kneehole bureau table (Boston) with Edmund Townsend's label is the only certain example of his work. Four examples of John Townsend's work, a breakfast and a card table, looking glass and side chair, are at Winterthur and three, a chest of drawers, clockcase and card table, are at the Metropolitan Museum of Art. A mahogany desk and bookcase made by John Goddard in 1761 is in a private collection, and a mahogany tea table by the same cabinetmaker was made for Jabez Bowen in 1763 (Winterthur). These pieces, other examples attributed to the two families, and the work of other Rhode Island craftsmen exhibit enough similarities to indicate that a regional school of craftsmanship was responsible for furniture produced in Rhode Island before 1790. The introduction of blockfront decoration was formerly assigned to the two families, but the earliest known American example is a desk and bookcase made in 1738 by a Boston cabinetmaker, Job

1. **Townsend-Goddard.** *Desk and book-case, mahogany, c.1770. Henry Francis du Pont Winterthur Museum, Winterthur, Del.*

Coit, Jr. Scholars agree, however, that the most beautiful colonial examples of this form were the shell-carved pieces produced in Newport.

Walnut and mahogany were their preferred woods, with pine, cedar, and chestnut secondary woods. The presence of the latter in a piece of Queen Anne or Chippendale furniture is often taken as evidence of its Rhode Island origin. The cabinetmakers of this family and school were basically conservative and clung to baroque design concepts for at least two generations. Ornament characteristic of Chippendale never took hold in Rhode Island. Good line, form, and proportions were their guiding standards. They added decoration in the form of bold convex and concave shells, stop-fluting, a spiral scroll finishing an ogee bracket foot, raised paneling in the pediments of case pieces, claw-and-ball feet with undercut talons, and a flat, classical urn finial with fluted sides and corkscrew flame. A feature peculiar to Rhode Island furniture was a pad foot at the rear combined with claw-and-ball feet at the front. Furniture of this school has been termed by its partisans "the best and the most logical of all American pieces."

Chippendale, 1755–90

Furniture of this period is in the style of the London cabinetmaker, Thomas Chippendale (c.1718–79). Basically a recorder of English taste, his book of furniture designs, *The Gentleman and Cabinet-Maker's Director* (1754), had a tremendous influence in the colonies. It contained plans for both "elegant and useful" pieces of "household furniture" that were "suited to the fancy and circumstances of persons in all degrees of life." Designs were in the "Gothic, Chinese, and modern taste," or a combination of all three. "Modern" referred to the ornamentation of surfaces in an asymmetrical and usually exaggerated arrangement of shells, foliage, and flowers that was called "rococo" (a term combining the French words for rock, *rocailles,* and shell, *coquilles*).

It should not be thought that all American Chippendale took on the exuberant appearance of French models. The influence of classical restraint in England and America affected both furniture forms and decoration. The *Director,* for example, contained many designs incorporating elements of classicism, and although some truly rococo furniture was produced in both countries, the new or "modern" fashion was most evident in the rococo surface decoration on traditional forms.

The direct impact of Chippendale's design on American craftsmen is more difficult to prove than is its indirect influence. Judging, however, from several advertisements in 1755 in Philadelphia and Boston offering furniture in "the newest fashions," and others offering current English books on furniture styles, there was little or no time-lag in the adoption of the "modern taste" in the colonies.

The most striking innovation in furniture of this period is the use of pierced splats (backs) and bow-shaped cresting rails on chairs. Piercing a solid splat yielded chairmakers an almost infinite variety of patterns. Cresting rails now rested on upright stiles and craftsmen created an asymmetrical effect with elaborately carved ears using shell or cabochon—a convex, peanut-shaped decoration. Claw-and-ball feet were the most popular type, although they were somewhat "old fashioned," none being illustrated in the *Director.* Blocklike Marlborough feet were often employed to terminate straight-legged furniture that had been introduced as part of the Chinese influence. On case furniture, ogee bracket feet were in common use and either a pierced cartouche or carved flowers and foliage decorated the center of pediments. Pierced frets of Chinese or Gothic derivation were part of the decoration of all furniture forms.

In keeping with a style mainly concerned with surface ornament, few new basic types of furniture were introduced. The high chest of drawers, a form that disappeared from use in England, was developed to its highest expression in America. Kneehole bureau tables, used for dressing and grooming, or as desks, while not an innovation of this period, came into popular use. New Pembroke, or breakfast tables with broad tops and narrow leaves, offered a sharp contrast to the narrow top and wide leaves of earlier drop-leaf tables. China tables, with pierced galleries around the edges of their rectangular tops to protect a display of ceramics, were a variant of the tea table. Small furniture forms such as stands to support basins, kettles, and candlesticks were developed, as were fire screens. Although certainly not common in America, the breakfront bookcase,

2

3

Chippendale
2. *John Cogswell (attributed). Desk with mirror, mahogany, bombe base with claw-and-ball feet, Corinthian pilasters, 1760–80.*
3. *Mirror, Philadelphia Chippendale, carved yellow pine, painted white and gold, 1760–80.*
4. *John Townsend. Drop-leaf breakfast table, one of a pair, mahogany with curly maple underframing, 1760–80. All, Henry Francis du Pont Winterthur Museum, Winterthur, Del.*

4

Furniture

called a "library bookcase" by Chippendale, made its appearance in New England and Charleston, S.C.

With the emphasis of Chippendale on carved decoration, it is not surprising that the close grain of mahogany made it the most popular furniture wood of this period. Following in a descending order of cost for furniture forms were walnut, cherry, maple, and pine. Regional preferences in wood and construction became intensified despite the widespread use of design books. Craftsmen in Massachusetts excelled in the use of the bombe, or kettle-shaped base, for case furniture. When combined with a serpentine-shaped front, the result was quite sophisticated furniture. Newport cabinetmakers retained the grace and beauty of the earlier baroque design of the Queen Anne style. When carving appeared on Newport furniture it was of a line or intaglio type, rather than the lush relief carving on much furniture made in Philadelphia. The side talons of Massachusetts claw-and-ball feet rake backward at a sharp angle. Those on Newport furniture often have an undercut talon. Though much fine furniture was produced throughout the colonies during this period, Philadelphia is generally regarded as the center for cabinetwork exemplifying the Chippendale style.

Windsor

The most prolific examples of the turner's skill in 18th-century America are the simple armchairs, side and writing-arm chairs, benches, and settees known as Windsor furniture. The style was unrelated to fashion trends. It has been assumed that it originated in England, but there is no documentation on its origin or its introduction to the colonies. Windsor chairs were known in England by the 1720s and were in use in America by the 1730s. Their early production centered around Philadelphia, where David Chambers advertised a Windsor chair shop in 1748. The greatest period of popularity and development of this type of furniture was between 1760 and 1800. Windsors were made with "high, low, sack, bow, and fan" backs for use in gardens, inns, public buildings, and homes. In 1796, for example, George Washington purchased twenty-four "oval back" Windsor chairs for Mount Vernon. One Philadelphia chairmaker had 1200 Windsors on hand, ready for sale, in 1775.

Each Windsor form was made of sev-

Chippendale
1. Side chair, Chinese style, with pierced splat and bow-shaped cresting rail, 1755–90. Metropolitan Museum of Art, N.Y.
2. Thomas Affleck. Satin-covered armchair. Chinese style, with straight legs ending in Marlborough feet, 1760–70. Henry Francis du Pont Winterthur Museum, Winterthur, Del.

Windsor
3. Thomas Gilpin. Windsor armchair, c.1775. Collection Mr. and Mrs. David Stockwell.
4. Round Windsor table with three turned legs, late 18th century. Henry Francis du Pont Winterthur Museum, Winterthur, Del.

eral species of unseasoned wood such as tulip wood, pine, ash, hickory, and maple. Because of the variety of wood color and grain in each piece, paint was used to cover these differences. Until about 1790 green was the most popular color, but white, yellow, black, and "mahogany" colors were also employed. Sometimes the plank seats of the chairs were upholstered in leather or moreen and finished with a row of brass-headed tacks.

Dunlap, 1769–1836

Students of American furniture have assigned cabinetwork to New Hampshire whenever it was impossible to show that it had come from Massachusetts or Connecticut. If the piece of furniture had been made before 1825, it was invariably attributed to the Dunlap family, country craftsmen whose work was first identified in 1937. Although at least 214 cabinetmakers were at work in New Hampshire between 1775 and 1835, thus far their products have not been as carefully identified as have those of the Dunlap family. The cabinetmakers in this family were Major John (1746–92), Lieutenant Samuel (1752–1830), Robert (1779–1865), Samuel II (1783–1853), John II (1784–1869), and Dan (1792–1866). James Dunlap (1787–1875), son of Lieutenant Samuel, is also known to have made furniture although he is designated a joiner in old records. Furniture forms made by this family include bedsteads; slatback, country Chippendale, and Windsor side chairs; chests-of-drawers, high chests, chests-on-chests, and chests-on chests-on-frames; also clockcases; slant-top desks; and a wide variety of tables and stands. Only a few of these forms are branded or bear a chalk signature to indicate which of the Dunlap craftsmen made them. A number of characteristics, however, enable cabinetwork to be assigned to the family: flowered ogee moldings, both S-scrolls, carved "spoon-handle shells" and "sunrise fans" on drawer fronts, and a "basketweave" cornice on high chests.

(C.F.H.)

Neoclassicism

While a far-reaching political revolution was stirring in the American colonies in the 1760s and early 1770s, a revolution in taste was occurring in Europe. A reaction to the exuberant excesses of the prevailing rococo style and a reassertion of the classic tradition, it was inspired by excavations at such sites as Herculaneum (begun 1738) and Pompeii (1748). From such original sources,

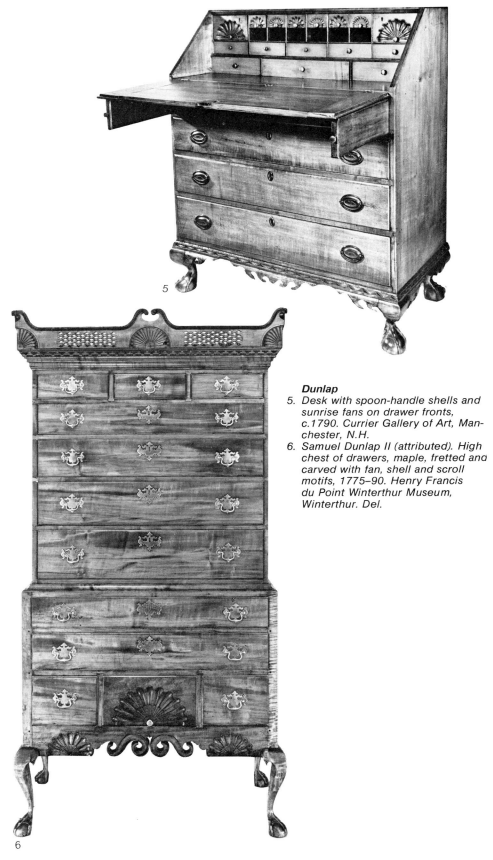

Dunlap
5. *Desk with spoon-handle shells and sunrise fans on drawer fronts, c.1790. Currier Gallery of Art, Manchester, N.H.*
6. *Samuel Dunlap II (attributed). High chest of drawers, maple, fretted and carved with fan, shell and scroll motifs, 1775–90. Henry Francis du Point Winterthur Museum, Winterthur, Del.*

rather than from Renaissance and baroque interpretations of antiquity, designers formulated a new vocabulary of ornament for architecture and furniture. The most important designer was the Scottish-born architect Robert Adam, who, at times in partnership with his brother James, began in the 1760s to create entire classical interiors, including furniture, for wealthy Englishmen. As his style evolved, Adam favored simple, light, even delicate forms, straight lines and compass curves, particularly the oval, and highly ornamented surfaces. These became the dominant characteristics of the first phase of late 18th- and early 19th-century neoclassicism in America as well as in England.

Plagued by difficulties in communication and torn by the war against Britain, the colonies felt little of this change in taste during the 1770s and 1780s. Furniture craftsmen continued to work in the American Chippendale tradition. Finally in 1789, the young nation, free of political bonds but not of other ties, turned again to English sources, and embraced neoclassicism. In Greece she found analogies to her democratic aspirations; in Rome, suggestions of economic grandeur. For half a century after the founding of the new republic, interiors and furniture were predominantly neoclassical. Three fairly distinctive but somewhat overlapping phases of neoclassicism can be distinguished: the early Federal (1790-1815), the late Federal (1810–25), and late classical or Greek revival (1825–40).

Early Federal, 1790–1815

Between 1790 and 1815, American cabinetmakers employed furniture forms and ornament drawn from English pattern books which had popularized the light, fragile style of the brothers Adam. Chief among these books were *The Cabinet-Maker and Upholsterer's Guide* (1788), published by the widow of George Hepplewhite, *The London Cabinet-Makers' Book of Prices* (1788) with designs by Thomas Shearer, and *The Cabinet-Maker and Upholsterer's Drawing Book* (1791–94) by Thomas Sheraton. Although all used some similar designs, each author has come to be associated with certain characteristics: Sheraton with turned, often reeded, legs used with square chair and sofa backs; and Hepplewhite with square tapered legs, sometimes terminating in spade feet, and oval-, shield-, and heart-shaped backs on chairs. Shearer, less

1

2

known today than the other two, contributed mainly in new mechanical devices. Consequently, American furniture of this period is often designated by the English style names of Sheraton or Hepplewhite.

As in the years before the Revolution, American ports enjoying trade with England were the major locations of the cabinetmaker's art. In New England, the Boston-Salem area superseded Newport, R.I., as the major style center; and Portsmouth, N.H., and Providence, R.I., became prominent. In the middle states, Philadelphia, long a center of sophisticated craftsmen, remained important, even as New York began its rise to preeminence. Fewer centers existed in the South, and the furniture there was imported from Europe and from other states. In Maryland, the well-to-do could turn to the often fine craftsmanship of Baltimore artisans, who also helped to furnish fashionable homes in the new federal capital of Washington.

Although the production in these cities followed English patterns, differences in regional interpretations persisted. Generally, New England continued to prefer slender, attenuated forms. In Boston the firm of John Seymour and his son, Thomas, made furniture of extraordinary sophistication, decorated with carving, painting, and veneering in contrasting woods. Sliding tambour, or reeded, fronts, made of narrow half-round strips of wood glued on canvas, sometimes inlaid with festoons of bellflowers, appear on Seymour desks, along with interiors painted blue in the English manner. This blue paint, as well as inlaid pilasters and demilune (crescent-shaped) stringing, which often decorated their case pieces, were also used by other cabinetmakers of the region. The suburbs of Boston boasted fine craftsmen in the Federal mode: Stephen Badlam in lower Dorchester Mills, Jacob Forster and Archelaus Flint in Charlestown. In the neighboring seaport of Salem, grown suddenly rich through the China and "triangle trade," the host of skilled cabinetmakers included William Hook, William Lemon, Elijah and Jacob Sanderson, Edmund Johnson, and Nehemiah Adams. The latter two are known to have made a popular form that combined desk, cabinet, and bookcase, and is now generally called a "Salem secretary." In addition, Salem's famed woodcarver, Samuel McIntire, designed

chairs and tables, and executed finely carved decoration of vines, cornucopia, flowers and garlands of fruits, often against a punchwork ground.

Philadelphia was no longer the center it had been in the Queen Anne and Chippendale periods, but it still had a hundred cabinetmakers in the 1790s. Among the most skilled were Henry Connelly and Ephraim Haines, known for their barback Sheraton chairs. Philadelphia Federal case pieces carrying the maker's label are rare, but a handsome desk and bookcase signed by John Davey uses a play of veneered mahogany and mirrored ovals on a rich satinwood ground to break up the surface of a heavy and rectilinear form.

The use of similar veneered or mirrored panels is found on Federal furniture of Baltimore, where glass with elaborate reverse painting in gilt, called *verre eglomisé,* was also employed for decoration. A piece of furniture with all these is the "Sisters Cylinder bookcase" made about 1810–11 after an 1803 Sheraton design. Baltimore card and pier tables were often inlaid with ovals containing floral sprays or flowers in pots. Straight tapering legs have a chain of pendant bellflowers, with a central elongated petal. Painted furniture in the Sheraton manner was also popular, and complete sets, including chairs, settees and tables, were made by the brothers John and Hugh Finlay and by Thomas Renshaw, whose work was decorated by John Barnhart.

Unlike their Philadelphia and Baltimore counterparts, New York furniture makers seldom used light woods, but favored case pieces with large fields of figured mahogany veneers, often enriched with light wood stringing and small panels of inlay. Chests were made with curving French front feet joined by a distinctive apron. Sideboards, an important new concept originated by Robert Adam and first published in designs of Shearer and Hepplewhite, usually had a "sweep" or curving center with a two-door cupboard beneath the middle drawer. They were supported on canted straight legs, sometimes inlaid with bellflowers in a chain or strung with intersecting ovals. Extensive use was made of quarter fans in corners of drawers and doors and of stringing to outline an entire form. Cabinetmakers who labeled New York furniture in this early Federal style include Michael Allison, Mills and Dem-

3

4

Early Federal
1. *Nehemiah Adams. Gentleman's secretary. Henry Francis du Pont Winterthur Museum, Winterthur, Del.*
2. *John and Thomas Seymour (attributed). Boston sideboard, inlaid mahogany with veneered tambour doors, ivory escutcheons and brass pulls, 1800–10. Metropolitan Museum of Art, N.Y.*
3. *Ephraim Haines (attributed). Barback armchair, mahogany with satin upholstery, 1800–10. Henry Francis du Pont Winterthur Museum, Winterthur, Del.*
4. *Samuel McIntire (attributed). Oval-backed chair, c.1796. Museum of Fine Arts, Boston.*

1

2

ing, George Shipley, Elbert Anderson, and Thomas Burling.

Not only in New York, but in all major American ports, the early Federal style persisted for about twenty-five years; and in rural areas, much longer. However, elements of a new taste began to appear before 1810, especially in New York. The War of 1812 created a brief hiatus, but by its conclusion another neoclassical style had taken over.

Late Federal, (1810–25)

Furniture of the latter Federal period was characterized by another kind of neoclassicism, a literal borrowing of Greco-Roman forms. Again the style had European sources, this time as much French as English. Influenced by archeological discoveries, the Frenchmen Charles Percier and Pierre Fontaine during the periods of the Directoire and Consulat (1795–1804) helped to create "le style antique," employing such classical forms as the Greek klismos and the curule, or "Grecian cross." The klismos chair had a rectangular seat on outflaring front and rear legs and a broad, curving horizontal backrest, or rail. The curule is an X-shaped support historically associated with the magistrate's stools of imperial Rome. There was also much use of carved acanthus leaves, and of animal supports, such as swans, dolphins, eagles, and a one-footed creature, often with lion head and paw. After Napoleon's Egyptian campaign, exotic motifs of lotus and sphinxes were added. In 1801 Percier and Fontaine published their influential work *Recueil de Decorations Interieures.* Soon the new style had reached England, and books by Sheraton (1803), by the connoisseur and dilettante designer Thomas Hope (1807), and by George Smith (1808) formulated the style known as English Regency (1811–20). Their books were known to American craftsmen, as were two important periodicals, The French *Journal des Dames et des Modes* (1796–1830) with engravings by Pierre de la Mésangère (later published as *Meubles et Objets des Gouts*), and the English *Repository of Arts* (1809–28) with plates by Rudolph Ackermann. American furniture of this late Federal period is often termed "Empire" when it is based primarily on French sources, but "Regency" if it derives more clearly from English work.

During the years before and after the War of 1812, New York became America's style capital. There, two foreign-born cabinetmakers exemplify the two new traditions now designated "late Federal." Of Scottish birth, Duncan Phyfe,* described by a contemporary as "The United States rage," had many imitators but few equals in his highly skilled interpretation of English Regency, while Charles Honoré Lannuier, after his arrival in 1803, advertised furniture in "the newest and latest French fashion." Phyfe's Regency furniture included chairs with single or double cross, ogee cross, lyre or harp, or eagle backs, saber or Grecian cross legs, and sometimes paw feet. Case pieces such as sideboards, secretaries, and dressing tables were distinguished by their rich mahogany veneers, smooth mechanical workings, and brass embellishments such as galleries, moldings, paw feet, and circular or lion head and ring pulls. Cresting rails of chairs and sofas often had carved motifs of leaves, ribboned reeds, or drapery and tassels, while the acanthus leaf in high relief on chair and table legs was a regional interpretation.

Lannuier made furniture in an Anglo-American style strikingly similar to Phyfe's, but he is better remembered for his Empire pieces, such as those ordered from him by Baltimore merchant James Bosley or New York socialite Stephen Van Rensselaer IV. On card and pier tables, chairs and window seats, and even beds, Lannuier used figural supports, of gilded swans or winged caryatids, and gilded and verd antique dolphins. Light wood veneers of amboina, satinwood, or maple contrasted with mahogany and rosewood. Both light and dark woods formed backgrounds for elaborate French gilt (ormolu) mounts in classic patterns. Brass inlay sometimes appeared as a Greek-key banding or a line of alternating stars and circles. Lannuier died in 1819, and no other New York cabinetmaker who worked in the French style ever achieved his mastery and preeminence. New York cabinetmakers who left labeled pieces in the style associated with Phyfe include Michael Allison, John Dolan, George Woodruff, and Moses Young.

Boston cabinetmakers faithfully interpreted English Regency, employing bold reeding on legs, ovolo (rounded) corners on tables and case pieces, and, after 1815, more extensive brass inlay than their New York contemporaries. In

Philadelphia, the firm of Joseph B. Barry made highly individual interpretations of late Sheraton styles, such as a pier table created for Louis Clapier in 1810–1815, with virtually all the period ornamentation: carving, veneering, inlaying, and ormolu mounts.

In Baltimore, the Regency-Empire taste had begun as early as in New York, for there the architect B. H. Latrobe* was given the responsibility for furnishing the White House. Consulting with the First Lady, Dolley Madison, he designed for the drawing room a suite of klismos chairs and Grecian sofas. With their extremely graceful scrolling arms, Grecian sofas had by the postwar period become a feature of fashionable parlors in any city. Sometimes they were lower on one end than the other, a form today often called Recamier after David's painting of the famous Madame Recamier. One of the most imaginative and successful interpretations of the Grecian couch, made about 1815–20, perhaps in New York, rests on legs in the form of dolphins whose bodies sweep up and out to form the arms. Like much other furniture of the late Federal period, the dolphin sofa has an element of the grotesque, but also the more ample proportions popular by this time. By the early 1820s the sometimes grotesque qualities of the early Empire style and the delicacy of the early Regency had given way to a new look which was influenced by but did not parallel developments in France and England.

Late Classical
or Greek Revival, 1825–40

The concluding phase of neoclassicism in America, usually termed late classical, featured massive furniture in scale with the high-ceilinged interiors of the dominant Greek revival* style of architecture. Designs were those of the latter years of the regency, and subsequently, of the French Restoration (1814–30), the period of the return of the Bourbon monarchy. English furniture styles illustrate many of the characteristics of American furniture of this period. Grecian sofas remained, but their graceful saber legs were replaced by heavy turned legs; their scrolling arms often became large, rolled ends, perhaps imitating the round cushions of earlier years. Case pieces were often supported by widely gadrooned (fluted) bun feet. Massive animal paw feet also appeared, particularly on New York so-

3

4

Late Federal
1. A corner of the "Blue Room" at the Henry Francis du Pont Winterthur Museum, Winterthur, Del.
2. Joseph B. Barry & Son. Pier table, veneered, carved and gilded mahogany with ormolu mounts, 1810–15, Collection Mrs. T. Wistar Brown, Ardmore, Pa.
Greek Revival
3. Empire-style parlor, c. 1839. Henry Francis du Pont Winterthur Museum, Winterthur, Del.
4. Duncan Phyfe (attributed). Pier table, carved mahogany with mirrored back and reed-edged marble top, c. 1830's. Metropolitan Museum of Art, N.Y. (L. E. Katzenback Fund).

Furniture

fas, pier tables, sideboards, and secretary bookcases, where they were sometimes painted. Such distinctive, rather baroque carving also appeared on New York mahogany card, drop-leaf, and center tables of the 1820s in the form of crisply detailed leaves above hairy paw feet. Supports took the form of columns with twisted reeding, or a single massive pedestal carved like a diamond-faceted pineapple, or encircled with cuplike leaves. Michael Allison, master of the earlier phases of neoclassicism, also worked in this style, as did Thomas Astens and the firm of Joseph Meeks.

In Boston, furniture of the 1820s was less baroque, more architectonic. A labeled pier table that was made by Emmons and Archbald, with characteristic Boston ebonized (stained black) ball feet ringed with brass beads, shows French influence in its pillared supports and ormolu mounts. Large numbers of French ormolu mounts from the workshop of Henry Kellam Hancock also survive; yet documented pieces by him, and labeled furniture by his younger brother, William Hancock, show a closer adherence to English precedents.

Philadelphia's most successful immigrant cabinetmaker of this era was Antoine-Gabriel Quervelle, working there by 1817. In 1829, he made furniture for the White House. Large gadrooning on aprons or table edges, bands of gilt trim, and, on case pieces, a convex radial fan, were among his decorative motifs. He often used baccarat glass pulls and ormolu mounts, indicative of his French heritage.

By the 1830s the more ornate pieces by these craftsmen were being supplanted by a simpler style based on forms favored during the restoration. Still dependent for its effect upon the skillful laying on of highly figured mahogany veneers, this furniture was produced both by the workshops of famed cabinetmakers such as Phyfe, and by factories mass producing it with new power-driven tools. The first published expression of this furniture was an advertisement for the New York firm of Joseph Meeks & Sons* appearing in 1833. In these pieces, drawn almost directly from Smith, the emphasis is on large expanses of veneered surfaces as well as extensive use of columns and scroll supports, which give the style its popular name of "pillar and scroll."

Far to the west of the original cabinetmaking centers, in places like Cincinnati, Ohio, and Grand Rapids, Mich., America's earliest large-scale efforts at furniture manufacture occurred in this style. In 1840 there appeared America's first pattern book, John Hall's *The Cabinet Maker's Assistant,* which was also one of the last gasps of the classical style, now so debased as to be unrecognizable. In it are forms almost completely supported by single and double scrolls, easily cut by machine. The age dominated by master craftsman, along with the half century dominated by neoclassicism, was drawing to a close.

Historic Revivals, 1840–76

By 1840, the use of machines made it easier for a carpenter to saw large expanses of veneer or make flatcut scrolls and fretwork, and furniture production was improved. However, mechanization throughout the mid-century tended to implement existing styles rather than initiate new ones. The existing styles were again those of France and England, where, beginning in the late 1820s, a series of historic revivals began. In 1833, Loudon's *Encyclopaedia* cited the classical or Grecian as the most widespread style, but also mentioned the Gothic, the Elizabethan, and the style of the age of Louis XIV.

Aware of the anachronisms implicit in these revivals, a group of reform-conscious critics grew up in England. One of their chief spokesmen was Henry Cole, who published, under the pseudonym Felix Summerly, the *Journal of Design* from 1848 to 1852. In it in 1849 he made his famous statement: "We all agree only in being wretched imitators." Cole and his circle were instrumental in bringing about the first great international art exposition, at the London Crystal Palace in 1851. This was followed by the international exhibitions of 1855 and 1867, and the London exhibition of 1862; in America, the New York Crystal Palace of 1853 and the Philadelphia Centennial of 1876, which heralded a new era. Despite the reform backers, the exhibition at the London Crystal Palace featured lavish furniture and objects derived from such a mixture of historic and exotic sources that critics were at a loss to find descriptive names for them. Exhibitors at the New York Crystal Palace followed suit, and in the two decades between that exhibition and the Centennial, more than half a dozen styles were popular. They were

1. **Louis XVI.** Leon Marcotte (New York City). Armchair, part of a suite, carved and turned maple and fruitwood with gilded bronze mounts and front-leg casters, deep-tufted gold damask upholstery, c.1860. Metropolitan Museum of Art, N.Y. (gift of Mrs. Chester D. Noyes).
2. **Gothic.** Easy chair, carved walnut with tufted upholstery, c. 1850. Metropolitan Museum of Art, N.Y. (Rogers Fund).
3. **Elizabethan.** Side chair, carved rosewood and mahogany with petit-point upholstery, mid-19th century. Museum of the City of New York.

variously and often inaccurately called Gothic, Elizabethan, Louis XIV, Louis XV, rococo, Louis XVI, Renaissance, and neo-Grec.

Gothic Revival

This style emerged in America about 1840, at least a decade after English designers had established its principles, and novelists like Sir Walter Scott had helped create its romantic aura. Its first great American proponents were landscape gardener and arbiter of taste Andrew Jackson Downing* and architect Alexander Jackson Davis.* The latter designed Gothic furniture for some of his houses, including the "Country Mansion in the pointed style" (1838–41, now Lyndhurst) at Irvington, N.Y., for William Paulding.

In 1842 a New York pattern book, Robert Conner's *The Cabinet Maker's Assistant,* first illustrated the style. Throughout the 1840s in numerous cities, fine Gothic furniture was made by noted cabinetmakers; Burns and Trainque, Alexander Roux, and the Meeks in New York, Paul in Boston, and John Jelliff in Newark. Downing's *The Architecture of Country Houses . . .* (1850) illustrated Gothic furniture and recommended it for hallways, bedrooms, and libraries. The style began to wane in the 1850s as cheaper versions were created, and it was no longer dominant in the 1860s, although it recurred throughout the 19th century as it had throughout the late 18th.

Elizabethan

Like the Gothic, this was a romantic style rooted in the English tradition of the picturesque. Beginning in England in the early 1830s with the books of T. F. Hunt and Henry Shaw, it did not appear as a popular style in America until more than a decade later. The salient characteristic was the use of spiral or bobbin turnings on stiles (or legs) of chairs, as well as on columns of case pieces. Such baroque turnings were actually typical of 17th-century furniture in the reign of Charles I and Charles II rather than in the time of Elizabeth. Although some American high-style furniture of the late 1830s and early 1840s—such as high-backed prie-dieu chairs —incorporated these turnings, the most widespread use was in decoration of suites of cheap painted "cottage" furniture, usually for the bedroom. Matching split spindles, also Elizabethan in character, were often applied to dressers and chests.

3

Rococo

The dominant furniture style of the mid-century, this was sometimes called "French modern" because in the reign of Louis Philippe (1830–48) it was the new style, and sometimes "French antique" because it revived motifs of mid-18th-century rococo: the cabriole leg, C- and S-scrolls, and naturalistic carving, often featuring the shell. Beginning in France after the restoration, and coming to England in the late 1820s as Louis XIV, it rapidly changed to the more curvilinear forms of Louis XV, and became popular in the United States in the 1840s. Despite its origins in historic styles, the rococo revival developed a character of its own. The scale of seating furniture was generally smaller. The cabriole leg, at times ending in the French scroll foot, also often terminated in a tapered cylinder. The rear leg of chairs and sofas was not usually the cabriole, but a reverse curve, for an appearance of stability. Backs of seating furniture were usually higher than on 18th-century pieces; padding of seat and back was more opulent. Indeed, it is in this period and this style that upholstery became of major importance, perhaps partly because of the perfecting of the coil spring, but more because of a new concern with comfort. Seats and backs were often deep-buttoned or "tufted." Favored woods for frames and case pieces were rosewood, mahogany, and black walnut. Marble was extensively used to top pieces on which objects were to be set: dressing bureaus and tables, center tables, and sideboards. The forms of wood furniture were often emulated in cast iron, some of which was intended for indoor use and painted to simulate wood; some for gardens, finished in black, green, or dark brown. Chiefly, however, the style was used for parlor and bedroom furniture, as Downing had advocated, because of its grace and lightness. The name most associated with the rococo revival in America is that of John Henry Belter of New York, whose distinctive laminated furniture was imitated by a number of his contemporaries, particularly Charles Baudouine. Equally masterly was Alexander Roux, noted for superb carved pieces. Other well-known cabinetmakers producing rococo revival furniture in mid-century included the Meeks, Bembe and Kimball, and E. W. Hutchings of New York City, Ringuet LePrince and Marcotte of

Furniture

Paris and New York, Elijah Galusha of Troy, John Jelliff of Newark, George Henkels and Daniel Pabst of Philadelphia, Auguste Eliaers of Boston, and Prudent Mallard and François Seignoret of New Orleans.

Louis XVI

Almost concurrent with the curves and cabriole of the rococo were the rectangular forms and straight lines of the neoclassical style of Louis XVI. Favored during the Second Empire (1848–70) by Napoleon III's empress, Eugénie, it gained impetus at the Paris exhibition of 1855. Louis XVI à L'Imperatrice reached its high point in America about 1860, and in this period was employed primarily by French-trained cabinetmakers such as New York's Leon Marcotte. Actually Marcotte's versions, like all Victorian interpretations of past styles, followed such styles superficially. For example, woods, instead of being painted pale colors, were usually ebonized, sometimes in combination with rich veneers and inlays. Following the Civil War, the style was again popular, but in an even more eclectic interpretation, with forms more closely related to the style that is now known as Renaissance revival.

Renaissance

Perhaps the most confusing of the revival styles, especially in the wide application of its name, was that called Renaissance. Although pattern books as early as the 1830s mentioned styles called "Cinque-cento" and "French Renaissance," the Renaissance revival did not appear in America as an important style until the early 1850s. Following many foreign designers at the London Crystal Palace of 1851, American designers and cabinetmakers exhibited Renaissance revival pieces, chiefly cabinets, buffets, and bookcases at the New York Crystal Palace of 1853. Early examples of the style had little to do with actual forms of the Renaissance; rather they were eclectic combinations of a multitude of styles from the 15th through the 18th centuries. They were usually massive and architectural in form, with a rounded or broken arch pediment, sometimes with a cartouche, heavy moldings, and deeply carved ornament. Often consoles or caryatids were a part of the design, or there were sculptural busts. The influence of English Elizabethan styles could be seen in the use of carved strapwork, or of fruit and game on

1

2

3

*1. **Eclecticism and Reform.** Grand Rapids bedroom suite shown at the 1876 Centennial Exhibition in Philadelphia, made by Berkey and Gay. Grand Rapids Public Museum, Mich.*
Rococo
2. Alexander Roux. Carved rosewood étagère, pier stand, mid-1860's. Brooklyn Museum, N.Y.
3. John Henry Belter. Center table, carved and laminated wood in a floral pattern with grapes, 1856–61. Museum of the City of New York (gift of Mr. and Mrs. Ernest Gunther Victor).

sideboards. Throughout the 1850s in America, Renaissance and rococo elements were often almost equally blended in furniture. Toward 1860 the Renaissance revival became increasingly mixed with forms and ornament of the Louis XVI revival. In this phase, certain new characteristics were added, some of them doubtless stemming from ornate furniture featuring porcelain and metal plaques made for Empress Eugénie. Case pieces, still heavy and rectangular in form, often had angular protrusions—scrolls, brackets, pilasters, pseudo supports—without structural meaning. Elaborate marquetry became important. Applied ebonized bosses, carved pendant acorns and tassels were popular, as was a stylized anthemion or "palmette." Carved human busts were still used, often as supports for the arms of chairs. Legs of seating furniture were often heavy turned versions of the Pompeian form; small tables had complex bases of curving supports around a central baluster.

Eclecticism and Reform, 1876 to 1918
Just as the Crystal Palace Exhibition in London in 1851 forms a logical point to consider styles at mid-century, so the Centennial Exhibition in Philadelphia in 1876 marks a turning point for design in the latter part of the century. Revivals continued, but for the first time reform, active in England for several decades, became evident. Although most furniture remained the overblown, extremely ornate interpretations of styles considered suitable for expositions, one American firm exhibited "the only examples of furniture designed after the canons of Eastlake . . . whether among the English or American exhibitors." Generally speaking, American reviewers were highly critical of the furniture shown. Nevertheless, both the pieces exhibited and visitors' interest in such varied exhibits as the New England Kitchen, the Japanese Pavilion, and the Turkish Bazaar presaged future developments. The three trends which the Centennial foreshadowed were: 1) continuance of older revivals, especially of the Renaissance, rococo, and Louis XVI styles; 2) new tastes and renewed revivals expressed primarily in exotic styles such as the Near Eastern (Persian, Moorish, or Turkish), as well as the Indian and oriental, and a revival of colonial styles; 3) reform styles growing out of the English Arts and Crafts* movement.

Near Eastern and Eastern
A favorite Centennial attraction was a Turkish Bazaar and Café, and one of the few room settings by an American furniture company featured a fireplace with "Moorish pillars." Interest in the Near East had been strong throughout the century, beginning with the domes and minarets of Nash's Brighton Pavilion in regency England, a fantasy emulated in America in such houses as P. T. Barnum's Iranistan (1848) and Samuel Colt's Armsmear (1855–62). In the early 1870s a precursor of this renewed interest was Olana, the Persianized home that painter Frederic Church built overlooking the Hudson. By the early 1880s the exoticism of the East had seized the imagination of many decorators and designers, among them Louis Comfort Tiffany,* whose drawing room offered "a simple suggestion of the ancient Moorish style," according to a New York publication of 1883–84. As usual, the style was highly eclectic, with "a dash of East Indian" and Japanese. An even more significant use of the Moorish taste in this period was a parlor decorated for Arabella Worsham's house (later the John D. Rockefeller residence) at 4 West 54th Street, New York City. This room, now in the Brooklyn Museum, has carved and polychromed Moorish decoration on woodwork and carving or inlay on ebonized art furniture of fine quality, apparently by custom cabinetmaker George Schastey, who had exhibited one of the "gems of the Centennial." In the homes of rich and poor, the influence of the Near East showed itself in a renewed interest in cushions and divans. The Moorish style was often recommended for smoking rooms, while pillowed and padded "Turkish corners" became popular everywhere. To complement the upholstered pieces, small objects from bazaars were used, such as inlaid hexagonal or octagonal tables, decorative chests and screens, and brass and copper accessories. Egyptian, which had been a substyle of Victorian Renaissance furniture, continued to appear in decorative motifs, and enjoyed renewed popularity after 1881, when the obelisk known as Cleopatra's Needle arrived in New York.

During the early 1880s, at the height of the taste for the exotic, the artist Lockwood deForest, one of Tiffany's partners, established a shop in Ahmadabad, India, to produce carved furni-

1

2

Near Eastern and Eastern

1. *George Schastey (attributed). Parlor decorated in the Moorish style, with carved and polychromed woodwork, carved and inlaid ebonized furniture, divans and cushions, c.1880. Brooklyn Museum, N.Y.*
2. *Imitation bamboo table and chair, c.1885. Metropolitan Museum of Art, N.Y.*

3. **Art Furniture.** *Christian Herter. Wardrobe, carved and ebonized cherry with marquetry flowers and petals, made for Lillian Russell, 1880's. Metropolitan Museum of Art, N.Y. (gift of Kenneth O. Smith).*

3

ture and woodwork. The favorite exotic wood of this period, however, was the bamboo of Japan. In Brooklyn, the firm of Nimura and Sato made furniture framed in genuine bamboo, with panels of matting on decorative painting to simulate lacquer work. Even more popular was imitation bamboo furniture, made of turned natural maple. Kimbel's *Album of Designs* (1876), a trade catalog, illustrates a chair of this type, and a photograph album (Cooper Hewitt Museum) of work by the firm of Kimbel & Cabus shows a pseudo-bamboo settee. George Hunzinger, another New York chairmaker, designed a set of bamboo-style furniture with woven wire seats. (Provincetown Museum). All of this furniture—as well as the case pieces with hand-painted Japanese tiles set into the wood to form decorative panels—was closely allied to art furniture.

Colonial Revival
Few colonial pieces were actually shown at the Centennial. One exhibit that charmed visitors was of an old New England kitchen. A few knowledgeable people had already begun to collect furniture of America's past; a comment in *Gems of the Centennial* (1877) noted that "extraordinary prices" of old furniture "indicate strongly how taste is tending." By 1884 *Cabinet Making and Upholstery* reported that "The manufacture of antiques has become a modern industry." Although many relatively faithful copies of Queen Anne and Chippendale styles were produced, by the end of the century pieces often incorporated elements of several styles. Even furniture emulating such late styles as Empire was customarily miscalled "colonial," and large manufacturers proudly advertised the "Furniture of our Forefathers."

Reform Styles
The boundaries between reform styles are sometimes unclear. Although terms were used interchangeably, sources of the reform movement are easily traced. As early as the 1830s in England, A. W. N. Pugin advocated honesty of construction as found in medieval furniture. Elements of his philosophy were also expounded by the critic John Ruskin, who condemned the excesses of the machine and urged a return to a handicraft system. Chief spokesman in England for the Arts and Crafts* ideal was William Morris, poet, craftsman, and utopian socialist, who had a pro-

found influence on all decorative arts, though he designed little furniture. His followers included painters of the pre-Raphaelite group, and architects such as William Burges, Richard Norman Shaw, and Philip Webb. From the work of these men there developed by the late 1850s and early 1860s a school of furniture based on medieval forms: it was strongly rectilinear, with honest, revealed construction, and decorated panels painted by well-known artists.

The firm Morris, Marshall, Faulkner & Company was founded in 1861. Another major influence on the reform movement was the Japanese section of the London International Exhibition of 1862, in which Burges saw "the real Middle Ages," the principles of craftsmanship that had all but disappeared from the Western world. Before the close of the 1860s an Englishman, Edward W. Godwin, was designing esthetic furniture in the Anglo-Japanese mode, while the philosophy of reform had been announced to a wide audience in the books of Bruce J. Talbert and Charles Lock Eastlake.*

Eastlake
Primarily interested in promulgating moral truths in style, Eastlake designed little furniture. His very popular book, *Hints on Household Taste* (London, 1868, and Boston, 1872), carried his message of "sincerity" of purpose. He recommended straight lines and simple forms and decried furniture that bulged. Wood was best left natural, he declared, but if stained, should be black. From Eastlake's illustrations and tenets American designers of the 1870s created a style to which they gave his name. For the most part, Eastlake was a term applied in America to modest, even cheap, factory-produced furniture of rectilinear form and incised line decoration. Clarence Cook in *The House Beautiful* stated that Eastlake furniture must not be judged "by what is made in this country and sold under the name. I have seen very few pieces of this that were either well designed or well made."

Art Furniture
In 1877 *American Architect* lamented that there were no great American "art furniture" manufacturers at the Centennial. The one truly significant piece of art furniture shown was English: a cabinet designed by T. E. Collcutt and first exhibited in London in 1871. At Philadelphia it aroused great admira-

tion. It presented most of the features of art furniture: rectilinear form, ebonized finish, and flat surface decoration within panels. On the Collcut cabinet the decoration was painted; on most American pieces it was carved or inlaid in elaborate marquetry. In large part, American art furniture (sometimes called Eastlake) stemmed from the designs of the Englishman E. W. Godwin, who had begun creating "Anglo-Japanese" furniture in the late 1860s. By 1877 Godwin had published *Art Furniture,* a catalog that provided designs that others adapted or quite literally copied. Most of Godwin's work was more progressive than that of his American followers. Art furniture in America was a luxury style and lasted only from the mid-1870s to the mid-1880s, when it was supplanted by other reform movements aimed at a broader market.

Architect Furniture
During the period from 1800 to 1875, the eastern seaboard, and particularly New York, dominated design. In the 1880s and 1890s progressive design in architecture shifted to two new centers, Chicago and California, and, to some extent, progressive furniture design also shifted west. Henry Hobson Richardson,* the first great architect to make an impression on furniture design, was originally based in New York, then in Brookline, Mass. He designed pieces that were, like his Romanesque buildings, massive and straightforward. Some of his chairs and tables for libraries and churches show the influence of progressive high-Victorian Gothic designers, while others, like a wheel-armed settee, are closer to the work of Godwin. Simple spindle-form chairs and benches, like those of the firm of William Morris, seem to derive from traditional vernacular forms. Allied to contemporary English reform design, the aim of these pieces was to make furniture fit its setting, a concept expanded by other architects. In Chicago, the Tobey Furniture Company produced for the Borden House a set of dining-room furniture with a table as monumental in form as any Richardson building, with carved scrolling ornament in the style of another great architect, Louis Sullivan.* In the prairie school of architecture centering around Chicago, men such as Frank Lloyd Wright,* George Maher, and Harvey Ellis created for their earth-bound "organic" houses furniture freed from the rigid-

1

2

ly compartmented rooms of earlier homes. The range was great. Maher's furniture was very sophisticated and highly finished, while Wright favored simple designs which could be followed by any competent carpenter. Wright himself, like many architects of the era, at one point lived with, and sometimes advocated, the craftsman furniture made by Gustav Stickley in New York and New Jersey. For a brief period after the turn of the century, Harvey Ellis designed furniture for Stickley, while in Pasadena, Cal., the brothers Charles and Henry Greene would recommend Stickley's furniture when their own custom cabinet designs were not feasible. For great houses such as the Gamble House, they established Peter Hall to make their elegant furniture, which was honestly constructed with ebony pegs and splines (thin wood strips), both functional and decorative. In these pieces, as in the work of other major progressive architects, there is continually evident the philosophy of the Arts and Crafts tradition, both of the English movement of the 1850s and 1860s and the resurgent movement of the late 19th and very early 20th century.

Arts and Crafts, Craftsman, and Mission
The ideals of the English Arts and Crafts movement never died out in England and America. In the closing years of the century, followers of William Morris sought to reestablish the beauty and dignity of hand labor, to create a unity of crafts, to work toward an art which all could share, and to draw upon the vitality of the vernacular arts. The problem in Morris' philosophy lay in making art for the masses while eschewing the product of the machine. As early as the late 1840s, men like Henry Cole had realized the need to reconcile manufacturing processes with principles of design. During the esthetic period when art furniture reigned, the critic and supreme esthete Oscar Wilde proclaimed the new "line of beauty" to be that of the machine. Similarly, although Frank Lloyd Wright owed a debt to Morris and followed Arts and Crafts principles in his early furniture designs (using natural finishes and realizing "the nature of the materials"), he came to praise "the clean-cut, straight-line forms that the machine can render far better than would be possible by hand." This basic dualism of machine versus hand production

created divisions in the Arts and Crafts movement in America, as it had in England. Perhaps the purest application of Morris' principles was made by local groups working in his tradition. In England a number of such groups were founded in the 1880s. Emulating them was the Art Workers Guild of Providence, R.I., whose leading members were Sydney R. Burleigh, Charles W. Stetson, and John G. Aldrich. Their furniture, which included cabinets and chests with painted panels highly reminiscent of the work of Burges and Webb, had no direct effect on American style, but was an expression of a philosophy that became part of the mainstream of 20th-century thought.

Less derivative but also more closely allied to Arts and Crafts than to the art nouveau* movement to which it has been linked was a small body of highly sophisticated, straight-line decorated furniture designed at the turn of the century. Clearly related to the work of such British designers as Charles Rennie Makintosh, Voysey, and Baillie Scott were the furniture designs of the enormously talented illustrator Will H. Bradley for Edward Bok's *Ladies' Home Journal.* Like the best art furniture, these fine handcraft products of the Arts and Crafts movement, though meant for a wide public, could be afforded only by a few. It remained for two men working in craft communities to bring simple reform furniture of high quality down to the price level of mass consumption. They were Gustav Stickley and Elbert Hubbard, whose furniture was in the craftsman, or mission, style. Stickley began designing and producing furniture in 1898 in Eastwood, N.Y., and before going bankrupt in 1915 had extended his enterprises to include the Craftsman Workshop near Syracuse, N.Y., the Craftsman Farms in Morris Plains, N.J., *Craftsman Magazine,* and the Craftsman Building in New York City. During the intervening years, his trade catalogs and magazine had made his designs available to countless amateur craftsmen across the country. He was widely copied commercially, not always in a quality he would have endorsed. Elbert Hubbard (1856–1915), best remembered for his Roycroft press and as author of *A Message to Garcia,* headed a craft community at East Aurora, N.Y. There the Roycroft shops produced "craft-style" furniture—not unlike Stickley's—simple

Architect Furniture
1. *Frank Lloyd Wright. Side chair, designed for the Imperial Hotel, Tokyo, c.1920. Cooper-Hewitt Museum of Design, N.Y.*
2. *Gustav Stickley. Armchair, oak, with leather seat and copper fastenings, c.1900. Collection Mr. and Mrs. Robert Mattison, Berkeley, Cal.*

oak tables, chairs, benches, and bookcases. Stickley's and Hubbard's furniture and the imitations in solid, sturdy oak came to be known as "mission" furniture because it had a mission of usefulness. In time, because of a renewal of interest in America's past and in indigenous forms, the name became associated with the Franciscan missions of California.

Vernacular Furniture

Throughout the 19th century, sometimes running with the stream of prevailing styles, sometimes against it, were several modes that presaged the functionalism of the 20th century. Perhaps the most important were vernacular furniture and patent furniture.

The term "vernacular" can be broadly applied to a large body of forms that met the everyday needs of common people. The vernacular furniture of the 19th century had its roots in earlier cultures, but utilized forms that had been adopted or had evolved over a long period of time. In addition to these native forms created throughout the young nation were furniture forms created by ethnic or religious sects set apart from the general community. The 19th century was the age of utopian experiments, and scores of model communities were founded in America. Only a few of these groups, however, became known for their crafts. Probably the most important was the Shakers.

Living in communal "families," the Shakers from the late 18th century through the 19th created utilitarian furniture, accessories, and tools of refined proportions and unadorned surfaces. Their crafts (see Shaker Crafts), like their lives, reflected their emphasis on order, cleanliness, simplicity, and economy. Their forms show the influence of the simple vernacular furniture of New England—Windsor and slat-back chairs, plain tables, stands, and chests—which were the original furnishing of Shaker buildings before a Shaker style evolved. As communities became established in eight states, Shaker furniture developed certain consistent characteristics, such as an absence of surface ornament and superfluous parts. Such furniture suited their setting: plain almost austere rooms, often featuring built-in cupboards and drawers. Large cupboards and chests often sat flush on the floor, and moldings were eliminated. Narrow doors were used on cupboards, dovetails

3

4

Vernacular Furniture
3. *Shaker dining room. Table made for Shaker ministers of the Enfield, Conn., Shaker community; pine benches from the New Lebanon, N.Y., community; and candle sconce from Hancock, N.Y. Museum of American Folk Art, N.Y. (Andrews Collection).*
4. *Shaker tripod stand from the New Lebanon, N.Y., community. Henry Francis du Pont Winterthur Museum, Winterthur, Del.*

were exposed, showy escutcheons and brasses were eliminated, the latter being replaced by simple wooden pegs. The smaller, movable pieces of furniture could appear somewhat fragile, since they were intended for "family" rather than wordly use. Turnings on stands, chairs, and even stairway balusters became more slender. In all smaller furniture there was an emphasis on mobility and functionalism. Chairs were often low or had low backs that allowed for them to be slid under tables. Beds were set on large wooden casters or rollers, and could be easily moved for cleaning. Early chairs had a ball and socket device on back posts so they could be tilted, and rocking chairs were favored. Side chairs had slender finials by which they could be easily grasped; they were often hung upon the peg boards that lined the rooms.

Mechanization and Patent Furniture

Although mechanization had little effect in changing the predominant furniture styles—the historic revivals which have been characterized as the "ruling taste"—it did have some effect on forms and the way furniture was made, especially in achieving cheaper substitutes for hand work. Mechanization thus contributed to one of the great visual problems of the 19th century, which was decoration bearing little or no relation to the forms it embellished. Of more positive importance was the new use of mechanization to "aid and support the human organism." This aspect is more obvious in American patent furniture (furniture with patented parts that could be mass produced). In addition to exploring new forms and new uses, furniture manufacturers also explored new materials. Although such exploration might be seen as part of the 19th century's unceasing search for variety and newness, it might also be partially attributed to the new technology. A final and little-recognized effect of mechanization, particularly in the 1860s and 1870s, was the creation of ornament and forms based on parts of machines.

Perhaps the most important aspect of innovative and patent furniture of the 19th century was the emphasis on movability. There were basically four kinds of movability: 1) movability of the whole, as in folding furniture; 2) movability of certain parts for conversion into another use, such as sofas convertible into beds; 3) movability for in-

1

2

1&2. Patent Furniture. George Hunziger. *Arm chair and rocking chair from an illustrated advertisement, 1876.*

creased comfort, as in revolving or reclining chairs; 4) movability of parts for specialized use, as in typing chairs and piano stools.

Along with an interest in new forms there appeared an interest in new techniques and materials. Two technical innovations were bending and laminating of wood, which reached a high point in mid-century with the bentwood chairs of the Austrian Michael Thonet and the laminated furniture chiefly associated with German-born John Henry Belter.* Both techniques, however, had been employed as early as the federal period. Bentwood seat rails appear on early 19th-century fancy chairs, while Boston cabinetmaker Samuel Gragg produced a group of remarkable bentwood seating furniture. Lamination, the principle of gluing together layers of wood, each layer at opposite grain to the preceding, is the principle of plywood. It was occasionally employed to shape curving parts of federal furniture and by mid-century for chair backs, table aprons, and carved areas by a number of cabinetmakers. By 1874 the combination of the two principles could be seen in the American patent for a bent-plywood chair.

Along with new techniques came the employment of new materials. An interest in the organic runs throughout the 19th century: thus, from mid-century on, furniture was made of animal horns, rattan, wicker, bamboo, and rustic wood complete with bark and the stumps of branches. There was also an interest in mineral substance and metals, and the potentials of brass, iron, and steel were all explored. In 1844 a brass bedstead was exhibited at the American Institute Fair, while in 1848 a brass bedstead and four iron bedsteads were shown, as well as two spring mattresses. The first spring bed was patented in 1848–49. This period was the age of cast iron; numerous manufacturers specialized in iron furniture, including Chase Brothers of Boston, and John Wickersham, J. L. Mott, and J. W. Fisk of New York. The potentials of wire were further expanded in the 1870s, when wire furniture, principally chairs, settees, and plant stands in fanciful, lacy shapes became prevalent.

Since 1920

The most radical changes in the history of furniture design have occurred since 1920. The modern movement began in the 19th century in Europe with William Morris, Michael Thonet, Edward Godwin, C. R. Mackintosh, Van der Velde, Joseph Hoffmann, and the art nouveau movement and in America with Gustave Stickley, Elbert Hubbard, various arts and crafts groups, and architects such as Frank Lloyd Wright.* Their desire to create furniture forms totally unrelated to the past, and yet both practical and comfortable, to simplify construction, and to fit the design to its surroundings, marked the beginning of a new thrust in furniture design and introduced some of the principle tenets of 20th-century design. It is significant that almost all important furniture of the modern movement was designed by architects and is characterized by strong delineation of forms, an understanding of engineering and new materials, and an overall integration of furniture and building.

In the 19th and early 20th centuries, furniture designers were unable to make use of the machine and large-scale machine production. The controversy over machine versus hand craftmanship had raged since the middle of the 19th century, and it was only in the 20th century that designers came to grips with technology's potential. The fifty years before 1918 had seen no substantial innovation in furniture materials, manufacturing, or marketing. The turning point came when World War I, shattering existing social and economic structures, brought an era of experimentation and change. By the 1920s modern designers had accepted the idea of mass-production and had begun to experiment with new materials and technology. They showed a preference for geometric forms and were influenced by modern art concepts featuring pure abstraction.

In 1917–18 a Dutch architect, Gerritt Rietveld (1888–1964), designed a chair consisting of flat, painted wooden rectangles simply joined. The members crossed one another, but did not penetrate, creating a feeling of lightness and clarity. It was totally original. De Stijl, a group which subscribed to constructivism* and to which Rietveld belonged, believed that total abstraction, simplication and integration of art and architecture would help to bring about social change. In Berlin, the Bauhaus* began in 1919 to deal practically and inventively with all aspects of art and industry; it became the most important force in design between the wars. In 1925

the young Marcel Breuer,* Bauhaus student and teacher, designed the Wassily armchair, the first chair made from chromed tubular steel. In 1926, both Mart Stam (1899–) and Mies Van Der Rohe* created cantilevered side chairs in tubular steel. Mies also designed the German Pavilion for the Barcelona International Exhibition of 1929 and the chair he created for its interior—made of chrome-plated steel frame and leather cushions—has become world famous. In France, another great architect, Le Corbusier, was also experimenting with metal furniture; in the Scandinavian countries traditional forms in wood had been adapted to industrialization. Alvar Aalto (1898–) of Finland experimented with the natural spring of plywood and in 1933 he designed a cantilevered chair with a birch frame and molded plywood seat and back.

Little progressive furniture design appeared in the United States before the early 1920s, as most American furniture manufacturers still produced machine-made period reproductions, such as Louis XV, Adamesque, Tudor, and Spanish Renaissance. Around the turn of the century, Americans had become enamored of their own heritage and had started the "colonial revival." But World War I brought many immigrants, among whom were furniture designers Paul Frankl,* Kem Weber,* Frederick Kiesler (1890–1965), Joseph Urban (1872–1933), Wolfgang and Pola Hoffmann, William Lescaze,* and Raymond Loewy (1893–), all of whom introduced new ideas in furniture. Even though the United States did not participate in the Paris exhibition of 1925 —"L'Exposition Internationale des Arts Décoratifs et Industriels Modernes"— Americans were influenced by the modern furniture shown there. From this exhibition came a new design movement, art deco.* Furniture developed a lower profile and became more rectilinear, and the transportation machine, in particular the automobile and the ship in the 1920s, and the airplane in the 1930s, emphasizing speed, became the symbolic design force (see Streamlined Moderne).

America's department stores deserve credit for acquainting the public with the new European styles and with the work of those few American designers who were expressing the new approach. In 1927, R. H. Macy & Company

sponsored an "art moderne" exhibition, showing work by Jules Bouey, Paul Frankl, and others. Frankl himself exhibited his "skyscraper furniture," an attempt to achieve a typically American design. Two department stores, Lord and Taylor's and B. Altman's, held displays of French decorative arts in 1928, but the important exhibition was again at Macy's, with only three Americans, Kem Weber, Eugene Schoen, and William Lescaze, among the three hundred exhibitors who were chosen to participate. The Metropolitan Museum of Art and the Museum of Modern Art also held industrial design shows. The latter was particularly influential in promoting the International style,* which evolved out of the Bauhaus tradition of steel, glass, and leather, and emphasized functional structure and decorative austerity. Early practioners of this style were Kiesler, Richard Neutra,* and the firm of Howe & Lescaze.* In the early 1930s a second wave of immigrants including Albers,* Gropius,* Breuer, Moholy-Nagy, and Mies van der Rohe, was to have a profound effect on modern design.

By 1928 manufacturers of furniture were producing a flood of modern styles, though there was great resistance to "the machine-for-living" look of steel and glass. An intense rivalry between modern and traditional styles ensued. Baker Company presented its "Connoisseur" line of careful English reproductions. At the same time pioneer modernists, such as Frankl, Weber, and Donald Deskey—famous for his interior design of New York's Radio City Music Hall—Russell Wright, Joseph Urban, Jules Bouey, Eugene Schoen, and others, were experimenting with new forms, new materials, mass-production, time- and space-saving devices. The industrial designer,* a peculiarly American phenomenon, greatly influenced furniture design, contributing practical ideas and functional innovations. The traditional role of the furniture designer—that is, as cabinetmaker—was enlarged and expanded. The Chicago World's Fair of 1933 further publicized the new developments. An avant-garde designer, Gilbert Rohde,* attracted much attention with his "Design for Living House," stressing practical, flexible, comfortable, well-constructed, machine-made furniture. In 1931 he persuaded Herman Miller, Inc., a company that made con-

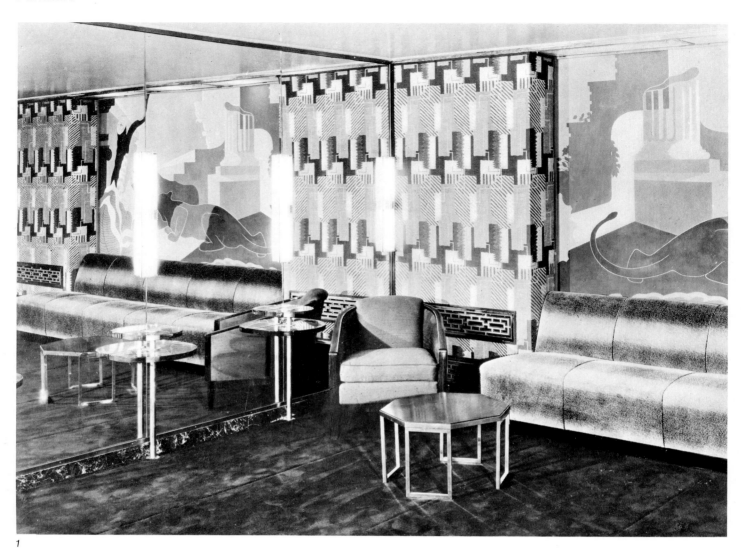

1

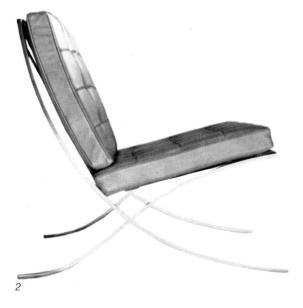

2

3

ventional, easily salable furniture, to change its total concept of design and marketability: it was not to worry about public taste and to allow the designer to experiment and retain complete control over the production of his designs. The firm became a pioneer in encouraging experimentation, including the work of such designers as Charles Eames* and George Nelson.* At the end of the decade Swedish modern became the rage after it was shown at the New York World's Fair of 1939.

In the 1940s America became a leader in technical innovations in furniture. Americans had always been concerned with inventing ways of reducing labor and saving time. The wardrobe that became a bed, and the chair that transformed into a table, were 19th-century expressions of this concern. Standardization of parts, an idea introduced for bookcases at the turn of the century, was an American development. After World War II, the drive towards simplification and experimentation was matched by technological know-how. Charles Eames, an American designer, and Eero Saarinen,* Finnish-born architect, designed a revolutionary chair, which won first prize in the Museum of Modern Art's Organic Design Competition in 1940. For the first time, the back, arms, and seat were joined in a single molded plywood form. The chair was never put into production but after the war Eames created one of the great chair designs of the 20th century. The seat and back are of plywood molded to fit the body. The parts are attached to plywood or metal frames by rubber shock mounts that give the chair greater resiliency. In 1948 Eames and a group from the University of California, Los Angeles, designed a chair of molded plastic reinforced with fiberglass—the first commercial use of fiberglass. Finally, an economical, single-shell, lightweight, indestructible chair had been designed; it was to lead to all kinds of new experiments with plastics.

Saarinen went his own way with an easy chair and ottoman made of a molded, one-piece shell. Designed for maximum comfort, it utilized molded plastic with fabric-covered latex foam upholstery, mounted on a chromium-plated tubular frame. Because of the chair's large, enveloping shape Florence Knoll Bassett* of Knoll Associates, another important manufacturing pioneer in modern furniture design,

dubbed it the "Womb Chair." Founded by Hans Knoll* in 1938, Knoll Associates has used many leading American and European designers, including the sculptor Harry Bertoia (1915–   ), who began in 1951 to design chairs and related furniture using welded steel rods, and Isamu Noguchi,* who created a free-form sculptural table of wood and glass in 1940. In 1950, Knoll also put back into production Mies van der Rohe's Barcelona Chair, which had an immediate influence on interior design.

There has been a continual drive in 20th-century furniture to reduce the number of parts of a piece of furniture and simplify the manufacturing process. Thus over the century, chairs have gone from four legs to one: Eero Saarinen's tulip pedestal chair (1956–57), made of molded plastic and fiberglass and supported on a single aluminum pedestal base. The demands of contemporary living require furniture that is adaptable, informal, and practical. One of those concerned with creating new forms which are relevant to the social realities of today is George Nelson,* who invented in 1945 the "storage wall," a storage system of interchangeable, flexible parts.

Though the direction of furniture has been towards experimentation and new materials, wood is still popular. The handcraft tradition has continued in the work of designers like Wharton Esherick* and George Nakashima.* In 1943, Mrs. Vanderbilt Webb founded the American Craftsman's Council and in 1956 she established the Museum of Contemporary Crafts. Both have helped foster American handcraftsmanship. Many designers have applied contemporary standards of functionalism and simplicity to the adaptability of wood. Robsjohn-Gibbings,* an American, and Jens Risom,* a Dane, are exponents of the Scandinavian tradition of well-designed, well-constructed, machine-made wood furniture. During the 1950s in particular, the Scandinavian influence was very strong in America.

The past decade has seen another flurry of activity in design. There has by no means been a universal acceptance of modern styles. Traditional sentiments are still strong, although there have been changes in size and scale to accommodate present-day life styles. Italian designers have influenced styles all over the world with dramatic new

4

5

Since 1920
1. Donald Deskey. Women's lounge, Radio City Music Hall, N.Y., in art deco style, 1932.
2. Ludwig Mies van der Rohe. "Barcelona" chair, c.1929, chrome-plated steel frame and leather cushions. Knoll International, Inc., N.Y.
3. Gilbert Rohde. Exhibit room from the "Design for Living" house at the 1933 Chicago World's Fair.
4. Charles Eames. Side chair, c.1946, molded plywood. Herman Miller, Inc., N.Y.
5. Wharton Esherick. Moveable library steps, 1935. Estate of Wharton Esherick, Paoli, Pa.

1

2

3

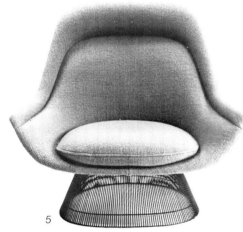

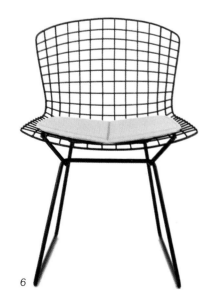

forms and shapes. Innumerable types of plastics have been developed but their real potential has only recently begun to be explored. A shortage of living space, more informal living patterns, and built-in furniture have drastically changed the concept and appearance of furniture. Many traditional pieces such as wardrobes, sideboards, bookcases, and storage units of all types are disappearing. Only the chair and table endure. And the chair has gone through a myriad of changes. It can now stack, like David Rowland's "40/4 Chair," for easier storing; it may come in units or modules for more flexible arrangements; and it can be made of wood, steel, or plastic, with or without upholstery. In this age of technological miracles the possibilities are endless.   (M.J.B. and D.H.P.)

Futurism.

An Italian movement in painting, sculpture, and literature conceived and organized by the poet Filippo Tommaso Marinetti, who wrote a futurist manifesto in 1909 calling for the destruction of traditional art forums such as museums and libraries. In 1910 the sculptor Umberto Boccioni and the painters Carlo Carra, Giacomo Balla, and Gino Severini signed manifestos espousing futurism, and the group launched a series of demonstrations. In *La pittura futurista,* a manifesto published in Milan in 1910, the futurists expressed their way of seeing: "Things in motion are so multiplied and distorted that they succeed each other like vibrations in the space through which they move." In their concern with subjects reflecting the contemporary, the futurists attempted to portray dynamism and energy, eschewing such traditional themes as landscape and still life. Their surfaces were fragmented into planes, recalling analytical cubism,* but they added strong color to cubism's bland palette, and used "force lines" to express the kinetics of movement and the thrust of machine power. Whereas the cubist painters portrayed subjects as seen from several points of view, as though the observer moved, the futurists depicted the subject itself as moving.

In 1911 the work of the futurists gained international exposure, and in Paris in 1912 they organized their first group exhibition. In 1914 Boccioni published a book defining the group's ideas, but then, with the outbreak of World War I and the death of Boccioni in 1916, the group dispersed. By 1920 the art of several of the futurists had taken on new metaphysical aspects that influenced the avant-garde movement known as dada.* Futurist concepts also had a lasting impact on architecture, photography and film, stage design, typography, and advertising.

The United States was introduced to the concept of the depiction of motion in painting when *Nude Descending a Staircase* (1912) by Marcel Duchamp* caused a sensation at the Armory Show* in 1913. Among American artists, Joseph Stella* was most closely connected with the futurists. However, their influence is reflected in many ways, including the "force lines" and symbols of movement in the works of John Marin* and Abraham Walkowitz.*
                              (D.W.S.)

Since 1920
1. Eero Saarinen. "Tulip" pedestal table and chairs in a Knoll Interior, 1957, molded plastic and fiberglass on aluminum base. Knoll International, Inc., N.Y.
2. Marcel Breuer. The "Wassily" armchair (the first chair made from chromed tubular steel), 1925, steel and leather. Knoll International, Inc., N.Y.
3. David Rowland. The "40/4 Chair," 1964, steel and plastic. G. F. Business Equipment, Inc., N.Y.
4. Eero Saarinen. "Womb Chair" (with ottoman, not shown), molded plastic with fabric-covered latex foam on a chrome-plated tubular steel frame, 1946.
5. Warren Platner. Easy chair, nickel finish steel rod with hand-woven wool upholstery, 1961.
6. Harry Bertoia. Armchair, 1952 welded steel and fabric-covered foam latex.
   All, Knoll International, Inc., N.Y.

Gabo, Naum (1890–   ).
Sculptor and theoretician who holds an important place in modern sculptural history, having developed new spatial theories early in the century and illustrated them in his works. Born Naum Pevsner in Briansk, Russia, Gabo shared with his brothers a deep interest in the revolutionary artistic ferment before and after the Russian Revolution of 1917. He studied in Munich between 1910 and 1914, first natural sciences, then engineering. At the outbreak of World War I, he went to Scandinavia, where he changed his name to Gabo (to distinguish him from his two brothers, also artists) and experimented with his first "constructions." While working on these—mostly highly abstract, rigorously analyzed heads—Gabo began to formulate his radical new vision of sculptural space. Together with his brother Antoine Pevsner, he published his views as the *Realist Manifesto* during their first public exhibition in Moscow in 1920. The principal statements in the manifesto—which has become a landmark in art history—are: space and time are the essential elements of real life; volume is not the only spatial element; static rhythms alone are not capable of giving expression to real time; art must cease being representational in order to become creative. The most important of these principles is the insistence that volume is not the only spatial element. Dispensing with the traditional solid volumes used even by the cubists, Gabo worked his way into transparent volumes, which were sometimes set in motion.

Gabo's vigorous vanguard stance met with quick resistance, and in 1922 he left Russia for Berlin, where he remained until 1932. He became well known to other European artists as an originator of the constructivist idea in sculpture. He insisted from early on that a work must be *constructed* rather than carved, modeled, or hewn, and that by using new materials, such as transparent plastics, the artist would construct a new philosophy of art. Later he explained constructivism* thus: "... in a constructive sculpture, space is not part of the universal space surrounding the object; it is a material by itself, a structural part of the object—so much so that it has the faculty of conveying a volume as does any other rigid material. ..." This vision of interpenetrating spaces is faithfully pursued throughout his work. Many of his sculptures juxtapose curves, executed in transparent synthetic materials and qualified by masses of slender threads that set up countercurrents in the shifting spaces. Early constructions in which he worked out his basic principles were first exhibited in 1926 in the United States, and in 1930 he had a one-man exhibition in Hanover, Germany. Two years later he left Germany for Paris, where he joined the group of geometrically inclined abstract artists called "abstraction-creation." Gradually his reputation assumed international proportions. In 1936 he and his brother Antoine Pevsner exhibited at the Chicago Arts Club, and in 1938 he had a one-man show at the Wadsworth Atheneum. Gabo spent the World War II years in London. He then settled permanently in the United States in 1946. He was cordially received and two years later the Museum of Modern Art held an exhibition of works by him and Pevsner. In 1955, Gabo was commissioned to create a monumental sculpture for the entry of the Bijenkorf Department Store in Rotterdam. He seized the opportunity to design a huge, eighty-foot-high realization of his principles. The steel-and-wire construction, with its slightly asymmetrical curves and its transparent central core, is regarded by many critics as the major constructivist monument.

Gabo has received many honors, among them a Guggenheim Fellowship, the American Art Institute's Logan Medal (1954), and the Brandeis Award (1960). In 1965–66, a retrospective exhibition of his work toured major European museums.   (D.A.)

Gallier, James, Sr. (1798–1868).
Architect. Born in Ravensdale, Ireland, he studied at the School of Fine Arts, Dublin (1815–16), worked as a joiner in Manchester, England, and then at building jobs in Ireland. From 1822 to 1832, he and his brother did building work in London, with James working for a time for William Wilkins, well-known architect of the Greek revival.* In search of a more lucrative practice, Gallier sailed for New York in 1832; there he worked for the firm of Town* and Davis. After a year in partnership with Minard Lafever,* Gallier and another architect, Charles Dakin, sailed in 1834 for Mobile, Ala., where they won a competition for the new City Hall (never built). They moved on to New Orleans and were joined by James Dakin to form the firm of Dakin, Gallier & Dakin. The young architects preferred the fashionable Greek revival style, which they used for their best works: the St. Charles Hotel (1834–36), built of Quincy (Mass.) granite, burned in 1850; Christ Church (1835–37); and the Merchant's Exchange (later the Post Office, burned 1960). Several plantation houses with classical columnar porticoes are credited to Gallier, such as Ashland (later called Belle Hélène), built in 1841 (now dilapidated) for Duncan Kenner, sportsman and politician.

About 1840 Gallier opened his own office. His best building in this period was the New Orleans City Hall (1845–50), using the Ionic order, and built of Quincy granite and Westchester, N.Y., marble. In the late 1840s his eyes weakened and, after seeking a cure in

England, he retired. He died in the wreck of the *Evening Star* off Cape Hatteras.

Gallier's contribution was to bring to the Louisiana area an intelligent use of the Greek revival style and to introduce architecture as a full-fledged profession. He compiled a handbook, *The American Builder's General Price Book and Estimator* (1833), and published an autobiography (1864), which gives much information on the practice of architecture at that time.   (P.F.N.)

Gallo, Frank (1933–   ).
Sculptor. Born in Toledo, Ohio, he is a graduate of the Toledo Museum of Art School and the Cranbrook Academy of Art in Michigan. Gallo employs cast epoxy to create figures with a sensual surface, which are incised and colored to give an interplay between flesh and clothing. Lounging in chairs or leaning against portions of architecture, Gallo's figures often emerge from their supports with an air of spontaneity. In the early 1960s, they were casually attired and had a strong domestic tone. By 1968, as Gallo concentrated almost exclusively on women, they grew more voluptuous in form and vivid in color. Drawing on recent fashion, he has gone from domesticity to pop-oriented glamor, as in his full-sized, extremely lifelike figure of the screen actress Raquel Welch. In a one-man show in New York City in 1972, his work showed the influence of a nostalgic art deco* eroticism, especially in heads of nubile girls whose faces emerge from enveloping, 1930s-style flower hats. In 1966, Gallo received a Guggenheim Fellowship and became acting head of the sculpture department at the University of Illinois.   (C.R.)

Gardiner, Sidney (c.1788–1827).
A Boston silversmith working about 1809, he was in partnership with Thomas Fletcher* by 1810 and moved with him to Philadelphia in 1811, where they became the leading makers of presentation silver after the War of 1812. Gardiner was the manager of the work in the shop. He died during a second business trip to Mexico to discuss the making of medals for the Mexican government.

Gardner, Alexander, (1821–82).
Photographer whose contribution to the visual history of the Civil War equals

1

2

1. *Naum Gabo.* Linear Construction, Variation, *1943, plastic and nylon thread. Phillips Collection, Washington, D.C.*
2. *Frank Gallo.* Man at Desk, *1967, epoxy. Graham Gallery, N.Y.*

1. *Alexander Gardner.* Execution of
the Lincoln Conspirators: Adjusting
the Ropes, *1865, photograph.*
2. *Alexander Gardner.* Lewis Payne,
*from the Washington police "Rogues'
gallery", c1873, photograph.
Both, Library of Congress,
Washington, D.C.

3. *Joseph Victor Gatto.* Times Square
at Night, *1943. Collection Roy
Neuberger, N.Y.*

and in some ways exceeds that of the better-known Mathew B. Brady.* He was born in Paisley, Scotland, and a thorough training in physics and chemistry led to an early interest in photography. The theories of the utopian-socialist, Robert Owen, brought Gardner to the United States in 1849 to establish a Utopian settlement, Clydesdale, near McGregor, Iowa. For the next seven years Gardner devoted himself to writing and lecturing in Scotland to persuade others to join the Iowa experiment. But when he and his family finally emigrated to the United States in 1856, they found that an epidemic had ravaged their intended home. They settled instead in New York City, and Gardner was soon employed in the plush Broadway studio of Mathew B. Brady. Brady, the most successful photographer in New York, recognized in Gardner a keen business sense as well as a photographer's sensitive eye and chose him to direct a new gallery in Washington, D.C. Gardner moved to an eighty-acre farm near downtown Washington in 1858. So capable was his management of the new gallery that its profits subsidized Brady's New York operation, and money he invested in real estate eventually brought him a handsome income.

The Civil War brought a radical expansion of Gardner's photographic activities. He joined the staff of Union General McClellan in early 1862. Although a civilian, he was known as "Captain" Gardner, Photographer to the Army of the Potomac. His official duties —making photographic copies of documents and maps—provided transportation for his equipment to the front, where he photographed posed portraits of officers and "instantaneous" views of the troops. The popularity of these photographs brought a serious disagreement with Brady, Gardner contending that photographs made on his own time and with his own equipment belonged to him, Brady insisting that all photographs made by his photographers were his property. As a result, Gardner opened his own Washington studio around the corner from Brady's late in 1862. More important, Gardner persuaded the most talented of Brady's photographers then documenting the war, T. H. O'Sullivan,* Guy Foux, D. G. Woodbury, and G. N. Barnard,* to work for him. This new association resulted in thousands of photographs of the war

—each meticulously credited to the photographer who made it—a vast visual document. The finest of these were issued in 1866 in two folio volumes, each containing fifty actual photographs with a text by Gardner. This work, *The Photographic Sketchbook of the War,* is his most significant contribution to American photography.

Although he continued to photograph for another fifteen years, his real estate holdings and his philanthropy took more and more of his time. He photographed statesmen, visiting dignitaries, and Indian delegates to Congress. It was he—and not, as is commonly thought, Brady—who documented the executions of the Lincoln conspirators and of Jacob Wirtz, head of the infamous prison at Andersonville. In 1867 he published two sets of stereoscopic views of the territory covered by the Union Pacific Railroad. In 1873, he organized a "Rogues' Gallery" for the Washington police.

Both Brady and Gardner petitioned Congress in 1869 to purchase the thousands of photographs they and their associates had made of the Civil War, but they were ignored. Fortunately, nearly ten thousand of these priceless negatives have been preserved and are now in the National Archives in Washington, D.C. (D.L.)

Gatch, (Harry) Lee (1902–68).
Painter. Born in a rural community near Baltimore, Md., as a child Gatch spent much time in the Chesapeake Bay region, where he developed a love of nature that was to provide the main theme of his work as an artist. He studied at the Maryland Institute of Fine Arts, particularly with John Sloan* and Leon Kroll.* In 1924 he won a year's fellowship at the American School in Fontainebleau; he also studied in Paris with André Lhote, returning to the United States in 1925. He had one-man shows in New York City in 1927 and 1932.

By the early 1930s, Gatch was involved in an effort to combine the insights of impressionism and cubism. He gradually eliminated the human figure from his work; at the same time, his style became more expressionistic, often employing religious and philosophical symbolism. As finally developed, his work is individual and contemplative, with a lyrical and mystical feeling for nature. Light and movement, vibrancy of color, paint textures, and

the elusive intimation of the object are major elements in his mature manner. An example is *Night Gothic* (1957, Boston). A perfectionist, he worked slowly and meticulously, and so his output was small. In 1957 he began to employ a kind of collage, using thick, glossy paint as a mortar for pasted pieces of canvas with frayed edges. In the 1960s, he experimented with "stone pictures," paintings incorporating thin slabs of flagstone among their collage elements.

Gatch set up his studio in Lambertville, N.J., in 1935 and lived there, more or less in seclusion, until his death. He was married to Elsie Driggs, a painter associated with the precisionist movement. Major exhibitions of his work have been held by the Phillips Gallery (1956) and the Whitney Museum (1960). (A.F.)

Gatto, Victor Joseph (1893–1965).
Self-taught artist who turned to painting in 1940 after illness forced him to look for less arduous work than boxing and steamfitting. Although a native of Greenwich Village, N.Y., Gatto's life was completely separate from that of the surrounding artistic community, and his first painting, the product of economic necessity, was inspired by a sidewalk exhibition in Washington Square, New York City. His total oeuvre probably did not exceed one hundred canvases, but the pictorial range is wide, including historic, biblical, topical, fanciful, and natural subjects—most of them depicted with little technical facility but painstaking concentration on each detail and an unusual gift for observation. (M.J.G.)

Gemini G.E.L.
Graphic Editions Limited (G.E.L.) is a commercial enterprise set up in 1966 by a former Tamarind Lithography Workshop technical director, Kenneth Tyler, to print and publish lithographs. It has issued lithographs by Josef Albers,* Jasper Johns,* Ellsworth Kelly,* Roy Lichtenstein,* Claes Oldenburg,* Robert Rauschenberg,* and Frank Stella* as well as of California artists such as Kenneth Price and Ed Ruscha. In 1968 Gemini moved into molding and casting, producing works in lead, plastics, brass, bronze, aluminum, and steel. These works, in larger editions than most sculpture, are categorized as "multiples." Besides conducting extensive research into the nature of

1

2

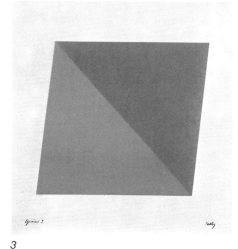

3

4

Gemini G.E.L.
1. *Jasper Johns.* Fool's House, *1971.*
2. *Robert Rauschenberg.* Banner, *1969.*
3. *Ellsworth Kelly.* Blue/Green, *1970.*
4. *Roy Lichtenstein.* Modern Head No. 5, *1970.*
   All, © *Gemini G.E.L.*

lithographic printing, developing large hydraulically operated presses and chemically stable papers and inks capable of printing the largest hand-pulled lithographs, Gemini has actively promoted the idea of prints and multiples as the dominant art of the 1960s. In 1971 "Technics and Creativity: Gemini G.E.L.," a traveling exhibition, documented the production of Gemini's first five years. (R.C.)

Genre.
Genre painting was a comparatively late development in American art. Paintings of everyday life reached a peak in the Low Countries in the 17th century, and in the work of such painters as William Hogarth and Thomas Rowlandson in England in the 18th century; however, their work had no direct influence on the art of the colonies. Art in America until well after the Revolution was largely limited to portraiture. A few artists after the Revolution made isolated experiments in the genre field. For example, what is probably the first American genre print, *Accident in Lombard Street,* a comic incident, was etched by Charles Willson Peale* in Philadelphia in 1787 (an example is in Winterthur). Eight years later, Jeremiah Paul exhibited at the Columbianum in Philadelphia what appears to have been the first American genre painting, *A Boy Holding a Cat to a Mouse* (c.1795, location unknown). After 1800, a number of painters, including Washington Allston,* Henry Sargent,* and Charles Bird King,* produced at least one genre scene.

These first strivings to broaden the acceptable range of painting in America, however, failed to receive public support, and the painters rarely repeated their attempts. The first American-born painter to specialize in genre was Alvan Fisher* who began to paint scenes of country life outside Boston as early as 1813. At about the same time, John Lewis Krimmel,* a young German immigrant, produced some charming scenes of life in the Philadelphia area. But Fisher and Krimmel were at least a decade ahead of the true beginning of popular interest in genre in America. This interest burgeoned in the late 1820s and was in full flower by the 1830s. The social climate was then for the first time sympathetic to such a development. The first native tradition of landscape painting, the

Hudson River School,* had been launched, and genre art—celebrating the homespun qualities of the common man, as the Hudson River School sang the peculiar beauties of the uncultivated landscape—was a parallel development. Both were a natural outgrowth of Jacksonian democracy. Americans were possessed by a chauvinistic enthusiasm which knew no bounds. They took pride in all the republican virtues and the classlessness of society and saw nothing undignified in holding up for admiration the native son or daughter attired in workaday clothes and engaged in the routine activities of the farmer, the store- or tavern-keeper, and the blacksmith. William Sidney Mount* was the recognized leader of this first wave of genre specialists, but he had a numerous company of colleagues, notably Francis W. Edmonds,* Charles Deas,* Richard Caton Woodville,* and William Ranney,* and in the next generation, George Caleb Bingham,* James Clonney,* James Henry Beard,* David G. Blythe,* Arthur Fitzwilliam Tait,* and Jerome B. Thompson* to name just a few. The latter often added other types of subjects.

Genre painting as first practiced in America was in no way a provincial version of foreign traditions. However, after its rise to popularity, most American painters went abroad to study, and the influence of foreign academic instruction in technique—if not in themes —and especially the rigorous academic discipline of the Dusseldorf Academy, became apparent. When Paris supplanted Dusseldorf as the center of art studies, an equally strong dependence upon French academicism, lasting until the end of the 19th century, could be detected.

Generally the genre paintings produced in America in the first half of the 19th century were characterized by directness, clarity of vision, and a refreshing simplicity. In the figures, emphasis was placed on appearance; warts, wrinkles, frayed and work-worn clothes were depicted with care, and all details were given a high finish. Frequently the painting was humorous or comic, and made gentle or broad fun of some unfortunate victim of circumstance.

This brand of what is a peculiarly American strain of realism lasted roughly up to the Civil War. After the freshness—or naiveté—of the works of the

5

6

Genre
5. *David Gilmour Blythe.* Corn Husking, *c. 1850–55. Metropolitan Museum of Art, N.Y.*
6. *George Caleb Bingham.* The County Election, *1852. Art Museum of St. Louis.*

first generation of American genre painters, there was a marked change in the manner of painting as well as in attitude. Americans emerged from the trauma of the Civil War with a loss of their earlier almost overbearing self-confidence and independence of mind. Suddenly they became citizens of an international power and were at a loss as to how to conduct themselves. Many turned to Europe, and especially to France, for training, and as a result American art became international. American painters absorbed the mannerisms and the palette of the French academicians to whose studios they flocked; and their work soon reflected the vogue for triviality, refinement, and sweetness characteristic of the Victorian era. Sentimentality rather than true sentiment became pervasive in genre paintings, even among such outstanding genre painters as John George Brown,* George Lambdin,* Thomas W. Wood,* and Eastman Johnson.*

The genre tradition has never ceased to be an important aspect of American painting. After 1900, the Ash Can School,* focusing on urban life, developed its own much more realistic mode of expression. Some American scene painters of the Depression years, such as John Steuart Curry,* Thomas Hart Benton,* and Grant Wood,* depicted scenes on midwestern farms. Still more recently, Edward Hopper* and others have kept the tradition alive with fresh vision and vigor. However, since 1960, the genre tradition has perhaps been strongest not in painting, but in sculpture, as in the realistic scenes created by such artists as George Segal* and Edward Kienholz.* (H.W.W.)

Gifford, Sanford Robinson (1823–80). Landscape painter of great sensitivity whose studies of light make him a founder of American luminism.* Gifford was born in Greenfield, N.Y. After attending Brown University for two years (1842–44), he withdrew to devote himself to painting. About 1845 he studied with the watercolorist John Rubens Smith and at the National Academy of Design* in New York. Turning to landscape during the summer of 1846, he made several walking tours among the Catskill and Berkshire mountains. A strong source of inspiration for him in this pursuit was Thomas Cole,* whom he admired. Though he

1. **Sanford Robinson Gifford.** Kauterskill Falls, *1862. Metropolitan Museum of Art, N.Y. (bequest of Maria de Witt Jesup).*

2. **Cass Gilbert.** *Detroit Public Library, Mich., 1917.*

had no formal training as a landscapist, by 1847 the American Art-Union* accepted one of his scenes for distribution, and in 1848 it took eight of them. In 1851 he was elected to the National Academy of Design.

Gifford traveled in Europe during 1855–57. He visited England and Scotland, calling on the critic John Ruskin,* and in Italy he traveled with another American painter, Albert Bierstadt.* Arriving back in New York, he moved into the Tenth Street Studio Building and soon exhibited his mature style. Shedding the static, dark composition of the early Hudson River School,* his new work showed the influence of the great English master, J. M. W. Turner, and of the Barbizon School.* His painting of *Lake Nami* (1856, Toledo), executed in Italy, demonstrates Gifford's technique: his brushwork is exact, the strokes are invisible, and his forms are clearly outlined; he paints the sun directly, and topography becomes less important to him than painting the effects of light on land and water. In his *Kauterskill Falls* (1862, Metropolitan), the artist has carried this approach to its culmination, dissolving form and painting light and atmosphere with great subtlety.

Although he never painted the heroic subject matter that was so important to some of his contemporaries, Gifford continued to travel widely. He made a second European trip in 1868–69, going as far afield as Egypt, Jerusalem, and Greece, and in 1870 he traveled to the Colorado Rockies with his fellow painters Worthington Whittredge* and John F. Kensett.* In the last decade of his life, his precise style gradually loosened; his pictures became more painterly but less effective. Gifford was one of the most popular members of his school, and was honored at his death by a memorial exhibition at the Metropolitan Museum and an accompanying catalog of his entire work.

(T.E.S.)

Gilbert, Cass (1859–1934).
Architect. He was the son of the first mayor of Zanesville, Ohio, where he received his early education. Later, he went to work as a surveyor in an architect's office in St. Paul, Minn. A talented draftsman and watercolorist, he was sent in 1878 to the Massachusetts Institute of Technology for one year. With money he earned as a surveyor,

he went abroad in 1880, and on returning entered the New York office of McKim, Mead & White* as an assistant to Stanford White. In 1882 he set up a partnership with James Knox Taylor in St. Paul and practised for a decade, designing the Endicott Building among other commissions.

Gilbert later practised alone, with an ever-increasing emphasis on classical architecture. In 1896 he won the competition for the Minnesota State Capitol which supports a dome similar to that of St. Peter's in Rome. He redesigned the upper portion and dome of the Arkansas State Capitol at Little Rock in 1908. In 1928, he also redesigned the West Virginia State Capitol at Charleston. All of these state capitols involved millions of dollars of costly materials, sculpture, and rich interior decorations. His design for the New York City Custom House, at Bowling Green, was very much in keeping with its heroic-sized sculpture by Daniel Chester French* and nine other sculptors.

An early attempt at a steel-framed building clad in terra-cotta was the West Street Building (1905), designed in Gothic eclectic* style. It was the forerunner to his Woolworth Building (1909–13), the highest building on the New York skyline until its eclipse in the late 1920s (see Skyscraper). He designed public libraries for St. Louis (1912) and Detroit (1917) and in 1933 crowned his career with the rather forbidding classicism of the Supreme Court Building in Washington, D.C. He did very little residential work. He was president of the American Institute of Architects in 1908 and president of the National Institute of Arts and Letters.

(A.B.)

Gill, Irving J. (1870–1936).
Architect, born in Syracuse, N.Y., where his father was a building contractor. He attended schools in Syracuse, but did not go to college. At the age of twenty he went to Chicago, where he became a draftsman in the firm of Adler & Sullivan.* Early in 1893 he left for San Diego and there formed a partnership with W. S. Hebbard. Like others who had worked for Sullivan, Gill was strongly influenced by Sullivan's philosophy and visual forms. Some of Gill's early work, for example, his Pickwick Theatre (San Diego, 1904), is pure Sullivanesque; other buildings, such as his Normal School (San Diego,

1895), built in Renaissance revival* style, demonstrated that even a champion of new indigenous architecture had to design occasionally in a traditional mode to obtain commissions. During the late 1890s and early 1900s Gill struggled to find an approach to architecture that would be personal, would express Sullivan's philosophy of an "American architecture," and still be successfully sold to clients.

It was in the mid-1900s that Gill felt the impact of the popular California Mission revival, with its tile roofs, plain white stucco walls, and its use of simple arches. By 1907, in the Laughton House (Los Angeles) and the Klauber House (San Diego), he had developed his own personal interpretation of Mission revival. In the years that followed he continued to refine and abstract his designs so that in their outward forms they came closer and closer to the buildings of the Viennese Adolf Loos and the early International style* buildings of the 1920s. His Acton Hotel (La Jolla, 1908) is a rectangular white stucco box punctured by horizontal groupings of windows, while his Dodge House (Los Angeles, 1916) and his Horatio West Apartments (Santa Monica, 1919) are "cubist" compositions which rank with the European International style buildings of the period. Also concerned with structural innovation, Gill used the concrete tilt-wall construction in a number of his larger buildings. Housing for people of low income was another of his interests. His Lewis Courts (Sierra Madre, 1910) and his housing for the new industrial city of Torrance (1916, laid out by F. L. Olmsted*) indicate how successful he was in providing a small-scale yet highly livable environment at low cost. Though much more puritanical than other "progressive" American architects at the turn of the century, Gill's work lies essentially within the framework of the Arts and Crafts* tradition.

Gill found it difficult to maintain his practice during the 1920s and early 1930s. His only substantial project during these years was the Civic Center and School at Oceanside (1929), which in its massing and vertical stripped windows is marginally expressionistic.

(D.G.)

Girard, Alexander H. (1907–   ).
As an architect specializing in interiors and furnishings, he brought into the

midst of the stripped International style* a richly ornamented and sumptuously colored collage of patterns and objects that fed the starved romantic eye. Born in New York, N.Y., and raised in Florence, Italy, he studied at the Royal Institute of British Architects, London, and the Royal School of Architecture, Rome. After working in architects' offices in Florence, Rome, London, and Paris, he opened his own office in New York (1932), later moved to Detroit (1937), and finally settled in Santa Fe, New Mexico (1953). In four decades of practice, he explored many areas of design, including museum exhibitions, textiles, graphics, china, glass, leather, furniture, shelving, hardware, and films. He created houses, showrooms, offices, hotel interiors. He was color consultant on the General Motors Research Center in Detroit (1951) with Eero Saarinen* and worked with I. M. Pei* designing interiors for the Denver Hilton Hotel (1956). His three exhibition designs for the Museum of Modern Art include "The Textile and Ornamental Arts of India" (1955). From 1952 on he designed innovative collections of textiles and wallpapers for Herman Miller Inc., in New York, as well as that firm's dazzling retail shop, Textiles and Objects (1961). In 1960 he and his wife, Susan, established the Girard Foundation to house an expanding collection of folk art objects, whose influence found its way into his elegant work. Girard has displayed a lively sense of orchestrating textures, manipulating pattern on pattern, and juxtaposing vibrating colors, paving the way for the immediate acceptance of optical art* techniques in the design of furnishings. In La Fonda Del Sol, a New York restaurant (1960), and in a total environmental and graphic design program for Braniff International Airlines (1965), he brought true elegance to the thin theatricality of much commercial design. (C.R.S.)

Glackens, William (1870–1938). Illustrator, graphic artist, and painter. Born in Philadelphia, Pa., Glackens joined the art staff of the Philadelphia *Record* in 1901. He later moved to the *Press,* where John Sloan,* George Luks,* and Everett Shinn* worked at various times. Glackens' formal art training was limited to night classes at the Pennsylvania Academy of the Fine Arts, where he studied with Thom-

as Anshutz.* He had decided to become a painter, and he was exposed to the enthusiasm of Robert Henri*—recently returned from Paris—when the two shared a studio in 1894. In 1895 Glackens took a cattle boat to France and spent more than a year in painting and travel.

Returning to the United States, he settled in New York City, where he worked on the *Herald,* and then with George Luks on the *World.* He began to do magazine illustrations, displaying a sure touch, a lively sense of drama, and an uncommonly keen observation —qualities that mark the vivid drawings he did for *McClure's Magazine* in 1898 while covering the war in Cuba. After his return, he ceased working as an artist reporter, accepting only commissions for illustrations and concentrating increasingly on his painting.

He realized that it would not be easy to win acceptance, for he aimed at a directness of approach then regarded by academic critics as vulgar or clumsy, and he admired the simplified, flattened shapes of James Whistler* and Manet. Indeed, the influence of Manet seems uppermost in his work, as he turned out park and cafe scenes, landscapes and figure compositions, working for the direct beauty of paint on canvas, as in *The Drive, Central Park* (1904, Cleveland) and *The Shoppers* (1908, private collection). He began in 1901 to exhibit in national shows and in group exhibitions with Henri, Sloan, and other friends, and, as a climax, with The Eight* in 1908. His work immediately attracted attention.

By 1905 he had achieved a first peak of confidence and power in his *Chez Mouquin* (1905, Chicago), winning an honorable mention at the Tenth Carnegie International. However, he suffered his share of attacks from conservative critics and juries. In contrast to Henri and Sloan, Glackens was a mild and tolerant man, untouched by the politics of the art world. He served as chairman for the selection of American art for the Armory Show* (1913) and was first president of the Society of Independent Artists.* He accepted influences without self-consciousness, feeling that the life he transmitted through his canvases was his personal contribution. Henri was undoubtedly the influence that turned him toward the darker manner of Manet. Glackens visited Alfred Maurer* in France in

1906, and he must have been aware of his friend's development toward fauvism.* But his own transition following the exhibition of The Eight was to the breezy, colorful shimmer of impressionist landscape. His admiration for Renoir became apparent in his *Nude with Apple* (1910, Brooklyn), but he also drew on such a variety of masters—including Degas, Pissarro, Vuillard, and Matisse—that one must look for his continuity in the frank, sensous, lyrical spirit of his work rather than in stylistic influences. He himself was indifferent to the criticism that he was overly imitative. The catholicity of his taste was demonstrated when he went to France in 1912 to buy paintings for his old friend, the collector Albert C. Barnes, and returned with works by Cézanne, Renoir, Manet, Degas, Gauguin, van Gogh, and Matisse, the start of the Barnes Foundation Collection in Merion, Pa.

About 1914 Glackens freed himself from work as an illustrator and concentrated wholly on his painting. Figure studies, nudes, and summer landscapes followed in profusion. From 1925 until 1932 he traveled often to France, painting around Paris and in the south, as for example *Fête du Suquet* (1932, Whitney). One of the most ambitious compostions among his later paintings, typical of the 1930s in style and subject, is *The Soda Fountain* (1935, Pennsylvania). His later work included many small still lifes of fruit or flowers in glowing, joyous color.   (D.W.S.)

Glarner, Fritz (1899–1972).
Painter, born in Zurich, Switzerland, he studied at the Academy of Fine Arts, Naples, and then lived in Paris. He moved to the United States in 1936. He was a friend of the Dutch abstractionist Piet Mondrian, and was deeply influenced by him, particularly in the field of mural painting. Glarner was trained in the tradition of geometric abstraction, particularly that of Dutch geometric school known as De Stijl, and was a pioneer in introducing this tradition to the United States in the 1930s. Throughout his career he had consistently used the primary color palette of Mondrian: reds, yellows, and blues with accents of white, gray, or black. He was different from Mondrian in that he moved away from the rigid vertical-horizontal patterns, slightly tilting his color planes, and also in that he

3

1. **William Glackens.** Chez Mouquin, 1905. *Art Institute of Chicago (Friends of American Art Collection).*
2. **Alexander H. Girard.** La Fonda Del Sol *(restaurant), N.Y., 1960.*
3. **Fritz Glarner.** Relational Painting, 1949–51. *Whitney Museum of American Art, N.Y.*

worked on a large architectural scale, as in *Relational Painting* (1949–51, Whitney). Among his most notable architectural commissions is that of the Time and Life Building lobby, New York, 1960. Major one-man exhibitions of his work have been held in Paris (1952 and 1955) and in New York during the 1940s. He was a member of the American Abstract Artists* association since the 1930s.

Glarner is important not only as a link between European and American geometric abstraction, but also as a pioneer in the tradition that has led to American color-field* painting of the 1960s.   (H.H.A.)

Glass

The first glass factory, indeed the first industry established on the North American continent, started in Jamestown, Va., in 1607 with the arrival of eight Polish and German glassmakers sent by the London Company to exploit the vast natural resources of the new colony. At some distance from the stockaded village they built a thatched-roof structure and several furnaces in which to fire the clay pots necessary for melting glass and annealing it. Although primitive in appearance, this factory was not too different from the numerous forest glasshouses of Central Germany and Bohemia or the Wealdon region of England.

The aim of the London Company was to provide a new source of glass to satisfy the growing demands of England at a time when natural resources, principally wood used as fuel, were becoming scarce and expensive. Beset by a hostile environment and a increasingly inhospitable Indian population, the colony hardly survived the winter of 1609, and the glass factory failed to produce any product that can be identified today. No doubt, simple containers and window glass were intended to be the main staples.

By 1615 England had developed successful methods for using coal instead of wood, and this reduced the appeal of importing fragile glass from a colony over 3000 miles away. Hence over a decade passed before a second factory was established (in 1621) near Jamestown. Manned by Italian craftsmen, it was plagued by internal dissension and Indian incursions; it failed by 1623, also without leaving any identifiable products. Enthusiasm for glass-

making waned; England had become increasingly self-sufficient, and new colonists either brought with them or imported the wares they needed.

To the north, in New Amsterdam, three factories are recorded as having been established—in 1645, 1654, and 1674—but their output has not been identified. Other factories are recorded in Salem, Mass., in 1641 (this one may have lasted until 1661), in Philadelphia, and near Jamestown at Green Springs, Va., but their output and profitability are unknown. The early colonists had other priorities and, seemingly, competent glassmakers were not induced to immigrate. Glassmaking requires few tools and inexpensive raw materials, but considerable knowledge is needed since glass is the result of a complex transformation of matter from a crystalline to a vitreous state. This change, to be stable, requires a delicate balance among composition, temperature, and time, and those capable of producing it on a consistent basis were relatively few until the 20th century. This may be the principal reason for the long delay before glass became a well-established industry in the colonies.

Glass was therefore imported in fair quantities, especially from England where, after the Restoration (1660), a consortium of sellers and producers sought to develop styles and formulas differing from the prevailing Venetian models. By 1675–76 George Ravinscroft had developed his lead glass formula, which imparted a new brilliance and weight to the product. The age of science had come, and as English glass improved in quality, it became even more difficult to develop a local industry in the colonies. Excavations of late 17th- and 18th-century houses, especially along the James River, prove that English lead glass of high quality (so-called flintglass) was imported. Those who could not afford this elegant fabric used earthenware and wood, and, apparently, did very little to foster a glass supply they could afford. Finally, in 1739, a German businessman-manufacturer, Caspar Wistar,* who had immigrated in 1717 and achieved financial success, brought over from the Netherlands four German glassmakers to found a factory in southern New Jersey. It prospered until 1780, first under Caspar's direction and, after his death in 1752, under that of his son, Richard.

This factory did not aim to supplant the elegant English imported wares, but rather to produce staples such as bottles, kitchen containers, and window glass. Wistar's products followed very closely in appearance the vernacular glass common in England and on the continent, and the wine bottles attributed to his factory are indistinguishable from those made in England at that time. Extensive advertisements compared his products favorably with those made in England.

From Wistar's factory, and other factories established in the late 18th century by his workers, has come the South Jersey* tradition in American glass. This is characterized by: the use of a crude glass, often dark green or aquamarine in color due to iron traces in the sand; applied decoration in the form of threads and pads; the very occasional use of molds; and individualistic shapes, each varying in size, form, color, and decoration. In short, Wistar's production was in a folk tradition, as opposed to the industrial systematization that was the principal aim of the second successful 18th-century glassmaker in America, Henry William Stiegel.* Stiegel, who was also German, immigrated in 1750, and after successfully engaging in the manufacture of iron, he established a glass factory at Elizabeth Furnace in central Pennsylvania in 1763. This was followed by a second factory in Manheim, Pa., in 1765, and a third in 1769. To compete with the fine tablewares imported from Europe, Stiegel recruited English and German workmen, and in advertising urged his customers to "buy American."

Stiegel's glass was refined, and he gradually developed a brilliantly crystalline lead formula as well as rich tones of sapphire blue, deep green, or amethyst. His glass was often engraved with shallow designs derived from Germanic prototypes that were especially appealing to the Pennsylvania Dutch. On the whole, his production followed so faithfully English and continental prototypes that it is virtually impossible to differentiate them. For the first time pattern molds were used in America to produce quilted or diamond designs similar to the ones used in the Bristol area. "Stiegel-type" pieces can only be attributed on the basis of their predominance in the region surrounding his factories. Some reveal their American origin by the combination of an English feature, such as the diamond design of the sugar bowl, and the twisted finial, a central European decorative device. Like Wistar's factory, Stiegel's was beset with financial difficulties, due primarily to the absence of a protective tariff or any general awareness that to "buy American" was a patriotic duty. In addition, his pretentious style of living was a constant drain on his resources. By 1774 his factories had closed.

In New Jersey, members of the Stanger family, who had worked for Wistar before he closed in 1780, founded a glass house in a place that became known as Glassboro. This continued to produce vernacular glass, similar to Wistar's and in the South Jersey tradition. With this factory, southern New Jersey became and has remained a recognized glassmaking center.

Contrary to what one might expect, the Revolution and the attendant antipathy toward England did not increase interest in local industries. Glass continued to be imported in vast quantities, especially the elegant English or Irish glass that met the requirements of an increasingly wealthy bourgeoisie.

Another attempt to establish a new local competitive source of good glass was made in 1784. Again, a German was involved, Johann Frederich Amelung.* He arrived from Bremen with ample financial support, sixty-eight glass workers and their families, and a deed to 2100 acres of land south of Frederick, Md., in a place that became known as New Bremen. By 1785 Amelung, who came from a well-known German glassmaking family, had established a factory and a self-contained community for his workers. In spite of financial difficulties, a disastrous fire in 1790, and foreign competition, his factories produced a full range of tablewares, many of which were among the most elegant so far made in the New World. Elaborate presentation pieces were engraved with various heraldic designs emulating, though on a very modest scale, the sophistication of mid-18th century central European engraved glass. In addition, a full range of utilitarian vessels, window glass, and possibly mirrors were made before the factory failed in 1795.

In the last quarter of the 18th century there were several other glass-making efforts. In 1787 the Boston Crown Glass Manufactory was formed

and the Pitkin family started a bottle factory in East Hartford, Conn., in 1783. It proved profitable, but the main center of glassmaking was gradually shifting West. Manufacture followed population, and as it did so, it increased the distance from ports of entry. Western Pennsylvania and particularly the Pittsburgh area, where coal was abundant and water transportation available, attracted industry. Glassmakers were among the first to explore these areas.

Albert Gallatin founded his factory in New Geneva in 1797. It was staffed by some of the workers who had left Amelung's floundering enterprise and it produced wares very comparable in quality to Amelung's. In 1797 James O'Hare and Isaac Craig founded a glass factory in Pittsburgh. It was staffed by experienced workers of English and German origin, and produced principally window glass, tablewares, and, of course, bottles, which were increasingly in demand.

Until about 1810 most factories in the United States concentrated on staple production, and only a few attempted to make elegant glass that could compete with imports from England and especially Ireland. Of the thirty-six factories started in New England before 1840, only six made tablewares, and when Benjamin Bakewell founded his glasshouse in Pittsburgh in 1808, it became the only one making fine glass. Bakewell began a tradition in Pittsburgh in the fine cutting and engraving of a pure lead glass that was to assure a leading role to that city until well beyond the Civil War. In 1810 Charles Ihmsen and associates founded another window-glass factory that also produced elegant engraved wares, continuing the tradition established by Amelung. By the 1830s Pittsburgh's cut glass was virtually indistinguishable in quality from the best made abroad, and was developing, in the Anglo-Irish vocabulary, variations that gave it an unmistakably American character. This was the glass that foreign travelers noticed and that was presented to General Lafayette when he made his triumphant tour in 1824–25.

The midwestern glass industry was now developing on a broad front. Commercial wares, heavily molded and in a clear lead metal, or in deep blues or greens, were traded along the Mississippi; window panes of increasingly large size were made by substituting the

Glass
1. Sugarbowl from Germany, late 18th century, colorless glass.
2. Sugarbowl from Caspar Wistar's glass factory, South Jersey, late 18th century, green glass.
Both, Corning Museum of Glass, Corning, N.Y.

cylinder method for the crown method. Further to the west, the South Jersey tradition was continued in window and bottle factories. In Zanesville, Mantua, and Kent, Ohio, local raw materials, rich in iron, imparted to the glass deep green and brown tones that were emphasized by the use of pattern-molding in ribs, swirls, and quilted diamonds.

The use of pattern molds occurs virtually everywhere in the history of glass. It is the easiest and most inexpensive way to impart a design. The full-sized mold also provides evenness in shape and content and makes for more rapid production. Exploiting the properties of the mold is perhaps the most important contribution of the American glass industry in the 19th century. It helped to standardize quality (although lowering it esthetically) and enormously increased the rate of production while keeping relatively stable the number of hands required. It also had important social implications, giving substance to the ideal of "more for less for the many."

Two-piece, full-size molds were used by 1815 to make whiskey or medicinal flasks,* to which a patriotic or commercial pattern or slogan was imparted as the glass was blown. Numerous factories in New England, Pennsylvania, and the Midwest employed this technique to produce these inexpensive containers. It was refined, however, by such firms as the New England Glass Company (1818) and the Boston & Sandwich Glass Company (1825) to emulate the deep geometric designs of cut glass. A full range of designs eventually developed that brought to the market place the "poor man's" cut glass. Though the original impetus for this may have come from Irish prototypes of the very early 18th century, its development can be considered an original American contribution. By the 1830s designs were no longer geometrical and had acquired a curvilinear complexity that could not be produced by other means; from being merely imitative and cheaper to produce, blown three-mold glass had developed its own styles.

Pressing soon followed. A technique virtually as old as glass itself, it took a new dimension in American hands. Stimulated perhaps by the pincer-shaped presses used in England at the end of the 18th century, it seems to have been first used in the Pittsburgh

area shortly before 1825 to make door-knobs. By 1827 several patents had been taken out in Pittsburgh and Sandwich for various technical improvements, and by 1830 it was the prime source of tablewares and decorative pieces, which were produced in large quantities in factories from Boston to Baltimore and from Philadelphia to Pittsburgh. Virtually no limit could be set on the intricacy of the ornamentation—whatever an engraver could gouge in a mold could be transferred to the glass. Indeed, the greater its intricacy, the more it was sought after, and the better for the glassmaker, since defects in composition, striations, and so on could be completely concealed by the design. This "improvement" had large esthetic consequences: it removed both the decoration and the shaping of the product from the glassmaker, making him an adjunct, if a necessary one, to the moldmaker. The final product was the result of a metal rather than a glass technique: the industrial revolution had come, and its effect on esthetics can be seen nowhere better than in glass. Technically perfect, but more and more ornate, larger in size, more tortuous in taste, pressed glass evolved first (1850–60) into pressed pattern glass of rather indifferent metal, then into the mass-produced premium ware of the turn of the century.

The number of glass factories increased. As technological complexity became greater, competition reduced prices, and the smaller, provincial glass factories that were continuing the South Jersey tradition in upstate New York, New England, Pennsylvania, and New Jersey had to change their modes or vanish. In their heyday, though, these produced some of the most engaging, sculpturally valid pieces made in America in the 19th century. However, specific attributions are often difficult since glassmakers continued to follow the custom of their forebears of moving from one locality to another. Hence it became very difficult to differentiate, for example, between a glass produced in Lancaster, N.Y., and one from Redford, N.Y., even though these places are over 200 miles apart.

Cutting and engraving, in spite of the strides of other techniques, continued to be practiced at the New England Glass Company (1818), the Boston & Sandwich Glass Company (1825), at

Glass

1. Sugarbowl from Henry Stiegel's glass factory, Manheim, Pa., c.1770, pattern-molded glass.
2. Covered tumbler from Johann Amelung's glass factory, New Bremen, Md., 1788, free-blown of smoke-gray glass and copper-wheel engraved to Carolina Lynne Amelung, illustrated with the apocryphal story of Tobias and the angel.
3. Group of drinking vessels made in both New England and Midwestern glass factories, mid-19th century, pressed in colorless glass in the "Horn of Plenty" pattern (marketed as the "Comet" pattern).
4. Serving dishes from the Boston & Sandwich Glass Company, mid-19th century, pressed colored glass in the "lacy" style.
5 & 6. Pair of decanters made at the Corning Glass Works, c. 1890, free-blown and engraved with the initial "R", horses, and flora.
7. Ewer from one of Christian Dorflinger's glass factories, Brooklyn, N.Y., mid-19th century, free-blown and cut glass.
All, Corning Museum of Glass, Corning, N.Y.

1

2

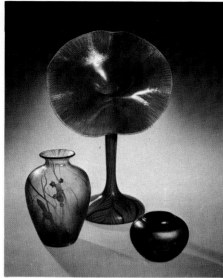

3

Glass
1. Art nouveau glass. Tiffany vase from the Steuben Glass Company, Corning, N.Y., c.1910.
2. Art Glass. Left to right: Burmese glass candlestick from Mt. Washington Glass Works, New Bedford, Mass.; "Peach Blow" glass bowl from Mt. Washington Glass Works; Swirled Amberina and "Wild Rose" glass vases (respectively) from New England Glass Company; "Coral" or "Peach Blow" glass cruet from Hobbs, Brockunier & Company, Wheeling, West Va.
   All, c. 1890, Corning Museum of Glass, Corning, N.Y.
3. Dominick Labino. Three forms, 1968, free-hand blown iridescent prunted glass.
4. Andre Billeci, Group No. 3, 1972, unknown glass. Collection of the artist.

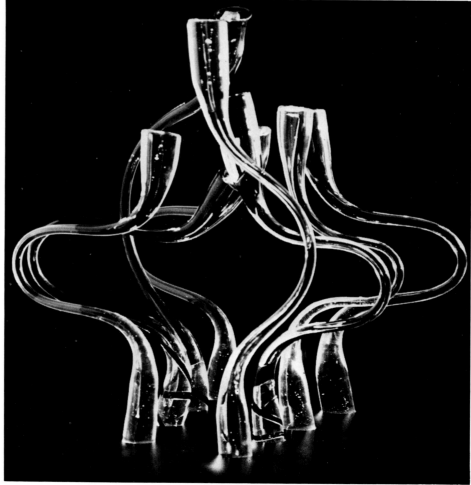

4

John L. Gilliland's Brooklyn Flint Glass Works (1823), at Bakewell, Page & Bakewell in Pittsburgh, and numerous other factories, particularly along the Ohio River. The impetus had come from Europe, but cutting styles now tended to develop indigenously. After the Civil War, the sparkling composition of the lead glass was exploited by the countless new designs which characterize the "brilliant" period of American cut glass. The level of technical perfection attained, for example, by Christian Dorflinger's factories in Brooklyn, N.Y., and White Mills, Pa., has never been surpassed, and American cut glass was successfully entered in the various world fairs that succeeded the Crystal Palace Exposition of 1851. Commercially, however, it is American pressing that was the more influential. Within less than six years after the technique had been perfected in America, it was copied abroad—leading to the creation of a host of forms and designs, the majority of which are immediately identifiable as French, Belgian, or English. America became renowned for her new glass technology, but this technology had similar consequences abroad: a lowering of taste and less dependence on individual craftsmanship.

In the United States the reaction against mechanization led to the search for new formulas and the combination of different techniques, most of them requiring the intervention of a skilled craftsman. Amberina, Pomona, Peach Blow, Burmese, Crown Milano are the trade names for these glasses. They were produced by many different companies: the New England Glass Company; the Mt. Washington Glass Company of New Bedford, Mass.; and Hobbs Brokunier of Wheeling, W.V., are but the principal ones. All shared the same concern: to restore uniqueness in texture, color, and shape, and do so by commercially feasible means. During the period of intense change that followed the Civil War, influences continued to be received from abroad, especially England, and the earlier generation of immigrating English glassmakers such as Thomas Leighton and his sons were followed by Joseph Locke, Frederick Shirley, and others; they brought with them a knowledge of experiments being carried out in England and of course developed them. Art glass* was produced in huge

quantity and varying quality. It reflected the desire of the late Victorian era for rich ornamentation and exotic texture. It used industrial means—that is, it was not marked by a dominating artistic philosophy or personality. That was to be the contribution of art nouveau* and, especially in the United States, of Louis C. Tiffany, who first introduced his experiment with lustrous iridescent, metallicized glasses in 1893 (see also Tiffany & Company). By 1896 Tiffany was exhibiting widely and donating pieces he considered outstanding to museums in the United States and abroad. Glass now became one of "the fine arts." The inspiration of tropical flora, Japanese art, and the mysterious beauty of partly decomposed glass recovered from classical archeological sites, combined with a concern for the organic growth of forms, are all superbly reflected in Tiffany's glass. It was to exert a profound influence abroad and in the United States. Tiffany, like his French counterpart Émile Gallé (1846–1904), became a leading exponent of the art nouveau style. He had many followers. Some had independently developed glasses similar to his, such as Frederick Carder,* who immigrated from England to found Steuben Glass in 1904, while others pirated, or at least were strongly influenced by, his techniques and forms. With Tiffany, American glass received international recognition as an artistic medium; he had no immediate successor, and only one outstanding contemporary: Carder.

By the 1920s, mediocre epigones had taken over. Second-rate commercialization of earlier ideas was being perpetuated in a wide variety of factories, many located in West Virginia. Commercial pressed glass was made in vast quantities, satisfying social, if not esthetic needs. While cut glass continued to be produced, often of high quality, it also was being debased by the increasingly frequent use of pressed forms, which were then more easily cut. There were exceptions, however, and the firms of Libbey, in Toledo, Ohio, and Steuben, in Corning, N.Y., continued to search for forms and techniques expressive of a contemporary esthetic. In 1933 Steuben was reorganized and a new formula was inaugurated. Glass design was now considered an artistic discipline and, calling upon architects and painters to contribute designs that could be translated into this medium

of unsurpassed brilliance, Steuben by the 1950s had become outstanding for the quality of its product and had attained a degree of international recognition unequalled since Tiffany.

In the mid-20th century glass took many different and some new directions. Mass-produced tableware by Libbey, Fostoria, and others was often freeing itself of "chichi" ornamentation and attaining the clean, streamlined shapes associated with the best contemporary "industrial" design. Similarly, the growth of the craft movement in ceramics, textiles, silver, and other materials had stimulated a number of artists to turn to glass as a vehicle for individual expression. Harvey Littleton,* at the University of Wisconsin, was a leader in this trend and the first to develop a glass program within a university. Today, over forty institutions have glassmaking facilities for undergraduate or graduate programs. Glass is being explored by numerous talented practitioners, among whom Dominick Labino,* André Billecci, Marvin Lipofsky, and Dale Chihuly are the best known. They are linked together by a passionate admiration for the ductility, optical brilliance, and depth of color which are inherent in glass and present such a great challenge to sculptors. For unlike other materials, glass reflects, absorbs, magnifies, and distorts light. Indeed, it is light become mass, and it is in the United States, after a history as old as the country itself, that its full artistic potential is coming closest to being realized. It is also in the United States that its economic and scientific roles have received the most important encouragement with the development of mass-production methods in the early 19th century and the systematic investigation of its properties in the early 20th century.　(P.N.P.)

Glass Cutting and Engraving.
A method of decoration in which the surface of the glass is cut away, either by a graving tool such as a diamond point, or by a revolving wheel. Most American engraved glass was cut by means of copper wheels, which force an abrasive against the glass; glass cutting was usually done with stone wheels.

Although very little engraved work was done in America in the 18th century, Stiegel's* glasshouse advertised

1

engraved wares, and Amelung's* short-lived New Bremen Glassmanufactory made very high quality engraved pieces. In the major eastern cities, immigrant English or German engravers probably cut designs on glass to order; but no examples of such work have ever been positively identified. The first known American glass cutter in the 19th century was William Peter Eichbaum, a German who was engaged by Benjamin Bakewell in 1810 and who is said to have cut the first chandelier made in the United States. Bakewell & Company of Pittsburgh, founded in 1808, was so well-known that most visitors to the western country went to see the factory. The style of cutting was closely related to the glass being imported from England and Ireland, and it is consequently often difficult to distinguish between American and imported wares of this period.

In the next few years several other firms began cutting, among them the New England Glass Company (founded 1818) and the Boston & Sandwich Glass Company (founded 1825) in Massachusetts, the Brooklyn Flint Glass Works (founded 1823), the Union Flint Glass Company (founded 1826) in Philadelphia, the Jersey Glass Company (founded 1824) in Jersey City and several firms in Wheeling and Pittsburgh. None used any sort of trademark, and in most cases family tradition is the only means of attributing pieces.

The Anglo-Irish geometric style of cutting was fairly standard from about 1820 to about 1850. Plain flute cutting or facet cutting became popular from about 1845–70. Also popular from about 1850 until the early 20th century was cased glass, i.e. colorless glass with one or more layers of colored glass over it. The casing was then partially cut away in a design which revealed the glass beneath. This was referred to as "Americo-Bohemian" glass and was much utilized in making lamp fonts and shades.

What is now called the "brilliant" style of cutting was developed during the 1880s. Heavy lead glass blanks were cut in allover patterns that took maximum advantage of the refractive properties of the lead glass. In this period, several large firms such as Corning Glass Works (from 1868), C. Dorflinger & Sons (from 1875), the Mt. Washington Glass Company (from about 1880) and the Union Glass Com-

pany (from about 1870), supplied high-quality blanks on which they and a number of small cutting firms turned out ever more elaborate patterns. These tended to migrate, with the workers, from one company to another. Dorfinger in White Mills, Pa., Hawkes & Hoare in Corning, N.Y., Pairpoint in New Bedford, Mass., and other companies brought this type of cutting to a peak of excellence; however, it was abruptly curtailed by World War I and the difficulty of obtaining raw materials for high-quality blanks. A final factor in the loss of popularity of this type of glass was the introduction of pressed blanks and of pressed patterns copied from cut glass.

Engraving, usually done on a lighter weight glass, flourished also in the Pittsburgh area early in the 19th century and later in New England. Simple engraved floral designs were characteristics of the early period, but mid-19th century pieces were apt to have elaborate pictorial engraving. In the last decades of the century engraved pieces with classical motifs were produced, along with wares that were light in comparison with the heavy cutting then popular. The turn of the century brought "rock crystal engraving," which emphasized flowing curves rather than geometric facets. This style remained popular until the 1920s brought the severe lines and angles of art deco.*

Cutting and engraving have never been American traditions and in general the cutters and engravers were immigrants. Louis Vaupel of the New England Glass Company arrived from Germany, John Hoare from England, and Thomas G. Hawkes from Ireland, and all were master craftsmen before they arrived in America. Cutters and engravers alike tended to migrate from factory to factory in search of better wages and working conditions, a situation that makes it difficult to attribute a specific piece to a specific factory.

At present, Steuben Glass, in Corning, N.Y., is producing copper-wheel engraving of high quality on free-blown or cast blanks with a very high lead content. They are the only American producers of such fine engraved wares, and several of their engravers have been trained in Europe.   (J.S.S.)

Godefroy, Maximilian (1765–c.1842). Architect, painter, and military engineer. Born in Paris, he was impris-

1. *Glass Cutting and Engraving.* Tumbler from Union Glass Work in Philadelphia, c.1830–40, free-blown. Corning Museum of Glass, Corning, N.Y.
2. *Maximilian Godefroy. First Unitarian Church, Baltimore, 1818.*
3. *Bruce Goff. Glenn Harder House, Mountain Lake, Minn., 1972.*

oned in 1793 under suspicion of Royalist tendencies, but he joined the cavalry and late in 1795 was discharged. He was again imprisoned in 1803, escaped, was recaptured, and then allowed to sail for America.

Godefroy never revealed whether he was trained as artist or architect; he was probably self-trained, though he had worked in the office of a military engineer. Arriving in America in 1805 he found a position teaching painting and architecture at St. Mary's College, a French school for boys in Baltimore. In 1806 Godefroy designed a Gothic chapel for the school that still stands, though altered to its detriment. It was probably the earliest Gothic revival* church in America after Trinity Church, New York.

When the British were expected to advance on Baltimore in 1814, Godefroy planned the defenses of the city; he also designed the Battle Monument erected after the war. The Baltimore Exchange (1815–20) was supposedly a collaborative effort by Godefroy and B. H. Latrobe,* but Latrobe made the designs and Godefroy, somehow offended, withdrew from the project. In the Unitarian Church, Baltimore (1817–18), which is still standing, Godefroy designed a building of considerable beauty, using a simple Tuscan order and plain wall surfaces. After some landscaping work and a few house designs in Richmond, Va., Godefroy left for England in 1819, poverty-stricken and angry with what he claimed was shabby treatment by Baltimoreans. Though he exhibited paintings and architectural views in London and had several jobs, he could not establish himself there. He moved to France in 1827 and finally obtained a position as architect for the Department of Mayenne at Laval, where he seems to have remained until his death. (P.F.N.)

Goff, Bruce (1904–   ).

Architect whose work since the early 1930s has represented the art-for-art's-sake attitude that prevailed at the turn of the century. From a traditional point of view, Goff's designs are outrageous, the purely emotional elements seeming to overwhelm all practical or rational considerations. Goff was born near Tulsa, Okla. Without formal architectural training, he was apprenticed at age twelve to the Oklahoma City firm of Rush, Endicott & Rush and advanced to

2

3

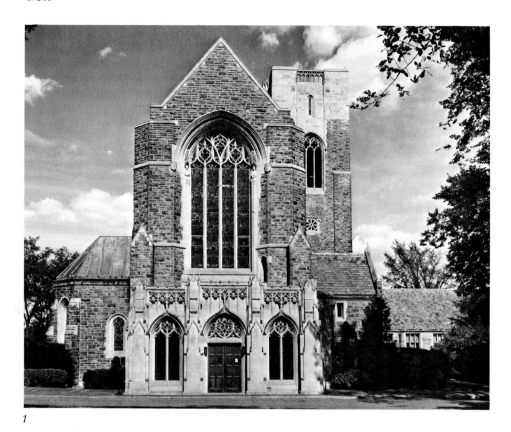

1

2

1. **Bertram G. Goodhue.** Christ Church, Cranbrook Academy, Bloomfield Hills, Mich., 1928.

2. **Sarah Goodridge.** Portrait of Gilbert Stuart. Metropolitan Museum of Art, N.Y. (Moses Lazarus Collection).

a partnership in 1928. During the Depression he moved to Chicago (1934), where he taught design and drawing. He also worked briefly as head of the design department of Libby-Owens-Ford Glass Company, where he became infatuated with glass. In 1947 he joined the faculty at the University of Oklahoma and from 1948 to 1957 was chairman of the School of Architecture. Since 1957 he has maintained his own practice, first at Bartlesville, Okla., then at Kansas City, Mo., and finally at Tyler, Tex.

Goff's earliest projects, in the early 1920s, were sensitive variations on Frank Lloyd Wright's* "prairie" houses. These designs were followed by expressionistic schemes reminiscent of the sketches for streamlined buildings by Erich Mendelsohn in Europe and of Wright's angular and jagged forms of the 1920s. Goff's first major statement was the Boston Avenue Methodist Church (Tulsa, 1929). The Church reflects both expressionism and streamlined moderne* in its encrusted and angular details and in its interior space, which bears a resemblance to a dated Hollywood science fiction stage set.

Much of his work of the late 1930s and early 1940s, such as his triangular-plan Usonian House in Park Ridge, Ill. (1940), was very much like Wright's. Other designs, such as his spread-winged Trisero House in Ferncreek, Ky. (1940), again suggest the science fiction world of Buck Rogers. This imagery of the world of the future continued after World War II in such works as the Ledbetter summer lodge in Texoma, Okla. (1947), where a glass box with an enclosed cylinder was suspended above the ground by a central pole with diagonal radiating wires. No two of his designs are alike. His Ford House in Aurora, Ill. (1950) is a squat, lumpy dome, while his Baringer House, near Tulsa, Okla. (1955–56), is formed of a spiral stone shaft from which is suspended a spiral roof with living and sleeping "pads" hung in the interior space. The Durst House in Houston (1958), with its row of large round windows thrust into the low horizontal roof, suggests a futurist rocket ship; while the Pollock House in Oklahoma City (1958) creates a fantastic world of perspective in its receding pattern of square-faced volumes, each with its own roof. Futurism,* expressionism,* and occasionally very distinctive design elements derived from Wright, have continued to characterize Goff's visual imagery. (D.G.)

Goodhue, Bertram G. (1869–1924). Architect, born in Pomfret, Conn. He did not attend an architectural school but at age fifteen entered the office of the famous 19th-century Gothic revivalist, James Renwick.* In 1891 he joined the office of Ralph Adams Cram, and soon became his partner. The firm of Cram, Goodhue & Ferguson became known as the most important and fashionable exponent of the Gothic revival* in the United States. It produced innumerable works in the Gothic mode, ranging from buildings at Princeton University and West Point to churches such as St. Thomas in New York (1905). Goodhue was not only an adroit designer, he also acquired a reputation as one of the most skillful delineators of architecture in American history. His *A Book of Architectural and Decorative Drawings* (1914) beautifully demonstrates his design and drafting skills.

In 1914 he separated from Cram and formed his own firm. This shift also marked a change in his point of view as a designer. Although he had produced buildings in the Spanish colonial revival style as early as 1905 (the Episcopal Cathedral, Havana, Cuba), it was in 1914–15 that he turned his full attention to the emerging fashion for things Spanish and Mexican. His buildings for the San Diego Fair of 1915 (designed with Carleton Winslow) were a major force in moving California architectural taste from the mission revival mode to the Spanish colonial, he himself doing a number of large country houses in Southern California in the latter style.

The second shift in Goodhue's architectural direction was due in part to his encounter with the San Diego pioneer modernist Irving J. Gill. The housing he designed in 1916–17 for the new mining town of Tyrone, N.M., has the same stripped quality as Gill's work. But the acceptance, and finally the advocacy, of a monumental modernism became fully evident in his winning design for the Nebraska State Capitol at Lincoln (1916–28), in his Central Library Building at Los Angeles (designed with Carleton Winslow, 1924), and in his entry in the widely publicized competition for the Chicago *Tribune* Tower (1922).

Goodhue's solution to the question of what style should prevail in the 20th century was an instance of having one's cake and eating it too. His late buildings have the solid authority of classical architectural traditions, while their uncluttered, clearly stated volumes and surfaces reflect the atmosphere of the machine. Goodhue's influence lingered on after his death. The "neo-Babylonian" quality of so much Federal architecture during the 1930s and even much of the more recent work of Edward Durell Stone* and of Skidmore, Owings & Merrill* could never have developed without the precedent of Goodhue's work of the late 1910s and early 1920s. (D.G.)

Goodnough, Robert (1917–   ). Painter. Born in Cortland, N.Y., he studied at Syracuse and New York universities. His earliest training consisted of drawing from casts, working from models, and painting portraits, but he soon became interested in Picasso's early cubist work. Goodnough's impulse toward structure was reinforced by the purist disciplines of the French art theorist and painter Amédée Ozenfant and a later interest in the Dutch abstractionist Piet Mondrian. However, his work was saved from ultimate rigidity by his energized forms—rectangular shapes given direction and "thrust" by their individual irregularities and calculated groupings. Although he studied with Hans Hofmann,* his work represents a reaction against the formlessness of much second-generation abstract expressionism.* He always starts with an object—in his earlier work, a figure, as in *Seated Figure with Gray* (1956–57, Whitney)—flattening and abstracting it, and fusing it with its background, producing tensions between abstraction and "reality" and between surface and depth. A series of "Boat Abstractions" of 1965–66 contained explicit references to figures. In his most recent work, a series of large mural-sized canvases, he has turned completely to abstraction, scattering rhythmic groupings of colored rectangles across wide areas of gray-white primed canvas. (E.C.G.)

Goodridge, Sarah (1788–1853). Miniature painter. A self-taught artist, daughter of a farmer in Templeton, Mass., she worked in Boston as early as 1812 and opened a studio there in 1820. Gilbert Stuart* took a liking to her, and she often brought him her work for criticism. A high moment in this friendship came when he said, "Goody, I intend to let you paint me." Not only that but, so it was said, he posed for her while he himself worked on a miniature intended to clarify for her his own feeling for miniature painting. There is, indeed, in her *Gilbert Stuart* (Metropolitan) a look of sharp concentration unlike Stuart's usually relaxed and humorous visage. It is an excellent example of her thorough, competent workmanship. Most of her career was spent in Boston, but she also painted in Washington, D.C., during 1828–29 and 1841–42. (C.C.S.)

Gorham Company. It was founded by silversmith Jabez Gorham of Providence, R.I., who began working about 1815. He formed various partnerships and gradually built a large firm utilizing factory methods. He retired in 1847, but the firm continued and was chartered by Rhode Island in 1863 and incorporated in 1865. In 1868 they adopted the sterling standard. During the period of eclecticism from 1870–1900, many of their designers, such as Thomas Pairpoint, were trained abroad, and some of their wares followed European fashions closely. About 1875 the firm produced "The Ice Berg" ice bowl (Bowdoin College, Me.) in rough-textured silver with cast polar bears and icicles; it was an inventive and artistic design. Gorham sent impressive exhibits to the Paris Exposition Universelle in 1889 and to the World's Columbian Exhibition in Chicago in 1893, the latter including a silver figure of Columbus after French sculptor Frédéric Bartholdi's statue. In addition to ecclesiastical silver, Gorham became noted for its naval presentation services, one of the earliest of which was made in 1891 for the U.S.S. *Maine.* (M.G.F.)

Gorky, Arshile (1904–48). Painter. Born Vosdanig Manoog Adoian in a small village in Armenia. He came to the United States in 1920. Among other institutions, he studied at the Polytechnic Institute in Tiflis, Russia (1916–18), and after 1920, the Rhode Island School of Design and the New School of Design in Boston. He taught at the Grand Central School, New York (1925–31) and painted in the WPA Federal Art Project* (1936–38). His mural commissions under the art pro-

1

2

1. **Arshile Gorky.** The Liver is the
   Cock's Comb, 1944. Albright-Knox
   Art Gallery, Buffalo, N.Y.
2. **Arshile Gorky.** Garden in Sochi,
   1941. Museum of Modern Art, N.Y.
   (gift of Mr. and Mrs. Wolfgang S.
   Schwabacher).
3. **Gothic Eclectic.** Cass Gilbert.
   Woolworth Building, N.Y., 1913.

ject included that of the Aviation Building at the New York World's Fair (1939). He exhibited in the international exhibition of surrealism* in 1942. Major exhibitions of his work were held in New York City and elsewhere between 1945 and 1962 culminating in a retrospective at the Museum of Modern Art. In 1946 fire destroyed twenty-seven of his paintings in his studio in Sherman, Conn., and the next year he had a serious auto accident. In 1948 he committed suicide.

Gorky was the principal translater of European modernism into a new American painting during the 1940s. He learned his vocabulary from the works in museums and from illustrations in art books and periodicals. More than any other American artist of his day he recognized the revolution that had taken place in the School of Paris from impressionism through the early 20th century, and he set himself the task of retracing this revolution generation by generation in his own works. Beginning in 1925 he studied impressionism* and then Cézanne (whom he considered the "greatest artist that has lived") and during the 1930s analytic and synthetic cubism.* At the same time he assimilated the lessons of the organic surrealists such as Miró and Masson; and he met many of these artists when they too migrated to New York during World War II.

To him Picasso was the greatest of contemporaries, and in painting after painting he followed Picasso's path with shameless enthusiam. Thus, his *Organization* (1932) is a literal transcription of Picasso's *The Studio* (1927–28, Modern Museum). But in such works of the 1930s, there is never a simple imitation. When Gorky was looking most intensely at Picasso, he was also studying other modern European masters, such as Mondrian, Léger, and Miró, and, among Americans, Willem de Kooning* and Stuart Davis.* In the series "Image in Xhorkam" he turned to a form of biomorphic abstraction similar to that of Miró, but with a heavy, rich paint surface such as Picasso was using in the early 1930s. This led, around 1941–42, to a much freer form of automatic painting, which was comparable to Kandinsky's early abstract expressionism* but demonstrating a more immediate influence from the surrealism of the Chilean artist Roberto Matta Echaurren, who had come to the United States in 1939.

It was primarily as a result of surrealism that Gorky made his individual contribution as a painter and that his unique style emerged during the 1940s. It began with the versions of *Garden in Sochi* (for example, 1941, Modern Museum) executed between 1940 and 1943 and continued in climactic works such as *The Liver Is the Cock's Comb* (1944, Albright). Although the late works may be rooted in the paintings of Miró, they are different in effect and unique. Gorky's late paintings are a mass of delicately drawn, visceral shapes floating in a tangible world of brilliant, transparent color. The shapes are suggestive of internal organs, brutally mutilated, or microscopic views of plants and flowers transformed into strange menacing beasts or embracing in an ecstasy of sexual fulfillment. They are at the same time living organisms, still lifes, or landscapes, all filled with an ecstatic and disturbing sense of physical vitality and psychological conflict.

Gorky was both a founder of American abstract expressionism and the painter above all others whose work made the transition from European to American modernism. (H.H.A.)

Gothic Eclectic Style.

An architectural style that offered a ready design solution for the skyscraper.* Tall buildings required light masonry veneers that could be carried on continuous steel brackets fastened at each floor to the structural frame. Early attempts to carry tiers of columns, one above the other, had proven unsuccessful. Working with the terra-cotta companies, the architects developed a lightweight exterior veneer for high buildings to which the soaring verticality of Gothic architecture was admirably adapted. The rich Gothic ornament was readily reproduced, in fine detail, in this versatile, self-washing material and any unit could be reproduced endlessly. The styles most favored derived generally from late English Gothic sources.

Commercial Gothic eclectic, which served for the skyscraper, served also as a veneer for the one-story office building, the motion picture theater, or the large department store. Cass Gilbert* set the highwater mark in this mode in the Woolworth Building in New York City, expressively adapting Gothic form to the needs of the high building.

Collegiate Gothic eclectic was a tra-

3

Gothic Revival

dition handed down from the English. The buildings were generally of stone, as at Yale University and the University of Chicago. Terra-cotta was also employed on many campuses, and an early instance of its use is in the buildings George B. Post (1837–1913) designed for the College of the City of New York. Despite the crisp profiles of these academic buildings, an attempt was made at Yale to give them an aura of antiquity quite aside from their ivy-clad character. James Gamble Rogers (1867–1947), who designed much of the campus at Yale, prided himself on the authenticity of his Gothic architecture; this quest for architecturally correct designs was typical of eclecticism* and the eclectic period.

Ecclesiastical Gothic eclectic, whether for an urban church or a country parish church, generally followed English prototypes. Fieldstone walls were trimmed with cut stone, which was necessary to produce the ribs and tracery of Gothic windows. Terra-cotta was also much in evidence, and when used as the only material was usually reserved for the urban church. Ralph Adams Cram (1863–1942), the great Gothicist, designed St. Thomas Church on Fifth Avenue in New York City as an all-stone church, displaying some of the finest carved detail in the country.   (A.B.)

Gothic Revival Style.

An architectural style popular from 1830 to 1875. It was brought to America by Benjamin Latrobe* (who also introduced the Greek revival*), and became popular partly because of Sir Walter Scott's novels. With its medieval allusions, Gothic was felt to be more suitable for church architecture than the "pagan" Greek. The books of A. J. Downing* showed how small houses could be fashionably transformed into Gothic cottages with the addition of fretwork ornamentation and pointed arches over the windows and doors. The style was also characterized by a steep roof and decorative asymmetry. (See also Architecture Since 1540.)

Goto, Joseph (1920–   ).

Japanese-American sculptor, born in Hawaii, who began his training, as did many other contemporary American sculptors, as an industrial welder. After World War II, he moved to the United States to study at the Art Institute of Chicago, working both in painting and

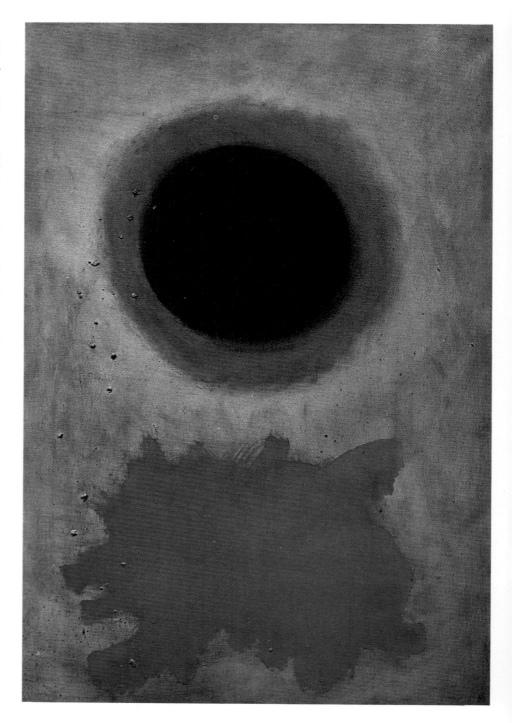

Adolph Gottlieb. Chrome, 1965. Collection Paul and Marianne Steiner, N.Y.

sculpture. While teaching at the University of Michigan, he developed a method of sawing thick chunks of steel, burnishing and welding them, and juxtaposing them with linear flourishes that gained him a national reputation. Moving away from the spidery, draftsmanlike quality that had characterized much steel sculpture of the 1950s, Goto used his materials for massive effects. In the mid-1960s, he interrupted his teaching at the Rhode Island School of Design in order to work in a steel fabricating plant near Providence. There he was able to use heavy gauge steel freely, building compositions to the height of twelve feet, and spreading in powerful thrusts into the surrounding space. One of these sculptures, *Tower Iron Sculpture #5,* is installed (on loan from the Carnegie Institute) in front of a Pittsburgh television station. Goto has exhibited widely, in New York City and other large American cities, and has several times participated in the Carnegie International Exhibition.　(D.A.)

Gottlieb, Adolph (1903–　　).
Painter. Born in New York, N.Y., Gottlieb studied at the Art Students League* with John Sloan* and Robert Henri,* at the Académie de la Grande Chaumière in Paris (1921), as well as in Berlin and Munich, and, back in New York in 1923, at the Parsons School of Design. He has received many awards, including first prize at the São Paulo Biennial (1936), and among his many exhibitions have been retrospectives at the Jewish Museum, (New York City, 1957) and the Walker Art Center (Minneapolis, 1963). In 1925 he joined with a group of avant-garde artists, known as "The Ten,"* that included Ilya Bolotowsky* and Mark Rothko.* His first New York one-man show was in 1930. In 1936 he worked as an easel painter on the WPA Federal Art Project.* During 1937 he lived in Tucson, Ariz., where he had the first inspiration for pictographic subject matter. In 1939 he returned to New York. During the 1940s Gottlieb was active in many artists' groups and participated in important forums by artists along with other pioneers of American abstract expressionism.* His important architectural commissions have included ark curtains for Congregation B'nai Israel in Millburn, N. J. (1951) and for Congregation Beth El in Springfield, Mass. (1953), and a stained-glass façade of 1300 square feet for the Milton Stein-

berg Memorial Center in New York (1952–55). He has taught at Pratt Institute and the University of California at Los Angeles (1958).

Emerging from American scene and social realism painting of the 1930s, Gottlieb experimented with a form of magic realism in the late 1930s and early '40s. A favorite magic realist subject, perhaps deriving from his western desert associations, was a strange and barren landscape fronted by boxes enclosing three-dimensionally painted forms of marine animal or plant life. These compartmentalized paintings may have inspired the basic shapes of his so-called pictographs of the 1940s with the important distinction that the pictographs were essentially vertical-horizontal arrangements of linear shapes and images on the surface of the canvas. They owed something to Piet Mondrian but more to Paul Klee and the Uruguayan constructivist painter Joaquin Torres-Garcia (1874–1949). In making his pictographs, Gottlieb of course was aware of European surrealism* and he was included as a surrealist in Sidney Janis' pioneer *Abstract and Surrealist Art in America* (1944). His pictographs have no conscious narrative scheme but include suggestions of fragments of human heads, snakelike animal forms, and other imagery from primitive art, as in *Dream* (1948, Delgado). His general direction in the late 1940s was toward a breaking down of the rectangular frame with freer brushwork.

By 1950 the compartmentalized pictographs had been compressed into single masses with a specific totemistic effect. There is a wide variety in Gottlieb's formulae in every phase of his career, and his handling of paint ranges from the heavily textured to the thinly transparent. Yet there is a remarkable consistency. Even when the greatest changes occur, as in the transformation of the 1940s pictographs into the imaginary landscapes of the 1950s, it is a steady process without abrupt departures.

The imaginary landscapes of the 1950s usually have a foreground suggestive of landscape and an open "sky" in which ovoid or rounded rectangular shapes like suns, moons, or planets hover in a void. The "foreground" may still echo the earlier pictographs, and the paintings maintain a vertical-horizontal frontality, as in *The Frozen*

Sounds, Number 1 (1951, Whitney). Although he is consistently grouped with the abstract expressionists, Gottlieb's space is that of nature and the universe, not simply that of two-dimensional canvas.

By 1957 the horizontally-arranged landscapes were transformed into more vertical arrangements entitled "Bursts." In a broad, unified ground there is a bursting shape like some cosmic explosion, above which floats a circular or ovoid sun, as in *Thrust* (1959, Metropolitan). This basic formula has taken many shapes during the 1960s, becoming at times precise and almost geometric, at other times loose and amorphous. In all of them the feeling for a symbolic content is explicit, with the artist seeming to explore over and over again the problems of man isolated in a vast, empty, and ever-changing universe. Although Gottlieb belongs with the abstract expressionism that grew out of surrealism, he may perhaps best be associated with the wing called abstract imagism. His paintings are in effect images whose abstract forms encompass definite naturalistic associations.

　(H.H.A.)

Gould, Thomas Ridgeway (1818–81).
Sculptor. A drygoods merchant in Boston, Mass., his hobby of modeling led him to a career as a sculptor. Among his earliest works is a bust of Ralph Waldo Emerson (1861, Concord Public Library). Gould went to Florence, Italy, in 1868 and, except for brief visits to America, lived there the rest of his life. Probably his best known work is *West Wind* (c.1874), a neoclassical personification that bears a marked similarity to *Hebe,* a work by the Italian sculptor Canova. Despite controversy over its originality and conception, seven replicas were commissioned. Although hampered by a lack of sculptural training and skill, Gould produced a number of ideal works in the romantic neoclassical style that dominated the art of sculptors in Italy from the 1850s to the 1870s, and he also continued to make portrait busts and statues.

Graham, John (1881–1961).
Painter. Born in Russia, he emigrated to America. Although he has left only a small body of work, Graham—like Hans Hoffmann *and Joseph Albers *and Piet Mondrian—was important as an influence on such artists as Jackson Pollock;*

it was Graham who in fact arranged Pollock's first exhibition (1941). A brilliant and eccentric figure on the New York avant-garde scene, he was a collector and a bibliophile, and had an ardent interest in the occult. His early paintings, influenced by Picasso, were cubistic in style, and he transmitted his grasp of the principles of cubism* and of surrealism* to the yonger generation of painters. In about 1940 Graham's work changed and he began to paint mysterious, symbolical figures. He is the author of *System and Dialectics of Art* (1937), a prophetic treatise on esthetics.

Graves, Morris (1910–)

Painter. Born in Fox Valley, Ore., Graves worked as a seaman on Orient-bound mail ships before taking up painting in the early 1930s. He was largely self-taught, although he studied briefly with Mark Tobey.* Tobey's work, along with his own interest in oriental painting and in Zen Buddhist and Vedanta philosophies, has formed a lasting influence on Graves' art. Between 1936 and 1939 Graves also worked with the WPA Federal Art Project.*

His earliest paintings were in oil, which was thickly applied and heavily handled. These gained him an award from the Seattle Art Museum in 1933 and a one-man show there in 1936. The following year, however, he turned to tempera, gouache, ink, and wax painted on thin papers in a technique reminiscent of Japanese and Chinese scroll paintings. He has returned to oil periodically since the early 1950s, but he remains best known for his smaller works on paper in muted tones of transparent tempera and watercolor.

Although his painting has affinities with western surrealism as well as orthodox oriental traditions, Graves has evolved a highly personal, symbolic art that has little relationship to other contemporary styles. Among his favorite and recurring images are those of birds —sometimes "blind," or "wounded" or "maddened by the sound of machinery in the air"—of snakes, minnows, hibernating bears, and of radiant chalices. Often they stand near the darkish forms of sea rocks bathed in a nocturnal glow, and are isolated in "windows" delineated by calligraphic white traceries that create mysterious interior spaces, as in his *Bird in the Spirit* (1940–41, Whitney). These works vary widely in style, from Sumi-like strokes executed

with a single flourish of the brush, to a deft, precisionist draftsmanship combined with misty dark washes. The quiet mood, ambiguous space, and evocative use of natural forms, however, remain constant. Since 1960 he has virtually abandoned representational imagery altogether in favor of abstract interpretations of motion and space. He had a one-man show at the Whitney Museum in 1956. His paintings are in major museum and private collections. (A.F.)

Gravestones.

Headstones and other grave markers are among the earliest ritual creations of European settlers on American soil, and they have now been recognized as the first expression of a national sculpture. Colonial stone carvers initially followed the folk traditions they brought with them, and the earliest stones adhered to the forms, symbols, and inscriptions of English and continental European models. Individual styles and regional preferences soon emerged, however, and the work of several distinguishable hands and some makers has been identified. Among the earliest of the known carvers is Joseph Lamson (active early in the 18th century), whose stones are in the Charlestown, Mass., graveyard. Anonymous, but just as readily identifiable, are the finely carved late 18th-century stones in the Rockingham, Vt., graveyard with their complicated compass scribings and low relief details. The Rockingham marker for the infants of Lovita and Elijah Bellows who died in 1799 is unusual in its depiction of the children as two lambs.

Among the more common design elements of 18th-century stones were angels, death's-heads, hourglasses, and even stylized likenesses of the deceased, often embellished with wings and foliage. The degree of relief of these carvings increased progressively in the 19th century, and the early slate material gave way to mica schist, sandstone, and marble. By the century's midpoint the individuality of the regional carver was overtaken by stock designs. At roughly the same time the churchyard itself was supplanted as the site of fashionable burial by the park-like cemetery, for which more ambitious markers based on European sculptural models were soon produced. In the 1960s interest in 18th-century

4

1. **Morris Graves,** Bird in the Spirit,
   c.1941. Whitney Museum of American Art, N.Y. (gift of the Friends of
   the Whitney Museum).
   Gravestones
2. Gravestone of Captain Coustan Hop-
   kin, Truro, Cape Cod, c.1800.
3. Gravestone of Nicholas Bows, Warren, Mass., c.1750.
4. Gravestone of Mary Harvey and
   Infant, Deerfield, Mass., c.1785.
   All, Rubbings by Avon Neal and Ann
   Parker from Museum of American
   Folk Art, N.Y.

gravestones was stimulated by a popular use of stone-rubbing techniques, and very fine professional rubbings were acquired by many American museums. (M.J.G.)

Gray, Henry Peters (1819–77).
Painter, born in New York, N.Y. He studied with Daniel Huntington* and in 1839 accompanied his teacher to Europe. Returning in 1841, Gray worked in New York and Boston before making a second European trip in 1845–46. Elected to the National Academy of Design* in 1842, he served as its president in 1870–71. Between 1871 and 1875 he worked in Italy, returning home in 1875. Gray's figure paintings were strongly influenced in compostion and palette by the Italian Old Masters, especially Titian. His classical and historical subjects won him popular acclaim during his life. Typical of his Italianate compositions is *The Judgement of Paris* (1861, Corcoran), which is suffused with a Titianesque golden glow. In his attempt to recreate Renaissance images he failed, producing only superficial, contrived canvases, very genteel in content but utterly lacking in vitality and individuality. His significance as an artist is as an example of one stratum of popular taste in American society at mid-century. (H.W.W.)

Greek Revival Style.
An architectural style popular from 1820 to 1860. Distinguished by spare lines and white classic porticos, usually Doric or Ionic, this style was used in every kind of building, from banks and cottages to plantation mansions. The early Republic had a romantic attachment to the ancient world, particularly Greece, as the birthplace of democracy, and Greek revival combined democratic allusions with a degree of dignity and stateliness that could be achieved quickly and with available materials. (See also Architecture Since 1540.)

Greene, Balcomb (1904–   ).
Painter. Greene was born in Niagara Falls, N.Y., the son of a Methodist minister whose work kept him moving through small towns in Iowa, South Dakota, and Colorado. Greene's interest in painting developed late. After graduating from Syracuse University, he also did post-graduate work in psychology in Vienna, some of it under Sigmund Freud, and published articles in European psychological journals. On his return to America in 1927, he studied English literature at Columbia University and taught that subject for several years at Dartmouth College.

In 1931, Greene moved to Paris, determined to become a painter; his transition to the new career was greatly assisted by his wife, Gertrude Glass, herself a painter and sculptor. Greene, who never had formal instruction in art, worked independently at the Académie de la Grande Chaumière. He returned to America in 1933, and after some journalistic work was employed by the mural division of the WPA Federal Art Project* (1936–39) designing a stained glass window for a school in the Bronx, and painting murals for the Hall of Medicine at the New York World's Fair. By 1935 Greene's style had settled into a severe, geometrically abstract mold; he was a founder of the American Abstract Artists* society and was its first chairman. He was also a founder and a president of the Artists' Union and the Federation of Modern Painters and Sculptors.* In 1943 he received a master's degree in art history from New York University, and he taught that subject, as well as esthetics, there until 1957.

In the early 1940s Greene introduced figurative elements into his painting but retained the hard edges and unmodulated colors of his abstract work. His style changed completely at the time of his first one-man show in New York City in 1947. Ambiguous images, seen in blinding light and with deep shadows, now dominated. The emphasis was on the human figure, usually nude, and the sea; and the palette concentrated on pearly whites, grays, gray-greens, gray-blues, and dull reds. An example is *The Wreck, No. II* (1958, Brooklyn).

Greene was a leading figure in the Museum of Modern Art's "New Images of Man" show in 1959 and was given a retrospective exhibition at the Whitney Museum in 1961. He has exhibited very widely throughout the United States and Europe and is represented in the collections of major museums. (A.F.)

Greene, Charles S. (1868–1957) and Henry M. (1870–1954).
Brothers who were born in Cincinnati, Ohio, educated in St. Louis, Mo., and studied architecture at the Massachusetts Institute of Technology. They both worked in architectural offices in Boston before establishing their own firm in Pasadena, Cal., in 1893. Their first houses brought together a number of the current styles of the 1890s, but their preferred mode was the shingle style,* sometimes colonial revival in feeling, as in the Swan House (Pasadena, 1894), and at other times half-timbered and English, as in the Culbertson House (Pasadena, 1902).

Architecture in the early 1900s in California was strongly influenced not only by the Arts and Crafts* movement, but by the mission revival and Japanese forms and details. The Greenes merged all of these with the late shingle style to produce one of the most popular styles of the 20th century in America—the California bungalow. Their Bandini House (Pasadena, 1903) was a single-floored, U-shaped house oriented around a courtyard; while their Ford House (Pasadena, 1904) grouped its two-story space around a completely enclosed patio. By 1907 in the Blacker House (Pasadena) and in 1908 in their famous Gamble House (Pasadena), they had fully established the style of the "woodsy" California bungalow, with its low-pitched, widely overhanging roofs, extensive porches and terraces, its "open" plan extending outdoors, and its use of "natural" material: shingles, untreated wood, brick, and stone. The style was seized upon by builders and developers and by the late 1910s, entire districts of American cities were covered with small and large versions of the California bungalow.

With the waning of the Arts and Crafts movement in the late 1910s, the Greenes found it difficult to obtain commissions and slowly withdrew from practice, Henry remaining in Pasadena, Charles moving to Carmel, Cal. Both continued to execute occasional commissions during the 1920s, for example, Charles Greene's James House in Carmel (1917–21). (D.G.)

Greenough, Horatio (1805–52).
Sculptor. Born in Boston, Mass., and reared in cultural surroundings, he determined, while at Harvard, to become a sculptor. Upon graduation in 1825 he sailed for Italy; in Rome he studied with the Danish sculptor Bertel Thorwaldsen, coming at once under the influence of neoclassicism.* He then worked under Bartolini in Flor-

ence, where he established permanent residence. At first there were only commissions for portrait busts, but in 1829 James Fenimore Cooper commissioned the marble group (now lost) called the *Chanting Cherubs,* which was sent on tour of eastern America and brought national attention to the young sculptor. When Congress voted appropriations in 1832 for a marble statue of George Washington for the Capitol rotunda, Washington, D.C. much pride was taken in the fact that the commission could be entrusted to a native son.

For several years Greenough worked on a heroic image of Washington patterned after the great statue of Zeus made by Phidias in the 5th century B.C. Italian stonecutters translated Greenough's plaster model into Carrara marble and in 1841 the colossus was shipped to America and installed in the rotunda. Its reception was mixed; the nation's intelligentsia praised it but the average American criticized its Jovian character, insisting that the figure, naked to the waist, bore no relationship to their beloved Washington. Greenough's disappointment over this reaction did not discourage him from undertaking symbolic or ideal subjects, and he did less and less portraiture. Another commission from Congress led to the group known as *The Rescue,* which was placed alongside the central stairs of the east front of the Capitol; it represents a pioneer struggling with an Indian to protect his wife and child from attack. Other ideal works in marble include the angel *Abdiel* (1838, Yale), a *Venus* (1841, Boston Athenaeum), and an oval relief of *Castor and Pollox* (1847–51, Boston). From such subjects it is evident that Greenough was inspired by the art of classical antiquity, with themes chosen from mythology, the Bible, and Romantic authors such as Byron. In his own writings on artistic theory, however, he was surprisingly modern, advocating the principle of "form follows function" well before its application to architecture later in the 19th century. He further advocated an "American art" that would reflect the spirit of the nation, as opposed to an imported, European art, but it is difficult to relate this theory to his actual practice. In 1850 he left the expatriate colony of Florence to return to Boston. He died two years later.   (W.C.)

1

2

1. **Horatio Greenough.** George Washington, *1841, marble. National Collection of Fine Arts, Smithsonian Institution, Washington, D.C.*

2. **Balcomb Greene.** The Wreck, No. II, *1958. Brooklyn Museum, N.Y.*

1

Greenough, Richard (1819–1904).
Sculptor. Born in Boston, Mass., he commenced studying sculpture in 1837, when he went to Italy to work with his older brother, Horatio Greenough.* Returning to Boston he opened a studio and specialized in portrait busts; in 1848 he went back to Europe and remained in American expatriate colonies in Rome and Paris. Influenced by Roman art, many of his works were of classical subjects, such as his *Shepherd Boy with an Eagle* (1853, Boston Athenaeum). His brand of neoclassicism,* influenced by ancient statuary and the work of the Danish sculptor Bertel Thorwaldsen, often took on the Victorian characteristic of romantic sentimentality at the expense of sculptural form. His portraits, such as the bust of Cornelia Van Rensselaer (1849, New York Hist.), also possess a Victorian love of surface decoration that fascinated with its virtuosity but failed to conceal weak sculptural form. In the 1870s he moved to Rome, where he created such examples of Victorian classicism as *Circe* (1882, Metropolitan).

Greenwood, John (1727–92).
Portrait and genre painter and engraver, whose life reveals a modest talent, combined with rough humor and a spirit of adventure. Born in Boston, Mass., he served as apprentice to the engraver Thomas Johnston, and began painting portraits at about the age of eighteen. His *Mrs. John Franklin* (c.1747–50, Brooklyn) and *Mrs. Welshman* (Washington) are typical of his wooden style, literal characterization, and dependence upon mezzotint prototypes.* In 1752 he voyaged to Surinam where, in the next five years, he painted over one hundred portraits and one Hogarthian satirical genre piece, *American Sea Captains Carousing* (1757–58, St. Louis). A mezzotint done of a Boston town character, *Jersey Nanny* (1748), is his best-known engraving. Greenwood next appeared in the Netherlands as an engraver, 1758–62. The rest of his life was spent as an art dealer in London, interspersed with occasional painting of landscape and portraits. During the American Revolutionary War he was active among the pro-American and other dissident groups. (C.C.S.)

Grooms, Red (1937–   ).
Painter, filmmaker, and a pioneer of happenings.* His most characteristic works are probably constructions or environments in which he peoples entire rooms with cutout figures and objects painted in brilliant and clashing colors, satirically depicting themes such as *Discount Store, Banquet for Henri Rousseau,* or *City of Chicago.* He was born in Nashville, Tenn., and studied at the Peabody College there, the Art Institute of Chicago, the New School for Social Research in New York, and the Hans Hofmann School on Cape Cod. Grooms frequently collaborates with his wife, the painter Mimi Gross, as well as with the filmmaker Rudolph Burckhardt. His paintings, environments, and films are characterized by wild fantasy and broad slapstick humor and are rather like three-dimensional comic strips that are rooted in a precise observation of contemporary popular culture. (H.H.A.)

Gropius, Walter (1883–1969).
Outstanding figure in 20th-century architecture and design, first in Germany and later in the United States. It was the group around him at the German design institute, the Bauhaus,* that brought together the various elements of avant-garde design of the 1920s and formulated the International style*—the most unified style since mid-18th century rococo. Gropius accomplished this by means of activities ranging from styling industrial products and buildings to writing, teaching, and administrative work.

Gropius was trained at the colleges of technology of Berlin and Munich. During 1907–10 he worked in the office of Peter Behrens (both Mies van der Rohe* and Le Corbusier also worked there). In 1910 he established his own practice in Berlin, and in 1911 he and Adolph Meyer (who collaborated with him on many projects) designed the Fagus factory at Alfeld, an epoch-making building. Its steel and glass curtain wall, hung independently of the frame of the building, is a perfect example of the imagery of the International style of the 1920s and 1930s. In his 1914 Model Factory and Office Building at the Werkbund Exposition at Cologne he created a design which not altogether successfully mixed details from Frank Lloyd Wright* with his own earlier stringent machine esthetic.

During World War I Gropius was appointed Director of the Arts and Crafts School at Weimar; after the war he

1. *Richard Greenough.* Shepherd Boy with an Eagle, *1853. Boston Athenaeum.*
2. *Red Grooms.* Discount Store, *1970, Walker Art Center, Minneapolis.*

combined this school with the Academy of Arts in Weimar, creating the Bauhaus. The early atmosphere of the Bauhaus, like that of William Morris' 19th-century Arts and Crafts* movement, was more closely allied to hand than machine production. Like Mies, Erich Mendelsohn, and others, Gropius was affected by German expressionism,* and a number of his designs and those of other members of the Bauhaus reflected the agitated, primitive feeling of this movement. But by the early 1920s Gropius had abandoned the Arts and Crafts direction and had fully committed himself and the Bauhaus to the production of industrial design. When the Bauhaus (because of conservative political pressure) moved to Dessau, Gropius designed its new buildings; his Bauhaus Building (1925–26), especially the glass-sheathed workshop wing, became the visual ideal for several generations of modern architects. In the late 1920s he resigned as director of the Bauhaus to concentrate on low-cost housing. His Siemenstadt Housing (Berlin, 1929) was composed of large-scale rectangular blocks of apartments, highly mechanical in feeling, which were placed in curved rows facing parklike greenery. His contribution to the famous Weissenhof Housing Exhibition, Stuttgart, 1927, was a completely paneled prefabricated house. It was during the late 1920s that he explored experimental designs for the theater, all of them suggesting a new close relationship between audience and the performer. With the advent of the Nazis, Gropius went to England, where he was associated with the English architect Maxwell Frey (1934–37). In 1937 he came to America as professor of architecture and later chairman of the department at Harvard University. Between 1937 and 1941 he was associated with his former Bauhaus colleague Marcel Breuer.* Out of this association came such houses as Gropius' own home (1937) at Lincoln, Mass., which sought to mellow the machine quality of the International style imagery with the more traditional wood of a New England house.

In 1949 he designed (with the Architects' Collaborative) the Harvard Graduate Center, Cambridge, which, compared to the imagery of his earlier designs, lacks visual precision and clarity. While continuing his close involvement with architectural education,

2

1

2

Walter Gropius
1. Chamberlain Cottage, Weyland, Mass., 1940.
2. The architect's residence, Lincoln, Mass., 1937. Both, with Marcel Breuer.
3. **Chaim Gross,** Girl on a Wheel, *1940*, wood. Metropolitan Museum of Art, N.Y. (Morris K. Jesup Fund).

Gropius formed his own firm, the Architects' Collaborative. During the 1950s and 1960s it received a number of commissions, including the classic concrete pavilion of the United States Embassy, Athens (1957–61), the University of Baghdad (1960–62), which tried to be both modern and exotic, and the Kennedy Federal Office Building (Boston, 1961), which tends to be dry and academic. Gropius served as an architectural advisor on a number of major projects. These included the controversial Pan Am Building (New York, 1958, with Emory Roth & Sons), which raised questions with its highly academic design and a location that appreciably increased the density of an overpopulated area.

Gropius can be credited with establishing almost single-handedly the imagery of the International style. From the late 1930s on his major concern was with education. In the realm of architectural practice he was especially interested in how designers and other specialists could work together constructively. Architecture and the whole of industrial design, he pointed out, is and must be a collaborative effort. The question he posed was how this collaboration could be organized to function creatively. (D.G.)

Gropper, William (1897–   ).
Painter, cartoonist, and lithographer. Gropper was born in New York and grew up in poverty. His father was a sweatshop garment worker, and young Gropper left high school to work as a dishwasher, delivery boy, and laborer. He had begun to draw at an early age, and eventually he saved enough money to study with Robert Henri* and George Bellows* at the Ferrer School (1912–13). He later attended the National Academy of Design* and the New York School of Fine and Applied Art.

Gropper began his career in 1919 as a political cartoonist for the Sunday New York *Tribune,* and he remained active as a cartoonist and illustrator throughout the 1920s, contributing to numerous periodicals. He accompanied the novelists Theodore Dreiser and Sinclair Lewis to Russia in 1927, and published a volume of drawings on the trip.

In 1921, Gropper began painting. He worked in a grotesquely distorted expressionistic style with themes of social concern: politicians, military figures, rural farm hands, Jewish villagers. The passionate satire of his work has led him to be called "the American Daumier." In the 1930s he was also active as a muralist, with commissions in the New Interior Building in Washington, D.C. (1938) and the Detroit Post Office (1939). In recent years, Gropper's art has moved from satire to themes of broader human concern. A group of pictures painted in 1963 after a walking trip through Yucatán, and a more recent series dealing with aged Jewish types, cast his figures in an almost biblical spirit. Typical of his work is the angry satire called *The Senate* (1935, Modern Museum).   (A.F.)

Gross, Chaim (1904–   ).
Sculptor. Gross was born in Austria and emigrated to New York City in 1921. After studying at the Art Students League* he attended the Beaux-Arts Institute, where he became a teacher. In 1927 he carved the *Mother and Child at Play* (Newark Museum) which has as a basic part of its esthetic the natural grain and "blockiness" of the wood and an interesting surface pattern made by the chisel. Although his work is frequently less than life-size, there is a monumentality in it, due primarily to the reduction of details in favor of the larger forms. All of these elements remained at the center of his style and indicated his concern for formal matters in his art. He belongs to the direct-carving group of sculptors but his work is more playful than that of such other members as José de Creeft,* John Flannagan,* and William Zorach.* During the 1930s and '40s he often took circus acrobats as his subject, as in his *Handlebar Riders* (1935, Modern Museum), *Lillian Leitzel* (1938, Metropolitan), and *Girl on a Wheel* (1940, Metropolitan). His woodcarving style was enlarged to heroic porportions in his *Alaskan Snowshoe Mail Carrier* (1935, Post Office Building, Washington, D.C.), which was cast in aluminum. From 1942 to 1959 Gross taught at the art school of the Brooklyn Art Museum. Dating from the later part of his career are *Adolescent* (1950) and *Happy Mother* (1958, Philadelphia). He is the author of an autobiography, *A Sculptor's Progress* (1938), and *The Technique of Wood Carving* (1957).   (W.C.)

Grosz, George (1893–1959).
Painter and caricaturist. Born in Berlin and reared in the small Pomeranian town of Stolp, Grosz displayed an early facility in drawing. Following his expulsion from school because of a revolt against Prussian discipline, he attended the Royal Saxon Academy of Fine Arts. He received thorough academic training there between 1909 and 1911 but was drawn to the German expressionist movement then current. The *Linienstil* of popular illustration and Italian futurism were other influences on his development.

Grosz served in the German infantry during 1914–16. A series of violently satirical drawings of the military which he did in Berlin following his discharge because of illness brought him wide notoriety. He was conscripted again in 1917 but was soon hospitalized with a nervous breakdown. In 1918 he returned to Berlin, joining the German dada* movement, and during the ensuing fourteen years he created the satirical drawings, watercolors, and oils on which his fame chiefly rests. These works catalog the moral decay of postwar Germany in a spare, linear style related to that of Otto Dix and the painters of the then current German movement called The New Objectivity. In the early years of this period Grosz was also involved in political propaganda and in the publication of dada magazines and broadsides.

Grosz was arrested three times and fined twice during the 1920s following the publication of portfolios of his satirical works. Although he was not Jewish, his position was increasingly threatened with the rise of Nazism. He therefore accepted an invitation to teach summer classes at the Art Students League* in New York in 1932, and in the following year he settled with his family in the United States.

In New York, Grosz embarked on a complex remaking of his art. For a time he continued to produce satirical drawings for magazines, and in 1936 he published *Interregnum,* a portfolio of sixty-five drawings that looked back on the German society he had left. But he was no longer primarily interested in satire and he sought to enrich his work in the light of European tradition, including that of the Old Masters and the 19th-century German anecdotal painters on whom he had been brought up. His first American works were drawings and watercolors of New York, related in style to his late German drawings, but tending toward a decorative ab-

3

straction of flat patterns and calligraphic line. In 1935 he turned to landscape, the nude, and still life, and began for the first time to exploit the rich and sensuous qualities of oil. Meanwhile, inspired by events in Europe, he created a series of watercolors that dealt with the butchery of war. Grosz's vision became increasingly cataclysmic during the years that followed, and he produced many oils wherein the impending catastrophe of war—and ultimately the war itself—were set forth in elaborately symbolic terms, with a baroque turbulence of movement and a sense of Gothic horror recalling Bosch and Grünewald. In 1947 Grosz created a series of "stickmen," elaborating a detailed mythology that formed a parable of postwar ruin, starvation, and suffering. Later he returned to landscape, the nude, and still life in a highly finished, sometimes overworked style. He continued to teach, both at the Art Students League and in his studio on Long Island, N.Y.

Grosz was a complex and paradoxical person. Although he achieved celebrity for his political satire, he had little to do with radical politics. In America he often played a dandified role, and for a time cherished the ambition of becoming an illustrator for the slick magazines. His working habits alternated between periods of impassioned intensity and fallow interludes, and his painting often verged on the garish shameless enthusiasm. Thus, his *Organi-* level. However, in his finest American work he succeeded in elevating the topical commentary that characterized his early career to a universal statement on human brutality and suffering.

(A.F.)

Grotell, Maija (1899–).
Best known for wheel-thrown ceramics with patterns built up with clay slips and metallic glazes over them—objects of great purity. Born in Helsinki, Finland, Grotell emigrated to the United States in 1927, teaching and working in New York City until 1938. She then joined the faculty of Cranbrook Academy of Art, Bloomfield Hills, Mich., where she was head of the Department of Ceramics until 1966. Her mastery of wheel-throwing and of glaze chemistry made her one of the most important ceramics teachers in this country. One of her techniques is to etch patterns and designs directly into a colored clay slip,

with iron oxide glazes painted on other areas to juxtapose the rough slip textures with the brilliant glazes. A favorite shape is an almost closed round pot, which seems like a mystical vessel because of the earthiness of its colors.

(R.S.)

Guermonprez, Trude (n.d.–).
Weaver of experimental tapestries in which loom construction for texture, depth, and composition is achieved purely through the yarn. Tension and thickness are varied for expressive effects while color is muted, emphasizing the material purity of the whole. Her teaching has been very important to the craft in the United States. Born in Austria, Guermonprez emigrated to America in 1939 and thereafter taught loom weaving at Black Mountain College in North Carolina and at San Francisco Art Institute, and presently at California College of Arts and Crafts in Oakland. She is able to weave a wide variety of shapes because of her mastery of warp and weft manipulation.

(R.S.)

Guggenheim, Peggy (1898–).
Art collector and patron who was highly influential in the promotion of modern painting and sculpture. Born into a wealthy New York family, she was the niece of the founder of the Guggenheim Museum, Solomon Guggenheim. She went to Europe in her early twenties and settled in Paris, where she became acquainted with the artists and writers of the postwar era. Moving to London, in 1938 she opened a gallery of modern art, Guggenheim Jeune, and with the help of Marcel Duchamp* organized pioneer exhibitions of abstract and surrealist artists, including Kandinsky, Brancusi, Alexander Calder,* Henry Moore, Jean Arp, and Max Ernst (whom she later married). Guided by the English critic Herbert Read, she planned to convert the gallery into a modern museum concentrating on cubism,* abstraction, and surrealism.* When the outbreak of World War II prevented her from doing so, she began collecting intensively and soon had an important group of modern paintings, including key works by Picasso, Brancusi, Miró, Klee, and other leaders of the School of Paris.

Upon the German occupation of France in 1941, Miss Guggenheim escaped to New York with her collection and in 1942 opened her gallery,

Art of This Century, designed by the architect Frederick Kiesler. Many of the leading European modernists, including Breton, Mondrian, Ernst, Lipchitz,* Léger, and others had just then migrated to New York. Art of This Century exhibited most of these artists, as well as many of the American pioneers of abstract expressionism,* perhaps the most significant original movement in modern American painting. Among the American artists exhibited were Jackson Pollock,* Mark Rothko,* Robert Motherwell,* Hans Hofmann,* Clyfford Still,* and Adolph Gottlieb,* as Peggy Guggenheim expanded her collection to include the American avant-garde. In 1946 she closed the gallery in New York and returned to Europe. She established her gallery in a palazzo in Venice. In 1969 she willed her collection and her Venice gallery to the Solomon R. Guggenheim Foundation.

(H.H.A.)

Guglielmi, O. Louis (1906–56).
Painter. Born in Egypt of Italian parents, he spent his early childhood moving from European city to city with his father, an orchestral musician. The family moved to New York City in 1914 and settled in the Italian slum in Harlem, and this experience permanently affected Guglielmi's outlook and work.

Guglielmi studied at the National Academy of Design* from 1920 to 1925. He attempted to assimilate the conservative principles of this education to the modernist ideas then current in American art circles. Later, he felt that the spirit of social criticism engendered by the Depression had much to do with releasing his own individuality, and he dated the start of his career around 1932. He worked on the WPA Federal Art Project* in the 1930s and served in the U.S. Air Corps during World War II. He taught at Louisiana State University from 1952–53 and later he taught at the New School for Social Research in New York City.

Guglielmi won his reputation with paintings that combine social commentary with strong elements of surrealism.* Typical of his style is *Terror in Brooklyn* (1941, Whitney), which presents a desolate street with three figures in black, huddled, weeping and protesting, under a bell jar; their terror seems to have been caused by the bones of a human pelvis suspended by bright ribbons across the surface of a blank wall at the right. The street moves endlessly into the exaggerated deep space of the surrealist tradition; the hallucinatory clarity and precision of all the images in the painting is also surreal. In the last years of his career, Guglielmi's imagery grew less specific, deep space was eliminated, and an abstract, somewhat decorative emphasis, still based on the imagery of the city, supervened.

Guglielmi won many prizes and awards, and his work is in the permanent collections of numerous museums.

(A.F.)

Gullager, Christian (1762–1826).

"Portrait and Theatrical Painter," as he described himself in 1797. A Dane, born to a prosperous family in Copenhagen, he studied there at the Royal Academy of Arts and won, in 1780, a medal and traveling scholarship. He studied in Paris and then traveled to Massachusetts; by 1789 he was established in Boston as a leading portrait painter. In 1797 he worked briefly in New York, then lived with his family in Philadelphia until 1806.

Gullager's portraits often reveal a flair unusual in early American art. It appears at times in a vigorous, breezy treatment of elements of costume, at times in a bright or jovial look on the face of the sitter, and sometimes even a look of slightly bibulous gaiety, which is a surprise, considering Gullager's largely Puritan clientele. His *George Washington* (Boston Hist.), which Gullager painted from life in 1789, seems to be watching his glass refilled, wearing a genial air like no other Washington portrait. In the next year, Gullager modeled and was exhibiting in New York a bust of the president. By 1797 his repertoire included miniatures, theatrical scenery, flags, and decorative painting of all sorts, an expanding field that suggests declining fortunes; little is known of the last twenty years of his life. (C.C.S.)

Gussow, Roy (1918–   ).

Sculptor. Born in Brooklyn, N.Y., he studied sculpture with the Hungarian artist Laszlo Moholy-Nagy and the Russian sculptor Alexander Archipenko at the Institute of Design in Chicago. His early works were free-form abstractions in terra-cotta and red sandstone. In the 1950s he welded metal rods and wire in linear constructions, some of

Louis Guglielmi. Terror in Brooklyn, *1941. Whitney Museum of American Art, N.Y.*

them kinetic sculptures in which the motion of the elements forms and reforms plane surfaces. Under the influence of José de Rivera* he produced works in polished or chrome-plated sheet steel, bronze, and aluminum. In 1967 he helped de Rivera construct a large sculpture, *Infinity,* for the mall of the Smithsonian Institution in Washington, D.C. Gussow has maintained the constructivist tradition, often expanding it to a public scale in commissions for large outdoor pieces. In 1969 he produced *Amity,* a monumental work designed for the plaza at the Civic Center in Tulsa, Okla. He has exhibited in numerous museums in New York, Chicago, and elsewhere since 1947. His first one-man show in New York took place in 1958. Since the mid-1960s his works have consisted of two or more chromed metal pillars, with curved indentations whose mirrored concavities create elegant variations on the pillars' flat surfaces.   (C.R.)

Guston, Philip (1913–   ).
Born in Montreal, Canada, he grew up in Los Angeles. He studied briefly at the Otis Art Institute in Los Angeles in 1930, but is largely self-trained. He collaborated on murals for the Public Works Administration in Los Angeles during 1934–35 and, moving to New York, was on the WPA Federal Art Project* between 1935 and 1940, executing murals for the 1939 New York World's Fair and for the Queensbridge Housing Project, Long Island, N.Y. (1940–41). He has received various grants and fellowships and has had many exhibitions, including those at the São Paulo Biennial (1959), the Venice Biennial (1960), and a major retrospective at the Guggenheim Museum (1962). He has taught widely, including the State University of Iowa (1941–45); New York University (1951–59); and Pratt Institute, Brooklyn (1953–57). He lives in Woodstock, N.Y.

Guston was perhaps unique among those artists associated with abstract expressionism* in that he was a successful figure and subject painter during the 1940s before he turned to abstraction. Although highly conscious of 20th-century cubism,* abstraction, and surrealism,* his first interests were in Renaissance masters such as Uccello, Mantegna, and Piero Della Francesca. His figure paintings of the 1940s combined Renaissance archi-

1

2

tectural structure with cubist simplification. Many dealt with children rendered in a romantic, dreamlike mood, evincing a strong personal poetry, as in *If This Be Not I* (1945, Washington University). During 1948–49 Guston began painting abstractly but his work continued his sense of architectural construction. This persisted during the early 1950s in a series of "white" paintings that combined a vertical-horizontal, Mondrian-like construction with impressionist color and brushstroke. The exhibition of these works in 1953 marked a milestone in his career. In the 1950s there was a gradual movement away from balanced symmetry toward a greater coloristic density and asymmetrical organization of heavily brushed shapes floating in an atmospheric void. Blacks become more important. Typical of this period is *The Clock* (1956–7, Modern Museum). Guston's abstract paintings never entirely lose the sense of specific subject—of mood, metamorphosis, fantasy, or conflict.

During the 1960s his paintings increased in scale. In 1966 he exhibited a group of large gray paintings (at the Jewish Museum, New York) pervaded by an overpowering mood of atmospheric darkness. In these he abandoned his mastery of color and technical virtuosity in favor of a somber expression and crudity of execution that seemed to reflect some inner torment and uncertainty. With his next exhibition, in 1970, a startling change was revealed, with Guston returning to a literal-expressionist subject matter: dingy interiors or urban landscapes suggesting seedy tenements. The scenes, painted with a coarse brush, garish color, in a primitive cartoon manner, are populated by hooded Ku Klux Klan figures smoking cigars, pointing fingers like guns, or wielding whips. These grisly scenes are reminiscent of some of Guston's paintings of the 1940s, in which children masked in paper bags and armed with wooden sticks and garbage-can covers play at war. The recent figure paintings represent a revival of earlier themes, but emerge directly from the abstract expressionist paintings of the 1960s with their suggestions of black shapes and brilliant colors struggling together.

Whether working abstractly or figuratively, Guston begins by sketching objects directly and literally and then seeing how far he can go in eliminating representational elements. In the most recent subject paintings he maintains the appearance of the studio objects but transforms them into a brutal world of gangsters and dismembered torsos portrayed in a primitive comic-strip technique. (H.H.A.)

Guy, Francis (c.1760–1820).
Landscape painter. One may speculate that his birth and childhood in the English lake district may have had some formative influence on his career. As a young man he became a silk dyer in London, emigrating to America in 1795 but failing to find there enough work in any city to sustain him in his trade. He moved from New York to Brooklyn to Philadelphia and then to Baltimore. At Baltimore, unemployed and desperate, he set out to become a painter of landscape. In order to take views with mechanical accuracy, he invented a sort of tent with a glass opening—a camera, as it were, with its operator inside. From this beginning, he developed an independent skill of hand and eye. He was soon successful in the practical line of making views of wealthy gentlemen's estates. His work has a feeling for open spaces rare in early American art, with a use of figures to add interest but never to dominate the scene. In 1817 he returned to Brooklyn as a painter. Two years later an exhibition of his work in New York, under special lighting and with a musical accompaniment, drew much public attention and praise, including that of Charles Willson Peale,* who, though they were unacquainted, seems to have influenced Guy's work through his own. Good examples of Guy's work are *Baltimore from Beech Hill* (Maryland Historical Society) and *Brooklyn* (1817, Brooklyn). (C.C.S.)

Gwathmey, Robert (1903–   ).
Painter and graphic artist. Born in Richmond, Va., Gwathmey studied at North Carolina State College, the Maryland Institute of Design, and the Pennsylvania Academy of the Fine Arts. He later traveled in Europe and the Caribbean. He painted murals (U.S. Post Office, Eutaw, Ark.) as well as easel paintings. His first one-man show was in 1939 in New York. He taught at Beaver College (1930–1937), the Carnegie Institute of Technology (1939–1942), and he has taught at Cooper Union since 1942.

Gwathmey draws his subjects from southern life, particularly the life of the rural Negro, as in *Singing and Mending* (1945, private collection). He simplifies and flattens figures and objects in bold, formal patterns, enclosing areas of intense, bright color within precise, dark outlines. His paintings alternate between strongly stated social commentary and more implicit messages. He has won several awards and his work is included in a number of public collections. (A.F.)

1. *Philip Guston.* Duo, *1961. Solomon R. Guggenheim Museum, N.Y.*
2. *Philip Guston.* Untitled, *1966. Marlborough-Gerson Gallery, N.Y.*

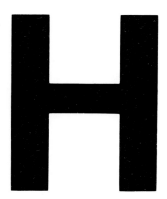

H

Haberle, John (1853–1933).
Still-life painter who was born in New Haven, Conn., and lived there all his life. Haberle began his career as a preparator in the paleontological museum of Yale University and was associated with Yale off and on for many years. A forerunner of pop art,* he exploited the same vein of vernacular humor and satire as the pop artists of the 1960s, but he was much more fanatically devoted than they to precise, illusionistic rendering and *trompe l'oeil.* One of his most remarkable inventions is his use of a painting not in *trompe l'oeil* style as the central object of a *trompe l'oeil* composition; in one instance (*Night,* New Britain Museum of American Art), he produced a completely finished picture of an unfinished picture.

Hadfield, George (1763–1826).
Architect, born of English parents in Leghorn, Italy. The family returned to England in 1779, where young Hadfield became a carpenter's apprentice. In 1781 he exhibited drawings made during a visit to Italy, and was admitted to study at the Royal Academy at a time when Thomas Sandby was Professor of Architecture. While a student he exhibited regularly at the annual Royal Academy exhibit, and in 1784 won the gold medal of the Academy. In 1790 he received a three-year traveling fellowship from the Academy, and spent most of his time abroad making drawings of classical antiquities in Italy.

In 1794 the American painter John Trumbull* recommended Hadfield to the Commissioners of the City of Washington, who were seeking an architect for the Capitol. Hadfield accepted an appointment and came to America in 1795. He worked at constructing the north wing. At the same time he made well-proportioned classical designs for the Treasury and Executive offices

1

2

1. *John Haberle.* The Bachelor's Drawer, *c.1892. Collection Mr. and Mrs. J. William Middendorf II, N.Y.*

2. *Raoul Hague.* Plattekill Walnut. *1952. Museum of Modern Art, N.Y. (Elizabeth Bliss Parkinson Fund).*

258

(1798, burned 1814). As a professional architect, he expected to supervise construction; when this was denied him, he refused to give the plans to the Commissioners and was dismissed. In 1800 Hadfield patented a brick-making machine. He then designed the Washington County Jail (1802) and the Arsenal (1803). The citizens of Washington elected him a councilman in 1803. In 1812 the distinguished architect B. H. Latrobe* hired him briefly as an assistant; a few more jobs came his way, but never enough to constitute a good living. Within the District of Columbia he designed the Commodore Porter House (1816–19), the Washington City Hall (finished 1819, refaced with stone 1917), the Washington Assembly Rooms (1822), Arlington House (1820) for G. W. Parke Custis (now in Arlington National Cemetery), and the Van Ness Mausoleum, Oak Hill Cemetery (1833).

Hadfield was trained in the era of the classical revival, and all his designs reflect this background. The severe classicism that appealed to him is well represented by the Arlington House colonnade, with its heavy unfluted Doric columns. Latrobe said of him: "All that he proposed proved him a man of correct tastes, of perfect theoretic knowledge, and of bold integrity. . . ."

(P.F.N.)

Hagen, Ernest (n.d.).
A skilled craftsman, Hagen is remembered primarily for the valuable notes he wrote about other 19th-century cabinetmakers. Born in Hamburg, Germany, he moved to New York City in 1844, working for a succession of furniture makers, including Charles Bauduoine. In 1858, in partnership with J. M. Meier, he bought shop property at 213 East 26th Street. Several prosperous New York families became his customers, some ordering copies of Duncan Phyfe* furniture. Hagen mastered the Phyfe style and began to collect information which in 1907 he included in an informal memorandum on Phyfe. In the manuscript, his "Personal Reminiscences of an Old New York Cabinetmaker" (now at Winterthur), he discusses styles, shop practices, and major furniture-makers of the 1850s–'80s.

(M.J.B.)

Hague, Raoul (1905–   ).
Sculptor. Best known for his massive wood sculptures, Hague was born in

Constantinople of Armenian parents. He emigrated to the United States in 1921 and attended Iowa State College and later the Art Institute of Chicago and the Art Students League in New York. During the 1930s he excelled in stone carving, which he had studied with William Zorach* at the League, but in 1943, after serving in the army, he settled in Woodstock, N.Y., where he began his long devotion to wood.

Hague's works became increasingly abstract during the 1950s, echoing in their rough-hewn contours the sinuous movements of natural forms but never precisely delimiting them. His first exhibition in New York City was privately sponsored in 1953. Three years later he was included in the Museum of Modern Art's "Twelve Americans." He was praised for his agility in handling extremely large forms that retained their treelike origins but suggested the sophisticated problems in sculptural abstraction that were current at the time. He received a Ford Foundation Grant in 1959, and had his first one-man show in a New York gallery in 1962. In 1964 his first museum exhibition was held at the Washington Gallery of Modern Art. Since then, his work has been exhibited both in the United States and in Europe in numerous group exhibitions. (D.A.)

Haidt, John Valentin (1700–80).
Painter of religious subjects and portraits. Born in Danzig, the son of a German goldsmith, he studied drawing at the Royal Academy in Berlin while learning his father's craft. Established in London as a goldsmith, he joined the Moravian church about 1740 and soon after entered its ministry. His ministry took him to Pennsylvania in 1750, where he devoted his life and art to his church for more than twenty years. Haidt was the earliest American painter of religious subjects. His works, rather imitative of Rembrandt and other Dutch painting, were primitive in composition, bright in coloring, but painted with feeling. Examples are preserved by Moravian congregations in Pennsylvania at Bethlehem, Lititz, and Nazareth, and at the Moravian Historical Society. His portraits are remarkably explicit likenesses, stiffly posed yet in expression relaxed and pleasant—a charming reflection of provincial culture. (C.C.S.)

Hall, George Henry (1825–1913).
Still-life painter. Born in Manchester,

N.H., he moved to Boston as a child. He began painting portraits and genre pieces about 1842. In 1849 Hall traveled with Eastman Johnson* to Düsseldorf, and studied there and then in Rome and Paris. Upon his return to America in 1852, he established himself in New York City, became an associate of the National Academy of Design* the next year, and began to paint the fresh, small still lifes for which he is now best known. Many of these depicted raspberries or other fruit tumbling from a container or lying on the ground. Other favorite subjects were life-size studies of single pieces of fruit and lush vases of mixed flowers. Hall exhibited regularly in Boston, Philadelphia, and New York, and he traveled widely, visiting Spain (1860 and 1866), Italy (1872), and Egypt (1875). By the time of his death he had been forgotten, as styles of painting changed, but he had a considerable reputation during his lifetime and was one of the few still-life specialists mentioned in H. T. Tuckerman's* *Book of the Artists* (1867). (T.E.S.)

Hamilton, James (1819–78).
Irish-born landscape and marine painter. At fifteen, Hamilton was brought to Philadelphia, where he lived and prospered for most of his career. He became a drawing teacher around 1840, and journeyed to London in the 1850s. His loose style, with strong romantic sensibility and his interest in light, shows the influence particularly of the English seascape painter, J. M. W. Turner, as in his *Capture of the Serapis by John Paul Jones* (1854, Yale). Although he specialized in ships on dark seas, he did not hesitate to portray places he had never seen, such as the American West and the Arctic. He was also a competent engraver and etcher. He typically inscribed, signed, and dated his paintings on the reverse side of the canvas.

Handcrafts, Contemporary.
The emergence of the American craftsman is a phenomenon of the last twenty-five years. Except for a limited expression in the Appalachians and American Indian cultures, crafts existed only briefly during the colonial period and were all but wiped out by the industrial revolution and the growth of machine mass production. Isolated craft and utopian community movements sprang up

here and there, but were all of short duration.

Contemporary craftsmanship in the United States is the paradoxical expression of an industrial culture in which the very technology that almost eliminated the craftsman's function has freed him to expand his creative scope. Once the machine-made product became available, he was no longer required to make things strictly for use. Craftsmanship is also the expression of the culture's resistance to the depersonalizing forces of technological and corporate power. It asserted itself in the late 1940s and was thereafter stimulated and nurtured by a university system peculiar to the United States. The growth of craftsmanship in America is not a renaissance or a nostalgic throwback to old methods and vocations; it is a completely new handcraft culture within an industrial power structure.

In the 1920s and 1930s American craftsmen were scarce, although it was not uncommon for painters and sculptors to make useful handmade objects as a way of supporting themselves while they practiced their art. Resolute and devoted studio potters who kept the craft alive in this country included Adelaide Robineau at Syracuse University, Arthur Binns at Alfred University, Charles Harder, specializing in reduction firing at Ohio State University, Glen Lukens,* working with surface textures at the University of Southern California, Arthur Baggs, working with salt glazes and stoneware, Henry Varnum Poor* as painter-potter, and Finnish-born Maija Grotell,* who became the head of the ceramics department at Cranbrook Academy of Art in Michigan and had a major influence on the development of an entire new generation of American potters.

With the advent of the Works Progress Administration in the 1930s, artists and craftsmen received their first encouragement and support as individuals who did work of value to society. At the same time, in an effort to help the unemployed of her community, Aileen Osborn Webb opened in Putnam County, N.Y., in 1940, a retail outlet to sell craft products made at home. Her shop became America House, the first firm to promote the work of American craftsmen. This was followed in 1941 by her establishment of the American Craftsmen's Educational Council,

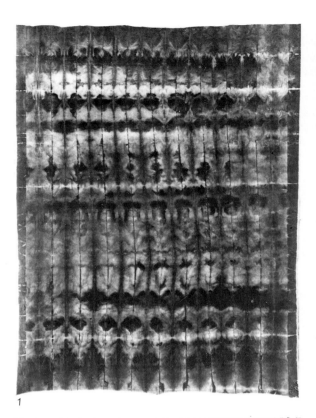

1

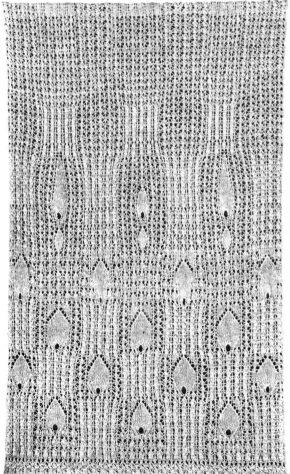

2

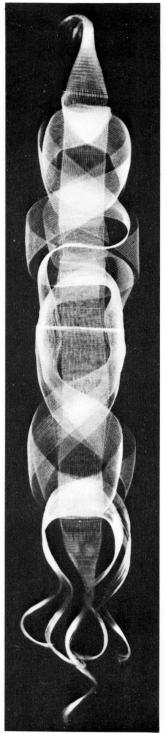

3

4

5

6

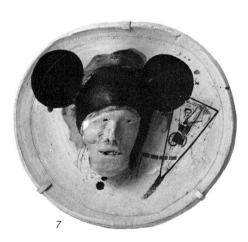

7

Handcrafts, Contemporary

1. *Jack Lenor Larson.* Chimu, *1965, length-of-fold dye on cotton velvet. Johnson Collection of Contemporary Crafts, Racine, Wis.*
2. *Mary Walker Phillips.* #K56, *1969, linen and synthetic yarn. Collection of the artist.*
3. *Kay Sekimachi. Untitled, 1965, clear nylon monofilament. Collection of the artist.*
4. *Alice Adams. Untitled, 1967, light steel cable looped on spiralling heavy steel cable. Museum of Contemporary Crafts, N.Y.*
5. *Michael Frimkess. Chinese-shape, decorated covered jar, 1965, stoneware, white underglaze. Museum of Contemporary Crafts, N.Y.*
6. *Gertrud and Otto Natzler. Bowl, 1956, earthenware with crater glaze. Johnson Collection of Contemporary Crafts, Racine, Wis.*
7. *James Melchert.* Ghost Plate with Mickey Mouse Hat, *1964, ceramic. Museum of Contemporary Crafts, N.Y.*

the national organization now known as the American Crafts Council, and of *Craft Horizons,* a magazine devoted to the hand arts in all media. Other stimuli to hand craftsmanship as a profession were the opening in the 1930s of art schools that offered craft courses, as at Alfred and Syracuse universities, the Cranbrook Academy of Art, and the Cleveland Institute of Art.

A major influence in the same direction were the émigré craftsmen from Germany and Austria, including potters Gertrud and Otto Natzler,* Marguerite and Franz Wildenhain,* and weavers Anni Albers* and Trude Guermonprez.* The Wildenhains established the now famous Pond Farm Pottery Workshop in Guerneville, Cal., while Anni Albers and her husband, the noted painter Josef Albers,* became directors of Black Mountain College in North Carolina. In 1946 Aileen Osborn Webb also organized the School for American Craftsmen of the Rochester Institute of Technology.

After World War II, the universities and professional schools, stimulated by the G.I. bill, which subsidized veterans who went back to school, established workshops and provided materials on an unprecedented scale, fostering a whole new generation of artists and teachers of art. By then the movement in American painting called abstract expressionism* had won attention throughout the western world and expressed the American esthetic of the time so well that its counterpart appeared in every visual and plastic medium.

American artists emerging from the university system did not make orthodox distinctions among media. Having been exposed to all disciplines, materials, and techniques in art and craft courses, they made their choices freely, unfettered by traditional craft limits. This explains, for instance, how Peter Voulkos,* studying painting at Montana State College, happened to encounter clay and made it the medium of his art.

Formerly buried in the home economics or design departments of universities, crafts were now included in the regular curriculum of art departments. By the end of the 1950s the university had become the patron of the arts and crafts, employing the most creative talents to teach and train artist-craftsmen. A flood of publications and galleries, and a postwar society overflowing with material abundance further encouraged the making of objects. Among the major centers of such work today are the University of Wisconsin, Southern Illinois University, and the branches of the University of California and especially those at Berkeley, Davis, and Los Angeles. In addition, the summer workshop at Haystack Mountain School of Crafts at Deer Island, Me., has been a significant influence, while the Penland School of Crafts in Penland, N.C., which provides a year-round working program for craftsmen and their students, has been a focal point of craft work.

In 1957, in Asilomar, Cal., craftsmen from all over the United States met each other for the first time in a national conference (organized by the American Crafts Council). It was a milestone in this field, and such conferences are now held triannually. In 1960, the Museum of Contemporary Crafts was established by the American Crafts Council as the major showcase for the exhibition of crafts as creative expression. Then, in 1964, Mrs. Webb organized the World Crafts Council, which has brought together craftsmen from over eighty countries in conferences held in New York, Switzerland, Peru, Ireland, Turkey, and Canada over the past ten years.

The New Craftsman

In diversity of materials, forms, and concepts American craftsmen have extended the traditional confines of craft and pushed into wholly new creative areas. Refusing to allow the machine to take the making of things out of the creative human orbit, the new craftsman points up the difference between submissive, uncommitted labor, serving the power of the machine with little responsibility to the product, and independent, responsible work committed to producing esthetically satisfying objects. Modern craftsmanship identifies work with the process of self-creation: it works toward the transformation of life into things and things into life. The craftsman recognizes fully the liberating power of the machine, but he treats the machine as a tool that must serve him, not he it.

As recently as 1950, crafts in the United States were still considered a form of superficial artiness. The rapid growth of technology had created an atmosphere of contempt for what was regarded as a rather precious exercise

1

3

2

in creativity. Scorned on the one side by the machine culture, which could produce more rapidly and cheaply, and on the other by the art world, which sanctified the artist and placed his quest above worldly considerations, the American craftsman had to establish the creative authenticity and worth of his art.

The craftsman's first steps, taken in the 1950s and 1960s, were to free his work from competition with the machine that produces useful commodities for the market and to expand his creative vocabulary. Having been freed to exercise his skills, the range of his expression expanded enormously and the distinction between artists and craftsmen faded.

Another decisive change took place when the craftsman began to produce for an anonymous market, in contrast to the early craftsman who was part of a stable agricultural community. As his mobility increased, the craftsman lost direct contact with those for whom he was making things. In the isolation of his workshop or studio, the contemporary craftsman began to create objects that related to himself alone and expressed only his own feelings in relationship to his material.

The craftsman also found himself in the quixotic position of producing objects for a society that already has more things than it needs, and where nothing need last very long. This contrasts sharply with the economics of scarcity in other parts of the world, where traditional design guards against waste, where exquisitely exacting techniques have evolved with a minimum of materials and tools, and where labor is plentiful. America's wealth and the availability of tools and materials has allowed the American craftsman to experiment freely and to emphasize expressive content rather than utility. This has led him to an involvement in the actual making of the object from beginning to end, as compared with the artist-craftsmen of other countries who do only the designing and finishing and leave the technology to peasant craftsmen. Aside from the fact that there are no peasant craftsmen in America, the American craftsman finds that intimacy with tools and materials is a source of creative power. Paradoxically, since there is little folk tradition in America, the craftsmen must go to an art school or a university to learn about a craft.

This has also led to a questioning of traditional techniques and to personal invention of new ways of handling materials, new application of tools, new materials, and new tools.

Unlike the traditional craftsman, the American craftsman, then, is the product of the university or specialized school and has a background in painting and sculpture as well as design and craft techniques. He does his research in books and by traveling and studying in countries with a craft tradition, and is thus the product of international experience.

Craftsmen Since 1950

The primary media in which American craftsmen have distinguished themselves are clay fiber, glass, metal, and wood. The following are outstanding among the many excellent craftsmen who have emerged since 1950.

In studio pottery, Peter Voulkos made the original breakthrough in the early 1950s from traditional wheel-thrown pottery forms to free, expressive manipulation of the material, stressing sculptural values rather than functional ones. Voulkos taught and influenced many younger ceramists. Among them are Ron Nagle, known for his arresting series of cups in luminous color and boxed in plexiglass-lined wooden boxes, and Michael Frimkess, who paints comic-strip style political and social commentary on the surfaces of classical Greek and oriental shapes. Others who have made distinctive contributions to ceramics in America are: Robert Arneson,* Rudy Autio,* Maija Grotell,* Hui Ka Kwong,* James Melchert,* Kenneth Price,* Daniel Rhodes,* Paul Soldner,* and Marguerite Wildenhain.*

The growth of the textile culture in America has taken many forms—from loom construction and direct fiber manipulation in off-the-loom technique, to machine-produced fabrics originally designed on the loom. It has become the most diverse of the crafts. In printed fabrics, silk screen, tie-dye, as well as batik, handblocked and painted techniques have predominated. Two of the major designers of mass-produced textiles are Jack Lenor Larsen (1929–   ) and Dorothy Liebes (1899–1972). Larsen is notable for his adoption of the power loom as the production tool of the hand loom, thereby enlarging the scope of creative textile production. Since 1952, when he produced the

draperies for Lever House, New York City's first important post-World War II office building, he has designed upholstery and drapery fabrics for buildings internationally. His research into textile cultures all over the world, the richness of design concept, the variety of natural and synthetic yarns, and color range have all made his fabric collections the most comprehensive of their kind. Dorothy Liebes, fabric designer, consultant, and stylist, began her long and distinguished career specializing in custom hand-woven work for architects and decorators. National recognition came to her in 1939, when she headed the decorative arts section of the Golden Gate Exposition. Shortly thereafter she became associated with mass-produced fabrics as a stylist for home furnishings with major firms. Known for her color range and texture, and the introduction of metallic yarns in production weaving, she has had numerous major commissions for both architectural and apparel applications and has received many awards.

Among the many notable hand craftsmen in fiber during the 1950s and 1960s are Alice Adams,* Anni Albers, Lili Blumenau,* Trude Guermonprez,* Sheila Hicks,* Mary Walker Phillips,* Ed Rossbach,* Kay Sekimachi,* Walter Nottingham,* Lenore Tawney,* and Claire Zeisler.*

In glass the pioneering efforts of Harvey Littleton* throughout the 1960s, preceded by Dominick Labino,* and before that by Frederick Carder,* gave impetus to a high level of experimentation in glassblowing, literally and figuratively the most volatile of all crafts. Among the noteworthy younger artists in the medium are Dale Chihuly, known for blown-glass sculptures in exotic twisted and coiled shapes containing neon and other gases ignited by electrodes; and Joel Myers, who is both a studio craftsman and a stylist in industrial production. Marvin Lipofsky's work is characterized by the control with which he blows and draws out the glass close to its limits.

In enameling, Kenneth Bates and Paul Hultberg head a long list of gifted artists. Bates has held a preeminent position in the field for many years, and is also important for his teaching and writing. An innovator in the techniques of champléve, basse-taille, grisaille, en résille, and cloisonné, he draws

Handcrafts, Contemporary
1. *Paul Soldner. Ceramic plaque (platter), 1972. Museum of Contemporary Crafts, N.Y.*
2. *Maija Grotell. Vase, stoneware, dark brown clay, raised white slip decoration, semi-opaque white glaze. Cranbrook Academy of Art, Bloomfield Hills, Mich.*
3. *Peter Voulkos. Black ceramic pot, 1972. Museum of Contemporary Crafts, N.Y.*
4. *Ron Nagle. Cup with silk-screened photograph of Peter Voulkos, 1963, clay with brown and green luster glazes.*
5. *Rudy Autio. Button Pot, 1966, stoneware with slip glaze over main body, opaque white and felds-pathic glaze on collar and lid. Johnson Collection of Contemporary Crafts, Racine, Wis.*

his imagery from another interest of his, horticulture. His books are *Enameling, Principles and Practice* (1951), *Basic Design, Principles and Practices* (1963), and *The Enamelist* (1967). Paul Hultberg is best known for large abstract expressionist, architecturally scaled panels.

Fresh forms and textures in metalwork and jewelry have been developed in the last 25 years by such artists as Irena Brynner (n.d.–   ) and Sam Kramer (1913–64). In 1950 the former began making distinctively three-dimensional jewelry and body adornments which reflect her training in sculpture, oriental background (she emigrated to San Francisco from Manchuria in 1926), and knowledge of Etruscan body ornaments. Kramer, known for his flamboyant surrealistic creations, was one of the first American craftsmen to use jewelry forms in an expressive—and often bizarre—way. His organic shapes of cast and forged silver were frequently set with such offbeat items as glass eyes, moose teeth, and old bones. He influenced many young jewelry-makers after World War I. In the early 1960s, Stanley Lechtzin (1936–   ) was one of the first jewelry craftsmen to work with the electroforming process in which a metal skin adheres (by electrochemical attraction) to a master form which is then removed to leave the lightweight shell. The process opened the way for combinations of metals and new structural and textural possibilities for jewelry.

A leading silversmith, and one of the first contemporary artists to be associated with industry, John Prip (1922–   ) was designer of flatware (1957–60) and design consultant (1960–70) at Reed and Barton Silversmiths, in Taunton, Mass. His recent pieces of small jewelry and sculptures of precious metals tend to juxtapose clean geometric shapes and puddle shapes, often with a pearl set at the end of a delicate, wavy tendril. Prip's intimacy with his materials enables him to push a modest technical process to the limit of its potential.

John Paul Miller (1918–   ), one of the foremost American goldsmiths, is known for his extreme refinement of granulation techniques. His imagery is derived from animal and crustacean forms, as in *Armored Polyp* (1969, Johnson Coll.). In this work, several small pieces of sheet gold rest shield-like over flowing tendrils to which the granulation has been applied.

Other distinguished innovators have been: Michael J. Brandt, Jr., Ronald Senungetuk, Tom Thomason, J. Fred Woell, Merry Renk, Ruth and Svetozar Radakovitch, Charles Loloma, Margaret De Patta, Sam Wiener, Art Smith, Ronald Pearson, Olaf Skoogfors, Margaret Craver, Alma Eickerman, Ramona Solberg, Imogene Bailey Geiling, Philip Fike, Eleanor Moty, Arline Fisch.

The outstanding mosaicist in America is Jeanne Reynal (1903–   ); she has contributed a unique, painterly approach to the medium, investing it with the freedom and gesture of abstract painting. In the late 1960s she created elongated figurelike mosaic sculptures in the round, most of them over nine feet high, in a plastic mass imbedded with brilliant tesserae of precious and semiprecious stones.

In the field of woodworking, the values of sculptural form and integrity of the material have been brilliantly accommodated to the demands of function in the work of, among others, Arthur Carpenter,* Wharton Esherick,* Sam Maloof,* Wendell Castle,* and George Nakashima.*   (R.S.)

Happenings.

Collaborative events in which elements of theater are combined with the other arts in relatively loose performance situations. Although there are forerunners of happenings—the spontaneous cabaret performances during the dada* period, for instance—the term is associated with the activities of a group of artists in New York City during the late 1950s and the 1960s. One of the most active in the movement at its beginning was the sculptor Claes Oldenburg.* He described the group's intentions as a desire "to work between painting and sculpture; to invite public action and involvement; to create an altered reality with the full power of reality."

Sculptor Allan Kaprow, who was the first to use the term "happening," is often credited with the initial performance in the medium. In 1956, Kaprow transformed an exhibition of his collages into what he called a collage-environment, in which viewers were regaled with blinking lights and had to peer through slashed curtains to see the works. Later, Kaprow conceived the idea of making collages of people and things in action. At the same time, Oldenburg, Robert Whitman,* Red Grooms,* and Jim Dine* were working along the same lines. Soon after, they formed a loose group, collaborating in events for the public.

The happenings that developed from this initial collaboration generally were based on a lean scenario and much improvisation. In a happening an artist could use human dancers, a short film, spoken words, and crudely executed sculptural structures. Chance entered in the unpredictable behavior of the audience, which was often invited to participate freely in the happenings in the arena. The acceptance of chance was influenced by the theories of the avant-garde composer John Cage, who had long advocated the integration of the fortuitous event in his own works. Many critics regard Cage as the first exponent of happenings, referring to a 1952 performance at Black Mountain College, North Carolina, in which the dancer Merce Cunningham, the artist Robert Rauschenberg,* and the pianist David Tudor, among others, participated. Cage had placed the audience midway in the room and the performers worked around the audience, dancing, projecting films on the ceiling, reading poetry simultaneously, and cranking out music on an old phonograph.

As happenings gained momentum toward 1960, the various practitioners attempted to define the specific nature of their art. Kaprow sought to give his works mythical overtones. He moved out of the storefront and loft situation into city and country landscapes, inviting the public to collaborate in the almost ritualistic succession of scored events. Whitman moved closer to theater, preparing sequences with different sets and planning actions within given settings. Dine moved toward the psycho-drama in happenings in which threatening and macabre effects were stressed. Oldenburg, a sculptor by temperament, concentrated on activating responses to objects in motion. "My aim," he has written, "is the perfection of the details of the events rather than any composition . . . the audience is considered an object and its behavior as events."

Happenings continue to interest the artists who prefer hybrid forms. They have emcompassed aspects of the dance, of composed music, and of vanguard modes of theater. To some

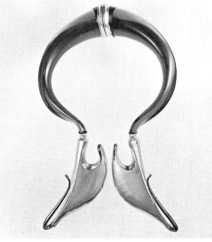

Handcrafts, Contemporary
1. *Jeanne Reynal.* Woman Clothed with Son, *mosaic. Collection of the artist.*
2. *Harvey Littleton.* Pile-up, 1972, *glass sculpture, offhand blue rods and crystal rods, ground, polished and bent gray plate glass. Toledo Museum of Art, Ohio.*
3. *Joel Philip Myers.* Hand forms, *glass, offhand blown, hot-tooled with applied base and thumb, trailed pattern. Toledo Museum of Art, Ohio.*
4. *Stanley Lechtzin.* Torque, 1972, *green polyester and electroformed silver. Collection of the artist.*

degree, discontinuity of imagery and the absence of the traditional linear progression of plot differentiate happenings from theater, but finally, a happening partakes more of theater than of any other art form. (D.A.)

Hard-Edge.

A term coined in the late 1950s to distinguish the work of many artists who had begun to oppose the tenets of abstract expressionism* by producing clean, precisely defined edges of forms. In reality there has always been "hard-edge" painting and sculpture, though the distinction is often couched in the term "classical" (hard-edge) as opposed to "romantic" (abstract expressionism). The 17th-century American "limners," as well as John Singleton Copley,* Ralph Earl,* William Harnett,* the "precisionists" Georgia O'Keeffe* and Charles Sheeler,* and Stuart Davis* could all be considered "hard-edge" painters. The Dutch abstractionist Piet Mondrian and the neo-plasticists, with their cool, geometric abstractions, are an obvious link to the "hard-edge" painters of the 1960s. Because of the overwhelming success of abstract expressionism, with its amorphous, loosely-brushed forms, we tend to forget that such prototypes of the hard-edge artists as Alexander Liberman* and Ellsworth Kelly* were also working during the 1950s. Their painting and sculpture, with its meticulously delineated flat planes of color, provided the groundwork for the extension of hard-edge into pop art,* op art,* "figurative" painting, color-field,* and "object sculpture." This original emphasis on "edge," with its clear definition of "area" and "boundary," was one of the factors that made it possible to fabricate art industrially during the 1960s. (See also Shaped Canvas, Minimal Art.) (E.C.G.)

Hardenbergh, Henry Janeway (1847–1918).

Architect. Born in New Brunswick, N.J., he attended Hasbrouck Institute in Jersey City and in 1865 began his architectural apprenticeship in the office of Detlef Lienau,* who had been trained in classical and neo-Grec* styles. In 1870 he set up practice in New York City, specializing in hotels, apartment houses, and commercial buildings. His design followed German and French Renaissance styles, rather freely interpreted, with considerable emphasis on the visible expression of structure. This was evident in his bold use of horizontal band courses, quoins (corner blocks), squat columns, and high roof gables. He generally favored brick, with stone trim and terracotta ornament.

His New York hotels were renowned for their bold exteriors and opulent interiors, beginning with the modest Hotel Albert (1883) on University Place, and progressing to the spectacular Waldorf Hotel (1892) at 33rd Street and Fifth Avenue. The addition of the Astor Hotel (1897) to the Waldorf (creating the Waldorf-Astoria) provided the wealthy of New York with a setting to display their furs and jewels to advantage. His other hotels, the Manhattan (1896) and the Martinique (1897), were also fine in their day, but the Plaza (1906) at 59th Street, facing Central Park, outstripped all in elegance. Two hotels in Washington, the Raleigh (1898) and the New Willard (1898), brought elegance to the capital, as did the low-lying Copley-Plaza to Boston.

His Dakota, an apartment house built in 1884 in the open spaces at 72nd Street and Central Park West, and still in use, was considered a marvel at the time. Only the technology of the great hotels that preceded it made possible its many innovations. Several fine commercial buildings, such as the handsome Astor Building (1885) on Wall Street, round out his architectural works of note. Hardenbergh served as president of the Architectural League of New York in 1901. (A.B.)

Harding, Chester (1792–1866).

Portrait painter born in Conway, N.H. His father brought his family from New Hampshire to New York City, where the boy grew up in poverty. After working as a laborer and house and sign painter, he learned portraiture from an itinerant artist. Seeking work, he made trips to Cincinatti, St. Louis, and Kentucky, where he joined his brother, Horace, as a cabinetmaker; then the two took up portrait painting together.

Chester found that he had a knack at this new trade and was overwhelmed by the ease with which he could find work at $25 a head. From there on, traveling around, he rode a slowly rising wave of success. Daniel Boone was his first sitter of eminence. He went to Boston, hoping, as so many did, for a word of encouragement from Gilbert Stuart.* Stuart was friendly, commissions were plentiful and in Boston Harding suddenly found himself becoming a successful painter. The best people came to be painted, fascinated by this huge, earnest frontiersman with his penetrating eye and sure hand. They called it "Harding fever," and the same excitement of fashionable patronage came again when he visited England in 1823. He returned three years later, painted in Boston for a few years, then toured other American cities. He produced over a thousand portraits, distinguished primarily by bluff, relentless honesty. His portraits of women are more sensitive to character than those of men, as can be seen in his *Mrs. Thomas Brewster Coolidge* (1828–30) and *Mrs. Blake* (c.1845–50, Metropolitan). His autobiography, *Egotistography*, describes his extraordinary rise from the western frontier to the salons of Boston and London. (C.C.S.)

Hardy, Jeremiah Pearson (1800–87).

Painter and engraver. Born in Pelham, N.H., he moved with his family to the Bangor, Me., area in 1811. He is said to have had some instruction in art in Boston in 1821 with David Brown and later in New York with Samuel F. B. Morse.* Although largely self-taught, he was far from being a primitive; he developed a personal and quite professional style which only occasionally showed the lack of thorough academic training. About 1827 he returned to Bangor, where he lived until his death.

As a portrait painter working in the isolation of the Penobscot River Valley, Hardy developed his natural acuteness of observation and expressed himself with sensitive draftsmanship, luminous color, and a feeling for mood. *Catherine Wheeler Hardy and Her Daughter* (c. 1842, Boston), typical of his more ambitious portraiture, illustrates his ability to create a feeling of melancholy detachment. His exotic bust-length portrait of *Sarah Molasses* (1825, Tarrantine Club, Bangor) shows the daughter of a chief of the Penobscot Indians decked out in all her primitive finery. A good portrait, it has the added interest of showing the costume of a Maine Indian early in the 19th century. *The Artist's Rose Garden* (1879, Colby College Art Museum) is at once a portrait, a landscape, and a genre painting, depicting the artist's daughter, Ann, seen full length as she waters flowers.

There are no known major genre paintings by Hardy, but he and his daughter were painters of fruit and flower still lifes, and many examples, mostly in private collections, attest to their skill.

(H.W.W.)

Hardy Holzman Pfeiffer Associates.
An architectural firm founded in 1963. It is among the most interesting of younger architectural groups in its exploration of permissive and so-called "nonarchitecture" forms and its building of uncommon architecture from standardized parts and from existing buildings. Hugh Hardy studied at Princeton (1954) and worked with Eero Saarinen* and Jo Mielziner; Malcolm Holzman studied at Pratt Institute (1963) and worked with John Graham & Company and Kelly & Gruzen; Norman Pfeiffer studied at the University of Washington and Columbia (1965) and worked with Kirk, Wallace & McKinley. Among the leaders of supermannerist architecture, Hardy Holzman Pfeiffer early explored mannerist optical devices such as supergraphics* in interior design and planning and also investigated "formless" and underground architecture. In a series of houses they broke away from rectangular spaces and designed contradictory and unexpected interiors with many diagonals belying the exteriors. Ultimately, this residential idiom was developed for a larger scale condominium complex, The Cloisters, in Cincinnati, Ohio (1971).

As their first ventures in public building, they showed what could be done with existing architecture, converting a former automobile showroom into a neighborhood children's museum (MUSE, Brooklyn, N.Y., 1968). For several performing arts facilities they converted older buildings: a park building (Shelter Theatre, Playhouse in the Park, Cincinnati, 1963), a school auditorium (Phillips Exeter Academy, 1969), and carriage houses (Taylor Theater, Lockport, N.Y., 1969); and for the Newark Community Center of the Arts, Newark, N.J. (1961). Meanwhile, they had also designed one of the significant regional theaters of the decade, the Cincinnati Playhouse in the Park (1968). Around 1970 they began to show a new kind of art work in architecture in the use of industrialized systems: in a school (Bartholomew County School, Columbus, Ind., 1972), in a projected museum design (Brooklyn Children's

1. **Henry Janeway Hardenbergh.** *Plaza Hotel, N.Y., 1906.*
2. **Chester Harding.** *Mrs. Blake, c.1845–50. Metropolitan Museum of Art, N.Y.*

Museum, Brooklyn, 1971), in an innovative theater facility (Tufts University, Medford, Mass., 1971), and in a master plan and initial buildings for an educational complex (Shaw University, Raleigh, N.C. 1970). (C.R.S.)

Hare, David (1917–   ).
He early gained recognition for his experimental color photography but soon turned to sculpture. Born in New York, N.Y., Hare studied briefly there and in Arizona and Colorado, returning to New York at a time when a number of European surrealists had taken refuge there during World War II. Hare's precocious knowledge of the arts recommended him to them and he was made editor (1940–42) of the surrealist journal *VVV*. During this period his sculpture developed along generally surrealist lines, with emphasis on metamorphosing forms in a threatening atmosphere. His admiration for the Swiss sculptor Alberto Giacometti was apparent in the works he showed during the late 1940s, and, like Giacometti, he won the attention of the existentialist philosopher and writer Jean-Paul Sartre, who wrote on his work. Hare's first exhibitions were at the exclusively surrealist gallery of Julien Levy. There his works were noticed by the Museum of Modern Art, which showed him in the important "14 Americans" exhibition in 1946.

During the 1950s, Hare retreated from the menacing symbols of his surrealist period and began working with modeled, figurative images. His nudes and heads were widely remarked and often exhibited. Always restless, Hare explored the possibilities of many media, including welding and mobile structures. In the mid-1960s he paused to devote himself for a few years to painting. Hare has often had one-man shows in New York, and his works have been included in many international exhibitions, including two São Paulo biennials (1951 and 1957), the International Sculpture show at the Musée Rodin in Paris (1956), and the Brussels World's Fair (1962). He is an agile writer and has published several essays. In 1940 he collaborated with Dr. Clark Whistler in producing a portfolio of color photographs on the American Indian. (D.A.)

Harnett, William Michael (1848–92).
Still-life painter, born in Clonakilty,

1. **William Michael Harnett.** After the Hunt, 1885. California Palace of the Legion of Honor, San Francisco.
2. **David Hare.** Sunrise, c.1954–55, welded steel. Albright-Knox Art Gallery, Buffalo, N.Y.

Ireland, but raised in Philadelphia. Harnett came of a family of artisans and he began his career as an engraver of table silver. This training helped develop the remarkable precision and surety in draftsmanship that distinguish his painting.

Harnett received some education at the Pennsylvania Academy of the Fine Arts and in 1871 moved to New York City, where he attended night classes at Cooper Union while working in the silver shops. In 1874 he left the silver trade and set up as a still-life painter. The following year he first exhibited at the National Academy of Design.* His career, which lasted only eighteen years, divides into three equal periods: 1874 to 1880, mostly in Philadelphia; 1880 to 1886, mostly in Munich; and 1886 to his death in 1892, entirely in New York.

In the first period he specialized in small, modest still lifes of mugs and pipes on table tops or of books, pens, and ink bottles; in these he continues the much earlier Philadelphia tradition of Raphaelle Peale.* His old-fashioned quality is, indeed, the clue to his entire career. In his own time criticism derided him for it and his appeal was primarily to old-fashioned and not very knowledgeable collectors. As a result, his career is very thinly documented, and when, in the 1930s, surrealism* and abstract art* caused a reevaluation of Harnett's precise, almost hallucinatory, and often fantastic style, there was little biographical information available. Inappropriate stylistic criteria for Harnett were therefore generally accepted, and the works of his contemporaries, notably John Frederick Peto,* were widely circulated as his, many of these works bearing forged Harnett signatures.

In addition to the mug-and-pipe pictures and the writing-table still lifes, there are a few larger canvases from Harnett's first period, notably *The Artist's Card Rack* (1879, Metropolitan). This work follows an old but not very common tradition: strips of tape are tacked to a door and hold a clutter of envelopes and cards to its surface. The almost total flatness of this pictorial device is what counts. Eye-fooling illusionism—*trompe l'oeil*—such as Harnett practices abhors deep space. The more shallow the space, the greater the illusion, and if the third dimension can be eliminated almost entirely, as it is in the card-rack motif, the success of the

illusion is greatly enhanced. That is the real reason why Harnett and his school so often painted paper money; there is nothing flatter than a five-dollar bill. So, likewise Harnett delights in subjects like *Music and Good Luck* (1888, Metropolitan) wherein fairly shallow but not completely flat objects, such as a violin and bow, are placed on a door or wall that holds the eye at the picture plane and prevents its further progress into space.

Harnett began his European career in 1880 by greatly reducing the scale of his tabletop still lifes; some are actually miniatures. Toward the end of his European sojourn, he went to the opposite extreme. His four paintings of weapons and game, collectively known as *After the Hunt,* are among the largest works of his life, and the last of them (1885, California Palace of the Legion of Honor, San Francisco) was both his largest and most celebrated work. It hung from 1886 to the Prohibition year of 1918 in Theodore Stewart's fancy saloon near the New York City Hall. Every other fancy saloon in the United States had to have a version of it, and for a quarter of a century the making of plagiarisms and paraphrases of *After the Hunt* became a major industry among American painters, including Haberle,* Peto, and Chalfant.*

Highly characteristic of Harnett in his last years is a tabletop still life set before a shallow space boxed in with paneling, with the objects on the table composed in pyramidal form. There are more Harnetts of this kind than of any other (see, for example, *Emblems of Peace,* 1890, Springfield Museum of Art, Mass.) but none before 1880. They recall still lifes of the 17th-century Dutch masters, especially in their emphasis upon rich and precious objects. But the last period also abounds in paintings of highly vernacular subjects, like those of horseshoes.

Harnett's reputation, practically nonexistent during his lifetime among those whose opinions mattered, revived by a single exhibition at the Downtown Gallery in New York City in 1939. Long neglect has also meant the loss of most of his works; of the 500 pictures he probably painted, only about 160 are now known to exist. (A.F.)

Harrison, Peter (1716–75).
Architect, merchant, and farmer. Born in York, England, but in 1739 he came to

Newport, R.I., in his brother's trading vessel. He outfitted another vessel and was active in trading until 1748, when he settled in Newport. While in England in 1747–48 he evidently studied building styles and bought the architectural books from which he gleaned most of his basic ideas. Hearing of his interest, founders of the Redwood Library in Newport asked him for plans, which he sent from England in 1748. The Library, completed in 1750, reveals Harrison's enthusiasm for the movement to convert English architecture to the Italian style of Palladio.

Other commissions soon followed, such as that for King's Chapel, Boston (1749–54), the first sizeable cut-stone structure in America. Owing to high costs, the portico and balustrade were not added until 1787 and the steeple was never built, but the interior, based on English pattern books, was elegant and much admired.

He spent the next decade in trading, real estate, and farming, all of which were lucrative until the financial collapse in the French and Indian War. During this period he designed only a stone lighthouse and the complicated fortifications for Fort George on Goat Island (the latter never completed). Mercantile friends in Newport selected him to design Touro Synagogue (1759–63), for which Harrison relied on designs in a book on the English architect Inigo Jones. The interior is well-proportioned and enhanced by elegant classical decoration. The merchants then asked Harrison to design the Brick Market near the Newport wharves. No common market house, it stood as a model of taste for many decades and is still intact. His last and richest interior design was that of Christ Church, Cambridge (1760–61). Here he combined elements from various architectural authorities to create a design of considerable originality. A contemporary described the interior as having "a beauty and elegance not unbecoming the majesty of religion." Records exist of other houses by Harrison, including his own, called Leamington Farm, Newport (1747); Governor Wentworth's in New Hampshire (1768–70); and Winthrop House, New London (1754). In debt and associated with the hated Tories, Harrison left Newport for New Haven in 1766; there he became collector of customs and died amidst a changing world.

The few buildings Harrison designed were surprisingly excellent considering that his architectural knowledge came solely from observation and books. He showed a sense of taste beyond that of any other American designer before the 1780s, and although he had little influence on other designers, and no pupils, his buildings were much appreciated. (P.F.N.)

Hart, George Overbury, nicknamed "Pop" (1868–1933).
Painter known for lively, informal watercolors, etchings, and lithographs. Born in Cairo, Ill., he traveled through Europe, Egypt, the South Seas, South America, and Mexico, studying briefly at the Chicago Art Institute and the Académie Julien in Paris. For many years he made his living by painting signs and movie sets. His undisciplined but warm, human sketches of genre scenes observed on his travels received little recognition before the 1920s, when his prints began to be included in museum collections.

Hart, Joel Tanner (1810–77).
Sculptor. Known primarily for his busts and statues of Henry Clay. Born on the Kentucky frontier, he was apprenticed to a stonecutter in Lexington, where he observed Shobal Vail Clevenger* modeling a bust. Hart began to model portraits; among these early efforts were busts of Henry Clay and Andrew Jackson. In 1845 he went east, where he obtained commissions for portrait busts, which he executed in a naturalistic style. His big opportunity came when a Virginia group commissioned him to do a full-length marble statue of Henry Clay. To produce the piece he went to Florence, Italy, in 1849, where he worked on little else for ten years.

In 1859 he returned briefly to America for the unveiling of the statue. It was acclaimed and replicas were ordered for Louisville and New Orleans; critics, however, felt the vitality and heroic quality of the head were diminished by excessive emphasis on detail and Clay's ill-fitting attire. In the 1850s Hart devoted himself to developing a pointing machine that would transfer the shape and proportions of a subject's head directly into clay, thereby saving much time in modeling portrait busts, but the device was never completely perfected. Although Hart's total production was not large and was faulty in

anatomy and perspective, he was one of the best-known American sculptors of the mid-19th century. (W.C.)

Hart, William (1823-94) and
James MacDougal (1828–1901).
Scottish-born brothers, brought to Albany, N.Y. in 1831, whose repetitive, pastoral landscapes and animal paintings brought them high praise in the 1860s and 1870s. William began as a portraitist, and after extensive travels opened a studio in New York City in 1854. He exhibited widely and became a member of the National Academy of Design* in 1855. His work, though rather primitive, was noted for its minute detail and a fresh unsentimental quality. His younger brother James apprenticed at fifteen to a sign painter, studied in Düsseldorf in 1850, and opened a studio in Albany in 1853 and in New York in 1857. He worked in a similar mode, often portraying cattle standing in rivers, yet during the 1860s he painted several impressive landscapes that depict specific topography and a quality of real light. During the 1870s the quality of their work declined. Like many other members of the Hudson River School,* they both also painted portraits. (T.E.S.)

Hartigan, Grace (1922–   ).
Painter. Born in Newark, N.J., she worked in 1942–47 as a mechanical draftsman in the war industry, while studying painting at night with Isaac Lane Muse. Since her debut in 1950, she has had eighteen one-man exhibitions and has appeared in numerous group shows, including the Museum of Modern Art's "Twelve Americans" (1956), São Paulo Biennial (1957), the Brussels World's Fair (1958), and Documenta II, Kassel (1959). In the struggle to find a personal manner, she turned to abstract expressionism.* As a member of the second generation of the "New York School" she sought, like Willem de Kooning,* to carry figurative art into abstraction, while employing brilliant expressive color both formally and psychologically. Nature has always been a fundamental point of departure in her work, from her earliest "collage still-lifes," through her abstract interpretations of lower Manhattan of the 1950s, to her latest work, which is even more specifically figurative. She writes: "I want an art that is not 'abstract' and not 'realistic' . . . my 'sub-

ject' concerns that which is vulgar and vital in American modern life, and the possibilities of its transcendence into the beautiful. I do not wish to *describe* my subject. . . . I want to distill it until I have its essence. Then the rawness must be resolved into form and unity." Such a painting is *The Grand Street Brides,* inspired by a window display of mannequins—studied from a series of photographs—and then recreated by the artist.

The impact of her work comes not from sheer size, but from her brilliant color (she often achieves mosaic or stained-glass effects by surrounding her forms with thick black outlines), her sensuous manipulation of paint, and from the formal resolution of conflicting forces. Typical of her paintings is *Billboard* (1957, Minneapolis).
(E.C.G.)

Hartley, Marsden (1877–1943).
Painter. He was born in Lewiston, Me., and his roots in that state provided continuity during a life of restless travel. In 1892 he went to Cleveland to study art, and then to New York City in 1898 to attend the William M. Chase* school and later the National Academy of Design.* By 1908 he was painting the Maine mountains in distorted, flattened shapes and nervous, broken color, expressively intensified to reflect his personal mysticism, as in *The Mountains* (1909, Columbus). The painter Maurice Prendergast* took an interest in his work, and he had a one-man show at Alfred Stieglitz'* Photo-Secession Gallery 291 in 1909. With the help of Stieglitz and of the perceptive Arthur B. Davies,* he went abroad in 1912. By this time his painting reflected his intense admiration for Albert Pinkham Ryder* and also his discovery of the work of the modern European masters Cézanne and Picasso.

Going to France and Germany, Hartley entered a period of some ten years of experimentation, influenced by fauvism* and cubism,* then by Kandinsky and the German expressionists, by the dada* movement and again by later forms of cubism. He returned from time to time to painting landscape heightened by expressionist or symbolist means, but his most original series of paintings stems from the period he spent in Germany at the start of World War I (1914–15). He formed a friendship with the painter Franz

Marc, who invited him to exhibit with the expressionists of *Der Blaue Reiter* group. Hartley's painting at the time was symbolist in form, although he insisted it had no symbolist meanings, being merely a recombination of images usually observed (*Painting No. 5*, 1914–15, Whitney), such as motifs derived from the signs and decorations of German military life, expressed with a vividness of color and a sensuousness of painted surface unique in his work.

Hartley was active in avant-garde exhibitions, including the pioneering "Younger American Painters" show of 1910, the Armory Show* of 1913, and the Forum exhibition of 1916. He traveled to Taos and Santa Fe, and during the 1920s he painted a number of pictures from his memories of New Mexico. Returning to Europe in 1921, he gradually worked away from cubism toward a rugged expressionism based on the forms of nature. During the late 1920s he painted in the south of France, entering a period of strong Cézanne influence. This he translated to New England subjects at the beginning of the 1930s. After a trip to Mexico in 1932 and a winter in the German Alps, he returned and began to work seriously with Northeastern subjects, his painting after 1937 centering around his yearly visits to Maine. He developed his final style, almost painfully brusque and direct, in which blocky, powerful forms are shaped and driven by an expressionist emotion. His themes run from waterfalls to mountains to breaking waves on the coast, as in *Evening Storm, Schoodic, Maine* (1942, Modern Museum); they also included still lifes of ropes and fishermen's gear and the fishermen themselves in the simple, stern ritual of their lives, as in *Fishermen's Last Supper—Nova Scotia* (private collection, 1940–41). The paintings of his last years, which form a Maine epic, climax his long struggle to find a style and theme to convey the strong current of his innermost feelings for nature.

(D.W.S.)

Harvey, George (1801–78).
A landscape, genre, and miniature painter. Harvey, a native of Tottenham, England, came to America at the age of twenty. For several years he lived in the West and in Ohio, Michigan, and Canada before beginning a career as an artist. He settled in Brooklyn before

1. *Grace Hartigan.* Hobby Shop Human, 1966.
2. *Marsden Hartley.* Painting Number 5, 1914–15. Whitney Museum of American Art, N.Y.

1828 and was elected to the National Academy of Design.* In 1829 he moved to Boston where he became successful as a miniature painter, completing four hundred likenesses. He made a trip to England to study, but was back in this country about 1833. He helped design Washington Irving's home, "Sunnyside," and he himself built a house nearby at Hastings-on-Hudson. There he started on the project for which he is best known, a series of "atmospheric views" of American landscapes. In 1838 he again visited London; two years later he returned with the intention of having forty of his delicate and charming watercolor landscapes engraved and published by subscription. The text was to be written by him and edited by Irving. The project failed for lack of sufficient subscribers, but four of the scenes were engraved and published in 1841. About twenty of the original paintings are now owned by the New York Historical Society. These watercolors (for example, *Hastings Landing—Palisades Rocks in Shadow*) reflect his early training as a miniature painter and are important for the study of luminism* in American landscape painting. He excelled in capturing the ever-varying atmospheric conditions of the American climate. While predominantly a watercolorist, he also occasionally worked in oil: *The Apostle Oak* (1844, New York Hist.), which depicts boys playing near a country school, demonstrates his skill in combining figures and landscape. In 1850 *Harvey's Illustrations of our Country* was published in Boston.

Records are lacking to document his career after 1850. He seems to have made his home in England but to have made trips to America until a couple of years before his death. His nephew of the same name (c.1835–after 1920), a pupil of his, was also a landscape and portrait painter. (H.W.W.)

Hassam, Childe (1859–1935).
Impressionist painter, born in Dorchester, Mass. He left high school to go to work in Boston, where his natural aptitude led him into wood engraving and then in the 1880s and '90s into illustration. Among the publications for which he illustrated were *Scribner's* and *Harper's* and books such as Howells' *Venetian Life*. In his spare time he took lessons at the Boston Art Club, then at the Lowell Institute, and finally with

1

2

1. *Childe Hassam.* Sunny Blue Sea, *1913. National Collection of Fine Arts, Smithsonian Institution, Washington, D.C.*
2. *Childe Hassam.* Boston Common at Twilight, *1885-86. Museum of Fine Arts, Boston.*

Ignaz Gaugengigl, a young German painter.

Hassam repeatedly tried new media and subject matter with encouraging success. He began doing watercolors, went on sketching trips to paint landscapes, and soon set up a studio next to that of George Fuller,* an established Boston artist who became a good friend. In 1883, when he had begun sending his paintings to exhibitions, he made an extended tour of Europe. His subsequent painting showed great assurance and skillful composition. Although his colors were quiet browns and grays, light played a major role in his pictures, as in *Boston Common at Twilight* (1885–86, Boston). In 1886 he went again to Europe, settling for three years in Paris, where he supported himself by illustrations and the sale of paintings. He studied briefly at the Académie Julien, but the principal influence on his work came from the paintings of the impressionists. By 1887 his *Grand Prix Day* (Boston) showed an entirely new and more sparkling application of color. Hassam stressed the English roots of his landscape art, but by the time he returned to the United States, the broken brushwork and high key of his sun-flooded landscapes bore an unmistakable debt to French impressionism,* and he quite naturally fell in with Edmund Tarbell,* Frank W. Benson,* Robert Reid,* J. Alden Weir* and John Twachtman,* with whom he joined in The Ten* of 1898. His early adoption of impressionism seemed to cause little difficulty to juries. Before leaving Paris in 1889 he received a bronze medal at the Exposition Universal—the first of thirty-five major prizes he was to win in an exceptionally successful career. From the mid-1890s to his death he missed hardly an annual exhibition at the National Academy of Design, the Carnegie International, or the Pennsylvania Academy of the Fine Arts, to name only three of the many organizations that awarded him honors.

Hassam, like other earlier American impressionists, painted his most lyrical and freely-brushed atmospheric works in the early 1890s, as in *The Room of Flowers* (1894, private collection). In his later style, though his technique varied from brusque to delicate, he was consistent in simplifying objects and forms, and in emphasizing flat patterns in shapes. His surfaces were built up of short, dry, positive strokes, and color areas tended to be massed together. Though he usually worked in a fresh, high key, he did not stress color vibration at the expense of form (*Sunny Blue Sea,* 1913, National Coll.). His painting, whether of landscape or interiors, was zestful and cheerful. He retained an illustrator's interest in descriptive setting and an American touch of realism that added substance to forms that shimmered in impressionist light. There was, in fact, an underlying conservatism in his viewpoint which, although it did not deaden his most vigorous work, resulted in an arid quality that became increasingly pronounced in his late years. He was represented in the Armory Show* in 1913 but was later outspokenly critical of its more radical tendencies.

Hassam is above all associated with landscapes of summer resorts in New England and views of New York's squares and streets—a notably colorful series shows displays of flags during World War I—and also apartment interiors, often with women standing against the glow of curtained windows. He painted portraits and nudes—sometimes as nymphs in his landscapes. He began serious work in etching in 1915, and in 1917–18 he turned out a number of lithographs. Much of his late work shows scenes around Easthampton, N.Y., where he spent his last seventeen summers.   (D.W.S.)

Hathaway, Rufus (1770–1822).
Born in Freetown, Mass., he was a self-taught portrait artist and carver. His highly stylized late-18th-century figures with feathered hats, and their arbitrary placement of floral and animal accoutrements, as his *Lady with Pets* (c.1790, Garbisch Coll.), suggest much earlier authorship. He settled in Duxbury, Mass., in 1795, and ultimately became the town doctor.

Haviland, John (1792–1852).
Architect. Born at Gundenham Manor, Somerset, England. Apprenticed to architect James Elmes, he supervised construction of at least one building, St. John's Church, Chichester (1812–13). The design was Greek-inspired, but the interior gallery was held up by cast-iron pillars such as Haviland often used in later buildings. An aunt had married a Russian count, and Haviland visited them in St. Petersburg in 1815 and promptly entered the Imperial Corps of Engineers. He then decided to travel to America. Arriving at Philadelphia in 1816, he formed a school of architectural drawing with the painter Hugh Bridport. He built his reputation, however, on the publication of *The Builder's Assistant* (3 vols., 1818–21), which was not only accurate but illustrated the Greek orders for the first time in an American book. He also published the *House Carpenter's Book of Prices and Rules* (1819).

Prisons were among Haviland's outstanding designs. Of the more than one hundred architectural projects he worked on, the most important in the prison category were the Eastern State Penitentiary in Philadelphia (1823–35), Western State Penitentiary in Pittsburgh, and New Jersey State, Rhode Island State, and Missouri State Prisons. He was recognized internationally when prison authorities from Europe visited America in the 1830s and found his radial plan and individual cells to their liking. He did two outstanding churches in Philadelphia: the First Presbyterian (1820–22), an early Greek revival* design, and St. Andrew's Episcopal (1821–24). Among his public buildings were the Pennsylvania Institute for the Deaf and Dumb (1824–25), now the Philadelphia College of Art; Miner's Bank, Pottsville, Pa. (1828), sheathed with iron over brick; Franklin Institute (1825), now the Atwater Kent Museum, Philadelphia; and the "Tombs," the Halls of Justice and City Prison, N.Y. (1836–38), with columns and coved cornice in the Egyptian style. In Haverhill, Mass., he built an early Greek revival house with recessed Ionic columns. Though Haviland's prison designs most impressed the public, it was his large practice and his architectural publications that made him one of the most prominent architects of his era. Twelve volumes of his notes and drawings are in the Somerset County Record Office in Taunton, Mass.   (P.F.N.)

Hawes, Josiah Johnson, see Southworth, Albert Sand.

Hawthorne, Charles Webster (1872–1930).
Figure painter. Born in Illinois, he studied art in New York with Frank Vincent DuMond and George De Forest Brush* before joining William Merritt

Chase* as a student and assistant. Hawthorne is primarily identified with Provincetown, Mass., where he established the Cape Cod School of Art in 1899 and painted rugged fishermen with a strength that caused him to be likened to the New York realists of The Eight* (*The Family,* n.d., Albright). His range also included deft, restrained portraits of women and children. His figures confront the viewer with quiet and refreshing directness. The academically disciplined drawing and composition added poise and strength when the works were not overly repetitive. He was influential as a teacher, conducting classes not only in Provincetown but also at the Art Students League,* the National Academy of Design,* and the Chicago Art Institute.　　(D.W.S.)

Heade, Martin Johnson (1819–1904). Romantic painter whose career was one of the longest and most varied of any American artist, Heade was born in Lumberville, Pa. Before he was twenty he had studied with his neighbor, the Quaker painter Edward Hicks.* His earliest works, dating from 1839, are portraits that recall Hicks' unsophisticated approach. During the 1840s, Heade slowly developed his portrait style until it approximated the popular academic mode. He also produced genre scenes, only one of which is known to have survived, and occasional landscapes that are crude reflections of the prevailing Hudson River School* style. Beginning in the 1840s, he exhibited his work at the leading artists' institutions in the east.

Heade traveled a great deal. As a young man, about 1837–40, he had taken a long trip to Italy, France, and England. In the next decade, he worked in New York, Brooklyn, Philadelphia, and Trenton, N.J. During the 1850s he was mainly a journeyman portrait painter whose commissions were largely for copies of works by better-known men. He traveled over much of America, painting, speculating in land, and probably trying other professions as well. In 1852, he was in St. Louis; in 1853, in Chicago; then in Trenton; and by 1857 his studio was in Rhode Island. At forty he had yet to produce a truly distinguished picture. In 1859 he made a fortuitous move to New York City, renting quarters in the Tenth Street Studio Building, which housed many leading landscape painters. Soon

Heade began to concentrate on landscapes and shore views. His style was influenced by the intensely colored, highly realistic canvases of Frederic E. Church,* who became a good friend. He was probably affected also by the coast scenes of John F. Kensett* and by the seascapes of Fitz Hugh Lane.*

By the mid-1860s, Heade had given up portraiture and genre and was painting sensitive marsh views and almost surreal seascapes. His favorite subject became salt marshes—at Newbury, Mass., and in Rhode Island during the 1860s; in New Jersey in the 1870s; and in Florida late in his life. He also had a lifelong interest in the sea, which he could portray as soft and misty or as chilling and terrible. Perhaps his single masterpiece is the supremely intense *Approaching Storm: Beach Near Newport,* (c.1860, Boston). Although he learned much from Church and the Hudson River School, he never shared their interest in popular places and sites. Rather, his concern, was in painting light and air, and he would always sacrifice topographical accuracy for compositional effect; thus he is often considered one of the masters of American luminism.* He was particularly interested in moments of natural drama and change, such as dawn and sunset, or the approach or lifting of a sudden storm. Beginning in the 1860s with a series of mixed flowers in Victorian vases, he went on in the next decade to do many rose and apple blossom subjects.

In 1863, he traveled to Brazil to make sketches for a book on the hummingbirds of that country. After painting a series of small hummingbird pictures, he went to London in 1865 to have them chromolithographed. Although the project was abandoned, a few trial proofs of the prints survive. He returned to South America in 1866 and in 1870, and after the last journey began a series of dramatic paintings of orchids and hummingbirds in a tropical landscape. These pictures are unprecedented in American art, both in their high-keyed richness and in their subject matter, which combined hummingbirds (previously used only in botanical illustrations) with orchids. The most powerful of these pictures date from the 1870s (an outstanding example is *Two Fighting Hummingbirds with Two Orchids,* 1875, Whitney), though Heade used the subject at least until 1901. He

1

2

1. ***Martin Johnson Heade.*** Approaching Storm: Beach near Newport, *c.1860.*
2. ***Martin Johnson Heade.*** Orchids and Spray Orchids with Hummingbirds, *c.1865.*
3. ***Martin Johnson Heade.*** Passion Flowers and Hummingbirds, *c.1865. All, Museum of Fine Arts, Boston (Karolik Collection).*

3

was thus perhaps the only 19th-century American whose work in both landscape and still life is of importance.

Heade was never popular either among other artists or patrons. His work gained occasional recognition, but when he left New York for Washington, D.C. in 1881, it was quickly forgotten. In 1885 he moved permanently to St. Augustine, Fla., and won his first great patron, the Florida developer Henry M. Flagler. Before 1890, he had produced several large Florida landscapes for Flagler, and he found new subjects in the Cherokee rose and the magnolia, using them in some of his finest still lifes. (T.E.S.)

Healy, George Peter Alexander (1813–94).

Portrait painter. Born in Boston, Mass., son of an Irish sea captain, he began his artistic career there at the age of seventeen. A slender, energetic youth, fortune was with him. One day in 1832 he knocked on the great front door of the Harrison Gray Otis house, telling the servant that "a gentleman" wished to see Mrs. Otis "on business." When she learned that this young man was an artist asking her to pose because "my ambition was to paint a beautiful woman," she laughed. But pose she did, and he painted her laughing. With this new friend and patron he earned enough money to go to France to study.

He worked in the studio of the melancholy Baron Gros until Gros's suicide in 1835, and there formed a lifelong friendship with the brilliant young painter Thomas Couture. Aggressive and eager, in two years Healy perfected a strong portrait style that brought him the patronage of the wealthy and powerful of Europe and England, including King Louis Philippe and other statesmen. Considering the great number of his paintings and the speed and facility with which he worked, his work is remarkable for originality, grace, and insight. Not content to be known as a portraitist only, he also painted genre and history, winning a medal at the Salon of 1855 with his huge *Franklin Urging the Claims of the American Colonies before Louis XVI* (destroyed in the Chicago fire of 1871). With this fresh triumph, he returned to the United States, where he remained through the Civil War and until 1867. His work was always as eagerly sought as it had been in Europe. His familiar

portraits of *Abraham Lincoln* (Washington), *The Peacemakers* (White House), *U. S. Grant* (Newberry Library), and the striking pair of *General and Mrs. William Tecumseh Sherman* (National Portrait Gallery) belong to this period.

Healy remained, for all his long European sojourns, assertively democratic and American, and in America chose to make his home base the new, sprawling, young metropolis of Chicago rather than any of the eastern cultural centers. Another protracted residence in Europe followed, 1867–72 in Rome, 1872–92 in Paris. The last two years of his life were spent in Chicago, where the World's Columbian Exposition (1893) served to emphasize, in a way, the achievements of this artist as creator of a memorable record of American life and character. (C.C.S.)

Held, Al (1928–   ).

Painter. He was born in New York, N.Y., and studied at the Art Students League and the Grande Chaumière, Paris (1949–51). He was most impressed by the paintings of Jackson Pollock* in the late 1940s, and in some of his own work of 1950–51 experimented with synthesizing the calligraphic ideas of Pollock and the classic, architectural space of the Dutch abstractionist Piet Mondrian. On his return to New York he became involved in abstract expressionism,* particularly that of Pollock, Willem de Kooning,* and Franz Kline.* His paintings were already characterized by heavy pigment and large, bold structure. During the 1950s, while continuing to apply paint in an almost brutally massive manner, he moved toward larger, simplified, geometric forms and bold, clear colors, while the scale of his paintings increased to mural dimensions. Although Held may be associated with color-field* painting during the 1960s, he has an individual expression that combines the European geometric abstraction of Mondrian and Léger with the abstract symbolism of American hard-edge* painters such as Kenneth Noland* and Ellsworth Kelly.* At the same time, he differs from these artists in his use of heavy pigment that gives the effect of a massive wall advancing toward the spectator rather than receding in depth. It is in this emphasis on the painting as an object, a reality in itself rather than an illusion of anything else, that Held considers himself a realist.

2

1

1. *Al Held.* Mao, 1967, Andre
   Emmerich Gallery, N.Y.
2. *Robert Henri.* Young Woman in
   White, 1904. National Gallery of Art,
   Washington, D.C. (gift of Miss Violet
   Organ).
3. *Robert Henri.* New York Street in
   Winter, 1902. National Gallery of Art,
   Washington, D.C. (gift of Chester
   Dale).

3

Held's concern with the painting as an object is most dramatically illustrated by his later works; in these he deserts color for a rigid black and white framework which at times suggest Renaissance experiments in perspective drawing. These, however, still emphatically continue his insistence on the painting as a physical object. (H.H.A.)

Henri, Robert (1865–1929).
Portrait, figure and landscape painter, born Robert Henry Cozad, in Cincinnati, Ohio. His father, once a professional gambler, founded the town of Cozad, Neb., where the family moved in 1873. In 1882 the elder Cozad shot a man in self-defense and then fled. Eventually the family was reunited in Denver, and later, when they moved to New Jersey, changed their names. Robert, reflecting his French ancestry, chose "Henri" as his new surname (but pronounced it "Hen'rye").

In 1886, Henri enrolled at the Pennsylvania Academy of the Fine Arts, where the tradition of Thomas Eakins* was passed on to him by Thomas Anshutz.* After two years in Philadelphia, Henri sailed for Paris to attend the Académie Julien, receiving criticism from the French painters Bouguereau and Robert-Fleury. His painting remained essentially academic, culminating in his admission to the École des Beaux-Arts in 1891. But soon his summer landscapes came under the influence of impressionism.* After returning to Philadelphia in 1891, he studied with the impressionist Robert Vonnoh* at the Academy, and in 1892 began, at the Philadelphia School of Design for Women, his long career as a teacher. Soon he became the guiding spirit at regular gatherings in his studio, where friends such as the sculptor A. Stirling Calder,* and younger painters, including John Sloan,* William Glackens,* Everett Shinn,* and George Luks,* listened as he expounded on Emerson, Thoreau, Whitman, independent creativity, and philosophical anarchism.

In the mid-1890s, Henri returned to Europe and abandoned impressionism (which he felt was becoming a superficial and academic style) to embrace a dark-toned and broadly brushed manner influenced by Velásquez, Manet, Whistler,* and especially Hals. In Paris he began developing this technique, and he was rewarded by the acceptance of portrait studies in the Salons of 1896 and 1897. A one-man exhibition of 87 works in Philadelphia in 1897 led to support from William M. Chase* and Arthur B. Davies* that helped introduce him to the New York art world. In Paris again, in 1899, he was greatly encouraged when a street scene, *La Neige,* was acquired for the Luxembourg Museum. In 1900, after a visit to Spain, he returned to the United States and established himself in New York. He rapidly became a leading painter and a spokesman for younger artists, advocating realism and freedom of expression. After painting a few strong New York scenes and summer landscapes, he concentrated on figure work, intent on a career as a portrait painter. As an instructor at the New York School of Art, founded by Chase, his popularity grew remarkably. He was soon a political force, receiving awards and serving on juries in the Society of American Artists,* the National Academy of Design,* the Art Institute of Chicago, and other institutions. Thus he became a member of the establishment even while he led the younger men in their struggle for independence. Henri had long been seeking ways of expanding exhibition opportunities when events in 1907 convinced him that the National Academy was altogether inadequate in representing the art scene. He took a leading role in planning the exhibition at the Macbeth Gallery, which the press dubbed the show of The Eight.* Again, in 1910, he led in arranging for the much broader show of the Independent Artists,* and in 1911 helped establish the small group exhibitions at the MacDowell Club. Henri, however, was not in tune with the more radical art developments that burst on the scene with the Armory Show* of 1913, although his work was in the exhibition.

His painting style, which had appeared unconventionally brusque and vigorous under the influence of Hals and Manet in the early 1900s, as in *Young Woman in White* (1904, Washington), became progressively more colorful after 1909, under the influence of the color system of Hardesty Maratta. Constantly striving for greater breadth and rapidity of execution, he developed a more superficial and sensational manner. From 1906 he traveled yearly to the West or Europe in search of picturesque types, working in Santa Fe, in Spain, or—especially in later years —in Ireland, where he found models for some of his most popular works, as in *Himself* and *Herself* (1913, Chicago).

Henri holds his place in American art by virtue of a number of strong paintings, especially from his earlier period. He was equally important as a spokesman for more liberal exhibition opportunities. His leadership was temporary because, during a period of change, he found himself a progressive in theory rather than practice; but he continued to stimulate students. Between 1902 and 1912 he taught at the New York School of Art and the Henri School, where George Bellows,* Stuart Davis,* Edward Hopper,* Rockwell Kent,* Yasuo Kuniyoshi,* and Paul Manship* were his students. In 1911–18 he taught at the educationally and politically radical Ferrer Center School with Moses Soyer,* Man Ray,* and even Leon Trotsky attending his classes. From 1915 to 1928 he taught at the Art Students League. His enthusiasm for painting was projected far beyond his classroom by the publication of a collection of his precepts, *The Art Spirit* (1923, often reprinted). (D.W.S.)

Henry, Edward Lamson (1841–1919).
Painter and illustrator of historical scenes of 18th- and early 19th-century American life. Born in Charleston, S.C., Henry was taken to New York as a child. He studied there in 1855 with the landscapist W. M. Oddie (c.1808–65) and after that at the Pennsylvania Academy of the Fine Arts in 1858. In 1860 he visited Paris and studied with Charles Gleyre, and then Gustave Courbet. Yet this training and his numerous later trips to Europe seem to have had little effect on his style. His paintings of carriages, houses, trains, and sentimental scenes seem specifically American. As the critic Samuel Isham pointed out in 1905, Henry's pictures are finished "minutely, with all the funny, quaint details given. . . ." He was elected to the National Academy of Design* in 1869. Examples of the genre* style on which his reputation was based are *Carriage Ride on a Country Lane* (1906) and *Philadelphia Interior* (1868, both Shelburne). (T.E.S.)

Herter, Christian (1840–83).
German-born designer and painter best known for his influence on American furniture and interior design. Son of a Stuttgart carver and cabinetmaker,

Christian became a student at the École des Beaux-Arts in Paris at fifteen. Some five years later he joined his older half-brother, Gustave, in New York, where the latter had already made a name as a silver and furniture designer. In the mid-1860s Gustave's furniture and decorating company on Broadway became Herter Brothers. In 1868 Gustave sent Christian to France to study with Pierre Victor Galland, a popular decorative artist. On his return to New York, about 1870, Christian bought out Gustave. In the next decade Christian made Herter Brothers the decorating firm of America's mercantile princes, including J. Pierpont Morgan, Mark Hopkins, and Jay Gould.

Although the firm employed numerous designers and craftsmen, its furniture and interiors maintained certain characteristics. Furniture forms owed something to the Renaissance revival until after the Philadelphia Centennial of 1876, when they showed the influence of the English Arts and Crafts* movement and its reform tradition of rectilinear forms and surface ornamentation. Herter's work culminated in 1882 in the Italian Renaissance twin houses he designed for W. H. Vanderbilt on Fifth Avenue at 51st Street. As both architect and decorator of the buildings, he imported sixty European sculptors and carvers to execute his designs and he employed 600 to 700 men for eighteen months on the interior decorations. Herter then retired to Paris to study painting; however, he contracted tuberculosis and died a year later.   (M.J.B.)

Hesselius, Gustavus (1682–1755).

Painter of portraits and religious and mythological subjects. After receiving academic training in his native Sweden, he came to the Swedish colony on the Delaware in 1711 with his brother, Andreas, a clergyman. Gustavus soon left the country parish to seek patronage at Philadelphia. He lived thereafter in that city and in Maryland, with occasional painting tours through the plantation country.

Hesselius brought a baroque style to America; in portraiture he was competent, honest, and direct—too much so to please certain patrons. Never a fashionable painter, he nonetheless became the leading artist of the middle colonies. His solid qualities appear admirably in his three best works, a late

self-portrait touched with thoughtful melancholy, and his portraits of two Indian chiefs, Lapowinsa and Tishcohan (all at Historical Society of Pennsylvania). The Indians, painted in 1735 shortly before the infamous "Walking Purchase" of their lands, have been valued as pioneering ethnological studies and are notable for their scientific realism. Actually, however, they represented a long-established convention of art and diplomacy, an official compliment paid to one head of state by another.

A devout man, Hesselius was early established as a painter of religious subjects, and is perhaps the first painter of such works in America. A *Last Supper* was commissioned in 1721 by St. Barnabas Church in Prince George's County, Md. A *Crucifixion* of 1748 attracted much attention in Philadelphia. In curious contrast to these are two surviving reflections of classical themes painted in a dramatic baroque style: *Bacchanalian Revel* (Pennsylvania) and *Bacchus and Ariadne* (c.1720–30, Detroit). In later years, in partnership with John Winter, he was offering the Philadelphia public "coats of Arms drawn on coaches, chaises, etc. or any kind of Ornaments; Landskips, Signs, Show-boards, Ship and House Painting, Gilding of all Sorts, Writing in Gold or Colour, old Pictures cleaned and mended, etc." Such diversified activities were typical of the colonial artist. Hesselius' work became increasingly realistic as he grew older. His approach, particularly in his Indian paintings, established a tradition that was continued in the works of many later artists including the Peale* family.

(C.C.S.)

Hesselius, John (1728–78).

Portrait painter. Trained by his father, Gustavus Hesselius,* he was influenced also by the Philadelphia work of Robert Feke* and later of John Wollaston.* He was most active in the decade 1750–60, and had a patronage spread over a wide area, including Philadelphia, Delaware, Maryland, and Virginia. His marriage to a wealthy widow in 1763 brought him better connections, though less incentive to work. He lived thereafter like a country gentleman at Bellefield plantation near Annapolis. It was there that he gave Charles Willson Peale* his first lessons in painting. His best-known portrait is *Charles Cal-*

1

1. *Christian Herter.* Shaving stand, N.Y., 1882. Collection Marilynn J. Bordes, N.Y.
2. *Edward Hicks.* The Peaceable Kingdom, c.1843. New York State Historical Museum, Cooperstown.
3. *Edward Hicks.* The Cornell Farm, 1849. National Gallery of Art, Washington, D.C. (gift of William and Bernice Chrysler Garbisch).

vert (1761, Baltimore), showing the five-year-old aristocrat attended by a favorite slave. His portraits, of which more than one hundred survive, have a rather polished smoothness although the figures are awkwardly posed; he was one of the last of the baroque colonial painters. (C.C.S.)

Hicks, Edward (1780–1849).

Quaker folk painter and preacher. Born in Bucks County, Pa., he was orphaned when he was three. Apprenticed to a carriage-maker, he went on to become a sign painter. He embraced the Quaker faith when he was twenty-one. Hicks created a rich pictorial record of Bucks County farm life and landscape and some one hundred visions of the biblical prophecy of God's peaceable kingdom on earth, such as *The Peaceable Kingdom* (c.1840–45, Brooklyn), in which the lion would lie down with the lamb and all creatures would be led in peace by a child. Here, as in all his biblical and historical paintings, he showed a fascination with the variety of animal form and coloring. In the theme of the peaceable kingdom he found ample opportunity to indulge this predilection as well as to incorporate messages of personal or historical significance, particularly in glimpses of William Penn signing his treaty with the Indians. His rural scenes captured the industry and prosperous serenity of his surroundings, as in the several versions of *The Residence of David Twining,* for example (c.1846, Abby Aldrich Rockefeller), based on his adult recollections of the scene of his own childhood. One of the best-known primitive artists, Hicks was a prominent Quaker minister; he chose religious and patriotic themes because he doubted the moral worth of art but needed its financial rewards. (M.J.G.)

Hicks, Sheila (1934–   ).

A pioneer in free-hanging nonloom weaving techniques. She was born in Hastings, Neb., studied painting with Josef Albers* and Rico Lebrun* at Yale, weaving with Anni Albers,* and anthropology with Junius Byrd. Her M.F.A. thesis, *Pre-Incaic Textiles* was followed by a Fulbright Grant in 1957 for research into the ancient fiber work of Peru, Bolivia, Ecuador, and Chile. In 1967, she moved to Paris and founded her weaving workshop, Atelier des Grands Augustins. She also worked and

2

3

1

2

3

1. **Lewis Hine.** Group of Breaker Boys
   inside the Breaker, c. 1910, photograph. George Eastman House,
   Rochester, N.Y.
2. **Lewis Hine.** Child Victim of an
   Accident in a Mill, c. 1910, photograph. George Eastman House,
   Rochester, N.Y.
3. **Thomas Hicks.** Oliver Wendell
   Holmes, 1858. Boston Athenaeum.

taught at the cooperative workshop of Hacienda Huaquen in Chile, as well as in Mexico, India, Morocco, and throughout Europe. Her favored nonloom techniques of twining, looping, wrapping, knotting, and braiding have precedents in Andean textiles, and they are sometimes combined with a loom-woven ground. But her most distinguished work, a combination of many elements distributed with much freedom in space, are her free-hanging elements and her architectural walls.

The Principal Wife Goes On (1969, Johnson Coll.) is an assemblage of eleven elements of linen, silk, wool, and synthetic fibers, spliced and grafted together, with each element 180 inches long. Unbleached natural fibers are wrapped with synthetic colors of Indian brightness. The spatial qualities of her works have involved her in architectural applications of her fiber sculptures.

(R.S.)

Hicks, Thomas (1823–90).
Portrait, genre, and landscape painter born in Newton, Pa. He received his first instruction in art as early as 1838 from his famous cousin, Edward Hicks.* He continued his studies at the Pennsylvania Academy of the Fine Arts and the National Academy of Design.* In 1845 he went abroad and worked in Paris with Thomas Couture, whose influence can be detected in much of his later painting. Returning to the United States in 1849, he established his studio in New York City and built up a respected position as a portrait painter.

Hicks received his fair share of official portrait commissions. That of *Hamilton Fish* (1852, City of New York) is typical of the heroic-sized, official portrait then popular. Although the paint quality is rather dry, the wealth of picturesque detail in the architectural setting and personal accessories give life to a portrait that is otherwise formal and dignified. Hicks was more at home with smaller, less ambitious works for private clients, as in his simple but appealing portrait, *Oliver Wendell Holmes* (1858, Boston Athenaeum).

The landscapes that Hicks painted of scenes in Venice, Rome, and the United States form only a small part of his total work and few have found their way into important public collections. Hicks' genre pictures, especially those done before he went abroad, are in their simplicity and directness superior

to his later efforts, which show the academic influence of his French training. The unsophisticated subject matter and straightforward approach of *Calculating* (1844, Boston), an early work, is in the genre tradition of William S. Mount* and George C. Bingham.* A typical late work, *Dropped in to Hear the News* (c.1875, Milwaukee Art Center), is more softly focused, less well drawn, and makes a far weaker impression.

(H.W.W.)

Hidley, Joseph H. (1830–72).
Woodcarver and self-taught folk painter and taxidermist of Poestenkill, N.Y. Hidley painted his home town and the villages of surrounding areas with the dynamic sweep of an airborne camera, recording distant mountains and rural vistas and cloud formations lying above and beyond the immediate subject. He also did some fanciful religious paintings, floral shadowbox pictures, and townscapes such as *Poestenkill-Winter* (c.1850, Abby Aldrich Rockefeller).

Hill, John William (1812–79).
A London-born landscape and topographical painter best known for the large lithographs of cities, public buildings, and private residences reproduced after his designs. His family moved to Philadelphia in 1819 and later moved to New York City. He served an apprenticeship with his father, John Hill (1770–1850), an early aquatintist who had engraved Joshua Shaw's *Picturesque Views of American Scenery* in 1819. In the mid-1830s young Hill became a topographical artist for the New York State Geological Survey. Later he drew views of many American cities, which were published as lithographs by Smith Brothers of New York. One of his most ambitious and attractive views is the aquatint *New York From Brooklyn Heights* (1837, engraved by William James Bennett after Hill's view).

Hill's later work was chiefly pure landscape but he also produced some flower and bird paintings in watercolor, ninety-four of which are in the Field Museum, Chicago. Typical of his highly finished watercolor landscapes is *The Waterfall* (undated, Corcoran), which probably represents a scene in the Adirondacks. It is an example of the new "naturalism," which the English critic Ruskin advocated in his *Modern*

Painters. Hill was considered the leading spirit of this movement in America. His landscape views were mainly of New Jersey and New York, especially along the Hudson River; however, he did work as far afield as the Androscoggin River and Portland, Me. He exhibited fairly regularly at the National Academy of Design* from 1828 to 1860. From 1836 on he made his home near West Nyack, N.Y.

(H.W.W.)

Hine, Lewis (1874–1940).
Documentary photographer. Hine was a teacher of nature studies at the Ethical Culture School in New York City in 1903 when he began to photograph. He received a degree in sociology from Columbia University in 1905 and began photographing with great compassion the vast number of immigrants arriving at Ellis Island in New York Harbor. A large number of these photographs, such as *A Madonna of Ellis Island,* have become famous. In 1908 he resigned from teaching to become an investigator-photographer for the National Child Labor Committee and made one of his first important photo documentations, "Neglected Neighbors of Our National Capital." Hine was also staff photographer for *Charities and Commons* magazine (later *Survey*), and a great quantity of his early work appeared in its pages. Many of his photographs also appeared in such magazines as *McClure's, World's Work,* and *Outlook.* Hine also worked for the Russell Sage Foundation and his photographs appeared in their books, including the six volumes of *The Pittsburgh Survey* (1909). He photographed army camps during World War I, went to France in 1918–19 as a captain in the American Red Cross, and was later part of a mission surveying war damage in southeastern Europe. In 1920, after his return to New York, the National Arts Club gave him a one-man exhibition.

Although Hine carried out many assignments after 1920, the period was unrewarding for him except for two projects: in 1930 he documented the construction of the Empire State Building and in 1933 he photographed the work of the Tennessee Valley Authority. Virtually forgotten, Hine died in poverty at Hastings-on-Hudson, N.Y. Since the late 1940s Americans have slowly become aware that he left an immensely rich visual record of the varied peoples that populated and helped build America in the first third of the 20th century. (T.F.B.)

Hinman, Charles (1932-   )
Painter. Born in Syracuse, N.Y., he is known for his shaped-canvas wall constructions, first exhibited in 1965. These wall-pieces represent the extension of color painting into the third dimension, sometimes projecting three feet or more into the space of the room. Alternately geometric and organic, Hinman's forms are sometimes reinforced, sometimes contradicted by color. In several large reliefs he achieves an almost buoyant, weightless effect through the use of clean, pale colors.

Hirshfield, Morris (1872-1946).
Self-taught artist born in Russian Poland, he began painting in 1937, after retiring from business as a coat and slipper manufacturer in New York. In his childhood in Central Europe Hirshfield had modeled wooden figures of Jewish biblical characters, but his artistic interests were put aside when he emigrated to the United States and settled in New York City at the age of eighteen. The paintings he later produced were usually characterized by a bold central figure (either human or animal) surrounded by a field in which detail was expressed as varying pattern. A general concern with symmetry has suggested to many critics that Hirshfield's invention stems from his earlier experience with tailor's patterns, and the linear and textured elements of his painting certainly suggest needlework. An example is *Girl before a Mirror* (1940, Modern Museum). In 1943 he had an exhibition at New York's Museum of Modern Art, an indication of the prominence, unusual for a primitive painter, that he attained. (M.J.G.)

Hoban, James (1762-1831).
Builder and architect. Born in County Kilkenny, Ireland, he studied in Dublin schools and received an award for architectural drawing in 1780. He then worked as an artisan on several buildings in Dublin. Hoban came to America in 1785 and advertised in the Philadelphia papers as a carpenter and joiner. In 1787 he moved to Charleston, S.C., and there designed the State Capitol at Columbia (finished in 1791, burned 1865), building it of wood, with a brick basement. He then entered a

competition for the president's house in Washington (then the Federal City), and won it with a Dublin-flavored design adapted from James Gibb's *Book of Architecture* (1728). He also supervised its construction (1793-1801). Hoban replaced George Hadfield* (who had been dismissed as superintendent of the Capitol) and remained until B. H. Latrobe* was appointed architect in 1803. Although he constructed a few other buildings in Washinton, his entire reputation as an architect rests with his exceptionally graceful Georgian design for the White House. He acquired a considerable amount of land and gradually retired from building, but did rebuild the White House after it was burned in 1814. He was a Washington city councilman from 1802 until his death. (P.F.N.)

Hoffman, Malvina (1887-1966).
Sculptor. She began as a student of painting but about 1909 turned to sculpture, studying with Herbert Adams* and Gutzon Borglum.* The next year she went to Paris, where she studied with Rodin, who impressed upon her the necessity of vital naturalism in portraiture, a boldness of sculptural form, and an expression in the features that projected the personality of the subject. It was in portraiture that she was to do her best work. For over fifty years— until she retired in 1963— she modeled likenesses of distinguished people, including *Paderewski* (1923), *Anna Pavlova* (1924), *Wendel L. Willkie* (1944), and *Katharine Cornell* (1961).

There were other aspects to her career; it was her spirited bronze *Bacchanale Russe* (1917, Luxembourg Museum, Paris) that first brought her international recognition. She also attempted large heroic groups, such as the medieval-style *The Sacrifice* (1920, Harvard), but these were never as successful as her portraits. In 1930 she was asked by the Field Museum in Chicago to tour the world making studies for the "Races of Man"; the results of this trip—heads and figures of men and women from Africa, Asia, Europe, Pacific islands, and North America—were cast in bronze and placed in the museum. She was the author of *Heads and Tales,* an autobiography (1936), *Sculpture Inside and Out* (1939), and *Yesterday is Tomorrow* (1965). (W.C.)

Hofmann, Charles C. (active 1872-78). Pennsylvania sign painter. As a voluntary poorhouse inmate, he recorded his own surroundings and the nearby rural landscape with crisp precision and bright colors, as in his *View of Montgomery County Almshouse Buildings* (1878, Abby Aldrich Rockefeller).

Hofmann, Hans (1880-1966).
Painter and teacher. Born in Bavaria, Germany, he studied science, mathematics, and music in Munich, and during 1896-98 he served as assistant to the director of public works of the state of Bavaria, inventing an electromagnetic comptometer. When his father sent him money to continue his scientific investigations, he enrolled in art school instead. In 1903 Hofmann went to Paris, where he attended evening sketch classes at the Académie de la Grande Chaumière along with Matisse.

At first he produced meticulously-painted portraits and figure studies. At the same time, he was absorbing the discoveries of such contemporaries as Delaunay, Picasso, and Braque, all of whom he knew personally. During this period he painted still lifes, landscapes, and figure pieces in the cubist style. Ultimately he would synthesize the spatial concepts of Cézanne and the cubists with the high-key color dynamics of fauvism* and of Kandinsky. At the outbreak of World War I, Hofmann returned to Germany, founding his first art school in Munich in 1915. Its aim was "to clarify the new pictorial approach of modern painting, which sought to create depth not as an illusion, but as a plastic reality, by means of the backward and forward animation of the whole picture surface through color, shapes, and rhythm." In 1930 and 1931 he taught summer sessions at the University of California at Berkeley, and the following year he moved to the United States permanently. By 1934 Hofmann had brought the gospel of modern art to New York City students. The Hans Hofmann School of Fine Arts, noting that young American artists were in an "isolated and unaided position," emphasized that creative expression grew out of the translation of inner states of being into "pure," nonrepresentational form. By stressing the dynamics of movement and counter-movement, positive and negative space, advancing and receding color, and composing in terms of flat planes, he was highly influential in the whole move toward "formalism" in American art.

By 1940 Hofmann's own work had begun to progress steadily toward abstraction. He was now abandoning recognizable motifs, converting his figures and still lifes into clashes of color and energy. He is generally considered a major figure in the development of abstract expressionism,* and such pictures as *Red Trickle* (1939) and *Spring* (1940) are sometimes considered "the first drip paintings." A series of "Landscapes" (1940–41), with their loosely-brushed and scumbled areas of bright color, might well be considered proto-abstract expressionist, while other paintings, such as *Palimpsest* (1946), show the influence of surrealism.* Hofmann never abandoned the spatial tenets of cubism,* however, and during the 1950s this influence again came to the fore. In his last work he attempted to fuse cubism and expressionism* by floating smoothly-painted rectangles of pure hues amid expressionistic fields of squiggles and splashes of color. Hofmann's first important show in America, in 1944 at Peggy Guggenheim's* Art of This Century gallery, was followed by innumerable other exhibitions, including retrospectives at the Baltimore Museum of Art (1954), the Whitney Museum (1957), and the Museum of Modern Art (1963). Hofmann was in his late seventies when he gave up teaching in 1958. He donated forty-five of his paintings to the University of California in gratitude for his first job in America.

Hofmann has written: "At the time of making a picture I want not to know what I'm doing; a picture should be made with feeling, not with knowing. . . ." However, he has been called "an academician of the modern tradition" and it was precisely in the techniques of picture-making that he excelled. He has remained a force in American art primarily through his teaching, first in New York City and then in Provincetown, Mass. His students comprise three generations of American artists and include Burgoyne Diller,* Louise Nevelson,* and Helen Frankenthaler.* Hofmann's quest for "the inner life of things"—his conviction that "art must not imitate physical life, but must create pictorial life"—is expressed in his book *The Search for the Real* (1967).

(E.C.G.)

1

2

1. **Hans Hofmann.** Autumn Chill and Sun, *1962, Collection James Tree, N.Y.*
2. **Hans Hofmann.** Fantasia in Blue, *1954. Whitney Museum of American Art, N.Y.*

1

2

Homer, Winslow (1836–1910).

Painter and graphic artist, a leading figure in 19th-century American naturalism. He was born in Boston, Mass., and from the age of about six he lived in nearby Cambridge, still a village, so that he had an active outdoor childhood. He grew up an independent young man, loving outdoor life, laconic in speech but with a dry humor. Without art training, he was apprenticed at about nineteen to the Boston lithographer J. H. Bufford. He loathed the drudgery of the job, and at twenty-one he became a free-lance illustrator for *Ballou's Pictorial,* Boston, then for *Harper's Weekly,* New York. In 1859 he moved to New York City and continued to draw for *Harper's.* He studied drawing briefly at the National Academy of Design,* and took a few lessons in painting from the nineteenth–century landscape painter, Frédéric Rondel; otherwise he was self-taught. During the Civil War *Harper's* sent him to the Virginia front several times. His war illustrations, marked by realism, sure draftsmanship, and absence of heroics, were the strongest pictorial reporting of the war.

Not until he was twenty-six did he begin to paint regularly—at first pictures of army life. After the war he turned to contemporary country life for subjects; these ranged from summer resorts with their fashionable young women to the simple world of the farm, in which children often played leading parts. These early paintings, such as *Long Branch* (1869, Boston) and *Snap the Whip* (1872, Butler), while remaining completely faithful to the native scene, nevertheless had an unsentimental poetry. They are the most authentic and attractive visual records of American country life in the 1860s and 1870s. The same themes appeared in his many illustrations, not only for *Harper's* but for other magazines and for books. These wood-engraved illustrations, with their strong graphic quality and handsome decorative values, are among the finest American black-and-white art of the period.

Homer's style from the beginning revealed little influence of other art or artists. It was the product of first-hand observation of nature and of direct recording of the artist's visual sensations, especially of outdoor light and color. This fresh, naturalistic vision was combined with a pronounced

1. *Winslow Homer.* The Look-Out: "All's Well," *1896. Museum of Fine Arts, Boston.*
2. *Winslow Homer.* Northeaster, *1895. Metropolitan Museum of Art, N.Y.*
3. *Winslow Homer.* Snap the Whip, *1872. Butler Institute of American Art, Youngstown, Ohio.*
4. *Winslow Homer.* Hurricane, Bahamas, *watercolor. Metropolitan Museum of Art, N.Y. (gift of George A. Hearn).*

3

4

decorative sense, a feeling for the sensuous qualities of color, tone, and line, and the patterns they created. In certain ways his early style resembled French impressionism, but without any possible influence. He made his first trip abroad when he was thirty, in 1866–67, and spent ten months in France. The only artistic effect of this stay was a somewhat higher color range in his work.

In 1873 Homer began the regular practice of watercolor, a medium well adapted to his graphic sense, and which he used thereafter as much as oil. His watercolors sold well at modest prices, and after 1875 he stopped illustrating, except on occasion.

A turning point in Homer's career came in two seasons (1881–82) in England, at Tynemouth, a fishing port on the North Sea. Here, painting almost entirely in watercolor, he began to picture the sea and the men and women who earned their living from it. These watercolors showed a new undertone of emotion, and an advance in depth of color, roundness of modeling, and atmospheric quality.

After his return, Homer left New York for good, in 1883, and settled on the coast of Maine at Prout's Neck. On this lonely, rocky shore he built a studio where he was to live thenceforth entirely alone, sometimes staying through the long Maine winters. Homer was extremely reticent, and his reasons for this move will probably never be known. There was a family tale of an unhappy love affair; in any case, he never married. Probably more important was that he had finally found the kind of subjects he wanted to paint. That his solitary existence was genuinely satisfying is proved by his personal letters. "The life that I have chosen," he wrote, "gives me my full hours of enjoyment for the balance of my life. The Sun will not rise, or set, without my notice and thanks."

In Maine, Homer's art underwent its greatest change. His subjects became the sea, the forest and the mountains, and the lives of outdoor men. His style took on a new strength, largeness, and mastery. The first products of this evolution were a number of oils of deep-sea sailors and fishermen, including *The Fog Warning* (1885, Boston), *The Herring Net* (1885, Chicago), and *Eight Bells* (1886, Addison), which established his reputation, and which have

become marine classics. Motivated by the success of these oils, in 1884 Homer undertook the medium of etching, producing eight large plates, all but one based on his marines and English watercolors. His improvements in composition, as in *Saved* (1889), made these among his best-designed works in any medium. But they did not sell, and after 1889 he gave up etching.

After a few years at Prout's Neck, face-to-face with the Atlantic, Homer's chief theme became the ocean itself, without human figures. His dominating theme now was the never-ending battle between the sea and the shore—the force of the wave, the solidity of the rock, the shock of their collision. These later marines, such as *The Northeaster* (1895, Metropolitan) and *Early Morning after a Storm at Sea* (1902, Cleveland), are among the most powerful modern expressions of the majesty and the beauty of the sea.

Homer's few recorded remarks on art express a purely naturalistic viewpoint. But his work itself reveals conscious artistry. The severe simplification, the concentration on large masses and movements, the strong linear rhythms, the full-bodied, earthly color harmonies, were evidently the result of planned design. His finest mature paintings achieved a synthesis between vigorous naturalism and the sensuous values of form and color.

Aside from these mature oils, he attained his purest artistic values in his later watercolors. An outdoor man all his life, every year he went on fishing and hunting trips to the northern woods—the Adirondacks and Quebec —or for winter visits to the Bahamas, Cuba, Florida, or Bermuda. These changes of scene resulted in many watercolors, such as *Adirondack Guide* (1894, Boston) and *After the Hurricane, Bahamas* (1899, Chicago). They were among his freshest, most vital works in their graphic sureness and strength, magnificent color, and unerring rightness of design. His West Indian watercolors achieved the greatest chromatic brilliancy of all his works. Homer's mature watercolors contain the essence of his genius: the pure visual sensation of nature, recorded by the hand of a master.

In old age Homer, though seldom seen in the art world, was generally regarded as the foremost painter living in America. He received many awards

and honors, none of which had any effect on his way of life or on his work. Homer was the most many-sided and colorful American artist of the later 19th century. His energy, his perennial freshness of vision, and the sensuous vitality underlying all his art, make his works as alive today as when he painted them.   (L.G.)

Hood, Raymond M. (1881–1934). Architect, born in Pawtucket, R.I. He attended Brown University and then studied architecture at the Massachusetts Institute of Technology, graduating in 1903. Just as the name of Louis Sullivan* has now become synonymous with the development of skyscraper* architecture during the 1890s, Hood's name dominated the skyscraper scene in the 1920s and early 1930s. His designs for high-rise office buildings mirrored the rapid changes in fashion during these decades. Like many major figures in American architecture, he vacillated between projecting an image of himself as the practical businessman-architect and as the high-art artist-designer.

His first great success, which put him in the forefront of American architecture, was winning the much-publicized Chicago *Tribune* competition of 1922. Hood, in partnership with John Mead Howell, clothed the building in a version of late Gothic details. Such details had been employed as early as 1913 by Cass Gilbert* in the Woolworth Building in New York, but the earlier versions were essentially horizontal, stacked layers (like their classical counterparts), with a series of Gothic buildings seemingly piled one on another. Hood developed a unified scheme which emphasized the vertical and successfully tied the three elements of base, shaft, and capital together. This tripart division (first used by Louis Sullivan) enabled the designer to make a series of bold statements where they count—the upper silhouette of the building when seen from a distance and the close-up view from the street level. The shaft, which housed the main usable space of the building, could then be left rather simple and plain.

From 1922 on, Gothic-clothed skyscrapers began to dot the skylines of all larger American cities, but Hood did not remain attached to this one image. In his 1924 American Radiator Building, on West 40th Street, New York City, he attired a moderately Gothic structure in black and gold, thereby bringing his designs into the realm of the early Parisian-inspired streamlined moderne.* As the 1920s wore on, he continued to strip historic details from his buildings and to adopt more of the moderne vocabulary, especially decorative ornament. This simplifying process culminated in his 1930 *Daily News* Building, on East 42nd Street in New York, where the exterior was a vertical shaft without base or capital; and in his black-sheathed National Radiator Building (designed in association with J. Gordon Reeves), London, 1928, which was a rather neutral box, emphasizing neither the vertical nor the horizontal.

By 1930 Hood began to feel the impact of the European International style,* with its predilection for horizontal spaces and for details such as band windows. The result was his horizontal-banded 1930 Beaux-Art Apartments and his 1931 stepped McGraw-Hill Building, on West 42nd Street, New York City. In 1932, he penetrated the world of high art, becoming one of the few American architects represented in the exhibition, "The International Style: Architecture Since 1922," at the new Museum of Modern Art. He was again represented in the Museum's show "Modern Architects" by a project for a horizontal-windowed "tower apartment" set out in its own park. As visual forms, the McGraw-Hill Building and his Tower Apartments are far less impressive than any of the projected skyscrapers of such European architects as Mies van der Rohe* or Walter Gropius,* but Hood's buildings are much stronger in the expression of machine technology.

Anticipating the dominant modes of the late 1960s and early 1970s, Hood painted the stucco surfaces of his 1930 Patterson House at Ossining, N.Y., with angular bands of color that purposely clash with the strict rectangular geometry of the design. And in two retail stores designed for Rex Cole (one in Bay Ridge, Brooklyn, 1931; the other on Long Island, N.Y., 1931) he leaped into the world of direct programmatic architecture, i.e., a building in the form of the object it sells—generally associated with southern California. He transformed buildings into an enlarged surrealist image of a product—in this case refrigerators. By the time of his death he had become a leading exponent of the new streamlined moderne style, which was to dominate United States architecture for decades to come. (D.G.)

Hooker, Philip (1766–1837).
Builder, architect, and surveyor. Not long after his birth in Rutland, Mass., his family moved to Albany, N.Y. Since he was never apprenticed to an architect, Hooker's designs reveal his dependence upon contemporary American architects such as Bulfinch,* McComb,* and Benjamin.* He probably had access to builders' books, particularly those of Benjamin.

When Albany became the capital of New York State, its population increased from 3,500 in 1790 to 24,000 in 1830. Of the twenty-four buildings built from Hooker's designs in these years, the following are extant or of particular importance: North Dutch Church, Albany (1797, altered 1858); New York State Capitol, Albany (1802–06, demolished 1883); First Presbyterian Church, Cazenovia, N.Y., (1804, altered 1870); Hyde Hall, Otsego Lake (1811, addition 1833); Albany Academy (1814–15); Ontario Branch Bank, Utica (1815); Hamilton College, Chapel, Clinton, N.Y., steeple and facade (1825); City Hall, Albany (1829); Miller House, John Street, Utica (1830). Having arrived at the right moment in Albany, Hooker was able to introduce good early Republican architecture to the little town. The most interesting aspects of many of his buildings are the interior ornaments—derivative, but plentiful, and not without a certain robust beauty.

Besides his work in architecture, he was an assessor, alderman, city superintendent (1821–27), and city surveyor (1819–32). (P.F.N.)

Hopper, Edward (1882–1967).
Painter and etcher. Born in Nyack, N.Y., Hopper had his professional training during 1900–06 at the New York School of Art, largely under Robert Henri,* whose influence he often acknowledged, although Hopper's work was always more detached than that of Henri and other Ash Can School* painters. In 1906 he went to Paris, where he painted city scenes and sketched city life. The paintings of this period employ a blond palette and exploit zestful brushwork somewhat in Henri's manner. He returned to Europe for brief visits in 1909 and 1910; meanwhile, he had been painting soberly realistic studies of the American scene but they met with little success. Although he was represented in the Armory Show* of 1913 and sold his first picture there, he did not sell another painting for ten years, and so he turned to commercial art and ultimately to the graphic arts. He scored his first success as an etcher, and most of his prints in this medium were made between 1915 and 1923. His first one-man show was at the Whitney Museum in New York City in 1920. They deal with the same type of subject that he was to exploit in many of his best-known paintings—women in interiors, heavy-shadowed night scenes in the city, houses by railroad tracks, lonely people in elevated trains, lighthouses set on remote rocks in New England.

Hopper's New England experience is reflected in his numerous watercolors and oils of lighthouses, great white Victorian mansions in small towns, and boating in New England harbors. These works are always monumental in character, with intense light modeling very powerful forms, as in *The Lighthouse at Two Lights* (1929, Metropolitan). The same monumentality expresses itself in Hopper's many paintings of the city. He had no love, however, for the Manhattan skyscraper world that so excited an artist like John Marin;* his New York is a place of old buildings with heavy masonry and beetling cornices, red and yellow brick soberly enriched by sunlight, and carefully calculated geometric forms. Often his city streets are totally empty of people; the human figure, when it appears, is lonely; almost invariably a long diagonal of curb, road, railing, or railroad track cuts across the bottom of the composition. as in *Manhattan Bridge Loop* (1928, Addison), thereby preventing the spectator from entering in imagination. His other typical subjects are a thin scattering of tired people in a theater; individuals equally isolated in barber shops, cafeterias, train compartments, and offices; nude women, not young and a little gaunt, welcoming the morning sunlight; and empty rooms full of geometrized patterns of sunlight on the walls. The transience of American life in many of its manifestations is suggested in paintings of hotel and motel rooms. gasoline stations, and empty roads.

He also did some monumental landscapes, such as *The Camel's Hump* (1930, Proctor), and at times would try subject matter very remote from his usual interests, such as his picture of Union soldiers resting by a roadside before the battle of Gettysburg; this is probably his only painting on a historic theme. His figure draftsmanship tended to be awkward and heavy, and except for a few self-portraits and studies of his wife, he seems never to have attempted a portrait.

Hopper's mastery of form and mood were such as to endear him, almost uniquely among the representational artists of his time, to the modernists and their critical exegetes. Typical of this was his selection for a special retrospective at the São Paulo Biennial of 1967; here he was shown with twenty-one younger painters, indeed, the whole idea was to suggest that the pop artists and neorealists among the younger men were his intellectual descendants.

Hopper received many honors, prizes, and awards, was elected to the National Academy of Design* in 1932 (but refused because the Academy's juries had turned him down too often), and was accorded retrospective exhibitions at the Museum of Modern Art (1933) and the Whitney (1950 and 1964). He accepted various honorary degrees and election to the National Institute of Arts and Letters in 1945 and the American Academy of Arts and Letters ten years later. (A.F.)

Hosmer, Harriet (1830–1908).
Sculptor. The leader of what Henry James called "the white marmorean flock," the expatriate American women in Italy who devoted themselves to sculpture. Her decision to become a sculptor shocked the Hosmers' neighbors in Watertown, Mass., for sculpture was not an accepted profession for women. Equally startling was her decision to study anatomy at the all-male medical school in Columbia, Mo. Her only encouragement came from her father and a few friends. In 1852 she went to Rome, where she began studying with the aged English neoclassicist John Gibson. Under the spell of Rome (which was to be her home most of her life) and the influence of Gibson, her sculpture developed along neoclassical lines, drawing for its themes on classical mythology. A free-spirited eccen-

1

2

1. *Edward Hopper.* The Lighthouse at Two Lights, *1929. Metropolitan Museum of Art, N.Y. (Hugo Kaster Fund).*
2. *Edward Hopper.* The Camel's Hump, *1930. Munson-Williams-Proctor Institute, Utica, N.Y.*
3. *Edward Hopper.* New York Movie, *1939. Museum of Modern Art, N.Y.*
4. *Thomas Hovenden.* Breaking Home Ties, *1890. Philadelphia Museum of Art.*

3

4

tric, she had a large circle of friends, including Elizabeth and Robert Browning and other notables of Roman expatriate society. The most famous of her sculptures were the impish *Puck* (1856) and the popular *Will-o'-the-Wisp* (c.1856). The many marble replicas made of these gave her financial independence. More serious works, showing a borrowed classical style and the excessive surface decoration of Victorian romanticism, include the heroic marble *Zenobia* (1858), the great queen in chains, an *African Sibyl,* and a *Pompeian Sentinel.*   (W.C.)

Hovenden, Thomas (1840–95).
Talented genre and figure painter who was killed in an accident just as he was reaching a late maturity as an artist. Hovenden was born in Ireland and studied at the Government Art School in County Cork. After emigrating to America in 1863, he attended night school at the National Academy of Design* in New York City. He was in Paris from 1874 to 1880, where he studied with Alexandre Cabanel. Hovenden worked at this time in an international realistic style that suggests the influences of both the French painter Gustave Courbet and the American expatriate J. A. M. Whistler.* On his return to America, he became a respected teacher at the Pennsylvania Academy of the Fine Arts in Philadelphia; among his students was Robert Henri.* Turning from the Brittany scenes he had been painting, Hovenden began a series of studies of Negro life and other American genre subjects. Best known of these is *Breaking Home Ties* (1890, Philadelphia), which was widely praised when exhibited at the World's Columbian Exposition in Chicago in 1893. It depicts a country boy leaving home to make his fortune, and was described by the critic Samuel Isham as "excellent in its craftsmanship and profound and sincere in its sentiment."   (T.E.S.)

Hubard, William James (1807–62).
Portrait painter and cutter of silhouettes, born in Whitchurch, Shropshire, England. A child prodigy, his skill in cutting silhouettes was exploited by a traveling showman who brought him to America in 1824. Shortly thereafter, encouraged by the painters Gilbert Stuart* and Thomas Sully,* he launched a career as a portrait painter when he exhibited three portraits at the Penn-

sylvania Academy of the Fine Arts in 1829. After 1841, having lived briefly in New York, Boston, Philadelphia, and Baltimore, he settled in Richmond, Va. In 1853 he established a bronze foundry to make casts of Houdon's statue of Washington. When Virginia seceded from the Union his foundry began to cast cannon and other munitions for the confederacy, and he was killed in an accidental explosion in the plant.

Hubard specialized in "small whole-length," a form of portrait rare in American painting. These delightfully informal cabinet-size portraits, painted on 20″ x 15″ wood panels, included likenesses of many celebrated southern personages of the period (for example, Charles Carroll of Carrollton, c.1830, Metropolitan; John C. Calhoun, c.1832, Corcoran). Carefully finished in almost miniaturist detail, they incorporate backgrounds and personal accessories associated with their subjects. Many depict dimly lit interiors, but some have outdoor settings. These works are much superior in quality and interest to the routine bust-length portraits he also produced. (H.W.W.)

Hudson River School.
Realistic landscape painters, most of them based in New York, who flourished between 1820 and 1880. The group was given its name, according to Worthington Whittredge,* "by a savage critic who wrote for the New York *Tribune*," and it was in general use by the late 19th century. It was unquestionably a school: its artists knew each other, often worked in neighboring studios, and used the same techniques for the portrayal of nature. Though their interests ranged far beyond the Hudson River Valley, the river and the Catskill Mountains along it remained their favorite subjects; moreover, many of the important painters, including Thomas Cole,* Frederic E. Church,* and Sanford Gifford,* lived along the Hudson itself.

Precursors of the group were the artists who began to paint landscapes in America about 1790. John Trumbull's* *Monte Video* (1791, Yale) is an important prototype, as are some of the works of Ralph Earl,* Charles Willson Peale* (particularly his drawings of the Hudson River of about 1801), Washington Allston,* and Samuel F. B. Morse.* These men helped create a general acceptance of painting itself and of

romanticism, both fundamental to the Hudson River School approach. Equally significant in popularizing landscape painting were the views of rich men's country seats by such Anglo-American artists as William Groombridge (1748–1811) and Francis Guy* (1760–1820), and the landscape prints of such artists as William Russell Birch (c.1760–1820).

It is generally thought that the movement began with the arrival of young Thomas Cole in New York in 1825, but it had actually begun by 1820, when both Thomas Doughty* in Philadelphia and Alvan Fisher* in Boston were already full-time painters of pastoral views. Moreover, in 1821 Joshua Shaw's *Picturesque Views of American Scenery* was published in Philadelphia, and William Guy Wall's *Hudson River Portfolio* (1820–25) followed shortly. From the beginning, the movement comprised both painters and printmakers: often the latter popularized the subjects the painters later explored.

The esthetic of the group was established by Cole, who taught the painters of the country to go out to nature with their sketchbooks. Those who followed his lead included his friend, Henry Cheever Pratt, as well as Henry Inman,* Charles Codman, and William Allen Wall. Cole and other members of this "first generation" of the school painted the wilderness in a passionate, picturesque manner that appealed to the American imagination and made earlier American views seem weak and unobserved. Cole particularly loved paint itself, and he applied it richly and often colorfully. Though he led the way toward the realism of mid-century, his own art expressed moral and religious views, the "romantic agony" of which Wordsworth wrote, as much as it did recognizable American scenery. Thus there was in his art an ongoing struggle between the real and the ideal; though he sketched from nature and took his vocabulary from observed phenomena, his finished paintings were the result of his waiting "for time to draw a veil over the common details" of a scene so that he could depict only its "great features." He loved the landscape, not only for its own sake but also for the heroic human associations that could be found in certain places. He also valued his didactic paintings, such as *Past* and *Present* (Corcoran) at least as highly as his realistic ones, like *The Notch of the White Mountains* (Wash-

1

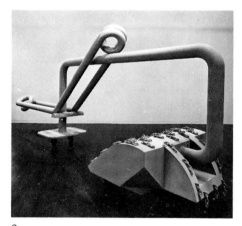

2

1. **Hudson River School.** Asher B. Durand, In the Woods. *1855. Metropolitan Museum of Art, N.Y.*
2. **Robert Hudson.** Untitled, 1968. *Allan Frumkin Gallery, N.Y.*

ington). His paintings and those of his followers thus parallel developments in American literature, both in the new interest in landscape, particularly wilderness, and in the conscious effort to create an American style; particularly comparable is Washington Irving's *The Sketch Book* (1819–20) and James Fenimore Cooper's *Leatherstocking Tales* (1823–41).

Cole died in 1848, and a "second generation" of the school led by Asher B. Durand,* John F. Kensett,* and Frederic E. Church began work during the 1840s. The style they perfected during the 1850s and 1860s followed Cole's lead with regard to picturesque wilderness subjects, but rejected his heavy brushwork, his idealizing, his tendency toward moralizing epics. They turned instead to Henry David Thoreau, author of *Walden* (1854) and *The Maine Woods* (1863), who had written that "the universe is not rough-hewn, but perfect in its details. Nature will bear the closest inspection. . . ." Durand became the theorist of the school, outlining the methods of the new realism in his letters on *Landscape Painting,* published in the art magazine *The Crayon** in 1855. He taught younger painters that they must learn from nature herself and from detailed engravings; that they should make careful sketches of details and scenes, never allow brushwork to become noticeable, and paint light and atmosphere as actually observed. By the late 1850s, Durand's closest follower, Kensett, had established the basic compositions for the school: the panorama (often the Hudson River itself), cool mountain and lake scenes, interior woodland, and simple coastal pictures.

The other leader of the school at mid-century, Church, found Kensett's paintings of popular eastern scenes too modest. He took the realistic style and the new interest in light and used them in heroic paintings of the great topographical wonders of the world: the Andes, the Arctic, the Near East, and Niagara Falls. Like most members of the school, Church worked in New York City. A distinction should be made between members of the school and the many painters across the country, varying widely in ability, who painted in the realistic Hudson River School style.

A "third generation" of the School, bringing another major stylistic change, came to maturity in the 1870s. By that time the major talents of the optimistic, high realism of mid-century had died or had lost much of their vigor. Moreover, in the post-Civil War years, as the wilderness disappeared under the onrush of civilization and industrialization, an increasingly pessimistic attitude developed toward the land itself. With the whole land under attack, it hardly seemed relevant for painters to celebrate every leaf and stone of a particular woodland glen. Moreover, the art patrons of the new period came to favor "the French style," which meant landscapes that were more imaginative, painted with the looser brushwork and more somber colors of the Barbizon School.* Some of the realists of the second generation never changed their styles: thus the work of Church, Bierstadt, and Gifford simply looked increasingly artificial and grandiose as times and tastes changed. Other painters, however, made the transition successfully and creatively, and can be considered a third and final generation of the school. Thus Inness,* Wyant,* Martin,* Blakelock,* and Whittredge,* who had begun in the tight Hudson River School style, each adjusted to the new way of seeing the land, and their continuing vigor—expressed through loose, almost impressionist brushwork and the poetry of mood rather than a sense of place—took the movement up to the very end of the 19th century   (T.E.S.)

Hudson, Robert (1938–   ).
Sculptor. Born in Salt Lake City, Utah, and educated at the San Francisco Art Institute, Hudson is a central figure in the development of California funk art. His works blend a surrealist allusiveness with cartoon-derived visual jokes. Often grotesque, his humor is founded on a strong sense of the interplay between optical and sculptural values. Trained as a painter, his eccentric metal forms are brightly painted and sometimes modified by inserts of plexiglass. Cantilevered beams, distorted polygons, crushed and twisted planes appear to be jumbled together randomly. Broad color areas give an overall cohesion, while local textures make allusions to landscape, architecture, and the body. Often a form is camouflaged by the color of its surface. Where a form is clear its impact is modified by color with decorative or sexual connotations.

Hudson has exhibited on the West Coast since the late 1950s and since 1965 in museums and galleries in New York and Chicago. In gallery shows in 1970–71 the frantic, obsessive quality of his work gave way to a more sober but still idiosyncratic concern with shape under structural tension. Bent tubing, chains, and wire are ordered by a visually clear but conceptually quirky logic.   (C.R.)

Hui Ka Kwong (1922–   ).
Ceramist known for formal interests, characterized by juxtapositions of abstract geometric shapes with bright glazes. Born in Hong Kong, he was an apprentice in a pottery during World War II, and moved to the United States in 1948. He studied with Marguerite Wildenhain* at Pond Farm Workshop in California and at Alfred University. During the 1950s his work was asymmetric and organic in form, with abstract brushwork and subdued earthy glazes. During the 1960s he was drawn by his formal interests to more defined shapes, principally wheel-thrown cylinders with hard-edge slab boxes and hemispheres interrupting the central form. In 1965 he collaborated for over a year with painter Roy Lichtenstein* on a series of pop art* ceramic sculptures, to which Hui credits the development of the clear, brilliant colors and the formal and technical precision for which he is known.   (R.S.)

Hull, John (1624–83).
The earliest American silversmith whose work has been identified, he was a partner of Robert Sanderson.* Born in England, he emigrated to Massachusetts in 1635. He learned the art from his half-brother Richard Storer, who returned to England shortly thereafter. In 1652 Hull was selected by the General Court as master of the mint, coining the famous pine tree shillings,* and becoming in the process a very wealthy merchant with shipping interests. Hull received one shilling out of every twenty minted, and when his daughter Hannah was married to the illustrious judge, Samuel Sewall, her father provided a dowry equal to her weight in pine tree shillings, according to a story told by Nathaniel Hawthorne in *Grandfather's Chair.*

Of the several dozen pieces of silver made by Hull, all but one beaker in the First Church, Boston, were made in

1. *Richard Humphreys.* Silver tea urn presented to Charles Thompson by the First Continental Congress, 1774. Collection Charles T. Chamberlain.
2. *Richard Morris Hunt.* Tribune Building, N.Y., 1875.

292

partnership with Sanderson. The earliest piece of American silver known today is a dram cup (Yale) made by them about 1651. Two examples of their church silver were a short granulated beaker (1659) and a standing cup on a well-shaped baluster shaft (1674, Yale).

While most of his silver was made for churches, Hull made several early straight-handled spoons and two tall beakers in the Dutch style for domestic use, as well as several paneled caudle cups, a tankard, and two porringers. Among his apprentices were Jeremiah Dummer* and John Coney.*   (M.G.F.)

Humphreys, Richard (1749–1832). Philadelphia silversmith, born of Quaker parents on the island of Tortola. He was sent for his education to Philadelphia, where he learned the art of the silversmith presumably from Philip Syng, Jr.,* whose house, shop, and business he took over in 1772 with Syng's public recommendation. In 1781 Humphreys moved his shop at the Sign of the Coffepot down Front Street to the Drawbridge area, where he offered a large assortment of silver wares from tea sets and table wares to sword hilts, buckles, and jewelry.

Until 1797 Humphreys was listed in city directories as a silversmith, after which he was called a "china merchant," so that his known work in silver can generally be dated 1772–97. The most ambitious extant example of his silver is also the earliest example of the fully developed neoclassical style in American silver: a tea urn presented by the Continental Congress (of which Humphreys was a member) to Charles Thomson in 1774. Now owned by a descendant (on loan at Philadelphia), the urn was engraved by James Smither. Humphreys made silver camp cups (Yale), tablespoons, and possibly salvers (Mount Vernon) for George Washington. In the Philadelphia Silver Exhibition (held in 1956) thirty examples and seventeen different forms of Humphreys' work were shown, including bowls, salts, tankards, and a tea caddy. Coffee pots in an inverted pear shape, with gadrooning and a bell-shaped finial, characterized his most representative work in silver.   (M.G.F.)

Hunt, Richard Morris (1828–95). First American architect to be trained in Paris, and one of the first to introduce high standards for materials and design to America at a time (the 1850s) when the profession lacked standing and prestige. He was born in Brattleboro, Vt., and when his family moved to Boston in 1838, he attended the Boston Latin School. When Mrs. Hunt took her family abroad in 1843, he began his life-long association with Europe. After two years in the atelier of Hector M. Lefuel, he was admitted in 1848 to the École des Beaux-Arts. After graduation in 1852, he traveled widely. In 1854 he was appointed "Inspecteur des travaux" of the Louvre under Lefuel, who had become architect to Napoleon III. He was later praised for his work on the Pavillon de la Bibliothèque.

In 1855, equipped with twelve years of training such as no other American had enjoyed, he returned to his country because, "There is no place in the world where they [the fine arts] are more needed or where they should be more encouraged." On his return he was called on by Thomas Ustick Walter* in 1856 to assist in adding the House and Senate wings to the Capitol in Washington, D.C. Hunt returned to New York in 1857 and opened his atelier, first on Washington Square, and then in the Studio Building, 51 West 10th Street, which he himself had designed in a modified version of French contemporary style. Here he trained students destined to become leaders in the profession.

Hunt's work reveals two overlapping phases. The first was influenced by the medievalism introduced in France by Viollet-le-Duc and by French neo-Grec* work. The second inaugurated the age of eclecticism* with its scholarly detail. In this phase, Hunt designed work in the French Renaissance style while moving closer to Italian Renaissance and classical themes. In his first phase, Hunt designed the first apartment house of note in New York City, on East 18th Street, in 1869. In 1871, a great apartment house (later the Hotel Victoria) on West 27th Street, with shops, balconies, and towering mansard roofs, brought Parisian elegance to the city. The Presbyterian Hospital on East 70th Street (1872) was medieval in structure, but Parisian in expression. The Lenox Library, built for James Lenox in 1873 on the site now occupied by the Frick Collection, was, in its massive simplicity, a pure evocation of the fashionable Parisian neo-Grec style.

The best example of the cast-iron building fronts he designed is the Dolly Varden Store (Roosevelt Building, 1873), which is neo-Grec in its details.

This first phase of Hunt's work overlapped the second, notably in the fine Romanesque revival* Ogden Mills House (1885) at 69th Street and Fifth Avenue, New York City. Probably his most typically neo-Grec structure was the base for the Statue of Liberty (1886), a simple, powerful design worthy of Bartholdi's great statue. Despite an unfortunate addition at its base, it has withstood the test of time. In Boston, Hunt's early work was represented by the three handsome neo-Grec town houses he designed, as a unit, for a Dr. Williams (1860) on the site now occupied by the Ritz Hotel. With their linear ornament, escutcheons, and mansard roofs, they epitomized the style of that time. In Newport, R.I., he designed frame cottages for J. N. A. Griswold (1862, now the Historical Society) and for Henry G. Marquand (1872). There was also Divinity Hall at Yale (1869), the Lenox Library and the Marquand Chapel at Princeton (1875), and the Hampton Industrial School buildings (1869–80) at Fortress Monroe, Va.

In his second phase Hunt was forced to meet the demands of rich clients seeking an elegance which, they hoped, would express culture and refinement—an architecture worthy of "royalty." Hunt's first essays in this direction in New York City were in the French Renaissance style, but at first more medieval than classical: town houses for William K. Vanderbilt (1879) and for Elbridge T. Gerry (1891), both on Fifth Avenue. The Vanderbilt House stirred a city of brick and brownstone into realizing that architecture could express the architectural ambitions of "the 400." Mrs. William Astor had Hunt design, at 65th Street and Fifth Avenue, a great double house (1893) which belonged to the later, more classical phase of the French Renaissance. Hunt repeated these triumphs in Newport, R.I., with "cottages" which, except for their cramped sites, amazed Americans by their sheer elegance as resort architecture. They include Marble House (1891), built for Mrs. William K. Vanderbilt in the French classic* style of Louis XV; Belcourt (1893), Oliver H. P. Belmont's stable-residence, a medieval house but with an exterior in

2

French villa style; Ochre Court (1895), a French Renaissance chateau for Ogden Goelet, with gardens extending to the sea; and finally, The Breakers (1895), Cornelius Vanderbilt's sumptuous Mediterranean villa of Italian Renaissance inspiration.

Hunt's most important private commission was for Biltmore (1896), the French Renaissance-style chateau, designed for George Washington Vanderbilt at Asheville, N.C. Here the setting—thousands of acres—was adequate, and the grounds, landscaped by Frederick Law Olmsted,* among the finest in the country. Among other important structures by Hunt were the Administration Building at the Chicago Columbian Exposition (1893) which, with its dome and spiky sculpture by Karl Bitter, exemplified the best in Beaux-Arts design; the restrained design of the United States Naval Observatory (1894) on Massachusetts Avenue in Washington, D.C., an instance of Hunt's sense of the appropriate; and finally, the monumental, almost Roman, central section of the Metropolitan Museum (completed by his son, Richard).

Hunt was a founder of the American Institute of Architects (1857) and received many awards from French, British, and American architectural societies. (A.B.)

Hunt, William Morris (1824–1879). Painter and cultural leader. Born in Brattleboro, Vt., he was the brother of Richard Morris Hunt,* a well-known architect. Hunt showed a precocious ability to draw. He enrolled in Harvard College and studied with the sculptor Henry Kirke Brown,* but left after his third year. Delicate in health, he was taken by his mother to France and Italy. In 1846 he entered the Düsseldorf Academy, but finding the training inflexible, left after a year. He then went to Paris, where he studied with the academic painter Thomas Couture. But the greatest influence on his painting and artistic theories came from his long friendship with the French painter of the Barbizon School,* Jean-François Millet. In 1855 he returned to the United States and after moving about, settled in Boston in 1862. From 1866 to 1868 he again traveled in Europe. He then opened an art school for young ladies in Boston and developed his theories on art education, later published as *Talks on Art* (1875). By his

1

2

1. **William Morris Hunt.** The Bathers, 1877. Worcester Art Museum, Worcester, Mass.
2. **Jacob Hurd.** Silver teakettle with coat of arms. Museum of Fine Arts, Boston.

charm, wit, and knowledge he exerted a considerable influence on society in Boston and led in the patronage that wealthy Bostonians extended to artists of the Barbizon School before they were widely collected in France.

Hunt's paintings clearly show the profound influence of his French masters, as does *The Drummer Boy* (c.1862, private collection). A versatile painter, Hunt did impressive portraits such as that of Francis Gardner, Master of the Boston Latin Public School (1871, Boston Latin School), and also produced charming little genre paintings in the French manner, such as *The Bathers* (1877, Worcester) and *The Ball Players* (c.1874, Detroit). The culmination of his career was a commission to paint two large murals for the Capitol in Albany, N.Y. Entitled *Anahita, Flight of Night* (c.1878), they were regarded as the best examples of American mural painting up to that date, but are now considered of slight esthetic or art historical significance. Dampness in the stone walls on which they were painted caused the paint to peel, impairing them drastically. The stress of completing this undertaking undermined his health. Hunt drowned the next year, perhaps a suicide. (H.W.W.)

Huntington, Daniel (1816–1906).
Portrait painter. Born in New York, N.Y., he entered Yale, but soon transferred to Hamilton College, where he met Charles Loring Elliott,* a portrait painter who encouraged him to become an artist. In 1836 he studied in New York with Samuel F. B. Morse* and Henry Inman.* He went abroad in 1839 and again in 1842 and spent almost three years in Rome. Returning to America, he established himself in New York City. Between 1851 and 1858 he painted in England.

Huntington was one of the most prolific painters of his time, producing some twelve hundred works, one thousand of which are portraits. There were few categories of painting he did not try. Although he acquired most prestige as a portraitist, he was unfortunately not one of the best of his generation in this field. His likenesses are generally somber in color, stiffly posed, and lack the spark of life a superior portraitist can supply. Typical of his solid but rather dull portraits is that of the first secretary of the Smithsonian Institution, *Joseph Henry* (1857, Corco-

ran). His group portrait of five figures against an Italian landscape, *The Field Family in a Garden,* (c.1870, National Coll.) has more pictorial appeal. He enjoyed considerable popularity for religious compositions, genre paintings, and incidents from literary sources, such as *Katrina Van Tassel and Ichabod Crane* (1861) from "The Legend of Sleepy Hollow" by Washington Irving (Sleepy Hollow Restorations, Tarrytown, N.Y.). Unquestionably his most widely known painting was *Mercy's Dream* (1842, Pennsylvania), of which there are two replicas (1850, Corcoran, and 1858, Metropolitan). The sentimentality of this painting (taken from *Pilgrim's Progress*) is cloying to current taste, but it was vastly esteemed from the 1840s to the 1860s and was often reproduced in engravings. Huntington's landscapes differ from typical Hudson River School* views in that he was more interested in general atmospheric effects than in finished studies of a particular landscape. *Trout Brook* (1848, Montclair Art Museum, New Jersey) has a rather sickly greenish cast and reveals a lack of detailed observation of nature.

He was elected to the National Academy of Design* in 1840 and served as its president (1862–70 and 1877–90). Unlike many painters, Huntington enjoyed great prestige, popularity, and financial rewards while he lived. The collapse of his reputation came after his death and today he seems much less important than many of his once less-esteemed contemporaries. (H.W.W.)

Hurd, Jacob, Nathaniel, and **Benjamin.**
An outstanding American silversmith, Jacob Hurd (1702/3–58) was born in Charlestown, Mass. He probably received his training from John Edwards* and established himself in business in Boston in 1724. A captain in the Boston regiment, he was commissioned to make the long silver mace of the Admiralty Court (Massachusetts Historical Society, on loan to Boston). His biographer located 296 examples of his work in 1939, and a number of other examples have since been recorded. Maker of ecclesiastical vessels as well as tutorial silver, he is especially noted for the large two-handled covered cups that Boston merchants presented to the ships' captains who had captured

French privateers. The earliest of these is the fifteen-inch grace cup (Yale) presented to the commander of the ship *Prince of Orange* in 1744. Its design closely follows that of a London-made cup owned in Boston at the time. It has a curvilinear body with an elaborately engraved cartouche above the midband, a high double-domed lid surmounted by a large knob finial, and a circular stepped base. In addition to the usual forms, Jacob Hurd made chafing dishes, sword hilts, and such rare items as candlesticks. His most unusual form is the large teakettle on stand (Boston) in the early rococo style with a round body engraved with a coat of arms.

Two of Jacob Hurd's sons became silversmiths. Benjamin (1739–81) left few examples of his silver, most of which were spoons. He has been noted as a heraldic artist as well as a silversmith, and also as an engraver of certificates for the masonic lodge.

Nathaniel Hurd (1729/30–77) achieved his reputation as an engraver. Twenty-four extant examples of his silver attest to his skill as a silversmith, most being engraved with a coat of arms, crest or initials. John Singleton Copley's* portrait (Cleveland) shows him with a copy of John Guillim's *Display of Heraldry* on the table beside him. He used this book for his armorial engraving on silver as well as for seals and bookplates. More than 110 varieties and states of bookplates engraved by Nathaniel Hurd, displaying fifty-five different coats of arms, have been located. Among the seals which he cut are those of the Boston Marine Society, 1754, Brown University, 1765, and Dartmouth College, 1773. (M.G.F.)

Impressionism (American).

American artists were generally first introduced to the French impressionist movement during the late 1880s. By the 1890s, an active group of American painters had adopted impressionist techniques in varying degree. Though the creative stimulation of impressionism lasted only a decade or so, the revolutionary implications of impressionist concepts influenced all later generations of painters. French impressionism emerged as a full-fledged style when a group of progressive French artists joined to exhibit as the "Société Anonyme" in 1874. The exhibition raised a storm of protest and the painters were dubbed "Impressionists" after the title of Monet's *Impression—Sunrise* (1872). The group, which included, among others, Pissarro, Sisley, Renoir, Degas, and eventually Mary Cassatt,* exhibited together eight times, the last in 1886, by which time their work had won general acceptance. They began at this time to influence younger American painters.

Impressionism involved the awareness that light is perceived as color sensations which constantly change, that form is perceived only as light reflected from a surface, while shadow is merely light of a lower intensity. The manner of painting light takes the place of subject matter. Subject, in turn, is no more than a motif drawn from landscape, still life, or perhaps a figure. Since only color is perceived, line is not used, and the customary chiaroscuro of studio painting is abandoned in the interest of portraying colored light. Likewise, effects of three-dimensional plasticity and deep space are subordinated to the effect of a continuous, flattened picture surface; changes in colored pigment on this surface indicate that form and space are perceived as colored light. Since light is depicted through color, it is analyzed into its constituent parts, and variations in hue and intensity are stressed. This leads to the application of color in small brushstrokes, which in turn heightens the effect of vibration and change of light. In the end, as Lionello Venturi says of Monet's painting, "When that effect of vibration was no longer felt to be merely a rendering of life but was considered a requirement of painting style, then impressionism was truly born."

Mary Cassatt was the first American associated with the impressionist movement. As early as 1874 she began to employ the high-key colors of the group, and her work caught the eye of Degas, whom she particularly admired. In 1879 she exhibited with the impressionists and also in the United States. It was at this period that her work took on, for a time, some of the vibration of impressionism proper, though she was never an impressionist in the narrowest sense. Although the early oils of John Singer Sargent,* dating from about 1875, seem to reflect something of the impressionist manner, he did not pursue impressionist techniques further until after his visit to Monet in 1887. Theodore Robinson* sought out Monet the next year, and he and Sargent were the first Americans to paint landscape under the direct influence of Monet. Meanwhile, Childe Hassam* was adapting impressionism to street scenes in Paris, and when he returned to the United States in 1889, he pioneered in bringing back the new style. He did not have to suffer as an innovator. Impressionism aroused little furor in this country. The Durand-Ruel gallery had presented a full-dress show of impressionists in New York City in 1886, and the exhibit was generally well received.

About 1890 J. Alden Weir* and Edmund Tarbell* began to adopt impressionist techniques, and they were soon joined by John Twachtman,* Robert Reid,* F. W. Benson,* Robert Vonnoh,* and others. By 1898, a group of these artists banded together to exhibit as The Ten*; by that time, the pioneering phase of American impressionism was past.

The various American impressionists evolved their styles independently and belonged to no definite school. In general, they did not carry the technique as far as did Monet and his associates; the Americans kept a firmer grasp on form and normally accepted appearances. On occasion, however, the American subjective tradition intervened, and such a painter as Twachtman used impressionist devices to achieve effects that were poetic rather than realistic.   (D.W.S.)

Independent Artists, The Exhibition of (1910).

The first large, unrestricted, no-jury and no-prize exhibition in the United States, it formed an important link between the exhibitions of The Eight* in 1908 and the Armory Show* in 1913. Robert Henri* and his friends felt that the independent character of their Macbeth Gallery show titled "The Eight" should be embodied in an exhibition of broader scope. Talks became frequent following the rejections by the National Academy's 1909 winter jury, with Henri proposing to organize the "Independent American Artists." Early in March, 1910, Henri and John Sloan* were stung by fresh rejections by the Academy jury. Within three days they worked out a plan with Walt Kuhn* to stage a large exhibition starting April 1. It was motivated by an element of pique, but also by a belief in a basic policy, as Henri made clear in an article in *The Craftsman:* it was intended to provide a chance for young artists to show "the independent personal evidence which each artist has to make and which must become a record of their time. . . ."

The organizational problem was

staggering and the expenses mounted sharply. Henri, Sloan, Kuhn, and Arthur B. Davies* assessed themselves $200 apiece, and others made smaller contributions. Sloan served as secretary-treasurer; William Glackens* and George Bellows* joined the others to help with the hanging. Exhibitors included all of The Eight except George Luks (who was preparing his own one-man show) and a number of Henri students. In all, more than a hundred artists were represented by some 500 works.

The exhibition proved a sensation. Over two thousand people caused such a jam at the galleries on the opening night that the police were called. The press, as usual, gave widely varying criticisms of the displays but contributed colorful publicity. Nevertheless, sales were almost negligible. The most important effect of the exhibition was its demonstration that the time was ripe for such broadly inclusive, independent ventures, and that a few dedicated artists could plan and stage them. The independents, not the Academy, had the spotlight, and the American art scene was profoundly altered by the exhibitions that followed. A sidelight of the exhibition was the polarization of the nontraditional painters of America into two distinct groups: Alfred Stieglitz'* avant-garde coterie at Gallery 291 did not show in the Independents' exhibition. Henri and his followers were not modernists nor sophisticates; their group represented a "third stream" much closer to the American popular tastes of the day than were either the academics or modernists.   (D.W.S.)

Independent Artists, The Society of. Founded in New York City in 1917, it established the large, liberal type of exhibition called for by the rapid increase in numbers of artists and changes in styles of the first two decades of this century. The National Academy had long held a near monopoly on exhibition opportunities, and it could not cope with this growth. Exhibitions such as those of the Independent Artists* in 1910, and the Armory Show* in 1913 were planned as outlets for younger and more progressive artists. Members of The Eight,* together with their friends and students, were deeply involved in both these shows and later in the Society, whose founders included Walter Pach,* William

1

2

Impressionism
1. *Childe Hassam. Nude Seated, 1912. National Gallery of Art, Washington, D.C. (Chester Dale Collection).*

2. *J. Alden Weir. The Red Bridge, 1895. Metropolitan Museum of Art, N.Y. (gift of Mrs. John A. Rutherford).*

Indiana

Glackens,* and Maurice Prendergast,* together with three French expatriates, Villon, Marcel Duchamp,* and Picabia. The model for the Society was the French Société des Artistes Indépendants, whose annual Salon des Indépendants the American society emulated, adopting the same motto: no jury, no prizes. The only requirement for membership was payment of a small initiation fee and annual dues. To avoid the abuses of the traditional picture-hanging committee, works were arranged in alphabetical order. The opening exhibition was held in April, 1917, at the Grand Central Palace, with over 1100 artists represented.

The following year, John Sloan* was elected president, and he held the office throughout his lifetime. Under his leadership, the Society supported the arts nationally, arranging traveling exhibitions and encouraging regional shows. During the 1920s the annual exhibitions in New York were among the liveliest events of the season. The exhibitions, of course, contained works of very uneven quality, but many serious and accomplished artists participated, and they afforded young painters of talent a first showcase. In the 1930s, exhibition opportunities began to increase generally, and the need for a complement to the National Academy declined. During World War II the exhibitions were discontinued and the Society became inactive. It had served its purpose in forming a bridge, as Sloan expressed it, between the Armory Show and the general acceptance of the modern movement.   (D.W.S.)

Indiana, Robert (1928–   ).
Painter and printmaker whose name is a pseudonym taken from his native state. He was born Robert Clark in New Castle, Ind., and received a B.F.A. from the Art Institute of Chicago. He may be said to belong to the wing of pop art* that has concerned itself with a form of sign painting based on familiar images of the American scene. He characteristically paints in bold, contrasting, and frequently clashing colors and with much use of black and white. His images are those of American road signs and billboards.

Of all the hard-edge public painters, Indiana is closest to the earlier American tradition of precisionist painting, particularly that of Charles Demuth.* This relationship is acknowledged in

3

4

5

1. **Robert Indiana.** The Demuth American Dream No. 5, *1963. Collection Mr. and Mrs. Robert Scull, N.Y.* **Industrial Design**
2. *Employee cafeteria, First National Bank of Chicago, 1969.*
3. *Executive offices, RCA Building, New York City, 1970.*
4. *Stacking cupholders, Fabrika Corp., Kalamazoo, Mich., 1970.*
5. *Credit Verification Terminal, Emerson Electric Co., St. Louis, 1971.*
6. *Series II Tractor-Shovel, Clark Equipment Co., Buchanan, Mich., 1962. All designed by Ford & Earl Designer Associates, N.Y.*

one of Indiana's best-known paintings, *The Demuth American Dream No. 5* (1963, private collection), which was inspired by Demuth's well-known *I Saw the Figure 5 in Gold* (1928, Metropolitan). Other well-known Indiana images are the paintings *Love, Eat, Die,* and so forth, in which the word, presented in large block letters and bold color, frequently within a light circle imbedded in a black or deeply colored rectangle, achieves a hypnotic effect and attempts to give a universal impact to the familiar or commonplace.

(H.H.A.)

Industrial Designer.
A present-day American phenomenon. With the 20th century came tremendous industrial expansion, mass production, and competition, stimulating a race to design the most attractive as well as efficient product. To achieve this goal, large companies began to hire people with art or architectural backgrounds. The industrial designer thus emerged toward the end of the 1920s, when purchasing power was at a peak. He had to be versatile—able to design everything from furniture, interiors, exhibitions, radios, and refrigerators to railroad trains and automobiles.

Design pioneers like Norman Bel Geddes* and Walter Dorwin Teague (1883–1960) did much to modernize our environment. Bel Geddes is credited with inventing the verb "streamline" to express the desire to reduce friction in an era when speed of movement is highly prized. He is also credited with changing the style of department store displays. Teague transformed the appearance of cameras, air-conditioning and optical equipment, caterpillar tractors, x-ray machines, and automobile service stations, and he helped to modernize automobile design as early as the Marmom Model 16 of the early 1920s. Other early leaders in design are Henry Dreyfus,* who remodeled trains, clocks, bathroom fixtures; Russell Wright (1905–), whose energies have been directed toward the home, especially furniture, dinnerware, flatware, drapery, upholstery, and lamps; Raymond Loewy (1893–), and John Vassos. Such designers have contributed functional improvements as well as beauty to everyday objects whose appearance had been taken for granted. Since the 1930s, these designers have so expanded their range of activities as to require international companies that pool the talents of architects, engineers, artists, and draftsmen, and many companies have made design staffs an integral part of their organization. (D.P.)

Ingham, Charles Cromwell (1796–1863).
Portrait and miniature painter. A native of Dublin, Ireland, he studied art there before emigrating to New York City with his parents at the age of twenty. His *Death of Cleopatra,* awarded a prize in Dublin, was much praised by American critics. He remained a New Yorker throughout his life, and was a founder and vice-president of the National Academy of Design,* and an important figure in the society and art worlds. His work is laborious, highly finished, and distinguished by an almost pre-Raphaelite rendering of precise detail, with a strong infusion of Victorian sentimentality. His *Amelia Palmer* (1830, Metropolitan) is a charming example of his style. (C.C.S.)

Inman, Henry (1801–46).
Painter. Born in Utica, N.Y., he moved with his family to New York City in 1812. Two years later he was apprenticed to John Wesley Jarvis,* with whom he remained for seven years as a favorite pupil and assistant. Toward the end of that time they worked in close collaboration, Jarvis taking the likeness and Inman finishing each canvas. During a successful visit to New Orleans in 1820–21, they completed six portraits a week, grossing $6000. The two were in Boston soon after, where Inman did better than his master, as his little watercolor portraits, made with great facility, caught the fancy of the public. Inman opened his own studio in New York City in 1824, and in 1826–28 worked in collaboration with a student of his own, Thomas S. Cummings.* Inman was a founder of the National Academy of Design* in 1826, and its vice-president until 1831, when he moved to a farm near Philadelphia and became a partner of Cephas Grier Childs (1793–1871) in the publication of lithographs. Inman's versatility fitted him well for this role, for he was successful with genre and landscape subjects as well as with portraits. By 1838 he was apparently the best-paid painter in America. But he returned to New York as a portrait painter in 1834. In

1

2

1. *George Inness.* Home of the Heron, 1893. Art Institute of Chicago (Edward B. Butler Collection).
2. *George Inness.* The Monk, 1873. Addison Gallery of American Art, Phillips Academy, Andover, Mass.

1844–45, in failing health, he visited England to fulfill commissions for two portraits: *William Wordsworth* (University of Pennsylvania) and *T. B. Macaulay* (Pennsylvania). He was well received, but he soon returned to New York and died a few months later.

Much loved and admired in his lifetime, Inman's work reflects the advancing taste of his time and his own attractive personality. His revealing *Self-portrait* (1834, Pennsylvania), a little painting turned out to illustrate a point under discussion with friends, is one of his best. His strongly characterized *John Wesley Jarvis* (Fogg) was a tribute to his teacher and friend. (C.C.S.)

Inness, George (1825–94).
One of the ablest and most prolific of 19th-century landscape painters. Inness spent his earliest years in New York City and in Newark, N.J. A sickly youth, he had little formal education and he soon decided to become a painter. His first brief instruction in art was with the itinerant painter John Jesse Barker (active 1815–56). He was then apprenticed for about two years to the engravers Sherman and Smith in New York.

Inness received moderate praise at the age of nineteen when he exhibited a landscape at the National Academy of Design* in New York; thereafter, he exhibited regularly at the Academy and at the American Art-Union* until it closed in 1852. His early landscapes reflect the influence of the prevailing Hudson River School* style, and particularly the detailed, vertical woodland views of Asher B. Durand.* Yet even at this point his work is distinguished by a compositional expressiveness and sophistication that suggest that he already knew something of European landscape prints.

Inness was a frequent European traveler, going to Italy about 1850 and to France in 1853–54, and sojourning in both countries during 1870–74. He appears to have been particularly impressed by the dramatic, freely painted landscapes of the Barbizon School* in France about 1853. Though he never became an imitator of foreign styles, he did not hesitate to use what he learned abroad. The result was a development from a tight early style to a poetic, almost abstract late manner— which earns him a place as one of the most creative of American landscape painters. The paintings that culminate his first mature period, such as *Peace and Plenty* (1865, Metropolitan), are still in the Hudson River* mode; they express the kind of expansiveness and optimism found in paintings by the best of Inness' contemporaries, such as Albert Bierstadt* and Frederic E. Church.* At the same time, his work glows with light and color, suggesting that he was already trying to go beyond the realistic, panoramic style of mid-century. As the critic Samuel Isham recognized, Inness "felt instinctively the weakness of the Hudson River School, and his foreign study and personal genius led him to an ampler, completer art."

Inness lived in New York until 1859, then moved to Medfield, Mass., and in 1864 settled in Eagleswood, N.J. In 1870 he and his wife and his son, George, Jr. (whose own later paintings can be confused with his father's) left for a four-year stay in Italy that resulted in considerable changes in his style: a new interest in the drama of color and form, gradual rejection of the topographical accuracy of the Hudson River School, and an increasingly "electric" brushwork through which the artist expressed his passions. A masterpiece of this period is the dark, brooding painting, *The Monk* (1873, Addison).

During the artist's late period, from about 1880 on, his powers increased and he turned further away from literal transcription of scenery and toward a personal vision of nature. Seldom working outdoors, almost never sketching, often repainting a single canvas many times as various frenzied visions occurred to him, Inness created some of the most powerful works in American art. These late paintings have been explained on various grounds: that he had been influenced by the loose brushwork of the French impressionists (which he vehemently denied); that he had become a disciple of the Swedish religious mystic, Emanuel Swedenborg; or that the frenzy of his late work reflects his own personality, and particularly a lifetime of poor health, including epilepsy.

Inness' example in moving from the Hudson River style to one of increased richness of tone and breadth of handling led such younger men as Alexander H. Wyant* and Homer D. Martin* in the same direction. Inness' development reflects an increasing disillusion concerning the future of the land itself in the post-Civil War years; it also parallels a shift in taste away from the native American school toward a more fashionable "French taste." One of the best known of Inness' late works is *The Home of the Heron* (1893, Chicago), a painting of rich glazes and glowing colors whose blurred, visionary mood is typical of his art in these years. At a time in the 1880s when the masters of realism, such as Church, were increasingly neglected, Inness found both critical appreciation and patronage for the first time. In this period he lived mainly in Montclair, N.J., though he continued to travel widely for his health. He died while visiting Scotland. (T.E.S.)

Insley, Will (1929–   ).
Sculptor whose vast projects for monuments recall the fantasies of 18th-century visionary architects, and combine his skills as draftsman, architect, painter, and sculptor. He studied at Amherst College and then took a degree in architecture at the Harvard Graduate School of Design. He worked primarily in painting during his first years in New York, and his first one-man exhibition, in 1965, included severe, geometrically designed abstractions. Soon after, he began studying the possibilities in extending his designs in three dimensions, producing numerous plans and drawings, as well as charts, graphs, and poetic texts which, taken together, formed a universe uniquely derived from fantasy. Models for Insley's monuments, which are often planned for vast spaces such as tundras and deserts, invariably suggest in their sculptural simplicity the sacred places of long-vanished civilizations. But they are sacred places, as he says, remembered from the future, and as such, seem grim and foreboding. They tend to be rendered in concrete, often with concentric sloping walls that are intended to extend for miles, and suggest mythical mazes. His drawings, with their slipping, arching spaces, confirm the complexity of his spatial imagery.

Insley has exhibited widely since 1965 and has had many one-man shows. (D.A.)

International Style.
The dominant architectural style in the United States since the late 1920s, it

has sought to reflect the machine esthetic, from the smallest piece of furniture to plans for entire cities. The ideal building in this style is independent of its site, often floating above the ground on stilts; the building is an unadorned box, often with white stucco walls punctured by horizontally repeated window units. The enclosing walls are separated from the structure; the interior space is open, with one area flowing into another, and a unity of interior and exterior is achieved through walls of glass. The materials used—steel, concrete, and glass—are those associated with the machine and its products.

The style originated in Europe in the early 1920s, and by 1930 was already codified. The three Europeans most responsible for it were the Swiss-French architect, Le Corbusier (1887–1965), and two German architects closely linked with the Bauhaus* (the famous German school of design), Walter Gropius* and Mies van der Rohe.* Of these, Le Corbusier exercised the strongest worldwide influence, both in the design of his buildings and through numerous plans for cities. It was he who most convincingly established the image of the modern city as freestanding skyscrapers* set in vast open parklands. Architects and urban planners in America and elsewhere have returned again and again to this image for urban renewal projects and new communities.

Although the style was basically a European import, many of its sources were American. The early prairie designs of Frank Lloyd Wright* were a major force in its development. And certain buildings by the southern California architect Irving Gill may be mistaken for early International style work from Europe. During the 1920s only a handful of buildings constructed in the United States could be considered examples of the International style, and they came from Rudolph Schindler* and Richard J. Neutra,* both Viennese in background and training. Schindler's concrete beach house for the Lovells (Newport Beach, 1922–26), and Neutra's steel-framed Los Angeles residence, also for the Lovells (1929), are the only buildings in the new style that are comparable to the work in Europe of Le Corbusier, Gropius, and Mies van der Rohe.

America became more receptive to the new style after 1930. In 1932 the new Museum of Modern Art in New York City organized its influential show, "The International Style: Architecture Since 1922." Soon after came Howe and Lescaze's Philadelphia Savings Fund Society Building (Philadelphia, 1932), which was both streamlined moderne* and modern—i.e., the International style—and A. Lawrence Kocher and Albert Fray's small steel-framed vacation house on Long Island (1934). Until the late 1930s, most American buildings were only marginally International style; American architects were far more interested in streamlined moderne. But Wright adopted the new style with true conviction and produced such masterpieces as the Kaufmann House at Bear Run, Pa. (1936). On the West Coast, both Neutra and Schindler were highly productive in the 1930s, but their work was almost exclusively residential. The only eastern designers who can be squeezed into the International style category were William Lescaze* and the Detroit firm of Albert Kahn,* the latter producing an impressive group of pre-World War II industrial buildings.

By the end of the 1930s the International style was only one of several competing styles in the United States. It was saved from eclipse partly by the immigration of several leading European exponents of the style. By 1940 Gropius, Mies van der Rohe, Marcel Breuer,* Laszlo Moholy-Nagy,* Herbert Bayer, and Erich Mendelsohn had come to America and soon occupied important positions in architectural education and in industry, Gropius as chairman of the School of Architecture at Harvard, and Mies van der Rohe in a similar position at the Illinois Institute of Technology in Chicago. Inspired by these major figures, American architects quickly took up the style and produced some creditable work. In the East, Hugh Stubbins seized on its visual geometry and clothed his buildings, as Gropius and Breuer had done, in wood sheathing. More stringent in his interpretation of the style was Philip Johnson.* His own courtyard house in Cambridge, Mass. (1942) was certainly comparable in quality to Mies van der Rohe's courtyard-oriented houses of the early 1930s. Equally adroit in handling the style in their pre-World War II designs were Eero Saarinen* and his father Eliel Saarinen.* Their winning project for the Smithsonian Gallery of Art (Washington, D.C., 1939) was a

Chauncey Bradley Ives. Egeria, 1876, marble. Virginia Museum of Fine Arts, Richmond.

successful blend of the International style with a modicum of streamlined moderne and the conservative modernism of contemporary Scandinavian architecture. In southern California the lessons of the style as expressed by Neutra were applied to many small buildings by Gregory Ain and Raphael Soriano; while in northern California, Ernest Kump (of Kranklin and Kump) began to produce school buildings such as that at La Fayette (1940–41), where various units of a school were spread loosely over the site but were connected by open passages.

The San Francisco Bay area of California was also the home of a popular woodsy, or "soft," version of the style. In the late 1930s and early 1940s, William Wurster, Gardner Dailey, John Funk, and the southern California designer Harwell H. Harris, combined elements of the style with the local vernacular wood tradition. While this combination was less expressive of the machine, it produced buildings that were more livable and much more related to American building technology than the symbolic, machine-oriented International style.

After World War II the International style, and variations thereof, became the prevailing style in America. Only domestic architecture remained untouched by it despite a vigorous effort by the Internationalists to encourage such a use. Johnson designed his "glass house" in New Canaan, Conn. (1949), and Mies van der Rohe produced his much publicized Farnsworth House in Plano, Ill. (1950). On the West Coast, John Entenza, publisher of *Arts and Architecture,* introduced his Case Study House program, with its evangelistic commitment to steel, glass, and modular planning. Out of this program came some of the most significant International style designs of the period, ranging from the Charles Eames* House on the Pacific Palisades (1949) to the beautiful and convincing high-art architecture of the Los Angeles houses of Craig Ellwood.

The period from 1945 through 1959 saw a resurgence of the skyscraper, but now under the aegis of the International style. The post-World War II skyscraper style quickly became a set formula. But in the hands of such gifted designers as Gordon Bunshaft* of Skidmore, Owings & Merrill* it resulted in impressive buildings such as Lever House (New York City, 1952) and the Pepsi Cola Building (New York City, 1958–59). Mies van der Rohe himself, working with Philip Johnson, designed what probably is the masterpiece in the academic International style—the Seagram Building (New York City, 1956–58). Equally impressive were Erich Mendelsohn's Maimonides Health Center (San Francisco, 1946–50) and Eliel and Eero Saarinen's General Motors Technical Center (Warren, Mich., 1951–57).

As with any popularly accepted style, most of the American buildings of the International style of the 1950s and 1960s were hardly brilliant examples of architecture. But since the style could be captured through a set formula, it could be repeated with reasonable success by the average architect.

(D.G.)

Ives, Chauncey Bradley (1810–1894). Sculptor. Born in Hamden, Conn., he learned woodcarving during his apprenticeship under a local craftsman and then began modeling portrait busts in New Haven. An early example of his work is the bust of David Daggett (1839, Yale). After working briefly in Boston and New York City, he left for Italy in 1844. Until 1851 he resided in Florence, where he produced portrait busts in the prevailing naturalistic style with a touch of neoclassicism* in the toga-like drape about the shoulders. His portraits displayed great refinement and were superior to most contemporary marble portraiture in their animation and beauty of sculptural form. Although he made brief trips to New York to dispose of his works, his home was in Rome from 1851 until his death. The classical influence of Rome inspired him to works on ideal themes, usually full-length marble figures from ancient mythology, literature, and the Bible. His greatest fame came from works such as *Undine* (1855, Yale) and *Pandora* (1854) and *Egeria* (1876, both Virginia Museum of Fine Arts). Touched by mid-century neoclassicism, they were really a romanticized version of that style. They were very popular and Ives continually received commissions for marble replicas of these works, producing as many as twenty of his *Sans Souci* (c.1855).

Around 1870 Connecticut commissioned Ives to do life-size, full-length statues of Roger Sherman and Jonathan Trumbull for Statuary Hall in the U.S. Capitol, where they were placed in 1872. But Ives had difficulties with anatomical proportions in these works and was more successful in statuary conceived in the romantic spirit, using picturesque and melodramatic images from the great literature of the past. He retired about 1875 on the modest fortune his art had brought him.   (W.C.)

Jackson, John Adams (1825–79).
Sculptor. A native of Bath, Me., he studied painting in Paris in the late 1840s. Returning to Boston, he decided to become a sculptor, and one of his earliest works is his portrait bust of Daniel Webster (1851). The stylistic basis of his work was naturalism; and he showed a refined sensitivity in the modeling and in capturing facial expression. His busts of George S. Hillard (1853, Boston Athenaeum) and William Lloyd Garrison (1858) are in the pseudoclassical manner of the time. Jackson went to Florence in 1853, and about 1860 he settled there permanently. He did attempt a few works on allegorical or ideal themes, including *Dawn* and *Morning Glory*. *Eve Mourning over the Dead Body of Abel* (1869) was much praised and is probably his most famous work.   (W.C.)

Jackson, William Henry (1843–1942).
Photographer. Jackson was born in Keeseville, N.Y., and devoted most of his long career to photographing the scenic wonders of the American West. At fifteen he became a retoucher for a photographer in Troy, N.Y., and at seventeen he apprenticed himself to Frank Mowrey, a photographer in Rutland, Vt. Jackson served as a cartographer during the first years of the Civil War. In 1863 he worked at Styles' Gallery of Art, a photograph studio in Burlington, Vt. In 1866 he traveled to California and in 1868 settled in Omaha, Neb., where he photographed the construction of the railroad and nearby Indian villages. During 1870–79 he was photographer to the U.S. Geological and Geographical Survey under Dr. Ferdinand Hayden. Some of Jackson's collodion negatives were a mammoth 20 x 24 inches, painstakingly transported by muleback into the Rocky Mountains. "These are," he wrote, "the largest plates ever used in field photog-

raphy in this country. They convey an impression of the real grandeur and the magnitude of mountain scenery that the smaller views cannot possibly impart." Nine of his photographs of the Yellowstone region were shown to both houses of Congress and were instrumental in having that area declared, in 1872, the first national park.

Jackson founded the Jackson Photo Company in Denver, Col., in 1879, and in 1898 he became a partner and chief photographer in the Detroit Publishing Company in Michigan. Administrative duties prevented him from photographing actively after 1902. Jackson died in New York City at the age of 99 and was buried in the National Cemetery in Arlington, Va.   (D.L.)

Jarves, Deming (1790–1869).
New England glass manufacturer. Jarves was clerk of the Boston Porcelain and Glass Manufacturing Company during its brief life (1814–17) and agent of the New England Glass Company, East Cambridge, Mass., from its inception in 1818 until he withdrew to direct the Boston & Sandwich Glass Company in Sandwich, Mass., in 1825. He was associated with the New England Glass Bottle Company, and in 1837 he was instrumental in founding the Mt. Washington Glass Works in South Boston. In 1858 Jarves left the Boston & Sandwich factory to organize the Cape Cod Glass Works, only a few blocks away, which he ran until his death. He thus helped in founding six glass factories, four of which made tablewares of high quality. Jarves is credited with three developments in glass pressing: he was granted a patent in 1828 for "pressing glass into moulds," one in 1829 for pressed glass knobs with a glass screw shank, and one in 1830 for pressed glass objects with attached handles. Although he was not a glassblower and is not thus associated with

the production of any individual pieces of glass, he was probably proficient in the technical aspects of glassmaking —for example, batch mixing, glass receipts, and moldmaking. He published *Reminiscences of Glass-making* in 1854. His fame rests on the quality of the glass he made, his business abilities, and his faith in glass as a material.

(J.S.S.)

Jarves, James Jackson (1818–88).
American author, art critic, and collector who was a pioneer in almost everything he did. Jarves began collecting Italian "primitives," mainly paintings of the trecento and quattrocento, during the 1850s, hoping to create the core for a future American national gallery. He failed in this plan due to public indifference and critical hostility, and eventually deposited his whole collection in the then-new Yale Art School as security on a loan; when he defaulted, Yale purchased the entire collection of 119 paintings at auction. He was indefatigable as a collector, and later groups of objects assembled by Jarves are now at the Cleveland Museum, at Wellesley College, and at the Metropolitan Museum.

Jarves was also an articulate and widely-read art critic, and here again he was well ahead of his time. In his book *The Art-Idea: Sculpture, Painting, and Architecture in America* (1864) he rejected the prevailing notion of realism in American landscape painting, and opted for the more painterly, moody works of George Inness* and others who had been influenced by the French school. He wrote many other books on art and travel, including *Art Hints* (1855), *Art Studies* (1861), *Art Thoughts* (1870), and *Italian Rambles* (1883).   (T.E.S.)

Jarvis, John Wesley (1780–1840).
Portrait and miniature painter who was

1

2

1. *John Wesley Jarvis.* Washington Irving, *1809. Sleepy Hollow Restorations, Tarrytown, N.Y.*
2. *William Henry Jackson.* Tower Creek, *Yellowstone National Park, 1871, National Archives, Washington, D.C.*

born in England and brought to Philadelphia in 1785. From 1796–1801 he was apprenticed to the painter and engraver Edward Savage.* Jarvis subsequently set up a studio in New York, and from 1802–10 produced portraits and miniatures in partnership with Joseph Wood (c.1778–1830), a specialist in small cabinet-size likenesses. In 1806–07 he gave home and friendship to the aging Thomas Paine, of whom he sculpted a remarkable bust (now at the New York Historical Society).

From 1814 to 1834 he was one of the leading portraitists in America. On the floor above his studio Jarvis assembled an exhibit of his own landscapes, copies of Old Masters, and some works of other artists. To these he added in 1814 the controversial and titillating *Danae* of Adolph Ulrich Wertmuller,* an investment which brought visitors flocking to his door, and added income. At this time, Henry Inman* and John Quidor* joined him as pupils and assistants. Inman finished the drapery and backgrounds of his portraits. After 1820, Jarvis traveled more widely (including sojourns in Baltimore and New Orleans) and always with a success reflecting the brilliance and speed of his painting and the humor of his conversation. A wit and raconteur, he spent his money and talent so freely and gave himself so willingly to high living that he stands out as the prototype of the carefree bohemian. In 1834 a paralytic stroke ended his professional career.

His mature work has a sturdy, painterly competence, revealing a free spirit, a firm clear hand, and ability to capture a likeness. His *Alexander Anderson* (1815, Metropolitan), an unfinished study of the founder of wood engraving as a fine art in America, is a noteworthy example. Among his major works are the full-lengths of military and naval heroes of the War of 1812, painted for New York's City Hall. Among his many notable sitters were Andrew Jackson, whom he painted in 1819, and Washington Irving, who sat for him in 1809. A son, Charles Wesley Jarvis (1812–68), a pupil of Henry Inman, also became a successful portrait painter. (C.C.S.)

Jay, William (1792–1837).
Architect. Born in Bath, England, an area of well-developed architecture which must have attracted his attention.

He was apprenticed to a London architect, and soon exhibited at the Royal Academy (1809–17). His only known design in England, Albion Chapel, in London (1815, demolished 1879), had a Greek Ionic entrance and low dome. In 1817, he moved to Savannah, Ga.

Several of Jay's buildings still stand in Savannah and Charleston, though some of the best have disappeared. Most were in the fashionable new Greek revival* mode. In Savannah, these were the Branch Bank of the United States (1820, demolished); the Owen-Thomas House; Scarborough House (now a school, with later alterations); Telfair House (now Telfair Academy, with later additions); and the Bullock House (demolished). The Ashley Hall School for Girls, 172 Rutledge Avenue, Charleston, is attributed to him. His Marine Villa, on Sullivan's Island (1819, demolished), was in the Gothic* style. His designs are original in the classical revival manner, always tasteful and free of the awkwardnesses of many more experienced architects.

Although he apparently accomplished much during his few years in Georgia, Jay returned to England about 1822. Nothing is known of his work for the next decade, but in 1836 he went to the colony of Mauritius as assistant chief architect and inspector of works. He died soon afterward. (P.F.N.)

Jefferson, Thomas (1743–1826).
Statesman, architect, writer, born in Albemarle County, Va. (This entry covers only his architectural activities.) While at William and Mary College, Williamsburg, Va., Jefferson became acquainted with a group of educated men interested in the beauty as well as the usefulness of architecture. This led to his desire to design his own house (Monticello, 1768) on his property at Charlottesville, Va. He first constructed a one-room brick building to serve as a law office, but when Shadwell, the family home, burned he was forced to live in the little building. As Monticello was gradually completed, the little building was incorporated in the total plan. Jefferson's first design for Monticello was inspired by engravings in books by the Italian Renaissance architect Palladio and by Robert Morris's *Select Architecture* (1755). Monticello was left unfinished when Jefferson went to France as ambassador. On his

return, inspired by contemporary French architecture like the Hôtel de Salm in Paris, he remodeled it, making the two-story house appear single-storied. He also retained an Italian influence by roughly imitating Palladio's Villa Rotunda, Vicenza. Built of red brick and white wood trim, Monticello, completed in 1808, remains one of the handsomest homes of the era. Its romantic setting on a hill overlooking Charlottesville, with broad gardens around it, adds greatly to its architectural effectiveness.

Keenly interested in all that might enhance America, Jefferson promoted the idea of good architecture for public buildings. "The first principles of the art of architecture are unknown," he said, "and there exists scarcely a model among us sufficiently chaste to give an idea of them." His first chance to set an example came when the Virginia legislature asked him, while he was in Paris, to provide a design for the new Capitol building in Richmond. Jefferson had been so taken with a Roman building called the Maison Carrée at Nîmes in southern France that he asked the French architect Clerisseau to design the Richmond Capitol based on the Maison Carrée. Jefferson also contributed his own ideas, so that the final design was a combined effort. It was the first American building directly inspired by classical architecture.

Jefferson laid down the conditions of the competition for the Capitol and White House, Washington, D.C., and even himself submitted a design for the president's house in case no other proved satisfactory. When Jefferson became president and the Capitol Building was still under construction, he pleaded for appropriations to continue building it, and appointed B. H. Latrobe* architect after other architects had been dismissed. Jefferson summed up his feeling about the importance of enduring architecture thus: ". . . when buildings are of durable materials, every new edifice is an actual and permanent acquisition to the State, adding to its value as well as to its ornament."

Although Jefferson was assisted by William Thornton* and Latrobe in designing the University of Virginia at Charlottesville (1817–26), the work is essentially his. The library on the axis of this village of learning symbolized a center of knowledge. Students lived in

1. **Thomas Jefferson.** Rotunda of the University of Virginia, Charlottesville, 1825.

2. **William Jennys.** Colonel Constant Storrs, 1802. Pennsylvania Academy of the Fine Arts, Philadelphia (gift of John F. Lewis).

single-story rooms between the two-story pavilions where their teachers lived and taught. The pavilions, each designed in a different classical manner, were themselves exemplars of tasteful architecture.

As his reputation in the area of public and private building grew, many began to seek his advice and often requested plans, which he gave whenever he could. Of the many buildings for which he made plans, we are certain of his responsibility for the following: Buckingham County Courthouse (1821); Charlotte County Courthouse (1823); Christ Church, Charlottesville (1824, demolished); Bremo (1817) for John H. Cocke; Barboursville, Orange County (1817), for James Barbour (burned 1884 but with walls and columns still standing); Poplar Forest (1806), built on his wife's estate; Edgehill (1799); Farmington (1803); and Redlands (1798–1808) for Robert Carter. These were all designed in the same style as Monticello, with the classical entrance colonnades and other white-painted decorative woodwork set off by neatly laid red brick walls.

Believing that any improvement in the arts in America would bring greater prestige to the country, raise economic levels, and provide better living conditions, Jefferson did his utmost to bring this about by his own example.   (P.F.N.)

Jennewein, Paul (1890–   ).
A leader of the academic tradition in sculpture from the 1920s through the 1940s, he was born in Stuttgart, Germany, and came to the United States in 1907. After studying at the Art Students League* he went to Europe (1913–14), won the Prix de Rome in 1916 and studied in Rome for five years. Like Paul Manship* before him, he was greatly influenced by the decorative aspects of Greco-Roman art, as may be seen in his *Cupid and Gazelle* (1919, Metropolitan). Returning to New York he commenced a career which led to the presidency of the National Sculpture Society and the vice-presidency of the National Academy of Design.* Since 1963 he has been president of Brookgreen Gardens in South Carolina where several of his works may be seen, among them *Nymph and Fawn* (1922) and *The Greek Dance* (1926).

Jennewein was often chosen by architects to execute sculptural pieces for their buildings; combining a classi-cal style with a decorative element not unlike art nouveau,* his rhythmic and stylized forms worked well with architecture. One of his most important commissions was for the pedimental figures of polychromed terra-cotta for the enormous temple-like Philadelphia Museum of Art (c.1930). He did a few portrait statues, such as *Governor Endicott* for Boston and *Puritan* for Plymouth, Massachusetts, and various war memorials. His decorative reliefs are found in the Justice Building in Washington, D.C., and his bronze doors were installed in the British Building in Rockefeller Center.   (W.C.)

Jennys, William (active 1790–1805).
Itinerant portraitist active in and around New Milford, Conn., in the 1790s, in New York City in 1797–98, and then through much of New England from 1800 to 1805. His pictorial style seems to have influenced a number of Connecticut Valley artists, including Simon Fitch* and Reuben Moulthrop.* Most of Jennys' sitters were depicted within an oval panel and were presented with unusual realism through the use of harsh direct light. They share an intensity of expression that is curiously like that of neorealistic painting of the 20th century—staring forward at the viewer although their heads are shown in three-quarter view. As with other folk portraitists, the painting of the sitter's hands presented a problem, and Jennys usually avoided showing them, as in *Hannah French Bacon* (1795, Abby Aldrich Rockefeller).   (M.J.G.)

Jewett, William (1795–1873).
Portrait painter. A farm boy in the Connecticut River Valley, he was apprenticed at sixteen to a carriage-maker and painter in New London. It was there that he met Samuel Lovett Waldo* and determined to become, like Waldo, an artist. When Waldo moved to New York, Jewett followed, becoming first his friend's assistant, and then partner. It became a close and lifelong association, brightened by trips afield together to paint landscape. As portraitists, they had one studio and worked together on the same paintings; they were extremely successful.

Johansen, John M. (1916–   ).
Architect who has continually rejuvenated and updated his directions and techniques since 1950. Born in New York, N.Y., and educated at Harvard under Walter Gropius* and Marcel Breuer,* he first worked in the offices of Breuer and of Skidmore, Owings & Merrill.* He opened his own office in 1948. During the structural experimentation of the 1950s he showed interest in reinforced concrete shells, sprayed reinforced concrete, and sculpturally expressive precast concrete members, as in his Dublin Embassy (1964). Following that, he designed a number of elegant and crisply articulated houses and schools, and several large-scale performance halls, such as Clowes Hall at Butler University (1963, Indianapolis, Ind.) and Morris Mechanic Theater (1967, Baltimore, Md.). Then he declared his revolt against the International style* in the Goddard Library of Clark University (1968, Worcester, Mass.) and in articles describing the project as "architecture for the electronic age." This strongly fragmented, tense, and angular design represented a restless breaking out of the bonds of rectangular purity and an exterior expression of interior function. Subsequently, he became even more radical, incorporating industrialized parts in seemingly incompatible, elegant settings and expressing circulation not only of people but of mechanical support systems and materials on a bold new scale for civic architecture (1969, L. Frances Smith Elementary School, Columbus, Ind.; 1970, Mummers Theater, Oklahoma City). Throughout these two decades, this innovative activity also showed itself in master plans for educational complexes and housing developments.   (C.R.S.)

Johanson, Patricia (1940–   ).
Painter and sculptor, born in New York, N.Y. By 1964 Johanson was painting the most minimal* of paintings—a single line of color on an expanse of raw canvas, eliminating shape and eliciting a relatively pure experience of a color. She then began placing color in real, rather than subjective or illusionistic, space. A later series of thirty-foot paintings attacked problems of visual perception and aerial perspective and pieces have been contrived so the spectator is given as many points of view as possible. In 1966 she began casting color into three-dimensional space. *Stephen Long* (1968), a 1600-foot, three-color piece, built on an

abandoned railroad track, was developed out of Leonardo's theories of perspective and Chevreul's theories of color optics.

In 1969 Johanson turned to landscape design, creating drawings for vanishing-point gardens and gardens for highways. Meanwhile, her construction of a linear marble, redwood, and cement-block piece (1968–72), low lying and winding unobtrusively through a private woodland park, led to commissions at the Indian Point (N.Y.) Nuclear Park—a sculpture nearly one mile long—and landscape designs for a dormitory complex at Yale University. Johanson has broken through the usual contradictions of architecture with fine art, pointing the way toward a viable integration of modern abstract concepts with principles acceptable to both humanists and ecologists. (E.C.G.)

Johns, Jasper (1930–).
Painter. Johns was born in Allendale, S.C., and attended the University of South Carolina. He moved to New York in 1949 but was drafted into the army, returning to New York in 1952. By the mid-1950s Johns was a close friend of the painter Robert Rauschenberg,* the dancer Merce Cunningham, and the composer John Cage. Dating from this period are his first paintings of flags and targets, painted with some precision and in strong colors. His choice of subject was interesting, and was in large part responsible for deflecting the course of abstract expressionism.* First, by selecting real objects that are flat, he was able to totally identify his subject with the picture plane. These were recognizable objects, but by removing them from their usual context, Johns was able to produce disconcerting reversals of our conventional responses to them. The American flag, calculated to arouse nationalistic feelings, suddenly became a pattern of stars and bands; the target only a pattern of concentric circles. Johns maintained that he was not interested in motifs, symbolism, or new formal discoveries, but just wanted to look at familiar objects with a fresh vision. All representational painting deals with transforming everyday objects into art, and yet Johns' return to the object at this juncture in art history had a great influence on his fellow artists. He is considered, along with Rauschenberg, one of the fathers of pop art;* and even

the schematized designs of artists such as Kenneth Noland* and Frank Stella* are related to Johns' targets and flags.

The first exhibition of one of Johns' targets came in 1957 at New York's Jewish Museum. This was followed by a one-man show in 1958 and inclusion in the Venice Biennial (1958). Johns' work was tremendously popular from the outset, although some considered it eclectic, frivolous, and gimmicky. He had always worked in encaustic and now he began to paint his subjects in the brushy, splashy, mannered technique of the abstract expressionists, often encrusting his forms in paint. This overall brushy activity set up a gently-pulsating surface that was reminiscent of action painting, and also stated the problem of flatness versus illusionism by first presenting a two-dimensional image that was then dissolved in paint. Other famous Johns subjects were numbers, letters of the alphabet, and maps. Stencilled letters and numbers were sometimes presented singly to be seen in terms of their individual shapes; at other times they were presented in series to form an overall pattern, as in *Numbers in Color* (1959, Albright). From the beginning Johns had produced a number of works in blacks, whites, and grays such as *White Flag* (1955, Metropolitan), alternating with pictures in other colors. In a series of works such as *False Start* (1959) he began to give conflicting visual and verbal information; thus an area painted red might be stencilled over with letters that spelled "blue," offering several levels of form and meaning. Another aspect of his work is his "sculpture," again dating from his earliest targets. These were sometimes topped by life masks or casts of parts of the body, each in its own compartment, thus achieving his usual ambiguity between art and life. Related to these are "objects," such as flashlights, lightbulbs, flags, a toothbrush cast in sculptmetal, plaster, or bronze; the most famous are his bronze Ballantine beer cans (1960), nearly facsimiles. Closer to assemblage* are his canvases with attached objects such as *Thermometer* (1959), and *Fool's House* (1962), featuring a real broom. Johns maintains that he was interested only in the formal qualities of these objects—the shiny handle and textured bristles of the broom, for example. However, one suspects

that he was also involved in his usual reexamination of meaning. A related, but somewhat different move toward process art is Johns' idea of continual modification: "Take an object. Do something to it. Do something else to it." His intellectualization has also pointed the way toward concept art,* from his earliest distinctions between painting and language, knowing and seeing, and seeing and believing. Always a prodigious draftsman, Johns has produced many drawings and lithographs. A retrospective of his work was held in 1964 at the Jewish Museum. (E.C.G.)

Johnson, David (1827–1908).
Landscape painter whose realistic drawings and paintings of pastoral scenes in New York State and New England make him a typical member of the Hudson River School.* Johnson was born in New York, N.Y., and he spent most of his life there, but often traveled through the eastern United States. He became a member of the National Academy of Design* in 1861. His fine draftsmanship reflects the influence of his teacher, Jasper F. Cropsey,* while his mature landscapes, impressive in their high detail and cool green tonality, are close to those of John F. Kensett,* as in his *Brook Study at Warwick* (1873, Proctor). He also painted a handful of fine still lifes and numerous portraits. After 1874, his landscape style grew looser and his compositions, falling under the somewhat static Barbizon School* influence, became monotonous. (T.E.S.)

Johnson, Eastman (1824–1906).
Important genre and portrait painter. Born in Lowell, Me., he spent much of his boyhood in Augusta, Me., because his father was secretary of state of Maine. In 1840 he went to Boston, where for about a year he was employed in the lithography shop of John H. Bufford (active 1835–71). He then took up black-and-white crayon portraiture, and had considerable popular and artistic success in this media, never venturing into the use of color. Between 1841 and 1849 he worked in Augusta, Cambridge, Newport, and Washington, D.C. In 1849, Johnson went to Düsseldorf, Germany, where he shared a studio with Emanuel Leutze.* He then studied for nearly four years at The Hague, where he became known as the "American Rembrandt." De-

1

2

3

1. *Jasper Johns.* Edingsville, 1965.
   Collection of the artist.
2. *Jasper Johns.* Target with Four
   Faces, 1955, encaustic on newspaper on canvas, with plaster and
   wood. Museum of Modern Art, N.Y.
   (gift of Mr. and Mrs. Robert C.
   Scull).
3. *Jasper Johns.* Painted Bronze,
   1964, painted bronze. Leo Castelli
   Gallery, N.Y.

1

2

clining the post of court painter to The Hague, he studied briefly in Paris, where he was influenced by the French Victorian genre style then popular. He returned to the United States in 1855. He then worked in Wisconsin, Cincinnati, and Washington, D.C., before settling in New York City in 1859. He quickly made his reputation there, winning election to the National Academy of Design* with his painting *The Old Kentucky Home* (1859, New York Hist.). Painting with the attention to detail and the story-telling sentimentality that marked much of his work, the artist succeeded in appealing to a nation that wanted to see only the sunnier side of southern slavery.

To many, Johnson's greatest accomplishments lie in two series of outdoor genre scenes he undertook during the 1870s: the maple sugar camp views, such as *The Shelter* (c.1870, Corcoran) which were based on sketches made near Fryeburg, Me., and the even more extensive series on cranberry harvests on Nantucket Island. There are over twenty versions on the latter theme; they vary widely in size and technique, and some are unsigned, suggesting that the artist saw them only as preliminary sketches. Working in the studio he maintained on Nantucket during this decade, Johnson painted the island and its cranberry pickers with quick, broad strokes. *In the Fields* (c.1870, Detroit) is almost impressionistic in its approach to light, color, and atmosphere. Johnson was also successful as a painter of the "portrait interior." With sharp realism and great attention to costume and interior decoration, he portrayed the wealthy families of New York at ease in their luxurious homes. Outstanding among these paintings is *The Hatch Family* (1871, Metropolitan). In his own time, Johnson was most often compared to Winslow Homer* and was highly regarded as a figure painter.

However, in the 1880s his reputation declined while Homer's was gaining. Finding few patrons for his genre scenes of the 1870s, he turned back to portraiture. During the last two decades of the century, he was a fashionable and successful portrait painter. His favorite subjects were the wealthy men of New York, whom he portrayed with dignity if not with insight, as in *The Funding Bill* (1881, Metropolitan).

(T.E.S.)

3

4

1. **Eastman Johnson.** The Cranberry Pickers, *c.1875. Kennedy Galleries, N.Y.*
2. **Eastman Johnson.** The Blodgett Family, *Collection Stephen W. Blodgett, Esq.*
3. **Philip Johnson.** New York State Theater, main lobby, N.Y., 1964.
4. **Philip Johnson.** Glass House, New Canaan, Conn., 1949.

Johnson, Philip (1906–   ).
Architect, born in Cleveland, Ohio. Johnson studied classics at Harvard in 1927, and returned to take his architecture degree in 1943. His career has been unique. He began in 1927 as a writer-critic and did not design his first building until 1942, when he was in his late thirties. As a critic-historian he occupies a highly significant place in the development of modern architecture in the International style.* From 1930–36 he was director of the department of architecture of the newly established Museum of Modern Art in New York City, and helped to establish this institution as the leading shaper of taste in the United States. In 1932, in collaboration with Henry Russell Hitchcock, he organized the famous exhibition at the Modern Museum, "The International Style: Architecture Since 1922," with a catalog that became a kind of bible of modern architecture. It was important because it illustrated the great works of those early modern architects, Le Corbusier and Mies van der Rohe* and of Walter Gropius,* whom he had met in Europe in 1930 and who was considered his mentor. The text advocated the International style, not because it was more functional or because it utilized new materials such as concrete, steel, and glass, but because it most perfectly reflected the new machine esthetic of the 20th century.

In 1943, Johnson turned his full attention to the practice of architecture. His own Cambridge house of 1942–43 is, like most of his work, both classic and modern. In this design he enclosed an entire city lot behind a high wall and then divided this space into an indoor and an outdoor area, which were divided only by a single glass wall. In his well-known "glass box" house (1949) in New Canaan, Conn., the exterior controlled space is that of a low grass platform or podium upon which the house and its accompanying guest house were placed. This classical theme, in part based on the work of Mies van der Rohe, is found in all of his domestic designs and most of his nondomestic work, down to the present. All of these buildings are set aloft from nature, are almost always symmetrical, often use columnar forms reminiscent of classical architecture, and employ traditional and expensive materials. The space within is elegant,

1

1. **Joshua Johnston.** The Westwood
   Children, 1807. National Gallery of
   Art, Washington, D.C. (gift of
   William and Bernice Chrysler
   Garbisch).
2. **Donald Judd.** Untitled, 1965, gal-
   vanized iron. Collection Henry
   Geldzahler, N.Y.

2

312

often the materials and detail are precious and expensive, and the space tends to be formal. This can be seen in such divergent buildings as the Wiley House (1953, New Canaan, Conn.), the Leonhardt House (1956, Lloyd's Neck, Long Island, N.Y.), and the Kline Science Center at Yale University (1962–66, New Haven, Conn.). Johnson's view has always been that architecture is essentially a high art. Like other 20th-century architects and artists, his designs and criticism overflow with historical and intellectual references and he does not seek to make them simple or easy to comprehend.   (D.G.)

Johnston, Henrietta (active 1705–29). America's first woman painter. She brought the art of the pastel from England to Charleston, S.C., arriving with her husband, Gideon Johnston (or Johnstone), an Anglican clergyman, in 1705. She had probably had academic training sometime before 1700, and although only her pastels are known, she may have also painted in oils. Her portraits are resolutely dainty but they lack strength of characterization. Johnston made at least one trip afield as an artist—to New York in 1725.

Johnston, Joshua (active 1796–1824). Baltimore, Md., artist credited with having been the first professional black portrait painter in the United States. Stylistic kinship to the work of the Peale* family has suggested that Johnston (or Johnson, as he is also recorded) received his training in that household, possibly as a slave although he is specifically listed in Baltimore city directories as a freeman. His early paintings of the highly civilized members of Baltimore's prosperous merchant families conform to an 18th-century English ideal in which softly painted, toylike figures are depicted against a dark background. Groups are often seated on a Sheraton settee with brass nailheads outlining the delicate curve of back or arm, as in his painting, *The Kennedy Long Family* (c.1805, private collection). Johnston's later figures loom larger, and refinement gives way to stronger expression of personality. His sitters are usually portrayed in rigid three-quarter poses with typically tight-lipped mouths, heavy-lidded eyes, and curiously formalized, lobeless ears, as in *The Westwood Children* (c.1807, Garbisch Coll.).

Johnston, Thomas (1708–67). Engraver whose prints included maps, trade cards, bookplates, music, currency, and views. Johnston was a versatile craftsman who applied japanned decoration to furniture, painted coats of arms, built organs, and published song books. His entire working career was spent in Boston. He was engraving as early as 1728, when he signed the copperplate of the map of Boston engraved by him after William Burgis' design. As his apprentice for several years after 1741, John Greenwood painted coats of arms and engraved bookplates. In 1749, after Greenwood had established himself as a successful portrait painter in Boston, Johnston was the engraver of the *Prospect of Yale College* after Greenwood's drawing. Johnston's engraving of 1755, after Samuel Blodgett's drawing, of *A Prospective Plan of the Battle Fought Near Lake George,* is part map, part depiction of the battle, and is·considered the earliest American historical print. Also among the best-known American 18th-century prints is his engraving *Quebec, The Capital of New-France* (1759), based on a French engraving of Quebec.   (S.H.)

Jones, Thomas Dow (1811–91). A sculptor, he grew up in Ohio and was working as a stonecutter in Cincinnati when in 1841 he first attempted a portrait bust. His career as a sculptor was launched and he remained a portraitist, working in a dry, undramatic, and unheroic naturalism.* In 1851 he settled in New York City, where he continued to produce portrait busts and numerous profile bas-relief medallion portraits, which were usually cast in plaster. He patented and mass-produced medallions of Henry Clay, Daniel Webster, and a bust of Abraham Lincoln (1861); however, each of these is weak formally and lacks the dignity associated with the subject. In 1865 Jones returned to Cincinnati, and shortly thereafter modeled one of his finest portraits—that of Griffin Taylor (Cincinnati Art Museum). Another superior specimen of his portraiture is his marble bust, *Chief Justice Salmon P. Chase* (c.1874, Supreme Court Building, Washington, D.C.). His career came to an end around 1880.   (W.C.)

Jouett, Matthew Harris (1787–1827). Painter. Born in Mercer County, Ky., he studied in Boston with Gilbert Stuart.* The first western painter to achieve prominence, among his more than 300 portraits are one of Lafayette (State Capitol, Frankfort, Ky.) and one of John Grimes (Metropolitan).

Judd, Donald (1928–   ). Sculptor. Born in Excelsior Springs, Md., he is a leading figure in the development of minimal art.* In the early 1960s, Judd produced paintings and low-relief constructions of plywood, masonite, galvanized metal, canvas, and paint. These works achieved a geometric severity that avoided both the personal rhetoric of abstract expressionism* and the idealized purity of constructivism.* Judd wrote criticism for several art magazines during 1959–65. He issued a number of general statements in this period, notably "The Specific Object," in which the aims of his art are set out. In 1963 he began fabricating boxes from metal, painting them with industrial pigments. These works sometimes included two sides of plexiglas to make their inner surfaces visible. Continuing to produce rectangular shapes, some resting on the floor, others stacked in series along the wall, Judd was given a large one-man show at the Whitney Museum, New York City, in 1968. Since 1970 he has designed pieces in response to the space in which they are to be exhibited. At the Guggenheim International in 1971 he set a large galvanized iron ring at a tilt within a slightly larger ring, thus echoing the structure of the museum building. In 1972 he produced outdoor works in which large geometric shapes are nestled within each other to reflect the surrounding topography. His concern has thus been to create works which occupy "real space" with a maximum of visual clarity. His outdoor sculpture reveals his ability to achieve this aim on a scale greater than that of traditional museum and gallery exhibitions.   (C.R.)

K

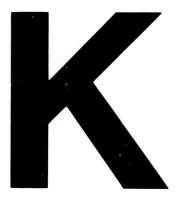

Kahn, Albert (1869–1942).
Architect. Born in Rhaunen, Germany, Kahn came to America in 1880. He obtained his professional education in a Detroit architectural office while studying drawing on the side. In 1891 he received a traveling architectural scholarship and spent a year studying in Europe. From 1892 until 1902 he was associated with several Detroit architectural firms and then set up his own practice. The following year he designed his first automobile plant—for the Packard Motor Car Company in Detroit. Thereafter his firm had almost a monopoly on the design of factories for automobiles and their components. His Packard Factory of 1905 represented the first use in Detroit of a reinforced concrete frame. The repetition of design elements inherent in concrete form construction was forcefully stated in his 1907 factory for the Chalmers Motor Car Company of Detroit and in many later factories. By 1909–10 he was producing buildings where all assembly-line production could take place under one roof, and by about 1913 he was designing factories where all production could take place on one floor.

From 1920 through the 1940s, his buildings caught beautifully the spirit of the machine and mass production, while at the same time discreetly mirroring the prevailing architectural styles, from the neoclassical through streamlined moderne* to the International style.* Thus, his factory units at the Ford River Rouge Plant at Dearborn, Mich., especially the Power House, 1921, and the Glass Plant, 1924, posed an imagery, like that of the automobiles of the 1920s, composed of parts kept quite separate from one another. During the late 1930s and the 1940s, his factories, such as the much-photographed Dodge Half-Ton Truck Plant of 1938 at Warren, Mich., are,

1

2

like other industrial designed objects of the 1930s, housed and sheathed in a single container.

Kahn's nonindustrial designs closely followed the changes in architectural taste during the first half of the century. Although he did produce designs in Georgian and other period styles, his favorite garb for houses was English Tudor. For the exterior of office buildings he often used the neoclassical mode of McKim, Mead & White* (for example, in the Detroit Athletic Club of 1915), while the Fisher Building in Detroit (1927) is moderately Gothic with a hint of early zigzag moderne.* By the late 1930s, he was producing streamlined moderne designs, the best known of which was the Ford Exposition Building at the New York World's Fair (1939). The impressive group of industrial buildings Kahn's firm built just before and during World War II, was a significant factor in the wide acceptance of the International style after 1945.　　　　　(D.G.)

Kahn, Louis I. (1901–　　).
American architect who was considered the prophet of the decade from the mid-1950s to mid-1960s. The first convincing rebel against the industrial doctrines of Mies van der Rohe,* he combined classical clarity in planning and massing with richly textured, heavily sculptural walls. Born on the Island of Osel in Estonia (now Russia), Kahn was brought to Philadelphia in 1905. He studied art and music but settled on architecture and received the prevailing Beaux-Arts architectural education from the University of Pennsylvania (1924). He worked in Philadelphia with architect Paul Cret, then with George Howe and Oskar Stonorov, producing houses, hospitals, and commercial structures. Until he was over fifty, he had built almost nothing known to anyone except his associates and students. He then began teaching at Yale University (1949) where his theories began to coalesce with his architecture. As a philosopher-poet-metaphysician he captured the attentive, eager minds of hundreds of architects whose dreams of ideal spaces and grand designs were constantly confronted by practical problems. Kahn led them into ever more visionary approaches to creation—methods for uncovering the significant factors in client programs and sites and in struc-

3

4

1. **Albert Kahn.** Dodge Half-ton Truck Plant, Warren, Mich., 1938.
2. **Albert Kahn.** Edsel Ford Residence, Grosse Pointe Shores, Mich., 1929.
3. **Louis I. Kahn.** Burnap-Post Residence, Chestnut Hill, Pa., 1961.
4. **Louis I. Kahn.** Kimbell Art Museum, Ft. Worth, Texas, 1972.

tural systems. He gave architects a "will" to search for what each building "wants to be."

At this time he began to produce one significant building after another. In the Yale University Art Gallery (1952–54, with Douglas I. Orr) he designed a tetrahedron concrete ceiling that permits great variety in exhibition planning and in the use of partitions and lighting. For the A.F.L. Medical Service Plan Building (Philadelphia, 1954–56) he designed exposed trusses with elongated hexagonal openings that showed an impatience with the rectangle and the square. In his plans for the Trenton Bath House (1955–56, Jewish Community Center, Trenton, N.J.), he returned to the Beaux-Arts idiom, designing a classical cross-axial scheme of pyramidal-roofed pavilions around an atrium. This tiny monument, with its strong but hollow corner piers, first expressed Kahn's philosophy of separating "servant" spaces for utilities from "served" spaces for human use. Next, his visionary project for "Tomorrow's City Hall" (1957), a study for the Universal Atlas Cement Company, with its vertical truss and structural diagonals, and its offset overhanging floors, was so divergent from the current architectural thinking that it could hardly be understood even by professionals, yet its imagery was unforgettable.

Then, in the Richards Medical Center (1957–61, University of Pennsylvania), he produced his first masterpiece: a series of rational, precast concrete and glass towers spinning off from a core of elevators and stairs with separate mechanical service towers located on the perimeter. These subordinate, brick-clad, windowless towers not only gave the project rhythm and sculptural strength, but also lent new impetus to modern architecture in their focus on separating and expressing mechanical systems. In the small plant of the Tribune Review Publishing Company, Greensburg, Pa., (1958–61), he constructed brick piers and concrete block walls with windows in the tense horizontal-square-and-thin-vertical-rectangle combination that he had used in a few of his houses about that time. In the projected United States Consulate at Luanda, Angola (1959–62), Kahn devised a double ventilating roof system and sunscreen walls in a giant keyhole-shaped window motif that became the trademark of his super-

scale geometry. In another masterwork, the First Unitarian Church (1959–64, Rochester, N.Y.) he separated service facilities from major "served" spaces, but this project was plagued by revisions, including Kahn's continual reworking of the decorative tapestry for the sanctuary. From 1959 to 1965 he worked on the Jonas Salk Institute for Biological Studies (San Diego, Cal.), where a classical courtyard plan shows separate office and laboratory spaces. Structure and mechanical systems are integrated to provide a separation of fresh air from "laboratory service air" by means of generous secondary mechanical levels between each floor. This scheme was to serve as the model throughout the next decade for flexible loft space in hospitals and other technical facilities. In a library and dining hall complex for Phillips Exeter Academy (1971, Exeter, N.H.), he created a monumental piece of "jewelry" architecture: a square fortress-keep with plum-colored brick piers that diminish as they ascend past larger windows on each higher floor; inside, a central court is open to upper floors through a vast four-story circular opening.

The peak of his creation of forms is the ruinlike complex of brick towers with massive circular and keyhole openings designed for Dacca, the capital of East Pakistan (now Bangladesh). In 1972 he designed the Kimbell Art Museum (Fort Worth, Tex.), a series of concrete, cycloid vaults that are split to provide natural illumination for the art works. The resulting atmosphere is poetic, while the entire design is a triumph of functionalism.

In his design theory, Kahn claims to strive for structural honesty and expression, for flexibility to accommodate future changes, in contrast to the rigid tidiness or regularity found in the "packaging" architecture of the previous decade. Critics later recognized that his forms were perhaps more vital, but still in many cases no more literal an expression of structure, than the architecture he disclaimed. His own geometry, although much more gigantic in scale, was as decorative as others. It was the very pattern-making he deplored that seized the public imagination. He was making larger details, but they were still details; only his approach to mechanical systems thrust him unquestionably beyond this 19th-century idiom.   (C.R.S.)

Kane, John (1860–1934).
Self-taught artist, best known for his paintings of the city of Pittsburgh, where he lived most of his life. Born in Edinburgh, Scotland, of Irish parents, Kane began as a mineworker at the age of ten and continued in the mines until he emigrated to America nine years later. In Pittsburgh, Pa., where he settled and married, he first supported his family by manual labor. By 1890 he was doing pencil sketches of local scenes. He did not use paint until after his fortieth year, when he became a painter of houses and freight cars. Although he experimented with color drawings on the sides of freight cars early in the century, Kane waited until he was sixty-four before he turned to Pittsburgh's Carnegie Institute for recognition. His first submissions to the Carnegie International were rejected as copies (which they were), but in 1927 a painting was accepted. In the seven years until his death, Kane achieved considerable celebrity, augmented by the publication of his life story, *Sky Hooks,* which he wrote with the assistance of a newspaper reporter. He continues to hold a position of eminence among self-taught artists of the 20th century for his detailed record of Pittsburgh as a developing industrial metropolis; and his insistently symmetrical frontal *Self Portrait* (1929, Modern Museum) was probably a key work in the development of American neorealism of the 1950s.   (M.J.G.)

Kantor, Morris (1896–   ).
Painter. Born in Minsk, Russia, he came to New York in 1911. Five years later, an ambition to become a cartoonist sent him to the Independent School of Art. While there he decided to become a painter. His early work was largely abstract. After he had studied the old masters in Paris in 1927, a more humanistic tendency entered his work. In 1928 he took an apartment on Union Square in New York, and his painting thenceforth was concerned mainly with the human scene observed through the windows of that apartment, with reflections from the interior to suggest both external and internal worlds. Curiously, these works seem to have the somewhat ominous psychological implication associated with surrealism,* as for example *Farewell to Union Square* (1931, Newark). Kantor has also painted many seascapes and large abstractions.   (A.F.)

Käsebier, Gertrude Stanton (1852–1934).

Photographer. Born in Des Moines, Iowa, of Quaker parents, she became a leading New York photographer and one of the most successful American women artists. It was her pioneer grandmother, a weaver of great imagination, who inspired Gertrude's interest in the visual arts. As a child she journeyed with her family in a covered wagon across the great plains to Colorado. After her father's death, she attended Moravian College for Women in Bethlehem, Pa., and then joined her family in New York City. There she married Eduard Käsebier, a native of Wiesbaden, Germany, an importer, and bore him three children. Motherhood, which was later to form a major theme in her photographic work, prevented her from pursuing her artistic studies for many years. Finally, about 1888, she entered Pratt Institute in Brooklyn to study portrait painting. In 1893, accompanied by her daughters, she went to France and continued to paint. Photography had been an incidental part of her studies. "But one day," she wrote, "when it was too rainy to go into the fields to paint, I made a time-exposure in the house, simply as an experiment. The result was so surprising to me that from that moment I knew I had found my vocation."

Like the great English Victorian photographer, Julia Margaret Cameron (1815–79), whose career parallels hers, Käsebier embraced photography with dogged devotion. "I had no conveniences for work, no dark-room, no running water in the house. . . . I had to carry my wet plate down to the river Brie to be washed. . . . It was often two o'clock in the morning, or almost dawn, when I had finished." To learn to control her newly adopted medium, she apprenticed herself to a photographic chemist. Finally, in 1897, she rejoined her husband in New York and opened a studio at a fashionable location on Fifth Avenue. Over the next thirty years, in studios that moved up Fifth Avenue in step with New York's development, she made over 100,000 photographs. The world of the professional photographer was, she recalled, that of "the painted background, the papier-mâché accessories, the high-backed chair, the potted palm, the artificial flowers in the studio." Käsebier's approach to portraiture was revolutionary. Encour-

1

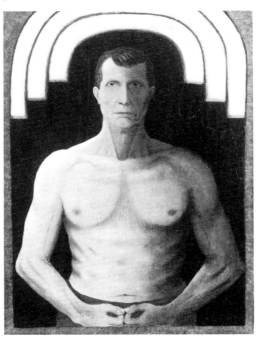

2

1. *Gertrude Stanton Käsebier.* Edward Steichen and Others, *c.1903, George Eastman House, Rochester, N.Y.*
2. *John Kane.* Self-Portrait, *1929. Museum of Modern Art, N.Y. (Abby Aldrich Rockefeller Fund).*

aged by her experiments in France, she placed her subjects, whether in her studio or in their own homes, in everyday surroundings. Natural light floods her pictures through real windows and doorways; her people engage in simple, natural activities; whole families are seen sharing moments of quiet intimacy. Mrs. Käsebier printed her negatives in platinum and gum bichromate—processes which permitted the subtle gradations of white and the rich, clear, dark tones of her finest work.

The critic Charles Caffin, reviewing a major exhibition of her work in 1906, wrote: "I know of no photographer at home or abroad who displays so much charm of invention. There is always . . . a perpetual freshness of conception, as extraordinary as it is fascinating." Her contemporaries agreed with his opinion. Mrs. Käsebier was a member of the English Linked Ring group and a founder and fellow of the Photo-Secession,* an organization of the leading American pictorialists. Their magazine, *Camera Work,* honored her by publishing several of her best-known photographs in its inaugural issue in 1903. Most widely reproduced of these is *Blessed Art Thou Among Women* (c.1900), one in a long series on motherhood.

The Indians that she had seen in her childhood on the plains and in Colorado resulted in a remarkable series of Indian photographs made around 1900 in her New York studio and later on the North Central Plains. These portraits (now in the Smithsonian Institution) transcend the merely documentary. Her initial subjects, members of Buffalo Bill's Wild West Troupe, were romantically transformed into what she imagined them to have been: ideal embodiments of nobility and strength. Published in *Everybody's Magazine* in January, 1901, these portraits, large, direct, tightly cropped, form one of the high points of Mrs. Käsebier's long career.

Mrs. Käsebier continued to work professionally up to the time of her last major exhibition, held in 1926 at the Brooklyn Institute of Arts and Sciences. Today the richest collections of her photographs are in the Museum of Modern Art, the Library of Congress, and at George Eastman House, Rochester, N.Y. She died in New York City.

(D.L.)

Kelly, Ellsworth (1923–   ).
Painter. Born in Newburgh, N.Y., he became interested in art at an early age. In 1943–45, while serving in the U.S. Army in France, he developed an interest in Romanesque churches and Byzantine mosaics. On his return to America he studied at the Boston Museum School (1946–48), where Karl Zerbe* introduced him to the work of the European expressionists. In 1948, eligible for the G.I. Bill educational program, Kelly returned to Paris, where he remained for six years, studying for a time at the École des Beaux-Arts. There he visited the sculptors Brancusi and Arp, and the Dutch painter Vantongerloo, although his own work remained stubbornly based on observed fact. His earliest works were representational: figure studies, portraits, and still lifes. However, soon his interest in the visual and formal characteristics of his subject caused his nature-derived forms to take on another quality—a combination of literalness with absolute abstraction, as in *Window* (1949, Museum of Modern Art, Paris), an exact representation of a museum window in oil on canvas. This anticipated his later involvement with the rectangle, with color shapes, and with the painting as object, which was often extended into shallow bas-relief, and later into flat, planar metal "sculpture." Similar works included the changing shadows on a staircase, and an hourglass-shaped painted wood panel—perhaps the earliest "shaped-canvases"—derived from the arch of a French bridge and its reflection in water. Kelly has commented on his continual search for forms and patterns in everyday objects, specifically mentioning "a fragment of a piece of architecture, or someone's legs, or sometimes the space between things. . . ." If Kelly's scrutiny of the object was a distinctly American trait, still he did not remain isolated from the Paris scene.

During the 1950s he produced many collages and began to experiment with "automatic drawings" and compositions produced by "chance," tearing up drawings, letting the pieces drop at random, and fixing them in place as Arp had done thirty-five years before. He also let thinned ink run down a page, guiding it by blowing on the liquid—a forecast, perhaps, of the spilled-paint technique of Morris Louis.* Kelly's object was to rid himself of preconceptions about art; his results relate more to the

1

2

1. **Ellsworth Kelly.** Two Panels: Blue, Red, 1968. *Sidney Janis Gallery, N.Y.*
2. **John Frederick Kensett.** Lake George, 1869. *Metropolitan Museum of Art, N.Y. (bequest of Maria de Witt Jesup).*

random patterns of natural phenomena than to an interest in combinations and permutations. A number of the "chance" compositions, such as *Brush Strokes Cut into 49 Squares and Arranged by Chance* (1951), look forward to the later panel paintings with their regular divisions. In 1951–54 he formed compositions by simply adding modular units. *Colors for a Large Wall* (1951, Modern Museum) consists of 64 panels, each painted one unmodulated color, all joined to form an 8-foot square. In other works, color panels are stretched side by side, to be "read" as one painting. Here Kelly literally turned color into subject matter: the modular panels allowed him to free color from subservience to form, while the innovation of one color to a panel gave each hue its own concrete "reality" and individuality. Kelly returned to New York in 1954, where the size of his canvases increased, and he began a reexploration of black and white curved shapes, fragments of images cut off by the edge of the canvas, and plays on the rectangle itself.

In his early shows in New York (1956, 1957, and 1959) he had become known as the purest representative of "hard-edge"* painting (although he has noted that he has no interest in "edges"). Throughout the 1960s Kelly simplified his shapes, as in *Blue Red Green* (1962–63, Metropolitan), ultimately returning to arrangements of the color panels, and severely limited his palette, often working with only the primaries or black and white. Recently he has been working with color panels of various sizes to form triangular, "T," and "erratic perimeter" groups, wherein the proportion and position of each color is of prime importance. As always, his object is to achieve maximum emotion with severely limited means using shape and sensuous color intuitively. (E.C.G.)

Kensett, John Frederick (1816–72). Engraver and landscape painter who was both a social and artistic leader among members of the second generation (about 1850–70) of the Hudson River School.* Kensett was born in Cheshire, Conn., the son of an immigrant English engraver, Thomas Kensett (1786–1829). He learned to draw and engrave in his father's New Haven firm, and after his father's death continued his training with an uncle, Alfred Daggett (1799–1872). Kensett worked as an engraver of maps, labels, and banknotes in New York City until 1841. In New York, Kensett met John W. Casilear,* a fellow engraver, who urged him to turn to painting. Receiving further encouragement in 1838 when he exhibited a landscape painting at the National Academy of Design, he determined to become a painter. Fortuitously, he was able to join three other artists —John Casilear, Asher B. Durand,* and Thomas P. Rossiter of New Haven— who were just then turning to landscape, and he set off with them on a European Grand Tour in June, 1840. Kensett left the others after visiting London and went to live in Paris with a young American painter, Benjamin Champney (1817–1907). It was only after several years there and a stay in London (1843–1845) that he finally gave up engraving completely and set off with Champney on a sketching tour of Germany, Switzerland, and Italy.

Finally returning to New York in 1847, Kensett was an almost immediate success. He was soon elected to the National Academy of Design* and later was a founder of the Metropolitan Museum of Art. The art critic Henry Tuckerman described him as "the most thoroughly amiable" of all artists; both his art and personality endeared him to a wide range of people, and many of the leading painters, writers, and businessmen of New York were among his friends.

From the beginning, Kensett's paintings demonstrated his care for detail and his fine draftsmanship. The relatively heavy impasto of his earliest English woodland scenes soon gave way, in Italy, to an increased interest in picturesque views reminiscent of the French 17th-century landscape painter Claude Lorrain. Kensett's early work, like that of almost all of his contemporaries, was influenced by Thomas Cole's richly-painted, stormy compositions. By the 1850s, however, he was following the dictates of the new leader of the Hudson River School, Asher B. Durand, who advised the younger men to make topographically realistic, detailed pencil sketches outdoors and then to "work up" the sketches into finished paintings in their studios. As the most talented of Durand's followers, Kensett had established by the mid-1850s his own mature style as well as his leadership of the school. He established a limited range of compositions that became most popular among both painters and patrons: the detailed woodland interior, such as *Bish-Bash, South Egremont, Mass.* (1855, Boston); the shoreline view, of which an early example is *Beacon Rocks, Newport Harbor* (1857, Washington); the view from above of a great expanse of mountains and water, as in his *View from West Point* (1863, New York Hist.); and the luminous, enclosed scene of a mountain lake seen from a low point of view, among which is his *Lake George* (1869, Metropolitan), are all outstanding.

Kensett's most appealing canvases are often those that portray popular scenes of the Eastern United States in modest size and sparkling, noontime clarity. His paintings are carefully composed, lightly painted, and normally make use of a subtle tonal range of blues and grays. He provided his generation with an alternative to the approach of Albert Bierstadt* and Frederic Church,* who were then producing heroic compositions of exotic scenery. The majority of the school followed Kensett, and his influence may be seen particularly in the work of Sanford Gifford,* Worthington Whittredge,* and Martin J. Heade.*

Like many of the school, Kensett worked in a New York City studio in winter and used the summers for sketching tours of his favorite areas of the Catskills and the White Mountains. At times he traveled farther afield, going to Niagara in 1851, up the Mississippi in 1854, and to Colorado in 1870. In his late paintings, particularly in the so-called "Last Summer's Work"—a group of thirty-eight views of Long Island Sound that he left to the Metropolitan Museum—he was increasingly concerned with the interaction of light in sea and sky, and he created some of the archetypal examples of American luminism.* At the time of his early death, Kensett was mourned throughout America. Shortly afterward, the contents of his studio—over five hundred paintings—were auctioned off for $136,312, an amazing sum at that time and further evidence of his popularity.

(T.E.S.)

Kent, Rockwell (1882–1971).
Painter, writer, and graphic artist. He was born in Tarrytown, N.Y., and studied with William Merritt Chase,* Abbott H. Thayer,* Robert Henri,* and Kenneth Hayes Miller.* While still in his twenties,

1

2

3

Kent developed his predilection for broadly massed compositions of open landscapes of the Far North. He was one of the organizers of the Exhibition of Independent Artists* (1910) and was subsequently active in such politically-oriented organizations as the American Artists' Congress. Kent practiced wood engraving in a manner that enjoyed great vogue in the 1920s and 1930s—boldly stylized, with strong patterns and dramatic characterizations. He wrote and illustrated a number of books, including accounts of his travels to Greenland, Alaska, and the Strait of Magellan. His later life was embittered by dissension stemming from his radical political sympathies and his consequent confrontations with congressional committees. He was given the Lenin Peace Prize in Moscow in 1967. (D.W.S.)

Kienholz, Edward (1927–).
Known for sculptured and assembled tableaux that often assimilate bits and pieces of local Americana. A self-taught artist, Kienholz was born into a farming family in Fairfield, Wash. He attended several colleges in the West, but never completed his formal education and had little association with the arts in his formative years.

When he went to Los Angeles in 1953, Kienholz began experimenting with wood constructions which he painted and to which he often gave humorous titles. Already his interest in the vernacular was evident. Many of the constructions made between 1954 and 1958 were composed of "found objects" and odd pieces of wood or metal. Occasionally, Kienholz alluded to topical events that disturbed him, such as miscarriages of justice in the prisons, or political persecutions. These he interpreted in burlesque terms and heightened with a comic title. Toward 1960, Kienholz began to evolve his tableau format. His first notable tableau, *Roxy's,* was an almost nostalgic recollection of a small-town brothel in 1943. He assembled an entire environment ranging from fringed, pink-bulbed lamps and the letters written by the prostitutes and hidden in drawers, to the calendars and patriotic photographs on the walls. The figures, modeled in wood and fiberglass, were appropriately clothed for the period, but their features were handled with fantasy. The "madam," for instance, was

equipped with the head of a boar while one of the girls had a clock set in her stomach. Kienholz's fusion of authentic props with outrageous fantasy set his work off from those of colleagues who dealt with environmental realism, or who drew on surrealistic sources. His insistent reference to American mores has led many critics to assign him a role as a social critic. To this evaluation he always replies that he is merely an artist-observer. Certain of his themes, such as the perils of illegal abortion, have strong overtones of violence; on the other hand, he demonstrates a sense of tragedy and sympathy in such works as *State Hospital,* in which he portrayed the pitiable inmates as victims of neglect, hopelessly abandoned.

Kienholz has exhibited widely, first in Los Angeles in the late 1950s, and later in New York. He has had several retrospective exhibitions, in both the United States and Europe. (D.A.)

Kinetic Sculpture.
Sculpture that expands the range of traditional materials and effects by employing motion. Its theoretical basis was established well before any works were produced. The futurist manifestos of 1909, 1910, and 1912 proposed sculpture that incorporated mechanical motion. This was part of the futurist call for a radically new art that would celebrate modern life, especially its technological aspects. The first kinetic sculpture was a so-called "ready-made" by Marcel Duchamp,* in which a bicycle wheel was mounted on a wooden stool. Although not produced in a spirit of futurist celebration, it helped break down the barrier between art objects and the objects of everyday life, and it opened the way to new processes, materials, and effects in art.

There are two ways of classifying kinetic sculpture: according to its energy source; and according to the spirit in which it is produced, which can be a desire to create pure form in motion or to express satire or whimsy. The former is derived from futurism* and constructivism,* and the latter from dada* and surrealism.* The energy sources employed in kinetic sculpture include: natural forces such as wind, magnetism, motors, and the viewer's own motion. In the futurist-constructivist tradition are the early mobiles of two Italians, Giacomo Balla and Fortunato Depero, both futurists. These

1. *Edward Kienholz.* Roxy's *(detail), 1970, mixed media. Collection of the artist.*
   Kinetic Sculpture
2. *Len Lye.* Fountain *(in motion), 1963, steel rods. Howard Wise Gallery, N.Y.*
3. *George Rickey.* Ten Rotors, Ten Cubes, Variation II, *1971, stainless steel. Collection of the artist.*

works, produced in 1914, were set in motion by currents of air. Two Americans, Alexander Calder* and George Rickey* are foremost among artists who have continued in this direction. The motorized sculpture of Naum Gabo* was developed directly out of his constructivist experiments with form. His *Virtual Space* (1930) is a vibrating steel spring that finds a latter-day counterpart in Len Lye's* *Tangible Motion Sculpture,* widely seen in the 1960s, in which clusters of steel rods are rapidly vibrated by a hidden motor. Others in the constructivist tradition who employed kinetic resources are Laszlo Moholy-Nagy, whose mechanized *Light-Space Modulator* (1930) cast a variable flood of light into surrounding space, and Thomas Wilfred, whose "clavilux performances," seen in America in the 1920s, projected changing patterns of light onto a screen by means of mirrors and colored lights. Wilfred's use of projection suggests the importance cinema has had for the development of kinetic sculpture. Both his works and Moholy-Nagy's *Light-Space Modulator* can be seen as ancestors of Nicolas Schöffer's *Cybernetic Tower,* exhibited at Liege, Belgium in 1961. Employing electronic as well as mechanical devices, it produced computerized music along with changing light patterns. Among kinetic works whose energy is the viewer's motion are pieces by Argentinian Jesus-Raphael Soto and Yacov Agam of Israel. Optical vibrations and changes in painted patterns of color occur as the viewer walks in front of their intricately designed panels. In the late 1960s, Soto filled large spaces with hanging plastic fibers, whose motion is created as the viewer-participant walks through them.

On the dada-surrealist side of kinetic sculpture are mobiles from the early 1920s by Man Ray* and the German artist Kurt Schwitters. Closely related to the pure forms of Calder and Rickey, these works employ the same natural source of motion, air currents, but elaborate pure form with imagery drawn from their dadaist works in traditional mediums. In 1920 Man Ray produced his *Destructible Object,* similar in spirit to his mobiles but employing mechanical means. The image of an eye was placed, with uncanny effect, on the bar of a metronome. Later kinetic sculpture in this tradition includes the work of the Frenchman Pol Bury, the

Swiss sculptor Jean Tinguely, and American Robert Breer. Bury's panels of fibers, wooden discs, and metal rods are made to pulsate by means of hidden motors. The mechanical seems to be evolving toward a state of quasi-biological life. Tinguely has created numerous bizarre machines that parody human actions, including *Homage to New York,* an immense machine which destroyed itself in the sculpture garden of the Museum of Modern Art, New York City, in 1961. Robert Breer, who has made animated films, turned in the 1960s to motorized slabs of polyurethene which creep over the floor at a rate almost too slow to be noticed. They make a witty comment on the pace of modern life—mechanized but sometimes impossible to grasp. In the late 1960s he expanded these floats, as he calls them, to larger than life size, drawing on the viewer's motion (one is sometimes obliged to get out of their way) as a source of kinetic effects. This recalls the kineticism in the happenings* of the late 1950s and early 1960s, where the actors' performances sometimes became threatening to the viewers, especially when such machines as power mowers were used. Duchamp's bicycle wheel was proto-dadaist in spirit and required the viewer to set it in motion, but kinetic sculptors in the dada-surrealist tradition prefer mechanical sources.   (C.R.)

King, Charles Bird (1785–1862).
Portrait and still-life painter. He was a native of Newport, R.I., where painter and nautical instrument-maker Samuel King (1749–1819) had been keeping alive the art tradition of the little town. He is said to have come as a runaway from home, at the age of fifteen, to the New York studio of Edward Savage.* During 1805–12 he was in London as a pupil and studio assistant of Benjamin West,* and in these years became a close friend of Washington Allston* and Thomas Sully.* Back again in America, he worked in Philadelphia, Richmond, and Baltimore before settling permanently at Washington in 1816, with sojourns in Newport in the summer.

William Dunlap* characterized him as lacking talent but making up for it in constant study and activity. His long residence in the capital brought him many distinguished sitters. John Quincy Adams, rarely satisfied with

an artist's work, described him as "one of the best Portrait Painters in this country. . . . He is also an ingenious thinking man, with a faculty of conversing upon almost every topic." In Washington he was frequently called upon to paint visiting Indians, and these works, at the Smithsonian Institution and elsewhere, form a notable part of his oeuvre; today they are considered important documentary material. His best-known picture, however, is his still life *The Vanity of the Artist's Dream* (1830, Fogg), which is often cited as a summary of his career. It shows a cupboard filled with books, papers, palette, a plaster cast, and other objects chosen to symbolize the struggles, perils, and tragedies of a life in art. It is one of the earliest American still-life paintings.   (C.C.S.)

King, John Crookshanks (1806–82).
Scottish-born sculptor who came to America in 1829 and settled in Cincinnati, where he worked as a machinist. About 1834, encouraged by Hiram Powers,* King turned to sculpture. Throughout his career his work consisted almost totally of portraiture; his likenesses were accurate enough but undramatic and sculpturally not very exciting. King never attained the highest rank in his profession, but he was competent and managed to eke out a living. In 1837 he moved to New Orleans, but finding insufficient patronage there, he moved to Boston in 1840. Select examples of King's work are the *Reverend Francis W. P. Greenwood* (1841, King's Chapel, Boston) and *John Quincy Adams* (1848, U.S. Capitol). In 1852 his studio burned, destroying all of his plaster models; he continued working, however, until about 1860.   (W.C.)

Kirk, Samuel (1793–1845).
Silversmith, born in Doylestown, Pa., of Quaker ancestry, Kirk was trained by James Howell of Philadelphia. In 1815 he opened a shop in Baltimore and about 1828 he began making the rococo revival silver with ornate repoussé decoration for which his firm was to become well known. In 1846 his son, Henry Child Kirk, became a partner under the firm name of Samuel Kirk & Son, which is today one of the oldest surviving silversmithing firms in the United States. It has made many important trophies and presentation

pieces, including the forty-eight-piece dinner service for the cruiser *Maryland;* designed in 1905 it depicts the history of the state. A traveling exhibit of antique silver, formed to show the history of silver and the company's development, circulates throughout the country. Included in it are sugar urn and vegetable dishes Kirk made for Betsy Patterson Bonaparte, wife of Napoleon's brother, Jerome. (M.G.F.)

Kline, Franz (1910–62).

Painter, born in Wilkes Barre, Pa., Kline grew up in coal country. He attended Girard College in Philadelphia, Boston University (1931–35), and Heatherly's Art School, London (1937–38). From England Kline moved to New York, where he exhibited in Washington Square's outdoor art shows and at the National Academy of Design.* His work through the decade of the 1940s consisted mainly of portraits and figure studies and street scenes, all done in a variety of styles. Even at this early stage Kline was moderately successful. He sold a few pictures to collectors, was commissioned to paint murals for the Bleecker Street Tavern in Greenwich Village (1940), and won two prizes at National Academy of Design exhibitions for his landscapes (1943 and 1944). The famous "bar murals"—each panel approximately four feet by four feet—show Kline at his figurative best. Scenes such as *Hot Jazz, Bubble Dancer,* and *Masquerade* are alive with singing waiters, musicians, and dancing girls, and both in subject matter and in fine composition they show how carefully he had studied the French café painters such as Toulouse-Lautrec and Degas.

It is said that Kline discovered his famous black-and-white image in 1949 when a slide of a figure sketch was projected in magnified and reversed form. Actually, the image had begun to develop several years earlier in some small figure drawings. Kline noted: "I kept simplifying the forms in black and white and breaking down the structure into essential elements." At the same time he was aware of the large automatic canvases Jackson Pollock* had begun to paint and he was also a close friend of Willem de Kooning.* In his first one-man show (1950) he achieved a major breakthrough in his work. His paintings were now totally abstract—often a single, centered black figure

Franz Kline. Orange and Black Wall, *1959. Collection Mr. and Mrs. Robert C. Scull, N.Y.*

on a white background. In this series Kline seems totally preoccupied with line and structure, building his images by drawing with black paint on white canvas. They have the quality of sketches (Kline always produced countless sketches, often on newspaper) and were compared to oriental calligraphy. Although Kline denied any such influence, when the sculptor Noguchi* took some of these drawings to Japan, they met with instant success.

Kline's earliest black-and-white paintings were sometimes tentative, mostly small (ranging from about one foot square to six feet square) and more involved in "image" than in dramatic tensions. Over the next few years his canvases grew gradually larger and he became increasingly involved in the struggle to produce these paintings, slashing the paint on in great broad strokes with a housepainter's brush. His black forms were now far more aggressive, and there was more interaction—often a clashing conflict and resolution—between black and white areas, as in *New York* (1953, Albright). Kline's exploration of dramatic tensions, his deliberately careless handling of paint, and the involvement of his whole body in his gestural brushstrokes put him in the forefront of the new abstract expressionist movement. In certain explanations of his work he notes: "I don't decide in advance that I'm going to paint a definite experience, but in the act of painting, it becomes a genuine experience for me." Kline's instantly recognizable image met with immediate success, and although he taught art—at Black Mountain College (1952), Pratt Institute (1953–54), and the Philadelphia Museum School of Art (1954)—he was now selling everything he produced and was represented in most major national and international shows including the São Paulo Biennial (1957) and the Brussels World's Fair. He now began experimenting with color, adding it to his familiar black and white image as in *Dahlia* (1959, Whitney). The results were seldom felicitous since his color was decorative and never a structural necessity. Kline's monumental and powerful canvases were particularly admired in Europe—possibly because they seemed to express all the raw energy and violence of America. At the height of his career, he fell ill and died, leaving behind a large number of works

that fulfilled his own criterion for great art—"whether or not the painter's emotion comes across." (E.C.G.)

Knaths, Karl (1891–1971).
Painter. Born in Eau Claire, Wis., Knaths spent his early life in the Midwest. In 1911 Knaths began studying at the Art Institute of Chicago. In 1919 he took up residence in Provincetown, Mass.; he remained there, never leaving the United States, for the rest of his life.

Knaths began painting in an impressionistic style, but in Provincetown he became acquainted with artists interested in the new ideas from Paris, especially cubism,* and this profoundly affected his mature production. Beginning about 1930, he planned all his pictures according to strict rules derived from the theories of Mondrian, Kandinsky, and others. He held that as there are measurable correspondences between musical intervals, so there are measurable intervals between colors and spatial proportions. In practice, he used only preselected colors and began by setting down structural lines. His work is essentially abstract— he is the heir of Juan Gris in plane structure and of Jacques Villon and Robert Delaunay in color—but he never completely abandoned subject matter; most of his subjects were derived from his environment at Provincetown, as for example *Duck Flight* (1948, Whitney.) At times, as in *The Sun* (1950, Phillips), he permitted himself to transcend his method in the interests of coloristic lyricism.

Duncan Phillips was Knaths' first— and for many years his only—patron, and did much to establish the artist's reputation. From 1937 to 1950, Knaths taught an annual six-week course at the Phillips Gallery in Washington; he also taught at Bennington College, Vt., and American University, Washington, D.C. (A.F.)

Knoll, Florence, see Bassett, Florence Knoll

Knoll, Hans G. (1914–55).
Modern furniture designer. Born in Stuttgart, Germany, he followed in the footsteps of his father, a pioneer furniture manufacturer, and received a thorough design education. Before emigrating to the United States in 1937, he was president of a small interior

design firm in England. In 1938 he established the Hans G. Knoll Furniture Company in New York City. Having been exposed to the work of the Bauhaus,* from which emerged the most advanced design ideas of the 1920s, Knoll determined to produce only modern furniture and textiles, while most of his competitors made traditional pieces to survive. As a result of his vision, today Knoll International is one of the most successful and progressive design forces in America. Florence Shust (see Florence Bassett), an architect, began to work for Knoll in 1943 and three years later they were married. Together they shaped the ultimate direction of the firm. Many prominent designers in America and Europe have been associated with Knoll, including Harry Bertoia, George Nakashima,* Isamu Noguchi,* Eero Saarinen,* and Mies van der Rohe.* When Knoll took over the Italian firm Gavina in 1968, other artists such as Marcel Breuer,* Sebastian Matta, Kazuhide Takahana, and Tobia Scarpa were added to the roster.

The firm's extensive work has been in the field of office planning. Working closely with the architects of various companies, institutions, and governments, Knoll Associates has helped to create new ways of organizing practical and well-developed office space. The influence of the Bauhaus and the International style* are reflected in the company's austere design and clean sense of detail. The Knoll look has been called "elegant and meticulous" whether the materials were wire, plastic, cherry, walnut, or rosewood. When Hans Knoll was killed in an accident, Florence Knoll carried on the firm's work until her retirement in 1965. (D.H.P.)

Kohn, Gabriel (1910–   ).
Sculptor who began experimenting, around 1954, with the techniques used by carpenters and shipbuilders. The resulting sculptures in wood gained him the reputation of being one of the few American artists capable of dealing with wood in a modern way.

Kohn was born in Philadelphia, Pa., and studied art at the Cooper Union and at the Institute of Design, New York City, from 1929–34. He won distinction in numerous competitive exhibitions during the 1930s. After the Second World War he joined the stream of veterans seeking to extend their art educations abroad and studied with the Russian-born sculptor Ossip Zadkine in Paris during 1946–48. There, Kohn concentrated on modeling, particularly in terra-cotta, and by 1948, he was ready for his first one-man show in Rome. When he returned to New York in the early 1950s he continued modeling, but eventually shifted over entirely into a technique of joinery unique to him.

His sculptures of laminated, bent wood shapes, joined unobtrusively, were frequently cantilevered, creating odd relationships to floor and wall. He was one of the first American sculptors to work with a concept that had eliminated the pedestal. Kohn has exhibited in New York frequently, and has been included in traveling exhibitions in Europe and South America.   (D.A.)

Krans, Olaf (1838–1916).
Swedish-born, self-taught genre painter whose family immigrated to the United States in 1850 to join a communal religious group at Bishop Hill, Ill. The community prospered initially but dissolved in 1862. Krans, who after serving in the Civil War worked as a house painter, decorator, and signmaker, is best known for a series of detailed, primitive paintings recording the community's history as he recalled it in later years, and for portraits of its founding members, probably painted from late photographs. The paintings remain in the Old Colony Church at Bishop Hill, and form an extraordinary record of communal folkways among 19th-century religious sects of the American Midwest. An example is *Planting Corn* (1875–95, Village of Bishop Hill).   (M.J.G.)

Krimmel, John Lewis (1787–1821).
Genre and portrait painter. He was a native of Würtemberg, Germany, who in 1810 emigrated to Philadelphia to join his brother in business. Much preferring the studio to the counting house, he very soon turned portrait painter. Krimmel taught himself art by copying, in oil, engravings by Hogarth and other Europeans. In the first Pennsylvania Academy exhibition in 1811, Krimmel was represented by four genre pieces, with both Philadelphia and German themes. Little genre scenes of the Dutch school were already popular in America, and this new painter, able to produce the same from American

1

2

1. **Knoll.** Florence Knoll Bassett. Knoll Interior, 1950s. Knoll International, Inc., N.Y.
2. **Karl Knaths.** Duck Flight, *1948.* Whitney Museum of American Art, N.Y.

life, combining decorative realism with friendly humor, had a promising future in a city which was becoming a center of book and print publishing. Success came gradually, partly because it depended on the slow process of engraving, but his work was exhibited in both Philadelphia and New York. Alexander Lawson (1773–1846) was the most eminent of his engravers. Krimmel was again in Germany, settling family affairs, in 1817–19. His short life ended tragically when he drowned. He had just been elected president of the Society of American Artists.*

Krimmel's best-known works are his *Election Day* (Historical Society of Pennsylvania) and his *Country Wedding* (1814, Pennsylvania). Noteworthy also is his painting, *Fourth of July in Center Square* (1819, Historical Society of Pennsylvania). (C.C.S.)

Kroll, Leon (1884–).
Painter, born in New York, N.Y. Kroll studied at the Art Students League* with John Henry Twachtman,* and at the National Academy of Design.* He later visited Paris and studied under Jean-Paul Laurens at the Académie Julien. Kroll had his first one-man show in New York in 1911 and was included in the Armory Show* (1913). His early paintings were primarily city landscapes and industrial scenes done in a heavily brushed style and related to the work of the New York realist artists. His more recent paintings center on still-life objects and the human figure and are done in a somewhat academic style with overtones of Cézanne and Renoir, as, for example, *Nude* (1933–34, Metropolitan).

Kroll was a member of the WPA Federal Art Project,* and his mural commissions include works in the Justice Department Building in Washington, D.C. (1936–37); the War Memorial Building in Worcester, Mass. (1938–41); and Johns Hopkins University. He has taught at the Art Students League and the Chicago Art Institute. A retrospective of his work was held in 1935 at the Carnegie Institute. (A.F.)

Krushenick, Nicholas (1929–).
Painter. A native of New York, N.Y., he studied at the Art Students League* and the Hans Hofmann School in New York City. During the 1950s Krushenick designed window displays, an experience that may help account for the

1

2

3

1. *John Lewis Krimmel.* Interior of an American Inn, *1813. Toledo Museum of Art, Ohio (gift of Florence Scott Libbey).*
2. *Yasuo Kuniyoshi.* Amazing Juggler, *1952. Des Moines Art Center.*
3. *Walt Kuhn.* Clown with Black Wig, *1930. Metropolitan Museum of Art, N.Y. (George A. Hearn Fund).*

bold color and imagery of his paintings. His works consist characteristically of images presented in the boldest of simplified colors, red, yellow, blue, or orange, defined by a heavy, black, frequently undulating line. He is a hard-edge* painter concerned with the presentation of abstract objects on the canvas with images that frequently have the impact of machine forms. His style, particularly in the use of color defined by black lines, owes something to the later works of Fernand Léger and in its collage effect to the late, monumental cutouts of Matisse. The sense of the painting as object is particularly evident in his concern with the three-dimensional relief projection. Using traditional perspective devices, he builds his forms out from the plane of the picture toward the spectator. During the 1960s he moved from undulating, curvilinear shapes increasingly toward a rigid geometry in which jagged triangles take on a violently expressionist quality. (H.H.A.)

Kuhn, Justus Engelhardt (active 1708–17).
Portrait painter and decorator. A native of Germany, Kuhn has left a legacy of large portraits of Maryland children, posed in a baroque splendor of flowers, gardens, and palaces. He was master of a charming candy-box yet personal style, of which his *Eleanor Darnall* (c.1710, Maryland Historical Society) is an excellent example. The inventory of his estate reveals a character in harmony with his art, a lover of music, good books, and fine dress. He augmented his income by painting coats-of-arms.

Kuhn, Walt (1880–1949).
Painter, draftsman, illustrator, and designer. Born William Kuhn in Brooklyn, N.Y., he adopted "Walt" about 1900. After a year at the Brooklyn Polytechnic Institute he opened a bicycle shop and spent several summers racing at county fairs. In 1899 he worked in San Francisco as a cartoonist. From 1901 to 1903 he was in Europe, studying at the Académie Colarossi in Paris and the Royal Academy in Munich. Returning to the United States, he developed a vigorous, impressionist-derived landscape style on summer excursions that took him from Florida to Nova Scotia. From 1905 he worked regularly as a cartoonist in New York, contributing to

Puck, Judge, and the New York *Sunday Sun* and *World.*

Becoming associated with The Eight,* Kuhn helped to precipitate the 1910 Exhibition of Independent Artists.* In December, 1911, he was one of four artists who initiated the planning that led to the Association of American Painters and Sculptors (of which he was secretary) and the subsequent 1913 Armory Show.* The impact of the Armory Show is particularly evident in Kuhn's painting. The work he displayed in his first one-man exhibition in 1911 was still impressionist-based, though with a fauve energy; his 1914 *Polo Game* moved toward fauvism,* and in his *Flowers and Forms* (c.1915, Kuhn Estate) he experimented with synthetic cubism.* His change in style ranged through flat color shapes, cubist and expressionist distortions, and technical approaches recalling the work of the French painters Rouault and Derain. Gradually, he arrived at his final personal manner, in which he placed a boldly outlined figure, light-struck, in monumental frontality, frozen against a dark background. The forms were simplified, flattened, but brusquely modeled by sharp dark accents. Colors and textures were strident, the mood intense—even disturbing.

These qualities were evident in Kuhn's studies of woman circus performers produced in the mid-1920s, such as *Dressing Room* (1926, Brooklyn). He continued, with increasing power, to portray clowns and acrobats in the 1930s (*Clown with Black Wig,* 1930, Metropolitan) and the 1940s (*Acrobat in Red and Green,* 1942, Metropolitan). As the series progressed, the chalky masks of the clowns only half concealed pent-up emotions, hinting at tragedy and clearly reflecting Kuhn's own growing bitterness. But the brutal power of his painting did not depend on subject matter; during the same years he injected comparable expressive force into a series of still lifes dramatically reduced to stark forms.

As a leitmotif throughout his work was a stream of relaxed, incisive drawings and watercolors that showed him a master of informal, economical characterization. At times the manner recalled that of his friend Jules Pascin, and at others, his years as an illustrator and cartoonist; it covers every sort of subject and many moods, always

revealing a tremendous vitality.

During the 1920s Kuhn earned his livelihood as a designer and director for musical revues, working six months of the year and painting during the remaining six. In the 1930s and '40s he turned his designing talents to such industrial products as railway club cars. His intense drive began to take its toll: he suffered a nervous breakdown and died in a mental hospital.
                                                           (D.W.S.)

Kuniyoshi, Yasuo (1893–1953).
Painter and graphic artist. Born in Okayama, Japan, he emigrated to the United States at the age of thirteen. He studied art at the Los Angeles School of Art and Design and, after moving to New York City, at the Art Students League* in 1916 with Kenneth Hayes Miller.* There he met Alexander Brook,* Peggy Bacon,* and Reginald Marsh.* He soon found a patron, Hamilton Easter Field, and he began exhibiting regularly in 1921.

His paintings from the 1920s were stamped with the highly individual imagination and the combination of oriental sensitivity and western sensuousness that characterize all his work. He painted landscapes, cows, and babies in distorted, flattened shapes, suggesting a wittily sophisticated primitivism, as in *Boy Stealing Fruit* (1923, Columbus). After trips to Europe in 1925 and 1928, he began to paint directly from the subject, and his works of the 1930s include still lifes—odd assortments of objects, united by a rich poetry of color and paint texture—and figure studies of half-clad girls caught in intimate moments of reflection, as in *I'm Tired* (1938, Whitney).

Kuniyoshi, a friend but not an imitator of the social realist painters, was sensitive to the tensions of the late 1930s and the grim impact of World War II. His painting progressively lost its softness and emphasized pattern and symbolic content. The overt human concern of such a painting as *Mother and Daughter* (1945, Carnegie) gave way in his last style to fantasy with ominous overtones: carnival figures with leering masks, painted in high-pitched color glazes and scumbles (*Amazing Juggler,* 1952, Des Moines). At the same time, his lifelong interest in drawing and lithography culminated in a series of harshly powerful wash drawings done during his last year.
                                                           (D.W.S.)

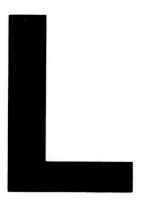

Labino, Dominick (1910–   ).
Leading glass craftsman with long industrial associations that have led to the development of a wide range of color possibilities. Labino was born in Clarion County, Pa., studied at Carnegie Institute of Technology and the Toledo Museum Art School of Design, and until his retirement in 1965 was director of research for Johns-Manville Fiberglass. He holds more than fifty patents for glass compositions, machines for forming glass fibers, and furnace design, and his technical knowledge is extensive in his field. Since 1963 he has worked with free-blown glass as an art form. His forms are determined by the metallic colors and the refractory potentials he wants to have dominate formal design. Many of his shapes are very regular in order for light to transmit colors clearly; others are pulled or have trapped air bubbles so that cobalt and copper colors are refracted with unusual shadow effects. His enlargement of the technical vocabulary of blown glass has had a specific effect on its revival as an art in the last decade.

(R.S.)

Lachaise, Gaston (1882–1935).
Sculptor. Born in Paris, he attended the École des Beaux-Arts, but soon rebelled against the academic tradition and joined the avant-garde circle active at the turn of the century. In 1906 he emigrated to the United States, which he described as "the most favorable place to develop as a creative artist." At first he worked in the Boston studio of Henry Kitson, but in 1912 he moved to New York, where he established his own studio and also assisted Paul Manship.* In 1912 he began his *Standing Woman* (Whitney), but his mature style —developed around bulbous, monumental female figures—did not appear until about 1920, as in his *Woman Walking* (1922, Modern Museum). By

1927, when he created his *Floating Figure* (Modern Museum) the essentials of his style had been formed and thereafter came a steady succession of interesting variations on the heroic female nude. Great sculptural masses united in dynamic rhythms overpower anatomical details; Lachaise's interest in the symbol of womanhood and her sexuality is expressed through distortion and the emphasis on plastic form and rich modeling. In later works of the early 1930s—such as *Kneeling Woman* and *Dynamo Mother*—the theme of sexuality is quite pronounced. A large exhibition of his work was held at the Museum of Modern Art in New York City in 1935; at that time Lachaise was a leader of America's avant-garde artists. He died that same year of leukemia.

(W.C.)

Lacy Glass, see Pressed Glass.

La Farge, John (1835–1910).
A still-life, portrait, landscape, and mural painter, thought in his own time to be one of the greatest American artists. Born in New York, N.Y., of wealthy French émigré parents, he received his first instruction in art from his grandfather, Binsse de Saint-Victor, a miniaturist. After graduation from St. Mary's College in Maryland, he studied law. In 1856 he went to Paris, where he studied painting briefly with Thomas Couture, and to London, where he came to know the work of the pre-Raphaelites. He finally decided to become a professional artist after studying with William Morris Hunt* in Newport in 1859, and in the following decade he produced a wide variety of paintings, including landscapes in the loosely painted, brown-toned manner of the Barbizon School,* and a series of softly-painted flower pictures—closer to the work of the French master Fantin-Latour than to any American style—which are

1. **Gaston Lachaise.** Woman Walking, 1922, bronze. *Museum of Modern Art, N.Y. (Abby Aldrich Rockefeller Fund).*
2. **John La Farge.** Afterglow, Tantira River, Tahiti, *1891. National Gallery of Art, Washington, D.C.*
3. **John La Farge.** Maua, Our Boatman, *1891. Addison Gallery of American Art, Phillips Academy, Andover, Mass.*

his masterpieces. Outstanding among these is *Flowers on a Window Ledge* (c.1862, Corcoran).

La Farge spent several years recovering from an illness, and then in 1873 he went abroad again. In 1876 he accepted a commission to decorate the interior of Boston's Trinity Church, designed by the noted architect H. H. Richardson.* La Farge spent much of his time up to 1890 working on designs for murals and stained glass, making use of his knowledge of the techniques of Renaissance tradition, and thus played an important role in the American revival of these arts. He was also one of the first American artists to travel to Japan (1886) and to the South Seas (1890–91), and he made many paintings of the exotic scenery and people he had seen on these trips, such as *Maua, Our Boatman* (1891, Addison). Perhaps most satisfying of all his work are his watercolors—both those of Tahitian subjects and earlier ones of still life and landscape; in this medium he expressed himself more fluently and more freely than in his more ambitious, larger works, which often appear labored. On both journeys across the Pacific, as well as on a trip to France in 1899, La Farge was accompanied by the writer Henry Adams; and throughout his life he was a friend of the most cultivated and cosmopolitan Americans. He himself wrote and lectured on art and travel, and his books included *Considerations on Painting* (1895) and *An Artist's Letters from Japan* (1897). Although he was very talented, his interests were probably too varied and his approach too self-conscious to allow him true greatness as an artist.

(T.E.S.)

Lafever, Minard (1798–1854).
Builder, architect, born near Morristown, N.J. In 1807 the family moved to Seneca Lake, N.Y., where Minard attended local schools. He had no formal architectural training, but probably learned the carpenter's trade. He moved in 1824 to Newark, N.J., where he worked as a carpenter and devoted his evenings to architectural drawing. Soon he moved to New York City (c. 1827), where he was listed as builder and carpenter until about 1829, when he began calling himself an architect.

The publication of Lafever's highly influential books began with *The Young Builder's General Instructor* (1829),

2

3

which contained the Greek and Roman orders. Next came *The Modern Builder's Guide* (1833), followed by *The Beauties of Modern Architecture* (1835), emphasizing ornamental features. His last book was *The Architectural Instructor* (1856).

In 1833 Lafever took James Gallier* as his partner, but Gallier left for Mobile, Ala., the following year. One product of their collaboration may have been the First Reformed Dutch Church, Brooklyn (1834–35, demolished). Its majestic Ionic colonnade recalled the great temples of Asia Minor. Lafever now shifted to the Gothic revival* style, borrowing design ideas mainly from English pattern books. His first success in this style was the Dutch Reformed Church, Washington Square, New York City (1839–40, demolished 1895). Other important churches in Brooklyn included the Pierrepont Street Baptist Church (1843–44); First Unitarian Church (1844); and First Universalist Church (1851, later the Swedenborgian Church). All these were variations on the Gothic style. He also designed some mansions, and the curious, somewhat Egyptian-styled Whalers' Church in Sag Harbor, Long Island, N.Y. (1843–44), which is still standing, minus its steeple.

Lafever is remembered mainly for the influence of his builders' books, with their clear and appropriate designs.

(P.F.N.)

Lambdin, George Cochran (1830–96). One of the first flower specialists among American painters. He was the son of James Reid Lambdin (1807–89), a successful Philadelphia portrait and miniature painter, who trained him. The younger Lambdin lived in Philadelphia all of his life except for two years in New York (1868–70) and two trips to Europe (1855 and 1870). Besides the paintings of roses and other flowers, seen both in vases and outdoors, *in situ,* he did sentimental portraits and genre scenes of the Civil War and other subjects. Typical of his work is *Vase of Flowers* (1873, Boston).

Landscape Architecture.
The shaping and arranging of a garden or tract of land. In America the art began very early when European settlers established vegetable and herb gardens, to which they soon added flowers. Late 17th-century gardens, such as

1

2

Landscape Architecture
1. Governor's Palace Garden, Williamsburg, Va., 18th century. Pre-revolutionary formal garden using geometrically pruned box-wood as the primary design element.
2. Plan of Mt. Vernon, late 18th century, showing bowling green with serpentine, representing a transition between the formal and picturesque styles.

that of the Whipple House, Ipswich, Mass., were formal—that is, plots were planted in squares or rectangles and executed in the Renaissance tradition. The Renaissance approach was also predominant in the 18th century, during which time the concept of the "pleasure garden" was expanded. These gardens were situated away from the house and served those who wanted to walk, talk, and enjoy scenic views. Splendid gardens of this type were created in the 18th century, particularly in the South. The most familiar example is that of the Governor's Palace, Colonial Williamsburg, Va., which has boxwood planted in a formal pattern. The most beautiful pre-Revolutionary garden remaining today is the unrestored garden at Middleton Place on the banks of the Ashley River, Charleston, S.C. A later example of the formal garden is Hampton, in Towson, Md., created in the 1780s and '90s. Also designed at this time was George Washington's garden at Mount Vernon, which is characterized by a formal plan except that it included a serpentine path, the first in the country. Toward the end of the 18th century, gardens contained a greater variety of plants, primarily because a number of Philadelphia and New York nurseries began offering customers a wider selection of such material.

Before 1800, the formal Renaissance, or classical, style of landscaping was the fashion. With the new century, English, or picturesque, style came slowly into vogue. The Renaissance style was distinguished by straight paths, rows of a single variety of trees, and by architectural devices or ornaments such as walls, steps, urns, and statues. The English style was identified by twisting paths, the irregularity and variety of planting, an extensive use of lawn, and the absence of architectural devices. An early harbinger of the new style was the serpentine path at Mount Vernon. Another was the landscaping of Monticello, near Charlottesville, Va., where Thomas Jefferson,* after leaving the White House in 1809, set out his trees on a sloping lawn in the so-called "natural" manner. The great change in landscaping occurred around 1830, with the triumph of the Romantic movement in poetry, fiction, and painting. William Cullen Bryant in his poetry and James Fenimore Cooper in his novels expressed the appeal of unspoiled nature as an ideal setting. A sufficient number of painters turned to landscapes to constitute what is known as the Hudson River School.* André Parmentier (1780–1830), a Brooklyn horticulturist, was the first American landscapist to assert the superiority of the "natural" over the "geometric" garden plan. But Parmentier was a very minor figure compared to Andrew Jackson Downing* of Newburgh, N.Y. In 1841, Downing heralded the virtues of the picturesque in his *Treatise of the Theory and Practice of Landscape Gardening, Adapted to North America.* The fashion that had begun in England early in the 18th century now swept the United States. It made the lawn, an English invention, a key part of American landscape design. Although Downing laid out the grounds of a number of estates, especially along the Hudson River, none is known to have survived. The best example in his style is Lyndhurst, at Irvington, N.Y., designed in the 1840s (now a property of the National Trust for Historic Preservations).

Downing's successors were Frederick Law Olmsted* and Calvert Vaux (1824–1895). Vaux, an English-trained architect, had been Downing's partner, and Olmsted was a gentleman farmer and a writer. They gave the picturesque a new dimension, adopting a style that had been confined to private estates and making it the style for public parks. In 1858 they won the competition for the design of Central Park in New York City. Whereas a formal landscape seeks to separate the ground into planes by using architectural effects, a picturesque landscape links varying grades by creating natural-seeming curved surfaces without the use of walls, terraces, or sharply-angled banks or steps. Central Park's terrain ranged from 4 feet to 137 feet above sea level. To cope with these varied grades Olmsted and Vaux situated lakes in the principal hollows, occasional lawns and meadows in the flatter areas, and trees and shrubs singly and—where a wooded effect was desired—in clusters. In addition, they kept many of the rock outcrops of the original landscape in their design. From the point of view of city planning, they made two important innovations: one was sunken roads to keep traffic across the park hidden from park users; the second was the separation of pedestrians, horseback riders, and carriages by a carefully planned system of paths, bridlepaths, and drives. Central Park, even before its completion in 1876, became New York City's proudest ornament.

Olmsted and Vaux themselves considered Prospect Park in Brooklyn, N.Y., laid out in 1866, their best design. It too was in the picturesque style, as were their many other parks (designed principally by Olmsted) from Boston to the West Coast. The picturesque became the standard form for parks and made the English lawn so popular that it was used even in the dry terrain of the Southwest. The American suburb, with its heavy shade trees and winding streets, was and still is influenced by this style.

Parks and gardens of the latter half of the 19th century profited from new plant material that was placed on the market by enterprising nurserymen. Explorers sent plants to America from all parts of the world, and horticulturists developed countless new plant varieties by hybridization. Startling changes now took place in the flower garden. Where formerly the blossoming season had been limited to springtime, it now stretched through to autumn, something unknown in the previous century. One conspicuous result was the use of raised flower beds, or carpet bedding, which consisted chiefly of cannas, coleuses, and geraniums. These were planted in star, crescent, and other geometric shapes, or used to spell out the name of a town or to form the American flag. The best surviving example of bedding dating from the 1860s is the Boston Public Gardens.

Toward the end of the 19th century, and the close of Olmsted's career, a shift in landscaping fashion occurred—the picturesque gave way to the formal and classical. Olmsted had anticipated this change in his design of an Italian garden for Biltmore, George Washington Vanderbilt's estate at Asheville, N.C., in 1888. More important, Olmsted and his partner, Henry Sargent Codman (1859–93), helped plan the World's Columbian Exposition of 1893. Held in Chicago, this event, more than any other, encouraged the American architectural renaissance (started by Richard Morris Hunt* and McKim and White of McKim, Mead & White*) and the second great era of American landscape architecture. Between 1890 and 1930, more time and money was spent

Landscape Architecture

to transform the American landscape into an ideal of beauty than at any other time in the nation's history. Among those who participated in this movement were the stepson and son of Olmsted, John Charles Olmsted (1852–1920) and Frederick Law Olmsted, Jr. (1870–1957); Charles Adams Platt* (1861–1933); Beatrix Farrand (1872–1959); Jacques Gréber (1882–1962); Bryand Fleming (1877–1946); Marian C. Coffin (1872–1957); Annette Hoyt Flanders (1889–1946); Vitale & Geifert (Ferruccio Vitale, 1875–1933; Alfred Geifert, Jr., 1891–1957); and Diego Suarez (b.1888). Most of their work has unfortunately disappeared, swallowed up by great metropolitan areas. Happily, a few beautiful examples do survive, such as the gardens of Villa Viscaya by Diego Suarez at the Dade County Museum of Art, Miami, Fla. These are among the finest classical gardens in the western hemisphere. Platt's work is represented by the garden of Faulkner Farm (Brandegee Estate) in Brookline, Mass., which has been preserved in its main features. Dumbarton Oaks in Washington, D.C., carefully maintains the gardens designed by Beatrix Ferrand. There are also Longwood Gardens at Kennett Square, Pa., whose magnificent fountain gardens are the work of its founder Pierre S. du Pont. The best example of the classical garden on the West Coast is the grounds of San Simeon, which were planned by Julia Morgan (1872–1948) for William Randolph Hearst.

After 1893, the use and variety of flowers changed: raised beds disappeared, replaced by straight formal beds and the herbaceous border where flowers were planted to achieve different color effects throughout the season. Many followed the concepts of English gardener Gertrude Jekyll, who placed borders in a formal setting wherein classical architectural devices were kept to a minimum and flowers were emphasized. Flowering shrubs were also sometimes placed in prominent positions. A good example of this can be seen in the gardens of the Henry Francis du Pont Winterthur Museum outside of Wilmington, Del., where azaleas and rhododendrons are set out in quantity in a picturesque landscape designed by Marian C. Coffin. An exception to the fashion for classical bedding and a herbaceous border was the work of Jens Jensen

1

2

Landscape Architecture
1. *Gardens of the Henry Francis du Pont Winterthur Museum, Winterthur, Del., with Sargent cherry trees, in the picturesque style.*
2. *Frederick Law Olmsted. Central Park, N.Y., picturesque style, 1876.*
3. *Viscaya Gardens of the Dade County Art Museum, Miami, Fla., in the modern formal style.*
4. *Viscaya Gardens of the Dade County Art Museum, Miami, Fla., showing steps and pool.*

3

4

(1860–1951) of Chicago, who created the "prairie style" in landscape. His picturesque gardens were limited to the use of native species, with an accent on horizontal forms.

The classical tradition in landscape architecture ended with the triumph of modern art in the 1930s. It was replaced with several styles, the most conspicuous being the "new picturesque," or, as it has been termed by some, "parkway picturesque." Much as modern art shook off classical traditions along with ornament and the glorification of the human figure, so landscape architecture in the 1930s shook off all attempts at formalized style. The new picturesque consists of lawn and the spotting of trees and shrubs here and there, as seen not only along parkways, but also around corporate headquarters and similar suburban buildings, and on college campuses. The style has in part been dictated by the demand from clients that maintenance costs be kept to a minimum. The best-known firm working in this manner is Clark & Rapuanoe (Gilmore D. Clarke, b. 1892 and Michael Rapuano, b.1904), long associated with parkway work.

Another modern school of landscape design is the abstract, stemming from recent fashions in art. The best-known professional in this style is Thomas Church, who is identified with the free-form pool. The emphasis here is on irregular plans, the use of evergreens, and paths of variegated gravel. In public work, such as the redesigning of Boston's Copley Square by Sasaki, Dawson, De May Associates (Hideo Sasaki, b.1919; Stuart O. Dawson, b.1935; Kenneth De May, b.1932), the emphasis is on irregular levels, eccentric architectural shapes, and a minimum of planting, instead of the flower beds that were formerly the chief feature. To avoid high maintenance costs, in public and corporate work, most landscape architects today lean toward designs where architectural effects predominate and planting is minimal. In private work, flowers and flowering shrubs remain very much in evidence. Designs are informal although there remains a continuing interest in the formal or classical among a minority. The Garden Club of America and its affiliated clubs, the Horticultural Societies of New York, Pennsylvania, and Massachusetts, in addition to the nurserymen, are the prime movers for horticulture. The American Society of Landscape Architects is concerned primarily with design.

The other significant change in the profession is its extension into city planning. The first step in this direction came when Frederick Law Olmsted, Jr., was appointed to the McMillan Commission of 1901, which brought back the L'Enfant* plan for Washington, D.C., and resulted in the capital city we know today. The second step came in the 1920s, when Jacques Gréber laid out Franklin Parkway in Philadelphia, linking City Hall and the Philadelphia Museum of Art and created one of the greatest urban vistas in America. As more landscape architects became involved in city planning, landscape architecture became established as a profession. In 1899, the American Society of Landscape Architects was founded. In the following year, Harvard University offered its first landscaping course, and in 1909 its school of architecture offered courses in city planning. Since then, many landscape architects have adopted the title of city planner. Today, as a result of the great concern with ecology and the environment, some even advocate "environmental landscaping" and "ecological planning" as part of landscape architecture. Ironically, as the range of the profession has expanded, the landscapes produced by the architects have become ever plainer. Although it is difficult to judge what landscape architecture in the future will stress, perhaps the next swing will be in the direction of joining design and horticulture, and flowers will once more appear prominently in the nation's parks and gardens. (H.H.R.)

Lane, Fitz Hugh (1804–65).
Master of marine painting and lithography, born in Gloucester, Mass. Partially crippled at an early age, Lane began to sketch the seashore of Cape Ann while still a child. His talent as a draftsman secured him an apprenticeship with William S. Pendleton's lithography firm in Boston, which constituted his only formal training in art. He remained with Pendleton's from 1832–37, and then joined the firm of Keith & Moore. From 1845 to 1847 he was in the lithography business with John W. A. Scott (1815–1907), a minor Boston painter, but returned to Gloucester in 1849 and

subsequently published his own lithographs. During his lifetime he produced almost fifty prints, ranging from tradecards, sheet music covers, and book illustrations to ambitious topographical views of New England coastal towns. His *Norwich from the West Side of the River* (c.1840, Leffingwell Inn Museum, Norwich, Conn.) is typical of his meticulous, early draftsmanship. As he gained greater mastery of the medium his lithographs became more sophisticated and he succeeded in rendering atmosphere and light with the same delicacy and brilliance that marks his achievements in paint.

As a neophyte painter Lane was influenced by Robert Salmon,* Englishborn marine artist who had earlier settled in Boston. Lane's oil painting, *Yacht "Northern Light" In Boston Harbor* (1845, Shelburne) is, in fact, after a sketch by Salmon. Lane painted about 150 oils as well as a few watercolors and numerous drawings. His paintings include shore scenes, ship portraits and harbor views, landscapes, a few portraits, parade decorations, and two naval engagements of the War of 1812; one of the latter, *The United States Frigate "President" Engaging the British Squadron* (1850, Corcoran), shows his skill in depicting a rousing naval battle. In his mature work, beginning in the late 1840s, Lane skillfully melded the draftsmanship of his lithographed topographical views, a knowledge of ship construction gained on frequent cruises, and a mastery of the nuances of water, light, and space under differing conditions of time and weather. His style, illustrated by such works as *Owl's Head, Penobscot Bay, Maine* (1862, Boston), was the culmination of years of observing and recording nature. He achieved the effect of arrested time, stillness, and heightened lucidity that characterized the work of his best period. Between 1848 and 1855 Lane achieved an increasing sensitivity to nature in coastal trips and especially through annual cruises to Castine, Me. He was fascinated by the special character of the light and air in the cold northern coastal waters around Mount Desert, Blue Hill, and Owl's Head. During the 1850s he embarked on longer voyages—to New York, Baltimore, and Puerto Rico—and these also resulted in paintings.

Although Lane established no school of marine painting, he did exert an in-

fluence on some of his contemporaries, especially on Frederic Church,* who also began to make painting trips to Maine. Lane provides yet another instance of a painter who achieved great popularity during his lifetime, only to fall into oblivion after his death. Although his emergence as a 19th-century American master dates back only a couple of decades, his high position is now firmly established. (H.W.W.)

Lange, Dorothea (1895–1965).
Photographer. Born in Hoboken, N.J., she worked briefly with photographer Arnold Genthe and in 1917–18 studied photography with Clarence White* at Columbia University. In 1919 she opened a portrait studio in San Francisco and worked in a camera store. After she married the artist Maynard Dixon, she traveled with him on his painting trips throughout the Southwest. In this period she photographed her family and friends, but without a distinctive point of view. During the Depression years of the early 1930s she realized that her camera could help shape the public's ideas about people and society in a period when thousands of homeless were pouring into California. In 1934 she became an assistant to Paul Taylor, University of California economics professor (whom she later married). Taylor used her photographs and recorded comments to broaden a report he was preparing on the plight of migrant labor. Willard Van Dyke, who with Ansel Adams* founded the f/64* group, recognizing that her sensitive treatment of people was related in its directness to the aims of the photographers in that group, invited her in 1934 to join them and exhibit her work in their gallery in Oakland. In 1935 she joined the Rural Resettlement Administration (later the Farm Security Administration*) and continued to photograph for this agency until it was disbanded in 1943. Her FSA pictures convey a genuine sense of concern. She emphasized the pathos of the displaced families seeking work in California and was acutely sensitive to details that would convey the character as well as the appearance of the migrants. They seemed instinctively to trust her and this enabled her to respond more fully to the situations she photographed. Her work shows both objectivity and concern, yet she used understatement to convey her ideas.

1

2

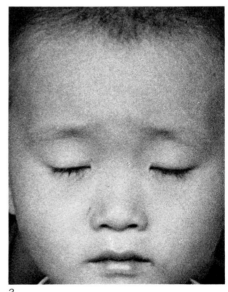

3

1. **Fitz Hugh Lane.** Owl's Head, Penobscot Bay, Maine, *1862. Museum of
   Fine Arts, Boston (Karolik Collection).*
2. **Dorothea Lange.** Nile Delta, Egypt,
   *1963, photograph. Oakland Museum,
   Cal.*
3. **Dorothea Lange.** Korean Child,
   *1958, photograph. Oakland Museum,
   Cal.*

During World War II, she worked for the Office of War Information and the War Relocation Authority, and took sympathetic photographs of the Japanese-Americans who were taken from the West Coast to relocation camps inland. She fell ill in 1945, and did not resume photographing again until 1951. In 1954, with Ansel Adams, she did a photographic essay, "Mormon Villages," for *Life* Magazine. In 1955 she photographed two very sensitive documentary essays, "The Irish Countrywoman" and "The Public Defender," also for *Life*. She was working on a major retrospective exhibition of two hundred of her prints for the Museum of Modern Art, New York City, when she died. (V.D.C.)

Lannuier, Charles Honoré, (1779–1819).
Furniture-maker. Born in Chantilly, France, he advertised as a cabinetmaker in New York in July 1803 and was listed in New York directories by 1805. Records reveal that his older brother, Nicholas, was a well-known Parisian cabinetmaker; possibly Charles Honoré was apprenticed to him. His early work in New York was in the Louis XVI style, with straight lines; restrained ornamentation of carving or ormolu mounts; and turned, tapering legs, often reeded or fluted. A fine gaming table of this period, stamped with his name, is in the Museum of the City of New York; and there are two matching labeled card tables with reeded legs, brass moldings, and ormolu mounts, one at the Metropolitan Museum of Art, and one at Winterthur. Also at Winterthur are a satinwood and mahogany pier table with fluted legs, and a night table of satinwood and rosewood. Lannuier's work soon showed the influence of the Empire style, and it is for furniture of this later Federal period that he is chiefly remembered. His labels are on a number of pieces in the Empire style, including a small stand called a gueridon (the White House); a pair of small corner pieces called encoignures (Albany Institute); several tables, both card and pier; and a bed with dolphin feet made for Stephen Van Rensselaer (Albany Institute of History and Art). Like the bed, a number of pieces attributed to Lannuier's shop feature supports in the form of caryatids, swans, eagles, or dolphins. A large group of such furniture was made for Baltimore merchant James Bosley (Maryland Historical Society). After Lannuier died, his shop was continued for a short time by his foreman, John Gruez. (M.J.B.)

Lasansky, Mauricio (1914–   ).
Printmaker. Born in Buenos Aires, Argentina, of Eastern European parents, he studied there, later directed an art school in a provincial town, and in 1939 became the director of the Taller Manualidades in Cordoba, Argentina. In 1943 he received a Guggenheim Fellowship; this allowed him to go to New York, where he studied the print collection of the Metropolitan Museum of Art and worked at Atelier 17.* In 1945 he was appointed visiting lecturer at the State University of Iowa, and has been a professor there since 1948. Before his move to the United States, Lasansky worked in the surrealist vein and his prints had been shown internationally. The group of surrealist artists who frequented Atelier 17 further stimulated him in the development of a dynamic attitude towards his preferred medium, intaglio (that is, etching, engraving, aquatint, etc.). Influenced by the works of Picasso and Goya, he often paints the horrors of war, and also reveals a brooding, Latin American religiousness in his work. Since the late 1950s Lasansky has produced large portraits and full figures, some of which are compilations of the attributes of the subject in a composite form rather than classic portraiture. More influential than his work is his teaching, which has fostered print workshops in most of the major American universities and given rise to most of the intaglio printmaking activity of the 1950s and 1960s. (R.C.)

Lassaw, Ibram (1913–   ).
Sculptor. Born in Alexandria, Egypt, Lassaw arrived in the United States in 1921. He was one of the founders of the American Abstract Artists* group and served as its president in 1946–49. After intense experimentation with new materials in the late 1940s, he arrived at his mature style. He bent, welded, and brazed copper and bronze wire, achieving what has been called "drawing in space," skeins of abstract form with strong organic overtones. He has always striven for "polymorphism," that is, form with multiple significance. This reflects his deep interest in biology, cosmology, and oriental religious thought, including Zen Bud-

1

2

1. *Benjamin Henry Latrobe.* Dickinson College, "Old West," Carlisle, Pa., 1803.
2. *Ibram Lassaw.* Galactic Cluster #1, 1958, bronze and silver. Newark Museum, N.J. (gift of Sophronia Anderson).

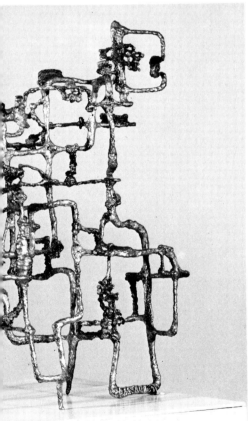

dhism. A charter member of the Artists Club in 1949, Lassaw shared with the abstract expressionists their early concern with biomorphic, mythologically tinged imagery. In his later work he turned from linear to more fully sculptural form, as in *Bird of Time* (1961), in which twisted strips of brazed metal rise from a rootlike cluster to suggest the growth of coral cells. His work has been widely exhibited since the 1940s, and was given a retrospective at the Massachusetts Institute of Technology in 1957. He was artist-in-residence at Duke University, Durham, N.C., in 1962–63, and at the University of California, Berkeley, Cal., in 1965–66.   (C.R.)

Latrobe, Benjamin Henry (1764–1820). Architect and engineer, born near Leeds, Yorkshire, England. His father was head of the English wing of the Moravian Church and young Latrobe was sent to Moravian schools. Arriving in London in 1784, he had various positions until, in 1788, he began working in the office of the architect Samuel Pepys Cockerell. In 1791 he opened his own office and gained a few commissions, notably Hammerwood Lodge and Ashdown House, both near East Grinstead, Sussex. These designs show dependence on the work of other London architects, but Hammerwood is one of the first residences in England to use the Greek Doric order. Ashdown House (now a boys' school) uses the Ionic order for its portico.

Disconsolate after the death of his wife, Latrobe emigrated to America. He arrived at Norfolk, Va., in 1796 and engaged in small architectural jobs. He then went to Richmond, Va., where he completed the design and supervised construction of the penitentiary. During a visit to Philadelphia, Latrobe met the president of the Bank of Pennsylvania, who requested a design for a new building. Erected in 1798, it was the first building in America to exhibit the Greek orders (here Ionic) in correct proportion. Public approval of the bank produced many commissions, both architectural and engineering. The most spectacular was his system for supplying Philadelphia with water, including a pumping station (in the Doric order), a storage tank, and the use of wooden pipes. Thus established as a professional architect-engineer, it was not surprising that Thomas Jefferson* chose him in 1803 to complete the

Capitol Building in Washington, D.C. By 1811 both wings were finished. When the British burned the Capitol in 1814, leaving the walls standing, Latrobe was hired (1815–17) to rebuild the interior. His plans were adopted, but the Capitol was not finished until 1829, and then by the architect Charles Bulfinch.*

Another of Latrobe's innovations was his use of the Gothic style for residences, such as Sedgeley Park near Philadelphia (1799). Other houses of his show the strong influence of London architect Sir John Soane; they were severe, but with a classical elegance supported by good proportions, making them superior to most contemporary houses. After a fire at Dickinson College, Carlisle, Pa., Latrobe designed (1803), without fee, the replacement now called "Old West." Not advanced in plan, it is nevertheless a superb demonstration of how stone can be used cheaply to produce a building of genuine character and good proportions.

The Baltimore Cathedral (1804–21) was, after the Capitol, Latrobe's largest project. It remains intact, with additions made to the chancel. Of designs in both classic and Gothic styles, Bishop Carroll chose the former, although Latrobe preferred the latter. The first church in the United States vaulted with stone, it is a masterpiece of the building art. The Bank of Philadelphia (1807–8, demolished) was Gothic, while Latrobe's design for additions to Dr. Herron's Presbyterian Church, Pittsburgh (1815), and his design for St. John's Church, Washington, D.C. (1815–16), were simplified Georgian. In an age of romanticism and no official style, Latrobe moved with ease from one style to another, though his own choice was usually Grecian. Commodore Decatur's house, Washington, D.C. (1817–18), though outwardly austere, represents the general excellence of his domestic designs, and the interior was beautifully adorned.

Latrobe's son Henry also became an architect and started his career in New Orleans, but he died in 1817 of yellow fever. Latrobe went there in 1818 to complete the young man's projects, and took some other commissions, the most important being the State Bank of Louisiana (1820); however, he also succumbed to yellow fever.

The first well-trained professional architect to practice successfully in the

United States (such men as Hallet* and Hadfield* were relatively unsuccessful and had little influence), Latrobe promoted a cultivated interest in architecture by the example of his own excellent designs. He introduced the Greek revival* style, built the first major waterworks, assisted (without fee) many colleges and churches with architectural problems, and trained William Strickland,* Robert Mills,* and other leading architects of the next generation.

(P.F.N.)

Laurent, Robert (1890–1970).
One of the earliest sculptors to experiment with abstraction in America, he was born in Concarneau, France. A prodigy, his talent was recognized by the American painter Hamilton Easter Field, who took the boy back to America and educated him. About 1905 he was sent to Paris as an apprentice art dealer; he met Picasso and learned of the work of the cubists, and also discovered primitive art. He experimented with abstraction in his own work. He began carving directly in wood, an early example of which is his bas-relief, *Negress* (1913). Two years later he had a one-man show in New York and thereafter was a major influence on American sculpture through his abstraction and stylization of natural form and his technique of carving directly in wood or stone. His first attempt at direct carving in stone came in 1923 in a head of his wife, Mimi; he was therefore developing this technique at the same time as William Zorach,* who also had his studio in Brooklyn. Laurent's abstract art met resistance, however, and in 1932 his *Goose Girl* was rejected after it had been commissioned for Rockefeller Center's Radio City (critical opinion eventually forced its acceptance). A good example of his work may be seen in *Seated Nude* (1940, Pennsylvania), with its abstraction of natural form into monumental masses. Laurent had begun teaching at the Art Students League* in 1925 and in 1942 he joined the faculty of the art department of Indiana University and taught there for over twenty-five years. His summers were spent at his home in Ogunquit, Me., where he conducted an art school. A late example of his work is the bronze *Venus* at Indiana University. (W.C.)

Lawrence, Jacob (1917–   ).
Black painter of social comment. Born in Atlantic City, N.J., Lawrence spent his early childhood in Easton, Pa., where his father was a coal miner. In 1920 he and his mother moved to Harlem in New York City. From 1932 to 1939 he studied with the black painter Charles Alston and attended the various Harlem gatherings that were generating interest in American Negro history. He painted under the WPA Federal Art Project* from 1934–38. In 1936, Lawrence embarked on his first series of paintings, based on the life of Toussaint L'Ouverture, the former slave who founded the republic of Haiti. In 1937 he won a scholarship to the American Artists School and studied there for two years studying under Anton Refregier.* His first major one-man exhibition was held in 1941 in New York City.

The majority of Lawrence's paintings were narratives of contemporary history executed in series, beginning with his "The Migration of the Negro" (1940–41, Modern Museum and Phillips), a group of sixty pictures in tempera on composition board. Other major series depicting the plight of the black man with posterlike cut-out figures in tortured expressionistic positions include twenty-six gouaches, "Life in Harlem" (1943), a "war" series, based on his experience as a Coast Guard officer in World War II; a John Brown series (1946); and "Sanitarium" (1950). In 1948, Lawrence did the illustrations for *One-Way Ticket,* a book by the black poet Langston Hughes. He did paintings based on desegregation in the South during the late 1950s and early '60s, and in 1964 he traveled to Nigeria, which became the subject for several works. His more recent works have tended to be more decorative than the earlier social comment paintings. But all of his work is characterized by the stylization of figures into strong, flat patterns; a frequent use of masks or masklike faces; and a use of vivid color and sharp contrasts, which give his social and historical themes an expressive, symbolic intensity, and make clear his strong social protest. (A.F.)

Lawrie, Lee (1877–1963).
Sculptor. He was born in Rixdorf, Germany, but was brought to the United States in infancy and raised in Chicago. He began his career about 1894 as an assistant in the studios of Augustus Saint-Gaudens* and other sculptors, and he was to become known primarily for his quasi-abstract decorative architectural sculpture. Lawrie created the sculpture for many of the buildings designed by Bertram G. Goodhue,* the best known of which is probably the Nebraska State Capitol in Lincoln (c.1922). He also did the architectural decorations for the Harkness Memorial Quadrangle at Yale University, where he had received a degree in 1910 and taught from 1908–18. He made the great reredos for St. Thomas' Church, New York City, and the decorations for the Los Angeles Public Library. Lawrie was special consultant for sculpture at the Century of Progress Exposition (1933, Chicago) and the New York World's Fair (1939). One of his best-known works is the heroic bronze *Atlas* in Rockefeller Center. (W.C.)

Lawson, Ernest (1873–1939).
Landscape painter and member of The Eight,* born in Nova Scotia, Canada. At sixteen he went to Mexico as an engineering draftsman. He moved to New York City in 1891, studied at the Art Students League,* and was decisively influenced by his teachers, J. Alden Weir* and John H. Twachtman.* In 1893 he went to Paris, where he attended the Académie Julien and made his debut the following year at the Salon des Artistes Française. In 1895 he met Alfred Sisley and was influenced toward a more vigorous impressionism.*

Returning to America, he settled in New York's Washington Heights. There he produced a number of paintings of upper Manhattan and the Harlem River, such as *Winter on the River* (1907, Whitney), in which he developed his characteristic richly colored, heavily pigmented style. In 1904 he met William Glackens* and two years later he moved down to Greenwich Village. He had an exhibition at the Pennsylvania Academy of the Fine Arts* in 1907, and joined The Eight in their epochal show in 1908. He subsequently exhibited with the Independent Artists* (1910) and in the Armory Show* in 1913, as well as with Canadian groups.

Lawson usually painted in heavy impasto laid on by palette knife, with more or less extensive areas of broken, intense color. This tougher adaptation of impressionism was in line with the movement toward stronger individual expressiveness in advanced art of the early 20th century. The critic James Hunecker praised Lawson's "palette of crushed jewels," a characterization that aptly describes his best work and has since been associated with it. In 1916 Lawson painted in Spain, and on later occasions traveled in Nova Scotia, the western United States, and the South. During the 1920s he taught in Colorado Springs and Kansas City. For reasons of health he settled in Florida in 1936. Adapting his technique to new landscape problems was not easy, and his late work was uneven. (D.W.S.)

Lebrun, Rico (1900–64).
Painter, sculptor, and printmaker. Born in Naples, Italy, Lebrun was educated at the National Technical Institute and the Naples Academy of Fine Arts. In 1922 he took a job as designer and supervisor in a stained-glass factory and moved to the United States two years later, when the factory opened a branch in Springfield, Ill. He returned to Italy repeatedly to study Renaissance and baroque masters, and his agonized, expressionistic style remained deeply influenced by memories of his native land. Lebrun soon moved to New York City, where he quickly achieved success as an advertising artist. He also embarked on mural projects, one of which won him a Guggenheim Fellowship. He began work on a mural, *River Flood,* for a post office, but this project was abandoned as the result of a dispute. In 1938 he moved to California. He taught at the Chouinard Institute in Los Angeles in 1939 and later taught animation at the Walt Disney studios and was instrumental in the production of *Bambi;* his cinematographic experience exerted a strong influence on his subsequent work. In 1944–46 he was artist-in-residence at the Santa Barbara Art Museum—and although he continued to travel extensively, teaching and painting in Mexico, the United States, and Europe, the rest of his life was centered in southern California.

Lebrun's mature style dates from the late 1930s, with paintings of cripples, beggars, and harlequins in the Spanish tradition of Velásquez, Goya, and Picasso. His work of the early 1940s ranged from "Spanish exercises" in realistic still life to a morbid surrealism.* A pivotal series during his first years in Santa Barbara interpreted farm imple-

Rico Lebrun. Genesis, *1960.*
Pomona College, Claremont, Cal.

ments as expressionistic parables of the human skeletal anatomy; a second series dealt with images from slaughterhouses. In 1947, Lebrun started on a "Crucifixion" series that eventually comprised more than 200 drawings and paintings and culminated in a gigantic triptych (now at Syracuse University). Basically monochromatic, it was conceived as a cycle of cinematographic "frames" and is characterized by a baroque sense of drama and convulsive movement joined to a contemporary use of abstract form. A new use of vivid color and strong light entered Lebrun's work in Mexico in 1953–54—largely monumental collages in dynamic, organically based compositions. The breadth and boldness of these collages carried over into a 1954–58 series based on the atrocities of Buchenwald and Dachau. In 1960, he completed his most ambitious single painting, the mural *Genesis* at Pomona College, Cal., and in the following years executed series of drawings and prints after Dante's *Inferno*, Brecht's *Dreigroschenoper,* and a *Crucifixion* by Grünewald. In his paintings of those years, the human figure was increasingly transformed into dark, brooding, spectral imagery. He was working on a series of some thirty sculptures at the time of his death.

Lebrun was the recipient of various awards and held numerous national exhibitions. His work and teaching exerted a major influence on figurative artists in southern California as well as in Mexico and on the east coast. His art was an intense reflection of the postwar spirit of destruction and despair, coupled with an impassioned sense of affirmation, of spiritual transformation and rebirth. (A.F.)

Lee, Arthur (1881–1961).
Sculptor. Born in Norway, he was brought to America when he was eight years old. In 1901 he studied at the Art Students League* in New York but then went to Paris (1905–10) and attended the École des Beaux-Arts. On his return to America he was represented in the Armory Show* of 1913 by four pieces, two of which—*Hercules* and *Aphrodite*—reveal his interest in classical art. He was a classicist in spirit rather than in any eclectic sense, however, seeking a reserved dignity, balance, and gracious rhythm in the human figure without resorting to diluted forms

of neoclassicism.* Although there is great poise in his figures in either marble or bronze, there is also a marked vitality, as may be seen in his *Volupté* (1915, Metropolitan). Lee worked in Paris from 1914–17; after returning to New York he became, during the 1920s and '30s, one of the most respected sculptors of the conservative school. His bronze *Rhythm* (1928) was acquired by the Whitney and his *Great Fortune* (c.1936) is in the Valentine Museum, Richmond, Va. In the latter work, Lee's comprehension of the nature of abstraction is evident, but he never deviated from realism beyond a slight abstraction of the human figure. (W.C.)

Lee, Doris (1905–   ).
Painter. Born Doris Embrick in Aledo, Ill., she graduated in 1927 from Rockford College, Ill., and then traveled and studied in Italy and France; one of her teachers in Paris was André Lhote. Returning to America in 1930, she studied at the California School of Fine Arts in San Francisco with Arnold Blanch, whom she married in 1939. Since 1931 the center of her activities has been Woodstock, N.Y., but she has traveled extensively. She has taught at the Colorado Springs Fine Art Center and at Michigan State College.

At the start of her career, Miss Lee's work was in abstract modes, but it soon developed into a whimsical, folksy, and anecdotal evocation of the American scene, as for example, *Thanksgiving* (1936, Chicago). This painting, depicting the preparation of a Thanksgiving feast in a farmhouse, was awarded the Logan Medal at the Art Institute of Chicago, but the vigor of its presentation so angered the donor of the medal, Mrs. Frank G. Logan, that she established the anti-modernist Society for Sanity in Art to carry on propaganda for "sweetness and light." Miss Lee has illustrated many books, and has executed commissions from *Life* to depict the folkways of Hollywood, of Central America, and of Africa. In 1936 she painted a mural in the headquarters of the Post Office Department in Washington, D.C. She is represented in many American museums. (A.F.)

L'Enfant, Pierre Charles (1754–1825).
Military engineer, architect, and city planner. Born in Paris, he came to America in 1777 to fight in the Revolu-

tionary War. Wounded at Savannah, Ga., in 1779 and captured by the British, he was exchanged in 1783 and promoted to major.

L'Enfant's first architectural work was to convert the City Hall, New York City, into Federal Hall (1789, demolished) for the first American Congress. He used a design based on the French Renaissance* mode, emphasizing the columnar second story with its numerous sculptured panels and iron railings. After Congress decided to build the Federal City on the Potomac, L'Enfant was selected by Washington to plan the city and design the public buildings (1791). He planned imaginatively, using his knowledge of the designs of European cities, and fusing a grid with a radial plan (probably influenced by the plan of Versailles) in which ease in transportation from one distant point to another was combined with an orderly arrangement of streets. The character of his plan has survived in spite of many encroachments, and remains as testimony to his great skill as a city planner. L'Enfant was dismissed by Washington in 1792 for overzealously guarding the partition and sale of city lots.

Of his architecture little remains but the memory of "Morris's Folly," Philadelphia (1793–97). Thoroughly French in style, it had a mansard roof, burgeoning bay windows, marble walls, and other extravagances. It was built for Robert Morris, a wealthy merchant who went bankrupt in 1798 and ceased payments on the unfinished house, which was promptly destroyed. Although offered other opportunities for work, L'Enfant's temperament usually offended his employers. Brilliant but unrestrainable, his talents were mainly wasted—except for his magnificent city plan of Washington. (P.F.N.)

Lescaze, William (1896–1969).
Architect, one of the first proponents of the International style* and streamlined moderne* architecture to practice in the United States. Born in Geneva, Switzerland, he studied architecture in Zurich. In 1920 he arrived in New York, where at first he designed mostly interiors and furniture. In 1929 he formed a partnership with the Philadelphia architect George Howe,* and almost immediately their firm, Howe & Lescaze, became the foremost exponent of the International style in the

1. **Doris Lee.** Thanksgiving, *1936. Art Institute of Chicago.*
2. **William Lescaze** *(with E. T. Heitschmidt). CBS Radio Building, Hollywood, Cal., 1938.*

United States. Their most widely publicized building was the Philadelphia Savings Fund Society Building (1932), which has long been cited as the first modern skyscraper* in the United States in part because of its horizontal bind windows, and partly because of the exterior exposure of the steel frame. It was one of the few American buildings included in the important exhibition, "The International Style: Architecture Since 1922," at the Museum of Modern Art in 1932. Although this building does exhibit many of the visual qualities of the International style, it is in fact as much moderne as it is modern. Thus the mezzanine banking floor with its dominant, curved, corner window and much of the interior detailing, are excellent examples of early streamlined moderne. Purer in its commitment to the International style were their Hessian Hill School at Croton-on-Hudson (1931) and, after Lescaze had established his own practice in 1934, the school he designed at Ansonia, Conn. (1936). The imagery of these two schools conveys some of the stripped qualities of the International style as one finds it in the work of Albert Kahn.* Lescaze in his writings, particularly in his *On Being an Architect* (1942), decried the idea of streamlining buildings, yet all of his pre-1941 designs for buildings as well as his furniture exhibit numerous elements of streamlined moderne. In his own New York studio-house (1934), he employed glass brick in curved wall sections and in his CBS Radio Building in Hollywood (designed with E. T. Heitschmidt, 1937–38), much of the interior detailing is more moderne than modern. This vacillation between the two modes persisted in his later work, as in his Aviation Building at the 1939 New York World's Fair and his Longfellow Building (1941), Washington, D.C.

Although Lescaze continued to design after 1945, he was no longer a major figure on the architectural scene. His death in 1969 was almost totally ignored. (D.G.)

Leslie, Alfred (1927–   ).
Painter. Born in New York, N.Y., Leslie attended New York University (1948–49) and began to paint in earnest. He received immediate recognition, exhibiting in the "New Talent" show (1949) organized by the critic

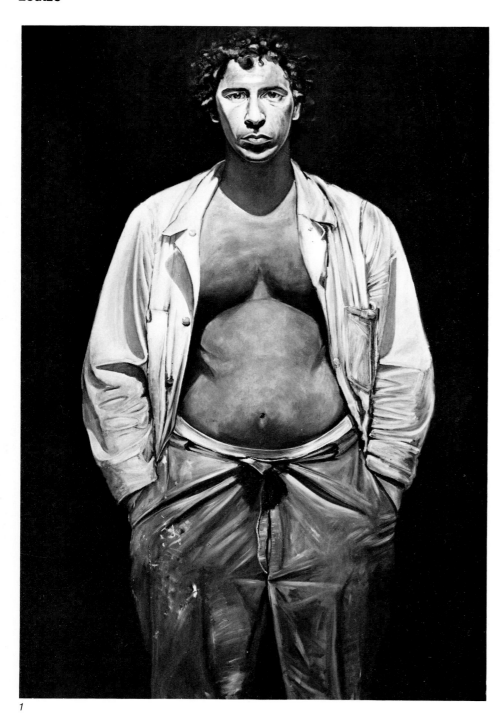

1

Clement Greenberg, and in numerous shows throughout the 1950s. A second-generation practitioner of abstract expressionism,* he quickly acquired the mannerisms of his predecessors, using wide, slashing brushstrokes and drips and splatters of paint to create a raw, angry, "unfinished" look, as in *The Red Side* (1961). Nevertheless, his paintings were tightly controlled and invariably had an underlying geometric structure. By putting several canvases together to form one large painting he produced literal divisions in a huge, blown-up image, resulting in a highly original insistence on the reality of the support itself. By the early 1960s his image had become "cleaner" and more geometric; this was followed by his abandonment of abstraction altogether. His subsequent heroic-sized figurative paintings are characterized by a hard-edged photographic realism reminiscent of the "blue" illustrations in such newspapers as *Police Gazette*. His work is in major collections.   (E.C.G.)

Leutze, Emanuel Gottlieb (1816–68). Historical, portrait, and landscape painter. He is remembered today as the creator of two monumental, popular, and pedantic works, *Washington Crossing the Delaware* (1851, Metropolitan) and the allegorical-historical mural in the Capitol, *Westward the Course of Empire* (begun in 1860). Unfortunately, his achievement in works of a more modest scale and character has been neglected. Born in Gmünd, Germany, as a child he was brought by his family to Philadelphia, where he eventually studied painting. At twenty he began painting portraits in Churchtown, Pa. A turning point in his career came in 1841, when he went abroad to study at Düsseldorf under a well-known German historical painter, Karl-Friedrich Lessing. He remained abroad for twenty years, studying also in Munich, Venice, and Rome, but living in Düsseldorf. He returned to America in 1859 to paint *Westward the Course of Empire* and to fulfill other commissions. During the last decade of his life he worked both in New York and in Washington.

Leutze, like his Düsseldorf colleagues, devoted himself to painting historical and literary reconstructions; these were carefully composed and researched, meticulously drawn, and markedly melodramatic in style. He

1. *Alfred Leslie.* Self-Portrait, *1967. Whitney Museum of American Art, N.Y.*
2. *Emanuel Gottlieb Leutze.* Washington Crossing the Delaware, *1851. Metropolitan Museum of Art, N.Y. (gift of John S. Kennedy).*
3. *Jack Levine.* The Feast of Pure Reason, *1937. Museum of Modern Art, N.Y. (on extended loan from the WPA Federal Art Program).*

painted a series of canvases drawn from American history, and occasionally literary subjects, such as *Cromwell and Milton* (1854, Corcoran). Despite their contemporary popularity, these now appear dull and academic. While Leutze has necessarily been judged on the basis of these tiresome and somewhat sentimental paintings, he occasionally did work that appeals to present-day taste. His portraits, for example *Nathaniel Hawthorne* (1862, National Portrait Gallery), are attractive and extremely well painted. His rare landscapes, such as *On the Banks of a Stream* (c.1860, Corcoran), reveal him to be a fine colorist. Probably done primarily for pleasure and not for exhibition, they show a different and more pleasing side of his work and deserve more attention than they have received.

(H.W.W.)

Levine, Jack (1915–   ).
Painter. Born in Boston, Levine began studies at the Boston Museum School in 1929 and at Harvard. He worked for the WPA Federal Art Project* in 1935, showing in the Museum of Modern Art's 1936 WPA show. Throughout his career he has remained aloof from schools, movements, academies, and the politics of the art world, maintaining his independence and a private studio. His first one-man show was in 1939; he has had many awards and exhibitions including retrospectives at Boston's Institute of Contemporary Art (1953) and the Whitney Museum (1955).

Levine is a painter of protest and social comment. The contrast between professed ideals and brutal realities is a favorite one with him, and reaches perhaps its most powerful statement in *Gangster Funeral* (1952–53, Whitney), wherein political leaders and police officers are gathered in mourning around a mobster's coffin. His work is filled with satires on the military (*Welcome Home*, 1946, Brooklyn) and on the administration of justice (*The Trial*, 1956, Chicago). He has done a series of parodies on the classic theme of *The Judgment of Paris*. However, he has also painted many straightforward portraits without satire; nor is there satire in his numerous paintings on Old Testament themes or on subjects drawn from modern Jewish life. Levine's style has parallels in the work of Chaim Soutine, Francisco Goya, and Georges Rouault; however, he has

2

3

made a totally personal synthesis, using distortion, enlarged heads, colored glazes, and the transluscent surfaces reminiscent of baroque painting.

(A.F.)

Levine, Les (1935–   ).
Environmental and process artist. Born in Dublin, Ireland, Levine developed an early interest in photography. In 1954 he moved to London, attended the Central School of Arts and Crafts, and began to design technical mechanisms and jewelry. Despite his success in England, Levine was attracted to American technology and moved to Canada (1957), which he felt offered the best of both worlds. Gradually he turned toward the fine arts, and the first exhibition of his painting and sculpture was at the University of Western Ontario in 1963. His interest in surrealism* was apparent in *Rocker Column* (1963), an eleven-foot tower that rocked back and forth, threatening to fall on the spectator.

His first move toward environmental art* occurred in 1964 in an "all silver" show in Toronto that brought him tremendous success. Here he attempted to change the space of the gallery, chiefly by placing objects jutting out into the room. The implications of this work were extended in *Slipcover,* "a place" exhibited at the Art Gallery of Ontario (1966). By covering walls, floor, and ceiling with mylar, and projecting slides of paintings onto the shiny plastic, Levine combined environmental art with theatrical performance. Other "effects" included vinyl bags that continuously expanded and deflated, and sounds picked up and reverberated by audio equipment. Levine had moved to New York City in 1964, and within two years his American success was assured. *The Star Garden,* exhibited at the Museum of Modern Art (1966), consisted of large, clear plastic bubbles with walkways through the middle which were intended to induce feelings of "giddiness" and "weightlessness" in the spectator. *The Clean Machine* was a six-foot-high, three-foot-wide walkway composed of white plastic modular units; as the spectator moved through this environment he would presumably become aware of the space as well as his own body. By 1968 Levine had turned to "disposables," obviously a comment on the built-in obsolescence

of American products. In a show called "The Process of Elimination," 112 vacuum-formed plastic curves were placed in a gallery; four were removed each day, so that by closing day the room was empty. As in many of his other works, the emphasis was on "process" and not on "form." He then turned to television-works. *Iris* (1969) consisted of three TV cameras and six monitors in an eight-foot-high "cabinet," presenting the spectator with simultaneous images of himself in close-up, medium, and long shot. Levine has had numerous shows throughout the world.

(E.C.G.)

Lewis, Martin (1883–1962).
Draftsman, printmaker, and painter, born in Australia, Lewis made his reputation in Manhattan as a chronicler of the exuberance of the city's street life in the 1920s. His drypoints display skilled, vigorous draftsmanship and an identification with the moods of New York. In the 1930s he captured the sombre and sometimes sinister mood of Manhattan and the loneliness of small-town America.

Lewitt, Sol (1928–   ).
Sculptor, known for his "serial compositions." Born in Hartford, Conn., and graduated from Syracuse University (1949), Lewitt had his first one-man show in New York City in 1965. His earliest white three-dimensional grids were acclaimed for their "minimal"* form and pristine purity. By 1966, in *Serial Project #1,* he was involved in a more complicated mathematical order —producing all the possible permutations for an alternately open and closed cube and rectangle, one set inside the other. He wrote: "Serial compositions are multipart pieces with regulated changes. . . . The artist would follow his predetermined premise to its conclusion avoiding subjectivity. Chance, taste, or unconsciously remembered forms would play no part in the outcome. The serial artist does not attempt to produce a beautiful or mysterious object but functions merely as a clerk cataloging the results of his premise." Exhibitions based on this theme were held in 1967 and 1968, the latter "46 three-part variations on three different kinds of cubes." Despite Lewitt's emphasis on conceptual aspects, his open space-frames were quite beautiful, and their simple perspective recession

probably influenced literalist art.

By 1969 he had abandoned architectural wood and painted aluminum constructions in favor of two-dimensional "wall drawings," executed in pencil right on the gallery walls. Again, the "subject matter" was a numerical series of permutations. One wall, for example, consisted of four horizontal rows of sixteen squares each, the squares presenting four variations of three superimposed lines. Such mathematical games could become tedious were it not for the delicacy and beauty of the work itself. By superimposing horizontal, vertical, and diagonal lines, secondary patterns began to emerge, forming geometric compositions much like Islamic decorative art. Lewitt continues to deny any interest in the final result, insisting that his pieces are made without regard for esthetics. And he has continued to make wall drawings that are destroyed at the close of each exhibition. By 1971 the drawings had evolved into pure texture: in Amsterdam one wall contained "10,000 evenly-distributed straight lines approximately 24 centimeters long"; the opposite wall contained 10,000 more pencil lines 12 centimeters long.

(E.C.G.)

Liberman, Alexander (1912–   ).
Painter, sculptor, and photographer. Liberman was born in Kiev, Russia, attended school in England, and then studied in France under André Lhote at the Sorbonne (1929–31), at the École Speciale d'Architecture, and at the École des Beaux-Arts. In 1933–37 he worked for *Vu,* one of the first illustrated magazines, and rose to managing editor. During the next four years he produced realistic paintings of Paris, made two-color films on French and English art, and won the gold medal for magazine design at the Paris International Exhibition (1937). With the advent of World War II, Liberman moved to New York and joined the staff of *Vogue,* becoming its art director in 1943 and eventually editorial director for all Condé-Nast publications.

It was not until 1945 that Liberman began to paint again, and then his work became increasingly abstract, flat, and concerned with overall pattern. By 1949 his pictures consisted of short, thick, juxtaposed brushstrokes. The following year he began his well-known circle paintings—at first drawn freehand but later constructed with a compass and painted with industrial enamels on sprayed masonite panels. His precision and geometry were notable at a time when the dynamic and romantic approach of abstract expressionism* held sway. Yet he continued to move from such perfected and minimal* paintings as *Minimum* (1950), a black enamel circle on a black enamel background, to ideas that would gain acceptance only ten to twenty years later. As Liberman became interested in reproduceable art, some of his paintings were executed by an assistant according to his precise instructions. By 1955 his work became increasingly complex, dealing not only with systems within systems, such as circles within circles within a circle, but also with afterimages—later a concern of op art.* He had also begun to explore the realm of accident and chance; the composition for *Six Hundred Thirty-nine* (1959), for example, was arrived at by tossing poker chips, one by one, onto the canvas.

Throughout this period Liberman made sculptures. These were small, white plaster "columns" set on a white plaster pedestal. An example is *Space* (1952). In 1959 he produced his first welded sculpture, and this was followed by a series of absolutely flat, "pictorial," painted aluminum works whose purity and geometrical shapes were related to his early painting. He then turned to assemblages* of junk metal and old boiler parts, many of which were huge. In 1963, just as hard-edge* abstraction was becoming fashionable, he turned to abstract expressionism in a series of passionate, gestural canvases. His latest paintings have explored the triangle, both as a shape in itself, and within a rectangular format. Since his first painting was shown at the Guggenheim Museum in 1954, he has had numerous shows, including a retrospective at the Corcoran Gallery, Washington, D.C. (1970). He is also known for his photographs, especially those of artists, which can be seen in his books, *The Artist in His Studio* (1960) and *Greece, Gods and Art* (1968).

(E.C.G.)

Liberty Bowl.

The most famous piece of early American silver, it was made by Paul Revere* of Boston in 1768 to commemorate June 30, 1768, when the Massachu-

1

2

1. **Sol Lewitt.** Modular Structure (Floor), *1966. Dwan Gallery, N.Y.*
2. **Liberty Bowl** by Paul Revere. Engraved: "To the Memory of the glorious NINETY-TWO Members of the Honbl. House of Representatives of the Massachusetts Bay, who, undaunted by the insolent menaces of Villains in Power, from a strict Regard to Conscience and the LIBERTIES of their Constituents, on the 30th of June 1768, Voted NOT TO RESCIND," 1768, silver. Museum of Fine Arts, Boston.

setts Bay House of Representatives voted against rescinding their complaints to the King of England even though it meant the dissolution of their body. Similar in design to contemporary ceramic punch bowls, circular in shape with a molded foot and slightly flaring lip, it is distinguished by its documentary engraving with symbols of liberty such as the Magna Carta, the Bill of Rights, and the Liberty Cap.

Lichtenstein, Roy (1923–   ). Painter. Born in New York, N.Y., Lichtenstein studied at Ohio State University. During the 1950s he had a series of one-man shows in New York City, working first in the prevailing abstract expressionist style, and then (1957) producing expressionist versions of such mundane subjects as machine parts, cogs, pulleys, dollar bills, Donald Duck, and Mickey Mouse. He wrote: "I had the idea of painting banal subject matter of some kind or other, very standard cliché work." It was not until 1961 that Lichtenstein began to produce seemingly objective versions of his cartoon subjects, developing painting techniques that imitated not only the effect of commercial printing, but also some of its processes as well: stencilling, Ben Day dots (a device by which images are produced in printing), and mechanically projected images. However, paintings such as *The Engagement Ring* (1961) were far from mere facsimiles of their mass-media prototypes. Starting with a comic strip, for example, the artist would recompose it; then use an opaque projector to cast the image onto his canvas, where further changes might be made; and finally stencil in the dots, filling in flat areas of color and comic-book black line. Because these early images were derived from commercial art and executed in an impersonal manner, seemingly indifferent to the values of "fine art," they were catalogued as pop art,* though in fact their sophistication went far beyond popular levels of taste. Like the best of contemporary abstract painting, Lichtenstein's work displayed elegant drawing, decorative color (usually restricted to primaries and complementaries plus black and white), a sense of large scale despite the fact that many of the paintings were quite small, and a flatness in the picture plane that resulted in an emphasis on surface pattern. Along with his fellow

Roy Lichtenstein. Drawing for a Modern Painting of New York State, *1968.*

pop artists, however, he reestablished an avant-garde interest in representational art, initiated earlier by Jasper Johns.* During the early 1960s Lichtenstein almost invariably selected images from reproduced sources. At a later stage he turned to landscape, "moderne" geometrical compositions, and the work of fellow artists—Picasso, Monet, Mondrian—for inspiration, executing his versions of these subjects in his usual mechanical manner. (He once noted that he would like his work to look "programmed.") He is far less of a social critic than many of his fellow pop artists, who emphasize the materialism, vacuity, and mechanization of American life. Rather, he seems a purely decorative stylist—a feeling reinforced by his brass and mirror *Modern Sculpture* (1967), with its revived tubular forms of the 1930s, his ceramic tableware manufactured by the Durable Dish Company (1966), and a host of graphics, often silkscreened on such materials as metallic plastic. Lichtenstein has had numerous one-man shows and he exhibited at the Venice Biennial in 1966. (E.C.G.)

Lie, Jonas (1880–1940).
Landscape painter and president of the National Academy of Design* (1934–39). His father was Norwegian and his mother American; he was born in Moss, Norway, and came to the United States in 1893. As a young man in New York he attended night classes at the National Academy of Design* and the Art Students League.* His painting, which was freshly and broadly executed, enjoyed early success, and for years he was a prolific exhibitor of high-keyed, picturesque views of rocky coves and harbors. Lie was deeply interested in encouraging younger artists (he was one of the organizers of the Armory Show* in 1913), but he was also an advocate of strong academic training and an energetic spokesman for conservative values in art. (D.W.S.)

Lienau, Detlef (1818–87).
Architect. Born in Schleswig-Holstein, he trained as a cabinetmaker in 1837–41, and his exceptional ability as a draftsman earned him a year at the Royal Architectural School in Munich. He went on to Paris, where he studied for five years under the architect Henri Labrouste, chief proponent of the neo-Grec* style. In 1847 he worked for the architect of the *Chemins de Fer Paris à Lyon* in Paris. He next went to London, and thence to the United States. On shipboard he met Henry Marcotte, well-known New York decorator, and they formed a partnership; but in 1849 he set up his own office and began the thriving practice he was to enjoy most of his life. One of his first commissions, from Hart M. Shiff, the French banker, was a Fifth Avenue town house, which had one of the first mansard roofs in America. Two great town houses for the Schermerhorn family on West 23rd Street gave New York City a further introduction to Parisian architecture. In 1869, the blockfront of town houses he designed for Rebecca Jones on Fifth Avenue at 55th Street, with their handsome pavilions crowned by mansard roofs, were other outstanding examples of the orderly elegance of Parisian architecture.

The LeGrand Lockwood mansion (1869), at South Norwalk, Conn., built for a railroad tycoon at a cost of over a million dollars, was described in glowing terms in contemporary accounts. Lienau also designed villas at Newport, R.I., and row houses both in New York City and in Jersey City. His office and loft buildings in New York were notable for their sedate designs. The National City Bank Building (1866) on Wall Street, with its three-centered arch windows and their wide openings at first floor and basement, was well ahead of its time. His designs for sugar refineries were notable for their frank acceptance of functional requirements, of which their exteriors are a logical expression. Lienau was one of the founders and a fellow of the American Institute of Architects. (A.B.)

Light Sculpture.
Light was one of the most important subjects in art of the 17th and 19th centuries. Such painters as Vermeer, Rembrandt, Georges de la Tour, and Monet all employed light as a central theme of their work. With the rise of abstract painting in the 20th century, color began to replace light as subject, although the color-fields of certain abstract expressionist painters such as Mark Rothko* seemed to have light emanating from within. By the 1960s, artists who were still interested in light had begun to use it literally. Dan Flavin,* perhaps the most original of the light artists, places ordinary fluorescent fixtures on the walls, floor, and ceiling, and in the corners of rooms, using light to restructure architectural space. Flavin's work is wholly environmental art,* and deals with reflections, shadows, and light as form. The work of Chryssa* is more decorative and object-like, employing curvilinear shapes made of neon-tubing that are sometimes placed in plexiglass boxes, where they may blink on and off. Chryssa claims that her work has been influenced by the brightly colored advertising signs of Times Square which, she notes, "have solved the basic problem of sculpture: how to be static, yet have motion." Stephen Antonakos has also used lengths of neon tubing to fashion decorative object-sculptures, and like Chryssa he has been entirely straightforward about the medium, often employing wires, plugs, sockets, and receptacles as an integral part of the work. During the 1960s a number of artists, including Robert Morris* and Donald Judd,* used light on occasion in their minimal* works, George Segal* and Edward Kienholz* in their figurative tableaux, and Isamu Noguchi* in his commercial paper lamps. Other artists, such as Robert Whitman,* began to employ the sophisticated technology of laser beams, while still another group turned to the manipulation of color-shadows by means of controlled lighting effects (for example, Robert Irwin). All of these works are highly theatrical—mainly because they are indoor gallery or museum works using artificial lighting. During the late 1960s, however, a whole generation of younger artists began to work out-of-doors, and these artists (Michael Heizer, Dennis Oppenheim, Peter Hutchinson, Patricia Johanson,* Robert Smithson*) have used the effects of natural light and shade to create literal landscape-sculptures. (E.C.G.)

Lindner, Richard (1901–   ).
Painter. Born in Hamburg, Germany, he first studied music but then enrolled in the Academy of Fine Arts in Munich. He went to Paris in 1933 and then to the United States in 1941. He was a successful magazine illustrator until 1952, when he began to paint seriously. He had his first one-man exhibition in New York in 1954. He taught at the Pratt Institute in Brooklyn from 1952 to 1965.

Although Lindner did not emerge as

a full-fledged painter until he was in his fifties, his personal images—figures rooted in reality but controlled by a mechanistic cubism* and marked by a haunting symbolism—were fully realized from the first. In a sense his entire career since then has involved the development of strange, erotic images filled with personal and literary associations and recapitulating his entire life. It is no accident that one of his rare portraits (1950) is a symbolic interpretation of Marcel Proust.

Lindner is one of the most individual and compelling figurative painters on the scene today. A fairly characteristic painting, *The Visitor* (1953, private collection, New York), is reminiscent of Giorgio de Chirico's work and the Italian metaphysical school of the early 1900s. *Ice* (1966, Whitney), a painting with harsh, flat, and geometric color shapes that frame an erotic but not sensual woman-robot, establishes a line between the metaphysical tradition and the pop art of the 1960s.

(H.H.A.)

Lipchitz, Jacques (1891–1973). Sculptor. Born in Druskienki in Lithuania, Lipchitz arrived in Paris in October, 1909, and studied at the École des Beaux-Arts and the Académie Julien. By 1911 he had established his own studio in Montparnasse and by 1913 had met Picasso and other cubists. He began to experiment with cubism* in 1914, producing such proto-cubist works as *Sailor with Guitar* (Philadelphia). By 1915 he had emerged as a full-fledged cubist and during the next few years he became one of the world masters of cubism. He was, thus, a pioneer of 20th-century art and during the early years in the century was closely associated not only with Picasso, who remained a lifelong friend, but with other masters such as Juan Gris, Amedeo Modigliani, and Chaim Soutine. Lipchitz' specifically cubist phase extended to the mid-1920s and was climaxed in the monumental *Joy of Life* (1927). Although his style has changed radically, the cubist sense of form has remained. In 1925 he began experimenting with transparent sculptures in which open space was defined by delicate, linear contours. These were important prototypes of open, constructed sculpture.

From the early 1920s the artist also explored specific expressive subjects

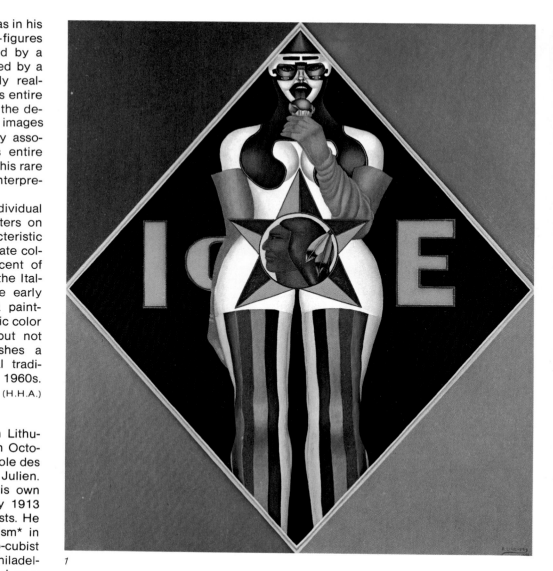

1

1. *Richard Lindner.* Ice, 1966, Whitney Museum of American Art, N.Y.
2. *Jacques Lipchitz.* Figure, 1926–30, bronze. Museum of Modern Art, N.Y. (Van Gogh Purchase Fund).
3. *Jacques Lipchitz.* Le Pont Vecchio, 1967, bronze. Marlborough-Gerson Gallery, N.Y.

in which the theme itself assumed a greater significance than did the Pierrots and standing figures of cubism. Aside from subjects with a personal significance, such as the *Embrace,* the *Mother and Child,* or the *Harpists,* he has drawn principally on the Old and New Testament and classical myths. His subjects always have a deep personal significance for him, which lends them their power. Thus, *Jacob Wrestling with the Angel* (1932) is a symbol of man's ability to defy even God to maintain his individuality—and to be blessed by God for so doing. The theme of *Prometheus Strangling the Vulture* (1936, 1944 and after) is for Lipchitz a symbol of man's struggle with the powers of darkness and ignorance. During the 1930s his sculpture became more freely expressive, evolving not only in major works but in innumerable improvisations and maquettes in which he captured his first ideas. Throughout his life he also continued to make portraits.

In 1940, with the German invasion of France, Lipchitz left Paris and in 1941 moved permanently to the United States. His works of the last thirty years have demonstrated a continually developing and increasingly youthful enthusiasm and fertility of imagination. During the 1960s he received commissions for monumental works, enabling him to carry out his ideas on the largest scale. Some of these include the statue of *Notre Dame de Liesse* (1948 and after), the *Peace on Earth* for the Los Angeles Music Center, and the statue of the explorer Duluth for the University of Minnesota at Duluth (1965). He was busy in the early 1970s finishing several huge sculptures: *Bellerophon Taming Pegasus* for the Law School, Columbia University; *Government of the People* for the city of Philadelphia; and a vast project, *Our Tree of Life,* for Mount Scopus in Israel. At the same time, he continued to create small lost-wax bronze improvisations such as the *Seven Madrigals—The Invisible Hand.*

Lipchitz' early work is a prime example of cubism in its early phase. Subsequently he became expressionistic, showing a devotion to religious and mythical subjects which he handled in a baroque curvilinear style. Moving from planes and geometric shapes to curving transparent forms, he became romantically expressive, using frenzied anthropomorphic shapes to convey liturgical themes. During the last twenty years Lipchitz received many honors from all over the world and he had one-man exhibitions in major museums throughout the United States and Europe. (H.H.A.)

Lippold, Richard (1915–   ).
Sculptor. Born in Milwaukee, Wis., he attended the University of Chicago (1933–37), majoring in industrial design. In 1937–41 he worked as a professional designer, but in 1942 he turned to sculpture and began to produce small constructions made of iron, brass, and copper wire. Most of Lippold's earliest pieces are carefully balanced, delicate little objects composed of linear (wire) elements—sometimes with metal shapes in between them. In 1944 he moved to New York City and in 1947 he had his first one-man show there. By this time his sculpture had grown larger and far more elegant, and he had begun to concentrate on the space delineated by his wire forms. He noted that he used "hair-thin wire" in order "to seduce the viewer to look into the space," and added that "the material for me becomes minimal and the space becomes maximal." He had also begun to employ simple geometric forms to give overall structure to his work. *Variation Number 7: Full Moon* (1949–50, Modern Museum) is a series of open-work squares set within each other, with wires, like shafts of light, radiating out to both floor and ceiling. Lippold claims to have derived these and similar works from the effects of moonlight filtering through mist, yet they seem to have little to do with nature, and fall wholly within the constructivist tradition (see Constructivism). Other pieces dating from the late 1940s and early '50s have stars as a theme, and a giant "Sun" *(Variation within a Sphere, Number 10: the Sun)* was commissioned by the Metropolitan Museum of Art in 1956. Lippold used fine gold wire for the latter, and like *Full Moon,* it was exhibited in semi-darkness against a black backdrop, giving a glittering, theatrical effect as light flooded the piece itself. The artist has noted that he wanted his work to seem to exist in limitless ("outer") space. Some critics have referred to these elegant, glistening gold constructions with their contrived lighting effects as "jewelry." Lippold's first large commission came in

2

3

1

1950, when Walter Gropius* asked him to design the *World Tree* to be placed outside his Harvard Graduate Center.

By the 1960s his spatial approach to sculpture and the increasing size of his work had lead to numerous collaborations with architects. His gigantic wire constructions now appeared in such major New York City edifices as the Seagram Building; Philharmonic Hall at Lincoln Center, where "Orpheus and Apollo" spanned 190 feet; the Pan Am Building; and Houston's Jones Hall for the Performing Arts. The majority of these pieces are suspended from the ceiling, where they hang like huge three-dimensional spiderwebs—sometimes symmetrical, sometimes exquisitely balanced. All are gossamer and sensual, owing to the lightness and delicacy of the polished gold wire. Even more architectural in feeling is his *Baldacchino,* a canopy over the altar of the Cathedral of St. Mary the Virgin in San Francisco. Lippold was artist-in-residence at Black Mountain College, N.C., in 1948 and taught at Hunter College, New York City, in the 1950s. (E.C.G.)

Lipton, Seymour (1903–   ).
Sculptor. His metal abstractions create mythological presences related to those in the paintings of William Baziotes* and the early Mark Rothko.* Born in New York, N.Y., Lipton was educated at the Brooklyn Polytechnic Institute and Columbia University in esthetics and art history. Lipton began in the 1920s to sculpt portrait heads in clay and wood. His first one-man show took place in a New York gallery in 1938. He exhibited at the World's Fair (1939) and the American Artists Congress (1940), both in New York. Turning to bronze casting and lead sheet construction in the 1940s, his work became progressively more abstract. In 1949 he began brazing and welding sheet steel, creating the rough, monumental forms that have characterized his work since that time. *Sanctuary* (1953 Modern Museum) shows hollow crescent shapes nestled within each other in an evocation of organic growth. The biomorphism of this period has slowly given way to allusions to specifically human and architectural form. Lipton accepts the weightiness of his materials as a challenge to be overcome by the delicacy of his com-

positions. He has appeared in every Whitney Sculpture Annual since 1946 and in many museums and galleries. His awards and grants include a Guggenheim Fellowship in 1960. As the scale of his works has expanded, he has undertaken numerous architectural commissions, among them *Laureate* for the Milwaukee Performing Arts Center in 1967. (C.R.)

Littleton, Harvey (1922–).
Glassblower, responsible for the upsurge of interest in experimental glassblowing for color and forms expressive of the material and for the esthetic nature of glass as a medium of sculpture. Widely influential as teacher and chairman of the art department at the University of Wisconsin at Madison, he has made that city a center for students of glass over the last ten years. He is himself a master technician, notable for the freedom, gracefulness, and purity of his work. Born in Corning, N.Y., his original craft was ceramics, which he studied at Cranbrook Academy in Michigan and at the Brighton School of Art in England.

By 1960 he was firmly established as a ceramist and teacher, but it was then that his interest in glassblowing emerged. After studying glass techniques at European factories and in the studios of a number of glass craftsmen in 1962, he established his own workshop with a grant from the University of Wisconsin. At the Toledo Museum's first glass seminar, he and Dominick Labino* virtually began the free-form glassblowing movement in America, and his workshop, expertise, and prodigious output have shaped the craft. Representative of his style is *Falling Blue* (1969, Johnson Coll.). This sculpture is composed of five slender tubes of varying blues—one end of each mounted on a base, the other open and cleanly cut—gracefully bend upwards as if windblown, the longest tube reaching a height of 21¼ inches. (R.S.)

Long, Robert Cary, Sr. (1770–1833).
Carpenter-architect. Apprenticed as a carpenter, Long learned the rudiments of architecture from books and experience. His designs tend to be pieced together rather than unified. Nevertheless, he had greater success than his predecessors in Baltimore, Md., where he did most of his work. He is best known for the Union Bank (1807, demolished, but the pediment sculpture is now at the Peale Museum, Baltimore); the Peale Museum (1813), the first museum building in America; the Medical Building, University of Maryland (1812); and St. Paul's Church (1814–17, burned 1854), with a fine Georgian tower.

Long's son, Robert Cary Long, Jr. (1810–49), first learned his architectural skills in his father's office, then with architect M. E. Thompson, New York. Dying of cholera at the peak of his career, his accomplishments were few, but his early ventures in Baltimore in the Gothic style are noteworthy: St. Alphonsus' Church (1843) and the Franklin Street Presbyterian Church (1844), both with details of design taken from books by the English architects Pugin and Richman. (P.F.N.)

Louis, Morris (1912–62).
Painter. Born Morris Bernstein in Baltimore, Md., he studied at the Maryland Institute of Fine and Applied Arts (1929–33) and worked on the WPA Federal Art Project* during the 1930s. Aside from four years (1936–40) in New York City, he lived in Baltimore and Washington, D.C., isolating himself from the New York art world, teaching, and concentrating on his personal experiments. At the beginning of the 1950s he was experimenting with spatial problems rooted in cubism,* attempting to adapt some of Jackson Pollock's* line and spatter techniques, and seeking a transition between Pollock's linear web paintings of the later 1940s and his own feeling for color-space.

In 1954 he was introduced to the paintings of the New York artist Helen Frankenthaler.* Louis was fascinated by her open color work and the process of staining in which all sense of foreground and background was elimated and a new kind of color-space emerged. He adapted these discoveries in a series of large paintings he called "Veils." In these, he spilled thin acrylic paint on sheets of unsized and unprimed canvas, which he had stapled on a vertical scaffolding and let hang free. The paint was flowed down over the surface in rhythmic, billowing curves, perhaps guided by folds the artist made in the canvas and by a stick wound with cloth. Brush drawing or any descriptive linear contours were abandoned. Using wash after wash of the extremely thin, quick-

2

1. *Richard Lippold.* Variation Number 7: Full Moon, *1950, brass rods, nickel-chromium, and stainless steel wire. Museum of Modern Art, N.Y. (Mrs. Simon Guggenheim Fund).*
2. *Seymour Lipton.* Oracle, *1966, bronze on monel metal. Marlborough-Gerson Gallery, N.Y.*

drying acrylic, he created transparent, pure color organizations involving complete integration of the paint and the canvas, as in *Saraband* (1959, Guggenheim). The later "Veils," executed principally during 1958–59, are inverted, flowing from bottom to top in a series of roughly fan shapes, and the color is generally more densely applied. Although he continued painting the "Veils" until 1959, he also embarked on another series of experiments during 1954–57. Called "Florals," these were roughly flower-shaped paintings radiating in thin washes from a dense center with equal emphasis given to movement in all four directions. Around 1960 he painted another series of "Florals," to which he gave the generic name "Aleph." This was followed by a series which he called "Unfurleds," huge canvases with blank centers and color in broken diagonal stripes across the ends, as in *Alpha-Pi* (1961, Metropolitan). Because he produced in a short time an enormous number of paintings on a few themes, while constantly moving from one theme to another as he explored his basic problems, their chronology is unclear.

During the last two years of his life Louis concentrated on a series of stripes in which the colors are densely massed in a vertical arrangement leading toward the center of the blank canvas. He seems to have been on the verge of entirely new explorations when he died.　　　　(H.H.A.)

Lukens, Glen (1887–1967).
Outstanding ceramist-teacher, noted for the virtuosity of his glazes and for having trained many of the first generation of American ceramists. Lukens was born in Cogwill, Mo., attended state colleges, and taught in the Midwest and California. During his years as professor of ceramics at the University of Southern California (1936–58) he made many discoveries that brought unusual colors to his earthenware and glazes, including the use of impure oxides and desert stones. His crackle glazes were unique, and he also revived the use of Egyptian paste and restated the art of slumping glass in his glass works. He was awarded prizes at the Syracuse Ceramic National from 1933 onward, and in 1945 he went to Haiti at the request of its government in order to develop ceramics as a home industry. In 1951 the Haitian govern-

ment decorated him for his services. He had made financial sacrifices to remain in Haiti, so that after his return to Los Angeles, he was forced to sell his home and studio. He worked as a consultant for glass firms, gave occasional workshops, and was involved in a Peace Corps project in 1964. Although himself never formally educated as a ceramist, he was indispensable to a generation of potters who benefited from his teaching.　　(R.S.)

Luks, George Benjamin (1867–1933). Graphic artist and painter. Luks was born in Williamsport, Pa., and grew up in coal mining country. His father, a physician, and his mother both painted as amateurs. Apparently he went with his brother to Philadelphia in 1883, performed in vaudeville, and then attended the Pennsylvania Academy of the Fine Arts* in 1884. He is believed to have spent the following decade in Düsseldorf, Munich, Paris, and London, studying at German and French academies en route. The record is clear from 1894 on, for that year he joined the art department of the Philadelphia *Press.* In 1894–95 he formed friendships with the newspaper artists who surrounded Robert Henri.* He was a talented amateur actor, but his pose as "Chicago Whitey" or as "Lusty Luks," an ex-boxer, apparently deceived nobody. Late in 1895 Luks went to Cuba as a war correspondent for the Philadelphia *Evening Bulletin.* He sent back drawings made a safe distance from the action, then went to New York and there joined the staff of the New York *World* in 1896. At that moment Richard Outcault, who had initiated the first comic strip, *The Yellow Kid,* took his strip to the *Journal,* and Luks was assigned to continue to draw *The Yellow Kid* for the *World.* For several years he worked as a cartoonist, also drawing *Hogan's Alley* and *McFadden's Flats.*

In 1897, his Philadelphia friends William Glackens* and Everett Shinn* joined him on the *World.* Glackens, working as an illustrator but committed to a career of painting, encouraged Luks to paint. Luks made rapid progress, filling sketchbooks with studies of colorful characters of every sort—dockworkers, slum children, and varied social outcasts. Soon he was turning out canvases which, although painted in a dark, strongly-brushed manner akin to that of Glackens and Henri,

1

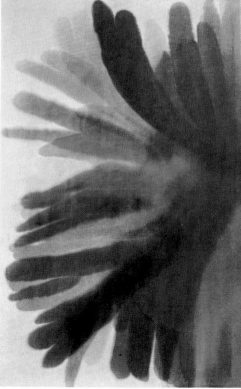

2

3

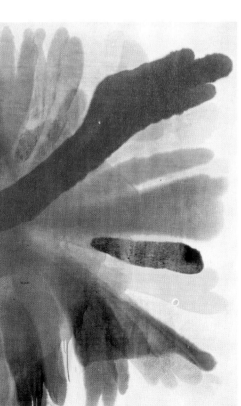

4

1. **Morris Louis.** Saraband, 1959. Solomon R. Guggenheim Museum, N.Y.
2. **Morris Louis.** Aleph Series I, 1960. Collection Mr. and Mrs. Paul Waldman, N.Y.
3. **George Benjamin Luks.** The Bersaglieri, 1918. National Gallery of Art, Washington, D.C. (gift of the Avalon Foundation).
4. **George Benjamin Luks.** The Spielers, 1905. Addison Gallery of American Art, Phillips Academy, Andover, Mass.

Luminism. *John F. Kensett*, Bish-Bash, South Egremont, Mass., *1855. Museum of Fine Arts, Boston (Karolik Collection).*

354

were more brutal than theirs, and more influenced by Hals and 17th-century Dutch realists. When he exhibited with his friends at the National Arts Club in 1904, his power was clearly evident. Some of the strongest work of his career soon followed: *The Spielers* (1905, Addison), *The Old Duchess* (1905, Metropolitan), and *The Wrestlers* (1905, Boston). Even before he exhibited with The Eight* in 1908, he was plainly the most powerful realist of the group, though deeply sympathetic toward his sitters and also quite unpredictable in technique. He worked on impulse, claiming "I can paint with a shoestring dipped in pitch and lard. . . . Guts! Guts! Life! Life! that's my technique."

In 1910 he declined to contribute to the exhibition of Independent Artists* in order to increase the impact of his first one-man show, then imminent. In 1913 he sent paintings and drawings to the Armory Show.* His later work moved into a more colorful key, often with light-filled passages. He varied his range of mood and expression, as in *Armistice Night* (1918, Whitney), but continued to emphasize figure and character studies, as in *The Miner* (1925, Washington), working boldly and, at his best, with a sure and personal touch. But he also turned out potboilers.

Luks taught for several years at the Art Students League,* then founded his own school, where his devoted students were stimulated by his working alongside them but sorely pressed to take care of the "rowdy oldster." Luks had a weakness for starting barroom rows. When his body was found in a doorway one morning, his friends assumed he had finally picked a fight once too often. The papers reported that he died sketching on the street.

(D.W.S.)

Luminism.

A landscape style of the mid-19th century in which the study of light was crucial. The term was coined in 1954 by John I. H. Baur, director of the Whitney Museum, and his description of the style is still valid: "a polished and meticulous realism in which there is no sign of brushwork and no trace of impressionism, the atmospheric effects being. achieved by infinitely careful gradations of tone, by the most exact study of the relative clarity of near and far objects, and by a precise rendering of the variations in texture and color produced by direct or reflected rays." Luminism was practiced both by artists of the Hudson River School,* such as John F. Kensett* and Sanford Gifford,* and by painters only on the periphery of the school, such as Fitz Hugh Lane* and Martin J. Heade.* Although there was no luminist movement per se, the qualities now seen in luminism were recognized by contemporary critics. Thus the leading biographer of the landscape school, Henry Tuckerman, commented that Heade, for example, was particularly successful with "peculiar atmospheric effects," and that Gifford was masterly in "depicting only sea and sky . . . with such truth . . . in light and perspective as to captivate the eye. . . . " Luminism was a major interest of the landscape painters during the reign of realism as practiced by the "second generation" of the Hudson River School, or from about 1850–75. The sources of the style may be traced back almost to the beginnings of American landscape, notably the marines of Robert Salmon and the "atmospheric views" by George Harvey (c.1800/01–78) during the 1830s. By 1844, Thomas Cole* had painted perhaps the first "luminous landscape"—his *Lake Scene* (Detroit). In this work, unique in his oeuvre, Cole paid little attention to his usual subject—the land and its symbolism—and instead painted a simple, tonally unified view of sky and lake, separated by small islands in the foreground and an indistinct shore in the distance. The implications of luminism were advanced in the following year by two important genre paintings: George Caleb Bingham's* *Fur Traders Descending the Missouri* (1845, Metropolitan) and William Sidney Mount's* *Eel-Spearing at Setauket* (1845, New York Historical Association). Both portray heroic figures against a luminous, hazy background of water and sky. Then in the later 1840s and early '50s, advanced studies of light were painted by the Gloucester painter, Fitz Hugh Lane, and by Cole's student, Frederic E. Church.* The latter played a vital role by introducing to the Hudson River School a brighter palette and a new interest in light in both its descriptive and emotional aspects. Although Church himself turned away from luminism in favor of portraying topographical wonders, such early pictures as *Sunset off the Maine Coast at Grand Manan* (1852, Wadsworth) are prototypes of the style.

The archetypal luminist paintings of the 1860s usually portray water and light and their tonal unification; they are delicate, realistic, and poetic. The luminist format is usually horizontal, as in Lane's glassy sunset scene, *Owl's Head, Penobscot Bay, Maine* (1862, Boston), or Kensett's serene, empty *Eaton's Neck* (Metropolitan). However, Gifford's golden, atmospheric *Kauterskill Falls* (1862, Metropolitan) shows that a luminist painting need have neither a body of water nor a horizontal shape. Most luminist paintings study the light of perfect days, but a few—notably those of Heade—are concerned more with the fleeting effects of mists and sudden thunderstorms, with clouds and atmosphere, than with light itself. Unifying all luminist paintings is a sense of awe as nature is viewed in her quietest, most poetic moments.

Luminism had a logical conclusion about 1870 in paintings which are almost abstract, portraying only water and sky. After this date, the style declines, paralleling the development of the Hudson River School itself. Some of the best of its practitioners died, as did Lane and Kensett, while others, including Gifford and Heade, became increasingly heavy-handed in their brushwork and in the increasingly histrionic brightness of their palettes. By 1880, the date of Gifford's death, the style had been largely outmoded by the new interest in French art.

(T.E.S.)

Lyrical Abstraction.

Despite the proliferation of countermovements, the influence of abstract expressionism* never wholly disappeared during the 1960s. By the early 1970s, in reaction to the precision and cerebration of such movements as minimal,* pop,* and hard-edge,* a new group of painters had arisen who were determined to reassert poetic and romantic values. This third generation of abstract expressionists places great importance on subjective and sensuous experiences, and frequently creates frankly beautiful, hedonistic pictures. There is a new love of nature and its effects: one often senses light filtering through trees, flickering shadows, or violent storm imagery, recreated in soakings and drips and splashes of paint. While there is a traceable lineage from Mark Rothko,* Jackson Pollock,* and Willem de Kooning,* through Helen Frankenthaler* and Jules Olitski* to these new, younger artists, they place a greater emphasis on minutiae—both in form, technique, and meaning. These are in fact lyric "poets," compared to the great epic compositions of the first generation.

(E.C.G.)

Lye, Len (1901–   ).

Sculptor and filmmaker. Born in Christchurch, New Zealand, he grew up with a great interest in the dances and rituals of the aborigines in Australia and the Oceanic Islands. In 1920 he went to live on Samoa, and there began working on kinetic* constructions. In 1926, he went to London, where he began experimental work with films, inventing a method of inscribing his design directly on the film. Settling in the United States in 1946, he again experimented with moving sculptures, obviously remembering his impressions of Australian boomerangs. He continued working as a director and originator of film and in 1958 won the silver award at the Brussels World's Fair for his film *Free Radicals*.

By 1961 Lye had perfected his sculpture enough to show his *Tangible Motion Sculpture* (at the Museum of Modern Art in New York City), a work which was electrically energized and controlled by the artist. Gradually, he developed electronic systems to control and program his large moving works, and in 1964 and 1965, when they were shown in a New York City gallery, he enraptured audiences with the unusual forms he set in motion. For instance, a piece called *Flip and Two Twisters* was described thus: "a suspended band of burnished steel lifts itself slowly upwards, hesitates as it reaches its apex, and then, as it turns itself inside out, suddenly collapses with a shimmering cascade of sound." Another piece, *The Loop*, was a twenty-two-foot strip of polished steel formed in a band resting on a magnetized bed. The magnets pulled the loop into various positions, from which it appeared to struggle for release. Out of this undulating motion, accompanied by odd musical sounds, came a bizarre and somehow anthropomorphic effect. Most of Lye's pieces differ from other kinetic works in his distinct interest in choreography and his ability to suggest associations with human movements. They are lyrical rather than mechanical images. Lye gave performances with his pieces at the Albright-Knox Gallery in Buffalo, N.Y., in 1965. In 1966, they were presented at the University Museum in Berkeley, Cal. His films are exhibited at the Museum of Modern Art.

(D. A.)

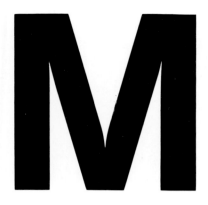

MacDonald-Wright, Stanton
(1890–   ).
Painter and teacher. A native of Virginia, Wright moved with his family to Santa Monica, Cal., in 1900. A precocious youth, he entered the Art Students League of Los Angeles in 1905, and in 1907 went to Paris, where he studied briefly at the Colorossi and Julien academies. He began painting in a freely impressionist manner while studying the work of Cézanne, the older masters, and the newer developments of Matisse and Picasso. About 1911 he met Morgan Russell* and with him undertook a study of color theory. By 1912 Wright was painting abstracted figurative subjects in pure color, as in *Portrait of Jean Dracopoli,* and exhibiting at the Salon des Indépendants. The following year he and Russell founded synchromism,* staging exhibitions in Munich and Rome. They brought their work to New York in 1913, and between 1914 and 1918 Wright exhibited at several New York galleries, including Alfred Steiglitz'* Gallery 291.

Wright spent the years 1914–16 in London with his brother, Willard Huntington Wright, whom he assisted in the writing of several books on art, including *Modern Art* and *The Future of Painting.* From London he went to New York, and in 1919 he returned to the Los Angeles area.

As Wright developed through his earlier synchromist phase, his work moved from figurative abstractions to paintings in which discs and fanlike passages of spectral colors were organized into diagonal and spiraling sequences, as in *Abstraction on Spectrum* (1914, Des Moines). By 1916, the figure reasserted itself as the motif behind the lines and color planes into which the surface was broken as, for example, in *Synchromy in Green and Orange* (1916, Walker), and soon Wright added landscape and still-life motifs in which

the methods of Cézanne and cubism* became increasingly apparent (*Canyon Synchromy,* c.1920, University of Minnesota). By 1920 he felt dissatisfied with "the orientation of modern art" and "the personal academicism of his own synchromism." He began a thirty-year period of study and experimentation, undergoing profound influences from oriental art in the 1920s, experimenting with color abstractions on film, and reflecting something of Braque's later cubism in the 1940s.

He was also active as a teacher, designer, and administrator. He was director of the Art Students League of Los Angeles (1922–30); he designed sets and wrote satires for the Santa Monica Theater Guild; he served as WPA director for Southern California (1935–37) and developed new mosaic techniques for WPA projects; and he taught art history and esthetics at the University of California at Los Angeles (1942–54). He then returned to painting full time, working for some years in a nonobjective style which at times approached his synchromist manner, but with more decorative colors, more rhythmic forms, and suaver textures, as in *Embarkation* (1962, Modern Museum). Wright's painting in his later sixties and seventies included some of the finest of his career. The impulsive vitality of his early experimental canvases was replaced by a mature, harmonious elegance.   (D.W.S.)

MacIver, Loren (1909–   ).
Painter. One of the forerunners of abstract expressionism,* MacIver was born in New York, N.Y., and she received her only formal training at the age of ten, when she spent a year in Saturday classes at the Art Students League.* Although she continued to paint through her teens, her earliest preserved work dates from 1929, and her paintings of the next few years are

characterized by childlike fantasy and naive drawing, as in *Winter Dunes* (1932) with its bird's-eye view of a town and a stick figure walking on a beach. From 1936–39 MacIver worked on the WPA Federal Art Project* and in 1938 she had her first solo show. During this period her work grew in stature and her poetic intentions became clearer. Her paintings are always meant to be read on several levels: first in terms of their formal arrangement—their color and design; next, specific objects might be recognized; and finally a personal symbolism is developed related to the mood of each subject. Thus *Hopscotch* (1940) is seen first as an abstract and slightly menacing pattern with chalk numbers on one side. Only later does one realize that this is blistered pavement, but the mystery has added another level of meaning to the image. She wrote: "Quite simple things can lead to discovery. This is what I would like to do with painting: starting with simple things, to lead the eye by various manipulations of colors, objects and tensions toward a transformation and a reward. . . . My wish is to make something permanent out of the transitory." During the 1940s she "transformed" such objects as an ashcan, a pushcart, a gas stove, a skylight, and a window shade. Her desire is to reveal the visual beauty of each, as well as its human significance, and she invests her objects with a fragile delicacy, and often a sense of wistfulness or poignancy. *Red Votive Lights* (1943), with its rows of candles in colored glasses, goes beyond mere geometry. *Window Shade* (1948) is totally different in mood, and prophetic with its *en fáce* view and meticulous realism that includes the carefully painted scratches on the shade. Because she has never felt hampered by esthetic theory or current styles, she has been free to follow her own intuition. Circuses and clowns have always been a favorite theme; her portraits of Jimmy Savo and Emmett Kelly (1947) are introspective and idealized, both of them displaying slightly blurred features.

MacIver's growing reputation during the 1940s led to a number of commissions, including magazine covers for *Town and Country* and *Fortune* and murals for the ship S.S. *Argentina* (1947) and four panels for American Export Line ships (1948). In 1948 she made her first trip to Europe, and on her return her paintings became larger, bolder, and more abstract. *Dublin and Environs* (1950), for example, is quite mysterious until we learn that the crossed lines are stone walls, the streaked greens are fields, and the bottle and shapes at the lower right are "Paddy's Whiskey" and "fish, or maybe potatoes." After 1950 there is a growing interest in luminous color and phosphorescent forms against a dark background. Her subjects range from the rainbow hue of an oil slick to the flicker of candles, forms bathed in moonlight, and rain on glass. Her pictures are always halfway between abstraction and reality. Her creation of soft-color areas that blend and often bleed into each other obscures the clear relation of forms, and adds to the elusive quality of her work—a rare blend of poetry, mystery, symbolism, and design.

(E.C.G.)

MacMonnies, Frederick (1863–1937). Sculptor. He was born in Brooklyn, N.Y., and became a studio assistant to Augustus Saint-Gaudens* when he was eighteen years old. He also studied at the Art Students League,* and in 1884 went to Paris, where he studied at the École des Beaux-Arts. After returning to Saint-Gaudens' studio for several years, he spent the next twenty-five years in Paris. From the outset his style was marked by a vibrant naturalism and rich modeling, never embracing the neoclassicism* of earlier generations of American sculptors. This is evident in his *Nathan Hale* (1890, New York City Hall) and his *Bacchante* (1893), where the surfaces reflect a lively play of lights and shadows, quite unlike the smooth contours of neoclassicism. Although its nudity seems harmless today, *Bacchante* aroused strong criticism in Boston. Also from 1893 dates his famous *Triumph of Columbia* for the World's

1

2

1. **Loren MacIver.** Window Shade, 1948. Phillips Memorial Gallery, Washington, D.C.
2. **Stanton MacDonald-Wright.** Abstraction on Spectrum (Organization 5), 1914. Des Moines Art Center, Iowa (Nathan Emory Coffin Memorial Collection).

Columbian Exposition in Chicago; made of staff (plaster and straw), it barely survived the exposition, but its colorful imagery and rich modeling did much to establish MacMonnies' reputation in America. Most of the many commissions that came to him were executed in his Paris studio; he so absorbed the French style that his work was almost indistinguishable from that of Parisian sculptors. Among his more important works are *Shakespeare* and a set of bronze doors for the Library of Congress, the spandrels for the Washington Arch in New York City, the sculpture for the Memorial Arch, Brooklyn, and the *Horse Tamers* for Brooklyn's Prospect Park. In 1905 MacMonnies opened an art school at Giverny, outside Paris. Ten years later he returned to America, where he spent the rest of his life, turning from sculpture to painting. (W.C.)

1

MacNeil, Hermon (1866–1947).

Sculptor. Born near Chelsea, Mass., he attended the State Normal Arts School and then taught briefly at Cornell University. In 1888 he went to Paris, studied at the Académie Julien and the École des Beaux-Arts and mastered the impressionistic Parisian style of modeling with lively surfaces. Back in Chicago, he created decorative sculptures for the World's Columbian Exposition of 1893. He then became interested in the American Indian and produced several important Indian statues and memorials such as the *Sun Vow* (1898, Metropolitan). After several years in Rome, where he was not at all influenced by neoclassicism,* he established a studio in New York. For Buffalo's Pan-American Exposition (1901) he created the *Despotic Age,* a group rich in Indian dress and ceremony, and for the city of Portland, Ore., he made *The Coming of the White Man* (1905), a bronze of two Indians. MacNeil did a few portrait statues, among the best of which is his *Ezra Cornell* (1915–17, Cornell University), and several war memorials, such as those in Albany, N.Y. (1917), and Columbia, S.C. (1932). (W.C.)

Macramé.

The art of creative knotting. The ornamental knotwork of the 19th century practiced as a nautical pastime by sailors and by Victorian ladies as a parlor art is now collected as an expres-

2

1. **Conrad Marca-Relli.** The Blackboard, *1961. Seattle Museum (Eugene Fuller Memorial Collection).*
2. **Paul Manship.** Actaeon *(from the sculptures* Diana *and* Actaeon*) 1924. Brookgreen Gardens, S.C.*

sion of American folk art. Its history is obscure because knotting has appeared as a highly developed craft form in many unrelated societies over a vast span of time. However, the word *macramé* is probably of Turkish or Arabic derivation, and the technique has been traced to the square-knotted fringe that traditionally terminated lengths of Turkish towel. Nineteenth-century American macramé objects range from belts and bracelets to huge bed and window handings. Knotwork picture frames embellished with ornate rosettes were a popular expression of the medium, and good examples are preserved in the collection of the Mariners Museum in Newport News, Va. In the 1970s macramé has enjoyed a lively resurgence as both a popular American craft and a creative art technique. (M.J.G.)

Maentel (or Maentle), Jacob (1763–1863).
Primitive watercolor portraitist and farmer who settled in New Harmony, Ind. Maentel's work had been erroneously attributed to a Pennsylvania publisher-bookseller, Samuel Endredi Stettinius, until 1965, when Mary C. Black was able to identify the artist properly and illuminate much of his career. His early portraits, executed in the Pennsylvania Dutch country, are typically profile figures with carefully worked faces such as *General Schumacker's Daughter* (c. 1812, Garbisch Coll.). In later Pennsylvania work (c. 1826) and in that done in Indiana he adopted a full-face convention. Maentel's sitters were likely to be shown in brightly colored costumes, and many of them were depicted in either indoor or outdoor settings rendered with considerable detail. As a result these small paintings provide abundant information on the domestic life of the early 19th century. The artist's unusual German inscriptions, his persistent short cast from subject toward viewer, and his isometric projection of chairs and tables all aid in identifying his work.

Malbone, Edward Greene (1777–1807).
Portrait and miniature painter. Born in Newport, R.I., he studied there with Samuel King. He painted portraits in Providence and Boston before meeting Washington Allston,* with whom he traveled to Europe. He studied at the Royal Academy with Benjamin West* and although West encouraged him to remain in London, he returned to America in 1801. An outstanding miniaturist, his work is graceful and delicate in tone.

Maloof, Sam (1916–   ).
Woodworker whose furniture designs are notable for graceful form, superb articulation of wood, and exquisite joinery. Maloof was born in Chino, Cal., and worked for a number of years in architectural drafting, graphic arts, and industrial design. He became a woodworker in order to furnish his own home in Alto Loma, Cal., and his first commissions resulted from his inventive and unique achievements for himself and his family. He works mostly with walnut, uses only beeswax and linseed oil for finishes, and is a master of joinery. His designs develop as he works, often from common-sense considerations of function. Although influenced by Wharton Esherick,* Maloof's furniture is characterized by clean, straight lines. He has never expanded his well-established custom furniture business beyond a family scope, and with his son, a nephew, and perhaps one apprentice, he produces about one hundred pieces a year. (R.S.)

Manship, Paul (1885–1966).
Sculptor. Raised in St. Paul, Minn., he attended the Institute of Art there. In 1905 he went to Philadelphia, where he worked with several sculptors before winning the Prix de Rome in 1909 and leaving for study at the American Academy in Rome. Ignoring Paris and the École des Beaux-Arts, Manship immediately fell under the spell of antiquity. The decorative stylizations of archaic Greek art in particular were to have a profound influence on his mature style, as is evident in his *Woodland Dance* (c.1912), while the classical phase of Greco-Roman style is reflected in his *Duck Girl* (1911, Fairmount Park, Philadelphia). Returning to America in 1912, Manship achieved immediate recognition with such pieces as *Centaur and Dryad* (1913, Metropolitan) and *Dancer and Gazelles* (1916, Corcoran).

Most of Manship's work was cast in bronze and was exceptional in its craftsmanship and finish. His subjects came from nature but the forms were stylized to obtain his characteristically delicate rhythms and flowing contours; abstraction came, however, from the study of ancient art rather than from the experimentation with form being carried on by the cubists and constructivists. Balance and order—two essential components of ancient art—were always a part of Manship's work. But a fresh spirit of creativity separated his art from the eclectic sculpture of most 19th-century neoclassicists. The archaic Greek style is evident in two of his most important works, the bronze *Diana* and *Actaeon* (1924, Brookgreen Gardens, S.C.). Probably his best-known work is the gilded bronze *Prometheus* (1933) for the fountain in New York's Rockefeller Plaza. In the 1930s Manship had several one-man shows and rose to the top of his profession. His work received numerous awards, and he was president of the National Sculpture Society. By 1940, however, as the tide of "modern" art swelled upon the American scene, his work was labeled as academic. (W.C.)

Marca-Relli, Conrad (1913–   ).
Painter. Born in Boston, Mass., of Italian parents, he studied briefly at Cooper Union in New York, but is largely self-taught. Perhaps because of his Italian background and many sojourns in Italy, his early mature works of the 1940s have analogies to the Italian wing of surrealism* and specifically to the metaphysical school of Georgio de Chirico, Carlo Carra, and Giorgio Morandi. These are cityscapes and still lifes painted with subdued palette and an architectural austerity that frequently, in their loneliness and emptiness, evoke a romantic desolation like that of de Chirico's early works. He spent four years in the U.S. Army and then settled in New York City, where he had his first one-man show (1948). He taught at Yale (1954–55 and 1959–60) and the University of California at Berkeley (1958). He has received many awards. He exhibited principally in New York galleries in the 1950s and has also shown often in Europe and Latin America. In 1967 he was given a retrospective at the Whitney Museum.

In the late 1940s Marca-Relli turned to collage and has become one of the American masters in this medium, frequently combining oil paint and collage on a monumental scale. The collage paintings have been characterized by figuration, which in the early 1950s was influenced by the puppet-like figures of de Chirico and Carra and Willem de Kooning's* figure studies. In the 1950s the figures merged into large abstract constructions with violent movement suggestive of battle scenes, as in *The Battle* (1956, Metropolitan). Although the collage elements continued to be carefully structured, the artist intensified his color and brush gesture to include bold hues, broken surfaces, and expressionistic spatter techniques. In the late 1950s and '60s he returned to classical abstraction in which collage elements were generally arranged in a predominantly vertical and horizontal manner, and color was subdued and often combined with an overall romantic atmosphere, as in *Sierra Madre* (1961). His principal direction of the 1960s has been toward a more sculptural relief use of collage achieved through heavier materials (such as vinyl plastics and cut-out aluminum) and shapes outlined with painted or actual nail holes emphasizing their three-dimensional plasticity. From this point it was a short step to relief and to free-standing minimal* sculpture that maintains the interlocking forms of the collages.

The figure emerged once more in painted collages of the late 1960s, now brushed in freely in a large architectural space suggesting the figure portraits of Giacometti. Marca-Relli also produces painted collages of the utmost abstract simplicity—large, black or ochre, roughly rectangular shapes isolated on a neutral ground. Despite his range from absolute abstraction to specific figuration, he has remained remarkably consistent. In the collage-constructions and sculptures of 1968–70, the integration of abstract figures and machine forms brings together all of his interests and illustrates their essential unity. Figures become machines which become abstract shapes. In all of them there is an insistence on the actuality of the object as a distinct entity.　　　　　　　　　(H.H.A.)

Marin, John (1870–1953).
Painter and leading watercolorist, born in Rutherford, N.J. At eighteen he began painting delicate tonal landscapes in watercolor, but he did not study art seriously until after several years as an architectural draftsman. In 1899 he entered the Pennsylvania Academy of the Fine Arts,* where

1

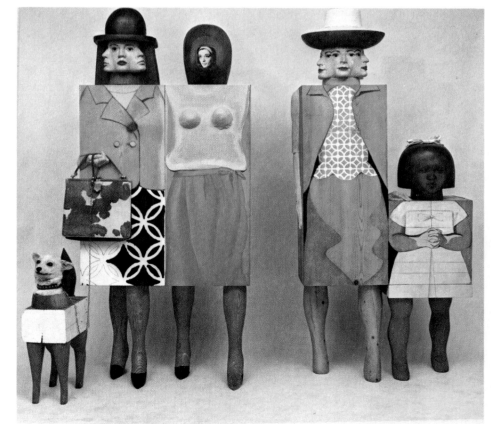

3

2

Thomas Anshutz* and Hugh Breckenridge were his teachers. He attended the Art Students League* briefly in 1905, and then he sailed for Paris—an artist who at thirty-five had little more to show than a few fragile watercolor sketches.

Marin spent almost five years working in Paris during the winters and taking sketching trips through Italy, Belgium, and Holland during the summers. He remained on the periphery of Parisian art groups but he associated with such experimental young Americans as Arthur B. Carles,* Max Weber,* and Alfred Maurer,* and he exhibited at the Salon des Indépendants and the Salon d'Automne. His landscapes, in watercolor and oil, were in spirit close to those of J.A.M. Whistler,* developed in restrained tonal areas which played up nuances of value and color. Gradually the brushwork became more patchy, stressing the overall pattern, until in a watercolor such as *London Omnibus* (1908, Metropolitan) he approached a freedom of surface like that of the fauve painters. Through the painter and photographer Edward Steichen* he met Alfred Stieglitz* in Paris in 1909, and later that year participated with Maurer in a joint exhibition at Stieglitz' Gallery 291 in New York. The critics found Maurer a "wild man" and Marin, by contrast, pleasantly reminiscent of Whistler, with just a dash of Matisse. In 1910 Marin had his first one-man show at Gallery 291. The influence of the dealer and his avant-garde coterie played an important part in Marin's development, and it was through Stieglitz' help that he was able to devote himself to painting during the next few years. His development toward abstraction was at first slow: the 1910 *Tyrol at Kufstein* (Metropolitan) is a delightful shorthand notation but basically naturalistic. But by 1912 he had plunged into depictions of the tensions and movements of New York crowds and skyscrapers, employing jagged twists and thrusts (*Movement, Fifth Avenue,* 1912, Chicago), akin to those of his French contemporary, Robert Delaunay. Marin's experimental work was shown at 291 in January, 1913, just prior to the Armory velopment toward abstraction was at Show,* in which he also exhibited.

During the next few years he began to project schematic lines of force boldly through all parts of his compositions. Most of his summers were spent

along the New England coast, and his simplified distillations of rock and wave themes reached a peak about 1917. At the same time, he experimented with total abstractions based on geometric motifs. By 1919 his paintings reflected an interest in recombining vividly observed landscapes with spontaneous pattern-making and abstract lines emphasizing structure and movement. For some twenty years his mature style was based on developments of these elements, always under the impulse of intuitive and emotional response to the rhythms and movements he felt in nature. He worked at first entirely in watercolor, becoming one of the foremost American masters of the medium. His subjects ranged from city scenes (*Lower Manhattan,* 1920, Modern Museum) to ships and the Maine coast. His *Maine Islands* (1922, Phillips) is a well-known example of his use of vigorous framing, perspective and force lines freely combined with an observed landscape and touches of personal symbolism.

During the summers of 1929 and 1930 Marin painted in Taos, his work reflecting the New Mexico landscape. In the 1930s he began to paint more oils and to introduce figures into his paintings, sometimes placing broadly characterized nymphs in beach settings. The oils are more turgid than the watercolors and had a mixed reception. They allowed him a wider range of texture development, however, as he began to place less emphasis on specific vistas and more on active brushwork that covered the pictorial surface. His late style (in both watercolor and oil) culminated in the later 1940s in paintings that at times were reduced to almost pure calligraphy laced with black lines, stylistically paralleling the abstract expressionism* developing in the same period. Marin's work, however, belonged to no school but was essentially individual, directly reflecting his imaginative and emotional reactions to the world around him.

(D.W.S.)

Marisol Escobar (1930–   ).
Sculptor. Born in Paris of Venezuelan parents, Marisol studied at the École des Beaux-Arts in Paris in 1949. Moving to New York City in 1950, she studied at the Art Students League and then, in 1951–54, at the New School and the Hans Hofmann School. Loose-

ly associated with the pop art* of the early 1960s, Marisol finds her subject matter in urban society. *The Party* (1965–66) consists of fifteen life-sized figures. Their bodies are formed of solid blocks of wood whose geometrical regularity suggests the rigidity of their poses. The meticulously decorated surfaces of the figures emphasize their obsession with apparel. The treatment of individual faces is revealing: a multiple profile suggests mechanical alertness; blank eyes show inpenetrable inwardness. *President Charles de Gaulle* (1967) has a tiny head with an immense body precariously balanced on a toylike carriage. By schematizing the manners and dress of her subjects, Marisol achieves sharp, sometimes acidulous satirical comments on public figures and the world of fashion. Her work has been seen widely in group shows since 1954. Her first one-man show was at a New York gallery in 1958. The Worcester Art Museum in Worcester, Mass. gave her a full-scale retrospective in 1971.   (C.R.)

Marsh, Reginald (1898–1954).

Painter. Born in Paris of American parents who were painters, Marsh was brought home at the age of two and grew up in New Jersey. He began his career during his student days as art editor and cartoonist for the Yale *Record,* and on graduation in 1920 was employed as staff artist for *Vanity Fair* and the New York *Daily News.* In 1924 he had his first one-man show at the Whitney Studio Club. In the following year he became a staff member of *The New Yorker,* but soon left for Europe to study. His life-long ambition was to depict contemporary life in Old Master style.

On his return from Europe in 1926, Marsh studied at the Art Students League* under John Sloan,* George Luks,* Kenneth Hayes Miller,* and Boardman Robinson,* all of whom exercised a major influence on his work. He painted murals for the Post Office Building in Washington, D.C., and for the New York City Customs House, but most of his mature effort went into paintings, etchings, and lithographs of New York City life: subways, burlesque houses, the bums of the Bowery, Coney Island, and everyday street activities, all rendered in a vigorous, baroque style in which his study of the Old Masters is evident.

1. **Reginald Marsh.** Why Not Use the "L"?, 1930. Whitney Museum of American Art, N.Y.
2. **Reginald Marsh.** Coney Island Beach, 1935. Collection Senator William Benton, N.Y.
3. **Reginald Marsh.** Tattoo and Haircut, 1932. Art Institute of Chicago.
4. **Reginald Marsh.** Taxi Dance Hall, 1947. Collection Senator William Benton, N.Y.

3

4

Outstanding examples are *Why Not Use the "L"?* (1930, Whitney), *In 14th Street* (1934, Modern Museum), *Coney Island Beach* (1935, private collection), and *Tattoo and Haircut* (1932, Chicago).

Marsh produced few oils. His favorite paint media were egg tempera and watercolor. He had a strong predilection for line and regarded drawing and printmaking as purer forms of art than painting. Consequently much of his best work went into Chinese ink drawings and etchings.

In his contribution to Peyton Boswell's *Modern American Painting* (1940) Marsh said: "The havoc caused by the tremendous influence of impressionism and expressionism must be overcome before America can go on and paint the substance, not the light and shadow. The struggle to free art from superficial impressionistic style or fantastic nonsense is probably harder now than in the old days when art was strong, simple, and real." Yet Marsh himself was far more of a fantasist than a realist. His New York is a world of phantasmagoria produced by the unlikely conjunction of contemporary urban subject matter and Old Master techniques; "strong, simple, and real" are strange words to find on the page in connection with his crowded, often violent, dreamlike or nightmare-like transformations of everyday urban happenings, as for example in *Taxi Dance Hall* (1947, private collection). The Chinese ink drawings are often quieter, more spacious, and the white of the paper to add its serenity. These drawings and his etchings, such as *Bread Line—No One Has Starved* (1932, private collection), often emphasize the tragedy of the maimed and the dispossessed.

A word should also be added about the Reginald Marsh woman, the most consistently represented member of his urban dramatis personae as found in the famous *High Yaller* (1936, private collection) and *In 14th Street*. Tall, buxom, self-confident, she strides alone, now blonde, now brunette, now black, now white, yet always the same.

Although his work is allied in subject with that of the realistic social protest artists of his time, Marsh remained aloof from all political entanglements, reserving his political statement for his art.   (A.F.)

Martelé.

The name given by William C. Codman and the Gorham Company* to silver

designed in a modified art nouveau*
style and produced entirely by hand,
scorning the machines that had completely dominated silver work throughout the 19th century. The designs were
characterized by flowing lines and
naturalistic motifs, such as flowers,
waves, sea nymphs, fish, tortoises,
shells, and clouds. The hammer marks
were not entirely planished out so
that the handcraftsmanship would be
apparent. Finer than sterling in silver
content, each piece was marked with
the Martelé stamp. This was one of the
first efforts on the part of a large company to offer essentially an art production. While development of this
expensive line began in 1895, Martelé
vases, tankards, and bowls were not
put on the market until 1901. Production continued for about twelve years.
At the 1902 Exposition in Turin, Italy,
candlesticks, an inkstand, a loving cup,
a tea set and a coffee set were shown.
The Louisiana Purchase Exposition
in St. Louis in 1904 included an enormous centerpiece and an outstanding
punch bowl entitled *Toilers of the Sea.*

(M.G.F.)

Martin, Agnes (1921–   ).
Painter. Born in Saskatchewan, Canada, she came to the United States in
1932, attended Columbia University,
and during the 1950s and 1960s had a
studio in New York. Her first one-man
show (1958) and succeeding exhibitions (1959, 1961, 1963) ran totally
counter to the prevailing spirit of abstract expressionism,* and were seen as
the work of a poetic and individual
geometrical-purist. Such a painting as
Bones Number 2 (1961), however,
with its double stacks of narrow, white
rectangles floating on a black background, found a context in the later
1960s with the advent of hard-edge*
and ·minimalism.* (This painting, in
fact, presents an exact two-dimensional
analogue for the stacked metal boxes
of Donald Judd.*) By 1963 Martin had
abandoned this rigid austerity, and was
producing large, delicate paintings
based on a grid format. *Night Sea*
(1963) contains such subtleties as a
six-foot-square canvas filled with cobalt
blue rectangles and defined by gold-
leaf lines. The majority of Martin's
paintings were less opulent, however,
sometimes consisting of simply a penciled grid on bare canvas. She has
produced vast numbers of drawings,

1

2

1. **Homer Dodge Martin.** Honfleur
   Light, *1892. Century Association,
   N.Y.*
2. **Alfred Henry Maurer.** Still Life with
   Doily, *c.1930. Phillips Memorial
   Gallery, Washington, D.C.*

and most of her paintings retain the delicacy and intimacy of this more personal medium.

Her use of a rigid format has, further, worked to increase the individuality of each of her paintings. In one of the early moves away from "composition," she abandoned the idea of figure-ground or "forms" and adopted a "structure"—the grid. This not only assured the unity of each picture, but left her free to explore the subtleties of chiaroscuro and the range of grays that could be obtained by placing the lines closer or farther apart. With a minimum of means Agnes Martin produced some of the richest paintings of the 1960s. The mystical quality of her work is similar to, but on a grander scale than, Mark Tobey's* "White Writing" series. She has had several one-man shows on the West Coast and was included in the "Responsive Eye" and "The Art of the Real" exhibitions at the Museum of Modern Art. (E.C.G.)

Martin, Homer Dodge (1836–97).
Landscape painter and draftsman whose stylistic development began in a tightly realistic Hudson River School* style and ended in something close to impressionism.* Born in Albany, N.Y., he studied there with James Hart;* his early landscapes are uninspired reminiscences of Hart's. In 1862 he moved to New York, his home for thirty years, and under the influence of John F. Kensett* he painted cool, detailed landscapes of the lakes, mountains, and waterfalls of New York State, such as *Honfleur Light* (Century Association, N.Y.). Although in this period his work resembled that of many of his contemporaries, he never gained great popularity, perhaps because of his uncongenial personality or the relative barrenness and lack of sentimentality in his paintings. He first went abroad in 1876, and in England became friendly with the expatriate American painter James M. Whistler;* he made several other trips, including a long stay in Normandy (1881–86). From these European experiences came a drastic change in style; his late work was influenced by French landscape painting, seemingly both by the dramatic landscapes of the Barbizon School* of the early 19th century and by the light-keyed tonalism of the French impressionists. After 1890, Martin's health declined and his vision became very

poor; yet some of his best-known paintings, including the semi-impressionistic *Harp of the Winds* (1895, Metropolitan) date from these years. (T.E.S.)

Maurer, Alfred Henry (1868–1932).
One of the first American painters to be influenced by fauvism* and cubism.* Maurer was born in New York, N.Y., where his father, Louis Maurer, was a successful Currier and Ives* lithographer and genre painter. After working as a lithographer and studying at the National Academy of Design,* he went to Paris in 1897 and briefly attended the Académie Julien. He was soon painting works such as *An Arrangement* (1901, Whitney), which combined firm academic technique and decorative pictorial arrangements, influenced by William M. Chase* and James M. Whistler.* He won the first prize at the Carnegie International in 1901 and his success appeared assured as other honors followed.

Within a few years, the influence of Parisian art decisively changed his style. He became a friend of Gertrude and Leo Stein in 1904. Soon he was stimulated by the example of Matisse and the fauves to paint landscapes and figures in thrusts of unusual raw color that conveyed an impulsive vitality. Alfred Stieglitz* exhibited this work at his Gallery 291 in 1909 and 1910, and it was by paintings of fauvist tendency that Maurer was represented at the Armory Show* in 1913 and the Forum Exhibition in 1916. Through his contacts in Paris he also arranged for many of the foreign entries in the Armory Show.

Maurer returned permanently to the United States in 1914. By the end of the war he was working in a cubist manner of flat, overlapping, and interpenetrating planes. He produced a number of female heads and bust-length figures, sometimes single and sometimes paired or interpenetrating, often with distorted features and intense staring eyes, such as *Twin Heads* (c.1930, Whitney). He also painted boldly colored and textured still lifes in which the forms were subjected to both cubist and expressionist distortions (*Still Life With Doily,* c. 1930, Phillips). Between 1920 and 1931 Maurer produced a large body of such works in oil, watercolor, and gouache. Uneven but frequently forceful, they received little attention in their day. After the

closing of Steiglitz' gallery in 1917, avant-garde artists such as Maurer found few opportunities to exhibit and little encouragement in America. Maurer was introverted and reticent, and he lived in the shadow of his father's strong personality and popular success. Following his father's death in 1932, he committed suicide. (D.W.S.)

Maybeck, Bernard (1862–1957).
Architect. The son of a German woodcarver who came to America in 1848, he entered the furniture business in which his father was employed. His father sent him to Paris to study furniture design but he soon discovered the École des Beaux-Arts and took up studies there in 1882. On his return to New York in 1886, he obtained a job with the architectural firm of Carrère & Hastings* and supervised work on the Hotel Ponce de Leon, St. Augustine, Fla., in 1887. In 1889, he went to San Francisco, where he worked for Ernest Coxhead, an English architect who combined the local shingle style* with the fashionable Queen Anne* style. He also became an instructor in drawing and descriptive geometry at the University of California at Berkeley. While there, he persuaded the mother of publisher William Randolph Hearst to finance a master plan for the campus. He designed Hearst Hall (1899), one of the earliest uses of laminated wood trusses for a building in this country, and the Men's Faculty Club (1900), whose wide expanses of wall were reminiscent of the California missions. In Wyntoon (1902), a miniature castle commissioned by Mrs. Hearst and set on the McCloud River, Maybeck combined high stone walls with a steep-roofed, cantilevered wooden superstructure. Maybeck believed in the visible expression of structural elements, and in his Outdoor Art Club House (1905, Mill Valley, Cal.), he carried widely spaced uprights through the roof and then horizontally across to meet the king-post trusses inside. His first experience with reinforced concrete came with the Lawson House (1907), Berkeley, where a plain, rather cubist structure was made dramatic by a deeply recessed porch above the main entry, and end pavilions with large semicircular openings facing outward. The First Church of Christ Scientist (1910–12), Berkeley, is considered by many to be Maybeck's masterpiece.

Its blocklike interior trusses are a powerful expression of structure, even though the spaces between truss members are filled with Gothic ornament.

Maybeck is also remembered for the colossal colonnade he designed for the Palace of Fine Arts at the Panama-Pacific Exposition in San Francisco (1915). It is a painter's concept, with Corinthian columns profiled against the sky and partially enclosing a lagoon containing a domed temple on an island. An exercise in Beaux-Arts virtuosity was his Packard Salesroom Building (1924), San Francisco. Maybeck's shingle style houses are of interest for their low-pitched roofs, trellises, and freely asymmetrical plans. These are typified by the Chick House (1913) at Berkeley and the large Bingham House (1917) at Montecito.

Generally disregarded by his colleagues, Maybeck was pleasantly surprised in the 1930s to hear himself referred to as a pioneer of modern architecture. He received several honorary degrees and in 1951, at the age of eighty-nine, the gold medal of the American Institute of Architects.

(A.B.)

McCobb, Paul (1917–69).
Furniture designer known for his elegant but simple styles for people of modest means. Ambitious to become a painter, he attended art school in his native city of Boston, Mass. His first job was as an interior designer at the large Boston department store, Jordan Marsh. With the advent of World War II, he enlisted in the Camouflage Corps of the Army. In 1945 he formed his own firm, Paul McCobb Associates, in New York. Joining with B. G. Mesberg, a furniture distributor, he started the Planner Group in 1950 to produce low-cost furniture that was simply designed and made of natural woods. He also designed other lines of furniture. In 1958 he introduced what he called a "Living Wall," consisting of free-standing tubular aluminum posts with channels to which desks and cabinets could be attached—an answer to the problem of more flexible living space in cramped quarters. McCobb won Good Design awards from the Museum of Modern Art in 1950, 1951, 1953, and 1954. He also received many other honors.

McComb, John, Jr. (1763–1853).
Architect. He was born in New York, N.Y., where his father, John McComb, was a reputable builder-architect who had built the Brick Church (1767), the North Dutch Church (1769), and the New York Hospital (1773) in 18th-century colonial style. John McComb, Jr., became his father's assistant in 1783. He had toured Europe before his first independent design for the façade of Government House, New York (1790). He built several lighthouses: Montauk (1795), Eaton's Neck (1798), and Cape Henry (1791). Combining with Joseph Mangin, French-born architect working in New York, he won the competition for the New York City Hall (1802), and was appointed to superintend its construction (1812). The City Hall displays the late 18th-century French (Louis XVI) interest in a prominent exterior massing of architectural form and in small-scale decoration. The classical portico and severe though handsome vestibule are in the English style of Sir William Chambers and James Paine.

Most of McComb's buildings were based on English Georgian style, with little decoration. The most notable were the New York Free School House (1808); Queens Buildings, Rutgers University (1809); Alexander Hall, Theological Seminary, Princeton, N.J. (1815); and the well-proportioned Bleecker Street Presbyterian Church, New York City (1825). A large collection of his drawings is at the New York Historical Society.

(P.F.N.)

McCracken, John (1934–   ).
Sculptor and painter. Graduated from the California College of Fine Arts, Oakland, in 1962, McCracken has since become a leading member of the southern California school of "finish fetishists." This group, which includes Larry Bell* and Billy Al Bengston, favors the lustrous but impersonal finishes created by industrial processes. Employing metallic paints and the elaborate technologies of plastics fabrication, these artists conceal all evidence of the individual hand. McCracken's best-known works are a series of thin polyester resin boards, often ten feet in length, which he leans against the wall instead of mounting on a traditional sculptural base. One of these pieces, *There's No Reason Not To* (1967), received much attention at "The Art of the Real," an exhibit at the Museum of Modern Art, New York City, in 1968. The impact of these sculptures is owed to their visual clarity, but they still present enigmas. E. C. Goossen, director of "The Art of the Real," said in the catalog: "As for John McCracken's slabs of sheer color, it is hard to tell whether one is confronting a painting or a sculpture." McCracken has also shown mandala-like paintings, in which rings of luminous color create subtle but intense visual vibrations. His work has been seen regularly in New York and Los Angeles since 1965. He is represented in numerous museum collections.

(C.R.)

McFee, Henry Lee (1886–1953).
Painter. Born in St. Louis, Mo., he studied at the Art Students League* and in Paris. He spent much of his life in Woodstock, N.Y., where (with George Bellows* and Eugene Speicher*) he helped to found the famous Woodstock art colony. From 1942 to his death he taught at Scripps College in Claremont, Cal.

Early in his career McFee devoted himself largely to still life, as in *Still Life with Striped Curtain* (1931, Metropolitan). His emphasis was on monumental structure, in the tradition of Cézanne, but with sumptuous color in addition to powerful forms. Later while continuing to paint still life, he turned to landscape and the human figure, working in a less abstract style than that of his early days.

McGarrell, James (1930–   ).
Painter. Born in Indianapolis, Ind., he studied at Indiana University, Skowhegan School in Maine, the University of California at Los Angeles, and the Academy of Fine Arts, Stuttgart. He has taught at Reed College in Oregon (1956–59) and is currently a professor at the University of Indiana. He has had many one-man exhibitions in New York City and throughout the United States and Europe and has exhibited widely in group shows. McGarrell is a pioneer expressionist-realist who paints the figure in an environment: it is depicted in a rough, explicit manner and rendered in rich and varied color. He is also a printmaker, and uses the same subjects and techniques in his etchings and lithographs as in his paintings.

(H.H.A.)

McIntire, Samuel (1757–1811).
Builder-architect. Born in Salem, Mass., he learned the building trade in his father's shop, and by 1779 was

building houses to his own designs. The designs were dignified, well-proportioned, finished with classical details, and superior to the work of all but a few other New England architects before 1800. He borrowed ideas from the books of English builders but did not copy complete designs.

McIntire's houses made Salem the handsomest New England town in the late 18th century. His skill in carving wood and using it as architectural ornament was unmatched. The scale of domestic architecture best fitted his abilities. He at first depended on the mid-18th-century builders' books for his version of colonial design. Elongated classical pilasters, quoins (raised cornerstones), and moderately bold classical ornament on the interiors mark his early style as found in such buildings as the Peirce-Nichols House (1779); Boardman House (1882–89); Joshua Ward House (1784–87), of brick; and the Benjamin Pickman House (remodeled 1786). His designs after 1790 are more advanced in style, comparable to the late Geogian, small-scale decorative patterns by London architects like Robert Adam. Charles Bulfinch* had already begun to use the Adam style in Boston, which probably stimulated McIntire to discard his earlier manner. The Adam style had delicate classical ornament inside and a refinement and elegance of proportion outside, as in the thin porch columns and delicate balusters, while narrow pilasters and quoins disappear. This style appears early in the Elias Hasket Derby House (elevation c. 1795 drawn by McIntire; now demolished); Lyman House, Waltham (1793–98); Pingree House (1805); and Jabez Baldwin House (1809–12), all in Salem.

The next generation of architects was better trained in their profession and better able to cope with the shift to the Greek revival* style, which required a considerable knowledge of ancient Greek architecture. Nevertheless, McIntire supplied Salem with the best woodcarving anywhere in the country.

(P.F.N.)

McKim, Mead & White (1879–1961). For many years the most influential architectural firm in New York City, it trained many young men destined to become leading architects. Charles Follen McKim (1847–1909) was born in Isabella Furnace, Pa. He entered

1

1. *John McComb, Jr.* New York City Hall, 1812.
2. *Bernard Maybeck.* Hearst Hall, University of California at Berkeley, 1899.

2

the Lawrence Scientific School at Harvard in 1866, but after a year became an apprentice in the New York office of Charles D. Gambrill and H. H. Richardson.* In 1872 he joined forces with William Rutherford Mead, and later with Stanford White, to form the firm of McKim, Mead & White in 1879. An exponent of Roman architecture, McKim fought for years to establish the American Academy in Rome, and worked to restore Washington, D.C., to some semblance of Major L'Enfant's* original axial scheme. William Rutherford Mead (1846–1928) was born in Brattleboro, Vt., and graduated from Amherst College in 1867. In 1868 he began his apprenticeship, like McKim, in the Sturgis office. In 1871 he went to Florence, Italy, where he lived for two years. Upon his return to America, he joined McKim and became the level-headed businessman in the firm. Stanford White (1853–1906) was born in New York City, son of Richard Grant White, a noted scholar and composer. He too entered the office of Gambrill & Richardson (in 1872) and there absorbed the Romanesque revival* influence. In 1878 he went to Europe and was joined by McKim in his travels. White, the Renaissance man of the firm, imported many objets d'art to furnish the houses he had designed. His brilliant career was later cut off when he was shot to death by a fellow clubman in the most sensational scandal of the time.

Much of the major work of the firm was done in New York City. It began auspiciously with two monuments. The first was the base for the proto-art nouveau* Farragut Monument in Madison Square, done in collaboration with the sculptor Augustus Saint-Gaudens* in 1879. It displayed a plastic fluidity of design that would not appear abroad for another ten years. The other monument was the Washington Arch at the foot of Fifth Avenue, built of staff and plaster in 1889 and rebuilt in stone, by popular demand, a few years later. The young firm had something new to offer, a refined classicism in an age of eclecticism.* In 1891 the firm used terra-cotta and yellow brick for the Century Association (Club) Building and for the multipurpose sports arena, Madison Square Garden, designed in the Italian Renaissance style. These buildings gave New Yorkers, accustomed to red brick and brownstone, a

refreshingly new architecture. With its high tower, loggias, roof garden, and diverse interior functions, Madison Square Garden proved the versatility of the new eclectic architecture. One of the most joyous structures ever erected in New York was the two-story New York *Herald* Building (1893). Located on a prowlike site at Broadway and 35th Street, and built in the Italian Renaissance style, its first-floor arches formed an open arcade along its west side.

Another commission, the New York University Bronx campus, designed in the classical Roman tradition (1894–1912), included a domed central library, half encircled at the rear by the open-galleried "Hall of Fame" and flanked by classroom buildings. At this time the firm also designed three outstanding clubhouses in Manhattan: the Metropolitan Club, at 1 East 60th Street (1894), modeled on an Italian Renaissance palace; the Harvard Club at 27 West 44th Street (1894–1915), a much smaller neo-Georgian structure of red brick with limestone trim; and the University Club at 54th Street and Fifth Avenue (1899), another Italian Renaissance palazzo. Among their other institutional work was their imposing classical Brooklyn Museum facing Eastern Parkway (1890), and, when Columbia University proposed to move to a new site at 116th Street and Broadway, their two-level plateau scheme for the campus, with Italian Renaissance classroom buildings of brick and limestone, and the centrally located, domed Low Library, won the commission (1895–97).

McKim, Mead & White did some of their finest work in commercial architecture. Their Pennsylvania Railroad Station in Manhattan formed an imperial gateway to the city (1903–10). It covered two city blocks, and in its use of classical columns was acclaimed for its monumental dignity. The main concourse, with its vaulted ceiling, resembled a great Roman public bath. The outer concourse, leading to the trains, was a functional expression of skylighted steel construction. Two splendid Fifth Avenue stores set a new level for excellence in design: Tiffany & Company at 37th Street (1906), was a large-scale but much simplified version of the Palazzo Grimani in Venice, while The Gorham Manufacturing Company building at 36th Street (1906), with

arcaded base, smooth shaft pierced by windows, and top-floor loggia effect, displayed beautiful proportions.

The firm's public buildings did much to establish a new high order of civic architecture. For the New York Public Library system they designed three small branch libraries (1905–08, at 115th, 135th, and 145 streets) in the Italian Renaissance style. The need for more office space outside of City Hall led to the commission for the Municipal Building (1912). The firm's ingenious solution of the problem was a stone-veneered skyscraper* straddling Chambers Street. A monumental screen of columns closed the western side of this U-shaped building, with a Roman triumphal arch motif at its center. The tower and other details were reminiscent of Italian Renaissance prototypes. In 1914 the firm designed the enormous General Post Office that, with its great frontal loggia, repeated the Roman theme of Pennsylvania Station facing it across Eighth Avenue. The clubhouses the firm designed included the Lambs Club at 128 West 44th Street (1905), a high, narrow, brick structure featuring a second-floor glazed loggia; the Colony Club at 120 Madison Avenue (1908), now the American Academy of Dramatic Arts; and the Racquet and Tennis Club at 370 Park Avenue (1915), with triple-arched loggia at the second floor, and its blank upper walls expressive of the tennis courts within.

J. P. Morgan asked the firm to design a library for his priceless books and manuscripts adjacent to his residence on 36th Street (1906). Severely plain, with large expanses of blank wall, this little stone building featuring a Palladian arched entrance loggia, set a high standard of design, often emulated but rarely equalled. One of the major works of the firm was the Savoy Plaza Hotel (1927). Facing the Plaza Hotel at 59th Street, it towered thirty stories with a high hipped roof crowned by two enormous chimneys, a very free interpretation of French Renaissance* precedent. The first notable town house the firm designed in New York was the large U-shaped group of mansions under one roof for the railroad magnate, Henry Villard, on Madison Avenue at 50th Street (1882–85), which introduced the Italian Renaissance style in their residential work. In the popular Romanesque revival* style, they designed a large residence for Charles L. Tiffany on Madison Avenue at 72nd Street (1884). The rock-faced stone base was surmounted by picturesque gabled wings and a corner oriel window. The firm also designed an interesting row of similar town houses on 139th Street between Seventh and Eighth avenues (1892), in Harlem, in simplified Italian Renaissance style. Perhaps the most beautiful Italian Renaissance town house ever built in New York was the one for John Innes Kane at 49th Street and Fifth Avenue (1907). It had the elegant restraint of the Palazzo Massimo in Rome.

McKim, Mead & White did much distinguished work in other cities, its most notable achievement being the Boston Public Library on Copley Square (1887–94). This stone building with its boldly grooved stonework base surmounted by rows of arched windows, richly detailed cornice and hipped tile roof, was inspired by the Bibliothèque Ste. Geneviève in Paris. An inner court with pool, surrounded by an arcaded loggia, provided a summertime amenity. In Washington, D.C., their remodeling of the White House (1903) and the addition of new Executive Offices in a low wing was a successful solution to a difficult problem. In the same year they designed a town house for Mrs. Eleanor Medill Patterson at 15 Du Pont Circle. C-shaped to conform to the circle, it is an impressive example of Italian Renaissance architecture. The rather pompous principal building of the Army War College, at 4th and "P" streets, S. W. (1908), was a compromise between Roman grandeur and a brick Georgian style.

One of the most interesting churches the firm designed was the all-stone Methodist Church in Baltimore (1882). Here, a central auditorium is set in a square building approached by arcades on two sides with an archaic tower at the corner. Philadelphia also had its share of their work with the brick "colonial" Germantown Cricket Club and the imposing Girard Trust Company in the heart of the city, a glistening white marble bank complete with dome and two porticoes. For the World's Columbian Exposition of 1893 in Chicago the firm designed the Agricultural Building, one of the largest facing the lagoon. For its long façades they established a rhythm of arched colonnades punctuated by rectilinear pavilions

1

2

1. **McKim, Mead & White.** *Bowery Savings Bank Interior, N.Y., 1884.*
2. **McKim, Mead & White.** *University Club, N.Y., 1899.*

which had a surprising amount of visual interest. They also designed the New York State Building, cleaving once again to Italian Renaissance precedent with a modified version of the 16th-century Villa Medici.

In their commissions for large country estates they set a new standard in elegance. Among the earliest was a large waterfront house with a picturesque combination of wood shingles and stone towers for Charles J. Osborn in Mamaroneck, N.Y. (1885), and a great low-lying shingle-style and stucco house for E. D. Morgan in Wheatley Hills, Long Island, N.Y. (1891). A great stone castle, "Ophir Court," for Whitelaw Reid in Purchase, N.Y., in 1893 (now Manhattanville College), was an unusual return to the picturesque at this late date. The palace designed for Frederick W. Vanderbilt in Hyde Park, on the Hudson (1899), was almost classical although it was Italian Renaissance in detail. The finest of these estates was the one for Clarence H. Mackay in Roslyn, Long Island (1902), a rather free version of the Chateau de Maison, near Paris.

In Newport, R.I., the firm did some of its finest resort architecture, designing "cottages" in the shingle style for Mrs. Frances L. Skinner (1882), Samuel Coleman (1883), and Isaac Bell (1883), not to mention The Casino on Bellevue Avenue (1881). One of the finest shingle-style houses ever designed was "Southside" for Robert Goelet on Narragansett Avenue (1883). The colonial revival was reflected in the great frame "cottage" for H. A. C. Taylor (1886) which, with its four brick chimneys and captain's walk, was a dominant feature on Annandale Road. In keeping with the new formality introduced by the Chicago Exposition, and reminiscent of the Grand Trianon at Versailles, was the seaside villa for Mrs. Herman Oelrichs (1902).

In the Berkshires of Massachusetts a stone and brick French Renaissance chateau for Joseph H. Choate in Stockbridge (1887), and an enormous sprawling stone mansion for Mrs. Mark Hopkins in Great Barrington (1885), gave the summer colony there a new taste of splendor. A brick Federal style* house for Thomas Jefferson Coolidge in Manchester, Mass. (1904), and a frame house with a porch like that of Mount Vernon for James Breese in Southhampton, Long Island (1906),

completes the roster.

In the age of eclecticism no other firm surpassed the level of work produced by McKim, Mead & White. It was one of those happy partnerships—it lasted about thirty years—in which each partner did the work for which he was best equipped. Their influence in the profession was pervasive and today is legendary, so that almost any fine building of the period is apt to be attributed to McKim, Mead & White.(A.B.)

McNeil, George (1906–   ).
Painter, born in New York, N.Y., McNeil studied at the Pratt Institute (1927–29), the Art Students League (1930–33), the Hans Hofmann School (1934–37), and Columbia University, where he earned a B.A. and D.Ed. degrees. McNeil has taught at Pratt Institute since 1948 and at the University of California (1955–56). He designed abstract murals for the WPA Federal Art Project* and has been a member of the American Abstract Artists* group since 1936. He has been a pioneer of American abstract expressionism* since the early 1950s, painting in a powerful, rough, and highly coloristic manner.

Mead, Larkin (1835–1910).
Sculptor, born in Brattleboro, Vt. In 1853 he went to New York City and became an assistant to Henry Kirke Brown.* Returning to Vermont, he was commissioned in 1857 to make a colossal personification of his native state as Ceres for the state capitol, as well as a marble statue of Ethan Allen (1861). Later he made a second version of Allen (1876) based on Michelangelo's *David,* for Statuary Hall, U.S. Capitol. Mead spent the Civil War years in Italy, and his marble statue, *Echo* (c.1863, Corcoran), shows the influence of ancient Roman statuary. He returned briefly to America but, receiving a commission for a large memorial to Abraham Lincoln for Springfield, Ill., Mead went back to Florence, Italy, and worked on the memorial throughout the 1870s. From the next decade dates his marble *Recording Angel* (All Souls' Church, Brattleboro, Vt.) and a pedimental group for the World's Columbian Exposition of 1893 in Chicago. He died in Florence.   (W.C.)

Meeks, The (active 1797–1868).
Furniture-makers. Active in New York

City, the Meeks firm was founded by Joseph Meeks (1771–1868) in partnership with his brother Edward. By 1800 Joseph had his own business, which continued under his descendants until 1868. Although the early productions (1787–1825) must have been in Federal* styles, no labeled or documented pieces are known for this period. A small group of Federal furniture appears in front of the Meeks shop on Broad Street in a view by architect A. J. Davis (Museum of New York).

The majority of their known furniture is of the period 1830–55 and is in a late classical or a historic revival style. An 1833 broadside of Joseph Meeks and Sons copies many plates from George Smith's *Cabinet-Maker and Upholsterer's Guide* (London, 1826). One of the earlier pieces, bearing the Meeks label of 1829 to 1835, is a gilt-stenciled pier table with paw feet below carved and gilded leaf brackets. A rosewood and satinwood secretary (Metropolitan) bearing Meeks' stenciled mark with their 1835–55 address has Gothic revival* arched muntins (wood dividing panes of glass) on the doors. A documented rococo revival* suite, made for the marriage of a Meeks daughter, bears a resemblance to other New York laminated rococo furniture and furnishes a basis of attribution of similar pieces (Metropolitan and Garvan Collection, Yale University).   (M.J.B.)

Melchers, Gari (1860–1932).
Figure and portrait painter, the son of a Parisian-trained woodcarver and decorator who emigrated from Germany to Detroit, Mich., where Melchers was born. The youth went to Düsseldorf in 1877, where he studied art until 1881; he then attended the Académie Julien in Paris. The following year he showed at the Salon, launching a career that soon brought him many awards. In 1884 he established a studio in Paris and one in Egmond, a fishing village on the coast of Holland. His portrayals of the villagers and their life, as in *The Communion* (Cornell University), won him an international reputation. His activities included visits to America to paint portraits and murals (Chicago World's Columbian Exposition, Library of Congress, and Missouri State Capitol); and five years in Weimar at the invitation of the Grand Duke of Saxe-Weimar (1909–14). He then returned to the United States.

Melchers often painted his Dutch subjects in a luminous, light gray tonality; at other times his brushwork and color ran to a higher key, in a kind of sturdy impressionism,* as in *Madonna* (c.1906–07, Metropolitan). His realism, which seemed in his day unaffected, now seems anecdotal and somewhat sentimental. Cosmopolitan and eclectic, he was a semi-expatriate, a semi-realist and a semi-impressionist, gifted with facility in characterization and a decorative flair in composition. Among his works were religious subjects, including a *Last Supper*. He has left some memorable paintings but few in proportion to the honors accorded him, including the signal one of election to the Institute of France. (D.W.S.)

Melchert, James (1930–   ).
Ceramist, sculptor, leader in the drive for new modes and media, and best known for the surreal wit of his ceramic sculptures. Born in New Bremen, Ohio, Melchert studied art history at Princeton University and received an M.F.A. from the University of Chicago. He became interested in ceramics only after being asked to teach it. Not long after, he was so impressed by a show of the work of Peter Voulkos* that he went to study with him in the early 1960s at the University of California, Berkeley. He received his second M.A. from that university.

His first important work was a series of "Leg Pots" in which limblike, wheel-thrown cylinders were joined to oddly shaped boxes, often with metal and cloth inlays, emphasizing the juxtaposition of opposing forms, the "encounter of two radical elements . . . evident in most of my work" and the introduction of contrasting materials. These were followed by the "Ghost Wares," a highly introspective and brooding series with heads and mysterious human images mounted on plates and jars. In recent years Melchert has adapted the imagery of surrealism,* creating a series of bitterly funny "Game Works," in which ceramic objects from everyday life such as coat-hangers and food shapes are distributed on plywood marked-off in oblique squares, inviting the viewer to "play" with them. His most recent project has been a series of letter A's, in which the shape of the letter is manipulated and distorted to the point where it takes on a life of its own. (R.S.)

Metcalf, Eliab (1785–1834).
A little-known but able portrait, still-life, and miniature painter and silhouette cutter, he was born in Franklin, Mass. Metcalf was based in New York from about 1810 to 1819, when he moved to New Orleans. His work appears to have been influenced by S. L. Waldo, with whom he studied, and by John Vanderlyn.* In 1824 he moved permanently to Havana, Cuba.

Metcalf, Willard Leroy (1853–1925).
Impressionist landscape painter. Born in Lowell, Mass., he received his first instruction there before attending the school of the Museum of Fine Arts, Boston. He was a student of the Boston landscape artist, George L. Brown* during 1876–77. He then studied at the Académie Julien in Paris and received an honorable mention in the Salon of 1888. Returning to the United States, he visited the Southwest as a naturalist and explorer for the Smithsonian Institution in 1881–82. He then tried his hand at illustration and painting figures and flowers, but eventually concentrated on the New England landscape. He won a medal at the World's Columbian Exposition in Chicago (1893) and showed with The Ten* when they began exhibiting in 1898.

Metcalf painted a variety of subjects —fields and hillsides, village streets and houses—in all seasons, under various effects of light. Like other impressionists, he chose the delightful aspects of nature, but he sought portrayal of a specific place, as in *The North Country* (1923, Metropolitan) rather than a generalized effect of enveloping atmosphere. He applied his paint precisely and somewhat drily, working methodically to achieve pleasantly convincing characterizations of the New England scene. (D.W.S.)

Mezzotint Prototypes.
A tone process of engraving. British mezzotint portraits were used by colonial artists as models for pose, costume, and ornamental detail. These prints of ladies and gentlemen of the court, and of political and theatrical figures, became popular in the late 17th century. They remained so from the time of Sir Godfrey Kneller into that of Sir Joshua Reynolds. They lent themselves readily to copying by a painter, and proved invaluable to inexpert artists in the American provinces. The house

painter and glazier who aspired to portraiture followed as best he could the stately composition of the print and then added the American face. American art historians, searching for native characteristics, were late in learning to what a large extent these foreign prints were embodied in colonial art. In America's earliest portraits they found what they believed to be the rough and sturdy spirit of the pioneer, whereas many of the pictures were only dim reflections from the court of Queen Anne or George I. The discovery was made by Waldron Phoenix Belknap, a Boston architect and art historian, whose conclusions were well developed by the time of his death in 1949. John Marshall Phillips of Yale brought it to public attention at the College Art Association meetings of 1952. This resulted in a fruitful redirection of the study of the foundations of American art away from the nativist emphasis and toward the identification of Old World influences.

Belknap's discovery may have begun with his study of a portrait he owned, *Johannes de Peyster* (1718, New York Hist.), which an unknown New York painter had derived from *Sir John Percival,* engraved by John Smith after Kneller (1708). The patroon painters* made very large use of the prints, but it is now known or assumed that every colonial artist had a collection of them in his studio, and quite possibly allowed patrons to look through it to select pose and costume. There was no plagiarism involved, since for one artist to imitate another was thought to be only an act of deference to a greater talent. European-trained artists were not dependent on the prints, but a talented colonial such as Robert Feke* used them freely. His *Mrs. Barlow Trecothick* (1748, Wichita) is based on a print of the actress Kitty Clive, and his *Mrs. William Bowdoin* (c.1740–48, Bowdoin College, Me.) on that of Anne Oldfield, another actress. Before Belknap began his study, only John Singleton Copley's* use of a print for his *Mrs. Jerathmael Bowers* (c.1763, Metropolitan) had been published, and had been regarded as a unique flaw in a great talent. Belknap showed, first, that Reynolds in painting the original of the print had himself borrowed details from a mezzotint of fifty years earlier and, next, that Copley had made fuller use of the prints than any other, repeatedly borrowing compositions and using them to keep abreast of the latest London mode in portraiture. (C.C.S.)

Midwestern Glass, see Pattern-molded Glass, Pressed Glass, Flasks, Glass Cutting and Engraving.

Mies van der Rohe, Ludwig (1886–1969).
Architect-designer. Of the major figures associated with the style-setting German Bauhaus,* it was he who most directly affected American architecture after 1945. His concept of the skyscraper* as steel-framed and thinly sheathed in metal and glass became the normal academic style after World War II. Mies was trained under two of Germany's most gifted designers of the turn of the century—Bruno Paul and Peter Behrens. His pre-World War I designs were classically oriented, with stripped volumes and restrained details. After the war he was caught up in the short-lived German expressionist movement and produced a jagged-volumed, all-glass skyscraper for Berlin (1921). By the mid-1920s he had returned to simple rectangular volumes and surfaces. He was active in producing housing in Berlin and Stuttgart. In 1929 he designed one of the great monuments of the International style,* the German Pavilion at the Barcelona Exhibition, which in its abstract manipulation of vertical and horizontal slabs appears to be as much pure sculpture as architecture.

During the crucial years 1930–33 Mies was director of the Bauhaus; however, Nazi pressure forced him to close it. In 1938 he emigrated to the United States and was appointed professor of architecture at the Illinois Institute of Technology. He designed the new campus for the Institute and in 1950 created the much-publicized Farnsworth House in Plano, Ill., which transformed the concept of his pavilion at Barcelona into an all-glass house. In Chicago and elsewhere Mies began to receive large commissions for skyscrapers. The most impressive of these was unquestionably the Seagram Building (New York, 1956–59), designed in collaboration with Philip Johnson.* Mies's ideal, "less is more," very early led him to simplify his forms and concentrate his full attention on the specific details—how sheathing and structure are put together—and to establish ideal proportions and ratios for his volumes and their defining surfaces. His use of industrial products, especially steel and glass, and his desire to mirror the machine forcibly in his architectural image, enabled him to create a style which could, with reasonable facility, be imitated by the average commercial architect in the United States. (D.G.)

Milkowski, Antoni (1935–   ).
Sculptor. Born in Evanston, Ill., he studied at Kenyon College. His sculpture is usually considered minimal* and he was included in the first exhibition of this kind of art in 1964. These early works were made of steel, and though often small in size they achieved monumentality through their simple geometrical volumes, their symmetry, and their monolithic quality. At a time when many artists were turning toward the superficial "balancing acts" and bright hues of "pictorial sculpture," Milkowski continued to explore the possibilities of three-dimensional form. In 1964–65 he worked in Poland on a Fulbright Fellowship, and on his return he began to produce even larger versions of his earlier works. Other series have employed basic modular units, such as cubes, which fit together to form both simple and more complex pieces. The solidity as well as the scale and directness of his large works allows his sculpture to compete with rather than "inhabit" architecture, and his work has appeared in a number of "sculpture in the city" exhibitions of the late 1960s and early 1970s.
(E.C.G.)

Miller, Kenneth Hayes (1876–1952).
Painter of the New York scene and an influential teacher. Born in Oneida, N.Y., Miller studied at the Art Students League* under Kenyon Cox* and Frank Vincent DuMond as well as at the New York School of Art under William Merrit Chase.* He traveled and studied in Europe and in 1899 joined the staff of the New York School of Art. In 1911 he moved to the Art Students League, where he taught intermittently until 1951. His students included George Bellows,* Edward Hopper,* Reginald Marsh,* and Isabel Bishop.*

His early work was in a romantic vein, strongly influenced by his friendship for Albert Pinkham Ryder* (*Recumbent Figure,* 1910–11, Columbus). After the 1913 Armory Show (where he exhibited four pictures) his painting became increasingly intellectual, based upon Renaissance compositional procedures and executed in underpainting and glaze. His subjects were the women of New York, salesgirls and shoppers; the frozen classical poses he gave them are combined incongruously with their everyday clothes and settings, as in *The Fitting Room* (1931, Metropolitan). His influence, both in subject and technique, was particularly strong on pupils such as Marsh and Bishop, but was also reflected widely through Greenwich Village painters of "the Fourteenth Street School" who portrayed the New York scene during the 1920s and '30s. (D.W.S.)

Milles, Carl (1875–1955).
Sculptor, born near Uppsala, Sweden. He studied at the Technical School of Stockholm before going to Paris. He remained there from 1897 to 1904, studying at the Académie Colarossi and exhibiting in the Paris Salon of 1899. He went on to Munich in 1904, but returned to Sweden in 1908 and sculpted monumental figures in a studio in Lidingo. This subsequently became the Milles Museum. Milles made his first visit to the United States in 1929; in 1931 he was appointed professor of sculpture at the Cranbook Academy in Michigan and remained in America.

Milles' sculpture, originally expressionistic, gradually moved toward classicism, but with large areas of his figures smoothed into boldy simplified forms. Major works include the onyx *Peace Monument* for the St. Paul, Minn., City Hall (1936) and *Man and Nature* (1940), which was executed in wood for the Time/Life Building in New York City.

Millet, Francis D. (1846–1912).
Illustrator and painter of genre scenes, murals, and portraits. Born in Mattapoisett, Mass., he attended Harvard, studied art in Antwerp, and traveled extensively, serving as a reporter during the Russo-Turkish and the Spanish-American wars, and residing at times in England. He is best known for popular depictions of historic genre, such as *Between Two Fires* (Tate), and for his role as an organizer of the mural painting at the 1893 World's Columbian Exposition in Chicago. He contributed decorations to a number of buildings, including Trinity Church in Boston.

1. **Ludwig Mies van der Rohe.** *Minerals and Metals Research Building, Illinois Institute of Technology, Chicago, 1943.*
2. **Kenneth Hayes Miller.** The Fitting Room, *1931. Metropolitan Museum of Art, N.Y.*

He was a leader in art societies and served as a trustee of the Metropolitan Museum. His active and varied career ended when he was lost at sea in the *Titanic* disaster. (D.W.S.)

Mills, Clark (1810–83).
Sculptor. His fame rests primarily on one work—the equestrian statue of Andrew Jackson in Lafayette Square, Washington, D.C. A tour de force of design and bronze casting, it was his first effort that went beyond a portrait bust and is as much a tribute to his skill as a mechanic and engineer as to his ability as an artist. Mills was born in upstate New York but spent his early life in the South, wandering about seeking employment as a carpenter and plasterer. He had no formal training in sculpture, and his earliest works were life-masks which he developed into portrait busts in the 1840s in Charleston, S.C. In 1845 he executed his first bust in stone, doing the carving himself; his bust of Calhoun (Corcoran) won him an award as well as support and commissions.

Three years later, Mills submitted an entry to the Jackson Memorial Committee and, despite his inexperience, was awarded one of the most challenging sculptural commissions of that era. It was the first equestrian statue in America, and the design, showing Jackson on a rearing horse supported only by its hind legs, was indeed a severe test. Mills worked on it for nearly five years, building in Washington one of the earliest foundries in America for casting bronze statuary. His masterpiece, unveiled in 1853, evoked the highest praise. As in all of Mills' work, the statue was a naturalistic one, but it had a dynamic quality that his portrait busts lacked. A grateful Congress voted him a commission for an equestrian statue of Washington; it was erected in 1860 on Washington Circle in the capital, but it was less successful than the *Jackson*. The cities of New Orleans and Nashville ordered replicas of the *Jackson*. He assembled the deceased Horatio Greenough's* marble *Rescue* group at the Capitol and he cast Thomas Crawford's* *Armed Freedom* for the Capitol dome. (W.C.)

Mills, Robert (1781–1855).
Architect and engineer. Born in Charleston, S.C., he attended Charleston College. He was the first American to get

professional architectural training (in the office of B. H. Latrobe*) in the United States. In 1800 James Hoban,* builder-architect, persuaded him to go to Washington, D.C. There he met Thomas Jefferson* and studied architecture with him. In 1804 the president sent Mills on a tour through the eastern states to examine the latest construction. Latrobe then hired Mills to work on the Capitol in Washington (1804–08), and in Latrobe's office Mills began practicing architecture. He designed the Sansom Street Church, Philadelphia (1804), with the first dome over a church in America. He settled in Philadelphia in 1808 and became well known as both architect and engineer. His designs were in the Greek revival* style, which Latrobe had introduced, presumed a knowledge of ancient Greek architecture and decorative form, particularly that of the temple. In Philadelphia, he designed the Unitarian Church (1811–13), and the Upper Ferry Bridge (1812, burned 1828) whose single span of 360 feet was the longest in the world. Washington Monument, Baltimore (1814–29), unifying the square at Charles and Monument streets, utilizes the Doric column as a symbol of honor.

Mills moved to Baltimore in 1817 and was appointed chief engineer for the city waterworks. He wrote a *Treatise on Inland Navigation* (1820), which led to several commissions to construct canals. Returning to Charleston in 1820, he designed the State Hospital for the Insane, Columbia, S.C. (1822), and the Record Office Building (1822). Money in South Carolina for the construction of public buildings becoming scarce, Mills returned to Washington, D.C., in 1830. President Jackson appointed him architect of public buildings (1836–51), and in this capacity he designed the Treasury Building (1836–39), the Patent Office (1936–40), and the Post Office (1839). These projects set the style for government buildings for many decades to come; all were gigantic, Greek-columned structures, scaled to the developing city. He wrote *The American Pharos, or Lighthouse Guide* (1832), and *A Guide to the Capitol of the United States* (1834). In 1836 he won the competition for the Washington Monument in Washington, D.C., with his design of a 555-foot obelisk, at that time the tallest structure in the world.

Mills' many buildings were almost all in the Greek revival style; indeed, the end of his career coincided with the end of public interest in the Greek revival. In defending his use of the style, he said that he never copied the Greeks, but adapted their principles to modern purposes. (P.F.N.)

Minimal Architecture.
The ultimate refinement of the International style* of Mies van der Rohe,* this style reached its peak from the mid-1960s into the 1970s. It was a pure distillation of Bauhaus* principles, yet because of its simplicity it went almost unnoticed as a distinct substyle. Few critics of the time made the comparison with minimal art.* In its course, it developed a sparse, elemental look, eliminating even the structural articulation that Bauhaus designers had devised as a decorative motif. It minimized or stripped off everything that might possibly be considered extraneous: joints, reveals, moldings, and the like. This technique looked effortless, but it concealed extremely complicated internal systems of structural, mechanical, electrical, and joining elements. Its exterior products were simple geometric structures of greatly increased scale, smoother surfaces over larger areas, thinner skins, and flatter profiles. It resulted in a mirror-wrapped and black-velvet quality, in buildings of such monumental clarity and elemental strength that they looked like a design scheme constructed just as it was originally conceived.

In interiors, the minimal style produced white plaster boxes with broad expanses of plain surfaces. Door and window openings were frameless and trimless—simply sliced into the planes. Window coverings were spare and ascetic. Only "natural" textures in deep wools and burl woods enriched the pure "clean" envelopes, and crisp, machine-age furnishings were placed in space like objects in a museum.

The most prominent exponents of this substyle were Gordon Bunshaft* of Skidmore, Owings & Merrill;* Kevin Roche* of Roche, Dinkeloo & Associates; the early Louis Kahn;* I. M. Pei;* and Edward L. Barnes.* It was an unlikely group and sometimes it shared only the aim of large scale and smooth concealment. The outstanding interior designers who first gave the sub-style distinction were Florence Knoll Bas-

1. **Robert Mills.** *The Washington Monument in Baltimore, 1829. Lithograph from Maryland Historical Society, Baltimore.*
2. **Minimal Architecture.** *I.M. Pei. Society Hill Apartments, Philadelphia, Pa., 1963.*

1

2

sett,* Alexander Girard,* Benjamin Baldwin,* and Charles Eames.*

Not only was the minimal style a final working out of older esthetic theories, but also it was a repudiation of a basic tenet of functionalism—that form follows function. By concealing all functional subsystems, it subverted the whole concept of industrialized, systematized architecture. The by-products of its regularity of parts, precise proportions, and general symmetry, were coldness, abstraction, and lack of individuality. The final forms were monolithic packages, which one critic called "superclassicism." Ultimately, this minimalist purity was rejected by a younger generation as a formality that was monotonous and sterile. Instead they developed supermannerism,* which was so to speak, decidedly unminimal. (C.R.S.)

Minimal Art.
A tendency, or direction, that by the early 1960s had become strong enough to be considered a style. While some critics have tried to relate it to European movements (especially Kasimir Malevich's suprematism), the "minimal" attitude, with its antipathy to composition, hierarchy, "beauty," "sentiment," and "personal emotion," is wholly American. In the early 1960s an astute art critic noted that "under the testing of modernism more and more of the conventions of the art of painting have shown themselves to be dispensable, unessential. . . ." Throughout the 1950s artists such as Ellsworth Kelly* and Alexander Liberman* had simplified their form and color, and developed methods of applying paint that eliminated the "hand of the artist," and Tony Smith* had worked with modular systems that tended to diminish the number of "arbitrary" decisions an artist had to make.

By the 1960s, a full-blown reaction to the subjectivity and romanticism of abstract expressionism* had set in. By 1964 enough younger artists had begun to reject personal mannerisms and to seek an art of anonymity and direct experience to warrant the arrangement of the first show of minimal art, called "8 Young Artists," at the Hudson River Museum in New York City. The sculptor Tony Smith had already reduced three-dimensional form to its essence in his remarkable six-foot cube, *Die* (1962), and other painters

and sculptors were beginning to employ primary forms in uninflected, "deadpan" ways. By 1964 Patricia Johanson,* the most explicit minimalist painter, had painted her pictures in a single line, and the sculptor Donald Judd* had begun to seek "wholeness" in simple three-dimensional volumes that he called "specific objects." Both had turned against "the relational character" (composition) of almost all painting, illusionism, and decorative sensuosity, in favor of simple "facts." Paradoxically, most minimal artists were later forced in the direction of visual perception when it was apparent that even the simplest form is highly complex as seen in the context of its total environment, lighting conditions, and the position of the spectator. Robert Morris,* meanwhile, influenced by the dancer Merce Cunningham and the composer John Cage, had begun to produce gray plywood objects that seemed even more impersonal than Judd's metal boxes. His "Notes on Sculpture" (1966–69) forms one of the prime documents of minimalism, and his work is typical of the style in its lack of dramatic incident and its "nonart" look. By the late 1960s minimal art was deemphasizing "talent," "technical virtuosity," and "ego," and much was industrially fabricated. Because almost all minimal works were conceived "a priori," and many of them illustrated processes of thought or ideas, it forms a direct link with process art and concept art.* At the same time, its involvement with the literal, physical object had led to such exhibitions as "primary structures" (1966) and The Museum of Modern Art exhibition, "The Art of the Real" (1968).

Because the spectator was not given a "biased," personal, "editorialized" vision of the world, but rather facts—to interpret however he would—the spectator now played as important a role as the artist. This new intrusion of the human being in turn led to such concepts as "presence" (the confrontation between spectator and work of art), "monumentality," and "theatricality." In brief, the simplification of form, the repetition of elements, and the new comparison between "body" size and the size of the work of art, all tended to lead to art on a vast scale (Robert Smithson's* *Spiral Jetty,* 1970; Patricia Johanson's sixteen-hundred-foot sculpture, *Stephen Long,* 1968). Additional meanings have begun to supplant the

1

Minimal Art
1. *Ellsworth Kelly.* Blue Red Green, *1963. Metropolitan Museum of Art (Arthur H. Hearn Fund).*
2. *John McCracken.* Rainmaker, *1965, wood and lacquer. Robert Elkon Gallery, N.Y.*
3. **Charles W. Moore.** Sea Ranch *Condominiums, Interior, Gualala, Cal., 1965.*

2

"purity" of the mid-1960s work, yet minimalism remains startling in its simplicity and its confrontation with "fact." Despite its cool, anonymous image, minimalism has from the beginning harbored a wealth of individual viewpoints; artists as diverse as Ronald Bladen,* Dan Flavin,* John McCracken,* Sol Lewitt,* and Les Levine* have all worked within the minimalist esthetic. As a philosophical attitude, minimalism has reached beyond the individual and affected every direction in recent art. Appearing at a moment when expressionism had run its course, minimalism reaffirmed that art needs a more universal base than purely personal values. It addressed itself to the problem of the relationship between the spectator and the reality of art itself. As such, it stimulated new attitudes in all the arts—music, dance, architecture, and landscape architecture, as well as in the visual arts of sculpture and painting. It brought about a reinvestigation of the role that art should and could play in making the public aware of the affective power of form, in and of itself. (E.C.G.)

Mitchell, Joan (1926–   ).
Painter. Born in Chicago, Ill., she attended Smith College and the Art Institute of Chicago (1944–47), after which she studied in Europe on an Art Institute fellowship. She also attended Columbia University and received an M.F.A. from New York University in 1950. She now lives and paints in Europe. She belongs to the second generation of the abstract expressionists, who emerged during the 1950s in the footsteps of Willem de Kooning.* During the 1950s she exhibited regularly at the Stable Gallery in New York, a center for the exhibition of abstract expressionism* and other avant-garde painting. During the 1960s she has had one-man exhibitions at the Massachusetts Institute of Technology, in New York, and in Europe.

Mitchell has painted since the early 1950s in a free, violent, brush-textured manner that owes much to de Kooning, but is nevertheless a personal form of expression. Typical is *George Went Swimming at Barnes Hole, but It Got Too Cold* (1957, Albright). She characteristically uses brilliant color and has consistently introduced accents of vertical paint drips. Her paintings of the early 1970s involve a greater sense of architectural structure. The paint is generally worked in impasto effects to create an overall light color texture broken up by large accents of contrastingly deep color. (H.H.A.)

Moore, Charles W. (1925–).
A leading architect in the design revolution called supermannerism.* Through his colorful and joyous works, he made the sterner theories of his more doctrinaire compeers accessible to the public. Born in Michigan, he received his Ph.D. from Princeton (1957). From 1960 on he taught at the University of California at Berkeley, and served as chairman of the architecture department (1962–65). At the same time, he was a partner in the firm of Moore, Lyndon, Turnbull & Whitaker. It was at this period that his name and that of his firm burst into prominence, first through an award for the design of his own house (Orinda, Cal., 1962), and then for a constant flow of other projects for the next five or more years. All showed a new vision and a complex view of geometry, of intricate, baroque forms, of already-existing architectural elements, of color, texture, and decoration, as well as unconventional means of opening interiors to the outside.

His firm produced the brightest, most continuous progression of works that developed the idiom of supermannerism.* At Yale University from 1965 to 1971 he was chairman of the architecture department, and then dean of the faculties of design and planning. His architectural practice was divided between offices in San Francisco and New Haven, Conn., but was then moved to Essex, Conn. Besides single-family houses, his firm designed condominium units (Sea Ranch, Gualala, Cal., 1965) and two small athletic clubs in which supergraphics* by Barbara Stauffacher Solomon* were major design elements (Sea Ranch, Swim Club I, Gualala, Cal., 1966; Faculty Club, University of California, Santa Barbara, 1968; dormitories, Pembroke College, Providence, R.I., 1969). At the beginning of the 1970s, he became interested in designing low-cost housing, some of it constructed out of prefabricated mobile units (The Housing Foundation, Orono, Me., 1971) and some of it using concrete blocks with sentry-box-like stripes for decoration (Church Street South Housing, New Haven, Conn., 1971). (C.R.S.)

3

Moore, Edward C. (c.1835–91).

One of Tiffany and Company's* fore-most silver designers, the son of John C. Moore, who manufactured silver for Marquand & Company and their successors, Ball, Tompkins & Black. Moore learned his trade in his father's shop and took over the business in 1851. He manufactured silver solely for Tiffany, and in 1868 his plant was bought by Tiffany. Early in the 1860s, realizing the need for better instruction in the decorative and industrial arts, he established a system of training based on the technical schools of Paris. It developed into the most thorough school of its kind. Drawing and modeling from natural objects, improvement of standards of silversmithing, and placing form and utility above decoration were prime concerns. It was Moore who introduced the "hammered silverware" exhibited by Tiffany at the Paris Exposition of 1878. Silver prior to the industrial revolution had been hand hammered, with the hammer marks removed by planishing. Moore's innovation was to leave the marks, to emphasize the blows by oxidizing, and to introduce natural objects such as insects, birds, and fish for decorative purposes. These decorative motifs were formed of different kinds of gold, copper, and other metals and then mounted on the silver. Inspired by Japanese metalwork, Moore perfected the amalgamation of metals, exhibiting a three-foot-high vase of several metallic compounds at the Paris Exposition in 1889. At this exposition he also introduced his Saracenic silverware, which included enameling and etched work.

(M.G.F.)

Morris, Kyle (1918–   ).

Painter. Born in Des Moines, Iowa. He studied at Northwestern University (1935–40), the Art Institute of Chicago (1935–39), and Cranbrook Academy in Michigan (1947), and since 1940 has taught painting and art history in many universities. He has been painting full time in New York City since 1954, but he was also lecturer, Cooper Union (1958); visiting critic, Yale Graduate School (1965); and guest artist, Carnegie Mellon University (1970).

Morris was a figurative painter until the early 1950s, working in a romantic mode that gradually became more spare and austere. In the 1950s he was associated with the second wave of abstract expres-

1. **Robert Morris.** Untitled, 1967, gray felt. Collection Ellen Johnson, N.Y.
2. **Edward C. Moore.** Hammered silver tea service exhibited by Tiffany and Company at the Paris Exposition of 1878.

sionism,* the efforts of a younger group to develop the achievements of the pioneers in new directions. In the 1960s, he worked first with large color shapes, sometimes balanced by expressively brushed areas. From this he moved gradually to a rigidly austere form of monochromatic hard-edge* painting, turning shapes around the edges of the stretched canvas, and frequently using serial groupings of three or five panels. This in turn has led him to an ultimate geometry of black ruled lines defining the spatial essences of series of white canvases. It is this continuing search for pictorial spatial relationships that is, perhaps, the unifying factor in his diverse work. He has been in many one-man and group shows since the early 1950s, and he is represented in major museums.   (H.H.A.)

Morris, Robert (1931–   ).
Sculptor and artist in mixed media. Born in Kansas City, Mo. His earliest paintings (1954) were strongly influenced by Jackson Pollock* in their overall patterning, loose brushwork, and understated color, and in 1957 and 1958 he had one-man shows in San Francisco. In the late 1950s Morris worked on theater improvisations in California until 1961, when he moved to New York City and made his first sculpture. *Box with the Sound of its Own Making* (1961), a nine-inch walnut cube on a high pedestal, has all the formal simplicity and elegance of a Brancusi sculpture; a three-hour tape recording of the sounds of the box's construction is hidden inside it. *Column* (1961), an eight-foot-high gray plywood shaft, moves from "process" to "unitary object," and points toward his later geometric sculptures. Morris meanwhile moved to a series of mixed-media works, some dealing with the subjectivity of measuring systems, as in *Three Rulers* (1963) presenting several rules of different lengths, yet each measuring 30 "inches."

All his exhibited sculpture had surrealistic, or at least enigmatic, overtones, until a 1964 show of large plywood objects established him as a minimal* artist. *Slab* and *Cloud* were simple wooden "boxes" painted battleship gray—one placed on the floor, the other hung from the ceiling. An inverted "L" cantilevered off the gallery wall, with its leg resting on the floor, while a triangular *Corner Piece* (1964)

occupied the intersection of two walls. All were based on four- by eight-foot sheets of plywood; all were related to (and structured by) the architecture of the room; and all were simple, geometric "gestalts"—"unitary objects" that could not be broken down into parts. One of the chief considerations in these pieces was to avoid relationships within the work itself; however, many observers could not see them as formalist development (or even as an aspect of pop art,* with its emphasis on the banal and ordinary), but concentrated on their lack of "craftsmanship," "expression," or "inspiration." From 1964–66 Morris produced a large number of similar works. Having eliminated color, texture, and dramatic incident in his work, by 1967 Morris was assembling groups of "unitary objects" into "permutable pieces." Here square, triangular, and wedge-shaped units were formed into larger geometric configurations. By rearranging the same fiberglass units periodically, he created many different pieces of sculpture out of the same elements.

Recently, Morris has abandoned these "boring" object-sculptures in favor of a more direct manipulation of material and a greater emphasis on the processes by which his works come into being. In 1967 he cut up bolts of felt and let them fall into self-determined configurations by hanging them on walls or dropping them in heaps on the floor. Such works were linked to the "anti-form" movement, which used soft materials to produce forms that could not be predicted in advance. Similar configurations resulted from his "earthworks" of 1968—literally heaps of dirt, often with bits of debris, integrated into the "composition." Far more striking are his "scatter pieces" (1968–69) in which the entire floor of a room is filled with pieces of metal (copper, aluminum, zinc, steel) and in another room colored thread, wire, and small mirrors.

Morris has long been interested in theater and the dance, and his work has become increasingly involved in "real life" situations. A series of steam pieces (1968–69) simply allows steam to escape from valves in the ground. A "process" work of 1969 involved riding a series of polo ponies back and forth over a given course until a path was worn in the grass; meanwhile a photographer recorded the "performance."

Morris' most recent works are an earth and sod "observatory" in Velsen, Holland, and several experimental film and videotape projects. His "Notes on Sculpture" (1966–69) and his articles on "Anti-Form" and "Notes on the Phenomenology of Making," all published in the art magazine *Artforum,* have given wide circulation to his ideas.   (E.C.G.)

Morse, Samuel Finley Breese (1791–1872).
Painter and inventor. Born in Charlestown, Mass., Morse went to England in 1811 to study painting under two Americans, Washington Allston* and Benjamin West.* Accepting the traditional attitude that history and literature furnished the artist's proper subject matter, he produced in 1813 a huge painting and a small sculpture, both entitled *The Dying Hercules* (both Yale). The sculpture has a nervous strength but the painting is a weakly drawn version of various Renaissance paintings. Neither work was well received in America, and Morse, returning in 1815, turned to portrait painting to support himself. Although he did not think highly of such painting, some of his best work was in this field, notably his *Lafayette* (1825–26, City Hall, New York City), in which the old soldier looms dramatically against a fiery sunset. Morse also did vigorous, colorful historical paintings with a meticulous accuracy of detail, as in *The Old House of Representatives* (1822, Corcoran), in which he portrayed eighty-six legislators and an Indian in the lofty hall. In 1826 he joined the architect Ithiel Town* and the landscape painter Thomas Cole* in founding the National Academy of Design.* In 1829 he went abroad with commissions to paint views and copies of Old Masters. One result of this trip was his painting *The Exhibition Gallery of the Louvre* (1832, Syracuse University), which shows a gallery hung with Rembrandts, Titians, and over thirty other identifiable masterpieces.

After his return to America in 1832, Morse turned to making the electrical experiments which led, in 1839, to his invention of the telegraph. As it began to bring him wealth and fame, he abandoned painting. He also introduced the daguerreotype process to America in 1839. Morse maintained his interest in art and remained president of the

1

2

National Academy of Design until 1845.

Although his fame as an inventor has eclipsed his accomplishments as a painter, Morse is nevertheless one of the major artists of the Romantic school. In addition to the hundreds of portraits that comprised the bulk of his oeuvre, and several historical canvases, he produced a few completely charming landscapes that are outstanding of their kind. An example is *The View From Apple Hill* (c. 1828).

(H.W.W.)

Moses, Anna Mary Robertson, known as "Grandma Moses" (1860–1961). Prolific, self-taught artist of Eagle Bridge, N.Y., who began painting at the age of seventy-seven, when her neuritis became too painful for her to make the yarn pictures that had regularly won prizes for her at country fairs. For almost a quarter of a century "Grandma Moses" ranked as the quintessential American folk painter, drawing her subject matter from the historic past of the rural area her family had inhabited for two centuries and celebrating the routine activities of a farm life that was rapidly giving way to 20th-century mechanization. In paintings such as *Hoosick Falls in Winter* (1943, Phillips) and *July 4th* (White House Collection) she demonstrated a native delight in color and pattern and an ability to communicate depth and distance in terms of formal relationships established on the picture plane without reference to pictorial perspective.

(M.J.G.)

Motherwell, Robert (1915–   ).
Born in Aberdeen, Wash., he grew up on the West Coast, but has lived most of his mature life in the East and has been associated with the New York school of painting since its inception early in the 1940s. He studied briefly at the Otis Institute in the 1920s and the California School of Fine Arts, San Francisco (1932). In 1937 he received a degree from Stanford University, and continued studying philosophy and esthetics at Harvard University (1937–38). During this period he painted on his own. In 1940–41 he studied art history at Columbia University, principally under Meyer Schapiro, who also introduced him to the European abstract and surrealist painters then congregating in New York City as a result of World War II, including Marcel

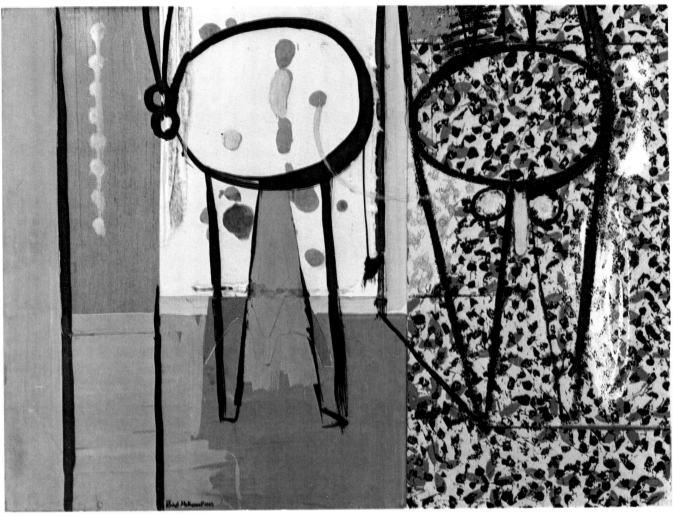

3

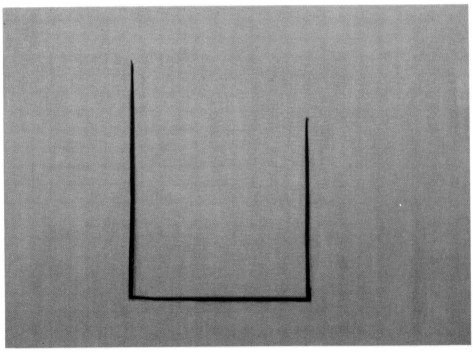

4

1. *Samuel Finley Breese Morse.* The Muse, 1827. *Metropolitan Museum of Art, N.Y. (gift of Herbert L. Pratt).*
2. *Anna Mary Robertson Moses (Grandma Moses).* The McDonel Farm, 1943. *Phillips Memorial Gallery, Washington, D.C.*
3. *Robert Motherwell.* Pancho Villa, Dead and Alive, 1943. *Museum of Modern Art, N.Y.*
4. *Robert Motherwell.* Open Study No. 22, 1968. *Collection Paul and Marianne Steiner, N.Y.*

Duchamp,* Max Ernst, André Masson, and Piet Mondrian. Particularly important was his friendship with the young Chilean surrealist (Roberto) Matta Echaurren, with whom he traveled to Mexico (1941). Through these associations and his travels in Europe, Motherwell became one of the most European-oriented of the American abstract expressionists. He settled in New York City in 1942 and began devoting himself professionally to painting, experimenting with surrealist automatism and exhibiting (1944) at Peggy Guggenheim's* gallery, Art of This Century.

During the early 1940s he became acquainted with leading American abstract expressionists, including Willem de Kooning,* Hans Hofmann,* William Baziotes,* Barnett Newman,* Adolph Gottlieb,* and Mark Rothko,* and with them conducted an art school in New York City, "Subjects of the Artist." He taught at Black Mountain College in North Carolina (1945, 1951), Hunter College (1951–58), and at Yale and Harvard universities.

Motherwell is rare among American abstract expressionists in that he was essentially an abstractionist from the beginning of his professional career. The *Little Spanish Prison* (1941, Modern Museum) and *Spanish Picture with Window* (1942, Modern Museum), his most important early surviving paintings, although suggestive of architectural scenes, are basically abstractions rooted in the vertical-horizontal organization of Piet Mondrian. In the paintings and collages of the 1940s (Motherwell, together with Jackson Pollock,* was one of the first American abstract expressionists to experiment with collage), the tendency toward geometric nonobjectivism persisted, although there were occasional excursions into a freer brush gesture and suggestions of figurative or landscape subjects deriving from literary associations, such as *Mallarmé's Swan* (1944–47, Cleveland) or his travels in Mexico (*Pancho Villa, Dead and Alive,* 1943, Modern Museum). The interest in figuration became more evident during the late 1940s; this was accompanied by a freely-brushed line and color structure. In 1948–49, almost by accident, he ventured upon a theme that was to become a signature for major works throughout the next twenty years: "Elegies to the Spanish Repub-

1

2

1. **Robert Motherwell.** Elegy to the Spanish Republic LV, *1960. Cleveland Museum of Art.*
2. **The Moultons.** Ebenezer Moulton, *silver pitcher presented to Isaac Harris, 1810. Museum of Fine Arts, Boston.*

lic." The elegies, of which he has executed well over a hundred, are generally monumental oil paintings—but also include small drawings and sketches in oil and gouache—predominantly painted in black on a white or light ground, in which black ovoid shapes are suspended between vertical panels.

While Motherwell, who is an immensely prolific artist, was producing innumerable elegies, he was also painting in a wide variety of styles and subjects, ranging from the freest drip and spatter expressionism to the most controlled color-field* combinations. Major paintings during the 1950s and 1960s have been accompanied by hundreds of drawings, collages, prints, and typographical experiments. Despite this range and variety, a consistency becomes evident if one compares the earliest paintings with the latest, the "Open" series. Although he has been affected by the automatism of the dadaists and the fantasies of the surrealists—as well as by aspects of Mondrian and the cubists—it is his debt to Matisse that is most evident in these recent works, which center on the themes of the wall and the window.

Motherwell began to exhibit in New York City during the 1940s. Since then he has had one-man exhibitions throughout the world, including a 1965 restrospective at the Museum of Modern Art in New York City. His paintings have been included in every major exhibition of American abstractionism and he has received many awards and honors. From 1958–71 he was married to the American painter Helen Frankenthaler.* (H.H.A.)

Moulthrop, Reuben (1763–1814).
Connecticut portraitist and wax-modeler. His waxworks were exhibited in Massachusetts, New York, and Pennsylvania, but his painting activities were apparently confined to Connecticut. Some of his canvases, such as the pendant portraits of *James Reynolds* and his wife *Mary Kimberly Reynolds* (both c.1790), are close in manner to the work of Winthrop Chandler, with large figures and abundant rendition of surrounding details. In others, the style changes drastically, often toward an intimate realism, as in the portrait of *Jonathan Edwards, Jr.* (Yale). In all of Moulthrop's work the sitter's personality was perceptively recorded, and a sculptural solidity, which may trace to

his wax modeling, was underscored by dark outlining of hands and other elements. Most of the work attributed to him shares a heavily crackled and alligatored surface due to his use of thick paint and an incompatible binding substance. (M.J.G.)

Moultons, The.
One of America's largest family of silversmiths, the Moultons began business in Newburyport in the 18th century and became the Towle Company* in the 19th century. Joseph (1694–1756) and his brother William (1720–c.1793) were the first to engage seriously in silversmithing. William moved to Marietta, Ohio, in 1788, but his son Joseph (1744–1816) continued the tradition, working in Newburyport in partnership with Theophilus Bradbury. Joseph's sons William (1772–1861); Ebenezer (1768–1824); Enoch (1780–1815), who moved to Maine; and Abel (1784–c.1840), who took over his father's business, all worked as silversmiths. Of these sons, William and Ebenezer produced the most interesting silver. William made jewelry in addition to supplying well-crafted church silver and other vessels, and his son Joseph (1814–1903) continued this business. Ebenezer worked in Boston until about 1820, when he returned to Newburyport; he is best known for his covered barrel-shaped pitcher (Boston) presented to Isaac Harris in 1810 and engraved with a view of Harris' heroic actions when the Old South Church was threatened by fire. (M.G.F.)

Mount, William Sidney (1807–68).
The outstanding genre painter of the 19th century. Mount was born in Setauket, Long Island, N.Y., and lived there and in the nearby villages of Stony Brook and Port Jefferson throughout his life, except for long sojourns in New York City. He came of a farm family, but his older brother, Henry Smith Mount, became a sign painter in New York City, and William Sidney became interested in art when he served as an apprentice in Henry's shop. In 1826 Mount became one of the first students at the newly established National Academy of Design,* remaining there one year. His earliest paintings were portraits and dramatic "history pieces" in a naive adaptation of the 18th-century grand manner. In 1830 he exhibited his first genre pic-

ture, *The Rustic Dance after a Sleighride* (private collection) which, although very immature in style and plagiarized from John Lewis Krimmel,* was an enormous success at the annual exhibition of the National Academy of Design (even winning him election as an associate), and it won the first prize in art at the annual trade fair sponsored by the American Institute of the City of New York. This success set Mount on the path of genre painting which, along with portraiture and some landscape, he followed for the rest of his career.

His development thereafter was very rapid, and he produced a steady flow of paintings of country types and incidents emphasizing the Long Island landscape. He was equally active as a portrait painter. His portraits are uneven and have been slighted by the critics, but at their best they are distinguished by the same precision and Ingres-like crispness that distinguish Mount's genre painting.

Disgruntled with the famous Art-Union,* whose annual lotteries did much for the recognition of American artists at home, Mount took up with William Schaus, a New York agent of a European dealer. Schaus had ten of Mount's paintings lithographed in Europe, where they were very widely circulated, so that Mount became the first American painter to be generally known to European collectors and art historians. Mount also repeatedly painted subjects that Schaus thought would sell abroad, especially black men playing musical instruments, such as *The Banjo Player* (1856, Suffolk Museum). Mount had, it is true, exhibited a predilection for black subjects before he ever met Schaus, and was, in fact, the first American painter to give blacks dignity and individuality in his art.

Mount was a typical country inventor. He was known for his fiddle playing, and he invented a "hollow-backed" violin that he felt was far superior to the Cremona model. He also created many innovations in boats. But most of his inventiveness went into the chemistry of painting. His diaries are filled with reports of experiments in pigments, brushes, studio lighting, and other aspects of the painter's craft.

The anecdotal, populistic aspect of Mount has been overemphasized. As a draftsman and painter he has not been given his due until recently. His

1. *Jan Müller.* Jacob's Ladder, 1958.
   Solomon R. Guggenheim Museum,
   N.Y.
2. *William Sidney Mount.* The Banjo
   Player, 1856. Suffolk Museum, Stony
   Brook, N.Y. (Melville Collection).
3. *William Sidney Mount.* The Truant
   Gamblers, 1835. New-York Histori-
   cal Society, N.Y.

4 & 5. *Mourning Pictures.* Artists unknown.
Both, Smithsonian Institution, Washington, D.C.

landscape drawings, particularly, are extraordinarily free in style and often unexpectedly summary and impressionistic; there are also a few paintings in the same manner.

Although leading museums (Boston, Chicago, Corcoran, Metropolitan, and others) have major works by Mount, nearly three-quarters of his known works are in one collection, that of the Suffolk Museum, founded by Ward Melville in Stony Brook, N.Y. At no other museum in the United States can the work of a single artist be studied in such detail. (A.F.)

Mourning Pictures.

Pictorial memorials burgeoned as an American folk art phenomenon that traces to the death of George Washington and continued into the 19th century as a "ladies art form" taught at female seminaries. The iconography remains remarkably constant regardless of the identity of the deceased or the technique employed—pencil, watercolor on paper or silk, and embroidery all having been popular media for such works. An elaborate example from about 1810 is the anonymous work, *Mourning Picture—Philo Day* (Abby Aldrich Rockefeller), in which typical elements of church, tomb, obelisk, urn, weeping willow, and bereaved mourner are all incorporated—in this case further embellished with a symbolic figure of Charity and clusters of grass that limply reflect the sorrowful form of the willow. (M.J.G.)

Mitchell, Joan (1926–).

Painter, born in Hamburg, Germany, and died, prematurely, in New York City. With the rise of Nazism, he and his family were forced to leave Germany in 1933, going to Czechoslovakia and then France. In 1941, with the invasion of France, he escaped to Spain, Portugal, and then the United States. After working at odd jobs during World War II, he began to study painting in 1945, first at the Art Students League and then with Hans Hofmann* between 1945 and 1950. Thus his career as a painter spans only ten years. He experimented first with cubism* and then with a form of abstract expressionism* influenced by Hofmann. In 1953 his work became more representational, first in the form of a kind of landscape with a suggestion of figuration. By 1956 the figuration had

4

5

taken over in a strange expressionist manner that owes something to early 20th-century German expressionism and something to late 19th-century symbolist painting. Within a somewhat abstract landscape made up of loose, rich color patterns, he presented conclaves of frontalized figures with mask-like faces suggesting the ghosts or demons of medieval mythology, as in *Jacob's Ladder* (1958, Guggenheim).

(H.H.A.)

Munday, Richard (c.1690–1739). Carpenter-builder. Known to have been in Newport, R.I., by 1713, and to have kept a tavern there. Changing his profession, he called himself "house-carpenter" on the deed of a house he bought in 1721, and he may even have built some houses. His first public commission was Trinity Church, Newport (1725–26). It was built of wood, with an elongated plan and interior decorative and structural members deriving from Christ Church, Boston, and ultimately from Sir Christopher Wren's London churches, though somewhat heavier in its classical proportions. His Old Colony House (1739), built of brick with brown rustic quoins (projecting cornerstones) and window surrounds, and white wood trim, is situated conspicuously in the center of Newport and has always been admired for its stateliness. The somewhat cumbersome, chopped-off pediment, without pilasters to rest upon, adds a provincial quality predictable for a carpenter without professional training.

(P.F.N.)

Murphy, J. Francis (1853–1921). Landscape painter, born in Oswego, N.Y. He was self-taught and his early work is in a dry, timid manner. But this gave way to a Barbizon*-influenced style during the mid-1880s, about the time he was elected an associate of the National Academy of Design* (1887). Fifteen years later he changed his style again and began to turn out "tonalist" works that were a tremendous success. He concentrated on a limited range; his bare autumnal fields with a suggestion of trees, as in *Frostbitten Wood and Field* (1914, Freer), were painted in a vigorous impasto that only hinted at natural forms, leaving much to accidents of brushwork and nuances of brownish hues. The results were sometimes praised as deeply subjec-

tive poetry, sometimes criticized as decorative at the expense of the true spirit of nature.

(D.W.S.)

Muybridge, Eadweard (1830–1904). Photographer. Born Edward J. Muggeridge near London, Muybridge emigrated to the United States in 1852. When he learned photography is not known, but in the late 1860s he was commissioned by the U.S. government to photograph the Pacific Coast area. In 1867 in Yosemite Valley he made a series of excellent large views (16 x 20 inches), which were exhibited in America and abroad and brought him wide recognition. In 1868 he photographed in Alaska for a government survey and in 1870 opened a studio in California.

At the instigation of Leland Stanford, a former governor of California and a prominent horseman, he undertook in 1872 a pioneering project in stop-action photography to determine if a horse when galloping ever lifts all four feet off the ground. He set up a battery of cameras with fast-acting shutters actuated by a moving horse, but the relative insensitivity of the wet plate negative process made the results inconclusive. After spending 1875–76 photographing in Central America, he returned to California and again applied himself to recording the movement of horses. With improved dry plates and electrically controlled shutters he successfully documented the action of a horse's legs at various gaits. He then invented the zoopraxiscope, which projected his photographs on a wall in rapid succession so that the subjects appeared to be moving. This work, enthusiastically received by scientists and artists everywhere, paved the way for cinematography.

In 1883 Muybridge was invited to the University of Pennsylvania to make studies of human and animal locomotion. During the two years he spent on this project he invented a sophisticated system of multiple cameras that could photograph a subject simultaneously from different angles. The results were published in *Animal Locomotion: An Electrophotographic Investigation of Consecutive Phases of Animal Movement* (1887) in eleven volumes containing 781 plates. These remarkable stop-action pictures have been widely distributed and have had a great influence on the way artists have represented action.

(V.D.C.)

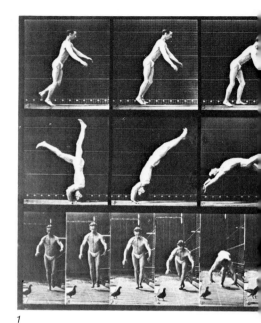

1

2

1. **Eadweard Muybridge.** Head-spring, a Flying Pigeon Interfering, *1885, plate 365 from* Animal Locomotion. *George Eastman House, Rochester, N.Y.*
2. **Richard Munday.** Trinity Church, interior, Newport, R.I., 1726.

Myers, Jerome (1867–1940).

A painter associated with portrayals of New York City's Lower East Side. He was born in Virginia and lived in Philadelphia and Baltimore before going to New York in 1886. He worked as a theater scene painter while studying at Cooper Union and at the Art Students League* under George De-Forest Brush.* In 1896 he visited Paris.

For years Myers drew city scenes in pencil and pastel. In 1900 William Macbeth became his dealer and encouraged him to use oil. Myers subsequently began to exhibit widely and joined the art circle of John Sloan.* He showed in the exhibition of Independent Artists* (1910) and helped to organize the Armory Show* (1913). Myers enjoyed only intermittent success in selling his paintings but received some recognition, including several prizes from the National Academy and the Carnegie Prize of the Carnegie Institute (1936). Shortly before his death he wrote his autobiography, *Artist in Manhattan.* Myers' typical paintings (and etchings) were sympathetic views of children and immigrants in slum settings, treated in a flattened, semidecorative style.

(D.W.S.)

Myers, Myer (1723–95).

Outstanding silversmith. Born in New York, he became a freeman in 1746 and was active in the Shearith Israel Synagogue, making a pair of rimonim (silver scroll bells used to ornament the wooden rollers on which the Torah is wound) for the congregation about 1765. Fashioned of pierced and repoussé bulbous shafts, they were surmounted by a gilt crown and encircled with three tiers of bells. He made similar rimonim about 1765 for Touro Synagogue in Newport and for Congregation Mikveh Israel in Philadelphia (see Church Silver). Myers also made alms dishes and a baptismal bowl for Presbyterian churches in New York.

During the revolution he went to Norwalk, Conn., and is believed to have spent some time in Stratford as well. From 1780–83 he was in Philadelphia, returning to New York after the evacuation of the British. He was selected chairman of the Gold and Silver Smith's Society.

Myers' domestic silver includes some unusual forms demonstrating his ability to keep up with changing taste. About 1765 he made a pair of candlesticks in the rococo style and a shell-footed stand and pair of snuffers for John and Catherine Reade (both Yale). A large pierced basket (Metropolitan) was made for Samuel and Susan Cornell, for whom he also made the only known dish ring (Yale) by an American silversmith. Other rare forms by Myers include a pair of coasters owned by the Schuyler family (New York Hist.), a dish cross (Yale), and a tea caddy fashioned in the shape of contemporary Chinese porcelain vases. Many of Myers' teapots, coffeepots, and sugar bowls are in the fully developed rococo style with inverted pear shapes, gadrooning or engraved borders, and a closely cropped circular base. A few mourning rings and a large gold shoe buckle survive to show his work in gold. (M.G.F.)

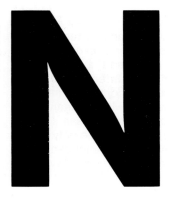

Nadelman, Elie (1882–1946).
Sculptor. Born in Warsaw, Poland, he studied at the Art Academy there. By 1903 he was in Paris, where he was first influenced by Rodin but soon became interested in avant-garde trends there. Nadelman's experiments with form appear to have been largely independent of the cubists, and he even claimed that in some of his drawings of about 1906 and a modeled head of around 1907 he was actually in advance of Picasso in the defraction and reorganization of natural form. His friends of these years—Leo and Gertrude Stein, André Gide, Picasso, and Matisse—recognized him as one of the leading forces in the modern movement. The originality of his experiments may be seen in the bronze *Standing Female Nude* (c.1909, Modern Museum) in which naturalism is sacrificed to a simplification and reorganization of natural form. The abstract beauty of curve and countercurve, mass and countermass, became exceedingly important to Nadelman; these stylistic elements dominated his art for the next thirty years. In reducing the human figure to a series of abstract curves, he sought to capture the essence of sculpture. This may be seen in his *Dancer* (1918). The refinement and reduction of human features to an abstract form of great elegance are visible in two of his best-known works— *Man in the Open Air* (c.1915, Modern Museum) and *Man in a Top Hat* (1927, Modern Museum). Both of these were produced in America, for with the outbreak of World War I in 1914, Nadelman had fled to London and then to New York. In America his work became popular, in part through the patronage of Helena Rubenstein, who commissioned numerous of his sophisticated marble heads for her beauty salons. In 1919 he married a wealthy widow and frequently took high society as

his subject. In the stock market crash of 1929, however, he suffered severe financial losses. He went into seclusion, and during the 1930s produced only a series of very small terra-cotta figures. In 1933 he lost his studio and kiln, and two years later some workmen accidentally destroyed many of his plaster and wooden pieces, bringing his brilliant career to an end. (W.C.)

Nakashima, George (1905–   ).
Woodworker, architect, and designer of furniture, best known for his excellent craftsmanship and the classical purity of his style. Of Japanese descent, Nakashima was born in Spokane, Wash., studied architecture and forestry at the University of Washington, attended the École Americaine des Beaux-Arts at Fontainebleau, and continued with architecture at the Massachusetts Institute of Technology. He studied wood craftsmanship while traveling in France, India, and Japan, returning to America in the early 1940s. He became critical of architectural practice in America as compared to the craftsmanship of Japanese masterbuilders, who designed as well as built their own structures. Woodworking became his primary occupation. After a period in a World War II internment camp, where he refined his techniques with a carpenter trained in Japan, Nakashima built a workshop and home in New Hope, Pa., and there he employs twelve assistants, many of whom are European-trained. By 1949 he was firmly established, and he has designed furniture for Knoll* Associates and Widdicomb. Nakashima personally oversees all steps of production, from the selection of woods to finishing. His work combines old traditions of workmanship with the recognition of modern design requirements. Details of wood coloration and grains are highlighted and he approaches the piece of wood

as if it were an uncut gem. His furniture is simple and severe, influenced both by Shaker* design and Japanese grace.
(R.S.)

Nakian, Reuben (1897–   ).
Sculptor. Born in Long Island, N.Y., Nakian studied in New York City at the Art Students League* and the Independent Art School. Apprenticed to sculptor Paul Manship* in 1916, Nakian became close friends with the French sculptor Gaston Lachaise and shared a studio with him in the 1920s. Influenced by Lachaise and another sculptor friend, William Zorach,* he produced bronze and marble portrait heads and full-length figures, including an eight-foot-high statue of Babe Ruth (1934). His work, with its full, rounded forms and highly finished surfaces, was widely accepted. He exhibited regularly at a New York gallery, at the Whitney Studio Club (later the Whitney Museum), the American Art Association, and the Museum of Modern Art. In the mid-1930s he met Arshile Gorky* and Willem de Kooning,* whose painting led Nakian to bring his own work closer to the aims of these leading avant-garde Americans. His works became more improvisatory and his surfaces less smooth. By the late 1940s he had achieved his mature style, a sculptural equivalent of action painting, in which roughly textured abstract forms achieve a spontaneous monumentality. In his "drawing in stone," improvisatory strokes made in a terra-cotta surface create an effect of high relief, often suggesting mythological subjects. In 1959 his large *Rape of Lucrece,* an abstraction in bronze, was acquired by the Museum of Modern Art. He had a retrospective there in 1966. (C.R.)

Nameboards.
Carved and painted or gilded wooden panels made to identify American

ships. A law at the close of the War of 1812 required identification at the stern of all sailing vessels; later legislation called for identification on both sides of the prow, and steamboats had to carry identification on the pilot house. Carved trailboards that swept back from the figurehead and carved stern decorations are recorded in American shipbuilding as early as 1689; but the actual appearance of such panels prior to the Revolution is unknown. American ship plans for the late 18th century show scrolls, foliage, flags, cannon, and national shields on the trailboards and occasionally human and animal figures as well. After the enactment of the identification laws, shipcarvers incised lettering to their skills and produced elegant work in a wealth of 19th-century letterforms, often terminating the panels with foliage scrolls or feathered flourishes. The tapered trailboards tend to be considerably more elaborate than the symmetrical sternboards (also called quarter boards). Good early 19th-century examples of the former are a board from the *B. L. Leach* and a somewhat later one from the *Frances S. Dubois* (Maryland Historical Society).

Nameboards retrieved from wrecks or abandoned vessels have been collected as an expression of American folk art and in Nantucket are popularly used as exterior building decorations. A considerable collection of nameboards carried by Chesapeake Bay ships, both sailing vessels and steamboats, is in the Mariners Museum in Newport News, Va.   (M.J.G.)

National Academy of Design, The.
The most important art institution in America throughout much of the 19th century. The Academy was founded in 1826 "under the exclusive control and management of the professional artists," in reaction to the management of the staid American Academy of the Fine Arts (1801–40) by businessmen and amateurs. First founded as the New York Drawing Society in 1825, the Academy was established by fifteen original members, including William Dunlap,* Asher B. Durand,* Samuel F. B. Morse,* and Ithiel Town,* the architect, who then chose an additional fifteen, including Thomas Cole,* Rembrandt Peale,* and John Vanderlyn.* Formation of the National Academy helped make New York the art

1

2

1. *Reuben Nakian.* The Dance of Death, *1967, plaster for bronze casting. Egan Gallery, N.Y.*
2. *Elie Nadelman.* Standing Female Nude, *c.1909. Museum of Modern Art, N.Y.*
3. *Elie Nadelman.* Man in a Top Hat, *c.1927. Museum of Modern Art, N.Y. (Abby Aldrich Rockefeller Fund).*

1

2

center of the country, and almost every ambitious artist of the period sought membership in it. Its annual spring exhibition, and their public reviews, were highlights of the New York art season, and for many years the Academy fostered the most advanced American art. Its presidents in its early days included Morse (1826–45), Durand (1845–61), Daniel Huntington* (1862–70, 1877–90), and Worthington Whittredge* (1874–77). However, the Academy too eventually came under attack, first from a younger group of Paris- and Munich-trained artists, who founded the Society of American Artists* in 1877. Although by 1906 the Society had merged into the Academy, even the "new" Academy remained conservative and under the control of such men as the muralist Edwin H. Blashfield.* Thus the formation of American modernism by The Eight* and by the Alfred Stieglitz* group at Gallery 291 occurred outside of the Academy. Even today the Academy remains a historic rather than an active institution. (T.E.S.)

Natzler, Gertrud (1908–71) and **Otto** (1908–   ).
Among the foremost American ceramists, best known for simple, elegantly proportioned shapes and an enormous variety and perfection of glazes. Both Natzlers, who were born in Vienna, had no formal training when they began their collaborations in 1933. Otto Natzler then began an intensive study of the chemistry of glazes; he became an authority on the subject, and eventually developed some 2500 glazes. Among them is the now-famous "crater" glaze, a pitted surface of subdued and subtle color. Gertrud Natzler created the ceramic shapes, developing a straightforward, classical style that was beautifully disposed toward the glazes her husband then applied. They moved to the United States in 1939 and settled in Los Angeles. They have received innumerable awards for their gemlike utilitarian pieces. *Teardrop* (1964, Johnson Coll.) is a perfectly shaped earthenware tear, rising 22¼ inches to a slightly open neck. A reduction-fired sang-mariposa glaze complements its shape. (R.S.)

Nauman, Bruce (1941–   ).
Sculptor and experimenter with mixed media. Born in Ft. Wayne, Ind., Nauman

1. *Bruce Nauman.* Untitled, *1967, rope and wax over plaster. Leo Castelli Gallery, N.Y.*

2. *John Neagle.* Pat Lyon at the Forge, *1829. Pennsylvania Academy of the Fine Arts, Philadelphia.*

390

studied at the University of Wisconsin and the University of California. After producing a series of anti-form works in such diverse materials as cloth and latex, he began in 1967 to present visual equivalents of familiar phrases; thus, *Waxing Hot* is a photograph of the artist waxing the wooden letters "H-O-T." *From Hand to Mouth* is a cast of the portion of the artist's body extending from his hand to his mouth. These and other Duchampian (see Marcel Duchamp) puns gave way in 1969 to films, video tapes, and holograms that show the artist grimacing, tumbling onto the floor, and performing repetitious motions. Since 1970 Nauman has constructed architectural alterations. Employing sound-proofing, intense lighting and video monitors, they isolate the senses from each other, giving a heightened if artifical physical awareness to the participant. Nauman's work has been seen regularly in one-man shows in New York City since 1968, and in numerous group shows in Europe and America. (C.R.)

Neagle, John (1796–1865).
Portrait painter. Although he worked for a time in New York and in early life traveled through the South as an itinerant painter, his career is identified with the Philadelphia art community. He began to paint professionally in 1818. In 1825 he received some friendly criticism from Gilbert Stuart,* whose portrait he painted and by whose work he was much influenced. In the next year he was commissioned by Patrick Lyon, a well-to-do Philadelphia manufacturer, to paint the picture for which Neagle will always be best remembered. *Pat Lyon at the Forge* (versions at Boston and Pennsylvania) is a full-length portrait in a startling variation of the formal tradition. Far from wanting to commemorate his success, Lyon wished to be remembered as the Irish locksmith who had been sent to prison on a trumped-up charge, his guilt too readily accepted by the city's respectable elements. Proved innocent, he had prospered, but was in no mood to be pictured as one of the class from whom he had suffered so much. Neagle's task, therefore, was to adapt the composition of the conventional portrait to this new point of view, and he has done so with intricacy and skill.

Within the accepted tradition, he could also compose a portrait with spirit and a measure of originality, as may be seen in his oft-repeated and acclaimed full-length *Henry Clay* of 1843 (Union League, Philadelphia and Capitol Building, Washington, D.C.). His large body of smaller, domestic portraiture won him praise as a brilliant colorist, and is distinguished by a perceptive, forthright delineation of character. He could paint women with charm, but excelled in his portraits of men. His *James Fenimore Cooper* (Yale) is a fine example of his mature style. (C.C.S.)

Neal, John (1793–1876).
Art critic and drawing teacher. He was born in Portland, Me., and traveled throughout the United States. He was a roving poet and novelist and a pungent, energetic commentator on the culture of his times. He contributed to leading magazines and was himself editor of *New England Galaxy, Brother Jonathan,* and *The Yankee.* In Britain, 1823–27, his articles appeared in *Blackwood's Edinburgh Magazine.* His sensitive and sound judgment and blunt, fluent style, combined with driving energy and a wide personal acquaintance among artists made him a figure of first rank in the development of American taste. (C.C.S.)

Nelson, George (1908–).
Furniture and industrial designer, and architect. He was born in Hartford, Conn., graduated from Yale University in 1931, and won the Rome Prize in Architecture a year later. After studying in Rome he became associate editor of *Architectural Forum* in 1935. At the same time he worked as an architect (Fairchild House, New York City, 1941). While collaborating on a book, *Tomorrow's House* (1945), he came to grips with the problem of storage, and invented the "storage wall," a system of interchangeable, flexible parts, architectural in appearance, but not built in. He left *Architectural Forum* in 1947 and opened his own office, working mainly on design problems. He also became director of design in the furniture firm of Herman Miller, Inc.,* and that year he published a devastating criticism of the furniture industry in *Fortune* magazine.

Nelson has designed furniture; exhibits (notably the American National Exhibition in Moscow, 1959, and the Chrysler Exhibition, New York World's Fair, 1964); graphics; products such as clocks; and residential, institutional, and commercial buildings. Always concerned with overall problems rather than individual pieces, he eliminated the boxy, bulky substructure of upholstery in 1963 by designing the "Sling Sofa" of continuous tubular chromed steel supported by a T-bar inserted in the tubing. That year he also designed a so-called Catenary Group of chairs and table, in which the chairs consist of horizontal pillows hanging from cables swung from a chrome-plated steel framework. In 1964 Herman Miller introduced Nelson's "Action Office" furniture group composed of interchangeable parts for a flexible and efficient use of working space.

Nelson has lectured at Yale University, Columbia College, and Pratt Institute, and his campaign for practicality and simplicity in design has been recorded in such books as *Industrial Architecture of Albert Kahn* (1939) and *Problems of Design* (1957), and as editor of *Chairs, Display, Storage and Living Spaces.* (D.P.)

Neoclassicism.
A style in painting, sculpture, and architecture based upon a revival of interest in the arts of Greece and Rome. Baroque* and rococo* were expressions of foreign elegance never accepted comfortably in early American taste. The classic revival that followed the rococo not only gained immediate popularity in Europe but became a prevalent American influence for a hundred years. The older forms had long been associated with an effete aristocracy—this one, with the straightforward, sturdy qualities of the ancient Roman republic, of Cato, Cincinnatus, and other heroes with whom the American of the Revolutionary era identified himself. One of the first exemplars of the new style in painting was an American, Benjamin West,* who had been stimulated by excitement over the discoveries of the Roman ruins at Pompeii and Herculaneum. He brought the style to England and established its popularity there, notably with his *Agripinna with the Ashes of Germanicus* (Yale). Precise, linear, more restrained in coloring, it was intellectual rather than emotional and appealed strongly to the revolutionary spirit of the times. It dominated

the art of Revolutionary and Napoleonic France, and the French version reached America in the art of John Vanderlyn* and others. In American painting after the turn of the century it was tempered by the new romanticism of the times, but remained a dominant influence in architecture and sculpture. (C.C.S.)

Neo-Grec Style.

An architectural style of the 1870s that developed out of the French Second Empire* style of the 1860s. It should not be confused with the Greek revival* style of the first half of the 19th century. Although it appeared in France in the 1840s, it did not reach our shores until Vermont-born Richard Morris Hunt,* graduate of the École des Beaux-Arts in Paris, designed the Lenox Library (at 70th Street and Fifth Avenue in New York City) in 1870. Other neo-Grec buildings by Hunt in New York City include the Roosevelt Building at 480 Broadway, and the base of the Statue of Liberty. It attempted to reconcile such modern materials as iron and glass with fine masonry materials. Its ornament was a much simplified and stylized version of Greek ornament. Low pediments cut from one block of stone served as door and window lintels, and a linear type of ornament was cut in the face of these lintels. Pilasters usually had widely spaced vertical grooves, and columns and pilasters had Ionic capitals derived from the Greek temple of Apollo Epicurius. Many commercial store fronts had cast-iron columns characterized by flat sides, with the plane facing the street profiled by moldings above and below vertical grooves.

The noted architectural critic Montgomery Schuyler said of neo-Grec: "It professed to offer the reconciliation of the classicism of the schools with the new romantic impulse." Like Victorian Gothic,* it did not long survive the financial panic of 1873; yet it continued to appear as a form of ornament in urban row houses until it was merged with the Queen Anne* style of the 1880s. (A.B.)

Neutra, Richard J. (1892–1970).

The only American architect who had a major share in developing the International style.* Born in Austria, he was educated at the Imperial Institute of Technology in Vienna and the University of Zurich. In Vienna he worked

under Adolf Loos, an early exponent of stripped architecture, and was exposed to the new "puritanism" in modern architecture. From 1921 to 1923 he served in the Berlin office of Erich Mendelsohn. He moved to the United States in 1923 and worked briefly in New York, in Chicago, and with Frank Lloyd Wright* in Wisconsin. In 1925 he went to Los Angeles, where he was at first closely associated with Rudolph Schindler.* These two architects, along with the planner Carol Arnovici, produced a number of designs, the most significant of which was the one for the League of Nations Building competition (1926). Neutra then began to work on an ideal city of the future. It included the streamlined imagery of the machine and deserves comparison with Le Corbusier's urban plans of the 1920s, and Wright's Broadacre city project of the 1930s. Neutra's first building in the United States was the Jardin Apartments (1927) in Los Angeles, a reinforced-concrete structure that was chosen for the famous 1932 exhibition, "The International Style: Architecture Since 1922," at the Museum of Modern Art. In 1929 his steel-framed Lovell House in Los Angeles (also included in the exhibition) ranks with Le Corbusier's Villa Savoye (Poissy, France, 1929–31) and the Bauhaus* Building (Dessau, Germany, 1926) of Walter Gropius* as a monument of the new style. In fact, with its thin steel frame, paperlike "gunite" surface, and extensive use of glass, Neutra's house fulfills the ideal of the new style more than does the work of any European of the 1920s. As image, the Lovell House was equally successful, for it was not, like the Savoye or Bauhaus buildings, exclusively an object of high art; it was also a remarkable balance between the art of pure form and the mechanistic imagery of the machine product. It established Neutra's international reputation.

Despite the Depression, Neutra maintained a successful practice during the 1930s and, together with Schindler, helped to establish Los Angeles as a center of modern domestic architecture. He designed a number of modular steel and plywood experimental houses in California during these years, the most impressive being the metal-sheathed Von Sternberg House (Northridge, 1936), the Beard House (Altadena, 1935), and the Miller House

(Palm Springs, 1938). In the late 1930s and early 1940s the stringency of his machine imagery mellowed and he began to use more wood, as in the Nesbitt House (Los Angeles, 1942). He also designed several impressive multiple-housing units, including the Strathmore Apartments, the Landfair Apartments (both in Los Angeles, 1938) and the extensive Channel Heights Housing Project (San Pedro, 1942). His Corona Avenue School (1935) at Bell continued the earlier California tradition of fully open-air schools.

After the war Neutra expanded his practice and began to receive large-scale commissions. He designed the United States Embassy (1960) in Karachi, Pakistan, and in 1962 in Los Angeles he designed the new Hall of Records in association with Robert Alexander, Honnold, and Rex, and others. Residential design continued to occupy his attention during the 1950s and 1960s; the best known of his single-family homes were the Tremaine House (Montecito, 1948) and the Yew House (Los Angeles, 1957). Like other proponents of the International style, Neutra lectured and wrote extensively. His 1927 volume *Wie Baut Amerika* ("How Does America Build") provided Europeans with a close look at American industrial and commercial architecture and at several early modern buildings on the West Coast. Later books, such as *Survival through Design* (1954) and *Building with Nature* (1971), are mainly theoretical. During his last years he divided his time between Vienna, where he lectured and supervised his European commissions, and Los Angeles, where he maintained his principal office. (D.G.)

Nevelson, Louise (1900–).

One of America's foremost contemporary sculptors, she was born in Kiev, Russia, and was brought to America at the age of five. Her childhood was passed in the rockbound coastal area of Maine, where she learned to observe the powerful natural forces that were later to enter her work as specific motifs.

When she moved to New York City at the age of twenty, Nevelson, with characteristic energy, threw herself into the study of painting and drawing, while at the same time taking lessons in voice and dramatics. After attending

1

2

1. **Richard Neutra.** *Von Sternberg House, Northridge, Cal., 1936.*
2. **Richard Neutra.** *United States Embassy, Karachi, Pakistan, 1960.*

the Art Students League* (1929–30), she went to Munich in 1931 to study with Hans Hofmann.* Returning to New York, she was chosen by the Mexican artist Diego Rivera to assist on a mural at the New Workers' School in 1932. She traveled extensively in Mexico and Latin America; her interest in the pre-Columbian past was partly inspired by her natural affinity for myth and legend. When she held her first one-man exhibition in 1941, her work was immediately identified with primitive sources. Her terra-cottas and wood pieces were handled with a knowing roughness, and alluded to ancient legends.

It was not until 1955, however, that her broad interests coalesced into a characteristic theatrical ensemble of symbolic forms. She exhibited her works under the general title of "Ancient Games and Ancient Places" and one critic thought she had created "a sculptural landscape that is ageless and permanent." The following year she exhibited black wood sculptures in an ensemble called *The Royal Voyage.* Complete with the personages of king and queen, it unified a host of metaphors by means of controlled dim lighting and the uniformity of dusty black surfaces. In 1958 she exhibited *The Moon Garden Plus One* in which the prototypes of her stacked-box style appeared. Soon after, she became interested in the ensemble of allusive forms, each in a composition within a rectangular container. These could be moved and rearranged at will, making her one of the first American sculptors to realize what has come to be called an "environmental" conception (see Environmental Art). These boxed reveries generated a great deal of excitement, resulting partly from her resourceful use of found materials—dadoes, bits of furniture, radio chassis, and finials from Victorian chairs—and partly in the veiled poetic meanings. Nevelson moved freely from her theatrical blacks to a period in which everything was dazzling white (perhaps a reminder of her New England background) and later into a "golden age" where all her sculptures were sprayed with gilt.

During the mid-1960s, she turned to other materials and more open forms, making plastic cubes through which the light could penetrate. Working first in formica and later in steel, she

1

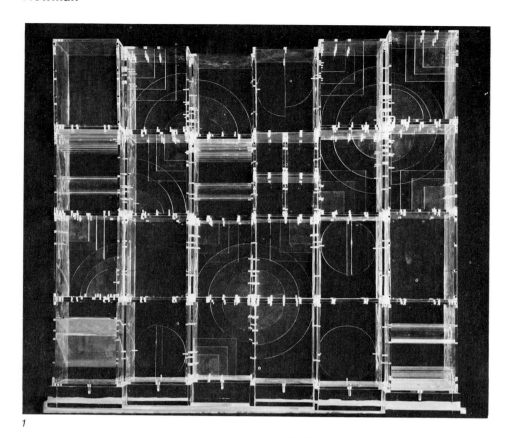

2

developed a more austere vocabulary, suited to the architectural uses the new huge pieces would serve. More recently, she has returned to wood, and ensembles of boxed images that hug the walls, but incorporating the great simplifications of her plastic experiments. Often there is a systematic modular schema within which only minute details differ.

Since the mid-1950s, her works have been exhibited all over the world, and have been acquired by institutions in numerous countries. In 1967 she had a major retrospective exhibition at the Museum of Modern Art in New York City, and in 1970, at the Whitney Museum. She has shown in the Venice Biennial, the Tate Gallery in London, Carnegie and Guggenheim Internationals, and Musée Rodin in Paris, and has received numerous honors. (D.A.)

Newman, Barnett (1905–70).
Painter. Newman was born in New York, N.Y., and he attended the Art Students League* during his last year of high school and while at City College. Upon graduation in 1927 he became a partner in his father's clothing manufacturing company. Although he remained in the business for ten years, he continued to visit galleries and museums with his friend Adolph Gottlieb* and was a substitute art teacher in public high schools. In 1944–45 he began a series of calligraphic, automatic, surrealist drawings. Out of these came his first paintings: "cosmic landscapes" such as *Gea* (1945) and *Genetic Moment* (1947). All dealt with the subject of genesis; however, the circular female forms and vertical male shafts were soon converted into circles and abstract stripes that acted no longer as shapes but as divisions. In 1948 with Mark Rothko,* William Baziotes,* and Robert Motherwell* he founded the school "Subjects of the Artist."

In 1946–49 Newman appeared in four group shows and wrote a number of catalog introductions for exhibitions. In one of these he indicated the kind of intellectual and emotional content with which he would thereafter be preoccupied: "The basis of an aesthetic act is the pure idea . . . the artist's problem is the idea complex that makes contact with mystery—of life, of men, of nature, of the hard black chaos that is death, or the grayer, softer

3

4

1. **Louise Nelson.** Model for Atmosphere and Environment, Ice Palace I, *1967, clear lucite. Pace Gallery, N.Y.*

2. **Louise Nelson.** Atmosphere and
Environment V, *1967, aluminum and
black epoxy enamel. Pace Gallery,
N.Y.*

3. **Barnett Newman.** Vir Heroicus Sub-
limis, *1951. Museum of Modern Art,
N.Y. (gift of Mr. and Mrs. Ben
Heller).*

4. **Barnett Newman.** Triad, *1965. Collection Kimiko and John G. Powers,
N.Y.*

chaos that is tragedy." Newman had become aware of the dilemma facing modern artists: where to go from the geometry and compositional balances of European abstractionists Malevich and Mondrian. Part of Newman's solution was always to seek meanings beyond mere formalism. The other half of his solution came in 1948 with a small painting called *Onement I.* In this painting an orange "stripe" cuts the red-brown canvas into two equal sections, with each part equally weighted, so that there is no sense of composition or foreground-background, but rather of pure color and classical harmony. During the next four years Newman developed this theme and produced some of the outstanding paintings of his career. Despite his reduction of the picture plane to areas of relatively flat color broken only by bands of other colors, as in *Purple in the Shadow of Red* (1963, Detroit), Newman was never involved in decorative art. Rather, he employed minimum means to achieve maximum meaning. He used his stripes sometimes to limit, sometimes to define, sometimes to inflect the color, and in his larger works the spectator is enveloped by shaped emanations of color and light. These paintings reveal his feeling for scale, proportion, and for an absolute quantity of a given color. Newman had his first one-man show in 1950, and it was a critical disaster; so was his second show (in 1951). His work was attacked by all segments of the art world, including friends and fellow artists, for being "decorative," "empty," and "fraudulent." It was felt that he had carried the "absurdity and purism" of Mondrian and Malevich too far—an opinion bolstered by the fact that his fellow abstract expressionists were producing passionate, gestural, "painterly" paintings.

Newman retreated into isolation, refusing all exhibitions until a retrospective of his work at Bennington College in Vermont in 1958. After this he began to emerge as a pioneer figure for a generation of younger artists, serving as a link between abstract expressionism* and the color-field* and minimal* painters. More than any other member of his generation Newman, with his vast areas of pure color, is responsible for establishing color-field painting. In 1966 he exhibited his *Stations of the Cross* at the Guggen-

heim Museum, fourteen black and white paintings that explored the nuances of Christ's passion without resorting to "anecdote" or "sentimental illustrations"—a continuation of his idea of the abstract shape as "a vehicle for an abstract thought-complex, a carrier of awesome feelings...." In 1950 Newman extracted his painted stripe and cast it into real space in the plaster sculpture *Here I (to Marcia)* (private collection). He produced two similar sculptures, as well as the twenty-foot-high *Broken Obelisk* (1967 in the Rothko Chapel, Houston, Tex.) related to such later triangular-shaped paintings as *Jericho* (1969). *Broken Obelisk* (1967), with its shaft balanced on a pyramid, perhaps summarizes Newman's involvement with classical stability, order, and permanence; while his sensuous color paintings, with their classical proportions and spiritual and heroic overtones, made him one of the most influential artists of his time.

(E.C.G.)

New York School, see Abstract Expressionism.

Niehaus, Charles (1855–1935).
Sculptor. A native of Cincinnati, Ohio, he began his studies at the McMicken School of Design there. In 1877 he attended the Royal Academy in Munich for four years; his style was to retain much of the German academic tradition. He returned to the United States, settling in Cincinnati, and was at once commissioned to make statues of the assassinated President Garfield, one in marble (c.1883) for Statuary Hall (U.S. Capitol) and one in bronze for the city of Cincinnati. To execute these works he returned to Rome, where, under the spell of antiquity, he worked in a neoclassical style (see Neoclassicism), ignoring the Parisian style that was by then the dominant influence on American sculpture. While in Rome (1883–85), he created several ideal works, among them the nude *Caestus* (Metropolitan) and *Athlete Scraping Himself with a Strigil,* both greatly influenced by Roman statuary. Returning to America in 1886, he established his studio in New York. He was elected to the National Sculpture Society in 1893 and received important commissions for a set of bronze doors and statues for the Library of Congress. One of Niehaus' finest works was the

full-length bronze of the scientist Hahnemann (1900) for Washington, D.C. His work was prominent at the Pan-American (1901, Buffalo) and Louisiana Purchase (1904, St. Louis) expositions. Niehaus was in constant demand for portrait statues; in these his style was a rather eclectic naturalism that achieved a likeness but failed to express the personality of his subjects.

(W.C.)

Nivola, Constantino (1911–).
Italian-American sculptor who has brought to his American career something of the civilization from which he came. Born in Orani, Sardinia, he early learned the art of masonry from his father, and later acquired such demanding skills as stucco decoration. This experience with simple materials and an old tradition has always informed Nivola's sculptures. The basic materials of his craft—lime, clay, brick, and sand—are to this day his favored means. Nivola won a scholarship to the Instituto Superiore D'Arte in Monza, Italy, a school often called the Italian Bauhaus, graduated in 1936, and was promptly appointed design director of the Olivetti Company. In 1939 he settled permanently in the United States, working first as a designer and later as independent painter and sculptor. He has exhibited regularly in New York since his first one-man show in 1950.

Nivola's chief works are his reliefs and free-standing sculptures fashioned by scooping out generous forms in the sands near his Long Island home and casting them in concrete. These sand sculptures are highly adaptable to architecture, and Nivola is one of the chief artists employed by progressive architects in the New York area. He began with an exceptional wall relief for the Olivetti show room in 1954, and since then has had innumerable school and business commissions. His major architectural commission came from the architect Eero Saarinen, whose dormitories at Yale University are embellished with thirty-five Nivola sculptures.

Nivola's works on a more intimate scale, frequently terra-cotta reliefs, have been widely praised for their distinctly lyrical quality. Their gently undulating contours are reminiscent of ancient Sardinian and Etruscan forms, but these are subordinate to a timeless poetic imagery. Nivola is also an accomplished portrait sculptor. Winner of numerous awards both in the United States and Italy, he has been honored both as a designer and an original artist.   (D.A.)

Noguchi, Isamu (1904–   ).
Sculptor and designer. Born in Los Angeles, he spent his childhood in Japan, and then returned to the United States, where he decided to study sculpture and served briefly as apprentice to Gutzon Borglum.* His earliest art training in New York City was academic; however, after seeing a shot of Constantin Brancusi's abstract sculpture he determined to turn to abstraction. In 1927 he went to Paris, sought out Brancusi and became his assistant. Here he "learned respect for tools and materials," studied the work of Picasso and the constructivists, and began to experiment with grooved joints held together by gravity or tension. On his return to New York in 1929 Noguchi exhibited his constructions, but found it necessary to return to academic portrait busts to support himself. The following year he journeyed to Peking, where he made brush and wash drawings, and then to Japan to study traditional terra-cotta and Japanese garden techniques. Noguchi's reworkings of the 1500-year-old *haniwa* figure, his "modern" Japanese lanterns, and his feeling for landscape and natural materials appear throughout his career. In 1933 he submitted a model of a "Play Mountain" to the New York City Parks Department. Here social values, sculptured earth, and architectural space combined to turn a vacant lot into a playground. The land was variously tilted into a pyramid to slide down or crawl into, a spiral for sleds in winter, and a shallow pool—all prototype earthworks (see Earth Art) and functional sculptures. The playground was unfortunately rejected. Noguchi's first big commission came in 1938 for a ten-ton stainless steel work for the façade of the Associated Press Building in Rockefeller Center, New York. Meanwhile, he had begun to design costumes and stage sets for such choreographers as Martha Graham and George Balanchine. Rejecting the idea of painted backdrops, he placed sculptural objects on the floor of the stage, creating a series of planes for the dancers to move through. His

1

2

1. *Isamu Noguchi.* The Gift, *1964, black, African marble. Collection of the artist.*
2. *Isamu Noguchi.* Bird E—Square Bird, *1958/66, marble. Collection Mr. Carl E. Solway, Cincinnati, Ohio.*

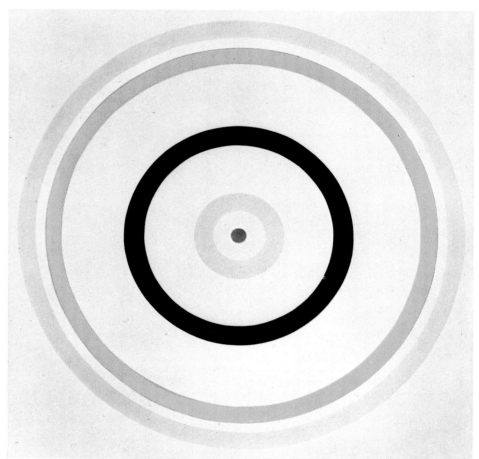

1

2

twenty "stagesets" for Martha Graham often consisted of delicately carved, totem-like objects suggesting the mysteries of prehistory, and she has commented on the challenge of working within Noguchi's spaces. Because he conceives of sculpture as "creating space," he has been extremely popular with interior designers and architects, especially with Gordon Bunshaft* of Skidmore, Owings & Merrill.* Noguchi has done entire gardens for the IBM headquarters in Armonk, N.Y., and the Connecticut General Life Insurance Company Building, Hartford, Conn., the latter consisting of four courtyards as well as a large group of monoliths on the grounds. His garden for Yale University Library uses three motifs: pyramid, circle, and cube, which he relates to "points of infinity, the disc of the sun, and the zero of nothingness." Less philosophical and more traditionally Japanese is his rock garden for Chase Manhattan Plaza, New York City.

Through the years, Noguchi has produced much commercial art, ranging from lamps to furniture. Especially popular were his round paper lamps (1966), which he spoke of as "illuminated sculpture." Although he periodically reverts to constructions, Noguchi is basically a stonecarver, and his work, while abstract, remains firmly grounded in nature. He speaks of his sculptures as "images of moods—moods of flowers, of the vegetative and nonvegetative aspects of nature." Occasionally his works are more explicit, as in his phallic symbols, his bonelike constructions of "heads," "legs," and "arms," and his variations on the biomorphic shapes of French abstract sculptor Jean Arp and the Spanish painter and sculptor Joan Miró. Directly out of the Japanese tradition are his involvement with materials (especially stone), his forms that are simultaneously primitive and sophisticated, and his tendency to strip his sculpture down to essentials. Whereas the minimalists are literal, Noguchi's work remains decorative, often with witty or surrealist overtones. His most famous New York City landmark is the 28-foot-high bright red cube with a hole in one side, which stands on one point in front of the Marine Midland Grace Trust Company. Noguchi has had numerous exhibitions since the 1930s, including a retrospective at the Whitney Museum in 1968.

(E.C.G.)

1. *Kenneth Noland.* Bend Sinister, 1964, Collection Joseph H. Hirshhorn, Greenwich, Conn.
2. *Kenneth Noland.* Turnsole, 1961. Museum of Modern Art, N.Y. (Blanchette Rockefeller Fund).

Noland, Kenneth (1924–   ).
Painter. Born in Asheville, N.C., he studied art at Black Mountain College and worked with Ilya Bolotowsky* (1946–48) and with Ossip Zadkine in Paris (1948–49). In 1949 he moved to Washington, D.C., where he taught painting at the Institute of Contemporary Art and later at Catholic University. Also painting in Washington at this time was Morris Louis,* and the two soon became friends, beginning the so-called "Washington Color School." During the next few years both were influenced by the soak-stain technique of Helen Frankenthaler.* Noland's first one-man show was in Paris in 1949 and his work was subsequently widely exhibited, including in the Venice Biennial (1964) and in a retrospective at the Jewish Museum in New York City (1964).

By 1958 Noland had discovered the target as a means of presenting concentric bands of pure color. These early target paintings often retained traces of abstract expressionism* such as splashed paint, dynamic brushwork, and ragged edges where paint had been scumbled or bled. By 1960, however, Noland had begun to clean up his targets, and produced a series featuring pristine color bands, each separated by a narrow width of white canvas, the whole floating on a field of unprimed canvas. In 1961 he moved to New York City, and began his chevron paintings, adopting a banal motif in order to feature color. It was, however, a new way of organizing the picture field, for Noland's "V's" of color moved off the edges of the canvas and were given directional thrust. These suspended bands of color seemed to be only a part of a much larger image, presumably hovering above the picture, and the drama created by the suggested but unknown image impinged on the primacy of color. To counter this, in 1964 Noland began a series of diamond-shaped pictures. Related to these were attenuated, diamond-shaped canvases and long rectangular paintings, both of which tended to become objects because what was going on *inside* the painting was an aspect of its exterior dimensions. Noland's color became considerably less sensuous and far more calculated than in his earlier work. Frequently he relied on a progression from darks to lights to inflect his bands

with movement (usually upward). In a series of nearly twenty-foot-wide diamonds, such as *Par Transit* (1966, Pasadena), Noland achieved maximum directional movement by dividing the canvas into broad color bands. Reportedly, he hoped to "cancel his shapes out with color"—an effect never fully realized until his stripe paintings, begun in 1967. Here many horizontal stripes ran across long rectangular canvases. Because the stripes were narrow and of various widths the spectator became aware of a kind of vertical stacking of color, and his eyes moved up and down the canvas. At the same time the color bands stretched out of the field of vision, providing a lateral movement. These paintings are structured totally by color, and Noland achieves vibrating optical effects. As in all of his work, the space is a result of the placement and sequence of colors. Like many painters who came after the abstract expressionists, Noland has chosen one element of painting and has forced it to carry the main burden of pictorial means and interest. As a formalist, his work is involved solely in its own economy; it carries no contingent meanings or associations.   (E.C.G.)

Notman, John (1810–65).
Architect. Born in Edinburgh, Scotland, he learned about building from his father, a mason. It is thought that he attended the School of the Arts, Edinburgh. He was apprenticed for four years to a builder and was briefly employed by an architect. He sailed for Philadelphia in 1831, and there may have studied architecture under William Strickland* at the Franklin Institute. His first work was his design for the Laurel Hill Cemetery (1836), which featured a classic gateway and a Gothic chapel (demolished). He then designed the chapel of St. Mary's Hall, Burlington, N.J. (1837), also Gothic, and this was followed by a host of commissions. He often employed his brother-in-law, John Gibson, as decorative painter. Of his innumerable churches and private dwellings, the following are the best known: in Burlington, N.J., Riverside (1839), a dwelling for an Episcopal bishop and the first building in the Italian Villa style in the United States; in Princeton, N.J., the Stockton House (1845), Woodlawn (1846), Ivy Hall (1847), and Prospect (1849) for Thomas Potter (now the home of the president

of Princeton University); and in Philadelphia, St. Mark's, Locust Street (1848–51), St. Clement's, Cherry Street (1855–59), and Church of the Holy Trinity, Rittenhouse Square (1856–59). He also built many houses in the suburbs of Philadelphia and churches throughout the United States. He was probably the first to use a mansard roof since the 1790s. Though he preferred the Gothic* and Romanesque* styles, he designed the Philadelphia Athenaeum (1845–47) to resemble a London club and patterned it after the Italian Renaissance style.   (P.F.N.)

Nottingham, Walter (1930–   ).
Fiber artist known for woven, crocheted, and macraméd hanging forms with totemic significance. Nottingham was born in Great Falls, Mont., and studied at Cranbrook Academy in Michigan. In the late 1960s he strove for an abstract imagery in his multiple weave hangings, which often had a compact, wrapped structure from which long hairlike fibers extended. In 1970 he finished a series of "ancestor image" hangings, based on magic forms from the Sioux and Oklahoma Indian tribes. In addition to his usual combination of nonloom techniques, he interworked beads, feathers, and bones, and two of the series included images on photosensitized cloth. More strongly structured than his previous work, they continued his obsession with mystical-poetic expression. (R.S.)

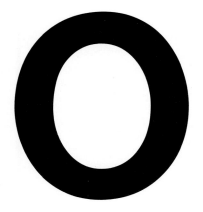

Ohlson, Doug (1936–   ).
Painter. Born in Cherokee, Iowa, he studied at the University of Minnesota. His earliest paintings were static, symmetrical designs, usually squares or rectangles floating in a field of color. After experimenting with joined canvases, Ohlson separated the parts of his painting in a series of panel pictures (1967). Each work comprised from three to twelve tall panels, all separated by a few inches of wall space; as counterpoint to these modular rectangles, squares were painted at intervals above and below some of the panels. Ohlson's color in these pictures ranged from the sensuous (as in *Cythera,* 1968) to the reticent. Recently he has turned to large spots—each painted a different hue and seemingly placed at random—to create paintings that throb with color and light. These are often divided into three or four "episodes" by painted boundaries. Ohlson's recent paintings have eliminated these interior divisions, and his color has grown more romantic and sensuous, the spots pulsating across fields that range up to thirty feet in width.   (E.C.G.)

O'Keeffe, Georgia (1887–   ).
Painter, born in Sun Prairie, Wis. She showed an early talent for drawing, and studied at the Art Institute of Chicago (1904–05) and the Art Students League in New York (1907–08), but the only teacher who seems to have had any influence on her development was Arthur Wesley Dow, with whom she worked at Teacher's College, Columbia University. A student of Gauguin, Dow rejected realism in favor of the simplification, flat patterning, and coloristic harmonies of oriental art—all of which became elements of Georgia O'Keeffe's mature style.

She spent four winters between 1912 and 1918 teaching school in the

1

2

1. **Georgia O'Keeffe.** Black Iris, *1926*
   Metropolitan Museum of Art, N.Y.
   (Alfred Stieglitz Collection).
2. **Georgia O'Keeffe.** Black Cross, New
   Mexico, *1929. Art Institute of*
   Chicago.

Texas Panhandle, and the southwestern landscape left in indelible impression on her art. She produced her first important works in 1915—a series of large abstractions in charcoal that evoke natural forms and movements, and a group of watercolors, most of them landscapes in broad, simple forms and vivid colors. Later that year, the drawings fell into the hands of Alfred Stieglitz,* who included them in a show the following spring at his avant-garde Gallery 291 in New York. She had her first solo show there in 1917. She married Stieglitz in 1924 and exhibited annually in his various galleries until his death in 1946. During this time Stieglitz produced his 500-print "portrait" of Georgia O'Keeffe.

Although closely associated with the circle of American modernists whom Stieglitz promoted—Charles Demuth,* Marsden Hartley,* Arthur Dove,* and John Marin*—O'Keeffe developed a style that was intuitively personal and had little relationship to modernist movements. Her paintings over the last half-century have ranged from pure abstraction to precisionistic realism. But all are characterized by elemental, three-dimensional forms projected rhythmically in ambiguous space and achieving a sense of disembodied, visionary presence. They are enigmas executed with absolute clarity but combining sensuousness with austerity.

Following her first abstract oils, O'Keeffe's paintings of the 1920s veered closer to naturalism. They included numerous landscapes, a series of highly magnified flowers, such as *Black Flower and Blue Larkspur* (1929, Metropolitan), and a group of relatively geometric New York scenes.

In 1929 O'Keeffe spent her first summer in Taos, N.M.; she returned there annually until 1949, when she settled permanently in a remote ranch outside the village of Abiquiu. During most of these years, her paintings have explored the natural and spiritual terrain of the southwestern desert—its mountains, canyons, and vast spaces; its bleached animal bones and rocks; the black crosses and other religious symbols peculiar to the Mexican-American population. Her work of the last twenty years often involves an abstraction in which highly simplified forms are set against vast color spaces. Since 1958, she has also done many paintings that have their source in

earth, clouds, and sky as viewed from an airplane. (A.F.)

Oldenburg, Claes (1929–   ).
Sculptor, painter, writer, and early contributor to the development of happenings,* Oldenburg is a major figure in American pop art.* Born in Stockholm, Sweden, he grew up in Chicago, Ill. After graduating from Yale University (1950), he worked as a reporter for the City News Bureau in Chicago and then (1952–54) studied painting, figure drawing, and anatomy at the Art Institute of Chicago. His earliest paintings were roughly brushed, expressionist nudes and portraits. In 1956 Oldenburg moved to New York, where he met other artists who were beginning to question the established boundaries between art and life. These included Jim Dine,* Red Grooms,* Allen Kaprow,* and George Segal,* all of whom would turn to environments and happenings.* In his first one-man show (1959) there was already an indication of his later intentions: during the exhibition he wore a large papier-mâché "elephant mask" through the streets of New York, both to express his own feelings and arouse the feelings of a larger public. Oldenburg's major influences during these years were primitive art, comics, graffiti, and children's drawings—all deeply involved with direct, physical manipulation of materials, caricature, and the symbolic object. In 1960 he presented two exhibitions of *The Street*—both total environments composed of such objects as tattered cars, grotesque figures, and billboards—all formed out of the detritus of the city: wrapping paper, cardboard, burlap, and newspapers. *The Store* (1961–62) recreated the world of commodities and commercial advertising in explicitly vulgar, unappetizing form. Here "merchandise" such as bread, cake, sausage, soda pop, and shoes, shirts, and dresses were fashioned out of plaster, muslin, and chicken wire; then these shoddy "products" were covered with drips and spatters of bright enamel house paint. With *The Store* Oldenburg achieved a complete breakdown of the barrier between art and life. He rented a real store; produced his "wares" in the back room; marketed them in the front; and displayed them in the show window. Later he would even present a series of happenings there, known as "The

1

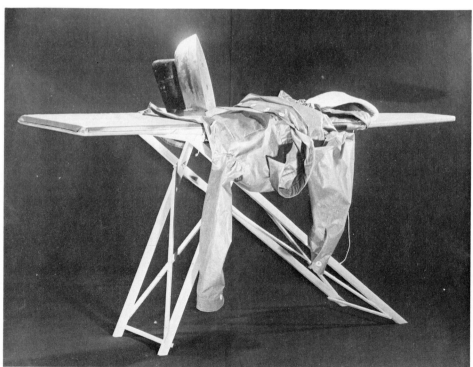

3

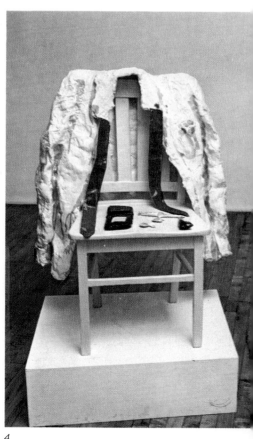

4

1. *Claes Oldenburg.* Soft Giant Drum Set, *1967, canvas, vinyl, and wood. Collection Kimiko and John G. Powers, N.Y.*
2. *Claes Oldenburg.* Soft Typewriter, *1963, vinyl, kapok, cloth, and plexiglass. Collection Allan Powers, London.*
3. *Claes Oldenburg.* Ironing Board with Shirt and Iron, *1964, mixed media.*
4. *Claes Oldenburg.* Chair with Shirt and Objects *and* Chair with Pants and Objects, *1962, plaster and enamel.*

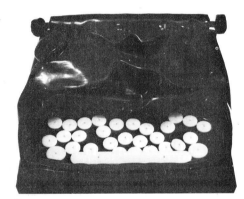

2

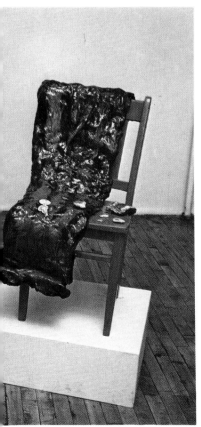

Ray Gun Theater." In writing about *The Store* in 1961 Oldenburg hinted at his distaste for "high art" and his basic respect for the artistic images of mass culture: "I am for an art that does something other than sit on its ass in a museum. I am for an art that grows up not knowing it is art at all. . . . I am for an art that involves itself with the everyday crap and still comes out on top. I am for an art that imitates the human, that is comic if necessary, or violent, for whatever is necessary. I am for an art that takes its form from the lines of life . . . and is sweet and stupid as life itself."

In 1962 the full scope of Oldenburg's fantasy, humor, and ironical wit became apparent when he exhibited his giant *Hamburger, Ice Cream Cone,* and an enormous *Pants.* The sculptures were all made of sewn canvas, stuffed with foam rubber, and painted with liquitex. The artist himself has likened these large, somewhat ludicrous sculptures lying on the floor of the gallery to the automobiles in the show window next door, and has commented on the "female" forms of the hamburger, bun, and pickle and the "phallic" quality of the ice cream cone. By 1964 Oldenburg's work had undergone a radical stylistic change, largely through the use of new materials. He was then producing works with anonymous, industrially finished surfaces, and even his new "soft" sculptures were made of synthetic materials such as vinyl, formica, and plexiglass. Gone was the "hand of the artist"; however, his scrutiny of everyday objects had intensified and his interest in sexual imagery remained in such works as *Electric Outlet with Plug* (1964) and *Bedroom Ensemble.* The latter, an almost surrealist "environment," reproduces a West Coast motel suite, whose vinyl-covered bed, imitation marble, and zebra-patterned furniture, and fake Pollock* paintings are sterile to the point of embalmment. Perhaps Oldenburg's most radical and original work were the "soft sculptures" begun in 1963. Most of the objects he selected to reproduce in vinyl—bathtubs, typewriters, drums—required rigidity in order to function; thus there was no confusion in distinguishing the artist's version from the real-life object (as there was in the work of many other pop artists). By subjecting his sculptures to the force of gravity he not only "humanized"

the products of industrial society but created an art with built-in permutations: whenever one touched or moved one of these pieces, it would simply settle into a new position. Just as Oldenburg's new work could assume many different forms, it could also support a host of meanings—sexual, ironic, witty, as well as serious social comment.

Because he is basically an expressionist, Oldenburg never just presents his objects; he always reinterprets them. In 1965 he began a series of drawings of proposed "colossal monuments" for New York. All showed common objects raised to enormous size and placed on a site in the city that he deemed appropriate for it, thus: a half-peeled banana for Times Square, a soft Good Humor Bar to sheathe the Pan Am building; a teddy bear for Central Park North, near Harlem. The inventiveness and depth of Oldenburg's thinking can be seen in his justification of the teddy bear, which he considers "a source of pathos, since it really doesn't have any hands or feet . . . as if they'd been chopped off . . . the helplessness of the city person and specifically of the Negro in New York." More witty (but ultimately serious) monuments were designed for London in 1966. These include a giant toilet float for the Thames and a lipstick for Piccadilly Circus. The latter was subsequently fabricated in America and installed at Yale University (1969). Mounted on tractor treads ("Isn't it terrible to have sculptures littering the landscape that are unremovable?") the lipstick can be extended and retracted in its sheath—an allusion to weaponry, with strong sexual overtones. Similar in spirit is his *Giant Icebag* (1970) which inflates to a height of seventeen feet by means of gears, hydraulics, and blowers. Seen by many as an attack on self-important monuments that "just sit there," it is typical of Oldenburg in its union of fantasy and technology, its inventive form and associative richness, and its ultimate social comment. Oldenburg's many exhibitions include the Venice Biennial (1964), the São Paulo Biennial (1967), and retrospectives at the Museum of Modern Art, New York City (1969), and the Tate Gallery, London (1970). (E.C.G.)

Olitski, Jules (1922–   ).
Painter. A native of Gomel, Russia, he was brought to America as an infant.

He received an M.A. degree from New York University and then studied portrait painting at the National Academy of Design.* From 1948–51 he studied in Paris, at the Académie Grande Chaumière and with Ossip Zadkine, where his work became increasingly abstract. He has taught art at C. W. Post College on Long Island (1956–63) and Bennington College (1963–67). By 1959 (the year following his first one-man show in New York) Olitski was producing thickly-impastoed surfaces featuring rounded blotch forms highly reminiscent of the French painter Jean Fautrier. Seeking a more original result, Olitski moved to the soak-stain technique and more opulent hues, painting balls and concentric rings in broad, flat areas of color, with unpainted bands in between. In 1961 one of the earliest of these pictures won second prize for painting at the Carnegie International. In 1965 he abandoned shapes and began spraying his paint. By using slight variations in value, and spraying different colors on top of one another, he inflected the surface and achieved subtle atmospheric effects. One critic has called these paintings "the first fully abstract version of impressionism," though in fact they are diametrically opposed to impressionism* since they are not based on a study of light and atmosphere.

In attempting to make a painting out of nothing but color, Olitski dissolved the surface of his canvas into an ambiguous mist, so that the structure of the picture reverted to the edges of the canvas, and the shape of the picture as a whole became all important. Many of the early spray paintings have tall, narrow formats. Later versions are often horizontal—sometimes as much as twenty feet long—and are held together by impasto bands of paint at the edges and corners which act as a frame for the illusionistic effects of the sprayed center. Olitski's paintings are chiefly successful on the level of pure sensuous experience. In 1968 he produced a group of low-lying sprayed aluminum sculptures (exhibited at the Metropolitan Museum in 1969) that again dissolved form in paint. (E.C.G.)

1. *Jules Olitski.* Green Goes Around, 1967. *André Emmerich Gallery, N.Y.*
2. *Nathan Oliveira,* Standing Man with Stick, 1959. *Museum of Modern Art, N.Y.*

Oliveira, Nathan (1928–   ).
Painter and printmaker, born in California, studied with Max Beckmann at Mills College, and received an M.F.A. from the California College of Arts

and Crafts in 1952. He has taught at the California School of Fine Arts (now the San Francisco Art Institute), and at Illinois, Cornell, and Stanford universities. He has exhibited throughout the United States, including many one-man exhibitions. Oliveira has a highly individual approach to figuration, influenced by the Swiss sculptor-painter, Alberto Giacometti. He presents a single figure or head isolated within a large blank space. The figures are painted in heavy impasto emerging crustlike from a dark, atmospheric ground, as in *Standing Man With Stick* (1959, Modern Museum). In the late 1960s he turned to a form of architectural landscape or views of room interiors in which he isolated a tiny figure or simply one or two pieces of furniture, such as a bed and a couch, within a vast, empty space with doors opening out into further emptiness. Shadowed pyramid forms appear in a number of these works and seem to have for him a particular symbolic significance. Since the early 1960s Oliveira has also experimented intensively with graphic media, drawings, gouaches, watercolors, and prints. These extend the mood of his figurative paintings and manifest the influence of Goya's macabre prints, which he discovered when he visited Spain. (H.H.A.)

Olmsted, Frederick Law (1822–1903). America's greatest landscape architect was born in Hartford, Conn., the son of a prosperous merchant. Because of poor eyesight, he abandoned his plan to attend Yale College and turned instead to scientific farming and from 1848 to 1854 he had a farm on Staten Island, New York, which included a fruit tree nursery. He took time off from farming to travel in Europe, and in 1850 he made the first of several tours through the South, sending back long letters to *The New York Times;* these were published in three books, *A Journey in the Seaboard Slave States* (1856), *A Journey Through Texas* (1857), and *A Journey in the Back Country* (1860), which constitute an outstanding view of the ante-bellum South. During a second trip to Europe he was able to give some attention to parks and gardens.

While his journalistic activities drew him away from his farm and nursery, he was never out of touch with them. As early as 1847 he contributed to *The*

Horticulturist, Andrew Jackson Downing's* publication. That same year Alexander Jackson Davis,* the leading architect of the pre-Civil War era, was advising him on architecture and landscaping. He was still at loose ends in 1857 when he was made "Superintendent of the Central Park," a job which consisted mainly of clearing the park site.

Shortly afterward, Calvert Vaux (1824–95), a partner of Downing's persuaded him to enter the competition for the park's design. Vaux, an architect born and trained in England, had come to America in 1850 at Downing's invitation. He did much of his work in various Hudson River towns and in New York City, where his best known buildings are the Jefferson Market Courthouse (1876) and the Samuel Tilden mansion (1874, now the National Arts Club). As Olmsted's partner in park design, Vaux planned all buildings and bridges as well as sharing in the landscaping. The two men submitted a plan which won the $2000 prize in 1858.

Olmsted continued to be associated with the park until 1887, except during the Civil War, when he was secretary to the United States Sanitary Commission, and later when he was subjected to municipal political machinations.

Central Park proved to be a landmark in its field. It was the first large park in the world—along with the Bois de Boulogne in Paris—specifically designed for public use. Also, it represented the climax of the picturesque tradition, which was distinguished by informality in landscape design—with twisting paths, a variety of planting, and an extensive use of lawn. What had begun in the early 1700s as a landscaping style for private estates in England became the standard for public parks in the United States. The style remains with us today in diluted form along many parkways.

Olmsted, despite the success of Central Park, might have forsaken landscape architecture for journalism had not Vaux persuaded him to join in designing Brooklyn's Prospect Park in 1865. Later, Olmsted was to consider Prospect Park his finest work. Among other projects the firm carried out was the still existing Riverside Park in Chicago (1869), the model of a suburb in the picturesque style. The partnership with Vaux ended in 1872, and

Olmsted went on his own triumphant way. Among his outstanding works are Mount Royal Park in Montreal, Canada; Franklin Park in Boston; the Boston Park System; the Chicago Park System; South and Delaware parks in Buffalo; the Leland Stanford University Campus; and the Capitol grounds in Washington. In addition, he helped to save what is now Yosemite Park and the area around the American side of Niagara Falls. All this work was supplemented by commissions for private estates.

Interestingly enough, Olmsted did not cling to the picturesque style if the situation dictated otherwise. In his most important architectural commission, the great west terrace of the national Capitol (1880), he took his cue from the building and worked in the classical mode. This was also true at Biltmore, George Washington Vanderbilt's great estate in Asheville, N.C., where, besides the extensive grounds, he laid out an esplanade and a large formal garden. He also had a major role in planning the World's Columbian Exposition (1893, held in Chicago), which had such an important influence on American art.

In recent years much has been made of Olmsted's social ideas, and he is presented as a kind of 19th-century prophet, sometimes at the expense of his farming and horticultural accomplishment. But this has been to some extent redressed by the major exhibition put on at the National Gallery of Art in 1972. It reaffirms Olmsted as, above all, an artist in shaping the landscape. Steeped in the English picturesque tradition, he helped to impose that style on the American urban park. Olmsted's son, Frederick Law Olmsted, Jr. (1870–1957), was also a noted landscape architect. (See also Landscape Architecture.) (H.H.R.)

Onckelbag, Gerrit (1670–1732). Silversmith, best known for two two-handled covered cups (Deerfield, Yale) similar in design to one made by Jurian Blanck, Jr.* Onckelbag worked in a bold, articulate style with strong baroque details and elaborate armorial engraving. In addition to caudle cups, tankards, and spoons, he is known to have made a saucepan, bowl, and casters; and for the Dutch Church of Flatbush, New York, in 1697 he made a pair of beakers engraved with figures of Faith, Hope, and Charity.

Optical Art

Optical or Op Art.

A "movement" dating from the early 1960s. It is deeply opposed to the static harmony and clear relationships of classical art, seeking instead a kind of dynamism that often depends on visual "devices." At worst it is a superficial mode that descends into titillation and formula. The roots of op art can be found in the dynamism of Italian futurism*—especially in works like Giacomo Balla's *Dog on a Leash* (1912) and Marcel Duchamp's* *Nude Descending a Staircase* (1912). Earlier, the French impressionists had experimented with perceptual effects, and their optical mixtures of color dots were based (like every "modern" theory of color) on the studies, published in 1839, of Michel-Eugene Chevreul. The work of Richard Anuszkiewicz* and Josef Albers,* for example, only demonstrate Chevreul's principles of simultaneous contrast and the interaction of color. However, it has been pointed out that optical art is basically not an art of color but of graphic design, and that most of its works would be equally successful in black and white.

Op art has had a greater following in Europe than in America. Its most influential figure is probably Victor Vasarely, a Hungarian painter working in France. One of the very few artists who has consistently managed to produce "optical" works of some depth is the English-woman Bridget Riley. In America, artists such as Alexander Liberman,* Ellsworth Kelly,* Gene Davis,* and Kenneth Noland* have produced paintings that depend in part on optical effects, though none is an "op" artist. Larry Poons* in his op period (1963–66) painted all-over patterns of vibrant spots that achieved viewer participation because one sensed the underlying grid, and these visual links made the spots appear to "jump." Viewer participation is essential in optical art, and the demands made on the spectator range from asking him to distinguish subtle color variations (Ad Reinhardt,* Robert Irwin) to subjecting him to spasmodic after-images that can bring on a near nausea (Richard Anuszkiewicz). The unsettling effect is rarely modified by subsequent viewings because such works depend on devices and these elicit a response that never changes. A number of op artists simply present "optical illusions" based on psychologists' diagrams. (Perceptual psychology

1. *Timothy H. O'Sullivan.* View on Apache Lake, Sierra Blanca Range, Arizona, *1873, photograph. George Eastman House, Rochester, N.Y.*

2. *Timothy H. O'Sullivan.* Bodies of Dead Federal Soldiers, *1863, photograph. Library of Congress, Washington, D.C.*

has been a major influence.) Such devices as spatially reversible images and moire patterns, formed by superimposing sets of parallel lines or concentric circles, are common. Other optical artists employ uniform patterns of small geometric units which the eye, seeking solutions to the "puzzle," groups and regroups. Still others achieve effects of light and shade by altering the spatial interval between units; as the spectator changes his viewing position, changes seem to occur in the work. Much optical art is based on theories originating in Chevreul or the work of John J. Gibson, a contemporary theorist in visual perception. Although these theories are often used merely to assault the spectator or devise a perceptual "game," some tendencies depend on sense impressions and visual illusions without devolving into the mechanical quality of much optical art. The abstract illusionism of painters like Ronald Davis, the emphasis on spectator participation and angles of observation in the work of Robert Morris* and Patricia Johanson,* and the glass boxes of Larry Bell* all involve the subjective experience of the viewer and go beyond the superficial "excitement" of an agitated surface. The chief optical art show, "The Responsive Eye," was held at the Museum of Modern Art in 1965. The real challenge posed by optical art—to produce an art of depth and meaning and develop new object-spectator (objective-subjective) relations—remains unanswered. (E.C.G.)

Orphism.

The term "orphic cubism" was coined in 1912 by the French poet Guillaume Apollinaire to describe the tonal or musical color variations in the paintings of the Parisian painter Robert Delaunay. Delaunay's paintings had clearly passed beyond analytical cubism by 1912, and the next year they moved into abstract geometric patterns creating light and space by the use of overlapped and juxtaposed planes of color, without reference to an object. As Delaunay attracted followers in 1913 and 1914, the group became known as "orphists" or "simultanistes." The American painter Patrick Henry Bruce* came directly under the influence of Delaunay's prismatic compositions, while Morgan Russell* and Stanton MacDonald-Wright* headed the re-

lated and parallel movement of synchromism.* (D.W.S.)

O'Sullivan, Timothy H. (1840–82).

Photographer. Documentor of the Civil War, the jungles of Panama, and the American West, O'Sullivan was born in New York, N.Y. A youthful association with the photographer Lewis Emory Walker in 1855 led him to an apprenticeship in the New York studio of the most famous photographer of the 19th century, Mathew B. Brady.* Sometime before 1860, O'Sullivan was transferred to Brady's Washington Gallery and photographed under the direction of Alexander Gardner.*

The Civil War brought O'Sullivan's studio days to an end. Outfitted by Brady with the elaborate equipment required for the wet collodion process then in use, O'Sullivan followed the northern troops into battle. By November, 1861, the army had penetrated deep into South Carolina, and O'Sullivan, calmly working through furious bombardments (it is said that his camera tripod was twice knocked down by shell fragments), documented the action. A photograph possibly made during this time shows him seated on the ground, leaning against the wheel of his buggy (it doubled as a portable darkroom), sharing a cold meal with his assistant. He gazes gravely at the camera, his bearded young face, thin and intense. Perhaps the most gifted of the dozen or so photographers who comprised Brady's "photographic corps," he soon became first lieutenant on the staff of Brigadier General Viele, but he continued his photography work until his honorable discharge in 1862.

In 1863 Gardner left Brady's employ and, taking O'Sullivan with him, established a rival company whose sole purpose was to document the progress of the war. O'Sullivan's most notable contribution to this undertaking was a harrowing series made in July, 1863, on the carnage at Gettysburg. Published in the two volumes of Gardner's Photographic Sketchbook of the War (1866), these photographs show, in Gardner's words, " . . . the blank horror and reality of war, in opposition to its pageantry. Here are the dreadful details! Let them aid in preventing such another calamity falling upon the nation." Of the one hundred albumen prints illustrating Gardner's text, O'Sullivan contributed forty-five.

With peace came the westward expansion. Because the vast territory west of the Rocky Mountains was still an unknown land, Congress ordered four great geographical and geological surveys of it. In 1867 O'Sullivan became the photographer for the first of these, the United States Geographical Explorations West of the 40th Parallel, led by the dynamic Clarence King. The King party spent three years exploring the uncharted Nevada Territory. Using an old army ambulance to haul his photographic equipment, O'Sullivan documented everything, even photographing the subterranean galleries of the Great Comstock Lode by the light of burning magnesium. The expedition resulted, according to one O'Sullivan biographer, Nancy Newhall, in "photographs still unsurpassed in their bold and sensitive grasp of huge motifs."

In 1870, O'Sullivan was appointed photographer to the Darien Surveying Expedition, a project to investigate routes for a canal across Panama. Jungle heat and humidity made photographing extremely difficult. The following year he joined the geographical and geological explorations commanded by George M. Wheeler of the corps of engineers. A trek across the burning sands of Death Valley was followed by a nearly disastrous boat trip up the Colorado River to the Grand Canyon. O'Sullivan braved death by drowning and starvation only to have almost all his glass negatives lost or broken in transit to Washington. But compensation came in the magnificent photographs he took in 1873 during the exploration of Arizona and New Mexico. Of these the modern master Ansel Adams* has written: "No modern photographs I have seen so successfully convey the mood of such noble scenes." O'Sullivan's photograph showing the mysterious ruins of an ancient Indian civilization nestled in the side of a sheer cliff in the Canyon de Chelly is one of the masterpieces of 19th-century photography.

O'Sullivan returned to the East in 1880 and was made a photographer for the Treasury Department. Ill health forced him to retire in 1881. (D.L.)

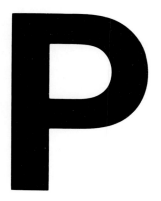

Page, William (1811–85).
Figure and portrait painter. Page was born in Albany, N.Y., and educated in New York City. His early teachers were James Herring and Samuel F. B. Morse.* In 1827 he exhibited his first oil at the National Academy of Design* (many years later, in 1871, he became its president). Between 1829 and 1832 he painted portraits and historical subjects in Northampton, Mass., and in Albany and Rochester, N.Y. From 1833–43 he lived in New York City and then for four years in Boston. In 1850 Page sailed for Italy and for the next decade was a prominent member of the Anglo-American colony in Rome. While there, he produced historical pictures and copies after Titian. When he returned home in 1860, he lived in New Jersey until 1866 and then on Staten Island.

Page was a personality unique among his artist contemporaries. Volatile and exuberant, and eloquent in expounding unorthodox compositional and technical theories, he was a somewhat controversial figure on the art scene. His technical experiments with the oil medium have won him a measure of respect in recent years. He developed a technique that contrasted heavy impasto with thin glazes of transparent pigment. As a colorist he achieved novel effects, using underpainting and an intermingling of pigments in his glazes, strikingly unlike the monotonous areas of local color created by his tradition-bound contemporaries.

Page's portraits were not bound by set formulas and his other figurative works in the grand manner were equally unorthodox. He considered each portrait a fresh problem in composition. *Mrs. William Page* (1860, Detroit), for example, with its quality of mystery and timelessness, is anything but a routine portrait. His *Cupid and Psyche* (1843, private collection), created quite a stir and offended some delicate sensibilities because of the sensuality of its two nude figures embracing. *The Young Merchants* (c.1834, Pennsylvania) was his only essay into genre painting, but even here he transcended stock formulas, and the delightful result was unique. Page was not a prolific painter and he received few commissions as compared with his peers. Works by Page are comparatively scarce and the number is further reduced by the fact that his experiments in imitating the cinquecento Venetians have caused many of his paintings to darken and deteriorate beyond recognition.

(H.W.W.)

Palmer, Erastus Dow (1817–1904).
Sculptor. Born in Onondaga County, N.Y., he worked as a carpenter in Utica before turning to cameo carving. In about 1848 he began modeling on a larger scale. Unlike most 19th-century American sculptors, Palmer did not go to Europe to study and he seldom traveled. Although some of his early marble sculptures bear such names as *Infant Ceres* and *Infant Flora* they are not neoclassical in style; Palmer had very little opportunity to become acquainted with such neoclassical works as those of the Italian master, Canova, and of the Norwegian sculptor, Thorwaldsen. His style is a simple naturalism blended with strong elements of romanticism, sentimentality, and morality, as for example, in his *Indian Girl, or The Dawn of Christianity* (1856, Metropolitan), a life-size marble statue.

The nude figure had hardly gained general acceptance in America when Palmer created his now most famous piece, *White Captive* (1858). The statue found acceptance, not primarily for esthetic reasons but because of the moral lesson it told—of a white girl whose Christian soul allowed her to triumph spiritually over the heathen Indians who had kidnapped her. Based on direct observation of the model, *White Captive* is thoroughly naturalistic; the proportions are not those of ancient Greco-Roman statuary nor are they idealized. As with much 19th-century sculpture, the work of art can not be separated from the story it tells; sometimes pamphlets accompanied such works to explain the subject in melodramatic prose.

Although Palmer never became one of the artists who gathered around the National Academy of Design,* then making New York City the hub of artistic activity in America, he was recognized by the 1860s as one of the nation's foremost sculptors. He preferred literary or pictorial subjects and only occasionally did portraits. His bust of Washington Irving dates from 1865 and his full-length bronze of Chancellor Robert Livingston was completed in 1874; the latter was executed during a stay in Paris but shows little influence of the rich modeling techniques taught at the École des Beaux-Arts. Again, naturalism is the basis of the style; when compared with other statues around it in Statuary Hall of the U.S. Capitol it seems small and unimpressive. Palmer's portraits never reached the level of his imagined or literary subjects.

(W.C.)

Paperweights.
The manufacture of glass paperweights reached a level of unsurpassed excellence in mid-19th century France when the Baccarat, Clichy, and St. Louis factories dominated production. Their weights consisted of colorless, flawless "domes" enclosing lampworked flowers of "millefiori" designs composed of colored glass canes cut in cross-section and arranged in patterns to look like many flowers. The weights were sometimes cased in one or more layers of colored glass cut through with facets

1. **William Page.** Mrs. William Page, 1860. Detroit Institute of Arts.
2. **Erastus Dow Palmer.** White Captive, 1858, marble. Metropolitan Museum of Art, N.Y. (gift of Hamilton Fish).

to reveal and magnify the interior design.

American weights throughout the second half of the 19th century were either factory productions or the work of individual gaffers who copied existing fashions or designed their own pieces. Few weights are marked or signed, and they are difficult to identify and date. Of American manufacturers, the New England Glass Company was noted for its life-size, hollow-blown fruit weights; and the Boston & Sandwich Glass Company and the Mt. Washington Glass Company, for flower weights. The Brooklyn Flint Glass Works is said to have made faceted millefiori weights. Each of these factories probably made more than one type of weight, however; and other American factories may have made them also. Nicholas Lutz, who worked at the Boston & Sandwich factory in the later part of the 19th century, was noted for his enclosed flower weights; and Ralph Barber, who worked in New Jersey in the early 20th century, for his "Millville Rose." (See also Glass.)

(J.S.S.)

Paris, Harold Persico (1925–   ).
Sculptor. Born in New York, N.Y., Paris began his art studies at the Atelier 17* under Stanley William Hayter in 1949. While at the Atelier 17, Paris experimented with various print techniques and excelled in new approaches to graphics. In 1953 he enrolled in the Academy of Fine Arts in Munich, where he remained until 1956. Later he traveled through Europe, worked for a time in Paris, and became well known for his experimental works on the plastic material, lucite.

When he settled down in San Francisco and began teaching at the University of California in Berkeley, Paris turned increasingly toward sculpture. From the beginning he showed a highly inventive spirit, and an ability to combine varied techniques. He developed a way of using cast rubber and plaster, which he sometimes used in conjunction with stretched canvas shapes. Gradually Paris enlarged his units of assembled firms until around 1964, when he began to shape an entire room. This was the first of many subsequent ensembles intended to fill a given enclosed space. Paris populated floor, walls, and ceiling with stark black and white forms. In his combinations of

rubber and plaster he contrasted soft and hard; in his shapes, he contrasted fragment and whole. White and black formica provided shiny platforms for this highly theatrical assemblage of sculptured objects, and the stagelike character of the imagery was emphasized by his use of soft, dark fabric on the ceiling. After this first room, Paris experimented with sound and movement, and eventually, even flowing water, in integrated contexts.

Paris has received several fellowships, including a Tiffany Grant in 1949, a Guggenheim, and a Fulbright in 1953. He has exhibited widely all over the world.   (D.A.)

Park, David (1911–60).
Painter, born in Boston, Mass. He studied at the Otis Art Institute in Los Angeles and taught at the California School of Fine Arts (1944–52), the University of California in Berkeley (1955–60), and elsewhere. Although best known as a painter, Park was also a theater designer. During the 1930s he executed murals under the WPA Federal Art Project.*

Park belongs with the California school of figure painters, but antedates them in that he was a figure painter in the 1930s and '40s. After experimenting with a form of abstract expressionism* in the early 1950s, he turned permanently back to figurative representation. His style of the late 1950s involves single figure or groups usually set within a unified color space and painted in heavy impasto outlined in bold black contours. The figures are frequently organized in highly atmospheric contrasts of light and shadow; the faces are blank masks with black blobs for eyes, nose, and mouth. In his earlier works there is a strong sculptural feeling reminiscent of Park's early experience in sculpture. In the last paintings, the color is bold and brilliant, the figures rendered loosely with violent immediacy in a few big strokes of the brush. Of all the California figure painters, Park is perhaps closest to the earlier tradition of German expressionism.*   (H.H.A.)

Parker, Raymond (1922–   ).
Painter, born in Beresford, S.D. He received an M.F.A. degree from the University of Iowa (1948), taught there in 1947–48, at the University of Minnesota in 1948–51, and since 1955 at

Hunter College, New York City. He has had one-man exhibitions at major museums throughout the United States. In New York he has been associated with abstract expressionism* and, subsequently, with color-field* painting. As a student, Parker painted in a precise, realistic manner reminiscent of Italian 15th-century style. In the late 1940s his painting became more abstract, although it still suggested recognizable objects, particularly machine forms. During the 1950s he moved to complete abstraction and developed a personal image in which he isolated large, roughly ovoid or rectangular color spaces within a unified color ground, as in *Untitled* (1959, Albright). The total impact of these works owes something to the painting of Mark Rothko* but is still highly individual. Parker's ovals and rectangles seem to float in space, closely approaching or barely touching one another as though drawn or repelled within a magnetic field.

By the mid-1960s his color shapes became more firmly rectangular and had crisp edges. Their impact as brilliant color objects, centralized and floating within a neutral ground and approaching and receding from one another, continued. In the late 1960s Parker developed a collage-like style in which the color shapes became freely biomorphic, and the uniform ground even more intense in color. The organic shapes continued to float around one another, but now at times overlapped and interlocked. (H.H.A.)

Parris, Alexander (1780–1852).
Architect-builder. Born in Hebron, Me., his family soon moved to Pembroke, Mass., where he was educated and then apprenticed to a carpenter and builder. About 1801 he moved to Portland, Me., and there built the Portland Bank (burned 1866), some residences in the 18th-century colonial style, and fortifications in the harbor. He left for Richmond, Va., in 1809, and built a number of residences, including the home of the governor. In 1812 Parris bought land in Boston, but his first known commission there was the David Sears House (now Somerset Club) on Beacon Street, in 1816. His early designs were colonial in style, but his buildings then became robust and classically precise, influenced no doubt by the Greek revival* buildings he saw in

Washington and Philadelphia.

Most important for the introduction of the Greek revival style to Boston was Parris' St. Paul's Cathedral (1819–20), with a colonnade like that of a classic temple. The largest and most distinguished design of his career was made for Faneuil Hall (Quincy) Markets (1824–26) and the adjoining buildings on North and South Market streets. An early example of good, income-making city planning, the market still flourishes. A central, Roman dome has connecting wings each terminated by a fine portico of Greek monolithic granite column. Here and in the commercial buildings to the north and south, Parris has used stones set vertically as pillars surrounding door and window openings. Though probably not his innovation, the device is noteworthy and effective. He also designed the Marine Hospital, Chelsea, and the Arsenal, Watertown; and in 1847 he was appointed civil engineer at the Navy Yard, Portsmouth, N.H. (P.F.N.)

Parrish, Maxfield (1870–1966).
Painter and illustrator, he was the son of Stephen Parrish, a successful Philadelphia painter who exposed the precocious youngster to European schools and art galleries at an early age. Young Parrish entered Haverford College intending to be an architect, but in 1889 he turned to the Pennsylvania Academy of the Fine Arts,* where he studied with Anshutz* and Vonnoh.* He was particularly drawn to the English artists of the pre-Raphaelite tradition, and he also sought instruction from the illustrator Howard Pyle at the Drexel Institute.

Parrish soon established himself as a painter and illustrator, exhibiting at the Pennsylvania Academy in 1894 and doing a cover for *Harper's Weekly* in 1895. His highly decorative, whimsical style won him commissions for book illustrations after his work appeared in L. Frank Baum's *Mother Goose in Prose* (1897). In the same year, he won a national poster competition. Thereafter, his range expanded steadily. In 1903 his first colored illustrations were published in Edith Wharton's *Italian Villas,* and in 1906 he painted his well-known mural decorations on the theme of Old King Cole for the Knickerbocker Hotel (later the St. Regis) in New York City. During the next decades he did several murals, dozens of covers for magazines, and advertisements that

established the public image of several major manufacturers. His greatest impact, however, came through color prints that sold literally by the millions and appeared as overmantels across the country. Typical of these were *The Garden of Allah* (copyright 1919) and *Dawn* (copyright 1920), which showed lounging maidens in idealized, semiclassical settings before romantic, natural backdrops. Parrish's draftsmanship was meticulous, his detail photographic, his finish impeccable, and his composition strikingly decorative. His combination of luminous, suavely glazed color and intricately drawn textures created the effect of a magical, almost surrealistic world.

After 1930, Parrish retired from the illustration field and turned to landscape painting, which he practiced for another thirty years. In 1964 there was a flurry of renewed interest in his work. A critic, Lawrence Alloway, proclaimed him "part of the invisible art world" beyond the pale of the art establishment. In the same year the Metropolitan Museum purchased his *Errant Pan* (c. 1915), a representative example of the curious mixture of naturalism, fantasy, and sentiment that for two decades had a popular appeal far greater than the work of any of the leading painters of the period. (D.W.S.)

Partridge, William Ordway (1861–1930).
Sculptor. He was born of American parents in Paris. After graduating from Columbia University, he studied sculpture in Florence, Rome, and Paris and then in 1889 established his studio in Milton, Mass. The lively, impressionistic manner of the Parisian sculpture style of the 1870s and '80s dominated his work from the beginning. Mainly a portrait sculptor, he made many full-length statues of contemporary and historic persons, including *Shakespeare* (1894, Lincoln Park, Chicago), *U.S. Grant* (1896, equestrian, Brooklyn, N.Y.), and *Alexander Hamilton* (1908, Columbia University), and portrait busts of such famous authors as Keats, Milton, and Shelley. Among his few symbolic works is the marble female head, *Peace* (1899, Metropolitan). From his later career dates *Pocahontas* (1921, Jamestown, Va.). Partridge was also a poet and critic, writing several perceptive articles about contemporary sculpture. (W.C.)

Patchwork.

The technique of piecing together in a regular pattern bits of fabric salvaged from worn clothing and furnishings originated in Europe, but it produced a particularly abundant expression as an American folk art, perhaps originally in response to the scarcity and cost of imported textiles. The primary application of the patchwork technique has been the quilt. After about 1840, the "pieced" patchwork quilt is supplanted by "appliqué" quilts in which small pieces of cloth are sewn onto muslin backing and the muslin sections later pieced together. The new technique liberated patchwork from small geometric designs forming an overall mosaic. It produced bolder and more imaginative design elements that might be repeated at spaced intervals in a large field but might just as readily be unique figures occupying uniformly bordered areas. A good example of the latter is the quilt (c.1850) at the Henry Ford Museum, Dearborn, Mich., with red-bordered rectangular panels containing mostly floral motifs but also a horse, a cat, houses, a church, and a ship.

To make a quilt, the completed patchwork fabric is lined with thin padding and stitched to a plain or patterned backing. The running intersecting stitches or "quilting" that affix the three layers may follow or contrast with the stitching of the patchwork cover, and in many quilts the elaborate artistry of the quilting equals or even surpasses the patchwork elements in decorative invention. To a considerable extent patchwork patterns were standardized and favorite named elements were repeated again and again. The *Sunburst* pattern and the *Festoon and Bowknot* border (as in the fine yellow, green, and red patchwork quilt with elegant feather-stitched quilting in the Brooklyn Museum) are readily identified motifs, as are the eight-pointed *Star of Bethlehem* or the *Rose and Tulip*. Other recurrent figures reveal much about the rural environment and social pattern of their makers' lives—among them *Log Cabin, Horseshoe, Bear's Paw, Bachelor's Puzzle, Hand of Friendship, Snowball,* and *Birds in the Air*.

In many rural areas the making of patchwork quilts has survived 20th-century mechanization, and quilting bees continue as cooperative work

Patchwork

1. Patchwork and Appliqué bedspread, cotton, 19th century. Collection Index of American Design, National Gallery of Art, Washington, D.C.

2. Princess Feather and Tulip, Pa., c.1825. Collection Jonathan Holstein, N.Y.

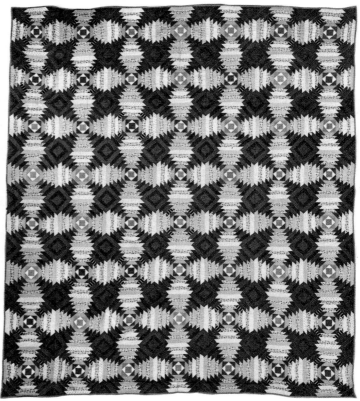

1

2

3

4

Patchwork

1. Log Cabin *blocks arranged in a pattern called* Barn Raising, *cotton, Pa., c.1880.*
2. Triangles, *cotton, Pa., c.1870.*
3. Star of Bethlehem, *cotton, Pa., c.1880.*
4. Pineapples, *cotton, N.J., c.1870. All, Collection Jonathan Holstein, N.Y.*

sessions in which one maker's accumulation of appliqué elements are joined together and lined. A new awareness of the decorative value of traditional patchwork patterns has also given rise to machine-made reproductions, the marketing of precut components, and the intensive development of patchwork quilts as an Appalachian cottage industry. (M.J.G.)

Patroon Painters.
The first clearly recognizable school in American art; the term applied to the naive artists (c.1675–1750), many unknown by name, who served the merchants and officials of New York and the Dutch manorial lords of the Hudson River Valley. Their work, although linear and flat, often quaintly out of drawing, and much dependent on mezzotint prototypes,* nevertheless reveals several markedly individual styles. An original sense of design and feeling for the subject is often apparent and sometimes amusingly so, as in *Mrs. Thomas Van Alstyne* (1721, New York Hist.), where the artist, signing himself "Aetatis Sue Limner,"* has, in his concentration upon an attractive arrangement of arms and a flower, given the lady two right hands. A very early masterpiece of the school is the full-length of the forceful and warlike patroon, *Pieter Schuyler* (c.1700–10, City of Albany, N.Y.). A "school" of artists in the sense of a coherent and continuing succession is rare in American art, adding interest to these works which the art historian E. P. Richardson has called "the earliest significant development of native-born talent in American painting." Their coherence comes not only from the baroque tradition, dimly but ardently reflected in their portraits, and from their patronage by a proud, aggressive New World aristocracy, but also from closeness of family ties and the traditional father-to-son transmission of skill and profession. Pieter Vanderlyn* was the father of another painter, and he was the grandfather of the well-known John Vanderlyn.* Evert Duyckinck (1621–1702) founded a dynasty that includes his son, Gerrit (1660–c.1710), a grandson, Evert (1677–1727), Gerrit's son, Gerardus (1695–1742) and grandson, also Gerardus (1723–97). Since patronage tended also to follow family patterns, genealogical research has aided in the still conjectural identification of artists

and the attribution of paintings. Thus the active "De Peyster Limner" has been tentatively identified as Gerardus Duyckinck I. Evert Duyckinck I had come from Holland as a young soldier. In his work, as well as that of others, some influence of Dutch painting might be expected, and can be discerned in the "Stuyvesant Limner's" *Peter Stuyvesant* and *Nicholas William Stuyvesant* (New York Hist.), done in the 1660s. Yet undoubtedly the most consistent stylistic influence was English, transmitted through the popular mezzotint portraits from the court of London. (C.C.S.)

Pattern-molded Glass.
A type of glass production in which the hot gather is forced into a patterned mold that imparts decoration to the glass; the gather is then removed and inflated to the desired shape, the design being expanded and distended to some extent. Henry William Stiegel* and Johann Amelung* employed this type of glass decoration in America in the 18th century. In the 19th century, it spread to all glass producing areas and especially the Midwest, where it is sometimes erroneously referred to as "Ohio Stiegel." Although pattern-molding was practiced in the New England factories, it became a specialty of the Pittsburgh area and factories up and down the Ohio River. The massive and often wide pieces with heavy ribbing are sometimes called by collectors "steamboat glass" from a belief that they were made especially heavy to prevent breakage when used on river boats. The factories in Zanesville, founded in 1815, and Kent (c.1823–34), Ohio, produced high-quality colored, ribbed, and diamond-patterned tableware of a lighter type. Attributions of this type of glass are tentative, and the wares of the various glasshouses are often much alike because of the general use of a few designs and the frequent moves of glassblowers from one factory to another. (J.S.S.)

Peabody, Robert Swain (1845–1917). Architect. He was an early leader in the colonial revival and a classicist who espoused a very formal Renaissance type of design. He graduated from Harvard in 1866 and went abroad, entering the École des Beaux-Arts in 1868. In 1870 he returned to Boston and formed a partnership, Peabody &

Stearns, with John Goddard Stearns (1843–1917) that lasted for nearly forty years. Stearns usually supervised the construction of buildings while Peabody was the designer. One of their first commissions in Boston was the Brunswick Hotel on Copley Square (1874), which, with its horizontal band courses and pointed stone arches at the main portal and roof gables, was the last word in Victorian Gothic* elegance. In 1878 they designed the Mutual Life Insurance Company Building on Milk Street. This grand exposition of the best Paris had to offer had a two-tiered mansard roof crowned by a high clock tower. The following year they won the competition for the Union League Club, built at 39th Street and Fifth Avenue, New York. It was designed in the fashionable Queen Anne* style, with high gables and steep roof. Peabody's interest in the colonial revival is visible in the gables, windows, and cupola of the Hemenway Gymnasium at Harvard University (1880). A notable creation of the firm was the Unitarian Association Building in Boston (1886). A rectangular Italian palazzo, it contrasts smooth-surfaced stonework at the base with rough-cut stonework on the floors above. The firm also designed Machinery Hall for the World's Columbian Exposition in Chicago in 1893; it presented a severely classical colonnaded front surmounted by rich baroque towers and domes.

The firm produced many town houses in Boston and a grand Romanesque revival* house for the railroad magnate James J. Hill in St. Paul, Minn. (1889). Their most interesting summer resort house was an asymmetrical shingle style* villa for George Nixon Black at Manchester-by-the-Sea, near Boston (1884). In 1915 they inserted a tower in the center of the old Greek revival* Custom House in Boston; it rose to a height of 495 feet and was Boston's first skyscraper. In Philadelphia they built two handsome Italian Renaissance town houses on Rittenhouse Square for George W. Childs Drexel (now Curtis Institute of Music) and for Alexander Van Rensselaer.

Peabody served for many years, without pay, as head of the city park department in Boston. He was the author of several sketchbooks of architecture. An early member of the American Institute of Architects, he was elected to fellowship in 1889. (A.B.)

Peale, Anna Claypoole (1791–1878). Miniature painter. A daughter of James Peale,* granddaughter and niece of the James Claypooles,* Anna grew up as one of a household and family of Philadelphia painters. She became proficient in both oils and watercolor. At the Pennsylvania Academy exhibition of 1811 she showed a "Fruit Piece (first attempt)," and in 1814 a "Frame containing three miniatures." Between 1817 and 1842 she entered 120 works at the Academy, almost all of them miniatures on ivory. She painted in Philadelphia, Baltimore, Washington, and in Boston, where she exhibited at the Athenaeum.

President James Monroe, Dolley Madison, General and Mrs. Andrew Jackson, and Commodore Bainbridge were among her sitters. Her ivories are painted with great skill and with a feminine tenderness appropriate to the art of the miniature. The portrait usually appears against a modulated but rather dark background. She retired in 1841. (C.C.S.)

Peale, Charles Willson (1741–1827). Portrait and natural history painter and museum proprietor. Peale became the leading representative in American art of the rationalism of the 18th-century Enlightenment. Eldest son of a Maryland country schoolmaster, he grew up in Annapolis as the main support of a widowed mother. As a saddler's apprentice, he showed a propensity for constant activity, experimentation, and an interest in many arts—traits that were to characterize his life. In Philadelphia he began painting lessons with John Hesselius.* By 1764 he was combining a medley of trades—saddler, chaisemaker, silversmith, clock and watch repairman, and portrait and sign painter —with political campaigning. This led to business failure and a flight to New England, where he painted a few portraits and received advice and encouragement from John Singleton Copley.* After his return, in 1766, wealthy Marylanders subscribed to a fund to send him to London to study art.

Working in the studio of Benjamin West* for a year and a half, Peale acquired a sophisticated style of portraiture. From others he gained facility in miniature painting, mezzotint,* and sculpture. He was influenced by Hogarth's *Analysis of Beauty,* and by Charles Du Fresnoy's poem emphasizing the relationship of painting to poetry. He returned to Maryland in 1769, and eventually became the leading portrait painter of the middle colonies. A single-minded dedication to art resulted in works composed with care and sensitivity, the element of poetry often expressed in linear rhythms. Technical difficulties hampered him, and his faces of this period have a yellowish cast due to impermanent flesh tints. Among his prominent patrons were John Beale Bordley, John Cadwalader, and George Washington; his portraits of the latter are regarded as the best likenesses of the general.

The Peales moved from Annapolis to Philadelphia in 1776. Peale again combined art with campaigning—in war as a captain of militia, in politics as a leader of the radical Whigs. Political propaganda had appeared in his art from the first, and it now blossomed out in allegorical transparencies celebrating victories, the French alliance, and American democracy. First shown in the windows of his own house, others were commissioned by Congress and the state of Pennsylvania. They mark the beginning of his dependence on popular rather than private patronage. In 1782 he added a skylighted gallery to his home, filling it with portraits of heroes of the war. Here he exhibited "moving pictures," a refinement of transparency painting. In 1786 began the museum of natural history which was to be his major concern for the next forty years.

"Peale's Museum," an expression of the deist philosophy of God in nature, was in whole and detail a work of art. As a naturalist Peale is a minor figure, but in scientific exposition he was far ahead of his time, notably in the exhibition of birds against painted backgrounds of natural habitat, and in mounting animals on carved wooden forms to reveal the muscular action of the pose. To support the museum's growth, Peale continued to paint for the museum portrait gallery, eventually completing more than 250 works. Over a third of the gallery is still preserved in the Independence Hall collection, Philadelphia. Peale's *trompe l'oeil* portrait of his sons on a staircase, *The Staircase Group* (1795, Philadelphia), was long an entertainment feature of the museum, and his *Exhumation of the First American Mastodon* (1801, Peale Museum, Baltimore) accompanied the exhibition of the mounted skeleton. The museum exhibited occasional paintings and sculpture by Peale's family and friends. Silhouettes, commonly attributed to Peale, were traced by a machine and cut by Moses Williams, a former Peale slave.

Peale's later portraits are more variable in quality than those of his earlier period. Throughout, he sought to catch the mood of the sitter most pleasing to him, and as a result his faces tend to reflect a rational, benign confidence. His canvases are solidly painted, without glazing, his chief technical difficulty coming from experiments with pigments. Almost all larger pieces are signed and dated but his miniatures are unsigned. In 1786 he left this branch of the art to his youngest brother, James Peale,* although he still occasionally pursued it.

Peale was the father of seventeen children, many either artists or naturalists, including Rembrandt Peale,* Raphaelle Peale,* Rubens Peale,* and Titian Ramsey Peale.* (C.C.S.)

Peale, James (1749–1831). Painter of portraits in miniature and oils, and of still life, landscape, and historical subjects. The youngest brother of Charles Willson Peale,* he was born in Chestertown, Md. During his youth he received painting lessons from his brother. From 1776–79 he served in the Continental Army, rising from ensign to captain, an experience which left him in delicate health but with a feeling for the military virtues. He resigned after the Battle of Monmouth, but was again with the army at the siege of Yorktown, returning with a view of the battle which he used in his full-lengths of General Washington. In 1782 he married and began an independent professional career. He was primarily a miniaturist for the next fifteen years, though he also painted in oils in Philadelphia and Maryland. He also assisted his brother in the family museum.

His portraits on ivory are deft and sturdy, though without sentiment and with the likeness generally marred by a stylized mouth. His early work on canvas is indistinguishable from his brother's, but a style of his own gradually emerged. He tended to pose his subjects stiffly upright in mid-canvas, yet he caught the romantic mood of the turn of the century, imparting an air of thoughtfulness to the sitter's face and bringing shadow and mystery into his landscape backgrounds. After his Yorktown scene of 1781, he produced some other historical pieces, notably *The Battle of Princeton* (Princeton University), *Defense of Fort Moultrie,* and *Allen McLane and the British Dragoons.* From 1819 until his death he painted occasional landscapes, moving from meticulous portraiture of place to large, slightly romanticized paintings such as *Pleasure Party at the Mill.* In his later years he did paintings of wild and stormy nature. Within the same period he became a successful painter of still life, mostly fruit pieces, forty-three of which appeared in exhibitions at the Pennsylvania Academy of the Fine Arts. They proved more popular, though less skillfully rendered, than those of his nephew, Raphaelle Peale.* In contrast to the diverse interests of other members of the Peale family, James' career in art was interrupted only by his years in Washington's army. He generally signed his work "I.P." along with the last two digits of the date. He was the father of Sarah M. Peale.* (C.C.S.)

Peale, Raphaelle (1774–1825).

Painter of still life and portraits. As the eldest son of Charles Willson Peale,* he grew up in a large family immersed in painting, music, and poetry and in the natural history museum which became their chief support. In 1796–97 he and his brother Rembrandt Peale* were in Baltimore painting portraits on canvas and in miniature and conducting a museum and picture gallery. He painted miniatures in Philadelphia and on the road, advertising his excellent work in the newspapers with humor, the lure of reduced prices, and the guarantee, "No Likeness, No Pay." After 1802, he occasionally toured the country with a physiognotrace, a copying device with which he made silhouettes by the thousand. He attempted to exploit some of his father's inventions, patented methods of his own for protecting ships' bottoms and purifying sea water, and, even explained the working of the solar system in a "theory of the universe."

In 1812 Raphaelle first exhibited a still-life composition, and continued to concentrate on this form with a technical perfection that set standards that were to dominate American still-life

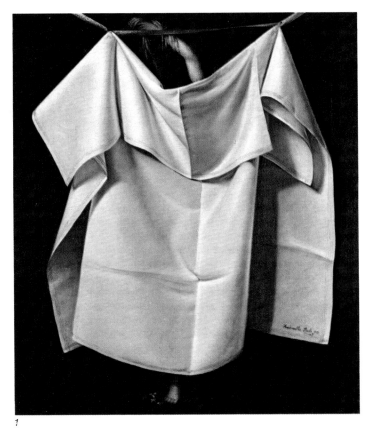

1

2

1. *Raphaelle Peale.* After the Bath, *1823. William R. Nelson Gallery of Art, Kansas City.*
2. *Charles Willson Peale.* The Staircase Group, *1795. Philadelphia Museum of Art (George W. Elkins Collection).*

painting for many years. His compositions are generally rather stark arrangements of fruits, dishes, and objects set on a table, along the edge of which his signature appears in varying forms, with the date. A punster, ventriloquist, and jokester, he was not beyond painting his signature in the form of an apple peel curling toward the viewer. The simplicity of his work is in contrast to the more popular still life of his uncle, James Peale,* who filled out his canvas with foliage and many objects. Though Raphaelle never went abroad, his work was close in spirit to 17th-century Dutch still lifes. He sometimes raffled off his vivid little pictures or gave them to settle a grocer's bill. His most famous work, a *trompe l'oeil* titled *After the Bath* (1823), is a large painting in which a freshly-ironed napkin is apparently pinned over the canvas to cover what seems to be, from the small bare feet below and the hand and hair above, a nude figure. It is painted over a portrait of Raphaelle himself, and its purpose was to confuse and dismay his long-suffering wife. Raphaelle died two years later, his last employment the writing of love poems for the party cakes made by a Philadelphia baker. This was a sad plight for an artist, he said, and especially for one who so much preferred the "comic" to the "lovesick." (C.C.S.)

Peale, Rembrandt (1778–1860).
Portrait and historical painter. A son of Charles Willson Peale,* he was born in Bucks County, Pa., while his family was in refuge from Philadelphia and his father was with the army at Valley Forge. More than any other of the children growing up in the Peale studio, Rembrandt dedicated himself to a life in art. The first American art academy, the short-lived "Columbianum," was founded by his father in 1794, largely as an encouragement to this son; and similarly, in 1795, Washington was persuaded to sit for the seventeen-year-old boy. Three other members of the family joined in that sitting—the occasion when the painter Gilbert Stuart* warned Mrs. Washington that her husband was being "Pealed all around." Eighteen years later, with the emergence of the cult of Washington worship, Rembrandt painted an idealized portrait, the basis of his many "porthole" versions, a strong likeness which had the endorsement of many of

1

2

1. **Rembrandt Peale.** Court of Death, *c.1820. Detroit Institute of Arts.*
2. **Philip Pearlstein.** Two Nudes on a Mexican Blanket with Mirror, *1972. Private collection, Washington, D.C.*

Washington's friends and family.

Rembrandt also shared his father's interest in natural history, using it to advance his career in art. He was in Baltimore with his brother Raphaelle in 1797, exhibiting portraits and natural history objects selected from his father's Philadelphia museum. He took part in the exhumation of the first complete mastodon skeletons in 1801, an event of sensational scientific and popular interest. In 1802–03 he exhibited one of the skeletons in England, taking advantage of that opportunity to paint portraits and attend Royal Academy classes. In 1805 he helped found the Pennsylvania Academy of the Fine Arts.* Three years later, and again in 1809–10, he visited Paris to paint portraits for the gallery of his father's museum, returning with a more individual and vigorous style, much influenced by neoclassicism* and the grandiose mythological and biblical paintings of the French. This sojourn, where his talent was recognized and he was offered a place among Napoleon's court painters, confirmed his ambition to be more than a portraitist. From a large equestrian portrait of Napoleon, strongly praised by the art critic John Neal,* he moved on to a classic theme, *Roman Daughter* (1812, Peale Museum, Baltimore). Criticism by the Russian artist Paul Svinin questioning the originality of this picture was directed more against Peale's admiration for Napoleon than the picture, but it so discouraged Rembrandt that he stopped painting and founded a museum of art and natural history in Baltimore in 1814. But it was only a digression from art, and in 1820 he at last achieved success with his very large painting, *Court of Death* (Detroit). He took it on tour from city to city, drawing crowds, and earning over $9000 in one year. He had been one of the first American artists to take up lithography, and a color lithograph by John B. and William S. Pendleton, whom he had trained, helped to publicize the picture.

Following his years at the Baltimore museum, Rembrandt Peale had studios in New York, Boston, and, finally, Philadelphia. His tour of Europe, 1829–30, is described in his *Notes on Italy.* He crossed the Atlantic for the fifth and last time in 1831–34. (These trips were financed in part by painting copies of Italian masters, in which he occasion-

ally felt free to make small variations.) In his later years he published his *Graphics,* a school text on the principle that skill in writing is the best introduction to drawing, and his *Portfolio of an Artist,* an anthology of favorite works including a few poems of his own. He also delivered on many occasions a lecture on the portraits of Washington, illustrated with paintings. His own masterpiece in portraiture, however, is undoubtedly his *Thomas Jefferson* (New York Hist.), painted from life in 1805. (C.C.S.)

Peale, Rubens (1784–1864).
Museum director and painter. Son of Charles Willson Peale,* he managed his father's Philadelphia museum, 1810–22, and was proprietor of museums in Baltimore, 1822–25, and New York City, 1825–37. Each had its gallery of portraits and other paintings. Through the last ten years of his life he painted still life and landscape characterized by a painstaking primitive charm, such as *Two Grouse in an Underbrush of Laurel* (1864, Detroit).

Peale, Sarah Miriam (1800–85).
Portrait painter. A daughter of James Peale,* she grew up in her father's studio, painting her first portrait for exhibition at the age of eighteen. An earlier self-portrait, full of youthful allure, was much praised, although her father is said to have commented, "Damn it, why didn't you do what I told you to do?" She was elected an academician of the Pennsylvania Academy of the Fine Arts* in 1824. In the next year, General Lafayette posed for her, and her likeness of him was highly praised. In 1831 she settled in Baltimore, where she became in time the city's leading portrait painter. In 1841–43 she was active in Washington, D.C., painting prominent figures in the government, and in 1847 was persuaded to move to St. Louis, where she remained for thirty years. She turned to still-life painting late in life, in St. Louis and after her return to Philadelphia, where she died. She never married, and it is a tribute to her talent that she could support herself entirely by her profession throughout a long life. (C.C.S.)

Peale, Titian Ramsay (1799–1885).
Painter of natural history. The youngest son of Charles Willson Peale,* he was trained as a naturalist at his father's

Philadelphia museum and at the University of Pennsylvania, and he accompanied exploring expeditions to Florida, the West, South America, and the Pacific Ocean as artist-naturalist. While primarily an illustrator of natural life, notably of Charles Lucien Bonaparte's *American Ornithology* (1825–33), his imaginative feeling for landscape and love of adventure was expressed in oils and watercolors. In his last twenty-five years he contributed to the development of photography as an active amateur. He became director of the Philadelphia Museum in 1833; in the same year he published *Lepidoptera Americana.* His naturalist paintings are distinguished by frosty tones, a restrained style, and decorative elegance. (C.C.S.)

Pearlstein, Philip (1924–   ).
Painter. He was born in Pittsburgh, Pa., and studied at the Carnegie Institute and New York University's Institute of Fine Arts. He has been a chief proponent of a return to realism in painting and his own stark portrayals of the human figure have been both highly original and influential. Pearlstein presents his nudes without idealization, just as one might find them in a domestic situation. He is relentless in painting what he sees, often verging on gauche or grotesque effects, and his harsh lighting and mannerist habit of arbitrarily cutting the image off (as in *Woman Reclining on Couch,* 1966, where half of the head and a foot are amputated by the edge of the canvas) add to the effect of candid photography. Technically, however, Pearlstein's figures and props are clearly constructed of paint and cannot be confused with mechanical images. Primarily a draftsman, his monochromatic paintings sometimes resemble pink- and gray-tinted drawings, which removes them even further from any sensuous concerns. Pearlstein has painted several portraits of college presidents—such as the academic-robed *Dr. Meng* of Hunter College—which carry forward the same qualities as his studies of the nude. If Pearlstein's pictures sometimes seem unflattering, or even semi-surrealistic, one nonetheless believes in them, and out of the clarity of his highly subjective and personalized vision one finds the reality and beauty of everyday life. Pearlstein is represented in major museum collections.

Pei, I(eoh) M(ing) (1917–   ).
An architects' architect in the 1950s
and early 1960s, by the end of the
1960s he was sought after for his large-
scale housing and educational projects
as well as for small, sculptural buildings
such as museums and monuments.
Born in Canton, China, he studied at the
Massachusetts Institute of Technology
(1940) and Harvard Graduate School of
Design (1946), where he taught (1945–
48). He became a naturalized citizen of
the United States in 1954. He began his
practice as architect for Williams Zeck-
endorf's real estate developments, and
showed that buildings of genuine distinction could be produced in such an
association: Mile High Center and Denver Hilton Hotel, Denver (1957); Kips
Bay Plaza Apartment, New York City
(1962); and Society Hill Apartments,
Philadelphia (1963). In the latter two
projects, as in the Center for Earth Sciences at the Massachusetts Institute of
Technology (1965) and a series of other
towers, including University Plaza,
New York City (1966), Pei developed
poured-in-place concrete systems that
are exceptionally refined and precise,
rhythmic without being overly chaste.
These projects, like the Place Ville
Marie center in Montreal (1963), were
also large-scale urban planning developments. In his National Center for Atmospheric Research in Boulder, Col.
(1967), and the academic center of the
State University at Fredonia, N.Y.
(1969), he displayed a plastic, sculptural sense in planning and massing. His
design of a graceful air traffic control
tower to be used by the Federal Aviation Agency at all United States airports
(1963) was a national recognition of his
skill in concrete sculpturing. Yet, what
brought him most acclaim was his
smaller, pavilion-like buildings: East-
west Center, University of Hawaii
(1964); Newhouse Communications
Center, Syracuse University (1965);
Des Moines Art Center Addition, Iowa
(1969); and the Everson Museum of Art,
Syracuse, N.Y. (1968), with its weighty
cantilevers.

At the beginning of the 1970s, his
National Airlines Terminal at Kennedy
International Airport, New York (designed 1961; completed 1971) displayed his mastery of the pavilion
idiom. Here round concrete columns
support a slim attic in a structure that
is otherwise enclosed in a transparent
skin of glass and glass fins. This build-

1

1. **I.M. Pei.** University Plaza, New York
City, 1966.
2. **Irving Penn.** Woman in Bed, 1949,
photograph. The Condé Nast Publications, Inc.

2

ing is one of the purest products of the minimal* style. With the East Building to the National Gallery of Art, Washington, D.C., the Choate School Fine Arts Center, and the John Fitzgerald Kennedy Library, Cambridge, Mass., his work seemed ever more purified, jewel-like, and costly.

His most significant contributions, however, are his large-scale urban plans and developments, such as Boston's Government Center (1963) in which he fixed the plans, massing, and roof lines of an enormous renewal area; and L'Enfant Plaza in Washington (1967), as well as others in Cleveland, Los Angeles, Providence, and Oklahoma City. (C.R.S.)

Pelham, Henry (1749–1806).
Engraver whose print of the "Boston Massacre" of 1770 was copied and made famous by Paul Revere.* Son of Peter Pelham* and half-brother of the painter John Singleton Copley,* Pelham painted portraits and miniatures and designed a large and beautiful *Plan of Boston in New England with its Environs.* Based on drawings made by him on the spot, before his flight from Boston with other Loyalists in 1776, the map was engraved in aquatint by Francis Jukes in London and published there by Pelham in 1777.

Pelham, Peter (c.1695–1751).
Engraver and portrait painter. He came from London to Boston in 1726, the first practitioner to bring to America the art of engraving mezzotint prototypes.* He worked also in Newport, R.I., but returned to Boston where, in 1748, he married as his third wife the widowed mother of John Singleton Copley.* His greatest influence in American art history is as,the encourager and teacher of his stepson. He was the father, by this marriage, of Henry Pelham,* painter and engraver. His portrait of Cotton Mather (1728) may be America's first graphic work.

Penfield, Edward (1866–1925).
Designer of striking posters, magazine covers, and advertising pages. Penfield was born and grew up in Brooklyn, N.Y.; he left school to study at the Art Students League* in New York. Beginning in 1890, he was art editor of *Harper's Magazine;* soon he took on the art editorships of *Harper's Weekly* and *Harper's Bazaar* as well. In 1901 he

resigned these jobs to devote all his time to painting and drawing. In his poster work, begun about 1890, he learned (as others were learning at the same time) to use commercial lithography for his own artistic purposes. He emphasized the elegant dress and surroundings of fashionable life in the United States, treated Ivy League collegiates with sympathetic humor, and returned again and again to the image of the tall, athletic, comely young American woman. Sometimes working in flat patterns of color influenced by the prints of Bonnard, sometimes in spatter techniques derived from the work of Toulouse-Lautrec, he based his designs on strong, sure, careful draftsmanship. He loved horses, collected carriages, and often incorporated horse-drawn equipages in his drawings. (S.H.)

Penn, Irving (1917–   ).
Photographer. Born in Plainfield, N.J., he attended the Philadelphia Museum School of Art, studying advertising design with Alexey Brodovitch. In the early 1940s he became art director of Saks Fifth Avenue department store. He tried painting in Mexico in 1943, but returned to New York and became a staff photographer for *Vogue.* In 1944 he joined the Quaker American Field Service and traveled to India and Italy as a photographer for this relief agency. After World War II he rejoined Condé Nast Publications and became well known for his fashion photographs and portraits of prominent personalities in society and the arts. He continued to travel and photograph in China, India, Peru, and Turkey. In 1953 he opened his own studio in New York. A one-man exhibition of his work was held in 1960 at a New York gallery.

His first book, *Moments Preserved* (1960), was a retrospective selection of his photographs. These are precisely composed and innovative in their treatment of themes. His photographs as a whole are optimistic and often convey a feeling of sensual joy. They celebrate the life of those who crave change and new experiences, who travel widely, and keep abreast of fashions in clothes and art. His color work is imaginative and he often uses color that is "unreal" in order to divorce his easily recognized subjects from their normal context. By such devices, subjects of limited or topical significance are rendered exotic. His portraits, characterized by distinctive poses, show penetration much beyond a pleasing likeness and often reflect a fascination with surrealism.*   (V.D.C.)

Pennsylvania Academy of the Fine Arts, The

America's second oldest public art gallery and art school. It was founded in 1805, largely through the efforts of Charles Willson Peale.* The Academy began by importing from the Louvre casts of antique sculpture and copies of Old Master paintings for the enlightenment of its students. For many years, this was the only collection of its kind at one of the only art schools in the United States. Beginning in 1806, the Academy for many years held annual exhibitions of American art. In 1870 it moved to its present location, into a building designed by Frank Furness.* The Academy, now an art school and museum, has an outstanding collection of early American painting, particularly examples by the Peale* family, as well as Robert Fulton's* collection of European art.

Pereira, Irene Rice (1907–71).

Painter. She was born in Chelsea, Mass., and after studying fashion design at the Traphagen School, attended the Art Students League* in New York City. In 1931 she studied in France with Amédée Ozenfant, adopting his theories of "unadorned functionalism." After traveling widely, she returned to New York, where she painted semi-abstract pictures of the machine and its effects on human life. In 1935 she taught in the design laboratory of the WPA Federal Art Project,* and this experience clearly influenced her turn toward geometric abstraction, a mode she practiced for the rest of her life. She described her effort as "seeking a system of plastic equivalents for the revolutionary discoveries in mathematics, physics, biochemistry, and radioactivity." Later she characterized her art in metaphysical terms. She experimented intensively with paint textures, as in *Oblique Progression* (1948, Whitney), and with painting on superimposed panes of glass and on parchment.   (A.F.)

Period Revival Style (1920–41).

A style of architecture, employed since the early 1890s, that continued to dominate the urban core and the suburban streets of America during the 1920s and 1930s. The favored imagery for governmental buildings continued to be a mixture of Roman and Renaissance. On the whole, these classical compositions were handled with confidence and sophistication, and it could be argued that the most impressive of America's neoclassic buildings date from these years: the National Gallery of Art (Washington, D.C., 1937) by John Russell Pope (1874–1937) and that ideal of the classical tradition, the colonnaded Thomas Jefferson Memorial (Washington, D.C., 1937), also by Pope. At the same time, the versatile Paul P. Cret (1876–1945) designed the classical Federal Reserve Building (Washington, D.C., 1937). On a state level, the beautifully sited Washington State Capitol by Wilder and White (designed in 1911) carried on the 19th-century predilection for central-domed structures.

Neoclassical imagery continued to be used in commercial structures, as in the Cunard Building (New York City, 1921) by Benjamin Wister Morris (1870–1944), but, in general, neoclassical buildings were increasingly stripped, and in many cases began to incorporate moderne details and ornament. Cleaned-up classicism of this sort ranged from the Nebraska State Capitol (Lincoln, 1916–1928) by Bertram Goodhue* to Paul Cret's Folger Shakespeare Library (Washington, D.C., 1930). The influence of the Paris Exposition of Decorative Arts of 1925 and of the Viennese Secessionists made a soft, delicate, boudoir version of the neoclassical style increasingly popular, particularly for the exterior of retail stores.

But the major commitment of the 1920s was to neo-Gothic, used for commercial skyscrapers* and other large nongovernmental buildings. The winning of the Chicago *Tribune* Competition by the gothicized design of Howell & Hood* in 1922–24 established the prestige of this mode, and it continued to be preferred for skyscrapers during the 1920s. As with neoclassical buildings, the later neo-Gothic designs were increasingly denuded of historic details, and in many instances moderne detail became an integral part of design. The neo-Gothic was also preferred for church and educational designs. The major exponent of the medieval style continued to be the Boston architect Ralph Adams Cram (1863–1942). In New England and elsewhere, the colonial revival style, i.e. American Georgian and Federal,* was very often used for churches, colleges, university buildings, and small-scale governmental structures such as post offices and libraries. In California the Spanish colonial revival mode was widely used for retail stores, motion picture theaters, churches, educational and governmental buildings; whole communities were remolded into this "indigenous" Mediterranean style. In New Mexico the "adobe revival," which had begun before the war, was fully realized, especially in the work of the Santa Fe architect John Gaw Memm (b.1894).

While commercial and even governmental architecture slowly began to absorb both the moderne and the modern, domestic architecture never wavered in its full commitment to period forms. In the East and Midwest (with the exception of Florida) the allegiance was primarily to the colonial. The large country houses of the 1920s and early 1930s abandoned the monumental scale of the pre-1918 period and substituted a more intimate massing of volume and smaller interior spaces of the colonial, Tudor, and French Provincial. Such high-style architects as Delano & Aldrich,* Hyman Embury, and David Adler created a relaxed, sometimes stage-set array of country houses across the United States.

In smaller houses all of these modes were used, but it was the white clapboard or brick colonial revival house that was looked upon with the greatest fondness. America's popular home magazines, *House Beautiful, House and Garden, American Home* and others, filled their pages with one-and-a-half-story and two-story versions of America's colonial past. Increasingly these small houses became closer to the scale and proportions of the originals. The acknowledged master of this imagery was the New England architect Royal B. Wills (1895–1962), who not only built in this mode prolifically and with real understanding, but also was a formidable propagandist through his many books such as *Houses for Good Living* (1940). Equally important in ensuring the correctness of colonial revival work in the 1930s was the publication of measured drawings of 18th-

1

2

Period Revival
1. *Richard Morris Hunt. Biltmore, Asheville, N.C., 1895.*
2. *Julia Morgan. San Simeon (William Randolph Hearst's California house), Neptune pool, 1947.*

and early 19th-century historic houses, the sketches and photographs of Samuel Chamberlain (b.1895), and the intense interest aroused by the Rockefeller restoration of Colonial Williamsburg (1927–1935).

California was the scene of a new regionalism: the Spanish colonial revival style, which by the end of the 1920s had reshaped the visual environment of almost all cities and towns. The most gifted exponent of the style was the Montecito architect George Washington Smith (1876–1930), who produced highly abstract compositions derived from the provincial Andalusian architecture of Spain and the provincial architecture of Mexico. In Florida, the more theatrical designs of Addison Mizner (1872–1933) at Coral Gables and elsewhere, implanted the image of Spain. The largest single monument in the style was San Simeon (1919–1947), William Randolph Hearst's castle, designed by Julia Morgan (1872–1957) and set high on the coastal mountain range of central California.

Though period architecture was bitterly criticized by exponents of the International style,* it proved to be as satisfactory a method of packaging a building as that of high-art International style or of low-art moderne. The period revival designers were as concerned with plumbing, heating, and other functional aspects as were the modernists. In fact, the period revival product often functioned far better as machines for working or living than any International style product. Like all versions of a past tradition, the period revival buildings of the 1920s and 1930s established their own characteristics, which in the long run turned out to be as peculiar to the period as those which were considered modern. (D.G.)

Peterdi, Gabor (1915–   ).
Printmaker and painter. Born near Budapest, Hungary, Peterdi received a Prix de Rome at fourteen. He studied in Rome and at Stanley Hayter's Atelier 17* in Paris before emigrating to the United States in 1939. In 1947 he rejoined Hayter's Atelier 17, by then established in New York City. Peterdi went on to establish printmaking workshops at the Brooklyn Museum Art School, Hunter College, New York University, and Yale University, where he has been a professor since 1960. He is the author of books on the tech-

1

2

niques and history of printmaking. His early work was almost totally figurative engraving. After working with Hayter he expanded his technical vocabulary while still concentrating on natural forms. As he developed away from the surrealist influence of the Atelier 17 circle of artists, he increasingly observed the minutiae of life in organisms and other phenomena of nature. Mixing intaglio techniques, which allow numerous possible combinations of line and color, he has depicted the miraculous landscapes, rock formations, ice-caps, and lava flows of the United States. (R.C.)

Peto, John Frederick (1854–1907).
Still-life painter, born in Philadelphia, Pa., and trained at the Pennsylvania Academy of the Fine Arts.* Peto began his career in his native city, doing anything of an artistic nature that came to hand—painting, sculpture, and photography. For lack of success at home, he moved in 1889 to Island Heights, N.J., where he had been offered a position as cornet player at the religious sessions known as camp meetings, and there he remained until his death. In the isolation of Island Heights, Peto developed his own distinctive style, characterized by softly radiant surface effects, heavy emphasis on worn-out, discarded, derelict objects, restless composition, and frequently a dark, even violent moodiness. An example is *Still Life with Lanterns* (c.1890, Brooklyn). Because Peto was very little known during his lifetime and was totally forgotten after his death, a number of his works were given the forged signature of William Harnett* and floated on the New York market as paintings by the older man. As such they attained considerable notice; at one time, indeed, Harnett was best known through these faked Petos. The problem was complicated by the fact that Peto admired Harnett and adapted some of his subjects and compositional devices, but he transformed them all into his own style. (A.F.)

Pewter.
Pewter is an alloy of which the chief constituent is tin. Smaller quantities of lead, copper, and antimony were added to the tin, the proportions depending largely upon the function of the finished article. The finer grades, consisting of over ninety percent tin

with little or no lead, were used for all forms requiring strength, a smooth finish, and a high lustre. Where these qualities were not required and a low cost of manufacture was important—as in candle molds, pipe organs, and inkwells—the lead content might run as high as forty percent.

Because of the problems faced by the colonial pewterer in obtaining tin, a difficulty not shared by his counterpart overseas, the quality of his pewter was not always as high as that of the ablest British or continental pewterers. His reputation had to stand instead upon the simplicity, dignity, and purity of line of the forms which he fashioned. By any such standard he was highly successful, for the finest American designs compare favorably with those of the pewterers of England and the Continent.

The 17th Century
The earliest of the colonial pewterers of record were emigrants from England. When they sailed for America they took with them, whenever possible, the molds and tools they had been using, and in America they continued to make vessels of the same designs as those to which they were accustomed. Only gradually did they or their apprentices and successors attempt innovations in form and decoration. Some of the new designs, when presented, were eminently satisfying, both functionally and esthetically.

Such success as the colonial pewterer achieved was gained in spite of handicaps and hardships that were, to a large extent, imposed upon him by the British government. One such difficulty was his inability to import tin from England. Cornwall, England, had the largest deposits of high grade tin in the western world, a source upon which the pewterers of Great Britain and western Europe were almost completely dependent. The British government, determined to prevent the colonies from manufacturing any product that could be made in England and sold in America, exported finished pewter wares to the colonies duty-free, but placed such a tax on tin bars that the colonial pewterer could not afford to import English tin. To practice his trade he had to depend upon his ability to gather up worn and damaged pewter for remelting. As a result, colonial pewterers learned early and with surprising accuracy how to determine the

1. *John Frederick Peto.* The Poor Man's Store, *1885. Museum of Fine Arts, Boston (Karolik Collection).*
2. *John Frederick Peto.* Ordinary Objects in the Artist's Creative Mind, *1887. Shelburne Museum, Shelburne, Vt.*

3

4

metallic composition of each damaged article brought to them and thus build up piles of graded stock that ranged from the finest quality, which was high in tin, to the poorest, which was high in lead.

In one other respect the American pewterer was at a disadvantage in competing with his English cousin. His business was not controlled, as in England, by an all-powerful guild that established standards of quality, ordered each pewterer to mark his metal with his own touchmark to identify it, and fined him for infringement of any of its regulations. Standards in each colonial shop were established only by the conscience of its master pewterer.

The earliest pewterers of record in the colonies were Englishmen by birth and training. At least fourteen can be identified by name as working in Boston or Salem, Mass., during the 17th century. Of work done by the earliest of those settlers, only some ten pieces, now in collections, are known to exist today. These are attributed with confidence to Edmund Dolbeare, who arrived in Boston about 1670, moved to Salem about 1684, and some fifteen years later returned with his family to Boston. There he died sometime between 1706–11. His surviving work includes a rose-water bowl, a plate, and eight large dishes, all of early design and all struck four times on each brim with a touchmark enclosing the initials E. D. Whether any or all of these items were made before 1700 cannot be determined now.

In Virginia pewterers were also at work during the 17th century. Probably older than the Dolbeare pewter are fragments of spoons found in excavations made on the site of Jamestown. On the handle of one such spoon is a still-decipherable touch that shows the name Joseph Copeland, his place of work, Chuckatuck, Virginia, and the date 1675. Copeland completed his apprenticeship as a pewterer in London in 1670 and apparently sailed for Virginia soon thereafter. He died in Jamestown about 1691.

The 18th Century
Boston was the first large center of pewter-making in America. We know the names of more than forty pewterers who were working in or near Boston before the American Revolution. However, some of those men were only journeymen and never operated shops

of their own. Existing shop inventories and newspaper notices prove that the larger shops were equipped to make a wide variety of forms and also carried extensive stocks of English pewter. However, for some unexplained reason Boston makers have left a much more limited range of marked shapes and designs than have those of New York or Philadelphia. Except for the few plates and dishes made by Dolbeare, very little Boston pewter made before 1750 has been found. The few distinctive early forms that have survived appear to be the work of just one shop. They are marked with a round touch featuring a coronet flanked by the initials R and B—a touch tentatively attributed to Robert Bonynge, apparently an obscure artisan active in Boston from about 1730–63 and probably later. Among the unusual forms bearing this touch are tall beakers of a design used later by many Connecticut pewterers; pint mugs of three different patterns, fitted with solid or hollow handles; porringers with two types of handle, both of great rarity; and, most distinctive of all, church cups that closely resemble English 17th-century caudle cups. The body of the cup was decorated in relief with rope banding and a pattern of gadrooning. Some of the cups were provided with two solid handles of gracefully modulated curved lines, embellished on top with a beaded motif of great charm.

A great quantity of marked Boston pewter made in the second half of the 18th century has survived, but its lack of variety in form and design is disappointing. Although account books show that John Skinner in Boston and Nathaniel Austin in Charlestown, for example, sold much pewter, their marked work includes little beyond plates, dishes, basins, and mugs. This criticism is true in a general way of all of New England. Its pewterers have left little evidence of imagination in design or ingenuity in developing new forms.

Newport in the 1730s and a decade later Providence, R.I., were pewter-making centers of some importance. However, during the Revolution many Rhode Island records were lost and the present listing of her pewterers may be far from complete. The earliest Rhode Island pewterer of record was an Englishman, Lawrence Langworthy, who settled in Newport about 1731. His few surviving pieces suggest that he may

Pewter
3. *Edmund Dolbeare. Hammered plate with multiple-reed brim, c. 1700. Collection Dr. James H. Kier.*
4. *Daniel Curtiss. Covered pitcher, 17th century. Gallery of Fine Arts, Yale University, New Haven, Conn. (Mabel Brady Garvan Collection).*

Pewter

1. Johann Christopher Heyne. Communion service of the Hill Evangelical Lutheran Church, Cleona, Pa., mid-18th century, flagons and covered chalice. William Penn Memorial Museum, Harrisburg, Pa.
2. Joseph Leddell. Chalice of Christ Church Parish, West Haven, Conn., 1744. New Haven Historical Society, Conn.
3. Francis Bassett. Teapot, mid- or late 18th century. Collection Charles V. Swain, Doylestown, Pa.
4. Philip Will. Church Flagon, mid-18th century. Collection Mr. and Mrs. Oliver W. Deming, Westfield, Mass.
5. Coffee pot on a square base, adapted from a silver pattern by Colonel William Will, late 18th century. Collection Dr. and Mrs. Robert Mallory III, N.Y.

424

have been a maker of superior ability. Benjamin Day of Newport, working during 1744–57 has been credited with four fine specimens of superior workmanship in rare forms. He may have been the ablest of the Rhode Island pewterers. Later craftsmen, such as the Melvilles in Newport and the Hamlins in Providence, were well-trained, but had little more range in design than their Boston contemporaries.

Early in the 18th century, merchants in Boston, New York, and Philadelphia were accumulating fortunes, a landed aristocracy was developing, Old World culture was being introduced, and a growing leisure class was in a position to indulge itself in the amenities of life. Connecticut, on the other hand, was largely a colony of farmers and small-tradesmen who were unable or unwilling to spend hard-earned savings on the more decorative trappings of life. So her pewterers provided their customers with little more than the essential house utensils and equipment. Her earliest pewterers of record were Ivory Lucas, who appeared in New London in 1732, and Thomas Danforth, who moved from Taunton, Mass., to Norwich, Conn., in 1733. Lucas left New London for Delaware about fifteen years later. Danforth, however, lived out a long life in Norwich and sired a clan of nineteen pewterers. The Danforths and their apprentices were responsible for practically the entire output of 18th-century Connecticut pewter; they also scattered as far west as Buffalo and south to Virginia, North Carolina, and Georgia. Although many of the Danforth dynasty were workmen of competence within a limited range of design, nothing that they made before 1800 warrants favorable comparison with the best work of the pewterers of New York or Pennsylvania.

Because pewter was so inexpensive in the 17th and 18th centuries, and because old damaged pewter could be turned in for replacement with pewter of newest design at a ratio of two pounds of old for one of new, there was little incentive for families to preserve for posterity even the finest of their pewter. Since little, if any, pewter made in New York and Pennsylvania before 1725 can be identified positively as such, we cannot compare the work of early New York and Pennsylvania pewterers with that of their contemporaries in Boston.

6

7

8

Pewter

6. *Colonel William Will. Communion service of the Lost Creek Presbyterian Church, Huntingdon, Pa., late 18th century.*

7. *Colonel William Will. Pitcher from the communion service of the Salem Lutheran Church, Aaronsburg, Pa., late 18th century.*

8. *Coffee urn with fluted body and baluster column on circular foot, from the Britannia Manufacturing Company (Taunton, Mass.), c.1832. Collection Dr. William P. Shelton, Dallas, Tex.*

Pewter

New York Pewterers

The first New York pewterer of record was Thomas Burroughs, who completed his apprenticeship in Bristol, England, in 1678, sailing soon thereafter for America. He settled first in Boston but moved to New York about 1684. There he opened what is believed to have been the town's first pewtermaking shop, becoming a successful pewterer and merchant as well as a prominent citizen. A partial list of the molds in his inventory shows that he was equipped to manufacture pewter in a wide variety of forms; but none of it has survived. The same is true of his immediate successors, Thomas Burroughs, Jr., William Digges, and William Horsewell.

However, pewter of the middle colonies from about 1725 until 1800 has been preserved in sufficient quantities and from enough shops to warrant the assertion that standards there were generally higher than in New England, and that the pewterers made a more diverse line of forms and designs, and showed greater imagination, taste, and ingenuity. The touches of at least ten or twelve pewterers working in New York City and Albany, N.Y., have been found on pewter of exceptional merit. The larger shops in New York, such as those of the Leddells, Bradfords, Bassetts, and Wills, were unquestionably stocked with large numbers of molds and a great variety of tools and equipment, as attested by the diversity of the surviving forms and the wide variation in details. The finish was usually excellent, and elegant engraving could be provided when desired. Such sophistication was rarely, if ever, found in New England.

One of the most coveted forms in pewter today is the lidded tankard, made with wide variation in details by every pre-Revolutionary New York shop of any size; yet it is almost unknown among surviving New England pewter. Of particular distinction are the tankards with flat-topped lids and crenate lip (that is, with rounded projections or teeth) as found on Stuart tankards in 17th-century England. No known example of this form has been recorded for any colony except New York. Other distinctive articles, peculiar to New York, were round-lidded powder boxes, unusually tall beakers, christening basins, wide-mouthed chalices, the so-called "Albany" chalices

with flaring lip of cup and stepped base, and foot-warmers. Only the Pennsylvania pewterers approached in range and beauty of design the work of the New York makers.

Pennsylvania Pewterers

Philadelphia's first pewterer was Thomas Paschall from Bristol, England, who arrived with Penn's earliest settlers in 1682, a year or two before his apprentice, Thomas Burroughs, opened what is believed to have been New York's first pewter shop. Thus the earliest pewter forms and designs in both New York and Philadelphia must have followed those of Bristol rather than London. However, Philadelphia's earliest existing pewter was made by a London-trained man, Simon Edgell (active 1713–42) and included a few plates, several fine dishes that were hammered all over, and one covered quart tankard.

By the latter date a large-scale immigration to Pennsylvania was under way from continental Europe, particularly from Germany and Sweden. At just this time, 1741, the Moravian Church was establishing in Bethlehem, Pa., what was to become the mother church in America for this sect. Among the first settlers who arrived in the "first Sea Congregation" was an able pewterer, Johann Christian Heyne, a Saxon by birth. In 1750 Heyne left Bethlehem, settling first at Tulpehocken, Pa., and moving later to Lancaster, where he died in 1780. Heyne's early work followed his German patterns, but with some of the designs modified later by his exposure to the more prevalent English designs. The result was a cosmopolitanism in form unknown in any other colony. Some of Heyne's most unusual pieces, particularly his communion flagons, altar candlesticks, and chalices with knopped stem, are so patently Germanic that they would have been so classified but for Heyne's touches stamped thereon. Heyne's younger contemporary, William Will, alone among Pennsylvania pewterers excelled him in range and diversity of form.

Two Swedish pewterers, Abraham Hasselberg and his son-in-law, John A. Brunstrom, working in Philadelphia, influenced the designs of native-born pewterers there. This is particularly apparent in a typically Swedish tankard design, with wide banding on the drum and a low-dome lid flattened to permit

the insertion of a coin. Just such a tankard bears Brunstrom's name touch and exact replicas have the touches of Parks Boyd and Robert Palethorp, Jr., native Philadelphians.

Pewter design and craftsmanship reached its peak in Pennsylvania—indeed in America—in the final quarter of the 18th century, in the work of William Will. Will was a son of the Rhineland pewterer, John Will, who moved with his family to New York in 1752, there to become one of New York's ablest pewterers. William had been born in Nieuwied on the Rhine in 1742. Soon after completing his apprenticeship in New York he moved to Philadelphia, opening his first shop there in 1764. During the Revolution he organized Captain Will's Company of Associators, rose to a colonelcy and commanded the Third New Jersey Regiment of Foot. After the war he was chosen a member of the Pennsylvania General Assembly. Despite these and other public offices in which he served with distinction, he not only managed to keep his shop in operation but he became the ablest, most gifted pewterer in the nation. Several hundred examples of his work in many forms and designs have survived, testifying to his many capabilities. He was a talented innovator, adapting silver designs to pewter, as witness his superb tall coffeepots. He kept abreast of the times, offering new and sometimes original forms. An example is his Aaronsbury Church pitcher, a vessel exemplifying his good taste which is impressive for its simplicity, dignity, and charm.

The close of the 18th century signalled the end of an era in American pewter. Pewter had been waging a losing battle with Staffordshire and other forms of China and crockery that were gayer in appearance, frequently cheaper, and just as readily replaceable. British pewterers had long sought a harder alloy, one that could be cast into thin sheets and then formed into hollow ware with thinner walls. Toward the close of the century pewterers in Sheffield, England, developed a metal that met these requirements. The new alloy, called Britannia, was actually a grade of pewter that was very high in tin content, free of lead, and with small admixtures of copper and antimony, the amounts depending on the purposes to which the finished wares would be put.

Ammi Phillips. Portrait of Harriet Leavens, *c.1816. Fogg Art Museum, Harvard University, Cambridge, Mass.*

The 19th Century

By the first decade of the 19th century, Britannia was being made in America. Almost certainly Thomas D. Boardman of Hartford, Conn., in 1806 turned out the first quality work in the new metal. The harder and more lustrous alloy was at first cast, just as pewter had been. But it soon became apparent that by casting the metal in thin sheets and then reworking it the cost of production could be cut and the manufacture of a much wider variety of forms and shapes could be facilitated.

Under one new method termed spinning, introduced into America about 1822, a thin sheet of cast metal was fastened in a lathe over a chuck that held in place blocks shaped to form the exact design of the part to be produced. As the chuck was revolved, blunt tools pressed against the metal and shaped it. Another new technique was stamping, whereby panels were stamped out of sheets on a press. Frequently a finished article was composed of assembled sections that had been made by three different methods. Britannia quickly supplanted the heavier and more costly pewter. Almost overnight the character of the business changed. Prospective Britannia-makers required little capital for their comparatively inexpensive equipment; not required to serve an apprenticeship, and with little or no training, they opened shops from as far north as Belfast, Me., south to Augusta, Ga., and as far west as St. Louis, Mo.

Railroads and faster mail circulated new styles ever more rapidly. In addition, Britannia appeared at a time when taste in craftsmanship design was moving away from the simple dignified designs of an earlier day. The new forms featured sharp angles and less evenly modulated curves. And, as the period advanced, the Victorian tendency toward overelaboration became more pronounced. Naturally, much shoddy and tasteless work was turned out.

After the beginning of the century, the demand for dishes, plates, basins, porringers, and mugs—the bread-and-butter business of the pewterer—dwindled and was replaced by the manufacture in great quantities of Britannia tall teapots, tea sets, coffeepots, water pitchers, spoons, small beakers, candlesticks, and lamps. In spite of the deserved criticism of many Britannia forms, some very fine shapes in handsome designs were evolved—compositions that would have done credit to the ablest pewterers of an earlier day. Such are the "light-house" teapots of Israel Trask and Eben Smith of Beverley, Mass., the footed baptismal bowls of Trask's brother, Oliver, and the communion flagons of the Boardmans of Hartford, to name but a few.

After 1840, designs became more florid, and the business in many shops was limited largely to the manufacture of plate for silverplating. A few shops continued to manufacture fine Britannia, some even to the end of the century, but by the time of the Civil War the demand had almost disappeared and the short-lived Britannia industry was all but finished. (L.L.)

Phillips, Ammi (1788–1865).
Itinerant portraitist who worked in the Berkshire area of New England. Because he used a succession of sharply defined styles, he has been variously identified as the "Kent Limner" and the "Border Limner," and many of his works were once erroneously attributed to miniaturist John Bradley (active 1837–45). Born and raised in Colebrook, Conn., Phillips may have been exposed to the painting of such earlier itinerants as Reuben Moulthrop* before 1811, when he executed his first two known portraits in western Massachusetts. These realistic and somber bust-length paintings are curiously at odds with paintings of the following eight years, when the artist may have come under the influence of J. Brown,* who also painted in the Berkshire area where Phillips' new style emerged.

Beginning in 1812 his work is characterized by a light and subtle coloration and linear details resulting in a translucent and a dreamlike quality. Many of the ethereal paintings of this "Border Limner" period of Phillips' career are three-quarter or full-length portraits such as that of Harriet Leavens (c.1816, Fogg). A dramatic departure from the style occurs in 1820, when the pearly tones of the Border period give way to dark gray and mulberry backgrounds against which faces and white linen stand forth clearly, and black dresses crisply display laces and muslins. The style, which suggests acquaintance with the work of the academically trained Ezra Ames of Albany, pervades Phillips' painting until 1829.

In the ensuing decade he adopted a highly stylized painting technique with women shown in graceful poses, men depicted with one arm casually resting on the crest rail of a stencilled chair, and an insistence on a total figurative contour that crowds against the confines of the canvas. This style, exemplified in *Woman in a Black Ruffled Dress* (Kaplan Coll.),is the one ascribed to the "Kent Limner." It disappears by 1840, giving way to less mannered likenesses and, toward the end of the decade, to a more fully developed interest in sculptural modeling. Phillips' late works are those of a competent artist tutored by many years of experience and, almost inevitably, influenced by the introduction of photography.

(M.J.G.)

Phillips, Mary Walker (1923–).
Leader in the field of nonwoven textitles, especially in the application of knitting and macramé techniques. She was born in Fresno, Cal., and studied weaving at the Cranbrook Academy in Michigan. She first came to attention with her long, symmetrical hangings knitted of linen, handspun yarns, asbestos threads, leather, and other materials. She favored the stockinette stitch and experimented with stitch removal combinations of yarns in a single strand. In recent years she has done similar exploratory work in macramé. She is the author of two books, *Step-by-step Knitting* and *Step-by-step Macramé.*

Photography.
Photography was introduced to the world in 1839. A Frenchman, L. J. M. Daguerre, one of the primary inventors, was, like many early phtographers, a prominent academic painter. The medium's history is in fact interwoven with the development of traditional art. It was influenced by painting, and it in turn influenced both painting and printmaking. For example, the luminist portrait painter George Fuller* was a daguerreotypist before he took up brush and palette John Mix Stanley,* known for oils of Indian life in the West, was also a daguerreotypist. The famous artist-inventor Samuel F. B. Morse* was one of America's first photographers. Morse taught the daguerreotype process to Mathew Brady,* among others. Brady, reversing the pattern, began his career as a painting student of William Page.* Moreover, a substan-

1

Photography
1. *Southworth and Hawes. Daguerreotype c.1860. George Eastman House, Rochester, N.Y.*
2. *Eadweard Muybridge. A stereographic study of Yosemite, 1867.*
3. *George W. Barnard. Ruins of the R.R. Depot, Charleston, S.C., c.1865.*
4. *Alexander Gardner. A Sharpshooter's Last Sleep, Gettysburg, Pa., 1863.*
All, George Eastman House, Rochester, N.Y.

tial number of the portraits painted by Page, Thomas Sully,* G. P. A. Healy,* and other prominent artists were based on photographs taken by Brady's studio rather than on life. Landscapists including Frederic Church* used stereo cards and other photographs as *aides-memoire* for their work. Thomas Eakins* was an innovative photographer of people in motion and used photographs as models for some of his paintings.

On the other hand, a considerable body of camera work was greatly influenced by paintings and painterly ideas. For instance, the allegorical daguerreotypes that Gabriel Harrison made in the 1850s were in a class with Currier and Ives* lithographs. Although sentimental and stiff, his daguerreotype of a young boy holding a large cross, a picture with obvious religious connotations, and his three figures posed to symbolize the three phases of a woman's life, represent a striving for esthetic effects inherited from academic painting.

Where Harrison sought to make pictures that looked like paintings, most photographers were merely tradesmen interested in the camera's money-making possibilities. They set up studios in the major cities, and daguerreotypists traveled the countryside in horse-drawn "daguerreian vans." Most of the early photographers and their patrons were satisfied if the camera managed to produce a recognizable likeness. Art was not the aim of these pioneer portraitists; this is understandable since the procedure required lengthy exposures. Paralyzing poses tended to destroy any sense of naturalness or vitality in most of their pictures. A few photographers, however, among the thousands operating in America in the last century, stand out by reason of the special "photographic" qualities of their work and their fine craftsmanship. In New York City in the 1850s Jeremiah Gurney frequently softly modulated his beautifully finished daguerreotype portraits with light to give them the pulse of life. Mathew Brady's studios in New York City and Washington, D.C., produced daguerreotypes and, later, paper prints that are often as interesting esthetically as for their documentation of historical personages. Probably the best American daguerreotypists were Albert Sand Southworth* and Josiah Johnson Hawes.

In 1841 Southworth opened a studio in Boston called the "Artist's Daguer-

2

3

4

reotype Rooms." He had become interested in working with the camera after seeing a demonstration of the daguerreotype process by François Gouraud, who represented himself as being Daguerre's American representative. In 1844 Hawes became Southworth's partner. By avocation a painter and miniaturist, he advertised "Superior Colored Daguerreotypes" even before joining Southworth. The partners had their studio in the same building as a number of Boston artists. Southworth and Hawes had the highest standards of any of our early photographers and took the pictures themselves rather than depending on "operators" in their employ as did Brady and most popular daguerreotypists. Their work avoids the rigidity of most daguerreotype portraits and subtle lighting effects give their pictures a high degree of clarity and tonal gradation. Aided undoubtedly by their study of painting, they achieved an unusual firmness in the features of their sitters and a light that was pleasing and natural.

The Civil War and the West

Another important early photographer, George N. Barnard,* was an accomplished daguerreotypist who became a master of the wet-plate process during the Civil War. His narrative daguerreotype *The Woodsawyer's Nooning,* known now only from a reproduction, is a very "photographic" picture, even though the figures were obviously posed. The slight imperfections, such as the man's blurred hand, make the scene seem lifelike. Attached to the Union Army during the campaigns in Tennessee and Georgia, Barnard, using the cumbersome wet-plate process, recorded with a sure command of his medium the details as well as a broad view of General Sherman's scorched-earth campaign. Some members of Brady's team of photographers, such as T. H. O'Sullivan* and Alexander Gardner,* also made remarkable records of the Civil War, but none took as consistently well-composed pictures as Barnard.

After the Civil War, O'Sullivan went on geographic survey parties in the virtually unknown West. His photographs of Arizona, Nevada, and New Mexico from 1871 to 1878 are clear, well composed, and informative. In some cases, as in his view of Canyon de Chelly, they are as fine as landscapes made by any means. Other noteworthy

1

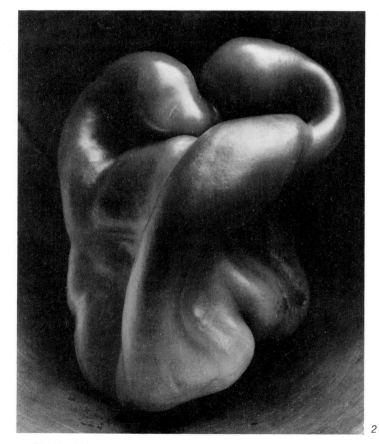

2

Photography
1. *Alfred Stieglitz.* Georgia O'Keeffe, *1922. George Eastman House, Rochester, N.Y.*

2. *Edward Weston.* Pepper, 1930. *Museum of Modern Art, N.Y.*

survey photographers who worked in the West were John Hillers and William Bell. The Civil War over, Gardner also photographed the West; so did S. J. Russell, who worked largely in Utah after a stint with the Union Pacific during the construction of the railroad. Their work has more documentary than artistic value, but it set the stage for successors who combined the two aspects of the medium. The best-known photographer of the West was William Henry Jackson.* His magnificent pictures of the Yellowstone area in 1872 so impressed Congress that land was set aside there as our first national park. Jackson, like most western photographers, eventually employed a team of cameramen to take many of the western views he offered for sale to tourists or for distribution by railroad companies selling land. Jackson's own work is often distinguished and he deserves his high place among 19th-century landscape photographers. But Eadweard Muybridge,* who made magnificent large-scale views of Yosemite Valley, deserves the highest place among early photographers of the West. Although not nearly as famous as his photographs of people and animals in motion, Muybridge's landscapes are his finest artistic achievement. There is a beautiful sense of atmosphere in his landscapes and a feeling of majesty worthy of the trees and mountains he photographed.

The Photograph as Art

Photographs of the West had great appeal as subjects in the last quarter of the 19th century, but they were rarely considered art. However, by the end of the century, the aim of a number of photographers was to produce photographs that would be accepted as works of art. They became very self-conscious, and in London a society, the Linked Ring, was formed in 1892 to further the cause of artistic photography. Alfred Stieglitz* was the best known American member; he had achieved an international reputation while studying with a famous photochemist in Berlin. He felt that photography with artistic character could be made with a hand-held camera, and his pictures of commonplace incidents in Europe and on the streets of New York were regarded as the highest expression of American photographic art. In 1902 under his leadership a group called the Photo-Secession* was

formed in New York. Among its members were Edward Steichen,* Clarence White,* and Gertrude Käsebier.* Steichen, who began his career as a painter, made soft-focus, indistinct pictures of people and landscapes, using warmtoned platinum paper. He also worked with the very popular gum-bichromate process, which permitted him to use textured paper and green, red, and blue tones to create large romantic photographs that resemble the hazy paintings of J. A. M. Whistler* and Eugène Carrière. After doing aerial photography for the army in World War I he changed to a more directly photographic type of representation and became famous as a fashion and portrait photographer for *Vanity Fair* and *Vogue.* Meanwhile, White and Käsebier continued even after World War I to do work that, while very charming, looked more like paintings or prints than photographs.

Among Stieglitz' associates, the photographer most clearly affected by prevailing concepts of modern art was Alvin Langdon Coburn. The photographs he made shooting straight down from New York skyscrapers were pioneer pictures of the walks in Central Park made in a straightforward manner. And in 1917 under the influence of vorticism, a cubist-related movement in England, he made "vortographs," a form of abstract photograph, using prisms that fractured the image into faceted planes. These photographs were a forerunner of the interest in ideas related to modern painting later seen in the work of Man Ray,* Francis Bruguière,* and a few other photographers. Bruguière, a somewhat neglected figure, was a venturesome photographer who made a significant contribution to the medium, especially in his vivid use of negative imagery and solarized negatives. Related to surrealism* in a way, he dealt with fantasy as one might find it in films or the theatre.

Documentary Photography

Although largely ignored by critics and those who sought to use the camera as a means of artistic expression, it is now clear that documentary photography was one of the most important uses of the medium. Some of the best of these photographs documented the lives of New Yorkers. At the same time that John Sloan* and other painters of the Ash Can School* were painting the raw and commonplace aspects of life in the

bustling metropolis, for which they had been hailed as daring innovators, three photographers—Jacob Riis, Lewis Hine,* and for a time, Paul Strand*— were doing far more realistic views of the city. Riis, a Danish immigrant who became a police reporter, used his photographs to illustrate strident articles about the dark realities of slum living and immigrant life. Hine was a sociologist whose photographs of child labor and other social abuses helped to bring about the amelioration of such conditions. Strand, a student of Hine, combined an acute artistic sensibility with a great sympathy for the outcasts of big city life. He produced in 1915–16 some of the most powerful photographs ever made of people living in poverty. While a student, Strand had seen photographs at Alfred Stieglitz'* famous art gallery, "291," in New York City, including some made by Stieglitz himself of city streets covered with snow or lighted by gas lamps at night. Made with a hand camera, a very unusual practice for a photographer who considered himself an artist, these pictures by Stieglitz inspired Strand to record everyday life. When Stieglitz saw Strand's photographs of a blind woman and of office workers hurrying to their jobs in the caverns of Wall Street, he recognized their power and immediately published a series in the 1915–16 issues of *Camera Work,* the prestigious periodical devoted to modern art and photography that he edited.

In contrast, Hine's photographs were published in informational books and reports. Stieglitz never saw them and even if he had, he would probably have found them too straightforward, too narrowly directed toward social reform. Today it is evident that Hine is the true father of all American photography meant to influence public opinion and expose the evils of our social system.

After his early pictures of the poor, Strand became interested in the theories of cubism.* He was one of the first to see machines as subjects that could be treated in a semiabstract manner. Charles Sheeler,* a painter-photographer and a close friend to Strand, was also stimulated by these ideas. In his photography he paid homage to the beauty of the precision of machines as well as to the work of American architects. His crisp, clean photographs emphasized the formal quality of clusters of factory buildings as well as of simple

1

2

3

Photography
1. *Jacob A. Riis.* Baxter Street Court, *1888. Museum of the City of New York (Jacob Riis Collection).*
2. *Walker Evans.* Barber Shop, Southern Town, *1936.*
3. *Lewis W. Hine.* Newsie, *1910. George Eastman House, Rochester, N.Y.*
4. *Russell Lee.* Negro Mother Teaching Children in Home of Sharecropper, Transylvania, La., *1939. Library of Congress, Washington, D.C.*

4

utilitarian objects such as stairwells.

Like Strand and Sheeler, Stieglitz was also influenced by the abstractionists. Thus, he made a series of impressive pictures of skyscrapers under construction; but his most important contribution in the 1920s was his "Equivalents." These were photographs of clouds that reflected in rather lyrical terms his feelings about life. Little understood when they were made, these photographs had a strong impact on a number of photographers during the 1950s.

During the early 1930s Strand went to Mexico and made sensitive photographs of people and buildings as well as several pioneering films, the most important being *The Wave.* In 1935 he returned to the United States and along with Ralph Steiner* photographed the powerful documentary film *The Plow That Broke the Plains* (1936). Steiner, like Strand, had begun his career as a documentary still photographer, usually photographing things rather than people, and creating pictures that have a distinctive coherence and clarity. Since 1929 he devoted his major efforts to documentary and experimental films.

While Strand and Sheeler were working in the East, in California a cluster of photographers formed in the 1920s and 1930s around Edward Weston.* Like Steichen, Weston had come into prominence as an impressionist, or soft-focus, photographer; but as a result of seeing an exhibition of European modern art in 1915 in San Francisco and his friendship with artistically aware people in southern California, he had shifted to a sharply defined form of imagery termed "straight photography." Weston joined forces with Ansel Adams* and other advocates of straight photography to form the f/64* group in 1932. Although Adams moved freely between the Weston and Stieglitz camps, his work and viewpoint is closer to the former. Adams has been very influential as a teacher owing to his magnetic personality, his spectacular interpretations of nature, and his technical knowledge.

The Social Document

In addition to these major creative photographers, there are a number of photographers who took all of American society, and especially the poor or forgotten, as their subject. Early in the 20th century, as the number of American Indians began decreasing and their

Photography

customs were being forgotten, two photographers undertook to document what was thought of as the "dying Redmen." Edward S. Curtis, a professional photographer from Seattle, Wash., devoted two decades to recording in a romanticized fashion the members of various tribes. His photographs are of great ethnological value and convey the spirit of his subjects as well as their appearance. Adam Clark Vroman, a bookseller from California and an amateur photographer, made photographs of the Indians of the Southwest that are less dramatic than Curtis' but unquestionably authentic, and display a special feeling for atmospheric light.

Walker Evans,* who worked for the Farm Security Administration* (FSA) in the 1930s, has also dealt beautifully with the effects of light on surfaces. In measured and lucid terms he demonstrated a regard for people and their architectural surroundings. His is a clinical rather than emotional involvement with his subjects; more directly concerned with people as personalities was Dorothea Lange.* Like Evans, she worked for the FSA during the 1930s and continuously demonstrated an ability to convey honestly but sympathetically the daily life of displaced sharecroppers and men in breadlines. Another dedicated FSA photographer, one with a sharp eye for pictures of the plight of small-town residents during the Depression, was Russell Lee. In an unpretentious but incisive way he documented the depressed life of most of the rural residents of Texas and the Southwest.

More recently, Bruce Davidson,* whose work is in a more romantic vein than that of Evans, Lange, and Lee, has carved out a special place for himself in documentary photography. His book, *East 100th Street* (1969), gives us a remarkable insight into what it means to live in a slum. Achieving a sense of belonging to the area, he was able to record the most intimate details of the life of blacks and Puerto Ricans residing on the single block in New York City. Davidson captures a sense of warm human relationships and a feeling of pride despite the wretched surroundings these people find themselves in.

Diane Arbus,* who died at the peak of her career, used the camera to document unusual people—midgets, transvestites, nudists, lesbians, and circus folk. Even when she photographed

1

2

"normal" people, a feeling of mystery permeates her pictures. However, it is not wholly the bizarreness of her subject that gives her work its power. In her photographs we can see the grotesque in everyone. To her, people were not good or bad, pretty or ugly; she simply confronts us with them as they are. In the history of photography her work stands somewhere between that of Robert Frank* and Lee Friedlander.* The latter is our liveliest and most discerning practitioner of "street" photography, a movement whose many followers use the slangy vernacular of the snapshot to chronicle life in an urban milieu. Friedlander is a diarist who sets down acerb notations on the passing scene. He catches signs or gestures that somehow challenge us to see the commonplace in a new way.

Photojournalism

When *Life* magazine appeared in 1936, a type of photography practiced in Europe by Felix Man and Erich Salomon but rarely seen in America captured the imagination of the American public: interpretive photo-essays about public and private events.

Margaret Bourke-White and Peter Stackpole were two of the photographers who pioneered what became known as photojournalism, Bourke-White with a 4 x 5 camera and flash, and Stackpole with a 35mm camera and natural light. The small camera and the array of lenses with which it could be equipped made it possible to photograph in low-level light conditions. The photojournalist set out to catch the action in sporting events and political gatherings, as well as to satisfy the public's vast appetite for brutally candid pictures of people. W. Eugene Smith,* working with a miniature camera, added greatly to the new language. He began his career as a distinguished war photographer. After World War II he became a master of the photo essay, doing for *Life,* in the late 1940s and early 1950s, a variety of subjects ranging from "Country Doctor" (1948) and "Spanish Village" (1951) to a dramatic and moving treatment of Dr. Albert Schweitzer ("Man of Mercy").

Smith's pictures speak to the heart. Robert Frank's* photographs challenge the mind. With an eye disciplined to capture the significant wink or shrug, Frank made an acute appraisal of American life in 1960 in his starkly candid book, *The Americans.* Frank had come

3

Photography
1. *Lee Friedlander.* Hillcrest, New York, *1970.*
2. *Bruce Davidson. From* East 100th Street, *1969. Magnum Photos, N.Y.*
3. *W. Eugene Smith. From "Klu Klux Klan," 1951, photo essay.* © *Eugene Smith.*

Photography

1. *Edmund Teske.* Untitled, *image combine, 1947.*

2. *Aaron Siskind.* Martha's Vineyard, *1954. Light Gallery, N.Y.*

to America from his native Switzerland, and, after Laszlo Moholy-Nagy, is the most influential photographer to settle in America as a mature artist. Unlike Smith, who continues to do photo-essays, Frank has turned to filmmaking, a not unusual shift.

Lyric and Symbolic

Looking back at the 1950s, we see that two main streams of poetic photography developed in America. Representing a fusion of Stieglitz, Adams, and Weston were such men as Minor White,* Wynn Bullock,* and Frederick Sommer.* All three have dealt with the vital forces that bind man and nature and nourish instinctive impulses. Working with a large camera on a tripod, each explored symbolism derived from nature in making characteristically precise and beautifully printed photographs. This intent is particularly evident in White's successful use of "Equivalents," a form that Stieglitz had originated. Something of life's mysteries are conveyed in the sensitive photographs White has made of rocks, water, trees, and sky. These men are poets, not reporters. They have created a body of work demonstrating that through the use of symbols and allegory, photography can express every level of esthetic experience. Sommer makes almost surreal photographs of assembled objects; these objects are constructed of such things as parts of dead chickens and torn old valentines. In addition to making ordinary photographic prints, he creates negatives by controlling the buildup of layers of smoke on glass, which yield prints that provide a hallucinogenic experience for viewers.

Portraits, formal and informal, probably make up at least 75 percent of all photographs. Few of these, however, penetrate much beyond a sitter's outward appearance, and even fewer are done with artistic style. However, at least two American photographers, Irving Penn* and Richard Avedon,* have consistently made portraits that convey something of the personality of a subject, and are also exciting as photographs. Penn and Avedon are primarily known as fashion photographers. The abiding necessity to "sell" tends to inhibit the freedom of such photographers, but this is not so true in the making of portraits. Both Penn and Avedon have taken original and arresting portraits of famous actors, authors, and politicians in unconventional settings. Whether faithful or caricaturish, their portraits are stamped with an artistic style and are startling as well as symbolically significant.

At an opposite pole from the work of these photographers is that of Val Telberg and Edmund Teske.* Their multiple imagery derives in part from the work Moholy-Nagy did in Europe and the ideas made popular by surrealism. They combine negatives, or negatives and transparent positives, to achieve new levels of imagination—ambiguities such as are experienced only in dreams.

Another vein in recent photography is represented by Aaron Siskind,* Harry Callahan,* and Jerry Uelsmann.* Siskind is an outstanding teacher as well as photographer. His early work was entirely documentary but in the last twenty-five years he has turned to a more personal kind of vision. He invests lichen-covered stone walls and fragments of billboards with talismanic values related to the passage of time on one ·hand and the human pageant on the other. Callahan has an uncanny grasp of the potential of the camera to record people's faces and to evoke emotions through photographs of buildings and people. Whether he does a figure in a softly lighted forest scene or a single blade of grass, he achieves a strange air of suspended animation and an overwhelming feeling of the oneness of man and nature. Uelsmann, through his sensitive use of imagery from three or four negatives combined in a single frame has added a new dimension to photography—a lyrical dimension that challenges reality to measure up to our dreams.

As we have seen, painting has had a marked influence on creative photography. In recent years this debt has been repaid as a new generation of artists freely borrows ideas from photography. At the same time, photographers have become increasingly aware of the unique qualities of their medium. As the work of most painters has become narrower in focus and often alienated from everyday life, photographers have assumed the role of conveying an ever widening range of visual experience relevant to contemporary life. Photographers have thrown off their self-consciousness for they now know that the camera, including film and television, provides a means of dealing not only with the face of our time but with the most intensely personal responses we experience. (V.D.C.)

Photo-Secession (c.1902–10).
An organization of American photographers founded and directed by Alfred Stieglitz.* Resentful of the attitude that photography was merely the handmaiden of art, Stieglitz, the leading amateur photographer in America, and those who rallied around him, determined to fight for the recognition of photography as a fine art. The story of their effort is, ultimately, the chronicle of the coming of modern art to America.

In 1902 Stieglitz was asked by the National Arts Club to arrange an exhibition of pictorial photography. Long eager to show in New York the kinds of photographs he had, with immense success, sent to European exhibitions, he agreed. The result, "An Exhibition of American Pictorial Photography Arranged by the Photo-Secession," was enthusiastically received by most critics. Taking their name from similar dissident groups in Europe, particularly Germany and Austria, the American Secessionists had as their goal the advance of "photography as applied to pictorial expression" and the drawing together of "those Americans practicing or otherwise interested in art." Stieglitz was the director of a council composed of John G. Bullock, William B. Dyer, Frank Eugene, Dallet Fuget, Gertrude Käsebier,* Joseph T. Keiley, Robert S. Redfield, Eva Watson Schütze, Edward Steichen,* Edmund Stirling, John Francis Strauss, and Clarence H. White.* Eventually 105 American and European photographers and critics were invited to join.

Perhaps the most remarkable result of their association was the publication in January, 1903, of a sumptuous quarterly, *Camera Work*. Described by Lloyd Goodrich, art historian and museum director, as "the most radical American magazine of arts and letters," *Camera Work* in its fifty issues included not only magnificent reproductions of the work of photographers Stieglitz believed important but also recorded events at "291," the informal name of the "Little Galleries of the Photo-Secession" founded at 291 Fifth Avenue in 1905. Critics such as Charles Caffin, and the erratically brilliant Sadakichi Hartmann found in it an open forum for their ideas, and George Bernard Shaw and Maurice Maeterlinck used it to champion the new in photography and art. And in a special number in 1912, Gertrude Stein was published for the first time in America—in two radically innovative prose portraits, one of Picasso and one of Matisse.

Beginning in 1907, Stieglitz put on at "291" the first of the exhibitions of nonphotographic works that were to introduce that bewildering phenomenon, "modern art." Five years before the famous Armory Show* of 1913, drawings by Auguste Rodin and watercolors and etchings by Henri Matisse were displayed at "291". Works by Marin,* Hartley,* Toulouse-Lautrec, Manet, Cézanne, Renoir, and Henri Rousseau followed. Paintings and drawings by Picabia, Picasso, and Braque brought cubism* to America. African sculpture, Mexican pottery and carvings, and children's drawings extended radically the boundaries of what then constituted an exhibition. Gallery 291 became, in short, a laboratory for the study of the whole spectrum of modern art in America.

For some members of the Photo-Secession, however, the attempt to define photography by associating it with the other visual arts was unwelcome. They accused Stieglitz of having abandoned the cause of photography. Therefore, in 1910, when the Albright Art Gallery in Buffalo, N.Y., asked Stieglitz to arrange an international exhibition of photography, he accepted enthusiastically. More than six hundred photographs were hung at the museum, and attendance was the highest ever reached there. A more important sign of success was the purchase by the Albright of fifteen prints for its permanent collection. The Photo-Secession had won its battle for the recognition of photography as a fine art. But in doing so, its very reason for being disappeared. In 1911, few members responded to notices for dues. Many of them devoted themselves to their own work; others returned to the conventional camera clubs. The triumph of the Albright show marks the end of the Photo-Secession and also of the esthetic viability of the pictorial photography it championed. Gallery 291 closed its doors after its seventy-ninth major exhibition, "Recent Work by Georgia O'Keeffe,"* in May, 1917, and *Camera Work* ceased publication. Both were victims of America's entry into World War I. (D.L.)

Phyfe, Duncan (1768–1854).
Furniture-maker. Born in Scotland, Phyfe emigrated to America in 1783 or 1784 and settled in Albany, N.Y. He moved to New York City about 1792, and in 1795 opened a shop on Partition Street (later Fulton Street). He began making furniture for the city's most prominent families and is remembered chiefly for designs created from 1807–20. Among the earliest products of his shop is a chair (made for William Bayard) with reeded frame and tapered reeded legs ending in a long bulbous foot (Museum of New York).

The cresting rail is carved with a bow-knot and thunderbolts, which, along with cornucopias, drapery swags, and branches of laurel, were motifs that often characterized Phyfe chairs and sofas. The design, based to some extent on that of Sheraton (see Furniture: Early Federal), anticipates such later Phyfe work as a set of "Grecian Cross" chairs made for Thomas Pearsall. Phyfe's shop also produced Grecian couches and many kinds of tables: card, work, pier, pembroke, drop-leaf, and dining room. The new pillar-and-claw style supplanted the four-reeded legs, the pillar usually having a vase-shaped support and the claws (legs) being reeded or carved with water leaves and terminating in carved or brass paw feet with casters. Although few case pieces are documented from this period, there are desks, desk and bookcase combinations, and wardrobes that probably were made in the Phyfe shop. A documented case piece is a "butler's" desk made as wedding furniture for Sophia Miles and George Belden about 1815. The matched flame grain panels framed by cross-banding show Phyfe's characteristic use of highly figured fine mahogany veneers.

By the late 1820's Phyfe's shop was producing the fauteuils (armchairs) and chaise gondoles of the French Restoration era. Furniture made for Phyfe's daughter, Elisa Vail, is in this style, as is an 1837 parlor set for a lawyer, Samuel Foot. The Foot furniture exhibits the scroll supports that have caused furniture of this type to be called "pillar and scroll." In the decade before he retired in 1847, Phyfe probably made furniture in the new historical revival styles; however, no documented furniture of his in any style except the classical is now known.

(M.J.B.)

Pickett, Joseph (1848–1919).
Self-taught artist who painted slowly, apparently for his own personal pleasure, behind the general store that he owned and operated in New Hope, Pa., where he was born. Several of his paintings are known to survive, and from these it appears that he devoted himself to depicting the surrounding Pennsylvania landscape and to local events from the American Revolution.

Picknell, William Lamb (1853–97).
Landscape painter born in Hineburg, Vt. An orphan, he was raised by an uncle in Boston, who, recognizing his talent sent him abroad to study art. In Rome young Picknell persuaded the expatriate painter George Inness* to take him as a student. After two years with Inness, he worked under Jean Leon Gérôme in Paris. Subsequently he moved to Brittany, where an international group of artists had gathered. There he attracted the attention of Robert Wylie (1839–77), the American expatriate painter noted for his pictures of Brittany peasants, who exerted a strong influence on his painting. In 1876 Picknell first exhibited in the Paris Salon. His reputation was given a boost when his large landscape *The Road to Concarneau* (1880, Corcoran) was given an award in the Salon of 1880. This academic canvas, strikingly simple in design, relied for its impact on broad masses of darks and lights, and most of all on the effect of brilliant sunshine and shadow. He returned to America in the early 1880s and settled in Annisquam, Mass. He later went back to the Riviera and Normandy, but returned to America again in 1897.

(H.W.W.)

Pine, Robert Edge (c.1730–88).
Painter of portraits and historical subjects. He moved to Philadelphia in 1784 as the most distinguished British emigrant artist after the Revolution, having been a leading portrait painter of London and Bath, some of whose subject pieces had been engraved. His work was in the rich rococo* style and luminous color of Sir Joshua Reynolds. He announced his intention of painting a series of historical pictures celebrating American independence, and undertook portraits and sketches of important Americans. He painted George Washington several times, spending three weeks at Mt. Vernon. His one

American historical piece, *Congress Voting Independence* (1788, Historical Society of Pennsylvania), remained unfinished and is of documentary value only, as it included portraits of Benjamin Franklin, Francis Hopkinson, and others.

(C.C.S.)

Pine Tree Shillings.
The first coins minted in the American colonies were struck in Massachusetts Bay by John Hull* and his partner Robert Sanderson* at the mint established in 1652. The first dies bore the initials NE for New England. In the first year of minting, a willow tree design was substituted. About 1662 oak tree coins were minted and about 1667 the pine tree design was first struck. It is by the latter name that all these early coins have been known.

Pinney, Eunice (1770–1849).
Self-taught watercolorist of Simsbury, Conn. She frequently used late 18th-century woodcuts, book illustrations, and printed textiles as models but developed a distinctive pictorial style in which two-dimensional figures were incorporated into a cohesive rhythmic composition. Her work is in many ways reminiscent of the work of the English artist Thomas Rowlandson (1756–1827) but no instance of direct reference to his prints has been found. Typical of her work is *Two Women* (c.1815, New York Historical Association.)

Pinprick.
A 19th-century decorative art technique popular in the United States that, like English quillwork of the 17th and 18th centuries, probably represents a bridge between the needlework and drawing taught at ladies' seminaries. In many instances pinprick figures appear as embellishments of watercolors. The pinprick technique simply involves piercing a piece of paper from behind to raise the surface that is toward the viewer. Pinpricks either outline a design or fill a defined area to represent a texture. A good example of the former may be found in the anonymous drawing of *Miss Liberty* (c.1815, Abby Aldrich Rockefeller). In the same collection is an example of the latter, a watercolor of *The Shepherd and His Flock,* in which pinpricking of varying boldness has been used to simulate the coat of sheep, the foliage of trees, and

1. **Duncan Phyfe.** Fireplace, mirror, and furniture from Moses Rogers House, New York City, 1806. Henry Francis du Pont Winterthur Museum, Winterthur, Del.
2. **Eunice Pinney.** Two Women, c.1815. New York State Historical Association, Cooperstown.

a shepherd's cloak. In other examples pinpricking simulates lace or embroidery, and it enjoyed considerable popularity as a medium for creating the lacy valentines that were common in the later 19th century.   (M.J.G.)

Pittsburgh Glass, see Glass, Pattern-molded Glass, Pressed Glass, Flasks, Glass Cutting and Engraving.

Platt, Charles A. (1861–1933). Architect and landscape architect who insisted that landscaping and architecture be developed simultaneously. He began his training at the National Academy of Design* and the Art Students League,* New York City. In 1882 he went to Paris, studied painting at the Académie Julien, and exhibited in the Salon of 1885. Returning to America in 1887, he worked mainly with the sculptor Augustus Saint-Gaudens* in Cornish, N.H. In 1892 he went to Italy to study Renaissance gardens. This trip had a decisive influence on his life, as reflected in his book *Italian Gardens* (1894). It led to his first major landscape commission, Faulkner Farm in Brookline, Mass. (1897). The design of gardens drew him quite naturally to the design of the houses to go with them. One of his early architectural commissions was High Court in Cornish, the nearest thing to an Italian villa that most Americans of the time had ever seen. He had an unerring sense of design and did not hesitate to take liberties with proportions, adapting them to an American way of life. His houses created an interest in Italian architecture in a garden setting, which was portrayed in the popular paintings of his friend Maxfield Parrish.* Set at the end of a landscaped driveway, Sylvania, the country place of John Jay Chapman at Barrytown, N.Y. (1904), was in the palladian style with an Ionic portico and a bull's-eye window set in a cartouche (a scroll-shaped tablet), the hallmark of a Platt design. In 1908, Harold F. McCormick commissioned a country house in Lake Forest, Ill. With its arched loggia facing a courtyard, it was impressive as well as livable.

In Washington, D.C., as a member of the National Commission of Fine Arts, he worked with Horace Peaslee on the development of Meridian Hill Park, modeled after an Italian hillside garden. Platt also designed the Freer Gallery of Art (1915–23) in Washington, D.C.,

1. ***Jackson Pollock.*** Full Fathom Five,
   1947, oil on canvas with nails, tacks,
   buttons, key, coins, etc. Museum of
   Modern Art, N.Y. (gift of Peggy
   Guggenheim).
2. ***Jackson Pollock.*** Ocean Greyness,
   1953. Solomon R. Guggenheim
   Museum, N.Y.
3. ***Jackson Pollock.*** Portrait and a
   Dream, 1953. Dallas Museum of
   Fine Arts (gift of Mr. and Mrs.
   Algur H. Meadows).

a symmetrical one-story building featuring a triple-arched loggia entrance leading into an inner courtyard. In the realm of academic architecture he designed buildings for Phillips Academy (1923–27) and Deerfield Academy (1930), both in Massachusetts. He made master plans for the University of Illinois (1919) and the University of Rochester and helped develop plans for Dartmouth College and John Hopkins University. His most significant commercial building was the *Leader-News* Building in Cleveland, Ohio (1911), and the Hanna Building 1914, both with Italian Renaissance detail.

Platt served as president of the Century Association, a club in New York, and of the American Academy in Rome.

(A.B.)

Pleinarism

A term derived from the French *plein air,* meaning open air. This was a movement, at its height in the 1880s, that endeavored to combine the atmospheric effects of outdoor light with precise, academic draftsmanship. It did not imply (as did "plein air impressionism") actually painting in the open air instead of in the studio. But it did attempt to reproduce the beauties of natural bright colors instead of the browns and grays of the academic tradition. Its leading practitioner in France, Jules Bastien-Lepage (1848–84), was a friend of J. Alden Weir* and the teacher of Robert Vonnoh* and Alexander Harrison (1853–1930), who won great acclaim in America for tonal sea studies such as *Le Crepuscule* (St. Louis) in the mid-1880s.

Pleinairism, like impressionism,* was a movement toward painting with a greater sense of luminosity and atmosphere, but it was essentially more conservative in technique, since it did not involve broken brushwork, separation of colors, and dissolution of line and form. Since pleinairism was closer to the Salon tradition and did not require painting from nature, pictures showing its influence tended to be larger, less spontaneous, and less intimate than impressionist works. A number of American painters reflected pleinairist characteristics in the mid-1880s as they evolved toward a more essentially impressionist style: John H. Twachtman* in *Arques-la-Bataille* (1885); Childe Hassam* in *Boston Common at Twilight* (1885–86); and John

Singer Sargent* in *Carnation, Lily, Lily, Rose* (1884–86). (D.W.S.)

Polk, Charles Peale (1767–1822).

Portrait painter. Left an orphan in 1777 when his father was killed on the quarterdeck of his privateer, *Black Joke,* he grew up in the home and studio of an uncle, Charles Willson Peale,* emerging as a painter with all of his seafaring parent's raw vigor and lack of imaginative talent. His portraits, painted in the Maryland and Philadelphia areas, are marked by stiff naiveté and harsh, bright coloring. He painted likenesses of Franklin and Lafayette and more than fifty portraits of Washington in uniform. Since Washington did not sit for. him, Polk seems to have copied the likeness from his uncle's 1787 portrait. In 1818 Polk abandoned his career and became a government clerk. (C.C.S.)

Pollock, Jackson (1912–56).

Painter. Born in Cody, Wyo., he grew up in Arizona and California. He began to study painting at the Manual Arts High School in Los Angeles, but then dropped out of school and moved to New York City, where he studied on and off with Thomas Hart Benton* at the Art Students League* (1926–33). Pollock's paintings of these years were influenced by Benton's heroic and mannered regional expressionism (see American Scene Painting), and even more by Albert Pinkham Ryder.* (Pollock later said that Ryder was the only American artist who interested him.) Even in his 1933–34 figure paintings and seascapes one notes that turbulent, rhythmic design, the all-over impasto of brushstrokes that is formed into a unified image—all characteristic of Pollock's later work.

During the 1930s Pollock made twelve sketching trips across the country, riding on freight trains or driving an old Ford. He also worked on the WPA Federal Art Project* (1935–42), and became interested in the work of the Mexican muralists, especially the blunt, angular forms and symbolism of Orozco and Siquieros. It has often been pointed out that Pollock's later heroic scale could have been stimulated by either the Mexican or WPA murals. At the same time other influences, such as Picasso and surrealism,* were asserting themselves. By the late 1930s Pollock was filling notebooks with black-ink line drawings related to cubism* (especially Picasso's *Guernica*), fantasy (dragons and monsters), and sexual imagery. Other drawings utilized the surrealist technique of "automatic writing," which presumably brought unpremeditated, subconscious thoughts into the open. With Pollock these "random," "undirected" drawings would ultimately lead to the all-over continuous linear rhythms of his "drip" paintings.

In the meantime, surrealism, with its spirit of revolt and "sacred disorder," along with its literary aspects and sexual imagery, had a deep effect on Pollock. Paintings such as *Birth* (1937) and *Male and Female* (1942), with their rounded, interlocked forms, were heavily influenced by Picasso's works such as *Girl Before a Mirror*. By 1943, however—the year of Pollock's first one-man show at Peggy Guggenheim's* influential Art of This Century gallery—Pollock was producing highly personal paintings on mythological themes. *The She Wolf, Guardians of the Secret,* and *Pasiphae* all have the quality of primitive art: seeming irrationality set within the most rigid formal structure—an attribute of all of Pollock's work. In all three paintings an underlying grid framework is buried in a welter of cabalistic signs and symbols that have been slashed on the canvas in thick brushstrokes. The overall impression is one of bacchanalian licentiousness. One feels that Pollock reached the subconscious in these paintings; that he was not illustrating these scenes, but ritually recreating them. The passion of his handling of the paint and the feeling of "ritual act" in the actual making of the picture were all carried forward into the famous drip paintings.

During 1943–47 Pollock received regular payments for his work from Peggy Guggenheim, which allowed him to paint uninterruptedly. The artist's move in 1945 to the Springs, on Long Island, N.Y., where he lived thereafter, was a turning point in his career. Prior to that, his pictures had been representational and anecdotal; now he began to paint such totally abstract works as *Shimmering Substance* and *Eyes in the Heat,* consisting of an all-over texture of squiggles of paint. With one blow Pollock had abandoned conventional pictorial composition, raised the technique of painting itself to the highest power, giving his painted surfaces such materiality as to

make them almost sculptural; he had begun a record of his moods and emotional responses equal to any great literary biography, and shown the beauty and order inherent in "chaotic" nature. Within a year he had intensified his involvement with the dynamics of painting and was dripping paint from a stick or can onto unstretched and unsized canvas tacked to the floor. The result was a painting such as *Full Fathom Five* (1947), with tangled webs of black, white, and aluminum paint against a green background with spots of bright yellow and orange and with objects such as cigarette butts, keys, nails, and tacks embedded in the paint for added texture. Pollock's method of achieving such works was ridiculed and attacked. Almost overnight he became the most publicized and one of the most influential artists in America. His expressionism had to be taken into account by his fellow abstract expressionists (see Abstract Expressionism), and he spawned a whole generation of imitators. He was able to produce works of such force because he was so totally committed to painting. There is a rightness and a meaning in his work that he attained by acting freely and in an unpremeditated way and that was never achieved by his imitators. In a famous statement Pollock discusses the unconscious as the source of his work, and the feeling of intimacy gained by tacking the canvas on the floor "since this way I can walk around it, work from the four sides and literally be *in* the painting. . . . When I am *in* my painting, I'm not aware of what I'm doing. It is only after a sort of 'get acquainted' period that I see what I have been about. I have no fears about making changes, destroying the image, etc., because the painting has a life of its own. I try to let it come through."

In 1948–50 Pollock produced ever larger drip paintings, including some, such as *Autumn Rhythm* (1950) and *One* (1950), that were nearly twenty feet wide. No matter how expansive his works became, Pollock maintained control, achieving an even greater fluency of line and lyricism in the larger works because his whole body was engaged in the act of painting. Similarly, the vast size of these paintings had an overpowering effect on the spectator, whose own body was seemingly engulfed by them. Although Pollock was now producing images that

had no visual equivalents in the real world, figures and residual links with nature were never far beneath the surface of his linear skeins. This provided his abstractions with an added dimension: an ambiguity that allowed the spectator to read his own thoughts into them, and another link with the fantasy world of surrealism. At the same time Pollock's work is extremely "physical." Allied to this was his feeling for paint as a material and his investigation of "nonart" colors such as aluminum paint and high-gloss enamels. The problem of figurative as opposed to nonfigurative art pursued Pollock throughout his career, and in 1951–52 he abandoned drip paintings and returned to a more representational image. Almost all of these pictures—heads and reclining figures—are painted in black and white, with an occasional touch of sepia, and are related to his earliest ink drawings. As with his other work, they are painted in a kind of rhythmic frenzy. During the last three years of his life Pollock left these large graphic webs to return to reworking earlier themes: ritual subjects in an impastoed, more violent, patterned version of the drip paintings. He was perhaps preparing to move off in a new direction when he was killed in an automobile accident.

Pollock's work is important partly because he succeeded in holding so many opposites together and because he was willing to risk so much of himself. Even the paintings of his student years reveal an intensity and a radical sense of freedom that put him beyond the world of mere pictorial values. And in his ultimate romanticism, coupled with his feeling for the material and the real, he could only have been an American. Pollock's work was an open assault on "cultivated" culture, yet its effects are not shocking but poetic. He was a master draftsman who knew how to control the speed of his lines by thinning them or flooding them with paint, and how to build form and space out of overlapping and intertwined lines. Pollock's images are always evocative and filled with content, although criticism usually dwelled on his paintings as "arenas for violent combat" ("action painting") and his radical methods of applying paint to canvas. Pollock had innumerable one-man shows during his lifetime. Other important exhibitions include the Venice Biennial (1950), "15 Americans" at the Museum of

Modern Art, New York City (1952), and a memorial exhibit at the same museum in 1956.   (E.C.G.)

Poons, Larry (1937–   ).
Painter. He was born in Tokyo, Japan, but was brought to the United States a year later. He studied at the Boston Museum of Fine Arts School. His first one-man show was in 1963, and in 1965 he exhibited at the São Paulo Biennial. By 1962–63 Poons was producing versions of his well-known optical art* image: round spots placed along diagonal and horizontal-vertical grids, seen against a field of pure color. The patterns in these early works were explicit and spatially unambiguous, possibly because one could still see the grid lines faintly penciled in between the dots. By the end of 1963, however, Poons had flattened his dots into ellipses, giving them direction and speed as they streaked across the canvas as in *Away Out on the Mountain* (1965, Allen Art Museum, Oberlin, Ohio). Added to this was high-keyed color, as in *Nixe's Mate* (1964), where brilliant green and blue dots are seen against a red-saturated background. By deliberately choosing colors that intensified each other, Poons produced all kinds of optical effects, after-images, and vibrations, with spots flickering and jumping across the canvas. He was never, however, primarily concerned with experiments in perception but with producing beautiful paintings. From the beginning his paintings had been large—a legacy from abstract expressionism*—and by 1968 he began to introduce other abstract expressionist effects. Whereas his color spots had been hard-edge and structured by the underlying grid, they now became amorphous, and seemed to drift aimlessly against a landscape type of background of washes of paint. This soft, floating quality with overtones of water and atmosphere is exactly opposite in feeling to his earlier relentless trajectories of high-speed dots. His return to a more painterly, ambiguous space, however, was perhaps a natural outgrowth of the "op" artist's flirtation with illusionistic effects. His color became subdued, with the spots often scumbled in varying textures, while other areas were soaked and bled. By 1970 Poons had moved toward an impasto style of swirling, almost topographical color intermixtures rem-

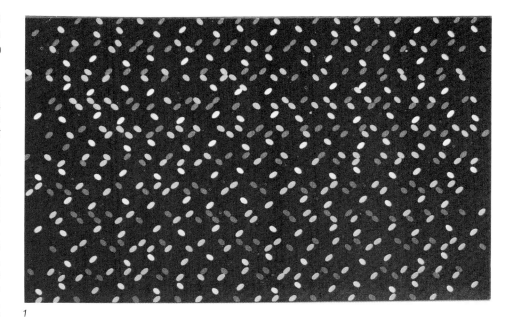

1

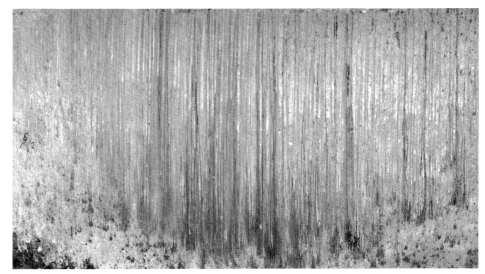

2

1. **Larry Poons.** Nixe's Mate, *1964.*
Collection Mr. and Mrs. Robert C. Scull, N.Y.
2. **Larry Poons.** Number 2, *1972. Rubin Gallery, N.Y.*

iniscent of photographs of planets taken from high altitudes.   (E.C.G.)

Poor, Henry Varnum (1888–1970).
Potter, ceramic muralist, painter, and designer of homes. Born in Kansas, Poor graduated from Stanford University and studied painting at the Slade School in London and the Académie Julien in Paris. Returning to teach at Stanford, he became a founder of the California School of Fine Arts (now the San Francisco Art Institute). After serving in World War I, Poor settled in New York City, where he designed and literally handcrafted his home, which was so unusual and beautiful that he was often commissioned to design and build for others. Living beside the Hudson River, he taught himself pottery using local clays and became one of the first American painter-potters. His painted decoration on ceramic forms featured human, floral, and animal imagery, as in his mural in the Klingenthal Pavilion at Mount Sinai Hospital in New York. He was author of *From Mud to Immortality* and *An Artist Sees Alaska*.   (R.S.)

Pop Art.
A movement that burst upon the New York art scene in the early 1960s, although elements of the pop attitude, with its interest in the banal, commercial, and vulgar had appeared much earlier, in Stuart Davis'* *Odol* and *Lucky Strike* themes and in Willem de Kooning's* pictures of Marilyn Monroe. Such isolated works, however, could not form a total esthetic point of view, and the man generally credited with laying the groundwork for pop is the aleatoric composer John Cage. During the early 1950s in lectures at Black Mountain College, North Carolina, and the New School for Social Research, New York City, Cage called on artists to efface the boundary between art and life, advocating ordinary street sounds as "music," and favoring the use of repetition and the elimination of the dramatic climax. By 1953–55 Robert Rauschenberg,* who had known Cage at Black Mountain, was producing his "combines," affixing real, three-dimensional objects to the surface of his paintings, and literally filling "the gap between art and life." Meanwhile, Jasper Johns,* a friend of both Cage and Rauschenberg, was making art works based on such commonplace subjects as flags, targets, coffee cups,

and coat hangers (1954–58). By 1960 Johns had produced two of the most famous pop icons: facsimile Ballantine ale cans and a Savarin coffee tin filled with paintbrushes—both cast in bronze.

Meanwhile, a whole group of younger artists had begun to reject the transcendental, and sometimes pretentious, attitudes of abstract expressionism*— its emotional subjectivity and loose painterliness—in favor of an art based on the anonymous, mechanized, mass-produced images of advertisements, billboards, comic books, and TV. In painting what they saw around them, these artists seemed to endorse the materialism, violence, vacuousness, and sexualized environment of affluent America. The pop artists also sought to obliterate the hand of the artist and reintroduce recognizable subject matter. (One of the reasons for the immediate acceptance of pop art—originally known as "The New Realism"—was that the public was again able to recognize what it was looking at.) But pop art did more than merely reproduce "popular" images; it transformed them into an art of ultimate sophistication. When an artist such as Andy Warhol* made facsimile Brillo boxes, he recreated them on a new level of reality, forcing the spectator to really look at them, and ultimately to see the supermarket in a new light. Similarly, his silkscreened (and mechanically reproduced) images of famous figures such as Jackie Kennedy and Marilyn Monroe approach social comment in their conversion of the "glamorous" into the vulgar and the saleable. Claes Oldenburg* achieves a similar vulgarity in his giant hamburger and his "soft" mechanical conveniences—typewriters, toilets, electric mixers. The viands he shapes are particularly unappealing, since they are obviously made of plaster and paint, while the "products" of industrial society are literally deflated, in a final touch of irony and editorial comment. In his paintings of comic strips Roy Lichtenstein* not only adopted America's stock heroes and heroines, but simulated the mechanical printing process with his meticulously painted Ben-Day dots (used in making engravings), while James Rosenquist* (like Lichtenstein, formerly a sign-painter) imitates the large scale and vapid smoothness of billboard advertisements. If the

work of artists like Warhol and Rosenquist frequently approaches "display art," George Segal's* tableaux of plaster figures in "real-life" settings often achieve genuine poignance. Because his "people" are cast from living models, their expressions and gestures are individually expressive, and his incorporation of real objects—beds, bicycles, and movie marquees—adds authenticity to his genre type of sculpture.

Like the abstract expressionist painters, each of the major pop artists developed his own style and image independently, though all share a common point of view. By exploring a level of reality existing beneath the glossy facade of American life they have attempted to challenge many of our assumptions, underscored the unique shapes and colors of the everyday world, explored the psychological overtones of visual cliches, and in the process affected our way of looking at the world around us.   (E.C.G.)

Pope, Alexander (1849–1924).
Animal painter and sculptor, best known for his large *trompe l'oeil* "door" still lifes. Pope was a successful "society" painter who spent all of his life near Boston. He studied sculpture with William Rimmer,* and his first works (1879–83) were carved wooden pieces of dead and live game. His best-known *trompe l'oeil* pictures were of "after the hunt" and military subjects, dark and precisely painted, while others portrayed live animals staring out from wooden crates. Less inspired were the portraits of people, dogs, and horses that he painted late in his career. Pope's painting was similar to that of William M. Harnett;* both painters were among the first to make still-life painting popular in 19th-century America. An example of his strikingly realistic style is *Emblems of the Civil War* (1888, Brooklyn).   (T.E.S.)

Porter, Fairfield (1907–   ).
Painter known for his carefully composed landscapes, still lifes, interior scenes, and portraits, which have remained stylistically much the same since 1948. Born in Winnetka, Ill., he graduated from Harvard University and studied art in 1928–30 at the Art Students League* with Boardman Robinson* and Thomas Hart Benton.* In 1949 he moved to Southampton, Long Island, N.Y. Porter has always worked

close to nature, and his pictures are reminiscent of impressionism,* and of the French painters Pierre Bonnard, and Édouard Vuillard without being as hedonistic or rigorous as theirs. Typically his landscapes are soft, relaxed, painted in pale, subdued pastel colors, and dappled with sunlight and greenery. His pictures always evoke a mood of nostalgia, and in fact he was one of the few artists to remain faithful to representational art during the heyday of abstract expressionism.* Porter was not, however, unaffected by the abstract art around him. In all of his paintings he employs shallow pictorial space; many of his pictures are composed of flat color-pattern areas, and in others his objects, on closer inspection, dissolve into strokes and dabs of paint. There is no attempt at *trompe l'oeil.* His lopsided bottles and jars and awkward figures are not "realistic." Rather, they are clearly made of paint and are part of the carefully worked out formal structure of the picture as a whole. Porter has painted a number of fine portraits, such as *Frank O'Hara* and a double portrait, *Andy Warhol and Ted Carey.* As art critic, his articles have appeared in the major art journals, and he has published a book, *Thomas Eakins.*   (E.C.G.)

Porter, Rufus (1792–1884).
Muralist, portraitist and silhouettist, and inventor. A New England farmer's son, he was born in West Boxford, Mass., was apprenticed to a local shoemaker at the age of fifteen, but subsequently embarked on a career in which he founded *Scientific American* magazine, designed an automobile, and became America's leading muralist. After token service in the War of 1812, Porter was briefly a Maine schoolmaster, built a number of wind-driven grist mills, and worked as a house and sign painter. In 1816 he embarked on a new career of portrait painting, which took him as far south as Virginia. Many of Porter's remarkable mechanical accomplishments date from the following eight-year period of itinerant portraiture.

It is for his subsequent activity as a muralist, however, that he commands most attention. American wall painting in the first half of the 19th century was almost exclusively dependent on European models, with the possible exception of work by Porter and his assistants.

Between 1825 and 1845 Porter worked on major fresco decorations in more than one hundred houses in Massachusetts, New Hampshire, Maine, and, in at least one instance, Vermont; and the decorations of at least another fifty houses, the great majority of them in Maine, can be attributed to his nephew, Jonathan D. Poor, or to other close followers. The early murals, like those at the Colburn Tavern in East Pepperell, Mass., are characterized by stippled or sponged foliage and a pictorial sparseness accentuated by a limited color range. In later work, like the murals executed for Captain Samuel Benjamin in Winthrop, Me., in the 1830s (now in the collection of the Maine State Museum, Augusta), Porter developed larger and looser handling with more varied foliage, an enriched palette, and the addition of architectural detail and genre incident. The general pattern is from the style of a folk decorator toward a considerably more sophisticated landscape painter, but throughout his career Porter celebrated the American scene around him. His mural painting appears to have ended abruptly in 1845 as he began editing and publishing *Scientific American.* He was also the author of several books, including one called *A Select Collection of Valuable and Curious Arts and Interesting Experiments.*   (M.J.G.)

Post-Painterly Abstraction.
The term "post-painterly abstraction" gained currency in 1964 from the title of an exhibition organized by the critic Clement Greenberg. Greenberg points out that abstract expressionism* had been not only "abstract" but also "painterly," and quotes the definition by the Swiss art historian, Heinrich Woelfflin, of *malerish* ("painterly") as "the blurred, broken, loose definition of color and contour." According to Greenberg, there were two reactions to abstract expressionism, with its strokes, blotches, and trickles of paint: one was pop art;* the other was post-painterly abstraction. The latter presumably moves toward "physical openness of design, or toward linear clarity, or toward both." Unfortunately, the definition was never a very precise one, and the term became a catchall for artists as diverse as Darby Bannard,* Gene Davis,* Thomas Downing, Helen Frankenthaler,* Al Held,* Alfred Jensen, Ellsworth Kelly,* Nicholas Krushenick,*

Kenneth Noland,* Raymond Parker,* Ludwig Sander, and Frank Stella.* Many of these artists were later claimed by other "movements" such as hardedge,* color-field,* and even lyrical abstraction*—perhaps because "openness," "clarity," "pure hues," and "geometrical formats" can be turned to many different ends. Post-painterly abstraction was never more than a general direction taken by a group of diverse individuals at a certain point in history (Greenberg calls it a "trend"), and most of these individuals have continued to develop in very different ways.   (E.C.G.)

Potter, William Appleton (1842–1909).
Architect. Son and brother of bishops, most of his work was in ecclesiastical and educational architecture. He specialized in chemistry at Union College in Schenectady, N.Y., and after graduation in 1864 became professor of chemistry at Columbia College. In 1866 he went to France to study chemistry but became interested in architecture; upon his return to America, he went to work for his older brother, Edward Tuckerman Potter (1831–1904), an architect. William's architecture, like that of his brother, was Victorian Gothic,* making much use of different colors in its stonework. Later, William was to develop a rather individualized Romanesque revival* style, influenced by the work of his contemporary, Henry Hobson Richardson.*

In 1872, he began his own architectural practice with two notable commissions. The first of these, the Chancellor Green Library in Princeton, N.J., had a polygonal central unit with flanking wings. It had tall slits for windows, surmounted by a trefoil window (an ornamental three-lobed unit), which filled the gable at each face. These gables gave the building a rather spiky appearance. The second commission was the South Congregational Church in Springfield, Mass. (1874), where he first stated his characteristic steeple theme. The rectangular steeple, set to one side of the gable of the nave, displayed high narrow side windows filled with Gothic tracery, producing a soaring effect crowned by a high pyramidal roof. One of his most interesting designs was the College of Sciences at Princeton (1873), a rock-faced stone building, very expressive of its structure. It was replete with gables and dormer windows and may best be described as High Victorian Gothic.

In 1875, Potter was asked to become supervising architect of the United States Treasury Department. He served for only one year but while in office designed several government buildings. These buildings, with their hipped roofs, low Gothic arches, rough-faced masonry, and human scale, were typified by the Custom House and Post Office, Nashville, Tenn. (1876) and the Post Office at Evansville. Ind. (1876). In the same year Potter formed a partnership with the very talented architect, Robert Henderson Robertson (1849–1919), and their work together began with the Grace Episcopal Chapel on East 14th Street, New York City (1876), a straightforward Victorian Gothic design with a large window facing the street. Their next commission was Saint Augustine's Protestant Episcopal Chapel on Houston Street, New York City. This elaborate Victorian Gothic chapel was a brave display of polychromy, for stones of different colors were alternated in the arches.

Potter's own designs after 1878 include the old Union Theological Seminary, Park Avenue at 70th Street, New York City (1883); Christ Church, Poughkeepsie, N.Y. (1888); St. Agnes' Chapel on West 91st Street, New York City (1889); Alexander Hall, Princeton, N.J. (1892); and Teachers' College, Columbia University, New York City (1894–97). Potter spent the last years of his life in Rome.   (A.B.)

Pousette-Dart, Richard (1916–   ).
Painter. Born in St. Paul, Minn., he spent his early years in Valhalla, N.Y., where he taught himself to paint. By the age of twenty he was a serious artist, and in 1938 he moved to New York City. Such early works as *Desert* (1940) display elements of cubism,* primitive hieroglyphs, and decorative signs and symbols in a taut abstract arrangement that stretches across six feet of canvas. Throughout the 1940s and 1950s he had numerous one-man shows, developing his private symbolism in a series of large, richly encrusted paintings. Typical of his work is *Number 11: A Presence* (1949, Modern Museum). These pictures have the same overtones of totem and ritual as Jackson Pollock's* early work. He believes that art is a process of self-discovery more than self-expression and his canvases

are usually much worked-over. Typically, one finds many layers of thinly-washed color, troweled areas of heavily built up pigment, surfaces that have been flecked and frosted, and subtly interwoven colors that alternately submerge and reveal form. During the 1960s Pousette-Dart's paintings became completely abstract, displaying evenly inflected dabs of color across the entire surface of the canvas. In many of these works he achieved effects of sensuous beauty; in others there is a sense of violent agitation. He exhibited at Documenta II, Kassel, Germany (1959) and the São Paulo Biennial (1961), and has taught at the School for Visual Arts, New York City.
(E.C.G.)

Powers, Hiram (1805–73).
Leading expatriate sculptor. Born near Woodstock, Vt., he grew up in Ohio, first working as a machinist in Cincinnati. He began making portrait busts around 1828 and attracted the interest of wealthy Nicholas Longworth, who was to become his patron and eventually send him to Italy. Powers had virtually no formal training, and while in Cincinnati had no exposure to neoclassicism* or any other European style. His talent for reproducing a likeness led to an uncomplicated naturalism that was to remain the basis of his style. In 1834 Longworth financed Powers' move to Washington, D.C., where the sculptor modeled the portraits of many eminent men of the government, including John Marshall, Daniel Webster, and Andrew Jackson. The latter advised Powers, "Make me as I am, Mr. Powers, and be true to nature always." This was an expression of the esthetic taste of the times in America, and Powers' naturalistic style matched it perfectly. After three successful years of portraiture in Washington, he and his family departed for Italy. Powers was greeted in Florence by the American sculptor Horatio Greenough,* who helped him establish a studio. He continued to do portraits throughout his career, but as early as 1838 he produced his first full-length nude figure in marble, *Eve;* this was followed in 1848 by his life-size *Fisher Boy* (Virginia Museum of Fine Arts). Although naturalism remained the basis of his style even in "ideal" works such as these, the influence of antiquity and neoclassicism is also apparent.

Hiram Powers. Greek Slave, c.1843, marble. Yale University Art Gallery, New Haven, Conn. (Olive Louise Dann Fund).

This is true as well of his most famous statue, *Greek Slave* (1841–43), which was based in part on the Florentine *Venus de' Medici.* It proved so popular in both England and America that six versions were produced in marble, and Powers became overnight one of the most acclaimed sculptors of his day. The statue was first seen in America in 1847, when it toured several large cities. Earlier attempts to introduce the American public to the nude figure in art had been unsuccessful, but Powers shrewdly explained in an accompanying pamphlet that her nudity was beyond her control, taken, as she was, a slave by the Turks and placed on the auction block; moreover, he wrote, she represented the triumph of Christian virtue over her horrible fate. Even the clergy urged their flocks to go see the statue and learn from it, and one clergyman wrote: "Brocade, cloth of gold could not be a more complete protection than the vesture of holiness in which she stands." The statue was the embodiment of 19th-century melodramatic romanticism.

Powers produced other allegorized statues and busts, but none achieved the success of his *Greek Slave.* His later portrait busts tended to be dry and prosaic, although the likeness was very accurate. He produced two life-size statues, the marble *John C. Calhoun* (c.1845–50, destroyed) and the bronze *Daniel Webster* (1858, State House, Boston). From about 1840–70 Powers was the most famous sculptor America had produced. (W.C.)

Pratt, Matthew (1734–1805).
Portrait painter. He served an apprenticeship under James Claypoole, Sr., general painter and dealer in colors, setting up as a portraitist in Philadelphia about 1758. Attracted to London by the success of Benjamin West,* he worked in West's studio, 1764–66, and there painted his best-known and most memorable picture, *The American School* (1765, Metropolitan), a group of five young artists in West's studio. Before sailing for home he painted portraits in Bristol. He crossed again to England and Ireland in 1770, was in New York in 1772, and Virginia in 1773. Settling in Philadelphia for the remainder of his life, he gained new fame as a painter of signs of unusual interest and attractiveness, an early example of popular advertising art. Relatively few

portraits are attributed to him with certainty, and it is probable that successful business involvement had stunted his development as an artist. His eldest son, Henry, born in 1761, became one of the city's wealthiest merchants.

Prendergast, Maurice (1859–1924).
Early modernist painter. He was born in St. John's, Newfoundland, but grew up in Boston, where he attended grammar school. As a young man he was apprenticed to a show-card painter. For more than ten years he worked on show cards, devoting his spare time to sketching landscapes in watercolor. His few surviving works of this period are restrained and conventional, but he had determined to become an artist, and his younger brother, Charles, decided to help him.

The key to his career lay in study abroad. In 1886 Maurice and Charles visited England (and perhaps France), working their way on a cattle boat, but it was 1891 before Maurice could afford a second trip. He remained in Paris three years, attending the Académie Colarossi and the Académie Julien. More important were the afternoons he spent sketching, the summer painting trips, and the stimulation of artistic friends. Prendergast arrived in Paris at a time when the impressionists had become established and the next generation—the symbolists, neo-impressionists, and Nabis—were moving on the scene. His Paris work reflects tonalities, patterns, and compositional arrangements reminiscent of James M. Whistler* and Édouard Manet, together with touches of Pierre Bonnard's more intimate quality. He filled notebooks and covered small panels with watercolors and oils, capturing in such works as *Dieppe* (1892) the gestures and picturesque silhouettes of the frequenters of the cafés, parks, and resorts. The stay in Paris established his direction: henceforth he was interested in the currents of the modern movement; his technique was aligned increasingly with those of the post-impressionists; and his subject matter centered on figures seen as color shapes placed in urban, park, or holiday settings.

Returning to the Boston area by 1895, he joined his brother, who was beginning a framing business. Charles' elegant frames led to the production of fine

gessoed panels, decorated with sensitively stylized and Persian-influenced scenes carried out in incised lines, gold leaf, and pigments. Maurice sometimes worked with Charles on the frames, but gradually in the later 1890s established himself more securely as a professional artist. He exhibited his work regularly and received an extensive commission for illustrations. In 1897 he had an exhibition in Boston and took a studio there. In 1898 he began a two-year sojourn in Europe. In Venice he painted watercolors with a new strength of form and pattern, inspired by the Renaissance masters, above all Carpaccio, as in *A Bridge in Venice* (1898, Cleveland).

His reputation grew rapidly after his return to the States. In 1900 he exhibited at the Chicago Art Institute and the next year he won a bronze medal for watercolor at the Buffalo Exposition. In New York he painted an important watercolor series, often using Central Park as a subject. The painter William Glackens* was sketching similar material and soon he and Prendergast established a firm friendship. When Glackens and his Philadelphia associates Robert Henri,* George Luks,* and John Sloan* decided to exhibit at the National Arts Club in 1904, they asked Prendergast and Arthur B. Davies* to join them. Reviewers found the breadth of Prendergast's work mildly disconcerting; apart from his lack of "finish," however, he was recognized as a master of delicate color and sure composition. Despite the criticism, Prendergast continued to broaden his application of paint, especially as he began to work regularly in oils, translating the themes of his watercolors into a patchwork of bold brushstrokes.

In 1905 Prendergast had a show at the Macbeth Gallery and in 1908 he exhibited there again with The Eight.* The press dramatized the exhibition as a revolt of the radicals. Although some of the more responsible critics praised Prendergast's lively and decorative qualities, he suffered attacks by sensationalists who described his work as "unadulterated slop" and "an explosion in a color factory." Prendergast remained perennially youthful and exploratory in his approach. Every few years he took a trip to Europe, which, together with the impact of the work displayed at the Armory Show* in 1913, brought

Pressed Glass

1

2

1. **Maurice Prendergast.** Central Park, 1900.
2. **Maurice Prendergast.** Promenade, Gloucester, c.1918.
   Both, Whitney Museum of American Art, N.Y.

about a period of intensive experimentation. He painted portraits, nudes, and imaginary landscapes inhabited by nymphs; and he tried his hand at mural decoration. On the technical side, he extended the mosaic-like application of paint, approaching the technique of Paul Signac; he introduced pastel and opaque white into his watercolors until they rivaled his oils in richness; and he painted still lifes which showed the influence of Cézanne in their study of space and form. The variety of subject matter and technique resulted in work that was uneven but always vital.

In 1914 the war brought Prendergast home from his last trip abroad. During his last years, he and Charles lived in New York City in a Washington Square apartment above Glackens' studio. In those years his enlarged vocabulary of colors, forms, and images became the basis of a richer and more evocative poetry, as *Promenade, Gloucester* (1918, Whitney). His painting expressed an increasingly visionary world of sensuous pageantry, weaving together tapestries of girls, parasols, swans, sailboats, park landscapes, river vistas, nymphs, and horses. (D.W.S.)

Pressed Glass.

A method of manufacture in which molten glass is dropped into a metal mold and pressed into the desired shape by means of a plunger. Small hand presses for making decanter stoppers and lamp, compote, and wineglass bases were in use in Europe in the late 18th century; however, the development of the hand-operated pressing machine is generally conceded to be an American invention. The earliest known patent for this process was taken out by J. P. Bakewell of Pittsburgh in 1825 for "an improvement in making glass furniture knobs." Subsequent patents were granted to Henry Whitney and Enoch Robinson of the New England Glass Company in 1826, to Phineas Dummer of the Jersey Glass Company in 1827, to Deming Jarves* in 1828, 1829, and 1830 for "pressing glass into moulds," for knobs with a glass screw, and for glass objects pressed with the handles attached; and to John M'Glann of Kensington, Philadelphia, in 1831 for "an improvement in the art of manufacturing all kinds of Bottles, Decanters and other pressed hollow glassware." Pressed glass rapidly became one of the mainstays of the glass industry because it was much faster and cheaper to produce.

Stylistically, the glass can be divided into four distinct periods. The earliest glass, made from 1826 until the early 1830s, tends to be simple in design and rather thick and clumsy. Contact with the metal molds caused the surface of the hot glass to contract slightly, and most of the luster and sparkle inherent in the material disappeared. To correct this, molds were cut with an all-over stippled background combined with more elaborate "lacy" patterns so that the entire surface was covered with decoration. The facets caused by stippling made the glass sparkle. The strippled molds were, however, time-consuming and therefore expensive to make; the so-called "lacy pressed glass" was popular probably until about 1840, when manufacturers discovered the foggy effect could be overcome by heating the molds and by fire-polishing the finished product. Patterns became simpler, after about 1840, and manufacturers began to produce glass in sets so that housewives could now afford a set of matching glasses and serving pieces. Some of the earliest glasses were made with pressed bowls or bases attached to blown stems or fonts. By mid-century, lamps, vases, and candlesticks were being pressed in two parts and joined while hot with a wafer of glass. In this way an infinite variety of lamps, candlesticks, and vases could be made with a limited set of molds for fonts, sockets, and bases. In 1864 the introduction of William Leighton's lime glass formula, which was cheaper than the "flint" or lead glass previously used, resulted in a decline in quality of the material among the firms that used it. Most of the glass firms in New England refused to cheapen their product in this way, and the center of pressed glassmaking gradually moved to the Midwest.

In New England, the Boston & Sandwich Glass Company (1825–88) and the New England Glass Company (1818–88) were the chief producers of pressed glass; but these wares were also made at the Providence Flint Glass Company (1831–33), the Mt. Washington Glass Works in South Boston (1837–69) and New Bedford (from 1869), the Portland Glass Works (1863–73), and the Phoenix Glass Works in South Boston (c.1820–1870). Dummer's Jersey Glass Company (1824–63)

must have made some quantity of pressed glass and a number of companies in Pittsburgh and Wheeling also made it: R. B. Curling's glass works (1827–63), Bakewell & Company (1808–82), the M'Kee firm (1850–89), the Wheeling Flint Glass Works (1835–45), Hobbs, Brockunier & Company (1845–91) and others. The Gillinder factory in Philadelphia also made a great deal of pressed glass in the later period. Since all of these various firms copied one another's designs, reliable attributions are virtually impossible except for occasional signed pieces.   (J.S.S.)

Price, Kenneth (1935–   ).
Ceramist influenced by abstract expressionism* in the late 1950s in Los Angeles, but later known for refined, precise shapes. Price was born in Los Angeles, Cal., and while studying at the University of Southern California in the late 1950s met the revolutionary ceramists gathering around Peter Voulkos.* His bullet-shaped pots of that period, while handled in a spontaneous manner, prefigured the smaller, carefully finished shapes with worm-like protrusions that he developed after receiving his M.F.A. from Alfred University. His work of the mid-1960s was characterized by refinements in shape, and marked by a series of slab cups with delicate and intricate carvings at the base and lyrical glazes.

Printmaking, Historical.
The first American printmakers were practical and ingenious craftsmen of varied skills. John Foster,* whose strong, primitive woodcut portrait of the Reverend Richard Mather was cut in Boston about 1670 and is the earliest American print, was a printer who also practised printmaking. John Coney,* engraver in Boston of some of the earliest colonial currency, was a silversmith active in the 1690s and during the first two decades of the 18th century.

Among the earliest colonial prints, in addition to currency, were symbols of authority (colony seals and royal arms), images of piety (including the first American copperplate portrait, a crude likeness of Increase Mather copied by Thomas Emmes from an English print about 1701), images of death (skulls, crossbones, crude funeral processions, and gallows scenes in the woodcuts on mourning broadsides and on the sensation-seeking broadsheets

4

Printmaking, Historical
3. Peter Pelham. Mather Byles, *1750, mezzotint.*
4. *Engraver unknown.* Captain Isaac Hull, *1813, mezzotint.*
   Both, Print Department, Boston Public Library.

Printmaking

1

2

hawked about the streets), images of science (woodcut and metalcut diagrams of eclipses in almanacs), and images of astrology and superstition (the man of signs which in tiny woodcuts linked parts of the body to signs of the zodiac).

First Professional Printmakers

Francis Dewing, arriving in Boston in 1716–17, brought with him what apparently was the first true copperplate press in the colonies. William Burgis, working in New York and Boston, 1716–31, possessed professional skills as a topographical draftsman and could also engrave, but most of his American views were sent to England for engraving and printing. Peter Pelham,* a London mezzotint* engraver who emigrated to Boston, produced and sold there during 1728–51 a series of fourteen mezzotint portraits, mostly of ministers, which are the most important group of prints produced in colonial America.

The beginnings of book illustration in British North America date from John Foster's almanac cuts of the 1670s, but more ambitious illustrations were cut on metal by the Boston printer, James Franklin, elder brother of Benjamin. James went to England to learn the trade of printing, and he returned not only with a stock of type and ornaments but also with the skill to engrave (beginning in 1717) frontispiece portraits and illustrations.

During the fifty years before the beginning of the American Revolution in 1775, there was a continuing need for maps, charts, and symbols of authority (royal and provincial arms), almanac and newspaper cuts, trade cards, bookplates, and views of towns and cities, as well as magazine and book illustrations. Among the most prolific printmakers of this period were Thomas Johnston* of Boston, James Turner* of Boston and Philadelphia, Nathaniel Hurd* of Boston, Henry Dawkins* of Philadelphia, and Paul Revere,* whose first engraving dates from about 1762. Only Peter Pelham, who painted a few portraits, and John Greenwood, successful portraitist at mid-century, might be called "painter-engravers." Greenwood's mezzotint of Ann Arnold, "Jersey Nanny," a Boston street character, advertised in 1748, is the first American genre print.

A mezzotint of Cotton Mather, which Pelham engraved in 1728, launched the series.

Printmakers and the Revolution

American printmakers in the years of revolution agitated against the British and pictured American heroes and victories. Paul Revere's *A Warm Place —Hell* (1768) was adapted from an English print. His other patriotic prints include the *Boston Massacre* and *Landing of the Troops,* both of 1770. Samuel Okey's mezzotints, *Mr. Samuel Adams* and *Major General Joseph Warren,* brought popular images to the American people. Amos Doolittle's four engravings (1775) of the battles of Lexington and Concord, after paintings by Ralph Earl, are prominent among American contributions to the pictorial reporting of the war. Robert Aitken, Bernard Romans, John Norman, and Joseph Callender all made prints supporting the American cause. The engraver James Smither, accused of loyalty to the British, fled from Philadelphia in 1778 and was able to return only after the war.

Prints from a New Nation

American patriotism received a higher artistic expression in prints by Edward Savage* and Charles Willson Peale.* Peale's small oval mezzotint portraits of Benjamin Franklin and the Marquis de Lafayette were issued in 1787. They are among the finest of all 18th-century American prints. Savage was one of the early contributors to the portraiture of George Washington, and in 1799 became one of the first Americans to use the aquatint process in his prints of the engagement between the *Constitution* and *L'Insurgent.* Another early practitioner was the Connecticut printmaker Abner Reed, whose *Six Views in Aquatint, Taken from Nature* were issued in 1810.

Philadelphia in these years became the major publishing and graphic arts center in the United States. There, Alexander Lawson engraved the plates for Alexander Wilson's *American Ornithology,* and William and Thomas Birch engraved and published their beautiful set of small *Views of Philadelphia,* 1800. Amos Doolittle, active in New Haven, produced numbers of patriotic prints, including a view of the inauguration of George Washington in New York City, 1789, and *A Display of the United States of America* (1791), showing state seals surrounding a portrait of Washington. John Norman's engraving and copperplate printing establishment in Boston after the Revolutionary War

produced maps, charts, and book illustrations, while Samuel Hill was active in the city in the 1790s as an engraver of book and magazine illustrations on copper.

In New York, Peter Rushton Maverick operated an engraving shop beginning in 1784. In the 1790s in New York, the physician Alexander Anderson took up wood engraving and introduced Thomas Bewick's white-line method to the United States. A generation of American wood engravers followed this style. Among the most productive were Abel Bowen in Boston, after 1805, and George Gilbert, in business in Philadelphia from 1816.

Among the new processes in use was stipple engraving, introduced to the United States before 1800 and used for copperplate portraiture by Tiebout, Houston, David Edwin, William Rollinson and others. The American invention of steel engraving in 1811 helped give the United States a later preeminence in banknote engraving.

Aquatint and Lithography

A group of experts in aquatint left England in the years of uncertain economic conditions after the Napoleonic wars and launched in the United States some of the great series of 19th-century American prints. John W. Hill* made and printed *Picturesque Views of American Scenery* (1820–21) after drawings by Joshua Shaw and *The Hudson River Portfolio* (1820–25) after watercolors by William Guy Wall. W. J. Bennett's folio prints of American cities based on his own drawings and those of other artists include New York, Philadelphia, Boston, Washington, Charleston, New Orleans, and Detroit and were made between 1828 and his death in 1844. Working from watercolors by George Harvey, he also made the four-print series of *Harvey's Scenes of the Primitive Forest of America.* Robert Havell, Jr., the English engraver of most of the plates for Audubon's *Birds of America,* was persuaded by Audubon to come to America in 1839; he aquatinted views of New York, Boston, Hartford, and Niagra Falls. Perhaps the most versatile of the English artist-immigrants was John Rubens Smith, who developed a theory of color, was active as a drawing-master, made portraits in stipple and mezzotint, and produced aquatint views, among them prints of Mount Carbon, Pa., Pawtucket, R.I. and Troy, N.Y. Earliest of the English practitioners

of aquatint to come to America, he was here by 1809 and was active for forty years in Boston, Philadelphia, and New York.

The first American experiment in lithography was carried out by Bass Otis in Philadelphia in 1818. In 1825 John and William Pendleton launched in Boston the first successful lithographic firm, employing artists like Rembrandt Peale,* David Claypoole Johnston, Alexander Jackson Davies,* and Fitz Hugh Lane* to draw designs on the stones. Several draftsmen, including Nathaniel Currier and John H. Bufford,* who were to make lithography into big business in later decades, learned the craft in the Pendletons' shop. The coming of lithography released a flood of pictures: lithographed sheet music covers, views of towns and cities, maps, forms, certificates, book illustrations, views of stores and hotels used as advertising, portraits, and drawing-manuals. Artists such as George Catlin,* Henry Inman,* and Eastman Johnson* tried their hand at the process, as did men who today are remembered only for their work in lithography: Moses Swett, Alfred Hoffy, Albert Newsam, and William Sharp, among others. Among the outstanding prints produced were Rembrandt Peale's big portrait of Washington (1826), Newsam's portraits beginning about 1830, including his portrait (1838) of Governor Ritner of Pennsylvania posing with one hand on his plow (based on J. F. Francis' painting); Osgood's portrait of David Crockett (1831), printed by Childs & Lehman in Philadelphia; Johnston's *Daniel Webster* (1834); Swett's lithographs for *Views on the Baltimore & Ohio Railroad* (1831); Lane's stark, primitive first lithographed view of Gloucester, Mass., (1831) as well as his *View in Boston Harbour* (c.1840); and William H. Brown's *Portrait Gallery of Distinguished Americans,* printed by E. B. and E. C. Kellogg and showing silhouettes of startling realism seen in meticulously detailed interiors or landscapes.

In the 1820s and 1830s, wood engraving grew into an industry. Many of the thousands of little cuts illustrating publications of the American Tract Society and the American Sunday-School Union, as well as almanacs and children's books, are unsigned; but in a naive and charming way they carry on the tradition begun by Bewick in England and popularized in America by

Printmaking

1

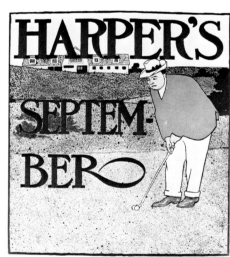

2

3

Alexander Anderson,* whose own work continued. He lived until 1870 and produced in his long life about 6000 wood engravings.

Prints for a Mass Audience

The painter-naturalist John James Audubon* spent most of the years from 1826–38 in Great Britain supervising the engraving and printing of the first editions of his *Birds of America, Quadrupeds of America,* and *Ornithological Studies.* His return to the United States was in part a recognition of the increasing technical skills which made possible, as one example, the fine folio lithographs, brilliantly hand-colored, of the *Quadrupeds,* issued by the Philadelphia lithographer J. T. Bowen from 1842 to 1848.

The discovery of photography by Daguerre in Paris in 1839 brought an immediate and intense response in the United States. In future decades many artists were to make use of the camera, and it was to have a strong impact on technology, too, with the beginnings of photo-lithography in America dating from the 1850s.

Wood engraving became more professionalized and more sophisticated, centering on reproduction of the fine pen lines of illustrators' drawings. An "American School" of book illustrators, served by the wood engravers, began to emerge. F. O. C. Darley was at work from about 1843. Other leading designers were John McLenan, David Hunter Strother (Porte Crayon), William Croome, H. W. Herbert (Frank Forester), and, in California after 1853, C. C. Nahl, and H. W. Arthur Nahl.

A mass audience was growing up. Among the first print publishers to reach it was Nathaniel Currier. For Currier, Napoleon Sarony put on stone an immensely popular lithograph, *Burning of the Steamboat Lexington* (1840), the first of the prints of disasters which found a wide audience. Sarony divided his long and distinguished career between lithography and photography, while Currier, later forming a partnership with his bookkeeper, James Ives, could proudly call the immensely productive firm of Currier & Ives* "Printmakers to the American People."

The new audience was reached in many ways. Viewmakers such as Edwin Whitefield (1816–92) traveled from city to city making careful drawings, rounding up subscribers, and issuing lithographic views of American communities in a period of intense growth. An interest in the already-vanishing Indian was fed by publications like George Catlin's *North American Indian Portfolio,* with its eye-filling, hand-colored lithographs. The American Art-Union,* pursuing the idea of a lottery with original works of art as prizes, commissioned and distributed engravings after some of the paintings it acquired.

Among them were James Smillie's engravings of Thomas Cole's* four scenes, *The Voyage of Life,* issued about 1846–47. They appealed to popular taste and found their way onto the walls of many American homes. Also popular were such genre subjects as *Mexican News,* engraved by Alfred Jones after Woodville, and *The County Election,* engraved by John Sartain after George Bingham's* painting.

Pictorial journalism began on a large scale with *Gleason's Pictorial Drawing-Room Companion* (1851–60), *Frank Leslie's Illustrated Newspaper* (from 1855), *Ballou's* (from 1855) and *Harper's Weekly* (from 1857). Each had its staff of wood engravers. Winslow Homer,* who received his early training in the Boston lithographic shop of J. H. Bufford, made his initial reputation beginning in 1857 when he obtained his first commissions for drawings for *Harper's Weekly.*

The Civil War Years

Winslow Homer's graphic art during the Civil War, including the drawings he sent back from the front to be engraved posthaste by engravers at *Harper's,* and the series of six lithographs, *Campaign Sketches,* published by Louis Prang in Boston about 1863, helped to make him more widely known. The lithographs, lively, full of humor, and well printed by Prang, have a freedom in the handling of figures that makes them unique in American printmaking up to then.

Also working for *Harper's,* beginning in 1862, was twenty-two-year-old Thomas Nast.* Unlike Homer, he made a career of magazine work, and his fame rests on his caricatures, engraved by staff engravers, of Boss Tweed and the Tweed Ring in the 1870s.

Mathew Brady* went to war with his camera. His visual record of the Civil War in thousands of photographs foreshadowed the primacy the photographer was later to have in pictorial reporting. His prints were distinguished for fine craftsmanship and for his own intensity of vision.

4

5

Printmaking

For some artists, business continued as usual. Some of Currier & Ives' best-known prints date from the war years. Arthur F. Tait,* the painter, did scenes of life in the West based on earlier pictures by Karl Bodmer,* George Catlin* and John Mix Stanley.* Charles Parsons' *Central Park, Winter—The Skating Pond* was published by Currier & Ives in 1862. Fanny Palmer drew for the firm some of the great romantic prints of the steamboat era, including *"Wooding Up" on the Mississippi* (1863) and *"Rounding a Bend" on the Mississippi, The Parting Salute* (1866).

Elihu Vedder* spent the war in New York. He and John La Farge* made the most daring of the illustrations, engraved on wood after their designs, for Ticknor & Fields' edition of *Enoch Arden* (1865). La Farge, during a stay in Paris years before, had looked at Japanese prints and found in them new approaches to design.

In Europe, James Whistler* had found the more congenial atmosphere he had left the United States to seek in the mid-1850s, and was well on his way to an international reputation. He dramatized the idea of the lone genius, temperamental and inspired, and was a leader in bringing acceptance of the artist's print issued in a signed limited edition for collectors. His first Paris etchings date from 1858, and his great Thames set was made in 1859—achievements that were not possible in the less sophisticated atmosphere of the United States of that era.

Industrialization and the Artist

As the graphic arts in the decades following the Civil War grew into a major American industry, more and more artists began to work independently as printmakers, obtaining results of a more personal kind. Louis Prang in his refinement of chromolithography attempted to mediate between industry and the artist; the chromos produced in his plant often used more than twenty colors, each printed from a different stone, to produce a glowing depth of color. Many were masterpieces of craftsmanship, reproducing oils or watercolors by Thomas Moran, John W. Hill, J. R. Key, Benjamin Champney, Alfred T. Bricher,* Winslow Homer, and others.

Some of the best opportunities for the American graphic artist after the Civil War lay in book and magazine illustration. Like Daumier in earlier years in Paris, Homer in New York learned to work with wood engravers and make them serve his artistic purposes in designs that reached a high point in *Harper's Weekly* and *Every Saturday* in 1873 and 1874. *Waiting for a Bite, Raid on a Sand-Swallow Colony,* and other wood engravings are unforgettable images of 19th-century America. W. J. Linton, Anthony, Juengling, Kruell, Closson, Timothy Cole, John P. Davis, and their fellow wood engravers, working in minutely detailed techniques, vied with each other in the pages of *Scribner's, Harper's, The Riverside Magazine for Young People,* and other journals. They engraved designs by Felix Darley,* Fenn, Augustus Hoppin, Homer Martin,* Thomas Nast, W. J. Hennessy, R. Swain Gifford, and, after 1880, Howard Pyle, Joseph Pennell,* and others. *Picturesque America* (1872–74) is a virtuoso display of wood engraving technique.

A leader in the increasingly vigorous American movement in caricature was Joseph Keppler, who emigrated to the United States in 1867, founded *Puck* as a German-language journal in 1876 in New York, and began an English edition the next year. Keppler was a talented draftsman and designer with exuberant humor and a responsiveness to new technology. His lithographed caricatures were originally printed in black and white, later had colors added from woodblocks, and later still were printed as chromolithographs.

Increasingly, photography was used as an art form. Men like John Gardner,* Timothy O'Sullivan,* and William Henry Jackson* went West with their cameras to record a landscape of immense space and grandeur. The new technology being evolved to reproduce photographs included development of light-sensitive gelatin coatings like collotype (for continuous-tone reproduction) and the screening of light through negatives to produce patterns on a sensitive plate that could then be etched as a half-tone reproduction, using densities of dots to convey varying degrees of dark tone. In time, these photo-mechanical reproductions were to put the professional wood engravers out of business.

Printer-printmakers such as Frank Duveneck,* Otto Bacher, J. Alden Weir,* Mary Cassatt,* and Joseph Pennell went to Europe in a successful quest for inspiration and access to special knowledge and craftsmanship in London studios and Parisian ateliers.

With the 1890s came a final flowering of chromolithography. There was an explosion of enthusiasm for the art of the poster and an invasion of advertising by uninhibited art nouveau* designers, which signalled a last alliance between artists and the increasingly standardized graphic arts industry of factory techniques and complex machine processes. There was an exuberance in design and a reaching out for new ideas. Howard Pyle and Charles Dana Gibson were among the artists taking advantage of the new photo-mechanical processes that reproduced drawings with precision of every detail. Will Bradley, Edward Penfield,* Louis Rhead, and Ethel Reed were among the leaders of the new movement in poster design. Maxfield Parrish,* John Sloan,* Charles Woodbury, and Ernest Haskell also tried their hands. Their works were effectively mass-produced by industrial lithography, which adapted well to designs with flat areas of color. Pictorial journalism, meanwhile, had not yet become the realm of the camera and half-tone, and aspiring artists could find jobs as newspaper draftsmen. In that capacity, William Glackens,* George Luks,* Everett Shinn,* and John Sloan worked for the Philadelphia *Inquirer* and the Philadelphia *Press* in the 1890s.

The Artist's Print, 1900–40

Only in the first years of the 20th century did the United States begin to offer the artist conditions for working that included the versatility and refinement of skills sought by Whistler in Europe more than four decades earlier. After 1900, there were many American painter-printmakers who treated printmaking as a major means of expression and communication.

John Sloan's early etchings, interpreting the crowded humanity of New York City, included *Man Monkey* (1905), *Turning Out the Light* (1905), and *Night Windows* (1910). Small in format, they are vigorous pictures, strongly drawn, with a deep-bitten etched line.

Pennell, returning from Europe in 1909 after an extended stay, made broad, virile lithographs—first of the coal towns of Pennsylvania (1910), then of the Panama Canal (1912) and of Greece (the "Land of Temples" series of 1913). John Marin,* initially a devotee of Whistler, returned from Europe in 1911 to make daring departures in style with a succession of increasingly expressionistic etchings. *Brooklyn Bridge* (1911) was followed in 1913 by two series of prints using the bridge and the Woolworth Building as themes explored in distortions, angles, and new envisionings.

The photographer and gallery-owner, Alfred Stieglitz,* meanwhile, was issuing *Camera Work,* taking advantage of the brief flowering of the gravure reproduction process as an art form. He and Edward Steichen* were finding a new vision in photography. The warmth and depth of tone of gravure was used to advantage by Edward S. Curtis in his monumental multivolume study, *The North American Indian,* and by Alvin Langdon Coburn in his books of photographic portraits of 1910–13.

Albert Sterner and Arthur B. Davies* were making prints. Childe Hassam* had begun the impressionistic etchings and lithographs that are among the important bodies of graphic work produced by any American artist. George Bellows* began lithography in 1916 and produced in the next decade, before his death in 1925, almost two hundred prints. Outstanding in draftsmanship and design, they were beautifully printed, often by the artist-lithographer Bolton Brown.

Bellows, Hassam, Sloan, Reginald Marsh,* and Edward Hopper* all have high rank among American artists who have been interested in printmaking. Hopper, using etching as one means of expressing his spare, eloquent views of America, steered a lone course. Marsh in the 1920s emerged with a bold, buoyant style, as in his lithograph *Penn Station* (1929), a satirical, almost Hogarthian closeup of hurrying businessmen and flappers.

Before 1920, Stuart Davis,* Abraham Walkowitz,* and Max Weber* were making lithographs. Charles Sheeler* later used the medium for precisionist lithographs that were lyrical in feeling. Another precisionist in style was Louis Lozowick. He began a career in lithography which was to extend for more than forty years. George "Pop" Hart* tried the medium; among others who were making use of it were Walt Kuhn,* Adolf Dehn, and Grant Wood.* Lyonel Feininger* gave America a share in German theories of abstraction. The austere geometry of his woodcuts makes much use of the white of the

1

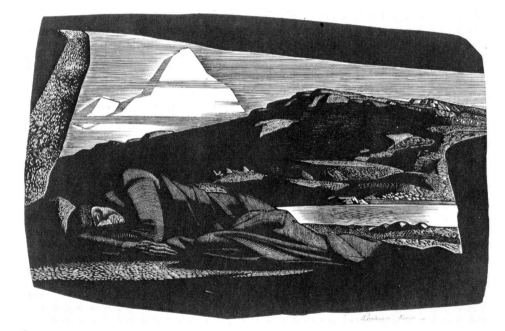

2

Printmaking, Historical
1. *Reginald Marsh.* Bread Line—No One Has Starved, *1932, etching. Collection Senator William Benton.*
2. *Rockwell Kent.* Northern Light, *c.1928, wood engraving. Philadelphia Museum of Art.*

Printmaking

paper and is sparing in placement of black lines and shapes. Lithographs by Dehn, Wood and many others, including John Steuart Curry,* William Gropper,* Thomas Hart Benton,* and Yasuo Kuniyoshi* were commissioned and published in the 1930s in New York by Associated American Artists, a major force in the patronage of art in that era.

Rockwell Kent's* stark, visionary wood engravings of the 1920s and 1930s had tremendous impact. His woodcut-like drawings for *Moby Dick* are among the most memorable of all American book illustrations. He worked in lithography as well. An outstanding example is his lithographic self-portrait, dramatic in its simple, uncluttered composition.

Rudolph Ruzicka, following his Czechoslovakian heritage of design, created small, meticulously executed wood engravings in color that gave outstanding pictorial quality to a number of well-designed, well-printed books, including *Newark* and *New York.* Thomas Nason cultivated wood engraving and expressed in it scenes of pastoral peace as well as the isolation, loneliness and decay of rural New England. J. J. Lankes worked broadly in woodcut and wood engraving, producing, like Nason, hundreds of prints that excelled in their poetic expression, technical mastery, and responsiveness to the special qualities of black and white possible in wood.

A group of men with strong ties to 19th-century European printmaking found themselves riding a boom in print collecting during the 1920s. All were accomplished draftsmen. Frank Benson,* picturing ducks in marsh and river and on the wing; Arthur Heintzelman with sensitive portraits and groupings of people; John Winkler with street scenes and city vistas; Kerr Eby with landscapes; and architectural etchers, including John Taylor Arms, Ernest Roth, and Samuel Chamberlain, pursued etching and sometimes drypoint, producing prints small in format, in black and white.

The 1920s are documented in graphic art full of high spirits, exemplified by John Sloan's etching of prancing flappers, *Easter Eve, Washington Square* (1926) and Martin Lewis' Manhattan street scenes. In the 1930s, a dark, brooding mood dominated American printmaking. Stow Wengenroth made somber lithographs of New York City

1

2

Printmaking, Modern
1. *Frank Stella.* River of Ponds III *(Newfoundland series), 1970.*

2. *Claes Oldenburg.* The Letter Q, *1972, 15-color lithograph. Both, Gemini G.E.L., San Francisco.*

456

and later of the New England coast, turning his attention to larger format and to the exploration of light and atmosphere along Maine shores as the decade of the 1940s began. Will Barnet and Federico Castellon were among the artists making lithographs of quality. George Biddle's* lithographs were bitter in satire and social protest. Marsh made powerful etchings of railroad yards, of tugs along the waterfront, of breadlines, of bums sleeping at the foot of Washington's statue. In eloquent lithographs, Raphael Soyer* pictured the loneliness of working women and the poverty, hunger, and despair of the unemployed. Lynd Ward's woodcut novels, inspired by the work of the Belgian, Frans Masereel, were shouts of anger. More serene, but still infused with the intense spirit of the decade, were the lithographed landscapes of Emil Ganso and the etchings—precise yet with warmth of texture and tone—in which Armin Landeck portrayed interiors as well as outdoor glimpses of city architecture.

In photography, Ben Shahn,* Walker Evans,* Dorothea Lange,* and others expressed much of the suffering of America. In caricature, now largely limited to editorial-page cartoons in the newspapers, Rollin Kirby, Boardman Robinson,* Daniel Fitzpatrick and other draftsmen carried forward the hard-hitting approach that Nast had done much to establish. (S.H.)

Printmaking, Modern.

During the Depression and the early 1940s the most popular printmaking medium was mass-producible lithography. The lithographs of Grant Wood,* Thomas Hart Benton,* William Gropper,* and Adolph Dehn were popularized by print clubs such as Associated American Artists and the Print Club of Philadelphia, and the annual print competitions of The Library of Congress and the Society of American Etchers. The silkscreen, a stencil technique that, like lithography, could produce large editions, was dubbed "serigraphy" by a group of artists in 1938 who wished to avoid the taint of its earlier commercial usage (see Serial Art). Ben Shahn* and Robert Gwathmey* were among those who made serigraphs, the flat style of the latter being nearest to the commercial silkscreen technique that was revived in the 1960s.

World War II and the resultant appearance in America of many of the well-established European artists changed the character of American art in all media. In New York, Stanley William Hayter opened his intaglio workshop, Atelier 17.* This became a place for Americans and younger European refugees to study and also meet Hayter's Parisian artist friends. Undoubtedly the surrealist etchings of Masson and Miró executed at the Atelier influenced a former student of Thomas Hart Benton, Jackson Pollock,* who made his only etchings there. Two younger artists, Mauricio Lasansky* of Argentina and Gabor Peterdi* of Hungary became the direct heirs of Hayter's American teaching. Absorbing the technical possibilities developed by Hayter, they made of intaglio a medium as complex as collage, combining etching, engraving, aquatint, special inking methods, and areas of high relief. Eventually, through their own workshops at the University of Iowa and Yale University, Lasansky and Peterdi changed the popular form of prints from lithography to intaglio, from narrative social realism to abstraction, incorporating color and relief elements.

During the late 1940s and the 1950s the mass appeal of cheaply produced black-and-white lithographs gave way to the special quality of these European-influenced prints. Woodcuts in the freely executed German expressionist tradition and exceptionally complex wood engravings reappeared with the work of Louis Schanker, the young Uruguayan Antonio Frasconi,* and the Chicago artist Misch Kohn. Two exhibitions, "Hayter and Studio 17" in 1944 at the Museum of Modern Art and "American Woodcuts 1670–1950" at the Brooklyn Museum of Art, influenced and reflected these changes. The free expression possible in these specialized techniques resulted in a group of artists who worked primarily in printmaking. Typical technical innovations were cellocuts, printing without ink (embossing), collographs (prints made from collages of miscellaneous materials), and engraving with dental tools. The skills generally were too complex for a painter to use only occasionally, so it is not surprising that the abstract expressionists of the 1950s made few prints during the period in which they developed the first internationally important American school. The most enduring artist-printmaker of the 1950s

was Leonard Baskin.* By utilizing his skill as a woodcarver he extended the dimension and directness of woodcuts into prints that could be seen only if hung on a wall. As paintings were growing in size, so the modern print had to react and expand in order to retain its artistic impact.

The European publishing tradition, encouraging prominent artists to make prints with the aid of skilled craftsmen, was developed in America by Mrs. Tatyana Grosman at her Universal Limited Art Editions,* and Miss June Wayne,* who directed the Ford Foundation-funded Tamarind Lithography Workshop.* Through the recognition by these workshops that many American painters and sculptors were well enough established to turn their attention to new media, the emphasis shifted from the predominantly printmaker's print to prints by well-known painters such as Josef Albers,* Sam Francis,* Jasper Johns,* Robert Motherwell,* Larry Rivers,* and Robert Rauschenberg.* Francis, the first abstract expressionist to produce a large body of work in lithography, began at Universal but did most of his early prints in Switzerland. Few of the lithographs done at Tamarind attained the recognition achieved by those from Universal because Tamarind prints had to be marketed by the artists themselves and few of their art dealers would sell prints. In addition, artists at Tamarind worked for only two months, while at Universal artists used the Workshop as an extension of their studios. Tamarind-trained printers who set up their own shops drew on the best elements of both workshops in their work with such artists as Willem de Kooning,* Claes Oldenburg,* and Frank Stella.*

The emphasis on printmaking in the 1960s was also made inevitable by the changing concept of painting, which began to include printed elements, or, as in the work of Warhol,* to be totally printed. The pop artist's insistence that paintings could be done with silkscreen (indeed, many of the images required it) removed the esoteric and the precious associations of printmaking. In his first lithographs Rauschenberg simulated silkscreened printing of newspaper photographs in the manner by which he incorporated those images in his paintings.

The first attempts by most pop artists to make prints was in silkscreen in rela-

457

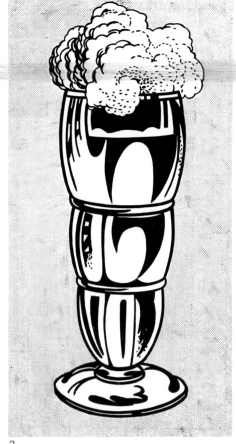

Printmaking, Modern
1. *Jasper Johns.* Numbers, *lithograph. Universal Limited Art Editions.*
2. *Roy Lichtenstein.* Ice Cream Soda, *1962. Private collection.*
3. *Robert Rauschenberg.* Landmark, *1968, lithograph. Universal Limited Art Editions.*
4. *Andy Warhol.* Green Coca Cola Bottles, *1962, silkscreen. Whitney Museum of American Art, N.Y.*

tively unlimited editions (Warhol's soup cans, Lichtenstein's comics, and Indiana's *Love*). As the size of their works grew, and as economic inflation and income tax structure changed, artists were assiduously scouted by publishers in the second half of the 1960s. Younger painters were able to obtain Tamarind grants, and students of all print media had opportunities to show their work in dozens of annual exhibitions devoted to prints. Individual prints of some living American artists had risen to 75 times their original price in eight years.

In addition to prints, a new art product evolved during the 1960s: multiples. Because many of the artists who were making prints sought means of making three-dimensional works other than classic sculpture in editions, much of American multiple art comes out of printmaking workshops. Rauschenberg's *Shades* from Universal Limited Art Editions in 1963, made of movable, lithographed plexiglass panels, was one of the first American multiples. A company, Multiples Inc., started with banners by Anuszkiewicz,* Krushenick* and Wesselmann,* among others, but was soon publishing print-engendered works. As in the previous decade, technical experimentation was widespread, particularly in the use of photographic materials and techniques. Photographic silkscreens, Xerox, photosensitized lithographic stones, reworked photo-offset, and photo-engraved plates were some of the means used to make prints. With the stylistic changes of the late 1960s, much of the primary works of art began to be printed. By 1970 large lithographs and silkscreens, three-dimensional multiples, and complex intaglio prints were challenged by the untranslatable and untransferrable typewritten or Xeroxed notebooks of the conceptualists and the photo-documentary materials of the process artists.
(R.C.)

Prior, William Matthew (1806–73).
Itinerant painter born in Bath, Me., who traveled through New England and as far afield as Baltimore, finally settling in Boston in 1841. Together with his wife and her brothers he set up a portrait studio that could supply likenesses that ranged from quite conventionally academic images to the primitive "flat picture . . . without shade or shadow for one half the price." It is for the numer-

ous paintings in the latter category that he is best known—large, brightly colored pictures featuring high foreheads, wide-set eyes, heavy brows, and lack of shadow, with scant attention to hands and other troublesome details. An example is *Portrait of a Young Man* (1844). He also made many copies on glass of the Gilbert Stuart* portraits of George Washington.
(M.J.G.)

Proctor, A. Phimister (1862–1950).
Sculptor. He was a native of Ontario, Canada, but was raised in Denver, Col., and the untamed, rowdy, and beautiful West remained the major subject of his sculpture throughout his life. In 1888 he went to New York to study at the Art Students League* and the National Academy of Design,* and between 1891 and 1893 he executed over thirty-five models of animals in staff (plaster and straw) material for the World's Columbian Exposition of 1893 in Chicago. After spending a year in Paris he returned to America to specialize in animal and Indian sculptures. The *Charging Panther* (c.1892, Corcoran) and the four monumental bison (1912–14) that adorn the Q Street Bridge, Washington, D.C., are among his best-known works. Other civic monuments include *Bronco Buster* (c.1915, Denver) and *Teddy Roosevelt as a Rough Rider* (1922, Portland, Ore.). For Proctor—as for other sculptors of the American West, such as Solon Borglum* and Cyrus Dallin*—only a rugged naturalism could do justice to the subject; and although all of these artists had gone to Paris, they rejected the decorative element and 19th-century academism of the École des Beaux-Arts.
(W.C.)

Purcell & Elmslie.
William Gray Purcell (1880-1964) was born in Wilmette, Ill., was educated in schools in Oak Park, Ill., and graduated from Cornell University's School of Architecture in 1903. He then served briefly as a draftsman in the Chicago office of Louis Sullivan,* and in 1904 worked with John Galen Howard in Berkeley, Cal., and then with several firms in Seattle. In 1906, he and George Feick, Jr., toured Europe and in the following year established a firm in Minneapolis. In 1909 they were joined by George Grant Elmslie; the firm of Purcell & Elmslie continued on until 1922.

George Grant Elmslie (1871–1952)

was born in Huntley, Scotland, however he was brought to Chicago in 1885.
In 1887 he was apprenticed to the successful Queen, Anne* revival architect Joseph L. Silsbee and from there went on to the office of Adler & Sullivan.* When Frank Lloyd Wright* left Adler & Sullivan, Elmslie became the chief draftsman and when the firm was dissolved in 1894, he remained with Sullivan (until 1909).

By the late 1890s Elmslie was in effect a co-designer with Sullivan; much of the ornament and detailing of the Carson, Pirie, Scott Store (Chicago, 1899–1903) and the earlier Bayard Building (Buffalo, 1894–5) was from his hand. The three major commissions of the Sullivan office after 1900, the Babson House (Riverside, Ill., 1907), the Bradley House (Madison, Wis., 1909), and the National Farmers' Bank (Owatonna, Minn., 1907–08), contain many elements by Elmslie.

As designers the Purcell & Elmslie firm brought together a number of current traditions, though strictly speaking they, like Wright, Greene & Greene,* and Gill,* should be thought of as essentially Arts and Crafts* architects. In their commercial buildings such as the Merchants Bank of Winona (Winona, Minn., 1911) they united their fondness for simple basic forms, developed out of the work of Richardson, Sullivan, and the European avant-garde such as H. P. Gerlage. Their larger public buildings, such as the Woodbury County Courthouse (Sioux City, Iowa, 1915–17), while Sullivanesque and Wrightian, are highly individual in character.

Their domestic work lies within the Midwest prairie style. Although houses like the Bradley Bungalow (Woods Hole, Mass., 1911) and Purcell's own house (Minneapolis, 1913), abound in Wrightian detail, their "open" plans, scale, and detailing readily distinguish them from Wright or any of the other Midwest exponents of the prairie style.

After 1922 both partners continued to practice independently, Purcell in Portland, Ore., and Elmslie in Chicago. Their work of the 1920s and 1930s reveals their awareness of current styles in America and Europe, especially the expressionism* of the early 1920s and the International style* of the mid-1930s.
(D.G.)

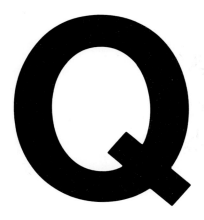

Queen Anne Style.

A style of architecture that came to America from England and flourished in the 1880s, along with Romanesque revival.* Nationwide in its influence, it was not a revival but derived directly from the contemporary work of Richard Norman Shaw (1831–1912) and others in England. It bore no particular relation to the pre-Georgian architecture of Queen Anne, but more nearly resembled the Elizabethan country manor house and the Flemish town house or guildhall.

Often referred to as the "Free Classic," it was classical in its details, but the buildings had picturesque profiles and the plans, very similar to those of Romanesque revival, were often asymmetrical, with large living halls featuring handsome staircases, woodwork, and paneling. Columns generally gave way to pilasters and, when the building was shingled, scallops and sawtooth patterns were used. Exterior wood panels displayed sunbursts or sunflower motifs. Brickwork, generally used for the city residence, might serve only for the first floor in the country or suburban house, with wood shingles or siding above. The town house often had curvilinear Flemish or pedimented gables and chimney flues were clearly expressed, on the exterior, by brickwork. Only brick of the finest finish was used. Black or red mortar joints were much in vogue. Like Romanesque revival, the double-hung windows often had the upper sash divided into small square panes, with the lower half a single sheet of plate glass. Copper-clad bay windows, which often extended through two or more floors, were to be found on city buildings. Building colors ran to dark reds, greens and browns. A reawakened interest in America's colonial heritage was apparent in the interior of the Queen Anne house in hand-railings of staircases and in broken pediments above doorways. Wrought iron was also reintroduced and was generally flat, twisted, or latticed.

The great appeal of this style was attributed to the quest for a cozy domesticity. In 1892, Montgomery Schuyler, in his book *American Architecture,* wrote: ". . . in an evil hour, and under a strange spell, the young architects of the United States followed the young architects of England in preferring the refinements of a fixed and developed architecture to the rudenesses of a living and growing architecture." Although the Queen Anne style was a *potpourri* of architectural details, the main theme was classical, like that of the World's Columbian Exposition of 1893, but with one important difference: the Queen Anne was a highly individualized style, whereas the classicism of the exposition lent itself to overall concepts, to uniformity, and to the dreams of town planners.   (A.B.)

Quidor, John (1801–81).

Painter. His life and art, the one long forgotten and the other largely lost or destroyed, were rediscovered in an exhibition at the Brooklyn Museum in 1942. The public awakened then to a figure painter wholly unlike the few others active in his time, one who was unique, original, American. In common with Thomas Cole* and others, his romanticism* had its close tie to literature. But Cole's romanticism, for all its personal quality, was essentially an import. Quidor's, tied strongly to the popular American authors Irving and Cooper, was more entirely his own— flamboyantly imaginative, as offbeat in color as in style and design. In a broad way Quidor may be compared to the later, equally original, Albert Pinkham Ryder* in his free response to literary allusion and rejection of reality, and in his untidy, impractical life.

He was born in Tappan, N.Y., and

1

1. *Queen Anne Style. McKim, Mead & White, The Gorham Building, N.Y. 1906.*
2. *John Quidor. Ichabod Crane Pursued by the Headless Horseman, c. 1828. Yale University Art Gallery, New Haven, Conn. (Mabel Brady Garvan Collection).*
3. *'John Quidor. Antony Van Corlear Brought into the Presence of Peter Stuyvesant, 1839. Munson-Williams-Proctor Institute, Utica, N.Y.*

2

3

studied in New York City under the brilliant, eccentric John Wesley Jarvis,* a relationship marred by mutual dislike. His earliest known picture, a scene from *Don Quixote,* is dated 1823. In 1827 he appears in the New York Directory as "portrait painter," a listing perhaps more hopeful than factual, since no portraits are known. He had, however, acquired a reputation in the city as a painter of banners and decorative panels for the engine and hose carriages of volunteer fire companies. James K. Paulding, the novelist, had come upon some of Quidor's scenes from Washington Irving in a shop window, arousing an interest in the artist, who had as yet no fashionable patronage.

In Illinois he undertook to buy a farm, to be paid for in cash and in a series of huge paintings on religious subjects that were to rival the famous productions of Benjamin West.* At the same time he showed the "Quidor Collection" of "Scriptural Paintings" at the National Academy of Design, New York City, in 1847 and may have realized something from the admission charge; but in the end he was bilked of cash, paintings, and farm. It was typical of his struggles, year after year; they ended in his retreat to his daughter's home in Jersey City.

Quidor was a romantic who painted fantastic grotesqueries, dreams, literary illustrations, and caricatures. His *Ichabod Crane Pursued by the Headless Horseman of Sleepy Hollow* (c.1828, Yale) seems to have attracted the most interest in his own day, perhaps because that story had so caught the fancy of the time. The most striking to modern eyes is his *Wolfert's Will* (1856), formerly one of several Quidor works in the large Philadelphia gallery of an inventor and locomotive builder, Joseph Harrison, the only prominent collector with an appreciation of his work. Today, Quidor brings us the humor and fantasy of young America distilled in his own imagination into forms as brightly original as those from which they are derived. (C.C.S.)

Ramage, John (c.1748–1802).
Miniature painter. An Irishman, trained at the Dublin School of Artists, he married and emigrated to Canada, where his presence at Halifax is recorded, 1772 and 1774, in suits for small debts. Soon after, he was active in Boston as a miniaturist. He returned to Halifax on its evacuation by the British army, and then in 1777 went to British-held New York,where he continued his profession until 1794. William Dunlap* met him there in 1787 and thought him "evidently declining through fast living." Yet the most notable of his works were done in these years. After a sheriff's sale of his effects, he retreated to Montreal, where he died. As a miniaturist he was precise and competent. Many of his ivories are in the form of an elongated oval, including his most distinguished piece, the full-face *George Washington* (Metropolitan), painted for Mrs. Washington in 1789.   (C.C.S.)

Ramée, Joseph Jacques (1764–1842).
Architect and landscape designer, born in the Ardennes, France. Nothing is known of his training, but at age sixteen he was appointed inspector of buildings for the Count of Artois. Suspected of royalist leanings, Ramée left Paris in 1792. From 1794 to 1811 he was in Germany and Denmark, practicing architecture and landscaping. The design for the Bourse in Hamburg is his. In Denmark he designed the chateaux of Sophiehold near Frederiksdal, and several country houses—all in classical style.
In 1811, David Parrish, a Philadelphia banker, persuaded Ramée to come to America to work on his estate near Ogdensburg, N.Y. A collection of Ramée's designs was published in Paris, including a plan for the Parrish estate on what is now Ogden Island in the St. Lawrence River. For Union College, Schenectady, N.Y. (1812–13) he made

a magnificent landscape plan and designs for some buildings, two of which were built in a subdued classical manner. He also designed the estate of Catherine Duane, Duanesburgh, N.Y. (1812–13), and Dennis A. Smith's estate, Calverton, in Baltimore (1816). When his design for the Baltimore Exchange failed to receive the first prize, he apparently returned to Europe. He worked in Belgium and Germany, and died in France. His son Daniel, whom he brought to the United States, later wrote extensively on architecture. Ramée deserves to be remembered for his well-constructed landscape plan for Union College, the first campus in America to be designed by an architect.
(P.F.N.)

Randolph, Benjamin (1737/38–91).
Philadelphia cabinetmaker who may be considered colonial America's equivalent to Thomas Chippendale. Born near Princeton, N.J., he probably went to Philadelphia about 1750, and served an apprenticeship in the shop of his cousin, Jedidiah Snowden (d.1797), a cabinetmaker.
Randolph received his training and entered the furniture-making business just as the new "rococo" fashions became popular in Philadelphia. As with many 18th-century American cabinetmakers, few documented pieces by Randolph have survived, but there is abundant evidence of his success and of the wealth and important social position he achieved. His establishment included carvers and upholsterers, and he himself was both a cabinetmaker and a carver, a combination of which he was quite proud. Because he owned a sawmill in Burlington County, N.J., he was able to keep a stock of local oak, pine, cedar, and walnut, in addition to imported mahogany, in order to supply local woodworkers. The names of more than thirty Philadelphia cabinetmakers,

carvers, and upholsterers appear in his accounts for 1768–87 and his receipt book for 1763–77. His customers included John Dickinson, Richard Bache, Andrew Hamilton, George Emlen, Jr., Samuel Mifflin, and Thomas McKean, and his business extended to New Jersey, Delaware, Maryland, and the Carolinas. Between 1765 and 1767, Randolph produced furniture valued at more than £200 for one patron alone, Colonel George Croghan, including a mahogany desk and bookcase, a commode bureau table, a carved mahogany tea table, and a clock bracket with carved cherubim's head. Randolph's shop also produced arm and side chairs; breakfast, card, dining, dressing, and slab tables; tea boards; chests of drawers; high chests; and wash stands. The most historic piece he produced was a portable writing desk for Thomas Jefferson, upon which the Virginian is said to have written drafts of the Declaration of Independence. Much of Randolph's reputation stems from a rococo trade card engraved by James Smither, six intricately carved "sample" chairs in the "modern taste" (Philadelphia, Williamsburg, Winterthur, Yale, and a private collection), several labeled chairs in American museums and private collections, and a labeled card table (Winterthur). The late architectural historian Fiske Kimball showed that designs for Randolph's trade cards were derived from England cabinetmaker's books of the 1760s.
Randolph, an ardent patriot, sold his shop tools in 1778 and retired from cabinetmaking. As a colonel he participated in the battles of Trenton and Princeton, and both Jefferson and Washington lodged at his house while they were in Philadelphia. Following the Revolution, Randolph went to live at an iron-making furnace that he owned in New Jersey. A man of wit and sophistication, he epitomizes the 18th-century

artisan's goal of using handcraft skill to move up the social scale from craftsman to merchant to "gentleman."

(C.F.H.)

Ranger, Henry Ward (1858–1916).

Landscape painter, born in Syracuse, N.Y. He attended art classes in the United States, France, and Holland, but developed his technique largely by himself. At first it was closely dependent on the Barbizon School* style, and his mature work still reflected its influence. He is best known for woodland interiors, often in rich, autumnal colors; majestic trees are arranged in decorative patterns, and the dark, textured masses of trunk and foliage help create a romantic mood. He painted a broad range of landscape subjects, from picturesque, tapestry-like trees to firmly modeled rocky hilltops, in various moods and seasons (*Spring Woods*, c.1910, Washington). He opened a New York studio in 1884 and was soon quite successful. His landscapes had great appeal at the turn of the century. He received important awards, critical acclaim, and eager support from collectors. A generous man and an idealist, he established the Ranger Fund at the National Academy of Design,* through which the works of younger artists are purchased and made available to museums.

(D.W.S.)

Ranney, William (1813–57).

Genre and historical painter, born in Middletown, Conn. His sea-captain father having been lost at sea, the boy was apprenticed to a tinsmith in Fayetteville, N.C. However, by 1833 he was studying drawing in Brooklyn, N.Y. Stimulated by the struggle for Texan independence from Mexico, he enlisted, and from March to November, 1836, served in the army of the short-lived Republic of Texas. He then returned to New York City and had a portrait studio there from 1843 to 1847. However, his work, judging from the few surviving examples, does not compare favorably with that of his many contemporaries who made it a specialty. Ranney settled in 1853 in Hoboken, N.J., and died of consumption at forty-four, leaving his family in extreme poverty. The members of the National Academy of Design,* to which he had been elected in 1850, arranged a memorial exhibition of all his unsold works to establish a fund for his widow. Thus,

his productive career as a genre painter was limited to the decade from 1845 to 1855.

Ranney was primarily a painter of the out-of-doors, and almost all his historical and genre pictures have open-air settings. His historical subjects, such as *The First News of the Battle of Lexington* (1847, North Carolina Museum of Art, Raleigh), were mostly related to the Revolutionary War. They suffer from a common weakness of many historical reconstructions: a failure to convey the spirit of the earlier period. Ranney's considerable reputation therefore rests on his genre subjects. These fall into two groups: western subjects, and scenes of hunting and fishing. Although Ranney's western experience was limited (as far as we know) to a few months in his youth, he drew upon it for some of his most important works. Many of these deal with aspects of frontier life, for example, *Hunting Wild Horses* (1846, Joslyn).

Most of Ranney's sporting paintings depict duck hunting in the vast marshes near his studio on the Jersey side of the Hudson River, but a few show fishing and crabbing scenes. *Duck Hunting on the Hackensack Meadows* (1849, Boston), and *Duck Shooting* (1850, Corcoran) combine a sensitive rendering of the atmospheric nuances of the landscape with a psychologically convincing situation.

(H.W.W.)

Rattner, Abraham (1895–   ).

Painter. Born in Poughkeepsie, N.Y., he was the son of a Russian immigrant. He studied architecture at George Washington University in Washington, D.C., and took night classes at the Corcoran School of Art, where he soon became a full-time art student. He transferred to the Pennsylvania Academy of the Fine Arts, but left in 1917 to join the army, serving as a camouflage artist in France in World War I. He returned to the academy, and in 1920 he won a traveling fellowship with which he went back to Paris, where he remained for the next two decades. There he studied at the École des Beaux-Arts, Académie Ranson, Académie Julien and the Grande Chaumière. He met Claude Monet during the latter's work on his water lily paintings, but the primary influences on his early work were cubism* and the painting of Picasso and Rouault, which he developed into a semi-abstract expressionist style char-

1

2

1. *Benjamin Randolph.* Trade card, engraved by James Smither. Library Company of Philadelphia.
2. *Benjamin Randolph.* Side chair, c.1770, mahogany. Henry Francis du Pont Winterthur Museum, Winterthur, Del.

acterized by distorted, severely angular figures, often of a religious nature, and by intricately patterned black lines and thick, mysteriously glowing colors. Romanesque art, Byzantine mosaics, and Greek Orthodox icons are other elements that Rattner absorbed into his mature style.

He had his first one-man show in 1935 and exhibited at the Salon des Tuileries and Salon des Indépendants, gaining recognition as a member of the Minotaur group. But in 1939, impelled by the Nazi threat in Germany, he returned to the United States, in the process losing twenty years of paintings. He then spent several months touring the United States by car with the novelist Henry Miller, drawing illustrations for Miller's account of the journey. With the outbreak of World War II, he produced such cataclysmic works as *City Still Life* (Walker), portraying the ruination of a town. He was also moved to rediscover his religious heritage, which led to numerous paintings on figures and themes from Scripture, as well as paintings dealing with vernacular imagery but infused with a sense of ritualistic mystery. Typical of his work showing the influences of Picasso and Rouault is his *The Emperor* (1944, Whitney).

In 1952, Rattner became artist-in-residence at the University of Illinois, and landscape themes have since appeared periodically in his art. His recent painting has moved further in the direction of abstract expressionism.* Rattner has taught in several American universities as well as the American Academy in Rome, and his paintings are in the collections of many American museums.

(A.F.)

Rauschenberg, Robert (1925–   ).
Born in Port Arthur, Tex., he is perhaps the most important painter in establishing the vocabulary of American pop art.* Rauschenberg studied at the Kansas City Art Institute, 1946–47, at the Académie Julien, Paris (1947), and at Black Mountain College in North Carolina (1948) with Joseph Albers* and the aleatoric composer John Cage. He studied at the Art Students League* with Morris Kantor* and Vaclav Vytlacil. He spent 1952–53 in North Africa and Europe. He was also associated with the avant-garde choreographer Merce Cunningham and since 1955 has been active in dance and theatre design.

Retrospective exhibitions have been held at the Jewish Museum (1963) and the White Chapel Gallery, London (1964), and he received first prize at the Venice Biennial in 1964.

Although he considers Albers his most important teacher, his paintings have little in common with Albers' austere geometric abstraction. The principal early influence on his thinking was John Cage, source of many of the ideas from which emerged pop art,* happenings,* environments, and the conceptual art of today. It was John Cage, more than anyone after Marcel Duchamp* and the European dadaists, who insisted that the end result of the creative act was not the object, the work of art itself, but rather the concept that went into its creation and the actual process of that creation (see Concept Art). It is this dialogue between the work of art as object and as concept that Rauschenberg pioneered and has explored since 1950 and which is the central concern of many leading younger artists today. His search for the inner nature of the work of art has led him into innumerable bypaths, making it difficult to trace a unified direction in his work.

Rauschenberg's earliest mature paintings, about 1950, stem principally from the abstract expressionism* of Willem de Kooning* but at the same moment he produced a monochromatic white painting consisting of seven identical vertical panels that paralleled Barnett Newman's* line paintings of that time. In the early 1950s he introduced photographic collage* elements in trompe-l'oeil effects comparable to those of the dadaists, Max Ernst, and the little boxes of the American surrealist Joseph Cornell.* At this point he was drawing on the entire range of modern fantastic experiment, from Duchamp and Picasso to contemporary pop culture. Compared to his predecessors, his works were characterized by a largeness of scale and a fertile and restless imagination. A collage painting might combine cutouts of academic photographic nudes, details of baroque, Victorian, or art nouveau* architecture, and clippings from newspapers or calendars, in intricate photomontages splashed with coloristic abstract expressionist brushstrokes. An example of this period is *Gloria* (1956, Cleveland). In an exhibition in 1955 he introduced what he called "combine" paintings, in which

he incorporated physical objects into the canvas. *The Bed* (1955) includes an actual pillow and quilt over which paint was splashed. The most spectacular combine was *Monogram* (1959), in which a stuffed ram was encompassed in an automobile tire standing on a painted collage base. Whereas Rauschenberg's combine collages may be traced to the constructions of the German dadaist Kurt Schwitters, his are different not only in their great size but in the large-scale use of topical theme and specific association. Innumerable, momentarily glimpsed and seemingly unrelated events flash by the eye of the spectator. In many of his mature works, cubist simultaneity of vision is combined with motion picture techniques to create visual impressions, the point of which is not what the spectator sees but the chaotic after-images left in his memory.

Since the 1960s Rauschenberg, like many other artists, has increasingly used silkscreen transfers to create a kaleidoscope of images deriving from the daily press and motion pictures. He differs from the younger pop artists not only in the fertility of his imagination but in his ability to create total harmonies from disparate elements. Despite his continuing concern with the painting as concept rather than as physical object, he has never lost his delight in the sheer act of painting, in creating color harmonies that spread over and unify the total surface. From his origins in abstract expressionism and early ventures in minimal* painting his work has enlarged to become contemporary expressionism in a much wider sense, incorporating every phase of the current scene expressed through all media of visual communication.

(H.H.A.)

Ray, Man (1890–   ).
Dadaist and surrealist artist, photographer, and filmmaker. He was born in Philadelphia, Pa., and studied architecture, engineering, and art at the National Academy of Design* in New York. By 1911 he had become interested in avant-garde movements, and following the Armory Show* in 1913, he began painting fauve and cubist-influenced works, which he first exhibited at the Daniel Gallery in 1915. In that year he met Marcel Duchamp,* and by 1916 his painting paralleled Duchamp's abstract and dadaist tendencies (*The*

2

1. **Robert Rauschenberg.** The Bed,
   1955, sheet, pillow, quilt and acrylic
   paint on canvas. Collection Mr. and
   Mrs. Leo Castelli, N.Y.
2. **Robert Rauschenberg.** Estate, 1963.
   Philadelphia Museum of Art (gift
   of the Friends of the Philadelphia
   Museum).

Rope Dancer Accompanies Herself with Her Shadows, 1916, Modern Museum). Ray took part in the Forum exhibition in 1916 and participated with Duchamp, the Parisian avant-garde artist Francis Picabia, and the collector Walter Arensberg in publications reflecting the European anti-art movement called dada.* Also with Duchamp he was involved in the founding of the Société Anonyme (1920) and in publishing the single issue of *New York Dada* in 1921. He created collages* and "objects" in the dada manner. His *Cadeau,* 1921, was a flatiron with a row of tacks glued to the smooth face. And in 1922 he also produced his first portfolios of "rayographs," prints that were made from film that had been exposed to light and objects directly, without use of a lens.

In 1921 Ray moved to Paris, where he became a member of the Paris dada circle. He joined the surrealists as that group developed from dada toward a more systematic exploitation of the effects of the unconscious, and he participated in their first exhibition in 1925. During the 1920s he was active as a professional and highly experimental photographer and made several surrealist motion pictures. His best-known surrealist painting is *Observatory Time—The Lovers* (1934). In 1940 he returned to the United States and lived in Hollywood until 1952. He then went back to Paris, where he has continued to produce objects which he assembled from wittily incongruous parts.

(D.W.S.)

Reed & Barton.

A leading American silver firm, it was the outgrowth of a partnership formed in 1824 in Taunton, Mass., between two jewelers, Isaac Babbitt and William W. Crossman. The manufacture of Britannia metal, an improved form of pewter,* was the main source of the firm's success. In 1840 Henry Reed and Charles Barton bought into the firm and by 1848 began to make plated silverware. In 1889 the firm started production of solid silver services. In 1909 they spent over a year making a forty-one piece service for the U.S.S. *Minnesota.* Designed in a Louis XV revival style, it made use of electric lights in the centerpiece. With several other silver firms, they have sponsored an annual student competition for the best contemporary silver design.

Refregier, Anton (1905–   ).

Painter and theatrical designer, born in Moscow and raised in the United States. Refregier first studied sculpture in Paris, then spent four years at the Rhode Island School of Design; he also worked for a time with Hans Hofmann* in Munich. He began his career as an interior designer in New York architects' offices. By 1928 he was also working for trade union journals as an illustrator, and during the 1930s he taught at the American Artists' School, designed the American version of Erika Mann's anti-fascist revue, *The Pepper-Mill,* and was employed periodically in the theatrical studios of Norman Bel Geddes.*

Refregier began his extremely active career as a mural painter with government commissions in the 1930s. His twenty-seven large mural panels for the Rincon Annex Post Office in San Francisco (1941) constitute one of the largest projects of its kind ever executed for the federal government. Illustrating many episodes in the history of California, including strikes, persecution of racial minorities, and miscarriages of justice, they fell afoul of the House Un-American Activities Committee in 1953 and were threatened with destruction, but ultimately were permitted to stand.

Refregier has also done murals for the Riker's Island Penitentiary in New York, the 1939 New York World's Fair, the Mayo Clinic, and for hotels, cafés, trains, steamships, and synagogues. He has been active as an easel painter, too, and as such is represented in the collections of the Metropolitan Museum, the Museum of Modern Art, and the Walker Art Center. He has taught at the University of Arkansas and the Cleveland Institute of Fine Arts.

(A.F.)

Regionalism, see American Scene Painting.

Reid, Robert (1862–1929).

Impressionist painter of figures and flowers. Reid was born in Stockbridge, Mass. He studied at the Boston Museum Art School, the Art Students League* in New York and at the Académie Julien in Paris. Returning in 1889 to America, he soon became known for his colorful and dashing personality and technique. He developed a decorative adaptation of impressionism,* interweaving sunny tapestries of flowers with the figures of pretty American girls (*Fleurs-de-lis,*

1

2

3

4

1. **Man Ray.** The Rope Dancer Accompanies Herself with Her Shadows, 1916. Museum of Modern Art, N.Y. (gift of G. David Thompson).
2. **Man Ray.** Cadeau, c.1958 (after a 1921 original), painted flatiron with metal tacks. Museum of Modern Art, N.Y. (James Thrall Soby Fund).
3. **Reed & Barton.** "King Francis" tea service, l965, silver-plated holloware.
4. **Robert Reid.** Fleurs-de-lis, c.1900. Metropolitan Museum of Art, N.Y. (George A. Hearn Fund).

1

c.1900, Metropolitan). The critic Sadakichi Hartmann saw him as the "poet of frivolity" and a potential master if he would avoid painting "ethereally."

Reid's decorative style adapted easily to murals, which he painted for the World's Columbian Exposition in Chicago (1893), the Library of Congress, the Appellate Court of New York, and in 1901 the Boston State House. He became a member of The Ten* in 1898. Along with a successful painting career (he is represented in most major museum collections), he taught at the Boston Museum School, the Arts Students League, and the Broadmoor Academy in Colorado Springs. Late in life he suffered paralysis of his right side and with a spirited effort trained himself to paint again with his left hand. (D.W.S.)

Reinhardt, Ad (1913–67).
Painter. Born in Buffalo, N.Y., he then moved to New York City. Reinhardt studied art history at Columbia University with Meyer Schapiro in 1931–35 and then intermittently at the New York University Institute of Fine Arts (1946–53). His principal interest was oriental art. During 1936 he studied painting with Carl Holty and Francis Criss, worked on the WPA Federal Art Project* (1936–38), and was associated with the American Abstract Artists* group during 1937–47. Reinhardt taught art history at Brooklyn College from 1947 until his death and also taught at many other schools, including Hunter College in New York, Yale, and the California School of Fine Arts. He worked as an illustrator and cartoonist for the newspaper *PM* and wrote criticism for various art journals. He held one-man exhibitions regularly from 1946 through the 1960s, was shown in major American and European exhibitions of avant-garde painting, and was given a large retrospective of some 120 paintings at the Jewish Museum in 1966. He traveled to Europe (1952) and Asia (1958).

Throughout his career Reinhardt was an abstractionist, early influenced by the paintings of Stuart Davis* but also by the nonobjective experiments of the Russian-born Kazimir Malevich and the Dutch painter Piet Mondrian. During the 1940s he moved into a free, coloristic, overall painting related to the calligraphic works of Mark Tobey,* but by 1948 he was abandoning this for a severely geometric manner rooted in Mondrian and a frontalized form of cubism.* Over the next few years he experimented with vertical-horizontal abstractions, but at the same time (1950–53) he was painting rigidly geometric vertical-horizontal shapes in solid colors of red and blue, as, for example, *Red Painting* (1952, Metropolitan). These led to the black paintings to which he devoted the last fifteen years of his life. The black paintings assumed various shapes; at first they were generally tall and narrow, but by 1960 his format had become square (60 x 60"). Executed in slightly varying values, they presented a cruciform shape within a square, dividing it into six smaller squares bisected by a horizontal band. To Reinhardt this was the "ultimate abstract painting," Malevich's black square on a white ground carried to its logical conclusion.

During his life Reinhardt was a prolific polemicist and critic of avant-garde painting. He was always seeking for absolutes, reiterating his conviction that "Art is Art. Everything else is everything else. Art is Art. Art from Art. Art on Art. Art of Art. Art for Art. Art beyond art. . . ." His "invisible" canvases were said to be associated with mystical states of mind related to Zen Buddhism. Through his paintings and writings Reinhardt had an enormous influence on the younger artists of the 1960s, particularly those subscribing to minimal* or conceptual art—artists to whom the concept of the work of art is more important than the work itself. Although in a sense he was preaching this doctrine throughout much of his life, he never ceased to be a painter for whom the actual painting maintained an absolute value. (H.H.A.)

Remington, Frederick (1861–1909).
Illustrator, painter, and sculptor of western subjects. Remington was born in Canton, N.Y., the son of a newspaper publisher. As a boy he worked at drawing and painting, but he had very little formal art instruction. At Yale (which he attended for two years) he dropped the art course to pursue athletics.

In 1880 he went West, riding through the country from Montana to Texas and the Indian territory, prospecting, cowpunching, and sketching. A picture was accepted and published, after being redrawn, by *Harper's Weekly* in 1882, and Remington conceived the ambition of recording the vanishing West. For several years he worked to

2

3

1. **Ad Reinhardt.** Red Painting, *1952. Metropolitan Museum of Art, N.Y. (Arthur H. Hearn Fund).*
2. **Frederick Remington.** Cavalry Charge on the Southern Plains, *1907. Metropolitan Museum of Art, N.Y. (gift of several gentlemen).*
3. **Frederick Remington.** Indian Warfare, *1909. Gilcrease Institute of American History and Art, Tulsa, Okla.*

establish himself as an illustrator, and finally, in 1886, began to place his drawings in *Harper's Weekly.* His development as a painter followed, and in 1887 he began to exhibit regularly at the National Academy of Design.* Before long, the burly, vigorous Remington was engaged in a variety of activities—painting in watercolor and oil, exhibiting at home and abroad, illustrating such works as young Theodore Roosevelt's *Ranch Life and the Hunting Trail,* traveling through Mexico, and writing articles of his own. He covered the Indian Wars of 1890–91 and the war in Cuba in 1898. Other travels took him to England, France, Germany, and North Africa. Meanwhile, he steadily advanced in his art career. He was elected to the National Academy, he began having one-man exhibitions and in 1895—encouraged by the conservative sculptor Frederic Ruckstull*—he tried his hand at sculpture (*Bronco Buster,* 1895, one model at Metropolitan). His small, animated bronzes met with immediate success.

Even more decisive in making Remington's name a household word was the popularity of his published print portfolios and double-page reproductions in *Collier's* and *Scribner's,* especially when these began to appear in full color about 1901. The demand for the prints led to a greater demand for his canvases and by 1905 Remington was turning his attention increasingly to easel painting and to broadened painting concepts, setting ever higher technical standards for himself. He began to do landscapes as well as western subjects, such as *Howl of the Weather* (1906, Remington Art Memorial, Ogdensburg, N.Y.). Collectors, critics, and museums united in paying him tributes.

Remington had a gift for simplification, emphasis, and drama—for conveying the sense of blinding sun or eerie moonlight, for establishing a landscape in a few strokes. He was a compelling illustrator, with his selective emphasis on action, characterization, and detail, as in *Fired On* (1907, National Coll.). His paintings are an outgrowth of his illustrations—frankly story-telling and eye-catching, but forthright and well-crafted. He embodied the image of the vanishing western frontier.   (D.W.S.)

Renaissance Eclectic Style.
An architectural style usually further

identified by the national source from which it was derived: Italian, German, Flemish, or Spanish. Most of the buildings in the classicism inaugurated by the World's Columbian Exposition of 1893, held in Chicago, were actually Renaissance in style. Most popular and adaptable of Renaissance styles was the Italian, with its open porticoes and loggias. The grooved or rusticated stonework, ornate pilasters, and handsome tile roofs of this style appealed to architects. The Spanish Renaissance was similar but more delicate, with its plateresque (resembling the work of a silversmith) type of low-relief ornament. The German and Flemish Renaissance styles tended to emphasize high roof gables, profiled with baroque curves or steps, and a mutiplicity of chimneys and dormer windows. The ornament favored grotesque carved figures and horizontal bands of stonework. (A.B.)

Renwick, James, Jr., (1818–95).
Architect. He was born in New York, N.Y. Through his father, a noted engineer and professor at Columbia College, he developed an interest in architecture and engineering. After graduating from Columbia in 1836, he joined the staff of the Erie Railroad. He superintended the construction of the Croton Water Distributing Reservoir on Fifth Avenue on the site of the present New York Public Library.

In 1843, he won the competition for Grace Church and Rectory at Broadway and 10th Street, New York (1846–47). With no formal training in architecture, but with a good knowledge of masonry construction, he produced a church that is considered one of the masterpieces of Gothic revival* in America. At the same time he did the Calvary Church at 21st Street and Fourth Avenue, New York City, and a Norman-styled Presbyterian church in Chicago. The Smithsonian Institution in Washington, D.C., begun the following year, achieved a picturesque quality with its Norman version of Romanesque revival* architecture, replete with towers, turrets, and crenellations. It was completed in 1856. In 1851, Renwick designed a striking Gothic revival house for C. T. Longstreet in Syracuse, N.Y., again using many towers, battlements and crenellations.

Renwick's greatest achievement was St. Patrick's Roman Catholic Cathedral on Fifth Avenue and 50th Street. In this great Gothic revival building he combined elements of French, English, and German Gothic most skillfully. The decision to build the vaults of the nave in staff and plaster instead of stone meant the elimination of flying buttresses which would have added immeasurably to its already imposing appearance. It was begun in 1858 and substantially completed by 1879. The spires of the two steeples on Fifth Avenue were completed about 1887.

In the 1860s, Renwick was appointed architect for the New York board of governors of Charities and Correction. For them he designed the City Hospital, the Work House, and the Smallpox Hospital on Blackwell's (Welfare) Island; and the Inebriate and Lunatic Asylums on Ward's Island, and the main building of the Children's Hospital on Randall's Island. Influenced by the French Second Empire,* Renwick designed the Corcoran Gallery of Art (1859) for W. W. Corcoran in Washington, D.C., and the main building of Vassar College (1865) in Poughkeepsie, N.Y. They are both symmetrical and have imposing central pavilions crowned by convex mansard roofs.

During the years 1869-70, Renwick traveled extensively through Italy and Egypt. In 1870, he took a partner, Joseph Sands (d.1880), and under the firm name of Renwick & Sands they built Saint Ann's Church in Brooklyn (1879), with its elegant Italian Gothic exterior. One of Renwick's finest designs was that for All Saints (R.C.) Church and Rectory on Madison Avenue and 129th Street (1887). The Church was designed in Italian Gothic, of brick and terra-cotta, with details from the Ca d'Oro, in Venice, at the Rectory.

Renwick owned two steam yachts, was a member of the Century Association and Union Club, and was a fellow of the American Institute of Architects. (A.B.)

Resnick, Milton (1917–   ).
Painter. He was born in Bratslav, Russia, but moved to New York in 1922. He studied at Pratt Institute (1934–35) and the American Artists School (1935–37), and then worked on the WPA Federal Art Project* in New York City (1939). After four years in the armed forces (1941–45) and two years in Paris (1946–48) he returned to New York, studied with Hans Hofmann* and was drawn into the storm center of abstract expressionism.* Resnick has taught at the University of California and at New York University.

By 1955, the year of his first one-man show, Resnick was painting passionate conglomerations of strongly marked shapes. Resnick's heavy impasto and obvious joy in manipulating paint gave these works a tremendous sense of solidity, though they were still marked by vestiges of cubist space. During the next five years his paintings became increasingly large (by 1960 they were mural size) and he moved toward lighter, featherly strokes and squiggles of color that covered the entire canvas. He had always admired Monet, and this group of paintings seems like a version of late impressionist works. There is a sense of total improvisation, of greater concern with the process of painting than with the result. Nevertheless, his best paintings are lyrical and evocative and call forth a train of nature images. (E.C.G.)

Retablos, see Santos.

Revere, Paul (1735–1818).
The best-known American silversmith. Born in Boston, Mass., the son of a French émigré, Apollos Rivoire, and his wife Debroah Hitchborn, Revere was trained as a silversmith by his father who had learned his trade from John Coney.* He took over the family silver business at the age of nineteen when his father died. His earliest work consisted of tea and table wares in the late rococo* style. A portrait painted by John Singleton Copley* (1768, Boston) shows Revere with a plain inverted-pear-shaped teapot in his hand and his engraving tools on the table beside him. In 1768 he made the most historic piece of American silver, the Liberty Bowl.* An ardent patriot, he fanned the flames of anti-British feeling by engraving and circulating prints showing the *Landing of the Troops* (1768) and the *Boston Massacre* (1770, both Winterthur). As a member of the Sons of Liberty, he carried dispatches from Boston to the other colonies, including the journey made famous in Longfellow's poem *The Midnight Ride.* During the war he served as a lieutenant-colonel in charge of Boston's Castle Island and was involved in efforts to manufacture gunpowder and to cast cannon. He was employed to engrave and print Massachusetts paper currency and treasurer's notes in 1775–76.

1

2

After the Revolution, Revere returned to his silver work, gradually changing from the old rococo style to the more fashionable neoclassical designs. His account books (Massachusetts Historical Society) show the large number of complete tea services he made, an elegant example of which is the fluted and engraved set at the Minneapolis Institute. He also made many small items, including surgical instruments, and he himself tried his hand at dentistry and making false teeth. As an engraver he cut many plates for printing bookplates, trade advertisements, newspaper mastheads, and magazine and book illustrations. A Grand Master of the Grand Lodge of Massachusetts, he made Masonic jewels and, after the death of Washington in 1799, fashioned the gold urn that contains a lock of the president's hair. In 1783 he opened a hardware store in Boston and in 1788 he established an iron foundry that manufactured cannon and church bells. In 1794 he was contracted to do all the brass and copper work on the frigate *Constitution.* This led to the building of a mill for rolling sheet copper in Canton, Mass. in 1800, furnishing copper for the State House dome in 1802, recoppering "Old Ironsides" in 1803, and providing copper boilers for Robert Fulton's Hudson River boats in 1809. The Revere Copper Company, which is still active, remained a family concern after his death, making, among many other products, cannon for the United States government during the Civil War.

The town of Revere, Mass., was named for him. A portrait showing him in advanced age was painted by Gilbert Stuart* (Boston). Revere's most successful design in silver was the presentation pitcher (Winterthur) fashioned after contemporary ceramic Staffordshire pitchers, several of which were presented to Massachusetts men about 1805. This classic form is still made and admired today. (M.G.F.)

Reverse Painting On Glass.
A technique of painting on a sheet of colorless glass so that one views the result *through* the glass. The highlights thus are painted first, and the background last. The technique is thus more properly considered a branch of the history of painting, especially of folk painting.

Reverse paintings were produced in Europe in the 16th century and later. American ones were influenced primarily by those made in central Europe, particularly Bohemia and adjoining regions. The more sophisticated English technique, which involved transferring the design from a mezzotint* onto the glass and filling in vacant areas with pigment, was scarcely practiced in the United States. American reverse paintings on glass tend to fall into three groups: those done in the "Pennsylvania Dutch" tradition, which often utilize tinfoil to give a sparkling effect; more formal studies done in New England and along the East Coast by traditional artists; and completely unsophisticated "folk" paintings, which often have great charm. (J.S.S.)

Rhodes, Daniel (1911–).
Potter, sculptor, teacher, and writer. Born in Fort Dodge, Iowa, Rhodes studied art history at the University of Chicago and painting and sculpture at the Chicago Art Institute and the Art Students League* in New York. He painted murals in public buildings from Washington, D.C., to Des Moines, Iowa. In 1941 he began experimenting with ceramics at the Fine Arts Center in Colorado Springs. He then went to Alfred University, where he studied ceramics under Charles Harder, and dedicated himself to studio pottery and reduction stoneware. For three years he did research in high-heat ceramics for Henry J. Kaiser Corporation, and then set up a full-scale studio in Menlo Park, Cal., producing thrown and cast ware for Gumps Department Store in San Francisco. Since 1947 he has been head of ceramics instruction at Alfred University, N.Y.

Rhodes' long-time interest in Japanese pottery is reflected in the tranquility of shape and the textured exterior of his wheel-thrown functional ware. During the early 1950s he created many hand-formed stoneware sculptures, usually small in scale and often including pieces of metal, wood, bone, and glass. He credits the new possibilities in these roughly figurative pieces with greatly enriching his functional work. In 1964 he developed a technique utilizing fiberglass in clay, which increased the possibilities of the material as a sculptural medium. When fired with stoneware, the fiberglass sheen melded with the earthiness of the clay. During the mid-1960s Rhodes

1. **Paul Revere.** John Singleton Copley, Portrait of Paul Revere. 1768. Museum of Fine Arts, Boston (gift of Joseph W., William B. and Edward H. R. Revere).
2. **Reverse Painting on Glass.** Vase with flowers, mid-19th century. Corning Museum of Glass, Corning, N.Y.

1. **Joseph Richardson.** *Repoussé tea-kettle on stand, c.1760. Yale University Art Gallery, New Haven, Conn.*
2. **Obadiah Rich.** *Vase presented to Daniel Webster for his "Defense of the CONSTITUTION of the United States" by the citizens of Boston (engraved), 1835. Boston Public Library.*

created sculptures he called "guardian figures," using a technique whose speed and spontaneity allowed him to leave lacelike openings in the sculptures, or to pull the clay upwards, giving the effect of hanging drapery—and to do this even in works three feet tall. His books *Clay and Glazes for the Potter, Stoneware and Porcelain, Kilns,* and *Tamba Pottery,* are impressive for both technical completeness and their insight into the handling of clay. (R.S.)

Rich, Obadiah (1809–88).
Boston's leading silversmith in the second quarter of the 19th century was born in Charlestown, Mass., and served his apprenticeship with Moses Morse. By 1830 Rich had established his own shop and from 1832 to 1835 worked in partnership with Samuel L. Ward. His career was cut short when he became blind about 1850. The most impressive example of his skill is the enormous vase (Boston Public Library) presented to Daniel Webster by the citizens of Boston in 1835. Based on the famous Warwick vase, it has repoussé rams' heads on the body, a heavy gadrooned border around the top, and intertwining handles. Rich also made two inkstands (Fogg and Yale) after a design by the sculptor Horatio Greenough,* and a pair of large salvers and pitchers presented to Uriel Crocker in 1842 by the Massachusetts Charitable Mechanic Association. Much of his tea and table silver is in the rococo revival style with floral repoussé decoration on exaggerated 18th-century forms. He continued the handicraft tradition in a period when most silver wares were being made by machine. (M.G.F.)

Richards, William Trost (1833–1905).
Marine and landscape painter and draftsman. Born in Philadelphia, Pa., Richards first went to work as a designer of gas fixtures. After studying painting briefly under Paul Weber (1823–1916), Richards decided to become a painter. In 1853 he traveled to Europe, studying in Paris, Florence, and Rome. By 1860 he was working in a pre-Raphaelite mode, making highly detailed pencil and watercolor sketches, and doing charming, precise woodland landscapes. After the Civil War, he traveled to Düsseldorf and Darmstadt, Germany, for a year, and on his return voyage began to make the marine studies which eventually led to his specialization in seascapes. Living in Philadelphia, he began summering in the 1870s at Cape May and Atlantic City. He became best known for a series of luminous paintings of the empty, rolling sea, exemplified by *On the Coast of New Jersey* (1883, Corcoran). Beginning in 1878, he made several trips to England, and thereafter the Channel Islands and Newport, R.I., provided many of his subjects. In 1890, he settled permanently in Newport, having gained considerable reputation for his precise marine paintings and watercolors. (T.E.S.)

Richardson, Francis, and Joseph, Joseph, Jr., and Nathaniel.
Philadelphia's leading dynasty of silversmiths was founded by Francis Richardson (1681–1729), who was brought by his mother and stepfather to the Quaker city about 1690 and established himself as a silversmith about 1701. Very little of his work has survived: buckles, patch boxes, porringers, a tankard, a mug, spoons, and a gold locket. The work of his son Francis (1705/6–1782) is even more limited (three porringers and a mug) since he worked as a silversmith only from 1729 to 1738. It was the second son, Joseph Richardson (1711–1784), who became one of America's finest silversmiths, working from 1729–77. In the 1956 exhibition of Philadelphia silver, sixty-six examples of his work were shown, including such items as coffeepots, creamers, sauce boats, snuff boxes, tankards, teapots, and trays. His masterpiece, and perhaps America's finest example of rococo silver, is an elaborate repoussé teakettle and stand (Yale). As his letter book (Winterthur) indicates, Richardson also imported and resold quantities of London-made silver. In addition, he made silver for ornamental objects for presentation to the Indians by the Quakers. His son Joseph, Jr., continued to do the same for the United States government in the years after the Revolution.

Joseph's sons, Joseph, Jr. (1752–1831), and Nathaniel (1754–1827), began their partnership in 1777 and continued until 1791, when Nathaniel became an ironmonger. Their work shows the development of the neoclassical style in American silver, particularly in the teasets they produced. Joseph, Jr., continued until 1801, when he devoted himself to his duties as assayer for the United States Mint in Philadelphia, having been appointed by George Washington in 1795. Richardson had made a teapot and slop bowl for the president as well as silver for the furnishings of the president's house.

Joseph Richardson, Jr., perfected his design for the large tea services in the Federal style, forming the vessels into urn-shaped, oval, or helmet-shaped objects. Decoration was restrained and orderly and consisted largely of delicate edges of beading, urn or pineapple finials, attenuated engraving of monograms, and a type of pierced gallery rim characteristic of the Philadelphia school of silver.   (M.G.F.)

Richardson, Henry Hobson (1836–86). Architect, born on a sugar-cane plantation outside New Orleans. After education in a private school and a year at the University of Louisiana, he went to Harvard. At college he was immensely popular. He graduated in 1859 and entered the École des Beaux-Arts in Paris in 1860. The Civil War cut off his funds and he was forced to seek part-time employment with an architect, Théodore Labrouste, in order to keep up his studies. After the war he returned to America (1865) without a degree but with an architectural training unusual for an American. He joined the New York office of Charles D. Gambrill (1832–80) in 1867 as a partner, serving as the designer of the firm. Although Richardson produced nothing of note in the New York area during his nine years there, he did begin the New England practice which led to his settling in Boston in 1874. Richardson's practice began with his winning a competition in 1866 for the Church of the Unity (Unitarian) at Springfield, Mass., a design that incorporated a broach spire, capricious window arrangements, and the picturesque profile associated with Victorian Gothic.* His North Congregational Church at Springfield (1873) begins to show his individuality in its outsize dormers and picturesque low tower. The next competition he won, for the Brattle Square Church in Boston's Back Bay (1872), brought him instant recognition. With its round-arch openings, it introduced the Romanesque revival* style in which he was to execute so many commissions. The beauty of the corner tower, with its frieze of figures high above the belfry and its

corner trumpeters, won the building the loving appellation "Church of the Holy Beanblowers."

His next church commission, Trinity Episcopal Church on Copley Square, Boston (1872–77), established him as the leading architect in Boston. In its overall massing, dominated by the huge tower over the crossing, it was the finest evocation of Romanesque revival up to that time. With its yellow-gray granite walls trimmed with red sandstone, it had a most lively appearance. The central tower was inspired by the old cathedral at Salamanca, Spain. Richardson was assisted by Stanford White, a young draftsman on his way to fame. Murals and stained glass windows by John La Farge* contributed to the glowing color scheme and made the interior one of the most notable in the country.

His public buildings began with the rather awkward Worcester, Mass., High School (1871), which was dominated by a high central tower. He next won an important competition for the State Hospital for the Insane at Buffalo, N.Y., with a group of buildings joined in the form of a "V." At the apex was a pavilion with two towers reminiscent of the French Renaissance style. The Hampden County Courthouse at Springfield, Mass. (1873), combined an early French Renaissance tower with a bold entrance of three arches in Richardson's best Romanesque revival manner. Working with Leopold Eidlitz (1823–1908) and Frederick Law Olmsted* on the completion of the State Capitol at Albany, N.Y., in 1876, Richardson created some handsome interior rooms, notably the Senate Chamber (1881), the Governor's Room, the Court of Appeals Room, and the great West Staircase. One of Richardson's finest buildings was the Romanesque revival City Hall (1882), facing the Capitol at the far end of the mall. Romantic in concept, with its open loggia (a roofed arcade at the second story), high clock tower, and picturesque profile, it has a unity rarely surpassed in his later work. Richardson's most notable group of public buildings was the Allegheny County Buildings complex in Pittsburgh (1884–87). This included the great courthouse with a high tower above its triple-arched entrance and a picturesque jail connected to it by an arched bridge at second-story level. In the jail he introduced some of the boldest rough-faced

masonry in this country—work which was to win the appellation "Richardsonian Romanesque." These buildings represent the epitome of his large-scale monumental work.

In the field of commercial structures, his Cheney Building in Hartford, Conn. (1876), is a fine Romanesque revival building, with great arches at the ground floor, each surmounted by a pair of two-story arched windows. Because of its impressive simplicity and the effective diminution in the size of its windows from floor to floor, the Marshall Field Wholesale House (Warehouse) Building in Chicago (1885–87) has been considered Richardson's masterpiece. There is virtually no exterior ornament, the architect relying solely on good proportions, the expressive use of rough-faced masonry, the batter (inward slope) of the first floor wall, and the crowning cornice.

It was in a series of libraries in Massachusetts that Richardson developed his Romanesque manner to the full. His first essay, and the boldest, was the Winn Memorial Library at Woburn (1878). This picturesque building, with its spiky tower set between a great gable and a low entrance porch, is rendered completely asymmetrical by the addition of a low wing at one end and an octagonal baptistry at the other. The key to this complex building is its coherent plan: a long narrow rectangle with one transverse element and the porch and tower set in the angle between them. Libraries for the Ames family at North Easton (1879) and the Crane Memorial Library at Quincy (1885) represent a gradual simplification of exteriors and some fine evocations of Romanesque revival architecture.

For Harvard, Richardson designed Sever Hall (1880), for classrooms, a symmetrical essay in brick, widely praised as a Romanesque revival building that harmonized with the earlier brick buildings in the Harvard "Yard." He also designed Austin Hall, the Law Library (1883), a stone building with a minor note of asymmetry in the tower to the right of the entrance loggia. The commission to build several stations in Massachusetts for the Boston & Albany Railroad met Richardson's desire to design some utilitarian structures in stone. The stations, low-lying and practical in design, were built at Auburndale (1881) and Chestnut Hill

1. **Henry Hobson Richardson.** *Marshall Field Wholesale House, Chicago, 1885.*
2. **Henry Hobson Richardson.** *Cheney Building, Hartford, Conn., 1876.*

(1884). Welcoming the practical challenge, he also designed a Business Car (1884) for the same railroad.

In the residential field, Richardson generally used an asymmetrical Romanesque revival architecture, of stone or frame construction. In Washington, D.C., he designed a large, comfortable house for N. Larz Anderson (1881) with two towers and a spacious stair hall, and in 1884 he provided adjoining houses for two famous friends, the historian Henry Adams and the statesman John Hay, facing Lafayette Square. The Adams house was a recreation of a medieval town house with broad, low arches at ground floor that provided a spacious entrance loggia. The Hay house had two towers with a low-arched entrance beneath a central gable. It is memorable for the beautiful staircase sweeping down into its entrance hall. One of his finest houses was built for J. J. Glessner on Prairie Avenue, Chicago (1887). In a fortress-like structure of rough-faced stonework with steep roofs and small windows facing the street, an inner courtyard, entered by a passageway from the street, provided privacy.

At Newport, R.I., Stanford White was Richardson's draftsman for a house for Frank W. Andrews (1872). This large, picturesque "cottage" reintroduced "colonial" wood shingles, dominated by a high central portion crowned by iron crestings. One of Richardson's most original creations was the small stone gate-lodge erected in 1881 for F. L. Ames at North Easton, Mass. It is built of boulders. To the right of the arch over the driveway is a two-story building that has a curved stair tower rising above the eaves of the roof. At the rear a well-head tower rises two stories with open loggia and balcony at the second floor. This building showed Americans how an indigenous architecture might develop out of a traditional style.

Despite a lifelong illness, Richardson maintained a charming disposition that won him many friends. Because his architecture was an all-masonry concept, rarely using steel, it was of limited potential in a world in which the steel frame was rapidly emerging as a structural necessity. But before he died he had the satisfaction of knowing that the style he had established, Richardsonian Romanesque, was already influencing an entire generation of architects. (A.B.)

Rickey, George (1907–   ).
A leading proponent and theorist of kinetic sculpture,* Rickey was born in South Bend, Ind., and educated in Scotland and England. After attending the Ruskin School of Drawing, Oxford, in 1928–29, he traveled in Europe. He was a painter during this period, studying with the leading cubist painters André Lhote and Fernand Léger, and the purist Amédée Ozenfant. While serving in the United States Air Corps during World War II, Rickey learned welding. He constructed his first mobile in 1945. His sculpture draws on the tradition of constructivism.* It employs spare, reduced forms such as pointed metal beams, light-reflecting metal strips, and small rotors. He has said: ". . . my technology is borrowed from crafts and industry. It has more in common with clocks than with sculpture." Delicately balanced, his forms move with the slightest current of air. Rickey is not interested in form in itself. As he puts it, "the visible motion is the design." In recent years he has been able to expand the scale of his works; his largest pieces, those employing metal beams, measure over forty feet high. Rickey has published numerous writings, among them a book-length treatment of the constructivist movement. He has also been active in organizing exhibitions of kinetic sculpture. He has taught at a number of schools since the 1940s, including the University of Indiana, the University of California at Santa Barbara, and Rennselaer Polytechnic Institute.   (C.R.)

Rimmer, William (1816–79).
Sculptor and painter, born in South Milford, Mass. One of the most enigmatic figures in American art, Rimmer lived most of his life with the delusion, acquired from his father, that he was the son of the lost Dauphin and heir to the throne of France. Raised in Boston, his early years were spent as an unsuccessful painter, while he held a variety of jobs to make a living. In 1847 he began to teach himself medicine; he practiced medicine for several years and in 1855 he was finally licensed as a physician. Not until 1860 did he take up sculpture seriously. As in painting and medicine, he was self-taught. Among his earliest pieces is the *Falling Gladiator* of 1861 (Boston), which in its richness of modeling, naturalism, and Romantic spirit foreshadows the art of Rodin. In 1864 he carved the granite statue of *Alexander Hamilton,* which was erected in Boston. In that year he published the first of several instructional books on drawing, *The Elements of Design.* Rimmer was to become famous as a teacher as well as an artist. During 1866–71 he was director of the School of Design for Women at Cooper Union in New York; thereafter he offered courses in anatomy and design in Boston and lectured widely on these subjects. Two fine examples of his work of later years are the *Fighting Lions* (Boston Art Club) and the *Dying Centaur* (Boston), both of 1871.   (W.C.)

Rinehart, William Henry (1825–74).
Sculptor. Born on a farm in Maryland, he became one of the foremost expatriate American sculptors working in the neoclassical style. After an apprenticeship in a stone quarry and work in a Baltimore stoneyard, he began taking courses at the Maryland Institute. His career as a sculptor thus commenced about 1850, and his portraits and ideal works quickly caught the attention of William T. Walters, wealthy Baltimore patron of the arts. With Walters' assistance Rinehart went to Italy in 1855, and after a brief period in Florence he settled in Rome. He continued the neoclassical tradition in sculptures, such as his *Clytie* (1870) and *Latona and Her Children* (1871–72, Metropolitan), inspired by classical mythology. The *Clytie* shows the influence of Praxiteles and comes as close to a pure classical style as any work of the period. But in other works he employed other styles: his portraits, for example, were thoroughly naturalistic and far from idealized, and their only trace of neoclassicism* is the toga-like drapery about the shoulders. Probably his most successful effort at portraiture was the seated bronze statue of *Chief Justice Roger B. Taney* (1872, State House, Annapolis). Occasionally he produced one of those sentimental or cute pieces for which the 19th century became notorious, such as the *Sleeping Children,* of which more than twenty replicas were made between 1859 and 1874. He also finished the bronze doors (which Thomas Crawford* had left incomplete at his death) for the U.S. Senate wing of the Capitol and made a second set for the House of Representatives wing (1861–66). After about 1865 Rinehart enjoyed the patronage of some of America's wealthiest men. He left the bulk of his estate to establish scholarships to send young American sculptors abroad to study.   (W.C.)

Risom, Jens (1916–   ).
Furniture designer noted for his respect for excellent craftsmanship and the beauty of natural woods. Born in Copenhagen, he was educated and served his apprenticeship in Denmark and Sweden. In 1939 he moved to New York City and became a free-lance furniture designer. His career was interrupted by service in the United States Army but was resumed in 1946, when he founded his own firm, Jens Risom Design, Inc. His firm enables him to have complete control of all aspects of manufacture, from the design to the finished product. He became one of the leading influences in the movement toward functional, simple modern furniture, emphasizing comfort, good proportion, sound construction, and the natural characteristics of wood, especially walnut. He still stands for elegantly wood-crafted, functional furniture.   (D.H.P.)

Rivers, Larry (1923–   ).
Painter and sculptor. A native of New York, N.Y., Rivers studied at the Juilliard School of Music and worked as a professional saxophonist in a jazz band before turning to painting in the mid-1940s. In 1947–48 he studied with Hans Hofmann,* and later with William Baziotes,* at New York University. He then toured England, France, and Italy. On his return, taking advantage of the techniques of abstract expressionism,* Rivers introduced illustrational material that allowed his paintings to appeal to a larger audience than that reached by pure abstraction. His portraits, landscapes, and figure studies of the early 1950s were considered "reactionary," and indeed they were structured by rigorous and realistic drawing and were often given a fragmented appearance by mannerist overlays of thin washes of transparent color.

In 1953 Rivers moved to Southhampton, Long Island, N.Y., and began a series of life-size outdoor figure sculptures. In the same year he painted *Washington Crossing the Delaware* (1953, Modern Museum), one of the earliest in his series on American history themes. Rivers' later representations of money and cigarette advertisements loosely associated him with the beginnings of pop art,* while his use of the same figure in two different poses, as in *Double Portrait of Birdie* (1955, Whitney), added another level of ambiguity to the central contest in all his work—the conflict between full-blown representationalism and the abstraction of the loosely-brushed areas of pure paint. His manner has been compared to Cézanne's watercolor technique: by leaving parts of his canvases bare and the rest in various stages of completion, he often gives his work a sketchy, "unfinished" quality and emphasizes the process of painting itself.   (E.C.G.)

Robb, Samuel A. (1851–1928).
New York City carver of wooden commercial sculpture. His career spans the three main branches of such work, ship, show,* and circus wagon* figures, all of considerable distinction. The figures produced in Robb's workshops are in a variety of sculptural styles, and since a succession of hands were responsible for both designs and execution, it is difficult to assign any stylistic qualities to Robb himself. A very smoothly modeled *Squaw and Papoose* (Old Museum Village of Smith's Clove, Monroe, N.Y.) provides a good example of his work for tobacconists, the neat profile and carefully executed lips of the figure having been seen by some as a Robb trademark. His work for circuses involved remarkable levels of sculptural imagination as exemplified by the fantastic monkeys and the muses from the tableaux dens of Ringling Brothers Barnum & Bailey Circus.   (M.J.G.)

Robinson, Boardman (1876–1952).
Illustrator, cartoonist, painter, and muralist. The son of a sea captain, Robinson was born in Nova Scotia and passed part of his youth in Wales. In 1895 he entered the Normal Art School in Boston. He spent much of the time between 1898 and 1904 in Paris, where he absorbed the art life, sampled the Académie Colarossi and studied with Jean-Léon Gérôme. He was much influenced by the drawings of French illustrators, especially Forain, but when he returned to New York seeking commissions, he found his concepts too advanced for the editors of the day. Needing work, he took a position as a social worker, an experience which directed his sympathies to the Socialist party.

1

1. *Larry Rivers.* Washington Crossing the Delaware, *1953. Museum of Modern Art, N.Y.*
2. *Larry Rivers.* Double Portrait of Birdie, *1955. Whitney Museum of American Art, N.Y.*
3. *Theodore Robinson.* Port Ben, Delaware and Hudson Canal, *1893. Pennsylvania Academy of the Fine Arts, Philadelphia (gift of the Society of American Artists).*

2

3

In 1906 he became art director for *Vogue,* and the next year moved to the *Morning Telegraph* (1907–10), where he had free rein to develop his own strong, direct style as artist-reporter and cartoonist. The climax of his newspaper period came during his years with the New York *Tribune* (1910–14) where he satirized political corruption brilliantly. The war ended the job but also occasioned a trip in 1915, along with journalist John Reed, as war correspondent to Eastern Europe and Russia. His drawings became strongly oriented toward political and social problems as he reported on the war, contributed to *The Masses* (1916–17), a radical magazine, and covered the Disarmament Conference (1921). The vigor and incisiveness of his drawings influenced a whole generation of rising artists, and inspired his older professional colleagues as well, as his friend John Sloan,* then art editor of *The Masses,* acknowledged.

In 1919 Robinson began teaching at the Arts Students League and held an exhibition of Old Testament drawings at a New York gallery. During the 1920s he turned increasingly to painting, working for a time with Thomas Hart Benton* on technique and formal organization. In 1927 he undertook his first major mural commission: ten panels depicting the history of commerce for the Kaufmann Department Store in Pittsburgh. Other murals followed, including one at Rockefeller Center (1930) and one for the Department of Justice in Washington (1937).

In 1930 Robinson moved to Colorado, where for many years he was the guiding spirit of the Broadmoor Art Academy. He painted murals and mountain landscapes, striving for a sense of the heroic, but he achieved this effect best in the smaller paintings he did as illustrations for such books as *The Brothers Karamazov* (1933), *King Lear* (1938), and *Moby Dick* (1943). These paintings have exceptional graphic force and assume their own life as works of art. (D.W.S.)

Robinson, Theodore (1852–96).
Pioneer American impressionist painter. He was born in Irasburg, Vt., but moved to Wisconsin while still a child. In 1874 he went to New York to attend the National Academy of Design;* two years later he traveled to Paris, where he studied with Gérôme and Carolus-

Duran. He exhibited at the Salon (1877 and 1879), with the Society of American Artists* from their first exhibition (1878), and with the National Academy from 1881. He had only moderate success in selling his pictures, and to support himself he worked as an assistant to mural painters (including John La Farge* in 1881) and taught private classes. Then, in 1884 he returned to France, settling first in Barbizon—where his style grew broader—and then, in a momentous move in 1888, in Giverny, where he became a neighbor and follower of Monet. His work, which was characteristically modest and somewhat intimate, developed from a dark tonal style (*Girl at Piano,* Pennsylvania) through a lighter tonality (*At the Piano,* painted just before he went to Giverny, in 1887, National Coll.) to a high-keyed impressionism,* as in *Church at Giverny* (National Coll.)—one of the early paintings in such tonality by an American landscape painter. Robinson, like other American impressionists, retained a greater emphasis on form and depth than did Monet. His forte was the sensitive transcription of a fragment of nature rather than pictorial organization. As he moved from his earlier interior scenes with their patterns of dark and light to high-keyed landscapes and studies of figures out of doors, the structure of his paintings became more tentative. In 1892 Robinson returned to America, where he struggled to adapt impressionism to the American landscape, as in *Port Ben, Delaware and Hudson Canal* (1893, Pennsylvania).   (D.W.S.)

Robsjohn-Gibbings, Terence Harold
(1905–   ).
Furniture designer and interior decorator. Throughout a long career, he has influenced furniture trends by combining classical forms with modern functionalism and simplicity. He has always rebeled against the domination of period decoration and the assertion that the home is a "machine for living."

Born in London, he was apprenticed to a draftsman at an early age. He studied at the University of Liverpool and London University, receiving a degree in architecture. After serving as head designer for Ashby Tabb Ltd. of London, he became art director for British International Pictures in 1927. Later he worked for Charles Duveen, well-known antique dealer. After a business trip

to New York in 1929 for Duveen, he moved to the United States permanently. He started his own firm, Robsjohn-Gibbings Ltd., in 1936, quickly establishing a reputation for modern furniture with a classical feeling. In 1943 he joined the Grand Rapids, Mich., firm of Widdicomb & Company, and was its designer until 1956. His first collection for Widdicomb, in 1946, when very little modern furniture of quality was being manufactured, was extremely successful. His architectural forms, with a minimum of detail and restrained in color, offered comfort and elegance not easily found elsewhere. His furniture had a custom-made look due to his designs and choice of woods, and the fine workmanship. He gained a reputation as an exponent of honest, straightforward design that was uncluttered, functional, and elegant, satisfied contemporary needs, yet had a warmth and comfort that he felt was lacking in earlier attempts at functionalism. A witty and caustic writer, he assailed the antiques industry, modern art, and interior design in various books: *Goodbye, Mr. Chippendale* (1944), *Mona Lisa's Mustache* (1947), and *Homes of the Brave* (1954). Because of his long interest in ancient Greek furniture design, he was asked in 1960 to recreate a group of "authentic" Greek furniture documented from sculpture, paintings, and pottery. The collection was shown in Europe and America. In 1962 he received one of the annual Elsie De Wolfe awards; it cited his ability to "combine a classical approach to design with a recognition of contemporary needs and thus capture the best of both worlds without ever resorting to a cliché."(D.P.)

Robus, Hugo (1885–1964).
Sculptor. Born in Cleveland, Ohio, he attended art school there before going to New York to study at the National Academy of Design.* He spent two years (1912–14) in Paris studying painting and it was not until 1920 that he turned to sculpture. Robus remained virtually unknown until the early 1930s, and until 1955 supported his family by working as a craftsman in precious metals, making table settings and jewelry. His usually small-scaled sculpture frequently has the flavor of finely crafted jewelry, as may be seen in his brass *Song* (1932, Metropolitan). The carefully controlled abstraction and

1

2

simplification of the human figure in *Song* is blended with characteristic charm and a metallic sleekness. After exhibiting his sculpture at the Whitney Museum, New York City, in 1933 Robus became better known. During this time one of his recurrent themes was that of women washing or combing their hair, as in *Woman Combing Her Hair* (1927, Corcoran) and *Girl Washing Her Hair* (1933, Modern Museum). Very simplified forms and long flowing contours characterize these works. From late in his career dates the rather grotesque *First Born* (1950). Large one-man shows of his work were held at the Whitney Museum in 1960 and 1963.

(W.C.)

Roche, Kevin (1922–   ).
Architect. Born in Dublin, Ireland, he attended Rockwell College in Ireland and in 1945 graduated in architecture from the National University of Ireland. Before coming to the United States in 1948, he worked in Dublin and later in England with Maxwell Frey. During 1948–49 he attended the Illinois Institute of Technology in Chicago, then under the directorship of Mies van der Rohe.* In 1950 he joined the firm of Saarinen, Saarinen and Associates. The first major commission upon which he worked after entering the Saarinen office was the General Motors Technical Center, Warren, Mich. (1951–57), which impressively summed up the post-World War II view of the International style.* With Eero Saarinen's* death in 1961, Roche and John Dinkeloo completed a number of this architect's major projects, including the Dulles International Airport Terminal near Washington D.C. (1961–62), the Trans World Airlines Terminal at Kennedy International Airport (1962), and the CBS Headquarters Building in New York City (1962–65). In 1966, as had been requested by Saarinen, the name of the firm was changed to Kevin Roche, John Dinkeloo & Associates.

Like Saarinen and others, Roche has not remained rigidly attached to the design canons of the International style, though numerous Miesian elements tend to dominate many of his buildings. Each of Roche's buildings tends, like Saarinen's, to be the result of a single theoretical planning concept. The strength of his buildings lies not only in their strong visual form, but equally in the vigor and complete-

ness of the intellectual principles that lie behind them. In his Ford Foundation Headquarters Building in New York (1968), he took the horizontal indoor garden theme of Paxton's 1851 Crystal Palace and stood it on end, with the garden extending up through vertical space.

In his Oakland Museum, Oakland, Cal. (1968), he created a nonbuilding, for from afar and from the street it reads not as a building but as a low, terraced garden. The Museum ends up functioning as an open green space in the city, rather than as a major monument, something, as critics have said, that might have more meaning in New York than in Oakland.

Recently Roche's work has begun to reveal an even greater fascination with basic geometric shapes—cubes, cylinders, segments of circles, etc. This elementary geometry asserted itself in his project (still unbuilt) for the National Fisheries Center and Aquarium in Washington, D.C. (1969–71, designed with Charles Eames*), where a segment of a concave circle is set on a classic rectangular podium. His twenty-three-story tower for the Knights of Columbus in New Haven, Conn. (1968–71), consists of four solid brick cylinders placed one each at the corner, with the windows and spandrels recessed behind them. In his New Haven Coliseum and Convention Center (1968–71), the elevated thin rectangle which houses the four-floored, 2400-car parking garage seems to be held in the air by the two brick cylinders containing the spiral car ramps. The exposed steel-frame box which houses the parking garage shows the influence of constructivism* and Mies van der Rohe, but its dramatic suspension in air and its abstract relation to the recessed vertical slabs below and the cylinders at the sides suggests that its design is the result of a concern for geometry instead of necessity.

(D.G.)

Rococo Style.
A style in art that emerged from the baroque style in Europe. A lighter, more delicate treatment of architectural and decorative design than the baroque, rococo was simplified in crossing the Atlantic. Its influence here is most marked in painting, appearing in more natural and intimate poses, with less attempt at ornate splendor. The two roving "drapery painters," John

1. **Kevin Roche,** *Oakland Museum, Cal., 1968.*
2. **Hugo Robus.** Song, *1932. Metropolitan Museum of Art, N.Y. (Rogers Fund).*

Wollaston* and Joseph Blackburn,* first brought the new feeling from London. John Singleton Copley,* influenced by Blackburn and by British prints, made it one of the foundations of his early success. It was a style appropriate to the 18th-century Enlightenment, and disappeared with the wave of Romantic feeling that followed in the 19th century.

Roesen, Severin (active in America 1848–71).
German porcelain painter who came to New York in 1848, Roesen is best known for flower and fruit paintings in a style recalling the late baroque tradition. His work varied considerably in quality; at its best it was luxurious and overflowing, and well reflected the Victorian aesthetic, as in *Still Life, Flowers and Fruit* (1848, Corcoran).

Rogers, Isaiah (1800–69).
Architect, born in Marshfield, Mass. His father, a shipbuilder, taught him the essentials of carpentry, and at sixteen he was apprenticed to a Boston carpenter. He went to Mobile, Ala. (1820–21), where he won a competition for a theater design (built by 1824). In 1822 he returned to Boston and worked for Solomon Willard, builder and architect. He is listed in the Boston directory by 1826, when he presumably opened his own office.

Rogers began his career with the commission for the Tremont Hotel, Boston (1828–29). The Tremont, grander and better equipped than any previous hotel, was only the first of his many magnificent hotels in the Greek revival* style. His next large undertaking was the luxurious Astor House, N.Y. (1834–36). While living in New York (1834–42), Rogers built banks, churches, an opera house, and the Third Merchants Exchange (1836–42, later the Customs House). About 1850 Rogers moved to Cincinnati, where he erected numerous large buildings, including the Burnet House (1850), considered the best hotel in the world. His other hotels include the Bangor House, Bangor, Me.; Battle House, Mobile, Ala.; Charleston Hotel, Charleston, S.C.; St. Charles Hotel, New Orleans (1851); Galt House, Louisville, Ky. (c.1865); and the Maxwell House, Nashville, Tenn. (1859), used as barracks in the Civil War.

Despite a very full career as architect, Rogers found time to improve the design of iron bridges and burglar-proof safes; and he was appointed supervising architect for the Treasury Department. (P.F.N.)

Rogers, John (1829–1904).
Sculptor. A native of Salem, Mass., he first worked as a mechanic; it was not until 1858 that he decided to become a sculptor. The next year he produced the first of his famous little plaster groups—*Checker Players.* That group proved very popular, as did the genre groups that followed; altogether he produced over eighty different groups during the next forty-four years. Like Currier and Ives* with their lithographs, Rogers had what amounted to a factory, producing sometimes as many as twelve thousand copies of a group from molds. Rogers always designed and modeled the groups himself, drawing on everyday scenes from mid-19th-century America, from the Civil War, literature, and sports. The groups are remarkable for the fine modeling of details and for their wit and humor or their display of feeling, whichever was appropriate to the subject. Naturalism was the basis of the style and this was something the often untrained eye of 19th-century Americans could admire. They could be purchased for as little as fifteen dollars in general stores around the country or ordered from a catalog. Rogers sold his business in 1893. In addition to his groups he produced a few portrait busts and ideal pieces, and a bronze equestrian statue of General John Reynolds for Philadelphia, but his fame rests on his plaster groups. (W.C.)

Rogers, Randolph (1825–92).
Sculptor. Born in Waterloo, N.Y., Rogers grew up in Ann Arbor, Mich., and worked as a dry-goods clerk in New York City before showing any interest in the arts. About 1848, however, he modeled a portrait bust of the son of his employer; it showed such promise that the employer financed him in a trip to Europe. By 1851 he had settled in Rome. He was destined to fall under the spell of ancient Rome and become famous for works such as *Nydia, the Blind Girl of Pompeii* (1853, Newark Museum), which stylistically were specimens of romantic neoclassicism.* His sculptures were as much oriented in literature as they were concerned with plastic form, but they suited perfectly the tastes of his patrons, and about one hundred marble replicas were made of his *Nydia.* Another idealized work was his biblical *Ruth* (1855, Metropolitan); about twenty replicas were made of it. Rogers also produced the great bronze doors (1855–61), illustrating the story of Columbus, for the Rotunda of the U.S. Capitol; these doors were greatly influenced by Ghiberti's celebrated *Gates of Paradise* of the Florentine Baptistry. For the Washington Monument in Richmond, Va., which had been left unfinished at the death of Thomas Crawford,* Rogers made several figures (c.1857–60) personifying events in Virginia's history. Among his few portraits are his bronze seated *Lincoln* (1870) for Philadelphia and his *Seward* (1875) for New York. In his portraits and his war memorials naturalism dominated, but in a late ideal work, *The Lost Pleiad* (Philadelphia), he reverted to romantic neoclassicism, a style faintly reminiscent of ancient statuary but incorporating a strong melodramatic element. He died in Rome, but left many casts of his works in Ann Arbor. (W.C.)

Rohde, Gilbert (1894–1944).
Avant-garde furniture and industrial designer. A native New Yorker and son of a cabinetmaker, he attended public schools and later the Art Students League and Grand Central School of Art. Interested in the technical aspects of art, he became a knowledgeable craftsman in various areas. Early in life he pursued such varied careers as political cartoonist and drama and music critic for New York newspapers, advertising man, photographer, and free-lance artist. These varied experiences proved ideal preparation for the new field of industrial design. He opened his own firm in 1929 and became a consultant for General Electric, Rohm & Haas, Hudson Motor Car, and other companies. In 1931 he persuaded Herman Miller, Inc., producers of standard furniture, to change its total concept of design and marketability. His idea was to create modern furniture with modern materials, to lead rather than to follow public taste, and to allow the designer complete control over the production of his designs. Herman Miller became a pioneer producer of modern American furniture; and Rohde's influence is still evident in the firm's philosophy.

At the 1933 Chicago World's Fair

Rohde gained widespread acceptance for modern furniture with his interior decoration of "The Design for Living House." Unit furniture, one of the innovations in this exhibit, illustrates his approach to design: furniture should be practical, convenient, comfortable, and flexible. He designed bookcases, cabinets, and shelves that could be shifted as needed, and "combination chairs" that could be used as a settee, a group of two, or individually. Most of this furniture retains a remarkably modern look even after forty years.

A concern with promoting better design of useful objects led Rohde to lecture widely and to serve from 1936 to 1938 as director of a free industrial art school, the Design Laboratory, established by the WPA. He taught at the New School for Social Research, and was head of the industrial design department of the school of architecture, New York University (1939–43). Rohde's conviction was that art belongs to everyone, everyday. In the 1930s he represented the progressive forces in furniture design. (D.P.)

Rohm, Robert (1934–   ).

Sculptor. Born in Cincinnati, Ohio, Rohm went to New York City to study at Pratt Institute. He received his M.F.A. from the Cranbrook Academy in Michigan in 1960 and had his first one-man exhibition in 1963 in Aspen, Col. Rohm's work with heavy ropes, usually knotted in ladder-like or hammock-like patterns, attracted the attention of critics during the late 1960s. The delicate shadow patterns his wall-hangings cast on their surroundings, and the associations with the seaman's art they inspire, earned him praises for his use of exceptional sculptural material and his lyrical gifts.

Roman Eclectic Style.

The most important of the eclectic architectural styles, it was used for large public buildings, state capitols, railroad stations, and commercial architecture, including banks and skyscrapers.* It was a purely classical style for which the fountainhead of inspiration was Rome. The scale was often overpowering, with high-columned porticoes crowned by pediments, serving as symbols of prestige for the buildings they adorned. The American Academy in Rome was established to train architects in adapting

Roman Eclectic. McKim, Mead & White, Pennsylvania Station, N.Y., 1910.

classical design to the new requirements of American architecture. Symmetry and formality were its most distinguishing characteristics. (A.B.)

Romanesque Eclectic Style.

An architectural style characterized by esoteric ornament, it was not popular with the average architect. Even its structural features were difficult to fit into the mold of 20th-century reality. In New York City the firm of York & Sawyer* made the style their own with a series of buildings, including the Bowery Savings Bank on East Forty-second Street, with its varicolored columns, mosaic walls, and tessellated marble floors. The Byzantine glories of low-domed St. Bartolomew's Church on Park Avenue exhibit further evidence of the beauty of this style. (A.B.)

Romanesque Revival Style.

An architectural style and the last of the revival styles, it spanned the last half of the 19th century. Its influence was eclipsed by the classicism introduced at the World's Columbian Exposition held in Chicago in 1893.

Romanesque revival can be divided into two phases. The first, an early, naive version, emerged in the late 1840s. Generally executed in brick, this style was used for industrial buildings and various commercial structures, as well as for churches—of which the earliest example was Richard Upjohn's* Church of the Pilgrims on Remsen Street in Brooklyn, N.Y.

The second, more mature phase was introduced to America in 1865 by the promising young architect Henry Hobson Richardson* and was often later referred to as "Richardsonian Romanesque." The fourth American to attend the École des Beaux-Arts in Paris, Richardson was greatly influenced by the rebellion against the classicism of the École that the architect-historian Viollet-le-Duc (1814–79) had aroused through his teachings and writings. Romanesque architecture, which had flourished from the 9th to the 13th century, had been reintroduced to the students and was being practised again in France as a contemporary style. Richardson returned to the United States in 1865 and began to develop that style that was to bear his name.

A rugged architecture that perpetuated the masonry tradition, in it the stone walls carried the structural loads.

Enormous stone arches spanned the principal entrances to buildings, sometimes supported on clusters of short, squat columns. By contrast, rows of small windows were often set high in the walls with continuous lintels supported on stone mullions between the windows. Its greatest contribution was an expressive use of fine masonry materials and the reintroduction of asymmetry, picturesque profiles, and a new romanticism. As in Victorian Gothic,* the use of varicolored stonework in the walls achieved interesting effects. A distinctive type of carved ornament was used for the keystones of arches and the capitals of columns. The color scheme for woodwork ran to dark reds, browns, and greens for doors and windows. Following the craftsman tradition, cast iron gave way to wrought iron, twisted or flat, and door hinges and locks were often recreated from medieval originals.

Another picturesque manifestation of the style was frame residential structures covered with wood shingles. Their color schemes were somber or, in houses built at seaside and mountain resorts, unpainted shingles and woodwork were simply allowed to weather.

Among the outstanding buildings in this style are Richardson's Trinity Church, Boston (1872–77); many of his small libraries; his great Allegheny County Courthouse and Jail in Pittsburgh (1884–87), a monument to the rugged strength of his designs; and his Marshall Field Wholesale Store Warehouse Building in Chicago (1885), which established a model for a generation of skyscraper* designs. (A.B.)

Romans, Bernard (c.1720–84).

Draftsman and designer of maps and views including a view of the Battle of Bunker Hill *(Exact View of the Late Battle at Charlestown June 17, 1775)* and *Map of the Seat of the Civil War in America.* His designs were engraved by himself and sometimes by others, including Paul Revere. Born in Holland, educated in England, Romans was a surveyor, botanist, and military engineer who emigrated to America in 1775.

Romanticism.

A late 18th- and 19th-century movement in the arts characterized, in general, by an emphasis on nature—often in its wilder aspects—and on the emo-

tional or the spiritual rather than the reasoned and intellectual. This attitude was far more pervasive in all the arts than either the rococo* or the baroque,* which preceded it. Like the other styles, it was late in reaching America from Europe, although its appearance was strengthened by the number of immigrant artists after the Revolution. The new mood was stimulated and spread by the French Revolution and the long turmoil of the Napoleonic Wars, which resulted in a sense of sinister powers beyond human control and obliterated much of the rationalism of the 18th-century Enlightenment. In portraiture—the predominant art of England and America—faces assumed an air of pensive concern, poses became simplified, and background shadows deepened. The landscape background, formerly often itself a portrait of the subject's home, became a symbolic element only. Landscape painting itself emerged as a distinct and favorite art. Even in sculpture and history painting, where monumentality tended to make tradition more stable, the romantic influence dominated in such works as Horatio Greenough's* marble *The Rescue* (1837, U.S. Capitol), complete with savage Indian, sturdy pioneer, pioneer wife and baby and the faithful dog, and in *Marius Musing Amid the Ruins of Carthage* (1807, de Young) by John Vanderlyn.* On a grander scale is Rembrandt Peale's* huge and shadowy painting, *Court of Death* (1819, Detroit), which toured America at an admission charge with immense success. Elements of romanticism are implicit in history painting, and in America this art greatly increased in favor as it shed the poetic conventions of former centuries. In the late 19th and early 20th century, its development eventually led to two other art forms, the American school of illustration and the motion picture. (C.C.S.)

Rosati, James (1912–).

One of the most versatile sculptors of his generation, he has experimented with all methods and materials, and excelled in several media. He was born in Washington, Pa., a coal-mining district. He studied the violin at an early age and perfected his style well enough to play with the Pittsburgh Symphony from 1928 to 1930. After seeing exhibitions at the Carnegie Museum, Rosati became deeply interested in sculpture

James Rosati. Interior Castle, Number I, *1959, sheet metal. Whitney Museum of American Art, N.Y.*

and began to teach himself modeling. In 1937 he worked in the WPA Federal Art Project* as a sculptor. When he arrived in New York in 1944, where he has remained, Rosati was a skillful carver and modeler.

During the late 1940s, Rosati was a member of a loosely defined group advocating a sharp break with tradition. He himself had begun to work with constructions of a geometric character in sheets of wax. But his chief preoccupation during the late 1940s and early 1950s was the development of fresh modes in stone carving. He had particularly admired the work of abstract sculptor Brancusi (1876–1957), and began working with very simple, curvilinear profiles in which the marble assumed only very indirectly the forms suggested by the human body. The perfection of his stone sculptures, with their evidence of his innate respect for living stone, gained him the esteem of such artists as Willem de Kooning,* Franz Kline,* and David Smith.*

During the late 1950s, Rosati's interest in welding led him to execute a group of relief sculptures in which he combined moderately curved volumes with rectilinear forms. He had already experimented with roughly square shapes in stone, and gradually he moved away from direct human allusions. His exhibitions in 1954 and 1957 heralded the direction of his work in the 1960s.

Working always with precisely finished models, Rosati established the scale he felt could represent his monumental aspirations. He then constructed huge steel sculptures in which every facet was highly controlled, and which are distinctly classical in their reserve. His play with diminishing lines and illusionistic perspective distinguished his works from the minimal* sculptures then gaining wide acceptance. By means of an almost imperceptible widening or narrowing of a rectilinear member, Rosati achieved a monumental effect even when the works were not gigantic. His masterly development was gradually acknowledged. In 1960 he won the Brandeis Creative Arts Award; in 1962 the Logan Medal at the Art Institute of Chicago; in 1964 a Guggenheim Fellowship; and in 1968 a National Arts Council grant. In 1969–70 a traveling exhibition showed his works at Brandeis, the Albright-Knox Gallery, Yale, and in New York City. He has

since had commissions for large outdoor sculptures, including one for Wichita, Kan. (D.A.)

Rosenquist, James (1933–).
Painter. Born in Grand Forks, N.D., and educated at the Minnesota School of Art and University of Minnesota beginning in 1952. In 1954 he painted advertising billboards in Minnesota. In 1955 he studied at the Art Students League* on a scholarship. He took a studio in New York in 1957 and met Richard Bellamy, a pioneer dealer in avant-garde American art, as well as such avant-garde painters as Jack Youngerman,* Robert Indiana,* Robert Rauschenberg,* and Jasper Johns.* Between 1958 and 1960 Rosenquist worked as a sign painter, painting the enormous billboards in Times Square as well as other theatrical displays, meanwhile becoming interested in the large paintings of Jackson Pollock* and Sam Francis.* His experience painting huge signs, involving extreme close-ups of gigantic details of the human face and figure and of industrial objects, supplied the basis of his particular version of pop art.* From sign painting he also drew his brilliant, often garish color palette. During the 1960s Rosenquist had regular one-man exhibitions at galleries in New York City, in 1964 in Paris and Los Angeles, and since 1968 widely in the United States and Europe.

Rosenquist presents his fragmented view of contemporary American popular culture—glamor girls, automobiles, airplanes, light bulbs, and Grand Rapids furniture—within the general limits of cubism* and sharp-focus realism. His most monumental work to date is *F-111* (1965), measuring 10 x 86 feet. Inspired by a new, monstrously expensive experimental bomber, he here documented his deeply-felt antagonism to the American arms buildup. *F-111* is a digest of contemporary American civilization, combining such everyday details as an automobile tire, electric light bulbs, and a happy child under an electric hair dryer with threatening fragments of the plane, atomic explosions, and other symbols of death and destruction. Rosenquist here moved from the documentation of the industrial commonplace to a symbolic commentary on war and the atomic bomb with their threats of total annihilation.

In the later 1960s he experimented

widely with different images, and he continues to reflect the tendency current in the so-called earth sculptures (see Earth Art) and conceptual work (see Concept Art) of organizing a work as a total room environment. One of the most impressive of these, *Horizon Home Sweet Home* (1970), fills a room, including an actual fog created by a dry-ice machine. (H.H.A.)

Rossbach, Edward (1914–   ).
Weaver, known for experiments with textile techniques utilizing a great range of materials from plastic strips to grasses. Born in Chicago, III., he studied painting, design, and ceramics at the universities of Washington, Seattle, and California at Berkeley. His production over the years has included upholstery, suiting, and rugs, but most of his objects are strictly nonutilitarian. During the 1950s the was interested primarily in raffia, tie-dye, and ikat techniques, but during the 1960s he experimented with hangings, solid woven walls, and anthropologically-derived basketry, using the most contemporary materials, singly and in combination. These have included polyethylene, mylar, anodized aluminum, vinyl tape, and plastic film, in addition to plastic tubing stuffed with paper. For example, the tubing was woven in an ancient Peruvian technique with four selvages. He is professor of design at the University of California at Berkeley.

Roszak, Theodore (1907–   ).
Sculptor and lithographer. Born in Poland, he emigrated to the United States when he was very young. After studying at the Art Institute of Chicago, he worked as a lithographer in a constructivist style until 1931. He then moved to New York City and attended the National Academy of Design.* A member of the faculty of Sarah Lawrence College in 1941–56, his first significant sculpture appeared in the late 1940s. His welded steel and brazed brass works of this period characteristically show a crescent shape set within a framework of bent rods. In the 1950s Roszak's vocabulary expanded to include semiabstract allusions to wings. bones, stems, and rocks. Outright figuration appears in 1957 with *The Basket Weaver,* which shows a deformed, birdlike creature surrounded by a skeletal framework. Roszak's sculpture combines haunting mythological refer-

ences with a biomorphism derived from surrealism.* He has said that the forms of his mature work "are meant to be blunt reminders of primordial strife and struggle, reminiscent of those brute forces that not only produced life, but in turn threatened to destroy it." His work has been seen in museum and gallery shows since the late 1940s. In 1956 the Whitney Museum, New York City, in collaboration with the Walker Art Center in Minneapolis, gave him a retrospective exhibition. He has received numerous appointments, including membership on the advisory council of the International Education Exchange Program. (C.R.)

Rothko, Mark (1903–70).
Painter. Born in Dvinsk, Russia, he went to Portland, Ore., at the age of ten. He attended Yale from 1921–23; then moved to New York City in 1925, where he studied with Max Weber* at the Art Students League.* Rothko's formal training was brief and he always considered himself self-taught. In 1929 he had his first exhibition and also began teaching art to children at the Center Academy in Brooklyn (a job he retained until 1952). Rothko's work of the 1930s stressed urban scenes—such as the loneliness of human beings who stand immobile and without contact with each other in his "Subway" series. In 1935 he and Adolph Gottlieb* cofounded The Ten*—a group of expressionistic painters (see Expressionism), and in 1936–37 he worked on the WPA Federal Art Project.* By the early 1940s, however, he had begun to be influenced by surrealism* and was producing paintings inspired by primitive myth and ritual, reinterpreted in Freudian terms. Although he had a number of shows during the 1930s, his first important exhibition came in 1945 at Peggy Guggenheim's* Art of This Century gallery. In 1948 he joined with Robert Motherwell,* William Baziotes,* and Barnett Newman* in founding the art school "Subjects of the Artist." Within a short time, however, his "biomorphs," such as *Entombment* (1946, Whitney), with their organic, sometimes linear, and always suggestive floating forms, had become completely abstract.

Rothko's symbolic "abstractions" had been painted in muted colors and often in watercolor and he carried this hazy, atmospheric quality into his 1947–48 pictures of soft rectangles

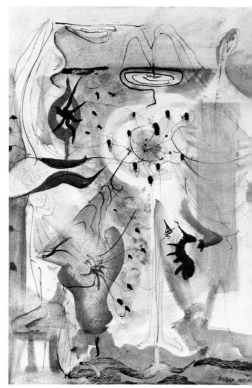

2

1. *James Rosenquist.* F-111 (partial view), 1965. Collection Mr. and Mrs. Robert C. Scull, N.Y.
2. *Mark Rothko.* Baptismal Scene, 1945. Whitney Museum of American Art, N.Y.
3. *Mark Rothko.* Four Darks in Red, 1958. Whitney Museum of American Art, N.Y. (gift of the Friends of the Whitney Museum).

1

3

gently nudging each other in an ambiguous space. These pictures attempted an internal balancing of forms, and often produced an asymmetrical effect. Within two years Rothko had added simplicity and monumentality to his image by using only two or three symmetrically placed rectangles that extended nearly to the edges of the canvas, and by painting much larger pictures, such as *Number 10* (1950, Modern Museum). He explained the large size of his canvases as part of his "impulse to deal with human values," noting: "I want to create a state of intimacy." The neutral nature of the rectangle allowed for the primacy of color, and its large size tended to disperse focus, so that seen close up—as these paintings were meant to be—the viewer was enveloped in emanations of light and color. Rothko had hated to abandon the human figure but he refused to "mutilate nature." He wrote: "It was with the utmost reluctance that I found the figure could not serve my purposes," and even after he had gone beyond surrealism into total abstraction he still sought to "deal with human emotion; with the human drama as much as I can possibly experience it." He disliked having his work discussed in formalist terms and noted that he was not concerned with art esthetically, but rather as a humanist and moralist. He wrote: "Only tragic and timeless subject matter is worthy of painting."

Rothko sought to achieve his ends chiefly through color, eliciting moods that ranged from serenity to pure joy, melancholy, and even foreboding and death. The rectangular format varied from painting to painting; thus the expansive, buoyant, blurry-edged forms of yellows and oranges (as in *Orange Brown*, 1963, Detroit) blues and pinks are completely different from his somber, more carefully delineated works in blacks, browns, maroons, and hot saturated reds (as in *Red Maroons #2, 1962,* Cleveland). His color could be dense or atmospheric, or radiant and luminous, achieved by superimposing veils of color. Throughout the period that Rothko was developing the style for which he was world famous by the late 1950s, he continued to teach: at the California School of Fine Arts in San Francisco (1947 and 1949), at Brooklyn College, (1951–54), and as visiting artist at the universities of Colorado (1955) and

Tulane (1956). In 1958 he began a major commission for murals for a New York restaurant. After completing the paintings—rectangular frames of somber colors against equally somber backgrounds—he decided they were not suitable for such a setting and refused to deliver them. These murals represent the beginning of a period of increasing austerity in which he aimed more and more at a transcendental, religious quality, culminating in the Rothko Chapel, commissioned by the de Menil family in Houston, Tex. Here fourteen large paintings are hung around the walls of an octagonal structure—all dark, and meant to invoke a meditative, inner world. Rothko considered the chapel the culmination of his career; he committed suicide shortly after these paintings were finished.

Rothko had a retrospective at the Museum of Modern Art, New York City, in 1961 and was included in virtually every international exhibition of his time. He was a pioneer of color-field* painting, although his work seems romantic and introspective compared to the generation of two-dimensional "pattern" painters that followed him. Rothko was considered a member of the abstract expressionist group, although he disliked the term and felt that his work had nothing to do with expressionism, impulse, or athletic gesture. Rather, he felt that art should be based on intelligence and not the senses alone, and yet he produced some of the most sensuous paintings of the period.   (E.C.G.)

Roux, Alexander (1813–86).
French-American cabinetmaker. "In New York, the rarest and most elaborate designs, especially for drawing-room and library use, are to be found at the warehouse of Roux in Broadway," proclaimed Andrew Jackson Downing,* an arbiter of American taste in the mid-19th century. Roux was born in Gap, France, and probably received his training in Paris. He first appeared in the New York City directories in 1837, being listed as an upholsterer at 472½ Broadway. From 1843 on he advertised himself as a cabinetmaker. One of the earliest known examples of his work, a set of four labeled Gothic chairs, can be dated as of 1848. A partnership with his brother Frederick lasted for only about two years (1847–49). The firm's last move, in 1877. was to 133 Fifth

Avenue. Roux and Company had a long and distinguished history (61 years) as a leading New York cabinetmaking and decorating establishment. Roux retired in 1881, but the firm continued until 1898 under the direction of his son, Alexander. According to credit rating sources, the elder Roux had a very prosperous business, employing 120 people as early as 1855 and reaching a peak in the 1870s when he made from $250,000 to $500,000 annually.

Reflecting the variety of styles that distinguished the 1840s and 1850s, Roux worked in Gothic, Elizabethan, rococo, Renaissance, or whatever was popular at the moment. His work is characterized not only by its diversity, but by fine craftsmanship and French sophistication.   (D.P.)

Ruckstull, Frederic Wellington (1853–1942).
Sculptor, born in Alsace, France. He was brought to St. Louis while an infant; he studied sculpture in Paris in 1882 and 1885–88, and had a studio there in 1890–91, his work receiving high praise at the annual salons. An example of his early work is *Evening* (1891, Metropolitan). By 1892 he had established a studio in New York, and the next year helped found the National Sculpture Society. Throughout his life Ruckstull had an exceptional ability to organize large sculptural programs, such as the Dewey Arch (1899, New York, destroyed), a collaborative effort of seven top sculptors. He also helped obtain the appropriation for the vast sculptural program of the Pan-American Exposition at Buffalo in 1901, and he provided the quadriga symbolizing *America Welcoming the Pan-American Nations.* Ruckstull's work was strongly influenced by Paris and, especially in his exposition sculpture, it had the flamboyant quality of the neobaroque style taught at the École des Beaux-Arts. In portraiture, however, an uncomplicated naturalism dominated. He also produced three marble portrait statues for Statuary Hall in the U.S. Capitol: *John C. Calhoun* (1910), *Uriah M. Rose* (1917), and *Wade Hampton* (1929). Late in his career he spent much time inveighing against insurgent modern art, which he called an "intellectual pest." His invective criticism was included in his book, *Great Works of Art and What Makes Them Great* (1925).
(W.C.)

Rudolph, Paul (1918–   ).
Architect whose designs of civil, residential, commercial, and institutional buildings from the 1940s to the present have aroused much controversy. His work displays ingenuity and drama on all levels of design, from planning, through building materials and interior spaces, to lighting and furnishings. Born in Elkton, Ky., and educated at Harvard under Walter Gropius,* he first practiced as a partner in the firm of Twitchell & Rudolph in Sarasota, Fla., and made a name for prize-winning small houses that utilized relatively unconventional construction systems (Healy House, 1948; Walker House, 1952). He then moved on to Boston and to larger buildings such as the Jewett Arts Center, Wellesley College, Massachusetts (1955), where he manipulated the building as a modern wall that harmoniously completes the fourth side of a neo-Gothic quadrangle. In his first high-rise structure, the Blue Shield Building (Boston, 1956), he designed an exterior concrete frame as a piece of large-scale sculpture. He continued to design houses and schools in Florida with elegant, Le Corbusier-inspired sun shades (Sarasota High School, Sarasota, Fla., 1958; Milam House, Jacksonville, Fla., 1960), and constantly broadened the geographic, esthetic, and functional range of his practice.

While chairman of the architecture department at Yale University (1958–65), Rudolph designed a mammoth, seemingly scaleless parking garage (1958–63), in concrete, for the city of New Haven, Conn. He also designed the Art & Architecture Building for Yale (1958–63), which became one of the most widely discussed buildings of the decade. In that work, Rudolph showed his revolutionary ideas: he rejected the smooth, refined packaging of the minimal style,* and espoused ambiguous planning that admitted the element of spatial discovery. He also revealed a breadth of vision in design vocabulary, imaginative expression of mechanical systems and lighting, and the accommodation of inspiration from historical architecture. He also used common materials in uncommon ways. This building, a precursor of supermannerist architecture, was later disfigured by fire—set, it was suspected, by younger revolutionaries who censured the building for being too "designed" and

1

2

1. **Paul Rudolph.** Art and Architecture Building, Yale University, New Haven, Conn., 1963.
2. **Paul Rudolph.** Tuskegee University Chapel, Alabama, 1969.

thus regimenting behavior and function.

Throughout the 1960s, Rudolph designed buildings that captured the interest of the architectural community: the Ford Foundation Ideal Theater project, announced in 1961, but never built, has a massive sculptural concrete exterior reminiscent of constructivist architecture; the roughly sculptured concrete Endo Laboratories on Long Island, N.Y. (1962–66) was a horizontal, round-cornered and turreted scheme that used the concrete texture of the Yale Art & Architecture Building. In high-rise housing for the elderly, Crawford Manor, New Haven, Conn. (1962–66), Rudolph designed a fluted concrete block that gave the structure texture and also reiterated the L-angle, pinwheel plan of the building. At each announcement, critics were both impressed and incredulous, doubting that he could actually have such flamboyant designs built. Yet he continued to do so, and on an ever-larger scale. A radiating concrete madder-plan chapel, designed in 1960 for Tuskegee University, was finally completed in 1969. Boston's Health Center (1962–72) grew to elaborate baroque dimensions, encompassing handiwork in concrete that could hardly be expected in a public building today. It contains a chapel that Rudolph considers his finest interior. A campus for Southern Massachusetts Technical Institute (1963–66) ultimately grew (1968) into a village center.

Affronted but undeterred by the disfiguration of his Art & Architecture Building at Yale, Rudolph continued to display a broad interest in the social goals of younger revolutionaries who were in fact following his lead. His interests focused on town planning (master plan for Stafford Harbor, Va. 1966), modular housing systems (Graphic Arts Center, New York City, 1967; New Haven housing, 1968), public housing (Tracey Towers, Bronx, N.Y., 1967–71; Urban Development Corporation housing, Buffalo, N.Y., 1969), and tension and inflatable structures (stadium for Saudi Arabia, 1968). (C.R.S.)

Rush, William (1756–1833).

First native American sculptor. He was born in Philadelphia, Pa., the son of a shipbuilder and public-spirited citizen. He was apprenticed to Edward Cutbush, woodcarver, and soon excelled his master in the design and production of figureheads and other decorative work for ships. Even before the close of the American Revolution he had a thriving business of his own, and in the years following it gained an international reputation as the prows of his vessels were seen and admired in foreign ports. Benjamin H. Latrobe,* the eminent architect, addressing the Society of Artists in 1811, gave due praise: "There is a motion in his figures that is inconceivable. They seem rather to draw the ship after them than to be impelled by the vessel. They are of exquisite beauty. I have not seen one on which there is not the stamp of genius."

During the Philadelphia campaigns Rush had been an ensign in the militia regiment in which Charles Willson Peale* was a captain. The two became lifelong friends. Rush's interest in the allegorical representation of virtues and national traits was shared by Peale, one applying it to ships, the other to transparency painting. Peale, who had studied sculpture in London, may have had a part in his friend's progress from ship carving to portrait sculpture, from wood to clay and terra-cotta. Joseph Wright* was probably even more of an influence here, and the work of the French sculptor Houdon, first seen in Philadelphia in 1786, was undoubtedly another. This development took place between 1787, the date of Rush's comparatively crude woodcarving of Benjamin Franklin (Yale), and his mature portraits of 1814 and after. Rush's success as a sculptor was sustained by his active citizenship as well as his original talent. For over a quarter of a century he was a respected member of the Philadelphia Common Council. He was among the founders of the Pennsylvania Academy of the Fine Arts* and, with Peale, one of the two artists on its original board of directors.

Rush's oeuvre falls into three principal categories: his figureheads and other marine work; his monumental sculpture, also in wood, for public buildings and civic projects; and his portraits in wood, plaster, and terra-cotta. Few of his figureheads have survived, but two notable full-length portrait examples are extant, *George Washington* (Independence Hall) originally intended for a ship but never so used, and *John Dickinson. Tamanend,* figurehead of the U.S.S. *Delaware,* holds an honored place on the Naval Academy campus at Annapolis. In the

1

1. **William Rush.** Comedy, 1808.
2. **William Rush.** Tragedy, 1808.
Both, The Forrest Home, Philadelphia Museum of Art.

2

realm of civic adornment his *Water Nymph and Bittern* is best known (c.1809, now badly damaged but reproduced in bronze, Fairmount Park, Philadelphia). It figures in the well-known view of *Center Square* by John Lewis Krimmel,* and in *William Rush Carving the Allegorical Figure of the Schuylkill* by Thomas Eakins.* His reclining figures of *The Schuylkill Chained* and *Schuylkill Freed* (c. 1828, Fairmount Park), may have been suggested by engravings of the ancient sculpture of the *Nile* (Vatican) and *Tiber* (Louvre). Standing figures, *Comedy* and *Tragedy* (1808, The Forest Home, Philadelphia) were carved for the Chestnut Street Theater. His *Wisdom* and *Justice* (Fairmount Park) were made for the triumphal arch celebrating the arrival of Lafayette, 1824. The Pennsylvania Academy owns a memorable group of Rush portraits, notably *Self-portrait* (c.1822) and *Lafayette* (1824).

Ruskin, John (1819–1900).
An English critic and esthetician who played a dominant role in the creation of American taste during the mid-19th century. The success of his writings beginning with his *Modern Painters* (1843, and shortly thereafter in the United States), was great and made him, as Ruskin himself wrote in 1855, more famous in America than in England. Such American journals as *The Crayon** (1855–1861) and the *New Path* (1863–1865) energetically promoted Ruskin's belief in pre-Raphaelite painting. He provided justification and defense for the naturalist tendencies in English art, particularly championing the landscape painter J. M. W. Turner and the pre-Raphaelite painters for their naive reverence for nature, their moralistic esthetic theories, and their meticulous observation of detail. His thoughts thus played a role both in American landscape and still-life painting, particularly around 1860. Moreover, Ruskin's admiration for the Italian Gothic also influenced architecture and decoration, and later the crafts movement in America. His theories of the morally uplifting and educating effects of art on society promoted art patronage, both in private collecting, as well as in the founding of American public museums. (T.E.S.)

Russell, Charles Marion (1864–1926).
Cowboy artist and recorder of the Old West. Russell was born in St. Louis, Mo., and formed an early ambition to see the frontier. In 1880 he went to Montana, where he lived with a trapper for two years, then worked as a cowboy for some ten years, riding as a night herdsman. During the winter of 1888–89 he passed several months with the Blood Indians, a primitive tribe of the Blackfeet in Canada.

Meanwhile, Russell took every opportunity to work at drawing and sketching. His earliest surviving oils date from about 1885, and one of these, *Caught in the Act* (Montana Historical Society), reproduced in *Harper's Weekly* in 1888, was his first published illustration. He was a keen observer, a gifted story-teller, and a poor businessman. Sales came slowly and prices were meager, but nevertheless by 1892 he began to work full time at painting. He was married in 1896 and the next year settled in Great Falls, Mont., where he built his studio. The rest of his career was spent making a record of the West he had known as a youth. Recognition came slowly; it was not until 1905—when Frederick Remington* was at the height of his fame—that Russell managed to make a significant impact on the New York market as a painter and illustrator. His works frequently appeared in *McClure's* and *Leslie's* magazines. In 1911 Montana commissioned him to paint a mural for its House of Representatives: *Lewis and Clark Meeting the Flathead Indians* (1911–12).

Russell, who remained a cowboy in the rough, was entirely self-taught. He had a native skill as a draftsman and painter, and was equally adept at pen-and-ink, watercolor, oil, and modeling. His subjects centered on the men and animals he knew best, shown as character studies or in lively action, but his sense of setting and landscape backgrounds added substantially to the continuing popular appeal of his paintings. Russell's work is as full of action as Remington's but more racy, homespun, and frankly illustrational. (D.W.S.)

Russell, Morgan (1886–1953).
American painter and pioneer abstractionist and theorist. Born in New York, N.Y., Russell studied with Robert Henri* and James Earle Fraser before settling in Paris (1909) and working with Henri Matisse. Russell was a founder of the movement called syn-

chromism,* issuing, with Stanton Macdonald-Wright,* a statement of their intentions during joint exhibitions in 1913. Russell's interest in pure color composition coincided with that of France's leading color theorist, Robert Delaunay. Russell's work became totally abstract by 1914 but in 1916 he returned for several years to figurative painting. As an abstractionist he was one of the first American innovators of this century. His typical "synchromies" were composed of simple geometric shapes, often circular, vigorously colored, and conveying a strong sense of form and mass.

Ryder, Albert Pinkham (1847–1917). Romantic painter of the 19th century, whose art anticipated certain aspects of modernism. He was born in New Bedford, Mass., at that time the chief whaling port in the world. His ancestors belonged to old Cape Cod families, and many of them had followed the sea. From childhood the sea played a large part in Ryder's mind. Because he suffered from oversensitive eyes, his education ended with grammar school. With no art instruction beyond advice from an amateur artist, he began painting landscapes around New Bedford.

With his family he moved in about 1867 to New York, where he lived thenceforth. After being turned down by the school of the National Academy of Design,* he received informal criticisms from portrait painter William Edgar Marshall, whose naive but original romantic and religious art influenced him. At the relatively late age of twenty-three Ryder was admitted to the Academy (1871), where he studied for four seasons, mainly drawing from the antique. Thus his art education was limited compared to that of most of his American contemporaries. His European experience was also limited, consisting of travel rather than study. In 1877 he made his first visit abroad, for a month in London. His next visit, and the longest, was in the summer of 1882, to London and Paris, then to Spain (with a brief trip to Tangier), Italy, and Switzerland. Another friend wrote later of "the comparative weakness of the impression made on him by the old galleries, and his almost complete rejection of modern art in Europe. To his companions this natural chauvinism was entertaining." Twice again he went abroad, in 1887 and 1896, but mainly for the sea voyage.

Ryder's first adult paintings, from the early 1870s, were small landscapes, usually with figures, or with horses, cows or sheep, reminiscent of the country around New Bedford. Although comparatively naturalistic in style, they already revealed a naive simplicity, a visionary quality, and strange, highly personal forms. They were usually rejected by the Academy exhibition juries, and when the younger liberal artists rebelled and established the Society of American Artists* in 1877, Ryder was one of its twenty-two founders, and exhibited in its shows for the next decade.

In his early thirties, about 1880, Ryder began to create more imaginative works. His sources were the Bible, classical mythology, and the great poetry of the English-speaking world: Chaucer, Shakespeare (his favorite poet), the early ballads, and the 19th-century Romantics, Byron, Campbell, Moore, Tennyson, and Poe. Wagner's operas inspired two major works, *The Flying Dutchman* (1880s, National Coll.) and *Siegfried* (c.1890, Washington) the latter based on *Götterdämmerung.* But these paintings were not "literary": they were not illustrations but pictorial dramas based on great themes and transformed by Ryder's imagination into intensely personal conceptions.

In all Ryder's works, nature played a central role. Throughout his life he was haunted by memories of the sea; his most frequent image was a lone boat sailing moonlit waters. But his principal paintings were more than simple nature poems. His art was essentially religious: he was one of the few 19th-century artists whose religion was not merely formal but profound belief. The basic theme of much of his art was the relation between the human and the superhuman. Often the human being was shown under the protection of divine powers, as in *Jonah* (c.1885, National Coll.), where God appears watching over his prophet; or *Constance* (c.1896, Boston), in which Chaucer's queen and her child, adrift on an empty sea without sail or rudder, are being miraculously guided toward home.

Ryder's style was as purely personal as his content. In a period when the prevailing viewpoint was naturalistic representation, he used nature's forms with great freedom, shaping them to his own conceptions. He once said: "What avails a storm cloud accurate in form and color if the storm is not therein?" To him painting was not mere representation but a creative language speaking directly to the senses through form, color, and tone. The originality and inner life of his forms, his sense of rhythmic movement, the depth and richness of his color harmonies, and above all, his sense of design, ranked him among the purest plastic creators of his time in any country.

He worked a long time over his pictures, applying layer on layer of pigment and glazes, and often painting on them for years. Hence his life's work totalled only about 165 paintings. Unhappily he lacked sound technical knowledge, and many of his pictures have chemically deteriorated to some degree. The small number of his works and their financial value in his later years were tempting to forgers, even in his lifetime, so that today the forgeries outnumber the genuine works by the deplorable ratio of about five to one. Among American artists only Blakelock* has been so extensively forged.

In his personal life Ryder was entirely unworldly. Reputation and money meant nothing to him. "The artist needs but a roof, a crust of bread and his easel," he said, "and all the rest God gives him in abundance. He must live to paint and not paint to live." He never married, and in later life he became a recluse, seeing only old friends and a very few younger ones. His living quarters on West 15th Street, New York City, reached a state of incredible disorder, filled waist-high with debris. In 1915 he had a serious illness and spent his last years with friends in Elmhurst, Long Island.

In some aspects Ryder can be looked upon as a belated but legitimate child of early 19th-century Romanticism.* But in others—his use of subconscious imagery, his freedom from literal representation, his intuitive methods of creation, his sense of design, and the purity of his plastic achievement—he was a forerunner of much in modern art.

(L.G.)

1

2

3

1. ***Albert Pinkham Ryder.*** Moonlight,
   *c.1885. National Gallery of Art,
   Washington, D.C.*
2. ***Albert Pinkham Ryder.*** Siegfried
   and the Rhine Maidens, *1891. National Gallery of Art, Washington,
   D.C. (Andrew Mellon Collection).*
3. ***Albert Pinkham Ryder.*** Mending
   the Harness, *c.1880. National Gallery of Art, Washington, D.C. (gift of
   Sam A. Lewisohn).*

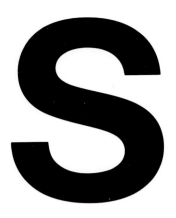

Saarinen, Eero (1910–61).
Architect, born in Kirkkonummi, Finland. Saarinen emigrated to the United States in 1923 with his famous father, the architect Eliel Saarinen,* and after graduating from Yale University (1934), traveled through Europe (1934–36). Saarinen grew up at Cranbrook, Mich., and entered into partnership with his father in the late 1930s. Although Eero was raised in an Arts and Crafts* environment, his early commitment was to the machine esthetic of the International style.* Working with his father, he stripped and internationalized the elder architect's designs, producing such buildings as the Tabernacle Church of Christ (Columbus, Ind., 1941–42) and the winning entry (1939) in the competition for the art gallery to be erected on the mall for the Smithsonian Institution (Washington, D.C., never built). After World War II he produced his most impressive essay in the International style, the General Motors Technical Center (Warren, Mich., 1951–57), which leaves the impression of an expensive machine product gently set down in a rural landscape. But like Philip Johnson,* Paul Rudolph,* and other American designers of these years, he eventually abandoned the stringent purity of the International style, and his work of the 1950s displayed a variety of approaches. In his auditorium and chapel at Massachusetts Institute of Technology (1955) he sought to impose two geometric shapes (an eighth of a sphere for the auditorium and a cylinder for the chapel) into a public space that was an extension of an existing neoclassical building style and layout. Though the small circular chapel, lighted from below by a reflecting pool, can be considered a gem of modern architecture, the two buildings do not seem to relate to one another, or to the older buildings near them.

In his furniture he remained faithful to the principles of machine esthetics in his use of materials and visual forms. This can be seen in the molded plywood chair that he and Charles Eames* designed in 1940, in his wire-framed "womb" chair of 1946, and his aluminum and fiberglass pedestal furniture of 1955–58, all of which have become classic pieces.

Saarinen's United States Embassy Building in London of 1965 (in contrast to his United States Embassy Building in Oslo of 1955–59) was from the beginning a subject of controversy. In its design he tried to be modern and yet take into account the 18th-century Georgian tradition of London. As critics both here and abroad pointed out, the building ended up being neither. Another group of his buildings departed from the precise rectilinear vocabulary of the International style and were more "expressionistic" in feeling; in several of these he used the structural system as a symbolic expression. The curved-wing, formed-concrete Trans World Airlines Terminal at Kennedy International Airport (1956–62) suggested a bird readying itself for flight, while the steel and wood Ingalls Hockey Rink at Yale (1956–58) implies the rigorous out-of-doors of a beached Viking ship. All of the buildings were highly successful in their interior space: the airline terminal not only functions well but also provides an impressive transition between the slower-paced world of the ground and the speed of air travel; while the interior of the Hockey Rink strikes an excellent balance between the verticalism needed for a large public space and an intimacy between the rink and spectators.

In the early 1960s Saarinen's buildings began to echo the historical: for example, his medieval, stone-bastioned Yale University College (1962), or his Columbia Broadcasting System Building (1962–65) in New York City, where he seemed to go back to the verticalism of the skyscrapers* of the late 1920s. Dramatic visual effects appeared to have become increasingly important for him in the years before his death. A concave-curved roof dominates his Dulles Airport outside of Washington, D.C. (1962), and his soaring Jefferson Memorial Arch at St. Louis (1948–67) is composed of a single elliptical form. At the same time he continued to explore the modular, rectangular vocabulary of the International style. His IBM buildings in Rochester, Minn. (1956) and in Yorktown, N.Y. (1956) are cold, corporate, and correct. His Deere and Company Building in Moline, Ill. (1962), with its exterior exposed steel frame, is almost Japanese in feeling. By the late 1950s the diversity of Saarinen's work illustrates how most modern architects were becoming dissatisfied with the restrictive canons of the International style.   (D.G.)

Saarinen, Eliel (1873–1950).
Architect and city planner, born in Rantasalmi, Finland. When Russia ruled Finland, his father, a Lutheran pastor, kept his congregation together in a church outside of St. Petersburg, and it was in the art galleries of this city that young Eliel decided to become a painter. In 1893 he enrolled in the Polytekniska Institutet in Helsingfors (Helsinki), where he studied both painting and architecture and set up an architectural partnership with two other students before graduating in 1897. The firm soon won competitions for apartments and market buildings and gained worldwide attention with their charming Finnish Pavilion for the Paris Exposition of 1900. The consolidation of the firm came in 1902 with the construction of their great studio-residence, Hvitträsk, in eastern Finland. In this picturesque house, the architects gave full rein to their love of craftsmanship. Loja Gesellius, who later

married Saarinen, wove the fabrics for the interiors.

In 1904 Saarinen won the competition for the Helsingfors Railroad Station, which was tantamount to a town-planning project. He created a beautiful and functional scheme that was to influence a generation of European architects. Saarinen's broad outlook led him, in 1910–11, into the field of town planning itself, including plans for Munksnäs-Haga, Finland; Reval, Estonia; and Budapest, Hungary. He then developed a comprehensive scheme for the decentralization of Greater Helsingfors. All of these plans and theories are described in *The City* (1944).

Probably the most significant single event in his career was winning second place in the competition for the Chicago *Tribune* Tower Building in 1922, which brought him, at the age of fifty, to America. Saarinen's simple design for the *Tribune* Tower, with its expression of the underlying steel construction and beautifully modulated setbacks, contrasted strongly with the prize-winning scheme in flamboyant French Gothic: the lesson it taught was that skyscraper* design would henceforth reflect a new simplicity.

In 1924, Saarinen became visiting professor at the University of Michigan. There a newspaper publisher, George G. Booth, interested in the Arts and Crafts* movement, commissioned Saarinen to design a school on his estate in Bloomfield Hills, a suburb of Detroit. In the Cranbrook School for Boys, the keynote was craftsmanship and the collaboration of artists. Sculpture and ceramics by Geza Maroti enlivened the handsome brickwork of the buildings, which were grouped around courtyards displaying sculpture by Carl Milles* and wrought ironwork by Oscar Bach. Saarinen's theme, "the nature of material decides the nature of form," was beautifully expressed in these buildings. The school and its design were so successful that Booth commissioned the Cranbrook Academy of Art in 1926. These studios formed the nucleus of the school to which Saarinen was appointed president in 1932. The school was completed in 1943 with the addition of the Art Museum and Library. In 1929, Saarinen added the buildings of the Kingswood School for Girls, which many regard as his masterpiece. Here his wife and two children collab-

1

2

Eero Saarinen. TWA Terminal at Kennedy International Airport, N.Y., 1962.
1. Exterior. front.
2. Interior. main lounge. ·

orated on interior design, furniture and fabrics. Saarinen emphasized natural plant forms in the exterior columns and other details. The beauty of the school is best expressed in the Dining Hall where all details combine to produce a notable effect of homogeneity.

In the 1930s Saarinen was joined by his son Eero Saarinen* in executing many commissions, including the Kleinhans Music Hall in Buffalo, N.Y. (1938–40), where one end of the expressive, violin-shaped structure was reflected in water; the multiple-unit Crow Island School in Winnetka, Ill. (1939–40), which set a precedent for an intimate type of school building; and the handsome Tabernacle Church of Christ at Columbus, Ind. (1941–42), where the pool theme again recurs, reflecting the high tower adjoining the church.

In 1939 Saarinen and his son were joined by Eliel's son-in-law, Swanson, and together they designed Willow Run Housing, town center and schools in Michigan (1941–42), a campus plan for Antioch College in Yellow Springs, Ohio (1945), and the Edmundson Memorial Museum for the Des Moines Art Center in Iowa (1948). In 1948, Saarinen wrote *Search for Form,* describing his theory of creativity and how it was exemplified through the ages. He was honored by many awards including gold medals from the American Institute of Architects in 1947 and the Royal Institute of British Architects in 1950.

(A.B.)

Saint-Gaudens, Augustus (1848–1907). Sculptor. He was born in Dublin, Ireland, but his father, a poor French shoemaker, brought the family to New York City while Augustus was still an infant. He served an apprenticeship with two cameo cutters and began taking lessons at the National Academy of Design.* The earliest surviving example of his work is a bust of his father, Bernard Saint-Gaudens (1867, at the artist's studio in Cornish, N.H.), made the year he departed to study in France. Young and impressionable, he was very receptive to the art at the École des Beaux-Arts and in the studios of Parisian sculptors; it was unlike the neoclassicism* that had dominated sculpture in the earlier part of the century, and its naturalism possessed a new vigor. He found the modeling richer and the surfaces alive with the play of lights and shadows; its spontaneity contrasted with the smooth, controlled surfaces and contours of neoclassical sculpture. After three years in Paris, he went to Italy in 1870 and yet another element was added to his emerging style—the influence of 15th-century Italian sculptors. In the work of the latter, such as Donatello, the two main forces were the vital naturalism and the delicate sensitivity in low-relief sculpture. All of these ingredients from Paris, Florence, and Rome, Saint-Gaudens blended into a powerful style of his own, which he introduced into the mainstream of American sculpture when he returned in 1874. He was the first to revitalize a naturalism that had reached its nadir in the lifeless banalities of 19th-century portraiture. His new style is evident in the bronze bust of *William Evarts* (c.1874, artist's studio) and made its first great impression in the famous bronze figure of *Admiral David Farragut* (1881, Central Park, New York City). From 1880 on, Saint-Gaudens was recognized as a leader of American sculptors and his style set the pattern for many of his contemporaries. Moreover, Paris rather than Italy became the center for young American sculptors who went abroad.

In contrast to Daniel Chester French,* who excelled in allegorical and personifying images, Saint-Gaudens' greatest achievement was in portraiture and memorials. In spite of the long periods he devoted to each work, he was a prolific artist, and only a few of his more prominent works can be mentioned. Among his portraits (all in bronze) are the *Shaw Memorial* (1884–97, Boston Commons); the standing *Abraham Lincoln* (1887) and the seated *Lincoln* (1907), both for Chicago; the equestrian *General Sherman* (1897–1903, New York), and the *Reverend Phillips Brooks Memorial* (1907, Trinity Churchyard, Boston). All are boldly naturalistic in style, but combine the real and the ideal in gripping pictorial sculpture. The delicacy is apparent in his bas-relief portraits, such as *Robert Louis Stevenson* (1887 and later versions) and *William Dean Howells and His Daughter* (1898). Saint-Gaudens occasionally left naturalism to venture into abstraction and personification, and his two best-known works of this type are the *Diana* (1892) and the *Adams Memorial* (1886–91, Rock Creek Cemetery, Washington, D.C.). The *Diana,* one of the sculptor's few nudes, stood atop the old Madison Square Garden arena in New York until 1925 and is now in the Philadelphia Art Museum. The *Adams Memorial,* evoking the tragic life of Henry Adams' wife, is a seated, enshrouded, sibyl-like figure representing the meditative qualities of oriental philosophies. It is one of the most original sculptures of the 19th century and anticipated modern expressionism by many years. Such works placed Saint-Gaudens at the very fore of American sculptors. He was active almost until his death, working summers in his studio at "Aspet," in the wooded hills of Cornish, New Hampshire, and the rest of the year on 36th Street in New York City. At "Aspet," which has become the Saint-Gaudens National Historic Site, casts of most of his works are preserved—a fitting memorial to his genius.

(W.C.)

Salmon, Robert (c.1775–c.1844). Marine, ship, and landscape painter. He went to Boston in 1828 as a mature artist, having been active in England and Scotland since 1800. With a studio in "a little hut" near the South Boston wharves, he was known in the town as an eccentric character, but nevertheless became established as a highly successful painter, particularly of ships. His work was largely on panels and in small size, but he also made a large panoramic view of Boston and a drop curtain for the Boston Theater. His rendering of sky, land, and water is free and luminous, while his portrait of a vessel always had the minute detail desired by her owners and crew. His delineation of the figures on board was considered remarkably well done. In 1835, Commodore Isaac Hull commissioned him to do a painting of Hull's capture of a French ship years before, and presented it to the Boston Athenaeum. Salmon's *Boston Harbor from Constitution Wharf* (1829) is at the U.S. Naval Academy. The successful union of historical accuracy with fluent artistic expression has brought him wide representation in museums.

(C.C.S.)

Samaras, Lucas (1936–   ). A versatile artist working in many media but known primarily for sculptured objects that often have fetishistic or fantastic overtones. Born in Macedonia, Greece, Samaras came to the United States in 1948. He studied from 1955–59 at Rutgers University, where he worked with both Allan Kaprow, the originator of "happenings,"* and George Segal.* Later, he studied in Columbia University's graduate program in art history. His early development was strongly influenced by encounters with artists working in unorthodox forms and media, such as Kaprow and Claes Oldenburg.* Both helped him to focus his own extravagant fantasy. Around 1960 he began to experiment with assembled objects, often enclosed in boxes that were swathed in strips of plaster or adorned with bits of feathers. By 1962, the boxed image took on menacing overtones. Sometimes Samaras covered them with sharp pins or included such objects as scissors, scalpels, and razor blades. He altered their interiors, or made accordion-like inserts, or suggested hidden chambers and mirrors, always producing startling effects. During the late 1960s he made other fantastic objects, among them a group of chairs, oddly balanced, or covered with colored yarn, spangles, and mirrors, revealing an intense interest in the bizarre potential of any familiar object. He has also experimented with photography, which he sometimes incorporates in his objects. Samaras has been included in many group exhibitions and has had more than a dozen one-man exhibitions in the United States. In 1972 Samaras had a retrospective exhibition at the Whitney Museum, New York City. (D.A.)

Samplers.

Formal demonstrations of embroidery stitches applied to letters, numerals, and the depiction of small figures by young girls as proof of their skill at needlework. In colonial America girls added to their samplers over a long period of time, working out their names and birth dates as well as mottos, biblical quotations, and decorative motifs in cross stitch and other more complicated stitchery on a square of linen or muslin. Since samplers were prized as proof of an important domestic accomplishment, but probably also because of their decorative quality, they were often framed. Thus preserved, they have constituted a source of historical and genealogical information in addition to providing an indication of changing tastes in embroidery technique and ornamentation. Eighteenth-century American samplers, like their

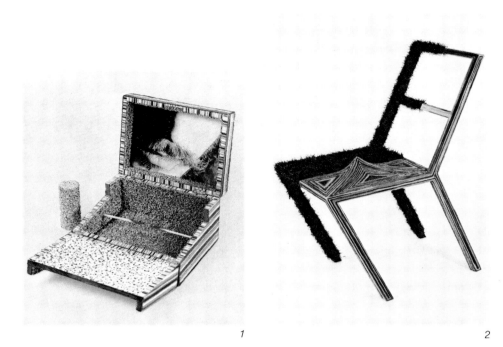

1

2

3

1. **Lucas Samaras.** Box #61, 1967, painted wood, wool, beads, photo, pins. Collection Dr. and Mrs. Martin Falxe, Cambridge, Mass.
2. **Lucas Samaras.** Untitled, 1965, pins, wool and paint on wood. Collection Robert Mayer, Chicago.
3. **Sampler.** Priscollia Nelson, "Sampler Wrought in the 14 Year of her Age," 1837, Index of American Design, National Gallery of Art, Washington, D.C.

Santos
1. *Jesus of Nazareth,* early 19th century.
2. *Mary with the Infant Jesus,* early 19th century.
   Both, Colorado Springs Fine Arts Center.

English prototypes, tended to be very fine, with carefully executed small figures. In the 19th century the technique became coarser and eventually even related to Berlinwork in wool (needlework on canvas of the Victorian era), as in the 1879 sampler made by Angeline Brown in the Valentine Museum, Richmond, Va. Examples of samplers of various 18th- and 19th-century styles are in the Essex Institute, Salem, Mass. (M.J.G.)

Sanderson, Robert (1608–93).
One of the earliest silversmiths working in New England, Sanderson was born in England and received his training from William Rawlins, registering his own mark at Goldsmith's Hall in London in 1635. He came first to Hampton, N.H., and in 1639 became a freeman in Massachusetts, moving to Watertown in 1642. By 1652 he was chosen as the partner of John Hull* to coin the first silver money in the colonies (see Pine Tree Shillings).

In a 1940 catalog of Hull and Sanderson's silver, 25 examples of their joint work and four pieces (three caudle cups and a tankard) marked by Sanderson alone are listed. Working in the late Renaissance style, utilizing chased panel designs and rectangular forms, Sanderson's silver was well wrought and well finished. The earliest tankard known in American silver was made by Sanderson; it is large with a straight-sided body, flat lid with engraved floral decoration, scrolled thumbpiece, widely scrolled handle with shield-shaped ending, and a very narrow base band (Boston). While most of the silver Sanderson made was ultimately presented to churches, he made silver for domestic use as well. (M.G.F.)

Sandwich Glass, see Pressed Glass; and Jarves Deming.

Santos.
Carved and painted saints' figures (more precisely referred to as *bultos*) and paintings of saints (frequently called *retablos*) created along the Rio Grande basin in what is now New Mexico, mainly between 1790 and 1840. Possibly originating as Spanish instructional figures, santos came to be fixtures in the home life of Christian converts, and a small group of itinerant native craftsmen *(santeros)* produced the images that served as central fea-

tures in each household's religious observance. As a fusion of Indian and Spanish traditions, they frequently depict saints with agrarian attributes—San Ysidro with his yoke of oxen, San Rafael the fisherman, and San Francisco with small birds at his feet or perched on his shoulders. Skeletons appear frequently in connection with the Day of the Dead, and the more gory aspects of the Passion are celebrated in connection with Good Friday. The most typical *bultos,* such as the one depicting *San Miguel, Arcangel* (Taylor Museum, Colorado Springs), are crudely carved figures from one to three feet high with gesso coating that smooths the rough surface before pigment is applied. *Retablos* were executed on fabric, leather, or board, again with a gesso undercoat laid down before the bright colors. The variation in size is considerable, ranging from the Taylor Museum's *Santa Veronica,* which is less than one foot high, to the huge *Reredos of the Chapel of Our Lady of Talpa* (from Duran, N.M.), also now in the Taylor Museum collection.

Sargent, Henry (1770–1845).
Painter of portraits, historical scenes, and genre subjects. Son of a prosperous Massachusetts merchant, he was twenty-three when he decided upon a career in art, and went to London for four years to study with Benjamin West at the Royal Academy. On his return to Boston, he took his place in the city as a thoroughly competent painter, but still without any compelling dedication. He pursued a military career, rising to the rank of colonel after the War of 1812. His paintings included a number of large religious subjects reminiscent of West's and a *Landing of the Pilgrims* (c.1813, Pilgrim Hall, Plymouth, Mass.), which added to his local reputation. Today his best-known works are his *Dinner Party* and *Tea Party* (Boston) of about 1820–25. Each is a strictly composed glimpse into the upper-class social life of Boston. They are among the earliest genre paintings in America.

Sargent, John Singer (1856–1925).
Portrait and landscape painter. His internationalism led to his being described as "an American born in Italy, educated in France, who looks like a German, speaks like an Englishman, and paints like a Spaniard." His father, a New England doctor, and his mother,

3. **John Singer Sargent.** Repose, 1911. National Gallery of Art, Washington, D.C. (gift of Curt H. Reisinger).
4. **John Singer Sargent.** The Daughters of Edward Darley Boit, 1882. Museum of Fine Arts, Boston (gift of daughters of E. D. Boit).

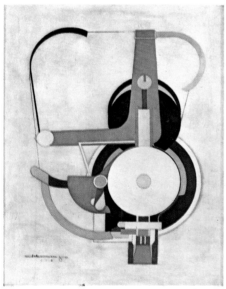

1. **John Singer Sargent.** Madame X, 1884. Metropolitan Museum of Art, N.Y. (Arthur H. Hearn Fund).
2. **Morton Livingston Schamberg.** Machine, 1916. Yale University Art Gallery, New Haven, Conn.

who painted watercolors, spent many years in Europe, often wintering in Florence, where Sargent was born. The boy showed an early interest in art and at fourteen enrolled in the Academia delle Belle Arti in Florence. In 1874 he went to Paris to study with Carolus-Duran. Sargent found his technique of painting directly with the brush, without preliminary drawing, entirely congenial to his temperament. Some of his early paintings suggest influences from another expatriate, James M. Whistler* (whom he had met in 1874), and from Edgar Degas and the impressionists. He quickly mastered an effective pleinair style (see Pleinairism) and his *Oyster Gatherers of Cancale* won an honorable mention at the Paris Salon of 1878.

During the early 1880s his work took on increasing strength and virtuosity. His *Portrait of Mrs. Charles Gifford Dyer* (1880, Chicago) rivals Whistler's work in the sensitivity of its tonality and brushwork. Trips to Spain and Morocco led to the sensational *El Jaleo* (Salon of 1882; Gardner) and *The Daughters of Edward Darley Boit* (1882, Boston), which echoes Velásquez' *Las Meninas.* Although Sargent made his first trip to America only in 1876, he quickly became the most sought after portrait painter in Boston and New York as well as in London. In the Paris Salon of 1884 he displayed one of the strongest and certainly one of the most audacious portraits of his career, *Madame X* (actually Mme. Gautreau; Metropolitan). This incisive characterization of a notorious beauty in décolleté and lavender-powdered skin caused such a scandal that Sargent was forced to shift his permanent studio from Paris to London, and to soften the realism of his portrait style.

The move to England brought Sargent into new circles of friends. He formed the habit of spending summers with Edwin A. Abbey,* and in the company of such other American expatriates as Frank Millet and Henry James. The countryside and gardens inspired studies in pleinairism such as *Carnation, Lily, Lily, Rose* (1886, Tate), a tour-de-force of color, tone and drawing, combining Japanese and impressionist influences. Sargent came even more directly into contact with the impressionist movement: he visited Monet at Giverny, where he sketched the French master and bought one of his paint-ings. Sargent's portraits and particularly his landscapes reflected his contacts with impressionism,* and the influence is clear in his later watercolors, where dancing sunshine, warm half-tones, and blue shadows are conveyed through quick washes and dashing brushstrokes.

Sargent's landscapes and watercolors were those of a compulsive sketcher who traveled and painted constantly during the intervals of a heavy schedule of portrait sittings. For some thirty years he worked assiduously at portraying the British and American upper classes with elegance and flair. He reflected what he saw, and his effects were selective; personality and character were revealed to those who looked carefully. The apparent ease and unhesitating flourish of his brushwork concealed an exacting standard that often required him to scrape out and rework a passage repeatedly before he was satisfied with it.

In the 1890s Sargent was at the peak of his activity, traveling and painting constantly, and winning the highest awards. Particularly demanding was a mural commission for the Boston Public Library, for which he adopted a symbolic style quite foreign to his realistic bent. The murals, which traced the development of religious thought, entailed trips to Egypt, Greece, and Jerusalem and engrossed him for some twenty-six years. When they were finally installed in 1916, they were highly praised, but Sargent's struggle to achieve a solemn monumentality was only partly successful.

By 1897 Sargent was a member of the National Academy of Design, the Royal Academy, and the Legion d'Honneur. He spent ten more years doing portraits, then began to disengage himself so that he could devote more time to landscape. In 1918 he began to serve the Imperial War Museum of London, sketching the troops in France. During his last years he spent more time on murals, carrying out compositions for the Boston Museum and the Widener Library of Harvard University.

At the time of his death, Sargent's reputation still retained much of the glamor that had led the art historian, Samuel Isham, to say in 1905 that Sargent held the position of "the first portrait painter since Reynolds and Gainsborough." By the 1930s a critical reaction had set in, and Sargent was being roundly condemned for superficiality. His exceptional talent has once again been recognized in recent years. He was, as he himself said, a chronicler. Though limiting himself in scope to observed facts and influenced by the socially accepted styles of his times, he stands above the host of his imitators. His pictures are right for what he set out to do, but the freshness and power of his earlier portraits make clear that he had lowered his goals by mid-career.

(D.W.S.)

Satin Glass.
A colored glass, popular from about 1880 to 1910, which had a nonglossy surface, produced by exposure to acid. See Art Glass.

Savage, Edward (1761–1817).
Portrait painter and engraver, born in Princeton, Mass. Little is known about him, but it is thought that he was a self-taught painter; however, he may have studied briefly with Benjamin West.* Savage lived and worked in Boston from 1794 to 1801, and from 1801 on he lived in New York City. His portraits of George and Martha Washington (Boston) and his *The Washington Family* (Washington) are his best-known works.

Savage, Eugene Francis (1883–   ).
Painter, sculptor, and teacher. Born in Indiana, he received his art education at the Corcoran Art School, the Chicago Art Institute, and in Munich. In 1912 he was awarded a fellowship to the American Academy in Rome, where he studied mural painting. He developed a style that was based on an academic, ideal symbolism but incorporated formal stylizations from early Renaissance, archaic Greek, and oriental sources. The result—an eclectic mannerism—brought him great success during the 1920s and into the 1930s. Critics praised his "elevated characteristics" and "great linear authority"; in 1931 the art historian Eugene Neuhaus termed his decorations for the Elks National Memorial Headquarters in Chicago "probably the most important decorative work yet completed in America." Savage taught painting at Yale from 1923–58, and created mural or mosaic decorations for buildings in Hawaii, Indianapolis, Ind., Harrisburg, Pa., Albany, N.Y., and Epinal, France. He continued painting murals and easel paintings well into his

eighties, retaining a style that now appears to belong to the art-deco *mode of the 1920s.

(D.W.S.)

Savery, William (1721–88).
Information about this Quaker craftsman is scant. In the 1740s he set up shop in Second Street, Philadelphia, and had a successful business there for over forty years. Working in the Queen Anne* and Chippendale styles, he made furniture that was simple and of a high quality, appealing to the taste of his fellow Quakers for objects that were "plain, but of the best sort." After a carved lowboy at Van Cortlandt Manor that bore his label was established as the first identified labeled piece of Philadelphia furniture, elaborate pieces of high-style furniture were attributed to his shop. Significantly, however, both of his known labels proclaim that Savery made "Chairs and Joiners Work." His first shop symbol was a chair, which he later changed to a "Chest of Drawers, Coffine, and Chair." Labeled examples of his furniture show that he manufactured mainly chairs. It is probable that, like other furniture makers in Philadelphia, Savery employed a carver to ornament the elaborate pieces bearing his label.

Savery's career warns us that not all simple furniture was country made. We now know that he produced much unsophisticated furniture for John Cadwalader, including six rush bottom chairs in 1770, and two stands painted green and a pine corner cupboard in 1771. In 1775, he made six plain "board bottom chairs" and "a kitchen table with a draw" for the daughter of James Pemberton, and, for Pemberton himself, "a mahogany clock case, scrole head and cullum corners." Obviously a furniture-maker of integrity and skill, he was able to attract numerous customers to his small shop near Market Street.

(C.F.H.)

Schamberg, Morton Livingston
(1882–1918).
Early abstract painter. Born in Philadelphia, Pa., he studied architecture at the University of Pennsylvania (1899–1903). After graduation, he attended the Pennsylvania Academy of the Fine Arts,* where he studied with William Merritt Chase* and met Charles Sheeler,* with whom he shared a studio. Schamberg made a number of trips abroad, the first in 1906, but the most

critical occurred about 1909, when, with Sheeler, he discovered the modern movement in Paris and in 1910–12 came under the spell of Matisse. His style was subsequently influenced by cubism* and the orphism* of the French painter Robert Delaunay. In 1915 his abstractions changed from the plastic and tactile development of color planes to the more linear and analytical study of specific forms. This led to his final phase, in 1916, in which he began to deal with abstracted machine forms in precisionist and dada* idioms. In these last works—watercolors, oils, and a few assemblages—he was the first American to develop the approaches of Marcel Duchamp* (whom he met in New York) and Francis Picabia. His training in architecture, his experience in photography, and his fastidious temperament all prepared him for this work in elegant, mechanical line and carefully arranged flat shapes, as in *Machine* (1916, Yale). He led an active career, exhibiting with the Independent Artists* (1910) and the Armory Show* of 1913, associating with the Alfred Stieglitz* circle at the gallery "291," and fostering the Society of Independent Artists.* His promising career was cut off prematurely when he died in the influenza epidemic of 1918.

(D.W.S.)

Schimmel, Wilhelm (1817–90).
German woodcarver who appeared in the Cumberland Valley of Pennsylvania after the Civil War and tramped through the countryside from farm to farm, often staying at jails or almshouses and meagerly supporting himself by selling his wooden figures for a few pennies. Schimmel's rough carvings of birds and animals and a few human figures were executed mainly as children's toys, but he also made some ornamental carvings for their elders. He died in a Pennsylvania almshouse and was buried in Potter's Field.

Schindler, Rudolph M. (1887–1953).
Architect. Born in Vienna, Austria, he studied architecture and painting at the Imperial Institute of Engineering and the Academy of Fine Arts. In Vienna he was exposed to two pioneers of modern architecture, Otto Wagner and Adolf Loos. Prompted by Loos, he accepted a position in Chicago in 1914 with the firm of Ottenheimer, Stern & Reichert. While with them he designed a number of provocative projects, including the

adobe Martin House in Taos, N.M. (1915). His first major building in the United States was the Buena Shore Club (Chicago, 1917–18); it combines his earlier interest in the work of Wagner and Loos with an intense interest in the designs of Frank Lloyd Wright.* Schindler had originally hoped to work with Wright, and he realized this ambition in 1917, joining Wright at Taliesin and then helping supervise construction of Wright's Hollyhock House (Hollywood, Cal., 1917–20). He set up his own practice in Los Angeles in 1921 and in that year built his Studio House on Kings Road, one of the great innovative buildings of the 1920s. Its walls were slabs of concrete, cast on the ground and then tilted into place. The interior space was grouped around several patio-courtyards to which the rooms were connected by sliding canvas doors. The interior arrangement was also revolutionary—each adult had his own enclosed living space and outdoor garden room. Sleeping porches were provided on the roof, and a common kitchen was to be used on a rotating basis.

Schindler next designed the Lovell Beach House (Newport Beach, Cal. 1922–26), a series of five concrete frames into which, and out of which, the enclosed volume of the house projected. In its use of reinforced concrete and its placement of the house a floor above the beach, this house has aspects in common with the early International style* in Europe, but its complex visual imagery sets it off as only marginally akin to that style. During the late 1920s Schindler cooperated on a number of unrealized projects with Richard J. Neutra.*

Schindler's contribution in the 1930s is his interpretation of the Dutch De Stijl mode of the early 1920s, which consisted of interpenetrating cubes. In his Wolf House (Catalina Island, Cal., 1929), and in three Los Angeles houses, the Elliot (1930), the Buck (1934), and the Rodakiewicz (1937), he interlocked and interpenetrated walls, the volumes and interior space and forms becoming agitated compositions. He further complicated these De Stijl forms by slanting the walls outward and employing shed, gable, and hipped roofs. His designs after 1945 became even more involved and agitated, as he posed a three-dimensional De Stijl composition as a façade

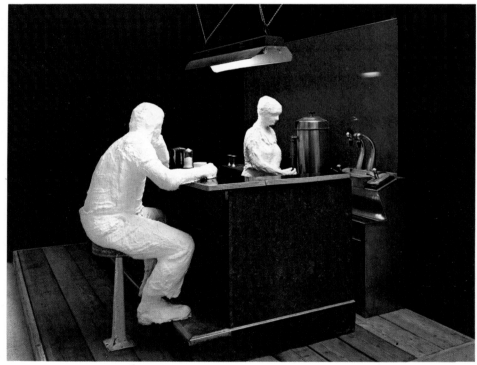

1

2

3

in front of a rectangular volume topped by a high-pitched gable roof of translucent blue fiberglass. His Janson House (Hollywood, 1949) rests precariously on toothpick-like supports.

Schindler wrote that the media for the 20th century architect was space, and this is the unifying theme in all of his buildings. He has remained a controversial figure in architecture. While his buildings were modern, they did not accept all of the major design elements of the International style. Instead of using simple volumes, his designs were highly complex, even employing shed roofs and slanted, angular walls. His interior spaces were never simply horizontal and his spaces thrust outward through projecting volumes and upward and downward by shifts in floor and ceiling levels. His work—like that of Bruce Goff*—was simply too self-conscious as art and too individualistic to fit with ease into any accepted style.

(D.G.)

Schrag, Karl (1912–   ).
Printmaker and painter. A native of Karlsruhe, Germany, Schrag studied art in Geneva and Paris, where he worked with Roger Bissière. After living in Belgium for two years, he moved to New York in 1938 and studied printmaking at the Art Students League. During the 1940s he established his reputation as a printmaker, working at the printmaking studio-shop known as Atelier 17,* with Stanley Hayter and having a one-man exhibition at the Smithsonian Institution. He became director of Atelier 17 in 1950. Primarily concerned with the truths of nature, Schrag develops his themes in a tachist style. His line is both Oriental in its frugality and expressionist in its vigor. Combined with brilliant color, his calligraphic line evokes a turbulent yet excitingly happy view of nature. He has since taught at Brooklyn College and Cooper Union. He has had a retrospective exhibition by the American Federation of Arts and has received a Tamarind* Fellowship.

(R.C.)

Scrimshaw.
Implements and decorative articles made from whalebone and whale ivory by 19th-century sailors. Whales' teeth with incised decoration are particularly prized specimens of this nautical folk art, a good example being the *Sighting Whales* tusk in the collection of the

Mariners Museum in Newport News, Va., in which the incised lines have been filled with colored pigment, in addition to the more common lamp black or tar, to clarify the drawing. Whalers used jackknives, needles, and awls for most such work, and in *Moby Dick* Herman Melville writes of "boxes of dentistical-looking implements, specially intended for the skrimshandering business." Among the objects most often fashioned for ladies ashore were the crimping wheel for pastry-making, typically with a serpentine handle, and the corset busk with sentimental etched patterns. Other popular items were yarn-winding swifts (reels), canes, workboxes, and sewing implements. Good examples of all of these are in the collection of the Whaling Museum, Nantucket, Mass.   (M.J.G.)

Segal, George (1924–   ).
Sculptor. He occupies a unique position in modern American sculpture, having developed a seemingly realistic mode of working during a period when the predominant idioms were abstract. Segal was born in New York, N.Y., where he lived until his sixteenth year, when his family moved to North Brunswick, N.J. He received a B.S. in art education from New York University and an M.F.A. in 1963 from Rutgers University.

He entered his professional career via an artists' cooperative in New York, the Hansa Gallery, exhibiting there in 1958 a group of his expressionist landscape paintings. The following year, he exhibited again, this time including several plaster figures—which were to be the point of departure for his future works. In 1960 Segal placed one of his plaster figures on a real chair and was struck by the tension the junction of the real and the created suggested. From then on, he sought to incorporate significant fragments from the real environment of his sitter, amplifying the context in such a way as to suggest both the habits and emotional attitudes of his subject, and the real obstacles or embellishments of his existence. On occasion Segal has incorporated bulky props such as dining-room tables, a movie marquee, part of a bus, and a complete butcher's counter into his work.

Segal's casting process is direct: he swathes his sitter in cloths that are dipped in industrial plaster and takes

1. **Rudolph M. Schindler,** *The Oliver Residence, Los Angeles, 1933.*
2. **George Segal.** The Diner, *1964-66, plaster, wood, chrome, formica, masonite, fluorescent lamp. Walker Art Center, Minneapolis, Minn.*
3. **George Segal.** Man in a Phone Booth, *1964, plaster and metal. Sidney Janis Gallery, N.Y.*

his impression in sections. It is while assembling the sections that his hand assumes the traditional function of the sculptor, accenting certain areas, blurring others. He avoids the similitude that characterizes the waxwork figure by means of these subtle alterations of the surface. Segal's work has often been cast together with that of pop* artists, although his intention was always to thrust into real space and (as he once said Brancusi did) to populate it with his own creations. Finally, the phantom-like figures he groups in suspended moments of silent communication have little in common with the burlesque or irony implicit in pop art. Rather, Segal works on the psychological plane which led such a predecessor as Degas to use a real tutu in his ballerina's portrait. The recent Segal ensembles emphasize his relationship to the history of expressive sculpture in which the attitudes of the human-scale effigy carried broad connotations.

Segal has participated in nearly all the major international exhibitions, such as the Venice and São Paulo biennials and Documenta. His first museum exhibition was in 1968 in Chicago's Museum of Contemporary Art. In New York he has exhibited regularly since 1965.

(D.A.)

Sekimachi, Kay (1926–   ).
Weaver of soft sculpture. She uses the loom to prepare the elements of her three-dimensional hangings. Born in San Francisco, Cal., she attended the California College of Arts and Crafts in Oakland. After training in graphic arts, she began loom weaving and in 1954 studied under Trude Guermonprez:* her radical development dates from that time. In the late 1960s she wove nylon monofilaments on the loom, and then composed them as transparent interconnected and interacting, free-hanging forms.

Seley, Jason (1919–   ).
Sculptor, noted for his use of welded automobile bumpers. After studying at the Art Students League* in New York with Ossip Zadkine, Seley spent three years teaching sculpture at Le Centre d'Art, Port-au-Prince, Haiti. During this period, 1946–49, he was influenced by the monumental, hollowed forms of the British sculptor Henry Moore. In the 1950s he began to see automobile bumpers as preformed abstractions.

Grouping them together in small configurations, he brought out their figurative connotations with plaster embellishments, casting the results in bronze. In 1961 he began to weld the bumpers, abandoning anthropomorphic effects for a severely abstract, extremely intricate deployment of rounded volume. Seley has said that he does not think of himself as an "automobile" or "junk" sculptor, or as an "assembler." He treats the automobile bumper as a "natural" form with which a modern artist can pursue traditional aims of harmony and balance. He returned to figuration with *Colleoni II* (1969–71), a full-scale rendering of Verrocchio's 15th-century equestrian statue; it employs only bumpers, testifying to the immense variety that he is able to draw from his chosen unit of form. (C.R.)

Serial Art.
In its simplest form, which is the mere reproduction of a popular work, it ranges from copies of antique statues to today's "multiples." In other cases works may be related by a common subject or theme, as in Barnett Newman's* *Stations of the Cross,* Kenneth Noland's* *Targets,* or Andy Warhol's* soup-can pictures. Sometimes all the works in a series are pre-planned and then executed, for example, Frank Stella's* eccentrically shaped canvases (1966). Here three versions of each canvas were produced by painting each "format" in a different color combination. Such series are often related to a market wherein demand exceeds supply, and makes it possible for more people to own highly popular works. Simpler series may progressively alter elements from work to work to note the effect on the original premise, as in John McCracken's* identical fiberglass planks (1966–67), each painted a different color. More complicated are those series conceived as a set. Here each of a fixed number of works satisfies given conditions, with the total number of works conceived as the whole, as in Sol Lewitt's* grid serial projects (1966–68). Younger, more mathematically minded artists employ such concepts as progression, permutation, rotation, reversal, to create works in "sets" or "series." In most cases each work is not complete in itself, but must be seen within the context of the group; sometimes the elements are even interchangeable. Whether an artist

produces the same work in an edition or in different materials (see Tony Smith), or a continuous image over a long period of time (see Paul Feeley), or where the overall structure takes precedence over each individual work, the thrust of serial art is the same: away from the uniquely conceived work of art—the "original," the "masterpiece." It replaces hierarchy with more democratic interrelationships. The works in a series interact and reinforce each other, so that the whole is greater than any part and is the sum of the parts.

(E.C.G.)

Serra, Richard (1939–   ).
Sculptor. Born in San Francisco, Cal., Serra attended the University of California in Berkeley and Santa Barbara. Working with various materials, he explores their qualities in works which, though they are not kinetic, abandon the fixed relationships traditional to sculpture for "provisional, non-fixed, elastic" relationships. In 1967 he set large sheets of vulcanized rubber on edge, allowing the weight of the material to determine the shape of the piece. In the following years he stacked, leaned, and propped heavy steel and lead sheets against walls or on top of each other in works whose "content" was their precarious balance. Other works from this period showed an emphasis on the process of art, as in a series of torn lead sheets scattered on the floor, a row of burning candles in a wooden rack, and tangles of fabric strips hanging from a wall. In 1968 Serra began to splash molten lead against the base of a wall. The first of these works appeared in a New York City gallery exhibition; he repeated it in Bern, Amsterdam, and at the Whitney Museum in the "Anti-Illusion: Procedure/Materials" exhibit in 1969. In the same year he exhibited giant sawed logs at the Pasadena Art Museum in California. He has had one-man shows in Rome, Cologne, and New York, but most of his work is too large for the gallery setting. His piece in the 1971 Whitney Museum Sculpture Annual was a steel ring, twenty-six feet in diameter, set in a pavement in the Bronx, N.Y. Since the late 1960s he has worked on a landscape scale, embedding large sheets of steel in the earth, permitting one corner to remain in view. In the same period he has produced several films investigating questions of process and perception in art. (C.R.)

Seymour, John and **Thomas.**
Cabinetmakers. Accompanied by his family, including a son Thomas (1771–1848), John Seymour (dates unknown), a highly skilled cabinetmaker, arrived in Portland (then called Falmouth), Me., in 1785 from Axminster, England. About 1794 he moved to Boston, setting up shop with Thomas on Creek Lane. In 1804 Thomas opened the Boston Furniture Warehouse, together with his father, and remained active until about 1816. The Seymours worked in a distinctive style, producing some of the most sophisticated furniture of the Federal* period. Characteristics generally associated with the Seymours include: extensive use of light wood veneers (satinwood, maple, or birch); tambour slides, often inlaid with festoons, on desks and sideboards; ivory key escutcheons, sometimes in classic urn pattern; greenish-blue paint on interiors of desks and bookcases; and demi-lune stringing (a line of inlay with repeated half-moon shapes). Many of these characteristics, however, mark other cabinetmaking of the region. Although over 400 pieces have been attributed to the Seymours, less than a half-dozen are labeled or documented. The best known of these is a semi-elliptical Sheraton (see Furniture: Early Federal) commode for which Thomas Seymour in 1809 billed Elizabeth Derby of Salem, Mass. Made of mahogany, satinwood, maple, and rosewood, it has carved floral motifs on its colonettes; brass lion-mask handles and paw-feet; and is decorated with a shell painted on the top by John Penniman.

Two labeled tambour desks have helped furnish a basis for further attributions. One of these (Winterthur), made between 1794 and 1800, is of figured mahogany with inlaid pilasters flanking the drawers, bellflowers in festoons on the doors and in a chain down the front legs, and pierced scroll brackets at the juncture of legs and case. The pulls are Bilston enamel and the keyhole escutcheons are ivory. A second desk of feathered satinwood veneer on mahogany has similar proportions and structure, though less inlay, and bears the same label.   (M.J.B.)

Shahn, Ben (1898–1969).
Painter, born in Kovno, Lithuania. His father had been sent to Siberia for revolutionary activities, but escaped and eventually came to the United

1. **Ben Shahn.** Sacco-Vanzetti *mural (detail), 1967. Syracuse University.*
2. **Ben Shahn.** Miners' Wives, *1948. Philadelphia Museum of Art (gift of Wright S. Ludington).*

States with his family in 1906. Shahn grew up in Brooklyn and began his career as apprentice to a commercial lithographer. He was involved in that trade from 1913–30, and his lifelong fascination with letters and numbers can partially be traced to his experience in designing labels for lithography. From 1919–22 Shahn studied at New York University and the City College of New York. After attending the National Academy of Design,* he went to Europe in 1925 and 1927; there he became acquainted with the work of Cézanne, which had much to do with the powerful simplification and abstraction of forms he ultimately practiced.

Shahn first attracted attention in 1931–32, when he exhibited his first social protest canvases: a sequence of twenty-three gouaches on the theme of the Sacco-Vanzetti case. These were done in an angry, deliberately awkward and primitivistic style, with razor-sharp characterizations. The case had ended in 1927 with the execution of the two philosophical anarchists accused of murdering a Massachusetts paymaster, but it was still a very sore subject in liberal and radical circles. In 1933 Shahn did a similar series on the trial of the San Francisco labor leader Tom Mooney, which had taken place in 1916. All these paintings are in many different collections, for example, one segment of the *Passion of Sacco and Vanzetti* is at the Whitney Museum, but the essential imagery of the Sacco-Vanzetti series is preserved in a large mosaic at Syracuse University executed under the artist's direction.

In 1933 Shahn assisted the Mexican muralist Diego Rivera on his frescoes for Rockefeller Center in New York City; these were later attacked and covered over because of their "radicalism" and their portraits of Russian Communist leaders. He did murals under the WPA Federal Art Project* in the 1930s and '40s, produced posters for the Office of War Information in the 1940s, and was employed by the Farm Security Administration* (1935–38) as a photographer to record the plight of agricultural workers. He was also active in the American Artists Congress, a left-leaning group representing art workers outraged by war and fascism abroad and Depression, poverty, and social injustice at home.

After World War II, Shahn's mood lightened. He rejected the social realism of earlier years in favor of a personal realism dealing with psychological rather than politico-social themes. His style remained, however, one of strong, quasi-abstract simplification, with brilliant color and homage to folk painting in the handling of forms and figures. An example is *Death of a Miner* (1949, Metropolitan). From 1948 on, he took great interest in Hebraic subjects, illustrated the Haggadah, book of the Passover service, and produced paintings and drawings based on the letters of the Hebrew alphabet.

In 1956, Shahn held the Charles Eliot Norton Chair of Poetics at Harvard. His lectures there, summarizing his humanistic, anti-abstract artistic philosophy, were published under the title *The Shape of Content*. A retrospective of his work was held at the Museum of Modern Art in 1947. (A.F.)

Shaker Crafts.
Popular name for the work of the United Believers in Christ's Second Appearing, a communal, celibate order that followed the precepts of Sister Ann Lee (1736–84), its leader in America. Establishment of Shaker communities began in 1787, the first in New Lebanon, N.Y., and by the time of the Civil War approximately 6000 members were assembled in eighteen communities in the Northeastern states, Kentucky, and Ohio. One community, at Sabbathday Lake, Me., has survived the passage of time and the limitations on continuity imposed by celibacy, and still has a handful of aged members.

In creating beautifully simple and utilitarian furniture for community use, as well as for what they called "the world's people," the Shakers became renowned for a remarkable degree of craftsmanship, which extended to their agricultural implements and their other domestic activities. The mass-produced Shaker chair, typically with ladder back and webbed seat, is now the most commonly encountered article of Shaker design and manufacture, but oval, wooden, covered boxes, tables, cupboards, benches, stoves, and chests of drawers are also widely collected and frequently reproduced. Fine examples of Shaker furniture and implements are assembled at the Shaker Museums in Old Chatham, Mass. and Sabbathday Lake, Me., the Shaker Historical Societies at Cleveland and Shaker Heights, Ohio, and Shakertown

at Pleasant Hill in Lexington, Ky.

A half century after Sister Ann's death, inspirational drawings made in several of the communities (notably Mt. Lebanon, N.Y. and Hancock, Mass.) recorded her testimony to the wonders of heaven. The most remarkable of these, as received and transcribed by Hannah Cahoon of the Hancock community, are preserved in the Hancock Shaker Village. While they incorporate some elements like birds, hearts, and stylized flowers that are reminiscent of Pennsylvania Dutch fractur,* the Shaker drawings are unique in their total graphic effect and remarkable for a consistency of style despite their widespread origin and various authorship. (M.J.G.)

Shaped Canvas.
Throughout art history painters have produced nonrectangular paintings such as tondos, altarpieces, and works done in conjunction with architecture, which often must assume odd shapes. In America, Georgia O'Keeffe* adjusted her canvases to her subject matter, as in the long rectangles for her "Canadian Barn" series. Perhaps the first shaped canvas of post-World War II America was Ellsworth Kelly's* *White Relief* (1952–55), which derived its hourglass shape from the arch of a bridge and its reflection in water. And Jasper Johns,* in his "Flag" paintings (1954–58), made the painting an "object" by making the total image congruent with the physical limits of the work. Abstract expressionists such as Barnett Newman* and Mark Rothko* had related their paintings to the shape of the canvas, and by the late 1950s much "pressure" was being put on the external edge of canvases.

In 1959, Frank Stella,* in order to totally identify "subject" and "object" (the painted image along with its support) began to notch out the superfluous parts of his designs. In a series of black and metallic paintings he attempted to reduce "illusionism" to a minimum by allowing the composition to determine the shape of the canvas. Stella is the only major artist who has continuously used the shaped canvas. He worked with L's, T's, U's, V's, triangles, pentagons, hexagons (1963–65), and eccentric shapes (1965–67), developing tensions between depicted shapes and the external shape of the canvas. Later he turned to circles and half-circles in his "Protractor" series.

1

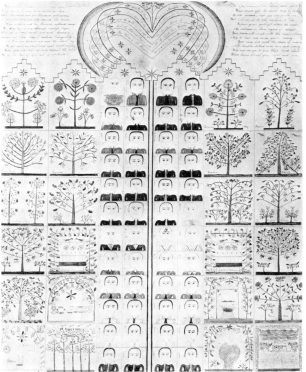

Shaker Crafts
1. *Shaker room in the Henry Francis du Pont Winterthur Museum, Winterthur, Del.*
2. *An Emblem of the Heavenly Sphere, c.1840. Hancock Shaker Village, Pittsfield, Mass.*

2

It was probably Stella who was most responsible for pushing easel painting to the point of "object-sculpture." Ultimately his pictures became so structural, his deep stretchers (the wooden framework) so physical, and his shaped canvases so object-like that it was a simple step for other artists to take their works off the wall and put them on the floor, thus transforming them into "primary structures." (A transitional step was John McCracken's* leaning "planks," which bridge the gap between wall and floor.) Among the other artists who have employed the shaped canvas are Alexander Liberman* in his tondos (1960–63); Barnett Newman in his triangle shape in the late 1960s; Kenneth Noland* in his diamond-shaped canvases (1966); and Ellsworth Kelly in his perspectival "rectangles" (1968).   (E.C.G.)

Shaw, Joshua (c.1777–1860).
English-born landscape painter, art teacher, and inventor. As an orphan, he was apprenticed to a country sign painter. Later he studied painting and drawing on his own, and between 1802 and 1817 he worked in Bath, painting flower pictures, still lifes, portraits, and landscapes. In 1817 Shaw arrived in Philadelphia, making his home there until he moved to Bordentown, New Jersey in 1843. He became a successful painter of landscape, genre, and Indian scenes, and he exhibited widely in the United States. He was well known for *A New and Original Drawing Book* (1819), a manual for artists, and for the landscape sketches which were engraved by John W. Hill* in *Picturesque Views of American Scenery* (1820–21). Shaw's landscapes are finely painted and show a sensitive use of light. However, with the exception of *The Deluge* (c.1813, Metropolitan), which was formerly attributed to Washington Allston,* they seem dry and repetitive. Illness prevented him from doing any painting after 1853.   (T.E.S.)

Sheeler, Charles (1883–1965).
Painter and photographer. Born in Philadelphia, Pa., Sheeler was trained at the Philadelphia School of Industrial Art (1900–03) and at the Pennsylvania Academy of the Fine Arts, where his principal teacher was William Merritt Chase.* Sheeler's earliest paintings rejoice in the bravura brushwork of the

1

2

1. *Charles Sheeler.* Ballardvale, *1946. Addison Gallery of American Art, Phillips Academy, Andover, N.H.*
2. *Isaac Sheffield.* Lady with Birthmark, *c.1835, Museum of American Folk Art, N.Y.*

Chase school, but several trips to Europe from 1904 to 1909 converted him to a more modern point of view, and the paintings he displayed in the Armory Show* of 1913 reveal a strong Cézanne influence.

Sheeler took up photography as a means of support in 1912. At first he specialized in architectural photography, and this doubtless had much to do with the emphasis on architectural themes that was shortly to manifest itself in his painting as well. Over the years, Sheeler did a great deal of independent photography. Several of his photographic portfolios, notably those devoted to the Ford Motor Company plant at River Rouge, Mich. (1927) and to Chartres Cathedral (1929) are landmarks in the history of the art of photography. Sheeler collaborated with Paul Strand* on *Manhatta* (1918), one of the earliest motion pictures devoted to the architectural atmosphere of New York, and one from which Sheeler derived a number of motifs later employed in his painting.

In the 1920s Sheeler's painting heavily emphasized early American handicraft, especially that of the Shakers, and the folk architecture associated with it. His own house in Doylestown, Pa., was a favorite subject at this period. Sharp edges, clearly defined planes, and a general sense of architectonic order related these pictures both to Sheeler's own photography and to the precisionist painting being practiced contemporaneously by such artists as Georgia O'Keeffe* and Charles Demuth.* An example is *Bucks County Barn* (1923, Whitney).

Gradually Sheeler's interest shifted from handicraft and historic Americana to the contemporary industrial scene. Retaining his low-keyed, cubist-inspired color, he took to recording the factories, ships, locomotives, and machines on which American industry was based, as well as the gigantic skyscraper architecture of New York. In the 1940s his color took a very dramatic turn: brilliant reds were counterpointed against equally brilliant blues, and along with this the architectural and industrial forms he continued to celebrate were handled in a far more abstract manner than formerly, often in interpenetrating planes and rays. Many of these paintings used old factory buildings in New England as a theme, as for example *Ballardvale* (1946, Ad-

dison). Brilliant color and abstract, overlapping forms continued to interest Sheeler to the end of his career; in his last years he returned to some of the bucolic subjects of the 1930s, but handled in his new style. Sheeler was awarded many prizes, for both his painting and his photography, and had major retrospective exhibitions at the Museum of Modern Art, New York City (1939), the University of California (1954), and the University of Iowa (1963).   (A.F.)

Sheffield, Isaac (1798–1845).
Itinerant Connecticut portraitist who was born in Guilford and lived in the whaling district of New London from about 1833. Sheffield's identified subjects are mainly sea captains or their wives and children. The subjects sat for miniatures and life-size portraits, in both of which adults are depicted in a three-quarter frontal position as though facing a pendant portrait (although only one pair of pendants is known). A drapery behind the sitter is drawn back —to reveal a sailing ship for the men or a harbor landscape behind the women. Sea captains typically hold large telescopes; their wives wear brooches and elaborate earrings that testify to the flourishing Connecticut whaling industry of the period. Most of Sheffield's sitters have a pensive or introspective expression that is rare in folk portraiture, and in both their clothing and surroundings the artist shows an unusual concern with colorful material and pattern, as in the penguin-skin coat worn by young *James Francis Smith* (1837, Lyman Allyn Museum, New London) or the rich mulberry dress and lace fichu of the so-called *Lady with Birthmark* (Abby Aldrich Rockefeller).   (M.J.G.)

Shingle Style.
A term popularized in the early 1950s by the architectural historian Vincent Scully. It is used to describe houses sheathed in wood shingles and built in the United States from the mid-1870s through the mid-1910s. At the time these houses were generally thought of as offshoots of the Queen Anne* revival, which was popular from the 1870s on. The houses were characterized by low, shingle-covered walls and roofs whose horizontality was accentuated by long bands of windows and often deep, overhanging roofs and wide,

extensive porches and verandas. Externally, these houses gave the feeling of large, almost primitive volumes. The same simplicity and clarity was strongly asserted within. The interior was usually divided into only a few rooms; these flowed into one another through wide openings. The detail of these houses reveals the wide variety of sources on which they drew. Living halls with inglenooks, leaded paned windows, towers and turrets, dormers and bays reveal the essential English background of the style. Equally prominent, as the style developed, were the colonial elements —shuttered windows, paneling, stair railings—all of which look back with nostalgia to 18th-century American architecture. Added to these were touches of the romantic and exotic: screens and wall paneling reminiscent of Japanese architecture; ogive windows and spindled screens echoing the Islamic world of the Near and Middle East.

The originator of the style was Henry Hobson Richardson* and the first building to express fully the style was his Watts Sherman House in Newport, R.I. (1874–76). In its picturesque half-timbering and brick infills it was modeled after the work of the late 19th-century English architect Norman Shaw. By the early 1880s Richardson had simplified his forms even more and clothed the entire structure in wood shingles, the roof and walls flowing into each other. By the mid-1880s the shingle style had reached its maturity; its plan was loose and open, and interior space flowed out-of-doors through numerous doors onto terraces and verandas. Such houses were built from Maine to California, and the chief practitioners of the style were the firm of McKim, Mead & White,* as well as John Calvin Stevens, Bruce Price, Harvey Ellis, and Ernest Coxhead.

At least three modes developed out of the shingle style in the 1890s: full-fledged colonial revival, expressed in numerous country and seaside houses of McKim, Mead & White, the West Coast bungalow tradition as seen in the turn-of-the-century work in California of Charles and Henry Greene; and finally the prairie style of the Midwest led by Frank Lloyd Wright.* Although shingle style country houses were indeed an escape from the pressing urban and social problems of the late 19th century, they may justly be considered America's first major contribution to modern architecture. (D.G.)

Shinn, Everett (1876–1953).
Painter, designer, and illustrator. Youngest member of The Eight,* Shinn, who was born in Woodstown, N.J., showed precocious ability in mechanics and drawing. He went to Philadelphia for mechanical drawing and shop training at the Spring Garden Institute, but in 1893 took a position as illustrator on the Philadelphia *Press* and enrolled at the Pennsylvania Academy of the Fine Arts.* He was associated with George Luks,* William Glackens,* Robert Henri,* and John Sloan* before moving to New York City to work on the *World* and *Herald.* In 1899 he turned to magazine illustration and also prepared drawings of New York scenes for a book by the novelist William Dean Howells, the American realist. Although unpublished, the drawings launched him as a city-life artist (*Herald Square,* 1951, Metropolitan) and led to commissions from *Harper's Weekly,* gallery exhibitions, and sales to private collectors. A trip to Paris in 1901 resulted in close contacts with the theatrical world, and his work extended to scenes of the stage, house decorations, and set designs (*London Hippodrome,* 1902, Chicago). His subject matter having shifted from the bleaker aspects of city life to the world of entertainment, his style, which was always facile, became progressively more nervous and sketchy. Pastels were particularly suited to his temperament, and his work reflected his admiration for Edgar Degas, though lacking the discipline of the latter's pictures.

Shinn showed scenes of the stage and theater at the exhibitions of The Eight* and the Independent Artists,* but his varied interests led him increasingly away from the career of an easel painter, and, unlike other members of The Eight, he did not send work to the Armory Show* in 1913. He painted murals for the Trenton (N.J.) City Hall and the Belasco Theater in New York City, worked as a playwright, and later served as an art director for several motion pictures. (D.W.S.)

Shirlaw, Walter (1838-1909).
Genre, portrait, and mural painter. Scottish born and Munich trained, he was known primarily for picturesque compositions of idealized female

1

3

4

2

5

nudes. He worked as an engraver until 1870, during which time he helped found the Art Institute of Chicago. After studying art in Munich from 1870–77, he exhibited at the National Academy of Design* and was instrumental in the founding of the Society of American Artists* and the Art Students League,* where he was an influential teacher.

Show Figures.
Large wood and metal street sculpture used to identify and advertise 19th-century American business establishments. American show figures derived from 17th- and 18th-century English prototypes, mainly small, polychromed, wooden figures of Black Boys, Indians, and Highland Laddies that signaled the availability of tobacco and snuff. Tobacconists were the primary users of such trade signs,* and Indians served most often as their identifying symbol. The American figures, however, were often life size or close to it, and the wheeled pedestals on which they were customarily mounted made them loom above pedestrian traffic.

Beginning in the 1850s, wholesale dealers in smokers' articles offered to the trade carved figures of Indian Chiefs and Squaws. These were joined by an ever-increasing tribe of Scotsmen, Turks, Punches, Dandies, and Ladies of Fashion, each proffering a symbolic bundle or box of cigars. The same and other figures with suitable identifying attributes were advertised by the same dealers for use by drugstores, clothiers, breweries, tea stores, theaters, banks, and insurance houses. By the 1870s, the New York City firm of William Demuth, which had become the principal national source of supply, was offering a wide variety of cast metal figures as well as the wooden models being produced for them by skilled New York shipcarvers, whose fortunes would otherwise have waned with declining shipbuilding.

It has been estimated that more than 5000 show figures once populated the streets of New York City alone, and expert carvers were producing many additional examples in Baltimore, Boston, Chicago, Detroit, Philadelphia, Providence, and Washington, D.C. Fewer than 400 of their works are known to survive, but the record of their activity has been resurrected by Frederick Fried, and is represented in major

1. *Everett Shinn.* London Hippodrome, 1902. Art Institute of Chicago (Friends of American Art Collection).
2. *Shingle Style House.* Berkeley, Cal., c.1900.
   Show Figures
3. *Cigar store figure of Punch*, 19th century, painted wood. Museum of American Folk Art, N.Y.
4. *Cigar store figure of Pocahontas*, mid-19th century, polychromed wood. Index of American Design, National Gallery of Art, Washington, D.C.
5. *Cigar store figure of seated* Indian, attributed to Charles J. Dodge, c.1858, stained and varnished wood. Long Island Historical Society, Brooklyn, N.Y.

American museums and collections.

The work of these men or, more properly, of their carving shops, varies considerably both in stylistic reference and quality of execution. Simplified, refined, and crisply colored forms like those of a *Racetrack Tout* and a *Lady of Fashion* (both, Abby Aldrich Rockefeller) even inspired the 20th-century sculpture of Elie Nadelman,* who was an early collector and champion of commercial woodcarving. At the opposite end of the field are works like the stained and varnished *Seated Indian* attributed to Charles J. Dodge (Long Island Historical Society, Brooklyn, N.Y.) and Julius Theodore Melchers' portrait figure of Keokuk (New York Hist.), both of which exhibit a remarkable degree of heroic realism that is achieved sculpturally rather than through the use of pigment. Among the collections of wooden show figures that best exemplify their variety are those at the Smithsonian Institution, the Shelburne Museum, and the Henry Ford Museum (Dearborn, Mich.).

(M.J.G.)

Shryock, Gideon (1802–80).
Architect. Born in Lexington, Ky., he learned the building trade from his father and then went to Philadelphia to study for a year with William Strickland,* successful Greek revival* architect. He returned to Kentucky, where most of his work was accomplished. In 1825 he won the design competition for the State Capitol at Frankfort (built 1827–29, now Kentucky State Historical Building). Although his earliest design, it is one of his best, with an exterior Ionic colonnade that is in proportion to the rest of the building, and an interior that has such unusual features as a central staircase with the dynamics of a true stone arch. The dome is handsomely decorated with cornucopias and rosettes. Other buildings by Shryock are the Orlando Brown House, Frankfort (1835); in Louisville, the Jefferson County Courthouse (1838–50), Board of Education Building, Bank of Louisville (1837), Waterworks (1861–67, of metal); in Lexington, Morrison College of Transylvania University (1833); and in Little Rock, Ark., the State Capitol (begun 1835, designed with Weigert). He relied on the builders' books of Minard Lafever* and generally preferred straightforward classical designs. (P.F.N.)

510

Silver.

The hope of finding silver and gold in the New World brought jewelers, refiners, and silversmiths aboard the first ships arriving in America. They found no precious ores, but as the colonists became more prosperous they began to take accumulated coins to the silversmith to be melted down and fashioned into useful and beautiful objects. In the absence of banks, this practice served a double purpose. Silver objects, unlike coins, could be identified in case of loss or theft, and at the same time served as visible evidence of the owner's prestige. It was also natural that the owners should desire their plate (as solid silver objects were called) to be made in the newest style. As a result, American silver kept pace with the major artistic movements in England and represented a fine art in the new country, receiving more patronage and progressing more rapidly than the arts of architecture, painting, and sculpture. American silver closely followed the fashions of English silver. Occasionally, however, Dutch settlers in New York and Huguenot refugees brought some direct continental influence to bear on colonial silver.

By 1650, when the first American silversmiths found encouragement, the late Renaissance tradition was still in vogue in England. With the restoration of Charles II in 1660, a rapid succession of innovations began. American silver in the last half of the 17th century was architectural in nature and rectilinear in form, with objects usually as broad as they were tall. Decoration included paneling, heraldic motifs, and simplified ornamentation. As in architecture and furniture, supporting members were balusters—tapering and swelling supports, shaped with a great deal of variation in girth. Chasing, the process of modeling the surface by hammering a punch and embossing the metal with a design, was one of the chief sources of surface decoration, as was pibling, whereby the surface was granulated. During the last quarter of the 17th century, engraving became sophisticated and the borders of beakers and plates might be engraved with elaborate designs of strapwork, running vines, flowers, and exotic beasts. In New York particularly, the use of elaborate engraved designs can be seen in the work of silversmiths following Dutch tradition. Increasingly

the use of repoussé decoration and gadrooning, ornamental borders of lobing, curved and convex or convex and concave, became more prevalent, as did elaborate cast handles.

In this period spoons were the first and perhaps only silver objects a family might have, but soon silver bowls, salts, cups, beakers, tankards, plates, and porringers were acquired. These objects were fashioned from a solid piece of metal, forged up from a flat disk of silver that was annealed repeatedly to keep the silver malleable. Handles, lids, and moldings were fashioned separately, soldered to the body, and then the piece was polished.

Baroque

At the end of the 17th century, the baroque style appeared in American silver. A bold, contrasting artistic style, it featured massive moving lines of curves and reverse curves, and florid three-dimensional details. In American silver the style was expressed with massive objects of noble proportions decorated with embossing, fluting, and gadrooning. Handles were formed of leafy elements with graduated beading or curvaceous caryatids. Often large areas were left smooth, highly polished and unornamented, in contrast to the richly worked areas of acanthus leafage or gadrooning. Bold finials or thumbpieces accentuated the richness of design. At this period the use of elaborate armorial engraving became more prevalent on plate. Sugar boxes, monteith punch bowls with scalloped rims, candlesticks, inkstands, large covered cups, standing salts, chafing dishes, and chocolate pots were added to the silversmith's repertoire.

Early Rococo

By 1720 the richness and heaviness of the baroque style had begun to give way to greater simplicity, lightness of line, and restrained ornamentation. American silver was modified with an emphasis on contour, plain surfaces, and rhythmic, continuous curves. Objects became basically circular with little surface decoration other than moldings and engraving. Octagonal forms were particularly well suited to the new tenets of taste. Variety was achieved by faceting and engraving. In contrast to the shiny smooth surfaces of the silver, engraving assumed great importance. In addition to decorative borders, engraved cyphers and roundly

Silver

1. *John Hull and Robert Sanderson. Dram cup, mid-17th century. Yale University Art Gallery, New Haven, Conn.*
2. *Jeremiah Dummer. Punch bowl, 1692. Yale University Art Gallery, New Haven, Conn. (Mabel Brady Garvan Collection).*
3. *John Coney. Covered Grace cup, 1701. Fogg Art Museum, Harvard University, Cambridge, Mass.*
4. *Edward Winslow. Sugar Box, c.1702. Henry Francis du Pont Winterthur Museum, Winterthur, Del.*
5. *John Edwards. Child's cup, c.1710. Henry Francis du Pont Winterthur Museum, Winterthur, Del.*
6. *Simeon Soumain. Covered sugar bowl, early 18th century. Yale University Art Gallery, New Haven, Conn. (Mabel Brady Garvan Collection).*

shaped script initials replaced the earlier block letters in the owner's initials.

At this time the effects of the introduction of new beverages into the western world were felt in the silversmith's shop. Teapots, coffeepots, sugar dishes, milk pots, all fashioned in circular, octagonal, or pear-shaped forms—as well as large tea trays, tea caddies, tea tongs, teaspoons, strainer spoons, and strainers—were among the new forms the silversmith was called upon to make. With the growing affluence of the colonists, sets of objects were made, such as casters, salt dishes, snuffers and trays, pairs of sauceboats, and sconces. Personal items such as buckles, buttons, snuffboxes, babies' rattles, and jewelry constituted a large part of the silversmith's production.

Late Rococo

While the emphasis in silver design of the second quarter of the 18th century was on form and line, by 1750 attention had turned to detail and superficial ornamentation. Many of the old basic forms remained or were elaborated into the inverted-pear shape, and were lightened by cast or repoussé naturalistic flowers, leaves, and ruffles, giving a gay and fanciful effect to silver. Outlines and handles that formerly had been simply curved now became doubly curved. C-scrolls in borders became broken C-scrolls. The earlier symmetrical scallop shell was superseded by an asymmetrical shell. Instead of smooth surfaces and engraving, there was a profusion of repoussé decoration, gadrooning, and cast ornamentation, leaving scarcely a spot of surface unembellished. Objects were raised up on curved legs with pad, shell, or claw-and-ball feet. Because of its malleability, silver was well suited to the rich, fully developed rococo style.

Silver tea sets were more abundant in this period and an occasional tea-kettle-on-stand was made. Several cruet stands were produced and such unusual forms as large pierced baskets, a dish ring, candlesticks, and inkstands are known to have been made. During this period many American silversmiths were importing large quantities of English plate for resale in order to augment the output of their own shops, taking advantage of the opportunity to keep abreast of English silver styles. Such imports included knives and forks and other items rarely made in American shops.

Silver

1. Myer Myers. Pierced basket, mid-18th century. Metropolitan Museum of Art, N.Y.
2. Paul Revere. Pitcher, 1806. Paul Revere Life Insurance Company, Worcester, Mass.
3. Paul Revere. Urn, 1800. Museum of Fine Arts, Boston.
4. John Chandler Moore. Tea Kettle, mid-19th century. Metropolitan Museum of Art, N.Y. (gift of Mrs. F. R. Lefferts).
5. Tiffany & Company. Cheese scoop and fish server, Metropolitan Museum of Art, N.Y. (gift of Mrs. D. Chester Noyes).

Neoclassical

After the Revolution, the naturalism and freedom of the rococo style was gradually replaced by order and regularity. The rational approach to design, popularized by Robert Adam in England, manifested itself in American silver in the use of classical oval and urn shapes marked by simplicity, symmetry, and proper proportion. Ornamentation was restrained and was used discreetly. Delicate beading, galleried borders, reeding, and flat acanthus leafage relieved the austerity of the design. Square or oval bases supported by ball feet or curved French feet replaced the rococo circular bases and shell feet. With large areas left smooth, engraving again assumed importance in the decoration of silver, with coats of arms emblazoned in shield-shaped enclosures festooned with floral swags or attenuated script initials within bow-knotted oval medallions. Engraved borders decorated the edges of objects and urn or pineapple finials were added to lids.

During this period Sheffield and Birmingham began exporting their silver-plated wares to the United States, and many American silversmiths both sold and repaired such wares. A few attempted to produce plated silver themselves. It became possible for the American silversmith to purchase rolled sheets of silver from refineries so that he no longer needed to melt down, refine, and forge objects from thick disks of metal. Instead he could more quickly raise the objects from the thinner uniform sheets or else fabricate them by soldering together pieces cut from the flat sheet. While more economical to produce, the result was less individuality from shop to shop. The large complete tea service, often in a fluted design, gained universal appeal in this period, while tea urns, pitchers, sideboard silver, and plateaux were among the newly introduced forms.

Antique

By the early 19th century, as interest in the neoclassic progressed, styles in silver became more strongly stated. Heavier forms of monumental Egyptian, Grecian, and Roman antiquities, popularized by the French during the Napoleonic era, began to appear in American silver. Using a heavier gauge of metal, the silversmith shaped objects in the form of antique urns, vases, and pitchers. An incredible mélange

4

5

of elaborately sculpted cast ornaments appeared, ranging from sphinxlike figures on heavy paw feet to ram's heads and asps. Milled borders of laurel, honeysuckle, or stars, machine-produced by the yard, decorated the edges of objects, and the egg-and-dart moldings of ancient architecture were chased into silver to form lobed borders and bases. The variety and size of silver objects now available was enormous. Whole dinner services were made with graduated sizes of silver plates, platters, and pitchers. Huge silver tureens and towering candelabra were introduced, along with new forms such as toast racks, mustard pots, wine coolers, and vases. Engraving was relegated to small-sized crests and arms, script initials, or presentation inscriptions.

Rococo Revival

By 1840 the antique style had finally begun to exhaust itself. The severity of neoclassicism gave way to romanticism. In silver this meant a return to naturalism and a revival of mid-18th century rococo decoration, and Gothic and naturalistic motifs. The forms ranged from bulky versions of 18th-century and classical shapes to melon shapes and archaic Empire forms. The industrial revolution had changed the making of silver from a handcraft performed in small shops to a factory operation where machines were developed for stamping silver and steam engines were introduced for power. Decoration could be milled or added by machine turning. The rise of the large silver firm coincided with an expanding economy. There was great demand for domestic silver in the rapidly expanding democracy.

Eclecticism

From 1860 to 1900 there was a rapid progression of revival styles. The rococo revival was succeeded in the 1860s by a Louis XVI revival and in the 1870s by Renaissance and Greek revivals. Combinations of different styles were also prevalent, melding Moorish and Persian elements with such disparate motifs as East Indian, Japanese, and Jacobean. Many large presentation pieces were made by American silver companies, often by designers and craftsmen trained in Europe. While these large testimonial pieces and trophies were ornate and were covered with mythological and symbolic figures, domestic plate tended to be angular

Silver

and somewhat simpler. Engraved and chased ornament replaced cast and repoussé decoration. Coinciding with the development of rapid production in industry, silver was characterized more by its economy of manufacture than by the quality of design or execution. With the exception of a few large firms like Gorham and Tiffany, who encouraged artistic designs, most companies turned out silver and plated silver of a motley nature. In addition to endless quantities of tea sets, flatware, and souvenir spoons, there were such new luxuries as silver pickle dishes, jardinières, puff boxes, and manicure sets. By 1900 designers borrowed indiscriminately from Byzantine, Egyptian, Celtic, and New Zealand motifs for the ornamentation of their wares.

Art Nouveau

While Louis Comfort Tiffany is credited with introducing the art nouveau* style to this country at the turn of the century, little silver in this fashion was made by Tiffany & Company.* It was the Gorham Company,* with its Martelé* line, which produced the finest art nouveau silver. In general, design was at a low point in the 1890s with endless copying of past styles and little originality. With its emphasis on creativity and the artist's personal expression, art nouveau was revealed in silver in freeflowing organic lines and undulating curves. The designs were imaginative and fanciful but at the same time based on nature, utilizing flames, waves, and smoke as well as tangled plant forms. One of the most recurrent motifs in art nouveau silver is that of a woman's head with dreaming eyes and flowing tresses. While Reed & Barton* and R. Wallace & Sons also made quantities of art nouveau silver, it was the smaller company like Unger Brothers of Newark or the Mauser Manufacturing Company in New York that took greatest advantage of the movement. Fish sets, claret sets, after-dinner coffee sets, small trays, cigar lighters, dresser wares, and vases were all adapted to the art nouveau expression.

Modern

In the 20th century, American silver has come to be identified with the large firm, although there are isolated examples of the work of individual artist-craftsmen, such as that of Margaret Craver and Fred Fenster. Functional

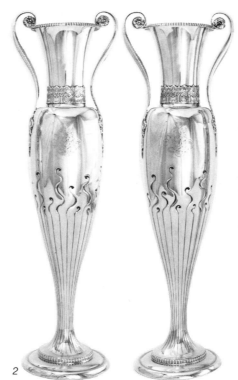

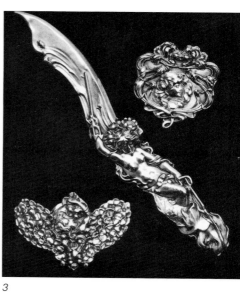

Silver
1. *Gorham Manufacturing Company. Vegetable dish, 1866. Museum of the City of New York (gift of Newcomb Carlton).*
2. *Tiffany & Company. Pair of art nouveau style vases, 1894. Museum of the City of New York.*
3. *Unger Brothers. Art nouveau style letter opener, brooch and belt buckle. Metropolitan Museum of Art, N.Y. (gift of Ronald Skane).*

forms, stripped of superficial ornament, following Georg Jensen's leadership, have dominated silver designs of the post-World War I era. With the emphasis on utility, cutlery has received the greatest attention of designers in the last quarter century. In recent years there has been revived interest in the old handcraft tradition of silversmithing due in large part to the restoration of a silversmith's shop at Colonial Williamsburg, where William de Matteo trains apprentices in time-honored techniques and perpetuates the tradition of the early American silversmith.

(M.G.F.)

Silver Marks.
American silversmiths usually stamped their silver with a maker's mark. The date letters, town marks, and quality marks found in English and European silver do not occur in American silver. However, in the third quarter of the 18th century, certain Philadelphia silversmiths added a scroll mark to the maker's mark and a few New York silversmiths added "NYork" to their touchmark. By 1800, a mark designating the place of manufacture became common, as did the use of pseudo-hallmarks. The earliest maker's marks consisted of the initials of the silversmith enclosed in a heart, shield, or trefoil and sometimes accompanied by a device. Early in the 18th century, an oval or circular enclosure for initials became common and in Boston a few silversmiths began to use a full last name in a conforming enclosure. In the last half of the 18th century, a rectangular mark became prevalent and in the early 19th century this shape was given a serrated edge. By this time full first and last names were given. Prior to 1800 marks generally appeared in relief, whereas after 1800 intaglio marks became more common. It was not until the early 19th century that a mark was added to indicate the quality of the metal. About 1820 silver was stamped COIN, and later C or D (dollar), to indicate that the metal was of the same quality as United States coins. The mark STERLING was used occasionally before 1860 but became common after 1868 when the Gorham Company* changed to the English standard and other companies followed.

(M.G.F.)

Simmons, Franklin (1839–1913).
Expatriate sculptor who was born in Webster, Me., but lived in Rome from 1867 to his death. He had some lessons in modeling from John Adams Jackson* in Boston about 1856 and then established a studio in Lewiston, Me., where he soon achieved recognition for several portrait busts. He remained primarily a portrait sculptor, except for a few ideal figures and memorials. His portrait style was a competent but unexciting naturalism. He worked briefly in Portland and Washington, D.C., where he specialized in busts of prominent officials and military men. After receiving the commission for a statue of Roger Williams for Statuary Hall, he left for Italy in 1867. The *Williams,* dedicated in 1872, was followed by a long series of similar commissions, including a Roger Williams memorial (1873–77, Providence, R.I.), a marble *William King* (1878, Statuary Hall, U.S. Capitol), a bronze *Longfellow* (1885–88, Portland, Me.), and the *Soldiers and Sailors Monument* (1891, Portland, Me.). He left many of his works to the city of Portland. The Portland Museum of Art owns several ideal works, among them a marble *Penelope* (c.1880) which reveals the influence of neoclassicism* on his work of this type.

(W.C.)

Siskind, Aaron (1903–   ).
Photographer and teacher. Born in New York, N.Y., Siskind graduated from the City College and taught English in New York City high schools. In 1932 he joined the New York Film and Photo League and began work on "Tabernacle City," a photographic document of the Camp Meeting Ground area on Martha's Vineyard. After 1936 he organized the Feature Group of the Photo League with the photographers Morris Engel, Jack Manning, Harold Corsini, and others, and spent the next three years with the group, producing such photographic essays as "Harlem Document," "Dead End: The Bowery," "Portrait of a Tenement," and "St. Joseph's House: the Catholic Worker Movement." He also did an independent photo essay, "Most Crowded Block in the World" in 1939. His work was shown in the Museum of Modern Art exhibition "Image of Freedom" in 1941.

The unique aspect of Siskind's photographs, which he developed in 1943–45, is his ability to work his subject matter (decaying walls, New England stone fences, timeworn statuary) into a picture plane that makes no use of traditional photographic perspective. His first one-man exhibition came in 1947 at a New York Gallery. He was also a member of a circle that included such avant-garde painters as Barnett Newman,* Adolf Gottlieb,* and Mark Rothko,* but the influence of these painters was overestimated by critics in the late 1950s. Siskind then took a sabbatical and during a western trip photographed such commonplace objects as weathered signboards, gloves, and walls of tarpaper shacks, composed them in highly subtle and complex images, and printed them beautifully. They have been widely exhibited and published. In 1951, he began teaching at the Institute of Design in Chicago, and was soon directing advanced students in a photographic survey of the architecture of Adler and Sullivan.* Continuing his association with painters, he was the only photographer who participated in the New York City "Ninth Street Show." In 1954 he made "Terrors and Pleasures of Levitation," a remarkable series of photographs of figures that appear to be floating free of gravity, in a dream state. Siskind's understanding of the unique visual aspects of photography, the ambiguity of scale relationships, fine delineation of detail and an almost limitless ability to isolate objects, coupled with his ability to produce quite large prints that retain a beautiful tonal range, have made his work a major influence on photographic esthetics since the mid-1950s.

He became head of the photography department of the Illinois Institute of Technology in 1961. In 1965 he was given a major retrospective exhibition at George Eastman House, Rochester, N.Y., and a one-man show at the Museum of Modern Art in New York City. He received a Guggenheim Fellowship the following year and he joined the faculty of the Rhode Island School of Design in 1971.

(T.F.B.)

Skidmore, Owings & Merrill.
The most influential architectural firm in the United States since 1945. Like the earlier neoclassical firm of McKim, Mead & White,* it has dominated the architectural scene not only through the quantity of its production but, even more, through the quality of its designs. It has major offices in New York, Chicago, and San Francisco. Louis Skidmore (1897–1953) was educated at Massachusetts Institute of Technology, and

Skidmore, Owings & Merrill

1

2

was a fellow at the American Academy in Rome. He was chief of design for the 1933 Chicago World's Fair, and in 1936 he joined with Owings and Merrill to form the present firm. Nathaniel A. Owings (b.1903) received his architectural education at the University of Illinois and Cornell University. He worked with Skidmore on the designs for the 1933 Chicago Fair. Edward A. Merrill (b.1900) attended the University of Minnesota and, like Skidmore, later went to the Massachusetts Institute of Technology.

The pre-World War II work of the firm was competent but not overly distinguished. Their designs reflected the International style,* as in their Little Traverse Hospital (Petosky, Mich., 1938), or in their version of the streamlined moderne,* Westinghouse Singing Tower of Light at the New York World's Fair of 1939. The firm solidly established its preeminence after World War II with its Lever Brothers Building on Park Avenue in New York City, arriving in one stroke at the specific imagery of the academic International style for the steel-framed and metal-sheathed skyscraper.* The designer was Gordon Bunshaft,* who had entered the firm in 1937 and later became chief designer for the New York office. The firm next did the equally successful Manufacturers Hanover Trust Building, New York (1951–52) and the small, handsomely detailed Pepsi-Cola Building on Park Avenue, New York City (1956–59). From the Chicago office, and under the direction of Walter Netsch (b.1920), another design partner, came the Inland Steel Building (1954). From their San Francisco office came such structures as the John Hancock Building (1959) and the Hartford Plaza (1967).

In the mid-1950s the firm won the commission to design the Air Force Academy near Colorado Springs (1956–60). Their solution was blocks of mechanistic, beautifully detailed International style buildings that contrast dramatically with the high-pitched, expressionistic design of the chapel. Like other American architects, they were eventually affected by the vogue of exposed concrete. In contrast to Le Corbusier or Kenzo Tange, the leading exponents of the new brutalism,* their buildings remain restrained. Whether in concrete or steel, the work of the firm during the late 1950s and 1960s became increasingly classical, controlled, and monumental. The Reynolds Metal Building

(Richmond, Va., 1958) was a classical pavilion similar in feeling to the pavilions of Edward Durell Stone.* The Beinecke Rare Book Library at Yale University (1963), with its modular sheathing of semitranslucent marble slabs, verges on the precious and merely opulent. Their imposing Lyndon Johnson Library at the University of Texas (Austin, 1971) is a striking mass situated on a high, dominant podium. These later buildings, with their strongly classical overtones, seem to augur a return to the kind of control evident in the best neoclassical work of McKim, Mead & White, of John Russell Pope, and others. (D.G.)

Skillin, Simeon, Sr. (1716–78).
Woodcarver, and the progenitor of a family of mid-18th-century to early 19th-century woodcarvers. One of the earliest American sculptors to emerge as a historical personality, he was the father of John (1746–1800) and Simeon Skillin, Jr. (1757–1806), both of them woodcarvers from the Boston area. The Skillin workshops were best known for their carvings for ships, especially figureheads; unfortunately no specimen of that work has survived. In fact, no example of the senior Skillin's work is known, but a number of pieces by John and Simeon, Jr., are known. The Skillin brothers evidently produced a considerable number of carved decorations for furniture, as may be seen in the three figures, *Agriculture, Liberty,* and *Plenty,* atop the Badlam Chest (1791) in Yale's Garvan Collection. Another example is the wooden figure of Liberty on the chest-on-chest in the Karolik Collection (1796, Boston). The brothers also produced several larger figures for the garden of Elias Hasket Derby, the wealthy Salem shipowner; one of these figures, *Pomona* (1793), is now in the Peabody Museum, Salem, Mass. The Skillins patterned their work after carvings on ships that called at the ports of Boston and Salem, and their furniture carvings were inspired by 18th-century design books, the most famous of which was Chippendale's. Stylistically, their work was a primitive or provincial version of rococo woodcarving. (W.C.)

Skyscraper, The.
An architectural form that had its first esthetic expression in Chicago and New York in the late 1880s and early 1890s, but whose heyday was the 1920s. For most people it symbolized man's ability to mold his environment and perhaps eventually even create his total environment. Magazines were filled with stories, drawings, and photographs revealing the fascination the skyscraper held for most Americans. The designer who did most to establish this image was Hugh Ferriss.*

The favored style for the skyscraper of the 1920s was Gothic revival,* which had been used as early as 1913 by Cass Gilbert* in his Woolworth Building (New York, 1913), and even more successfully in 1918 by Helmle & Corbett in the Bush Terminal Building in New York City. Awarding the prize in the Chicago *Tribune* Tower (1922–24) competition to the Gothic design of Howell & Hood* established the preeminence of this skyscraper mode. This was reinforced by Eliel Saarinen's* well-publicized second prize design, which was less historic in its reference, but still a Gothic revival design. By the mid-1920s the perpendicular Gothic mode had absorbed a full quota of zigzag moderne* elements. Out of this synthesis came such landmarks as the American Radiator Building (New York, 1924) by Howell & Hood, and the Richfield Building (Los Angeles, 1928) by Morgan, Walls & Clements.

The solidity and monumentality of the neoclassic image cropped up here and there during the 1920s and into the 1930s. Even the authority of Bertram Goodhue* and his skyscraper-dominated Nebraska State Capitol in Lincoln (1916–28) was not able to compete with the light and much more airy verticalism of the Gothic revival or even with zigzag moderne. Among other stylistic images of the 1920s were Miller & Pfleuger's 450 Sutter Street Building (San Francisco, 1930) which was pre-Columbian in flavor, and the Foshay Tower (Minneapolis, 1928) by Magney & Tusler, which, like the Washington Monument, took the form of an Egyptian obelisk. All of the avant-garde architects projected skyscraper designs at this time, but none of these was built. Modern and moderne designs, however, were realized by other designers, as in Howell & Hoods' *Daily News* Building (New York, 1930), which took the Gothic and made a vertical indented shaft of it, while their McGraw-Hill Building (New York, 1931) was moderately committed to the horizontality of the International style.* The two skyscrapers that most caught the public's fancy were the William Van Alen (1883–1954) Chrysler Building (New York City, 1930) in the zigzag moderne* mode and the Empire State Building (New York City, 1931) by Shreve, Lamb & Harmon. The only skyscraper design that was welcomed into the 1932 high-art exhibition of the Museum of Modern Art and was considered modern was Howe & Lescaze's* Philadelphia Savings Fund Building (Philadelphia, 1932), but even it has an admixture of streamlined moderne.*

The only important skyscrapers designed during the 1930s were those of the Rockefeller Center complex (1931–39) by Reinhard & Hofmeister, Corbett, Harrison & MacMurray, and Hood & Foulhoux. These buildings sought a compromise between the stripped verticalism of Howell & Hood's *Daily News* Building and the monumentalism of Bertram Goodhue. Their specific imagery was not so impressive as the utilitarian and visual site-planning of the whole seventeen-acre complex.

A second major revival of the skyscraper took place from 1945 to 1959 in the center of almost every large American city. The imagery was Mies van der Rohe's* version of the International style—the light-steel-frame building sheathed in paper-thin walls of metal and glass. The Lever Brothers Building (New York, 1949) of Skidmore, Owings & Merrill* fixed the style, while the Seagram Building (New York, 1958) of Mies and Philip Johnson* was its most elegant statement. Other significant skyscrapers of the 1950s were Mies's twin-towered, meticulously detailed Lake Shore Apartments (Chicago, 1951), the Equitable Life Insurance Building (Portland, 1948) designed by Pietro Belluschi,* where the glass and the exterior frame were kept precisely on the same plane, and Harrison & Abramowitz's Alcoa Building (Pittsburgh, 1955) with its sheathing of prefabricated bent metal and glass panels. Frank Lloyd Wright* finally built two small skyscrapers that embodied his "organic" trunk-and-branches concept of the 1920s: the Research Tower of the Johnson Wax Company (Racine, Wis., 1951) and his "tower in the prairie"—the Price Tower (Bartlesville, Okla., 1955). Just before his death in 1959 Wright's love-hate affair with the city culminated in his proposed pyramidal Mile High skyscraper city for Chicago.

The "glass box" developed by the academic internationalists of the 1950s

continued to be the most popular form for the skyscraper during the 1960s and early 1970s. Skidmore, Owings & Merrill staunchly continues to create office towers that maintain the high level of their designs of the 1950s. Their 140 Broadway Building (New York, 1967) is more formal in its site plan and composition, but its thin skin covering goes directly back to their Lever House. Throughout the country all of the large and most of the smaller architectural firms have continued to design within this tradition. The best of these "glass boxes" introduced variations on the central theme. The Atlantic-Richfield Building (Los Angeles, 1970–72) of Albert Martin & Associates was divided into two identical towers with a plaza between; the Bank of America Building (San Francisco, 1970) of Wurster,* Bernardi & Emmons; and Skidmore, Owings & Merrill, has a metal and glass skin that has been angled in and out to form the traditional San Francisco bay window; and the Ford Foundation Building (New York, 1968) of Roche,* Dinkeloo & Associates is a traditional "glass box" set between heavy vertical piers and cut away at one corner to provide for an enclosed garden.

Increasingly during the 1960s reenforced concrete came into use for the frames of American skyscrapers, and coupled with this has been the exposure of the bulky quality of the concrete frame and its rougher surfaces. The source of this approach is the European new brutalists, above all Le Corbusier, and also the work of such Japanese designers as Tange. But the design esthetics of the new brutalism* never caught on in the American skyscrapers; instead, the style has been the classical formalism and delicacy of Edward Durell Stone,* I. M. Pei,* and Minoru Yamasaki.* This formalism, coupled with a concern for mass and ideal shapes and forms, can be seen in the Knights of Columbus Building (New Haven, 1968–71) of Roche, Dinkeloo, & Associates, with its great vertical monolithic drums that support the floors; or in the Kansas City Office Building (Kansas City, Mo., 1971–72) of Louis Kahn,* where pairs of vertical piers placed close to each corner of the building perform a similar function.

The spate of skyscrapers of the early 1970s, exemplified by the twin-towered New York World Trade Center (1964–72) of Minoru Yamasaki, is going up at

2

a moment when for the first time faith in technology and man's ability to solve his urban environmental problems is failing. But with the number of skyscrapers being built or projected, the next decade will surely constitute another important chapter in the history of the building form which most fully expresses 20th-century architecture.

(D.G.)

Sloan, John (1871–1951).
Painter and graphic artist. He was born in Lock Haven, Pa., and raised in Philadelphia. After high school, he worked with a bookseller and as a commercial artist, learning etching in the process. From 1892 until 1903 he worked on the Philadelphia *Inquirer* and the *Press,* doing decorations and illustrations, and eventually full-page puzzle drawings in color. Most of this work was in the flat, decorative poster style popular in the mid-1890s; the puzzles were an art nouveau* elaboration of that style. His poster style was sufficiently innovative and accomplished to attract national attention. Meanwhile, Sloan's development as an artist was furthered by a year's study (1892–93) with Thomas Anshutz* at the Pennsylvania Academy of the Fine Arts,* and by the stimulation of fellow newspaper illustrators who became lifelong friends, notably William Glackens,* George Luks* and Everett Shinn,* whom he joined in meetings at the studio of Robert Henri.*

Sloan's earliest paintings included both city views and figure studies; their style was described as "in darkest Henri." From 1900 on he exhibited in major shows in Philadelphia, New York, Pittsburgh, and Chicago. His works were strong and solid, but reserved in treatment and at first attracted little attention. Meanwhile, he established himself as an etcher. During 1902–05 he did fifty-three etchings of genre scenes for a deluxe edition of the novels of a minor 19th-century French author, Paul de Kock. Moving to New York City in 1904, he was inspired to adapt the style of these illustrations to scenes of city life. The fresh realism of his vignettes of Fifth Avenue and the Tenderloin district was revolutionary, and four etchings of the ten he sent to the American Water Color Society's 1906 exhibition were returned as "too vulgar."

The sense of directly-observed, unvarnished city life that Sloan had captured in his etchings he soon transferred to his oils. The National Academy juries were at best uncertain about and at worst hostile to the realistic style of Sloan and his friends. He and seven associates (The Eight*) staged a show at the Macbeth Gallery in 1908 that brought them to national attention overnight. Sloan in particular exemplified the new realism, and he was henceforth associated with the New York scene depicted in such paintings as *Sixth Avenue and Thirtieth Street* (1907, private collection) and *Election Night, Herald Square* (1907, Rochester). Always a believer in liberal exhibition opportunities for artists, Sloan helped with a number of projects (including the exhibition of The Eight and the Independent Artists* exhibition of 1910) and was president of the Society of Independent Artists,* serving from 1918 until his death.

In 1912 he joined *The Masses,* a socialist magazine, as art editor and produced some of his finest drawings as depictions of the human comedy or as attacks on social injustice, as in *Ludlow, Colorado* (cover for *The Masses,* July, 1914; drawing coll. Dartmouth College). But he always insisted on presenting realism rather than propaganda, and ideological disputes with the magazine's policy caused his resignation in 1916. He later dropped his membership in the Socialist party, though he always retained actively liberal sympathies.

Following the showing of The Eight, Sloan became increasingly interested in problems of formal organization and in the color system of Hardesty Maratta. In 1914–18 Sloan summered in Gloucester, Mass., painting canvases in which there were reflections of the expressionism of van Gogh and, later, the structural qualities of Cézanne. Beginning in 1919, he spent his summers in Santa Fe, where he became deeply interested in survivals of Indian and Spanish culture and in the landscape.

His paintings of the mid-1920s—landscapes, figure subjects, and nudes—are firmly realized but do not further the abstract devices discernible in some of his work of 1917–22, such as *The City from Greenwich Village* (1922, Washington). Becoming progressively more dissatisfied with representing visual or surface reality, he entered in 1929 a decade of sustained work from the nude during which he developed a

Skyscraper
1. *Midtown Manhattan, 1964.*
2. *Harrison & Abramovitz, Alcoa Building, Pittsburgh, 1955.*

highly personal technique and viewpoint. His teaching precepts and concerns are summed up in his *Gist of Art* (1938), in which he stressed using "foreshortening rather than visual perspective in signifying spacial projection and recession; the use of color as a graphic tool; emphasis on realization rather than realism as the essential character of reality in art." To "realize" the form established in his underpainting, Sloan superimposed color-textural glazes, sometimes reinforced with hachure lines. The result was powerfully plastic, as in *Nude and Nine Apples* (1937, Whitney), but the public and critics alike found it difficult to reconcile the realistic figures with the arbitrary hatchings. His final phase was characterized by a more abstract organization of planes, high-keyed colors, and surface textures and brought a new expressiveness to his studies in "realization" (*Model with Red Hand Mirror*, 1950, private collection). The Whitney Museum presented a retrospective exhibition of his work in 1952.

Sloan had a gift for telling images and phrases—blunt, incisive, and sometimes witty, or biting. His impact on the art scene came not only through his art but also through his quick tongue, dedication to causes, leadership of organizations, and popularity as a teacher. His assocation with the Art Students League lasted from 1916 to 1938. In their very diversity his students reflect his encouragement of individuality: Alexander Calder,* David Smith,* Reginald Marsh,* Lee Gatch,* Adolph Gottlieb,* and Barnett Newman.*   (D.W.S.)

Sloan, Samuel (1815–84).
Architect. Born in Chester County, Pa., he first appears about 1833 as a carpenter at Philadelphia's Eastern State Penitentiary, then being built by John Haviland.* Sometime between 1836–41 he was a foreman at the Pennsylvania Hospital for the Insane, built by Isaac Holden. His first independent design was the courthouse and jail in Media, Pa. (1849). During the 1850s, he was flooded with commissions, building more than eighty residences, four jails, six civic buildings, eighteen public schools, several private schools, five hospitals for the insane, thirteen Protestant churches, and at least fifteen commercial buildings. A model of eclecticism,* Sloan designed in many styles, including Gothic, Georgian, Tu-

1

1. *John Smibert.* The Bermuda Group, *1729. Yale University Art Gallery, New Haven, Conn. (gift of Isaac Lothrop).*
2. *John Sloan.* The City from Greenwich Village, *1922. National Gallery of Art, Washington, D.C. (gift of Helen Farr Sloan).*
3. *John Sloan.* Nude and Nine Apples, *1937. Whitney Museum of American Art, N.Y.*

2

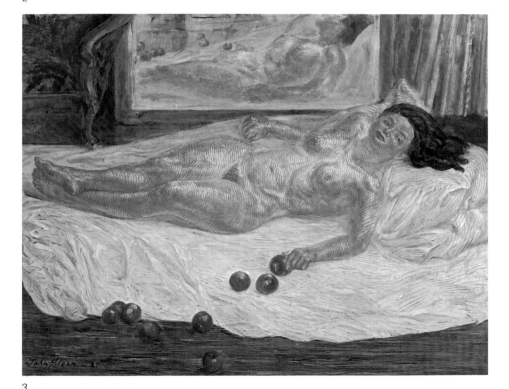

3

dor-Renaissance, Oriental, and Italianate Romanesque. When sufficient money was available, his designs were often splendid, picturesque, and exciting; but he also did a number of schools and houses that are quite uninspired. From 1852–57 he was in partnership with Thomas S. Stewart. In 1864, he took Addison Hutton as a partner, gave up almost all residential work, and concentrated on hospitals, churches, and commercial buildings, but still without keeping to any one style. He moved to Raleigh, N.C., in 1874, but only half a dozen projects are assignable to his last years.

In the Philadelphia area, Sloan's influence was enormous not only because of the many buildings he designed but also due to the number of books and articles he wrote. His first book, *The Model Architect* (1852), was the most successful, his picturesque designs suiting public taste perfectly. He also wrote *City and Suburban Architecture* (1859); *Sloan's Constructive Architecture* (1859); and *American Houses* (1861). His short-lived *Architectural Review and American Builder's Journal* (1868–69) was the first American journal devoted entirely to architecture. (P.F.N.)

Smibert, John (1688–1751).
Portrait and landscape painter. A thrifty, ambitious, and adventurous Scot, he served out an apprenticeship with an Edinburgh house painter, traveling to London at the age of twenty to seek his fortune. There he worked as coach painter and painter's assistant, and attended a drawing school. In 1717, he traveled to Italy, where he matured his portrait style, found ample employment, and filled his studio with copies of subject pieces that would come with him to America. After a period of successful portrait painting in London, 1722–28, Smibert sailed for Newport, R.I., in 1729.

He moved to Boston in 1730 and married well, thereby acquiring social prestige and the best patronage of any artist in the colony. Later, he opened a shop dealing in artists' materials and fine engravings, and organized the first art exhibition held in America. Smibert was the architect of Boston's well-known Faneuil Hall, 1742. Famous, too, was the exhibition of Old Master copies, sculpture, and original landscapes in his studio above the shop, which re-

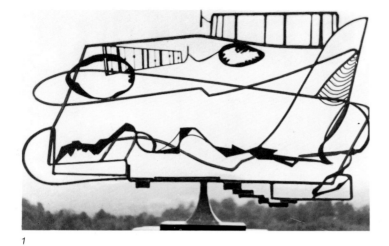

1

3

2

4

David Smith
1. Hudson River Landscape, *1951, steel.*
2. Zig II, *1961, steel painted.*
3. Cubi XIX, *1964;* Cubi XVII, *1963;* Cubi XVIII, *1964, all stainless steel.*
4. Bec-Dida Day, *1963, steel painted.*
All, courtesy David Smith Estate and Archives of American Art, Smithsonian Institution, Washington, D.C.

mained an influence on other American artists long after his death.

Smibert's most famous painting, *The Bermuda Group* (1729, Yale), contains a self-portrait (at left), of the artist gazing out upon the spectator. Smibert's portraits are in general solid likenesses in the dignified baroque style, with less sensitivity in characterization than one finds in those of the younger Robert Feke.* As with other immigrant artists, his style became simpler and more direct in response to the less demanding taste of his American patrons. Late in life, when failing eyesight impeded his work, he turned again to landscape which he had always loved. The standard of excellence in his work was unprecedented in colonial America, although by European standards it was imitative of the academic traditions of Sir Godfrey Kneller and the Italian Old Masters.   (C.C.S.)

Smith, David (1906–65).

Sculptor. Born in Decatur, Ind., he attended Ohio University (1924), Notre Dame (1925), and George Washington University (1926). In 1926 he moved to New York City to study painting at the Art Students League* with John Sloan* and Jan Matulka. The latter taught him the rudiments of cubism* and constructivism,* and Smith was further exposed to abstract art through his friendships with the painters Stuart Davis* and Jean Xceron, and the surrealist painter-art dealer John Graham.* Although he continued to paint through the early 1930s, the transition to sculpture was inevitable. He notes that his impasto became thicker and thicker. Finally, "the painting developed into raised levels from the canvas. Gradually the canvas was the base and the painting was a sculpture . . ." Smith had also begun to attach "found" and shaped wooden objects to the surfaces of his paintings, and in 1931 he produced his first free-standing painted wooden constructions. Two years later, after seeing reproductions of Gonzalez' and Picasso's iron constructions he borrowed welding tools and began working in forged iron. His first metal sculpture was a small Picassoid *Head* (1933), made of scrap iron and boiler plate which he annealed, cut into shapes, and welded together.

As a young man Smith had worked as a riveter on the assembly line of an automobile plant, and his instincts in sculpture led toward the solid craftsmanship of heavy industry, no matter how delicate his work might seem. Thus he found a perfect studio for himself at the Terminal Iron Works, a shipfitting establishment in Brooklyn, and with compulsive energy began to produce small abstract metal sculptures. Smith's earliest works show no faltering or indecision; each composition is a little masterpiece of forms in space—complex, yet economical; small in size, yet monumental. In 1935–36 the artist traveled through Europe, the Middle East, and Russia. In Greece he experimented with bronze castings, and on his return he began a series of fifteen bronze *Medals of Dishonor* (1937–40). Partially inspired by glyptic art and cylinder seals, these bas-relief medallions were more related to social-realist painting than to his earlier abstract sculptures, and won him a reputation as a "social surrealist." This attack on war and social injustice gave Smith's work a expressionistic force long after he had abandoned distinct figurative imagery.

His first one-man show was held in 1938, and during these years he also worked on the WPA Federal Art Project.* In 1940 he moved to Bolton Landing, N.Y., a village near Lake George, where he set up his studio as a machine shop and "factory" for making sculpture. Smith's love of technology is well documented. He once wrote: "The equipment I use, my supply of material comes from factory study, and duplicates as nearly as possible the production equipment used in making a locomotive. . . . What associations the metal possesses are those of this century: power, structure, movement, progress, suspension, destruction, brutality." Unfortunately he produced little sculpture during the next five years. At the outbreak of World War II he became a welder of army tanks in a defense plant. The sculpture he did produce during the last half of the 1940s struck out in many directions. One series of expressionist-surrealist "Interiors" seems directly based on Giacometti's *The Palace at 4 A.M.* Other works, such as *Cello Player* (1946), seem more inspired by cubism; while a whole group of "primitive," fetishistic objects, such as *Pillar of Sunday,* employ central vertical cores to which all manner of objects are appended. These forms are often imbued with literary, organic, symbolic, and even ritualistic meanings. Perhaps most significant for his future development, however, were the open, welded steel constructions that were frequently as two-dimensional as a painting and as linear as a drawing. The rhythmic silhouettes of such works as *The Royal Bird* (1948) and *Hudson River Landscape* (1951) are related to the "automatic writing" of surrealism* and Jackson Pollock's* lyrical line. During the 1950s Smith's method of "drawing in space" with forged metal became increasingly spontaneous. Never before had "sculpture" been so open, or so meant to be seen from a single, frontal view. He also began to conceive his images in related series. Both the "Agricola" and the "Tank Totem" series were based on the human figure, seen in varying degrees of abstraction. Most of these works were vertical, about seven feet high, and many incorporated "found objects." In 1955–56 Smith produced even more remarkable "Verticals"—some of them simply two-inch steel bars, inflected at certain points to provide rhythmic relationships. These minimal* works were untypical, however, and during the 1960s his work moved toward greater complexity. The "Voltri-Bolton" series reinterpreted the human figure in the flat planes of cubism. The "Zig" series continued the move toward geometry—a development paralleled by the new hard-edge* painting. Many of these assemblages of flat, cutout shapes were overly fanciful and painted in bright colors. Although overcomplicated and synthetic, with an undue emphasis on surface, they influenced many lesser talents. Smith's last series, the "Cubi," returned to three-dimensional volume, but he retained the emphasis on surface by scoring the sides of his stainless-steel units. Thoroughly abstract, these are perhaps his most architectonic and carefully composed works.

Smith was one of the most influential and prolific sculptors of the 20th century. He combined the qualities of the major European artists Picasso, Giacometti, and Gonzalez with an American freshness of vision. He carried the formal ideas of such European concepts as constructivism, surrealism, and cubism to new heights. If his sculpture suffers from pictorialism it nevertheless injects into pictorial sculpture a sense of hardness, a reality of the materials, which was denied in the re-

finements of European art and in the work of his many followers everywhere. Smith was basically a formalist who managed to unite romanticism and technology in a kind of heroic sculpture that paralleled the heroic painting of abstract expressionism.* His work has been widely collected and has been shown in major exhibitions throughout the world, including the São Paulo Biennial (1951 and 1959), the Venice Biennial (1954 and 1958), the Brussels World's Fair (1958), and the Kassel Documenta (1959 and 1964).   (E.C.G.)

Smith, Robert (c.1722–77).
Builder-architect, probably born in Glasgow, Scotland, of Quaker parents. He was soon brought to America, but there is no record of him until he became a carpenter in Philadelphia about 1750. In 1754 he built Nassau Hall, the first large structure for Princeton University (then College of New Jersey). He also designed the president's house, a rather modest 18th-century colonial building.

By the time Smith designed St. Peter's Church, Philadelphia (1758–61), he was called architect. This simple, rectangular building relied for effect on the window and door ornaments, about which Smith learned in architectural books such as Langley's *Builder's Treasury* and Palladio's *Four Books on Architecture*. His Zion Lutheran Church (1766–69, demolished 1869) was more imposing than St. Peter's because of the giant-size brick pilasters surrounding it, but it is similar in decoration. For the Carpenters' Company, Smith designed a graceful hall (1770–75) that still stands. The Walnut Street Jail (1773–76, demolished c.1835) looked like Princeton's Nassau Hall; it became notorious when cells for solitary confinement were added to it.

During the American Revolution, Smith served on a committee of Philadelphia mechanics in support of the embattled citizens of Boston. In 1775 he designed a channel block in the Delaware River near Fort Mifflin to obstruct English shipping and communications, and a similar device for Billingsport, N.J., in 1776. His architectural practice was undoubtedly considerably larger than the records show.
                                              (P.F.N.)

Smith, Thomas (active c.1650–85).
Portrait painter. On June 2, 1680.

"Major Thomas Smith" received payment for a portrait painted for Harvard College. That entry and his remarkable *Self-portrait* (Worcester) alone document one of the most tantalizing mysteries of the founding years of American art. A portrait of his daughter also descended with his in family ownership, and a small group of others has been attributed to him on the basis of style. Studies of the *Self-portrait* by Louisa Dresser and Waldron P. Belknap suggest a career in Cromwell's army, service with Blake's fleet in the Mediterranean, and possible connections with the sinister Sir George Downing, chief of Cromwell's spies. A portrait of Downing (Harvard University) has been attributed to Smith, and a Thomas Smith is mentioned in Downing's will. The *Self-portrait* (c.1690), a meticulous old-age summary of the artist's life, shows a naval battle with ships assailing a fort, while the artist holds a skull under one hand, and under it a poem of his own composition.   (C.C.S.)

Smith, Tony (1912–   ).
Sculptor and designer of environments. Born in South Orange, N.J., the son of a wealthy manufacturer, he attended the Art Students League* in 1931, went briefly to Georgetown University in Washington, D.C., and then in 1933–36 studied drawing and painting at the League at night while working as a toolmaker and draftsman. In 1937 he entered the New Bauhaus in Chicago, intent on becoming an architect, but, disappointed in his progress, soon withdrew. He got a job as a laborer on Frank Lloyd Wright's* "Ardmore Experiment" (1938–39), ultimately becoming clerk-of-the-works for this project and several residences, and working on drawings and estimates for forty of Wright's homes. During the next twenty years Smith designed and built about two dozen residences. He also became one of the most influential teachers of art: at New York University (1946–50), Cooper Union (1950–53), Pratt Institute (1950–53 and 1957–58), Bennington College (1958–61), and Hunter College (1962–   ). His students have included Robert Goodnough,* Larry Rivers,* Alfred Leslie,* and Patricia Johanson.* During the 1940s and '50s he was closely associated with such avant-garde artists as Jackson Pollock,* Clyfford Still.* Mark Rothko,* and Barnett Newman.*

1. **Tony Smith.** Smoke *(Installation at the Corcoran Gallery of Art, Washington, D.C.), 1967, plywood. Fischbach Gallery, N.Y.*
2. **Tony Smith.** Free Ride, *1962. Fischbach Gallery, N.Y.*

Smith notes that he has "always" painted and made sculpture, and that he has long thought of his work as a private pursuit and purely experimental. He considers an interlude in Germany (1953–55) particularly fruitful: he worked on small sculpture-constructions and modular drawings and paintings based on circles and "peanut" shapes. Because of his background in architecture, he is well versed in mathematics and modular systems of building. By 1960, weary of the capriciousness of clients, he intensified his sculptural explorations, making many maquettes for sculptures that were to be manufactured. Among his earliest and simplest pieces are *The Black Box, Die,* and *Free Ride,* all fabricated in steel in 1962. The first was modeled after an ordinary card-file box. Smith has always been fascinated by containers, and the mystery of what may be in the box gives it a surrealist undertone. *Die,* a six-foot cube, is both surrealistic and startlingly real. Neither object nor monument, it becomes a module for the space around it, while achieving powerful presence through its sheer existence. *Free Ride,* the third of Smith's classical and elemental propositions about form, articulated the three axes—height, width, and depth—of the cube. He had also begun to work with more complicated geometric modules: tetrahedra and octahedra. By combining these units, whole or "sliced," Smith produced a wide range of personal statements. These pieces, he says, "almost come into existence by some kind of spontaneous generation." Each modular system produces a different order of forms, and because the basic units have so many axes, the forms move in unexpected ways. They are "difficult to draw," so Smith works directly from models. *Cigarette* (1961) and *Spitball* (1961), the former an open arch, the latter a compact triangular "pyramid," indicate the range of possibilities.

Although Smith has often been classified with the minimal* sculptors, his involvement with modular design goes back to his youth. Among his influences he lists Jay Hambidge's book on *Dynamic Symmetry,* D'Arcy Thompson's *On Growth and Form,* the Japanese tatami mat system, and Alexander Graham Bell's tetrahedral tower and kites. Regularity combined with flexibility gives the organic world its multifarious forms, and it is precisely this that Smith achieves in his later experiments with three-dimensional close-packing and space-frames. His work also represents a return to the plasticity of traditional sculpture. He has reunited structure and form in powerful statements of monumentality and mass that the "pictorial" sculptors and constructivists only vaguely understand.

At first Smith's work was seen only by a few friends. In 1964 a single piece was exhibited at the Wadsworth Athenaeum in Hartford, Conn., followed by large one-man shows at that institution and in Philadelphia in 1966. It would be hard to overestimate the impact of Smith's massive plywood structures painted with a black automotive undercoat—all mock-ups for sculpture to be executed in steel. Their sheer size—they ranged up to 15 feet high by 26 feet wide by 18 feet deep—and the fact that many were placed outdoors, gave to American sculpture a new sense of scale and a new interest in the environment. Smith's pieces are always an experience. They sometimes act as landmarks; sometimes create the environment by their presence; sometimes form part of a spatial continuum, as positive elements interlocked with the structured world from which they are derived.

Since 1967 Smith has developed the implications of his work and added a host of new ideas. *Stinger* (1967), a rhomboidal "wall" 32 feet on a side, becomes a square "courtyard" that envelops the viewer once he has entered it. *The Wandering Rocks* (1967) are smaller pieces, each having its own identity but also constituting a group. Because there are no fixed spatial relationships, the "rocks" are different every time they are shown. In *Smoke* (1967), Smith articulated the atrium of the Corcoran Gallery in Washington, D.C., with a dramatic space-lattice, 22 feet high by 50 feet long. Other collaborations between sculpture and architecture include his *Bat Cave*, exhibited at the World's Fair in Osaka, Japan (1971); here thousands of corrugated cardboard components were taped together to form an immense, gloomy "cave" pierced by shafts of light. With its emphasis on internal space and its disregard of volume, it is his most "environmental" work to date. Each of Smith's pieces has a logic of its own; each is a different expression of

his imagination, and he thus achieves a wide range of emotional impacts and meanings. Unlike the literalists, his work transcends its own mere physicality. His sculpture cannot be reduced to the pictorial or the decorative. Rather, by returning to the most elemental forms and then showing how they could be extended, Smith has turned the tide in 20th-century sculpture, reuniting structure, form, scale, and meaning in a wholeness unrealized before in abstract sculpture. (E.C.G.)

Smith, W. Eugene (1919–).
Photographer, born in Wichita, Kan. In high school he became interested in photography and at seventeen began to photograph for local newspapers. He entered the University of Notre Dame on a photography scholarship but remained only a year before joining the staff of *Newsweek*. He was dismissed when he insisted on using a miniature (35 mm) camera because it gave him greater freedom than the large-format press camera. Using a miniature camera, frequently with multiple flash, he free-lanced and had his work reproduced in *Life, Colliers, American Magazine, Harper's Bazaar,* and *The New York Times.* In 1939 he joined *Life* magazine, but was dissatisfied with his assignments and resigned to free-lance again. During World War II he was a photographer in the Atlantic theater and the Pacific Islands campaigns. In 1944 he rejoined *Life* and covered the Saipan, Guam, and Iwo Jima invasions. His best war photographs caught the effect of the war on individuals and portrayed the agonies of the wounded and the despair experienced in the presence of death. He was wounded seriously in Okinawa. After two years of convalescence, Smith began a series of photo essays for *Life,* the most notable being "Folk Singers" (1947), "Trial by Jury" (1948), "Country Doctor" (1948), "Spanish Village" (1951), and "Nurse Midwife" (1951). Using a simple narrative form, the photographs in these essays involve us intimately in the everyday life of his subjects; he adds poignancy with touches of sentimentality.

In 1954 he again resigned from *Life.* During 1955–58 he was a member of Magnum Photos, a cooperative photojournalist picture agency. Guggenheim fellowships in 1956 and 1957 helped him carry forward a large-scale essay on Pittsburgh, thirty-eight pages of

which appeared in the 1959 *Photography Annual.* Smith's most extensive treatment of a single theme, it deals in humanistic terms with the people of the city and the impact on them of their environment. In 1957 he used his loft-studio in New York City in a series of pictures published by *Life* as "Drama Beneath a City Window." Despite poor health and financial difficulties, he began teaching photography at the New School for Social Research in 1958; and in the 1960s he participated in conferences ranging from the University of Oregon to the Rochester Institute of Technology. Exhibitions of his work were held at George Eastman House, the Museum of Modern Art, Expo '67 in Montreal, and in Germany at "Photokina." He spent 1961 in Japan on an essay on Japanese life commissioned by the large manufacturing firm of Hitachi Limited. Since then he has taught and photographed in New York City. In 1971 he was given a retrospective exhibition at the Jewish Museum, New York City.

Smith has exercised a great influence on young photographers drawn to photojournalism. His dedication to the concept of honest reporting and his insistence on the responsibility of photojournalists to have a distinct viewpoint has made him almost a living legend. He has a romantic side, which is conveyed in most of his work by concentrating on moments of pathos and a dramatic use of picturesque extremes of light and dark. By skilled use of side illumination, both natural and flash, and finishing techniques that artificially evoke the sense of light in dark areas, he has made deeply affecting photographs of a wide variety of subjects. (V.D.C.)

Smither, James (active 1768–97).
Philadelphia engraver. His prints include many book and magazine illustrations, among them small portraits, maps, and plates of machinery. He also engraved certificates, bookplates, and a large map of Philadelphia, published in 1786, which includes views of various buildings. Suspected of treason, he fled Philadelphia in 1778.

Smithson, Robert (1938–).
Born in Passaic, N.J., he studied at the Art Students League* in New York. One of his earliest works, *Enantiomorphic Chambers* (1965), consisted of two boxlike steel frames containing mirrors. The title refers to mirror-image pairs,

as for example the right and left hands, and Smithson's continued interest in reflected "pairs" can be seen in *Doubles* (1966) and in his mirror works in Yucatán (1969), where various groupings of small mirrors literally reflect nature. In his first one-man show (1966) he seemed more concerned with "serial" imagery, repetition, mathematical progression, and perspective: *Alogon #2* and *Plunge* consist of ten units each—each unit one-half inch smaller than the preceding one, giving a telescoped effect that suggests infinite extension in time and space. At this point his main influences were mathematical and minimal;* however, he was moving toward a more radical involvement with "mind and matter."

Smithson's nonformal approach to art is documented in articles that have appeared almost semiannually since 1966. In poetic terms he presents some of the most avant-garde ideas about art: "The most beautiful world is like a heap of rubble tossed down in confusion" (anti-form); and "A great artist can make art by simply casting a glance . . . but the society continues to cheat the artist . . . by only valuing 'art objects' . . . (thus) defrauding the work and mind of the artist . . ." (a prophecy of concept art*). Elsewhere Smithson speaks of "the primary process of making contact with matter" and "the dislocation of craft and fall of the studio." As early as 1966 he had proposed a *Tar Pool and Gravel Pit*—a square sink of tar surrounded by a square sink of gravel—and in 1968 he began a series of "sites" and "non-sites," displaying photographs of various quarries next to metal containers filled with specimens of rock from each location. These works tended to make explicit the distinction between gallery exhibitions and "raw matter in its original unbounded state." Smithson is considered one of the founders of the earthworks movement (see Earth Art); however, in *Spiral Jetty* (1970) he achieves a monumentality that transcends the work of most of that group. Here a spiral "road," fifteen feet wide, made of rocks and debris, has been built into the Great Salt Lake, Utah. Fashioned after the tail of the Great Serpent Mound in Ohio, it is typical of this artist in evoking past ages. In 1971 Smithson created a *Spiral Hill*—a conical mound with a "road" winding up to the top—near Emmen, Holland. A companion piece,

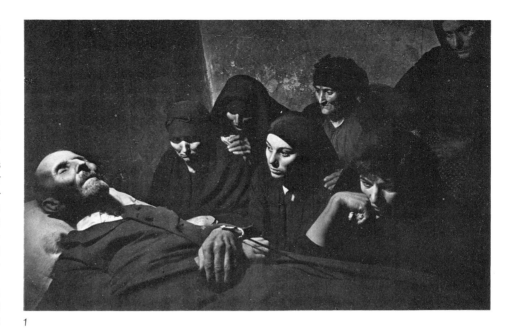

1

2

1 & 2 **W. Eugene Smith.** *Both from the* Spanish Village *photographic essay, 1951.* © *W. Eugene Smith.*

527

1

Broken Circle, is 140 feet in diameter; half land and half water, it has a huge boulder marking the center. Smithson's lack of concern for "quality" and "refinement" in the construction of his works may be open to criticism. It demonstrates the heavy emphasis placed by many artists of the late 1960s on conceptualization rather than on the work of art itself.　(E.C.G.)

Snelson, Kenneth (1927–　　).
Sculptor. Snelson was born in Pendleton, Ore., and studied with Buckminster Fuller* at Black Mountain College, North Carolina (1948) and with French artist Fernand Léger. At Black Mountain he produced several swinging-pendulum sculptures; then decided to separate his forms from one another, retaining them rigidly in space by means of metal cables. Snelson points out that this kind of structure was "completely novel to Fuller"; that the word "tensegrity" (which deals with free-floating compression members) was not coined until 1955; and that Fuller "absorbed my idea into his spherical geodesic domes." In New York Snelson became friendly with the abstract expressionist painters and continued to develop his ideas about space and structure, but his work was seen in terms of technology and engineering rather than art.

His first one-man show was not until 1966. He has justly observed that "none of the sculptures in the 'Primary Structures' exhibition were structures—they were constructions or assemblies." "Structures" are in fact involved with forces; the stressing of pieces together. Snelson's most daring structure was shown at the Los Angeles County Museum in 1968. Thirty feet long and weighing only 52 pounds, it was cantilevered off a wall with no other supports. Such a structure can stand only because it is highly stressed internally, that is, its members are bound together under tremendous tension and compression. Prototype stress structures include the kite, the bicycle wheel, and airplane fuselages.

Although Snelson discusses his work in technical terms, he thinks of himself as an artist. His primary objective is to express form; and in fact his most recent structures are indeterminate (they can not be mathematically calculated) and therefore must be arrived at by means of geometry and intuition.

His free-standing networks of cables and aluminum tubing, with the tubes often left seeming to float in midair, have moved toward the dematerialization of sculpture. Many of his pieces, deceptively simple, are composed of just a few elements. Others are visually perplexing, with the cables and tubes of various polyhedra difficult to sort out into their proper configurations. Recently he has enlarged his structures for exhibition outdoors. A show of his huge, tense "drawings in space" was held in Bryant Park, New York City, in 1968.　(E.C.G.)

Soldner, Paul (1921–　　).
Eminent ceramist and teacher, best known for his mastery of firing, salt-glazing and raku techniques, and kiln structure. Soldner was born in Summerfield, Ill., and received degrees in art education, his occupation until 1954, when he first studied ceramics. He attended Los Angeles County Art Institute (now Otis) to study under Peter Voulkos* and was the first of the young ceramists inspired by Voulkos. As a teacher of ceramics at Scripps College, Clarement, Cal., Soldner revitalized the Scripps ceramics program. In the last three years he has become involved with salt-glazing techniques which he has extended through his own unique inventiveness. In 1960 he began working in raku, developing an approach that had more in common with primitive pottery, especially that of the American Indian, than with the Japanese tradition. His unglazed raku pieces are characterized by strong rounded shapes, textured surfaces, and implications of accident and spontaneity in their startling color, bold brushwork, and mysterious smoke patterns. He has designed a kick wheel and power wheel (which he also manufactures and sells) and is a master of kiln construction. His work is represented in several major museum collections including the Smithsonian Institution and the Oakland Art Museum.
　(R.S.)

Soleri, Paolo (1919–　　).
Architect. Born in Torino, Italy, Soleri has worked in the United States since 1947, initially for Frank Lloyd Wright,* who strongly influenced him. In 1958 he began the design of Mesa City—one of the elaborate, multileveled buildings that he has conceptualized as a complete metropolis. Soleri has proposed to con-

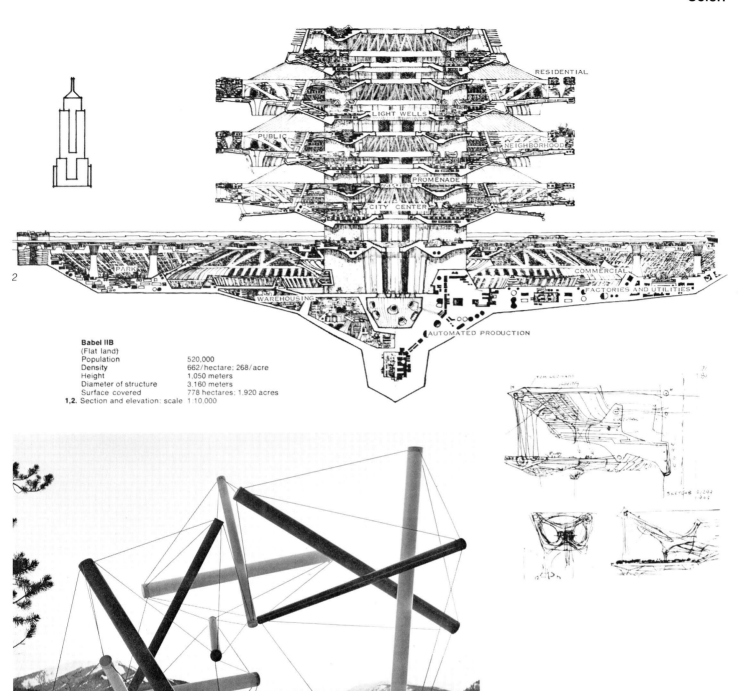

Babel IIB
(Flat land)
Population 520,000
Density 662/hectare; 268/acre
Height 1,050 meters
Diameter of structure 3,160 meters
Surface covered 778 hectares; 1,920 acres
1,2. Section and elevation: scale 1:10,000

RESIDENTIAL
LIGHT WELLS
PUBLIC
NEIGHBORHOOD
PROMENADE
CITY CENTER
PARK
COMMERCIAL
WAREHOUSING
FACTORIES AND UTILITIES
AUTOMATED PRODUCTION

2

3

1. **Robert Smithson.** Plunge, 1966.
Collection Kimoko and John G.
Powers, N.Y.
2. **Paolo Soleri.** Babel IIB, proposed
arcology, cross section drawing
and sketches, 1963. Empire State
Building shows scale of size.
3. **Kenneth Snelson.** Audrey 1, 1965,
porcelainized aluminum and steel
wire. The Cleveland Museum of Art.

centrate cities more closely, eliminating urban sprawl and leaving uncontaminated countryside between them. His plans for the many-layered city-buildings (some intended to house more than 50,000 people) have had a wide influence on contemporary planners and architects because of their allowance for the inhabitants' work and social activities, and for the cities' integration with the total environment. Soleri calls his plans "arcologies," a portmanteau word combining "architecture" and "ecology." He has constructed Cosanti, a model community in Arizona. So far, however, no major arcologies have been built, and Soleri remains, primarily, a seer in the desert.

Solomon, Barbara Stauffacher
(1932–   ).
Graphic designer of colorful, large-scale signage (signs, and the program of designing signs) and decorative programs based on abstractions strongly disciplined by Swiss graphic techniques. Born in San Francisco, Cal., she was a pioneer in supergraphics* and a teacher of the new graphics technique to architects at Yale and other colleges. She studied painting and sculpture at the San Francisco Art Institute, the Art Students League* in New York, and the University of California at Berkeley. She later studied at the Institute of Graphic Design in Basel, Switzerland, and was influential as a teacher of graphics and a designer of supergraphics. She has been graphics designer for architectural projects by Charles W. Moore,* I. M. Pei,* Lawrence Halprin, Mario Chiampi, and for numerous shops at San Francisco's Ghiradelli Square. She has also designed printed graphics and street signage.   (C.R.S.)

Sommer, Frederick (1905–   ).
Photographer and painter, born in Angri, Italy. In 1913 his family moved to Rio de Janeiro, where his father was a landscape architect. He came to the United States to study at Cornell University and received his Master of Landscape Architecture degree in 1927. He returned to Brazil, where he practiced landscape architecture until tuberculosis forced him to spend the winter of 1930–31 in Switzerland and in travel in Europe.

In 1931 Sommer settled in Tucson, Ariz., and began painting and drawing

1. *Frederick Sommer.* Coyotes, 1945, photograph. Light Gallery, N.Y.
2. *South Jersey Glass.* Sugarbowl from Suncook Glass Works, Suncook, N.H.; sugarbowl from Redford or Redwood Glass Works, N.Y.; mug from a South Jersey Glass house; all mid-19th century. Corning Museum of Glass, Corning, N.Y.

in a rather geometric style; these paintings were exhibited in a Chicago gallery in 1937. By 1938 he had begun making photographs. Two years later he met the painter Charles Sheeler* and in 1941 the surrealist artist, Max Ernst, the beginning of a friendship that has had a distinct effect on Sommer's imagery. This was the period of his horizonless Arizona landscapes, embryos, pieces of man and animals, and junkyard series. In the mid-1940s he began to make assemblages* of so-called "found objects" which he constructed and then photographed, the result being a print rather than the construction itself. By 1950 he had begun to work with "cameraless" photo-imagery, using cellophane and glass as a ground for pigment-laden oils or grease stained by smoke. These were then contact-printed or enlarged. His work during the 1960s explored three distinct areas: blurred (through camera movement) portraits and human figures; large sheets of paper that are quickly cut in a drawing-like rhythm, then hung vertically and photographed; and highly detailed photographs of accordion-folded reproductions of the wood engravings of Albrecht Dürer.

A one-man show of his photographs and drawings was held in New York City in 1949. His photographs were also included in exhibitions at the Museum of Modern Art, New York City (1949, 1951, and 1952), the Los Angeles County Museum (1950), George Eastman House (1964), Rochester, N.Y. and elsewhere. (T.F.B.)

Sonnier, Keith (1941–   ).
Sculptor. Born in Louisiana and graduated from the University of Louisiana in 1963, he lived in France for a year, returning for his M.F.A. at Rutgers University 1966. He first exhibited at a New York gallery in a show entitled "Eccentric Abstraction" (1966). These works were organic, nongeometric sculptures; made of fabric, they rested on the floor and inflated themselves at regular intervals. Later works employed sheet glass, neon tubing, latex, and flocking. They combined an elegant pictorialism with a concern for process; a configuration of glass and neon would be related compositionally to an expanse of flocked latex, attached to the wall and partially torn away. Works of this kind were included in the Whitney Museum's "Anti-Illusion: Procedures/Materials" exhibit

in 1969. Since then, Sonnier has expanded his art to an environmental scale. In one-man shows at a New York gallery, at the Museum of Modern Art, New York City, and at the van Abbe Museum in Eindhoven, the Netherlands, he has employed video, lighting systems, architectural alterations, and electronically produced sound to alter and intensify perceptual experience. (C.R.)

South Jersey Glass.
A style of glassware made in the late 18th and early 19th centuries in the lower half of the province of Jersey, the first glassmaking center in America. In the early and mid-19th century, glass of this type was also made in quantity in New England and New York. The pieces in this style are offhand products of individual glassmakers, produced from the glass left in the pots at the end of the day. Created principally in window and bottle glasshouses, they are generally made of nonlead glass and are aquamarine, greenish, or amber in color. They are characterized by boldness of form and applied decoration in the form of fancy threading, arranged in loops or lacy patterns called rigaree, and a peculiarly American decoration called the "lily-pad." Although these decorative devices and forms have their origin in the European backgrounds of their makers, they became transformed in this country into a uniquely American style. Glass of this type was probably produced at most of the South Jersey factories and in New England at Keene, Stoddard, Lyndeboro, and Suncook, N.H.; Chelmsford, Mass.; New London, Coventry, Pitkin, Willington, and Westford, Conn. New York factories include Peterboro, Geneva, Lancaster, Lockport, Redwood and Redford, Ellenville, Woodstock, Mt. Vernon, and Saratoga. (See also Wistar Caspar.) (J.S.S.)

Southworth, Albert Sands (1811–94) and **Josiah Johnson Hawes** (1808–1901).
Daguerreotypists. Preeminent in the history of American photography, their work combined the new sensibilities of the photographer with the high ideals of serious artists. This fusion—all the more amazing considering that photography was in its infancy—produced the finest portraits of Americans, celebrated and unknown, in the daguerreian period, about 1840–60.

Southworth was born in West Fairlee, Vt., and was a student at Phillips Academy in Andover, Mass. In 1840, he attended a daguerreotype demonstration in Boston by François Gouraud, a pupil of Daguerre's who had come to America to popularize the new process. Southworth was fascinated by the beauty of the microscopically detailed images on the silver-plated copper sheets. When a former schoolmate, Joseph Pennell, wrote him from New York City that he was studying daguerreotyping with Samuel F. B. Morse,* the pioneer American daguerreotypist, painter, and inventor, and suggested that they form a partnership, Southworth accepted. After a brief course under Professor Morse, the two friends established a studio in Cabotville (now Chicopee), Mass., but moved to Boston in 1841. Pennell left the partnership in 1843. His place was taken by Josiah Johnson Hawes, and in 1845 the firm name became Southworth & Hawes.

Hawes was born in the farming community of East Sudbury (now Wayland), Mass., and apprenticed at seventeen to a carpenter. He longed to be an artist, and was, it appears, entirely self-taught. "I practiced miniature painting on ivory in oil, landscapes, etc., with no teacher but my books." Like Southworth, he had been present at Gouraud's Boston demonstration. The result: "I gave up painting and commenced daguerreotypy." A fruitless quest for gold took Southworth to California from 1849–51 and his health appears to have suffered from the rigors of the mining camps. He retired from an active interest in portrait photography in 1861. But during the years they worked together Southworth and Hawes produced a body of work unique in American art. Into their studio on Tremont Row came almost every Bostonian of note, as well as many foreign celebrities, including Oliver Wendell Holmes, Henry Wadsworth Longfellow, John Quincy Adams, Charles Dickens, Jennie Lind, Lola Montez, Harriet Beecher Stowe, and Daniel Webster.

Southworth and Hawes approached their sitters, the celebrated and the ordinary citizen alike, with an insight into human personality not unlike that of the best portrait painters. "The artist," wrote Southworth, "is conscious of something besides the mere physical, in every object in nature. He feels its expression, he sympathizes with its

1. **Raphael Soyer.** Farewell to Lincoln Square, 1959. *Joseph H. Hirshhorn Foundation, N.Y.*
2. **Theodoros Stamos.** Aegean Sun-Box No. 12, 1968. *André Emmerich Gallery, N.Y.*

character, he is impressed with its language; his heart, mind, and soul are stirred in its contemplation. It is the life, the feeling, the mind, the soul of the subject itself." In addition, the artist-photographer must capture his perception effortlessly. In a passage that reminds one of Edward Weston's* theory of "previsualization" and Henri Cartier-Bresson's concept of "the decisive moment," Southworth wrote: "What is to be done is obliged to be done quickly. The whole character of the sitter is to be read at first sight; the whole likeness, as it shall appear when finished, is to be seen at first, in each and all its details, and in their unity and combinations." That these precepts informed their work can readily be seen in two strikingly different portraits made about 1851, now in the Metropolitan Museum of Art. In one, Lola Montez, Irish-born courtesan and entertainer, lounges like a languorous cat, head inclined toward the sun, sensual eyelids heavy, and gloved fingers holding an unlit cigarette. In the other, Harriet Beecher Stowe, author of *Uncle Tom's Cabin,* sits tensely erect in shadow, her eyes averted, her hands demurely resting upon her lap; on the table beside her, symbolically, is a delicate plant.

Away from their studio, Southworth and Hawes made daguerreotypes under conditions that pushed the medium to its limits: the operating theatre of the Massachusetts General Hospital in Boston (about 1850, location of the original unknown); a girls' schoolroom (about 1855, Metropolitan); and the interior of the Boston Athenaeum of about the same time (International Museum of Photography, Rochester, N.Y.). Ships at sea and in Boston Harbor, scientific studies of the eclipse of the sun and moon, and a series made of Niagara Falls in winter—all were recorded by their camera. But it is for their portraits that their unique collaboration will continue to be known. The finest examples of their work are in the Metropolitan Museum and the Boston Museum. The International Museum of Photography at George Eastman House has several hundred portraits of unidentified sitters together with the firm's business letters and account books.

Southworth spent his latter years employing photography to analyze handwriting. Hawes continued to photograph in his studio until his death at the age of ninety-four. (D.L.)

Soyer, Isaac (1907–   ).
Painter. Born in Russia, he emigrated to America in 1914, arriving after his older brothers, Moses Soyer* and Raphael Soyer.* He studied at Cooper Union (1920–24), the National Academy of Fine Arts (1924–25), the Educational Alliance Art School (1925–28), and spent a year in Paris and Madrid.

Like his brothers, Soyer is a painter of quiet social-realist and genre scenes, typified by his *Employment Agency* and *Girl Embroidering* (Whitney Museum) and by paintings in the Brooklyn Museum, the Dallas Museum, and other public collections. He has shown in international expositions in San Francisco, Paris, and New York City.   (A.F.)

Soyer, Moses (1899–   ).
Painter. At the age of 14 he and his twin brother, Raphael Soyer,* exiled from czarist Russia, emigrated to New York City in 1912. There Moses studied at Cooper Union Art School and the National Academy of Design.* George Bellows* and Robert Henri* were strong influences on his career. Moses Soyer is connected historically with the "little masters" of the realist tradition. His work exhibited a strong dependence upon the moods and the subject matter of Degas' seamstresses, ballet dancers, actresses, and models, but he also used a vein of hard reportage in the tradition of John Sloan*. He has exhibited nationally and his work is owned by many major museums and private collectors.   (A.F.)

Soyer, Raphael (1899–   ).
Painter. Born in Tombov, Russia, he was brought to New York City in 1912. As children, he and his twin, Moses Soyer,* and their brother Isaac, all of whom have had distinguished careers as artists, were encouraged to draw and paint by their parents. Raphael's command of English was so limited that he did not enter school until 1915. The Soyer brothers worked at factory jobs and sold newspapers to make a living. Raphael also studied in night classes at Cooper Union, for four years at the National Academy of Design,* and finally, for five months at the Art Students League.*

Throughout the 1920s and '30s, Soyer portrayed the daily life of New York's Fourteenth Street and Lower East Side: Bowery bums, working girls, shoppers, dancers, seamstresses, and other such types—all carefully portrayed—were among his favorite subjects. Probably Soyer has also painted more self portraits than any American artist since Charles Willson Peale.* In recent years he has taken to depicting the young, including the "hippies." He admits to special admiration for Goya, Thomas Eakins,* and Winslow Homer* among his predecessors and has painted an *Homage to Eakins* (1964–65, Hirshhorn Foundation), setting forth an assemblage of the New York realist painters presumably descended from Eakins. His style also owes a great deal to Degas.

Soyer has taught at the Art Students League and has won a remarkable number of prizes and awards throughout the country.   (A.F.)

Sparrow, Thomas (c.1746–?).
Engraver who worked in Annapolis, Md., from 1764 until at least 1784. His engravings on wood and copper include currency, bookplates, title pages for books and small cuts for books, his earliest being the woodcut arms of Maryland on the title page of Bacon's *Laws of Maryland,* 1765. He also worked as a silversmith and jeweller.

Speicher, Eugene (1883–1962).
Painter. Born in Buffalo, N.Y., he began his studies there at the Fine Arts Academy. In 1906 he entered the Art Students League* working under William M. Chase,* and with Robert Henri.* In 1907 he helped to found the Woodstock Art Colony. He became an academician of the National Academy of Design in 1927 and a director of the American Academy of Arts and Letters in 1945. Speicher was primarily a portraitist, paying court to girls and women in a monumental, yet lyrically expressive style, with hints of Cézanne in the powerfully simplified forms of his figures. A good example is *Marianna* (1937, Whitney). He also painted still life and landscape. A one-man exhibition of his work was held by the Denver Art Museum in 1948.

Spencer, Niles (1893–1952).
Painter. Born in Pawtucket, R.I., Spencer attended the Rhode Island School of Design (1913–15). During a visit to New York in 1915, he studied with George Bellows* and Robert Henri* at the Ferrer School, and the following year he moved to New York. However, he sojourned frequently in New England, first in the artists' colony at Ogun-

quit on the Maine coast, and later in Provincetown, Mass. He repeatedly traveled to France and Italy in the 1920s.

Spencer's earliest paintings were inspired by views of New England seacoast towns, their buildings simplified into geometric components that stand out against landscapes done in close-keyed, wintry tonalities of silvery gray. "Contact with the winter scene, when the underlying structure of the whole landscape stood out so clearly, affected the whole direction of my future work," he once wrote.

Beginning in the 1920s, he shifted his emphasis from landscape to the urban architecture of New York City. His unpeopled views of factories, skyscrapers, warehouses, and bridges reduced their subjects to abstract patterns in a cubist-realist style, using muted color in transparent planes in a way resembling the more architectural paintings of Charles Demuth.* Spencer's paintings of the late 1940s and '50s became increasingly abstract and two dimensional; such a work as *In Fairmont* (1951, Modern Museum) suggests that he had arrived at his own form of synthetic cubism. However, his puristic, abstract forms retain roots in the man-made geometry of the American city, and his somber, close-keyed color harmonies have an almost earthen richness. His paintings are in major museums throughout the United States. His mural commissions include the Post Office Building in Aliquippa, Pa., completed in 1937.   (A.F.)

Stamos, Theodoros (1922–   ).
Painter. Born in New York, N.Y., Stamos left high school at the age of fourteen after winning a scholarship to the American Artists School (1936). By 1939 he had turned to painting and only four years later, at the age of twenty-one, he had his first one-man show. He taught at Black Mountain College in North Carolina (1950) and the Art Students League* (1958). Among his many exhibitions was a retrospective of his work at the Corcoran Gallery of Art (1958–59) and he was awarded a prize at the Tokyo Biennial (1961).

His earliest paintings evolved out of a personal vision of surrealism* and his regard for the work of Arthur Dove.* Throughout the 1940s he employed biomorphic forms as a vehicle for the personal symbolism and mythical content of his work, as in *Echo* (1948, Metropolitan), a vision that may have influenced artists such as Barnett Newman* and Mark Rothko* and is similar to that of William Baziotes.* Paintings like *Archaic Vista* (1947) contain a whole complex of associations beyond the underlying geometric structure. They have both formal order and an ultimate sense of mystery. By the early 1950s Stamos had abandoned his more explicit mythological images and had moved toward a greater degree of abstraction. There was a stronger sense of composition, the earlier biomorphic shapes evolving into loosely brushed balls and rectangles structured by slashed lines of paint. Soon Stamos built his forms entirely of slashed and scumbled brushstrokes, which produced ragged-edged shapes seen against a hazy, atmospheric background, as in *Greek Orison* (1952, Whitney). The allusions were to landscape, with indefinite fluctuations of light and color across the canvas and the hazy quality of smoke. His painterly technique and his early move toward total abstraction made him one of the progenitors of abstract expressionism,* and he was closely associated with the leading figures of this style even though he was younger than most of them. In recent years his chief source has continued to be nature, so that one senses in his work more than just an arrangement of abstract color-shapes on a two-dimensional surface.

(E.C.G.)

Stankiewicz, Richard (1922–).
Sculptor. As one of the first to introduce "found" materials in metal sculpture, he has earned a special place in American sculptural history. His artistic development occurred at a moment when the United States was responding with tremendous excitement to new forms in art. After his Philadelphia childhood, Stankiewicz went to New York City to study with Hans Hofmann,* from whom he imbibed the principles of artistic freedom that characterized his generation. In 1950 he went to Paris, studying first in Léger's atelier and later in the studio of the Russian-born sculptor Ossip Zadkine. Returning to New York City in 1952, he experimented with carving and modeling for a short time, but soon found the discarded parts of old machines that became his primary materials. That year he became one of a pioneering group of

young artists that opened the cooperative Hansa Gallery, and the following year he exhibited his assemblages* of junk parts there. They were instantly acknowledged as witty and well-coordinated sculptures that extended the surrealist tradition.

For the next few years, Stankiewicz continued experimenting with such materials as rusted old bicycle chains, large screws and bolts, and parts of washing machines, radios, and carburetors. He felt that "visual puns, mechanical analogies and organic resemblances in machinery provide a large and evocative vocabulary for sculpture. . . ." Toward 1963, however, Stankiewicz began to limit the descriptive function in his work, using found parts in more severe arrangements and often in purely formal relationships. His lean, closely articulated forms took on new force as he added curving sheets of sheared metal and quasi-geometric forms at various levels in his spaces.

Stankiewicz has exhibited widely, although in recent years more rarely. From 1953 through 1965 he exhibited annually in New York. In 1958 he was represented in the Venice Biennial; in 1959 he was in "Sixteen Americans" at the Museum of Modern Art, New York City; in 1961 at the São Paulo Biennial: and in 1963 in London's Battersea Park exhibition.

(D.A.)

Stanley, John Mix (1814–72).
Painter best known for pictures of the American Indian. Born in Canandaigua, N.Y., he was orphaned at fourteen and was apprenticed to a wagon-maker. At twenty he went to Detroit, became a sign painter, and then began his career as a landscape and portrait painter. While living in Chicago and Galena, Ill., in 1838–39 he began to paint the Indians encamped around Fort Snelling. Thereafter painting occupied much of his time. During 1840–42 he worked in New York City, Philadelphia, and Baltimore, then traveled through Arkansas and New Mexico to California, making drawings and paintings of Indian life. In 1843 he went with the Indian agent, Pierce Mason Butler, to a council of chiefs of the Cherokee nation, and in 1846 he exhibited western paintings in Cincinnati and St. Louis. In that year he visited Keokuk, famous war leader of the Sauks, and painted portraits of various other Sauk chiefs as

well as the wife of Chief Black Hawk. In 1847–48 he accompanied the military expedition led by General Stephen Watts Kearny overland to California, then went on to Oregon, traveling by canoe on the Columbia River and making sketches along the way. He then sailed to Hawaii, where he painted the royal family (Royal Palace Museum, Honolulu).

In 1850–51 he exhibited his Indian paintings in the East, and then deposited his collection—about 150 paintings depicting forty-three Indian tribes—at the Smithsonian Institution in the vain hope that the government would buy them. (Unfortunately, all but five were destroyed by a disastrous fire in 1865.) In 1853 he was designated to accompany an expedition to find a railroad route from St. Paul, Minn. to Puget Sound. On this trip he made both daguerreotypes and paintings of Indians, especially of the Piegans. He lived in Washington, D.C., from 1854 to 1863 and then went to Buffalo; there he began his most ambitious painting, *The Trial of Red Jacket* (1868, Buffalo Historical Society), a dull and tedious effort, which contains some hundred figures.

His western landscapes are skillfully painted and compare favorably with similar work by his contemporaries. For example, *Western Landscapes* (c.1847, Detroit) is an attractive and well-organized picture, the glossy water in the foreground contrasting with the rugged mountains in the back distance. His reputation, however, was built on his Indian portraits and scenes. *The Disputed Shot* (1858, Corcoran), one of his few western paintings depicting only white men, is somewhat better in composition than *Trial of Red Jacket,* but it is stiff, awkward, and too obviously posed, however well it may document an aspect of frontier life. Less objective or scientific than the work of George C. Bingham,* Stanley's pictures with their rather sentimental, white-robed women and savage Indians were popular stereotypes in their own day, and seem only melodramatic in ours.

(H.W.W.)

Steichen, Edward J. (1879–1973).
Photographer, painter, and exhibition director. A gifted artist, whose decision to express his talent in photographs as well as in paintings had a profound influence on modern art in America.

2

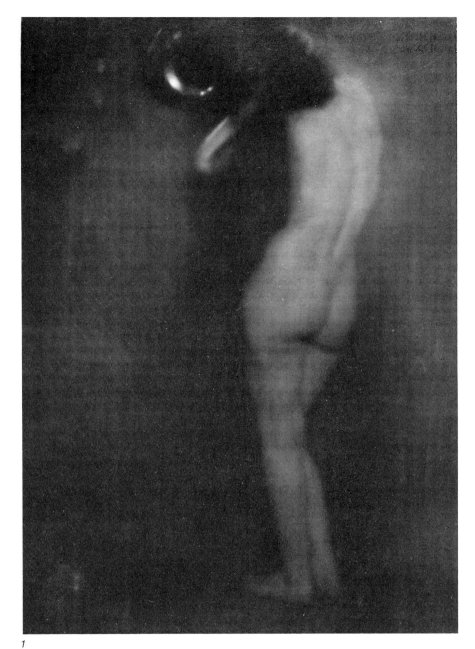

1

1. **Edward Steichen.** The Little Round
   Mirror, *Paris, 1902. Museum of
   Modern Art, N.Y.*
2. **Edward Steichen.** Greta Garbo,
   *Hollywood, 1928. Museum of
   Modern Art, N.Y.*

Steichen

Steichen was born in Luxembourg. His parents brought young Eduard (the spelling was later Americanized) to America in 1881, settling eventually in Milwaukee, Wis. He left school at fifteen to become an artist, apprenticed himself to a lithographic firm, and studied art in his spare time. He began to photograph in 1895 and in 1899 he submitted work to the Second Philadelphia Salon, where he came to the attention first of Clarence H. White,* and then of Alfred Stieglitz,* the most influential photographer in America. They encouraged Steichen by accepting his photographs for the Chicago Photographic Salon, held at the Art Institute of Chicago a year later.

In 1900 Steichen decided to go to Paris for further study. That autumn, a Boston photographer, F. Holland Day, included his work in an important London exhibition, "The New School of American Photography." Steichen's success led him to membership in the Linked Ring, an association of British photographers dedicated to photography as a fine art. This was the model upon which Alfred Stieglitz based his organization, the Photo-Secession,* which was established in 1902 with Steichen as a founding member. That year, in Paris, Steichen had his first one-man exhibition; it included both paintings and photographs. It was his ability to paint as well as to photograph that recommended young Steichen to Stieglitz and his fellow Secessionists. His work was vivid proof of their thesis that photography could be a medium of personal expression as meaningful as any other. His photograph *Self Portrait with Brush and Palette, Paris, 1901* (Chicago), expresses his dual role perfectly.

In 1905 Steichen suggested to Stieglitz that his old studio at 291 Fifth Avenue, New York City, would make an ideal gallery for fine photography. Eventually Stieglitz agreed and these modest rooms became the Little Galleries of the Photo-Secession, later known simply as "291". To "291" came not only the finest pictorial photography by Gertrude Käsebier,* Clarence White, Alvin Langdon Coburn, George Seeley, Steichen, Stieglitz, and Paul Strand,* but also the most vital examples of modern European art—from Rodin and Matisse to Brancusi and Picasso. And it was Steichen, moving between New York and a home in France,

1

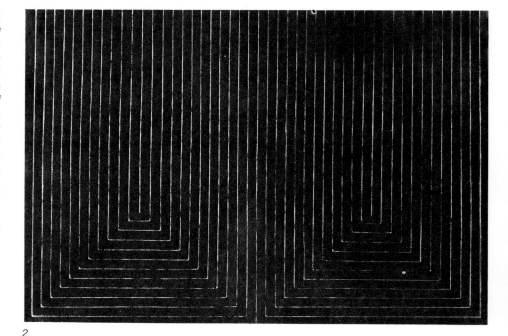

2

1. *Frank Stella.* Hagmatana III, *1967. Collection David Whitney, N.Y.*
2. *Frank Stella.* The Marriage of Reason and Squalor, *1959. Museum of Modern Art, N.Y. (Larry Aldrich Foundation Fund).*

536

who was primarily responsible for these important exhibitions. With America's entry into World War I, "291" was closed, and Steichen enlisted as a first lieutenant and was sent to France. His job, to establish aviation photography, brought about a fundamental change in his attitude toward the photographic medium. His early work had been concerned with hazy atmosphere and "poetic" effect. Now, he wrote, "The wartime problem of making sharp, clear pictures from a vibrating, speeding airplane ten to twenty thousand feet in the air had brought me a new kind of technical interest in photography completely different from the pictorial interest I had had as a boy in Milwaukee and as a young man in Photo-Secession days. Now I wanted to know all that could be expected from photography." After the armistice Steichen began a three-year period of intense investigation in three areas: plant forms, the technique of photography, and himself. The result was a dramatic affirmation of himself as a photographer. With the help of his French gardener he made a huge bonfire of all the paintings in his studio.

Steichen returned to New York City in 1923 and opened a photographic studio at 80 West 40th Street. An article in *Vanity Fair* magazine praising his portraits led him to an association with its publisher, Condé Nast, which lasted from 1923–38. For both *Vanity Fair* and *Vogue* Steichen created a remarkable series of fashion photographs and celebrity portraits including those of John Barrymore, Katherine Cornell, Lillian Gish, Martha Graham, Gloria Swanson, Maurice Chevalier, and Charlie Chaplin. Most striking, perhaps, is his 1928 Hollywood portrait of Greta Garbo. Dressed entirely in black, Garbo confronts the camera directly, her hands pressed against her hair, and presenting, with a kind of infinite resignation, a face of flawless alabaster, passive and cold.

Steichen closed his studio in January 1938 to devote himself to a lifelong interest in botany. (He had exhibited his hybrid delphinium at the Museum of Modern Art in 1936.) By 1941 America was again at war and Steichen was invited to form a unit to photograph naval aviation. In 1942, Lieutenant Commander Steichen, with the help of his brother-in-law, the poet Carl Sandburg, directed the exhibition "Road to Victory." In 1944 he supervised the United States Navy film, *The Fighting Lady.* He became the director of the department of photography of the Museum of Modern Art in 1947 and, until his retirement in 1962, he directed more than fifty important photographic exhibitions. Most influential was his exhibition "The Family of Man" (1955). Steichen and his staff painstakingly selected 503 photographs from more than two million that had been submitted. These photographs, the work of 273 photographers from sixty-eight countries, were structured to reveal the essential oneness of mankind throughout the world. Called the greatest of all photography exhibitions and seen by millions of people in more than seventy countries including the Soviet Union, "The Family of Man," remains, as Steichen himself agreed, the most challenging undertaking of his career.

(D.L.)

Steiner, Ralph (1899–   ).
Photographer and documentary filmmaker. Steiner's precise, visual statements of the objective world influenced a generation of documentary photographers. Born in Cleveland, Ohio, Steiner began photographing in 1917. He graduated from Dartmouth College in 1921, and after a year at the Clarence H. White* School of Photography he became an advertising photographer, winning the first prize in the 1928 New York Art Director's Show. His first successful film, *H₂O,* a study of water in motion, won the first prize in the 1929 *Photoplay* amateur contest. Grants from the Whitney Fund enabled him to make three additional short films: *People Playing Croquet* (c.1929), *Mechanical Principles* (1930), and *Surf and Seaweed* (1931). With Paul Strand,* Steiner photographed Pare Lorentz's classic documentary, *The Plow That Broke the Plains* (1936). In 1939 he became president of American Documentary Films, Inc., and with codirector Willard Van Dyke he made *The City,* first shown at the 1939 New York World's Fair. After World War II, Steiner spent two years in Hollywood as a production assistant. Only a number of short subjects and an unsuccessful fictionalized biography of the musicians Clara and Robert Schumann, *A Song of Love* (1947), resulted. Steiner's photographs have appeared in *Life, Fortune, Vanity Fair,* and *Theatre Arts* magazines and his exhibitions include "Realism in Photography" (1949) and "Photo Eye of the Twenties" (1970), both for the Museum of Modern Art.

(D.L.)

Stella, Frank (1936–   ).
Painter, born in Malden, Mass., and educated at Phillips Academy and Princeton University. He became interested in art in college, and after graduation moved to New York City, where he rented a studio and supported himself by working as a house painter. His first exhibition was in 1959, and since then he has exhibited in nearly every major national and international show of contemporary abstract painting. Despite the fact that abstract expressionism,* with its frenetic brushwork and personal and emotional approach was at its peak, Stella was determined to create an art that was rational and orderly. His earliest paintings of the famous "pin-stripe" series, such as *The Marriage of Reason and Squalor* (1959, Modern Museum), had a symmetrical central motif that extended out to the edges of the canvas in a series of 2½-inch-wide black stripes. The absolute flatness of these early works, their "monotonous" unit of composition, and the fact that they were designed prior to execution brought a mixed reaction of revulsion and praise. Stella explained that he wanted to "eliminate illusionistic space" and that a painting was "a flat surface with paint on it—nothing more."

By the following year he had carried the literalness of the black paintings—four of which had been in the Museum of Modern Art's "16 Americans" show—a step further. In a series of pictures using aluminum and then copper paint (1960–61) Stella began to cut notches out of the center, corners, and sides of his canvases so that the internal pattern of stripes would be totally identified with the shape of the picture as a whole. Thus the "image" and the canvas became an inseparable unit, and the painting itself became an object. Other pictures in this series assumed forms that departed radically from the traditional rectangular format: L's, T's, U's, and geometrical figures such as triangles, pentagons, and hexagons. These pioneering "shaped canvases,"* often painted with purple metallic paint, soon gave way to the "Running V" and "Notched V" series (1964–65) such as *Adelante* (1964, San Francisco), in which V's were lined up in varying configurations—sometimes for as great a length as twenty feet. The V's were sometimes all the same color, sometimes painted in different colors (reds, greens, and blacks) but the internal units of measurement, the stripes, always echoed the shape of the picture as a whole. In 1965 Stella began a group of eccentrically shaped canvases such as *Tuftonboro II* (1966) in which he developed tensions between depicted geometrical shapes and the literal shape of the framing edge.

In another radical departure from his earlier work he gave color a primary role, with geometrical shapes painted in brilliant shades of fluorescent paint. He produced four versions of each picture in this series, which allowed him to experiment with different color choices and combinations, and for the first time his pictures were structured as much by color as by format. Paradoxically these paintings, though employing flat shapes, represented a return to three-dimensional illusionism because the internal geometrical figures suggested various perspectival effects as they thrust forward and back in space. In the "Protractor" series (1967–68) he developed even further his interest in illusionism and color optics. Here geometrically shaped canvases based on the circle and half-circle are dissolved into interlaced bands of fluorescent color. These kaleidoscopic, almost psychedelic designs are heightened by their large size—usually about ten by twenty feet; in them Stella seems to be moving more and more in the direction of complexity and hedonism. His work has been called "a programmed attack on the problems of pictorial structure."   (E.C.G.)

Stella, Joseph (1877–1946).
A painter noted for his early adoption of European abstract idioms, especially futurism.* He was born near Naples and moved to New York in 1896. After spending a year at the Art Students League,* he studied at the New York School of Art with William Merritt Chase.* From 1905 to 1906 he worked as a magazine illustrator; during this period he produced dark, powerful drawings of aspects of the coal and steel industry at Pittsburgh. On a trip to Europe, 1909–12, he came in contact with avant-garde movements in Italy

1. *Joseph Stella.* Battle of Lights, Coney Island, *1913. Yale University Art Gallery, New Haven, Conn. (gift of Collection Société Anonyme).*
2. *Maurice Sterne.* Bali Bazaar, 1913–14. Whitney Museum of American Art, N.Y.

and France. Returning to this country, he began to paint high-keyed, semi-abstract figures and still-life studies and was represented in the Armory Show* in 1913. But that year he changed abruptly, becoming inspired by the forms and lights of industrial-age America, which he depicted in large, colorful, agitated, futurist-influenced canvases such as *Battle of Lights, Coney Island* (1913, Yale). Subsequently, he painted a series of panels abstracting the rhythms and monumental verticality of New York (*The Bridge,* 1926, Newark Museum). In the mid-1920s, again changing direction, he began to work in a more representational but primitivizing manner, charging his art with religious or sexual symbolism. A man of vivid and mercurial temperament, he worked in the widest variety of styles, but created in the process several pictures that stand as landmarks of modernism in America.   (D.W.S.)

Sterne, Maurice (1878–1957).
Painter, sculptor, and graphic artist. Born in Latvia, he emigrated to New York with his widowed mother in 1889. Two years later he began to work as a designer's helper in an engraving firm, and soon thereafter he studied mechanical drawing at Cooper Union. Between 1894–99 he was enrolled at the National Academy of Design,* where he studied anatomy in the weekly class offered by Thomas Eakins.* His professional career began with sustained work in etching and his first exhibition of oil paintings (1902). He won a National Academy traveling scholarship in 1904, and began a long period of far-flung travels to Europe and the Orient. In Europe he came under the influence of Manet and Cézanne, and then the masters of the Italian Renaissance. In Greece in 1908 he became interested in sculpture. In 1911 he visited Egypt and then went on to India, Burma, and Bali. At the approach of the war, he returned to Italy and finally to the United States. He lived in New Mexico in 1917, and from 1934 to 1936 in San Francisco, where he taught at the California School of Fine Arts.

Sterne's style was thoroughly grounded in academic draftsmanship. During his travels to the Orient he adopted a somewhat flattened and faceted modern idiom, and he first became widely known for portrayals of rituals of India

and Bali in this style (*Bali Bazaar,* 1913–14, Whitney). Later an enthusiasm for pure line and simplified forms became his chief characteristic. During the 1920s and '30s he was highly praised as a draftsman and received a number of major awards and honors, including commissions for monumental sculpture and the first one-man exhibition accorded an American by the Museum of Modern Art (1933). Official recognition came in a commission for a mural at the Department of Justice in Washington (1935) and appointment to the National Commission of Fine Arts (1945).

During the early 1940s Sterne became seriously ill. About 1945 he began summering on the waterfront of Provincetown, Mass., resumed his painting, and produced seascapes in a colorful, luminous, and richly pigmented style. These were as spontaneous and intuitive as his earlier manner had been controlled and formal.
                         (D.W.S.)

Steuben Glass Works, Corning, New York, 1903–present, see Art Nouveau Glass.

Stiegel, Henry William (1729–85).
American glass-manufacturer of German origin. Stiegel emigrated to Philadelphia in 1750. In 1752 he married Elizabeth Huber, daughter of the owner of an iron furnace in Lancaster County, and from then until 1763 he was engaged in the operation of the Huber furnace. He also acquired Charming Forge about twenty miles away, and it was from these properties that he drew sufficient income to support his ventures in glassmaking.

Stiegel began blowing operations at Elizabeth Furnace in September, 1763, and closed it down when he began operations at a second glasshouse in Manheim, Pa., in 1765. German workmen at both of these factories produced mainly window glass and bottles. In 1769, Stiegel opened an even larger factory at Manheim, the American Flint Glass Manufactory, employing more than a hundred men and advertising extensively all along the eastern seaboard. Many of the workmen for this factory were English, and their products were principally tablewares of fine flint (lead) glass.

Stiegel's glasshouses attempted to serve two markets, and so he made two

types of glass. The English workmen whom he had imported made flint (lead) glass, clear and colored, free-blown and pattern-molded, for the city dwellers in Philadelphia, New York, and other cities. For his Pennsylvania German neighbors, Stiegel produced glass in the German and Bohemian folk traditions, plain and probably engraved and/or enameled with the hearts, flowers, and birds that are associated with Central European folk design. No signed piece of Stiegel glassware has ever come to light, and a great deal of controversy therefore exists about attributions to this factory. The colored flint wares are virtually indistinguishable from their English counterparts, and the engraved and enameled pieces are similarly close to the German wares he copied. Two pattern-molded designs which have so far not been found in Europe and may thus be exclusive to Stiegel are the "daisy in hexagon" and the "diamond-daisy" design, both found in the form of pocket bottles. A small group of glasses with enameled inscriptions in English, "We two will be true," "My love you like me do," and "Friendship and Amity," also exist and probably can be attributed to the second Manheim factory.

Stiegel's contributions to American glassmaking lie in the fact that his was the second successful glassmaking venture in the colonies, and the first to make glass tablewares on a large scale. Stiegel attempted unsuccessfully to appeal to the patriotism of American buyers, but he went bankrupt and the glasshouse was closed in 1774. After spending a brief term in a debtors' prison, he died at a fairly early age.

Stiegel's ambition and grand scale of living during his prosperous years earned him the sobriquet of "Baron" from his neighbors, but he was not actually a member of the German nobility. His colorful life made him a legendary figure to early glass collectors, and in the 1920s and '30s a number of European and 19th-century American glasses were attributed to his factories. Lacking reliable evidence as to their place of manufacture, present-day collectors of this glass are inclined to label all of their pieces as "Stiegel-type."
                         (J.S.S)

Stieglitz, Alfred (1864–1946).
Photographer, editor, and art gallery director. In an effort to make photog-

1. **Alfred Stieglitz.** The Terminal, *1893, photograph.*

2. **Alfred Stieglitz.** Grape Leaves and House, Lake George, *1934, photograph. Both, George Eastman House, Rochester, N.Y.*

raphy a respected medium of artistic expression, Stieglitz established four revolutionary periodicals and a succession of art galleries. Born in Hoboken, N.J., of wealthy immigrant parents, he was educated at the City College of New York and the University of Berlin. His first photographs were made in Germany in 1883, and the process so fascinated him that he began to study photographic chemistry there with the world's leading photo-scientist, Dr. Herman Wilhelm Vogel. He returned to New York City in 1890 and lived there until his death.

From 1890 to 1895 Stieglitz managed a photoengraving company and explored photographic possibilities—the lantern slide and the use of simple hand-held cameras. Singled out for his freshness of vision as early as 1887 by Dr. Peter Henry Emerson, a giant of 19th-century photography, by 1900 Stieglitz became the world's leading amateur photographer. Through his editorship of the *American Amateur Photographer* (1893–96) and *Camera Notes* (1897–1902), the magazine of the Camera Club of New Work—an organization he helped to found in 1896—Stieglitz championed the work of such innovative pictorialists as Frank Eugene, Joseph Keiley, Gertrude Käsebier,* Alvin Langdon Coburn, Edward Steichen,* and Clarence H. White. These photographers formed the nucleus of the Photo-Secession,* which he founded in 1902. The effect of this organization on American photography was electric. Stieglitz welded an organization that drove into the American consciousness his conviction that photography, long considered only a handmaiden of art, was the first new medium of personal expression to have evolved in five thousand years. *Camera Work,* the lavish quarterly he issued in fifty numbers from 1903–17, brilliantly argued this point, using the critical writings of Charles Caffin, Roland Rood, Sadakichi Hartmann, Maurice Maeterlinck, and George Bernard Shaw. Its illustrations, superb hand-pulled gravures, documented photography's esthetic resources. But Stieglitz did not limit himself to photography. The newest in painting, architecture, and sculpture was presented in *Camera Work* and in the Little Galleries of the Photo-Secession, the avant-garde gallery he and Edward Steichen established at 291 Fifth Avenue in New York City in 1905. Conceived of as an esthetic laboratory, "291," as it was known, presented almost eighty exhibitions of modern art before it closed in 1917. Stieglitz launched two additional publications: *291* (1915–16), a dadaist magazine influenced by the French painter Francis Picabia, and *MSS* (Manuscripts, 1922–24) designed by Georgia O'Keeffe,* the American painter whom Stieglitz married in 1924.

Stieglitz was sixty, O'Keeffe, thirty-seven. For Stieglitz the marriage signaled his rebirth as a creative artist. His "Portrait of O'Keeffe," a stunning series of more than four hundred photographs made over almost twenty years, is one of the landmarks of photography. O'Keeffe's face, eyes, hair, body, and especially her hands; her activities, such as painting, sewing, working; her moods—pensive, imperious, seductive, enigmatic—all are seen through a lover's eyes and rendered with the subtle skill of the mature artist. No portrait in any art medium compares with it in scope and concept.

Of equal esthetic importance was another series of photographs begun in 1923: of clouds above his summer home on Lake George, New York. Exhibited the following year, these "Songs of the Sky" were the visual equivalent of a profound emotional response to great music. This concept of equivalency—that a photograph may evoke an emotion totally unrelated to its subject matter—has had a profound effect on serious photographers ever since, and has been most eloquently explored, perhaps, in the work of Paul Caponigro and Minor White.*

Stieglitz championed American artists in the two galleries he directed at the end of his career. The work of painters John Marin,* Arthur Dove,* Charles Demuth,* Georgia O'Keeffe, and the photographer Paul Strand* were shown at his Intimate Gallery (1925–29). Nearly seventy-five exhibitions of American art, including the work of photographers Eliot Porter and Ansel Adams,* were held at An American Place (1929–46). The finest collections of Stieglitz' own photographs are at the National Gallery, the Metropolitan Museum, the Boston Museum, the Chicago Art Institute, and George Eastman House, Rochester, N.Y.   (D.L.)

Still, Clyfford (1904–   ).
Painter. Born in Grandin, N.D., he lived

3

4

3. *Clyfford Still.* 1960-F, *1960. Marlborough-Gerson Gallery, N.Y.*
4. *Clyfford Still.* Painting, *1951. Museum of Modern Art, N.Y. (Blanchette Rockefeller Fund).*

until 1950 in Alberta, Canada, and Spokane, Wash., where the "nobility, cleaness and bigness" of the landscape impressed him deeply. Interested in art, he made a trip to New York in 1924 to survey the art scene. Returning to the West, he graduated from Spokane University and received an M.A. from Washington State College, where he also taught art history, painting and sculpture (1933–41). In 1943 he exhibited twenty-two canvases at the San Francisco Museum of Art and in 1946 he had a one-man show at Peggy Guggenheim's* Art of this Century gallery in New York City. In 1946–50 Still taught in California.

Still's early figurative paintings, such as *1936-N,* resemble Picasso's and yet are prophetic of his own later work with frontal, interpenetrating forms. By the early 1940s his pictures had become more surrealistic (a classification he bitterly rejected) with semi-abstract, demonic phantoms and sun and moon forms symbolic of "the Earth, the Damned and the Recreated." For example, *1943-J,* and *1944-A* are turbulent, dark, and foreboding, with writhing forms ultimately resolved in pictorial harmony. From the beginning, Still's paintings were realized gauchely with awkward, often "ugly" impasto effects and sickly monochromatic color. By ignoring the academic techniques, he hoped to reach beyond the world of easy competence into a more dramatic, powerful, and primitive realm. Still's distaste for the refined, sensuous art of Europe is well-documented. He notes that the Armory Show* "dumped upon us the combined and sterile conclusions of Western European decadence" and refers to "the nightmare of its labyrinthine evasions" and its "banalities and trivia."

Clearly, Still considered himself both a loner and a visionary like Albert Pinkham Ryder* or William Blake, and he tried to create his own world and give it a higher spiritual purpose. He wrote: "I held it imperative to evolve an instrument of thought which would aid in cutting through all cultural opiates, past and present, so that a direct, immediate, and truly free vision could be achieved . . ." and he affirms his "profound concern to achieve a purpose beyond vanity, ambition, or remembrance." His high-blown objectives and his denial of European or American influences ultimately gave him a reputation for cantankerousness. Outraged by the suggestion that his work might owe a debt to surrealism,* he railed against his "appropriation by the 'mythmakers' group," and expunged any vestige of figuration from his work. As early as in *1943-A,* Still had produced totally abstract paintings with ragged-edged, flamelike forms. Soon he was producing these exclusively, converting his earlier chthonic figurations into abstractions. His heavily-impastoed surfaces tended to make his paintings palpably real, rather than surreal or allusive, although his "relief-map" effects, with their suggestion of ravines and crevices, added to the implication of nature as his ultimate source. Paradoxically, his later work remains totally abstract, while at the same time echoing the browns and yellows of Canadian earth and ripening wheat and the vast space of the American West, as in *Painting* (1951, Detroit).

It was precisely during these years that his influence was felt most as one of the pioneers of abstract expressionism.* In 1947 he exhibited at a New York gallery, displaying dynamic, interlocking patterns. At the time his paintings seemed violent, raw and "expressionistic," with their impenetrable surfaces and aggressive textures, as in *1957-D No. 1* (Albright). Gradually Still had moved away from somber earths and blacks toward much brighter, but equally original color combinations, and throughout the 1950s his paintings became larger and more open as he simplified his forms—sometimes separating them by expanses of unpainted, sized canvas. His paintings had always been large, but now, like the other abstract expressionists, he overwhelmed the spectator by the sheer size of his work, and their flat, weighty surfaces. By the 1960s he had turned from drama to lyricism in a series of freer, more atmospheric and sensuous color-fields. But even as his work became brighter and more open, he himself withdrew into deeper isolation. From 1952 to 1967 he refused to exhibit in New York City, considering it too corrupt for his art. The major exhibition of his work was at the Albright-Knox Art Gallery in Buffalo (1959), and in 1964 he gave that museum thirty-one paintings.   (E.C.G.)

Stock, Joseph W. (1815–55).
Self-taught portraitist of Springfield, Mass., who was confined to a wheelchair as a result of a childhood accident. At his doctor's suggestion, Stock turned to painting in 1832 as a means of support, and his own records show that he produced more than nine hundred portraits—many of children, typically depicted on a boldly patterned carpet, and often with a cat or toys alongside the sitter, as in *Jane Henrietta Russell* (1844, Boston). A specially designed wheelchair permitted him to travel, and he is known to have worked as far afield as Rhode Island. Stock's diary, owned by the Connecticut Valley Historical Museum, provides unusual insight into the life of the 19th-century portraitist; it also lists all his works and the prices paid for them.   (M.J.G.)

Stone, Edward Durell (1902–   ).
Since the late 1930s, one of America's most successful architects. He was educated at Harvard and the Massachusettes Institute of Technology. During the 1930s he was recognized as a major exponent of the International style,* although his work was just as committed to the streamlined moderne.* Characteristic of his work in those years were the Mandel House in Mt. Kisco N.Y. (1935) and the Goodyear House in Old Westbury, N.Y. (1941). Both of them are a succession of connected white stucco boxes with curved, streamlined walls, glass-brick and steel-frame windows, and chrome trim. He first received international notice as the associate designer of the Museum of Modern Art (New York City, 1939).

After 1945 his work, like that of Minoru Yamasaki* and others, became increasingly decorative and classical Roman in feeling. In fact, he can be credited with the creation of a major post-World War II style—that of the classic pavilion, a simple rectangular box surrounded by a colonnaded porch on three or more sides. He used this motif in his American Embassy in New Delhi (1958–59), his United States Pavilion at the 1958 Brussel's World's Fair, the auditorium of the California Institute of Technology (Pasadena, 1963), and in numerous other buildings. His John F. Kennedy Center for the Performing Arts (Washington, D.C., 1965–71) is ornate in its decoration, conveying the impression of a lavish stage set which, with its colonnaded façades, is classical in feeling. Stone has been criticized by those who have adhered to the puritanical tenets of the

International style of the 1930s, but there can be little question that his very considerable popularity rests on the widespread desire for classical order, complete with Roman elegance.

(D.G.)

Stone, Horatio (1808–75).

Sculptor. A native of rural New York, he practiced medicine for several years before turning to sculpture. His work consisted almost totally of portraiture, such as his bust, *Chief Justice Roger B. Taney* (1857, Supreme Court Building, Washington, D.C.). The U.S. Capitol has three of his full-length marble statues in Statuary Hall: *John Hancock* (1858), *Alexander Hamilton* (c.1868), and *Edward D. Baker* (1873). His style is characterized by a prosaic naturalism, accurate in its likeness but devoid of much drama or sensitivity. During the 1850s much of Stone's energy was spent in a campaign to improve the arts of the national capital by the establishment of a Federal Arts Commission. This was finally accomplished in 1859 but President Buchanan dissolved the Commission the following year. Stone remained active as an artist in Washington until his death.

Storrs, John (1885–1956).

Sculptor who made daring experiments in abstract art* in the early 20th century. Born in Chicago, Ill., he lived most of his life in France. As a young man he studied in Berlin, then in Chicago, Boston, and Philadelphia before going to Paris, where he became a favorite pupil of Rodin. In 1913 his work showed the powerful influence of Rodin's style, but he soon became interested in cubism* and began experimenting with abstract form and the organization of planes and contours. Titles of works from the years 1917–19 reveal their abstract nature—*Panel with Black Marble Inlay,* and *Abstract Forms #1* and *#2;* a series called "Forms in Space" dates from 1920–25. Sometimes there is a slight suggestion of naturalistic form, as in his *Gendarme Seated* (1925), but in his *Composition around Two Voids* (1932, Whitney) the form is nonobjective, a study in planes, contours, and volumes. As innovative and esthetically successful as his sculptures were, they were not well received in America during his lifetime. An independent income allowed him to pursue his work, however. His art was highly

1

2

1. **Edward Durell Stone.** U.S. Embassy, New Delhi, India, 1959.
2. **John Storrs.** Composition around Two Voids, 1932, stainless steel. Whitney Museum of American Art, N.Y. (gift of Monique Storrs Booz).

regarded in France, but his career ended when he was imprisoned by the Nazis in a concentration camp in World War II. He died in Mer, France. (W.C.)

Story, William Wetmore (1819–95). Sculptor. The son of Supreme Court Justice Joseph Story, he was born in Boston, Mass., and after graduation from Harvard he pursued a career as a lawyer. He was also an amateur litterateur and artist; when his father died, William, although he had no professional experience, was invited to submit a design for a statue of the jurist. The result, the statue now owned by Harvard University, launched Story on his career as a sculptor. He gave up his law practice and moved to Rome, where he and his wife quickly became a part of the expatriate circle of artists and intellectuals. The couple had a large apartment in the Palazzo Barberini, where their neighbors were Robert and Elizabeth Browning; among their other friends were Nathaniel Hawthorne, Margaret Fuller, William Makepeace Thackeray, and the sculptor Thomas Crawford.* Story's literary interests had a profound effect on his work: his sculpture was usually more concerned with the illustration of literature than with the pursuit of interesting sculptural form. He has, in fact, been called a "literary sculptor," and his works generally possess an anecdotal quality with an emphasis on details, as if they were being described verbally in a novel. Except for his portraits, his subjects were usually taken from the Bible, ancient history, and classical mythology. His heroic *Cleopatra* (1869) brought him international fame; this was followed by his equally acclaimed *Libyan Sibyl* (c.1861, National Coll.). Story often chose the great women of antiquity for his subjects; among such works were *Medea* (1864), *Delilah* (1866), and *Salome* (1870). There were also heroic marble images of men such as his *Saul* (1863). Story has been labeled a neoclassicist, but the term applies primarily to his choice of classical subjects; in style his neoclassicism* was strongly conditioned by Victorian romanticism with its melodrama, historical eclecticism, and anecdotal details, rather than by purely sculptural beauty and plastic form. Story produced several portrait busts, including a self-portrait, and one of Elizabeth Barrett Browning (1866, original 1861,

1. *Paul Strand.* Town Hall, New England, *1946, photograph.*

2. *Paul Strand.* The White Fence, *1917, photograph.*
Both, © *Paul Strand.*

Boston Athenaeum). He also made several full-length portrait statues, notably *Josiah Quincy* (Harvard University), *Professor Joseph Henry* (1881, Smithsonian), and *Edward Everett* (1866, Boston). Story was one of the most famous American sculptors in his day.

(W.C.)

Strand, Paul (1890–   ).
Photographer, born in New York, N.Y. While a student of Lewis Hine,* at the Ethical Culture School in New York, Strand was taken to Alfred Stieglitz'* famous "291" gallery of photography and painting on Fifth Avenue. By 1915 he had completed a series of unusually strong pictures of the people and buildings of his native city. He showed these to Stieglitz, who in 1916 put them on exhibition at "291" and reproduced examples in *Camera Work,* the periodical Stieglitz edited that was devoted to creative photography and modern art. Thus launched, Strand quickly became a major figure in avant-garde photography. At Stieglitz' gallery he became acquainted with cubism* and met the painters Francis Picabia and Marcel Duchamp.* Their machine-oriented semi-geometric pictures helped to clarify Strand's style. In straightforward but measured terms he has since photographed machines and machine parts, rock formations, architecture, clouds, and people. He treats his subjects in a lyrical fashion that increases our awareness of the nature of surfaces, the roundness or roughness of forms, the special characteristics of walls and windows that are unique to a particular place. His photographs are carefully composed, usually in geometric terms, with special attention paid to the nature of the environments of his subjects.

Strand has also worked as a cinematographer. In collaboration with Charles Sheeler,* he made the poetic documentary film *Manhatta* (1918), and in 1936 he worked as a cameraman for *The Plow That Broke the Plains* (1936). From 1930 to 1932 he was chief photographer and cinematographer for the Mexican government. In 1940 a portfolio of still photographs he made of Mexico was published.

Strand has photographed in many parts of this hemisphere, including Europe and North Africa. One of his earliest trips was to the Gaspé Peninsula. There he developed the visually sophisticated approach to nature he has

applied to similar subjects on three continents. He collaborated with Nancy Newhall on *Time in New England* (1950). In 1950 he moved to France. Photographs made there were included in the book *La France de Profil* (1952). This was followed by *Un Paese* (1954), about the village of Luzzara in northern Italy; *Tir A'Mhurain, Outer Hebrides* (1962), which dealt with an island off the coast of Scotland; and *Living Egypt* (1969).

A major one-man exhibition of his work was held at the Museum of Modern Art in 1945. In 1971 the Philadelphia Museum of Art organized a retrospective exhibition, which later was shown in major museums in the United States, including the Metropolitan Museum in New York. In connection with the exhibition, *Paul Strand: A Retrospective Monograph* was published (1971). This is the definitive book on Strand's work.

(V.D.C.)

Streamlined Moderne.
A design formula, 1930-41, marked mainly by streamlining. In response to the aim of speed that increasingly dominated the 1920s and 1930s, designers developed the streamlined shape, first applying it to the transportation machine—ships, trains, automobiles, airplanes. In architecture, the shape first emerged in some of the horizontal, "hovering" prairie houses of Frank Lloyd Wright,* and in houses by William Gray Purcell* and George Grant Elmslie. But it was not until 1910–20 that the streamlined form made a genuine impact on architecture, first in the sketches of the futurist architect, Antonio Sant'Elia, later in the drawings of Erich Mendelsohn* and Kem Weber,* and finally in Mendelsohn's Einstein Tower in Neubabelsberg, Germany in 1917–21.

The streamlined image did not actually prevail until about 1930; even the transportation machines were not cast into teardrop or ovoid forms until the mid-1930s. The streamlined motif was a major shift in architectural and design fashion; instead of basing a design on the function of each part, it presented a single form within which all the parts were hidden. The complex was reduced to a simple, easily comprehensible form. Because of its aerodynamic implications, streamlining became synonymous with the airplane, which symbolized the future.

Streamlining became a nearly universal design formula in America due largely to the emergence of the industrial designer.* The Bauhaus* design ideal—or, to go back further, the turn-of-the-century Arts and Crafts* movement—of uniting art and industry became a reality in the late 1920s. All the great product designers, Walter Dorwin Teague, Norman Bel Geddes,* Raymond Loewy, and Henry Dreyfus, emerged at that time.

The streamlined architectural styling of the 1930s, with its flat roof, machine-smooth surfaces, curved bays, steel railings, horizontal lines, and glass brick windows, reflected the same view of style as did the automobile, train, camera, or toy "ray gun." It was the automobile of the early 1930s that most strongly imposed the new image, especially the Dymaxion Car of Buckminster Fuller,* Bel Geddes' Motor Car Eight, and several designs for trucks and buses by Loewy. In 1933, the designer Carl Breer produced the Chrysler "Air Flow," with its single-curved body, swooping tail lines, slanted windshield, and skirted wheels. In 1936 the classic of automobile streamlining, the Cord, designed by Gordon Buehrig, appeared; and by 1937, all mass-produced American automobiles were streamlined. Ocean liners, ferry boats, and passenger trains adopted similar styling; the late 1930s brought the Milwaukee Road's "Hiawatha," designed by Kuhler; the Pennsylvania Railroad's "Broadway Limited" by Loewy; and the New York Central's "Mercury" and "20th Century Limited," both by Dreyfus.

In architecture, variations on the theme were carried out by George Howe, William Lescaze,* Edward Durell Stone,* Stiles Clements, and many other architects, interior decorators, and building contractors. Even the major figures of American architecture—Frank Lloyd Wright,* Richard J. Neutra,* and R. M. Schindler*—succumbed to the fashion. The most sophisticated streamlined building of the 1930s was Wright's S.C. Johnson Wax Company Administration Building in Racine, Wis. (1936–39). Notwithstanding romantic overtones, it is the perfect example of the industrial-styled building. The culmination of the streamlined moderne occurred in the buildings, displays, and objects at the New York World's Fair of 1939; and it was the industrial designers—especially Bel Geddes and Loewy—not the architects, who established the character of the Fair. World War II signaled the end of the streamlined moderne as the dominant mode in American architecture, but elements of its vocabulary continued to crop up in the 1950s and 1960s. (D.G.)

Strickland, William (1788–1854).
Architect, engineer, and painter, probably born in Navesink, N.J. His father worked in Philadelphia as a carpenter on the Bank of Pennsylvania (1798–1801), designed by B. H. Latrobe.* Strickland was apprenticed to Latrobe in 1803, but, undependable and indolent, he was dismissed in 1805. However, by 1808 he had gathered himself together and designed the Masonic Hall, Philadelphia (1809–11), using the Gothic style. He also did oil paintings, engravings, theater scenery, book illustration, surveying, map-making, and during the War of 1812 he constructed ramparts required for the defense of Philadelphia.

Strickland designed the Swedenborgian Church, Philadelphia (c.1815). He won a competition for the Second Bank of the United States, Philadelphia, and built it (1818–24) in Greek revival* style, which became his favorite. As agent for the Pennsylvania Society for the Promotion of Internal Improvement, he sailed for England to investigate British commerce. On his return he published his *Report on Canals, Railways, and Roads* (1826), was consulted by canal and railway companies and retained to build a lighthouse in the Delaware River. In the following years his most important architectural commissions were the United States Naval Asylum, Philadelphia (1826–29), and, after a long tour of Europe, the famous Philadelphia Exchange (1832–34). The latter owes its classic appearance to the style of the Villa Tivoli, Italy, and to the Choragic Monument of Lysicrates, Athens, which Strickland knew from books. He also built the United States Mint, New Orleans (1835–36), later converted to other uses, and the Athenaeum, Providence, R.I. (1836), in the Greek revival style. For the next few years Strickland drew up many plans, but few were accepted, leaving him financially distressed. When in 1844 he was asked to design the State Capitol, Nashville,

Tenn. (1845–59), he moved to Nashville. Again he relied on classical precedent, placing the Choragic Monument of Lysicrates atop a Parthenon-style temple—not a happy solution. In Nashville he received commissions for various private houses and for the First Presbyterian Church (1848–51), which he did in Georgian style but with Egyptian ornament.

Strickland was elected to various professional organizations of artists and engineers as well as architects. Although he tried other styles, he is best known for his designs in the classical manner, especially with Greek forms. By the time his career ended, the popular enthusiasm for the styles of Greece and Rome had waned. (P.F.N.)

Stuart, Gilbert (1755–1828).
Leading portrait painter of the Federal period. His father ran a snuff mill in Newport, R.I., for Dr. Thomas Moffatt, who was a nephew of the painter John Smibert.* When a roving Scottish artist, Cosmo Alexander,* came to Newport he took a liking to the spirited, mischievous boy and took him back to Edinburgh as a pupil. With Alexander's sudden death in 1772, Stuart dropped from a cultivated circle in the northern capital into abject poverty. He worked his way home to Newport as a seaman, and there tried to support himself by painting. The threat of war limited commissions, and he sailed to Britain from Boston in June, 1775, the day before the Battle of Bunker Hill. In London his poverty was only partially relieved by employment as a church organist. When portrait commissions did begin to come, he lost them by accepting an advanced payment but failing to complete the work.

At last, humbly and desperately, he appealed to Benjamin West* for help, for West's studio and purse were open to every aspiring American artist. In his five years with West, Stuart worked on parts of his master's large historical compositions and helped turn out state portraits. Only portraiture interested him,. and in portraiture only the face. He had never learned to draw skillfully, and did not build up his work from linear studies or foundation. Instead, he developed on the canvas what seemed, as he described it, a clouded mirror image, gradually bringing into clear vision the face as he saw it. As he worked in this personal way, he would

keep up a steady patter of conversation, stories, jokes, and puns, to ensure animation in his model.

This style matured under the sympathetic eye of West, who was a very different sort of painter. Working with West, Stuart's rash, exuberant self-confidence returned. He had exhibited occasionally at the Royal Academy and needed only a successful picture to launch an indpendent career. This he achieved in 1781 with his full-length of William Grant, *The Skater* (1782, Washington). Portrait commissions poured into his new studio and Stuart lived in style, painting brilliantly and spending freely. Leaving debts and angry patrons behind, he moved on to new triumphs in Dublin, collecting first-payments on portraits he had no intention of finishing. He sailed for America in 1792.

In America he was immediately at the top of his profession, in New York until 1794, in Philadelphia and neighboring Germantown until 1803, in Washington until 1805, and then for the remainder of his life in Boston. His work revealed a remarkable ability to express character, as in his *General Horatio Gates* (c. 1794, Metropolitan). His style was noted for quick, deft brushstrokes, surface effects, and pale flesh tones. His sitters were idealized, in an impressionistic way, and as such continued the tradition of "idealized" portraiture made popular in England by the masters Sir Joshua Reynolds and George Romney. The total effect was one of nobility or romantic interest and quite different from the literal American style of portraiture. This made his first *Washington* (1795, Washington) immediately more acceptable than any other, a greater portrait, perhaps, than his more famous "Athenaeum" *Washington* (Boston) of the next year. These quickly led to portraits of other well-known public figures, with Americans eager to be shown as only Stuart could show them; but his career was marred again by broken promises. Even the famous "Athenaeum" portrait and its companion piece of Mrs. Washington, paid for in part, were never delivered. Through the last years in Boston, with his eccentricities and double-dealing accepted as marks of genius, he enjoyed more stability and produced much fine work, though not in the same lively Georgian style of his earlier painting.

Stuart accepted no regular students,

but gave instruction to some young artists to whom he had taken a liking, among them Mather Brown,* John Trumbull,* and Samuel F. B. Morse.*

(C.C.S.)

Sugarman, George (1912–   ).
One of the rare American sculptors who has been able to bend wood to his will, making a statement which is thoroughly contemporary and at the same time based on the simple skills of the wood craftsman. Sugarman's polychrome wood sculptures, increasingly simplified of late, have won him international renown. Born in New York, N.Y., Sugarman began to paint in 1950. However, the following year, he went to Paris on the G.I. Bill program, studied with the Russian-born sculptor Ossip Zadkine, and began intensive work in sculpture. He remained in Paris until 1955, when he returned to New York and settled down to develop his unique vision of wood sculpture. His first exhibition in New York City (1960) revealed the liberality of his fantasy. Great, sprawling forms of laminated wood, reaching out into space in unexpected and highly informal relationships, indicated the degree to which he adhered to the abstract expressionist principles of his generation. The following year he exhibited again, this time composing zigzagging and curvilinear forms in even more complicated sequences, and compounding the complexities by introducing color. By stressing the stacatto breaks in line, he enforced his central principle of discontinuity.

Sugarman was one of the first American sculptors to regard the entire surrounding space as integral to his sculpture. By 1964 he was developing huge sequences of smallish forms that wandered freely over the length of the gallery, but by miraculous force managed to form a single work. By 1967 he had begun to reduce the elements in his work, retaining the unexpected curves and elisions of forms, yet keeping them in large, open configurations. His uncanny ability to poise his forms on the ground in such a way as to suggest that they exist independent of the floor support was remarked by numerous critics. When, in 1969, he showed very large and very open structures, still wittily polychromed, he was hailed as one of America's most inventive sculptors whose fantasy had not been erased by

1

2

1. *Gilbert Stuart.* Mrs. John Adams, *1815, National Gallery of Art, Washington, D.C.*
2. *Gilbert Stuart.* George Washington, *1796. Museum of Fine Arts, Boston.*

the prevailing minimalist tendency.

Sugarman exhibits regularly in New York, and has had large one-man exhibitions in Amsterdam, Berlin, and Basel. He won second prize in the 1961 Carnegie International, and has received grants from the Longview Foundation, the Ford Foundation, and the National Council on the Arts.   (D.A.)

Sullivan, Louis Henri (1856–1924). Architect. Born in Boston, Mass., son of the proprietor of a dancing academy, he attended local schools. In 1872 he entered the Massachusetts Institute of Technology, the first notable school of architecture in America. After graduation, Sullivan went to Philadelphia and worked for Furness & Hewitt until the panic of 1873. He then joined his family in Chicago and entered zestfully into the reconstruction of the city, which had been devastated by the great fire of 1871. Apart from a year's study in Paris (1874), his career centered in Chicago. There, in the engineering architectural office of William Le Baron Jenney (1832–1907), he met Dankmar Adler (1844–1900), who would become his partner.

Adler was born in Lengsfeld, Germany, the son of a rabbi, and had come to Chicago in 1861, beginning his engineering apprenticeship in the office of Augustus Bauer. After several years in Detroit and Ann Arbor, and Civil War service as an engineer, he went to work for Edward Burling (1819–1892). In 1871 the firm became Burling & Adler, and then, in 1878, Dankmar Adler & Co. Sullivan joined Adler in 1879 as chief draftsman, and in 1881 they formed the firm of Adler & Sullivan. Adler was the engineer and businessman, while Sullivan devoted himself to design.

One of the first buildings Sullivan worked on with Adler was the Borden Block (1880) in Chicago, a clearly articulated (that is, expressing its structure) masonry bearing-wall office building in which narrow brick piers rose up to the slablike roof cornice. An innovation in construction was the use of cast-iron window mullions and I-beam lintels. Forming a new firm, Adler & Sullivan soon began a series of commissions destined to awaken architects to the fact that ornament could assume a highly individual character, expressive of structure and unhampered by classical rules. The firm's Rothschild Store, at 210 West Monroe Street (1881), was

1

2

3

4

Louis Henri Sullivan
1. *Carson, Pirie & Scott Building, Chicago, 1906 (with Dankmar Adler).*
2. *Walker Warehouse, Chicago, 1889 (with Dankmar Adler).*
3. *People's Savings Bank, Sidney, O., 1918.*
4. *Carson, Pirie & Scott, Detail of main entry, Chicago, 1906.*

a distinctly articulated design, with the clearly defined verticals of the cast-iron window mullions rising uninterrupted from the first floor to the top floor. The ornament, an array of Egyptian lotus blossoms, was highly original. The Ryerson Building, at 16-20 East Randolph Street (1884), had three bays between structural masonry verticals, and also used ornament reminiscent of the Egyptian. The Troescher Building at 15-19 South Market Street (1884) exhibited a feature anticipating skyscraper construction: horizontal I-beams serving as lintels, bearing directly on the masonry piers.

Influenced no doubt by Richardson's* remarkable Marshall Field Warehouse of 1885–87, Sullivan's Walker Warehouse at 200-214 South Market Street (1889) is a parallel solution to the same problem, and had in it the seeds of his successful skyscraper* designs. It, too, had vertical piers that were clearly defined as structural supports. A large temporary structure, an auditorium in the Interstate Exposition Building (1885), led to one of the firm's greatest commissions. So perfect was the acoustics of the auditorium that Ferdinand W. Peck, one of its sponsors, conceived the idea of a permanent auditorium building at Michigan Boulevard and Congress Street, combining a hotel and business offices. Sullivan designed the bold, rather forbidding, Romanesque revival* building (1889) with a single blocky tower. In the splendid interiors of the auditorium and the hotel, Sullivan introduced those highly individual details which made the building so outstanding. Again the acoustics was superb, and established Adler as the foremost acoustical engineer in the country.

At this time Sullivan also designed the Standard Club on Michigan Avenue and 24th Street (1888). A rather restrained essay in rock-faced Romanesque revival, it was relieved in 1893 by the addition of a two-story loggia that was poetic in its finely detailed suggestion of Oriental antecedents. Several office buildings and hotels kept the firm busy from 1890–93. These included the low-lying Opera House Block(1890) in Pueblo, Col., a square, combination office and theatre building of rock-faced stone in Romanesque revival style; and the St. Nicholas Hotel in St. Louis (1893), a bold, high-roofed building with striking gable ends pierced by

large arched windows, all rather German in manner. At the 1893 World's Columbian Exposition in Chicago, the "Great White City" was a classical mirage. Sullivan's Transportation Building, with its "Golden Door," was the only building at the fair which had the validity of contemporaneity. Resplendent with color, its long ranges of arched windows flanked the great central doorway. In the frame of the "Golden Door," Sullivan displayed some of his finest ornament, mingling organic nature forms with basic geometric forms.

In the residential field, Sullivan designed some very interesting houses on Chicago's south side, beginning with the large John Borden House on Lake Park Avenue (1880), a steep-roofed masonry building with brick walls horizontally banded with stone. Sullivan also did the Sol Bloomenfeld House on West Chicago Avenue (1883), with its Egyptian ornament; and for Max Rothschild, three uniform row houses with Moorish overtones, on Indiana Avenue. The great town house for James Charnley, at 1365 Astor Street, on the "Gold Coast" (1892), although Sullivanian in its ornament, showed the hand of a young draftsman in the office, Frank Lloyd Wright*—especially in the arrangement of its front door and flanking windows.

In a series of mausoleums, Sullivan was able to concentrate his design talents as never before. The Ryerson Tomb in Graceland Cemetery, Chicago (1889), with its battered (inward sloping) walls and cavernous doorway, expresses sorrow in visual form. Conversely, the little Eliza Getty Tomb, also in Graceland (1890), exudes a feeling of joyous assurance, with the ornament of its upper half contrasted with the smooth stone of the lower half.

Sullivan evolved a beautiful and original system of ornament to clothe buildings in which form followed function. He applied similar ornament in his most significant contribution, the high-rise office building. The first of these was the ten-story Wainwright Building in St. Louis (1891). Freed of every vestige of classicism, it was a unique creation. It had a smooth two-story base surmounted by a seven-story vertical shaft in which evenly spaced pilasters ran up between the windows to an effulgence of floral ornament at the top floor. After the Wainwright Building

1

2

1. *Patrick J. Sullivan.* A-Hunting He
   Would Go, *1940. Museum of Modern
   Art, N.Y.*
2. *Thomas Sully.* Mrs. Edward Hudson,
   1814. Detroit Institute of the Arts.

came the Schiller Building in Chicago (1892), an office tower superimposed upon a theatre. An arcaded loggia across the width of the building marked the entrance to the theatre, while the tower was crowned by a series of arcaded loggias with roof slab and a cupola on top. The Stock Exchange Building at 30 North LaSalle Street (1894), the first to sink caissons down to hardpan for support, was a large thirteen-story building that made use of the "Golden Door" theme. In his design for the Guaranty (later Prudential) Building in Buffalo, N.Y. (1895), Sullivan returned to the Wainwright Building theme with equally spaced verticals separated only by single windows. Adler left the firm in 1895 because of the lack of work after the panic of 1893, and the Guaranty Building was the last major work under the firm name.

One of the finest buildings Sullivan ever designed expressed the nature of steel frame construction—a cage wherein verticals are no more important than horizontals. This was the Schlesinger & Meyer Department Store (now Carson, Pirie & Scott), at State and Madison Streets (1899–1906). It had a strong corner tower, from which bay-width plate glass windows streamed away in either direction. A wealth of organic ornament adorned the first two floors of iron facings, and a recessed loggia at the top emphasized the slab-like quality of the roof.

Commissions had fallen off drastically after the dissolution of the firm, and Sullivan felt that his new architecture of democracy had been defeated by the classical revival that swept America after the 1893 Chicago Exhibition. He turned more and more to writing, hoping to awaken young draftsmen with his pleas for an organic architecture. Even in his lonely last years he was still able to create a series of gemlike small buildings for banks in outlying communities: the National Farmer's Bank (1908) in Owatonna, Minn.; the Peoples' Savings Bank (1911) in Cedar Rapids, Iowa; the Merchants' National Bank (1914) in Grinnell, Iowa; the Peoples' Savings & Loan Association Bank (1918) in Sidney, Ohio; and the Farmers' & Merchants' Union Bank (1919) in Columbus, Wis. The blank wall surfaces of these small rectangular buildings were enriched by an efflorescence of ornament at doors and windows.

Late in life he published the story of his life, *The Autobiography of an Idea* (1924), and finally, his beautiful drawings, in folio form, in *A System of Architectural Ornament According with a Philosophy of Man's Powers* (1924). Few architects—with the exception of his disciple Frank Lloyd Wright, who always referred to him as *Lieber Meister*—were able to express themselves in their writings in a more telling and sensitive way than Sullivan. He died at a low ebb in his career, but ample recognition of his greatness has since been accorded him. (A.B.)

Sullivan, Patrick J. (1894–1967).
Self-taught West Virginia artist. He first worked in a printing company and in the mills of industrial Braddock, Pa., where he was born, but he began to experiment with drawing and painting after some experience with house painting. He was apprenticed as a house painter in Wheeling, West Va., and apparently began painting in earnest during the Depression, when he found little income-producing work. During military service he was influenced by the design and symbolism of Ethiopian primitive art. Sullivan's artistic productivity spanned about a decade, but the few paintings he laboriously completed show him to be a highly original allegorist. His richly textured picture surfaces, achieved through repeated application of pigment followed by sandpapering that retains the pattern of individual brushstrokes, appear to have been cast in a mold. Subject matter ranges from the broadly philosophical *A-Hunting He Would Go* (1940, Modern Museum) to *An Historical Event* (private collection), painted in 1937 to celebrate the romance of King Edward VIII and Mrs. Wallis Simpson. In all of his work each element—including figures, forms, and colors—is assigned a specific, and often original, symbolic meaning, so that comprehension demands close study and some interpretive assistance from the artist. (M.J.G.)

Sully, Thomas (1783–1872).
Leading portrait, miniature, and figure painter. He was born in England, and went to Charleston, S.C., in 1792. There, a schoolmate, Charles Fraser,* instilled in him an interest in art. Later, he received lessons from his older brother, Lawrence (1769–1804), a miniature painter, and his brother-in-law,

Jean Belzons (active 1794–1812), a miniaturist, drawing teacher, and theatrical scene painter. Sully's professional career began at Norfolk, Va., in 1801.

His career was always close to the theater, aided in these difficult early years by the friendship of the distinguished actor Thomas Abthorpe Cooper. On Cooper's advice, Sully moved to New York in 1806, where he did some painting, but two years later he settled in Philadelphia, known as an art and publishing center. Artists were going abroad in those years of economic depression, and Sully was in England in 1809–10, receiving, as so many did, the friendly advice of Benjamin West.* However, he was far more influenced by Britain's leading portrait painter, Sir Thomas Lawrence, whom he came to know. Some of the fluent aristocratic verve of Lawrence's portraits is thereafter present in Sully's work, modulated to American taste yet equally appealing to a socially prominent patronage. Noted for a fluency of brushstroke, and dramatic use of light and shadow, Sully's work had the freshness and charm that enabled him to capture a mood or a pose. He became primarily a portraitist.

Returning to Philadelphia, he occupied the rooms in Philosophical Hall on Independence Square vacated by Charles Willson Peale.* Peale's death left him without serious rivals and he was soon highly successful. At the height of his career in 1838 he again went to England and painted *Queen Victoria* (private collection; sketch, 1838, Metropolitan) on commission of the Society of the Sons of St. George in Philadelphia. His portraits include works of Lafayette, Jefferson, Monroe, Madison, Jackson, and Washington, as well as members of Washington and Philadelphia society. Of major importance among his subject paintings were *Washington at the Passage of the Delaware* (1819, Boston) and *Mother and Son* (1840, Metropolitan), a painting of his daughter and grandson composed with rhythmic and poetic charm.

Of Sully's life work, some two thousand portraits are recorded, and over four hundred subject pieces—a monument to an enduring talent and to the popularity of his style in 19th-century America. (C.C.S.)

Supergraphics.
Gigantic design fragments painted or applied to architectural surfaces to pro-

1

2

Supergraphics
1. *Charles Moore. Church Street South housing complex, New Haven, Conn., 1971.*
2. *Ford and Earl Associates. RCA Consumer Electronics Division Design Center, Indianapolis, 1972.*

duce an effect of expanding space or volume. Such designs, executed by exponents of supermannerism* from 1962–71, were abstracts of two-dimensional typefaces, flat outlines of geometric forms—circles, cones, or cylinders—or fragments of photomurals from billboard advertising.

Generally they create abstract, optical effects. destroying architectural planes, distorting corners, and consequently changing architectural scale. Since the forms are so huge that they cannot be contained within the frame of a single architectural plane, they extend onto adjacent or opposite planes—from wall to wall to floor or ceiling—or beyond the planes themselves. By leading the viewer to complete these forms in his own mind's eye, supergraphics expand vision beyond a building or beyond the size of a room. They therefore change the viewpoint of the viewer as well as the scale of the building or room. For example, arcs on a wall can suggest huge wheels somewhere outdoors, as in the work of Charles Moore and Hugh Hardy. Stripes in reverse perspective can shorten a hallway, as one design commune showed. Many of these designs, applied primarily to existing buildings, are, however, so literary in their approach that they are not immediately understandable. But once the designer's intention is known, the design can be seen only in the intended way. Supergraphics was the most flamboyant and popular of the explorations into scale by the exponents of supermannerism.*   (C.R.S.)

Supermannerism.
In architecture a revolutionary design movement beginning in the 1960s as a counteraction to the minimal* style of the 1940s and 1950s. It is characterized by a manipulation of scale, as in 16th-century mannerist style, and by a broader range of allowable design elements. It accepts the pop art* device of using objects and materials out of context and out of scale. Because it uses an all-inclusive design vocabulary, it has been called the design of "inclusion" and "accommodation." Its social goal is to suggest that the design professions should help to create new life-styles and environments. Young designers, especially, encourage an involvement in social and political issues even though these are not related to formal design and esthetics. The formal goal of

3

4

Supermannerism
3. Hardy Holzman Pfeiffer Associates. Cloisters Townhouses, Cincinnati, 1969, exterior.
4. Hardy Holzman Pfeiffer Associates. Cloisters Townhouses, Cincinnati, 1969, interior.

supermannerism is to allow the physical and psychological needs of people to determine design. This presumes a more active participation in design by clients and users—an actual owner manipulation of his surroundings. To those who object to such concessions to chance and indeterminacy, the answer has been that there is no totally determined object and that art should be a discovery.

As part of the expansion in design goals, supermannerists included in their design vocabulary the diagonal as well as the pure rectangle and square that were hallmarks of the International style;* in fact, the supermannerist period could be called the decade of the diagonal. Supermannerists include historical traditions excluded by the internationalists—preservation, decoration, applied pattern, and ornament—as in the work of Charles Moore* and those who use graphics. Supermannerisms also include pop art allusions to commercial, synthetic, and roadside environments, as in the architectural billboards of Robert Venturi.* Also accepted by supermannerism are accidental developments that occur in the design process. Office landscape, a system of office planning, accepts an unorganized furniture arrangement if it is a functional order based on workflow and office circulation patterns. Supermannerism also sanctions whimsy and humor, and accepts ambiguity as a design element. Supermannerism destroys rectilinear spaces, relying for effect on dislocation and even alienation. It camouflages and confuses with unexpected textures, colors, perspectives, and lighting. It aims at a dematerialization of architecture through invisibility, multiple function, and reflection.

Finally, supermannerism adopts a superscale. In the decade of moon flight, sculptors and architects developed an esthetic measure of space that gave a dual vision—one of the earthbound volume they actually saw, and another as if in orbit. The effect is illustrated in megascale buildings such as the New Haven Parking Garage by Paul Rudolph* and the Knights of Columbus Building, also in New Haven, Conn., by Kevin Roche.* This superscale is also seen in deliberately ambiguous painted emblems, known as supergraphics,* which aim at a similar expansion of space.

Other exponents of some aspect of this movement are architects Hugh Hardy, John M. Johansen,* Philip Johnson,* Ulrich Franzen,* Walter Netsch, and graphic designers such as Barbara Stauffacher Solomon* and Barrie Briscoe.

Many critics reject the movement as frivolous and superficial, and opposition to its permissiveness and to the pop art inclusions has been vehement. Nevertheless, the movement grew from a series of optical, textural, and formal games that amused designers into a wrenching effort toward a transition to a space-age world. (C.R.S.)

Surrealism.

The roots of surrealism have been traced wherever the subjective, intuitive, and imaginative elements in art have been stressed above rational and conscious control. Precedents can be found in the romantic and symbolist movements, and the romantic-symbolist tradition affected a number of 20th-century artists (including Russian-born Marc Chagall and the Italian Giorgio di Chirico) who influenced the surrealist movement without actually joining it. The immediate predecessor of the movement was the loosely-allied dada* group of anti-rational and anti-esthetic writers, painters, and sculptors, many of whom congregated in Paris after World War I. By 1922 dada was losing its cohesion; essentially negative, it was exhausting itself.

The French poet André Breton, who was schooled in Freudian theory, sought to channel the movement in a constructive direction, as proclaimed by his "Surrealist Manifesto" of 1924: "Surrealism is based on the belief in the superior reality of certain forms of association heretofore neglected, in the omnipotence of the dream, and in the disinterested play of thought. It leads to the permanent destruction of all other psychic mechanisms and to its substitution for them in the solution of the principal problems of life." Where dada had been nihilistic, surrealism proposed to achieve a positive resolution of "dream and reality into a sort of absolute reality, a surreality, so to speak."

The surrealists as a group exhibited first in Paris in 1925; numerous other exhibitions followed, including showings in the United States in the 1930s and as late as 1960. Included in these exhibitions were internationally influ-

ential artists of very diverse styles, among them the German painter Max Ernst, who often worked in collage* and frottage (random rubbings); the Spaniard Salvador Dali, painter of sharply focused nightmarish visions; and the Swiss painter Paul Klee, contriver of deceptively childlike symbols. In the United States, too, the formative stage of surrealism was intermingled with the maturity of dada. Marcel Duchamp,* Francis Picabia, and Man Ray* were active in this phase. These artists, however, left for Paris after World War I; thus, when surrealism proper evolved, it was slow to gain adherents in America. In the 1930s Peter Blume* and Joseph Cornell* were among the first to reflect its influence. In 1939, however, the French Yves Tanguy, the English printmaker William Stanley Hayter and the Chilean Roberto Matta Echuarren arrived in America, soon followed by Dali and Ernst. The impact of their diverse surrealist styles came just as the war brought a new wave of subjectivism in art.

Such pioneers of abstract expressionism and action painting as Arshile Gorky* and Jackson Pollock* emphasized a completely spontaneous, irrational approach. During the 1940s and 1950s painters like Loren MacIver* and William Baziotes* evoked dreamlike associative images while arranging selected abstract forms. The calmly meticulous elaboration of nightmarish situations was carried on by George Tooker,* while, at the other extreme, the most incongruous juxtapositions of painted surfaces and "found objects" were arranged by Robert Rauschenberg.* Pop art,* happenings,* and much recent technological art spring from an anti-esthetic bias and leave order largely to chance. (D.W.S.)

Symbolism.

A movement in France during the last two decades of the 19th century, with manifestations in literature, music, and the fine arts. The poets Verlaine and Mallarmé, the dramatist Maeterlinck and the composer Debussy were among those who sought new techniques to convey sensations and inner emotions more directly. Among the painters, Paul Gauguin was the principal theorist at the outset, stressing by 1885 the importance of an intuitive, "primitive" approach in order to express deeper emotions. By 1888 he and his friends (including Vincent van Gogh) were working in a style that took new liberties in distorting nature for force and breadth of effect. Meanwhile, a more dreamlike vision was created by the French painter Odilon Redon, who declared that the symbolists aimed to "put the logic of the visible at the service of the invisible." The symbolist exploration of the intrinsic expressive potential of line, form, and color helped shape art nouveau* and stimulated the next generation of painters, including Henri Matisse and the fauves. In America, art nouveau influenced the decorative arts (as in the work of Louis Tiffany*) and illustration (see John Sloan). Painters such as Alfred Maurer* were deeply affected by fauvism.* The highly individual styles of Albert Pinkham Ryder* and Arthur B. Davies* combine the symbolists' concern for intuitive, expressive form with allegorical subject matter. (D.W.S.)

Synchromism.
The only one of the early "isms" in international modern art originated by Americans, it was introduced in two exhibitions held jointly by Morgan Russell* and Stanton Macdonald-Wright* in 1913. The word "synchromy" ("with color"), suggesting harmonized colors, was coined by Russell on the analogy of the word "symphony." Between 1908 and 1911 both Russell and Wright had developed their painting along parallel lines. Both were young Americans working in Paris, stimulated by the revelations of Monet, Cézanne, and Matisse. By 1910 both were experimenting with heightened color in their figurative work. They became friends and began to study books on color theory together. Meanwhile in Europe, Robert Delaunay and Frantisek Kupka were moving toward nonfigurative color painting, leading a trend so pronounced in the Paris exhibitions of 1912 that the French critic Guillaume Apollinaire introduced the term "orphic cubism" (see Orphism) to describe it. Russell and Wright were thus not the leaders of this direction in 1912, but they had been pursuing a similar course fairly independently. Russell has left notes and letters that show he felt Delaunay was not carrying his color experimentation far enough, while he himself aimed to ". . . do a piece of expression solely by means of color and the way it is put down, in showers

and broad patches . . . with force and clearness and large geometric patterns, the effect of the whole as being constructed with volumes of color." It was a year before he realized this aim.

Russell exhibited *Synchromie en Vert* (destroyed) at the Salon des Indépendants of 1913, and in June he and Wright exhibited together in Munich. Their paintings exhibited at the Bernheim-Jeune gallery in Paris that Fall developed toward more abstract form, better integrated with color. The tenets of synchromism were expressed in the catalogs to these exhibitions and in *Modern Art,* a book by Wright and his brother, Willard Huntington Wright, in 1915. By late 1913, Russell was painting total abstractions. His surfaces were broken into abrupt planes of strong colors that served to convey effects of light and recession. The organizing movement derived from a general dynamic theme, but not a specific motive in nature. Wright, however, preferred to base his movement on a figure theme, and painted few totally abstract works. His planes of modulated color follow sequences of fanlike or disk shapes that form rhythmic progressions.

With the outbreak of the war, Russell and Wright parted, but they spread the influence of synchromism. Wright's friend Thomas Hart Benton* used "synchromy" in the titles of his paintings, and Andrew Dasburg* painted "improvisations" strongly affected by Russell's style. All four artists exhibited synchromist-influenced work in the important Forum exhibition in New York in 1916. Russell and Wright continued using "synchromy" in the titles of their work into the 1920s, but Wright had by that time moved into an essentially different style. (D.W.S.)

Syng, Phillip, Jr. (1703–89).
Silversmith, born in Ireland, son of a silversmith who came to Philadelphia in 1714. A distinguished craftsman and active citizen, he was a founder of the Library Company and the American Philosophical Society, an original trustee of the academy that became the University of Pennsylvania, and a friend and co-inventor with Benjamin Franklin. The electrical machine used by Franklin in 1747 was contrived by Syng. In 1752 he was commissioned to make the silver inkstand purchased by the Provincial Assembly and used

at the signing of the Declaration of Independence and the Constitution of the United States (Independence Hall, Philadelphia). Fashioned in the rococo style, the tray has an elaborately scrolled border decorated with asymmetrical shells and is supported by four cast, scrolled feet. The containers for the quill pens, the ink, and the sand have cyma-curved sides and pierced tops. In the same style is a shell-footed snuffer tray by Syng (Metropolitan). In 1750 he cut the official seals for the counties of York and Cumberland, and provided the Common Council of Philadelphia with the die for medals presented in 1757 to Colonel John Armstrong of Carlisle. Syng was also a maker of silver ornaments presented to Indians. In 1772 he retired, turning his business over to Richard Humphreys.* Syng was represented by sixty-two pieces of silver in a 1956 exhibition of Philadelphia silver, the majority of which were canns, tankards, coffeepots, and trays. (M.G.F.)

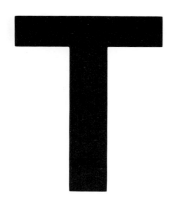

Taft, Lorado (1860–1936).
Sculptor, author, and lecturer. He was born in Elmwood, Ill., and after graduating from the University of Illinois went to Paris (1880) and attended the École des Beaux-Arts. By 1886 he had established his studio in Chicago, and he became an instructor and lecturer (1886–1929) at the Art Institute. Taft became a well-known sculptor in his day, but he is remembered chiefly as the first historian of American sculpture. His *History of American Sculpture* was first published in 1903, and his *Modern Tendencies in Sculpture*—a defense of the academic tradition and an attack on the abstractionists—appeared in 1921. His best-known sculptures are the *Fountain of Columbus* (1912, Washington, D.C.), the *Fountain of the Great Lakes* (1913, Chicago), and the *Fountain of Time* (1922, Washington Park, Chicago). Taft worked in the grand manner of the academic tradition, producing large-scale symbolic works that were characteristic of the École des Beaux-Arts. (W.C.)

Tait, Arthur Fitzwilliam (1819–1905).
Highly popular and prolific English-born painter of sporting scenes. Tait was born near Liverpool, England, and went to school in Lancaster. He later worked in a picture store in Manchester and studied from casts at the Royal Manchester Institution. In the 1840s, he sketched widely in England, and lithographs were made from a number of his drawings.

In 1850 Tait emigrated to the United States and settled in New York City. From this time on, he worked in a studio on Broadway, while usually summering at his camp in the Adirondacks, although he did on occasion travel as far west as Chicago. His favorite subjects, and the ones which made him one of the most popular painters of his day, were Adirondack scenes. These were rugged pictures of mountains and lakes, animals and game birds, and their hunters; the artist often depicted a dramatic moment, such as the instant before the hunter's shot. *American Frontier Life* (1852, Yale) is typical of a series of western scenes in which he depicted frontier and Indian life. A number of his paintings were printed by the famous lithographers Currier & Ives,* and his popularity grew along with theirs. During the 1850s, he also painted a number of still lifes of dead game.

Tait was a skillful craftsman who knew and capitalized on the taste of his time. Although his style developed very little after 1860 and his subjects were repetitive, he deserves recognition as an excellent animal and genre painter.
(T.E.S.)

Takaezu, Toshiko (1922–   ).
Ceramist known for the quality of her thrown forms, the subtlety of brush decoration, and the range of her glaze coloration. Born in Pepeekeo, Hawaii, she studied at the University of Hawaii and in 1951 went to the Cranbrook Academy in Michigan to study under Maija Grotell.* She has taught at Cranbrook, the Cleveland Institute of Art, and other schools and is now at Princeton University. She works with stoneware on the wheel and favors a closed, round form, which she shapes off the wheel. Her Buddhist upbringing and interest in Zen are evident in the concentration with which she works at the wheel and in the freedom and spontaneity with which she brush decorates. Although she can produce intense colors from high-fired cobalt-zinc glazes, her most typical colors are somber cobalt and copper blues, greens, and blacks. Her work is included in such major collections as the Cleveland Museum of Art and the Detroit Institute of Art.
(R.S.)

Taliaferro, Richard (1705–79).
Builder-architect. Probably born in York County, Va. So little is known of him that his importance is difficult to assess. If he designed the large southern mansions attributed to him, he was indeed remarkable. He is documented as a justice of the peace in Williamsburg in 1737, and as sheriff in 1740. He repaired the Governor's Palace, Williamsburg (1749–51), particularly the "Ball Room Wing." He built his own house in Williamsburg (1755), later bequeathed to his son-in-law, George Wythe, professor at William and Mary College. He also built a country house three miles outside of Williamsburg. He made repairs to the president's house, William and Mary College, in 1756. In 1774 he was elected to the Virginia Assembly.

If Taliaferro was the architect that some scholars suppose, he must be credited with designing a group of the finest brick buildings in 18th-century America. These would be Nelson House, Yorktown (c.1740) for Thomas Nelson; Elsing Green (1748) for Carter Braxton; Westover (c.1730) for William Byrd II; Wilton (1753) for William Randolph III; Carter's Grove (1750–53) for Carter Burwell; and Cleve (c.1750) for Charles Carter. Details of design for these houses derive mainly from William Salmon's *Palladio Londinensis* (1734). All are simple rectangular blocks of brick, some with outbuildings, and are decorated with an assortment of classical motifs, most elaborately on interiors where the woodwork approaches elegance. (P.F.N.)

Tamarind Lithography Workshop.
Founded in 1960 by June Wayne,* and funded by the Ford Foundation, this Los Angeles workshop served for ten years as the training ground for many lithographers, and a place where over 150 artists made original prints. In the

556

program devised by Miss Wayne, a committee selected artists to be awarded grants allowing them to work at the shop for a two-month period. Among the artists who made prints at Tamarind were Josef Albers,* Richard Diebenkorn,* Sam Francis,* Antonio Frasconi,* William Gropper,* Philip Guston,* Nicholas Krushenick,* Rico Lebrun,* and Louise Nevelson.* Each artist carried away from Tamarind not only editions of every print, but a knowledge of lithography that in many cases stimulated them and other artists to continue making prints. Miss Wayne's workshop also carried out research in aluminum-plate lithography, paper and ink stability, business methods for private workshops and print galleries, and preservation of remaining lithographic limestone. Printers undertook their preliminary study at the University of New Mexico (since July, 1970, the location of the workshop of Tamarind Institute) and then worked at Tamarind. Several then started their own workshops: Irwin Hollander's shop in New York City and Kenneth Tyler's Gemini G.E.L.* in Los Angeles have been in operation the longest time. From 1960 through June, 1970, over 2900 lithographs were printed in editions of twenty, plus nine Tamarind impressions. Publications on research programs as well as exhibition catalogs were issued.   (R.C.)

Tanguy, Yves (1900–55).
Painter, born in Paris. Tanguy's father was a French government official who summered in Brittany. The sand, the vast plateaus, and the prehistoric dolmens and menhirs of the latter region later played a major part in forming the younger Tanguy's art. It was not until he was twenty-three years of age, and after serving as a merchant marine officer and a soldier, that Tanguy, inspired by the work of Giorgio de Chirico, decided to become a painter. He was entirely self-taught.

Tanguy joined the surrealist movement in 1925, and exhibited with the surrealists at the Palais des Beaux-Arts in Brussels (1937). His surrealism* was entirely a matter of subject; technically his work was orthodox and involved no experiment. His mature manner, heightened by the experience of a trip to Africa, involved the surrealist "nostalgia of space" in the form of an endless plain merging with an equally endless sky; on the plain appear fantastic, often

extremely involved constructions suggesting bones and metallic forms, with much emphasis on pearly surface effects and precisely defined contours. Tanguy came to the United States in 1939 with his wife, Kay Sage, also a surrealist painter. The American West affected him as strongly as had Africa, and his later canvases, such as *Fear* (1949, Whitney), are larger in size and bolder in color than those done in France. Tanguy never sketched, but worked directly on the canvas, discovering his painting as he created it.

Tanner, Henry Ossawa (1859–1937).
Painter of religious subjects and landscape. Considered the most able black artist to emerge in the United States in the 19th century, Tanner grew up in Pittsburgh and Philadelphia, where his father was a distinguished African Methodist Episcopal bishop. As a boy he determined to become an artist. He studied under Thomas Eakins* at the Pennsylvania Academy of the Fine Arts* (1880–82), then worked as an illustrator while painting works that were exhibited at the Pennsylvania Academy and the National Academy of Design* in New York City. In 1888 he moved to Atlanta, Ga., where he taught for a year at Clark University. In 1891 he went to Paris and attended the Académie Julien for two winters, studying with Benjamin Constant and Jean-Paul Laurens. He soon began exhibiting in the Salon, receiving an honorable mention for *Daniel in the Lion's Den* (1896, Los Angeles) and a medal for *The Raising of Lazarus* (1897, purchased by the French government for the Luxembourg Gallery). Tanner painted landscapes and genre paintings, as, for example, *The Banjo Lesson* (1893, Hampton Institute), but he was above all identified with religious painting. His travels to the Holy Land in 1897 and 1898 inspired paintings on religious themes which enjoyed broad success in both Europe and the United States. He received a number of major prizes between 1900 and 1915 and was elected to the National Academy. A resident of France for most of his life, Tanner visited the United States in 1902, but after two years returned to Paris and remained there.

Tanner's earlier paintings reflect the dark brown tones and painstaking realism of Eakins. By the later 1890s his style became broader and more gener-

1

2

1. *Yves Tanguy.* Fear, 1949. Whitney Museum of American Art, N.Y.
2. *Henry Ossawa Tanner.* The Banjo Lesson, c.1893. Hampton Institute, Hampton, Va.

alized, and he often employed a bluish tonality. His work was founded on careful drawing in the academic tradition but was richly overlaid by layers of paint and glaze that developed an abstract, subjective poetry, at times reminiscent of the work of Albert Ryder.*   (D.W.S.)

Tarbell, Edmund C. (1862–1938). A leading Boston impressionist painter, born in West Groton, Mass. Tarbell's career paralleled Frank W. Benson's*: they attended the Boston Museum School and Académie Julien together; both were long-time teachers at the Boston Museum School, beginning in 1890; and both became members of The Ten* in 1898. There was a moment when Tarbell, working out of the darker, tighter manner of his French training, moved into a broadly conceived, glowing impressionism,* as authoritative as any in America, as in *In the Orchard* (1891, National Coll.). His friends and followers were nicknamed "Tarbellites" and described as virtuosos of the "dot style." The exploitation of this manner, however, was left to men like Benson and Robert Reid.* Tarbell turned to calm, light-filled interiors, where young ladies read or sewed in gracious sitting rooms with gleaming tables and floors. His beautifully drawn and executed paintings, such as *Mother and Mary* (1922, Washington), owed much to Vermeer. Tarbell received many marks of recognition, including the Clarke prize at the National Academy in 1900.

Along with his upper-middle-class genre scenes, Tarbell painted a few still lifes, marked by careful finish, and many portraits, done with sober craftsmanship. The latter were so in demand after World War I that Tarbell moved to Washington for a time, painting presidents Wilson and Hoover, and other figures of that epoch. He continued exhibiting his refined figure studies well into the 1930s, a calm and dignified Boston conservative.   (D.W.S.)

Taufscheine.
Decorated illuminated baptismal certificates made by the Pennsylvania Dutch and constituting a considerable body of the decorative lettering known as fractur.* These are valued as sources of history and genealogy because they customarily provided, not only a child's name and the date and place of baptism, but parents' and sponsors' names

1

2

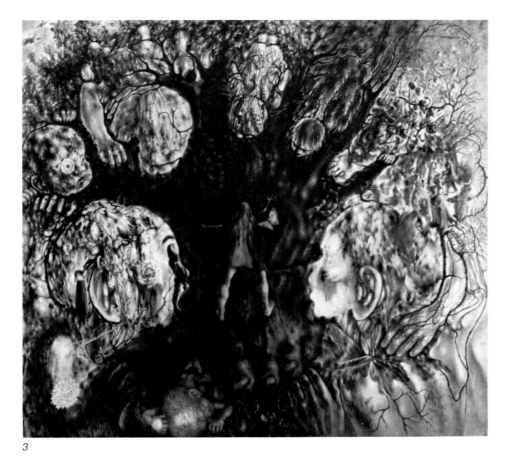

3

as well. Like other examples of fractur, *taufscheine* (meaning baptismal certificates in German) incorporated stylized symbols reminiscent of Near Eastern decorative motifs, as in the one by an unknown maker commemorating the baptism of Alexander Tanner (Abby Aldrich Rockefeller). (M.J.G.)

Tawney, Lenore (n.d.–).
Among the first weavers to expose the warp for spatial and expressive purposes. Born in Lorain, Ohio, she studied to be a sculptor but began weaving in 1948. She was soon producing linen hangings that ignored traditional functions or the wall. She used multiple techniques, binding, twining, knotting, and braiding the linen, in addition to plain weave and gauze weave. The free-hanging forms were given their rhythms of expansion and contraction by the weaving process itself. The forms were characterized by vertical slits which were reunited towards the base of the hanging. Often the hangings were on a monumental scale, in such as the one shown at the Seattle World's Fair in 1962, which was 27 feet high. Her works in the 1960s tended more and more toward the condition of sculpture: constructions in boxes incorporating drawings and found objects, and collages of paper built up like bas-reliefs. The imagery of those works was striking and poetic, the delicately balanced relationship of materials often assuming almost mystical significance. Her work is represented in major collections including the Museum of Modern Art in New York City and the Art Institute of Chicago. (R.S.)

Tchelitchew, Pavel (1898–1957).
Painter. Born of Russian aristocrats in Moscow, Tchelitchew was drawing at the age of two. As a child he was influenced by the romantic book illustrations of Gustave Doré. In 1918 he fled the political upheaval in Moscow, went to Kiev, and enrolled at the Kiev Academy. There he fell under the influence of Alexandra Exter, who had been a pupil of Léger, and worked on theater posters and stage design in a cubist-constructivist style.

After two years in Berlin as a stage designer, Tchelitchew moved to Paris in 1923, and almost at once he renounced his cubist manner. He painted a series of landscapes and another of portraits, associated with Gertrude

1. **Edmund C. Tarbell.** Mother and Mary, *1922. National Gallery of Art, Washington, D.C. (gift of the Belcher Collection).*
2. **Edmund C. Tarbell.** In the Orchard, *1891. National Collection of Fine Arts, Smithsonian Institution, Washington, D.C. (lent by Dr. Albert Cannon).*
3. **Pavel Tchelitchew.** Hide-and-Seek (Cache-Cache), *1942. Museum of Modern Art, N.Y. (Mrs. Simon Guggenheim Fund).*

Ten

Stein and her circle, and through Miss Stein was introduced to the blue- and pink-period pictures of Picasso, by which he was much influenced. He began to paint subjects with similarly tragic overtones, and reduced his palette for a time to earth colors and black and white.

In 1926 he showed with the group known as the neoromantics and began to experiment with showing successive views of a single face or figure simultaneously in his work, and, ultimately with violent distortions of foreshortening and perspective. He had his first solo show in London in 1928, and in the following year he designed the scenery and costumes for two Diaghilev ballets, *Ode* and *l'Errante*.

In the early 1930s Tchelitchew painted clowns, inspired by those of Toulouse-Lautrec. His first American show was held by the Museum of Modern Art, New York City, in 1930. By 1934, when he came to America, his interest had shifted, so far as subject was concerned, to bullfighters and tennis players. In the late 1930s he began the sketches for one of his most important works, *Hide-and-Seek (Cache-Cache)* (1942, Modern Museum), which combined children's heads, hands, trees, and other organic phenomena in a metamorphic web suffused with violent emotion. He also produced metamorphic landscapes at this time, and designed more ballets. By 1954 he was an international celebrity; but he was also ill and tired, and he moved to Frascati, Italy, where he died.

Tchelitchew underwent many changes of style and point of view. A ceaseless experimenter, particularly in exaggerated perspective, double images, and other variations of depth and plasticity, his romanticism was of a tormented kind that had more in common, as the critic James Thrall Soby put it, with Grünewald than with Raphael. He believed in the occult and the mystical and imagined himself to possess magical powers. (A.F.)

Ten, The (The Ten American Painters).
A group of well-established New York and Boston artists who joined together to exhibit their paintings in 1898. The members were Frank W. Benson,* Joseph De Camp, Thomas W. Dewing,* Edmund C. Tarbell,* Childe Hassam,* Willard L. Metcalf,* Robert Reid,* E. E. Simmons, John H. Twachtman,* and J.

Alden Weir.* Together, as E. P. Richardson observes, they formed "a kind of academy of American Impressionism."* They withdrew from the Society of American Artists,* feeling that the atmosphere of the Society was no longer "congenial to their views and purposes of art," and arranged with the Durand-Ruel gallery for space, which they divided into equal portions and assigned by lot.

The Ten continued to exhibit together annually for some twenty years. In 1902, following the death of Twachtman, William M. Chase* was chosen in his place. During the early years of the century the more vigorous and original members assured an exhibition of unusual interest, but in later days the group seemed united mainly by "a predeliction for exquisiteness in painting." Their organization, which served as an instrument for mutual advancement, hoped to call attention to American rather than French impressionists. It foreshadowed such ventures as those of The Eight* and the Macdowell Club. (D.W.S.)

Teske, Edmund. (1911–   ).
Photographer. Born in Chicago, Ill., he began photographing seriously in 1931, and did commercial work from 1933 to 1935. In 1937 he established a photographic workshop at Frank Lloyd Wright's* country home and school, Taliesin, in Spring Green, Wis. In Chicago during the early 1940s he taught at Jane Addam's Hull House and at the New Bauhaus School of Design founded by Laszlo Moholy-Nagy, a teacher and artist from Berlin's Bauhaus.* In 1944 he worked in the still photography department of Paramount Motion Pictures. Since that time he has taught at Chouinard Art Institute, Los Angeles, and the University of California at Los Angeles. In 1960 he was included in the "Sense of Abstraction" exhibition at the Museum of Modern Art, and he has had important one-man exhibitions in Los Angeles (1963), New York (1971), and Rochester (1971).

Teske's most characteristic photographs are unique prints (he calls them "duo tone") that are chemically stained in tones ranging from earth reds to purple. The prints are flashed with light during their development and this causes areas to appear negative in what would otherwise be a positive picture. The content of these prints is

generally one of a poetic, dreamlike nature, involved multiple images assembled from "stills" of movie stars, miscellaneous objects, and everyday interiors. (T.F.B.)

Thayer, Abbott Handerson
(1849–1921).
Painter. He was born in Boston, Mass., the son of a physician who moved his family to Keene, N.H., where the boy formed a lifelong appreciation of the countryside around Mount Monadnock. He moved to Brooklyn, N.Y., in 1867, and attended the Brooklyn Art School and National Academy of Design from 1868. In 1869 he opened a studio in Brooklyn, painting animals, especially dogs, along with occasional portraits, until 1875, when he went to Paris. There he studied briefly at the École des Beaux-Arts and then in the studio of Gérôme. By the time he returned to America in 1879, he had begun to concentrate on figure painting, and during the 1880s he developed the idealized female type with which his art became associated.

Nothing brought Thayer more popularity during the 1890s than his idealized women—including madonnas, young virgins striding forward flanked by children, and girls with angel's wings and flowing robes. And nothing has hurt his reputation more since that time, his concepts calling to mind not idealism but sentimentality. His famous *Caritas* (1897, Boston) may display unconvincing putti, but other allegorical figures such as *"Stevenson Memorial" Angel* (1903, National Coll.) are as sculptural as the statues of his friend Augustus Saint-Gaudens,* an artist of somewhat similar style and concept. In some of Thayer's figure studies and portraits, his strong, simple flesh forms, vigorously realized draperies, and tough, semiabstract backgrounds combine in an individual style of exceptional painterly force, as in *Girl Arranging Her Hair* (1918–19, National Coll.).

Thayer kept a studio in New York until 1901, when he moved to Dublin, N.H., and became a semirecluse. He was a student of nature, and his paintings of flowers and landscape, as in *Mount Monadnock* (Freer) reveal his love of the subject as well as his facility as an artist. His forms were depicted broadly, at times (especially in his watercolor landscapes) almost abstractly, as he sought to make economical brush symbols convey a vivid, honest visual impression. His concern for animals and study of nature, together with his painter's analysis of visual phenomena, led to his formulation of the principles of protective coloration in wildlife. One of these principles—that parts in the light are colored darker and that under parts are lighter—is known as "Thayer's Law." His studies were published in *Concealing Coloration in the Animal Kingdom* (1909), and camouflage techniques in both world wars were based on Thayer's theories.

(D.W.S.)

Theus, Jeremiah (c.1719–74).
Portrait painter. He moved to South Carolina from Switzerland with his parents about 1735. In 1740 he advertised his removal to new quarters in the Market Square at Charleston, "where all Ladies and Gentlemen may have their Pictures drawn, likewise landskips of all sizes, Crests and Coats of Arms for Coaches or Chaises. Likewise for the Convenience of those who live in the Country, he is willing to wait on them at their respective Plantations." He was active until his death, producing bright, pleasing likenesses, many in small sizes. His portraits of *Mr. Cuthbert* and *Mrs. Cuthbert* (c.1765, Washington) and *William Wragg* (c.1740–45, Detroit) are fine examples.

Thompson, Cephas Giovanni
(1809–88).
Primarily a portrait painter. Born in Middleboro, Mass., he studied with his father, Cephas Thompson (1775–1856), and later, in Boston, with David C. Johnston (1799–1865), a printmaker, illustrator, and sometime painter of humorous anecdotes. He started his career in Plymouth in 1827 and then, after short periods in Boston, Providence, and Philadelphia, settled in New York City in 1837. In 1849 he returned to Boston, but in 1853 went to Rome for a seven-year sojourn. He then returned and settled in New York City.

Thompson was a friend of such prominent literary figures as William Cullen Bryant and Nathaniel Hawthorne, many of whom he portrayed. One of many talented portrait painters in the mid-19th century, his portraits show him to have been a careful craftsman whose attractive likenesses must have satisfied well-to-do clients. They do not, however, show that he possessed a penetrating eye for character or any marked individuality in coloring and composition. He was the most fashionable portrait painter of New York in the decade after 1837. While most of his portraits were bust-length, such as that of *Grace Greenwood Lippincott* (undated, University of Michigan, on loan to the National Portrait Gallery), he did a few full-length portraits of children and elaborate compositions involving family groups. His brother, Jerome B. Thompson,* was a well-known genre painter.

(H.W.W.)

Thompson, Jerome B. (1814–86).
Portrait, landscape, and rural genre painter born in Middleboro, Mass. Although his father, Cephas Thompson, and his brother, Cephas Giovanni Thompson,* were painters, his father sought to make him a farmer, but he left home and went to Barnstable, Mass., where he tried his hand as a sign, ornamental, and portrait painter. At twenty-one he moved to New York City, opened a studio and began to build a reputation as a portrait painter. In 1852 he went to England and for several years studied the paintings of Joseph Turner, William Hogarth, and Claude Lorrain. Returning to America, he lived on a farm in Mineola, Long Island. There he illustrated a series of popular poems and songs, "Pencil Ballads," which had a wide circulation as engravings and lithographs. Subsequently he settled on a farm in Glen Gardner, N.J.

It was not until 1850 that Thompson broke away from portrait work. In that year he exhibited at the National Academy of Design* A *"Pic Nick," Camden, Maine* (c. 1850, Boston), one of his first important rural genre scenes. For these scenes, on which his reestablished reputation now rests, his formula was to combine genre and landscape elements.

In 1850–60 he created a series of these integrated genre-landscapes. In *The Haymakers* (1859, private collection), the toiling figures are made to appear completely at home in the landscape, which has an independent life of its own. The work possesses a luminous quality and a sensitive appreciation of nature that place it in the forefront of 19th century landscapes. Other paintings in the series, such as *Apple Gathering* (1856, Brooklyn), are almost as effective. Almost forgotten until quite recently, Thompson has begun to receive long overdue critical recognition.

(H.W.W.)

Thompson, Launt (1833–94).
Sculptor. He was born in Queens County, Ireland, but was brought to America by his widowed mother when he was fourteen. In Albany, N.Y., Erastus Dow Palmer* made him his assistant, but by 1858 Thompson had established his own studio in New York City. At first he carved cameos and profile medallions but moving quickly into the highest social circles, he obtained commissions for portrait busts in marble or bronze, such as the *William Cullen Bryant* (1865, bronze 1867, Metropolitan). After working in Europe in 1868–69 he returned to New York and produced a number of busts and full-length statues. The salient characteristics of his work were an uncomplicated naturalism blended with a reserved dignity, as may be seen in his bust of his fellow artist, Sanford R. Gifford (1871), or his statue of General John Sedgwick (1869, West Point). In 1874 he was elected vice-president of the National Academy of Design.* The next year he went to Florence, where he remained for six years. When he returned to America he was virtually unable to work due to alcoholism, and by 1890 he was confined to a mental hospital, where he died a few years later.

(W.C.)

Thornton, William (1759–1828).
Architect and inventor. Born in the Virgin Islands of Quaker parents. At age five he was sent to England for schooling. He attended the University of Edinburgh (1781–84) and received his M.D. degree from the University of Aberdeen (1784). After a stay in Paris, he sailed for Tortola, V.I., where he presumably had family property. He went to New York in 1787, and from 1778–90 worked on the invention of steamboats. Many years later, after Fulton's invention, Thornton wrote a treatise reminding the public of his own efforts.

Without having studied architecture, Thornton won the competition for the Library Hall, Philadelphia (1789–90, demolished 1880), with a design taken mainly from Abraham Swan's *Designs in Architecture* (1757). In 1790 he went back to Tortola for two years. While there, he entered the competition for the Capitol Building in the Federal City and won first prize. Thornton was glad

1

to have a professional, Stephen Hallet, modify his plans in order to make construction possible. However, after Thornton moved to Washington to become one of the Commissioners of the city, he discovered that his plans had been modified excessively. His objections brought about Hallet's dismissal. In 1802 Jefferson ordered the posts of commissioners abolished and in 1803 appointed B. H. Latrobe* architect of the Capitol. Latrobe's contempt for Thornton's architectural efforts led to a lifelong enmity between them.

Although educated as a physician, Thornton hated the practice of medicine. He preferred raising race-horses, painting, drawing, and writing novels. In 1802 Jefferson appointed him superintendent of the newly-formed Patent Office, a post he held until his death. As an architect he designed several houses for prominent citizens of Washington in the early Republican style, emphasizing smooth, brick surfaces, symmetry, and refined decoration. He built the Octagon House, Washington (1798–1800, now occupied by the American Institute of Architects) for John Taylor; Woodlawn, Fairfax County, Va. (1800) for Lawrence Lewis; Tudor Place, Georgetown (1812); and, in 1817, he gave Jefferson advice on designing the University of Virginia at Charlottesville.

Involved in many business enterprises that invariably failed, Thornton was a highly intelligent man deeply interested in the improvement of society, as shown in such publications as his book on political economy calling for the abolition of slavery, his essay suggesting a capital city in Panama "where a canal may be made from sea to sea, by locks," and his book on teaching the deaf to speak. (P.F.N.)

Tiffany & Company.
Leading American silver firm. Although Tiffany & Company did not actually manufacture silver until 1868, when they bought the shop and the silverware of Edward C. Moore,* the company was started in 1837 when Charles Lewis Tiffany (1812–1902) came from Connecticut to New York and opened a stationery and fancy goods store. He and his partner, John B. Young, purchased almost all of their silverware from Edward Moore's father, John C. Moore, who had worked as a silversmith in New York since 1827. Charles

Tiffany became one of the world's leading gem merchants, and opened a Paris branch in 1850 and a London branch in 1868. In 1852 he introduced the English sterling standard to America for Tiffany silver. His was the first American firm whose silversmiths won an award from an international jury—in Paris in 1867. The previous year he had introduced the pronged setting for diamond solitaires that became known as "The Tiffany Setting." Tiffany was one of two American silver manufacturers who exhibited products in most of the international expositions in the last half of the 19th century. During the Gold Rush era, John W. Mackay sent three tons of silver from the newly discovered Comstock lode in Nevada to Tiffany, which the company made into over one thousand pieces of silverware. Among these was the 28-piece set (University of California) made for James E. Birch, owner and operator of a stagecoach line in the 1850s. Designed in the florid rococo revival style, the service is etched and embossed with scenes of early California, such as stagecoaches and miners. Finials for the tea set are figures of miners panning gold. On the cover of the large tureen is a carefully modeled early stagecoach.

During the Renaissance revival, Tiffany's chief designer, Paulding Farnham,* and James H. Whitehouse established reputations for quality design and workmanship. At the Paris Exhibition in 1900 and the Louisiana Purchase Exposition in St. Louis in 1904, Tiffany exhibits such as the Adams Gold Vase and Florentine toilet sets attracted much attention. Tiffany was one of the first companies to use materials and designs native to America. At the World Columbian Exposition in Chicago in 1893 and at the Paris Exhibition in 1900 their display included Indian-inspired articles made from native metals and semiprecious stones. Tiffany's most important presentation piece of the late 19th century was the William Cullen Bryant Vase (Metropolitan) designed by James H. Whitehouse in 1875. A Greek vase in form, it was ornamented with American flowers and plants. Within medallions were a portrait bust of the poet and scenes of his life and works.

Louis Comfort Tiffany (1848–1933), son of the founder, made his reputation with his opalescent "Tiffany glass" dur-

Tiffany & Company. Vase, Magnolia, c.1893, silver, gold, enamels, and opals. Metropolitan Museum of Art, N.Y. (gift of Mrs. Winthrop Atwell).

ing the art nouveau* movement at the turn of the century. He also designed altar crosses, candlesticks, and other church silver of note. In 1955 Walter Hoving assumed control of Tiffany & Company from the Tiffany and Moore families. Among his present designers is Jean Schlumberger. (M.G.F.)

Tiffany, Louis Comfort (1848–1933). American glass manufacturer who popularized iridescent glass. See Art Nouveau Glass, and Tiffany & Company.

Tinsel Painting.
A popular 19th-century decorative art form (in its heyday also called oriental painting and crystal painting) related to reverse painting on glass.* In tinsel-work, figures are drawn on glass with lampblack and then lightly painted with pigments well diluted in Damar varnish so that light can pass through them. Simplified floral forms are most common, but birds, animals, and even some complex human figures occur. The completed figures are silhouetted with opaque paint, usually black but occasionally a light color or white, and the glass is backed with crinkled tinfoil, which reflects the light that passes through the transparent colored areas. Tinsel painting is now actively collected as an expression of American folk art,* and several contemporary craftsmen have revived the technique for their own creative work as well as for imitations of earlier production. Examples of various kinds of silhouettes can be seen in the Essex Institute, Salem, Mass. (M.J.G.)

Tinware.
Utilitarian and fanciful articles made of sheet metal that has been coated with tin to prevent rusting; also sheet metal articles, often called "tole" or "tole-ware," that are painted and decorated. The earliest American tinware has been somewhat speculatively assigned to the Weathervane*-maker, Deacon Shem Drowne, who was working in Boston in 1712, as well as to Edward Pattison, who in 1740 opened a tin shop in Berlin, Conn., that served as a center for both apprentice training and regional distribution. Utilitarian products of the work of Pattison and later tinsmiths—pans, kettles, ladles, skimmers, candlesticks, lamps, and lanterns —have been collected by antiquarians,

and the representational aspects of their work as found in cookie-cutters and molds has long been recognized as a folk art. In the 19th century, tinkers also created highly imaginative pieces to commemorate a tenth, or tin, wedding anniversary. Typical of such work are a lady's bonnet and a man's top hat, both in the collection of the Old Museum Village at Smith's Clove, in Monroe, N.Y., and the same collection also contains a much more unusual tin replica of a marriage certificate. Among other recurrent anniversary forms are bouquets and slippers.

The 19th-century tinker also indulged his creative fancy in the design of trade signs,* particularly the robot-like tin men that advertised their own trade, and in toys made from scrap metal. After 1800 New England tinsmiths began the practice of "japanning" or applying and kiln-drying glossy varnish and "flowering" their tin, and soon blank forms for trays, apple baskets, coffee pots, shakers, and boxes were being mass produced for such decoration in a number of regional centers. To a considerable extent the styles of geographic areas and particular workshops have since been reconstructed. In Maine, the Stevens Plains tin shop of Zachariah Stevens and the later ornamentation by the women in tinker Thomas Briscoe's family were distinctive for light backgrounds and a wide variety of relatively realistic floral forms. In Connecticut, and later in Elizabeth, N.J., Lansingburgh, N.Y., and St. Louis, Mo., Oliver Filley and his relatives produced and sold pieces with decorations according to a formalized brushwork, and in East Greenville, N.Y., members of the Reuben Butler family executed abundant colorful ornamentation that recalls much earlier Dutch painted furniture. Pennsylvania painted tin predictably relates to some of the stock floral designs of fractur.* Other distinctive styles have been identified in New York State and especially along the New York–Vermont border. Much of the information about 19th-century tin decorating techniques has been recovered through the efforts of members of the Historical Society of Early American Decoration, who continue to practice and teach this very specialized art according to rigid formulae. The Society has also assembled at Cooperstown, N.Y., an excellent collection of 19th-century tin work.(M.J.G.)

Tobey, Mark (1890–   ).
Painter. Born in Centerville, Wis., he worked as a commercial artist in Chicago in 1907 while attending classes at the Chicago Art Institute. He studied briefly with Kenneth Hayes Miller* in New York, and worked there intermittently during 1911–17. In 1923 he was taught some Chinese brushwork and during the 1920s he was introduced to the Bahai World Faith and began his extensive travels in Europe, the Near East, and the Far East. During 1931–38 he was resident artist at Dartington Hall, a progressive school in Devonshire, England, where he met many literary figures such as Aldous Huxley, Arthur Waley, and Rabindranath Tagore, who furthered his interests in oriental art, literature, and mysticism.

Until 1940, Tobey was principally a figurative painter earning his living from teaching, commercial illustration, and interior decoration. But as early as 1935 he improvised a small painting consisting of white, circular lines masked in a network with flashes of color showing through the light calligraphy. Although this work may have been suggested by his interest in Persian and Far Eastern drawing, the specific association was a recollection of Broadway lights flashing on and off at night. Thus, his initial venture into abstraction was a curious combination of the American scene translated into a free calligraphy. Although he had explored Renaissance perspective space and cubist simultaneous vision, he now began to abandon these spatial traditions and to create a world of space based on the movement of linear patterns through a void. The scene of Broadway lights was made explicit in a number of small paintings of the late 1930s, for example *Broadway* (1935, Chicago), whose dense linearism led to the artist's most characteristic style, called "whitewriting." It is interesting that Tobey and the Dutch painter Piet Mondrian, converging from the opposite poles of representation and abstraction, should have been fascinated by the same subject, the lights of Broadway translated into "multiple space" and "moving focus" on the surface of the canvas.

Tobey built his entire later career on these efforts in dynamic line, light, space, and motion. Since 1940, Tobey has continued to work in a narrow calligraphic range, avoiding extremes of

1. **George Tooker.** The Subway, *1950,
   Whitney Museum of American Art,
   N.Y.*
2. **Bradley Walker Tomlin.** Number 20,
   *1949, Museum of Modern Art, N.Y.
   (gift of Philip Johnson).*
3. **Mark Tobey.** Broadway, *1935. Art
   Institute of Chicago.*

color in favor of an atmospheric tonality that is shot through with flashes of light, as, for example, *Above the Earth* (1953, Chicago). Despite the conscious limitation in effects, his paintings are immensely complicated and filled with mystery. Although seemingly an isolated figure in American painting of the last thirty years, his works are central to most avant-garde experiments.

Although he has been painting successfully since early in the century, his principal contributions were made with the abstract expressionists after 1940. Although his use of a free calligraphy anticipated American abstract expressionism* and undoubtedly influenced Jackson Pollock* and others of the New York school, he remains essentially an individualist, with a very personal vision rooted in oriental mysticism.   (H.H.A.)

Tomlin, Bradley Walker (1899–1953).
Painter. Tomlin was born in Syracuse, N.Y., and graduated from Syracuse University in 1921. While still in college he illustrated children's books, designed posters, and executed two "Mother Goose" murals for the children's ward in Syracuse Memorial Hospital. He then moved to New York City, where his ability to adapt the art styles of others to his own work and his innate elegant taste brought him immediate success: he designed magazine covers for *Vogue* and *House and Garden* until 1929 and had his first one-man show in 1923. He spent a year in Europe in 1923–24 and again in 1926–27, studying painting at the Grande Chaumière and Académie Colarossi in Paris. His work went through innumerable stylistic changes. He continued to support himself through magazine work, sales, and portrait commissions until the Depression forced him to turn to teaching: at Sarah Lawrence College (1932–41) and at preparatory schools (1932–34). He had numerous shows in the United States and Europe, and a memorial exhibition was held by the Whitney Museum in 1957.

During the 1930s Tomlin began seriously to question himself as an artist and destroyed much of his early work. He was tremendously impressed by an exhibition of fantastic art, dada,* and surrealism* in 1937, and from 1939 to 1944 he moved from a modified realism into a decorative cubism.* Tomlin was never as interested in the intel-

lectual aspects of cubism as in its formal relations and aura of fantasy. To this was added, in 1941, the influence of Adolph Gottlieb's* compartmented pictographs; from this point on he began to identify himself with the abstract expressionist avant-garde, although it was not until 1948 that he painted his own first calligraphic symbols. Initially, these took the form of automatic writing: swirling linear shapes, brushstroke width, on gray backgrounds. Soon these were worked into overall geometrical patterns that wove across the canvas and forward and back in space, as in *No. 10* (1952–53, Proctor).

Tomlin's late work is remarkable in that he was able to combine spontaneity with rigorous structure; symbolism with abstraction; and expressionism with design. *Number 9: In Praise of Gertrude Stein* (1950, Modern Museum), for example, sets up a repeated rhythm of curved, vertical, and angular "symbols" in his typically muted colors—drab olive, mustard, black, and white. His ability to bring order out of the complexity of his overlapping, interpenetrating forms reached its peak in his last paintings of 1952, where a seemingly random scattering of rounded color shapes is brought into ultimate harmony.   (E.C.G.)

Tooker, George (1920–   ).
Painter. Born in Brooklyn, N.Y., he studied at Phillips Academy (1936–38) and graduated from Harvard in 1942. He also worked at the Art Students League* with Reginald Marsh* and later with Paul Cadmus.* Cadmus, a leader of American magic realism, was probably the single greatest influence on Tooker. Tooker has continued the tradition of social realism, painting on a miniature scale scenes of contemporary America transformed into a haunted world in which the most familiar, commonplace activities become nightmares, as in *The Subway* (1950, Whitney). Tooker is a traditionalist who paints in egg tempera such as that used in the early Renaissance but is concerned with contemporary issues of mechanization, urban isolation, and the facelessness of bureaucracy.   (H.H.A.)

Towle Company.
A firm of silversmiths founded by Anthony F. Towle and William P. Jones, who had served their apprenticeship with William Moulton.* They began

business in 1857 under the name of Towle & Jones, later buying the business of William and Joseph Moulton. In 1873 Edward F. Towle joined his father. The Towle Company, in addition to producing fine flatware and hollowware, often in traditional patterns, has emphasized the artistic side of silversmithing and has established an exhibition gallery where the work of modern artist-silversmiths as well as historic silversmiths can be shown.

Town, Ithiel (1784–1844).
Architect and engineer, born in Thompson, Conn. His father died when he was eight, and he was sent to live with an uncle in Cambridge, Mass. He became a carpenter and also taught school briefly. Town may have studied with Asher Benjamin,* Boston architect and writer of builders' books. His first important architectural work, designed with Benjamin, was Center Congregational Church, New Haven (1812–14). It had a graceful Georgian style, with the steeple constructed before it was raised to the tower. This commission doubtless led to the one for Trinity Church, New Haven (1814–15), but there his design was Gothic. For the next few years Town built mainly wooden bridges (more than fifty), many of them with Isaac Damon of Northampton, Mass. The first with Damon was a toll bridge across the Connecticut River at Springfield (1816). An inventive builder, he produced a device known as the Town lattice truss (patented 1820) that did not require arch support, was cheaper, and led to the use of metal trussing of similar form. It is contained in his *Description . . . of Bridges for Roads, Railroads, and Aqueducts* (1839).

Town's Eagle Bank, New Haven (1824, never finished), was his first work in the Greek revival* style. Thereafter most of his public and private buildings showed Greek influence. The many residences designed by Town are more interesting than his larger buildings because of his ability to adapt a Greek clarity and precision, as well as ornamental forms, to an intimate scale. Typical of these successes are the Hillhouse Estate (1828), Skinner Villa (1830), Town's own villa (1830), and the Whitney Estate (1835), all in New Haven. In 1827 Town formed a firm in New York City first with Martin E. Thompson and then, in 1829, with A. J. Davis, a young draftsman.

1

1. **Ithiel Town.** *Center Congregational Church, New Haven, Conn., 1814.*
2. **Ernest Trova.** Study: Falling Man Series, Six Figures, *1964, chrome-plated bronze. Whitney Museum of American Art, N.Y.*
   Trade Signs
3. *Tavern sign, 1797. Concord Antiquarian Society, Concord, Mass.*
4. *D, Beeme Inn, 1815. Smithsonian Institution, Washington, D.C.*

Town traveled in Europe in 1829–30, building up a library of 11,000 books and thousands of prints. Among the firm's important designs were: Connecticut State Capitol, New Haven (1827–31, demolished); Indiana State Capitol, Indianapolis (1831–35, demolished); North Carolina State House, Raleigh (1831); Custom House, New York (1832–42, later the U.S. Sub-Treasury Building); Illinois State Capitol, Springfield (1837, altered 1866); and the Wadsworth Athenaeum, Hartford, Conn. (1842).

He visited Europe again in 1843–44 and died shortly after. He was a founder of the National Academy of Design* and leader in his profession. His willingness to allow free use of his library provided many young architects with ideas, and from his office came many of the foremost architects of the next generation. (P.F.N.)

Trade Signs.
Pictorial signs symbolizing names or illustrating crafts and services. Such signs played an important part in the development of American commerce from early colonial days. In a society that was still far from taking literacy for granted, painted or sculptured identifications of a business or craft were a necessity in a wide range of activities, but they were especially abundant and ambitious as advertisements for inns and taverns. Paintings on boards executed by itinerant limners frequently took on heraldic aspects by virtue of sawn crestings or turned vertical supports, as in the 1815 sign (reworked in 1828) for D. Beeme's Inn (Smithsonian). An unusual marble sign in low relief in 1816 identifies J. Williams, Jr.'s Hotel in Ashfield, Mass. (New York Historical Association). Pictorial trade signs continue to be made in the United States in the 20th century, although they are rare as compared to mass-produced, lettered signs. Photographers have compiled a record of such signs in rural and urban settings, and their work suggests that the tradition continues most strongly in relation to midwestern cattle breeding, with itinerant sign painters still traveling from farm to farm and rendering idealized versions of a variety of breeds as entrance signboards. The same photographers have also called attention to a popular 20th-century form, the pictorial neon sign.

Three-dimensional carved wooden trade signs—a boot for a shoemaker, lambs and pigs for butchers, fish for seafood merchants—have also been actively collected as expressions of American folk art. As the 19th century progressed, they tended to increase in size, as exemplified by the giant pair of scissors made to advertise a New York City cutlery shop. Most celebrated of all the late 19th-century American trade signs were the large wooden show figures* that stood outside shop doors, in particular the life-size Indians that identified tobacconists' establishments. (M.J.G.)

Trova, Ernest (1927–   ).
Painter, sculptor, and creator of assemblages.* Born in St. Louis, Mo., he began his career as a department store display designer. His paintings, exhibited as early as 1953, were largely influenced by Willem de Kooning.* Gradually, Trova abandoned abstract expressionism* and began to produce collages and assemblages made from junk and old clothing. His first true success came with the "Falling Man" series, exhibited in Boston in his first one-man show (1963). Trova's famous featureless, armless, pot-bellied figure was derived from two aspects of his earlier work: assemblages made of humanoid parts culled from children's dolls, and a painting based on Leonardo's proportional drawing of a nude man in a circle. Trova's automation figure and the theme of precariousness stem from his view of man in modern society: "a flawed, fallen, imperfect and unfit creature who constantly needs technological boosts to maintain his equilibrium in space on the Wheel of Fortune, where he is alternately rising and falling." The man, ranging from six inches to seven feet, is made of polished brass, chrome-plate, clear plastic, or polished black epoxy—materials that add to the dehumanized effect. Cast from molds, they are all precisely alike and impersonal. Trova does, however, place them in various sculptural settings such as platforms or clear plastic boxes. Frequently they are embellished with found objects or sinister mechanical devices such as gas masks; one man becomes the chassis of a racing car; another, the axle between two huge rotating wheels. Despite his aim of commenting on the human condition, he has produced

2

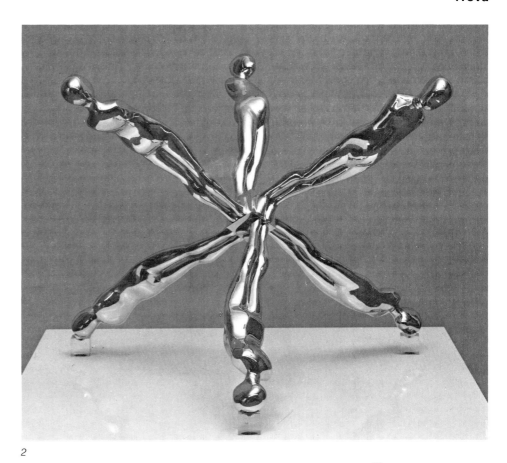
3

4

decorative objects: his sleek, "machine-made," anonymous "man" was one of the popular images of the late 1960s.

(E.C.G.)

Truitt, Anne (1921–   ).
Sculptor. Born in Baltimore, Md., she graduated from Bryn Mawr (1943) and studied art at the Institute of Contemporary Art, Washington, D.C. (1948–50), and the Dallas Museum of Fine Arts (1950). During the 1950s she exhibited in a number of group shows in the Washington, D.C., area but did not have a solo show in New York until 1963. By that time she was producing three-dimensional geometrical forms painted in dark colors. Because her rectangles, trapezoids, and cubes are often not quite regular and are subdivided into several areas in different colors, they have a strong element of illusionism. By 1964 she had turned to bright and pastel color combinations that added to the effect of dematerialization. Her work has been described as "mild neoplasticism," though actually her architectonic, low-lying shapes—some as much as eight feet long and less than three feet off the ground—are more in tune with pictorial sculpture. She used aluminum structures as surfaces on which to paint, dissolving their volume in color and optical effects. She lives and works in Tokyo, Japan.

(E.C.G.)

Trumbauer, Horace (1868–1938).
Architect. Born in Philadelphia, Pa., he attended public school there and at sixteen became office boy for G. D. & W. D. Hewitt, architects. Working his way up as a draftsman, he was able, without any formal training, to open his own office by the age of twenty-four. In 1894 he received a spectacular commission from William Welsh Harrison, a wealthy sugar refiner, for a large country seat at Glenside, Pa. He created a crenellated masonry mansion reminiscent of Windor Castle; it was later taken over by Beaver College. Attuned to the baronial aspirations of the newly-rich, he was soon receiving many commissions for country estates, especially from notable Philadelphia families.

Apparently Trumbauer never did a drawing after setting up his own office, but turned over commissions to Frank Seeburger, his chief designer. In 1898 the firm designed a neo-Italian palace

for Peter A. B. Widener, with gardens laid out by the noted French landscape architect, Jacques Gréber, and Elstowe Park for William Lukens Elkins, both in Elkins Park. Also in the Philadelphia suburbs, at the turn of the century, he designed the James W. Paul and George W. Elkins estates as half-timbered and stone English manor houses, and a stone mansion for John Gribbel in the English Tudor style. Probably the most magnificent commission he received for an estate was for Whitemarsh Hall, a palace for E. T. Stotesbury near Chestnut Hill (1916) with gardens also laid out by Gréber. As seen from the end of its long axial driveway, it was the nearest thing in America to Versailles.

In Philadelphia the firm designed, among others, two town houses: one for E. C. Knight, Jr., at 1629 Locust Street, very much in the French Beaux-Arts manner, and another for George A. Heun, at 16th and Walnut Street, a modified neo-Italian Renaissance palazzo. His public buildings there included the Widener Memorial Training School for Crippled Children (c.1904) and Jefferson Medical College. Adorning the new Parkway were the Philadelphia Free Library, at Logan Circle (c.1927), reminiscent of the Ministère de la Marine in Paris, and the terminal feature of the Parkway, the great Pennsylvania Museum of Art, by Zantzinger & Borie and Horace Trumbauer, completed in 1928. These buildings were inspired by Greek temples and were raised on their own acropolis. The full-size statuary (by C. Paul Jennewein* and John Gregory) in one of the pediments, utilizing colored ceramic, was one of the first attempts in this country to reproduce the color used by the Greeks in their temples and statuary. Among commercial buildings designed by the firm in Philadelphia were the Public Ledger Building (c.1922), counterpart, in the neo-Federal style, of the Curtis Publishing Company facing Independence Square, and the neo-Federal Ritz Carlton Hotel (1912). For the Racquet Club (c.1908) they designed a neo-Georgian façade in the Philadelphia tradition.

In New York City, Trumbauer's office designed several outstanding buildings in travertine, showing the influence of the French architect Jacques Ange Gabriel (1698–1782), a style introduced into the office by a very talented black

architect, Julian Abele, chief designer of the firm after Seeburger left in 1908. These included the very handsome Duveen Brothers Gallery at Fifth Avenue and 56th Street (1911), and the Wildenstein Gallery at 19 East 64th Street (1931). Among the Fifth Avenue residences they designed were those of George J. Gould at 67th Street (1907), the James B. Duke mansion at 78th Street (1909), now New York University Institute of Fine Arts, the James Speyer mansion with drive-in entrance, at 87th Street (1914), and the Herbert N. Straus house, with its superb sculptures at the roof, at 9 East 71st Street (1932).

On Long Island the firm designed estates for William K. Vanderbilt, Herbert Brokaw, Henry Phipps, and J. B. Grace. In New Jersey, in the early 1900s, they designed a palace for Martin Maloney at Spring Lake, and St. Catherine's Chapel, of which he was the donor. One of the most imposing mansions ever built by the firm was Shadow Lawn for Hubert T. Parsons at Elberon (1928, later occupied by Monmouth College). At Newport, R.I., The Elms, for E. J. Berwind (1900), was French classic Louis XV in style, while the Villa Miramar, for Alexander Hamilton Rice (1916), in the same style, was enhanced by gardens by Gréber.

In the South, in the early 1900s, splendid town houses were constructed in Washington, D.C., for Mrs. E. H. G. Slater and Perry Belmont, the latter in collaboration with the architect E. Sanson of Paris. In 1924 the office began to develop plans for Duke University in Durham, N.C., beginning with the neo-Georgian style Women's College in 1925, followed by the neo-Gothic Men's College in 1927.

Trumbauer's career, like those of many other American architects, was based on an efficient organization for which he obtained the commissions, while delegating the actual design of buildings to talented associates under his direction. The great wealth of Trumbauer's clients and their desire to emulate the palaces of Europe gave his office the opportunity to use the finest materials and the handsome, if derivative, designs for which it became known.

(A.B.)

Trumbull, John (1756–1843).
Painter of portraits and history. He was a son of "Brother Jonathan," Revolu-

tionary War governor of Connecticut, who sent the sickly, one-eyed boy to Harvard, where he graduated in 1773, the youngest in his class. The boy, over parental protest, wished to be a painter. Taking John Singleton Copley* as his model, he denied that it was a career unfit for a gentleman. With the outbreak of war, the governor placed his son as aide-de-camp, where his skill at drawing maps made him valuable to generals Washington and Gates. Always hypersensitive, he resigned his colonel's commission in 1777 and went to study art in Boston, occupying the former studio of John Smibert.* He saw action as a volunteer with the forces in Rhode Island in the next year, tried his hand at dealing in army supplies and then, in 1780, went to London by way of France, again to study art. In London, however, he was arrested in reprisal for the execution of John Andre, and it was not until after the war and a return to America that he was established in the London studio of Benjamin West.* It was the influence of West that caused him to modify the New England primitive style he brought to England.

There he began, in 1785, what was to become his life work, a series of historical paintings memorializing the events of the Revolution. West had planned to do this, but could not do so without losing the patronage of the king. Instead, West gave every encouragement to Trumbull, and the first, *The Battle of Bunker Hill* (1789, Yale) and *Death of General Montgomery at Quebec* (1786, Yale), show West's influence and are freer in composition, stronger in dramatic impact than later pieces painted in America. Pursuing what he now called his "national work," he returned to his own country in 1789 to paint small portraits of American generals and prominent political figures, to study the locales, and to get subscriptions to engravings of the pictures. It was to be a long effort which, abandoned at times, taken up again, brought him both fame and discouragements, all crowned at last by the Act of Congress, 1817, commissioning four large historical murals for the rotunda of the Capitol at $8000 each. They were completed in 1824.

In 1794 Trumbull had returned to England as secretary to John Jay, remaining until 1804. There he married Sarah Hope Harvey (1774–1824), an

1

2

1. *John Trumbull.* Death of General Montgomery at Quebec, *1786. Yale University Art Gallery, New Haven, Conn.*
2. *Horace Trumbauer.* Office Building, Julian Abele drawing, 1930.

1

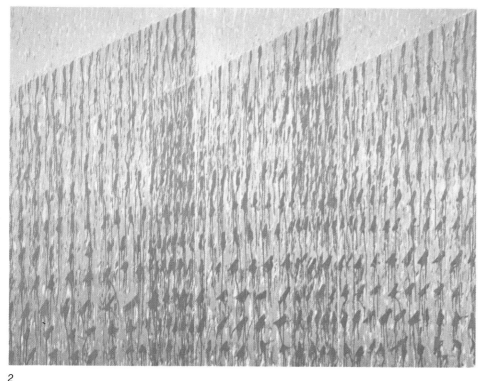

2

amateur painter. Home again (1804–08), he settled in New York as a portrait painter rather than compete with Gilbert Stuart* in Boston. A return to London in 1808 was prolonged until 1816 by the War of 1812. He was active in New York for the next twenty-one years. In 1817, he was elected president of the revived American Academy of Fine Arts. His partiality to the gentlemen patrons of the Academy rather than the young artists eager to study, capped by his statement that "beggars are not to be choosers," brought in 1826 the founding of the National Academy of Design* by dissident younger artists and the eclipse of the older group.

In 1831 Colonel Trumbull assigned all works in his studio to the Yale University Art Gallery in return for an annuity. There they remain as the chief monument to his career. Of his architecture only one building survives, the Congregational Church in Lebanon, Conn. His historical paintings, reproduced in countless illustrations, have become a part of American tradition. They combine a serious effort at accuracy with the poetic art conventions of the time. There is some updating in his uniforms, and the later works are marred by a tendency to line up rows of faces in order to bring in as many actual portraits as possible. The miniatures in oil on wood, painted for use in these large scenes, are among his best works. His larger portraits tend to be precise, dignified, but lacking in warmth and introspection; they reflect, as portraits often do, something of the character of the artist. (C.C.S.)

Tryon, Dwight William (1849–1925). Landscape painter. Born in Hartford, Conn., he made his mark as a poetic interpreter of his native New England countryside. In 1876 he went to France, where he was influenced by James M. Whistler,* sought advice from the French landscape painters Charles Daubigny and Henri Harpignies, and attended the drawing school of Jacquesson de la Chevreuse, a student of Ingres. He thus acquired a French style that stressed both the careful study of nature and the harmonious design of the broad masses of composition. Returning to this country, he began to win recognition during the 1880s. Meanwhile he developed his personal style, moving from a dark brown tonality toward a

1. **John Henry Twachtman.** Arques-la-Bataille, 1885. Metropolitan Museum of Art, N.Y. (Morris K. Jesup Fund).
2. **Jack Tworkov.** Partitions, 1971. French & Company, N.Y.

richer, impressionist-influenced coloration, deepening the subjective emotion and refining the composition. Characteristically, he began his painting with a simple, firm, horizontal landscape stretching to a row of trees against a cloudy sky; this he overlaid with an enveloping veil of luminous atmosphere, constantly modulating and adjusting to achieve effects that contemporary critics saw as essentially musical relations of lines and nuances of tone. On occasion he painted a moon caught in the clouds with a feeling approaching Albert Ryder's,* as in *Lighted Village* (Freer), and again he used the vertical accents of tree trunks to create an arrangement of a delicacy approaching Whistler's,* as in *Twilight, Early Spring* (Freer). However, Tryon lacked the deep fire of these artists, and over the years painted many similar themes, however with gradually diminishing intensity. (D.W.S.)

Tuckerman, Henry Theodore (1813–71).
Leading American art critic of the mid-19th century. Born in Boston, Mass., he went to the Boston Latin School and Harvard. Ill health caused him to leave college after two years, and thereafter he devoted himself to foreign travel and to writing poetry, biography, and essays on literature and art. Moving to New York City in 1845, he became friends with the leading American painters and sculptors working there. His *Artist-Life, or Sketches of American Painters* (1847) was the forerunner of his major work, the *Book of the Artists: American Artist Life* (1867). Beginning with such early painters as John Watson and John Smibert,* its biographical essays traced the rise of American art to what he saw as its culmination in his own time in the realistic landscapes of Frederic E. Church* and Albert Bierstadt.* Like other 19th-century critics, he overlooked artists outside of New York and whole genres such as still-life painting, and he often wrote as if personal virtue and "truth to nature" were the only tests of artistic ability. Nevertheless, his book stands as the major work of American art criticism of the time. He knew many of the artists well and he provided invaluable biographical information about them; moreover, a careful reading of his judgments show that time has often borne out his opinions. (T.E.S.)

Turner, James (active 1744–59).
Boston and Philadelphia engraver. His work included bookplates, seals, maps, and book illustrations. Citing Turner's cuts for an edition of Aesop's *Fables,* Isaiah Thomas wrote of him, "He was the best engraver which appeared in the colonies before the Revolution, especially on type metal." Turner moved to Philadelphia about 1752–53. His copperplate engravings included the *Chart of the Coasts of Nova-Scotia and Parts adjacent* which he published in Boston in 1750 and Lewis Evans' *A general Map of the Middle British Colonies, in America* (Philadelphia, 1755). He died in Philadelphia.

Twachtman, John Henry (1853–1902).
One of the most important and original of American impressionist painters. Twachtman was born in Cincinnati, Ohio, where he began his career painting floral decorations on window shades for his father's business while studying evenings at the Ohio Mechanics Institute. Subsequently he studied at the Cincinnati School of Design with Frank Duveneck,* with whom he went to Germany (1875) to attend the Munich Academy for two years. In 1877 he joined Duveneck and William Merritt Chase* in Venice, and later he made a two-year sojourn in Paris (1883–85), where he studied with Boulanger and Lefebvre at the Académie Julien. Returning to the United States in 1885, he went to Connecticut; in 1889 he purchased a farm and established a studio near Greenwich, where he spent the greater part of his life painting landscapes.

His early paintings reflect the dark, warm tonality of Duveneck and the Munich school. In France he came under the spell of the delicately toned, carefully arranged work of James M. Whistler.* His *Arques-la-Bataille* (1885, Metropolitan) shows his original adaptation of this influence, which he carried from a broadly, thinly washed technique into a highly personalized, richly brushed impressionism* during the last years of his life. His oils were often tonal, atmospheric landscape studies, flattened and simplified to the point of abstraction. Their apparent reticence half masks their underlying vigor, subjective depth, and inwardly-glowing color.

Twachtman, who was also an etcher of note, spread his influence through his teaching at the Cooper Union Institute and Art Students League* in New York City, and also through his association with The Ten,* a group of American painters he helped found in 1898. His work was early appreciated and soon included in most major American collections. (D.W.S.)

Tworkov, Jack (1900–   ).
Painter. Born in Biala, Poland, he came to America in 1913. He was trained at Columbia University (1920–23) and the National Academy of Design* (1923–25), working with such traditionalists as Charles Hawthorne* and Boardman Robinson.* He worked on the WPA Federal Art Project* (1937–41). He became an artist-teacher early and has been associated with many schools, including Queens College (1948–55), Pratt Institute, New York (1955–60), and Yale University (since 1963). He has exhibited widely ever since his first New York exhibition in 1940, has received many awards, and has been included in most group exhibitions of leading American abstractionists, notably at the Museum of Modern Art (1958–59) and the Guggenheim Museum (1961). He has had retrospective exhibitions at the Whitney Museum, New York City (1964, 1971).

Tworkov was early influenced strongly by the figurative paintings of Willem de Kooning,* with whom he shared a studio in the late 1950s. Throughout the 1950s and 1960s he developed his own pattern of abstract expressionism* involving heavily brushed, gestural painting organized largely in vertical strips of bold, off-key color or in large centralized panels usually framed with open space, as, for example, in *The Wheel* (1953, Modern Museum). His abstract expressionist style remained remarkably consistent and individual in its approach until the works of 1969 and 1970, wherein an apparently radical change may be noted. These paintings are characterized by an overall pattern of modulated small brushstrokes seemingly set within large linear triangles, diamonds, or squares. Colors are usually limited to consistent patterns of greens, blues, violets, and so on. The linear structure gives some sense of abstract perspective illusion. (H.H.A.)

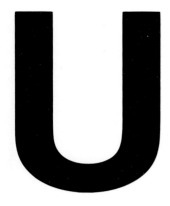

Uelsmann, Jerry N. (1934–   ).
Photographer and teacher, born in
Detroit, Mich. One of a growing number
of younger photographers with an
academic rather than practical background. At the Rochester Institute of
Technology (B.F.A., 1957), he was
influenced by Minor White* and Ralph
Hattersley. He received an M.S. degree
from Indiana University in audio-visu-
al communications (1958), but then
moved to the art department. There,
Henry Holmes Smith, teacher and editor, became one of his major influences. At this time he also worked with
the photographer Jack Welpott on five
photography programs for educational
television. His first successful combination print (made by projecting or con-
tact-printing a succession of negatives
on a sensitized surface), *The Nut Man,*
appeared in 1959. He became an instructor in art at the University of Florida in 1960 and a professor in 1970. By
1963, combined prints had become his
primary mode, and he soon began to
realize the importance in his work of
the "darkroom as a visual research lab."
In 1967 he had a one-man exhibition at
the Museum of Modern Art, New York
City, and received a Guggenheim Fellowship for experiments in multiple
printing techniques.

Uelsmann is the first photographer
since the 19th-century photographer
H. P. Robinson to make extensive use
of combined printing; however, he has
put far more emphasis on the psychological content and its implications than
would have been acceptable in the
Victorian period.

Uelsmann's imagery is notable for its
almost mystical utilization of the Florida
landscape, hanging moss, half-com-
pleted buildings left in the wake of a
land boom, and unusual vegetation.
Such forms are blended into a highly
personal landscape of reverie, despair,
and vague foreboding.   (T.F.B.)

Universal Limited Art Editions.
Founded in 1957 by Tatyana Grosman,
the wife of the painter Maurice Grosman, this lithography workshop in West
Islip, N.Y., has pioneered in the introduction to printmaking of some of the
most prominent painters of the 1960s.
Working with Larry Rivers,* Universal's
first important publication was a portfolio, "Stones," which combined the images of Rivers with the poetry of Frank
O'Hara. Jasper Johns* and Robert
Rauschenberg* made their first lithographs at Universal, and printmaking
came to dominate much of their creative time during the late 1960s. The
Swiss-born Fritz Glarner* produced
both individual prints and a book there,
and Helen Frankenthaler* and Robert
Motherwell* have been making lithographs at Universal since 1961. In 1967
Mrs. Grosman received a grant from
the National Foundation on the Arts
and Humanities to establish an intaglio
workshop. There, Frankenthaler, Jasper Johns,* Marisol,* Motherwell, and
Barnett Newman* worked for the first
time on etchings and aquatints. Seeing
paper as an inseparable part of the artist's composition and printing editions
limited to the amount that can be printed in a day, Grosman sponsored publications known for their sensitive combination of image and paper.   (R.C.)

Upjohn, Richard (1802–78).
Architect, born in Dorsetshire, England.
Upjohn was apprenticed in 1819 to a
cabinetmaker for five years. He then
worked as an independent cabinetmaker but fell heavily into debt. He
sailed for America, and by 1830 was
settled in New Bedford, Mass. There he
was listed as a carpenter. By 1833 he
was designing buildings, the first being
a house (1833–36) in the Greek revival*
style for Isaac Farrar, lumberman of
Bangor, Me. This was followed by the
Church of St. John's, Bangor (1836–38,

demolished), in the Gothic style, which
became Upjohn's favorite for practically all of his churches.

Commissioned to design Trinity
Church, New York (1839–46), Upjohn
moved to New York. His finest church,
Trinity, identified him with the construction favored by English churchmen who
advocated a return to medieval liturgy
and the Gothic style. The Episcopalians
were particularly pleased with Upjohn's
approach. Among the churches he designed were: Christ Church, Brooklyn
(1841–42); Grace Church, Providence,
R.I. (1847–48); Grace Church, Utica,
N.Y. (1856–60); St. Peter's, Albany
(1859–60); and St. Thomas', New York
(1868–70), all of Gothic design.

Upjohn's commercial buildings and
private residences were often derived
from Italian Renaissance styles. Although they had elegant interiors, they
do not match the quality of his Gothic
churches; for those he clearly had a
special affection. Upjohn was a founder
in 1857 of the American Institute of
Architects and was its first president.
He published one book, *Rural Architecture* (1852), mainly an advertisement of his own versatility. His son,
Richard M. Upjohn,* became a distinguished architect.   (P.F.N.)

Upjohn, Richard Michell (1828–1903).
Architect and son of Richard Upjohn.*
Richard Michell was the father of
Hobart Upjohn, an ecclesiastical architect who continued the Gothic tradition
into the third generation. In many ways,
Richard Michell was the most creative
of the three. He departed from the
correct Gothicism of his father and
espoused Victorian Gothic,* which permitted freer design forms. Except for
the contrasted color schemes of his
slate roofs, he did not overindulge in
horizontal-band courses or in alternating colors in the stones around doors
and windows, a practice popular with

the followers of the English critic John Ruskin,* who had introduced Italian Gothic to England.

Upjohn entered his father's office in 1845 and served as a draftsman until 1851, when he became a partner. In 1857 a group of distinguished architects met in the Upjohn office and formed the American Institute of Architects. The early commissions on which he worked, such as the Madison Square Presbyterian Church (Dr. Parkhurst's, 1854) and the Mechanic's Bank at 33 Wall Street (1856), both in New York City, introduced him to the high quality of his father's work, but do not bear the marks of his own style. After 1860, his work began to display his interest in Victorian Gothic. It included the tower of St. Peter's Church in Albany, N.Y., which was begun by his father as a conventional Gothic revival* building but has, in the upper belfry section (added in 1876) the spiky, linear quality of Victorian Gothic. Two other churches done in a Victorian manner were Grace Church, Manchester, N.H. (1860), and Trinity Church, New Rochelle, N.Y. (1863), where gables on four sides of the steeple enliven the whole composition. The finest building of the late Gothic revival is his main gateway for Greenwood Cemetery in Brooklyn (1861–65). Here the masonry gate lodges, unified by a great openwork stone feature above the roadways, and with the polychromy of the roofs, are transitional to Victorian Gothic. He also designed St. Chrysostom's Chapel in Manhattan (1869) and St. Peter's Church, Geneva, N.Y. (1872) in Victorian Gothic. He also designed an impressive Victorian Gothic country seat of stone for William Matthews in Rye, N.Y.

Quite without precedent was Upjohn's design for the State Capitol at Hartford, Conn. (1872–85), dominating Bushnell Park. With its high central tower crowned by a gilded dome and statue, it was the epitome of High Victorian Gothic design in the United States. In their quest for a crisp linear quality, Victorian architects, as in this building, turned to early 13th-century French Gothic prototypes, reviving spiky bud-capitals, squat marble columns, overall wall patterns, and plate-tracery (pierced stone) for windows. Much admired when built, and only recently rediscovered, this building alone ranks Upjohn as one of the high apostles of this style in America. (A.B.)

1

2

1. **Jerry N. Uelsmann.** Journey into Self, 1967, photograph.
2. **Richard Michell Upjohn.** State Capitol, Hartford, Conn., 1885.

Van Brunt, Henry (1832–1903).
Architect. Born in Boston, Mass., he graduated from Harvard in 1854 and worked briefly for George Snell (1820–93), architect. In 1856 he went to New York City and studied with Richard Morris Hunt* for several years. In 1863 he formed a partnership with William R. Ware in Boston, and their office became an atelier for architectural apprenticeships. Van Brunt's firm championed Victorian Gothic* architecture, with emphasis on the rich Italian polychromy advocated by John Ruskin,* English art critic. One of their early commissions was for the First Church (Unitarian) in Boston's fashionable Back Bay area (1867). It was squat and massive and had a low corner tower. In 1868 they designed the base for the High Victorian Gothic Ether Monument, with romantic sculpture by J. Q. A. Ward,* in the Boston Public Gardens. Weld Hall (1872), a dormitory for Harvard, was five stories high, with a multiplicity of Flemish gables. In 1874 they undertook a large building for Harvard: Memorial Hall, a monument of Victorian Gothic architecture, was surmounted by a high tower and led into an amphitheater, Sanders Theater, on one side, and the rectangular Dining Hall on the other. The firm also designed an east wing for Gore Hall, the library at Harvard, in 1877; its crisp rectangularity was of a type not seen in America before 1900. A spectacular railway station for Worcester, Mass. (1877), provided a contrast between its slender tower, 212 feet high, and its low-arched trainsheds. The firm also designed one of the most original creations of the Victorian Gothic period, St. Stephen's Church at Lynn, Mass. (c.1881).

In 1881 Ware became head of the new school of architecture at Columbia University, and two years later Van Brunt formed a new firm with Frank M. Howe (1864–1931). In 1885 Howe

opened an office for the firm in Kansas City, Mo., and most of their work was henceforth done in the West. They designed several stations for the Union Pacific, the most notable being the Romanesque revival* station at Cheyenne, Wyo. (1887). They also did the Electricity Building at the World's Columbian Exposition in Chicago (1893), an enormous neo-Italian Renaissance structure with an array of small domed towers. In 1904 they designed the Varied Industries Building for the Louisiana Purchase Exposition in St. Louis, Mo., in Beaux-Arts style.

Something of a scholar, Van Brunt was the author of *Greek Lines and Other Architectural Essays* (1893). He was president of the American Institute of Architects in 1899.   (A.B.)

Van der Burch, Cornelius (c.1653–99).
One of New York's earliest silversmiths, best known for the beaker he made for presentation to Robert Sandersen in 1685 (Yale). In Dutch tradition, the tall beaker is elaborately engraved, with strapwork borders and vignettes enclosing designs derived from the allegories of Jacobus Cats that were published in Amsterdam in 1655 and 1658. He also made traditional Dutch ceremonial spoons with cast handles for the funerals of prominent persons (Yale).

Vanderlyn, John (1775–1852).
Painter of portraits, historical subjects, and landscape. Descended from colonial craftsman painters, he was born in Kingston, N.Y., and began his career with three years of study under miniaturist and landscape painter Archibald Robertson (1765–1835). Aaron Burr, convinced of the young man's genius, arranged for him to study (1795–96) in the Philadelphia studio of Gilbert Stuart,* and then in Paris (1796–1801), under Antoine Paul Vin-

John Vanderlyn. Ariadne Asleep on the Isle of Naxos, *1814. Pennsylvania Academy of the Fine Arts, Philadelphia (Joseph and Sarah Harrison Collection).*

cent. He emerged a mature painter in the smooth, authoritative style of the French neoclassicists, and with a determination to rise above any dependence upon portraiture. After two years in New York, he returned to Europe. He lived mostly in France and, stimulated by the art life around him, produced what was to be his best work. There Joel Barlow chose him as illustrator of his poem, *Columbiad,* though Vanderlyn finished only one piece, called *The Death of Jane McCrea* (1804, Wadsworth). Vigorous and masterly, it shows that he might have added a genuine dramatic quality to the poet's turgid epic. His *Marius on the Ruins of Carthage* (1807, de Young), painted in Rome, was awarded the gold medal of the French Salon by fiat from the Emperor Napoleon. Vanderlyn's best work, his neoclassic *Ariadne Asleep on the Isle of Naxos* (1814, Pennsylvania), was painted in Paris. In 1815, preparing for his return to America after this long sojourn, he moved into the art of the cyclorama with his *Palace and Gardens of Versailles* (1816–19, Metropolitan) on 3000 square feet of canvas.

Back in New York, the city aided in the erection of a rotunda in the park, where his *Versailles* and other cycloramas could be shown. Vanderlyn shared also in outstanding portrait commissions memorializing Jackson, Madison, Monroe, and other great figures of the era. Yet his talent, nurtured abroad, never became acclimated to America, and his friendship with the unpopular Burr ruined his chances for acceptance and success. His remaining years were marked by disappointments, bitterness, and decline. The New York Rotunda failed financially and he was evicted from it by the city in 1829. He repeatedly pawned the Napoleonic gold medal and saw it redeemed by friends. Competing with John Trumbull* in seeking a government commission for paintings in the rotunda of the Capitol at Washington, he was, after twenty years of frustration and poverty, awarded one in 1837, *The Landing of Columbus.* He returned to Paris to paint it, spending from 1842–44 on it. When it was discovered that he had employed an assistant (in accordance with the usual practice on large pictures), the rumor spread that the work was not truly his own. More fair-minded critics gave him credit for a major work but could not praise it as a

great one. His career remained in shadow, and he died penniless and alone. (C.C.S.)

Vanderlyn, Pieter (c.1687–1778).
Dutch-born portrait painter who came to the province of New York in 1718. More than twenty portraits of Kingston and Albany residents, probably painted between 1720–45, have been attributed to him. Because the earliest work portrays members of the Gansevoort family of Albany, the artist is sometimes referred to as the "Gansevoort Limner." The consistently two-dimensional, thinly painted, finely detailed works, although unsigned, are inscribed with information about the sitters in a hand that corresponds to documents that Pieter Vanderlyn signed. In addition, the artist's residence in the upper Hudson River area neatly accommodates the sitters' ages. Pieter was the father of Nicholas Vanderlyn, an artist and sign painter, and grandfather of the well-known painter John Vanderlyn.* (M.J.G.)

Van Dyck, Peter (1684–1750).
Silversmith. He served his apprenticeship as a silversmith with Bartholomew Le Roux of New York and married Le Roux's daughter in 1711. He held several local offices, including serving as a constable in 1708 and 1715. His finest work is exemplified by a tankard (Yale) with ornate baroque cast mounts, richly gadrooned, and repoussé lid, elaborately engraved coat of arms, and characteristic New York cocoon-shaped thumbpiece and cut-card work. In addition to tankards, Van Dyck is noted for his early rococo teapots with smooth pear-shaped or octagonal bodies, curved spouts, and deeply domed lids (Yale; Metropolitan). Frequently Van Dyck's silver was engraved with thinly designed cyphers indicating the owner's initials. A rare egg-shaped mustard pot and a gold necklace (both Yale) were also made by Van Dyck. (M.G.F.)

Vedder, Elihu (1836–1923).
Figure painter, illustrator, and poet, now recognized for the unique vein of fantasy in his work. Descendant of an old Dutch family, he was born in New York, N.Y. At the age of twelve he began to study art. After a short time in an architectural office, he studied with the genre painter Tompkins H. Matteson in

1. **Robert Venturi** (with John Rauch). Fire Station No. 4, Columbus, Ind. 1969.
2. **Elihu Vedder.** The Questioner of the Sphinx, 1863. *Museum of Fine Arts, Boston (gift of Mrs. Martin Brimmer).*

Sherbourne, N.Y. In 1856 he sailed for Europe and studied painting in Paris, Florence, and Düsseldorf. Returning to America in 1861, he set up his studio in New York and made a precarious living designing greeting cards and comic valentines and illustrating books and magazines. He returned to Europe in 1866 and settled in Rome, but made frequent trips back to America to execute commissions for murals and mosaics.

During the Civil War, while barely managing to earn enough to keep alive, Vedder conceived some of the most imaginative paintings produced in that inhibited era. *The Questioner of the Sphinx* (1863, Boston), *The Lair of the Sea Serpent* (1864, Boston), and *The Lost Mind* (1864–65, Metropolitan) are the manifestations of a startlingly original mind, doubly surprising amidst the academically oriented art of complacent Victorian America.

On his return to Italy, Vedder produced a number of landscapes in oil of the hill towns and villages of the campagna. These have a quiet charm and an effect out of proportion to their small size. He continued in his later years to create mysterious and often haunting fantasies, as, for example, the moving *In Memoriam* (1879, Corcoran), a memorial to a son who had died in 1875. But Vedder's style underwent a change as he grew older. His once warm and luminous color became pale and chalky, and finally cold and repellent. His use of line, which in his middle years had been capable of intricate patterns and movement, became in his last period little more than a mannerism. Thus the bleak, contrived style of the murals and a mosaic done for the Library of Congress (1896–97) and the mural for the Bowdoin College Art Gallery in Maine (1894) did not add to his reputation.

Vedder fits into no neat category, and this has kept him from gaining recognition as one of the rare breed of creative spirits who do not conform to the fashion of the day. He was an artist of intellect who created images of rare strength and haunting beauty. Long overlooked, his work has recently come to be recognized as an early precursor of surrealism* in its use of symbolism and the bizarre juxtaposition of strange objects, which are painted in a sharply focused, realistic style.

(H.W.W.)

Venturi, Robert (1925–   ).
Architect whose theories were the most original and provocative of the 1960s. His writings, lectures, and architecture created a major controversy. In contrast to architects who had "prim dreams of pure order," he looked at a wider range of our built-up environment and pointed out "vitality as well as validity" in the "vulgar and disdained"—in roadside advertising, "ordinary buildings," the undesigned, the ornamented, and in history. He accepted the vitality and flashiness of the roadside strip and of the ordinary building as economically viable and usually successful; and he asked if architects should not learn from those structures. He called his supermannerist architecture "the architecture of accommodation."

Born in Philadelphia, Pa., Venturi studied architecture at Princeton (B.A. 1947, M.F.A. 1950) and then worked with Eero Saarinen* and Louis Kahn.* He opened his own office in Philadelphia in 1958, formed a partnership with William Short (1961–64), and then with John Rauch (Venturi & Rauch, 1964). He taught at the University of Pennsylvania (1955–63) and then achieved prominence while teaching at Yale University (1963–70). In his architecture he showed an early interest in using common materials in uncommon contexts (Duke House renovation, Institute of Fine Arts, New York University, 1959, with Cope & Lippincott). This led to a pop art* use of elements from roadside strips, as in the diner-café idiom of Grand's Restaurant (West Philadelphia, 1962, since destroyed). Among commercial motifs he favored billboards and large-scale lettering; in Grand's Restaurant a large graphic wall decoration (painted in mirror-image on the opposite wall) was one of the first supergraphics.* Concurrently, he incorporated elements from 17th-century mannerist and baroque English and Italian designers; entryways and principal façades were treated as symbolic, ceremonial portals (North Penn Visiting Nurse Association, Ambler, Pa., 1963; and a residence, Chestnut Hill, Pa., 1964). In an apartment house for the elderly, the Guild House, Philadelphia, he first combined all these motifs: an everyday, "ugly," red-brick apartment house idiom—a pop art approach—was joined with historical allusions in the screenlike façade. It was his first architectural billboard.

With the publication of his book *Complexities and Contradications in Modern Architecture* in 1966, Venturi became nationally known. In 1967 he married Denise Scott Brown, a city planner who then became a partner in the firm. The firm continued to manipulate the conventional building idiom, symbolized in white billboards and large lettering, combined with a historical entry portal (Football Hall of Fame competition, 1967; Fire Station 4, Columbus, Ind., 1969; Lieb House, Long Beach Island, N.J., 1969). A diagonally sited, but "ordinary" small brick building (Medical Office Building, Bridgeton, N.J., 1969) was designed with an entrance like an ancient oriental moongate in an occidental back fence. Such allusions and devices were so unorthodox that a number of the firm's designs were cancelled or destroyed. The Fine Arts Commission of Washington, D.C., rejected several of his designs for the Transportation Square Office Building (1967–   ). The congregation of a renovated church (St. Francis de Sales Roman Catholic Church, Philadelphia, 1970) removed an uncovered cold cathode lighting tube that the architects had used to focus on furnishings—resembling works by Claes Oldenburg*—for the new liturgy. A storm of professional protest was aroused by their "ordinary-looking" design for Yale's Mathematics Building (1970). However, by the early 1970s, the acceptance already accorded Venturi's writings was being extended to the buildings of Venturi & Rauch. They were working on more and larger commissions (Humanities Building, State University at Purchase, N.Y.), planning studies for the South Street Rehabilitation, Philadelphia, a study of suburban housing, and a book called *Learning from Las Vegas* (1972). Still, Venturi's wry, scandalizing humor—he has used the terms boring, ordinary, dumb, banal, and ugly about his own designs—continue to confuse and provoke public and professionals alike.

(C.R.S.)

Vicente, Esteban (1906–   ).
A native of Segovia, Spain, he enrolled in a Madrid painting academy, where he drew from casts and studied in the Prado Museum. Later he was awarded a fellowship for study in France and Germany, and then moved to New York City in 1936. He taught at the Univer-

sity of California (1954–55), Black Mountain College in North Carolina, and New York University. Although Vicente is usually identified with the abstract expressionist group, his work is more rigidly structured and his impasto effects are more calculated. He once noted that "painting should be detached from personality," and this attitude may account for the lack of immediacy, directness, or acceptance of accident in his work. Because the essential qualities of abstract expressionism* are missing, his work seems more European in its traditionalism and is similar to the Spanish version of modern expressionism. Vicente delights in powerful, brilliant color, and he is particularly interested in the luminosity of Velásquez. His painting has remained consistently abstract, although he claims no manifesto or program.

(E.C.G.)

Victorian Gothic Style.
A style of architecture introduced in the United States in the 1860s by transplanted English architects. It superseded the Gothic revival* of the 1850s, but also advocated a high level of craftsmanship in the costly masonry tradition. It appeared principally in ecclesiastical structures and some commercial and public buildings. In its use of colored stonework in the walls and in its clear expression of structure and materials it exemplified the Venetian architecture described by John Ruskin* in his influential book *The Stones of Venice* (1851–53). Because Ruskin's inspiration was Italian, this style is sometimes referred to as Italian or Venetian Gothic. Another influence was French medievalism, which had reintroduced 12th- and 13th-century Gothic architecture.

Victorian Gothic was a pointed-arch style, like the English ecclesiastical Gothic, but it enlivened this earlier style through the introduction of varicolored stonework in walls and in the polished pink granite colonnettes used at door and window openings. The new emphasis on the visible expression of structure produced such features as colonnettes set out from the wall, carrying the ends of trusses or of gables, thus proclaiming their strength for all to see. Tall, narrow, lancet-type windows followed the rise of interior stairs, and corner turrets were often carried on projecting supports well above

1

2

1. *Esteban Vicente.* Afternoon, 1971. André Emmerich Gallery, N.Y.
2. *Leonard Wells Volk.* Abraham Lincoln *(executed from a life mask), 1860, bronze.* Metropolitan Museum of Art, N.Y. (gift of Theodore B. Starr, Inc.)

street level—a visual expression of function. Victorian Gothic coexisted with neo-Grec,* and like it, often found a new expression for modern materials such as iron and glass.

The panic of 1873 curtailed the construction of buildings executed in this costly tradition, but isolated examples of the style continued to appear for some years. Its principal exponents in America were: Peter B. Wight (1838–1925), who introduced the style to the United States in 1862 with his National Academy of Design in New York City, a building reminiscent of the Doge's Palace in Venice; Frederick C. Withers,* whose Jefferson Market Courthouse and Prison (1874–77), was an outstanding example of High Victorian Gothic; William A. Potter,* and Richard Michell Upjohn.*　　　　　　　　(A.B.)

Volk, Leonard Wells (1828–95).
Sculptor, known primarily for one piece, his bust of Abraham Lincoln. Born in Wellstown, N.Y., Volk was a stonecutter before turning to sculpture. After studying in Rome (1855–57) he established his studio in Chicago, and there in 1860 he took the life-mask of Lincoln from which he produced his famous portrait. The original life-mask is owned by the Smithsonian, but replicas of the bust are in numerous collections. Volk produced a number of other portrait busts of well-known men, including Ulysses S. Grant and William Henry Seward, using plaster, marble and bronze; all were characterized by a rather prosaic naturalism. Volk was a founder of the Chicago Academy of Design and was its president for eight years.　　　　　　　　(W.C.)

Vonnoh, Bessie Potter (1872–1955).
A sculptor who dwelt primarily on one theme—the warm relationship of mother and child. Leaving her native St. Louis, Mo., she studied with Lorado Taft* at the Chicago Art Institute. From an early stage in her career her small bronze family groups achieved a great popularity and were accepted for exhibition both in this country and abroad. The *Young Mother,* for example, was shown at the Paris Exposition in 1900, where it won a bronze medal. Stylistically, her work shows the influence of the impressionistic, flickering surfaces of the late 19th-century French school, a style that lent itself to intimate domestic scenes. In 1899 Bessie Potter mar-

ried Robert Vonnoh,* the painter, and thereafter lived and worked in New York.

Vonnoh, Robert William (1858–1933).
Impressionist painter. Born in Hartford, Conn., he grew up in Boston, where he attended the Massachusetts Normal Art School. He spent much of the decade 1881–90 in Paris, first as a student of Bastien-Lepage and at the Académie Julien, later assimilating the technique of impressionism.* In 1891 he joined the staff of the Pennsylvania Academy of the Fine Arts,* where Robert Henri* studied with him. His later landscapes and portraits are skillful examples of American impressionism, in which fresh brushstrokes of pure color describe forms more tangible and less atmospheric than those of the French painters. His wife, Bessie Potter Vonnoh,* student of Lorado Taft,* was also an artist.

Voulkos, Peter (1924–　　).
Sculptor, born in Bozeman, Mon., and educated at Montana State College and the California College of Arts and Carfts, Oakland, where he received a M.F.A. A painter and ceramist until the late 1950s, he received the only gold medal awarded to an American at the International Exposition of Ceramics at Cannes, France, in 1955. Under the influence of abstract expressionism,* he soon turned to sculpture, heaping cylinders and mounds of clay into monumental forms. Many of these works were unable to withstand the firing process. Those which survived reflect the gestural energy of such painters as Franz Kline* and Jackson Pollock.* Among them is *Feather Rock* (1959), a craggy, looming work that shows his innovative change from traditional ceramic slip to acrylics in the application of color. In the early 1960s, Voulkos turned his experience as a foundryman to the casting of large bronze pieces from bolted slabs of sculptor's wax. The rough textures and shapes of these works had given way by 1964 to smooth platforms, pedestals and tubes of polished, reflective metal. This sculpture combines monumentality with elegance. Voulkos has taught at the University of California, Berkeley. He has been instrumental in founding ceramics and sculpture workshops in collaboration with Kenneth Price and John Mason, who also helped turn the

craft of ceramics into a fine art. His work is included in such major collections as the Museum of Modern Art, New York City, the Los Angeles County Museum, and the Baltimore Museum of Art. (C.R.)

Waldo, Samuel Lovett (1783–1861).
Portrait painter. A native of Windham, Conn., he first learned his craft in Hartford, about 1799, from the painter, silhouettist, and museum operator, Joseph Steward (1753–1822). After gaining experience as an itinerant portrait painter, roaming as far south as Charleston, S.C., he went to London with letters to the American expatriates Benjamin West* and John Singleton Copley,* and studied there (1806–08). With this background he settled in New York and remained a successful portraitist for more than fifty years. After 1820, he worked in close partnership with William Jewett.* Outstanding characterizations in his large oeuvre are his *Self-portrait* (1817, Metropolitan) and *The Independent Beggar* (1819, Boston Athenaeum).   (C.C.S.)

Walker, Horatio (1858–1938).
Canadian painter of peasant life who enjoyed great popularity in the United States at the turn of the century. Walker was born in Ontario, Canada, and after traveling to Europe in 1882 he settled near Quebec, where the French Canadian farmyards and pastures lent themselves to a broadly romanticized treatment reminiscent of Millet, as in *The Harrower* (Metropolitan). Walker visited New York in 1885. His skillfully painted scenes of farm animals won an impressive series of honors, including awards at the expositions in Paris, 1889; Buffalo, 1901; St. Louis, 1904; and San Francisco, 1915.

Walkowitz, Abraham (c.1880–1965).
Painter and draftsman. He was born in Siberia and came to New York City as a child of about nine. He studied at the National Academy of Design* and the Artists' Institute, and regarded Walter Shirlaw* as his most influential teacher. Between 1900 and 1906 he taught at the Educational Alliance, exhibiting paint-

1

2

1. ***Thomas Ustick Walter.*** *Girard College, Founder's Hall, Philadelphia, 1847.*
2. ***Abraham Walkowitz.*** *New York, 1917. Whitney Museum of American Art, N.Y. (gift of the artist in memory of Julian Force).*

580

ings there and at the National Academy, and began doing freely rhythmic drawings from life. He visited Paris during 1906–07, studying with Jean-Paul Laurens at the Académie Julien and being exposed to the new currents in art through association with Max Weber* and with Gertrude and Leo Stein. He met the French painter Henri Rousseau and Pablo Picasso, and attended the Cézanne retrospective of 1907. His oils after his return to New York in 1907 reflected the influence of fauvism,* but he began to place more emphasis on drawing than on painting, and it is for his graphic work that he is known as one of the pioneers of modernism in America.

Walkowitz held his first one-man exhibition in 1908, a modest show that nevertheless caught the discerning eye of Arthur B. Davies.* Alfred Stieglitz* also became interested in his work and gave him several shows at his gallery "291," starting in 1912. Walkowitz also exhibited in the Armory Show* (1913) and in the Forum exhibition (1916). During this period he did thousands of drawings trying to convey motion through line (and occasionally watercolor wash) used more or less abstractly. His treatment was sometimes spontaneously rhythmic, sometimes reminiscent of Rodin and Matisse, sometimes cubist or futurist in effect, and on occasion charged with expressionist tension. One series of drawings portrayed Isadora Duncan, whom he had seen dance in Paris, in hundreds of dance gestures; other series reflected the energies he perceived in the life and architecture of New York City (*New York,* 1917, Whitney).

During the 1920s Walkowitz shifted his emphasis to oils, usually portraying figure groups, sometimes of fishermen, or in works with overtones of social concern. In the 1930s he suffered from eye trouble that forced him to stop painting. He remained, however, a colorful and garrulous figure on the New York art scene. He had served on the board of the Society of Independent Artists;* in 1934 he became president of the Société Anonyme, and he was accorded retrospectives by the Brooklyn Museum (1939) and the Jewish Museum (1949). He persuaded a hundred artists to do his portrait and arranged an exhibition of the resulting works at the Brooklyn Museum in 1944. In 1962 he was accorded a late moment of recognition when he received the Marjorie Peabody Waite award of the American Academy of Arts and Letters.

(D.W.S.)

Walter, Thomas Ustick (1804–87). Architect, born in Philadelphia, Pa. He was apprenticed to his father, a bricklayer and stonemason. He then studied architecture with William Strickland* at the Franklin Institute. By 1825 he was classed as master bricklayer, but moved into the architectural profession upon entering Strickland's office (1828–30). He then began his own practice.

Walter won the competition for Moyamensing, the Philadelphia County Prison (built 1832–35, demolished c.1963). The prison was castellated Gothic, but Walter's addition of a Debtor's Prison (1836) was in the Egyptian style. Two years later he won a contest for the Founder's Hall, Girard College, Philadelphia (1833–47). The result was the epitome of Greek revival* style on the exterior but totally unsuitable inside. The building, intended for the education of orphan boys, was required to have four rooms, fifty feet square, on each of three floors. Surrounded by a Greek colonnade, this veritable temple had to enclose spaces in no way related to Greek usage, and the halls had echoes and lacked sufficient outside light. Nevertheless, in imitating the monumentality of the Temple of Zeus in Athens, it was an outstanding achievement of the Greek revival age. Other important buildings by Walter were Hibernian Hall, Charleston, S.C. (1835); the Philadelphia Contributionship (1836); Philadelphia Savings Fund Society Building (1839–40); Preston Retreat, Philadelphia (1837); and the Crown Street Synagogue (1849), also in Philadelphia.

In 1851 Walter, one of four winners of a competition, was asked by President Fillmore to prepare plans for an extension of the Capitol (1851–65). He designed the new legislative wings and a cast-iron dome. He also worked on the Treasury from the designs of architect Robert Mills.* His large practice also included many private dwellings. He wrote two books, *A Guide to Workers in Metal and Stone* (1846), and with J. Jay Smith, *Two Hundred Designs for Cottages and Villas* (1846). Walter was a founder of the American Institution of Architects in 1836 and second president (1876–87) of its successor, the American Institute of Architects.

(P.F.N.)

Ward, John Quincy Adams (1830–1910). Portrait sculptor. Born in Urbana, Ohio, he first studied sculpture as assistant to Henry Kirke Brown* in New York, and in the mid-1850s he helped model Brown's equestrian *Washington* for Union Square, New York. Unlike most other sculptors, he never went to Europe to study, but his forthright naturalism made him the dean of American sculptors from about 1875 on. He was seldom without commissions for life-size bronze portrait statues and he was extremely prolific. His work was generally not dramatic or exciting, but highly competent in its craftsmanship and with a good feeling for sculptural form. Ward's work frequently appears somewhat dry in comparison to the lively surfaces and decorative effects of such sculptors as Saint-Gaudens,* Daniel Chester French* or MacMonnies.* Examples of his early work are the bronze statuette, *The Freedman* (1865, New York Hist.) and *Indian Hunter* (1867, Central Park, New York). Among his better-known portrait statues, all in bronze, are the *Washington* (1883, Wall Street, New York), *Pilgrim* (1885, Central Park), *President Garfield* (1887, Washington, D.C.), and *Henry Ward Beecher* (1891, Brooklyn). He produced several equestrian statues, such as the *General Philip Sheridan* (1908, Albany). Ward created sculpture for the Dewey Arch (destroyed) in 1899, and for the pediment of the New York Stock Exchange (1903). He was elected president of the National Academy of Design* in 1874 and was also the first president of the National Sculpture Society.

(W.C.)

Warhol, Andy (1930–   ). The painter who, through his paintings, objects, underground movies, and personal life, stands more than any other for pop art* in the public imagination. He was born in Pittsburgh, Pa., studied at the Carnegie Institute of Technology, and moved to New York City in 1952. He had one-man shows at various galleries in the early 1960s and a retrospective at the Moderna Museet, Stockholm, in 1968. Like several other pop artists, Warhol was first a successful commercial artist. His blown-up comic strip paintings of Dick Tracy were

1

2

used as a 1961 window display for Lord and Taylor's department store in New York. It is reported that Warhol "painted" his first stencil pictures of dollar bills around 1961 on the suggestion of an art dealer; when she asked him what was the most important thing in his life, his answer was, "money." "Well, then," she reputedly advised, "paint it!" He began his Campbell Soup tin-can "paintings" because "I used to drink it. I used to have the same lunch every day, for twenty years, I guess; the same thing over and over again."

Warhol's most characteristic manner is repetition—endless rows of bottles, as in *Green Coca Cola Bottles* (1962, Whitney), Campbell Soup cans, painted flowers, Brillo boxes, photographs of celebrities and of himself. Beginning with the objects on supermarket shelves as they might pass in review on a television commercial, Warhol turned to the contemporary American folk heroes such as Elvis Presley and Marlon Brando, and love goddesses such as Elizabeth Taylor and Marilyn Monroe. Using silkscreen processes for mechanical repetition, he further emphasized his desire to eliminate the personal signature of the artist, to depict life and the images of our time without comment. It is said that Warhol, who is surrounded by an entourage, at times simply gives a subject to one of his followers and permits him to execute it.

During the later 1960s, referring to himself as a "retired artist," he turned more and more to the making of films—so-termed "underground" films. Using his principle of monotonous repetition, which gradually becomes hypnotic in its effect, he documents the world in which he lives. Although these films and even the process of making them contain strong elements of parody of the commercial film world and are sensationally erotic, they are a serious and sometimes important venture on the part of the artist. The story line, particularly as it deals with erotic themes, has gradually become stronger, and some of the films have become (for experimental movies) substantial financial successes. Warhol's turning to the films is also symptomatic of the synthesis of mediums (termed mixed-media) that has entered into the work of pop artists. Among Warhol's more notable films are *Chelsea Girls* (1966), *Lonesome Cowboys* (1967–8), *Blue Movie*

(1968), *Trash* (1971), and *Heat* (1972).

(H.H.A.)

Warneke, Heinz (1895–   ).
Sculptor, born in Bremen, Germany. He attended the Academy of Art in Bremen and in 1913 studied at the Academy of Art in Berlin. He came to America in 1923, settling first in St. Louis and then, in 1927, in New York City. An exhibition of his work in 1927 established him immediately as a leading sculptor of the semiabstract group. Warneke's work is based on nature—especially animals—but the form undergoes a process of simplification and abstraction similar in theory to that of William Zorach* or Robert Laurent.* Although he was in Germany in the years preceding World War I and in Paris in the early 1930s, his art was never lured very far from nature by the experiments of the cubists or constructivists. One of the early sculptors to carve directly in stone, he also worked in other media, such as brass. Examples of his work are *Hissing Geese* and *Wild Boars* (both c.1930–32, Chicago), *Orangutan Thinking* (c.1932, Addison) and *Prodigal Son* (c. 1938, Washington Cathedral, Washington, D.C.)

(W.C.)

Warner, Olin (1844–96).
Sculptor. A native of Suffield, Conn., he was one of the first to introduce the Beaux-Arts style to America sculpture. He went to Paris in 1869, studied at the École des Beaux-Arts, and became acquainted with the leading French sculptors of the 1870s and '80s. Warner learned the Parisian techniques of modeling, with the resulting lively surfaces and spontaneity of composition so unlike the neoclassicism* being practiced in Rome and Florence. He returned to America in 1872, established his studio in New York, and for several years did only portrait busts and medallions; one of his finest busts in the *J. Alden Weir* (1880, Metropolitan), which clearly shows the Parisian influence. His ideal works were also executed in the Paris style; an example is his bronze *Diana* (1898, Metropolitan), which in spite of its classical subject is rendered in a nonclassical style. Another important piece is the full-length bronze, *William Lloyd Garrison* (c.1885, City of Boston). He had also completed the first panel, representing *Oral Tradition*, for the bronze doors (c.1895–96) of the Library of Congress when he was

3

4

1. *Andy Warhol.* Marilyn Monroe, *1962. Collection Mr. and Mrs. Burton Tremaine, Meriden, Conn.*
2. *Andy Warhol.* Campbell's Soup, *1965. Leo Castelli Gallery, N.Y.*
3. *Olin Warner.* Diana, *1887, bronze. Metropolitan Museum of Art, N.Y. (gift of the National Sculpture Society).*
4. *Heinz Warneke.* Orangutan Thinking, *c.1932. Addison Gallery of American Art, Phillips Academy, Andover, N.H.*

killed in a carriage accident; Herbert Adams* completed the commission.

(W.C.)

Warren, Russell (1783–1860).
Architect and engineer. Born in Tiverton, R.I. It is uncertain where he received his training. He worked first as an architect in Bristol, R.I., where he designed several sumptuous mansions such as the William DeWolf House (1808) and the Gen. George DeWolf-Colt House (1810). By the 1820s he had shifted his practice to Providence and often worked there with James Bucklin. With the exception of the Gothic style of the Congregational Church (now Unitarian), New Bedford, Mass. (1836–38), done with A. J. Davis, Warren concentrated on the Greek revival* style, though often of a highly ornamental variety. His monumental colonnades, solid stone construction yet frequently playful detail make his buildings outstanding in southern New England. In Providence most of his buildings of consequence have been demolished, but the glass-roofed arcade, with Bucklin (1828), is still in use and is considered by many the finest arcade in the country. The immense Ionic colonnades of the façade contributed by Warren (on Weybosset Street) are of granite and have great dignity and strength. In New Bedford more of his buildings are still standing: the Free Public Library (1856); Institution of Savings (1853, now a machine shop); Merchants' and Mechanics' Banks Building (1831–35, originally two separate banks); the Mark Duff House. The John Avery Parker House (1834), in the Greek revival style, is the most distinguished and fashionable of his New Bedford houses.

Warren's engineering work was mainly on bridges, one of which crosses the Great Pedee River, S.C. The "Warren truss," used extensively for steel bridge construction, was supposedly named after him.

(P.F.N.)

Watson, John (1685–1768).
Scottish portraitist who settled in Perth Amboy, N.J., about 1714, and became one of its well-to-do citizens, lending money to his own patrons. His work includes both oils and small plumbago drawings. His home contained a collection of paintings he brought from Scotland in 1730, possibly the earliest art collection in America.

4

His portraits, such as *Governor William Burnet* (New York Hist.), are expert but stilted in the manner of the times and under the influence of mezzotint prototypes.*

Waugh, Frederick Judd (1861–1940). Marine painter. Waugh was born in Bordentown, N.J., and attended the Pennsylvania Academy of the Fine Arts and the Académie Julien in Paris. From 1892 to 1907 he remained in Europe, where he enjoyed success as an illustrator and painted figure compositions in a turn-of-the-century decorative manner. Subsequently, he began painting seascapes in England, then settled in Provincetown, on Cape Cod. His colorful, appealing, skillfully realistic views of waves and rocks brought him to national prominence by the 1930s, when he won the popular prize at the Carnegie International Exhibition for a number of years in succession.

Wayne, June (1918–   ). Painter, printmaker, and founder of Tamarind Lithography Workshop in Los Angeles. Born in Chicago, Ill., she was an industrial designer from 1939–41 and a radio writer until 1943. She has worked in lithography since 1948, and her prints are known for their technical excellence and variety. Her themes are generally symbolic, treated illusionistically, and occasionally incorporate the geometric forms of light refraction or the amorphous shapes of abstract expressionism.*

Weathervanes.
Wind-direction indicators, usually on rooftops, which have been decorative elements in Western architecture since the Middle Ages. Old continental and English vanes often incorporated flat birds (in particular, the rooster), animals, heraldic devices or banner-like forms that either surmount or terminate a directional arrow. American vanes based on these models date from the late 17th century, and these and other richly inventive examples produced here during the next two centuries have been recognized as widely dispersed examples of folk art expression.

The rooster, alleged to be prevalent among European weathervanes as the result of a 9th-century papal decree, was the most popular early American form. But in time the legless silhouette of the European prototype gave way

to realism, and American rooster vanes of the 19th century reveal the diversity of breeds known to American farmers. They are joined by some more ornamental birds, in particular the peacock, the swan and, almost inevitably, the national eagle. The 19th century produced a rich variety of vanes in the shapes of horses, deer, foxes, cows, grasshoppers, and (especially along the seaboard) fish and whales; and American vanes depicting Indians, trumpeting angels, ships, and wheeled vehicles (carriages, sulkies, and locomotives and, after the turn of the century, automobiles) have also been popular.

Although some of the individually made early American vanes are hollow, most are flat silhouettes made first of wood or wrought iron and later of flat sheet metal. The majority of late 19th-century examples are hollow figures, mass produced in molded sheet metal, usually copper or zinc that was likely to be gilded. A good example of the flat type is the *Angel Gabriel* (Folk Art, N.Y.). In the same collection is the largest known American weathervane, a hollow sheet-metal representation of Chief Tammany found in East Branch, N.Y., and probably dating from the mid-to-late 19th century.

Of the identified weathervane-makers, the earliest is Deacon Shem Drowne (1683–1774) of Boston, who produced in 1742 the Faneuil Hall grasshopper weathervane made of copper, and the New Brick Church cockerel vanes between 1716 and 1742. In the late 19th century, mass-produced vanes of distinction were manufactured in Waltham, Mass., by L. W. Cushing and Sons and by the firm of J. W. Fiske, which is still active in Paterson, N.J.

(M.J.G.)

Weaving.
In western civilizations weaving on the loom was, until the 20th century, inseparable on the one hand from pictorial tapestry and on the other from the production of utilitarian fabrics for garments or furnishings. Dorothy Liebes and Jack Lenor Larsen were pioneers in liberating utilitarian weaving from the limitations of the power loom and mass production. Both designed fabrics on the hand loom where control and invention are possible, and these fabrics were then mass produced on power looms. As designers and con-

Weathervanes
1. *Man with trumpet, 19th century, wood. Museum of American Folk Art, N.Y.*
2. *Angel with trumpet, gilded iron, 1840, made by Gould and Hazlett, Boston. People's Methodist Church, Newburyport, Mass. Index of American Design, National Gallery of Art, Washington, D.C.*
3. *Fish-man with trumpet, iron. Smithsonian Institution, Washington, D.C.*
Weaving
4. *Anni Albers. Black, White, Red, 1927, double weave silk and cotton wall hanging.*

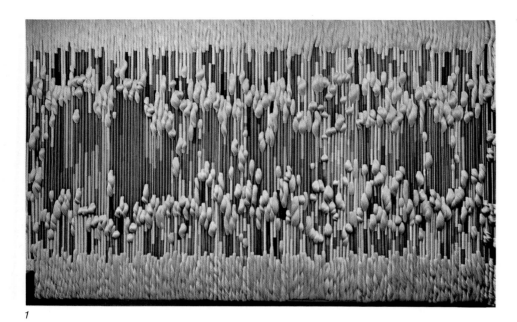

1

2

sultants to the textile industry, they introduced synthetic and metallic yarns and a color sense that has changed utilitarian fabrics and their effect on American life.

However, the mainstream developments in weaving as an art form resulted from a rejection of the pictorial tapestry. Most important to American weaving have been the influence of Anni Albers* and Trude Guermonprez,* both of whom brought to America the sense of design and material in weaving developed at the Bauhaus* in Germany between 1922 and 1930. For them, weaving was the creating of a fabric to be viewed as a nonutilitarian composition of colors and textures. This became the new tradition of American weaving. Design of loom-woven fabrics became more spontaneous, no longer following a cartoon as in the tapestry tradition. This in turn led to innovations in the use of the loom itself—manipulations of warp and weft and attention to the textural qualities of synthetic, manufactured, or hand-spun yarns. Weavings as art became known as wall hangings. But by the mid-1950s the same crisis that had struck the younger generation of ceramists affected weavers, leading to three-dimensional fabric hangings and the widespread utilization of nonloom techniques. These were credited to Lenore Tawney,* soon followed by such other innovators as Claire Zeisler,* Sheila Hicks,* and Alice Adams.* Weaving, like ceramics, became a sculptural medium, and off-the-loom construction was the major development of weaving in the 1960s and 1970s.

This was reflected in an exhibition, "Woven Forms," in 1963 at the Museum of Contemporary Crafts in New York City; it brought together sculptural hangings that had been woven on the loom. It included loose warps that were knotted, woven passages interrupted by slits, openings, and folds, and shapes that were reinforced through the use of metal or wood. The hangings actually had interiors, and foldings that let the object, when hung, shape itself. (See also Handcrafts, Contemporary.) (R.S.)

Weber, Kem (1889–1963).
Architect, furniture and industrial designer. Born in Berlin, he left school in

1904 to become apprenticed to the royal cabinetmaker at Potsdam. From 1908 to 1912 he studied at the Berlin Academy of Applied Arts with Bruno Paul. Under Paul he worked on the design of the German section at the International Exposition in Brussels in 1910. By 1914, when Weber arrived in the United States to design the German section of the Panama-Pacific Exposition in San Francisco, he was familiar with all the modern European movements. He remained in the United States during World War I and eventually settled in Los Angeles. In 1921 he worked in the design studio of Barker Brothers as a draftsman and from 1922–27 as art director. His commitment to modern styles, at a time when they were not popular, was encouraged by his friendship with such well-known architects as R. M. Schindler,* Richard Neutra,* Frank Lloyd Wright,* and Paul T. Frankl.* In 1926 he opened a shop, "Modes and Manners," in Barker Brothers. It was the first modern establishment of its kind in southern California, and by 1927 he was listing himself as an industrial designer.

Weber made such a reputation for himself with his designs for houses, interiors, and furniture that he was one of three Americans included in "The First International Exposition of Arts and Trades" held at Macy's New York City department store in 1928. Three years later he helped to organize the first exhibition of AUDAC (American Union of Decorative Artists and Craftsmen) at the Brooklyn Museum. He designed furniture for several large manufacturing companies and movie sets for Paramount Studios. Throughout the years he became known for his commercial work, such as that done for the Sommer and Kaufmann Shoe Store in San Francisco, which he referred to as "a merchandising machine for the purpose of selling shoes." He worked in wood and metal, designing lamps, silver, pewter, and clocks. His designs ranged from Spanish colonial to very sophisticated American versions of French art moderne, frequently with a dash of the International style.* After moving to Santa Barbara in 1945, he went into partial retirement.   (D.P.)

Weber, Max (1881–1961).
Painter and sculptor. He was born in Bialystok, Russia, the son of a tailor. When he was ten years old, his parents

3

4

Weaving
1. *Sheila Hicks.* Fugue Rothschild, 1970, linen, silk, cotton, and nylon. Collection Rothschild Bank, Paris.
2. *Claire Zeisler.* Red Preview, knotted jute and wool. Museum of Contemporary Crafts, N.Y.
3. **Max Weber.** Chinese Restaurant, 1915. Whitney Museum of American Art, N.Y.
4. **Max Weber.** Spiral Rhythm, 1915 Collection Joseph H. Hirshhorn, Greenwich, Conn.

moved to Brooklyn, New York. After a year at Boys' High School, he entered the teacher's course at the Pratt Institute. His courses ranged from manual training, where he learned sound craftsmanship, to the theory and practice of design under the inspiring Arthur Wesley Dow,* a believer in harmonious space relations. A year after receiving his diploma in 1900, Weber began his professional career by teaching at Lynchburg, Va., for two years and at the State Normal at Duluth, Minn., from 1903 to 1905.

During three student years in Europe (1905–08), Weber developed rapidly as a painter in the modern idiom. After working briefly at the Académie Julien under Jean-Paul Laurens, he began to draw and paint independently. He came under the spell of Cézanne, and his work reflected an increasing boldness of color and form as he became one of the organizers of a painting class conducted by Henri Matisse. He entered the circle of the young avant-garde, including Picasso and Robert Delaunay, and became a close friend of the aging primitive painter, Henri Rousseau. He exhibited with the Independánts (1906 and 1907) and at the Salon d'Automne (1907 and 1908). Returning to New York in 1909, he painted vigorous pictures influenced by Cézanne, the fauves, and Picasso. By 1911–12, he began to adopt cubist devices in a number of works, though others were basically primitive or expressionist. The cubist-related idiom predominated during the next few years, and he also assimilated aspects of futurism,* orphism,* and synthetic cubism into a colorful and dynamic style that culminated in such works as *Chinese Restaurant* (1915, Whitney) and *Athletic Contest* (1915, Metropolitan). He exhibited at Gallery 291 of Stieglitz* in 1910 and 1911 and with the Grafton Group in London (1913). As a pioneer modernist, he refused an invitation to show only two paintings at the 1913 Armory Show,* but his exhibition in 1913 at the Newark Museum was followed by more than three one-man shows in 1915. No other American avant-garde painter of the time exposed his work more widely, or received harsher attacks from the critics, who found his distortions of form and color bewildering and ugly.

During 1914–18, Weber taught art appreciation at the White School of photography. His lectures were published in 1916 as *Essays on Art*. In 1918 he began a series of boldly simplified woodcuts reflecting his long admiration for primitive art. Meanwhile, in his painting he turned to realistic elements, becoming progressively involved with mood-filled figure compositions and scenes from Jewish life. About 1920 Weber dropped the devices of synthetic cubism entirely. His richly painted compositions of nudes took on some of the stark monumentality of Picasso's contemporary work, as in *Alone* (1926). His still lifes sometimes reflected Cézanne, and at other times achieved a lyrical and sensuous spontaneity, as in *Zinnias* (1927, Newark Museum). This phase of Weber's art also included dramatic landscapes, such as *Winter Twilight* (1938, Santa Barbara), and continued well into the 1930s. He had begun staging regular exhibitions in 1923 and soon was widely accepted as one of the strongest of the progressive artists. During the 1920s he taught for a few years at the Art Students League.*

In the 1930s, moved by social problems at home and abroad, Weber became active in the American Artists' Congress and was its honorary national chairman (1938–40). His paintings often reflected his social concern, showing refugees and laborers. About 1940, his art moved into a late phase. Although its range was broad, it was characteristically colorful, highly graphic, inventive and even fantastic in its distortions of subject matter. His paintings were suffused with nervous energy, while the mood ranged from gay to vividly emotional or sober, as in *Flute Soloist* (1955, Museum, University of Iowa). Once again, there are overtones of Picasso's parallel development, but an underlying, personal expression of color and feeling gave coherence to Weber's entire work.

Although known primarily as a painter, Weber also worked in three-dimensional media and was in fact one of the first Americans to attempt abstract and nonobjective sculpture. His first pieces of sculpture were made in 1910 and some show the influence of the primitive art of Africa and Central America. By 1915 he was making completely nonobjective works, such as *Spiral Rhythm* (1915, Joseph H. Hirshhorn). He produced about thirty sculptures altogether, about half of them dating from 1915. He soon gave up sculpture to concentrate on painting, but in the early 1940s he again experimented with plastic form, usually creating pieces in plaster on a small scale and sometimes polychroming them; several were later enlarged and cast in bronze.

(D.W.S.)

Weese, Harry (1915–   ).
A leading Chicago architect from the mid-1950s on, he produced buildings that are rational, lean, and elegant but free of purism. In his designs for education, commerce, and the arts he consistently showed brightness, élan, and a deft pragmatism in each solution. Born in Evanston, Ill., he studied at Massachusetts Institute of Technology (1938), Yale University, and Cranbrook Academy in Michigan (1939). After a year in the Chicago office of Skidmore, Owings & Merrill,* he opened an office with his brother-in-law, Benjamin Baldwin.* Service in the navy (1941–46) interrupted his practice, but in 1947 he opened his own office in Chicago. He produced distinguished houses and housing developments, but first received international acclaim for his United States Embassy in Accra, Ghana (1959), which gave an African air to an uncompromisingly modern scheme.

For the Arena Stage Theater (Washington, D.C., 1961), he produced a rugged pavilion with constructivist overtones—containing one of the half-dozen significant regional theaters of the decade. Then in 1966 he led a team in restoring the Auditorium Theater in Chicago, created by Adler & Sullivan in 1886–89, which saved a treasure of American architecture. He continually updated his approaches, as in the design of his own offices (1967) and in the window treatment and detailing of ancillary areas for an otherwise classical building, the Seventeenth Church of Christ Scientist (Chicago, 1968). There he also showed a permissive attitude and playful use of angles which were to reappear later. In a high-rise office tower in Chicago, the Time/ Life Building, 1968, he used new cladding materials in a richly colorful way that added greatly to the cityscape and he developed the first successful installation of two-story elevator cabs. He executed performing arts centers (in Milwaukee, Wis., in 1969, and at the University of Wisconsin in Madison, Wis., in 1970), educational buildings, and campuses designed as horizontal structures that he called "linear" or "street buildings." He also designed an advertising-free and posterless subway system for Washington, D.C.

(C.R.S.)

Weir, John Ferguson (1841–1926).
Painter and teacher best remembered as the long-time director of the Yale School of Fine Arts. Weir was educated at West Point and received art instruction from his father, Robert W. Weir.* In 1861 he moved to the Tenth Street Studio Building in New York, where he came to know the leading American painters. During this decade he was at his height as an artist; in 1866 he was elected to the National Academy of Design on the basis of one of the first American industrial pictures, *The Gun Foundry* (1866, Putnam County Historical Society, Cold Spring, N.Y.), a boldly painted view of men at work in the hot, glowing interior of a factory. After spending a year in Europe and painting a number of charming small oil sketches of landscape views that suggest the influence of Frederic Church,* he took on the Yale directorship in 1869 and held the post until 1913. Though he continued to paint in his later years, his output consisted of academic portraits and increasingly impressionist landscapes, and his most important achievements stem from his administrative efforts, such as the acquisition in 1871 of the James Jarves* collection of early Italian paintings.

(T.E.S.)

Weir, Julian Alden (1852–1919).
Figure and landscape painter, the youngest son of Robert W. Weir,* who for forty-two years was the drawing instructor of the U.S. Military Academy. Like his older brother, John Ferguson Weir,* a painter of industrial scenes, J. Alden Weir received his first training from his father. Following a stint at the National Academy of Design* (during which he began a lifelong friendship with Albert P. Ryder),* he went to Paris in 1873, where he studied with Jean-Léon Gérôme and was influenced to work directly from nature by Bastien-Lepage. During the next ten years he made several trips to Europe, seeking out Édouard Manet (three of whose paintings he purchased) and J. A. M. Whistler* (whom he called "a first-

1

2

1. **Harry Weese.** U.S. Embassy, Accra, Ghana, 1959.
2. **Harry Weese.** Arena Stage Theater, Washington, D.C., 1961.

589

class specimen of an eccentric man").

Always interested in broadening the opportunities for the exhibition of paintings, Weir was a founding member of the Society of American Artists,* but he also worked within the framework of the National Academy, which he joined in 1885 and served as president in 1915–17. About 1890 Weir began to experiment with the technique of impressionism* and two years later to teach summer classes at Cos Cob, Conn., with John Twachtman,* his closest friend, and also an impressionist. Weir was a member of the "academy of American impressionism," The Ten*, from their first exhibition in 1898. Despite his association with the establishment, his work was personal and experimental, and he remained receptive to the newer movements in art. Late in 1911, as the Association of American Painters and Sculptors laid plans for the Armory Show* of 1913, he was elected president in the hope that such an eminent figure would unite the many factions. When the press played up the hostility of the Association to the Academy, Weir resigned, although he contributed to the exhibition in 1913.

Weir's work was stamped with what the collector and art writer Duncan Phillips termed a "reticent idealism"; at the same time it reflected the variety of an inquiring, liberal mind. He painted portraits, figure studies and landscapes, contributed a mural decoration to the World's Columbian Exposition in 1893 (held in Chicago), and worked in stained glass, etching, and watercolors. His *Idle Hours* (1888, Metropolitan) shows a relaxed but carefully composed interior flooded by light from the windows; the smoothly applied pigment contrasts with the broken brushwork and higher key of such impressionist works as *The Red Bridge* (1895, Metropolitan). Throughout his painting, ranging from the subdued grayed harmonies of *A Gentlewoman* (National Coll.) to the sun-flecked impressionism of *Visiting Neighbors* (1900–09, Phillips), the integrity of his quiet, individual vision is manifest. (D.W.S.)

Weir, Robert Walter (1803–89).
Romantic painter of landscapes, portraits, and literary and religious scenes. Best known as a teacher, Weir spent forty-two years (1834–76) as professor of drawing at the U.S. Military Academy

1

2

1. *Julian Alden Weir.* Idle Hours,
   *1888. Metropolitan Museum of Art,
   N.Y. (gift of several gentlemen).*
2. **Tom Wesselmann.** Big Brown Nude,
   1971. Sidney Janis Gallery, N.Y.

at West Point. His students there included such varied figures as generals Grant and Lee, the painter J. A. M. Whistler,* and his own two artist sons, John Ferguson Weir* and Julian Alden Weir.* Born in New York, N.Y., Weir was about twenty when he had his first instruction in art from John Wesley Jarvis* and from an English heraldic artist, Robert Cook. In 1824 he traveled to Italy for three years of study. He worked in Florence with the historic and portrait painter Pietro Benvenuti (1769–1840), and in Rome he lived with Horatio Greenough,* the American sculptor.

Weir's reputation grew quickly, and in the years before he went to West Point he worked in the company of leading American artists and exhibited regularly at the National Academy of Design.* He was artistically among the best educated of American painters. Yet he seldom achieved true success as an artist: his work is eclectic and he seems never to have settled on a style or a type of subject which he could develop fully. He saw himself primarily as a history painter in the tradition of Benjamin West,* and he is best known for his *Embarkation of the Pilgrims,* painted for the rotunda of the Capitol in Washington, D.C. However, his craftsmanship is better seen in more modest paintings such as *Microscope* (1849, Yale) and *View of the Hudson* (1869, Fruitlands Museum, Harvard, Mass.). After retiring from teaching in 1876, he returned to New York City and continued to paint until his death. (T.E.S.)

Wertmuller, Adolph Ulrich
(1751–1811).
Portrait and figure painter. He was a native of Stockholm who had studied at Paris and who brought to Philadelphia in 1794 a mature style influenced by French neoclassicism.* He returned to Sweden in 1796, but in 1800 was again in Philadelphia, where he married a granddaughter of the painter Gustavus Hesselius* and remained for the rest of his life. He was never successful as a portraitist, partly because of the competition of other capable artists and partly because respectable Americans looked askance at his main work, painted abroad, *Danae and the Shower of Gold* (National Museum, Stockholm). This picture, the first nude exhibited in America, however, long remained both an outstanding example of figure

painting, and a financially successful exhibition piece, upon both counts influencing Rembrandt Peale,* John Vanderlyn,* and other artists of the time. (C.C.S.)

Wesselmann, Tom (1931–).
Painter, born in Cincinnati, Ohio. He studied at Hiram College, Ohio, the University of Cincinnati, the Art Academy of Cincinnati, and Cooper Union, New York City. He has had one-man exhibitions regularly in New York since the early 1960s.

Wesselmann followed Andy Warhol* in the early 1960s in the depiction of supermarket canned products but differed in that he composed these with an emphasis on formal relations. Like Warhol, his depiction of the objects— canned or bottled food, corn cobs, processed raspberries—intermingled with photographic landscapes, emphasizes a sharp-focus realism. In his collage paintings Wesselmann adhered to rigid, formal structure combining actual objects—such as a window frame and a window opening on a landscape photograph, television sets, radios, tables, all of which emphasize the reality of the room occupied by the nude— with the nude herself painted flatly. During the later 1960s he has concentrated increasingly on erotic themes, the "Great American Nude," foot fetishes, and explicit bedroom paintings of breasts and genitalia. These works isolate details like the open mouth with protruding tongue or dangling cigarette, rendered in full erotic modeling. In these works, there seems to be a total assertion of realistic sexual imagery. (H.H.A.)

West, Benjamin (1738–1820).
Painter of historical subjects and portraits, born in Philadelphia, Pa. Once regarded as the towering genius of his time, he still stands as one of the most attractive figures in art history. Coming to Philadelphia in 1747, the painter-adventurer William Williams* gave him books and advice. By 1756 he was painting professionally as a portraitist and sign painter, but he was eager to paint the classic scenes of history and scripture. William Allen, a Philadelphia merchant, provided funds for him to travel to Italy, and in 1759 West set sail—the first of the many American art students who would go to Europe to study in the centuries that followed.

Arriving in Rome, he was received with enthusiasm and immediate deference to native genius from the faraway wilderness. But West knew he could not succeed without study and took full advantage of his opportunities in Italy. With the end of the war between England and France (1763), he moved to London. There his first large biblical and classical scenes brought immediate praise and the patronage of prelates of the Anglican Church. His *Agrippina with the Ashes of Germanicus* (1769, Yale), painted for the Archbishop of York, led to the patronage of the young King George III, and an intimate relationship which, despite West's frank American patriotism, lasted more than forty years.

"History painting," then regarded as the highest art form, had long been dominated by the French. Now the English felt they had found in West a champion to triumph over the French in art. In his work they saw all the nobility and splendor, yet within a style far more chaste and more true to the classic spirit. In the excitement surrounding this newly risen star, the Royal Academy was founded in 1768. Capping it all, the most sensational work of West's early career, his *Death of Wolfe* (1771, National Gallery of Canada) celebrated with moving realism Britain's first great victory of the French and Indian War. West's leading patrons, pleading for art in its loftiest style, had urged him to show the figures in Roman costume, advice he had wisely refused to take.

His salary as historical painter to the king assured financial independence. As president of the Royal Academy almost continuously from 1792, he had a commanding influence on the arts. This he used consistently to advance the careers of others, and particularly of the many young Americans who followed him to London year after year, among them Matthew Pratt,* C. W. Peale,* Mather Brown,* William Dunlap,* Gilbert Stuart,* Rembrandt Peale,* John Trumbull,* S. F. B. Morse,* Washington Allston,* and Thomas Sully.* Three generations of American painters would remember him as master and friend.

Constantly painting new pictures of historical or biblical events, and too often overpraised, West's reputation began to fade before the end of his career. Yet he remained at the top of his profession, continuing a vigorous

1

2

development. His *Death on a Pale Horse* (1802, Pennsylvania), painted with a fresh romantic fury, was shown in Paris and influenced the development of the French romantic school. The life-size version of fifteen years later, together with his *Christ Rejected* (1815), were taken on tour in America after his death, and are now shown with appropriate theatricality in the gallery of the Pennsylvania Academy of the Fine Arts. His portraits, relatively few in number, often have a dramatic, monumental cast, as in his *Sir Guy Johnson* (Washington), a seated figure with attendant Indian chief. West's *Self Portrait* (c.1771, Washington) painted early in his career and Sir Thomas Laurence's painting *West Lecturing at the Royal Academy* (Wadsworth) show the artist at the beginning and end of his career. (C.C.S.)

Westermann, H(orace) C(lifford), Jr. (1922–).
Sculptor and printmaker. Born in Los Angeles, Cal., he was educated at the Art Institute of Chicago. His art displays a bizarre, highly individual wit. He has been peripherally associated with the Chicago "monster school," and has always worked under the distant influence of surrealism.* Among his earliest pieces are glass-paneled boxes with enigmatic contents—toys, old-fashioned shoes, unidentifiable creatures cast in metal, worn photographs, and so on. Other works show wooden figures, reminiscent of children's stick drawings, set on panels amid cactus-like forms of wood. He has turned a series of pumpkin-sized rocks into jack-o-lantern heads. He often reveals a primal capacity to make things: a wooden chain will be suspended from the inner walls of a box, or dozens of wooden forms will be set in an elaborate rack, each one minutely different from the others. His work, especially that from the 1960s on, shows him to be a meticulous craftsman with a great respect for his materials. Westermann's prints are rough, cartoon-like lithographs showing the exploits of "The Human Fly" and other characters, especially cowboys and Indians. He uses ordinary materials and processes to create secret images from childhood and dreams. His work forms a body of private, peculiarly American mythology. He has been in numerous group exhibits here and abroad, and regularly

1. *Benjamin West.* Death on a Pale Horse, *1802. Pennsylvania Academy of the Fine Arts, Philadelphia.*
2. *Benjamin West.* Death of Wolfe, *1771. National Gallery of Canada, Ottawa (gift of the Duke of Westminster).*

in one-man shows in Chicago, Los Angeles, and New York since 1958. The Los Angeles County Museum gave him a large retrospective in 1968. His awards include a Campana Memorial Prize from the Art Institute of Chicago (1964) and a Tamarind Fellowship (1968). (C.R.)

Weston, Edward (1886–1958). Photographer, born in Highland Park, Ill. Fascinated by photography, he left school in 1906 to go to California, but he returned in 1908 to attend the Illinois College of Photography. He then went to Glendale, Cal., and began earning his living as a photographer by soliciting commissions from house to house. He opened a portrait studio in 1911 and from 1914 to 1917 he was given awards for his soft-focus photographs. Influenced by friends in the modern art movement in California and by avant-garde art at an exhibition in San Francisco, he began to turn from romantic, soft-focus photography to a straightforward, rather purified realism in which form as form became of utmost importance.

In 1922 he went to New York to meet such well-known photographers as Alfred Stieglitz* and Paul Strand* and the artist-photographer Charles Sheeler.* Their response to his sharp 8 x 10-inch contact prints was mixed. In 1923 he went to Mexico where he had a portrait studio until 1926. There he met such leading revolutionary painters as Siqueiros, Rivera, and Orozco, who strengthened his interest in the formal aspect of art. He returned to the United States in 1927, and in 1929 established a studio in Carmel, Cal. with his son Brett, who had been with him in Mexico. Such was his stature by this time that he was asked, along with Edward Steichen,* to organize the American section of the famous "Film und Foto" exhibition held in Stuttgart, Germany in 1929. A one-man show of 150 Weston prints was held in 1931 at the de Young Museum in San Francisco and in 1932 he helped found the f/64* group.

It was Weston more than any other photographer who exemplified the idea of pure photography as a means of using the unique characteristics of the medium for creative purposes. He was awarded a Guggenheim Fellowship in 1937 (the first to a photographer) to make pictures of California and the West. Over 1500 negatives

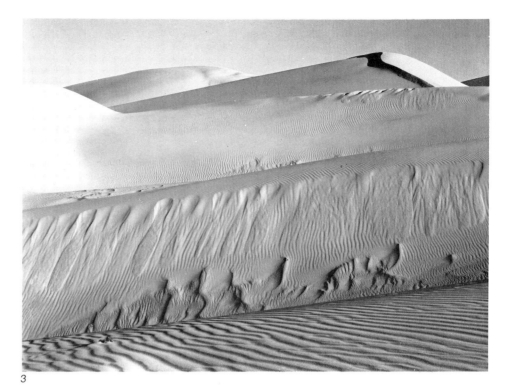

3

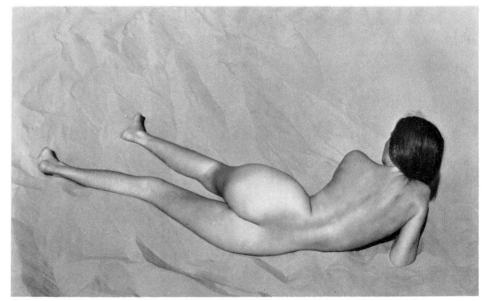

4

3. **Edward Weston.** Oceano, *1936, photograph.*
4. **Edward Weston.** Nude on Sand, Oceano, *1936, photograph.*

were made on this major project. He then traveled through the southern and eastern United States in 1941, making photographs for a special edition of Whitman's *Leaves of Grass.* The precision of the placement of elements in his landscapes and still-life compositions at this period was very distinctive and represents the final flowering of his style. He returned to Carmel when the United States entered World War II and continued to photograph around his home and on nearby Point Lobos until 1948, when he was stricken with Parkinson's disease. In 1946 a major retrospective of his work was held at the Museum of Modern Art.

A great photographer, Weston had a rare understanding of the power of pure form and could evoke deep emotional responses through his simple and carefully composed pictures of shells, peppers, kelp, roots, and rocks. His landscapes and portraits, always fresh and effectively arranged, are equally admirable. He felt that photographers should explore the unique aspects of their medium even though they could learn much about form from the traditional arts. He once wrote in his "Daybooks," "The painters have no copyright on modern art! . . . I believe in, and make no apologies for, photography: it is the most important graphic medium of our day. It does not have to be, indeed cannot be—compared to painting—it has different means and aims."

(V.D.C.)

Whirligigs.
Outdoor sculpture, created as toys or whimsies with movable parts that can be activated by the wind. In Europe, such figures are recorded as early as the 15th century. Late 18th- and early 19th-century examples have suggested that the American whirligig developed from models made by Hessian soldiers who fought with the British during the Revolution. The earliest known American whirligigs are simplified wooden military figures, such as *Revolutionary Soldiers* (Folk Art, N.Y.). Such examples are usually about one foot high with arms in opposed up-and-down positions, connected by an axle-like pin that passes through the shoulders, and terminating in paddle-like appendages. Later figures are more fanciful and complicated and often incorporate metal parts, especially in the activating blades. Some stand atop umbrella-like

structures with ribs terminating in blades that spin the figure horizontally while the arms flail vertically. Later in the 19th century, whirligigs activated by separate vertically mounted propellers depicted household chores, such as the *Scrubwoman* (Shelburne). In the 20th century, whirligigs have been mass produced as a cottage industry and brightly colored standardized forms like a windmill, a farmer milking, and a flying duck or goose are commonly offered for sale along rural roads.

(M.J.G.)

Whistler, James Abbott McNeill (1834–1903).
Portrait, figure, and landscape painter and printmaker, considered one of the most important of 19th-century artists. However, the extent to which he should be thought an American artist is debatable. Born in Lowell, Mass., Whistler spent his childhood in a prosperous New England setting. He was in Russia during 1843–49, where his father was an engineer overseeing construction of the Moscow to St. Petersburg railroad. In 1849 his father's death left the family in reduced circumstances and led to his return to the United States, where he attended the Pomfret School in Connecticut. He entered the U.S. Military Academy at West Point in 1851, but after three years as a cadet, he was dismissed for failing a chemistry course. He then worked briefly for the U.S. Coast and Geodetic Survey in Washington, D.C., receiving training in both drawing and etching, and serving as a cartographer.

Whistler had been sketching since his mid-teens and had long wanted to be an artist. It was natural for him to go to Paris, which had become the center of avant-garde art; he sailed in 1855, and never returned to the United States. After studying briefly in the atelier of the academic painter Charles Gabriel Gleyre (1808–74), Whistler set off on his own in Paris—sketching, painting, and soon becoming known as one of the most flamboyant personalities in the bohemian world of the art students. He became friendly with two of the ablest of the young French painters, Henri Fantin-Latour (1836–1904) and Alphonse Legros (1837–1911), with whom he formed a "Society of Three." He was soon also introduced to some of the leading personalities in modernist French art, including the re-

alist painters Gustave Courbet (1819–77) and Édouard Manet (1832–83), the poet Charles Baudelaire (1821–67), and the critic Théophile Gautier (1811–72). Exposure to the two artists, as well as to such Old Masters as Velásquez, helped Whistler form his own mature style, while the critics' theories influenced his ideas about the primacy of art for its own sake apart from nature or any moralizing ideals.

As early as 1859, Whistler reached a high level of accomplishment in his figure piece *At the Piano* (Taft Museum, Cincinnati), which shows the influence both of Fantin-Latour and of Edgar Degas (1834–1917), later one of the founders of impressionism.* In 1863 his reputation—both as a painter and an eccentric—was fully established when *The White Girl* (1862, Washington) became one of the great attractions of the Paris Salon des Refusés after being refused at the official Salon. The model for the painting was Joanna Heffernan, an Irish beauty who was Whistler's mistress. She is represented dressed all in white, standing on a bear rug, her "bridal" bouquet fallen at her feet. Critics considered her "an apparition," and Whistler became involved in the first of many *causes célèbres*. It was only a decade later that the artist was pleased when a critic compared his painting to musical forms, and thus gave the picture its full title: *Symphony in White No. 1: The White Girl.* London had become Whistler's permanent home in 1859; however, he continued to travel between England and the continent, and his art always retained both English and French elements. Although drawn to the leading figures of French modernism, who were his friends, he was equally influenced by the English pre-Raphaelite brotherhood, and particularly by a leading member of that group, the painter-poet Dante Gabriel Rossetti (1825–82). Thus the languid, idealized facial features of *The White Girl,* for example, specifically recall the pre-Raphaelite mode.

Whistler's later figure pieces—like *The White Girl*—were seldom portraits, but were rather conceived as purely artistic, ideal compositions; in them the artist sought the same qualities of tonalism and of delicacy of mood that he did in his landscapes. It was particularly in the paintings of the 1860s that Whistler demonstrated his interest in oriental art: he portrayed young women in

1

2

3

1. ***James A. M. Whistler.*** Caprice in
   Purple and Gold No. 2: The Golden
   Screen, *1864. Freer Gallery of Art,
   Washington, D.C.*
2. ***James A. M. Whistler.*** Nocturne in
   Black and Gold: The Falling Rocket,
   1875. Detroit Institute of Arts.
3. ***James A. M. Whistler.*** Symphony in
   White No. 1: The White Girl, *1862.
   National Gallery of Art, Washington,
   D.C. (Harris Whittemore Collection).*

595

Japanese costumes, often including rare Chinese porcelains in his compositions, and in both figure paintings and landscapes he experimented with compositions clearly influenced by Japanese woodcuts. Whistler's most famous portrait exhibits many of these qualities: it is the *Arrangement in Grey and Black No. 1: The Artist's Mother* (Louvre, Paris)—one of the best-known of all paintings—where the artist created a symbol of motherhood within a delicate, abstract composition.

Whistler had been interested in landscape ever since his days with the Geodetic Survey. His paintings of the early 1860s, such as *The Blue Wave: Biarritz* (1862, Hilstead Museum, Farmington, Conn.) are sharply realistic and brightly colored. As with his figures, his landscape development was toward the ethereal, the tonal—the subjective rather than the objective. In 1874 he shocked the English public in his first one-man exhibition by hanging a whole series of landscapes that bore the titles of "Nocturnes," "Arrangements," and "Symphonies." In 1875 he went on to paint an even more abstract nighttime impression of fireworks bursting in the sky, calling it *Nocturne in Black and Gold, The Falling Rocket* (Detroit). When this picture was exhibited in 1877, the leading English critic John Ruskin* responded with wrath, writing of the artist's "cockney impudence" in showing the painting, which he likened to "flinging a pot of paint in the public's face." In one of the most celebrated court cases of the period, Whistler sued the critic for libel. The trial resulted in a moral victory for the artist, who was, however, awarded only one farthing in damages; as a result, he was driven into bankruptcy by the costs of litigation. Nevertheless, he continued to paint, and in 1890 he published a book of his letters, *The Gentle Art of Making Enemies,* which reveals his egotistic nature, his deep commitment to art, his humor, and his profundity. During the last two decades of the century—and particularly with his retrospective exhibition in 1892—he began to receive serious public recognition and patronage both in the United States and abroad. American critics and painters thought of him as an American artist who happened to reside in London, but the English considered him one of their own, and in the mid-1880s he was honored with the presidency of the venerable Society of British Artists; and France, which could always lay claim to him on the basis of style, made him a chevalier of the Legion d'Honneur in 1889, and honored him even more with its purchase of *The Artist's Mother* in 1891.

Whistler was also one of the most original, sensitive printmakers in history. Beginning in 1858 with a group of twelve etchings known as "The French Set," which had been inspired by a trip through northern France and the Rhineland, he went on to produce among others, the "Thames Series" in 1871 and the "First Venice Set" in 1880. In all, he made over four hundred etchings, including landscapes, portraits, and figure pieces; he used line as a natural medium, and was constantly experimenting with new techniques of both etching and printing his plates. He was a lithographer as well, and after his introduction to this medium in 1878 he made over 160 lithographs. In his prints of such subjects as the Thames, of London's Chelsea district, of the Luxembourg Gardens in Paris, his feeling for tone and light is recorded with unique artistry.

Whistler's wife, Trixie, died in 1896 and left him grief-stricken. He traveled widely in Europe and northern Africa after her death, and moved from one London hotel to another.   (T.E.S.)

White, John (active, 1584–93).
Expeditionary artist. His careful watercolors, preserved in the British Museum, are the earliest authentic pictorial record of the Indians and the plant and animal life of the North American coast, and as such are very valuable. He was at Sir Walter Raleigh's Roanoke Island colony in 1585, was there again as governor in 1587, and returned for the third and last time in 1590. White's drawings were engraved for Thomas Hariot's *Brief and True Report of the New Found Land of Virginia* (1588), by Theodore De Bry, who also engraved the American scenes of Jacques Le Moyne de Morgues.

White, Minor (1908–   ).
Photographer, editor, and teacher. Born in Minneapolis, Minn., White became interested in photography at an early age, but did not explore it seriously until 1937–38, when he was stranded in Portland, Ore., on a trip West. Joining the Oregon Camera Club, he made documentary photographs of architecture in the urban core of Portland for a group from Reed College. In 1938 he was appointed a "creative photographer" for the Works Progress Administration and documented the old ironfront buildings still standing in Portland. In 1940–41 he was first a teacher of photography, then director of the WPA's Le Grande Art Center in Oregon. After spending 1942–45 in the army, he moved to New York City and began graduate work at Columbia University in art history while working part time as a photographer at the Museum of Modern Art and receiving training in museum methodology from photo historians Beaumont and Nancy Newhall.

In 1946 White met Alfred Stieglitz,* pioneer avant-garde photographer, and the Columbia University art historian Meyer Schapiro, both of whom influenced his thinking about photography as a means of creative expression. In the same year White joined the photography faculty at the California School of Fine Arts (now San Francisco Art Institute) in a program directed by the distinguished West Coast photographer Ansel Adams.* White's close friendship with Edward Weston,* another famous innovative photographer, began at this time. White's "sequencing" of photographs (a method that broke with the traditional linear display of visual material) began in 1942 with a series of pictures covering a YWCA ski trip; the technique was at first didactic but it has grown into a representation of metaphysical concepts through photographic and poetic images. His sequence "Songs Without Words" used photographs of the fog, sea, and mountains around San Francisco interspersed with portraits and was shown at the San Francisco Museum of Art in 1948. After attending the seminar "Camera and Reality" in Aspen, Col., in 1951, he helped found the quarterly *Aperture* and was named its editor and production manager. From 1953 to 1957 he was on the staff of the International Museum of Photography at George Eastman House, edited its journal *Image* (1956–57), and was responsible for various exhibitions. During 1955 he developed "Sequence 10/Rural Cathedrals" and began extensive reading in Zen Buddhism and mysticism. From 1957 to 1959 he developed the sequence called "Sequence 13/Return to the Bud."

During the early 1960s he expounded his ideas in various photographic workshops around the country, influencing many young photographers. Since 1965, White has been a professor at the Massachusetts Institute of Technology and has directed three major exhibitions, "Light 7" (1968), "Being Without Clothes" (1970), and "Octave of Prayer" (1972). He continues his investigations into Gurdjieff philosophy and oriental religions, which has been reflected in the titles of such sequences as "Steely the Barb of Infinity" (1960), "Sound of One Hand" (1960), and "All the Way to Heaven is Heaven" (1967). He continues as president of *Aperture,* the most influential photography periodical since Stieglitz' *Camera Work.*

White's most effective work has generally been done in "straight" or unmanipulated photography, although he has made use of infrared negative material and extended exposures that cause blurring in the negative. His portraiture, either within a sequence or in an individual print, arrests moments that usually escape documentation, as in his portrait of Valentina Oumansky (1953). Much of the later work (1960–72) in the sequences is nonrepresentational and achieves its effects through the calculated juxtaposition of carefully chosen pictures. Images that may not be effective by themselves often become singularly appropriate in one of White's sequences. The pictures themselves are only a part of this spiritually and intellectually complex man's contribution to photography. (T.F.B.)

White, Stanford, see McKim, Mead & White.

Whitman, Robert (1935–   ). Painter. He attended Rutgers University and had his first one-man show in New York City in 1959. During the next few years he turned to "happenings"* or "theater pieces"—an art form that had grown out of the emphasis on performance implicit in "action painting." Using real people and elaborate "stagesets"—papier mâché animals, plastic curtains, loudspeaker sounds, lights, and film projections—he presented "The American Moon" (1960), "Mouth" (1961), and "Flower" in a New York gallery and "Water" (1963) in Los Angeles. He notes: "I intend my

1

2

1. *Minor White.* Cobblestone House, Avon, N.Y., *1958, photograph.*
2. *Minor White.* Two Barns and Shadow, Dansville, N.Y., *1955, photograph.*

works to be stories of physical experience and realistic, naturalistic descriptions of the physical world." A participant in "Nine Nights of Theater and Engineering" (1966), an exhibition put on by E.A.T. (Experiments in Art and Technology), the following year Whitman presented laser projections in a darkened New York gallery. Recently he has concentrated on "cinema environments": windows, dressing tables, sinks, and shower stalls, each with a motion picture insert. These films often deal with intimate and normally overlooked routines and extend his earlier interest in the real world and literal time.   (E.C.G.)

Whitney, Anne (1821–1915).
One of the earliest of the women sculptors of the 19th century. Born in Massachusetts, she first did only portraits in a style of refined naturalism, but by 1861, as in her *Lady Godiva* (private collection), she was doing symbolic or ideal works. Her *Africa* (1863–64, destroyed), a heroic female personification, was created out of sympathy for the abolitionist cause. In 1867 she went to Rome, where she created the *Lotus Eater* (Newark Museum), which was much influenced by neoclassicism.* In 1871 she returned to America, opened a studio in Boston, and soon received a commission from the State of Massachusetts for a marble statue of Samuel Adams (Statuary Hall, U.S. Capitol); a bronze version (1880) was made for Boston's Adams Square. Two of her finest pieces are also full-length portraits—the *William Lloyd Garrison* (c.1880, plaster statuette, Smith College) and the *Charles Sumner* (1900, Harvard Square, Cambridge). In these, as well as in her many portrait busts she employed an uncomplicated naturalism which, if undramatic, did bestow a certain dignity on the subject.   (W.C.)

Whittredge, Worthington (1820–1910).
Landscape, portrait, and still-life painter who became a leading member of the Hudson River School.* Whittredge was born on a farm near Springfield, Ohio, and about 1837 left for Cincinnati to become a house painter. He advanced to sign painting, to making daguerreotypes, and then, around 1840, to portrait painting. About 1843 he turned to landscape, in which he was essentially self-taught; however, his earliest surviving pieces, dating from about 1845, reflect the influence of Thomas Cole* and Thomas Doughty.*

Whittredge traveled abroad to study in 1849, spending five years at Düsseldorf and then, after a sketching tour through Switzerland, five more years primarily in Rome. Many of the paintings he sent back to patrons in Ohio reflect the hard, relatively colorless Düsseldorf manner (until about 1855, they were signed "T. W. Whittredge," but thereafter "W. Whittredge."). On his return to America, he settled in New York in the popular Tenth Street Studio Building. He was elected to the National Academy of Design* and later (1874–77) served briefly as its president. He occasionally painted genre scenes (sometimes in collaboration with his friend Eastman Johnson)* and still lifes, particularly of branches of fruit, but he made his reputation as a landscape painter. Although Whittredge traveled widely in America and made three trips to the West (in 1866, in 1870 in the company of J. F. Kensett* and Sanford Gifford,* and in 1877), his favorite area remained the Catskill Mountains of New York. Many of his most successful paintings are interior woodland views of this region, and he excelled in depicting sunlight filtering into deep woods, as in his *Trout Brook in the Catskills* (Corcoran). He continued to paint these quiet forest scenes and other favorite subjects—such as the shore at Newport—throughout his life in a style that saw no radical changes but rather a gradual development as his brushwork became looser and more "painterly." His landscapes of the 1860s can be confused with Kensett's in their detailed realism; those of the 1880s, on the other hand, are characterized by the use of richer tones and an increasing control over the poetry of light. At his best, Whittredge ranks among the leading painters of the landscape school; his later work suffers from none of the emptiness of such contemporaries as Sanford Gifford and Frederic Church,* while unlike Inness* he remained true to the realist approach.

In 1880, Whittredge moved from New York to the countryside of Summit, N.J. Continuing to travel, he went to Mexico in 1893 and 1896. His *Autobiography* (1905) remains a key source of information about himself and the whole Hudson River School.   (T.E.S.)

Wiener, Isidor (1886–1970).
Self-taught artist who began painting in his sixties and usually signed his work "Pop" or later "GrandPa" Wiener. Wiener emigrated to the United States from Romanian Russia in 1903, supporting himself and his family by working as hatmaker, milkman, welder, gravedigger, and storekeeper. His first work, in watercolor, explored memories of Moldavian legend and countryside; later work, in oil, was devoted mainly to Old Testament episodes and the recording of contemporary seashore and mountain resort life. There are also some striking floral compositions and several paintings based on national and international current events. The animals he created in his biblical and rural pictures eventually led him to produce small, three-dimensional counterparts in plastic wood.   (M.J.G.)

Wildenhain, Marguerite (1896–   ).
Major influence for over thirty years as a teacher of ceramics at her famous studio, the Pond Farm Workshop in Guerneville, Cal. She is known for classical shapes treated in contemporary manner. Born in Lyons, France, she worked as a designer of porcelain for a factory in Thuringia until 1919, when she was apprenticed at the Bauhaus* in Weimar, Germany. After seven years of intensive training, she taught at the municipal School for Arts and Crafts in Halle-Saale, Germany, during 1927–33, and created models for the Royal Berlin Porcelain Factory. Forced by the Nazis to leave Germany in 1933, she set up a studio in Holland, and then in California in 1940. Her personal philosophy of craftsmanship influenced many of the major artists who emerged in the next two decades and her book *Name?* is a testament of her faith in education. Her simple forms are decorated in her characteristic range of surface tooling and muted earthy glazes.   (R.S.)

Wilmarth, Chris (1943–   ).
Sculptor. A graduate of Cooper Union in New York City, Wilmarth's earliest works were fetishistic sculptures in wood strongly influenced by Brancusi. In 1968, in his first one-man show in New York City, he combined cylinders and half-cylinders of wood with discs of plate glass. Soon abandoning wood, he began to elaborate the glass elements, leaving some clear, scoring

some with grids, or frosting others. His interest has gone more and more toward the interplay of reflection, translucence, and transparency with the smooth, often curved surfaces of his material. Held together by wire or suspended from a wall by nails, Wilmarth's pieces present an elegant, self-evident balance. By working with juxtapositions of curved and straight line, arc and plane, he has extended the constructivist approach to a material new to sculpture, though familiar and essential to modernist architecture. The architectural aspect of his work has been especially evident since 1972, when he included sheet metal, permitting an expansion in scale and a solider sense of structure. His work has appeared widely in museum and gallery shows since 1968. He received a Guggenheim Fellowship in 1970.

(C.R.)

Williams, Micah (active c.1815–30). Self-taught painter of watercolor, pastel, and a few oil portraits of subjects who were predominantly residents of Monmouth and Middlesex counties of New Jersey. His stiff figures are relieved by the use of somewhat florid color in both skin tones and clothing, and, in the pastels, by a general softness of contour, as in *Woman with a Book* (c.1820, Boston). (M.J.G.)

Williams, Neil (1934–). Painter. Born in Bluff, Utah, he took his B.F.A. at the California School of Fine Arts (now the San Francisco Art Institute) in 1959. Williams has had regular one-man exhibitions in New York since early in the 1960s. At first he used eccentrically shaped canvases as a vehicle for brilliantly-colored geometric patterns that generally followed the contours of the canvas. In the later 1960s he turned to a form of delicate lyrical abstraction, floating soft areas of delicately toned color over canvases that are less aggressively shaped. He frequently controls his color shapes by vertical and horizontal linear subdivisions.

Williams, William (1727–91). "Mariner and painter," as he described himself at the end of his odd career. Born in Bristol, England, son of a sailor, he yearned to be an artist but was sent out instead as apprentice seaman. At twenty he turned up in Philadelphia,

1. **Worthington Whittredge.** The Trout Pool. *Metropolitan Museum of Art, N.Y. (gift of Colonel Charles A. Fowler).*

2. **Isidor Wiener.** Crossing the Red Sea, 1967. *New York State Historical Association, Cooperstown.*

1

2

friend and first teacher of young Benjamin West.* He was in New York about 1757–60. There followed a sojourn as a painter in Jamaica, but at the end of the decade he was back on the mainland in New York. Along with these varied activities, he wrote an autobiographical novel, *The Journal of Llewellyn Penrose, a Seaman*. In 1776, Williams returned to Bristol.

Williams painted over two-hundred works in America. He was a master of English conversation-pieces. His few known portraits are vivid in coloring, unsophisticated but imaginative. He delighted in elegant accessories and landscape backgrounds with castled hills. These elements are quaintly naive, but when a ship appears it is drawn with accuracy. He dared to show his figures in action within the picture, something rarely attempted by colonial limners. His full-lengths of *David Hall* (Winterthur) and *Deborah Hall* (1766, Brooklyn) are outstanding examples. A revealing *Self-portrait* (Winterthur) was painted in his last years at the Merchants' and Sailors' Almshouse in Bristol.   (C.C.S.)

Wimar, Karl (1828–62).
Painter of the western frontier. Born in Siegburg, Germany, he emigrated to America at fifteen with his parents. They arrived in St. Louis, where the youth was enthralled by the boisterous life of that thriving frontier trading post. He was apprenticed to a landscape painter, Leon Pomarede (c.1807–92), whom he assisted in painting a panorama of the Mississippi River. A bequest enabled Wimar to go to Düsseldorf in 1852. There he studied with Emanuel Leutze.* He apparently arrived in Düsseldorf with sketches made in St. Louis, for some of his best-known western paintings, such as *The Attack on an Emigrant Train* (1856, Museum, University of Michigan, Ann Arbor) and *The Captive Charger* (1854, St. Louis), were completed there.

When Wimar returned to St. Louis in 1856, he found the city changed and the Indians no longer regular visitors. To renew his familiarity with the Indians, he made trips on American Fur Company river boats to distant trading posts on the upper Missouri and Yellowstone rivers, accumulating sketches and photographs as well as weapons, utensils, and clothing for use in his paintings. He painted portraits of local

1. *Garry Winogrand.* New York World's Fair, *1964, photograph.*
2. *Garry Winogrand.* Zoo, New York, *1962, photograph.*
3. *William Williams.* Deborah Hall, *1766. Brooklyn Museum, N.Y. (Dick A. Ramsay Fund).*

3

citizens to support himself, but his main subject was Indian life.

Wimar was thoroughly grounded in the academic tradition of the Düsseldorf School, which stressed precise draftsmanship, careful research on details, formal composition, high finish, and controlled, subtle color harmonies. His paintings were among the most attractive of those done of the western frontier, being carefully composed, dramatic—unfortunately, sometimes melodramatic—and studiously exact. *Indians Approaching Fort Benton* (1859, Washington University, St. Louis) is perhaps his masterpiece—a moody scene, combining landscape with figures, which has more emotional content than he usually achieves.

His last commission, four historical panels for the dome of the old courthouse at St. Louis, the first murals painted west of the Mississippi, has since been ruined by unscientific restoration. He died shortly after completing it. (H.W.W.)

Winograd, Garry (1928–).
A photographer whose amusing, ironic, and mysterious images have redefined the nature of American documentary photography. Born in New York, N.Y., he began to photograph casually while in the Air Force in World War II. Afterward, he studied painting at the City College of New York and Columbia University (1947–48). At Columbia he discovered the excitement of developing and printing his photographs himself. He soon turned permanently to the camera and studied documentary photography with Alexey Brodovitch at the New School for Social Research in 1951. As a free-lancer, Winogrand made photographs that were widely reproduced in many magazines. Edward Steichen* first showed his work at the Museum of Modern Art in the exhibition "The Family of Man" (1955). Inspired in 1955 by Walker Evans'* book *American Photographs* (1938), Winogrand began to record the American scene. Robert Frank's powerful study, *The Americans* (American edition, 1959), was further stimulus to this interest in his environment, and in 1964 he won a Guggenheim Fellowship for photographic studies of American life. Some of these photographs were shown in the George Eastman House exhibition, "Toward a Social Landscape" (1966) and at the Museum

1. **Frederick Clarke Withers.** St. Luke's Church, *Beacon, N.Y., 1868.*
2. **John Wollaston.** Lieutenant Archibald Kennedy, *c.1750, National Gallery of Art, Washington, D.C. (Mellon Collection).*

of Modern Art in 1966. John Szarkowski, director of the Modern exhibition, wrote: "Winogrand's jokes, like those of Rabelais, are no less serious for being funny, and, in the best sense, vulgar. His taste for life, being stronger than his regard for art, makes him equal even to the task of confronting the comedy of his own time." Comic confrontations between people and animals in a zoo became the subject of a book, *The Animals,* published in 1969, the year of his second Guggenheim Fellowship. Although the foibles and follies of urban life enliven Winogrand's work, its artistic vitality rests upon his fundamental respect for the photographs as a new thing in the world, not merely a comment about the world. "I photograph," he has said, "to find out what something will look like photographed." (D.L.)

Winslow, Edward (1669–1753).
A third-generation American silversmith, he was born in Boston, Mass. He may have received his training from Jeremiah Dummer,* becoming a freeman in 1702 at the age of thirty-three. From 1728 to 1743 he was sheriff of Suffolk County, in 1733 a colonel in the Boston Regiment, and finally judge of the Inferior Court of Common Pleas.

Most of the silver he made can be dated about 1700–25 and is in the baroque* or early rococo* tradition. His most elaborate productions were oval sugar boxes with lavishly gadrooned and repoussé lids, and with decorated medallions and hasps on the fluted sides of the bodies. Three of the boxes are dated 1702, one of which was made for Winslow's own use (Yale). Another was owned by Governor Saltonstall of Connecticut (Boston). Also in the rich baroque style are two armorial chocolate pots (Yale; Metropolitan) which Winslow made about 1700–10, and a gadrooned two-handled covered cup engraved with a coat or arms. Winslow silver was presented to churches in Massachusetts, Connecticut, and Rhode Island, and included such items as beakers, a baptismal basin, and tankards. One of the most unusual forms made by Winslow was a trefoil-shaped salver. (M.G.F.)

Wistar, Caspar (1696–1752).
Glass manufacturer of German origin. Wistar moved to Philadelphia in 1717,

and by the 1730s had become a successful businessman noted especially for his brass buttons. In 1739 he opened a glass factory in Salem County, N.J., on the southwestern shore. This plant operated for forty-two years until it was closed by Wistar's son, Richard, in 1781. The few contemporary advertisements of the glass works that have been found mention window glass, lamp glass, and various types of bottles; it seems clear that these were the staple products of this factory. Four German or Dutch workmen were brought from Rotterdam in 1739 to teach the Wistars the secrets of glassblowing and to operate the works. They probably made tablewares and decorative pieces for themselves and their families; but since none of these were signed, no single piece can be reliably attributed to this factory. Wistar's works was, however, the first successful glass factory in the American colonies. (J.S.S.)

Withers, Frederick Clarke (1828–1901). Architect. Born in Somersetshire, England, he attended school at Sherborne. In 1844 he was indentured to an architect-builder for five years. Later he worked in the London office of Thomas Henry Wyatt (1807–80), a well-known church architect. In 1852 Withers emigrated to America and worked briefly for Andrew Jackson Downing.* He then joined Calvert Vaux, another Englishman, and designed a series of country houses with him under the firm name of Vaux & Withers. In 1857 he worked with Frederick Law Olmsted* on the creation of Central Park, New York. In 1860 Withers enlisted in the Civil War but, after being wounded, returned to partnership with Vaux in 1862.

Withers was then appointed architect of the Department of Public Charities and Correction of New York City. In this capacity he designed (with Vaux) the Jefferson Market Courthouse and Prison (1874–77) at 10th Street and Sixth Avenue, a high-water mark of Victorian Gothic* in America. Tailor-made for its triangular site, it combined a courthouse, a fire water-tower and a prison. Under his own name, Withers designed some of the buildings of the Columbia Institution for the Deaf and Dumb (later Gallaudet College) between 1867 and 1877 in Washington, D.C., and the Hudson River State Hospital for the Insane at Poughkeepsie,

N.Y., both in Victorian Gothic. His design for the little Van Schaick Free Reading Room (1882), Westchester, N.Y. (now remodeled as the Huntington Free Library), had an attractive, distinctly medieval flavor. With Walter Dickson (1834–1903) Withers designed the New York City Prison (1897–1902) on Center Street to replace the old "Tombs." Ten stories high, this long narrow building with curved ends crowned by high, conical roofs, resembled a French château.

Withers is best known as an ecclesiastical architect, and his churches, generally of stone, cover a period of some forty years: First Presbyterian Church, Newburgh, N.Y. (1857); St. Michael's Church, Germantown, Pa. (1858); Reformed Dutch Church, Fishkill, N.Y. (1859); St. Mark's Church, Shreveport, La. (1867); First Presbyterian Church, Highland Falls, N.Y. (1868). A very important commission was the Clergy and Choir Rooms addition to the Trinity Church, New York (1878), which he designed in perfect harmony with the existing church. Utilizing his English background, Withers was instrumental in introducing Victorian Gothic to the United States. (A.B.)

Wollaston, John (active 1736–67). Portrait painter. He is believed to have begun, like his father, as a "drapery painter," one of those minor, but expert, specialists in the London art world who added costumes to portraits done by a more eminent hand. He came to America in 1749, working as a portraitist in New York (until 1752), in Annapolis (1753–54), Virginia (1755–57), and Philadelphia (1758). His career was interrupted by a position with the British East India Company, with whom he went to Bengal. There he is said to have acquired, as so many did, a fortune. In 1767 he returned to Charleston, S.C., where he painted some twenty portraits, and then left for London, apparently never to return. In America he completed some three hundred portraits, which had a marked influence on Benjamin West,* Matthew Pratt,* Gustavus Hesselius,* and other native artists. His professional background is revealed in his skillful rendering of costumes and these, with his repertoire of elegant poses, were the foundation of his American success. His faces are in a mannered pattern of his own, rarely revealing character. *Lieutenant*

Archibald Kennedy (c.1750, Washington), painted in New York, is an outstanding example. (C.C.S.)

Wood, Grant (1892–1941). Born on a farm near Anamosa, Iowa, Wood never forgot the rural surroundings of his early childhood. In 1910 he began studying at the Handicraft Guild in Minneapolis, and from 1913 until his enlistment in the army in 1918, he was occupied in a variety of ways: as metalworker, schoolteacher, interior decorator, and art student, studying at the Art Institute of Chicago. He returned to civilian life in 1919, taught art in a Cedar Rapids school, and during the next nine years made four trips to Europe.

In 1928 the Daughters of the American Revolution commissioned Wood to design and execute a large stained-glass window for the Cedar Rapids Memorial Coliseum. Wood went to Munich to have the work executed, and the DAR was incensed that it was made in a country with which the United States had recently been at war. At this point emerges the great paradox of Grant Wood's career: in his own time and in his beloved native Iowa, he was regarded as a political and social radical; elsewhere he has almost universally been bracketed with the chauvinist right, thanks in no small part to the views of the artist Thomas Hart Benton* and the critic Thomas Craven, who, rejecting European modernist influences on American art, set up a triumvirate of American regionalists—Benton, Wood, and John Steuart Curry*—as an antidote to the alleged foreign influences.

The irreverent Wood was a particularly poor choice for standard bearer in an American nationalist cause. One source of his style is ultimately Chinese—the famous "willow" plate pattern once found on inexpensive chinaware in most American homes. Wood's mother had a set of this china; it made a great impression on her son as a boy, and its clumped, neatly rounded hills, trees, and bushes are to be seen quite generally in his landscapes, such as *The Midnight Ride of Paul Revere* (1931, Metropolitan). The other major influence on Wood was that of 16th-century Flemish painting, which he discovered on his early trips abroad. Its painstaking realism, meticulously described detail, and high color are reflected in all his work, especially his figures. Wood's use of old Flemish techniques also accounts for the slowness of his method, and his small output. *Daughters of Revolution* (1932, Cincinnati)—one of whose *dramatis personae* holds a teacup in the willow pattern—is Wood's witty reply to the ladies of Cedar Rapids who disapproved of his using German technicians for his stained glass window. But Grant Wood's most celebrated work, and one of the key American paintings of this period, is *American Gothic* (1930, Chicago). Here an analogy is drawn between midwestern carpenter Gothic in the house and the faces of the couple, the forms of the pitchfork in the man's hand, and the stitching of his overalls; the faces of the man and woman, and their clothing, are set down with Van Eyckian clarity, and the continuity of a great tradition is affirmed with as much humor as virtuosity.

In his last years, Wood taught at the University of Iowa, founded a colony of artists at Stone City in that state, and traveled extensively as a lecturer.

(A.F.)

Woodville, Richard Caton (1825–55). Genre painter. Born in Baltimore, Md., he was educated at St. Mary's College. Intending to become a physician, he enrolled at the University of Maryland in 1842, but sometime before 1845 he decided to become a painter; in that year he exhibited *Scene in a Bar-room* (1845, location unknown) at the National Academy of Design, New York City. In 1845 he sailed for Europe and settled in Düsseldorf, where he studied for a year at the academy and then for five years with the German genre painter Carl Ferdinand Sohn. From 1851 on, Woodville lived in Paris and London, where he died at the age of thirty from an overdose of morphine.

Woodville's rising reputation rests on the handful of genre paintings of Baltimore scenes he produced during the single decade of his tragically brief career. While he also did a few portraits and historical reconstructions, they add little to his reputation. It is such paintings as *Politics in an Oyster House* (1848, Walters) that appeal to current taste. The similarity in their attitudes and achievement invites a comparison of Woodville and his older contemporary, William Sidney Mount.*

1

3

Unlike Mount, who never studied abroad, Woodville's native perception was refined by the sophisticated training he received from the Düsseldorf academicians, and is apparent in his subtle color harmonies and almost classical Dutch use of modulated light and shadow, as in his last completed work, *The Sailor's Wedding* (1852, Walters). While Mount's sense of humor was rather earthy, Woodville's was urbane. Woodville also appeared to have a more consistent grasp of the psychological relationships between his actors, as in his handling of blacks, who frequently appear in the works of both. Rather than the stereotype of "the Happy Negro," Woodville presents them as individuals with dignity and a sharply observed character. His range of subject matter was limited, essentially urban interior scenes related to Baltimore —which is remarkable since almost all of his productive career was spent abroad. His zeal for detail, his selection of still-life objects appropriate to his subjects, and the true-to-life characterizations assured his contemporary popularity. Outstanding among his other works are *Waiting for the Stage* (1851, Corcoran), its wealth of still-life details handled skillfully, and *War News From Mexico* (1848, National Academy of Design), in which the character of the central figure is, for once, disconcertingly overstated. Despite his small output, Woodville ranks as one of the outstanding American genre painters of his time. (H.W.W.)

Wormley, Edward J. (1908–   ). Furniture and interior designer. Born in Oswego, Ill., he spent his childhood in Rochelle, Ill. After high school, he enrolled in the Art Institute of Chicago for a year, then worked for the Marshall Field Department Store in Chicago, designing lavish interiors for Lake Shore Drive apartments. His real interest had always been furniture and after three years he became a designer for Berkey and Gay, a leading period furniture manufacturer; but the Depression struck and he was soon let go. He then joined the Dunbar Furniture Company, an Indiana firm seeking a designer who could modernize their furniture line. Thus began an association which lasted until the mid-1960s.

Throughout the years Wormley has designed furniture of immense variety, regularly presenting two collections a

2

1. *Grant Wood.* Daughters of Revolution, *1932. Cincinnati Art Museum (Edwin and Virginia Irwin Memorial).*
2. *Grant Wood.* American Gothic, *1930. Art Institute of Chicago (Collection of the Friends of American Art).*
3. *Richard Caton Woodville.* Waiting for the Stage, *1851. Corcoran Gallery of Art, Washington, D.C.*

year. He and his staff have designed and built store and showroom interiors in New York, Chicago, Boston, and other cities. He has also designed carpets, fabrics, and globe stands. Along with Robsjohn-Gibbings,* he was honored with the annual Elsie DeWolfe award in 1962. He consistently designs contemporary furniture that is comfortable, well-proportioned, elegant, and appropriate for modern living. He is not limited by fads and readily turns to the past, as well as to new materials and techniques, for inspiration. Concerned with every need within an interior space, he always designs furniture as part of a visual and functional whole. (D.P.)

WPA (Works Progress Administration) Federal Art Project.

An experimental program established in December, 1933, by President F. D. Roosevelt to help artists caught in the economic doldrums of the Great Depression. The Public Works of Art Project, as it was called, employed almost four thousand artists during its brief existence. They produced some fifteen thousand works, at a total cost to the government of $1,312,177.; their weekly wages varied from $26.50 to $42.50. This experiment ended in June, 1934, but the administration was encouraged by its success, and shortly two major agencies were created to take over and expand the work of the PWAP.

The first of these was the Section of Painting and Sculpture of the Treasury Department, established in October, 1934. The Treasury Department had long been responsible for the construction of public buildings; now the SPS was assigned the adornment of these buildings. This was not a relief project; the artists were paid only when their designs were accepted. In 1938 the SPS was renamed Treasury Section of Fine Arts and in the following year it became the Public Buildings Administration. This new agency encouraged the circulation of works produced under its parent arms of the Treasury, continued work on public buildings, contributed to the architecture and adornment of the New York World's Fair, recorded defense and war activities, and extended art programs to the Civilian Conservation Corps. But many artists were dissatisfied with it because it failed to provide the scope and the freedom they desired.

Meanwhile, in May of 1935, the Works Progress Adminstration was formed under Harry Hopkins. Part of its program was the establishment of projects for the employment of artists, musicians, writers, and actors. The Federal Art Project, directed by Holger Cahill, had four goals: employing artists, educating art students, expanding art programs into rural areas, and research into and recording of the cultural heritage of the United States. From its establishment to its dissolution in 1943, the Federal Art Project employed five thousand artists who created 108,000 paintings, 18,000 pieces of sculpture, 11,300 original prints, and 2500 murals.

The largest section of the FAP was the easel division. Once a painter had passed an examination to prove his capability and established that he was in need, he was placed on a payroll at twenty-three dollars a week. He was permitted to work in his own studio and to select his own subjects, but was required to submit his work every four to eight weeks. There was no pressure from the government regarding style or content, but the works produced were taken for the adornment of public buildings and for public exhibition. The project provided a magnificent opportunity for painters like Stuart Davis,* Ben Shahn,* Arshile Gorky,* Jackson Pollock,* and many others to develop their styles. The print division produced over 200,000 copies of the eleven thousand designs, and greatly improved the techniques for the mass production of lithographs and silk-screen prints in the process.

One of the most important aspects of the Federal Art Project was the Index of American Design, which recorded the history of decorative and applied art in America in a series of twenty thousand plates. Several hundred artists painted and drew furniture, utensils, architectural decorations, fabrics, and so on, produced in this country before the opening of the present century. The historic archive they established is now preserved at the National Gallery of Art in Washington, D.C.

In 1939 the WPA art projects came under criticism from both the press and Congress because of a fear of subversive propaganda from a program offering its artists total freedom of expression. In local areas, notably New York City, many WPA works were destroyed at the discretion of local di-

rectors. The project declined after 1939, and the outbreak of World War II brought it to an end.

In assessing the achievement of the effort of the Roosevelt Adminstration to assist the American artist, a clear distinction should be made between the work done under the Treasury Department and that done under the Works Progress Administration or, as it was later called, the Works Projects Administration. The major weakness of both was that they were less concerned with the creation of art than with providing employment for needy artists. The Treasury placed restrictions on subject matter, had the authority to reject the artists' work, and its jury system was no great success; the submitted designs were frequently the high point of the artist's achievement, and the actual execution of the project was often disappointing. In contrast, the WPA artist was unrestricted and nurtured his talent as he pleased. The Treasury concentrated on murals, whereas the WPA's major emphases were on easel painting and the Index of American Design. (A.F.)

Wright, Frank Lloyd (1869–1959).

The outstanding and most influential 20th-century American architect. Wright was born in Richland Center, Wis., son of a Baptist minister (later a music teacher) who left his family in 1885. At sixteen, Wright took a job with Allen D. Conover, a local builder, meanwhile studying civil engineering part time at the University of Wisconsin. In 1887 he left Madison for Chicago, where he worked for Joseph Silsbee, an architect who worked in the Queen Anne* style. Attracted by the work of the newly-founded firm of Adler & Sullivan, Wright joined it in 1887. He attracted the attention of Louis Sullivan* and in 1889 Wright was given an office next to Sullivan's, where he executed most of the firm's residential work. Wright worked on designs for Sullivan's shingled cottages (1891) in Biloxi Bay, Miss., and in Chicago for the Charnley House (1892), the Albert Sullivan House (1892), and the Victoria Hotel (1893). During this period Wright designed houses at night for his own practice. Although his "bootlegged houses," as he called them, were not prohibited by contract, Sullivan took offense at this work and in 1893 they ended their association. Despite the separation,

Wright, greatly influenced by Sullivan, continued to refer to him as *Lieber Meister,* beloved master.

The first houses Wright designed on his own represented a spectacular series of developments. Probably the low horizontality of Japanese architecture, with its plane surfaces and widely overhung eaves, influenced his designs; but the cubistic forms they displayed were probably derived from the system of blocks designed for children by Frederick Froebel, kindergarten founder.

Wright's own house on Forest Avenue, in suburban Oak Park, Ill. (1889), was ostensibly just another shingle style* house, except that the large end gable had been carried out over two projecting bays, at the first floor, in an unusual manner. The addition behind it of a barrel-vaulted playroom. and of a studio on the Chicago Avenue side, in 1895, belonged to the cubist formality of design he later developed. A house for Dr. Allison W. Harlan on Greenwood Avenue in 1892—with its wide eaves, low roof, ample fenestration, curved terrace, and wide balcony —displayed many of the characteristics of Wright's later designs.

A replica of a Japanese wooden temple that Wright undoubtedly saw at the World's Columbian Exposition in Chicago in 1893 probably influenced his design for the Winslow House in River Forest (1893), which gave Chicago a taste of things to come. This two-story house was symmetrical, low-lying, and stressed the horizontal in the shape of its windows and in its wide-eaved, hipped roof. It heralded the prairie style even before Wright gave it a name. The stable with its arched entrance, low wings forming a forecourt, and many roof levels, had an almost Japanese character.

Wright avoided the strictly urban style of structure but where he did design one, he generally set a precedent. The four Tudor-style row houses he designed for Robert W. Roloson on Calumet Avenue, Chicago (1895), were in this category. The Francis Apartments (1895) had a narrow opening extended through to the street, a scheme which, with its wide, plate-glass windows and strong horizontals, was widely copied. In the realm of low-income housing, Wright generally built low, using two stories, around large central courtyards as in San Francisco Terrace, Francisco Avenue (1895).

What we note most is the sense of dignity Wright managed to impart to these structures despite their low cost.

The high, brick, suburban houses Wright designed for Isidor Heller on Woodlawn Avenue (1897) and for Joseph W. Husser on Buena Avenue (1899) were a prelude to the horizontality of the prairie style house. The Husser House introduced Wright's rather continental scheme of a high basement with the principal rooms above it.

In 1901 the *Ladies' Home Journal* published Wright's plans and elevations for "A Home in a Prairie Town," which officially heralded the prairie style. Two stories high, with low, wide-eaved, hipped roofs, the house was a study in horizontals, with wing walls and strips of leaded casement windows. A second article, "A Small House with Lots of Room in It," presented the same two-story house but with gables instead of hipped roofs. Wright also projected the ridge pole beyond the ends of the eaves, creating a prowlike effect. Two of these gable-ended houses had already been built by Wright in 1900: the Warren Hickox House and the B. Harley Bradley House, both on South Harrison Ave. in Kankakee, Ill.

As early as 1900, Wright made a significant town plan: in his "Quadruple Block Plan for the Prairie" the houses were set out in groups of four with wide spaces between groups. Unfortunately, neither the house nor his town plan brought him any noteworthy commissions.

In 1904–08 Wright designed Unity Temple (Unity Universalist Church) on Kenilworth Avenue in Oak Park, Ill. A square building of purely cubist concept, built of reinforced concrete. it had horizontal, cantilevered, slablike projections above the massive piers that separated the windows. With its textured surface of exposed pebble aggregate, it achieved a monumental feeling of repose and dignity. The interior was a capacious square room, skylighted and with windows set above balconies at the sides. Stained glass was the principal ornament.

With the prairie style established, Wright in the next twenty years executed a series of commissions reflecting its principles. For the Arthur Heurtley House on Forest Avenue, Oak Park (1902), he again designed a high basement with the principal rooms on the second floor, anticipating some aspects of the split-level house of today. Classical in its monumentality, without the use of any conventional ornament, Wright's Ward W. Willitts House in Highland Park (1902) introduced the theme of a high central block from which low wings radiated. Most monumental, and comprehensive in its interior appointments, was the Susan Lawrence Dana House at Springfield, Ill. (1903), a fascinating example of the clear-cut articulation of building materials. Next came a commission from Buffalo for the Darwin D. Martin House, on Jewett Parkway (1904). Here, the low-lying hipped roof horizontality was enhanced by wing walls and a long covered walkway connecting with a conservatory and a garage.

Another major commission was a large house with outbuildings for the Avery Coonleys at Riverside, Ill. (1908). Wedded to its level site by terraces and wing walls, the Coonley House appears as a series of interconnected pavilions. In its elaborate detail, within and without, it is the greatest of Wright's prairie style houses. It served the living requirements of its owners without the ostentation prevalent in comparable houses of the time. The archetype of the smaller prairie style house was Wright's Frederick C. Robie House on Woodlawn Avenue (1909) in Chicago. With a high central mass, from which brick wings extended outward, it achieved a low-lying horizontality that belied its actual height. Here again was Wright's innovation—the high basement with principal rooms above it.

Wright's first large industrial commission was the Administration Building of the Larkin Company on Seneca Street in Buffalo, N.Y. (1904). This modern office building with full-height interior court was virtually unprecedented in concept. Wright had even designed its steel office furniture and light fixtures and included an early form of air conditioning and a restaurant on the top floor. The cubist appearance of the brick exterior was a logical expression of the interior in which stair towers rose up in four corner pylons. A fountain greeted the employees at one side of an offset entrance where plate-glass doors opened on the sky-lighted interior court. Another commercial commission, similar to those Louis Sullivan was executing in the last years of his life, was the City National Bank Building and adjoining ho-

1

2

3

tel, the Park Inn, in Mason City, Iowa (1909). The brick bank, like many of Sullivan's, was a rectangular box with blank lower walls. The Park Inn, to the rear of the bank, was three stories high and prophetic, in miniature, of the Imperial Hotel Wright later built in Japan. Both buildings relied for effect on their blocklike monumentality.

The epitome of the prairie style was Taliesin, the rambling studio-residence Wright built for himself in Spring Green, Wis. There Wright trained young architects, resident in the fellowship he established in the early 1930s. The stonework of Taliesin's exterior was freely carried into the interiors, and huge fireplaces graced many of the principal rooms. The interior had furniture designed by Wright. He spent the rest of his life at Taliesin except for winter sojourns in Taliesin West in the desert at Paradise Valley near Phoenix, Arizona.

Wright's first break with the prairie style came with his Midway Gardens in Chicago (1914). The brittle right-angle geometry of the walls and decorative details of this building were more abstract than in any of his prairie style work. The wealth of detail displayed in Midway Gardens foreshadowed the opulent forms he was to use in his celebrated Imperial Hotel in Tokyo, Japan (1922).

Wright lived in Japan from 1916–22, and with his great interest in that country, it might be expected that he would reflect Japanese influence in the ornament of the Imperial Hotel. But although the overall impression made by the hotel was oriental, its ornament was highly original and its axial plan was based on classical European tradition. A major structural innovation was the use of spread concrete footings carried on piles, which were allowed to float in a cushion of earth so that the sectionalized building units of the hotel could respond readily to the wavelike action of an earthquake. As a result, the hotel was one of the major structures in Tokyo to withstand the devastating earthquake of 1923.

The Midway Gardens, the Imperial Hotel, and much of Wright's other work of the 1920s shared with the European expressionism* of the period 1917–23 a delight in agitated forms. The world of the Mayans and Aztecs may have provided Wright with the architectural forms and ornament he used in Holly-hock House on Olive Hill, Hollywood, a kind of pre-Columbian fortress designed for Aline Barnsdall (1917–20). Similarly, the Charles Ennis House in Los Angeles (1924), using Wright's system of precast masonry blocks, was reminiscent of a small Mayan temple set on its own terraces. Contradictions characterized the block houses for John Storer (1923) and Samuel Freeman (1924); they were at once intimate and cold, monumental, and domestic. They represented excellent utilitarian solutions but displayed some highly arbitrary details. As with so many of Wright's designs, these houses were not necessarily intended to provide a quiet backdrop for the lives of their owners, but to achieve Wright's objective of high art, to impinge to the fullest on one's visual sense.

By the late 1920s Wright had begun to use elements in his house designs which, although original, were in tune with the contemporary art deco* style and with the verticalism of the skyscraper.* The Richard Lloyd Jones House, in Tulsa, Okl. (1929), was one of these. With its deeply recessed windows, set between piers of precast block construction, it provided no sense of scale; from a distance it could easily have been mistaken for a warehouse.

The project that Wright designed for a "House on the Mesa" in Denver (1932), and his renowned house, Falling Water, for Edgar J. Kaufmann in Bear Run, Pa. (1936), which cantilevered out over a waterfall, illustrated the fact that, despite denials, he was influenced by the International style.* In this weekend house he skillfully contrasted rough stone with cubist concrete horizontals. The S. C. Johnson Wax Company Administration Building in Racine, Wis. (1936–39), with its curved and interlocking forms, owed little to the International style, but had a certain kinship with contemporary streamlined moderne* architecture. It was probably the most sophisticated industrial building in the United States at that date.

Wright's numerous wood, stone, and brick Usonian dwelling houses of the 1930s and 1940s demonstrate that he was changing with the times. The greater use of wood and native materials in these houses marked a diminution in Wright's interest in cubism and in a mechanistic regularity of design. His own Taliesin West (1938–48), with its exposed timbers and form-cast stonework was remarkably sculpturesque in character. Despite this involvement with the rustic, which continued after World War II in houses he built from coast to coast, there were designs of non-domestic architecture that suggested the world of the 21st century. Among these, his chapel at Florida Southern College, Lakeland, Fla. (1940), with its central tower composed of spidery openings and its interior of hanging plants and light globes, represented a world of pure fantasy. Transcending the present was the ascending spiral of the Guggenheim Museum in New York City (1959). There are also the projecting prow of the Unitarian Church in Madison, Wis. (1947), and the spiky triangular-roofed Beth Sholem Synagogue in Elkins Park, Pa. (1959). All of Wright's late buildings, ranging from the Greek Orthodox Church at Madison, Wis. (1956), to the Civic Center for Marin County, Cal. (1971) appeal to the imagination.

With the exception of Le Corbusier, no architect of this century approached Wright in stature, yet he encompassed an astonishing set of contradictions. He was, in many ways, representative of 19th-century ideals but achieved some remarkable triumphs in the 20th century with schemes that often anticipated the future. Although a continuity is discernible in his work, no other architect was so able to adapt to the changing ideals of the times while mirroring the successive phases of his own architectural development. Prophetic by nature, Wright, both in his writings and in his architecture, expressed an ever-continuing development. Throughout a long life, whether it was the square, the circle, the hexagon, or the cube that inspired his design, he made that design his own. His mind worked to a modular system where order and certain laws of architecture, as he conceived them, had a regular place in the scheme of things.

As he guided his architectural projects with loving care, so he guided the young men around him, as when he said (in his *Modern Architecture*): ". . . to the young man in architecture, the word *radical* should be a beautiful word. Radical means 'of the root' or 'to the root'—begins at the beginning and the word stands up straight. Any architect should be radical by nature

because it is not enough for him to begin where others have left off."

Wright was the recipient of countless honors. (A.B. and D.G.)

Wright, Joseph (1756–93).
Portrait painter and sculptor. He was born at Bordentown, N.J., only son of the masterly sculptor in wax, Patience Wright.* Taken to London by his mother in 1772, he soon showed great promise as a painter. At the Royal Academy he exhibited (1780) a portrait of his mother that aroused a storm of public protest because she was shown modeling a head of Charles I. This was taken, rightly, as an allusion to the fate of tyrannical kings. Joseph took refuge in Paris, where he painted a well-known portrait of Benjamin Franklin before sailing for the United States. He painted portraits of Washington, 1783–84, again in 1790, and modeled a likeness in wax. His skill as a medalist led to his appointment in 1792 as designer and die-sinker of the new U.S. Mint, some of its early coinage being presumably his work. He is seen, with his wife, in an attractive *Self-Portrait of the Artist with his Family* (c.1793, Pennsylvania). Both died in the yellow fever epidemic of 1793.
(C.C.S.)

Wright, Patience Lovell (1725–86).
Sculptor in wax. A woman of startling simplicity and force of character, she stands unique as America's first professional portrait sculptor. Her father, a prosperous Quaker farmer, kept his large family upon a strict vegetarian diet and insisted that they dress entirely in white, Perhaps in reaction to this, his children early took to mixing colors, painting pictures, and fashioning little figures in dough or clay. Patience married and moved to Philadelphia in 1748. In 1769, she was left a widow with five children and no sufficient support, and her career as creator of a traveling waxwork exhibition began. Small wax profiles have been attributed to her, but all of her firmly recorded works are life-size heads and hands, done with amazing accuracy and minute detail. These were generally attached to clothed figures, making an image distinguishable from the living person only in its lack of motion. Mrs. Wright would begin a likeness with the hollow wax form on her lap covered by her apron (to keep the material warm and malleable), her eyes fixed on the sitter,

her loud voice and flow of anecdote holding his attention while her hands were busy shaping the wax. Afterward, she would add eyes, eyelashes, veins under the skin, and skin coloring. Having toured the eastern seaboard with much success, she sailed for England in 1772, leaving her sister Rachel to manage their American business.

In London, she won immediate renown, not only for her virtuosity in wax, but as a "sibyl" from the American wilderness whose intensity of eye and voice had an almost hypnotic effect. Vociferously American, she scoffed at rank and titles. When the King and Queen posed for her they were "George" and "Charlotte." At the outbreak of the Revolutionary War people of rank and title continued to visit her rooms, and hearing much in their conversation that could be valuable to General Washington, she passed it on to Rachel in Philadelphia concealed in wax heads of Lord North and other British celebrities. In 1781 she was in Paris, where she modeled Benjamin Franklin and, in London, she gave shelter to American prisoners of war.

Before her work, earlier waxwork shows had presented crude manikins of mythical figures, criminals, and kings, with little attempt at likeness. Her exhibition was a forerunner of the movement toward extreme realism at the end of the 18th century, which reached a climax with De Loutherbourg's landscapes in motion with sound effects such as C. W. Peale's* "moving pictures" and Robert Barker's cyclorama. Only one example of Mrs. Wright's works has survived: a somewhat damaged figure of William Pitt, it is preserved among the funeral effigies in Westminster Abbey. (C.C.S.)

Wurster, William W. (1895–   ).
Architect linked to regionalism and redwood. The *locus classicus* of the woodsy California ranch house, shingled or sheathed in redwood, is the San Francisco Bay area where Wurster has worked. He was born in Stockton, Cal., and received his architectural education under John Galen Howard at the University of California, Berkeley. He has divided his time between the practice of architecture and architectural education. For many years he taught at the University of California and following World War II was dean of its architecture school. He has also been dean

of the architectural school at the Massachusetts Institute of Technology, and was a fellow at the graduate school of design at Harvard. His independent practice began in 1926; in 1943 he formed a partnership with Theodore C. Bernardi and in 1944 with Donn Emmons. The firm of Wurster, Bernardi & Emmons has been a major force on the American architectural scene.

Wurster's first notable commission, the Gregory ranch house (1927) near Santa Cruz, Cal., firmly established his approach. Here and in later buildings, he brought disparate elements of the modern (sometimes the moderne) together with a strong sense of the builder's vernacular and of period architectural modes. The Gregory House is a mixture of the vertical board and batten-walled, informal (nondesigned) 19th-century California ranch house, with a touch of colonial revival style and a very slight sprinkling of the modern.

In the late 1930s and in the 1940s Wurster's buildings very closely approached the forms of the International style,* but such modern elements as horizontal strip windows and machine images were always abruptly contrasted with vernacular features—apparently ungainly proportions, vertically divided double-hung windows, and simple, seemingly unsophisticated ways of putting a building together. This approach can be seen in the Stovens House (San Francisco, 1941), and even in an office building such as that of the Schuckly Canning Company (Sunnyvale, Cal., 1942). During the 1950s and 1960s, the period architectural quality in his work increased, as if he were returning to his colonial-regency designs of the early 1930s. His Pope House (Madera, Cal., 1958) is a delicate, highly refined, contemporary version of the mid-19th century Larkin House in Monterey. Wurster has had great influence for forty years both as educator and designer. He received the gold medal of the American Institute of Architects in 1971.　(D.G.)

Wyant, Alexander Helwig (1836–92). Landscape painter who was a friend and follower of George Inness.* Wyant was born in Evans Creek, Ohio, the son of an itinerant farmer. After apprenticeship to a harness-maker, he turned to sign painting during the 1850s. In 1858 he visited New York

1

2

1. *Alexander Wyant.* Forest Stream: A Study from Nature, *Minneapolis Institute of Arts (William Hood Dunwoody Fund).*
2. *William W. Wurster. Redwood Shingle Beach House, 1955.*

1

2

City, where he met Inness; with the support of Nicholas Longworth, a Cincinnati collector of art, he returned to New York to study in 1860.

Wyant's earliest known works, dating from the early 1860s, are meticulous woodland scenes in the Hudson River School* style. Few of these fine paintings survive, because many were reportedly destroyed after the artist's death by his wife, who preferred his late work. His realism was reinforced when he traveled to Karlsruhe, Germany, in 1865 to study with Hans Friedrich Gude (1825–1903). In 1866 he went to England and Ireland, and in the latter made sketches for a number of later landscapes. Upon his return in 1867, he settled in New York. In 1873 he joined an expedition to Arizona and New Mexico, during which he suffered a stroke that paralyzed his right arm. Over the following two decades, Wyant developed a loose, painterly technique with his left hand, and his popular, gray-toned paintings of the time often recall the French Barbizon School* and particularly the subtle, luminous works of Corot (1796–1875). Wyant's development paralleled that of his lifelong mentor, Inness; though his own work was more repetitive and less vigorous than that of Inness, Wyant was still a major figure in the late Hudson River School. He often summered in Keene Valley in the Adirondack Mountains until he moved to Arkville in the Catskill Mountains in 1889.   (T.E.S.)

Wyeth, Andrew (1917–   ).
Painter, born in Chadds Ford, Pa. Wyeth's earliest training came from his father, a well-known illustrator, N. C. Wyeth, but he remains primarily a self-taught artist, observing, "I worked everything out by trial and error." Wyeth's first one-man show was in 1937 in New York—a series of bright Maine watercolors that were sold out within twenty-four hours. Apparently the nineteen-year-old Wyeth was somewhat disturbed by his immediate success, and determined to create an art of greater "substance." Gradually his colors became more subdued (he turned to tempera two years after his first show), and a new mood of seriousness began to pervade his work.

Wyeth's pictures are usually thought of as intensely realistic—even "photographic"—whereas actually they are highly subjective and often sentimental. Even in his carefully painted portraits he is concerned with underlying character traits and judiciously selects sitters for their moral courage and human dignity; their triumph over life's trials is frequently etched in the lines of their faces. At times he resorts to outright symbolism, as in *A Crow Flew By* (1949–50, Metropolitan) wherein a black man, his tattered garments hanging behind him, seems to interpret a bird as the coming of death. This "genre" quality in Wyeth's work is related both to 19th-century American painting and to the American "regionalists" (see American Scene Painting) of the 1930s and '40s. A number of his pictures have an ominous, tragic, or disquieting note, as in his most famous painting, *Christina's World* (1948, Modern Museum). Here Wyeth extracts maximum emotional impact from a female polio victim who seems to be crawling up a hillside (actually she is picking berries). Such psychological dramas often border on surrealism,* and he employs a full range of literary devices and odd visual angles to achieve such effects.

Wyeth is probably the most popular painter in America today, partly because of his "grass roots" image and partly because his realism represents "old values" to Americans suspicious of abstract art. His austere New Englanders, gentle blacks, frail children, battered wagons, unpainted houses, and lonely beaches evoke a nostalgia for a lost America. Most art critics consider Wyeth a reactionary—a loner who has neither impeded nor advanced the course of modern art. Certainly his work runs counter to contemporary trends, and yet when seen in the context of anecdotal painting and illustration it is superior. Technically his work is excellent. Because he is essentially a draftsman there is a strong linear quality and an emphasis on graphic pattern in his work, and his use of egg tempera allows for a subtle color range and infinite fine brushstrokes that capture the minute texture of grass, shingles, and lace curtains. Wyeth himself has noted that he wants to submerge technique "and make it the rightful handmaiden of beauty, power and emotional content," and at his best his paintings are powerful, poetic, and highly factual. He was the first artist to appear on the cover of *Time* magazine, and other magazines have devoted special issues to his work. He has consistently commanded the highest prices paid for the work of a living American artist, and in 1970 a book on his work was a huge success. He has had numerous retrospective exhibitions; these have usually drawn record-breaking crowds.   (E.C.G.)

1. *Andrew Wyeth.* Christina's World, *1948, Museum of Modern Art, N.Y.*
2. *Andrew Wyeth.* A Crow Flew By, *1949–50. Metropolitan Museum of Art, N.Y. (Arthur H. Hearn Fund).*

Yamasaki, Minoru (1912–   ).
Architect who belongs, like Gordon Bunshaft* and leoh Ming Pei,* to the generation that achieved prominence after World War II, when the forms and ideology of the International style* had at last been accepted. Their task was not so much to provide a really "new" architecture as to accommodate the style to the realities of need and the corporate imagery of America in the 1950s and 1960s.

Born in Seattle, Wash., Yamasaki studied at the University of Washington and did his graduate work at New York University. After working in several architectural offices, he became a partner in the firm of Leinweber, Yamasaki & Hellmuth (1949–55), reorganized as Yamasaki, Leinweber & Associates (1955–59), and finally (1959) as Minoru Yamasaki & Associates. His first well-publicized design, that of the Lambert-St. Louis Airport Terminal Building (1956), conveyed a constructionist, highly rational quality in its succession of domelike forms. But by the late 1950s, and especially in his work of the 1960s, he began, like other designers, to abandon the ascetic form of the International style for richer forms, details, and materials. In such work as the McGregor Conference Center, Wayne State University (Detroit, 1958) and in the Science Pavilion at the Seattle World's Fair (1962), the cold, hard, machine-like quality of the International style became light, delicate, and even tinsel-like, and the site planning of these buildings became increasingly Beaux-Arts and classical. The theme of the classical colonnaded pavilion began to appear in his work, as it had a few years earlier in the designs of Edward Durell Stone* and Philip Johnson.* Yamasaki's Northwest Life Insurance Building (Minneapolis, 1964) illustrates how refined and classically formal much of the archi-

tecture of the 1960s had become. The same visual qualities dominate his twin-towered 1350-foot high New York World Trade Center (1964–72); but the very size of this project poses serious questions as to our ability to reconcile technology with the needs of individuals who must live and work in a high-density urban environment.

(D.G.)

York & Sawyer.
Architectural firm formed in 1898 by Edward Palmer York (1865–1928) and Philip Sawyer (1868–1949). York was born in Wellsville, N.Y., and studied architecture at Cornell University. From 1890–97 he worked for McKim, Mead & White.* Sawyer, of New London, Conn., studied civil engineering before 1888 and then did field service as an engineer. He later entered Columbia University School of Architecture and completed his studies at the École des Beaux-Arts in Paris before joining McKim, Mead & White in 1891. He remained there until he and York formed their lifelong partnership in New York City.

Their hallmark was their knowledgeable use of the Italian Renaissance* and Romanesque* styles. The firm specialized in the design of banks and hospitals, with a lesser share of public, commercial, and college buildings. One of their first bank commissions resulted in the ornate Franklin Savings Bank at 42nd Street and Eighth Avenue, New York City (1899). Here, Sawyer gave full rein to his Beaux-Arts training, using boldly rusticated masonry. Also in 1899 they designed the classical Riggs National Bank at 1503 Pennsylvania Avenue, N.W., Washington, D.C. A richly adorned pediment crowns a wide entrance flanked by fluted Ionic columns. One of their handsomest classical buildings was the Guaranty Trust Company in New York City at 140 Broadway (1913). The last of their

1

1. **Minoru Yamasaki.** McGregor Conference Center, Wayne State University, Detroit, 1958, interior.
2. **Minoru Yamasaki.** McGregor Conference Center, Wayne State University, Detroit, 1958, exterior.
3. **York & Sawyer.** Bowery Savings Bank, N.Y., 1923, interior.

2

3

important classical banks was the Greenwich Savings Bank at Broadway and West 36th Street, New York City (1924), which displays imposing Corinthian colonnades on three sides.

In the Italian Renaissance style of the age of eclecticism,* typified by rusticated stonework, arched windows, and wrought ironwork were the Brooklyn Trust Company at 177 Montague Street (1915), the enormous Federal Reserve Bank of New York at 33 Liberty Street (1928), and the large-scale Central Savings Bank building at 73rd Street and Broadway (1928). Probably their finest bank design was the Bowery Savings at 110 East 42nd Street (1923), with its great neo-Romanesque main room and its varicolored marble columns and inlaid marble floor.

The firm is said to have designed some fifty hospitals, including the Lenox Hill at 107 East 76th Street (c.1913) and the Hospital Building at the Rockefeller Institute at 66th Street on the East River (before 1912). In 1932 the firm won the competition to execute the huge Department of Commerce Building on 14th Street and Constitution Avenue in Washington, D.C. This rectangular, classical building with its carefully spaced colonnades was in character with Washington's so-called federal triangle. Three notable office buildings by the firm include the Postal Life Insurance Company building at Fifth Avenue and 43rd Street, New York City (1919), with an Italian Renaissance façade; the Rhode Island Hospital Trust Company, Providence (1919), with a classical colonnade at the ground floor; and the Pershing Square Building, 100 East 42nd Street, New York City (1923), designed with the architect John Sloan in a modified Romanesque style. Outstanding among their residential designs was the town house of William W. Cook at 14 East 71st Street, New York (1913), where the doorway is surmounted by a large window crowned by a loggia.

York & Sawyer has distinguished itself by the highly individual quality of its Italian Renaissance and Romanesque buildings.   (A.B.)

Young, Ammi Burnham (1798–1874). Architect. Born in Lebanon, N.H., he received training from his father, a carpenter and builder. Early in the 1820s Young was in Boston, probably getting further training with Alexander

1

2

3

Parris.* His first architectural work, in and near Lebanon, was in the outmoded style of the previous century; it included the Congregational Church, Lebanon (1828), and Wentworth Hall (1828) and Thornton Hall (1829), both at Dartmouth College. He received the commission for the State Capitol, Montpelier, Vt. (1833–36, burned 1857), giving it a fine Doric portico (reused for the new Capitol). Young appears to have lived in Montpelier until 1838. He designed St. Paul's Church, Burlington, Vt. (1832), in the Gothic style approved by Bishop Hopkins of Burlington, who wrote a book on this style. He also designed the house of President Wheeler of the University of Vermont (1840). Having won the competition for the Customs House, Boston, in 1837, Young moved there, and remained until 1852. His design for the Customs House (1837–47) leaned strongly toward the Greek revival* style. Its immense, noble columns and domed interior carried the use of classic elements to a new peak, but a later architect's substitution of a central tower for the dome marred its grandeur. While in Boston he designed the Bromfield Street Methodist Episcopal Church (by 1853) in Romanesque.

In 1852 Young moved to Washington, D.C., to become a supervising architect in the Treasury Department, entailing designs for post offices, customs houses, courthouses, and hospitals. The vast number of buildings he did led to a standardizing of designs, but the buildings were almost always more than adequate for their purpose. Large cities were given more monumental designs, often in majestic Greek revival; smaller towns were accorded more delicate designs of an Italianate character. After a decade of federal work, in which he erected seventy buildings, he retired in 1862.　　(P.F.N.)

Young, Art (1866–1943).
Painter and cartoonist. Born on a farm in Illinois, he grew up in Monroe, Wis., where his family ran a general store. As a boy he made caricatures of all the town's leading characters. At eighteen he went to Chicago to study at the Academy of Design, and he began his professional career as a free-lance cartoonist. Shortly afterward he studied at the Art Students League* in New York and at the Académie Julien in Paris. On his return to the United States he joined the staff of the Chicago

Inter-Ocean, and is said to have been the first artist in history to draw a daily political cartoon.

In his mid-thirties, Young went to New York, where he became increasingly concerned with inequities in American political and economic life. He became a regular contributor to *The Masses* and other left-wing publications, employing a style of drastic, powerful, but essentially quizzical and humorous simplicity. He used his draftsman's pen in campaigns for women's suffrage, the abolition of child labor, racial equality, and the recognition of unions. He was arrested as a pacifist during World War I. Twice he ran for public office on left-wing tickets. Late in life he moved to Bethel, Conn., where he ran a small gallery of his own work. He wrote an autobiography, *Art Young: His Life and Times* (1939). (A.F.)

Young, Mahonri (1877–1957).
Sculptor. A grandson of the Mormon leader Brigham Young, he was born in Salt Lake City, Utah. In 1899 he went to New York to study painting at the Art Students League;* he then spent two years in Paris and Italy and began doing sculpture. Soon after returning to America he created his *Stevedore* (1904, Metropolitan), which brought him national recognition. Young was drawn to the theme of the workingman throughout his life, as in his early *Shoveler* and *Man Tired* or his *Bovet Arthur—A Laborer* (1904, Newark Museum) and *Man with Pick* (c.1912–17, Metropolitan). Usually under twenty-four inches in height, such works have a monumentality that belie their small size. They were modeled with a vigor befitting the subject, with a rich play of lights and darks on the surfaces, a massiveness of forms and a minimum of detail. Other subjects included Indians, modeled on a trip to Arizona in 1912, and prize fighters. His bronze statuette *The Rigger* (1922) is at Brookgreen Gardens in South Carolina, and a very late work is the marble statue of his famous grandfather, placed in Statuary Hall (U.S. Capitol) in 1950. Stylistically, Young's work had a powerful and rugged naturalism, yet it also possessed a sensitivity in its arrangement of masses. (W.C.)

Youngerman, Jack (1926–   ).
Painter. He was born in Louisville, Ky. and studied at the University of North Carolina. During 1944–46 he served in the navy; he then graduated from the University of Missouri (1947). In 1947–56 he lived in Paris, studying at the École des Beaux-Arts, where his earliest work was influenced by constructivism.* His first exhibition was at the Galerie Maeght in Paris (1950). In 1952–56 Youngerman traveled in Europe and the Near East, working on architectural projects in Lebanon and Iraq with the architect Michel Ecochard. In 1956 he returned to the United States and settled in New York, where one of his earliest projects was the design for *Deathwatch,* Jean Genet's play (1958). Confronted by the large forms, dramatic brushwork, and sheer size of American abstract expressionist pictures (see Abstract Expressionism) he began to modify his own work, and produced a series of highly original, powerful, ragged-edged images that seemed to burst beyond the limits of the canvas. Initially Youngerman's shapes were agitated and aggressive, owing to an expressionist handling of paint and the interpenetration of sawtoothed forms along their mutual edges. Since then he has simplified his shapes and flattened them even further. His color combinations—bright yellows and oranges, blues and whites, and greens and whites—have always been both raw and original, though his forms seem more and more related to the late cutouts of Matisse and the nature images of Georgia O'Keeffe.* A retrospective of his work was held at the Worcester Museum in 1965. (E.C.G.)

Yunkers, Adja (1900–   ).
Painter and printmaker. He was born in Riga, Latvia, studied in Leningrad, Berlin, Paris, and London, and lived in Paris for more than a decade. During World War II he lived in Sweden, where he edited and published the avantgarde art magazines *ARS* and *Creation.* Since 1947 he has lived in the United States, where he has moved from an abstract expressionist manner of gestural brush painting to a highly simplified form of color-field* painting. As a leading printmaker since the 1920s, his large, simplified, and spacious woodcuts, lithographs, and serigraphs have a particular pertinence in the recent revival of experimental printmaking. (H.H.A.)

1. *Ammi Burnham Young. Vermont State Capitol, Montpelier, 1836.*
2. *Jack Youngerman. Black, Yellow, Red, 1964. Finch College Museum of Art, N.Y.*
3. *Mahonri Young. Bovet Arthur: A Laborer, 1911, bronze. Newark Museum, N.J.*

Z

1

Zeisler, Claire (n.d.-).
Weaver-sculptor, among the first to introduce off-the-loom techniques to create free-standing, fiber-constructed forms. Born in Cincinnati, Ohio, she studied at Columbia University and the Institute of Design in Chicago. In the early 1960s she created small hangings in which stones, Christmas balls, or other "found materials" were enclosed in pouch or pocket networks of cotton lace. The surface achieved its variety of textures through the use of multiple techniques—tapestry, tabby and leno weaves, in addition to stuffing, braiding, and crocheting. In the late 1960s her works became larger—often six to eight feet high—with strands of fiber wrapped into networks of ribbing, often in radiating flanges, and the loose mass of warp ends cascading down and splayed out loosely around the base. She has also made small amulet-like objects of threads crocheted and wrapped around stones.

(R.S.)

Zigzag Moderne.
In American architecture, the dominant new imagery of the 1920s (called art deco* in Europe). Its exponents aimed to retain a grip on the past but to be of the present and future, particularly through the use of machine imagery. Typical of the mode was Morgan, Walls & Clement's Richfield Building (Los Angeles, 1928). Its vertical striations and sculptured group above the main entrance and along the parapets were Gothic in feeling, but the exterior black and gold terra-cotta surface and ornament, the metal windows and doors, and the basic simplicity of the massing were modern; so too was the interior layout, with floors devoted to automobile parking.

Generally, zigzag moderne buildings boasted ornamentation, but the patterns and often the way the ornament was used was only incidentally historic. Basically, the designs—triangles, zigzags, spirals, fragmented circles, often accompanied by sea shells, leaves, and flowers—were derived from modern painting and sculpture. Of three-dimensional forms, the cube and the rectangle predominated. When two or more volumes were brought together in the composition for a building or a piece of furniture, each volume retained a separate identity. The surfaces of buildings, interior and exterior, tended to be two-dimensional, plain, and smooth, but there was a fondness for rich-appearing materials: rare woods and stone, and new materials of alloy metal, and plastics such as Bakelite or Vitrolite.

The primary source of early moderne was the architecture and decorative arts of the 1925 Paris Exposition of Decorative Arts. A supplementary source was the simple geometric angularity of the work of those who, like the architect and stage designer Joseph Urban (1872–1933), continued the delicate surface tracery associated with the Viennese Secessionists of pre-World War I. Probably the characteristic that most strongly marked American zigzag moderne was a fascination with the machine and machine symbols. Transportation machines in particular enthralled Americans during the 1920s: the ship, then the automobile, and finally the airplane. As in the automobile and airplane of the period, each part of a moderne building or chair retained its independent identity.

Literally every major American architect, from Frank Lloyd Wright* to Bertram Goodhue* and Ralph Adams Cram, was affected by zigzag moderne. The large architectural firms applied the style to every sort of building, from small retail stores and gasoline stations to skyscrapers. The major monuments of the style were the Los Angeles Rich-

field Building, Howell & Hood's* American Radiator Building (New York, 1924), Miller & Pflueger's 450 Sutter Street Building (San Francisco, 1929), and William Van Alen's Chrysler Building on 42nd Street (New York City, 1929–30).

Zigzag moderne early associated itself with the multilevel city of the future and was most convincingly expressed in the widely published urban designs and renderings of Hugh Ferriss.* Like streamlined moderne* it became a truly universal style by the end of the 1920s. Every conceivable object, from perfume bottles to advertising, expressed it. Like other strong styles, it did not die out suddenly, for buildings in this mode continued to be erected throughout much of the 1930s, although by then its imagery was old fashioned. (D.G.)

Zorach, William (1887–1966).
Sculptor. He was born in Lithuania but was brought to America in 1891. He grew up in Port Clinton, Ohio, and attended the Cleveland Art School before going to New York City in 1907 to study at the National Academy of Design.* On his first trip to Paris in 1910 he discovered the experiments of the cubists and the fauves. Returning to New York, he and his wife, Marguerite, were among the avant-garde in American painting; they were both represented at the Armory Show* of 1913. It was not until 1917 that he turned to sculpture by carving directly a wood panel very much in the cubist style. Cubism* led him to abstraction but he soon renounced its theories to develop his own personal style—an outgrowth of direct carving. Using traditional themes, his style was characterized by monumentality (even in small pieces) and a simplification and abstraction of natural form. His restrained, dignified style is influenced by Egyptian and archaic Greek sculpture. It was about 1924 that he began, like his friend, Robert Laurent,* carving directly in stone, a technique and medium that led to his mature style. Among his best-known pieces are *Child with Cat* (1926, Modern Museum) and *Mother and Child* (1927–30, Metropolitan), in which his style was carried to a monumentality of scale as well as form. In the early 1930s Zorach became a center of controversy when his heroic nude female figure, *Spirit of the Dance* (1932), com-

missioned for Radio City Music Hall, New York City, was rejected. Public pressure eventually forced its acceptance, however.

Zorach's refinement of natural form may be seen in his black granite *Head of Christ* (1940, Modern Museum); and the recurring theme of the affection of a child and an animal or a mother and child are evident in his *Affection* (1933, Proctor) or *Future Generation* (1942–47, Whitney). During the 1930s Zorach became a leader of the modern movement in America, but following World War II the abstract expressionists and the heirs of constructivism led the way into a new art. Zorach continued to work in his own style throughout the 1950s and early 1960s. Examples of his late work are the granite *Head of Moses* (1956, Columbia University) and *Cat with Long Whiskers* (1966, private collection). Beginning in 1929, Zorach taught for over thirty years at the Art Students League.* He was the author of two books, *Zorach Explains Sculpture* (1947) and *Art is My Life* (1967). (W.C.)

Zox, Larry (1936–).
Painter. Born in Des Moines, Iowa, he was educated at Oklahoma University, Drake University, and the Des Moines Art Center and studied with George Grosz* and Louis Bouche. Zox is a color-field* painter who organizes his canvases in geometric configurations, utilizing sets and models. He uses strong, aggressive color, repetition of geometric shapes, and precise linear patterns. A white line or stripe frequently separates color areas to create intervals of rest and a directional structure within the color shape. During the late 1960s Zox painted on an increasingly monumental scale, diminishing or abandoning the white-line intervals in favor of vast, unified, and interrelated color areas. (H.H.A.)

1. *Zigzag Moderne. Chrysler Building, N.Y., 1930.*
2. *William Zorach. Mother and Child, 1927–30, marble. Metropolitan Museum of Art, N.Y. (Fletcher Fund).*

Guide to Entries by Arts

Gravestones
Hicks, Edward
Hidley, Joseph
Hofmann, Charles C.
Jennys, William
Kane, John
Krans, Olaf
Maentel, Jacob (or Maentle)
Moses, Anna Mary Robertson (Grandma Moses)
Moulthrop, Reuben
Mourning Pictures
Nameboards
Patchwork
Phillips, Ammi
Pickett, Joseph
Pinney, Eunice
Pinprick
Prior, William Matthew
Retablos
Reverse Painting on Glass
Robb, Samuel A.
Samplers
Santos
Schimmel, Wilhelm
Scrimshaw
Shaker Crafts
Sheffield, Isaac
Show Figures
Skillin, Simeon, Sr.
Stock, Joseph W.
Sullivan, Patrick J.
Taufscheine
Tinsel Painting
Tinware
Trade Signs
Weathervanes
Whirligigs
Williams, Micah

Furniture
Architect Furniture (see Furniture)
Art Deco
Art Furniture (see Furniture)
Art Nouveau
Arts and Crafts, Craftsman, Mission Furniture (see Arts and Crafts Movement
Baroque in American Art
Bassett, Florence Shust Knoll
Bauhaus
Belter, John Henry
Carpenter, Arthur
Castle, Wendell
Chippendale (see Furniture)
Colonial Revival (see Furniture) Furniture
Dennis, Thomas
Dunlap Furniture (see Furniture)
Eames, Charles
Early Federal (see Furniture)
Eastlake Furniture (see Furniture)
Elfe, Thomas, Sr.
Elizabethian Revival (see Furniture)
Esherick, Wharton
Evans, Edward
Frankl, Paul T.
Frothingham, Benjamin, Jr.
Furniture Since 1650
Gothic Revival (see Furniture)
Hadley Chests (see Furniture)
Hagen, Ernest
Herter, Christian
Industrial Designer
Knoll, Hans (see also Bassett, Florence Shust Knoll)
Lannuier, Charles Honoré
Late Classical or Greek Revival (see Furniture)
Late Federal (see Furniture)
Louis XVI (see Furniture)

Maloof, Sam
McCobb, Paul
Meeks, The
Miller, Herman, Inc.
Nakashima, George
Near Eastern & Eastern (see Furniture)
Nelson, George
Phyfe, Duncan
Queen Anne (see Furniture)
Randolph, Benjamin
Reform Styles (see Furniture)
Renaissance (see Furniture)
Risom, Jens
Robsjohn-Gibbings, Terence Harold
Rococo (see Furniture)
Rohde, Gilbert
Roux, Alexander
Savery, William
Seymour, John and Thomas
Shaker Crafts
Townsend-Goddard (see Furniture)
Tulip-and-Sunflower Chests (see Furniture)
Vernacular Furniture (see Furniture)
Weber, Kem
William & Mary (see Furniture)
Windsor Furniture (see Furniture)
Wormley, Edward J.

Glass
Amelung, Johann Friedrich
Art Deco
Art Glass
Art Nouveau
Blown-three-mold Glass
Carder, Frederick
Cut Glass
Flasks
Glass Cutting and Engraving
Glass Since 1607
Jarves, Deming
Labino, Dominick
Littleton, Harvey
Midwestern Glass
Paperweights
Pattern-molded Glass
Pittsburgh Glass
Pressed Glass
Reverse Painting on Glass
Sandwich Glass
Satin Glass
South Jersey Glass
Steigel, Henry
Steuben Glass Works
Tiffany & Company
Tiffany, Louis Comfort
Wistar, Casper

Handcrafts, Contemporary
Adams, Alice
Albers, Anni
Blumenau, Lili
Ceramics
Guermonprez, Trude
Handcrafts, Contemporary
Hicks, Sheila
Macramé
Nottingham, Walter
Phillips, Mary Walker
Rossbach, Edward
Sekimachi, Kay
Soldner, Paul
Takaezu, Toshiko
Tawney, Lenore
Weaving
Zeisler, Claire

Painting: Colonial to 1830
Aetatis Sue Limner

Alexander, Cosmo
Allston, Washington
Ames, Ezra
Audubon, John James
Badger, Joseph
Baroque in American Art
Bascom, Ruth Henshaw
Beardsley Limner, The
Benbridge, Henry
Birch, Thomas
Blackburn, Joseph
Brewster, John, Jr.
Bridges, Charles
Brown, J.
Brown, Mather
Chandler, Winthrop
Claypoole, James, Sr.
Codman, Charles
Cole, Thomas
Cooper, Peter
Copley, John Singleton
Dunlap, William
Durand, John
Earl, Ralph
Eichholtz, Jacob
Emmons, Nathaniel
Feke, Robert
Fisher, Alvan
Fisher, Jonathan
Fitch, Simon
Fraser, Charles
Fulton, Robert
Genre
Godefroy, Maximilian
Goodridge, Sarah
Greenwood, John
Gullager, Christian
Guy, Francis
Haidt, John Valentin
Harding, Chester
Harvey, George
Hathaway, Rufus
Hesselius, Gustavus
Hesselius, John
Hicks, Edward
Hubard, William James
Hudson River School
Ingham, Charles Cromwell
Inman, Henry
Jarvis, John Wesley
Jennys, William
Johnston, Henrietta
Johnston, Joshua
Jouett, Matthew
King, Charles Bird
Krimmel, John Lewis
Kuhn, Justus Engelhardt
Malbone, Edward Greene
Metcalf, Eliab
Morse, Samuel F. B.
Moulthrop, Reuben
Neagle, John
Neal, John
Neoclassicism
Page, William
Patroon Painters
Peale, Anna Claypoole
Peale, Charles Willson
Peale, James
Peale, Raphaelle
Peale, Rembrandt
Peale, Rubens
Peale, Sarah Miriam
Peale, Titian Ramsay
Pelham, Henry
Pelham, Peter
Pennsylvania Academy of the Fine Arts
Phillips, Ammi
Pine, Robert Edge
Pinney, Eunice
Polk, Charles Peale
Porter, Rufus
Pratt, Matthew
Quidor, John

Ramage, John
Rococo Style
Romanticism
Salmon, Robert
Sargent, Henry
Savage, Edward
Shaw, Joshua
Sheffield, Isaac
Smibert, John
Smith, Thomas
Stuart, Gilbert
Sully, Thomas
Theus, Jeremiah
Trumbull, John
Vanderlyn, John
Vanderlyn, Pieter
Waldo, Samuel Lovett
Watson, John
Wertmuller, Adolph Ulrich
West, Benjamin
White, John
Williams, Micah
Williams, William
Wollaston, John
Wright, Joseph

Painting: 1831–1912
Abbey, Edwin Austin
Abstract Art
Alexander, Francis
Alexander, John White
Allston, Washington
American Art-Union
American Artists, The Society of
Anshutz, Thomas
Art Nouveau
Art Students League
Ash Can School
Audubon, John James
Barbizon School
Bard, James and John
Bascom, Ruth Henshaw
Beard, James Henry & Beard, William Holbrook
Beaux, Cecilia
Bellows, George Wesley
Benson, Frank Weston
Bierstadt, Albert
Bingham, George Caleb
Blakelock, Ralph Albert
Blashfield, Edwin Howland
Blythe, David Gilmore
Bodmer, Karl
Bradford, William
Bricher, Alfred Thompson
Brown, George Loring
Brush, George De Forest
Buttersworth, James E.
Carles, Arthur B.
Casilear, John William
Cassatt, Mary
Catlin, George
Chalfant, Jefferson David
Chambers, Thomas
Chapman, John Gadsby
Chase, William Merritt
Church, Frederic Edwin
Church, Henry
Clonney, James Goodwyn
Codman, Charles
Cole, Thomas
Colman, Samuel, Jr.
Cope, George
Cox, Kenyon
Crane, Bruce
Crayon, The
Cropsey, Jasper Francis
Cubism
Cummings, Thomas Seir
Davies, Arthur Bowen
Davis, Joseph H.
Deas, Charles
Decker, Joseph
Dewing, Thomas Wilmer
Doughty, Thomas

Guide to Entries by Arts

Dove, Arthur G.
Du Bois, Guy Pène
Duchamp, Marcel
Duncanson, Robert S.
Durand, Asher Brown
Durrie, George Henry
Duveneck, Frank
Eakins, Thomas
Eastman, Seth
Eaton, Wyatt
Edmonds, Francis William
Eichholtz, Jacob
Eight, The
Eilshemius, Louis Michel
Elliott, Charles Loring
Ellsworth, James Sanford
Elmer, Edwin Romanzo
Fauvism
Feininger, Lyonel
Field, Erastus Salisbury
Fisher, Alvan
Fisher, Jonathan
Francis, John F.
Fuller, George
Futurism
Genre
Gifford, Sanford Robinson
Glackens, William
Goodridge, Sarah
Gray, Henry Peters
Haberle, John
Hall, George Henry
Hamilton, James
Harding, Chester
Hardy, Jeremiah Pearson
Harnett, William Michael
Hart, George Overbury
Hart, William and Hart, James
  MacDougal
Hartley, Marsden
Harvey, George
Hassam, Childe
Hawthorne, Charles Webster
Heade, Martin Johnson
Healy, George P. A.
Henri, Robert
Henry, Edward Lamson
Hicks, Edward
Hicks, Thomas
Hidley, Joseph
Hill, John William
Hofmann, Hans
Homer, Winslow
Hopper, Edward
Hovenden, Thomas
Hubard, William James
Hudson River School
Hunt, William Morris
Huntington, Daniel
Impressionism
Independent Artists, The
  Exhibition of
Ingham, Charles Cromwell
Inman, Henry
Inness, George
Jarves, James Jackson
Jewett, William
Johnson, David
Johnson, Eastman
Kensett, John Frederick
Kent, Rockwell
King, Charles Bird
Kuhn, Walt
La Farge, John
Lambdin, George Cochran
Lane, Fitz Hugh
Lawson, Ernest
Leutze, Emanuel Gottlieb
Lie, Jonas
Luks, George
Luminism
Marin, John
Martin, Homer Dodge
Maurer, Alfred Henry
Melchers, Gari

Metcalf, Willard Leroy
Miller, Kenneth Hayes
Millet, Francis D.
Morse, Samuel F. B.
Mount, William Sidney
Murphy, J. Francis
Myers, Jerome
National Academy of Design
Neagle, John
Neal, John
Neoclassicism
Orphism
Page, William
Parrish, Maxfield
Peale, Anna Claypoole
Peale, Rembrandt
Peale, Rubens
Peale, Sarah Miriam
Peale, Titian Ramsay
Penfield, Edward
Pennsylvania Academy of the
  Fine Arts
Peto, John Frederick
Pickett, Joseph
Picknell, William Lamb
Pinney, Eunice
Pleinairism
Poor, Henry Varnum
Pope, Alexander
Porter, Rufus
Prendergast, Maurice
Prior, William Matthew
Quidor, John
Ranger, Henry Ward
Ranney, William
Reid, Robert
Remington, Frederick
Richards, William Trost
Robinson, Boardman
Robinson, Theodore
Roesen, Severin
Romanticism
Ruskin, John
Russell, Charles Marion
Russell, Morgan
Ryder, Albert Pinkham
Salmon, Robert
Sargent, Henry
Sargent, John Singer
Schamberg, Morton Livingston
Shaw, Joshua
Sheeler, Charles
Sheffield, Isaac
Shinn, Everett
Shirlaw, Walter
Sloan, John
Speicher, Eugene
Stanley, John Mix
Steichen, Edward J.
Stella, Joseph
Sterne, Maurice
Stock, Joseph W.
Sully, Thomas
Symbolism
Tait, Arthur Fitzwilliam
Tanner, Henry Ossawa
Tarbell, Edmund C.
Ten, The
Thayer, Abbott Handerson
Thompson, Cephas Giovanni
Thompson, Jerome B.
Tryon, Dwight William
Tuckerman, Henry Theodore
Twachtman, John Henry
Vanderlyn, John
Vedder, Elihu
Vonnoh, Robert (William)
Waldo, Samuel Lovett
Walker, Horatio
Walkowitz, Abraham
Ward, John Quincy Adams
Waugh, Frederick Judd
Weber, Max
Weir, John Ferguson
Weir, Julian Alden

Weir, Robert Walter
Whistler, James Abbott McNeil
Whittredge, Worthington
Wimar, Karl
Woodville, Richard Caton
Wyant, Alexander Helwig
Young, Art

Painting: 1913 to date

Abstract Art
Abstract Expressionism
Action Painting
American Abstract Artists
Albers, Josef
Albright, Ivan Le Lorraine
American Scene Painting
Anuszkiewicz, Richard
Armory Show, The
Art Deco
Art Students League
Assemblage
Automatism
Avery, Milton
Bacon, Peggy
Bannard, Darby
Baziotes, William
Beaux, Cecilia
Bellows, George Wesley
Benton, Thomas Hart
Berman, Eugene
Biddle, George
Bischoff, Elmer
Bishop, Isabel
Blume, Peter
Bohrod, Aaron
Bolotowsky, Ilya
Brook, Alexander
Brooks, James
Bruce, Patrick Henry
Brush, George De Forest
Burchfield, Charles
Cadmus, Paul
Carles, Arthur B.
Cavallon, Georgio
Charlot, Jean
Collage
Color-Field Painting
Concept Art
Constructivism
Crawford, Ralston
Cubism
Curry, John Steuart
Dada
Dasburg, Andrew
Davies, Arthur Bowen
Davis, Gene
Davis, Stuart
de Kooning, Willem
Demuth, Charles
Dickinson, Edwin
Dickinson, Preston
Diebenkorn, Richard
Diller, Burgoyne
Dine, Jim
Dove, Arthur G.
Du Bois, Guy Pène
Duchamp, Marcel
Eilshemius, Louis Michel
Environmental Art
Evergood, Philip
Expressionism
Fauvism
Feeley, Paul
Feininger, Lyonel
Francis, Sam
Frankenthaler, Helen
Frost, John Orne Johnson
Funk Art
Futurism
Gatch, (Harry) Lee
Gatto, Victor Joseph
Genre
Glackens, William
Glarner, Fritz

Goodnough, Robert
Gorky, Arshile
Gottlieb, Adolph
Graham, John
Graves, Morris
Greene, Balcomb
Grooms, Red
Gropper, William
Grosz, George
Guggenheim, Peggy
Guglielmi, O. Louis
Guston, Philip
Gwathmey, Robert
Haberle, John
Hard-Edge Painting
Hart, George Overbury
  or "Pop"
Hartigan, Grace
Hartley, Marsden
Hassam, Childe
Hawthorne, Charles Webster
Held, Al
Henri, Robert
Hinman, Charles
Hirshfield, Morris
Hofmann, Hans
Hopper, Edward
Independent Artists, The
  Society of
Indiana, Robert
Johanson, Patricia
Johns, Jasper
Kane, John
Kantor, Morris
Kelly, Ellsworth
Kent, Rockwell
Kline, Franz
Knaths, Karl
Krans, Olaf
Kroll, Leon
Krushenick, Nicholas
Kuhn, Walt
Kuniyoshi, Yasuo
Lawrence, Jacob
Lawson, Ernest
Lebrun, Rico
Lee, Doris
Leslie, Alfred
Lewis, Martin
Levine, Jack
Liberman, Alexander
Lichtenstein, Roy
Lie, Jonas
Lindner, Richard
Louis, Morris
Luks, George
Lyrical Abstraction
MacDonald-Wright, Stanton
MacIver, Loren
Marca-Relli, Conrad
Marin, John
Marsh, Reginald
Martin, Agnes
Maurer, Alfred Henry
McFee, Henry Lee
McGarrell, James
McNeil, George
Melchers, Gari
Metcalf, Willard Leroy
Miller, Kenneth Hayes
Minimal Art
Mitchell, Joan
Morris, Robert
Moses, Anna Mary Robertson
Motherwell, Robert
Müller, Jan
Murphy, J. Francis
Myers, Jerome
National Academy of Design
New York School
Newman, Barnett
Noland, Kenneth
Ohlson, Doug
O'Keeffe, Georgia
Oldenburg, Claes

Olitski, Jules
Oliveira, Nathan
Optical Art
Orphism
Park, David
Parker, Raymond
Pearlstein, Philip
Penfield, Edward
Pennsylvania Academy of the
    Fine Arts
Pereira, Irene Rice
Pollock, Jackson
Poons, Larry
Pop Art
Pope, Alexander
Porter, Fairfield
Post-painterly Abstraction
Pousette-Dart, Richard
Prendergast, Maurice
Rattner, Abraham
Rauschenberg, Robert
Ray, Man
Refregier, Anton
Regionalism
Reid, Robert
Reinhardt, Ad
Resnick, Milton
Rivers, Larry
Robinson, Boardman
Rosenquist, James
Rothko, Mark
Russell, Charles Marion
Russell, Morgan
Sargent, John Singer
Savage, Eugene Francis
Schamberg, Morton Livingston
Schrag, Karl
Serial Art
Shahn, Ben
Shaped Canvas
Shinn, Everett
Sloan, John
Soyer, Isaac
Soyer, Moses
Soyer, Raphael
Speicher, Eugene
Spencer, Niles
Stamos, Theodoros
Stella, Frank
Stella, Joseph
Sterne, Maurice
Still, Clyfford
Sullivan, Patrick J.
Surrealism
Synchromism
Tanguy, Yves
Tanner, Henry Ossawa
Tarbell, Edmund C.
Tchelitchew, Pavel
Tobey, Mark
Tomlin, Bradley Walker
Tooker, George
Tryon, Dwight William
Tworkov, Jack
Vicente, Esteban
Vonnoh, Robert William
Walker, Horatio
Walkowitz, Abraham
Warhol, Andy
Waugh, Frederick Judd
Weber, Max
Wesselmann, Tom
Wiener, Isador
Williams, Neil
Wood, Grant
WPA (Works Progress Adminis
    tration) Federal Art Project
Wyeth, Andrew
Young, Art
Youngerman, Jack
Yunkers, Adja
Zorach, William
Zox, Larry

Pewter

Photography
Abbot, Berenice
Adams, Ansel Easton
Arbus, Diane
Avedon, Richard
Barnard, George N.
Bauhaus
Brady, Mathew
Bruguière, Francis
Bullock, Wynn
Callahan, Harry
Conner, Bruce
Cunningham, Imogen
Daguerreotype
Davidson, Bruce
Evans, Walker
f/64
Farm Security Administration
    (FSA)
Frank, Robert
Friedlander, Lee
Gardner, Alexander
Hawes, Josiah Johnson
Hine, Lewis
Jackson, William Henry
Käsebier, Gertrude Stanton
Lange, Dorothea
Liberman, Alexander
Muybridge, Eadweard
O'Sullivan, Timothy H.
Penn, Irving
Photo-Secession
Photography
Ray, Man
Sheeler, Charles
Siskind, Aaron
Smith, W. Eugene
Sommer, Frederick
Southworth, Albert Sands
Steichen, Edward J.
Steiner, Ralph
Stieglitz, Alfred
Teske, Edmund
Uelsmann, Jerry N.
Weston, Edward
White, Minor
Winogrand, Garry

Printmaking
Abbey, Edwin Austin
Anderson, Alexander
Aquatint and Lithography (see
    Printmaking)
Art Deco
Art Nouveau
Art Students League
Artists' Prints (see Printmaking)
Arts and Crafts Movement (see
    Furniture)
Atelier 17
Bacon, Peggy
Baskin, Leonard
Bellows, George Wesley
Biddle, George
Burgis, William
Cadmus, Paul
Casilear, John William
Chapman, John Gadsby
Claypoole, James, Jr.
Currier & Ives
Darley, Felix Octavius Carr
Dawkins, Henry
Doughty, Thomas
Durand, Asher Brown
Emmes, Thomas
Expressionism
Fisher, Jonathan
Foster, John
Franklin, Benjamin
Franklin, James
Frasconi, Antonio
Gemini, G.E.L.
Gropper, William
Grosz, George
Hardy, Jeremiah Pearson

Hart, George Overbury
Hill, John William
Homer, Winslow
Hopper, Edward
Indiana, Robert
Johns, Jasper
Johnston, Thomas
Kensett, John Frederick
Kent, Rockwell
Kuhn, Walt
Lane, Fitz Hugh
Lasansky, Mauricio
Lebrun, Rico
Lewis, Martin
Luks, George
Marsh, Reginald
Mezzotint Prototypes
Millet, Francis D.
Motherwell, Robert
Neal, John
Oldenburg, Claes
Oliveira, Nathan
Pelham, Henry
Penfield, Edward
Peterdi, Gabor
Printmaking, Historical
Printmaking, Modern
Rauschenberg, Robert
Remington, Frederick
Richards, William Trost
Robinson, Boardman
Romans, Bernard
Romanticism
Roszak, Theodore
Schrag, Karl
Shahn, Ben
Shaker Crafts
Shinn, Everett
Sloan, John
Smither, James
Solomon, Barbara Stauffacher
Sparrow, Thomas
Sterne, Maurice
Tamarind Lithography Workshop
Turner, James
Universal Limited Art Editions
Warhol, Andy
Wayne, June
Westermann, Horace Clifford, Jr.
WPA (Works Progress Adminis-
    tration) Federal Art Project
Yunkers, Adja

Sculpture: Colonial to 1912
Abstract Art
Adams, Herbert
Art Deco
Art Nouveau
Art Students League
Augur, Hezekiah
Ball, Thomas
Barnard, George Grey
Bartlett, Paul Wayland
Bissell, George Edwin
Bitter, Karl Theodore
Borglum, Gutzon
Borglum, Solon Hannibal
Boyle, John J.
Brackett, Edward Augustus
Browere, John Henri Isaac
Brown, Henry Kirke
Bush-Brown, Henry Kirke
Calder, Alexander Milne
Calder, Alexander Stirling
Calverley, Charles
Church, Henry
Clevenger, Shobal Vail
Cogdell, John
Connelly, Pierce Francis
Crawford, Thomas
Crayon, The
Dallin, Cyrus Edwin
Dexter, Henry
Frazee, John

French, Daniel Chester
Futurism
Gould, Thomas Ridgeway
Greenough, Horatio
Greenough, Richard
Hart, Joel Tanner
Hosmer, Harriet
Ives, Chauncey Bradley
Jackson, John Adams
Jones, Thomas Dow
King, John Crookshanks
Lachaise, Gaston
Lawrie, Lee
MacMonnies, Frederick
MacNeil, Hermon
Manship, Paul
Mead, Larkin
Mills, Clark
Nadelman, Elie
Neoclassicism
Niehaus, Charles
Palmer, Erastus Dow
Partridge, William Ordway
Pennsylvania Academy of the
    Fine Arts
Powers, Hiram
Proctor, A. Phimister
Remington, Frederick
Rimmer, William
Rinehart, William Henry
Rogers, John
Rogers, Randolph
Ruckstull, Frederic Wellington
Rush, William
Saint-Gaudens, Augustus
Simmons, Franklin
Skillin, Simeon, Sr.
Sterne, Maurice
Stone, Horatio
Story, William Wetmore
Taft, Lorado
Thompson, Launt
Volk, Leonard
Vonnoh, Bessie Potter
Warner, Olin
Whitney, Anne
Wright, Patience Lovell
Young, Mahonri

Sculpture: 1913 to date
Abstract Art
Agostini, Peter
André, Carl
Antonakos, Stephen
Apple, Billy
Armory Show, The
Art Deco
Art Students League
Assemblage
Automatism
Barnard, George Grey
Bartlett, Paul Wayland
Baskin, Leonard
Bell, Larry
Bladen, Ronald
Bontecou, Lee
Borglum, Gutzon
Borglum, Solon Hannibal
Bourgeois, Louise
Breer, Robert
Bush-Brown, Henry Kirke
Calder, Alexander
Calder, Alexander Stirling
Chamberlain, John
Chryssa
Collage
Concept Art
Conner, Bruce
Constructivism
Cornell, Joseph
Dada
Dallin, Cyrus Edwin
Davidson, Jo
de Creeft, José

Guide to Entries by Arts

de Rivera, José
Diller, Burgoyne
Di Suvero, Mark
Earth Art
Environmental Art
Ferber, Herbert
Flannagan, John Bernard
Flavin, Dan
French, Daniel Chester
Funk Art
Futurism
Gabo, Naum
Gallo, Frank
Goto, Joseph
Gross, Chaim
Gussow, Roy
Hague, Raoul
Happenings
Hard-Edge
Hare, David
Hoffmann, Malvina
Hudson, Robert
Insley, Will
Jennewein, Paul
Judd, Donald
Kienholz, Edward
Kinetic Sculpture
Kohn, Gabriel
Lachaise, Gaston
Lassaw, Ibram
Laurent, Robert
Lawrie, Lee
Lebrun, Rico
Lee, Arthur
Levine, Les
Lewitt, Sol
Liberman, Alexander

Light Sculpture
Lipchitz, Jacques
Lippold, Richard
Lipton, Seymour
Lye, Len
MacMonnies, Frederick
MacNeil, Hermon
Manship, Paul
Marisol Escobar
McCracken, John
Milkowski, Antoni
Milles, Carl
Morris, Robert
Nadelman, Elie
Nakian, Reuben
Nauman, Bruce
Neoclassicism
Nevelson, Louise
Niehaus, Charles
Nivola, Constantino
Noguchi, Isamu
Oldenburg, Claes
Paris, Harold Persico
Pennsylvania Academy of the
    Fine Arts
Pop Art
Proctor, A. Phimister
Rhodes, Daniel
Rickey, George
Robus, Hugo
Rohm, Robert
Rosati, James
Roszak, Theodore
Ruckstull, Frederic Wellington
Samaras, Lucas
Savage, Eugene Francis
Segal, George

Seley, Jason
Serial Art
Serra, Richard
Smith, David
Smith, Tony
Smithson, Robert
Snelson, Kenneth
Sonnier, Keith
Stankiewicz, Richard
Sterne, Maurice
Storrs, John
Sugarman, George
Taft, Lorado
Trova, Ernest
Truitt, Anne
Vonnoh, Bessie Potter
Voulkos, Peter
Warneke, Heinz
Weber, Max
Westermann, Horace Clifford, Jr.
Whitman, Robert
Wilmarth, Chris
WPA (Works Progress Administration) Federal Art Project
Young, Mahonri
Zorach, William

Silver
Antique Silver (see Silver)
Art Deco
Art Nouveau (see Silver)
Baroque (see Silver)
Black, Starr & Frost
Blanck, Jurian, Jr.
Burt, John, Samuel, William,
    and Benjamin

Church Silver
Coin Silver
Coney, John
Dummer, Jeremiah
Eclecticism (see Silver)
Farnham, Paulding
Fletcher, Thomas
Gardiner, Sidney
Gorham Company
Hull, John
Humphreys, Richard
Hurd, Jacob, Nathaniel, and
    Benjamin
Kirk, Samuel
Liberty Bowl
Martelé
Modern Silver (see Silver)
Moore, Edward C.
Moultons, The
Myers, Myer
Neoclassical Silver (see Silver)
Onckelbag, Gerrit
Pine Tree Shillings
Reed & Barton
Revere, Paul
Rich, Obadiah
Richardson, Francis, Joseph,
    Joseph Jr., and Nathaniel
Rococo (see Silver)
Rococo Revival (see Silver)
Silver Marks
Syng, Philip, Jr.
Tiffany & Company
Towle Company
Van der Burch, Cornelius
Van Dyck, Peter
Winslow, Edward

Abbreviations of Museums and Collections

Abby Aldrich Rockefeller	Abby Aldrich Rockefeller Collection of American Folk Art, Williamsburg, Va.
Addison	Addison Gallery of American Art, Phillips Academy, Andover, Mass.
Albany	Albany Institute of History and Art, Albany, N.Y.
Albright-Knox	Albright-Knox Gallery, Buffalo, N.Y.
Baltimore	Baltimore Museum of Art, Baltimore, Md.
Boston	Museum of Fine Arts, Boston, Mass.
Brooklyn	Brooklyn Museum, Brooklyn, N.Y.
Butler	Butler Institute of American Art, Youngstown, Ohio
Carnegie	Museum of Art, Carnegie Institute, Pittsburgh, Pa.
Carter	Amon Carter Museum of Western Art, Fort Worth, Texas
Chicago	Art Institute of Chicago, Chicago, Ill.
Cincinnati	Cincinnati Art Museum, Cincinnati, Ohio
Cleveland	Cleveland Museum of Art, Cleveland, Ohio
Columbus	Columbus Gallery of Fine Arts, Columbus, Ohio
Corcoran	Corcoran Gallery of Art, Washington, D.C.
Corning	Corning Museum of Glass, Corning, N.Y.
Dallas	Dallas Museum of Fine Arts, Dallas, Texas
Delgado	Isaac Delgado Museum of Art, New Orleans, La.
Des Moines	Des Moines Art Center, Des Moines, Iowa
de Young	M. H. de Young Memorial Museum, San Francisco, Cal.
Fogg	Fogg Art Museum, Harvard University, Cambridge, Mass.
Folk Art	Museum of American Folk Art, New York, N.Y.
Fort Worth	Fort Worth Art Center Museum, Fort Worth, Tex.
Freer	Freer Gallery of Art, Washington, D.C.
Garbisch Coll.	Garbisch Collection, National Gallery of Art, Washington, D.C.
Gardner	Isabella Stewart Gardner Museum, Boston, Mass.
Guggenheim	Solomon R. Guggenheim Museum, New York, N.Y.
Harvard	Harvard University, Cambridge, Mass.
Heyward-Washington	Heyward-Washington House, Charleston, S.C.
Hirshhorn	Joseph H. Hirshhorn Collection, New York, N.Y. and Washington, D.C.
International Museum of Photography	George Eastman House, Rochester, N.Y.
Johnson Coll.	Johnson Collection of Contemporary Crafts, Racine, Wis.
Joslyn	Joslyn Art Museum, Omaha, Neb.
Los Angeles	Los Angeles County Museum, Los Angeles, Cal.
Louvre	Louvre Museum, Paris, France.
Museum of New York	Museum of the City of New York, N.Y.
Metropolitan	Metropolitan Museum of Art, New York, N.Y.
Minneapolis	Minneapolis Institute of Arts, Minneapolis, Minn.
Modern Museum	Museum of Modern Art, New York, N.Y.
National Coll.	National Collection of Fine Arts, Smithsonian Institution, Washington, D.C.
New York Historical	New York State Historical Association, Cooperstown, N.Y.
New York Hist.	New-York Historical Society, New York, N.Y.
MESDA	Museum of Early Southern Decorative Arts, Winston-Salem, N.C.
Pasadena	Pasadena Museum of Modern Art, Pasadena, Cal.
Peabody	Peabody Museum, Salem, Mass.
Pennsylvania	Pennsylvania Academy of the Fine Arts, Philadelphia, Pa.
Philadelphia	Philadelphia Museum of Art, Philadelphia, Pa.
Phillips	Phillips Memorial Gallery, Washington, D.C.
Proctor	Munson-Williams-Proctor Institute, Utica, N.Y.
Santa Barbara	Santa Barbara Museum of Art, Santa Barbara, Cal.
San Diego	San Diego Fine Arts Gallery, San Diego, Cal.
San Francisco	San Francisco Museum of Art, San Francisco, Cal.
Seattle	Seattle Art Museum, Seattle, Wash.
Shelburne	Shelburne Museum, Shelburne, Vt.
Smithsonian	Smithsonian Institution, Washington, D.C.
St. Louis	City Art Museum of St. Louis, St. Louis, Mo.
Tate	Tate Gallery, London, England.
Toledo	Toledo Museum of Art, Toledo, Ohio.
Wadsworth	Wadsworth Atheneum, Hartford, Conn.
Walker	Walker Art Center, Minneapolis, Minn.
Wallace	Wallace Collection, London, England
Walters	Walters Art Gallery, Baltimore, Md.
Washington	National Gallery of Art, Washington, D.C.
Whitney	Whitney Museum of American Art, New York, N.Y.
Wichita	Wichita Art Museum, Wichita, Kan.
Williamsburg	Colonial Williamsburg, Williamsburg, Va.
Winterthur	Henry Francis du Pont Winterthur Museum, Winterthur, Del.
Worcester	Worcester Art Museum, Worcester, Mass.
Yale	Yale University Art Gallery, New Haven, Conn.

Guide to Museums and Public Collections

Andover, Mass. Addison Gallery of American Art, Phillips Academy.
Opened 1931. The permanent collection is exclusively American and includes furniture, silver, glassware, figureheads, and signs as well as paintings. The paintings begin in the colonial period with Smibert and include West, Allston, Stuart, Morse, and members of the Hudson River School. There are also outstanding holdings of Eakins, Homer, and Ryder and works by Bellows, Glackens, Hassam, Hopper, Luks, Prendergast, and Whistler. Among 20th-century artists are Pollock, Andrew Wyeth, and Sheeler.

Baltimore, Md. Baltimore Museum of Art.
Founded 1916; present building opened 1929. The extensive collection of the work of American artists and craftsmen, with emphasis on objects produced in Maryland, is exhibited in period rooms. Included are paintings by Hesselius, members of the Peale family, and Wollaston, as well as the works of various cabinetmakers and silversmiths. Among the non-Maryland painters are Allston, Burchfield, Cassatt, Eakins, Feininger, Hartley, Hofmann, Homer, Inness, Knaths, Marin, Motherwell, Still, Shahn, Tobey, and Weber; among the sculptors are Flannagan, Lachaise, Lipchitz, Nadelman, and David Smith. There is also a large collection of American prints. On the grounds is a spring house designed by the early American architect Latrobe.

Baltimore, Md. Peale Museum.
Established in 1814 as "Peale's Baltimore Museum and Gallery of Fine Arts." It became the Municipal Museum of the City of Baltimore in 1931. It contains maps, engravings, lithographs, paintings, and artifacts relating to the history of Baltimore, but it is most famous for its paintings by members of the Peale family, including C. W. Peale's *Exhuming of the Mastodon,* Rembrandt Peale's *Roman Daughter,* and Sarah Miriam Peale's *Self Portrait.*

Baltimore, Md. Walters Art Gallery.
Founded 1931. In addition to its notable collection of European medieval art, it has paintings and sculpture by Durand, Elliot (4), Eastman Johnson, Rinehart (9), Stuart, Woodville (5), and others, and glass by Tiffany.

Boston, Mass. Isabella Stewart Gardner Museum.
Opened 1903. It is best known for its collection of European paintings, prints, sculpture, furniture, and the decorative arts originally acquired by Mrs. Gardner, but it also has works by a number of American artists, notably Sargent (20) and Whistler (11). Other American artists in the collection include Blackburn, Cox, Dewing, Hassam, Hunt, La Farge, Manship, Sully, and Twachtman, and the cabinetmaker Duncan Phyfe.

Boston, Mass. Museum of Fine Arts.
Established in 1870 as an outgrowth of the fine arts collections of the Boston Athenaeum. In 1876 the collections were installed in a building on Copley Square designed in the Gothic tradition. The present building was completed in 1909. A major acquisition (in 1945) was the Karolik Collection of American paintings covering the period from 1815 to 1865. Today the museum has great strength in American art from the colonial portraitists almost until the present. The paintings, in addition to fifty Gilbert Stuarts, include works by Allston, Alexander, Bard, Bierstadt, Birch, Blackburn, Brush, Cassatt, Copley, Cropsey, Doughty, Durrie, Field, Francis, Hardy, Harnett, Heade, Homer, Hunt, Inman, Eastman Johnson, Lane, Neagle, Peto, Pelham, Rimmer, Henry Sargent, J. S. Sargent, Sully, Sloan, Thompson, Trumbull, Vedder, and Whittredge. There is sculpture by Rickey and Rimmer, among others; architectural drawings by Alexander Jackson Davis in the print collection; and furniture by Goddard, Seymour, McIntire, and H. H. Richardson. The silver includes work by Coney and a room devoted to native son Paul Revere. The period rooms of American decorative art range from 1673 to 1800.

Brooklyn, N.Y. Brooklyn Museum.
Opened 1897. Best known for its American art, the collection includes the early anonymous *Van Cortland Boys* and works by such 18th- and 19th-century painters as Bingham, Blakelock, Blythe, Church, Cole, Copley, Eakins, Feke, Guy, Edward Hicks, Homer, Inness, Johnson, Peale, Peto, Quidor, and Ryder. Among the 20th-century artists represented are Benton, Glackens, Hartigan, Hopper, Knaths, Levine, Nevelson, Rivers, Shahn, Sheeler, and Sloan. It also has more than 200 watercolors, with 18 Homers among them, as well as prints and drawings by Baskin, Cassatt, Feininger, Gorky, Homer, John Paul Jones, Marin, and Peterdi. The sculpture includes work by Hiram Powers, such moderns as Lachaise and Lipton, and a sculpture garden for

American architectural ornaments from demolished buildings. Among the decorative arts is a complete Dutch Colonial house (Schenk House, 1675), an 18th-century dining room, a 19th-century parlor, and a wide range of glass (especially Tiffany), silver, pewter, and ceramics. The Victorian rooms include a "Moorish parlor" from a Rockefeller mansion.

Brunswick, Me. Bowdoin College Museum of Art.
The original collection of American portraits was established in 1811 by James Bowdoin III. The Walker Art Building, designed by McKim, was erected in 1894 and has murals by Cox, La Farge, Thayer, and Vedder. The collection contains portraits (many of the Bowdoin family) by Badger, Blackburn, Copley, Earl, Feke, Joshua Johnston, King, Malbone, Smibert, Stuart, Sully, and Trumbull.

Buffalo, N.Y. Albright-Knox Gallery.
The Albright Gallery opened in 1905; the Knox wing, designed by Gordon Bunshaft of Skidmore, Owings & Merrill, was added in 1962. It has one of the largest collections of late 19th- and 20th-century art in America. The museum owns works by such 19th-century artists as Bierstadt, Edward Hicks, Homer, Inness, and Ryder, and such early 20th-century painters as Bellows, Burchfield, Demuth, and Spencer. The contemporary painting collection includes Baziotes, Gottlieb, Gorky, Guston, Kline, Marca-Relli, Motherwell, Pollock, Rothko, Still, and Tworkov. Contemporary sculpture includes works by Baskin, Dine, Lachaise, Lipchitz, Marisol, Milkowski, Nakian, Nevelson, Noguchi, and Tony Smith.

Cambridge, Mass. Fogg Art Museum, Harvard University.
The first museum built to hold Harvard's art collection, which had been assembled over 250 years, was opened in 1895. It moved to its present site in 1927. A passage now links it to the art school, which was designed by Le Corbusier, the only work he did in America. It is the largest university art collection in the world. Its print division contains 50,000 pieces and is second, in the United States, only to the Metropolitan Museum of Art. Among the paintings are many of J. S. Copley's finest works.

Chicago, Ill. Art Institute of Chicago.
Organized in 1882, the museum moved in 1893 into a building erected for the World's

Columbian Exposition. The American painting and sculpture collection starts with Feke, Copley, Stuart, and Sully and includes such significant 19th- and early 20th-century artists as Cassatt, Eakins, Glackens, Harnett, Hartley, Hassam, Homer, Inness, Neagle, Remington, Sargent, Vedder, and Whistler. The modern and contemporary collection has work by Albright, Blume, Alexander Calder, de Kooning, Gorky, Hofmann, Hopper, Kent, Levine, O'Keeffe, Pollock, Rothko, Still, Wood, and Andrew Wyeth. Among the decorative arts are various period rooms and examples of silver by Vanderburgh.

Cincinnati, Ohio. Cincinnati Art Museum.
Opened in 1886, this is the oldest general art museum west of the Alleghenies. From its beginning, the museum has emphasized American art, with a strong emphasis on 19th-century painting, sculpture, and decorative arts. It contains paintings by Blakelock, Cassatt, Chase, Hassam, Homer, Inness, C. W. Peale, Sargent, West, and Whistler; with sculpture by Clevenger, Gutzon Borglum, John Rogers, and Saint-Gaudens. It has an outstanding collection of Ohio glassware and ceramics. The 20th-century collection includes work by Barnett and Hofmann, and sculptures by Alexander Calder, Lipchitz, and David Smith. There is a collection of Cincinnati-related artists including Dine, Duncanson, Duveneck, Henri, Powers, Twachtman, and Wesselman.

Cincinnati, Ohio. Taft Museum.
Opened 1932. It contains paintings by J. W. Alexander, Duncanson (8), Duveneck, Sargent, and Whistler, sculpture by Barnard and Powers (3), and 25 pieces of furniture by Duncan Phyfe.

Cleveland, Ohio. Cleveland Museum of Art.
Opened 1916. A new wing, designed by Marcel Breuer, was opened in 1968. Almost every important American painter and sculptor is represented, including 18th- and 19th-century figures such as Allston, Blackburn, Cassatt, Chase, Church, Cole, Copley, Duveneck, Eakins, Feke, Heade, Edward Hicks, Homer, Inness, Johnson, Kensett, La Farge, Smibert, Stuart, Sully, West, and Whistler. From the 20th century there are paintings by Bellows, Burchfield, Cornell, Stuart Davis, de Kooning, Edwin Dickinson, Feininger, Glackens, Graves, Guston, Hart, Hartley, Hassam, Hofmann, Hopper, Keller, Kelly, Lindner, Luks, Marin, Motherwell, Noguchi, Prendergast, Rothko, Sloan, Sommer, Tworkov, Weber, and Weir, and sculpture by Flannagan, Lipchitz, and Roszak. Among the silver in the museum are pieces by Burt, Hurd, and Winslow, and a pair of spurs by Paul Revere.

Columbus, Ohio. Columbus Gallery of Fine Arts.
Opened 1931. The American collection is particularly strong in works of modernists of the 1910–30 period. It features a large group of paintings by George Bellows, a native of Columbus, and a group of early 20th-century watercolors, with 28 by Marin, 28 by Demuth, and 14 by Prendergast.

Corning, N.Y. Corning Museum of Glass.
Housed in the Corning Glass Center, this is one of the world's most comprehensive collections of glass, with nearly 13,000 pieces. The American collection includes work by Amelung, the Boston & Sandwich Glass Company, Tiffany, and Steuben. The museum also has an extensive library on the art of glassmaking and the history of glass.

Dallas, Tex. Dallas Museum of Fine Arts.
Opened 1936. It contains works by some early American painters but the strongest American section is from the 20th century: it includes works by Bellows, Bontecou, Dine, Gottlieb, Hopper, Motherwell, and Andrew Wyeth, and sculpture by Nevelson.

Denver, Col. Denver Art Museum.
Founded 1893. Its American Indian collection covers tribes from the Southwest to the Northwest coast. There is also a large gallery of the religious folk art works called *santos*. The colonial American art includes Copley, C. W. Peale, Stuart, West, and the 19th century is represented by Bierstadt, Homer, Ryder, and Whistler, among others.

Des Moines, Iowa. Des Moines Art Center.
Founded 1948. Its American collection emphasizes 20th-century painting and sculpture, with representative works by Bellows, Chase, Davis, Dove, Hartley, Hassam, Henri, Hopper, Kelly, Johns, Kuniyoshi, Lichtenstein, MacDonald-Wright, Marin, Oldenburg, Prendergast, Rauschenberg, Rivers, Shahn, Sloan, Storrs, and Weber. Among the 19th-century artists are Cassatt, Homer, and Stuart. There are also works by such contemporary sculptors as Alexander Calder and David Smith.

Detroit, Mich. Detroit Institute of Arts.
Founded 1885; present building opened 1927. It is one of the two municipally owned, major art museums. The American collection has approximately 1500 paintings, 200 sculptures, 200 pieces of furniture, 270 of silver, 50 of pewter, 330 of glass, and 270 of ceramics—exhibited chiefly in period rooms. Noteworthy among the museum's 18th- and 19th-century holdings are: Allston (4), Badger (3), Bierstadt (9), Bingham (3), Cassatt, Catlin, Chase (11), Cole (19), Copley (10), Dewing (3), Duncanson (6), Durand, Duveneck (3), Eakins (5), Flannagan (4), Fuller, Heade (3), Hesselius (3), Homer (7), Hunt (3), Hurd (4), Inness (5), Jarvis (4), Eastman Johnson (3), Kensett, La Farge (5), Martin (3), Myer Myers (3), C. W. Peale (3), Rembrandt Peale (6), Powers, Revere (5), Randolph Rogers (3), Saint-Gaudens (4), Sargent (7), Smibert, Stanley (14), Stuart, Sully (3), Tiffany, Trumbull (3), Tryon (4), Twachtman (4), Vedder, J. A. Weir, R. Weir (4), West (4), Whistler (5), Whittredge, and Wyant (4). The 20th-century painters and sculptors include Bellows, Gutzon Borglum (3), Solon H. Borglum (7), Burchfield (4), Alexander Calder, Davies, Demuth, Eilshemius, Feininger (9), Glackens, Graves (11), Hartley, Hassam, Henri, Hofmann, Kuhn, Lachaise, Lipchitz, Luks, MacIver (3), Manship (5), Marin (10), Melchers (13), Jerome Myers, Nadelman, Prendergast, Shahn, David Smith, Sloan, and Weber (6).

Fort Worth, Tex. Amon Carter Museum of Western Art.
Founded 1961. The original collection consisted primarily of works by Remington and Russell, along with a number of lesser western artists. It has been broadened to include many of the visual frontiers in American art as well as in American history, and now contains paintings by such 20th-century artists as Baskin, Dove, Hartley, Kuhn, O'Keeffe, Shahn, and Sheeler.

Fort Worth, Tex. Fort Worth Art Center Museum.
Building completed 1954. It has over 150 American paintings including works by such 19th-century artists as Inness and Eakins, and, from the 20th century, Sloan, Avery, Cadmus, O'Keeffe, Rothko, Shahn, Still, and Weber. It also has 500 prints, including works by Albers (12), Hassam (30), Johns (10), and Warhol (10); and contemporary sculpture by Judd and Oldenburg.

Hartford, Conn. Wadsworth Atheneum.
Opened in 1844, it is one of the oldest continuously operated museums in the United States. The original Tudor Gothic building was designed by Ithiel Town and Alexander Jackson Davis at the instigation of Daniel Wadsworth, brother-in-law to the painter, John Trumbull. In addition to a large collection of European work, the museum houses work by Earl, Copley, Cole (15), and Bierstadt. It also has outstanding collections of 17th-century furniture, inn signs, and pottery.

Indianapolis, Ind. Indianapolis Museum of Art.
Founded 1883; opened 1906. New building, 1970. A representative collection of more than 600 American paintings by artists ranging from the colonial period to the present. Notable are works by Bellows, Cassatt, Chase, Eakins, Homer, Indiana, C. W. Peale, Sargent, Shahn, Sloan, and Twachtman.

Ithaca, N.Y. Cornell University, The Herbert F. Johnson Museum of Art.
Formerly the Andrew Dickson White Museum, the name was changed in 1973, when the museum was moved to a new building designed by I. M. Pei. The print collection numbers 2200 and includes Baskin (210), Hassam (81), Marin (11), Pennell (168), and Whistler (89). There are paintings by Avery, Bierstadt, Davies, Dove, Eilshemius, Gottlieb, Hofmann, Kensett, and Rauschenberg, among others, and sculpture by Baskin, Bontecou, Lipton, Rhodes, Saint Gaudens, and Zorach. The glass collection includes 115 pieces by Tiffany and 2 stained glass windows by Frank Lloyd Wright.

Los Angeles, Cal. Los Angeles County Museum
Organized originally in 1913, it was moved in 1965 to a new complex of buildings designed by William Pereira. William Randolph Hearst made the museum a significant foundation with his contributions during the 1940s. Today the museum has paintings by Bellows, Stuart Davis, Hartley, Lebrun, Motherwell, Rothko and Pollock, as well as three mobiles by Alexander Calder, among its 20th-century works.

Milwaukee, Wis. Milwaukee Art Center.
Opened 1957. In a building designed by Eero Saarinen, collections from two smaller Milwaukee art institutes were combined, bringing together paintings by Rembrandt Peale, Blakelock, Inness, Homer, Henri, Demuth, and Shahn, among others, as well as a large collection of contemporary European artists.

Minneapolis, Minn. Minneapolis Institute of Arts.
Opened 1915. The museum contains a representative collection of more than 100 American painters, including works from the 19th-century by Copley, Eakins, Jarvis, Parrish, Peto, Sargent, Stuart, Twachtman, and West: and from the 20th century by Bellows, de Kooning, Feininger, Guston, Lawson, Prendergast, Rivers, Stella, and Wesselmann. The museum's print collection contains approximately 750 prints, including examples by Revere, Cassatt, Whistler, Bellows, Shahn, Dine, Rauschenberg, and Warhol. There is sculpture by Flannagan and Powers, a Calder mobile, and work by Rickey. The museum also has the only complete silver tea service by Paul Revere.

Minneapolis, Minn. Walker Art Center.
Opened 1926; new building, designed by Edward Larrabee Barnes, opened 1970. Known for its temporary exhibitions and its contemporary collection, this museum holds works by Stuart Davis, Brooks, Frank Stella, Gottlieb, and Baziotes, with sculpture by Noguchi, David Smith, Tony Smith, and Chryssa.

New Haven, Conn. Yale University Art Gallery.
The oldest university art museum in America. Yale was collecting American painting as early as 1750, although it had no museum building until the Trumbull Gallery was founded in 1832. This gallery was designed by the painter John Trumbull, who also donated a large group of his works. The Yale Art School was founded in 1864. The gallery went into its latest building in 1928. A wing, designed by Louis Kahn, was added in 1953. Its collection is particularly rich in colonial and early 19th-century art, including work by Blackburn, Earl, Morse, Smibert, Stuart, West, Wollaston, as well as many paintings by Eakins, Homer, and Sargent. Twentieth-century artists include Bellows, Hopper and Motherwell, among others. It also houses an outstanding collection of silver (the Garvan) and furniture.

Newark, N.J. Newark Museum.
Founded 1909; opened 1926. It has a representative collection of approximately 2000 paintings, 250 sculptures, 600 pieces of furniture, 450 of silver, 50 of pewter, 700 of glass, 1000 of ceramics. It includes paintings by Bierstadt (6), Cropsey (3), Durand, Earl, Heade, O'Keeffe, C. W. Peale, James Peale (3) and Joseph Stella (8), and sculpture by Gutzon Borglum.

New Orleans, La. Isaac Delgado Museum of Art.
Opened 1911. Its American collection includes works by such painters as Baziotes,

G. L. Brown, Davies, Durand, Gottlieb, Hare, Henri, Hofmann, Speicher, and Tanner. Also on exhibition is an extensive collection of American glass.

New York, N.Y. Solomon R. Guggenheim Museum.
A major museum of modern art, it is located on Fifth Avenue at 89th Street. The building, designed by Frank Lloyd Wright, is one of the most discussed examples of 20th-century museum design, with galleries organized on a continual flowing spiral ramp around a central courtyard. In the mid-1920s, influenced by a young German painter, Baroness Hilda Rebay, Mr. Guggenheim put together one of the first notable groups of 20-century European paintings in the United States. In 1939 the Solomon R. Guggenheim Collection of Nonobjective Paintings was opened on East 54th Street. It was moved to its present location in 1959. During the 1950s and 1960s important work by European and American abstract artists were purchased. The American collection includes works by Albright, Baziotes, Bolotowsky, Brooks, Alexander Calder, Chamberlin, Cornell, Crawford, Gene Davis, Stuart Davis, de Kooning, Demuth, Dine, Dove, Eilshemius, Feeley, Feininger, Ferber, Flavin, Francis, Gatch, Gottlieb, Graves, Balcomb Greene, Guston, Hare, Hartley, Hofmann, Inness, Kelly, Kline, Knaths, Lichtenstein, Louis, McCracken, MacIver, Marca-Relli, Kyle Morris, Robert Morris, Jan Muller, Noguchi, Noland, Oliveira, Parker, Pereira, Pollock, Rauschenberg, Ray, Samaras, Sargent, Serra, David Smith, Stankiewicz, Joseph Stella, Trova, Tworkov, and Warhol.

New York, N.Y. Metropolitan Museum of Art.
Founded 1870; opened 1880. The American Wing of the Metropolitan is the prototype of all museum installations of the American decorative arts. Originating with the Museum's exhibition of "American Art to 1815," organized for the Hudson-Fulton Celebration of 1909, the Wing now consists of 35 chronologically arranged period rooms containing approximately 950 pieces of furniture, 850 of silver, 200 of pewter, 1900 of glass, and 650 of ceramics. All major American craftsmen are represented. The Wing also contains some early American paintings and sculpture; the Museum's total holdings of these works represent most of the artists in this encyclopedia.

In the Department of Painting and Sculpture, major holdings (more than three) of works created before 1900 include: Alexander (4), Bartlett (6), Bierstadt (5), Blakelock (7), Brush (4), Cassatt (9), Chase (11), Cole (6), Copley (10), Cropsey (5), Durand (9), Eakins (10), Earl (4), Elliott French (5), Fuller (4) Harding (4), Harnett (5), Hassam (8), Healy (5), Homer (17), Hunt (9), Huntington (9), Inman (5), Inness (11), Jarvis (7), Eastman Johnson (7), Kensett (22), La Farge (4), MacMonnies (5), Martin (5), Mount (6), Powers (4), Proctor (5), Remington (14), Richards (4), Rogers (3), Ryder (10), Saint-Gaudens (20), Sargent (38), Smibert (4), Stuart (26), Sully (16), Thayer (4), Theus (4), Trumbull (7), Tryon (4), Twachtman (4),

Vanderlyn (7), Vedder (4), Waldo (14), Ward (4), Warner (8), J. A. Weir (4), West (10), Whistler (8), Wollaston (4), Wyant (7).

Major holdings (more than three) of works created since 1900 include: Albers (16), Bellows (13), Blume (4), Burchfield (7), Alexander Calder (4), Davies (12), Demuth (22), Dove (34), Du Bois (6), Eilshemius (11), Feininger (5), Grosz (10), Hartley (18), Henri (5), Hopper (8), Kuhn (6), Kuniyoshi (4), Lachaise (12), Manship (10), Marin (73), Marsh (7), Motherwell (17), O'Keeffe (42), Shinn (8), Speicher (17), Sloan (6), Stamos (4), Joseph Stella (6), Tobey (6), and Andrew Wyeth (7).

New York, N.Y. Museum of American Folk Art.
The opening of this museum in 1963 indicated the revived interest in American painting, sculpture, and the decorative arts of the common man. The museum houses portraits by colonial limners, Pennsylvania Dutch furniture, weathervanes (including that of Chief Tammany), New Mexican *santos,* New England gravestone rubbings, Shaker craft whirligigs, decoys, and samplers. It also has a large library on American folk arts.

New York, N.Y. Museum of the City of New York.
Founded 1923; opened 1931. Devoted to the social, economic, and political history of New York City. It contains paintings, prints, sculpture, and photographs. Outstanding among the holdings are 2885 Currier and Ives prints. It also has paintings by Ames, Audubon, Birch, Stuart, and Wollaston; sculpture by Beecher and MacMonnies; furniture by Belter, Blank, Lannuier, Phyfe, and Wynkoop; and glass by Tiffany.

New York, N.Y. Museum of Modern Art.
Founded in 1929 to acquire "the best modern works of art." Its permanent holdings now run to more than 3000 paintings and sculptures, 1600 drawings, 10,000 prints, 800 books illustrated by modern masters, 250 theatrical designs, and uncounted posters, architectural drawings and models, photographs, films, and objects in the design collection. The museum's building was erected in 1939 but has since been greatly expanded.

Among the painters included in the collection are: Albright, Albers, Avery, Baziotes, Bellows, Benton, Berman, Blume, Brook, Brooks, Burchfield, Cadmus, Davies, Gene Davis, Demuth, Edwin Dickinson, Preston Dickinson, Dine, Dove, Du Bois, Duchamp, Eilshemius, Francis, Frankenthaler, Feininger, Gabo, Gatch, Glarner, Gorky, Gottlieb, Graves, Greene, Gropper, Gross, Grosz, Gorky, Guston, Hart, Hartigan, Hartley, Hirshfield, Hofmann, Hopper, Johns, Kane, Kantor, Kelly, Kline, de Kooning, Knaths, Kuhn, Kuniyoshi, Lawrence, Lebrun, Lichtenstein, Louis, MacDonald-Wright, MacIver, Marca-Relli, Marin, Motherwell, Newman, Noland, O'Keeffe, Pereira, Peto, Pickett, Pollock, Pousette-Dart, Prendergast, Rattner, Rauschenberg, Ray, Refregier, Reinhardt, Rivers, Rothko, Russell, Shahn, Sheeler, Spencer, Stamos, Stella, Still, Tchelitchew, Tomlin, Tworkov,

Walkowitz, Warhol, Weber, Wesselmann, Andrew Wyeth, and Yunkers. It has sculpture by Bourgeois, Calder, Cornell, Davidson, de Creeft, de Rivera, Ferber, Flavin, Hare, Judd, Lachaise, Laurent, Liberman, Lipchitz, Lipton, Nadelman, Nakian, Nevelson, Noguchi, Oldenburg, Roszak, Segal, David Smith, and Tony Smith.

The pioneer photography department of the museum, organized by Edward Steichen, has work by Abbott, Avedon, Callahan, Eakins, Evans, Frank, Hine, Käsebier, Lange, Muybridge, Siskind, Steicher, Stieglitz, Strand, Weston, Clarence White, and Minor White.

New York, N.Y. New-York Historical Society.

Founded in 1804, the society moved into its present building in 1908. It has a very rich collection of early American art, including far more than just New York state. The collection comprises approximately 5000 paintings, 75,000 prints, furniture, silver, glass, and ceramics. Major holdings include paintings by Audubon (400), Bierstadt, Cole (21), Durand (74), Jarvis (25), Kensett, the Peale family, Stuart, Trumbull (7), and Wollaston (10); sculpture by Powers and John Rogers; silver by Hull and Sanderson, including the famous "pine tree shilling" of 1652; Duncan Phyfe furniture; a folk art collection consisting of paintings, weathervanes, cigar store Indians, and other objects; and a photography collection.

New York, N.Y. Whitney Museum of American Art.

Mrs. Gertrude Vanderbilt Whitney, a sculptor, first held informal exhibitions of American art and artists in her Greenwich Village studio in 1908. In 1914 she opened a gallery to exhibit the work of promising artists. Out of this grew the Whitney Studio Club, and, in 1930, the Whitney Museum of American Art, with Mrs. Whitney's collection of some 600 works as its nucleus. In 1954 the museum moved to a building adjoining that of the Museum of Modern Art; and in 1966 into its present building, designed by Marcel Breuer, located on Madison Avenue and 75th Street.

The Whitney's collection of 20th-century American painting, sculpture, and the graphic arts, close to 2600 items, is the largest of its kind. Among the painters represented are: Albers, Albright, Anuszkiewicz, Avery, Bacon, Baskin, Baziotes, Bellows, Benton, Berman, Bischoff, Bishop, Blume, Bohrod, Bolotowsky, Brook, Brooks, Burchfield, Cadmus, Carles, Curry, Dasburg, Davidson, Davies, Stuart Davis, Demuth, Edwin Dickinson, Preston Dickinson, Diebenkorn, Dine, Dove, Du Bois, Eilshemius, Esherick, Feininger, Ferber, Frankenthaler, Gatch, Glackens, Glarner, Gorky, Gottlieb, Graves, Gropper, Grosz, Guglielmi, Guston, Gwathmey, Hare, George O. Hart, Hartigan, Hartley, Henri, Hofmann, Hopper, Johns, Kane, Kantor, Kelly, Kent, Kline, Knaths, Kroll, Kuhn, Kuniyoshi, Laurent, Lawson, Leslie, Levine, Lewis, Lichtenstein, Lindner, Lipton, Luks, MacDonald-Wright, MacIver, Marca-Relli, Marin, Marsh, Kenneth Hayes Miller, Motherwell, Müller, Myers, O'Keeffe, Olitski, Peterdi, Pollock, Porter, Pousette-

Dart, Prendergast, Rattner, Rauschenberg, Ray, Refregier, Rivers, Robinson, Robus, Rosenquist, Roszak, Rothko, Schrag, Shahn, Shinn, Sheeler, Sloan, Isaac, Moses, and Raphael Soyer, Speicher, Spencer, Stankiewicz, Frank Stella, Sterne, Still, Tanguy, Tobey, Tomlin, Tworkov, Walkowitz, Warhol, Weber, Wood, Andrew Wyeth, Young, Yunkers, and Zox. The sculptors in the collection include Bell, Bontecou, Bourgeois, Alexander Calder, Chryssa, Cornell, de Creeft, Flavin, Gabo, Gross, Lachaise, Lebrun, Lipchitz, Nakian, Nevelson, Noguchi, Oldenburg, and Zorach.

Northhampton, Mass. Smith College Museum of Art.

Purchases of works of art began with the founding of the college in 1871. It now has over 570 paintings and drawings, including, among earlier American artists, Bierstadt, Church, Copley, Cropsey, Davies, Doughty, Durand, Eakins, Elmer, Heade, Homer, Innes, Kensett, Ryder, Sargent (8), and Tryon, and, in 20th-century art, Albers, de Kooning, Gottlieb, Hassam, Henri, Hopper, Kline, Marin, Maurer, Motherwell, Newman, O'Keeffe, Olitsky, Sheeler, Stella, and Andrew Wyeth. Its 400 prints range from early American to Albers, and the 37 pieces of sculpture include works by Saint-Gaudens, Baskin, and Calder. The museum also has a significant collection of Tiffany glass.

Oakland, Cal. Oakland Art Museum.

This museum, housed in a building designed by Kevin Roche, concentrates on the history of art in California. Its collection ranges from topographical drawings for railroad surveys of 1857 to landscape paintings by such 19th-century artists as Bierstadt. It also has work by contemporary California painters such as Bischoff and Diebenkorn.

Oberlin, Ohio. Allen Memorial Art Museum.

Opened 1917. The teaching museum of Oberlin College, it exhibits visual arts from ancient times to the present, including 71 American paintings and sculptures. Notable from the 19th century are works by Cole, Cropsey, Harnett, Kensett, Powers, and West; and in the 20th century, works by Diebenkorn, Gorky, Hart, Kline, and Poons.

Omaha. Neb. Joslyn Art Museum.

Opened 1931. Although it has European and other American works, its emphasis is on American artists of the western region, such as Catlin, Eastman, and A. J. Miller; Indian paintings are represented, as well as the complete set of watercolors done by Bodmer on an 1834 expedition among the Indians, led by Prince Maximilian of Wied. There are also paintings by Benton, Copley. Pollock, and Grant Wood.

Philadelphia, Pa. Historical Society of Pennsylvania.

Founded 1824. Approximately 4000 paintings, drawings, and prints, including work by Copley, Hesselius, members of the Peale family, Sully, and West. It also has sculpture, Philadelphia furniture, and 500 pieces of silver, chiefly by members of the Richardson family of silversmiths.

Philadelphia, Pa. Independence National Historical Park (Independence Hall).

Its 18th-century collection includes paintings by West, C. W. Peale, Rembrandt Peale, and Sully; prints by Birch, and sculpture by William Rush and Bellamy. It also has a fine collection of 18th-century furnishings, including 60 signed Windsor chairs, 80 pieces of silver by Syng and Richardson, wine bottles and glass decanters; and ceramics, including Pennsylvania slip ware, Queen's ware, and Chinese export porcelain.

Philadelphia, Pa. Pennsylvania Academy of the Fine Arts.

Founded 1805, it was the first art school in the United States. The present building was opened in 1876. In its collection (largely American) of 2500 paintings, 60,000 prints, and 20 sculptures are: paintings by Allston, Birch, Cassatt, Chase, Cropsey, Doughty, Durand, Eakins, Henri, Lawson, Luks, Neagle, the Peale family (51), Sloan, Stuart (28), Sully, John Vanderlyn, and West, and sculpture by Crawford, Greenough, Powers, and Rush.

Philadelphia, Pa. Philadelphia Museum of Art.

Built and opened over the years 1919 to 1928. Its major holdings are based on large, significant private collections that have been kept intact as they were donated, such as the J. G. Johnson Collection, the Gallatin Collection, and the Arensberg Collection. The last was started when Mr. and Mrs. Walter C. Arensberg were sufficiently impressed by the Armory Show of 1913 to buy work from it. The museum's collection of American painters concentrates on those relating to Philadelphia. Outstanding works are those by the Peale family and Eakins (over 60 paintings and drawings) and, from the 20th century, by Demuth, Kelly, Kline, Louis, Rauschenberg, and Sheeler. The museum owns three colonial Philadelphia houses—Mt. Pleasant, Cedar Grove, and the Letitia Street House—and has an extensive decorative arts collection. There are period rooms especially rich in Tucker china and Philadelphia Chippendale furniture, and the Geese Collection contains Pennsylvania Dutch folk art. Examples of American dress from the 18th to the 20th centuries are also on display.

Richmond, Va. Virginia Museum of Fine Arts.

Opened 1936. The American collection includes portraits from colonial Virginia, among them the Ambler collection of portraits, and other 18th-century works, such as J. S. Copley's *Mrs. Isaac Royall*. The 19th century is represented by sculpture by Powers and paintings by Doughty and Morse. Among the 20th-century painters are Stuart Davis, Hopper, Guston, and Shahn; and among the sculptors, Lipchitz and Zorach. The museum also houses a set of Victorian Belter furniture.

Rochester, N.Y. Rochester Memorial Art Gallery, University of Rochester.

Opened 1913; one wing added in 1926 and another in 1968. The American collection began with primitive and colonial painters.

Guide to Museums and Public Collections

Its 19th-century collection contains works by such artists as Copley, Homer, Eakins, Ryder, and a painting done by George Catlin for a Colt firearms advertisement. From the 20th century it has paintings by members of The Eight and such artists as Weber, Hofmann, and Stuart Davis, and sculpture by Nadelman and Noguchi.

San Diego, Cal. Fine Arts Gallery of San Diego.
Opened 1926. Its collection of more than 700 paintings and drawings is strong in paintings by members of the Ash Can School. Represented in its 19th-century art are works by Bingham, Blackburn, Chase, Eakins, Johnson, Ammi Phillips, and in the 20th century by Bellows, Burchfield, Lawson, O'Keeffe, Prendergast, and Sloan. Its collection of 500 prints includes 25 works by Whistler, and among its 150 pieces of sculpture are works by Lachaise, Proctor, Remington, and David Smith. The silver collection contains pieces by Jacob Hurd.

San Francisco, Cal. California Palace of the Legion of Honor.
Patterned after the Palace of the Legion of Honor in Paris, the building was given to the city in 1924 by Mr. and Mrs. Adolph B. Spreckels. Its 19th-century American paintings include works by Bierstadt, Bingham, Blakelock, Chase, Church, Copley, Duveneck, Eakins, Eilshemius, Fuller, Harnett, Hassam, Homer, Hunt, Inness, Eastman Johnson, Prendergast, Sargent, Twachtman, and Whistler, and its 20th-century collection includes Avery, Bellows, Berman, Benton, Grosz, Knaths, Kuhn, Levine, Luks, Sheeler, Shahn, Weber, and Andrew Wyeth.

San Francisco, Cal. M. H. de Young Memorial Museum.
Founded 1895 by M. H. de Young, publisher of the San Francisco *Chronicle*. Its 19th-century American paintings include works by Ames, Badger, Blakelock, Cassatt, Copley, Cole, Cropsey, Doughty, Healy, Inness, Metcalf, Morse, Neagle, James Peale, Rembrandt Peale, Ryder, Stuart, Sully, Thayer, John Vanderlyn, and West. From the 20th century it has paintings by Bellows, Glackens, Hartley, Hassam, Henri, Maurer, Prendergast, Shinn, and Andrew Wyeth.

San Francisco, Cal. San Francisco Museum of Art.
Opened in its present location in 1935. Its strength is in contemporary painting, sculpture, and graphics. It is known for its temporary exhibitions but it has paintings by Pollock, Still, Calder, and Gene Davis in its permanent collection.

Sarasota, Fla. John and Mable Ringling Museum of Art.
Opened in 1930 in the former Ringling mansion, this collection includes much European baroque art, but also work by Bierstadt, Chase, Hassam, Huntington, Remington, Tobey, and West. It has a large collection of prints ranging from Homer and Whistler to Baskin, Alexander Calder, and Warhol. It also houses American circus objects dating back to 1793.

Seattle, Wash. Seattle Art Museum.
Opened 1923. Its chief holdings are works by artists from the area, such as Graves (73) and Tobey (28). Also represented are Cassatt, Chase, Church, Cropsey, Doughty, Sargent, and Twachtman from the 19th century, and Albers, Frankenthaler, Hartley, Marca-Relli, Marin, and Pollock from the 20th century.

Shelburne, Vt. Shelburne Museum.
Opened 1947. This group of old New England village structures consists of 33 buildings such as a schoolroom, a grocery, and a jail, and an authentic sidewheel paddleboat, assembled to show early American architecture and crafts. In one of its two new art museums, the Webb Gallery, it has over 200 American paintings, starting with Pieter Vanderlyn and an anonymous painting of George Washington. The 18th- and 19th-century collection includes works by Bierstadt, Church, Cole, Copley, Homer, Morse, C. W. Peale, Quidor, and Wollaston. It also has an outstanding folk art collection containing figureheads, weathervanes, signs, carousel figures, carved American eagles, and carved decoys.

Springfield, Mass. Museum of Fine Arts.
The American collection includes Field's *Historical Monument of the American Republic* and works by Homer as well as an important selection of 19th-century American prints.

Sturbridge, Mass. Old Sturbridge Village.
Opened 1946. A recreated rural New England village of the period 1790–1840, it consists of nearly forty major buildings, including homes, shops, and mills, furnished with both useful and decorative objects. The houses contain examples of furniture, glass, folk paintings and carvings, embroidery, costumes, and metalwork.

Toledo, Ohio. Toledo Museum of Art.
Opened 1912. Notable among more than 300 American paintings are works by such 18th- and 19th-century artists as Bierstadt, Chase, Cole, Copley, Doughty, Duveneck, Eakins, Earl, Greenwood, Harnett, Homer, Inness (6), La Farge (11), Morse, Smibert, Stuart (4), and Waldo, and by such 20th-century painters as Baziotes, Feininger, Hopper, Knaths, Reinhardt, Frank Stella, and Andrew Wyeth. Also on exhibit is the large Libby Collection of American glass.

Tulsa, Okla. Gilcrease Institute of American History and Art.
Opened 1949. Approximately 5000 paintings and drawings, chiefly by artists of the Old West, such as Bierstadt, Bodmer, Catlin (77), A. J. Miller, Remington (22), and Russell. It also has works by other 19th-century painters such as Church and Eakins as well as a number of sculptures by Remington, Russell, and others.

Tulsa, Okla. Philbrook Art Center.
Founded 1938. Its emphasis is on American Indian art, with more than 6000 ethnic items. It also has paintings by Copley, Hassam, and Lawson.

Utica, N.Y. Munson-Williams-Proctor Institute.
Founded 1935. It has nearly 1000 American paintings, prints, and sculptures from the 18th to 20th centuries. Its holdings include paintings or drawings by Baskin, Baziotes (5), Burchfield (22), Cole (4), Copley (5), Davies (21), de Creeft, Demuth (4), Dove (5), Gatch (4), Graves (5), Hopper, Kline, Marsh (5), Pollock (3), Powers, Prendergast (3), Rothko, Sheeler (3), Stamos (17), Tobey (7), Vedder (5), and sculpture by Calder, Lachaise, Lipchitz, Nadelman, and Zorach.

Washington, D.C. Corcoran Gallery of Art.
Opened 1871. It contains mainly American painting and sculpture from the pre-Revolutionary period to the present. There are two Gilbert Stuart portraits of George Washington and 13 portraits of other presidents. The paintings from the 18th and 19th centuries include works by Bierstadt, Copley, Eakins, Homer, Morse, James Peale, Sargent, Smibert, and members of the Hudson River School. Among the 20th-century artists are Anuszkiewicz, Bellows, Bontecou, Gene Davis, Diller, Glackens, MacIver, Lebrun, Prendergast, and Olitski. Notable among the 19th-century sculpture is Hiram Powers' *The Greek Slave*. The collection of drawings ranges from Copley in the early 19th century to contemporary examples.

Washington, D.C. Freer Gallery of Art.
Founded 1906; opened 1923. It is a bureau of the Smithsonian Institution. It is best known for its oriental art, acquired by the Detroit industrialist, Charles Lang Freer (1856–1919), under the stimulus of his artist friend, J. A. M. Whistler. Its American paintings and prints are also notable, including Whistler's *Peacock Room* and more than half of his life work (279 paintings and drawings, and 889 prints), and paintings by Dewing (44), Homer (4), Sargent (3), Thayer (16), Tryon (72), and others.

Washington, D.C. National Collection of Fine Arts
The National Collection of Fine Arts, a bureau of the Smithsonian Institution, derives from the Smithsonian's original art collection, established in 1846. In 1906 the collection was designated the National Gallery of Art. The title was transferred to the present National Gallery in 1937, and the older collection was renamed the National Collection of Fine Arts. Since 1968 it has been housed in the Old Patent Office Building (begun in 1836), which it shares with the National Portrait Gallery, another Smithsonian bureau. The collection, over 8000 pieces, consists chiefly of American art (painting, sculpture, graphic arts, miniatures, and some examples of the decorative arts) from the colonial period to the present. There are works by Blakelock (5), Hassam (17), Healy (8), Homer (3), Ryder (18), Saint-Gaudens (5), Thayer (23), and Twachtman (12). There are also large deposits of works by Moran, Manship, and Zorach, as well as the estate of Hiram Powers and 445 Catlin drawings and paintings. The collection of 102 paintings given by S. C. Johnson and Sons includes many postwar artists.

Washington, D.C. National Gallery of Art.
The National Gallery of Art, established by act of Congress in 1937 in response to a gift by Andrew Mellon, was opened in 1941. Its name was transferred from the bureau of the Smithsonian Institution, which became the National Collection of Fine Arts. The National Gallery's collections represent European and American painting, sculpture, and graphics from the Renaissance to the 20th century, with a secondary emphasis on the decorative arts. The American painting collection includes works by some two hundred artists from the colonial period to the present; its particular strength is in portraiture of the 18th and 19th centuries, and in naive painting. There are extensive holdings in the graphic arts, including lithographs from the Tamarind Press. American decorative arts are depicted in approximately 22,000 renderings and photographs in the Index of American Design. American painters represented by more than three works include: Badger (4), Bellows (6), Cassatt (7), Catlin (351), Chambers (4), Copley (10), Du Bois (4), Eakins (5), Earl (4), Field (6), Harding (4), Henri (4), Homer (4), Neagle (6), Rembrandt Peale (4), Phillips (7), Sargent (8), Stuart (33), Sully (16), Trumbull (4), West (7), Whistler (9), and Wollaston (4).

Washington, D.C. National Portrait Gallery.
A bureau of the Smithsonian Institution, it was established by Congress in 1962 as a museum for the exhibition of portraits and statues of men and women who have made significant contributions to American history and culture. Since its opening in the former Patent Office Building (which it shares with the National Collection of Fine Arts), it has acquired paintings or prints by Bingham, Catlin, Copley, Healy, Hesselius, Huntington, Jarvis, David Johnson, Eastman Johnson, King, Leutze, Neagle, Page, C. W. Peale, Rembrandt Peale, Pine, Pratt, Sargent, Sully, John Vanderlyn, West and others, and sculpture by Davidson, French, Greenough, Powers, Rush, and Saint-Gaudens.

Washington, D.C. Phillips Memorial Gallery.
Called "A Museum of Modern Art and its Sources," the building is the enlarged former home of Mr. and Mrs. Duncan Phillips and houses their collection of European and American painting and sculpture. Among works by the majority of significant American artists since 1900, the major holdings are: Avery (11), Burchfield (9), Davies (13), Dove (23), Eilshemius (16), Graves (7), Hartley (7), Knaths (23), Lawson (10), Marin (23), Jerome Myers (9), Prendergast (9) Sloan (12), and Weber (7).

Washington, D.C. United States Capitol Art Collection.
Contains approximately 744 works of American art. The paintings include portraits of two presidents, Jackson and Jefferson, by Sully, portraits of Washington by C. W. Peale, Rembrandt Peale, and Gilbert Stuart; and an anonymous portrait of Pocahontas. In addition to 128 portraits, there are 54 other paintings, 75 marble and bronze busts (including the Gutzon Borglum bust of Lincoln), 95 other statues (including one of Jefferson by Hiram Powers), and 165 frescoes, murals, and lunettes dealing with American history.

Wichita, Kan. Wichita Art Museum.
Opened 1935 on the basis of a bequest of Louise Caldwell Murdock for the purchase of American art. This collection has grown from 16 paintings in 1940 to nearly 1000 paintings, prints, sculptures, and works of decorative art. Its holdings include works by J. S. Copley, de Creeft (4), Demuth, Dove, Eakins, Grosz, Hartley, Hopper (4), Kuhn, Kuniyoshi (4), Marin (6), Poor, Prendergast (4), Shahn, Sheeler, and Sloan (4), and glass by Tiffany (15).

Williamsburg, Va. Abby Aldrich Rockefeller Collection of American Folk Art.
In 1939 Abby Aldrich Rockefeller donated her collection of American folk art to Colonial Williamsburg, where it had been on exhibition since 1935. In 1957 a building designed to house the collection was completed. Today it contains over 2000 objects from the 18th, 19th, and 20th centuries, including paintings, calligraphs, and fracturs, wood and metal sculptures, weathervanes, figureheads, and embroideries. Paintings include works by Edward Hicks, Hidley, and Ammi Phillips. There are also several reconstructed period rooms. In addition to the permanent collection, there are special folk art exhibitions each year.

Williamsburg, Va. Colonial Williamsburg.
Williamsburg was originally laid out between 1698 and 1705, and represented the emergence of the Georgian style in architecture while it retained medieval characteristics in terms of the height and decoration of buildings. In 1927 restoration was begun on this 18th-century capital of Virginia, financed by John D. Rockefeller, Jr. About 600 inappropriate buildings have been torn down or removed from the restoration area, 88 have been repaired and restored, and 300 have been completely rebuilt on their original sites. Fifty gardens have been designed according to 18th-century standards. Today Colonial Williamsburg represents the most

complete "living" museum in the world. (See also Abby Aldrich Rockefeller Collection of American Folk Art)

Williamstown, Mass. Sterling and Francine Clark Art Institute.
Opened 1955. The American collection was increased by purchases (including Homer's *The Bridle Path*) from the Whitney Museum when that museum restricted itself to 20th-century American art. The silver collection is the most distinguished in the country, including five pieces by Revere and a George III jug presented to Benjamin Franklin when he went to England to plead the cause of the colonies.

Winterthur, Del. Henry Francis du Pont Winterthur Museum.
Originally built in 1829 as a country residence for Antoine Biderman, it was inherited in 1927 by Henry Francis du Pont, who, enlarging it and adding greatly to his collection of American antiques, converted it into a public museum in 1951. It contains 125 period rooms and alcoves furnished with more than 50,000 objects made in or imported to America between 1640 and 1840. It houses a very large collection of furniture, glass, silver, pewter, and ceramics by America's leading craftsmen. In its rooms hang the work of such American painters and printmakers as Audubon, Badger, Birch, Copley, Claypoole, Durand, Feke, Greenwood, Guy, Hesselius, Edward Hicks, Hurd, C. W. Peale, James Peale, Pelham, Savage, Seymour, Stuart, Trumbull, West, William Williams, and Wollaston.

Worcester, Mass. Worcester Art Museum.
Opened 1898. It has more than 250 American paintings, prints, drawings, and sculptures from the 18th to 20th centuries. Its holdings in the earlier periods include Badger, Bierstadt, Blackburn, Blakelock (3), Durand (8), Earl, Gullagher, Homer (19), Hunt (4), Huntington, Inness (5), La Farge (5), Morse (2), C. W. Peale, Ryder (2), Sargent (16), Savage, Thomas Smith, Stuart, Whistler (7), and Wollaston, and in the 20th century, Davies (3), Hassam (5), and Hopper (4).

Youngstown, Ohio. Butler Institute of American Art.
Founded 1919. The collection comprises nearly 4000 paintings, drawings, prints, sculptures, and pieces of glass and ceramics. Major holdings in the 19th-century section include Cassatt, Eakins, and Whistler, and in the 20th century, Avery, Burchfield, Hopper, Kuniyoshi, Marsh, and Sloan.

Glossary

Acrylics. Water-based polymer paint. Compared to oil paint, acrylic paint is relatively odorless, dries rapidly, and because it is a plastic, has a great resistance to deterioration.

Amboina. A light, reddish-brown wood from the East Indies, used for veneers and inlay.

Annealing. In silvermaking, the reheating of the metal to keep it malleable while it is being shaped. In glassmaking, the gradual cooling of hot glass to render it less brittle.

Anthemion. A flower-and-leaf design derived from ancient Greek art; used as an ornamental motif in Greek revival architecture and on Empire furniture, silver, and glass.

Appliqué. In needlework, a decoration made by applying pieces of one material to the surface of another.

Aquatint. A method of engraving which, like etching, uses acid for biting into a metal plate; aquatint, however, is used to render tonal instead of linear effects.

Armature. Metal framework used in sculpture as a foundation or skeleton for clay or plaster modeling.

Assemblage. A work of art made up of an arrangement of various found objects and materials.

Atrium. In architecture, an open central court.

Axial proportions. Proportions that are symmetrical about an axis.

Axial vistas. In architecture, views laid out so that they are balanced on either side of a central line or axis.

Baccarat glass. Fine crystal glass from the factory of La Compagnie des Cristalleries de Baccarat in France.

Ball turning. The turning or shaping of a piece of wood to resemble a series of ball forms.

Balloon frame. A building frame in which the vertical structural elements extend from the foundation sill to the roof plate and hold all joists.

Baluster. One of a series of short supports of a balustrade or stair rail.

Band window. Windows forming a continuous band across one side of a building.

Banister chair. A chair with a back consisting of vertical spindles or rods and a horizontal top curving outward like the handrail on a banister.

Baroque. A 17th-century style characterized by an intensified naturalism, often florid, exuberant, and emotional, and by heavy and even grotesque ornamentation. In painting, the style emphasized the play of light on forms. It continued into the 18th century.

Batten shutter. A shutter made up of boards held by cleats or long strips of wood (battens).

Batter. In architecture, the receding upward slope of a wall.

Bearing-wall. In architecture, a wall which supports the structure.

Berlin work. Wool embroidery, so called from the patterned background and soft worsteds imported from Berlin.

Billethead scroll. A scroll or ornamental carving used in place of a figurehead at the bow of a ship.

Bind window. Windows forming a horizontal band around two or more sides of a building, thus "binding" it.

Bitumen. Mineral pitch formerly used in some pigments. It causes cracking and tends to soften in higher temperatures.

Black letter. A heavy-faced Gothic style of type or lettering used in early English and in German books.

Block and cylinder shape. A piece of wood shaped so that it has lengths that are cylindrical and lengths with flat sides.

Block-front piece. A chest of drawers or a desk characterized by a sunken center panel between raised panels.

Blown-three-mold glass. Glass with a design impressed by a three-part, hinged mold.

Board and batten. In architecture, a type of wood sheathing with the boards placed vertically and a thin strip nailed across the crack between one board and the next.

Bobbin turning. The turning or shaping of a piece of wood to resemble a series of spools or bobbins.

Bombe. The lower part of case furniture when it has a kettle shape.

Bone china. A hard, white, translucent chinaware, made from clay and containing much bone ash.

Boss. An ornamental knob or stud.

Bottle glass. Non-lead glass, turquoise or amber in color, used in liquor flasks.

Bow-shaped cresting rails. The top rail of a chair back having the shape of a violin bow.

Braze. To join two pieces of metal by means of a hard solder that has a high melting point.

Breakfront. In furniture, a large case piece with a projecting center section usually surmounted by a pediment.

Broach spire. In architecture, an octagonal spire on a square tower that has no parapet.

Bubble inclusion. Small bubbles of air that have been deliberately or accidentally trapped in glass during manufacture.

Bull's eye window. A small circular or oval window; or a window with panes of bull's eye glass, a primitive type of blown glass with a knob in its center formed by the blower's rod.

Burl veneer. A veneer that has been cut from the swellings on trees and therefore exhibits a swirling or mottled grain.

Butterfly table. A drop-leaf table with leaves supported by brackets shaped like a butterfly's wings.

Cabochon. A plain round or oval surface in furniture or silver.

Cabriole leg. A curved, tapering leg (usually in Queen Anne and Chippendale furniture) that ends in an outward-curving, ornamental foot.

Caliper stage. A stage with curved extensions jutting out on each side of the audience.

Calligraphic line. In graphics or painting, a line with the variety and flexibility of handwriting.

Cane. The inner pith of a palm, often woven and used as the back or as seat material in furniture forms.

Cann. An early term for a lidless, one-handled silver drinking vessel.

Canted leg. A chair leg that slopes outward.

Cantilever. In architecture, a projecting beam or other structure supported only at one end, ideally by a downward force behind a fulcrum.

Capital (of a skyscraper). The top stories of a skyscraper, comparable, decoratively, to the top, or capital, of a column.

Caryatid. A supporting column in the form of a female figure; developed in ancient Greece and since used in architecture and furniture.

Cartouche. A decorative motif in the form of a shield or partially unrolled scroll.

Case piece. In furniture, any form that serves as a container, such as a desk, a bookcase, or a dresser.

Cased glass. Glass with one or more layers of differently colored glass ground away in decorative patterns and revealing the underlying glass.

Cast. In sculpture, the metal or plaster poured into a mold.

Castellated. Pierced in a regular pattern, as on the parapets of fortified structures; used also as an ornamental device on Gothic revival furniture.

Casting. In sculpture, the process of duplicating a clay, wax, or plaster original in a metal such as bronze, by the use of a mold made from the original.

Caudle cup. A two-handled, deep bowl. Often gourd-shaped, it is used to serve a wine concoction called "caudle."

Chaise gondole. In furniture, a side chair with open back, solid center splat and top rail, and uprights curved forward to rest on the seat.

Chasing. A decoration on metal surfaces produced by a relatively blunt instrument that indents but does not cut into the surface.

Chamfer. To cut grooves or fluting; also to bevel.

Chest-on-frame. A chest of drawers, standing high off the floor on legs.

Chiaroscuro. In painting, the treatment of light and shadow and the contrast between them.

Chipcarving. In furniture, to decorate by carving soft wood with a knife or similar instrument.

Chromolithography. The process of printing multicolor lithographs with a different stone or plate for each color.

Chuck. A device for holding pewter while it is shaped into a form.

Cladding. A metal coating bonded onto another metal.

Claw-and-ball foot. In furniture, a foot shaped to resemble a claw clutching a ball.

Cloisonné. A kind of enamelware in which the decoration is formed by thin wires set on edge and separating the different colors of enamel.

Collage painting. A pictorial technique in which elements such as newsprint, photographs, hair, fabric, etc., are pasted on a surface; these are often combined with painting.

Collagraph. A print made from a block on which the design is built up in the manner of a collage.

Colonettes. In architecture, slim columns whose circumference is slight in proportion to their height.

Commercial vernacular. Architecture built by contractors rather than by architects, for commercial use.

Compass curve. In furniture, a curve that is part of a perfect circle made by a compass.

Console. A side table without back legs, but supported by one or more brackets fixed to a wall.

Copperplate. An engraving process in which a print is made from a design engraved on a copper plate; also the print made by this process.

Cornice. A projecting horizontal band of masonry, often carved or otherwise elaborated, that crowns or completes a building or wall.

Crackled. The surface of a painting which has developed a network of cracks because of deterioration of binding elements in the paint.

Crackle glaze. In ceramics, a glaze that has a pattern of cracks deliberately induced as a design effect.

Crenate lip. A rim of a cup or pitcher cut into rounded scallops.

Crenelated. In architecture, having a parapet with square indentations, as on a fort or castle.

Crest rail. The top rail of a chair back.

Cresting. An ornamental finish along the top of a wall or roof, often perforated.

Crocket. A carved, projecting ornament of curved and bent foliage, used on the sloping edge of spires and gables in Gothic revival architecture; sometimes also used to decorate furniture.

Cross bond. Bricks in a row laid alternately lengthwise and endwise.

Crown method. A glassblowing technique in which the glass is spun rapidly at the end of a rod and forms a disk with a knob of glass remaining in the center.

Curtain wall. A wall having no supportive function, but which divides the space in a building.

Curule chair. A chair or stool with a cross-base support, derived from the folding stool of a Roman magistrate.

Cutcard work. Decoration cut from thin silver sheets and applied to the surface of a piece of silver.

Cyclorama. A large composite picture shown on the walls of a cylindrical room or hall.

Cylinder method. A glassmaking method in which a cylinder is blown, the ends severed, and the cylinder then split and flattened to form a rectangular pane.

Cyma. A double curve used as ornament in architecture or furniture. A *cyma-recta* is concave above and convex below: a *cyma-reversa* is convex above and concave below.

Dado. The separately decorated lower portion of the wall of a room.

Daguerreotype. A photographic process, developed in France by Louis Daguerre, in which a silver or silver-covered copper plate is made sensitive to light by the action of chemicals.

Daub and wattle. Intertwined sticks and branches covered with clay and used as a wall filling.

Demilune stringing. In furniture, thin bands of wood in crescent shapes (*demilune*= half-moon), used as inlay.

Desk-on-frame. A desk standing on open legs, with no drawers below the working surface.

Dish cross. An 18th-century device for supporting dishes above a small flame while on a table.

Disk turning. A shaping or turning of a piece of wood to resemble a series of disks placed flat against each other.

Dovetail. To make an interlocking joint between two pieces, as in a mortise-and-tenon joint.

Drypoint. An engraving on copper plates made with a stout needle that produces furrows with raised edges that print with a characteristic soft line.

Dry plate. In photography, a plate sensitized with an emulsion of silver and dried before exposure.

Ebonized. Stained black, in imitation of ebony.

Egg-and-dart molding. A convex molding with a design resembling alternately an egg and a dart.

Embossing. Raised figures or designs on the surface of paper, silver, or leather.

Entablature. In architecture, any raised horizontal member, particularly above a classical pillar.

Epoxy. A thermosetting resin that is tough, adhesive, and resistant to corrosion; used in coatings and adhesives.

Facet cutting. Cutting lead glass in a pattern of geometric facets for maximum refractive properties.

Farthingale chair. A 17th-century English style of broad-seated chair without arms.

Fenestration. In architecture, the design and placement of windows.

Ferro-concrete. Concrete reinforced with steel bars.

Finial. An ornament capping another form, as on the gable of a house or the top of a post.

Fire-polishing. Making glass smooth or glossy by reheating in a flame.

Flint glass. Glass of a heavy brilliant quality, containing lead; also called lead glass.

Flocking. Strewing pulverized cloth over a surface coated with paste to create a velour effect.

Fluting. Closely spaced parallel grooves used as decoration in architecture.

Folio. A book or manuscript of the largest common size, usually about fifteen inches in height.

Footing. The supporting base or groundwork (usually concrete) of a structure.

Foreshortening. In painting or drawing, the distortion of a figure or an object (or parts of objects) by contracting the lines of the long axis in order to achieve a dimensional or a perspective effect.

Found objects. Objects from everyday life incorporated into a collage or a sculpture.

Fret. An ornamentation in classical and Renaissance architecture consisting of patterns formed by straight lines that intersect each other at right angles.

Gadroon. Ornamentation on silver and furniture formed by fluting or reeding and often in a spiral design.

Gallery. Open fretwork or small balustrade forming a railing around the top of an article of furniture or silver.

Gambrel roof. A ridged roof having two slopes on each side, with the lower slope having the steeper pitch.

Gather. In glassmaking, a mass of molten glass collected and ready to be blown.

Gazebo. An open, often round or octagonal pavilion set in a garden and intended for use as a summerhouse.

Genre. The depiction of scenes or anecdotes, often humorous, from everyday life.

Gesso. A preparation of plaster of Paris, or a plaster-like paste, and glue that is applied to a surface to prepare it for paint. Gesso is applied, for example, to raw linen or cotton canvas in order to prime and size it.

Glass blanks. Heavy lead glass articles that are to be engraved with a pattern.

Glaze crystals. The crystalline pattern formed in a certain dry ceramic glaze.

Gouache. A kind of watercolor painting using opaque colors. The effect may be closer to oil painting than to watercolor.

Grace cup. A cup used in drinking "a health" after the grace at the end of a meal.

Gravure. A method of printing with etched plates or cylinders; an intaglio printing process.

Grecian order. The formal arrangement of columns, and the design of their bases, shafts, capitals, and entablatures, as developed in ancient Greece. The three orders were Doric, Ionic, and Corinthian.

Grisaille. A monochromatic painting in shades of gray.

Glossary

Guilloche. In architecture, an ornamental border made up of two or more bands or lines interlacing with each other.

Hachure. Shading with fine parallel lines.

Half-timbered. In architecture, a wooden framework with the spaces filled with plaster, brick, or other masonry, and the wood left visible on the exterior.

Half-tone. In photoengraving, a picture in which the gradations of light are achieved by the density of fine dots produced by photographing a subject through a screen.

Hexafoil. A geometrical shape with six lobes; used as the form of a silver platter or a wooden decorative panel.

Hip roof. A roof that slopes at each end as well as at the sides.

Hoop-back crest rails. The top rail of a chair, or other seating piece, which curves concavely.

Houndhandle pitcher. A pitcher with a handle shaped in the image of a dog.

Ideal figure. The human figure represented in accordance with a preconceived esthetic ideal, as opposed to a naturalistic rendering of the figure.

Illusionistic. In painting, the creation of an illusion of reality, as in *trompe l'oeil* painting.

Imbrication. A decoration consisting of thin plates overlapping each other in rows, in a fish-scale design.

Impasto. A thick application of paint which, by contrast with thinly painted areas, often imparts character and robustness to an oil painting.

Inglenook. The area formed by a piece of furniture set at right angles to a fireplace.

Inlay. Decoration formed by contrasting materials set into the surface of a piece.

Intaglio. In furniture, a figure or design depressed below the surface of the material. Also, a method of making a print from a face in which the parts that take the ink are incised into the surface.

Ionic. The second of the classical orders of pillars, distinguished by a scrolled capital.

Isometric projection. A geometrical drawing in architecture to show a building in three dimensions, without the foreshortening of visual perspective.

Keyhole escutcheon. The metal plate surrounding a keyhole.

Klismos. A side chair in an ancient Greek style; it has seat and rail uprights flowing in a continuous line into the leg.

Knopped stem. In pewter, a stem with a small knob on the end of it.

Lamp font. In an oil lamp, the bowl that holds the oil.

Lampwork. The technique of shaping glass over a burner without blowing the glass.

Lead glass. Glass of a heavy, brilliant quality containing lead.

Life mask. A plaster cast from a mold fashioned on the face of a sitter.

Lime glass. An inferior glass made with lime instead of lead.

Loggia. An arcade above the ground floor.

Lost-wax process. A method of casting metal by surrounding a wax model with clay, baking the clay, and pouring metal into the space left by the melted wax.

Macramé. Coarse lacework made by weaving and knotting cords into a pattern.

Madder. In painting, a transparent, ruby-red pigment; also known as rose madder.

Malerish ("Painterly"). Derived from the German term *maler*, meaning painter, and signifying the dominance of tonal masses over line as a means of defining form.

Mandala. A mystical symbol of the universe that usually takes the form of a circle enclosing a square.

Mannerism. A 16th-century style that departed from the classicism of the Renaissance to use strained and distorted figures, color heightened almost to garishness, and a generally self-conscious manner of presentation.

Mansard roof. A roof having two slopes on all sides, with the lower slope steeper than the upper one.

Maquette. In sculpture, a wax or clay model of a planned piece of sculpture; in architecture, a model of a building.

Marquetry. Decorative inlay in which a pattern formed of various woods or other materials is glued to a groundwork.

Matte finish. A dull, flat surface on a painting, print, or photograph; without gloss or sheen.

Millefiori. Colored glass canes arranged to look like flowers and encased in clear glass.

Modular. Planned or constructed on the basis of a standard scale or pattern. In furniture, easily joined to or arranged with other parts or units.

Moiré pattern. The effect produced by superimposing one design on the same or a different design.

Monteith punch bowl. A large bowl with a notched rim for chilling drinking glasses.

Mortise-and-tenon joint. A joint in wood or stone in which a projection (tenon) of one piece fits snugly into a cavity (mortise) in another piece.

Mount. In furniture, decorative hardware on a piece of furniture.

Mullion. A vertical strip or bar dividing the panes of a window or door.

Multiple. A print or object reproduced in quantity but with specific quality controls.

Muntin. A strip of wood dividing panes of glass horizontally in a window or door.

Mylar. Trade name of a polyester plastic used as a facing to prevent sticking.

Naturalism. A characteristic of any style in which subjects are reproduced so as to give the effect of truth to life, as opposed to "idealized" or "stylized."

Neoplasticism. An art movement, primarily Dutch, involving pure geometric-abstract forms. It was defined by the Dutch painter Piet Mondrian in the early 1910s.

Nonlead glass. Any glass which is produced without the use of lead oxides.

Nonobjectivism. Painting or sculpture that does not recognizably represent any element in nature.

Octavo. A book composed of sheets folded into eight leaves, the pages measuring from 5 x 8 inches to 6 x 9½ inches.

Ogee bracket foot. In furniture, a foot reinforced by brackets shaped in an S-curve, or ogee.

Ogive. A pointed arch, characteristic of Gothic architecture.

On-and-off-the-loom technique. A method of weaving in which the material is woven partially on a loom and partially by other methods, such as braiding.

Oriel window. A bay window projecting from a wall and supported by a bracket.

Outside-inside forms. Architectural forms that have the same character both inside and outside a building, such as a dome.

Palladian. In the style of the 16th-century Italian architect, Andrea Palladio, who used symmetrical, classical designs for domestic architecture, and who influenced British architecture of the 17th and 18th centuries.

Palmette. Stylized palm leaf patterns used ornamentally.

Pediment. In architecture, a low, triangular gable surrounded by a projecting cornice.

Pier glass. A tall mirror for use in the space between two adjacent windows or doors.

Pier table. A table designed to stand against a pier, that is, a section of wall between two windows or doors.

Pilaster. A squared column jutting from a wall, usually with a base and capital patterned in classical style.

Planar limits. The limits to which a plane can be visually extended.

Planishing. Light hammering of metal to produce a smooth surface.

Plastic form. A three-dimensional form in a plastic medium such as sculpture or pottery; The sense of form achieved by the artist through molding the materials of painting or the graphic arts.

Plate tracery. In architecture, decorative tracing in the slab or masonry above a Gothic window.

Plateau. A long, short-legged decorative centerpiece for the dining table, usually of silver.

Plinth. A square base or block upon which a column or statue rests.

Plumbago. A black lead of varying degrees of softness used in the manufacture of lead pencils.

Polychromy. The practice of coloring statuary or architectural decorations, usually with several colors and gold.

Presentation silver. A silver service or piece made for presentation on a formal occasion, usually to a dignitary.

Press cupboard. A 17th-century cupboard with drawers or doors below the main shelf.

Quoin. In architecture, a corner stone at the exterior angle where two walls meet.

Raked. Inclined or slanted from the perpendicular.

Rat-tail. A hinge with a tapered, curved extension running downward, resembling a rat's tail; also, in silver, an ornamental reinforcement on the back of a spoon.

Redware. Ancient Greek pottery, or a modern imitation of it, with red decorations on a black background.

Reeding. In architecture and furniture, a motif in semicircular relief, resembling straight, stylized reeds.

Repoussé. Ornamental work on metal in which the decoration is hammered into relief from the reverse side.

Representationalism. Painting or sculpture that attempts to reproduce the physical appearance of objects.

Reredos. An ornamental screen behind a church altar.

Roman brick. A building brick measuring 1½ inches high and 12 inches long.

Rusticated. In architecture, ornamentally roughened surfaces and recessed joints in stonework.

Salt glaze. A rough glaze produced by introducing rock salt to the kiln during the firing of earthenware or stoneware.

Santero. Maker of santos. See Santos entry.

Scumble. To soften the color or outlines of a painting by applying smoothly or rubbing on a thin film of opaque or semi-opaque pigment.

Segmental arch. An arch having the shape of a true arc, or segment of a circle.

Serigraph. Print made by the silkscreen process. See glossary under Silkscreen.

Sheathing. A layer of boards or other materials applied to the outer studs and rafters of a building to serve as a base for an exterior, weatherproof covering.

Shed roof. A single pitch roof, as on a one-story shed placed against a taller building.

Signage. The craft of making posters or decorative signs.

Silkscreen. A stenciling process in which a design is fixed on stretched silk, the blank areas around it are coated with an impermeable substance, and ink is then pressed through the design onto a printing surface; also, a print made by this process.

Slab and sideboard tables. Long, narrow tables for serving food, usually placed against a wall.

Soak-stain. In ceramics, a technique where a glaze is permitted to "soak" into clay at a lower temperature before the kiln is brought to full firing heat.

Spandrel. A triangular space adjoining the exterior curve of an arch.

Spindled screen. A screen made of a series of parallel spindles or rods set in a frame.

Splat. The upright center support in a chair back.

Splay-leg table. A table with legs that are farther apart at the base than at the top.

Split spindle. Slender, shaped, decorative shafts that have been split longitudinally.

Staff material. A material with a plaster-of-Paris base, used for temporary exterior sculpture and ornamental buildings.

Standing salt. Any piece created to hold table salt, especially one with a sculptured form.

Standish. A stand for writing materials.

Sterling standard. Originally, the exact amount of pure silver required by English law in silver articles; now a certain proportion of silver to copper in fine silver.

Stile. A vertical member of a furniture frame, as in the back of a chair.

Stipple engraving. Engraving in which the design areas are made up of small dots or flecks.

Stoneware. An opaque, durable ceramic ware, generally used for heavy-duty pieces such as crocks and bowls.

Stop-fluting. In furniture, rounded parallel grooves in which the lower parts of the grooves are fitted with reeding.

Storage wall. A room divider containing cupboard space and shelves.

Strapwork. Carved bands forming interlaced, repeated designs.

Stretcher. A horizontal member that connects and braces the legs of a piece of furniture.

Suprematism. An art movement, founded by Kasimir Malevich in Russia in 1913; it advocated strictly nonobjective art, and experimented with basic geometric forms and the simple colors.

Swag. Decoration representing swinging or suspended drapery or garlands of fruit on furniture and architecture.

Tambour. In furniture, a kind of door, as of a roll-top desk, consisting of strips of wood glued side by side on canvas.

Tempera. A method of painting in which pigments are mixed or tempered with a water-soluble binding medium such as egg yolk or egg white.

Tole. Painted tinware.

Tonalism. In painting, the use of closely related tones or "shades" of color to create form and mood in a picture.

Tondo. A circular painting, plaque, or medallion.

Transparent painting. Painting with transparent pigments as opposed to opaque ones, as achieved with glazes or in watercolor painting.

Travertine. In architecture, a light-colored limestone used as a facing material.

Trefoil. An ornament or architectural form resembling a threefold leaf.

Trestle table. A table supported by several trestles held together by a longitudinal bar.

Trifid foot. In furniture, a three-toed foot.

Triptych. A painting or sculpture on three panels placed side by side; the panels are often joined by hinges.

Trompe l'oeil. Literally, to deceive the eye. A painting which creates the illusion that it is actually what it depicts.

Trumpet turning. In furniture, a leg with the profile of an upturned trumpet.

Truss. In architecture, a system of timbers or supports joined together to bridge a space; often used to distribute the weight of the roof onto walls or piers.

Vase turning. A turning or shaping of a piece of wood into a vase form.

Vernacular architecture. The native architecture of a given place at a given time, such as the pueblo or log cabin.

Verre églomisé. Painted glass used as decorative inserts on furniture.

Vitrified. Having glasslike properties, such as high gloss and hardness, as in hard-glazed porcelain.

Volute. A spiral, scroll-like ornament.

Wainscot chair. Chairs with backs constructed of vertical strips of wood joined tongue-in-groove to resemble wainscoting.

Wet plate. A photographic negative made with a glass plate coated with a chemical solution and exposed while still wet.

Yoke-back crest rail. The top rail of a chair back that is shaped like a yoke.

Bibliography I. General Bibliography

Prepared under the supervision of Professor Eugene C. Goossen, Hunter College.

Painting and Sculpture: General Surveys and Reference

Barker, Virgil. *American Painting, History and Interpretation.* N.Y., 1950.

—. *A Critical Introduction to American Painting.* N.Y.,1931.

Born, Wolfgang. *American Landscape Painting: An Interpretation.* New Haven, 1948.

—. *Still-Life Painting in America.* N.Y., 1947.

Brown, J. Carter. "The American Vision" (film). Distributed by National Gallery of Art, Wash. D.C.,1966.

Burroughs, Alan. *Limners and Likenesses: Three Centuries of American Painting.* Cambridge, 1936.

Caffin, Charles. *The Story of American Painting.* N.Y.,1907.

Cahill, Holger and Alfred Barr, Jr. *Art in America, A Complete Survey.* N.Y., 1939.

A Catalogue of the Collection of American Paintings in the Corcoran Gallery of Art. Wash. D.C., 1966.

Craven, Wayne. *Sculpture in America.* N.Y., 1968.

Davidson, Marshall. *Life in America.* Boston, 1951

Eliot, Alexander. *Three Hundred Years of American Painting.* N.Y., 1957.

Fairman, Charles. *Art and Artists of the Capitol.* Wash. D.C., 1917.

Fielding, Mantle. *Dictionary of American Painters, Sculptors and Engravers.* N.Y., 1965.

Gardner, Albert, *American Sculpture, A Catalogue of the Collection of The Metropolitan Museum of Art.* N.Y., 1965.

Goodrich, Lloyd. *Three Centuries of American Art.* N.Y., 1967.

—. "Art of the United States," exhibition catalogue, Whitney Museum, N.Y., 1966.

Green, Samuel. *American Art, A Historical Survey.* N.Y., 1966.

Groce, George and David Wallace. *The New York Historical Society's Dictionary of Artists in America, 1564–1860.* New Haven, 1957.

Harris, Neil. *The Artist in American Society.* N.Y., 1966.

Hartmann, Sadakichi. *A History of American Art.* Boston, 1932.

Isham, Samuel and Royal Cortissoz. *The History of American Painting.* N.Y., 1968.

Kouwenhoven, John. *Made in America.* N.Y., 1962.

La Follette, Suzanne. *Art in America.* N.Y., 1929.

Larkin, Oliver. *Art and Life in America.* N.Y., 1960.

Lipman, Jean (ed.). *What is American in American Art.* N.Y., 1963.

Maine and Its Role in American Art, 1740–1963. N.Y., 1963.

Mather, F. J., C. R. Morey and W. J. Henderson. *The American Spirit in Art.* New Haven, 1927.

McCoubrey, John. *American Art, 1700–1960, Sources and Documents.* N.J., 1965.

Mendelowitz, Daniel. *A History of American Art.* N.Y., 1970.

Pierson, William, Jr. and Martha Davidson (eds.). *Arts of the United States: A Pictorial Survey.* N.Y., 1960.

Porter, James. *Modern Negro Art.* N.Y., 1943.

Prown, Jules. *American Painting, From Its Beginning to the Armory Show.* Cleveland, 1969.

Richardson, E.P. *American Romantic Painting.* N.Y., 1944.

—. *Painting in America.* N.Y., 1965.

—. *The Way of Western Art, 1776–1914.* Cambridge, 1939.

Soby, James T. and Dorothy Miller. "Romantic Painting in America," exhibition catalogue, Museum of Modern Art. N.Y., 1943.

Taft, Lorado. *History of American Sculpture.* N.Y., 1930.

17th and 18th Century

Bayley, Frank. *Five Colonial Artists of New England.* Boston, 1929.

Belknap, Waldron, Jr. *American Painting, Materials for a History.* Cambridge, 1959.

Bolton, Charles. *Portraits of the Founders.* Boston, 1919.

Drepperd, Carl. *American Pioneer Arts and Artists.* Springfield, Mass., 1942.

Dresser, Louisa. *Seventeenth Century Painting in New England.* Worcester, Mass., 1935.

Dunlap, William. *History of the Rise and Progress of the Arts of Design in the United States.* N.Y., 1834 and 1969.

Flexner, James. *America's Old Masters: First Artists of the New World.* N.Y., 1967.

—. *First Flowers of Our Wilderness.* Boston, 1947.

—. *The Light of Distant Skies.* N.Y., 1954.

Gardner, Albert and Stuart Feld. *American Paintings: Painters Born by 1815.* Greenwich, Conn., 1965.

Gottesman, Rita. *The Arts and Crafts in New York 1726–1776.* N.Y., 1937.

—. *The Arts and Crafts in New York 1777–1799.* N.Y., 1954.

Hagen, Oskar. *The Birth of the American Tradition in Art.* N.Y., 1940.

Lee, Cuthbert. *Early American Portrait Painters,* New Haven. 1929.

"Old and New England: An Exhibition of American Painting of Colonial and Early Republican Days," exhibition catalogue, Rhode Island School of Design. 1945.

Quimby, Ian (ed.). *American Painting to 1776, a Reappraisal.* Charlottesville, Va., 1971.

Sadik, Marvin. *Colonial and Federal Portraits at Bowdoin College.* Brunswick, Me., 1966.

Sweet, Frederick and Hans Huth. "From Colony to Nation," exhibition catalogue, Art Institute of Chicago. 1949.

Wright, Louis, George Tatum, John Mc Coubrey and Robert Smith. *The Arts in America: The Colonial Period.* N.Y., 1966.

19th Century

Baur, John. *American Painting in the Nineteenth Century.* N.Y., 1953.

Benjamin, Samuel. *Art in America: A Critical and Historical Sketch.* N.Y., 1880.

—. *Our American Artists.* Boston, 1879.

Bolton, Theodore. *Early American Portrait Painters in Miniature.* N.Y., 1921.

Callow, James. *Kindred Spirits, Knickerbocker Writers and American Artists, 1807–1855.* Chapel Hill, N.C., 1967.

Clement, Clara and Lawrence Hutton. *Artists of the Nineteenth Century and Their Work.* Boston, 1879.

Dickson, Harold (ed.). *Observations on American Art: Selections from the Writings of John Neal, 1793–1876.* Pennsylvania State College Studies, No. 12, 1943.

D'Ooge, Martin. *Catalogue of the Gallery of Art and Archaeology of the University of Michigan.* Ann Arbor, 1892.

Flexner, James. *That Wilder Image, The Painting of America's Native School from Thomas Cole to Winslow Homer.* Boston, 1962.

Frankenstein, Alfred. *After the Hunt: William Harnett and Other Still Life Painters, 1870–1900.* Berkeley, 1969.

Gardner, Albert and Stuart Feld. *American Paintings: Painters Born by 1815.* Greenwich, Conn., 1965.

Gardner, Albert. *Yankee Stonecutters, The First American School of Sculptors.* N.Y., 1945.

Garrett, Wendell, Paul Norton, Alan Gowans, and Joseph Butler. *The Arts in America, The Nineteenth Century.* N.Y., 1969.

Huth, Hans. *Nature and the American.* Berkeley, 1957.

Lanman, Charles. *Haphazard Personalities, Chiefly of Noted Americans.* Boston, 1886.

——. *Letters from a Landscape Painter.* Boston, 1845.

Lester, Charles. *The Artists of America.* N.Y., 1846.

McCracken, Harold. *Portrait of the Old West.* N.Y. 1952.

M. and M. Karolik Collection of American Painting: 1815–1865. Cambridge, 1949.

M. and M. Karolik Collection of American Water Colors and Drawings: 1800–1875. Boston, 1962.

Mc Spadden, Joseph. *Famous Sculptors of America.* N.Y., 1924.

Miller, Lillian. *Patrons and Patriotism.* Chicago, 1966.

"Nineteenth Century America; Paintings and Sculpture," exhibition catalogue, Metropolitan Museum of Art. N.Y., 1970.

Novak, Barbara. *American Painting of the Nineteenth Century.* London, 1969.

Peat, Wilbur. *Pioneer Painters of Indiana.* Indianapolis, 1954.

Rathbone, Perry. "Westward the Way," exhibition catalogue, City Art Museum. St. Louis, 1954.

Richardson, E. P. and Otto Wittmann, Jr. "Travelers in Arcadia, American Artists in Italy, 1830–1875," exhibition catalogue, Detroit Institute of Arts. 1951.

Sheldon, George. *American Painters.* N.Y., 1879.

Sweet, Frederick. "The Hudson River School and the Early American Landscape Tradition," exhibition catalogue, Art Institute of Chicago. 1945.

Thorp, Margaret. *The Literary Sculptors.* Durham, N.C., 1965.

Taft, Robert. *Artists and Illustrators of the Old West: 1850–1900.* N.Y., 1953.

Tuckerman, Henry. *Artist-Life, or Sketches of Eminent American Painters.* N.Y., 1847.

——. *Book of the Artists.* N.Y., 1867.

Williams, Hermann Warner, Jr. *Mirror to the American Past.* Greenwich, Conn., 1972.

Wilmerding, John. *History of American Marine Painting.* Boston, 1968.

20th Century

"American Sculpture of the Sixties," exhibition catalogue, Los Angeles County Museum. 1967.

Arnason, H. H. "American Abstract Expressionists and Imagists," exhibition catalogue, Guggenheim Museum. N.Y., 1961.

——. *History of Modern Art.* N.Y., 1968.

Ashton, Dore. *The Unknown Shore: A View of Contemporary Art.* Boston, 1962.

Battcock, Gregory (ed.). *The New Art.* N.Y., 1966.

Baur, John. *New Art in America: Fifty Painters of the Twentieth Century.* N.Y., 1957.

——. *Revolution and Tradition in Modern American Art.* Cambridge, 1951.

Brown, Milton. *American Painting from the Armory Show to the Depression.* Princeton, 1955.

Bryant, L. M. *American Pictures and Their Painters.* N.Y., 1917.

Burnham, Jack. *Beyond Modern Sculpture.* N.Y., 1968.

Cahill, Holger and Alfred Barr, Jr. *Art in America in Modern Times.* N.Y., 1934.

Cheney, M. C. *Modern Art in America.* N.Y., 1939.

"Contemporary Sculpture," *Arts Yearbook.* 1965.

Cortissoz, Royal. *American Artists.* N.Y., 1923.

——. *Art and Common Sense.* N.Y., 1913.

Cox, Kenyon. *The Classic Point of View.* N.Y., 1911.

Craven, Thomas. *Modern Art; The Men, the Movements, the Meaning.* N.Y., 1934.

Ely, C. B. *The Modern Tendency in American Painting.* N.Y., 1925.

Friedman, B. H. (ed.). *School of New York, Some Younger Painters.* N.Y., 1959.

Friedman, Martin. "The Precisionist View in American Art," exhibition catalogue, Walker Art Center. Minneapolis, 1960.

Gallatin, A. E. *American Watercolorists.* N.Y., 1922.

——. *Certain Contemporaries.* N.Y., 1916.

Geldzahler, Henry. *American Painting in the Twentieth Century.* Greenwich, Conn., 1965.

——. *New York Painting and Sculpture: 1940–1970.* N.Y., 1969.

Giedion-Welcker, Carola. *Contemporary Sculpture: An Evolution in Volume and Space.* N.Y., 1955.

Goodrich, Lloyd and John Baur. *American Art of Our Century.* N.Y., 1961.

Goossen, E. C. "The Art of the Real, U.S.A., 1948–1968," exhibition catalogue, Museum of Modern Art. N.Y., 1968.

——. "The End of the Object," *Art International,* vol. 3. 1959.

Gordon, John. *Geometric Abstraction in America.* N.Y., 1962.

Greenberg, Clement. *Art and Culture; Critical Essays.* Boston, 1961.

——. "Modernist Painting," *Art and Literature.* Spring 1965.

Hess, Thomas. *Abstract Painting: Background and American Phase.* N.Y., 1951.

Hunter, Sam. *American Art of the Twentieth Century.* N.Y., 1972.

Index of Twentieth Century Artists. N.Y., 1933-1937.

Kootz, Samuel. *Modern American Painters.* N.Y., 1930.

——. *New Frontiers in American Painting.* N.Y., 1943.

Kuh, Katharine. *The Artist's Voice: Talks with Seventeen Artists.* N.Y., 1960.

Mather, Frank. *Estimates in Art.* N.Y., 1931.

——. *Modern Painting: A Study of Tendencies.* N.Y., 1927.

McShine, Kynaston. "Primary Structures," exhibition catalogue, Jewish Museum. N.Y., 1966.

Mellquist, Jerome. *The Emergence of an American Art.* N.Y., 1942.

Miller, Dorothy and Alfred Barr, Jr. "American Realists and Magic Realists," exhibition catalogue, Museum of Modern Art. N.Y., 1943.

——. "12 Americans," exhibition catalogue Museum of Modern Art. N.Y., 1956.

——. "15 Americans," exhibition catalogue, Museum of Modern Art. N.Y., 1952.

——. "Fourteen Americans," exhibition catalogue, Museum of Modern Art. N.Y., 1946.

——. "Sixteen Americans," exhibition catalogue, Museum of Modern Art. N.Y., 1959.

Motherwell, Robert and Ad Reinhardt (eds.). *Modern Artists in America.* N.Y., 1951.

Pach, Walter. *Modern Art in America.* N.Y., 1928.

Protter, Eric (ed.). *Painters on Painting.* N.Y., 1963.

Richardson, E.P. *Twentieth Century Painting.* Detroit, 1936.

Ritchie, Andrew. "Abstract Painting and Sculpture in America," exhibition catalogue, Museum of Modern Art. N.Y., 1951.

——. "Sculpture of the Twentieth Century," exhibition catalogue, Museum of Modern Art. N.Y., 1952.

Rose, Barbara, *American Art Since 1900.* N.Y., 1967.

——. *American Painting: The Twentieth Century.* Switzerland, 1970.

Rosenberg, Harold. *The Tradition of the New.* N.Y., 1959.

Rosenfeld, Paul. *Port of New York.* N.Y., 1924.

Rubin, William. "Younger American Painters," *Art International.* Jan. 1960.

Soby, James. *Contemporary Painters.* N.Y., 1948.

Wright, Willard. *The Future of Painting.* N.Y., 1923.

——. *Modern Painting.* N.Y. 1915.

Zigrosser, Carl. *The Artist in America.* N.Y., 1942.

Architecture: General

Surveys and Reference

Andrews, Wayne. *Architecture, Ambition and Americans.* London, 1964.

——. Architecture in America. N.Y., 1960.

Bell, Ervin (ed.). *Architectural Index.* Sausalito, Calif.

Burchard, John and Albert Bush-Brown. *The Architecture of America.* Boston, 1961.

Condit, Carl. *American Building.* Chicago, 1968.

Downing, Antoinette and Vincent Scully. *The Architectural Heritage of Newport, Rhode Island, 1640–1915.* N.Y., 1965.

Early, James. *Romanticism and American Architecture.* N.Y., 1965.

Fitch, James. *American Building: The Forces That Shape It.* Boston, 1948.

Giedion, Sigfried. *Space, Time and Architecture.* Cambridge, 1947.

Gifford, Don (ed.). *The Literature of Architecture.* N.Y., 1966.

Gowans, Alan. *Images of American Living.* Philadelphia, 1964.

Hamlin, Talbot. *The American Spirit in Architecture.* New Haven, 1926.

Hitchcock, Henry R. *Rhode Island Architecture.* Cambridge, 1968.

Hoak, E.W. and W.H. Church. *Masterpieces of Architecture in the United States.* N.Y., 1930.

Jackson, Huson. *A Guide to New York Architecture, 1650–1952.* N.Y., 1952.

Jackson, Joseph. *Early Philadelphia Architects and Engineers.* Philadelphia, 1923.

Kimball, Fiske. *American Architecture.* Indianapolis, 1928.

Kirker, Harold. *California's Architectural Frontier.* San Marino, Cal., 1960.

Kubler, George. *Religious Architecture of New Mexico.* Colorado Springs, 1940.

Mumford, Lewis. *Sticks and Stones; A Study of American Architecture and Civiliation.* N.Y., 1924.

Olmsted, Roger and T.H. Watkins. *Here Today: San Francisco's Architectural Her-*

itage. San Francisco, 1968.

Pierson, William, Jr. *American Buildings and Their Architects: The Colonial and Neo-Classical Styles.* N.Y., 1970.

——. and Martha Davidson (eds.). *Arts of the United States: A Pictorial Survey.* N.Y., 1960.

Reau, Louis. *L'Art Français Aux États-Unis.* Paris, 1926.

Reps, John. *The Making of Urban America; A History of City Planning in the United States.* Princeton, 1965.

Roos, Frank, Jr. *Writings on Early American Architecture and an Annotated List of Books and Articles on Architecture Constructed Before 1860.* Ohio, 1943.

Sanford, Elwood. *The Architecture of the Southwest.* N.Y., 1950.

Scott, Mellier. *American City Planning.* Berkeley, 1969.

Tallmadge, Thomas. *The Story of Architecture in America.* N.Y., 1936.

Tatum, George. *Penn's Great Town.* Philadelphia, 1961.

Tuthill, Louisa. *History of Architecture from the Earliest Times.* Philadelphia, 1848.

Whiffen, Marcus. *American Architecture Since 1780: A Guide to the Styles.* Cambridge, 1959.

Whitehill, Walter. *Boston: A Topographical History.* Cambridge, 1959.

Withey, H.F. and E. R. Withey. *Biographical Dictionary of American Architects Deceased.* Cal., 1956.

17th and 18th Century

Baer, Kurt. *Architecture of the California Missions.* Berkeley, 1958.

Bailey, Rosalie. *Pre-Revolutionary Dutch Houses and Families In Northern New Jersey and Southern New York.* N.Y., 1936.

Bennett, G.F. *Early Architecture of Delaware.* Wilmington, 1932.

Briggs, Martin. *Homes of the Pilgrim Fathers in England and America.* N.Y., 1932.

Brock, Henry. *Colonial Churches in Virginia.* Richmond, 1930.

Congdon, Herbert. *Old Vermont Houses.* Brattleboro, 1940.

Dillard, Maud. *Old Dutch Houses of Brooklyn.* N.Y., 1945.

Donnelly, Marian. *New England Meeting Houses of the Seventeenth Century.* Middletown, Conn., 1968.

Downing, Antoinette. *Early Homes of Rhode Island.* Richmond, 1937.

Eberlein, Harold and Cortland Hubbard. *American Georgian Architecture.* Bloomington, Ind., 1952.

——. *The Manors and Historic Homes of the Hudson Valley.* N.Y., 1942.

Forman, Henry. *The Architecture of the Old South: The Medieval Style.* Cambridge, 1948.

Early Manor and Plantation Houses of Maryland, 1634–1800. Easton, Md., 1934.

——. *Jamestown and St. Mary's.* Baltimore, 1938.

Garvan, Anthony. *Architecture and Town Planning in Colonial Connecticut.* New Haven, 1951.

Gowans, Alan. *Church Architecture in New France.* New Brunswick, 1955.

Howells, John. *The Architectural Heritage of the Merrimack.* N.Y., 1941.

——. *The Architectural Heritage of the Piscataqua.* N.Y., 1938.

——. *Lost Examples of Colonial Architecture.* N.Y., 1931.

Isham, Norman and Albert Brown, *Early Connecticut Houses.* Providence, 1900.

Kelly, J. F. *Early Connecticut Meeting Houses.* New Haven, 1948.

——. *Early Domestic Architecture of Connecticut.* New Haven, 1924.

Kimball, Fiske. *Domestic Architecture of the American Colonies and the Early Republic.* N.Y., 1922.

Mason, George. *Colonial Churches of Tidewater Virginia.* Richmond, 1945.

Morrison, Hugh. *Early American Architecture.* N.Y., 1952.

Newcomb, Rexford. *Old Mission Churches and Historic Houses of California.* N.Y., 1916.

——. *Spanish Colonial Architecture in the United States.* N.Y., 1937.

Nichols, Frederick. *Early Architecture of Georgia.* Chapel Hill, N.C., 1957.

Raymond, Eleanor. *Early Domestic Architecture of Pennsylvania.* N.Y., 1931.

Reynolds, Helen. *Dutch Houses in the Hudson Valley Before 1776.* N.Y., 1929.

Shurtleff, Harold. *The Log Cabin Myth.* Cambridge, 1939.

Stoney, Samuel. *Plantations of the Carolina Low Country.* Charleston, S.C., 1938.

Tatum, George. "Architecture," *The Arts in America: The Colonial Period.* N.Y., 1966.

Wallace, P.B. and W.A. Dunn. *Colonial Churches and Meetinghouses, Pennsylvania, New Jersey and Delaware.* N.Y., 1931.

Waterman, Thomas and J.A. Barrows. *Domestic Colonial Architecture of Tidewater Virginia.* N.Y., 1932.

——. *The Dwellings of Colonial America.* Chapel Hill, N.C., 1950.

——. and Frances Johnson. *Early Architecture of North Carolina.* Chapel Hill, N.C., 1941.

——. *Mansions of Virginia, 1706–1776.* Chapel Hill, N.C., 1951.

Wertenbaker, T.J. *The Foundations of American Civilization: The Middle Colonies.* N.Y., 1938.

Whiffen, Marcus. *The Eighteenth Century Houses of Williamsburg.* N.Y., 1960.

Wilson, Samuel, Jr. *A Guide to the Early Architecture of New Orleans.* New Orleans, 1951.

19th Century

Badger, Daniel. *Illustrations of Iron Architecture Made by the Architectural Iron Works of the City of New York.* N.Y., 1865.

Birkmire, William. *The Planning and Construction of High Office-Buildings.* N.Y., 1898.

Brown, Glenn. *History of the United States Capital.* Wash. D.C., 1900–1903.

Bryan, Wilhemus. *History of the National Capital.* N.Y., 1914–1916.

Bunting, Bainbridge. *Houses of Boston's Back Bay, 1840–1917.* Cambridge, 1967..

Condit, Carl. *American Building Art, 19th Century.* N.Y., 1960.

Coolidge, John. *Mill and Mansion: A Study of Architecture & Society in Lowell, Massachusetts, 1820–1865.* N.Y., 1941.

Field, M. *City Architecture.* N.Y., 1854.

Field, Walker. "A Re-examination of the Invention of the Balloon Frame," *Journal of the American Society of Architectural Historians.* Oct. 1942.

Hamlin, Talbot. *Greek Revival Architecture in America.* N.Y., 1944.

Hitchcock, Henry R. *Architecture. Nineteenth and Twentieth Centuries.* Baltimore, 1958.

Kennion, John. *The Architect's and Builder's Guide.* N.Y., 1868.

Kilham, Walter. *Boston After Bulfinch.* Cambridge, 1946.

Lancaster, Clay. "Oriental Forms in American Architecture," *Art Bulletin.* Sept. 1947.

Maass, John. *The Gingerbread Age.* N.Y., 1957.

Mc Coy, Esther. *Five California Architects.* N.Y., 1960.

Mumford, Lewis. *The Brown Decades.* N.Y., 1955.

Newcomb, Rexford. *Architecture of the Old Northwest Territory.* Chicago, 1950.

New York Sketch Book of Architecture. N.Y., 1874–1876.

Norton, Paul. "Architecture," *The Arts in America: The Nineteenth Century.* N.Y., 1969.

Owen, Robert Dale. *Hints on Public Architecture.* N.Y., 1849.

Pelletreau, William. *Historic Homes and Institutions, 1840–1918.* N.Y., 1918.

Schuyler, Montgomery. *American Architecture.* N.Y., 1892.

Smith, J. Frazier. *White Pillars.* N.Y., 1941.

Weisman, Winston. "Commercial Palaces of New York, 1854–1875," *Art Bulletin.* Dec. 1954.

White, Theophilus (ed.). *Philadelphia Architecture in the Nineteenth Century.* Philadelphia, 1953.

20th Century

Banham, Reyner. *The Architecture of the Well-Tempered Environment.* London, 1969.

——. *Los Angeles: The Architecture of Four Ecologies,* London, 1971.

Behrendt, Walter. *Modern Building: Its Nature, Problems, and Forms.* N.Y., 1937.

Blake, Peter. *The Masterbuilders.* N.Y., 1961.

Cheney, Sheldon. *The New World Architecture.* N.Y., 1930.

Cheney, Sheldon and Martha. *Art and the Machine.* N.Y., 1936.

Coles, William and Henry Hope Reed, Jr. (eds.). *Architecture in America, A Battle of Styles.* N.Y., 1961.

Condit, Carl. *American Building Art, The Twentieth Century.* N.Y., 1961.

Edgell, George. *The American Architect of Today.* N.Y., 1928.

Fitch, James. *Architecture and the Esthetics of Plenty.* N.Y., 1961.

Gebhard, David. *George Washington Smith.* Santa Barbara, 1964.

Hitchcock, Henry R. *Modern Architecture.* N.Y., 1929.

——. *Architecture Nineteenth and Twentieth Centuries.* Baltimore, 1958.

——. and Arthur Drexler (eds.). *Built in U.S.A.: Post-War Architecture.* N.Y., 1952.

Hudnut, Richard. *Architecture and the Spirit*

of Man. N.Y., 1949.

Jacobs, Jane. *The Death and Life of Great American Cities.* N.Y., 1961.

Jacobus, John, Jr. *Twentieth Century Architecture: The Middle Years, 1940–1965.* N.Y., 1965.

Jones, Cranston. *Architecture Today and Tomorrow.* N.Y., 1961.

Jordy, William. *American Buildings and Their Architects: Progressive and Academic Ideals at the Turn of the Twentieth Century.* N.Y., 1972.

McCallum, Ian. *Architecture U.S.A.* N.Y., 1959.

McCoy, Esther. *Modern California Houses; Case Study Houses, 1945–1962.* N.Y., 1962.

Michaels, Leonard. *Contemporary Structure in Architecture.* N.Y., 1950.

Mock, Elizabeth (ed.). *Built in U.S.A., Since 1932.* N.Y., 1944.

Mid-Century Architecture in America: Honor Awards of the American Institute of Architects, 1949–1961. Baltimore, 1961.

Mumford, Lewis. *From the Ground Up.* N.Y., 1956.

—— (ed.). *Roots of Contemporary American Architecture.* N.Y., 1952.

Peter, John. *Masters of Modern Architecture.* N.Y., 1958.

Pevsner, Nikolaus. *Pioneers of Modern Design.* N.Y., 1949.

"Philadelphia," *Journal of the American Institute of Planners.* Aug. 1960.

Reed, Henry Hope, Jr. *The Golden City.* N.Y., 1959.

Scully, Vincent. *American Architecture and Urbanism.* N.Y., 1969.

——. *Modern Architecture.* N.Y., 1961.

Sexton, R.W. *The Logic of Modern Architecture.* N.Y., 1929.

Sharp, Dennis. *A Visual History of Twentieth Century Architecture.* Greenwich, Conn., 1972.

Teague, Walter. *Design This Day.* N.Y., 1940.

Folk Art: General

Black, Mary and Jean Lipman. *American Folk Painting.* N.Y., 1966.

Cahill, Holger. *American Folk Art, the Art of the Common Man in America 1750–1900.* N.Y., 1932.

Christensen, Irwin. *The Index of American Design.* N.Y., 1950.

Drepperd, Carl. *American Pioneer Arts and Artists,* Springfield, Mass., 1942.

Ford, Alice. *Pictorial Folk Art, New England to California.* N.Y., 1949.

Gardner, Albert. *101 Masterpieces of American Primitive Painting From the Collection of Edgar William and Bernice Chrysler Garbisch.* N.Y., 1962.

Janis, Sidney. *They Taught Themselves; American Primitive Painters of the Twentieth Century.* N.Y., 1942.

Kauffman, Henry. *Pennsylvania Dutch American Folk Art.* N.Y., 1946.

——. *Decorative Arts of Victoria's Era,* N.Y., 1950.

——. *Folk Art Motifs of Pennsylvania,* N.Y., 1954.

——. *Folk Art of Rural Pennsylvania,* N.Y., 1946.

Lipman, Jean. *American Primitive Painting.* N.Y., 1942.

——and Eve Meulendyke. *American Folk Decoration.* N.Y., 1951.

——and Alice Winchester (eds.). *Primitive Painters in America, 1750–1950, An Anthology.* N.Y., 1950.

——. *The Abby Aldrich Rockefeller Folk Art Collection, A Descriptive Catalogue.* Boston, 1957.

Polley, Robert (ed.). *America's Folk Art,* N.Y., 1968.

Sears, Clara. *Some American Primitives.* Boston, 1941.

Stoudt, John. *Early Pennsylvania Arts and Crafts.* N.Y., 1964.

——. *Pennsylvania Folk Art.* Allentown, 1948.

Wright, Richardson. *Hawkers and Walkers in Early America.* Philadelphia, 1927

Furniture: General

English Background

Chippendale, Thomas. *The Gentleman and Cabinet-Maker's Director.* N.Y., 1966 (reprint of 1762 edition).

Edwards, Ralph. *The Dictionary of English Furniture.* 3 vols., London, 1953.

—— and L. G. G. Ramsey (eds.). *The Connoisseur's Complete Period Guides.* N.Y., 1968. (Reprint of six volumes bound as one.)

Fastnedge, Ralph. *English Furniture Styles from 1500–1830.* Baltimore, 1955.

Ward Jackson, Peter. *English Furniture Designs of the Eighteenth Century.* London, 1955.

American Background

Bjerkoe, Ethel Hall. *The Cabinetmakers of America.* N.Y., 1957.

Comstock, Helen. *American Furniture: Seventeenth, Eighteenth, and Nineteenth Century Styles.* N.Y., 1962.

Downs, Joseph. *American Furniture, Queen Anne and Chippendale Periods.* N.Y., 1952 and 1967.

Hipkiss, Edwin J. *Eighteenth-Century American Arts. The M. and M. Karolik Collection.* Boston, 1941.

Randall, Richard H., Jr. *American Furniture in the Museum of Fine Arts, Boston.* Boston, 1965.

Winterthur Museum. *Country Cabinetwork and Simple City Furniture.* Winterthur, De . 1970.

Regional Studies

Albany Institute of History and Art. *New York Furniture Before 1840.* Albany, 1962.

Baltimore Furniture: The Work of Baltimore and Annapolis Cabinetmakers from 1760 to 1810. Baltimore, 1947.

Burton, E. Milby. *Charleston Furniture, 1700–1825.* Charleston, S.C., 1955.

Carpenter, Ralph E., Jr. *The Arts and Crafts of Newport, Rhode Island,* Newport, 1954.

Dorman, Charles G. *Delaware Cabinetmakers and Allied Artisans, 1655–1855.* Wilmington, Del., 1960.

Elder, William Voss, II. *Maryland Queen Anne and Chippendale Furniture of the Eighteenth Century.* Baltimore, 1960.

Fales, Dean A., Jr. *Essex County Furniture.*

Documented Treasures from Local Collections. Salem, Mass., 1965.

Hornor, William Macpherson, Jr. *Blue Book, Philadelphia Furniture.* Philadelphia, 1935.

Hummel, Charles F. *With Hammer in Hand. The Dominy Craftsman of East Hampton, New York.* Charlottesville, Va., 1968.

Kirk, John. *Connecticut Furniture: 17th and 18th Century.* Hartford, Conn., 1967.

Luther, Clair Franklin. *The Hadley Chest.* Hartford, 1935.

Ott, Joseph K. *The John Brown House Loan Exhibition of Rhode Island Furniture.* Providence, 1965.

Parsons, Charles S. *The Dunlaps and Their Furniture.* Manchester, N. H., 1970.

Virginia Museum of Fine Arts. *Southern Furniture, 1640–1820.* N.Y., 1952.

White, Margaret E. *Early Furniture Made in New Jersey, 1690–1870.* New, N.J., 1958.

Glass: General

Belknap, E. McCamly. *Milk Glass.* N , 1949.

Davis, Pearce. *The Development of the American Glass Industry.* Cambridge, 1949.

Knittle, Rhea. *Early American Glass.* N.Y. 1927.

Lee, Ruth Webb. *Antique Fakes and Reproductions.* Wellesley Hills, Mass., 1938.

McKearin, George S. and Helen. *American Glass.* N.Y., 1950.

——. *Two Hundred Years of American Blown Glass.* N.Y., 1966.

Peterson, Arthur. *400 Trademarks on Glass.* Takoma Park, Md., 1968.

Revi, A. Christian. *Nineteenth Century Glass: Its Genesis and Development.* N.Y., 1967.

Watkins, Lura Woodside. *American Glass and Glassmaking.* N.Y., 1950.

Specific Glasshouses and Areas

Harrington, J.C. *Glassmaking at Jamestown America's First Industry.* Richmond, V , 1952.

Herrick, Ruth. *Greentown Glass.* Grand Rapids, Mich., 1959.

Hunter, Frederick W. (ed., Helen McKearin). *Stiegel Glass.* N.Y., 1914 and 1967.

Innes, Lowell. *Early Glass of the Pittsburgh District.* Pittsburgh, 1949.

Jefferson, Josephine. *Wheeling Glass.* N.Y., 1947.

Lee, Ruth Webb. *Sandwich Glass.* Wellesley Hills, Mass., 1947 and 1966.

Maryland Historical Society. *Amelung Glass: An Exhibition.* Baltimore, 1952.

Toledo Museum of Art. *Libbey Glass, A Tradition of 150 Years.* Toledo, 1968.

——.*New England Glass Company, 1818–1888.* Toledo, 1963.

Watkins, Lura Woodside. *Cambridge Glass 1818–1888.* Boston, 1930 and 1953.

Wilson, Kenneth M. *Glass in New England.* Sturbridge, Mass., 1968.

——. *New England Glass & Glassmaking.* N.Y., 1971.

Cut Glass

Daniel, Dorothy. *Cut and Engraved Glass 1771–1905.* N.Y., 1965.

Pearson, J. Michael and Dorothy T. *American Cut Glass For the Discriminating*

General Bibliography

Collector. N.Y., 1965.
——. A Study of American Cut Glass Collections. Miami Beach, 1969.
Revi, A. Christian. American Cut and Engraved Glass. N.Y., 1965.

Pressed Glass

Kamm, Minnie W. Pattern Glass Pitchers. Books 1-8. Michigan, 1940-1954.
Lee, Ruth Webb and James H. Rose. American Glass Cup Plates. Northboro, Mass., 1948.
Lee, Ruth Webb. Early American Pressed Glass. Wellesley Hills, Mass., 1960.
Revi, A. Christian. American Pressed Glass and Figure Bottles. N.Y., 1964.
Rose, James H. The Story of American Pressed Glass of the Lacy Period, 1825-1850, A Special Exhibition. Corning, N.Y., 1954 (photomechanical reprint, 1967).

Bottles and Flasks

McKearin, Helen. Bottles, Flasks and Dr. Dyott. N.Y., 1970.

—— The Story of American Historical Flasks. Corning, N.Y., 1953 (photomechanical reprint, 1968).
Van Rensselaer, Stephen. Early American Bottles and Flasks. Part I and II. Peterborough, N.H., 1926.
Watson, Richard. Bitters Bottles. N.Y., 1965.
——. Supplement to Bitters Bottles. N.Y., 1968.

Photography: General

Caffin, Charles H. Photography as a Fine Art. N.Y., 1972.
Camera Notes. July 1899.
Camera Work. January 1903.
Coke, Van Deren. The Painter and the Photograph. Albuquerque, N.M., 1964.
Craftsman. April 1907.
Documentary Photography. N.Y., 1972.
Focal Encyclopedia of Photography. London, 1956.
Friedman, J.S. History of Color Photography. Boston, 1944.
Gernsheim, Helmut and Alison. Creative Photography. Detroit, 1963.

"H₂O," National Board of Review Magazine. Dec. 1929.
Hicks, W. Words and Pictures; An Introduction to Photo-journalism. N.Y., 1952.
Newhall, Beaumont. The Daguerreotype in America. N.Y., 1961.
——. The History of Photography. N.Y., 1964 and 1971.
Newhall, Beaumont and Nancy. Masters of Photography. N.Y., 1968.
Photo Era. March 1929.
Photography. London, March 19, 1904.
Rotha, Paul, and others. Documentary Film. N.Y., 1963.
Rudisill, Richard. Mirror Image. N.Y., 1971.
Scharf, Aaron. Art and Photography. London, 1968.
Szarkowski, John (ed.). The Photographer and the American Landscape. N.Y., 1963.
Taft, Robert. Photography and the American Scene. N.Y., 1938 and 1964.

Bibliography II Bibliography According to Entries

Abbey, Edwin Austin
Lucas, E.V. *Edwin Austin Abbey, Royal Academician.* 1921.
Abbott, Berenice
Abbott, Berenice. *Photographs.* N.Y., 1970.
Abbott, B. and H.W. Lanier. *Greenwich Village Today and Yesterday.* N.Y., 1949.
"Berenice Abbott," *Current Biography.* N.Y., 1942.
McCausland, Elizabeth. "Berenice Abbott, Realist," *Photo Arts.* Spring 1948.
Abstract Art
American Abstract Artists. Annual Exhibition Catalogues. 1937- present.
Barr, Alfred H., Jr. "Cubism and Abstract Art," exhibition catalogue, Museum of Modern Art. N.Y., 1936.
Breeskin, Adelyn. "Roots of Abstract Art in America, 1910-1950," exhibition catalogue, National Collection of Fine Arts. Wash. D.C., 1965.
Hess, Thomas. *Abstract Painting; Background and American Phase.* N.Y., 1951.
McNeil, George. "American Abstractionists Venerable at Twenty," *Art News.* May 1956.
Ritchie, Andrew. *Abstract Painting and Sculpture in America.* N.Y., 1951.
Schapiro, Meyer. "The Liberating Quality of Abstract Art," *Art News.* Summer 1957.
Abstract Expressionism
Artforum. Summer 1965.
"The New American Painting," exhibition catalogue, Museum of Modern Art. N.Y., 1959.
"New York School," exhibition catalogue, Los Angeles County Museum. 1965.
Sandler, Irving. *Triumph of American Painting: A History of Abstract Expressionism.* N.Y., 1970.
Adams, Alice
Linville, Kasha. "Whitney 1970 Sculpture Circus," *Arts.* Feb. 1971.
Slivka, Rose (ed.). *Crafts of the Modern World.* N.Y., 1968.
Adams, Ansel
Newhall, Nancy, *Ansel Adams: The Eloquent Light.* San Francisco, 1963.
Adams, Herbert
The Craftsman, vol. 2. 1898.
Metropolitan Museum of Art Bulletin, old series 6. 1911.
Taft, Lorado. *History of American Sculpture.* N.Y., 1930.
Adler, Dankmar
Adler, Dankmar. "The Chicago Auditorium," *Architectural Record.* June 1892.
Schuyler, Montgomery. "A Critique of the Works of Adler and Sullivan, D.H. Burnham and Company, and Henry Ives Cobb,"

Architectural Record. 1896.
Aetatis Sue Limner
Wheeler, Robert and Janet MacFarlane. *Hudson Valley Paintings, 1700–1750, in the Albany Institute of History and Art.* Albany, 1959.
Agostini, Peter
"Peter Agostini: The Sea and the Sphere," *Art News.* March 1959.
"Plaster Cornucopia," *Time.* Nov. 13, 1964.
Albers, Anni
Albers, Anni. *Anni Albers: On Weaving.* N.Y., 1965.
"Josef and Anni Albers," exhibition catalogue, Wadsworth Athenaeum. Hartford, 1953.
Albers, Josef
Albers, Josef. "The Interaction of Color," *Art News.* March 1963.
Hamilton, George H. "Josef Albers: Paintings, Prints, Projects," exhibition catalogue, Yale University Art Gallery. New Haven, 1956.
Namuth, Hans and Paul Falkenberg. "Homage to the Square" (film), distributed by Museum-at-Large, N.Y., 1969.
Albright, Ivan Le Lorraine
Kind, Joshua. "Albright: Humanist of Decay," *Art News.* Nov. 1964.
Alexander, Cosmo
Goodfellow. "Cosmo Alexander in America," *Art Quarterly.* Autumn 1963.
Alexander, Francis
French, Henry. *Art and Artists in Connecticut.* Boston, 1879.
Pierce, Catharine. "Francis Alexander," *Old-Time New England,* Oct.–Dec. 1953.
Alexander, John White
Caffin, Charles. "John White Alexander," *Arts and Decoration.* Feb. 1911.
"Catalogue of Paintings. John White Alexander Memorial Exhibition," exhibition catalogue, Carnegie Institute. Pittsburgh, 1916.
Allston, Washington
Allston, Washington. *Lectures on Art and Poems.* N.Y., 1950.
Flagg, Jared. *The Life and Letters of Washington Allston.* N.Y., 1892.
Richards, E.P. *Washington Allston, A Study of the Romantic Artist in America.* N.Y., 1967.
Amelung, Johann Friedrich
"Amelung Glass," exhibition catalogue, Maryland Historical Society. Baltimore, 1952.
American Art-Union
Cowdrey, Mary Bartlett. *American Academy of Fine Arts and American Art-Union.* N.Y., 1953.

American Scene Painting (Regionalism)
"A Half-day in the Studio of Reginald Marsh, Virile Painter of the American Scene," *American Artist.* June 1941.
Gunther, Charles. "1900: The American Scene," *Toledo Museum News.* Autumn 1964.
Janson, H.W. "Benton and Wood, Champions of Regionalism," *Magazine of Art.* May 1946.
——. "The International Aspects of Regionalism," *College Art Journal.* May 1943.
Schapiro, Meyer. "Populist Realism," *Partisan Review.* Dec. 1937–May 1938.
Ames, Ezra
Bolton, Theodore and Irwin Cortelyou. *Ezra Ames of Albany.* N.Y., 1955.
Anderson, Alexander
Burr, Frederick. *Life and Works of Alexander Anderson.* N.Y., 1893.
Hamilton, Sinclair. *Early American Book Illustrators and Wood Engravers, 1670-1870.* Princeton, 1950.
Scrapbooks with proofs of Alexander's engravings, New York Public Library, N.Y.
André, Carl
Bourdon, David. "The Razed Sites of Carl André," *Artforum.* Oct. 1966.
Tuchman, Phyllis. "An Interview with Carl André," *Artforum.* June 1970.
Anshutz, Thomas Pollock
"Thomas Anshutz. 1851–1912," exhibition catalogue, Graham Gallery. N.Y., 1963.
Antonakos, Stephen
"New Talent USA: Stephen Antonakos," *Art in America.* July-Aug. 1966.
"Stephen Antonakos," exhibition catalogue, Fresno State College, Calif. 1972.
Apple, Billy
Apple, Billy. "Live Stills," *Arts.* Feb. 1967.
Arbus, Diane
"Five Photographs by Diane Arbus," *Artforum.* May 1971.
Szarkowski, John. "Photographs by Diane Arbus," exhibition catalogue, Museum of Modern Art. N.Y., 1972.
Thornton, Gene. "Diane Arbus: The Subject was Freaks," *New York Times.* Aug. 22, 1971.
Architecture Since 1540
See General Bibliography
Armory Show
Brown, Milton. *The Story of the Armory Show.* Princeton, 1963.
Kuhn, Walt. *The Story of the Armory Show.* N.Y., 1938.
Mellquist, Jerome. "The Armory Show Thirty Years Later," *Magazine of Art.* Dec. 1943.

Bibliography According to Entries

Pach, Walter. "The Point of View of the Moderns," *Century Magazine*. April 1914.

Arneson, Robert

O'Brien, George. "New Uncrafty Crafts," *Art in America*. May-June 1966.

Selz, Peter and Brenda Richardson, "California Ceramics," *Art in America*. May-June 1969.

Art Deco

Hillier, Bevis and David Ryan. "Art Deco," exhibition catalogue, Minneapolis Institute of Arts. 1971.

Hillier, Bevis. *Art Deco*. London, 1968.

Pincus-Witten, Robert. "Art Deco,"*Artforum*. Dec. 1970.

Scherer, Herbert. "Minneapolis' Art Deco Extravaganza," *Arts*. Summer 1971.

Art Glass

Art's Master-Piece. London, 1710.

Davis, Derek and Keith Middlemas. *Colored Glass*. N.Y., 1968.

Smith, R. Weaver. "The Art of Glass," *Antique Dealer and Collector's Guide*. Oct. 1948.

Watkins, Lura, "Animals in Victorian Glass," *Antiquarian*. July 1926.

Art Nouveau (Architecture)

Grady, James. "Bibliography of the Art Nouveau," *Journal of the Society of Architectural Historians*. May 1955.

Guimard, Hector. "An Architect's Opinion of l'Art Nouveau," *Architectural Record*, vol. 12. 1902.

Madsen, S. Tschudi. *Art Nouveau*, N.Y., 1967.

Pevsner, Nikolaus. *Pioneers of Modern Design*. N.Y., 1949

Selz, Peter. *Art Nouveau*. N.Y., 1959.

Art Nouveau (Glass)

Grover, Ray and Lee. *Art Glass Nouveau*. Rutland, 1967.

Revi, A. Christian. *American Art Nouveau Glass*. Camden, 1967.

Art Students League of N.Y.

Landgren, M. E. *Years of Art: The Story of the Art Students League of N.Y.* N.Y., 1940.

Ash Can School

Glackens, Ira. *William Glackens and the Ashcan Group*. N.Y., 1957.

"New York Realists, 1900-1914," exhibition catalogue, Whitney Museum. N.Y., 1937.

Assemblage

Factor, Donald. "Assemblage." *Artforum*. Summer 1964.

Kultermann, Udo. *The New Sculpture: Environments and Assemblages*. N.Y., 1968.

Seitz, William. "Art of Assemblage," exhibition catalogue, Museum of Modern Art. N.Y., 1961

——. "Assemblage: Problems and Issues," *Art International*. Feb. 1962.

Atelier 17

"Atelier 17," exhibition catalogue, Museum of Modern Art. N.Y., 1944.

Atterbury, Grosvenor

Price, C. Matlack. "The Work of Grosvenor Atterbury," *Arts and Decoration*, vol. 12. 1912.

Audubon, John James

Ford, Alice. *John James Audubon*. Norman, Okla., 1964.

Herrick, Francis. *Audubon the Naturalist. A History of his Life and Time*. N.Y., 1917.

Original Watercolor Paintings by John James Audubon for the Birds of America. N.Y., 1966.

Augur, Hezekiah

French, Henry. *Art and Artists in Connecticut*. Boston, 1879.

"New Haven Sculptors," *Bulletin of the Associates in Fine Arts at Yale University*. June 1938.

Austin, Henry

Meeks, C. L. V. "Henry Austin and the Italian Villa," *Art Bulletin*. June 1948.

"A Victorian Mansion," *Hobbies*. Sept. 1944.

Autio, Rudy

Slivka, Rose (ed.). *Crafts of the Modern World*. N.Y., 1968.

Automatism

Kris, Ernst. *Psychoanalytic Explorations in Art*. N.Y., 1964.

Rubin, William. "Notes on Masson and Pollock," *Arts*. Nov. 1959.

Avedon, Richard

Avedon. Minneapolis, 1970.

Avedon, Richard and James Baldwin. *Nothing Personal*. N.Y., 1963.

Avery, Milton

Guest, Barbara. "Avery and Gatch: Lonely Americans," *Art News*. March 1960.

"Milton Avery," exhibition catalogue, Baltimore Museum of Art. 1952.

Bacon, Peggy

McBride, Henry. "Peggy Bacon," *Arts*. May 1931.

Murrell, W. *Peggy Bacon*. N.Y., 1922.

Badger, Joseph

Park, Lawrence. "An Account of Joseph Badger, and a Descriptive List of his Work," *Proceedings of the Massachusetts Historical Society*. Dec. 1917.

——. "Joseph Badger of Boston, and His Portraits of Children," *Old-Time New England*. Jan. 1923.

Ball, Thomas

Ball, Thomas. *My Threescore Years and Ten*. Boston, 1891.

Gardner, Albert. *Yankee Stonecutters: The First American School of Sculpture, 1800-1850*. N.Y., 1944.

Partridge, William. "Thomas Ball," *New England Magazine*. May 1895.

Bannard, Darby

Bannard, Darby. "Color, Paint and Present Day Painting," *Artforum*. April 1966.

Krauss, Rosalind. "Darby Bannard's New Work," *Artforum*. April 1966.

Barbizon School

Herbert, Robert. "Barbizon Revisited," exhibition catalogue, California Palace of the Legion of Honor. 1962.

Bard, James

Lipman, Jean and Alice Winchester. *Primitive Painters in America, 1750–1850*. N.Y., 1950.

New York Historical Society Quarterly Bulletin. Oct. 1924.

Sniffen, Harold. "James and John Bard, Painters of Steamboat Portraits," *Art in America*. April 1949.

Barnard, George Grey

Dickson, Harold. "Log of a Masterpiece, Barnard's 'Struggle of the Two Natures of Man,'" *Art Journal*. Spring 1961.

"George Grey Barnard, 1863, Centenary Exhibition," exhibition catalogue, Pennsylvania State University Library, 1963–1964.

Barnard, George N.

Newhall, Beaumont. *The Daguerreotype in America*. N.Y., 1961.

Barnes, Edward Larrabee

"Walker Art Center 1971," *Design Quarterly 81*. Minneapolis, 1971.

Bartlett, Paul Wayland

Bartlett, Ellen. "Paul Bartlett: An American Sculptor," *New England Magazine*, vol. 33. 1905.

Wheeler, Charles. "Bartlett, 1865-1925," *American Magazine of Art*. Nov. 1925.

Bascom, Ruth Henshaw

Dods, Agnes. "Connecticut Valley Painters," *Antiques*. Oct. 1944.

Lipman, Jean and Alice Winchester. *Primitive Painters in America, 1750-1850*. N.Y., 1950.

Sears, Clara. *Some American Primitives*. Boston, 1941.

Baskin, Leonard

Kaplan, Sidney. "Portraits of Artists by Leonard Baskin," *Massachusetts Review*. Autumn 1963.

O'Doherty, Brian. "Leonard Baskin," *Art in America*. Summer 1962.

Roylance, Dale. *Leonard Baskin: The Graphic Work 1950–1970*. N.Y., 1970.

Bassett, Florence Shust Knoll

Drexler, Arthur and Greta Daniel. *Introduction to Twentieth Century Design*. N.Y., 1959.

Pierson, William, Jr. and Martha Davidson (eds.). *Arts of the United States*. N.Y., 1960.

Bauhaus

Welsh, Robert. "The Bauhaus Show in Toronto," *Artforum*. March 1970.

Werner, Alfred. "The Bauhaus: An Impossible Dream," *Arts*. Dec.-Jan. 1970.

Wingler, Hans. *The Bauhaus*. Cambridge, 1969.

"50 Years Bauhaus," exhibition catalogue, Illinois Institute of Technology. 1969.

Baziotes, William

Alloway, Lawrence. "William Baziotes," exhibition catalogue, Guggenheim Museum. N.Y., 1965.

"The Magical Worlds of Redon, Klee, Baziotes," exhibition catalogue, Contemporary Arts Museum. Houston, 1957.

Sandler, Irving. "Baziotes: Modern Mythologist," *Art News*. Feb. 1965.

Beard, James Henry

Smith, S. Winifred. "James Henry Beard," *Museum Echoes*. April 1954.

Beaux, Cecilia

Beaux, Cecilia. *Background with Figures*. Boston, 1930.

Bell, Mrs. Arthur. "The work of Cecilia Beaux," *International Studio*, vol. 8, 1899.

Drinkers. Henry. "The Paintings and Drawings of Cecilia Beaux," exhibition catalogue, Pennsylvania Academy of the Fine Arts. Philadelphia, 1955.

Beaux Arts Eclectic

Harbeson, John. *The Study of Architectural Design with Special Reference to the Beaux-Arts Institute of Design*. N.Y., 1926.

Hastings, Thomas. "How the Beaux-Arts Institute Has Helped Our Architectural Schools," *Architecture*, vol. 37. 1918.

Bel Geddes, Norman

Bel Geddes, Norman. *Horizons*. Boston, 1932.

——. *Magic Motor Ways.* Boston, 1940.
Bell, Larry
Daniele, Fidel. "Bell's Progress," *Artforum.* Summer 1967.
Plagens, Peter. "Larry Bell Reassessed," *Artforum.* Oct. 1972.
Bellows, George Wesley
Boswell, Peyton, Jr. *George Bellows.* N.Y., 1942.
"George Bellows, Paintings, Drawings, Prints," exhibition catalogue, Art Institute of Chicago. 1946.
"Memorial Exhibition of the Work of George Bellows," exhibition catalogue, Metropolitan Museum of Art. N.Y., 1925.
Morgan, Charles. *George Bellows.* Scranton, 1965.
Belluschi, Pietro
Stubblebine, Jo (ed.). *The Northwest Architecture of Pietro Belluschi.* N.Y., 1953.
Belter, John Henry
"Victorianism as John Henry Belter Expressed It," *Arts and Decoration.* April 1934.
Vincent, Clare. "John Henry Belter's Patent Parlour Furniture," *Furniture History,* vol. 3. 1967.
Benbridge, Henry
Rutledge, Anna Wells. "Henry Benbridge (1743–1812?) American Portrait Painter," *American Collector.* Oct. 1948.
Benjamin, Asher
Benjamin, Asher. *The Country Builder's Assistant.* Boston, 1798.
Thompson, Florence. "More About Asher Benjamin," *Journal of the Society of Architectural Historians.* Oct. 1954.
Benson, Frank Weston
Downes, William. "Frank W. Benson and His Work," *Brush and Pencil,* vol. 6. 1900.
Smith, Minna. "The Work of Frank W. Benson," *International Studio,* vol. 35. 1908.
Benton, Thomas Hart
"The Arts of Life in America: A Series of Murals by Thomas Benton," exhibition catalogue, Whitney Museum. N.Y., 1932.
Benton, Thomas Hart. *An American in Art.* Lawrence, Kansas, 1969.
Craven, Thomas. *Thomas Hart Benton.* N.Y., 1939.
Berman, Eugene
"Stage and Artist in the Television Era," *Art News.* Feb. 1952.
Biddle, George
Biddle, George. *An American Artist's Story.* Boston, 1939.
George Biddle's War Drawings. N.Y., 1944.
Bierstadt, Albert
"Albert Bierstadt," exhibition catalogue, Whitney Museum. N.Y., 1972.
Hendricks, Gordon. "The First Three Western Journeys of Albert Bierstadt," *Art Bulletin.* Sept. 1964.
Spieler, Gerhard. "A Noted Artist in Early Colorado: The Story of Albert Bierstadt," *American-German Review.* June 1945.
Bingham, George Caleb
Bloch, E. Maurice. *George Caleb Bingham; The Evolution of an Artist and a Catalogue Raisonne.* Berkeley, 1967.
——. "George Caleb Bingham," exhibition catalogue, National Collection of Fine Arts. Wash. D.C., 1967.
Birch, Thomas
M. and M. Karolik Collection of American Painting: 1815–1865. Cambridge, 1949.

Bishop, Isabel
Johnson, Una. *Isabel Bishop, Prints and Drawings, 1925–1964.* N.Y., 1964.
Bissell, George Edwin
Mallett, Daniel. *Mallett's Index of Artists.* N.Y., 1935.
Bitter, Karl
Dennis, James. *Karl Bitter.* Madison, Wis., 1967.
Black, Starr & Frost
Rainwater, Dorothy. *American Silver Manufacturers.* Hanover, Pa., 1966.
Blackburn, Joseph
Baker, C.H.C. "Notes on Joseph Blackburn and Nathaniel Dance," *Huntington Library Quarterly.* Nov. 1945.
Morgan, John Hill and Henry W. Foote. "An Extension of Lawrence Park's Descriptive List of the Works of Joseph Blackburn," *Proceedings of the American Antiquarian Society.* April 1936.
Park, Lawrence. "Two Portraits by Blackburn," *Art in America.* Feb. 1919.
Bladen, Ronald
Baker, Kenneth. "Ronald Bladen," *Artforum.* April 1972.
Sandler, Irving. "Ronald Bladen," *Artforum.* Oct. 1966.
Blakelock, Ralph Albert
Daingerfield, Elliott. *Ralph Albert Blakelock,* N.Y., 1914.
"Ralph Albert Blakelock Centenary Exhibition," exhibition catalogue, Whitney Museum. N.Y., 1947.
Young, J. W., "Catalogue of the Works of R. A. Blakelock, NA, and of His Daughter Marian Blakelock," exhibition catalogue, Young's Art Galleries. Chicago, 1916.
Blashfield, Edwin
Blashfield, E. H. *Mural Painting in America.* N.Y., 1914.
——. "The Painting, of Today," *Century Magazine.* April 1914.
Blown-three-mold Glass
McKearin, George and Helen. *Two Hundred Years of American Blown Glass.* Garden City, N.Y., 1950.
McKearin, Helen. "Three Mold Glass," *Antiques,* vol. 6. 1924.
——. "Fictions of Three-Mold Glass," *Antiques,* vol. 16. 1929.
Blume, Peter
Godsoe, R. U. "Peter Blume, A New Vision," *Creative Art.* Sept. 1932.
Blume, Peter. "After Superrealism," *New Republic.* Oct. 3, 1934.
Soby, James Thrall. "Peter Blume's Eternal City," *Museum of Modern Art Bulletin.* April 1943.
Blumenau, Lili
Blumenau, Lili. *The Art and Craft of Hand Weaving.* N.Y., 1955.
——. *Creative Design in Wall Hangings.* N.Y., 1967.
Blythe, David Gilmore
Miller, Dorothy. *The Life and Work of David Gilmour Blythe.* Pittsburgh, 1950.
Bodmer, Karl
"Carl Bodmer Paints the Indian Frontier; A Traveling Exhibition," exhibition catalogue, Smithsonian Institution. Wash. D.C., 1954.
Draper, Benjamin. "Karl Bodmer, An Artist Among the Indians," *Antiques.* May 1944.
Wied-Neuwied, Maximilian. *Maximilian, Prince of Wied's Travels in the Interior of*

North America, 1832–1834. Cleveland, 1906.
Bogardus, James
Bannister, Turpin. "Bogardus Revisited," *Journal of the Society of Architectural Historians.* Dec. 1956 and March 1957.
Bogardus, James. *Cast Iron Buildings: Their Construction and Advantages.* N.Y., 1856.
"James Bogardus," *Scientific American.* May 2, 1874.
Bohrod, Aaron
Bohrod, Aaron. *A Pottery Sketchbook.* N.Y., 1959.
——. *A Decade of Still Life.* N.Y., 1966.
Bolotowsky, Ilya
Stiles, Knute. "Ilya Bolotowsky," *Artforum.* April 1970.
Borglum, Gutzon
Borglum, Gutzon. "The Revolt in Art," *Lotus Magazine.* Feb. 1918
McSpadden, Joseph. *Famous Sculptors of America.* N.Y., 1924.
Borglum, Solon Hannibal
Borglum, Solon. *Sound Construction.* N.Y., 1923.
Goodrich, A. "The Frontier in Sculpture," *World's Work,* vol. 3. 1902.
Sewall, Frank. "Sculptor of the Prairie: Solon Borglum," *Century Magazine,* vol. 68. 1904.
Bourgeois, Louise
"Annual Exhibition of Contemporary American Sculpture, Watercolors and Drawings," exhibition catalogue, Whitney Museum. N.Y., 1954
Robbins, Daniel. "Recent Still-Life," *Art in America.* Jan.–Feb. 1966
Brackett, Edward Augustus
Lee, Hannah. *Familiar Sketches of Sculpture and Sculptors.* Boston, 1854.
Bradford, William
New York Times. April 25, 1892 (obituary).
Wood, Edmund. "William Bradford," *Old Dartmouth Historical Sketches,* XXVI. 1909.
Brady, Mathew
Cobb, Josephine. "Mathew B. Brady's Photographic Gallery in Washington," *Columbia Historical Society Records,* vol. 53–56.
The Gallery of Illustrious Americans. N.Y., 1850.
Horan, James. *Mathew Brady, Historian with a Camera.* N.Y. 1955.
Meredith, R. *Mr. Lincoln's Camera Man, Mathew B. Brady.* N.Y., 1946.
Milhollen, Hirst. "The Brady-Handy Collection," *Library of Congress Quarterly Journal of Current Acquisitions.* May 1965.
Breer, Robert
"Motionless Motion," *Art News.* Nov. 1967.
Breuer, Marcel
Argan, G. C. *Marcel Breuer: Disegno Industriale E Architettura.* Milan, 1957.
Blake, Peter. *Marcel Breuer: Architect and Designer.* N.Y., 1949.
Jones, Cranston. *Marcel Breuer: Buildings and Projects, 1921–1961.* N.Y., 1963
"Recent Work of Marcel Breuer," *Architectural Record.* Jan. 1960.
Brewster, John, Jr.
Little, Nina. "John Brewster, Jr., 1766–1854, Deaf Mute Portrait Painter of Connecticut and Maine," *Connecticut Historical Society Bulletin,* vol. 25. 1960.
Bricher, Alfred Thompson

Bibliography According to Entries

Preston, John. "Alfred Thompson Bricher, 1837–1908," *Art Quarterly.* Summer 1962.

Bridges, Charles
Foote, Henry W. "Charles Bridges: Sergeant Painter of Virginia, 1735–1740," *Virginia Magazine of History and Biography.* Jan. 1952.

Brook, Alexander
Jewell, E. A. *Alexander Brook.* N.Y., 1931.
Murrell, W. *Alexander Brook.* Woodstock, 1922.
Watson, F. *Alexander Brook.* N.Y., 1930.

Brooks, James
Hunter, Sam. "James Brooks," exhibition catalogue, Whitney Museum, N.Y., 1963.
"James Brooks," *Magazine of Art.* Jan. 1953.

Browere, John Henry Isaac
Bennet, James. *The Mask of Fame.* Highland Park, Ill., 1938.
Hart, Charles. *Browere's Life Masks of Great Americans.* N.Y., 1899.
Millard, Everett. "The Browere Life Masks," *Art in America.* April 1950.

Brown, George Loring
Clement, Clara and Laurence Hutton. *Artists of the Nineteenth Century and their Work.* Boston, 1884.
M. and M. Karolik Collection of American Paintings: 1815–1865. Cambridge, 1949.

Brown, Henry Kirke
Boston Transcript. July 12, 1886 (obituary).
Lee, Hannah. *Familiar Sketches of Sculpture and Sculptors.* Boston, 1854.
Taft, Lorado. *History of American Sculpture.* N.Y., 1925.

Brown, Mather
Coburn, Frederick. "Mather Brown," *Art in America.* Autumn 1923.
Hart, Charles. "Portrait of Thomas Dawson, Painted by Mather Brown," *Art in America.* Oct. 1917.

Bruce, Patrick Henry
"Catalogue of the Société Anonyme," Yale University Art Gallery. New Haven, 1950.

Bruguière, Francis
Chappell, Walter. "Francis Bruguière," *Art in America,* no. 3. 1959.

Brush, George De Forest
"A Catalogue of an Exhibition of Paintings and Drawings by George de Forest Brush," exhibition catalogue, American Academy of Arts and Letters. N.Y., 1933.
Ely, Catherine. "George de Forest Brush," *Art in America,* vol. 11. 1923.
Merrick, Lula. "Brush's Indian Pictures," *International Studio,* vol. 76. 1922.

Buckland, William
Beirne, Rosamond, "William Buckland, Architect of Maryland and Virginia," *Maryland Historical Magazine.* Sept. 1946.
—— and John Scarff. *William Buckland 1734–1774, Architect of Virginia and Maryland.* 1958.

Buffington, Leroy Sunderland
Cristison, Muriel. "How Buffington Staked his Claim," *Art Bulletin.* March 1944.
Morrison, Hugh, "Buffington and the Invention of the Skyscraper," *Art Bulletin.* March 1944.
Upjohn, E. M. "Buffington and the Skyscraper," *Art Bulletin.* March 1935.

Bulfinch, Charles
Bulfinch, Ellen. *The Life and Letters of Charles Bulfinch.* Boston, 1896.
Kirker, Harold. *The Architecture of Charles Bulfinch.* Cambridge, 1969.
Place, Charles. *Charles Bulfinch: Architect and Citizen.* Boston, 1925.

Bullock, Wynn
Bullock, Barbara. *Wynn Bullock.* San Francisco, 1971.
"Wynn Bullock," exhibition catalogue, San Francisco Museum of Art.

Bultos
Boyd, E. *Popular Arts of Colonial New Mexico.* Santa Fe, 1959.
Christensen, Erwin. *Early American Wood Carving.* N.Y., 1952.

Bunshaft, Gordon
Jacobs, David. "The Establishment's Architect-Plus," *New York Times Magazine.* July 23, 1972.

Burchfield, Charles
Baur, John. *Charles Burchfield.* N.Y. 1956.
"Charles Burchfield: A Retrospective Exhibition of Watercolors and Oils, 1916–1943," exhibition catalogue, Buffalo Fine Arts Academy. 1944.
"Charles Burchfield: Early Water Colors (1916–1918), exhibition catalogue, Museum of Modern Art. N.Y., 1930.
McBride, Henry. "Burchfield," *Creative Art.* Sept. 1928.

Burgis, William
Dow, George. *The Arts and Crafts in New England, 1704–1775.* Topsfield, Mass. 1927.
Stokes, I. N. Phelps and Daniel Haskell. *American Historical Prints.* N.Y., 1933.

Burnham, Daniel H.
Architectural Work of Graham, Anderson, Probst & White, and Their Predecessors, D. H. Burnham & Company. London, 1933.
Moore, Charles. *Daniel H. Burnham.* Boston, 1921.
Schuyler, Montgomery, "A Critique of the Works of Adler and Sullivan, D. H. Burnham and Company, and Henry Ives Cobb," *Architectural Record.* 1896.

Burt, John and Samuel, William and Benjamin
Phillips, John. *Early American Silver Selected from the Mabel Garvan Collection at Yale University.* New Haven, 1960.

Bush-Brown, Henry Kirke
Mechlin, Leila. "The Bush-Brown's Exhibition at the Arts Club," *Art and Archaeology,* vol. 13. 1922.

Buttersworth, James E.
Panorama, vol. I. 1946.
Peters, Fred. *Clipper Ship Prints.* N.Y., 1930.

Cadmus, Paul
Johnson, Una. *Paul Cadmus: Prints and Drawings, 1922–1967.* Brooklyn, 1968.

Calder, Alexander
Arnason, H. H. *Calder.* N.Y., 1966.
Calder, Alexander and Jean Davidson. *Calder, An Autobiography with Pictures.* N.Y., 1966.
Gray, Cleve. "Calder's Circus," *Art in America.* Oct. 1964.
Sweeney, James J. "Alexander Calder," exhibition catalogue, Guggenheim Museum. N.Y., 1964.

Calder, Alexander Stirling
Gardner, Albert. *American Sculpture.* N.Y., 1965.

Callahan, Harry
Paul, Sherman. "Harry Callahan," exhibition catalogue, Museum of Modern Art. N.Y., 1967.

Calverley, Charles
Egbert, Donald. *Princeton Portraits.* Princeton, 1947.
National Academy of Design, Catalogue of the Permanent Collection. N.Y., 1911.

Carder, Frederick
Bardrof, Frank. "Frederic Carder: Artist in Glass," *The Glass Industry,* vol. 20. 1939.
Gardner, Paul. *The Glass of Frederick Carder.* N.Y., 1971.

Carles, Arthur B.
Marin, John. "On My Friend Carles," *Art News.* April 1953.

Carousel Figures
Christensen, Erwin. *Early American Wood Carving.* N.Y., 1952.
Fried, Frederick. *A Pictorial History of the Carousel.* N.Y., 1964.

Carrère and Hastings
Gray, David. *Thomas Hastings, Architect.* Boston, 1933.
Hastings, Thomas. *Six Lectures on Architecture.* Chicago, 1917.
"The Work of Messrs. Carrère and Hastings," *Architectural Record.* Jan. 1910.

Casilear, John William
"American Art Notes, Hudson River School," *Connoisseur.* April 1932.
Stauffer, David. *American Engravers Upon Copper and Steel.* N.Y., 1907.

Cassatt, Mary
Breeskin, Adelyn. *The Graphic Work of Mary Cassatt, a Catalogue Raisonné.* N.Y., 1948.
Sweet, Frederick. *Miss Mary Cassatt, Impressionist from Pennsylvania.* Norman, Okla., 1966.

Castle, Wendell
O'Brien, George. "New Uncrafty Crafts," *Art in America.* May–June 1966.

Catlin, George
Catlin, George. *Letters and Notes on the Manners, Customs, and Condition of the North American Indians.* London, 1841.
Haberly, Lloyd. *Pursuit of the Horizon: A Life of George Catlin, Painter and Recorder of the American Indian.* N.Y., 1948.
Thomas, W. Stephen. "George Catlin, Portrait Painter," *Antiques.* Aug. 1948.

Cavallon, Georgio
O'Hara, Frank. "Cavallon Paints a Picture," *Art News.* Dec. 1958.

Ceramics
Barber, Edwin. *The Pottery and Porcelain of the United States.* N.Y., 1902.
Barret, Richard. *Bennington Pottery and Porcelain: A Guide to Identification.* N.Y., 1958.
Clement, Arthur. *Notes on American Ceramics, 1607–1943.* Brooklyn, 1944.
Henzke, Lucile. *American Art Pottery.* N.Y., 1970.
Our Pioneer Potters. N.Y., 1947.
Peck, Herbert. *The Book of Rookwood Pottery.* N.Y., 1968.
Ramsay, John. *American Potters and Pottery.* Clinton, Mass., 1939.
Spargo, John. *Early American Pottery and China.* N.Y., 1926.
Watkins, Lura. *Early New England Potters and Their Wares.* Cambridge, 1950.

Chalfant, Jefferson David
Frankenstein, Alfred. "The Reality of Appearance," exhibition catalogue, National Gallery of Art. Wash. D.C., 1970.

Chamberlain, John
"Seven Sculptors," exhibition catalogue, Institute of Contemporary Art. Philadelphia, 1966.
Tuchman, Phyllis. "An Interview with John Chamberlain," *Artforum.* Feb. 1972.
Chambers, Thomas
Ford, Alice. *Pictorial Folk Art, New England to California.* N.Y., 1949.
Little, Nina. "Earliest Signed Picture by Thomas Chambers," *Antiques.* April 1948.
——. "Thomas Chambers, Man or Myth," *Antiques.* March 1948.
Chandler, Winthrop
Flexner, James. "Winthrop Chandler: An 18th Century Artisan Painter," *Magazine of Art.* Nov. 1947.
Little, Nina. "Recently Discovered Paintings by Winthrop Chandler," *Art in America.* April 1948.
——. "Winthrop Chandler," *Art in America.* April 1947.
Chapman, John Gadsby
Chamberlain, Georgia. *Studies on John Gadsby Chapman, American Artist.* Annandale, Va., 1963.
Chapman, John Gadsby. *American Drawing Book.* N.Y., 1847.
Davis, Curtis. "A Legend at Full Length, Mr. Chapman Paints Col. Crockett, and Tells About It," *Proceedings of the American Antiquarian Society.* Oct. 21, 1959.
"John Gadsby Chapman. Painter and Illustrator," exhibition catalogue, National Gallery of Art. Wash. D.C., 1962–63.
Charlot, Jean
Charlot, Jean. *Art-Making from Mexico to China.* N.Y., 1950.
Claudel, Paul. *Jean Charlot.* Paris, 1933.
Dodd, Lamar. *Charlot Murals in Georgia.* Athens, Ga., 1945.
Chase, William Merritt
Roof, Katharine. *The Life and Art of William Merritt Chase.* N.Y., 1917.
Van Rensselaer, M. "William M. Chase," *American Art Review,* vol. 2. 1881.
"William Merritt Chase," exhibition catalogue, University of California Art Gallery. Santa Barbara, 1964.
Chicago School of Architecture
Andrews, Wayne. *Battle for Chicago.* N.Y., 1946.
Condit, Carl. *The Chicago School of Architecture.* Chicago, 1964.
Schulze, Franz. "The New Chicago Architecture," *Art in America.* May–June 1968.
Tallmadge, Thomas. *Architecture in Old Chicago.* Chicago, 1941.
Chryssa
Calas, Nicolas. "Chryssa and Times' Magic Square," *Art International.* Feb. 1962.
Church, Frederic Edwin
Huntington, David. *The Landscapes of Frederic Edwin Church.* N.Y., 1966.
"Frederic Edwin Church," exhibition catalogue, National Collection of Fine Arts. Wash. D.C., 1966.
Church, Henry
Antiques. Sept. 1951.
Lipman, Jean and Alice Winchester. *Primitive Painters in America, 1750–1850; An Anthology.* N.Y., 1950.
Church Silver
Curtis, George. *American Church Silver of the Seventeenth and Eighteenth Centuries.* Boston, 1911.

Jones, E. Alfred. *The Old Silver of American Churches.* Letchworth, England, 1913.
Circus Wagons
Austin, A. E., Jr. *The Museum of the American Circus.* Sarasota, Fla., n.d.
Fox, Charles. *Circus Parades.* Watkins Glen, N.Y., 1953.
Fried, Frederick. *Artists in Wood.* N.Y., 1970.
Whitehall, Virginia. "American Circus Carvings," *Magazine of Art.* 1943.
Claypoole, James, Jr.
Sellers, Charles. "James Claypoole: A Founder of the Art of Painting in Pennsylvania," *Pennsylvania History.* April 1950.
Clevenger, Shobal Vail
American Collector. May 1946.
Cist, Charles. *Cincinnati in 1841.* Cincinnati, 1841.
Clonney, James G.
M. and M. Karolik Collection of American Painting: 1815–1865. Cambridge, 1949.
Codman, Charles
"Maine Artists," *Maine Library Bulletin.* July–Oct. 1927.
M. and M. Karolik Collection of American Paintings: 1815–1865. Cambridge, 1949.
Cogdell, John
Rutledge, Anna. "Cogdell and Mills, Charleston Sculptors," *Antiques.* March 1942.
Cole, Thomas
Cole Papers (manuscript). New York State Library, Albany.
Noble, Louis L. *The Life and Works of Thomas Cole.* Cambridge, 1964.
Seaver, Esther. "Thomas Cole, 1801–1848, One Hundred Years Later," exhibition catalogue, Wadsworth Athenaeum. Hartford, 1948.
Collage
Greenberg, Clement. "The Pasted Paper Revolution," *Art News.* Sept. 1958.
Janis Harriet and Rudi Blesh. *Collage,* N.Y., 1962.
Colman, Samuel, Jr.
Art News. April 3, 1920 (obituary).
Clement, Clara and Laurence Hutton. *Artists of the Nineteenth Century and their Work.* Boston, 1884.
Color-Field Painting
Henning, Edward. "Color and Field," *Art International.* May 1971.
Concept Art
Burnham, Jack. "Alice's Head: Reflections on Conceptual Art," *Artforum.* Feb. 1970.
"Conceptual Art," exhibition catalogue, New York Cultural Center. N.Y., 1970.
Kozloff, Max. "The Trouble with Art-as-Idea," *Artforum.* Sept. 1972.
Lippard, Lucy. "557,087," exhibition catalogue, Seattle Art Museum. Wash., 1969.
Meyer, Ursula (ed.). *Conceptual Art.* N.Y., 1972.
Coney, John
Bulletin of the Yale Associates in Fine Arts. July 1948.
Clarke, H. F. *John Coney, Silversmith.* Boston, 1932.
Stauffer, David. *American Engravers Upon Copper and Steel.* N.Y., 1907.
Connelly, Pierce Francis
Gardner, Albert. *Yankee Stonecutters.* N.Y., 1944.
Conner, Bruce
Leider, Philip. "Bruce Conner: A New Sensibility," *Artforum.* Nov. 1962.

Constructivism
Circle. London, 1937.
Hunt, Ronald. "The Constructivist Ethos," *Artforum.* Oct. 1967.
Kozloff, Max. "Constructivism in Buffalo," *Artforum.* May 1968.
McAgy, Douglas. "Plus x Minus," exhibition catalogue, Albright-Knox Art Center. Buffalo, 1968.
Rickey, George. *Constructivism, Origins and Evolution.* N.Y., 1967.
Cooper, Peter
"American Processional, 1492–1900," exhibition catalogue, U.S. National Capitol Sesquicentennial Commission. Wash. D.C., 1950.
Scharf, John and Thompson Westcott. *History of Philadelphia. 1609–1884.* Philadelphia, 1884.
Cope, George
Frankenstein, Alfred. "The Reality of Appearance," exhibition catalogue, National Gallery of Art. Wash. D.C., 1970.
Copley, John Singleton
Copley-Pelham Letters. Massachusetts Historical Society Collections, 1914.
Parker, Barbara, and Anne Wheeler. *John Singleton Copley; American Portraits in Oil, Pastel, and Miniature.* Boston, 1938.
Prown, Jules. *John Singleton Copley.* Cambridge, 1966.
Cornell, Joseph
Ashbery, John. "Cornell: the Cube Root of Dreams," *Art News.* Summer 1967.
Goossen, E. C. "The Plastic Poetry of Joseph Cornell," *Art International,* vol. 3. 1959–60.
Waldman, Diane. "Joseph Cornell," exhibition catalogue, Guggenheim Museum. N.Y., 1967.
Cox, Kenyon
Cox, Kenyon. *The Classic Point of View: Six Lectures on Painting Delivered at the Art Institute of Chicago.* N.Y., 1911.
——. *Concerning Painting.* N.Y., 1917.
Crane, Bruce
"The Landscape of Bruce Crane," *Art in America,* vol. 14. 1926.
Lawrence, H. J. "A Painter of Idylls: Bruce Crane," *Brush and Pencil,* vol. 11. 1902.
Trumble, Alfred. "A Poet in Landscape," *Modern Illustrator,* vol. 1. 1893.
Crawford, Ralston
Dwight, Edward. "Lithographs by Ralston Crawford," *Art in America.* Oct. 1955.
——. "Ralston Crawford," exhibition catalogue, Milwaukee Art Center. 1958.
Sweeney, James J. "Ralston Crawford," exhibition catalogue, Louisiana State University Art Gallery. Baton Rouge, 1950.
Crawford, Thomas
Art Journal. 1857 (obituary).
Hillard, George. "Thomas Crawford: A Eulogy," *Atlantic Monthly.* July 1869.
Lee, Hannah. *Familiar Sketches of Sculpture and Sculptors.* Boston, 1854.
Crayon, The
The Crayon: A Journal Devoted to the Graphic Arts and the Literature Related to Them. N.Y., 1855–1861 (monthly).
Crewelwork
Davis, Mildred. *The Art of Crewel Embroidery.* N.Y., 1962
Hedlund, Catherine. *A Primer of New England Crewel Embroidery.* Sturbridge, 1963.

Bibliography According to Entries

Stearns, Martha. *Homespun and Blue, A Study of American Crewel Embroidery.* N.Y., 1963.

Cropsey, Jasper Francis

Bermingham, Peter. "Jasper F. Cropsey, 1823–1900, Retrospective View of America's Painter of Autumn," exhibition catalogue, University of Maryland Art Gallery. 1968.

Cowdrey, Mary B. "Jasper F. Cropsey, 1823–1900, The Colorist of the Hudson River School," *Panorama.* May 1946.

New York Times. June 24, 1900.

Cubism

Barr, Alfred, Jr. "Cubism and Abstract Art," exhibition catalogue, Museum of Modern Art. N.Y., 1936.

Dasburg, Andrew. "Cubism—Its Rise and Influence," *Arts.* Nov. 1923.

De Zayas, M. "Cubism?", *Arts and Decoration.* April 1916.

Eddy, Arthur J. *Cubists and Post-Impressionism.* Chicago, 1914.

Fry, Edward. *Cubism.* N.Y., 1966.

Golding, John. *Cubism, A History and an Analysis 1907–1914.* London, 1959.

Habasque, Guy. *Cubism.* Cleveland, 1959.

Rosenblum, Robert. *Cubism and Twentieth Century Art.* 1961.

Winans, W. "The Ugly Side of the Cubist-Futurist, Vorticist Craze," *Lotus Magazine.* Feb. 1918.

Cummings, Thomas Seir

Cummings, Thomas S. *Historic Annals of the National Academy of Design.* Philadelphia, 1865.

Lossing, Benson. "The National Academy of the Arts of Design and its Surviving Founders," *Harpers New Monthly Magazine.* May 1883.

New York Daily Tribune. Sept 26, 1894.

New York Historical Society Quarterly. Oct. 1947.

Cunningham, Imogen

"Imogen Cunningham," *Aperture,* vol. 14. 1964.

Mann, Margery. *Imogen Cunningham: Photographs.* Seattle, 1970.

Currier and Ives

Peters, Harry. *Currier and Ives, Print Makers to the American People.* Garden City, 1929–31.

Simkin, Colin (ed.). *Currier and Ives' America.* N.Y., 1952.

Curry, John Steuart

Craven, Thomas. "John Steuart Curry," *Scribner's Magazine.* Jan. 1938.

"Retrospective Exhibition of Works by John Steuart Curry", exhibition catalogue, Syracuse University. N.Y., 1956.

Schmeckebier, Laurence. *John Steuart Curry's Pageant of America.* N.Y., 1943.

Dada

Barr, Alfred, Jr. *Fantastic Art, Dada, and Surrealism.* N.Y., 1936.

Baur, John. "The Machine and the Subconscious: Dada in America," *Magazine of Art.* Oct. 1951.

Motherwell, Robert (ed.). *The Dada Painters and Poets, An Anthology.* N.Y., 1951.

Rubin, William. *Dada and Surrealist Art.* N.Y., 1968.

Daguerreotype

Gernsheim, H. and A. *L.J.M. Daguerre.* London, 1956.

Newhall, Beaumont. *The Daguerreotype in America.* N.Y., 1961.

Dallin, Cyrus Edwin

Downes, William. "Mr. Dallin's Indian Sculptures," *Scribner's Magazine,* vol. 57. 1915.

Hodges, Katherine. "Dallin the Sculptor," *American Magazine of Art,* vol. 15. 1924.

May, M. S. "The Work of Cyrus E. Dallin," *New England Magazine,* vol. 48. 1912.

Darley, Felix Octavius Carr

Bolton, Theodore. "The Book Illustrations of F. O. C. Darley," *Proceedings of the American Antiquarian Society.* April 1951.

Old Print Shop Portfolio. Jan. 1954.

Weitenkampf, Frank. "F. O. C. Darley, American Illustrator," *Art Quarterly.* Spring 1947.

Dasburg, Andrew

"Andrew Dasburg," *Art News.* March 28, 1931.

Brook, A. "Andrew Dasburg," *Arts.* July 1924.

Davidson, Bruce

"Bruce Davidson," *Contemporary Photographer,* no. 3. 1961.

Davidson, Bruce. "What Photography Means to Me," *Popular Photography.* May 1962.

Davidson, Jo

Davidson, Jo. *Between Sittings.* N.Y., 1951.

Gregg, F. J. "The Extremists: An Interview with Jo Davidson," *Arts and Decoration.* March 1913.

Davies, Arthur B.

"Arthur B. Davies. "A Centennial Exhibition," Munson-Williams-Proctor Institute. Utica, N.Y., 1962.

"Catalogue of a Memorial Exhibition of the Works of Arthur B. Davies," Metropolitan Museum of Art. N.Y., 1930.

Cortissoz, Royal. *Arthur B. Davies.* N.Y., 1931.

Davis, Alexander Jackson

Andrews, Wayne. "Alexander Jackson Davis," *Architectural Review.* May 1951.

Davis, Alexander Jackson. *Rural Residences.* N.Y., 1837.

Newton, Roger Hale. *Town and Davis, Architects.* N.Y., 1942.

Davis, Gene

"Gene Davis," exhibition catalogue, Gallery of Modern Art. Wash. D.C., 1968.

Rose, Barbara. "A Conversation with Gene Davis," *Artforum.* March 1971.

Davis, Joseph H.

Lipman, Jean and Alice Winchester. *Primitive Painters in America, 1750–1850; An Anthology.* N.Y., 1950.

Spinney, Frank. "Joseph H. Davis," *Antiques.* Oct. 1943.

——. "The Method of Joseph H. Davis," *Antiques.* Aug. 1944.

Davis, Ronald

Fried, Michael. "Ronald Davis: Surface and Illusion," *Artforum.* April 1967.

Davis, Stuart

Blesh, Rudi. *Stuart Davis.* N.Y., 1960.

Davis, Stuart. "Self-Interview," *Creative Art.* Sept. 1931.

Goossen, E. C. *Stuart Davis.* N.Y., 1959.

Dawkins, Henry

American Collector. Feb. 1945.

Decatur, Stephen. "The Conflicting History of Henry Dawkins, Engraver," *American Collector.* Jan. 1939.

Reid, Robert. "Some Early Masonic Engravers in America," *Transactions of the American Lodge of Research, Free and Accepted Masons,* vol. III, no. 1. 1838–39.

Deas, Charles

McDermott, John. "Charles Deas: Painter of the Frontier," *Art Quarterly.* Autumn 1950.

Decker, Joseph

Prown, Jules. "The Rediscovery of America," *Art News.* May 1968.

Decoys

Barber, Joel. *Wild Fowl Decoys.* N.Y., 1954.

Earnest, Adele. *The Art of the Decoy: American Bird Carvings.* N.Y., 1965.

Webster, David and William Kehoe. *Decoys at the Shelburne Museum.* Shelburne, Vt., 1961.

de Creeft, José

Campos, Jules. *José de Creeft.* N.Y., 1945.

de Kooning, Willem

Hess, Thomas. *Willem de Kooning.* N.Y., 1959.

——. "Willem de Kooning," exhibition catalogue, Stedelijk Museum. Amsterdam, 1968.

Kozloff, Max. "The Impact of de Kooning," *Arts Yearbook.* 1964.

Namuth, Hans and Paul Falkenberg. "Willem de Kooning" (film), distributed by Museum-at-Large. N.Y., 1969.

Delano & Aldrich

Bottomley, W. L. "Delano & Aldrich," *Architectural Record.* July 1923.

Delano and Aldrich. *Portraits of Ten Country Houses.* N.Y., 1924.

Demuth, Charles

"Charles Demuth Memorial Exhibition," Whitney Museum. N.Y., 1937.

Gallatin, Albert. *Charles Demuth.* N.Y., 1927.

Mc Bride, Henry. "Water Colors by Charles Demuth," *Creative Art.* Sept. 1925.

Ritchie, Andrew. "Charles Demuth," exhibition catalogue, Museum of Modern Art. N.Y., 1950.

de Rivera, José

Ashton, Dore. "La Sculpture Americaine," *XXe Siecle.* Dec. 1960.

Dewing, Thomas

Dewing, Thomas. "Letter to Abbott Thayer," *Arts.* June–July 1921.

Ely, Catherine. "Thomas W. Dewing," *Art in America,* vol. 10. 1922.

Tharp, Ezra. "Thomas W. Dewing," *Art and Progress,* vol. 5. 1914.

White, Nelson. "The Art of Thomas W. Dewing," *Art and Archaeology,* vol. 27. 1929.

Dexter, Henry

Albee, John. *Henry Dexter, Sculptor.* Cambridge, 1898.

Dickinson, Edwin

Clark, Eliot. "Edwin Dickinson," *The Studio.* Oct. 1961.

Goodrich, Lloyd, *The Drawings of Edwin Dickinson,* New Haven, 1963.

Goodrich, Lloyd. "Edwin Dickinson," exhibition catalogue, Whitney Museum. N.Y., 1965.

Dickinson, Preston

"Preston Dickinson," *Art News.* Dec. 20, 1930.

Watson, F. "Preston Dickinson," *Arts.* May 1924.

Diebenkorn, Richard

Chipp, Herschel. "Diebenkorn Paints a Picture," *Art News.* May 1957.

Diller, Burgoyne

Larson, Philip. "Burgoyne Diller," exhibition catalogue, Walker Art Center. Minneapolis, 1972.

Dine, Jim
"Jim Dine," exhibition catalogue, Whitney Museum. N.Y., 1970.
Jim Dine; Complete Graphics. Berlin, 1970.

Di Suvero, Mark
Ratcliff, Carter. "Mark Di Suvero," *Artforum.* Nov. 1972.
Rosenstein, Harris. "Di Suvero: The Pressures of Reality," *Art News.* Feb. 1967.

Doughty, Thomas
Doughty, Howard. "Life and Works of Thomas Doughty" (manuscript), New York Historical Society. N.Y.

Dove, Arthur
Frank, W. "Art of Arthur Dove," *New Republic.* Jan. 27, 1926.
Phillips, Duncan. "Arthur G. Dove, 1880–1946," *Magazine of Art.* May 1947.
Rosenfeld, Paul. "The World of Arthur G. Dove," *Creative Art.* June 1932.
Wight, Frederick. "Arthur G. Dove," exhibition catalogue, University of California. Berkeley, 1958.

Downing, Andrew Jackson
Downing, Andrew Jackson. *The Architecture of Country Houses.* N.Y., 1858.
——. *A Treatise on the Theory and Practice of Landscape Gardening.* N.Y., 1860.
Pattee, Sarah. "Andrew Jackson Downing and His Influence on Landscape Architecture in America," *Landscape Architecture.* Jan. 1929.

Du Bois, Guy Pène
Cortissoz, Royal. *Guy Pène du Bois.* N.Y., 1931.
Du Bois, Guy Pène. "Despotism and Anarchy in Art," *Arts and Decoration.* Jan. 1915.
Medford, R. C. "Guy Pène du Bois," exhibition catalogue, Washington County Museum of Fine Arts. Maryland, 1940.

Duchamp, Marcel
"A Complete Reversal of Art Opinions by Marcel Duchamp, Iconoclast," *Arts and Decoration.* Sept. 1915.
"The Almost Complete Works of Marcel Duchamp," exhibition catalogue, Arts Council of Great Britain. 1966.
Schwarz, Arturo. *The Complete Works of Marcel Duchamp.* N.Y., 1969.

Dummer, Jeremiah
Bayley, Frank. "An Early New England Limner," *Old-Time New England.* July 1921.
Bulletin of the Associates in Fine Arts at Yale University. June 1938.
Clarke, Hermann and Henry W. Foote. *Jeremiah Dummer. Colonial Craftsman and Merchant, 1645–1718.* Boston, 1935.

Duncanson, Robert S.
Dwight, Edward. "Robert S. Duncanson," *Museum Echoes.* June 1954.
Porter, James. "Robert S. Duncanson, Midwestern Romantic-Realist," *Art in America.* Oct. 1951.

Dunlap, William
Coad, Oral. *William Dunlap.* N.Y., 1917.
Dunlap, William. *History of the Rise and Progress of the Arts of Design in the United States.* N.Y., 1834 and 1965.

Durand, Asher Brown
Durand, John. *The Life and Times of Asher B. Durand.* N.Y., 1894.
Durand Papers, (manuscript). New York

Public Library, N. Y.
Sweet, Frederick. "Asher B. Durand, Pioneer American Landscape Painter," *Art Quarterly.* Spring 1945.

Durand, John
Antiques, vol. LI. 1947.
Kelby, William. *Notes on American Artists, 1754–1820.* N.Y., 1922.
Thorne, Thomas. "America's Earliest Nude?", *William and Mary Quarterly.* Oct. 1949.

Durrie, George Henry
Cowdrey, Mary B. "George Henry Durrie, 1820–1863, Connecticut Painter of American Life," exhibition catalogue, Wadsworth Atheneum. Hartford, 1947.
Durrie, Mary. "George Henry Durrie, Artist," *Antiques.* July 1933.
Peters, Harry. "George Henry Durrie, 1820–1863," *Panorama.* Dec. 1945.

Duveneck, Frank
"Exhibition of the Work of Frank Duveneck," exhibition catalogue, Cincinnati Art Museum. 1936.
Heermann, Norbert. *Frank Duveneck.* Boston, 1918.

Eakins, Thomas
Goodrich, Lloyd. *Thomas Eakins: His Life and Work.* N.Y., 1933.
Mc Henry, Margaret. *Thomas Eakins Who Painted.* 1946.
Porter, Fairfield. *Thomas Eakins.* N.Y., 1959.
Schendler, Sylvan. *Eakins,* 1967.

Eames, Charles
"Charles Eames," exhibition catalogue, Museum of Modern Art. N.Y., 1946.
Drexler, Arthur and Greta Daniel. *Introduction to Twentieth Century Design.* N.Y., 1959.
Peter, John. Masters of Modern Architecture, N.Y., 1958

Earl, Ralph
Goodrich, Lloyd. "Ralph Earl," *Magazine of Art.* Jan. 1946.
Sawitzky, William. "Connecticut Portraits by Ralph Earl, 1761–1801," exhibition catalogue, Yale University Art Gallery. New Haven, 1935.
——. "Ralph Earl, 1751–1801," exhibition catalogue, Whitney Museum. N.Y., 1945.

Earth Art
Hutchinson, Peter. "Earth in Upheaval," *Arts.* Nov. 1968.
Tillim, Sidney. "Earthworks and the New Picturesque," *Artforum.* Dec. 1968.

Eastlake Style
Eastlake, Charles. *Hints on Household Taste.* Boston, 1876.

Eastman, Seth
Bushnell, D. I., Jr. "Seth Eastman. The Master Painter of the American Indian," *Smithsonian Miscellaneous Collections.* April 1932.
Mc Dermott, John Francis. "The Art of Seth Eastman," exhibition catalogue, Smithsonian Institution. Wash. D. C., 1959.
——. *Seth Eastman, Pictorial Historian of the Indian.* Norman, Okla., 1961.

Eaton, Wyatt
Hellman, George. "Wyatt Eaton," *Art World,* vol. 3. 1917.
Sherman, Frederic F. *American Painters of Yesterday and Today.* N.Y., 1919.

Eclecticism
Kidney, W. C. "Another Look at Eclecticism," *Progressive Architecture.* Sept. 1967.
"Nineteenth Century New York Interiors,

Eclecticism Behind the Brick and Brownstone," *Antiques.* June 1943.

Edmonds, Francis William
Mann, Maybelle. "Francis William Edmonds, Mammon and Art," *American Art Journal.* Fall 1970.

Eichholtz. Jacob
Beal, Rebecca. *Jacob Eichholtz, 1776–1842, Portrait Painter of Pennsylvania.* Philadelphia, 1969.

Eight, The
Dinnerstein, H. and Burt Silverman. "New Look at Protest: the Eight Since 1908," *Art News.* Feb. 1958.
"The Eight," exhibition catalogue, Brooklyn Museum. N.Y., 1943–44.
Pach, Walter. "The Eight Then and Now," *Art News.* Jan. 1944.
Perlman, Bennard. *The Immortal Eight.* N.Y., 1962.

Eilshemius, Louis
Farber, Manny. "Eilshemius: Artist behind Mahatma," *Art News.* April 1959.

Elfe, Thomas, Sr.
Burton, E. Milby. *Thomas Elfe, Charleston Cabinetmaker.* Charlestown, 1952.

Elliott, Charles Loring
Bolton, Theodore. "Charles Loring Elliott, An Account of his Life and Work and a Catalogue of the Portraits Painted by Charles Loring Elliott," *Art Quarterly.* Winter 1942.

Ellsworth, James Sanford
Mitchell, Lucy. "James S. Ellsworth, Miniature Painter," *Art in America.* Autumn 1953.

Elmer, Edwin Romanzo
Frankenstein, Alfred. "The Reality of Appearance," exhibition catalogue, National Gallery of Art. Wash. D.C., 1970.

Emmes, Thomas
Middlebrook, L. F. "A Few of the New England Engravers," *Essex Institute Historical Collections.* Oct. 1926.
Stauffer, David. *American Engravers Upon Copper and Steel.* N.Y., 1907.

Emmons, Nathanial
Antiques. Feb. 1947.
Dow, George. *The Arts and Crafts in New England, 1704–1775.* Topsfield, Mass., 1927.

Environmental Art
Goossen, E. C. and Herbert Ferber. "Environmental Sculpture," *Art International.* May 1960.
Kultermann, Udo. *The New Sculpture: Environments and Assemblages.* N.Y., 1968.

Esherick, Wharton
Pierson, William, Jr. and Martha Davidson (eds.). *Arts of the United States.* N.Y., 1960.

Evans, Walker
Evans, Walker and J. Agee. *Let Us Now Praise Famous Men.* N.Y., 1941.
Kirstein, Lincoln. "Walker Evans, American Photographs," exhibition catalogue, Museum of Modern Art. N.Y., 1962.
Szarkowski, John. "Walker Evans," exhibition catalogue, Museum of Modern Art. N.Y., 1971.
Szarkowski, John. *Walker Evans, Photographs.* Greenwich, Conn., 1972.

Evergood, Philip
Baur, John. "Philip Evergood," exhibition catalogue, Whitney Museum. N.Y., 1960.
McCausland, Elizabeth. "The Plastic Organi-

zation of Philip Evergood," Parnassus, vol. 11. March 1939.
Twenty Years of Paintings by Philip Evergood. N.Y., 1947.

Expressionism
Cheney, Sheldon. *Expressionism in Art.* N.Y., 1934.
Myers, Bernard. "Expressionism: The Emotional Approach," *American Artist.* March 1952.
——. *Expressionism: A Generation in Revolt.* London, 1963.

Farm Security Administration (FSA) Historical Division
Photographic Negatives, 1935–1943. Library of Congress, Wash. D.C.
Photographic Prints, 1935–1943. New York Public Library, N.Y.

Farnham, Paulding
The Adams Gold Vase. N.Y., 1896.

Federal Art Project
See WPA.

Feeley, Paul
Baro, Gene. "Paul Feeley, Memorial Exhibition," exhibition catalogue, Guggenheim Museum. N.Y., 1968.
Goossen, E. C. "Paul Feeley," *Art International.* Dec. 1964.

Feininger, Lyonel
"Feininger; Hartley," exhibition catalogue, Museum of Modern Art. N.Y., 1944.
"Lyonel Feininger," exhibition catalogue, Pasadena Art Museum. Calif., 1966.

Feke, Robert
Bolton, Theodore and Harry Binsse. "Robert Feke, First Painter to Coloniel Aristocracy," *Antiquarian.* Oct. 1930.
Foote, Henry W. *Robert Feke.* Cambridge, 1930.
Goodrich, Lloyd. "Robert Feke," exhibition catalogue, Whitney Museum. N.Y., 1946.

Ferber, Herbert
Goossen, E. C, Robert Goldwater,and Irving Sandler. *Three American Sculptors: Ferber, Hare, Lassaw.* N.Y., 1959.
Tuchman, Phyllis. "An Interview with Herbert Ferber," *Artforum.* April 1971.

Ferriss, Hugh
Ferriss, Hugh. *The Metropolis of Tomorrow.* N.Y., 1929.
——. *Power in Building: An Artist's View of Contemporary Architecture.* N.Y., 1953.

Field, Erastus Salisbury
Dods, Agnes. "A Check List of Portraits and Paintings by Erastus Salisbury Field," *Art in America.* Jan. 1944.
Lipman, Jean and Alice Winchester. *Primitive Painters in America, 1750–1850, An Anthology.* N.Y., 1950.
Robinson, Frederick. "Erastus Salisbury Field," *Art in America.* Oct. 1942.

Figureheads
Brewington, M. V. *Shipcarvers of North America.* Barre, Mass., 1962.
Pinckney, Pauline. *American Figureheads and Their Carvers.* N.Y., 1940.
Stackpole, Edouard. *Figureheads and Ship Carvings at Mystic Seaport.* Mystic, 1964.

Fisher, Alvan
Burroughs, Alan. "A Letter from Alvan Fisher," *Art in America.* July 1944.
Johnson, Charlotte. "The European Tradition and Alvan Fisher," *Art in America.* Spring 1953.

Fisher, Jonathan
Chase. Mary. *Jonathan Fisher, Maine Par-*

son, 1768–1847. N.Y., 1948.
Winchester, Alice. "Rediscovery: Parson Jonathan Fisher," *Art in America.* Nov.–Dec. 1970.

Fitch, Simon
Warren, William. "Captain Simon Fitch of Lebanon, 1758–1835, Portrait Painter," *Connecticut Historical Society Bulletin,* vol. 26. 1961.

Flagg, Ernest
Burnham, Alan. "Ernest Flagg: Forgotten Pioneering," *Architectural Forum.* April 1957.
"The Works of Ernest Flagg," *Architectural Record.* April 1902.

Flannagan, John B.
Forsyth. Robert. *John B. Flannagan.* South Bend, Ind., 1963.
Miller, Dorothy. "The Sculpture of John B. Flannagan," exhibition catalogue, Museum of Modern Art. N.Y., 1942.

Flavin, Dan
Burnham, Jack. "A Dan Flavin Retrospective in Ottawa," *Artforum.* Dec. 1969.
Flavin, Dan. "Some Remarks," *Artforum.* Dec. 1966.
Wilson, William. "Dan Flavin: Fiat Lux," *Art News.* Jan. 1970.

Fletcher. Thomas
Ormsbee. Thomas. "Gratitude in Silver for Prosperity," *American Collector.* April 1937.
Wood. Elizabeth. "Thomas Fletcher, a Philadelphia Entrepreneur of Presentation Silver," *Winterthur Portfolio,* vol. 3. 1967.

Foster, John
Green, Samuel A. *John Foster, the Earliest American Engraver and the First Boston Printer.* Boston, 1909.

Fractur
Kauffman, Henry. *Pennsylvania Dutch American Folk Art.* N.Y., 1946.
Little, Nina. *Abby Aldrich Rockefeller Folk Art Collection.* Boston, 1957.
Shelley, Donald. *The Fraktur-Writings, or Illuminated Manuscripts of the Pennsylvania Germans.* Allentown, 1961.

Francis, John F.
Frankenstein, Alfred. "John F. Francis," *Antiques.* May 1951.

Francis, Sam
Read, Sir Herbert. "Sam Francis," *Quadrum,* no. 5. 1958.
"Sam Francis," exhibition catalogue, Moderna Museet. Stockholm, Sweden, 1960.
"Sam Francis," exhibition catalogue, Albright-Knox Art Gallery. Buffalo, 1972.

Frank, Robert
Frank, Robert. *The Americans.* N.Y., 1961 and 1968.
Frank, Robert. *The Lines of My Hand.* N.Y., 1972.

Frankenthaler, Helen
Goossen, E. C. "Helen Frankenthaler," exhibition catalogue, Whitney Museum. N.Y., 1969.
Rose, Barbara. *Helen Frankenthaler.* N.Y., 1972.
——. "Painting within the Tradition: the Career of Helen Frankenthaler," *Artforum.* April 1969.
Rosenstein, Harris. "The Colorful Gesture," *Art News.* March 1969.

Frankl, Paul
Frankl, Paul. *New Dimensions.* N.Y., 1928.

Franklin, Benjamin
Franklin, Benjamin. *Autobiography of Benjamin Franklin.* N.Y., 1951.
Sellers, Charles. *Benjamin Franklin in Portraiture.* New Haven, 1962.

Franzen, Ulrich
"Interpretive Facilities Building, Harpers Ferry, West Virginia," *Architectural Forum.* July–Aug. 1971.

Frasconi, Antonio
"Annual Exhibition of Contemporary American Sculpture, Watercolors and Drawings," exhibition catalogue, Whitney Museum. N.Y., 1954.

Fraser, Charles
"Catalogue with a Short Sketch of Charles Fraser and List of Miniatures Exhibited," exhibition catalogue, Carolina Art Association. Charleston, 1934.
Smith, Alice and D. E. H. Smith. *Charles Fraser.* N.Y., 1924.
Tolman. Ruel. "The Technique of Charles Fraser, Miniaturist," *Antiques.* Jan. 1935.

Frazee, John
Caldwell, Henry. "John Frazee, American Sculptor," M.A. Thesis, New York University. 1951.
Frazee, John. "Autobiography," *North American Magazine.* April and July 1835.

French, Daniel Chester
Adams, Adeline. *Daniel Chester French: Sculptor.* Boston, 1932.
Cresson, Margaret. *Journey Into Fame, The Life of Daniel Chester French.* Cambridge, 1947.
French, Mary. Memories of a Sculptor's Wife. Boston, 1928.

Friedlander, Lee
Devree, Charlotte. "Is This Statuary Worth More Than a Million of Your Money?", *Art News.* April 1955.

Frothingham, Benjamin, Jr.
Spalding, Dexter. "Benjamin Frothingham of Charlestown, Cabinetmaker and Soldier," *Antiques,* vol. 14. 1928.

Fuller, R. Buckminster
Fuller, Buckminster. *Ideas and Integrities.* N.Y., 1963.
McHale, John. *R. Buckminster Fuller.* N.Y., 1962.
"The World of R. Buckminster Fuller," *Architectural Forum.* Jan.–Feb. 1972.

Fulton, Robert
Flexner, James. "Robert Fulton and Samuel F. B. Morse," *Art News Annual.* 1958.

Funk Art
Belz, Carl and Kurt Von Meier. "Funksville: The West Coast Scene," *Art and Australia.* Dec. 1965.
Perrault, John. "Metaphysical Funk Monk," *Art News.* May 1968.
Zack, David. "That's Saul, Folks," *Art News.* Nov. 1969.

Furness, Frank
Campbell, William. "Frank Furness, An American Pioneer," *Architectural Review.* Nov. 1951.

Furniture
Bjerkoe, Ethel. *The Cabinetmakers of America.* Garden City, 1957.
Boger, Ade. *The Complete Guide to Furniture Styles.* N.Y., 1969.
Butler, Joseph. *American Antiques 1800–1900, A Collector's History and Guide,* N.Y., 1965.
Cheney, Sheldon and Mary. *Art and the*

Machine. N.Y., 1936.

Comstock, Helen. *American Furniture: Seventeenth, Eighteenth, and Nineteenth Century Styles.* N.Y., 1962.

Cook, Clarence. *The House Beautiful, Essays on Beds and Tables, Stools and Candlesticks.* N.Y., 1878.

Davis, Felice. "Victorian Cabinetmakers in America," *Antiques.* Sept. 1943.

Downes, Joseph. "The Greek Revival in the United States," *Antiques.* Nov. 1943.

Drepperd, Carl. *First Reader for Antique Collectors.* N.Y., 1946.

Edwards, Ralph and L. G. G. Ramsey (eds.). *The Connoisseur's Complete Period Guide.* N.Y., 1968.

Frankl, Paul. *New Dimensions,* N.Y., 1928.

"Furniture by New York Cabinetmakers 1650 to 1850," exhibition catalogue, Museum of the City of New York. 1956–57.

Hall, John. *The Cabinet Makers Assistant.* Baltimore, 1840.

Hayward, Helena (ed). *World Furniture.* N.Y., 1965.

Horner, William, Jr. *Blue Book, Philadelphia Furniture, William Penn to George Washington,* Philadelphia, 1935.

Ingerman, Elizabeth. "Personal Experiences of an Old New York Cabinetmaker," *Antiques.* Nov. 1963.

Jourdain, Margaret. *Regency Furniture 1795–1820.* London, 1949.

Lea, Zilla (ed.). *The Ornamented Chair, Its Development in America.* Rutland, Vt., 1960.

"A Loan Exhibition of New York State Furniture," exhibition catalogue, Metropolitan Museum of Art. N.Y., 1934.

Loudon, J. C. *An Encyclopedia of Cottage, Farm, and Villa Architecture and Furniture.* London, 1835.

Modern Chairs 1918–1970. Boston, 1970.

Montgomery, Charles. *American Furniture, The Federal Period, in the Henry Francis du Pont Winterthur Museum.* N.Y., 1966.

Moody, Ella. *Modern Furniture.* London, 1966.

Ormsbee, Thomas. *Field Guide to American Victorian Furniture.* Boston, 1952.

Otto, Celia. "Pillar and Scroll: Greek Revival Furniture of the 1830's," *Antiques.* May 1962.

——. *American Furniture of the Nineteenth Century.* N.Y., 1965.

Palmer, Brooks. *The Book of American Clocks.* N.Y., 1950.

Ralston, Ruth. "The Style Antique in Furniture: Its Sources and Its Creators," *Antiques.* May 1945.

——. "The Style Antique in Furniture: Its American Manifestations," *Antiques.* Oct. 1945.

Randall, Richard, Jr. *American Furniture in the Museum of Fine Arts, Boston.* Boston, 1965.

Rice, Morman. *New York Furniture Before 1840 in the Collection of the Albany Institute of History and Art.* Albany, 1962.

Roe, F. Gordon, *Victorian Furniture.* London, 1952.

Roth, Rodris. "American Art, The Colonial Revival and Centennial Furniture," *Art Quarterly,* no. 1. 1964.

Sironen, Marta. *A History of American Furniture.* N.Y., 1936.

Smith, Robert. "Late Classical Furniture in the United States, 1820–1850," *Antiques.* Dec. 1958.

——. "Gothic and Elizabethan Revival Furniture 1800–1850," *Antiques.* March 1959.

——. "Rococo Revival Furniture, 1850–1870," *Antiques.* May 1959.

——. "Furniture of the Eclectic Decades 1870–1900," *Antiques.* July 1959.

Spofford, Harriet. *Art Decoration Applied to Furniture.* N.Y., 1878.

Teague, Walter. *Design This Day.* N.Y., 1940.

Tracy, Berry. "19th Century American Furniture in the Collection of the Newark Museum," *The Museum.* Fall 1961.

Futurism

Carrieri, Raffaele. *Futurism.* Milan, 1963.

Clough, Rosa. *Futurism.* N.Y., 1961.

Kozloff, Max. "The Futurist Campaign," *Artforum.* Feb. 1972.

Laurvik, J. N. *Is It Art? Post-Impressionism, Futurism, Cubism.* N.Y., 1913.

Martin, Marianne. *Futurist Art and Theory 1909–1915.* Oxford, 1968.

Parker, E. S. "An Analysis of Futurism," *International Studio.* April 1916.

Saarinen, Aline. "Collecting Modern Masters On a Master Plan," *Art News.* Oct. 1957.

Taylor, Joshua. *Futurism.* N.Y., 1961.

Gallier, James, Sr.

Gallier, James. *Autobiography of James Gallier.* Paris, 1864.

Gardiner, Sidney

Buhler, Kathryn. *American Silver 1655–1825 in the Museum of Fine Arts, Boston.* Greenwich, Conn., 1972.

Gardner, Alexander

Cobb, Josephine. "Alexander Gardner," *Image.* June 1958.

Photographic Sketch Book of the War. N.Y., 1959.

Garver, Thomas

Garver, Thomas. "Just Before the War," exhibition catalogue, Newport Harbor Art Museum. Balboa, Cal., 1968.

Gatch, (Harry) Lee

Guest, Barbara. "Avery and Gatch: Lonely Americans," *Art News.* March 1960.

Gatto, Victor Joseph

Salpeter, Harry. "Gatto: Little Primitive," *Esquire.* May 1946.

Sargent, Winthrop. *Geniuses, Goddesses, and People.* N.Y., 1949.

Gemini G.E.L.

"Gemini G.E.L.," exhibition catalogue, Museum of Modern Art. N.Y., 1971.

"Museums," *Arts.* Summer 1971.

Genre

"American Genre: The Social Scene in Paintings and Prints, 1800–1935," exhibition catalogue, Whitney Museum. N.Y., 1935.

"Art in New England: New England Genre," exhibition catalogue, Fogg Art Museum. Cambridge, 1937.

Bode, Carl. *The Anatomy of American Popular Culture, 1840–1861.* Los Angeles, 1959.

"Exhibition of American Genre Painting," exhibition catalogue, Carnegie Institute. Pittsburgh, 1936.

Gifford, Sanford Robinson

Cikovsky, Nicolai, Jr. "Sanford Robinson Gifford, 1823–1880," exhibition catalogue, University of Texas Art Museum. 1970.

"Memorial Catalogue of the Paintings of Sanford Robinson Gifford, N.A.," Metropolitan Museum of Art. N.Y., 1881.

Selkowitz, Judith. *Sanford R. Gifford.* Pittsfield, Mass., 1966.

Gilbert, Cass

Gilbert, Julia (ed.). *Cass Gilbert, Reminiscences and Addresses.* N.Y., 1935.

Girard, Alexander

Pierson, William, Jr. and Martha Davidson (eds.). *Arts of the United States.* N.Y., 1960.

Glackens, William

Gallatin, A. E. "Art of William J. Glackens," *International Studio.* May 1910.

Glackens, Ira. *William Glackens and the Ashcan Group.* 1957.

"William Glackens in Retrospect," exhibition catalogue, City Art Museum. St. Louis, 1966.

Glarner, Fritz

Ashton, Dore. "Fritz Glarner," *Art International.* Jan. 25, 1963.

Godefroy, Maximilian

Davison, C. "Maximilian Godefroy," *Maryland Historical Magazine.* Sept. 1934.

——. "Maximilian and Eliza Godefroy," *Maryland Historical Magazine.* March 1934.

Goff, Bruce

Murphy, William and Louis Muller. *Bruce Goff: A Portfolio of His Work.* 1970.

"The Seabee Chapel," *Architectural Design and Construction* (London). May 1946.

Goodhue, Bertram

Schuyler, Montgomery. "Works of Cram, Goodhue and Ferguson," *Architectural Record.* Jan. 1911.

Whitaker, Charles (ed.). *Bertram Grosvenor Goodhue: Architect and Master of Many Arts.* N.Y., 1925.

Goodnough, Robert

"New Work: Robert Goodnough," exhibition catalogue, Tibor de Nagy Gallery. N.Y., 1960.

Goodridge, Sarah

Parker, Barbara. "New England Miniatures, 1750 to 1850," exhibition catalogue, Museum of Fine Arts. Boston, 1957.

Gorham Company

McClinton, Katharine. *Collecting American Nineteenth Century Silver.* N.Y., 1968.

Gorky, Arshile

Rosenberg, Harold. *Arshile Gorky: The Man, the Time, the Idea.* N.Y., 1962.

Schwabacher, Ethel. *Arshile Gorky.* N.Y., 1957.

Seitz, William. "Arshile Gorky: Paintings, Drawings, Studies," exhibition catalogue, Museum of Modern Art. N.Y., 1962.

Gothic Revival

Andrews, Wayne. "America's Gothic Hour," *Town and Country.* Nov. 1947.

Donnell, Edna. "Alexander Jackson Davis and the Gothic Revival," *Metropolitan Museum Studies.* September 1936.

History of the Gothic Revival. London and N.Y., 1872.

Lancaster, Clay. "Three Gothic Revival Houses of Lexington," *American Collector.* Dec. 1948.

Myer, John. "Gothic Revival in New York," *Bulletin of the Museum of the City of New York.* April 1940.

Stanton, Phoebe. *The Gothic Revival and American Church Architecture.* Baltimore, 1968.

Bibliography According to Entries

Goto, Joseph
Malone, Patrick and Peter Selz. "Is There a New Chicago School?", *Art News.* Oct. 1955.
Sahlins, Bernard. "Nationwide Exhibitions: Chicago: Joseph Goto," *Arts.* Nov. 1959.

Gottlieb, Adolph
"Adolph Gottlieb," exhibition catalogue, Guggenheim Museum and Whitney Museum. N.Y., 1968.
Friedman, Martin. "Adolph Gottlieb," exhibition catalogue, Walker Art Center. Minneapolis, 1963.
Siegel, Jeanne. "Adolph Gottlieb: Two Views," *Arts.* Feb. 1968.

Gould, Thomas Ridgeway
Gardner, Albert. *Yankee Stonecutters.* N.Y., 1944.

Graham, John
Kokkinen, Eila. "Ioannus Magus Servus Domini St. Georgii Equitus," *Art News.* Sept. 1968.

Graves, Morris
Wight, Frederick, John Baur, and Duncan Phillips. *Morris Graves.* Berkeley, 1956.

Gravestones
Forbes, Harriette. *Gravestones of Early New England.* N.Y., 1967.
Ludwig, Allan. *Graven Images.* Middletown, Conn., 1966.

Gray, Henry Peters
Clement, Clara and Laurence Hutton. *Artists of the Nineteenth Century and Their Work.* Boston, 1884.
Magazine of Art. Nov. 1946.

Greene, Balcomb
Greene, Balcomb. "The Fourth Illusion, or Hunger for Genius," *Art News.* Sept. 1957.

Greenough, Horatio
Bender, Horace. *Travels, Observations, and Experiences of a Yankee Stonecutter.* N.Y., 1852.
Greenough, Frances Boott (ed.). *Letters of Horatio Greenough to his Brother Henry Greenough.* Boston, 1887.
Greenough, Horatio. *Form and Function.* Berkeley, 1947.
Tuckerman, Henry. *A Memorial of Horatio Greenough.* N.Y., 1853.

Greenough, Richard
Brumbaugh, Thomas. "The Art of Richard Greenough," *Old-Time New England.* Jan.–March 1963.

Greenwood, John
Burroughs, Alan. *John Greenwood in America, 1745–1752.* Andover, 1943.
Weitenkampf, Frank. "John Greenwood," *Bulletin of the New York Public Library.* Aug. 1927.

Grooms, Red
Berrigan, Ted. "Red Power," *Art News.* Dec. 1966.

Gropius, Walter
Giedion, Sigfried. *Walter Gropius: Work and Teamwork.* N.Y., 1954.
Gropius, Walter. *The New Architecture and the Bauhaus.* N.Y., 1937.
Gropius, Walter. *Scope of Total Architecture.* N.Y., 1955.

Gropper, William
Brace, E. "William Gropper," *Magazine of Art.* Aug. 1937.
Pearson, R. M. "His First Twenty Years as Cartoonist and Painter," *Forum.* May 1940.

Gross, Chaim
Lombardo, Josef. *Chaim Gross, Sculptor.* N.Y., 1949.

Grosz, George
Grosz, George and Herbert Bittner (ed.) *George Grosz.* Boston.
Lewis. Beth I. *George Grosz: Art and Politics in the Weimar Republic.* Madison, Wis., 1971.

Grotell, Maija
Pierson, William, Jr. and Martha Davidson (eds.). *Arts of the United States.* N.Y., 1960.
Nordness, Lee. *Objects: USA.* N.Y., 1970.

Guermonprez, Trude
Slivka, Rose (ed.). *Crafts of the Modern World.* N.Y., 1968.
Nordness, Lee. *Objects: USA.* N.Y., 1970.

Guggenheim, Peggy
Guggenheim, Peggy. *Confessions of an Art Addict.* N.Y., 1960.
"The Peggy Guggenheim Collection," exhibition catalogue, Tate Gallery. London, 1946-65.

Guglielmi, O. Louis
Guglielmi, O. L. "I Hope to Sing Again," *Magazine of Art.* May 1944.

Gullager, Christian
"Christian Gullager. 1759–1826," exhibition catalogue, Worcester Museum. Mass., 1949.
Dresser, Louisa. "Christian Gullager," *Art in America.* July 1949.

Gussow, Roy
Porter, Fairfield. "Meeting Ground at the Whitney," *Art News.* May 1956.

Guston, Philip
Ashton, Dore. *Philip Guston.* N.Y., 1959.
Hess, Thomas. "Inside Nature," *Art News.* Feb. 1958.
Hunter, Sam. "Philip Guston," *Art International.* May 1962.
Sandler, Irving. "Guston: A Long Voyage Home," *Art News.* Dec. 1959.

Gwathmey, Robert
Salpeter, Harry. "Gwathmey's Editorial Art," *Esquire.* June 1944.

Haberle, John
Frankenstein, Alfred. "The Reminiscent Object, Paintings by William Michael Harnett, John Frederick Peto and John Haberle," exhibition catalogue, La Jolla Museum of Art. Cal., 1965.

Hadfield, George
Cunningham, H. F. "The Old City Hall of Washington D.C.," *Architectural Record.* March 1915.
Townsend, George. *Washington Outside and Inside.* Hartford, 1873.

Hagen, Ernest
Ingerman, Elizabeth. "Personal Experiences of an Old New York Cabinetmaker," *Antiques.* Nov. 1963.

Hague, Raoul
Nordland, Gerald. "The Slow Emergence of Star Sculpture," *Art News.* Oct. 1964.
"Raoul Hague," exhibition catalogue, Gallery of Contemporary Art. Wash. D.C., 1964.

Haidt, John Valentine
Howland, Garth. "John Valentine Haidt, a Little Known 18th Century Painter," *Pennsylvania History.* Oct. 1941.
Morman, John. "The Painting Preacher: John Valentine Haidt," *Pennsylvania History.* April 1953.

Hall, George Henry
American Art Annual. XI (obituary).
Panorama. Dec. 1945.

Hamilton, James
Baur, John. "A Romantic Impressionist: James Hamilton," *Brooklyn Museum Bulletin.* Spring 1951.
Old Print Shop Portfolio. June–July 1952.

Happenings
Kaprow, Allan. "Pinpointing Happenings," *Art News.* Oct. 1967.
——. *Assemblage, Environments and Happenings.* N.Y., 1966.
——. *Some Recent Happenings.* N.Y., 1966.
Kirby, Michael. *Happenings.* N.Y., 1965.

Hard-Edge
Alloway, Lawrence. "Systemic Painting," exhibition catalogue, Guggenheim Museum. N.Y., 1966.
Goossen, E. C. "The Art of the Real," exhibition catalogue, Museum of Modern Art. N.Y., 1968.

Hardenbergh, Henry Janeway
Schuyler, Montgomery. "The Works of Henry Janeway Hardenbergh," *Architectural Record.* Jan.–March 1897.

Harding, Chester
Harding, Chester. *My Egotistography.* Boston, 1866.
White, Margaret. *A Sketch of Chester Harding, Artist, Drawn by his Own Hand.* Boston, 1929.

Hardy Holzman Pfeiffer Associates
"Pre-Engineered Buildings at Shaw University, North Carolina and East New York Community Resources Center," *Architectural Forum.* April 1971.

Hardy, Jeremiah Pearson
Eckstorm, Fannie. "Jeremiah P. Hardy: A Maine Portrait Painter," *Old-Time New England.* Oct. 1939.
Simpson, Corelli. *Leaflets of Artists.* Bangor, Maine, 1893.

Harnett, William Michael
Frankenstein, Alfred. *After the Hunt: William Harnett and Other American Still Life Painters 1870-1900.* Berkeley, 1953.

Harrison, Peter
Bridenbaugh, Carl. *Peter Harrison, First American Architect.* Chapel Hill, 1949.

Hart, George Overbury
Cahill, Holger. "George O. 'Pop' Hart," exhibition catalogue, Downtown Gallery. N.Y., 1928.
"George O. 'Pop' Hart, 1868–1933," exhibition catalogue, Newark Museum. N.J., 1935.

Hart, Joel Tanner
Coleman, J. W., Jr. "Joel Tanner Hart, Kentucky Sculptor," *Antiques.* Nov. 1947.
Hart, Charles. "Life Portraits of Henry Clay," *Mc Clure's Magazine.* Sept. 1897.

Hart, James Mac Dougal
American Art Annual, VI.
Panorama. May–June 1949.

Hart, William
Antiques. Aug. 1943.
Stiles, Henry (ed.), *The Civil, Political, Professional, and Ecclesiastical History of the County of Kings and the City of Brooklyn, N.Y.* N.Y., 1884.

Hartigan, Grace
"Documenta II," exhibition catalogue. Kassel, Germany, 1959.

Hartley, Marsden
"Feininger-Hartley," exhibition catalogue, Museum of Modern Art. N.Y., 1944.

McCausland, Elizabeth. *Marsden Hartley.* Minneapolis, 1952.

Phillips, Duncan. "Marsden Hartley," *Magazine of Art.* March 1944.

Harvey, George

Shelley, Donald. "George Harvey, English Painter of Atmospheric Landscapes in America," *American Collector.* April 1948.

Hassam, Childe

Adams, Adeline. *Childe Hassam.* N.Y., 1938.

Hathaway, Rufus

Little, Nina. "Dr. Rufus Hathaway, Physician and Painter of Duxbury, Massachusetts, 1770–1822," *Art in America.* Summer 1953.

Haviland, John

Haviland, John. *A Communication to the County Commissioners,* Philadelphia, 1849.

Teeters, Negley. "The Early Days of the Eastern State Penitentiary," *Pennsylvania History.* Oct. 1949.

Hawthorne, Charles Webster

Hoeber, Arthur. "Charles W. Hawthorne," *International Studio.* vol. 37. 1909.

McCausland, Elizabeth. *Charles W. Hawthorne.* N.Y., 1947.

Sadik, Marvin. "The Paintings of Charles Hawthorne," exhibition catalogue, University of Connecticut. Storrs, 1968.

Heade, Martin Johnson

"Martin Johnson Heade," exhibition catalogue, Whitney Museum. N.Y., 1970.

Mc Intyre, Robert. *Martin Johnson Heade.* N.Y., 1948.

Healy, G. P. A.

De Mare, Marie. *G. P. A. Healy, American Artist.* N.Y., 1954.

Healy, G. P. A. *Reminiscences of a Portrait Painter.* Chicago, 1894.

Held, Al

Burton, Scott. "Big H." *Art News.* March 1968.

Green, Eleanor. "Al Held," exhibition catalogue, San Francisco Museum. 1968.

Henri, Robert

Henri, Robert. *The Art Spirit.* Philadelphia, 1923.

Homer, William Innes. *Robert Henri and His Circle.* 1969.

Read, H. A. "Robert Henri and Five of His Pupils," exhibition catalogue, Century Association. N.Y., 1946.

Yarrow, W., and L. Bouche (eds.). *Robert Henri: His Life and Works.* N.Y., 1921.

Henry, Edward Lamson

Cowdrey, M. B. "Edward Lamson Henry, An American Genre Painter," *American Collector.* July 1945.

McCausland, Elizabeth. *The Life and Work of Edward Lamson Henry.* Albany, N.Y., 1945.

Herter, Christian

"Christian Herter," *New York Daily Tribune.* Nov. 3, 1883. (obituary).

Hesselius, Gustavus

Brinton, Christian. "Gustavus Hesselius, 1682–1755," exhibition catalogue, Philadelphia Museum of Art. 1938.

Hart, Charles. "Gustavus Hesselius," *Pennsylvania Magazine of History and Biography.* April 1905.

Richardson, E. P. "Gustavus Hesselius," *Art Quarterly.* Summer 1949.

Tolles, Frederick. "A Contemporary Comment on Gustavus Hesselius," *Art Quarterly.* Autumn 1954.

Hesselius, John

Bolton, Theodore and George Groce. "John Hesselius, An Account of his Life and The First Catalogue of his Portraits," *Art Quarterly.* Winter 1939.

Sawitzky, William. "Further Notes on John Hesselius," *Art Quarterly.* Autumn 1942.

Hicks, Edward

Ford, Alice. *Edward Hicks, Painter of the Peaceable Kingdom.* Philadelphia, 1952

Held, Julius. "Edward Hicks and the Tradition," *Art Quarterly.* Summer 1951.

Hicks, Sheila

Slivka, Rose (ed.). *Crafts of the Modern World.* N.Y., 1968.

Hicks, Thomas

Hicks, George. "Thomas Hicks, Artist, a Native of Newtown," *Bucks County Historical Society Papers,* IV. 1917.

Hidley, Joseph H.

Lipman, Jean. "Joseph H. Hidley (1830–1872), His New York Townscapes," *American Collector.* June 1947.

MacFarlane, Janet. "Hedley, Headley, or Hidley, Painter," *New York History.* Jan. 1947.

Hill, John William

Hill, J. H. *John William Hill, An Artist's Memorial.* N.Y., 1888.

Hine, Lewis

Gurman, Judith. *Lewis W. Hine and the American Social Conscience.* N.Y., 1967.

Hinman, Charles

Johnson, Ellen. "Three Young Americans: Hinman, Poons and Williams," *Oberlin College Bulletin.* Spring 1965.

Hirshfield, Morris

"Morris Hirshfield," exhibition catalogue, Museum of Modern Art. N.Y., 1943.

Hoban, James

Kimball, Fiske. "The Genesis of the White House," *Century Magazine.* Feb. 1918.

Hoffman, Malvina

Hoffman, Malvina. *Heads and Tales.* N.Y., 1937.

——. *Yesterday Is Tomorrow.* N.Y., 1965.

"Racial Types in Sculpture by Malvina Hoffman," *London Studio.* May 1934.

Hofmann, Hans

Greenberg, Clement. *Hofmann.* Paris, 1961.

Hofmann, Hans. *Search for the Real.* Cambridge, 1967.

Hunter, Sam. *Hans Hofmann.* N.Y., 1963.

Wight, Frederick. "Hans Hofmann," exhibition catalogue, University of California. Berkeley, 1957.

Homer, Winslow

Downes, William. *The Life and Works of Winslow Homer.* Boston, 1911.

Goodrich, Lloyd. *Winslow Homer.* N.Y., 1944.

——. *The Graphic Art of Winslow Homer.* N.Y., 1968.

Hoopes, Donelson. "Winslow Homer Watercolors," exhibition catalogue, Brooklyn Museum. 1969.

Hood, Raymond

Hood, R. *Raymond M. Hood.* N.Y., 1931.

North, Arthur. *Raymond M. Hood.* N.Y., 1931.

Hooker, Philip

Root, Edward. *Philip Hooker.* N.Y., 1929.

Hopper, Edward

Du Bois, Guy Pène. *Edward Hopper.* N.Y., 1931.

"Edward Hopper Retrospective Exhibition," exhibition catalogue, Whitney Museum. N.Y., 1950.

Goodrich, Lloyd. "Edward Hopper," exhibition catalogue, Whitney Museum. N.Y., 1964.

——. *Edward Hopper.* N.Y., 1971.

Hosmer, Harriet

Carr, Cornelia (ed.). *Harriet Hosmer, Letters and Memories.* N.Y., 1912.

Terry, Robert. "Recalling a Famous Pupil of McDowell's Medical College: Harriet Hosmer, Sculptor," *Washington University Medical Alumni Quarterly.* St. Louis, 1943.

Hovenden, Thomas

American Art and American Art Collections, vol. 2. 1889.

Last Moments of John Brown, Painted by Thomas Hovenden. Philadelphia, 1885.

Hubard, William James

Gardner, Albert. "Southern Monuments: Charles Carroll and William James Hubard," *Metropolitan Museum of Art Bulletin.* Summer 1958.

"William James Hubard 1807–1862," exhibition catalogue, Valentine Museum and Virginia Museum of Fine Arts. 1948.

Hudson River School

Howat, John. *The Hudson River and its Painters,* N.Y., 1972.

Jones, Agnes. "Hudson River School," exhibition catalogue, State University of N.Y. Geneseo, 1968.

Kellner, S. "Beginnings of Landscape Painting in America," *Art in America.* Oct. 1938.

Sears, Clara. *Highlights Among the Hudson River Artists.* Boston, 1947.

Sweet, Frederick. "The Hudson River School and the Early American Landscape Tradition," exhibition catalogue, Art Institute of Chicago. 1945.

Hudson, Robert

Danieli, Fidel. "Robert Hudson: Space and Camouflage," *Artforum.* Nov. 1967.

Leider, Philip. "Three San Francisco Sculptors: Robert Hudson," *Artforum.* Sept. 1964.

Hull, John

Bulletin of the Associates in Fine Arts at Yale University. June 1937.

Clarke, H. F. *John Hull.* Portland, Maine, 1940.

Hunt, Richard Morris

Burnham, Alan. "The New York Architecture of Richard Morris Hunt," *Journal of the Society of Architectural Historians.* May 1952.

Schuyler, Montgomery. "The Works of the Late Richard Morris Hunt," *Architectural Record.* Oct.–Dec. 1896.

Hunt, William Morris

Angell, Henry. *Records of William Morris Hunt.* Boston, 1881.

Hunt, William Morris. *Hunt's Talks on Art.* Boston, 1875.

Knowlton, Helen. *Art Life of William Morris Hunt.* Boston, 1899.

Huntington, Daniel

Catalogue of Paintings by Daniel Huntington N. A. Exhibiting at the Art Union Building. N.Y., 1850.

Hurd, Jacob, Nathaniel, and Benjamin

French, Hollis. *Jacob Hurd and His Sons, Nathaniel and Benjamin, Silversmiths,*

Bibliography According to Entries

1702–1781. Cambridge, 1939.

Impressionism (American)
"The American Impressionists," exhibition catalogue, Hirschl and Adler Galleries. N.Y., 1968.
Baur, John. "Leaders of American Impressionism," exhibition catalogue, Brooklyn Museum. 1937.
Huth, Hans. "Impressionism Comes to America," *Gazette des Beaux-Arts.* April 1946.
Pomeroy, Ralph. "Yankee Impressionists," *Art News.* Nov. 1968.
Wright, Willard. "Impressionism to Synchromism," *Forum.* Dec. 1913.

Independent Artists, The Exhibition of (1910)
"The Independents' Exhibition," *American Magazine of Art,* vol. 8. 1917.

Indiana, Robert
"Richard Stankiewicz, Robert Indiana," exhibition catalogue, Walker Art Center. Minneapolis, 1963.
"Robert Indiana," exhibition catalogue, Institute of Contemporary Art, University of Pennsylvania. 1968.
Swenson, Gene. "The Horizons of Robert Indiana," *Art News.* May 1966.

Industrial Design
Drexler, Arthur and Greta Daniel. *Introduction to Twentieth Century Design.* N.Y., 1959.
Pierson, William, Jr. and Martha Davidson. *Arts of the United States.* N.Y., 1960.
Silliman, Benjamin and C. R. Goodrich. *The World of Science, Art and Industry Illustrated from Examples in the New-York Exhibition, 1853–54.* N.Y., 1854.
Smith, Walter. *The Masterpieces of the Centennial International Exhibition, Volume II: Industrial Art.* Philadelphia, 1875.

Ingham, Charles Cromwell
Gardner, Albert. "Ingham in Manhattan," *Metropolitan Museum of Art Bulletin.* May 1952.
Strickland, Walter. *A Dictionary of Irish Artists.* Dublin, 1913.

Inman, Henry
Bolton, Theodore. "Henry Inman, An Account of his Life and Work" and "Catalogue of the Paintings of Henry Inman," *Art Quarterly.* Autumn 1940 and Supplement.

Inness, George
Inness, George, Jr. *The Life, Art, and Letters of George Inness.* N.Y.
Ireland, Le Roy. *The Works of George Inness, An Illustrated Catalogue Raisonné.* London, 1965.

International Style
Barr, Alfred, Jr. Henry Russell Hitchcock, Jr., Louis Mumford and Philip Johnson, "Modern Architecture International Exhibition," exhibition catalogue, Museum of Modern Art. N.Y., 1932.
Hitchcock, Henry Russell and Philip Johnson. *The International Style: Architecture Since 1922.* N.Y., 1932.
Scully, Vincent, Jr. "Wright vs. the International Style," *Art News.* March 1954.

Ives, Chauncey Bradley
French, Henry. *Art and Artists in Connecticut.* Boston, 1879.
"New Haven Sculptors," *Bulletin of the Associates in Fine Arts at Yale University.* June 1938.

Jackson, John Adams
Clement, Clara and Laurence Hutton. *Artists of the Nineteenth Century and Their Work.* Boston, 1884.
Taft, Lorado. *History of American Sculpture.* N.Y., 1925.

Jackson, William Henry
Hafen, Le Roy (ed.). *The Diaries of William Henry Jackson.* Glendale, Cal., 1959.
Jackson, Clarence. *Picture Maker of the Old West, William Henry Jackson.* N.Y., 1947.
Jackson, William Henry. "Field Work," *Philadelphia Photographer.* March 1875.
——. *Time Exposure.* N.Y., 1940.

Jarves, James Jackson
Jarves, James Jackson. *Art-Hints, Architecture, Sculpture, and Painting.* N.Y., 1855.
Jarves, James Jackson. *The Art-Idea.* N.Y., 1864.
Steegmuller, Francis. *The Two Lives of James Jackson Jarves.* New Haven, 1951.

Jarvis, John Wesley
Dickson, Harold. *John Wesley Jarvis.* N.Y., 1949.

Jay, William
Jay, Reverend William. *The Autobiography of the Reverend William Jay.* N.Y., 1855.

Jefferson, Thomas
Frary, I. T. *Thomas Jefferson, Architect and Builder.* Richmond, 1931.
Kimball, Fiske. *Thomas Jefferson, Architect.* Boston, 1916.
——. *Thomas Jefferson and the First Monument of the Classic Revival in America.* Harrisburg, Pa. 1915.

Jennewein, C. Paul
Cunningham, John. *C. Paul Jennewein.* Athens, Ga., 1950.

Jennys, William
Dods, Agnes. "Newly Discovered Portraits by J. William Jennys," *Art in America.* Jan. 1945.
Warren, William. "A Checklist of Jennys Portraits," *Connecticut Historical Society Bulletin.* April 1956.
Warren, William. "The Jennys Portraits," *Connecticut Historical Society Bulletin.* Oct. 1955.

Jewett, William
Evans, Elliot. "William S. and William D. Jewett," *California Historical Society Quarterly.* Dec. 1954.
Nelson, Helen. "A Case of Confused Identity: Two Jewetts Named William," *Antiques.* Nov. 1942.
——. "The Jewetts, William and William S.," *International Studio.* Jan. 1926.

Johansen, John M.
"Mummers Theater, Oklahoma City," *Architectural Forum.* March 1971.

Johanson, Patricia
Goossen, E. C. "The Art of the Young," *Vogue.* Aug. 1, 1968.
"Patricia Johanson: Stephen Long" (film), distributed by Museum-at-Large, N.Y. 1968.
Tillim, Sidney. "New York: Pat Johanson," *Artforum.* Jan. 1968.

Johns, Jasper
"Jasper Johns," exhibition catalogue, Jewish Museum. N.Y., 1964.
Kozloff, Max. *Jasper Johns.* N.Y., 1967.
Rose, Barbara. "The Graphic Work of Jasper Johns," *Artforum.* March 1970.
Steinberg, Leo. *Jasper Johns.* N.Y., 1963.

Johnson, David
American Art Annual, VII (obituary).

Clement, Clara and Laurence Hutton. *Artists of the Nineteenth Century and Their Work.* Boston, 1884.

Johnson, Eastman
Baur, John. "An American Genre Painter: Eastman Johnson, 1824–1906," exhibition catalogue, Brooklyn Museum. 1940.
Crosby, Everett. *Eastman Johnson at Nantucket.* Nantucket, Mass., 1944.
Heilbron, Bertha. "A Pioneer Artist on Lake Superior," *Minnesota History.* June 1940.

Johnson, Philip
Hitchcock, Henry-Russell. "Philip Johnson," *Architectural Review,* CXVII. 1955.
Jacobus, John, Jr. *Philip Johnson.* N.Y., 1962.
Johnson, Philip. *Architecture, 1949–1964.* London, 1966.

Johnston, Henrietta
Keyes, Homer. "Coincidence and Henrietta Johnston," *Antiques.* Dec. 1929.
Rutledge, Anna. "Who Was Henrietta Johnston?", *Antiques.* March 1947.
Willis, Eola. "Henrietta Johnston, South Carolina Pastellist," *The Antiquarian.* Sept. 1928.

Johnston, Joshua
Pleasants, J. Hall. *Joshua Johnston, The First American Negro Portrait Painter.* Baltimore, 1942.

Johnston, Thomas
Coburn, Frederick. "The Johnstons of Boston," *Art in America.* Dec. 1932 and Oct. 1933.

Jones, Thomas Dow
American Art Review, II, Part I. 1880 (obituary).
Boston Transcript. Feb. 28, 1881 (obituary).

Jouett, Matthew Harris
Jonas, Edward. *Matthew Harris Jouett, Kentucky Portrait Painter.* Louisville, 1938.
Martin, Mrs. William. *Catalogue of All Known Paintings by Matthew Harris Jouett.* Louisville, 1939.
Wilson, Samuel. "Matthew Harris Jouett, Kentucky Portrait Painter, A Review," *Filson Club History Quarterly.* April 1939.

Judd, Donald
Agee, William. "Donald Judd," exhibition catalogue, Whitney Museum. N.Y., 1968.
Baker, Elizabeth. "Judd the Obscure," *Art News.* April 1968.
Coplans, John. "An Interview with Don Judd," *Artforum.* June 1971.
Judd, Donald. "Specific Objects," *Arts Yearbook 8.* 1965.

Kahn, Albert
Nelson, George. *The Industrial Architecture of Albert Kahn.* N.Y., 1939.

Kahn, Louis I.
Braudy, Susan. "The Architectural Metaphysic of Louis Kahn," *New York Times Magazine.* Nov. 15, 1970.
Green, Wilder. "Louis I. Kahn, Architect; Richards Medical Research Building," exhibition catalogue, Museum of Modern Art. N.Y., 1961.
"Louis I. Kahn, Architect" (Film), Distributed by Museum-at-Large, N.Y. 1972.
Rowan, Jan. "Louis I. Kahn", *Progressive Architecture.* April 1961.
Scully, Vincent. *Louis I. Kahn.* N.Y., 1962.

Kane, John
Beam, Lura. *Development of the Artist.* Wash. D.C., 1940.

Kane, John. *Sky Hooks: The Autobiography of John Kane.* Philadelphia, 1938.
Millard, Charles. "Hicks/Kane/Pippin," *Artforum.* March 1967.

Kantor, Morris
Kantor, Morris. "Ends and Means; Autobiography," *Magazine of Art.* March 1940.
Shepherd, R. "Morris Kantor 1946," *Art News.* July 1946.

Käsebier, Gertrude
"Gertrude Käsebier," exhibition catalogue, Brooklyn Institute of Arts and Sciences." 1926.

Kelly, Ellsworth
Goossen, E. C. *Ellsworth Kelly.* Paris, 1958.
——. "Ellsworth Kelly," exhibition catalogue, Museum of Modern Art. N.Y., 1973.
"Paintings, Sculpture and Drawings by Ellsworth Kelly," exhibition catalogue, Washington Gallery of Modern Art. Wash. D.C., 1963–64.
Rose, Barbara. "The Sculpture of Ellsworth Kelly," *Artforum.* June 1967.
Waldman, Diane. *Ellsworth Kelly: Drawings, Collages, Prints.* Greenwich, Conn., 1971.

Kensett, John F.
Howat, John. "John Frederick Kensett," exhibition catalogue, American Federation of Arts. N.Y., 1968.
Kensett Papers (manuscript). New York State Library, Albany.
Kettlewell, James. *John Frederick Kensett.* Saratoga Springs, N.Y., 1967.

Kent, Rockwell
Armitage, M. *Rockwell Kent.* N.Y., 1932.
Rockwell Kent. N.Y., 1945.

Kienholz, Edward
Tillim, Sidney. "The Underground Pre-Raphaelitism of Edward Kienholz," *Artforum.* April 1966.
Tuchman, Maurice. "Edward Kienholz," exhibition catalogue, Los Angeles County Museum, 1966.

Kinetic Sculpture
"Kinetic and Optic Art Today," exhibtion catalogue, Buffalo Fine Arts Academy. 1965.
"Kinetic Currents," exhibition catalogue, San Francisco Museum of Art. 1966.
Kirby, Michael. "The Experience of Kinesis," *Art News.* Feb. 1968.
Leider, Philip. "Kinetic Sculpture at Berkeley," *Artforum.* May 1966.
Rickey, George. "The Kinetic International," *Arts.* Sept. 1961.
Selz, Peter and George Rickey. "Directions in Kinetic Sculpture," exhibition catalogue, University of California. Berkeley, 1966.

King, Charles Bird
Ewers, John. "Charles Bird King, Painter of Indian Visitors to the Nation's Capital," *Smithsonian Institution Annual Report for 1953.*

King, John Crookshanks
Hart, Charles. "Life Portraits of Daniel Webster," *Mc Clure's Magazine.* May 1897.
Lee, Hannah. *Familiar Sketches of Sculpture and Sculptors.* Boston, 1854.

Kirk, Samuel
The Story of the House of Kirk, the Oldest Silversmiths in the United States, Founded 1815. Baltimore, 1939.

Kline, Franz
"Franz Kline, 1910–1962," exhibition cata-

logue, Whitney Museum. N.Y., 1968.
"Franz Kline Memorial Exhibition," exhibition catalogue, Washington Gallery of Modern Art. Wash. D.C., 1962.
Goodnough, Robert. "Kline Paints a Picture," *Art News.* Dec. 1952.

Knaths, Karl
"Karl Knaths," *Art and Understanding.* Nov. 1929.
Mocsanyi, Paul. *Karl Knaths.* Wash. D.C., 1957.
"Paintings by Karl Knaths," exhibition catalogue, Art Institute of Chicago. 1942.

Knoll International
"Knoll Au Louvre," exhibition catalogue, Musée des Arts Decoratifs, Paris. N.Y., 1971.

Kohn, Gabriel
Petersen, Valerie. "Gabriel Kohn Makes a Sculpture," *Art News.* Oct. 1961.
Tillim, Sidney. "Month in Review: Gabe Kohn," *Arts.* Feb. 1963.

Krans, Olaf
Lipman, Jean and Alice Winchester. *Primitive Painters in America, 1750–1850; An Anthology.* N.Y., 1950.

Krimmel, John Lewis
Art in America. Dec. 1922.
Jackson, Joseph. "Krimmel, the American Hogarth," *International Studio.* June 1929.

Kroll, Leon
Gutman, W. "Leon Kroll," *Art in America.* Oct. 1930.
"Leon Kroll: An Interview," *American Artist.* May 1942.

Krushenick, Nicholas
Perrault, John. "Krushenick's Blazing Blazons," *Art News.* March 1967.
Robins, Corinne. "The Artist Speaks, Nicholas Krushenick," *Art in America.* May–June 1969.

Kuhn, Walt
Bird, P. *Fifty Paintings by Walt Kuhn.* N.Y., 1940.
Kuhn, Walt. *The Story of the Armory Show.* N.Y., 1938.
"Painter of Vision: Walt Kuhn," exhibition catalogue, University of Arizona Art Gallery. 1966.

Labino, Dominick
Slivka, Rose (ed.). Crafts of the Modern World. N.Y., 1968.

Lachaise, Gaston
Goodall, D. "Gaston Lachaise, 1882–1935," *Massachusetts Review.* Summer 1960.
Kirstein, Lincoln. "Gaston Lachaise: Retrospective Exhibition," exhibition catalogue, Museum of Modern Art. N.Y., 1935.

La Farge, John
Cortissoz, Royal. *John La Farge; A Memoir and a Study.* Boston, 1911.
"John La Farge," exhibition catalogue, Graham Gallery. N.Y., 1966.
La Farge, Henry. "John La Farge, Oils and Watercolors," exhibition catalogue, Kennedy Galleries. N.Y., 1968.

Lafever, Minard
Brown, Roscoe. *Church of the Holy Trinity.* N.Y., 1922.
Lafever, Minard. *The Architectural Instructor.* N.Y., 1856.
Lafever, Minard. *The Beauties of Modern Architecture.* N.Y., 1835.

Lambdin, George C.
Bolton, Theodore. *Early American Portrait*

Draughtsmen in Crayons. N.Y., 1923.
M. and M. Karolik Collection of American Paintings: 1815–1965. Cambridge, 1949.

Landscape Architecture
Downing, Andrew Jackson. *A Treatise on the Theory and Practice of Landscape Gardening, Adapted to North America.* London, 1841.
Fabos, Julius, Gordon Milde and V. Michael Weinmayr. *Frederick Law Olmsted, Sr., Founder of Landscape Architecture in America.* Amherst, 1968.
Hubard, Henry and Theodora Kimball. *An Introduction to the Study of Landscape Design.* N.Y., 1931.
Schuler, Stanley. *America's Great Private Gardens.* N.Y., 1967.

Lane, Fitz Hugh
Wilmerding, John. *Fitz Hugh Lane 1804–1865, American Marine Painter.* Salem, Mass., 1964.
Wilmerding, John. "Fitz Hugh Lane, the First Major Exhibition," exhibition catalogue, De Cordova Museum, Lincoln, Mass., and Colby College, Waterville, Me.

Lange, Dorothea
Dixon, D. and Dorothea Lange. "Photographing the Familiar," *Aperture,* no. 2. 1952.
Elliott, George. *Dorothea Lange.* N.Y., 1966.
Taylor, Paul and Dorothea Lange. *An American Exodus: A Record of Human Erosion.* N.Y., 1939.
Van Dyke, Willard. "The Photographs of Dorothea Lange, A Critical Analysis," *Camera Craft.* Oct. 1934.

Lannuier, Charles Honoré
"Lannuier in the President's House," *Antiques.* Jan. 1962.
Pearce, Lorraine. "The Work of Charles-Honoré Lannuier, French Cabinetmaker in New York," *Maryland Historical Magazine.* March 1960.
Waxman, Lorraine. "The Lannuier Brothers, Cabinetmakers," *Antiques.* Aug. 1957.

Lasansky, Mauricio
Frost, Rosamund. "Lasansky and the Hayter Circle," *Perspective,* vol. 1, no 5. 1947.

Lassaw, Ibram
Campbell, Lawrence. "Lassaw Makes a Sculpture." *Art News.* March 1954.
Goossen, E. C., Robert Goldwater and Irving Sandler. *Three American Sculptors: Ferber, Hare, Lassaw.* N.Y., 1959.

Latrobe, Benjamin Henry
Hamlin, Talbot. *Benjamin Henry Latrobe.* N.Y., 1955.
Kimball, Fiske. "The Bank of Pennsylvania," *Architectural Record.* Aug. 1918.
Latrobe, Benjamin. *The Journal of Latrobe.* N.Y., 1905.

Laurent, Robert
Gardner, Albert. *American Sculpture.* N.Y., 1965.

Lawrence, Jacob
Porter, James. "The Negro in American Art," exhibition catalogue, University of California. Los Angeles, 1966.

Lawrie, Lee
Devree, Charlotte "Is This Statuary Worth More Than a Million of Your Money?", *Art News.* April 1955.
Gardner, Albert. *American Sculpture.* N.Y., 1965.

Lawson, Ernest

Bibliography According to Entries

Du Bois, Guy Pène. *Ernest Lawson.* N.Y., 1932.

Gallatin, Albert. "Ernest Lawson," *International Studio.* July 1906.

Lebrun, Rico

Bear, Donald. "Rico Lebrun," *Pacific Art Review.* vol. 1. 1942.

"Rico Lebrun, Paintings and Drawings of the Crucifixion," exhibition catalogue, Los Angeles County Museum. 1950.

Soby, James T. *Rico Lebrun Drawings.* Berkeley, 1961.

Lee, Arthur

Gardner, Albert. *American Sculpture.* N.Y., 1965.

Lee, Doris

Blanch, Arnold and Doris Lee. *Painting for Enjoyment.* N.Y., 1947

Doris Lee. N.Y., 1946.

L'Enfant, Pierre Charles

Kimball, Fiske. "Origin of the Plan of Washington, D.C.," *Architectural Review.* Sept. 1918.

Kite, Elizabeth. *L'Enfant and Washington.* Baltimore, 1929.

L'Enfant, Pierre Charles. "L'Enfant's Memorials" and "L'Enfant's Reports to President Washington," *Records of the Columbia Historical Society,* vol. 2. 1899.

Lescaze, William

Lescaze, William. *On Being an Architect.* 1942.

Peter, John. *Masters of Modern Architecture.* N.Y., 1958.

Leslie, Alfred

Friedman, B. H. (ed.). *School of New York: Some Younger Artists.* N.Y., 1959.

Tyler, Parker. "Al Leslie," *Prisme des Arts.* Nov. 1956.

Leutze, Emanuel Gottlieb

"Catalogue of Exhibition of Works by Emanuel Leutze," Century Association. N.Y., 1946.

Levine, Jack

"Jack Levine," exhibition catalogue, Institute of Contemporary Art. Boston, 1953.

"Jack Levine, Retrospective Exhibition," exhibition catalogue, Whitney Museum. N.Y., 1955.

Levine, Les

Levine, Les. "The Artist Speaks," *Art in America.* Nov. 1969.

Perreault, John. "Plastic Man Strikes," *Art News.* March 1968.

Lewis, Martin

Salaman, Malcolm. *Modern Masters of Etching: Martin Lewis.* London, 1931.

Lewitt, Sol

Lewitt, Sol. "Serial Project #1," N.Y., 1966.

Lippard, Lucy. "Rejective Art," *Art International.* Oct. 20, 1966.

Liberman, Alexander

"Alexander Liberman: Painting and Sculpture 1950–1970," exhibition catalogue, Corcoran Gallery. Wash. D.C., 1970.

Blake, Peter. "Alexander Liberman: Beauty and Precision in Aluminum Sculpture," *Architectural Forum.* April 1963.

Hunter, Sam. "Alexander Liberman, Recent Sculpture," exhibition catalogue, Jewish Museum. N.Y., 1966.

Liberty Bowl

See Paul Revere

Lichtenstein, Roy

Alloway, Lawrence. "Roy Lichtenstein," *Studio International.* Jan. 1968.

Boatto, Alberto. *Lichtenstein.* Rome, 1967.

"Roy Lichtenstein, Graphics, Reliefs, and Sculpture," exhibition catalogue, University of California, Irvine. 1970.

Lie, Jonas

Berry, Rose. "Jonas Lie: The Man and His Art." *American Magazine of Art,* vol. 16. 1925.

"Jonas Lie's Paintings of the Panama Canal," *Pan American Union Bulletin,* vol. 38. 1914.

Price, F. Newlin. "Jonas Lie, Painter of Light," *International Studio,* vol. 82. 1925.

Lienau, Detlef

Kramer, Ellen. "Detlef Lienau," *Journal of the Society of Architectural Historians.* March 1955.

Light Sculpture

Baker, Elizabeth. "The Light Brigade," *Art News.* March 1967.

Kepes, Gyorgy. "Light as a Creative Medium," exhibition catalogue, Harvard University. Cambridge, 1965.

Piene, Nan. "Light Art," *Art in America.* May–June 1967.

Lindner, Richard

Ashton, Dore. *Richard Lindner.* N.Y., 1970.

Lipchitz, Jacques

Goldwater, Robert. *Lipchitz.* N.Y., 1959.

Hammacher, A. M. *Jacques Lipchitz: His Sculpture.* N.Y., 1961.

Lipchitz, Jacques, with H. H. Arnason. *My Life in Sculpture.* N.Y., 1972.

Sweeney, James J. "Jacques Lipchitz, Sculpture and Drawings, 1914–1950," exhibition catalogue, Portland Art Museum. Oregon, 1950.

Lippold, Richard

Campbell, Lawrence. "Lippold Makes a Construction," *Art News.* Oct. 1956.

Lippold, Richard. "Variation Number Seven: Full Moon," *Arts and Architecture.* May 1950.

Lipton, Seymour

Elsen, Albert. "The Sculptural World of Seymour Lipton," *Art International,* vol. 9, no. 1. 1965.

Lipton, Seymour. "Experience and Sculptural Form," *College Art Journal,* vol. 9, no. 1. 1949.

——. "Extracts from a Notebook," *Arts.* March 1971.

Littleton, Harvey

Slivka, Rose (ed.) *Crafts of the Modern World.* N.Y., 1968.

Long, Robert Cary, Sr.

Hall, Clayton (ed.). *Baltimore, Its History and Its People.* Chicago, 1912.

Hamlin, Talbot. *Greek Revival Architecture in America.* N.Y., 1964.

Louis, Morris

Fried, Michael. *Morris Louis.* N.Y., 1970.

——. "Morris Louis 1912–1962," exhibition catalogue, Museum of Fine Arts. Boston, 1967.

Greenberg, Clement. "Louis and Noland," *Art International.* May 1960.

Robbins, Daniel. "Morris Louis; Triumph of Color," *Art News.* Oct. 1963.

Lukens, Glen

Pierson, William, Jr. and Martha Davidson (eds.). *Arts of the United States.* N.Y., 1960.

Luks, George

Cary, E. L. *George Luks.* N.Y., 1931.

"Paintings, Watercolors and Drawings by George B. Luks: Public Auction Sale," Parke-Bernet Galleries. N.Y., 1950.

Spargo, Jr. "George Luks: An American Painter of Great Originality and Force," *Craftsman.* Sept. 1907.

Luminism

Baur, John. "American Luminism," *Perspectives U.S.A.* Autumn 1954.

"Luminous Landscape: The American Study of Light, 1860–1875," exhibition catalogue, Fogg Art Museum. Cambridge, 1966.

Lyrical Abstraction

Baur, John. "Nature in Abstraction," exhibition catalogue, Whitney Museum. N.Y., 1958.

Domingo, Willis. "Color Abstractionism." *Arts.* Dec.–Jan. 1971.

"Lyrical Abstraction," exhibition catalogue, Whitney Museum. N.Y., 1971.

Lye, Len

Dandignae, Patricia. "Arts in Architecture: The Visionary Art of Len Lye," *Craft Horizons.* May 1961.

Lye, Len. "Tangible Motion Sculpture," *Art Journal.* Summer 1961.

MacDonald-Wright, Stanton

"The Art of Stanton MacDonald-Wright," exhibition catalogue, National Collection of Fine Arts. Wash. D.C., 1967.

Wright, W. H. "Synchromism," *International Studio.* Oct. 1915.

MacIver, Loren

Art Now: New York. March 1971.

Baur, John. "Loren MacIver: I. Rice Pereira," exhibition catalogue, Whitney Museum. N.Y., 1953.

MacMonnies, Frederick

Gardner, Albert. *American Sculpture.* N.Y., 1965.

McSpadden, Joseph. *Famous Sculptors of America.* N.Y., 1924.

MacNeil, Hermon

Chapin, H. W. "Hermon Atkins MacNeil," *Pacific Monthly.* April 1906.

Kelly, F. F. "American Bronzes at the Metropolitan Museum," *Craftsman,* vol. 11. 1907.

Macramé

Graumont, Raoul and John Hensel. *Encyclopedia of Knots and Fancy Rope Work.* Cambridge, Md., 1952.

The Imperial Macramé Lace Book. N.Y., 1882.

Maentle, Jacob

Peat, Wilbur. *Pioneer Painters of Indiana.* Indianapolis, 1954.

Manship, Paul

Murtha, Edwin. *Paul Manship.* N.Y., 1947.

Marca-Relli, Conrad

Agee, William. "Marca-Relli," exhibition catalogue, Whitney Museum. N.Y., 1967.

Arnason, H. H. *Conrad Marca-Relli.* N.Y., 1963.

Marin, John

Helm, Mac Kinley, *John Marin.* Boston, 1948.

"John Marin; Watercolors. Oil Paintings, Etchings," exhibition catalogue, Museum of Modern Art. N.Y., 1936.

Norman, Dorothy (ed.). *The Selected Writings of John Marin.* N.Y., 1949.

Reich, Sheldon. John Marin. *A Stylistic Analysis and Catalogue Raisonne.* 1970.

Marsh, Reginald

Blossom, F. A. "Reginald Marsh as a Painter." *Creative Art.* April 1933.

Goodrich, Lloyd. *Reginald Marsh.* N.Y., 1972.

——. "Reginald Marsh," exhibition catalogue, Whitney Museum. N.Y., 1955.

Marsh, Reginald. "Let's Get Bak to Painting," *Magazine of Art.* Dec. 1944.

"Paintings and Drawings by Reginald Marsh," exhibition catalogue, Museum of Art of Ogunquit, Maine. 1970.

Sasowsky, Norman. *Reginald Marsh: Etchings, Engravings, Lithographs.* N.Y., 1956.

Martelé
Mc Clinton, Katharine. *Collecting American Nineteenth Century Silver.* N.Y., 1968.

Martin, Agnes
Alloway, Lawrence. "6 American Abstract Painters," exhibition catalogue, Arthur Tooth and Sons. London, 1961.

Linville, Kasha. "Agnes Martin: An Appreciation," *Artforum.* June 1971.

Martin, Homer Dodge
Carroll, Dana. *58 Paintings by Homer D. Martin.* N.Y., 1913.

Martin, Elizabeth. *Homer Dodge Martin, a Reminiscence.* N.Y., 1904.

Mather, Frank, Jr. *Homer Martin, Poet in Landscape.* N.Y., 1912.

Maurer, Alfred Henry
Godsoe, R. U. "Memorial Exhibition; Works of the Late Alfred Maurer; Oils and Gouaches Covering Work of Thirty-five Years," exhibition catalogue, Continental Club. N.Y., 1934.

Mc Causland, Elizabeth. "Alfred H. Maurer," exhibition catalogue, Walker Art Center. Minneapolis, 1949.

——. *Alfred H. Maurer.* N.Y., 1951.

Maybeck, Bernard
Bangs, Jean. "Bernard R. Maybeck, Architect, Comes Into His Own", *Architectural Record.* Jan. 1948.

Maybeck, Bernard. "Selections from the Writings of This Year's Gold Medalist", *Journal of the American Institute of Architects.* May 1951.

McComb, John, Jr.
McComb, John. "Notebooks" (manuscript), New York Historical Society. N.Y.

Schuyler, Montgomery. "The New York City Hall-A Piece of Architectural History," *Architectural Record.* May 1908.

Wilde, Edward. "The New York City Hall," *Century Magazine.* April 1884.

McCracken, John
Coplans, John. "Art News from Los Angeles: John McCracken," *Art News.* Dec. 1965.

Goossen, E. C. "The Art of the Real", exhibition catalogue, Museum of Modern Art. N.Y., 1968.

McFee, Henry
Barker, Virgil. *Henry Lee McFee.* N.Y., 1931.

"Henry Lee Mc Fee," exhibition catalogue, Fine Arts Foundation of Scripps College, Claremont, Cal. 1950.

Mc Fee, Henry. "My Painting and Its Development," *Creative Art.* March 1929.

McGarrell, James
Langsner, Jules. "Art News from Los Angeles," *Art News.* March 1957.

McIntire, Samuel
Cummings, Abbot. *Samuel McIntire, A Bicentennial Symposium.* Salem, 1957.

Kimball, Fiske, *Mr. Samuel McIntire, Carver, The Architect of Salem,* Portland, 1940.

Swan, Mabel. "A Revised Estimate of Mc-

Intire," *Antiques.* Dec. 1931.

McKim, Mead and White
Baldwin, Charles. *Stanford White.* N.Y., 1931.

A Monograph on the Work of Mc Kim, Mead and White. N.Y., 1925.
Moore, Charles. *Charles Follen Mc Kim.* Boston, 1929.

Reilly, C. H. *Mc Kim, Mead and White.* London, 1924.

Sturgis, Russell. "The Works of Mc Kim, Mead and White", *Architectural Record.* May 1895.

McNeil, George
Burton, Scott. "George McNeil and the 'Figure," *Art News.* Oct. 1967.

"George McNeil," *Quandrum 8,* 1960.

Mead, Larkin
Sartain, John. *Reminiscences of a Very Old Man, 1808-1897.* N.Y., 1899.

Meeks, The
Pearce, John and Lorraine and Robert Smith. "The Meeks Family of Cabinetmakers," *Antiques.* April 1964.

Pearce, John and Lorraine. "More on the Meeks Cabinetmakers," *Antiques.* July 1966.

Melchers, Gari
Brinton, Christian. "The Art of Gari Melchers," *Harper's Monthly Magazine,* vol. 114. 1907.

Gari Melchers, Painter. N.Y., 1928.

"Retrospective Collection of Paintings Representative of the Life Work of Gari Melchers," exhibition catalogue, Buffalo Fine Arts Academy. 1930.

Melchert, James
O'Brien, George. "New Uncrafty Crafts," *Art in America.* May–June 1966.

Selz, Peter and Brenda Richardson. "California Ceramics," *Art in America,* May–June 1969.

Metcalf, Eliab
Bolton, Theodore. *Early American Portrait Painters in Miniature.* N.Y., 1921.

Kelby, William. *Notes on American Artists, 1754–1820.* N.Y., 1922.

Piers, Harry. "Artists in Nova Scotia," *Nova Scotia Historical Society Collections,* XVIII. 1914.

Metcalf, Willard Leroy
Cortissoz, Royal. "Willard L. Metcalf," *American Academy of Arts and Letters Publication,* no. 60. 1927.

Ely, Catherine. "Willard L. Metcalf," *Art in America,* vol. 13. 1925.

"Special exhibition of landscapes by Mr. Willard L. Metcalf," exhibition catalogue, Cincinnati Museum. 1911.

Mezzotint Prototypes
Belknap, Waldron. *American Colonial Painting.* Cambridge, 1959.

Chaloner-Smith, John. *British Mezzotinto Portraits.* London, 1884.

Phillips, John, Barbara Parker and Kathryn Buhler (eds.). *The Waldron Phoenix Belknap Collection of Portraits and Silver, with a Note on the Discoveries Concerning the Influence of the English Mezzotint on Colonial Painting,* Cambridge, Mass., 1955.

Sweet, Frederick. "Mezzotint sources of American Colonial Portraits," *Art Quarterly,* vol. 14, no. 2. 1951.

Mies van der Rohe, Ludwig
Bill, M. *Ludwig Mies van der Rohe.* Milan,

1955.

Blake, Peter. *The Master Builders.* N.Y., 1960.

Hilbersheimer, L. *Mies van der Rohe.* Chicago, 1956.

Johnson, Philip. *Mies van der Rohe.* N.Y., 1947.

Milkowski, Antoni
Goossen, E. C. "Distillation," *Artforum.* Nov. 1966.

Miller, Kenneth Hayes
Burroughs, A. *Kenneth Hayes Miller.* N.Y., 1931.

Goodrich, Lloyd. *Kenneth Hayes Miller.* N.Y., 1930.

Millet, Francis D.
Baxter, Sylvester, W. A. Coffin, et al. "Francis D. Millet," *Art and Progress,* vol. 3. 1912.

Mechlin, Leila. "Ships of All Ages in Millet's Mural Decorations in the Baltimore Custom House," *Craftsman,* vol. 15. 1909.

Price, C. M. "The Late Francis D. Millet: Notes on the December Panels in the Cleveland Post Office," *International Studio,* vol. 48. 1912.

Mills, Clark
Rutledge, Anna. "Artists in the Life of Charleston," *Transactions of the American Philosophical Society.* Nov. 1949.

Rutledge, Anna, "Cogdell and Mills, Charlestown Sculptors," *Antiques.* March 1942.

Mills, Robert
Gallagher, H. M. P. *Robert Mills.* N.Y., 1935.

Hoyt, William, Jr. "Robert Mills and the Washington Monument in Baltimore," *Maryland Historical Magazine.* June 1939.

Minimal Architecture
Scully, Vincent, Jr. "The Precisionist Strain in American Architecture," *Art in America,* vol. 48, no. 3. 1960.

Minimal Art
Battcock, Gregory (ed.). *Minimal Art.* N.Y., 1968.

"Black, White and Gray," exhibition catalogue, Wadsworth Atheneum. Hartford, 1964.

"Cool Art," exhibition catalogue, Larry Aldrich Museum. Ridgefield, Conn., 1967.

Goossen, E. C. "The Art of the Real," exhibition catalogue, Museum of Modern Art. N.Y., 1968.

——. "8 Young Artists," exhibition catalogue, Hudson River Museum. Yonkers, N.Y., 1964.

McShine, Kynaston. "Primary Structures," exhibition catalogue, Jewish Museum. N.Y., 1966.

Rose, Barbara. "ABC Art," *Art in America.* Oct.–Nov. 1965.

Mitchell, Joan
Sandler, Irving. "Mitchell Paints a Picture," *Art News.* Oct. 1957.

Schneider, Pierre. "From Confession to Landscape," *Art News.* April 1968.

Moore, Charles W.
Aspinwall, C. A. *Security Storage Company, Washington D.C.* Wash. D.C., 1935.

Moore, Edward C.
"The Edward C. Moore Collection," *Collector.* May 1, 1892.

"The Edward C. Moore Collection," *Metropolitan Museum of Art Bulletin,* old series 2. 1907.

Morris, Robert
Burnham, Jack. "A Robert Morris Retro-

spective in Detroit," *Artforum.* March 1970.

Morris, Robert. "Anti-form," *Artforum.* April 1968.

——. "Some Notes on the Phenomenology of Making: The Search for the Motivated," *Artforum.* April 1969.

Tucker, Marcia. "Robert Morris," exhibition catalogue, Whitney Museum. N.Y., 1970.

Morse, Samuel F. B.
Larkin, Oliver. *Samuel F. B. Morse and American Democratic Art,* Boston, 1954.

Moses, Anna Mary Robertson
Grandma Moses, American Primitive, N.Y., 1946.

Kallir, Otto (ed.) *Grandma Moses, My Life's History.* N.Y., 1952.

——. "Grandma Moses," *Holiday.* Feb. 1947.

Motherwell, Robert
Goossen. E. C. "Robert Motherwell and the Seriousness of Subject. *Art International.* vol. 3, 1959

O'Hara, Frank. *Robert Motherwell,* N.Y., 1966

"Robert Motherwell, A Retrospective Exhibition," exhibition catalogue, Pasadena Art Museum. Cal., 1962.

Moulthrop, Reuben
New York Evening Post. Aug. 3, 1814 (obituary).

Sawitzky, William and Susan. "Portraits by Reuben Moulthrop," *New York Historical Society Quarterly.* Oct. 1955.

Mount, William Sidney
Cowdrey, Bartlett and Hermann Warner Williams, Jr. *William Sidney Mount, 1807–1868, An American Painter.* N.Y., 1944.

Frankenstein, Alfred. "William S. Mount," exhibition catalogue, National Gallery of Art, Wash. D.C., 1968.

Mourning Pictures
Little, Nina. *Abby Aldrich Rockefeller Folk Art Collection.* Boston, 1957.

Müller, Jan
"Jan Müller, 1922-1958," exhibition catalogue, Guggenheim Museum. N.Y., 1962.

Munday, Richard
Isham, Norman. "The Colony House at Newport, Rhode Island," *Old-Time New England,* vol. 8. 1917.

Murphy, J. Francis
Clark, Eliot. *J. Francis Murphy.* N.Y., 1926.

Buchanan, Charles. "J. Francis Murphy: A Master of American Landscape," *International Studio,* vol. 53. 1914.

Muybridge, Eadweard
Brown, Lewis (ed.). *Animals in Motion.* N.Y., 1957.

Jessup, Mary. "Eadweard Muybridge's Yosemite Valley Photographs, 1867–1872," *California Historical Society Quarterly,* XLII. 1963.

Muybridge, Eadweard. *Animal Locomotion.* Philadelphia, 1887.

Taft, Robert. *The Human Figure in Motion,* N.Y., 1957.

Myers, Jerome
"Jerome Myers Memorial Exhibition," exhibition catalogue, Whitney Museum. N.Y., 1941.

Myers, Jerome. *An Artist in Manhattan.* N.Y., 1940.

Phillips, Duncan. "Jerome Myers," *American Magazine of Art.* Oct. 1917.

Myers, Myer
Bulletin of the Associates in Fine Arts at Yale University. June 1937.

Rosenbaum, Jeanette. *Myer Myers, Goldsmith, 1723-1795.* Philadelphia, 1954.

Nadelman, Elie
Kirstein, Lincoln. "The Sculpture of Elie Nadelman," exhibition catalogue, Museum of Modern Art. N.Y., 1948.

Nakashima, George
Pierson, William, Jr. and Martha Davidson (eds.). *Arts of the United States.* N.Y., 1960.

Nakian, Reuben
Hess, Thomas, "Introducing the Steel Sculpture of Nakian: The Rape of Lucrece," *Art News.* Nov. 1958.

O'Hara, Frank. *Nakian.* N.Y., 1966.

Rose, Barbara. "Nakian at the Modern," *Artforum.* Oct. 1966.

Nameboards
Fred, Frederick. *Artists in Wood.* N.Y., 1970.

Natzler, Gertrud and Otto
Drexler, Arthur and Greta Daniel. *Introduction to Twentieth Century Design.* N.Y., 1959.

Nauman, Bruce
Raffaele, J. and Elizabeth Baker. "The Way Out West: Interviews with Four San Francisco Artists," *Art News.* Summer 1967.

Tucker, Marcia. "PheNAUMANology," *Artforum.* Dec. 1970.

Neagle, John
Lynch, Margaret. "John Neagle's Diary," *Art in America.* vol. 37, no. 2. 1949.

Neal, John
Dickson, Harold (ed.). *Observations on American Art: Selections from the Writings of John Neal, 1793–1876.* Pennsylvania State College Studies, No. 12. 1943.

Nelson, George
Pierson, William, Jr. and Martha Davidson (eds.). *Arts of the United States.* N.Y., 1960.

Neo-Grec Style
Souvenirs d'Henri Labrouste. Paris, 1928.

Neutra, Richard
Boesiger, W. (ed.). *Richard Neutra: Buildings and Projects.* Zurich, 1951.

Mc Coy, Esther. *Richard Neutra.* N.Y., 1960.

Neutra, Richard. *Survival Through Design.* N.Y., 1954.

Zevi, Bruno. *Richard Neutra.* Milan, 1954.

Nevelson, Louise
Glimcher, Arnold. *Louise Nevelson.* N.Y., 1972.

Kramer, Hilton. "The Sculpture of Louise Nevelson," *Arts.* June 1938.

"Louise Nevelson," *Art International.* Nov. 1963.

Roberts, Colette. *Nevelson.* Paris, 1964.

Newman, Barnett
Goossen, E. C. "The Philosophic Line of B. Newman," *Art News.* Summer 1958.

Hess, Thomas. *Barnett Newman.* N.Y., 1969.

Rosenberg, Harold. "Barnett Newman," *Vogue.* Feb. 1, 1963.

"VIII Sao Paulo Biennial," exhibition catalogue. National Collection of Fine Arts. Wash. D.C., 1966.

Niehaus, Charles
Gardner, Albert. *American Sculpture.* N.Y., 1965.

Niehaus, Charles Henry. "Autobiography; List of Works and Awards " (manuscript).

Metropolitan Museum of Art. N.Y., 1902.

Nivola, Constantino
Gerdts, William. "A Survey of American Sculpture," exhibition catalogue, Newark Museum. N.J., 1962.

Noguchi, Isamu
Ashton, Dore. "Isamu Noguchi," *Arts and Architecture.* Aug. 1959.

Edgar, Natalie. "Noguchi: Master of Ceremony," *Art News.* April 1968.

Michelson, Annette. "Noguchi: Notes on a Theater of the Real," *Art International.* Dec. 1964.

Noland, Kenneth
Fried, Michael. "Three American Painters: Noland, Olitski, Stella," exhibition catalogue, Fogg Art Museum. Cambridge, 1965.

Greenberg, Clement. "Louis and Noland," *Art International.* May 1960.

"Kenneth Noland," exhibition catalogue, Jewish Museum. N.Y., 1965.

Notman, John
Smith, Robert. *John Notman and the Athenaeum Building.* Philadelphia, 1951.

Smith, Robert. "John Notman's Nassau Hall," *Princeton University Library Chronicle.* Spring 1953.

Ohlson, Doug
Burton, Scott. "Doug Ohlson: In the Wind," *Art News.* May 1968.

Delahoyd, Mary. "Concept," exhibition catalogue, Vassar College Art Gallery. Poughkeepsie, N.Y., 1969

O'Keeffe, Georgia
Goossen, E. C. "O'Keeffe," *Vogue.* March 1, 1967.

Rich, Daniel C. "Georgia O'Keeffe," exhibition catalogue, Art Institute of Chicago. 1943.

Wilder, Mitchell. "Georgia O'Keeffe," exhibition catalogue, Amon Carter Museum. Fort Worth, 1966.

Oldenburg, Claes
Coplans, John. "The Artist Speaks: Claes Oldenburg," *Art in America.* March 1969.

Johnson, Ellen. *Claes Oldenburg.* Middlesex, England, 1971.

Rose, Barbara. *Claes Oldenburg.* N.Y., 1970.

Saarinen, Eric. "Sort of a Commercial for an Ice Bag" (film), distributed by Cine Art Productions, Calif.

Olitski, Jules
Fried, Michael. "Jules Olitski's New Paintings," *Artforum.* Nov. 1965

"Jules Olitski: Paintings, 1963–1967," exhibition catalogue, Corcoran Gallery. Wash. D.C., 1967.

Moffett, Kenworth, "Sculpture of Jules Olitski," *Art and Artists.* Sept. 1969.

Olmsted, Frederick Law
Broadus, Mitchell. *Frederick Law Olmsted,* Baltimore, 1924.

Olmsted, Frederick L., Jr., and Theodora Kimball. *Frederick Law Olmsted.* N.Y., 1922–28.

Onckelbag, Gerrit
Bulletin of the Associates in Fine Arts at Yale University. June 1937.

Optical Art
Arnheim, Rudolf. *Art and Visual Perception.* Calif., 1967.

Hess, Thomas. "You Can Hang It in the Hall," *Art News.* April 1965.

"Kinetic and Optic Art Today," exhibition

catalogue, Buffalo Fine Arts Academy. 1965.

Seitz, William. "The Responsive Eye," exhibition catalogue, Museum of Modern Art. N.Y., 1965.

Tillim, Sidney. "Optical Art: Pending or Ending?", *Arts.* Jan. 1965.

Orphism

Chipp, H. B. "Orphism and Color Theory," *Art Bulletin.* vol. 40. 1958.

O'Sullivan, Timothy

Baumhofer, H. M. "Timothy H. O'Sullivan," *Image.* April 1953.

Horan, James. *America's Forgotten Photographer; The Life and Work of Timothy O'Sullivan.* 1966.

Newhall, Beaumont and Nancy. *Timothy H. O'Sullivan, Photographer.* N.Y., 1966.

Page, William

McCoy, Garnett. "William Page and Henry Stevens: An Incident of Reluctant Art Patronage," *Journal of the Archives of American Art.* July–Oct. 1967.

Taylor, Joshua. *William Page: The American Titian.* Chicago, 1957.

Palmer, Erastus Dow

Chester, Anson. "Erastus Dow Palmer," *Cosmopolitan Art Journal.* vol. 2. 1858.

Palmer, Erastus Dow. "Philosophy of the Ideal," *Crayon.* Jan. 1856.

Richardson, Helen. "Erastus Dow Palmer," *New York History.* July 1946.

Webster, J. Carson. "A Check List of the Works of Erastus Dow Palmer," *Art Bulletin.* June 1967.

Paris, Harold

Pugliese, Joseph. "Work in Progress," *Artforum.* Jan. 1964.

Selz, Peter. "The Final Negation—Harold Paris' Koddesh-Koddashim," *Art in America.* March–April 1969.

Park, David

"San Francisco Painters, Poets, and Sculptors," *The Artist's View.* Sept. 1953.

Parker, Ray

Friedman, B. H. (ed.). *School of New York: Some Younger Artists.* N.Y., 1959.

Parker, Ray. "Intent Painting," *It Is.* Autumn 1958.

"Ray Parker," exhibition catalogue, Washington Gallery of Modern Art. Wash. D.C., 1966.

Parris, Alexander

Hamlin, Talbot. *Greek Revival Architecture in America.* N.Y., 1964.

Journal of the Franklin Institute. March 1841.

Parrish, Maxfield

Adams, Adeline. "The Art of Maxfield Parrish," *American Magazine of Art,* vol. 9. 1918.

Vincent, George. "Maxfield Parrish," exhibition catalogue, Smith College Museum. Northampton, Mass. 1966.

Partridge, William O.

Partridge, William O. "Development of Sculpture in America," *Forum.* Jan. 1896.

Patchwork

Colby, Averil. *Patchwork.* London, 1958.

Miall, Agnes. *The Woman's Magazine of Patchwork Old and New.* London, 1937.

Patroon Painters

Belknap, Waldron. *American Colonial Painting.* Cambridge, 1959.

Wheeler, Robert and Janet MacFarlane. *Hudson Valley Paintings, 1700–1750,* in the Albany Institute of History and Art. Albany, 1959.

Peabody, Robert Swain

Peabody, Robert Swain. *Address of Robert Swain Peabody, President of the American Institute of Architects.* Wash. D.C., 1902.

——. *Note Book Sketches by Robert Swain Peabody.* Boston, 1873.

Peale, Anna Claypoole

Born, Wolfgang. "The Female Peales: Their Art and Its Tradition," *American Collector.* Aug. 1946.

Peale, Charles Willson

"Checklist of Portraits and Miniatures by Charles Willson Peale," *American Philosophical Society Transactions.* vol. 42. 1952.

Hunter, Wilbur. *The Story of America's Oldest Museum Building.* Baltimore, 1964.

Sellers, Charles Coleman. *Charles Willson Peale.* N.Y., 1969.

Peale, James

Baur, John. "The Peales and the Development of American Still Life," *Art Quarterly.* Winter 1940.

Brockway, Jean. "The Miniatures of James Peale," *Antiques.* Oct. 1932.

Sherman, Frederick F. "Two Recently Discovered Portraits in Oils by James Peale," *Art in America.* Oct. 1933.

Peale, Raphaelle

Bury, Edmund. "Raphaelle Peale (1774–1825), Miniature Painter," *American Collector.* Aug. 1948.

"The Peale Family: Three Generations of American Artists," exhibition catalogue, Detroit Institute of Arts. 1967.

Peale, Rembrandt

"Catalogue of an Exhibition of Portraits by Charles Willson Peale and James Peale and Rembrandt Peale," exhibition catalogue, Pennsylvania Academy of the Fine Arts. Philadlephia, 1923.

Peale, Rembrandt. "Reminiscences," *The Crayon.* I–III. 1855–56.

Peale, Rubens

Detroit Institute of Arts Bulletin. April 1944.

M. and M. Karolik Collection of American Paintings: 1815–1865. Cambridge, 1949.

Peale, Sarah Miriam

Born, Wolfgang. "The Female Peales: Their Art and its Tradition," *American Collector.* Aug. 1946.

"Richmond Portraits in an Exhibition of Makers of Richmond, 1737–1860," exhibition catalogue, Valentine Museum, Richmond. 1949.

Peale, Titian Ramsay

Mc Dermott, John. "Early Sketches of Titian Ramsay Peale," *Nebraska History.* Sept. 1952.

Pearlstein, Philip

Art Now: New York. March 1971.

Midgette, Willard. "Philip Pearlstein: The Naked Truth," *Art News.* Oct. 1967.

Nochlin, Linda. "Philip Pearlstein," exhibition catalogue, Georgia Museum of Art. Athens, Ga., 1970.

Pei, I. M.

"Cleo Rogers Memorial Library, Columbus, Indiana," *Architectural Forum.* Nov. 1971.

"Essays: I. M. Pei" (film), distributed by Museum-at-Large, N.Y.

Huxtable, Ada. "Mr. Pei Comes to Washing-ton," *New York Times.* July 11, 1971.

"National Airlines Terminal, Kennedy Airport, New York City," *Architectural Forum.* Oct. 1971.

Pelham, Henry

Letters and Papers of John Singleton Copley and Henry Pelham, 1739–1776. Boston, 1914.

Slade, Denison. "Henry Pelham, the Half-Brother of John Singleton Copley," *Publications of the Colonial Society of Massachusetts; Transactions, 1897–98, vol. V.*

Pelham, Peter

Allison, Anne. "Peter Pelham, Engraver in Mezzotinto," *Antiques.* Dec. 1947.

Coburn, Frederick. "More Notes on Peter Pelham," *Art in America.* June–Aug. 1932.

Penfield, Edward

Jones, Sydney. "Edward Penfield," *Studio.* July 15, 1925.

Penfield, Edward. *Holland Sketches.* N.Y., 1907.

——. *Spanish Sketches.* N.Y., 1911.

Stone, Herbert. "Mr. Penfield's Posters," *Chap-Book,* vol. 1. 1894.

Penn, Irving

Penn, Irving. *Moments Preserved: Eight Essays in Photographs and Words.* N.Y., 1960.

Pereira, Irene Rice

Baur, John. "Loren MacIver; I. Rice Pereira," exhibition catalogue, Whitney Museum, N.Y., 1953.

Period Revival

Clifford, C. R. *Period Furnishings,* N.Y., 1927.

Menzies, William. *Period Furniture for Everyman.* London, 1939.

Peterdi, Gabor

Longo, Vincent. "Peterdi as Printmaker," *Arts.* Dec. 1959.

Peterdi, Gabor. *Printmaking.* N.Y., 1959.

"Prints and Drawings by Gabor Peterdi," exhibition catalogue, Cleveland Museum of Art. 1962.

Peto, John Frederick

Frankenstein, Alfred. "Harnett, True and False," *Art Bulletin.* March 1949

Frankenstein, Alfred. "John Frederick Peto," exhibition catalogue, Smith College Museum. Northampton, Mass., 1950.

Goodrich, Lloyd. "Notes:Harnett and Peto: A Note on Styles," *Art Bulletin.* March 1949.

Pewter

Hirsch, Richard. *Early American Pewter, The John J. Evans, Jr. Collection.* Allentown, 1966.

Hood, Graham. *American Pewter in the Garvan and Other Collections at Yale.* New Haven, 1965.

Jacobs, Carl. *Guide to American Pewter.* N.Y., 1957.

Jacobs, Celia. *Pocket Book of American Pewter.* Springfield, 1960.

Kerfoot, J. B. *American Pewter.* N.Y., 1924.

Phillips, Ammi

Black, Mary. Ammi Phillips, Portrait Painter, 1788–1865," exhibition catalogue, Museum of American Folk Art. N.Y., 1969.

Photo-Secession

Hartmann, Sadakichi. "The Photo-Secession; A New Pictorial Movement," *Craftsman.* April 1904.

Hinton, A. Horsley. "The Work and Attitude of the Photo-Secession of America." *Am-*

Bibliography According to Entries

ateur Photographer (England). June 2, 1904.

Poore, H. R. "The Photo-Secession," *The Camera*. 1903.

Stieglitz, Alfred. *Photo-Secessionism and Its Opponents*. N.Y., Aug. 1910 (pamphlet).

Phyfe, Duncan

Mc Clelland, Nancy. *Duncan Phyfe and the English Regency. 1795–1830*. N.Y., 1939.

Musgrave, Clifford. *Regency Furniture 1800 to 1830*. London, 1961.

Picknell, William Lamb

Chennevieres, Marquis de. "Le Salon de 1800," *Gazette des Beaux-Arts*. July 1880.

Downes, William. "William Lamb Picknell," *Dictionary of American Biograqhy*. N.Y., 1928–1958.

Pine, Robert Edge

Morgan, John H. and Mantle Fielding. *The Life Portraits of Washington and Their Replicas*. Philadelphia, 1931.

Prime, Alfred. *The Arts and Crafts in Philadelphia, Maryland, and South Carolina, 1786-1800*. Topsfield, Mass., 1932.

Pine Tree Shillings

Clarke, Hermann. *John Hull, A Builder of the Bay Colony*. Portland, Me., 1940.

Pinney, Eunice

Lipman, Jean. "Eunice Pinney, An Early Connecticut Watercolorist," *Art Quarterly*. Summer 1943.

—— and Alice Winchester. *Primitive Painters in America, 1750–1850; An Anthology*. N.Y., 1950.

Pinprick

Lipman, Jean. *The Abby Aldrich Rockefeller Folk Art Collection*. Boston, 1957.

Polk, Charles Peale

Kimball, S. F. *Life Portraits of Jefferson and Their Replicas*. Philadelphia, 1944.

Morgan, John and Mantle Fielding. *The Life Portraits of Washington and Their Replicas*. Philadelphia, 1931.

Prime, Alfred. *The Arts and Crafts in Philadelphia, Maryland, and South Carolina, 1786–1800*. Topsfield, Mass., 1932.

Pollock, Jackson

Greenberg, Clement. "Jackson Pollock: Inspiration, Vision, Intuitive Decision," *Vogue*. April 1, 1967.

Namuth, Hans and Paul Falkenberg. "Jackson Pollock" (film), distributed by Museum-at-Large, N.Y. 1950

"Jackson Pollock," exhibition catalogue, Museum of Modern Art. N.Y., 1956.

O'Hara, Frank. *Jackson Pollock*. N.Y., 1959.

Robertson, Bryan. *Jackson Pollock*. N.Y., 1960.

Poons, Larry

Champa, Kermit. "New Paintings by Larry Poons," *Artforum*. Summer 1968.

Coplans, John. "Larry Poons," *Artforum*. June 1965.

Tuchman, Phyllis. "An Interview with Larry Poons," *Artforum*. Dec. 1970.

Poor, Henry Varnum

Campbell, Lawrence. "Poor Makes a Ceramic Mural," *Art News*. Oct. 1954.

Pop Art

Amaya, Mario. *Pop as Art: A Survey of the New Super Realism*. London, 1969.

Coplans, John. "Pop Art USA," exhibition catalogue, Oakland Art Museum. Cal., 1963.

Lippard, Lucy. *Pop Art*. N.Y., 1966.

Rublowsky, John. *Pop Art*. N.Y., 1965.

Russell, John and Suzi Gablik. *Pop Art Redefined*. London, 1969.

"The Spirit of the Comics," exhibition catalogue, Institute of Contemporary Art. Philadelphia, 1969.

Swenson, G. R. "What is Pop Art?: Interviews with Eight Painters," *Art News*. Nov. 1963.

Pope, Alexander

Frankenstein, Alfred. "The Reality of Appearance," exhibition catalogue, National Gallery of Art. Wash. D.C., 1970.

Porter, Fairfield

Cummings, Paul. "Fairfield Porter," *Archives of American Art Journal*, vol. 12, no. 2. 1972.

Schuyler, James. "Immediacy is the Message," *Art News*. March 1967.

Porter, Rufus

Lipman, Jean. *Rufus Porter, Yankee Pioneer*. N.Y., 1968.

——. "Rufus Porter, Yankee Wall Painter," *Art in America*. Oct. 1950.

—— and Alice Winchester. *Primitive Painters in America, 1750–1850, An Anthology*. N.Y., 1950.

Post-Painterly Abstraction

Greenberg, Clement. "Post Painterly Abstraction," *Art International*. Summer 1964.

——. "Post Painterly Abstraction," exhibition catalogue, Los Angeles County Museum. 1964.

Potter, William A.

Schuyler, Montgomery. "The Work of William Appleton Potter," *Architectural Record*. Sept. 1909.

Pousette-Dart, Richard

Kroll, Jack. "Richard Pousette-Dart: Transcendental Expressionist," *Art News*. April 1961.

Perreault, John. "Yankee Vedanta," *Art News*. Nov. 1967.

Powers, Hiram

Gardner, Albert. "Hiram Powers and William Rimmer, Two Nineteenth Century American Sculptors," *Magazine of Art*. Feb. 1943.

Lester, Charles. "The Genius and Sculpture of Hiram Powers," *American Review*. July 1845.

Powers' Statue of the Greek Slave. Boston, 1848.

Roberson, Samuel and William Gerdts. "The Greek Slave," *The Museum*. Winter-Spring 1965.

Pratt, Matthew

Sawitzky, William. *Matthew Pratt, 1734–1805*. N.Y., 1942.

Prendergast, Maurice

"Maurice Prendergast Memorial Exhibition," exhibition catalogue, Whitney Museum. N.Y., 1934.

Phillips, Duncan. "Maurice Prendergast," *Arts*. March 1924.

Rhys, Hedley, *Maurice Prendergast*. Cambridge, 1960.

Price, Kenneth

"Robert Irwin, Kenneth Price," exhibition catalogue, Los Angeles County Museum. 1966.

Printmaking, Historical

Adhemar, Jean. *Graphic Art of the Eighteenth Century*, N.Y., 1964.

American Printmaking; The First 150 Years, N.Y., 1969.

Brinkley, John and John Lewis. *Graphic Design*, London, 1954.

Craven, Thomas. *A Treasury of American Prints*, N.Y., 1939.

Drepperd, Carl. *Early American Prints*, N.Y., 1930.

Fielding, Mantle. *American Engravers Upon Copper and Steel*, Philadelphia, 1917.

Gross, Anthony. *Etching, Engraving, and Intaglio Printing*, London, 1970.

"Language of the Print, A Selection from the Donald H. Karshan Collection," exhibition catalogue, Bowdoin College Museum. Brunswick, 1968.

Ivins, William, Jr. *How Prints Look*. Boston 1969.

Johnson, Una. *American Woodcuts, 1670–1950*. Brooklyn, 1950.

Karshan, Donald. "American Printmaking, 1670–1968." *Art in America*. July-Aug. 1968.

Mayor, A. Hyatt. *Prints and People*. N.Y., 1971.

Sotriffer, Kristian. *Printmaking: History and Technique*. London, 1966.

Stauffer, David. *American Engravers Upon Copper and Steel*. N.Y., 1907.

Zigrosser, Carl. *The Expressionists: A Survey of the Graphic Arts*. N.Y., 1957.

——(ed.). *Prints*. N.Y., 1962.

—— and Christa Gaehde. *A Guide to the Collecting and Care of Original Prints*. N.Y., 1965.

Printmaking, Modern

Adhemar, Jean. *Twentieth Century Graphics*. N.Y., 1970.

Furst, Herbert. *The Modern Woodcut*. London, 1924.

Gilmour, Pat. *Modern Prints*. N.Y., 1970.

Hayter, Stanley William. *About Prints*. London, 1962.

Heller, Jules. *Printmaking Today* N.Y., 1972.

Sachs, Paul J. *Modern Prints and Drawings*. N.Y., 1954.

Stubbe, Wolf. *Graphic Art of the Twentieth Century*. N.Y., 1963.

"Twenty-eight Contemporary American Graphic Artists," exhibition catalogue, Rijksakademie van Beeldende Kunsten. Amsterdam, 1968.

Prior, William Matthew

Little, Nina. "William Matthew Prior, the Traveling Artist, and his In-laws, the Painting Hamblens," *Antiques*. Jan. 1948.

Lyman, Grace. "William Matthew Prior, the Painting Garret Artist," *Antiques*. Nov. 1934.

Sears, Clara. *Some American Primitives*. Boston, 1941.

Process Art

"Art in Process," exhibition catalogue, Finch College Museum. N.Y., 1966.

Bochner, Mel. "Art in Process—Structures," *Arts*. Sept.–Oct. 1966.

Sharp, Willoughby. "Place and Process," *Artforum*. Nov. 1969.

Proctor, A. Phimister

Gardner, Albert. *American Sculpture*. N.Y., 1965.

Remington, P. *Metropolitan Museum of Art Bulletin*, old series 34. 1939.

Queen Anne Style

Downes, Joseph. *American Furniture, Queen Anne and Chippendale Periods*.

N.Y., 1952.

Elder, William. *Maryland Queen Anne and Chippendale Furniture of the Eighteenth Century.* Baltimore, 1960.

Quidor, John

Baur, John. "John Quidor," exhibition catalogue, Brooklyn Museum. N.Y., 1942.

——. "John Quidor," exhibition catalogue, Munson-Williams-Proctor Institute. Utica, N.Y., 1965.

Ramage, John

Morgan, John H. *A Sketch of the Life of John Ramage.* N.Y., 1930.

Ramée, Joseph Jacques

Hislop, C. and Harold Larrabee. "Joseph-Jacques Ramée and the Building of North and South College," *Union College Alumni Monthly.* Feb. 1938.

Larrabee, Harold. "How Ramée Came to Schenectady." *Union College Alumni Monthly.* Feb. 1937.

Randolph, Benjamin

Kimball, Fiske. 'The Sources of the Philadelphia Chippendale," *Pennsylvania Museum Bulletin.* Dec.-Jan. 1927–28.

Woodhouse, S. W., Jr. "Benjamin Randolph," of Philadelphia," *Antiques,* vol. 11. 1927.

——. "More About Benjamin Randolph," *Antiques,* vol. 17. 1930.

Ranger, Henry Ward

Bell, R. H. *Art-Talks with Ranger.* N.Y., 1914.

Bromhead, Harold. "Henry Ward Ranger," *International Studio,* vol. 29. 1906.

"Henry Ward Ranger Centennial Exhibition, 1858–1958," exhibition catalogue, Smithsonian Institution. Wash. D.C., 1958.

Ranney, William T.

Grubar, Francis. "William Ranney, Painter of the Early West," exhibition catalogue, Corcoran Gallery. Wash. D.C., 1962.

Rattner, Abraham

Getlein, Frank. *Abraham Rattner.* N.Y., 1960.

Weller, Allen. *Abraham Rattner.* Urbana, Ill., 1956.

Rauschenberg, Robert

Forge, A. *Rauschenberg.* N.Y., 1970.

"Robert Rauschenberg: Paintings, Drawings and Combines," exhibition catalogue, Whitechapel Gallery. London, 1964.

Solomon, Alan. "Robert Rauschenberg," exhibition catalogue, Jewish Museum. N.Y., 1963.

Ray, Man

"Man Ray," exhibition catalogue, Los Angeles County Museum. 1966.

Ray, Man. *Self Portrait.* Boston, 1963.

Ribemont-Dessaignes, G. *Man Ray.* Paris, 1924.

Reed & Barton

Gibb, George. *The Whitesmiths of Taunton; A History of Reed and Barton, 1824–1943.* Cambridge, 1943.

The History of the Spoon, Knife and Fork by Reed and Barton and Dominick and Haff. Taunton, Mass., 1930.

Sniffin, Philip. *A Century of Silversmithing.* Taunton, Mass., 1924.

Refregier, Anton

Refregier, Anton. *Natural Figure Drawing.* N.Y., 1948.

Regionalism

See American Scene

Reid, Robert

Porter, James. "The Negro in American Art," exhibition catalogue, University of California. Los Angeles, 1966.

Reinhardt, Ad

"Ad Reinhardt," exhibition catalogue, Marlborough Gallery. N.Y., 1970.

"Ad Reinhardt," exhibition catalogue, Jewish Museum. N.Y., 1966.

Muller, Gregoire. "After the Ultimate: Ad Reinhardt," *Arts.* March 1970.

Reinhardt, Ad "Ad Reinhardt on His Art," *Studio International.* Dec. 1967.

Remington, Frederick

"Frederick Remington. A Retrospective Exhibition of Painting and Sculpture," exhibition catalogue, Paine Art Center. Oshkosh, Wis., 1967.

McCracken, Harold. *Frederick Remington, Artist of the Old West.* Philadelphia. 1947.

——. *The Frederick Remington Book.* N.Y., 1966

Renwick, James, Jr.

McKenna, Rosalie. "James Renwick, Jr. and the Second Empire Style in the United States," *Magazine of Art.* March 1951.

Stewart, William. *Grace Church and Old New York.* N.Y., 1924.

Resnick, Milton

Campbell, Lawrence. "Resnick Paints a Picture," *Art News,* Dec. 1957.

"Six Highlights This Winter," *Art News.* Feb. 1960.

Retablos

See Santos

Revere, Paul

Brigham, Clarence. *Paul Revere's Engravings.* Worcester, 1954.

Forbes, Esther. *Paul Revere and the World He Lived In.* Boston, 1942.

Rhodes, Daniel

Rhodes, Daniel. *Clay and Glazes for the Potter.* N.Y., 1957.

——. *Stoneware and Porcelain, The Art of High-Fired Pottery.* Philadelphia, 1959.

Rich, Obadiah

Fales, Martha. "Obadiah Rich, Boston Silversmith," *Antiques.* Oct. 1968.

Richards, William Trost

American Art Annual, VI (obituary).

Morris, Harrison. *Masterpieces of the Sea: William Trost Richards, A Brief Outline of his Life and Art.* Philadelphia, 1912.

Richardson, Francis and Joseph, Joseph, Jr., and Nathaniel

Dego, Raymond. "Portrait of Joseph Richardson, Sr.," *American Collector.* Dec. 1941.

Gillingham, Harrold. "Indian Trade Silver Ornaments Made by Joseph Richardson, Jr.," *Pennsylvania Magazine of History and Biography,* vol. 67. 1943.

Richardson, Henry Hobson

Brooks, Phillips. "Henry Hobson Richardson," *Harvard Monthly.* Oct. 1888.

Hitchcock, Henry R. *The Architecture of H. H. Richardson and His Times.* N.Y., 1936.

——. *Richardson as a Victorian Architect.* Baltimore, 1966.

Townsend, Horace. "H. H. Richardson, Architect," *Magazine of Art.* 1894.

Van Rensselaer, Marianna. *Henry Hobson Richardson and His Works.* Boston, 1888.

Rickey, George

"George Rickey: Kinetic Sculpture," exhi-

bition catalogue, Institute of Contemporary Art. Boston, 1964.

Secunda, Arthur. "Two Motion Sculptors: Tinguely and Rickey," *Artforum.* June 1962.

Selz, Peter. "George Rickey: Sixteen Years of Kinetic Sculpture," exhibition catalogue, Corcoran Gallery. Wash. D.C., 1966.

Rimmer, William

Bartlett, Truman. *The Art Life of William Rimmer, Sculptor, Painter, and Physician.* N.Y., 1968.

Force, Juliana and Lincoln Kirstein. "William Rimmer, 1816–1879," exhibition catalogue, Whitney Museum. N.Y., 1946.

Rimmer, William. *Elements of Design.* Boston, 1864.

Rinehart, William Henry

Ross, Marvin and Anna Rutledge. *A Catalogue of the Work of William Henry Rinehart, Maryland Sculptor, 1825-1874.* Baltimore, 1948.

Rusk, William. *William Henry Rinehart, Sculptor.* Baltimore, 1939.

Rivers, Larry

Bowling, Frank and Larry Rivers. "If You Can't Draw, Trace." *Arts.* Feb. 1971.

Hunter, Sam. "Larry Rivers," exhibition catalogue, Jewish Museum. N.Y., 1961.

Rosenberg, Harold. "Rivers' Commedia dell' Arte," *Art News.* April 1965.

Robinson, Boardman

Biddle, George. "Boardman Robinson: 93 Drawings," exhibition catalogue, Colorado Springs Fine Arts Center. 1937.

Christ-Janer, Albert. *Boardman Robinson.* Chicago, 1946.

Robinson, Boardman. *Cartoons of the War.* N.Y., 1915.

Robinson, Theodore

Baur, John. *Theodore Robinson, 1852–1896,* Brooklyn, 1946.

"Theodore Robinson, American Impressionist," exhibition catalogue, Kennedy Galleries. N.Y., 1966.

Robb, Samuel A.

Christensen, Erwin. *Early American Wood Carving.* N.Y., 1952.

Robsjohn-Gibbings, Terence Harold

Robsjohn-Gibbings, Terence. *Good-bye, Mr. Chippendale.* N.Y., 1944.

——. *Homes of the Brave.* N.Y., 1954.

"Snapshots: The Growth of a Modernist," *Interiors.* April 1946.

Robus, Hugo

Gardner, Albert. *American Sculpture.* N.Y., 1965.

Roesen, Severin

Mook, Maurice. "Severin Roesen, the Williamsport Painter," *The Morning Call* (Allentown, Pa.). Dec. 3, 1955.

Stone, R. B. "Not Quite Forgotten, A Study of the Williamsport Painter, Severin Roesen", *Proceedings and Papers of the Lycoming County Historical Society.* Nov. 1951.

Rogers, Isaiah

Eliot, W. H. *A Description of Tremont House.* Boston, 1830.

Schuyler, Montgomery. "The Old New York Custom House," *Architectural Record.* Dec. 1908.

Williamson, Jefferson. *The American Hotel.* N.Y., 1930.

Rogers, John

Bibliography According to Entries

Barck, Dorothy. "Rogers Groups in the Museum of the New York Historical Society," *New York Historical Society Quarterly Bulletin.* Oct. 1932.

Smith, Mr. and Mrs. Chetwood. *Rogers Groups Thought and Wrought by John Rogers.* Boston, 1934.

Wallace, David. *John Rogers, The People's Sculptor.* Middletown, Conn., 1967.

Rogers, Randolph

Fairman, Charles. *Art and Artists of the Capitol of the United States of America.* Wash. D.C., 1927.

Taft, Lorado. *History of American Sculpture.* N.Y., 1925.

Rohde, Gilbert

"Gilbert Rohde," *Nuestra Arquitectura* (Buenos Aires). April 1941.

"Unit Furniture of Gilbert Rohde," *Decoration,* new series no. 9. 1936.

Rohm, Robert

Pomeroy, Ralph. "An Interview with Robert Rohm," *Artforum.* April 1970.

Romanesque Revival

Koch, Robert. "Medieval Castle Revival: New York Armories," *Journal of the Society of Architectural Historians.* Oct. 1955.

Meeks, C. L. V. "Romanesque Before Richardson in the United States," *Art Bulletin.* March 1953.

Schuyler, Montgomery. "The Romanesque Revival in America," *Architectural Record,* vol. 2. 1892.

——. "The Romanesque Revival in New York," *Architectural Record,* vol. 1, no. 1. 1891.

Wyatt, J. B. N. "Modern Romanesque Architecture," *Architectural Review,* vol. 6. 1896.

Romans, Bernard

Old Print Shop Portfolio. Aug.–Sept. 1947.

Stauffer, David. *American Engravers Upon Copper and Steel.* N.Y., 1907.

Rosati, James

Kunitz, Stanley. "Sitting for Rosati the Sculptor," *Art News.* March 1959.

Rosenquist, James

"James Rosenquist," exhibition catalogue, National Gallery of Canada. 1968.

Swenson, G. R. "Social Realism in Blue: An Interview with James Rosenquist," *Metropolitan Museum of Art Bulletin.* March 1968.

Roszak, Theodore

Arnason, H. H. "Theodore Roszak," exhibition catalogue, Walker Art Center. Minneapolis, 1957.

Griffin, Howard. "Totems in Steel," *Art News.* Oct. 1956.

"Theodore Roszak," exhibition catalogue, Whitney Museum. N.Y., 1956.

Rothko, Mark

Gossen, E. C. "Rothko: The Omnibus Image," *Art News.* Jan. 1961.

"Mark Rothko," exhibition catalogue, Marlborough Galleries. London, 1964.

Selz, Peter. "Mark Rothko," exhibition catalogue, Museum of Modern Art. N.Y., 1961.

Roux, Alexander

Hauserman, Dianne. "Alexander Roux and His Plain and Artistic Furniture," *Antiques.* Feb. 1968.

Ruckstull, Frederic Wellington

New York World. Dec. 30, 1894.

Ruckstull, Frederic. *Great Works of Art and What Makes Them Great.* N.Y., 1925.

Rudolph, Paul

Moholy-Nagy, Sibyl. *The Architecture of Paul Rudolph.* N.Y., 1970.

Piene, Nan. "Paul Rudolph Designs a Town," *Art in America.* July–Aug. 1967.

Rudolph, Paul. "Pavilion—The Galaxon," *Art in America,* no. 3. 1962.

Rush, William

Gilliams, E. Leslie. "A Philadelphia Sculptor," *Lippincott's Magazine.* Aug. 1893.

Marceau, Henri. "William Rush, 1756–1833, The First Native American Sculptor," exhibition catalogue, Pennsylvania Museum of Art. Philadelphia, 1937.

Ruskin, John

Evans, Joan. "John Ruskin: New Conclusions," *Art News.* Sept. 1954.

Ruskin, John. *The Seven Lamps of Architecture.* N.Y., 1909.

——. *The Stones of Venice.* N.Y., 1851.

Stein, Roger. *John Ruskin and Aesthetic Thought in America, 1840-1900.* Cambridge, 1967.

Russell, Charles M.

McCracken, Harold. *The Charles M. Russell Book.* Garden City, 1957.

Renner, Frederic. *Charles M. Russell, Paintints, Drawings, and Sculpture in the Amon G. Carter Collection.* Austin, 1966.

Russell, Charles. *Good Medicine.* 1929.

Russell, Morgan

Mac Agy, Douglas. "Five Rediscovered from the Lost Generation," *Art News.* Summer 1960.

Wright, W. H. "Modern Art and isms," *Mentor.* Oct. 1921.

Ryder, Albert Pinkham

Goodrich, Lloyd. *Albert Pinkham Ryder,* N.Y., 1959

Goossen, E. C. "Albert Pinkham Ryder, Student of the Night," *Vogue.* Aug. 15, 1970.

Sherman, Frederic Fairchild. *Albert Pinkham Ryder.* N.Y., 1920.

Saarinen, Eero

"Four New Buildings: Architecture and Imagery," exhibition catalogue, Museum of Modern Art. N.Y., 1959.

"General Motors Technical Center Revisited," *Architectural Forum.* June 1971.

Temko, Allan. *Eero Saarinen.* N.Y., 1962.

Saint-Gaudens, Augustus

Cortissoz, Royal. *Augustus Saint-Gaudens.* Boston, 1907.

Saint-Gaudens, Homer. *The American Artist and His Times.* N.Y., 1941.

—— (ed.). *The Reminiscences of Augustus Saint-Gaudens.* N.Y., 1913.

Thorp, Louise. *Saint-Gaudens and the Gilded Era.* Boston, 1969.

Salmon, Robert

Wilmerding, John. "Robert Salmon, The First Major Exhibition," exhibition catalogue, De Cordova Museum. Lincoln, Mass., 1967.

Wilmerding, John. *Robert Salmon, Painter of Ship and Shore.* Boston, 1968.

Samaras, Lucas

Levin, Kim. "Samaras Bound," *Art News.* Feb. 1969.

Solomon, Alan. "An Interview with Lucas Samaras," *Artforum.* Oct. 1966.

Waldman, Diane. "Samaras: Reliquaries for St. Sade," *Art News.* Oct. 1966.

Samplers

Bolton, Mrs. Ethel and Eva Coe. *American Samplers.* Boston, 1921.

Earle, Alice. "Samplers," *Century Magazine,* vol. 83. 1912.

"Eighteenth Century American Samplers," *Art in America,* vol. 9. 1921.

"History in Needlework," *Historical New Hampshire.* April 1946.

Sanderson, Robert

Bulletin of the Associates in Fine Arts at Yale University. June 1937.

Santos

Boyd, E. *Saints and Saint Makers of New Mexico.* 1946.

Wilder, Mitchell and Edgar Breitenbach. *Santos: The Religious Folk Art of New Mexico.* Colorado Springs, 1943.

Sargent, Henry

Addison, Julia. "Henry Sargent, a Boston Painter," *Art in America.* Oct. 1929.

Sargent, John Singer

Hoopes, Donelson. "The Private World of John Singer Sargent," exhibition catalogue, Corcoran Gallery. Wash. D.C., 1964.

McKibben, David. *Sargent's Boston.* Boston, 1956.

Mount, Charles. *John Singer Sargent, a Biography.* N.Y., 1955.

Ormond, Richard. *J. S. Sargent.* N.Y., 1970.

Savage, Edward

Dresser, Louisa. "Edward Savage, 1761–1817," *Art in America.* Autumn 1952.

Morgan, John and Mantle Fielding. *Life Portraits of Washington and Their Replicas.* Philadelphia, 1931.

Savage, Eugene (Francis)

"Eugene Savage N.A.," *Columbia University Quarterly,* vol. 27. 1935.

Powell, Mary. "The Expulsion, a Painting by Eugene Savage," *American Magazine of Art,* vol. 15. 1924.

Price, F. Newlin. "An Apostle of Unity," *International Studio.* April 1924.

Savery, William

Cescinsky, Herbert. "William Savery of Philadelphia," *International Studio.* Oct. 1928.

Halsey, R. T. H. "William Savery, the Colonial Cabinet-Maker and His Furniture," *Arts and Decoration,* vol. 10. 1919.

Hornor, W. M., Jr. "William Savery: Chairmaker and Joiner," *Antiquarian.* July 1930.

Schamberg, Morton Livingston

Pach, Walter. "The Schamberg Exhibition," *Dial.* May 17, 1919.

Wolf, Ben. *Morton Livingston Schamberg.* Philadelphia, 1963.

Schimmel, Wilhelm

Flower, Milton. "Schimmel the Woodcarver," *Antiques.* Oct. 1943.

Little, Nina. *Abby Aldrich Rockefeller Folk Art Collection.* Boston, 1957.

Schindler, Rudolph

Gebhard, David. *Schindler.* N.Y., 1972.

Schindler, Rudolph. Collected Papers (manuscript). New-York Historical Society, N.Y.

Schrag, Karl

Gordon, John. "Karl Schrag," exhibition catalogue, American Federation of Arts. N.Y., 1960.

Scrimshaw

Lipman, Jean. *American Folk Art in Wood, Metal and Stone.* N.Y., 1948

Segal, George

Geldzahler, Henry. "George Segal," *Quadrum 19.* 1965.

Johnson, Ellen. "The Sculpture of George Segal," *Art International.* March 1964.

Perreault, John. "Plaster Caste," *Art News.* Nov. 1968.

Sekimachi, Kay

Slivka, Rose (ed.). *Crafts of the Modern World.* N.Y., 1968.

Seley, Jason

Gerdts, William. "A Survey of American Sculpture," exhibition catalogue, Newark Museum. N.J., 1962.

Serial Art

Bochner, Mel. "The Serial Attitude," *Artforum.* Dec. 1967.

Coplans, John. "Serial Imagery," exhibition catalogue, Pasadena Art Museum, Cal. 1963.

Coplans, John. "Andy Warhol and Elvis Presley: Social and Cultural Predictions of Warhol's Serial Image," *Studio International.* Feb. 1971.

Lee, David. "Serial Rights," *Art News.* Dec. 1967.

Serra, Richard

Krauss, Rosalind. "Richard Serra: Sculpture, Redrawn," *Artforum.* May 1972.

Pincus-Witten, Robert. "Slow Information: Richard Serra," *Artforum.* Sept. 1969.

Seymour, John and Thomas

Stoneman, Vernon. *John and Thomas Seymour, Cabinetmakers in Boston, 1794–1816.* Boston, 1959.

Shahn, Ben

Shahn, Ben. *The Shape of Content.* Cambridge, 1957.

Soby, James Thrall. *Ben Shahn.* N.Y., 1947.

——. *Ben Shahn: His Graphic Art.* N.Y., 1957.

Shaker Crafts

Andrews, Edward. *The People Called Shakers.* N.Y., 1963.

——. "Shaker Handicrafts," exhibition catalogue, Whitney Museum. N.Y., 1935.

——. "The Shaker Manner of Building," *Art in America,* vol. 48, no. 3. 1960.

—— and Faith Andrews. *Shaker Furniture,* N.Y., 1950.

Storey, Walter. "Native Art from Old Shaker Colonies," *New York Times Magazine.* Oct. 23, 1932.

Shaped Canvas

Alloway, Lawrence, "The Shaped Canvas," exhibition catalogue, Guggenheim Museum. N.Y., 1964.

Fried, Michael. "Shape as Form: Frank Stella's New Paintings," *Artforum.* Nov. 1966.

Lippard, Lucy. "The Third Stream: Constructed Paintings and Painted Structures," *Art Voices.* Spring 1965.

Shaw, Joshua

Christian Intelligencer. Sept. 20, 1860 (obituary).

Shaw, Joshua. *A New and Original Drawing Book.* Philadelphia, 1816.

——. *Picturesque Views of American Scenery,* Philadelphia, 1820–21.

Sheeler, Charles

"Charles Sheeler," exhibition catalogue, Museum of Modern Art. N.Y., 1939.

"Charles Sheeler, American Photographer," *Contemporary Photographer,* vol. 6, no. 1.

Friedman, M., B. Hayes and C. Millard. *Charles Sheeler.* Wash. D.C., 1968.

Rourke, Constance. *Charles Sheeler, Artist in the American Tradition.* N.Y., 1938.

Sheffield, Isaac

French, Henry. *Art and Artists in Connecticut,* Boston, 1879.

Sherman, Frederick F., "Unrecorded Early American Portrait Painters," *Art in America.* Dec. 1933.

Shingle Style

Scully, Vincent. *The Shingle Style.* New Haven, 1955.

Shinn, Everett

Gallatin, A. E. "Everett Shinn's Decorative Paintings," *Scrip.* Aug. 1906.

——. "Studio Talk: Everett L. Shinn," *International Studio.* Nov. 1906.

Kent, N. "The Versatile Art of Everett Shinn," *American Artist.* Oct. 1945.

Shirlaw, Walter

American Art Annual. VIII (obituary).

Dreier, Dorothea. "Walter Shirlaw," *Art in America.* Autumn 1919.

New York Times. Dec. 30, 1909.

Show Figures

Fried, Frederick. *Artists in Wood.* N.Y., 1970.

Lipman, Jean. *American Folk Art in Wood, Metal and Stone.* N.Y., 1948.

Shryock, Gideon

Andrews, Alfred. "Gideon Shryock, Kentucky Architect and Greek Revival Architect in Kentucky," *Filson Club History Quarterly,* vol. 18. 1944.

Field, Elizabeth. "Gideon Shryock," *Kentucky Historical Society Register.* April 1952.

Newcomb, Rexford. "Gideon Shryock; Pioneer Greek Revivalist of the West," *Architect.* Oct. 1928.

Silver

Avery, C. L. *American Silver of the Seventeenth and Eighteenth Centuries. A Study Based on the Clearwater Collection.* N.Y., 1920.

——. *Early American Silver.* N.Y., 1930.

Brix, Maurice. *List of Philadelphia Silversmiths and Allied Artificers from 1682 to 1850.* Philadelphia, 1920.

Buhler, Kathryn. *American Silver 1655–1825 in the Museum of Fine Arts, Boston.* Greenwich, Conn., 1972.

Dauterman, Carl. *Checklist of American Silversmiths' Work 1650–1850 in Museums in the New York Metropolitan Area.* N.Y., 1968.

Fales, Martha. *Early American Silver.* N.Y., 1970.

Gourley, Hugh III. *The New England Silversmith, Seventeenth Century to the Present.* Providence, 1965.

Miller, Isabelle. *New York Silversmiths of the Seventeenth Century.* N.Y., 1963.

Rice, Norman. *Albany Silver, 1652–1825.* Albany, 1964.

Buhler, Kathryn and Graham Hood. *American Silver in the Yale University Art Gallery: Garvan and Other Collections.* New Haven, 1970.

McClinton, Katharine. *Collecting American 19th Century Silver.* N.Y., 1968.

Phillips, John M. *American Silver.* N.Y., 1949.

Silvermarks

Currier, Ernest. *Marks of Early American Silversmiths with Notes on Silver, Spoon Types and List of New York City Silversmiths, 1815–1841.* Portland, Me., 1938.

Ensks, Stephen. *American Silversmiths and Their Marks.* N.Y., 1948.

Wyler, Seymour. *The Book of Old Silver.* N.Y., 1965.

Simmons, Franklin

American Art Annual. XI (obituary).

Clement, Clara and Laurence Hutton. *Artists of the Nineteenth Century and Their Work.* Boston, 1884.

Siskind, Aaron

Aaron Siskind: Photographs. N.Y., 1952.

Aaron Siskind: Photographer. Rochester, 1965.

Skidmore, Owings & Merrill

American Can Company Headquarters, Greenwich, Connecticut," *Architectural Forum.* Jan.–Feb. 1971.

"Johnson Library, Austin, Texas," *Architectural Forum.* July–Aug. 1971.

Skillin, Simeon, Sr.

Pinckney, Pauline. *American Figureheads and Their Carvers.* N.Y., 1940.

Swan, Mabel. "Boston's Carvers and Joiners," *Antiques.* March 1948.

——. "Simeon Skillin, Sr., the First American Sculptor," *Antiques.* July 1944.

Thwing, Leroy. "The Four Carving Skillins," *Antiques.* June 1938.

Skyscraper

Condit, Carl. *The Rise of the Skyscraper.* Chicago, 1952.

Schuyler, Montgomery. "The Skyscraper Up to Date," *Architectural Records.* Jan.–March 1899.

Schuyler, Montgomery. "Some Recent Skyscrapers," *Architectural Record.* Sept. 1907.

Starrett, William. *Skyscrapers and the Men Who Build Them.* N.Y., 1928.

Weisman, W. "New York and the Problem of the First Skyscraper," *Journal of the Society of Architectural Historians.* March 1953.

Sloan, John

Brooks, Van Wyck. *John Sloan, A Painter's Life.* N.Y., 1938.

Morse, Peter. *John Sloan's Prints.* New Haven, 1969.

Scott, David and John Bullard. *John Sloan.* Wash. D.C., 1971.

Sloan, John. *Gist of Art.* N.Y., 1939.

Sloan, Samuel

Sloan, Samuel. *The Model Architect.* Philadelphia, 1852.

Smibert, John

Belknap, Waldron. "Feke and Smibert, A Note on Two Portraits," *Art Bulletin.* Sept. 1953.

Foote, Henry W. *John Smibert: Painter.* Cambridge, 1950.

Smith, David

Cone, Jane. "David Smith 1906-1965," exhibition catalogue, Fogg Art Museum. Cambridge, 1966.

Goossen, E. C. "David Smith," *Arts.* March 1956.

Kramer, Hilton. "David Smith, A Memorial Exhibition," exhibition catalogue, Los Angeles County Museum. 1965.

Krauss, Rosalind. *Terminal Iron Works, The Sculpture of David Smith.* Cambridge, 1972.

Smith, Robert

Smith, Robert. "John Notman's Nassau Hall," *Princeton University Library Chronicle.* Spring 1953.

Smith, Thomas

Bibliography According to Entries

Dresser, Louisa, *Seventeenth Century Painting in New England.* Worcester, Mass., 1935.

Hagen, Oskar. *The Birth of the American Tradition in Art.* N.Y., 1940.

Smith, Tony

Goossen, E. C. "Tony Smith," exhibition catalogue, Newark Museum. N.J., 1971.

Lippard, Lucy. *Tony Smith.* N.Y., 1972.

"Tony Smith," exhibition catalogue, Wadsworth Atheneum. Hartford, 1966.

Wagstaff, Samuel, Jr. "Talking with Tony Smith," *Artforum.* Dec. 1966.

Smith, W. Eugene

Kirstein, Lincoln. *W. Eugene Smith.* N.Y., 1969.

Mack, E. A. "The Myth Named Smith," *Camera 35.* Dec. 1959–Jan. 1960.

Smither, James

Prime, Alfred. *The Arts and Crafts in Philadelphia, Maryland, and South Carolina, 1721-1785.* Topsfield, Mass., 1929.

Weiss, Harry. "The Growth of the Graphic Arts in Philadelphia 1663–1820," *Bulletin of the New York Public Library.* Feb.–March 1952.

Smithson, Robert

Robbin, Anthony. "Smithson's Non-Site Sights," *Art News.* Feb. 1969.

Smithson, Robert. "Incidents of Mirror-Travel in Yucatan," *Artforum.* Sept. 1969.

Snelson, Kenneth

Battcock, Gregory. "Kenneth Snelson," *Arts.* Feb. 1968.

Snelson, Kenneth. "How Primary Is Structure?" *Art Voices.* Summer 1966.

Sommer, Frederick

Nordland, Gerald. "Frederick Sommer," exhibition catalogue, Philadelphia College of Art. 1968.

Sonnier, Keith

Baker, Kenneth. "Keith Sonnier at the Modern," *Artforum.* Oct. 1971.

Sharp, Willoughby. "Keith Sonnier at Eindhoven: An Interview," *Arts.* Feb. 1971.

Southworth, Albert Sands and Josiah Johnson Hawes

Hawes, J. J. "Stray Leaves from the Diary of the Oldest Professional Photographer in the World," *Photo-Era,* vol. 16, no. 2.

Southworth, Albert. "An Address to the National Photographic Association of the United States," *Philadelphia Photographer,* vol. 8, no. 94.

Stokes, I. N. Phelps. *The Hawes-Stokes Collection of American Daguerreotypes by Albert Sands Southworth and Josiah Johnson Hawes: A Catalogue.* N.Y., 1939.

Soyer, Isaac

Soyer, Moses. "Three Brothers," *Magazine of Art.* April 1939.

Soyer, Moses

Smith, B. *Moses Soyer.* N.Y., 1944.

Soyer, Moses. "Three Brothers," *Magazine of Art.* April 1939.

Soyer, Raphael

Goodrich, Lloyd. *Raphael Soyer.* N.Y., 1967.

Gutman, W. "Raphael Soyer," *Creative Art.* April 1930.

Watson, E. W. "The Paintings of Raphael Soyer," *American Artist.* June 1948.

Sparrow, Thomas

Arthur, Helen. "Thomas Sparrow, an Early Maryland Engraver," *Antiques.* Jan. 1949.

Speicher, Eugene

Barker, Virgil. "Eugene Speicher: Painter and Artist," *Arts.* Dec. 1924.

"Eugene Speicher: A Retrospective Exhibition of Oils and Drawings," exhibition catalogue, Buffalo Fine Arts Academy, 1950.

Mather, Frank J. *Eugene Speicher.* N.Y., 1931.

Spencer, Niles

Cahill, Holger. "Niles Spencer," *Magazine of Art.* Nov. 1952.

Mannes, M. "Niles Spencer, Painter of Simplicities," *Creative Art.* July 1930.

Miller, Dorothy. "Niles Spencer," exhibition catalogue, Akron Art Institute. Ohio, 1954.

Watson, E. W. "Niles Spencer: Interview," *American Artist.* Oct. 1944.

Stamos, Theodoros

Pomeroy, Ralph. "Stamos' Sun-Boxes," *Art News.* March 1968.

"Stamos: Abstracting the Ocean," *Art News.* Feb. 1947.

Stankiewicz, Richard

Miller, Dorothy. "Sixteen Americans," exhibition catalogue, Museum of Modern Art, N.Y., 1959.

"Richard Stankiewicz; Robert Indiana," exhibition catalogue, Walker Art Center. Minneapolis, 1963.

Stanley, John Mix

Draper, Benjamin. "John Mix Stanley, Pioneer Painter", *Antiques.* March 1942.

Kinietz, William. *John Mix Stanley and His Indian Paintings.* Ann Arbor, 1942.

Stanley, John M. "Portraits of North American Indians," *Smithsonian Miscellaneous Collections,* vol. 2. 1862.

Taft, Robert. *Artists and Illustrators of the Old West, 1850–1900.* N.Y., 1953.

Steichen, Edward

Sandburg, Carl. *Steichen the Photographer.* 1929.

Steichen, Edward. *A Life in Photography.* Garden City, N.Y., 1963.

—— (ed.). *The Bitter Years: 1935–1941.* N.Y., 1962.

——. *The Family of Man.* N.Y., 1955.

Steiner, Ralph

"Realism in Photography," exhibition catalogue, Museum of Modern Art. N.Y., 1949.

Steiner, Ralph. "H₂0" (film), 1929.

—— and Willard van Dyke. "The City" (film), 1939.

Stella, Frank

Fried, Michael. "Three American Painters: Noland, Olitski, Stella," exhibition catalogue, Fogg Art Museum. Cambridge, 1965.

Glaser, Bruce. "Questions to Stella and Judd," *Art News.* Sept. 1966.

Rubin, William. *Frank Stella.* N.Y., 1970.

Stella, Joseph

Baur, John. "Joseph Stella," exhibition catalogue, Whitney Museum, N.Y., 1963.

Jaffe, Irma. *Joseph Stella.* Cambridge, 1970.

Stella, Joseph. "The Brooklyn Bridge (A Page of My Life)," *Transition.* June 1929.

Sterne, Maurice

"Maurice Sterne, Retrospective Exhibition (1902–1932), Paintings, Sculpture, Drawings," exhibition catalogue, Museum of Modern Art. N.Y., 1933.

Sterne, Maurice. *Shadow and Light.* 1965.

Stieglitz, Alfred

Bry, Doris. "Exhibition of Photographs by Alfred Stieglitz," exhibition catalogue, National Gallery of Art. Wash. D.C., 1958.

Doty, Robert. *Photo-Secession: Photography as a Fine Art.* Rochester, 1960.

Frank, Waldo, et al. *America and Alfred Stieglitz.* N.Y., 1934.

Norman, Dorothy. *Alfred Stieglitz, Introduction to an American Seer.* N.Y., 1960.

Still, Clyfford

"Clyfford Still, Paintings in the Albright-Knox Art Gallery," exhibition catalogue, Buffalo Fine Arts Academy. N.Y., 1966.

Goossen, E. C. "Painting as Confrontation: Clyfford Still," *Art International.* Jan. 1960.

Kuh, Katharine. "Clyfford Still," *Vogue.* Feb. 1, 1970.

"Paintings of Clyfford Still," exhibition catalogue, Albright-Knox Art Gallery. Buffalo, 1959.

Stock, Joseph W.

"American Folk Art: The Art of the Common Man in America," exhibition catalogue, Museum of Modern Art. N.Y., 1932.

American Folk Art: A Collection of Paintings and Sculpture. The Gift of Mrs. John D. Rockefeller to Colonial Williamsburg. Williamsburg, Va., 1940.

Lipman, Jean and Alice Winchester. *Primitive Painters in America, 1750–1850; An Anthology.* N.Y., 1950.

Stone, Edward Durell

Bruning, Fred. "A Monument in Stone," *Newsday* (Long Island, N.Y.). Oct. 18, 1972.

Stone, Horatio

Clement, Clara and Laurence Hutton. *Artists of the Nineteenth Century and Their Work.* Boston, 1884.

Fairman, Charles. *Art and Artists of the Capitol of the United States of America.* Wash. D.C., 1927.

Storrs, John

Bryant, Edward. "Rediscovery: John Storrs," *Art in America.* May–June 1969.

Story, William Wetmore

James, Henry. *William Wetmore Story and His Friends.* Boston, 1903.

Phillips, Mary. *Reminiscences of William Wetmore Story.* Chicago, 1897.

Streamlined Moderne

Smithson, Robert. "Ultramoderne," *Arts.* Sept.–Oct. 1967.

Strickland, William

Gilchrist, Agnes. *William Strickland: Architect and Engineer.* Philadelphia, 1950.

——. "Additions to William Strickland," *Journal of the Society of Architectural Historians.* Oct. 1954.

Strickland, William. *Reports on Canals, Railways, Roads, and Other Subjects.* Philadelphia, 1826.

Stuart, Gilbert

Morgan, John Hill. *Gilbert Stuart and His Pupils.* N.Y., 1939.

Mount, Charles. *Gilbert Stuart, a Biography.* N.Y., 1964.

Park, Lawrence. *Gilbert Stuart; An Illustrated Descriptive List of His Work.* N.Y., 1926.

Richardson, E. P. "Gilbert Stuart, Portraitist of the Young Republic," exhibition catalogue, National Gallery of Art. Wash. D.C., 1967.

Sugarman, George

Glaser, Bruce, Lyman Kipp, George Sugarman and David Weinrib. "Where Do We

Go From Here?'', *Arts Yearbook 8.* 1965.

''Recent American Sculpture,'' exhibition catalogue, Jewish Museum. N.Y., 1964.

Sullivan, Louis
Morrison, Hugh. *Louis Sullivan.* N.Y., 1935.
Sullivan, Louis. *The Autobiography of an Idea.* N.Y., 1949.
——. *Kindergarten Chats.* N.Y., 1947.

Sully, Thomas
Biddle, Edward and Mantle Fielding. *The Life and Works of Thomas Sully.* Philadelphia, 1921.
Hart, Charles (ed.). *A Register of Portraits Painted by Thomas Sully, 1801–1871.* Philadelphia, 1908.
Sully, Thomas. *Hints to Young Painters.* Philadelphia, 1873.

Supergraphics
''Soft Sell on Walls,'' *Life.* Oct. 6, 1972.

Surrealism
Alexandrian, Sarane. *Surrealist Art.* N.Y., 1970.
Barr, Alfred, Jr. *Fantastic Art, Dada, Surrealism.* N.Y., 1936.
Cardinal, Roger and Robert Short. *Surrealism, Permanent Revelation.* London, 1970.
Janis, Sidney. *Abstract and Surrealist Art in America.* N.Y., 1944.
Levy, Julien. *Surrealism.* N.Y., 1936.
Rubin, William. *Dada and Surrealist Art.* N.Y., 1968.
Sandler, Irving. ''The Surrealist Emigres in New York,'' *Artforum.* May 1968.

Symbolism
Pincus-Witten, Robert. ''The Iconography of Symbolist Painting,'' *Artforum.* Jan. 1970.
Taylor, S. W. ''Symbolist Art in Toronto,'' *Arts.* Nov. 1969.

Synchromism
Agee, William. ''Synchromism and Color Principles in American Painting,'' exhibition catalogue, Knoedler Galleries. N.Y., 1965.
Chevreul, M. E. *De la Loi du Contraste Simultane des Couleurs.* Paris, 1839.
Seuphor, Michael. ''Synchromies,'' *L'Oeil.* Jan. 1958.
Wright, Willard. ''Impressionism to Synchromism,'' *Forum.* Dec. 1913.
——. ''Synchromism,'' *International Studio.* Oct. 1915.

Syng, Philip, Jr.
Eberlein, Harold and C. Hubbard. ''Philadelphia Silver by Ghiselin and Syng,'' *American Collector.* Aug. 1937.

Taft, Lorado
Taft, Lorado. *The History of American Sculpture.* N.Y., 1903.

Tait, Arthur Fitzwilliam
''Arthur F. Tait,'' *Cosmopolitan Art Journal.* March and June 1858.
Cowdrey, M. B. ''Arthur F. Tait, Master of the American Sporting Scene,'' *American Collector.* Jan. 1945.
Keyes, Homer. ''Arthur F. Tait in Painting and Lithograph,'' *Antiques.* July 1933.

Tamarind Lithography Workshop
Antreasian, Garo and Clinton Adams. *The Tamarind Book of Lithography: Art and Techniques.* N.Y., 1971.
Secunda, Arthur. ''Tamarind,'' *Artform,* vol. 1, no. 3. 1962.
Simon, Rita. ''The Tamarind Workshop and June Wayne,'' *Arts.* May 1969.

Tanguy, Yves
Cunningham, Charles. ''Yves Tanguy; Kay Sage,'' exhibition catalogue, Wadsworth Atheneum. Hartford, 1954.
Soby, James Thrall. ''Yves Tanguy,'' exhibition catalogue, Museum of Modern Art. N.Y., 1955.

Tanner, Henry Ossawa
''The Art of Henry O. Tanner,'' exhibition catalogue, Frederick Douglas Institute. 1969.
''Henry O. Tanner,'' *Art News.* Dec. 1967.
Matthews, Marcia. *Henry Ossawa Tanner.* 1969.

Tarbell, Edmund
Coburn, Frederick. ''Edward C. Tarbell,'' *International Studio.* Sept. 1907.
Price, Lucien and Frederick Coburn. ''Frank W. Benson; Edmund C. Tarbell,'' exhibition catalogue, Museum of Fine Arts. Boston, 1938.

Tchelitchew, Pavel
Kirstein, Lincoln. ''Pavel Tchelitchew,'' exhibition catalogue, Gallery of Modern Art. N.Y., 1964.
''Pavel Tchelitchew. 1898–1957,'' *Art News.* Sept. 1957.

Ten, The
Aston, Dore and Thomas Messer. ''10 Independents: An Artist-Initiated Exhibition,'' exhibition catalogue, Guggenheim Museum. N.Y., 1972.

Teske, Edmund
Wholden, Rosalind. ''Edmind Teske, The Camera as Reliquary,'' *Artform.* Feb. 1964.

Thayer, Abbott H.
Abbott H. Thayer. N.Y., 1923.
Barker, Virgil. ''Abbott H. Thayer Memorial Exhibition,'' exhibition catalogue. Corcoran Gallery, Wash. D.C., 1922.
White, Nelson. *Abbott H. Thayer.* Hartford, 1951.

Theus, Jeremiah
Dresser, Louisa. ''Jeremiah Theus: Notes on the Date and Place of his Birth and Two Problem Portraits Signed by Him,'' *Worcester Art Museum Annual,* vol. 6. 1958.
Middleton, Margaret and Jeremiah Theus. *Colonial Artist of Charles Town.* Columbia, S.C., 1953.

Thompson, Cephas Giovanni
Antiques. Feb. 1942.
M. and M. Karolik Collection of American Paintings: 1815–1865. Cambridge, 1949.

Thompson, Jerome B.
M. and M. Karolik Collection of American Paintings: 1815–1865. Cambridge, 1949.
Thompson, Jerome. *A Critical Guide to the Exhibition at the National Academy of Design.* N.Y., 1859.

Thompson, Launt
Gardner, Albert. *American Sculpture.* N.Y., 1965.
Taft, Lorado. *History of American Sculpture.* N.Y., 1925.

Thornton, William
Brown, Glenn. ''Dr. William Thornton, Architect,'' *Architectural Record.* July–Sept. 1896.
Clark, Allen. ''Dr. and Mrs. William Thornton,'' *Records of the Columbia Historical Society,* vol. 18. 1915.

Tiffany & Company
Koch, Robert. *Louis Comfort Tiffany, Rebel in Glass.* N.Y., 1964.
Robinson, Elton. ''Rediscovery: A Tiffany Room,'' *Art in America.* July–Aug. 1969.
Tiffany, Louis. *The Art Work of Louis Tiffany.* N.Y., 1914.

Tinsel Painting
Art Recreations. Boston, 1860.
Little, Nina. *Abby Aldrich Rockefeller Folk Art Collection.* Boston, 1957.

Tinware
Brazer, Esther. *Early American Decoration.* Springfield, Mass., 1940.

Tobey, Mark
''Mark Tobey,'' exhibition catalogue, Musée des Arts Decoratifs, Paris. 1961.
Seitz, William. ''Mark Tobey,'' exhibition catalogue, Museum of Modern Art. N.Y., 1962.

Tomlin, Bradley Walker
Ashbery, John. ''Tomlin: The Pleasures of Color,'' *Art News.* Oct. 1957.
Baur, John. ''Bradley Walker Tomlin,'' exhibition catalogue, Whitney Museum. N.Y., 1957.
''Bradley Walker Tomlin,'' *Magazine of Art.* May 1949.

Towle Company
Rainwater, Dorothy. *American Silver Manufacturers.* Hanover, Pa., 1966.

Town, Ithiel
Newton, Roger. *Town and Davis: Architects.* N.Y., 1942.
Sigourney, Lydia. ''Residence of Ithiel Town, Esq.,'' *Ladies Companion.* Jan. 1839.

Trade Signs
Chapin, Howard. *Early American Signboards.* Providence, 1926.
Harlow, Thompson. *Morgan B. Brainard's Tavern Signs.* Hartford, 1958.
Little, Nina. *Abby Aldrich Rockefeller Folk Art Collection.* Boston, 1957.
Swan, Mabel. ''Early Sign Painters,'' *Antiques.* May 1928.

Trova, Ernest
Amaya, Mario. ''Trova: Elegy for Mechanical Man,'' *Art and Artists.* April 1966.
Van der Marck, Jan. ''Idols for the Computer Age,'' *Art in America.* Nov.–Dec. 1966.

Truitt, Anne
Forgey, Benjamin. ''Washington,'' *Art in America.* Jan.–Feb. 1972.
Judd, Donald. ''New York Exhibitions: In the Galleries: Anne Truitt,'' *Arts.* April 1963.

Trumbauer, Horace
''A New Influence in the Architecture of Philadelphia,'' *Architectural Record.* Feb. 1904.

Trumbull, John
Sizer, Theodore (ed.). *The Autobiography of Col. John Trumbull.* New Haven, 1953.
——. *The Works of Col. John Trumbull, Artist of the American Revolution.* New Haven, 1950.
Turner, Evan and Theodore Sizer. ''John Trumbull, Painter-Patriot,'' exhibition catalogue, Wadsworth Atheneum. Hartford, 1956.
Trumbull, John. *Address Before the Directors of the American Academy of Fine Arts.* N.Y., 1833.

Tryon, Dwight William
White, Henry. *The Life and Art of Dwight William Tryon.* N.Y., 1930.

Tuckerman, Henry Theodore
Tuckerman, Henry. *Book of the Artists.* N.Y., 1867.

Twachtman, John Henry

Bibliography According to Entries

Boyle, Richard. "John Henry Twachtman," exhibition catalogue, Cincinnati Art Museum. 1966.
Clark, Eliot. *John Twachtman.* N.Y., 1924.
Tucker, Allen. *John H. Twachtman.* N.Y., 1931.

Tworkov, Jack
Finkelstein, Louis. "Tworkov: Radical Pro," *Art News.* April 1964.
Porter, Fairfield. "Tworkov Paints a Picture," *Art News.* May 1953.

Uelsmann, Jerry
Edson, Russell. *Jerry N. Uelsmann.* N.Y., 1970.
Parker, William. "Uelsmann's Unitary Reality," *Aperture.* vol. 13, no. 3. 1967.

Universal Limited Art Editions
Davis, Douglas. "Rauschenberg's Recent Graphics," *Art in America.* July–Aug. 1969.
Motherwell, Robert. "A La Pintura: The Genesis of a Book," exhibition catalogue, Metropolitan Museum of Art. N.Y., 1972.

Upjohn, Richard
Upjohn, E. M. *Richard Upjohn, Architect and Churchman.* N.Y., 1939.
Upjohn, Richard. *Upjohn's Rural Architecture.* N.Y., 1852.

Van Brunt, Henry
Van Brunt, Henry. *Greek Lines, and Other Architectural Essays.* Boston, 1893.

Van Der Burch (Vanderburgh), Cornelius
Bulletin of the Associates in Fine Arts at Yale University. June 1937.

Vanderlyn, John
Gosman, Robert. "Biography of John Vanderlyn" (manuscript). New-York Historical Society, N.Y.
Miller, Lillian. "John Vanderlyn and the Business of Art," *New York History.* Jan. 1951.
Mondello, Salvatore. "John Vanderlyn," *New York Historical Society Quarterly Bulletin.* April 1968.
Schoonmaker, Marius. *John Vanderlyn, Artist, 1775–1852, Biography.* Kingston, N.Y., 1950.

Van Dyck, Pieter
Bulletin of the Associates in Fine Arts at Yale University. June 1937.
Bulletin of the Associates in Fine Arts at Yale University. June 1938.

Vedder, Elihu
"Elihu Vedder Memorial Exhibition," exhibition catalogue, Buffalo Fine Arts Academy. 1929.
Soria, Regina. *Elihu Vedder, American Visionary Artist in Rome, 1836–1923.* N.J., 1970.
Van Dyke, John. "The Works of Elihu Vedder," exhibition catalogue, American Academy of Arts and Letters. N.Y., 1937.
Vedder, Elihu. *The Digressions of V.* Boston, 1910.

Venturi, Robert
Huxtable, Ada. "Celebrating Dumb, Ordinary Architecture," *New York Times.* Oct. 1, 1971.
Venturi, Robert. *Complexity and Contradiction in Architecture.* N.Y., 1966.
——, Denise Scott-Brown, and Stephen Izenour. *Learning from Las Vegas.* Cambridge, 1972.
"Venturi and Rauch," exhibition catalogue, Whitney Museum. N.Y., 1971.

Vicente, Esteban

Ashton, Dore. "Esteban Vicente," *Arts and Architecture.* Feb. 1960.
"Five Shows Out of the Ordinary," *Art News.* March 1958.

Victorian Gothic
Kimball, Fiske. "Victorian Art and Victorian Taste," *Antiques.* March 1933.
Stanton, Phoebe. *The Gothic Revival and American Church Architecture.* Baltimore, 1968.
"Texas Victorian," *Art in America.* July–Aug. 1969.
"Victoriana: An Exhibition of the Arts of the Victorian Era in America," exhibition catalogue, Brooklyn Museum. 1960.

Volk, Leonard
Clement, Clara and Laurence Hutton. *Artists of the Nineteenth Century and Their Work.* Boston, 1884.
Wilson, Rufus. *Lincoln in Portraiture.* N.Y., 1935.

Vonnoh, Bessie Potter
McSpadden, Joseph. *Famous Sculptor of America.* N.Y., 1924.
Monroe, Lucy. "Bessie Potter," *Brush and Pencil.* April–Sept. 1898.
"A Sculptor of Statuettes," *Current Literature.* June 1903.

Vonnoh, Robert William
Clark, Eliot. "The Art of Robert Vonnoh," *Art in America.* Aug. 1928.
"Vonnoh's Half Century," *International Studio.* June 1923.
Vonnoh, Robert. "The Relation of Art to Existence, A Noted Painter Voices Some Common-Sense Concerning Everyday Beauty," *Arts and Decoration.* Sept. 1922.

Voulkos, Peter
Nordland, Gerald. "Peter Voulkos, Bronze Sculpture," exhibition catalogue, San Francisco Museum. 1972.
"Peter Voulkos," exhibition catalogue, Los Angeles County Museum. 1965.
Secunda, Arthur. "Exhibitions: Peter Voulkos," *Craft Horizons.* July–Aug. 1965.

Waldo, Samuel Lovett
Crayon, VII. 1861 (obituary).
New York Evening Post, Feb. 18, 1861 (obituary).
Sherman, Frederick. "Samuel Lovett Waldo and William Jewett, Portrait Painters," *Art in America.* Feb. 1930.
Wehle, H. B. "Two Portraits by Waldo," *Metropolitan Museum of Art Bulletin.* N.Y., March 1923.

Walkowitz, Abraham
Bluemner, O. "Walkowitz," *Camera Work.* Oct. 1913.
McBride, Henry. John Weichsel, C. Vildrac and W. H. Wright, *One Hundred Drawings by Abraham Walkowitz.* N.Y., 1925.
Walkowitz, Abraham. *Art from Life to Life.* Girard, Kan. 1951.

Walter, Thomas Ustick
Biddle, Edward. "Girard College," *Proceedings, Numismatic and Antiquarian Society of Philadelphia.* 1916–1919.
Newcomb, R. G. "Thomas U. Walter," *The Architect.* Aug. 1928.
Walter, Thomas U. *Two Hundred Designs for Cottages and Villas.* Philadelphia, 1846.

Ward, John Quincy Adams
Adams, Adeline. *John Quincy Adams Ward, An Appreciation.* N.Y., 1912.
Sheldon, G. W. "An American Sculptor,"

Harper's Magazine. June 1878.
Thorp, Margaret. *The Literary Sculptors.* Durham, N.C., 1965.

Warhol, Andy
"Andy Warhol," exhibition catalogue, Whitney Museum. N.Y., 1970.
Coplans, John. *Andy Warhol.* N.Y., 1970.
——. "The Early Work of Andy Warhol," *Artforum.* March 1970.
Swenson, G. R. "Interview with Andy Warhol," *Art News.* Nov. 1963.

Warnecke, Heinz
Devree, Charlotte. "Is This Statuary Worth More Than a Million of Your Money?", *Art News.* April 1955.

Warner, Olin
Eckford, Henry. *Century Magazine,* vol. 37. 1889.
"Olin Levi Warner, Memorial Exhibition," exhibition catalogue, National Sculpture Society. N.Y., 1898.
Wood, C. E. S. "Famous Indians, Portraits of Some Indian Chiefs," *Century Magazine,* vol. 46. 1893.

Warren, Russell
Hamlin, Talbot. *Greek Revival Architecture in America.* N.Y., 1964.
Hitchcock, Henry R. *Rhode Island Architecture.* Cambridge, 1968.

Watson, John
Boston, Theodore. "John Watson of Perth Amboy, Artist," *Proceedings of the New Jersey Historical Society.* Oct. 1954.
Morgan, John. "Further Notes on John Watson," *Proceedings of the American Antiquarian Society.* April 1942.
——. "John Watson, Painter, Merchant, and Capitalist," *Proceedings of the American Antiquarian Society.* Oct. 1940.

Wayne, June
Simon, Rita. "The Tamarind Workshop and June Wayne," *Arts.* May 1969.

Weathervanes
Little, Nina. *Abby Aldrich Rockefeller Folk Art Collection.* Boston, 1957.
"Museum of Early American Folk Arts," exhibition catalogue, Time and Life Exhibition Center. N.Y., 1962.
Whipple, J. Rayner. "Old New England Weather Vanes," *Old-Time New England.* Oct. 1940.

Weber, Kem
Gebhard, David and Harriette Von Breton. *Kem Weber: The Moderne in Southern California, 1920 Through 1941.* Santa Barbara, 1969.

Weber, Max
Cahill, Holger. *Max Weber.* N.Y., 1930.
Goodrich, Lloyd. "Max Weber," exhibition catalogue, Whitney Museum. N.Y., 1949.
"Max Weber, The Years 1906–1916," exhibition catalogue, Bernard Danenberg Galleries. N.Y., 1970.
"Max Weber," exhibition catalogue, University of California. Santa Barbara, Cal.
Weber, Max. *Essays On Art.* N.Y., 1916.

Weir, John Ferguson
Sizer, Theodore. *The Recollections of John Ferguson Weir, Director of the Yale School of the Fine Arts 1869–1913.* N.Y., 1957.

Weir, Julian Alden
Coffin, William. "Memorial Exhibition of the Works of Julian Alden Weir," exhibition catalogue, Metropolitan Museum of Art. N.Y., 1924.

Millet, J. B. (ed.). *Julian Alden Weir, An Appreciation of His Life and Works*. N.Y., 1921.

Young, Dorothy. *The Life and Letters of J. Alden Weir*. New Haven, 1960.

Weir, Robert Walter

Weir, Irene. *Robert W. Weir, Artist*. N.Y., 1947.

Wertmuller, Adolph Ulrich

Benisovich, Michel. "Roslin and Wertmuller, Some Unpublished Documents," *Gazette des Beaux Arts*. April 1944.

——. "The Sale of the Studio of Adolph U. Wertmuller," *Art Quarterly*. Spring 1953.

Wesselmann, Tom

Swenson, G. R. "Interview with Tom Wesselmann," *Art News*. Feb. 1964.

West, Benjamin

Galt, John. *The Life, Studies, and Works of Benjamin West*. London, 1820.

Erffa, Helmut Von. "Benjamin West Reinterpreted," *Antiques*. June 1962.

Evans, Grose. *Benjamin West and the Taste of His Times*. Carbondale, Ill., 1959.

Sawitzky, William. "The American Work of Benjamin West," *Pennsylvania Magazine of History and Biography*. Oct. 1938.

Westermann, H. C.

Friedman, Martin. "Carpenter Gothic," *Art News*. March 1967.

Weston, Edward

Armitage, Merle. *The Art of Edward Weston*, N.Y., 1932.

Newhall, Nancy (ed.). *Edward Weston*. N.Y., 1965.

Weston, Edward. *The Daybooks of Edward Weston*. Rochester, 1962.

Whistler, James Abbott McNeill

Pennell, J. and E. R. *The Life of James McNeill Whistler*. London, 1908.

Sutton, Denys. *Nocturne: The Art of James McNeill Whistler*. London, 1908.

Sweet, Frederick. "James McNeill Whistler," exhibition catalogue, Art Institute of Chicago. 1968.

Whistler, James McNeill. *The Gentle Art of Making Enemies*. London, 1890.

Young, Andrew. "James McNeill Whistler," exhibition catalogue, M. Knoedler, N.Y. and Arts Council of Great Britain. London, 1960.

White, John

Bushnell, David, Jr. "John White: The First English Artist to Visit America, 1585," *Virginia Magazine*. Oct. 1927, Jan. 1928, and April 1928.

Lorant, Stefan. *The New World: The First Pictures of America Made by John White and Jacques Le Moyne and Engraved by Theodore De Bry*. N.Y., 1946.

White, Minor

White, Minor. *Camera* (Lucerne). Aug. 1959.

——. *Mirrors, Messages, Manifestations*. N.Y., 1969.

White, Stanford

See McKim, Mead & White

Whitney, Anne

American Art Annual, XII (obituary).

Gardner, Albert. *Yankee Stonecutters: The First American School of Sculpture 1800–1850*. N.Y., 1944.

Whittredge, Worthington

Baur, John (ed.). "The Autobiography of Worthington Whittredge, 1820–1910," *Brooklyn Museum Journal*. 1942.

Dwight, Edward. "Worthington Whittredge

(1820–1910), A Retrospective Exhibition of an American Artist," exhibition catalogue, Munson-Williams-Proctor Institute. Utica, 1969.

M. and M. Karolik Collection of American Paintings: 1815–1865. Cambridge, 1949.

Williams, Micah

American Provincial Paintings, 1680–1860, from the Collection of J. Stuart Halladay and Herrel George Thomas. Pittsburgh, 1941.

Cortelyou, Irwin. "A Mysterious Pastellist Identified," *Antiques*. Aug. 1954.

——. "Henry Conover: Sitter, Not Artist," *Antiques*. Dec. 1954.

Williams, Neil

Johnson, Ellen. "Three Young Americans: Hinman, Poons, and Williams," *Oberlin College Bulletin*. Spring 1965.

Williams, William

Flexner, James. "The Amazing William Williams: Painter, Author, Teacher, Musician, Stage Designer, Castaway," *Magazine of Art*. Nov. 1944.

Sawitzky, William. "Further Light on the Work of William Williams," *New York Historical Society Quarterly Bulletin*. July 1941.

——. "William Williams, First Instructor of Benjamin West," *Antiques*. May 1937.

Wimar, Karl

Hodges, William. *Carl Wimar*. Galveston, Tex., 1908.

Rathbone, Perry. "Charles Wimar 1828–1862, Painter of the Indian Frontier," exhibition catalogue, City Art Museum. St. Louis, 1946.

Wilmarth, Christopher

Ashton, Dore. "Radiance and Reserve: The Sculpture of Christopher Wilmarth," *Arts*. March 1971.

Winogrand, Garry

Goldsmith, Arthur, Jr. "Garry Winogrand," *Popular Photography*. Oct. 1954.

Longwell, Dennis (ed.). "Monkeys Make the Problem More Difficult: A Collective Interview with Garry Winogrand," *Image*. July 1972.

Winogrand, Garry. *The Animals*. N.Y., 1969.

Winslow, Edward

Bulletin of the Associates in Fine Arts at Yale University. June 1935.

Bulletin of the Associates in Fine Arts at Yale University. June 1936.

Wollaston, John

Bolton, Theodore and Harry Binsse. "Wollaston, an Early American Portrait Manufacturer," *Antiquarian*. June 1931.

Groce, George. "John Wollaston: A Cosmopolitan Painter in the British Colonies," *Art Quarterly*. Summer 1952.

Wood, Grant

Janson, H. W. "Benton and Wood, Champions of Regionalism," *Magazine of Art*. May 1946.

Woodville, Richard Caton

Canaday, John. "Richard Caton Woodville: New Stature for a Little Master," *New York Times*. March 3, 1968.

Cowdrey, B. "Richard Caton Woodville; An American Genre Painter," *American Collector*. April 1944.

Grubar, Francis. "Richard Caton Woodville, An Early American Genre Painter," exhibition catalogue, Corcoran Gallery. Wash. D.C., 1967.

Woodville, Richard C., Jr. *Random Recollections*. London, 1914.

Wormley, Edward J.

Pierson, William, Jr. and Martha Davidson (eds.). *Arts of the United States*. N.Y., 1960.

WPA Federal Art Project

Agee, William. "The Thirties," exhibition catalogue, Whitney Museum. N.Y., 1968.

Bruce, Edward and Forbes Watson. *Mural Designs, 1934–1936*. Wash. D.C., 1936.

Documents, Manuscripts, and Tape-Recorded Interviews with Government Officials and Artists, Archives of American Art. Wash. D.C., Detroit, and N.Y.

O'Conner, Francis. *Federal Art Patronage, 1933–1943*. College Park, Md., 1966.

——. "New Deal Murals in New York," *Artforum*. Nov. 1968.

Osnos, Nina. "New Deal for New Deal Art," *Art in America*. Jan.–Feb. 1972.

Wright, Frank Lloyd

Farr, Finis. *Frank Lloyd Wright*. N.Y., 1961.

Hitchcock, Henry-Russell. *In the Nature of Materials: 1887–1941: The Buildings of Frank Lloyd Wright*. N.Y., 1942.

Manson, Grant. *Frank Lloyd Wright to 1910*. N.Y., 1958.

Scully, Vincent. *Frank Lloyd Wright*. N.Y., 1960.

Wright, Frank Lloyd. *An Autobiography*. N.Y., 1932.

——. *Frank Lloyd Wright: Writings and Buildings*. N.Y., 1960.

——. *The Natural House*. N.Y., 1954.

Wright, Joseph

Kimball, S. F. "Joseph Wright and His Portraits of Washington," *Antiques*. May 1929 and Jan. 1930.

Perrine, Howland. *The Wright Family of Oyster Bay*. N.Y., 1923.

Wright, Patience Lovell

Hart, Charles. "Patience Wright, Modeller in Wax," *Connoisseur*. Sept. 1907.

Lesley, Everett. "Patience Lovell Wright, America's First Sculptor," *Art in America*. Oct. 1936.

Wall, A. J. "Wax Portraiture," *New York Historical Society Quarterly Bulletin*. April 1925.

Wurster, William

Wurster, W. W. "The Architectural Life," *Architectural Record*. Jan. 1951.

——. "The Outdoors in Residential Design," *Architectural Forum*. Sept. 1949.

Wyant, Alexander Helwig

"Alexander H. Wyant, 1836–1892," exhibition catalogue, Museum of Fine Arts, University of Utah, 1968.

Clark, Eliot. *Alexander Wyant*. N.Y., 1916.

Sixty Paintings by Alexander H. Wyant, Described by Eliot Clark. N.Y., 1920.

Wyeth, Andrew

"Andrew Wyeth," exhibition catalogue, Museum of Fine Arts. Boston, 1970.

"Andrew Wyeth," exhibition catalogue, Pennsylvania Academy of the Fine Arts. Philadelphia, 1966.

McBride, Henry. "Wyeth: Serious Best-Seller," *Art News*. Nov. 1953.

"The World of Andrew Wyeth" (film), distributed by International Film Bureau. Chicago, 1968.

Wyeth, Andrew. *Andrew Wyeth*. Boston, 1968.

Yamasaki, Minoru

Bibliography According to Entries

Collins, Glenn. "Notes on a Revolutionary Dinosaur," *New York Times Magazine.* Aug. 6, 1972.

"World Trade Center, New York City," *Architectural Forum.* May 1971.

York & Sawyer

Edward Palmer York, Personal Reminiscences by Philip Sawyer and Royal Cortissoz. N.Y., 1951.

Young, Ammi Burnham

Young, Ammi. *Plans of Public Buildings in Course of Construction, Under the Direction of the Secretary of the Treasury, Including the Specifications Thereof.* Wash. D.C., 1855.

Young, Art

Beffel, J. N. (ed.). *Art Young, His Life and Times.* N.Y., 1939.

Young, Art. *On My Way: Being the Book of Art Young in Text and Picture.* N.Y., 1928.

Young, Mahonri

"Mahonri M. Young, Retrospective Exhibition," exhibition catalogue, Addison Gallery of American Art. Andover, Mass., 1940.

Youngerman, Jack

Benedikt, Michael. "Youngerman: Liberty in Limits," *Art News.* Sept. 1965.

Roberts, Colette. "Jack Youngerman," *Archives of American Art Journal,* vol. 12, no. 2. 1972.

Rubin, William. "Younger American Painters," *Art International,* vol. 4. 1960.

"Sixteen Americans," exhibition catalogue, Museum of Modern Art. N.Y., 1959–1960.

Yunkers, Adja

Leeper, J. P. *Adja Yunkers.* N.Y., 1952.

Sawin, Martica. "Adja Yunkers," *Arts.* April 1957.

Sawyer, Kenneth. "Adja Yunkers: Recent Paintings," exhibition catalogue, Baltimore Museum of Art. 1960.

Zorach, William

Baur, John. "William Zorach," exhibition catalogue, Whitney Museum. N.Y., 1959.

Wingert, Paul. *The Sculpture of William Zorach.* N.Y., 1938.

Zorach, William. *Art is My Life.* Cleveland, 1967.

Zox, Larry

Campbell, Lawrence. "Larry in the Sky with Diamonds," *Art News.* Feb. 1968.

Photo Credits

We wish to thank the libraries, museums, galleries, and private collections named in the picture captions for permitting the reproduction of works of art in their collections, and for supplying the necessary photographs. Photographs from other sources are gratefully acknowledged below.

The numbers following each photographer's name refer to the page and illustration, respectively; thus, 30–1/1,2 refers to pages 30 and 31, illustrations 1 and 2.

Museum of American Folk Art: 178–9/4; 494–5/2
Wayne Andrews: 30–1/1,2; 32–3/2,4; 36–7/1; 90–1/1; 228–9/2; 252–3/2; 266–7/1; 294–5/1; 306–7/1; 314–15/1,2; 366–7/2; 368–9/2; 386–7/2; 490–1/1,2; 602–3/1
Morely Baer: 42–3/1; 376–7/2
Oliver Baker Associates, Inc.: 136–7/2; 282–3/2; 324–5/2; 500–1/3
Richard Bellamy Gallery: 146–7/3
E. Irving Blomstrann: 14–15/2; 158–9/1; 472–3/1
Ferdinand Boesch: 260–1/2; 394–5/1,2; 492–3/1,2
Brooklyn Public Library: 32–3/1
Rudolph Burkhardt: 172–3/1; 222–3/2; 308–9/3; 312–13/2; 378–9/1; 458–9/1,3; 582–3/2
Carl Byoir Associates: 260–1/1; 262–3/5,7
University of California, Santa Barbara: 36–7/2
Museum of the City of New York: 366–7/1; 460–1/1; 480–1/1
Leo Castelli Gallery: 78–9/1,2; 308–9/3; 312–13/2; 378–9/1; 582–3/2
Geoffrey Clements: 112–13/1; 140–1/1,2; 144–5/1,3; 146–7/1,2; 166–7/1; 170–1/1; 184–5/3; 270–1/2; 282–3/1; 342–3/1; 348–9/1,2,3; 350–1/2; 396–7/1; 398–9/2; 484–5/2; 504–5/2; 538–9/2; 542–3/2; 558–9/1;

566–7/2; 580–1/2; 586–7/3,4
Chicago Historical Society: 34–5/1; 114–15/2; 474–5/1; 548–9/1,2
Colonial Williamsburg: 20–1/1; 138–9/2; 330–1/1
Don Cook: 8–9/1
Cordier & Ekstrom Gallery: 396–7/1,2
George Cserna: 42–3/2; 186–7/1; 374–5/2
George M. Cushing: 250–1/1; 280–1/3; 328–9/3
Dade County (Fla.) Art Museum: 332–3/3,4
Jospeh de Valle: 260–1/7
Richard di Liberto: 260–1/1; 262–3/5
Alexandre Georges: 310–11/4
Bob Hanson: 262–3/3; 586–7/2
Hedrich-Blessing: 614–15/1,2
Ambur Hiken: 32–3/5,6
David Hirsch: 576–7/1
Historical Society of Pennsylvania: 28–9/5; 336–7/1
Evelyn Hofer: 518–19/1; 618–9/1
Sidney Janis Gallery: 146–7/1
Luc Joubert: 412/1
Peter A. Juley & Son: 352–3/4
Joseph Klima, Jr.: 16–17/1
Balthazar Korab: 44–5/1; 588–9/2
LaBel's Studio: 428–9/2
Paulus Lesser: 4–5/1
Library of Congress: 22–3/1,2; 24–5/4,5; 26–7/1
Lodder Photo Service Co.: 74–5/3
Lubitsh & Bungarz: 110–11/1
Robert E. Mates & Paul Katz: 570–1/2
Norman McGrath: 552–3/3,4
J. Mengis: 138–9/1
Miami-Metro: 332–3/3
Joseph W. Molitor: 44–5/2; 56–7/2; 486–7/1
Mount Vernon Ladies' Association: 330–1/2
John D. Murray: 300–1/1,2
Museum of Modern Art: 166–7/2
Samuel A. Musgrave: 518–19/2
Clay Nolan: 420–1/1

Philadelphia Museum of Art: 154–5/3
Phillips Studio: 476–7/3
Photo Researchers: 38–9/2
Photographis: 586–7/1
Pixit: 244–5/1; 380–1/2
Eric Pollitzer: 8–9/2,3; 298–9/1; 308–9/1; 318–19/1; 322–3/1; 444–5/2; 532–3/2; 590–1/2
Nathan Rabin: 388–9/1
Stephen Radich Gallery: 8–9/1
Rockefeller Center: 36–7/3,4
Walter Rosenblum: 58–9/3; 142–3/2
Walter Russell: 14–15/4
John D. Schiff: 140–1/3; 344–5/1
Ben Schnall: 82–3/1
Elton Schnellbacher: 74–5/4
Julius Schulman: 392–3/1
Marvin Schwartz: 100–1/1,2
Mark Sexton: 20–1/2,3; 28–9/2,3,4
Smithsonian Institution: 332–3/2
Eric Southerland: 250–1/2; 200–1/3
Ezra Stoller Associates, Inc.: 38–9/1,3; 40–1/1,2; 42–3/4; 58–9/2; 82–3/2; 94–5/1; 310–11/3; 314–15/3,4; 478–9/1; 516–17/1; 608–9/2
Soichi Sunami: 328–9/1
Joseph Szaszfai: 570–1/1
Talmar: 24–5/1.2,3
David Van Riper: 178–9/1
Malcolm Varon: 8–9/2,3; 224–5/2; 226–7/5; 318–19/2; 364–5/1; 394–5/4; 598–9/1; 616–17/2
Herbert P. Vose: 176–7/1
Wagner International Photo, Inc.: 368–9/1; 614–15/3
Susan Weiley: 418–19/1
Whitney Museum of American Art: 310–11/2
Wildenstein and Co.: 104–5/3
Willett Art Studios: 152–3/3
H. F. du Pont Winterthur Museum: 26–7/2; 332–3/1
Alfred J. Wyatt: 288–9/4; 414–15/2; 464–5/1,2; 502–3/2

This encyclopedia was set by University Graphics, Inc., Shrewsbury, N.J., in 9 pt. Claro (Helvetica) on 11 point line feed. Claro is a contemporary typeface of Swiss origin. Although typefaces without serifs were used in the 19th century, it was not until the 20th century that they became widely used. Helvetica was introduced in 1957 by the Haas Typefoundry and was first presented in the United States in the early 1960s. Because of its clean design, it is a very readable typeface.

The black and white reproductions and the color separations were made by Amilcare Pizzi, S.p.A., Milan, who also did the printing on a four-color Roland 160 press. The paper, of Italian origin, was manufactured by C.I.R. Stabilimento di Chieti (CH); the weight by American standards is 80 pounds. The book was bound in Italy in Canvas Extra cloth for the trade edition and Buckram for the library edition.